LITERATURE AND SOCIETY

AN INTRODUCTION TO FICTION, POETRY, DRAMA, NONFICTION

PAMELA J. ANNAS

University of Massachusetts/Boston

ROBERT C. ROSEN

William Paterson College

PRENTICE HALL

Englewood Cliffs, New Jersey 07632

Annas, Pamela J.
    Literature and society : fiction, poetry, drama, nonfiction /
Pamela Jeanne Annas, Robert C. Rosen.
    p. cm.
  ISBN 0-13-538182-7
  1. Literature—History and criticism. 2. Literature and society.
I. Rosen, Robert C.,   II. Title.
PN51.A55 1990
808.8—dc20   89-28012
                                                  CIP

Editorial/production supervision and
  interior design: **Margaret Lepera**
Cover design: **Ben Santora**
Manufacturing buyer: **Ray Keating**
Cover Photo: **James M. Via**/Memorial Art Gallery of the University of Rochester Marion
Stratton Gould Fund.
Credits and copyright acknowledgments appear on pp. 1458–1467, which constitute an
extension of the copyright page.

©1990 by Prentice-Hall, Inc.
A Division of Simon & Schuster
Englewood Cliffs, New Jersey 07632

Printed in the United States of America

10 9 8 7 6 5 4 3 2 1

ISBN   0-13-538182-7

Prentice-Hall International (uk) Limited, *London*
Prentice-Hall of Australia Pty. Limited, *Sydney*
Prentice-Hall Canada Inc., *Toronto*
Prentice-Hall Hispanoamericana, s.a., *Mexico*
Prentice-Hall of India Private Limited, *New Delhi*
Prentice-Hall of Japan, Inc., *Tokyo*
Simon & Schuster Asia Pte. Ltd., *Singapore*
Editora Prentice-Hall do Brasil, Ltda., *Rio de Janeiro*

CONTENTS

  The Director leads a tour through the hatchery, where elaborate
machinery makes babies in several different models, and through the
Conditioning Rooms, where hypnopaedia and shock treatment teach infants to like and dislike the right things.

POETRY   159

DRAMA 209

Three women in a maternity ward have strikingly different experiences with pregnancy and childbirth.

An aging king learns the hard way which of his three daughters really loves him.

A comic and pathetic old man listens to and talks back at tape recordings about his life that he made when he was younger.

NONFICTION 364

A Chinese-American girl tries to cope with a terrifying story her mother tells her about what it means to be a woman.

An American girl reaches puberty and discovers something about her West Indian heritage.

WOMEN AND MEN 384

During the worst years of the Great Depression, a chronically unemployed man hunts for "three hots and a flop."

College-educated Miss Moore takes a group of ghetto kids to an
expensive toy store to teach them a lesson about the society they live
in.

An important highway engineer gets some help he needs but doesn't
want starting his big car.

A mother has to decide which of two very different daughters should
get the family quilts.

POETRY 742

DRAMA   793

ARTHUR MILLER, *Death of a Salesman*, **793**
Aging Willy Loman, failing in his job, disappointed in his sons, tries
to make things work out better.

ALICE CHILDRESS, *Florence*, **876**
An encounter between a black woman and a white woman in a
segregated Southern train station affects the career of an aspiring actress.

NONFICTION   888

MERIDEL LeSUEUR, *Women on the Breadlines*, **888**
Writing in the 1930s, Le Sueur speculates about what women do and
where they go when they're out of work.

RICHARD WRIGHT, *The Man Who Went to Chicago*, **895**
Wright describes his work experiences in Chicago, from washing
dishes to selling burial insurance.

AGNES SMEDLEY, *Silk Workers*, **921**
An American journalist in China in 1930 visits a group of young
women silk workers who tell her, without words, how they won a ten-
hour work day.

PEACE AND WAR

INTRODUCTION

FICTION

POETRY

DRAMA   1046

Life in New York City today intersects with life in Hiroshima the day the bomb fell.

NONFICTION   1089

An old medicine man tells the story of the famous 1890 massacre of Native American men, women, and children by U.S. soldiers.

Duras describes her husband's return from a Nazi concentration camp.

HOW FICTION WORKS   1396

HOW POETRY WORKS   1412

HOW DRAMA WORKS   1438

HOW NONFICTION WORKS   1451

ALTERNATE CONTENTS

FICTION

POETRY

DRAMA

NONFICTION

PREFACE

We have organized *Literature and Society* around five major social issues or themes, and have selected for each one literary works—stories, poems, plays, and works of nonfiction—that embody a wide diversity of perspectives and bring to life a variety of experiences. The five sections, Growing Up and Growing Older, Women and Men, Money and Work, Peace and War, and Varieties of Protest, represent five important areas of social experience.

Growing Up and Growing Older are, of course, universal human experiences. But they are also profoundly particular social experiences, different, for example, for people of different gender, race, or social class, as the wide variety of literary works in this section reveal. On the theme of Women and Men, the selections range from love poems to poems of protest, from "problem" drama to satiric essay and comic fiction, but all illuminate the ways society shapes an individual's experience and identity as a woman or as a man. Money and Work are nearly universal in human experience but, as the literature in this section illustrates, the social conditions within which a person labors can make work fulfilling or alienating, exciting or tedious, life-sustaining or life-destroying, and the manner in which society uses and distributes wealth shapes the lives of those who have money and those who do not in subtle as well as obvious ways. We devote a section to Peace and War because war, and the need for peace, are so central to modern existence; even those who have never experienced war directly are profoundly affected by the legacy of past wars, by the militarization of culture, and by the nightmare prospect of nuclear war. Finally, in every society, people have engaged in protest, whether spontaneous or planned, whether as individuals or in groups, against what they have perceived as injustice; the selections that explore Varieties of Protest are not simply works *of* protest but works *about* protest, about the act of standing up (or, perhaps, sitting down) for what one believes is right.

The stories, poems, plays, and works of nonfiction grouped around these five themes provide a broad and accessible introduction to the ways literature can enrich one's understanding of self and society. The themes, of course, overlap. Literary works are complex; they are rarely about just one thing. Arthur Miller's play, *Death of a Salesman*, is about Growing Up and Growing Older as well as Money and Work; Pamela Zoline's science fiction story, "The Heat Death of the Universe," explores relationships between Women and Men as well as a very interesting Variety of Protest. The thematic categories are meant not to limit but to stimulate thinking and discussion.

Within each thematic category, *Literature and Society* offers a heterogeneous selection of literary works, representing a diversity of experiences and perspectives. We have included a full range of selections by women, black, gay, ethnic, and other writers who have traditionally found little welcome in the canon of works considered most worthy of academic study, but whose presence in a literature course will not only mean class discussions that are more varied and more exciting, but also an introduction to literature that truly reflects the extraordinary diversity of the society students live in. Virtually half of the selections in *Literature and Society* are by women and roughly one fourth by "minorities," both figures exceptionally high for an anthology of this kind. Alongside a well-known work by Faulkner or Keats or Hemingway students will find an important but less known work on the same theme by Alice Childress or Owen Dodson or Judy Grahn. The thirty-seven stories, two hundred seven poems, ten plays, and eighteen works of nonfiction included will enable students to hear a wide range of voices, differing from one another in gender, age, sexual orientation, race, ethnicity, social class.

The editorial apparatus of *Literature and Society* is designed to help students understand both the social meanings and the formal elements of the literary works included. Though we have organized the book by theme rather than by literary genre and literary concept, we give serious attention to matters of form, to the ways literary technique serves larger purposes—the recreation of experience, the testing of ideas, the exploration of social issues. Four detailed chapters—on fiction, on poetry, on drama, and on nonfiction prose—introduce key literary concepts and approaches, and develop them through lively examples. A long and (we think) exciting chapter on Literature and the Writing Process offers a number of extended metaphors to help students think about their own writing process and uses sample student papers, paragraphs, and journal entries to guide students through the stages of that process, from generating ideas to revising and editing.

A preface to each of the five thematic sections introduces the theme that unifies the section and raises some of the key questions the works included explore. Study and discussion questions, writing exercises, and author biographies accompany all short stories, plays, and works of nonfiction, and about one fifth of the poems in each section. The study and discussion questions are more or less objective, sometimes very specific; they lead students toward a basic understanding of the works. The writing exercises (meant to take from five to thirty minutes each) are more subjective and open-ended, intended to stimulate thinking about the larger meanings of the works and to encourage students to explore their own responses in creative ways and to articulate their own opinions. At the end of each thematic section appear a number of suggested topics for longer papers, usually involving a comparison of two or more works; these questions offer students the chance to integrate what they have learned.

Despite its careful structure, *Literature and Society* is quite flexible. Though designed specifically for an introductory literature course, the book could easily be used in a writing course, for its five thematic sections and many writing exercises can generate a wide range of formal and informal writing assignments, and its process-oriented chapter, Literature and the Writing Process, is engaging, accessible, and thorough. There are far more selections in *Literature and Society* than one could ever use in one or even two semesters of a literature or writing course, so an instructor will find a great deal of freedom to adapt the text to his or her own purposes. There is a careful mix of well-known, canonical works and equally teachable and formally interesting non-canonical works, so the familiar and the new can be combined in any proportion desired. As well as selecting among the works gathered around each theme, an instructor might decide to choose among themes, opting for a more thorough exploration of any one or more of the five offered. In addition, there is an Alternate Table of Contents, should one wish to organize a course by literary genre rather than by theme. However it is used, we think *Literature and Society* introduces students to a wide and exciting variety of literature in a way that will consistently engage their interest, that will help them understand that literature is about the very things—whether money or work or growing up or what it means to be male or female—that matter in their own lives.

* * *

We could never have done this book without the suggestions, help, and support of many people. We owe thanks to Barbra Apfelbaum, Michael Conlon, Robert Crossley, Lennard Davis, Mary Anne Ferguson, Marilyn Frankenstein, Bruce Franklin, Steve Golin, Linda Hamalian, Russ Hart, Jim Hauser, Jay Jordan, Louis Kampf, Mary Jane Karp, Stan Karp, Suzanne Kistler, Kathy Koch, Paul Lauter, Robert Lee, Lucye Millerand, Richard Ohmann, Susan O'Malley, Donna Perry, Susan Radner, Carolyn Rothschild, Pancho Savery, Ron Schreiber, Stephen Rosskamm Shalom, Roger Shatzkin, Wally Sillanpoa, George Slover, Leonard Vogt, Jack Weston, and all the other friends who rarely let on how tired they were of hearing about this project.

Special thanks to students in the following courses at the University of Massachusetts/Boston: Introductory Composition, Practical Criticism, Nature of Literature: Poetry, Writing as Women, The Modern Period, and Literature of the Working Class.

We would also like to thank a few people at Prentice Hall: Phil Miller, who gave us encouragement and valuable criticism; Margaret Lepera, who managed production; and Jane Baumann.

LITERATURE AND THE WRITING PROCESS

When you are first learning how to read and write about a work of literature, its very completeness and solidity might be intimidating, rather as though you are standing at the edge of a dense, green tropical jungle. Its facade is a solid and tangled mass of leaves. It smells of rain and shadows. You hear as yet unidentified creatures calling to each other from branch to branch and crashing through the undergrowth. How are you going to find or make a path into the jungle of the text? What are you going to discover there? Will you be able to make sense of it and describe it when you come out the other side? Whatever you bring back from your adventure—orchids, emeralds, tree frogs, or a load of leaf mold—you're bound to bring back something and to have been changed, however slightly, by the experience. And here the analogy ends, for no one has been lost inside and failed to emerge from a work of poetry or prose.

In some ways, reading and writing about a work of literature—a poem, a story, a novel, a play, an autobiography or other form of nonfictional but nevertheless literary prose—is easier than working on most nonliterary subjects. At least your subject, the literary text, is right there in front of you in all its glorious and annoying entirety, on your desk or on the kitchen table or maybe on your lap as you ride home from school on the subway. It often has a beginning, a middle, and an end; it certainly has a shape. It offers a world for you to visit and describe.

BEGINNING, DISCOVERING, INVENTING, PLANNING, DRAFTING

Ideally, you have had time enough to read the story, poem, essay, or play once through for enjoyment before you had to begin work on it. Now read it again, looking for a way in. This time, read with a pen or pencil in hand. Mark passages (lines, scenes, images, words) that particularly strike you. Perhaps this is where some insight about the whole clicks into place for you. Perhaps you notice recurrences and connections that will add up to a pattern you will be able to write about, like images of automobiles and children in Carolyn Chute's "Tall Woman Love"

(p. 729), or the repeated use of sibilant sounds ("s") in Langston Hughes's poem "Harlem" (p. 1262). Maybe you have noticed an aspect of this text that reminds you of another literary work you've read, perhaps one about a similar type of social experience, such as growing up immigrant and female in America or fighting on a battlefield, and you can note where and how the writers deal similarly and differently with various aspects of that experience. Or you might mark passages that remind you of something in your own life such as beginning school, looking for a new job, or falling in love. And you should certainly note any part of a literary work that particularly moves you, that evokes an emotional response or a sudden increase in attention that strongly pulls you into the words, even if you can't yet say why.

Generally speaking, your first impulses are good and can be trusted. If you are drawn to an image or a scene or an exchange of dialogue, the chances are very good that either: (1) it is an important passage, you are meant to notice it, and most other readers will too; or (2) it catches your particular interest because of who you are, and so you will probably have something original, unusual, and particularly your own to say about it. Either way, you have (to return to our opening metaphor) discerned a break in the wall of leaves that may well be a path into this literary jungle.

Taking Notes

So here you sit or stand or lie, reading the text for the second, or twelfth time, pen in hand. As well as marking parts of the text with a check, an asterisk, or brackets or using whatever notational system you like, you will also want to be making notes about your associations and reactions—personal, political, social, and literary. Some people make marginal notes in the text itself, but margins can very quickly become cluttered and hard to read. You might instead keep a note pad next to you and write down your reactions and insights as you read, identifying them by page number or key word or phrase from the text. Some people prefer note cards; 5 × 8 cards provide more room to write than 3 × 5 cards, and it's a good idea to write only on one side of the card. Have confidence; assume you will fill the cards up with brilliant or at least usable insights. The advantage of note cards is that you can shuffle them around until you find an order which makes organizational sense to you; then your deck of cards can either substitute for or help you to write an outline.

Exploratory Writing

You might want to do exploratory writing at this point in the writing process. Try *freewriting*, or free associating, on the topic for five to ten minutes. Simply write whatever comes into your mind, without worrying about grammar, spelling, organization, or logic. This form of uncensored writing usually has the effect of loosening you up and getting words onto the page, and so is of particular use to writers who block at the point in the writing process when they are first faced with a blank sheet of paper. Your freewriting may be mostly about your struggles with the text. That too is useful, if only to get those struggles out of the way now so that they don't creep into the paper itself. Much of what you freewrite may turn out to be garbage; often, though, you will produce valuable insights or the beginnings of an approach to the work. Besides, even garbage, if you compost it, is useful. Some association or fragmentary comment that initially seems irrelevant may turn out to be the key to your paper. Since freewriting is exploratory writing, not the paper itself but potential material for the paper, you need not care at all about this sounds or how grammatically or formally "correct" it is. Kick your critical, editorial self out of the room during the initial stages of writing. You can also use the initial freewriting to express any feelings you might be having about the text, the topic, the instructor, your boss, your boyfriend/girlfriend, or the weather, so that, refreshed and relaxed, you can get on with the job at hand. You might even discover, in the process of venting what you probably thought of as remarks inappropriate to the task of writing an essay, that there is some provocative connection between, for example, your current job situation and the story about which you are trying to write an essay.

In addition to freewriting, which you can do again at any point in the writing process where you feel stuck or blocked, another helpful exploratory exercise is to *divide* the topic into parts or categories and to make lists of characteristics about each one. You might do this with the characters in a story. As well as dividing, you might *connect*—make notes about the relations between the parts into which you have previously divided the topic. Your exploratory writing is still that part of the process where you are gathering material for your paper. Here the material is perhaps less centered on the text than on your own thoughts, responses, associations to the poem, story, play, or work of nonfictional prose with which you are engaged. If your paper is to come alive and to have your voice, it needs to have a great deal of you in the writing and behind the writing. In order for your paper to be engaging *to* your readers, it must be engaged *with* the literature you are writing about. If the paper is not in some way a record of your passionate relationship with the text, it's likely to be a dull and detached piece of writing.

Inventing an Approach

Have you been given a paper topic by your instructor or are you inventing one of your own? If you have been given a topic, then your reading, note taking and organizing of your material will be influenced by that topic. In some ways, having a topic given to you makes life easier because it aids you in the necessary task of limitation. You needn't say everything there is to say about a play or poem; you need only address yourself to the specific question.

Here is an example. How do Denise Levertov's images in her poem "Life at War" (p. 992) add up to an argument about war and what is that argument? Such a question gives you clues about what to look for and how to organize your paper. You have been given certain information: (1) that there *is* an argument about war in the poem, and that the poem is making a point; and (2) that the images in the poem, that is, the representations of visual or other sense perceptions, are in the service of its argument. You are given certain directions about what to look at, the images, and what to look for, the argument. You might want to begin by listing the various images of war in the poem: disasters like pebbles in the brain, a feeling like "lumps of raw dough" in a child's stomach, the mutilation of breasts, eyes, penises, the smell of "burned human flesh." Also list the images of human potential when we are at peace, such as "delicate Man, whose flesh/responds to a caress, whose eyes/are flowers that perceive the stars." Now, what are your own visceral and emotional responses to these two sets of images? We can venture a fairly solid guess, even from the few images we've listed here, that this is an antiwar poem. But why is Levertov against war, specifically the Vietnam War? What is it she says we are losing or perverting when we engage in this war, in any war?

It is more difficult and fraught with potential dangers to come up with your own topic for a literary work, but it can also be more fun. As with any other paper you write, a paper about a work of literature needs to have a central point, a thesis, that is large enough to engage something important and exciting in the text but small enough that you don't get lost in it. Most of us are far more likely to choose too large a topic, thinking in our modesty or lack of confidence that we will never find enough to say to fill up the required number of pages. A sense of what size topic fits what size essay is a skill that you will develop with practice. In the meantime, if you have two ideas for a paper, it is generally safer to choose the smaller, more limited topic. One simple way to limit yourself is to choose a formal aspect of the work to write about: with poetry, perhaps the image pattern, the sounds, the speaker of the poem; with fiction, the style, atmosphere, setting, the function of one of the characters, not necessarily the main character; with drama, the tension or conflict between two of the characters, how a subplot illuminates the main plot, the stage directions; with nonfictional prose, the rhetorical or narrative devices the writer uses to build an argument, the tone and the audience of the piece. In writing about any kind of literature, a good way to provide a workable limitation is to pick a passage to analyze in detail, and show

how that small part sheds light on or is representative of the work as a whole.

If you are free to come up with a topic of your own, you might well take this opportunity to explore a social or personal issue that interests you. Try ten minutes of freewriting your personal responses to the text. If Hemingway's attitude toward women annoys you when you read "The Short Happy Life of Francis Macomber" (p. 421), then you might want to explore just what Hemingway's attitude is and how formal elements like character and point of view express that attitude. What did he say that made you particularly angry? Point to specific examples in the text. Or you might want to write about his notions of male bravery and honor and how this story presents a particular conception of what it means "to be a man." Or you might choose two literary works on a similar theme and compare/contrast them—perhaps T. S. Eliot's "The Love Song of J. Alfred Prufock" (p. 165) and Irena Klepfisz's "they did not build wings for them" (p. 175), both about aging, identity, and self-esteem, but written from different gender perspectives. Any of these approaches might be of use to you in working out your own ideas on a subject that has relevance to your own life. If you choose a topic that interests you and to which you have some personal connection, you are more likely to enjoy writing the paper, to learn something from writing it, and to find time in your life to do it. Also, the paper is likely to be better.

Outlining

O.K. You have provided yourself with or been given a focus for your essay on a literary work, you've read and reread the text carefully (and if it is a poem, read it out loud), you've made notes and gathered evidence, you've had some insights and perhaps you've made a brief outline or in some other way begun to arrange your material. This outline is not necessarily the elaborate, detailed kind that you perhaps have been trained to make, but a brief *notational outline* that lists what you think are the most important insights you've come up with so far, with evidence under each point in the form of a page number or a few words to remind you where in the poem or story or play you found something to support that insight. Then you can experiment with arranging those insights in the order in which you think, at least for now, that it makes most sense to proceed.

Drafting

The chapters in this book on how fiction, poetry, drama, and nonfiction work suggest questions and approaches to each of the genres. There is, alas, no formula for writing about literature, or any other subject, that will work for everyone or that will inevitably produce a good paper. At some point you, personally, have to put pen to paper or fingers to keyboard and begin. Perhaps it would help if you discarded the notion that there is a right answer, a "correct" reading or interpretation of any given literary text. In fact, the more you reproduce the actual meeting, friendship, love affair, or confrontation between you and the text, the stronger your paper is likely to be. (Of course you do need to back up what you're saying with textual evidence.) While a book like this can offer you suggestions about gathering evidence and generating ideas, about revising and editing, the actual production of a piece of writing, sentence by sentence, is creative, mysterious, and depends a great deal on the kind of experience you are having with your subject. You may have a general idea of what you plan to say before you start, but what you actually *do* say may very well surprise you because writing is exploring a new country composed of you and your subject.

A few cautions. Do not wait until the night before the paper is due to begin writing it. While it is true that many of us work better under pressure, you are less likely to be satisfied with what you turn in if you leave no time to revise. Most people begin to have ideas as soon as the assignment is given. Take five minutes right then and write those ideas down before you lose them. Read (or reread) the work you are going to be writing about early in the space of time given for the assignment so it will be available for thinking about while you are driving, riding the subway or bus, walking, working, making dinner. When you have ideas, make a note of them immediately. You may find when you do begin to write that your accumulated notes and thoughts about the text add up to quite a bit of work already done.

Writing Block Syndrome can happen when the first (or rough) draft of your paper has to carry too much weight, especially: 1) if you have left yourself no time to revise, so that your first draft is of necessity also your last draft, and everything is riding on this one version, which is quite stressful; or 2) if you have done very little thinking or prewriting about your subject, so that, when you confront the blank page, your mind is also blank.

Even under the best conditions, sitting down to the task of the first complete draft of your paper is often accompanied by a certain amount of apprehension: Can I pull it off this time? Do I really have anything worthwhile to say? Hasn't it all been said before—and better? Is what I think this story is about what it really is about? How do I start? How do I end? How many words was this supposed to be anyway? This nervous anticipation, a sort of writing stage fright, is quite normal and happens to experienced writers as well as to relative beginners. The trick is to harness the nervous energy to the task of making sentences, and prevent it from escalating into panic. If you have allowed yourself some time to write and then to revise, and if you have gifted yourself with the time to think about your subject, to discuss it with whomever will listen, to freewrite some responses, to reread the text and mark passages that interest you, and to make a brief notational outline, then writing your first draft will not feel so much like a scary first step, but rather like just one more stage in the writing process.

In the first draft, you find, explore, and settle on the main focus of your paper. Some people have a fairly clear idea of their thesis when they begin the first draft; other people find themselves modifying their hypothesis as they think through their subject. You may find yourself writing for a while before you write a sentence that seems to be your true beginning, where you, your subject, and language finally connect. Don't fret if the first few paragraphs of your draft feel more like freewriting than formal writing. Keep writing.

As you move through your first draft, write as long as the words are flowing; when they stop, take a break, move around, then sit back down again and refer 1) to your notational outline to remind you of the next major section of your paper, 2) to your notes for your main points on that aspect of the subject, and 3) to the text for evidence and examples to support your points. Keep doing this until you reach the end. You will have the chance to rewrite everything that needs revising, including the introduction and conclusion.

Writers (that means you) sometimes find it demystifying and empowering to think very specifically about their writing process, either imaginatively and metaphorically or practically and realistically. What follow are (1) several metaphors for the writing process and (2) one student's day-to-day account of her experience writing a paper.

METAPHORS FOR THE WRITING PROCESS

Just as there is no one correct "answer" to any literary text, there is no one correct way to write about literature or any other subject. Depending on your temperament and on the topic, one method or another may prove more productive and comfortable for you. The metaphors that follow characterize some possibilities you might want to consider. You may find that one of them sounds most like what you already do. Or you might want to come up with a metaphor of your own that better captures your own particular writing process and helps you visualize its successful completion.

Oyster. The paper begins with a stimulating irritant, a central insight of your own or a provocative passage from the text, and you secrete successive layers of words around it. Each draft is longer and more complete, has more luster and depth. The first one probably contains the core of the finished piece, to which you find yourself adding anecdote, quotation, response, and analysis as you go along.

Flower. The paper gradually grows and unfolds from a seed to a bud to a full-blown opened flower. The original intuition or insight will take on different aspects as it unfolds but, as the seed "contains" the flower, you've captured the essence of your paper in the original epiphany or flash of insight, which is in itself probably a synthesis of a number of observations that had fallen into place. The gathering together (of notes, evidence, observations) culminates in an intuitive whole which then generates, as you make it clearer, new possibilities. Though as you form the piece of writing, you may use some of the details that got you to the insight in the first place, there will also be fresh insights as you search for better images or arguments. The process is similar to but is somewhat more generative than the oyster method.

Walnut. Some people feel more comfortable writing a lot in their rough or first draft, sprawling all over the page and the subject, putting down everything that seems even remotely relevant. The subsequent drafts then reduce the paper to a manageable size and a discernible shape. The reverse of the flower and oyster, when your paper is like a walnut you are working from the outside in, from larger to smaller. A walnut has three layers. When it drops off the tree, it is enclosed in a green pulpy covering, a thick skin which gradually, as the walnut lies on the ground, turns black, decays, dries up, and falls away. You wouldn't know they were walnuts if you saw them hanging in the trees, green, or lying on the ground, looking like debris. Writing can be like this. The first layer, the first draft, might not look much like the edible finished center. The next layer, the shell, looks wiser and more experienced; it's formally more interesting and aesthetically pleasing. But it's still not the center. You have to keep writing and discarding until you reach the kernel itself, until the paper seems the same substance all the way through.

Silkworm. If the previous methods of creation have a circular or concentric quality, then spinning out your thoughts in the silkworm method is more linear. This method works better for some people than for others and better for some projects than for others, and it is more traditionally "disciplined." You divide your subject into parts. You make an outline, however detailed you feel comfortable with. You compartmentalize your thinking, working on one part until you feel finished with it, until that part is as complete and polished as you can make it. Then you move on to the next part. Some people do this section by section in a paper; others do it paragraph by paragraph, needing the security and sense of satisfaction of something completed step by step in the process of writing.

Making soup. This method is as much about the writer's relation to his or her materials as it is about the process of writing. When we make soup, different sets of ingredients go in at different times. You have an overall image of the final soup based on your previous experience with the process of making soup (or writing a paper) and your knowledge of each ingredient you have at hand this time, and you need to be able to project each ingredient into a future based on its relation with other ingredients. So if you have left-over broccoli, you don't usually put it in black bean soup. You might choose to make some other kind of soup, possibly minestrone. Or you might decide that the broccoli can't be used. Too bad. The process here is a negotiation between the materials and the framework, between the overview and the collection of details, between the critical and the creative. Soup makers have to be easy going, flexible, adaptable and courageous. They need to know their ingredients, taste as they go, be capable of leaps of faith and be able to take risks—you don't *know* that chunks of potato will work in lentil soup, but the result might be delicious.

Quiltmaking. Like making soup, this is a negotiation between available materials and your vision of the final product. Quiltmakers piece together usable scraps to make a new and interesting whole. Though traditional patterns exist, there is much scope for creativity in the selection and placement of materials and in how you frame them. Further, making a quilt is often a communal rather than an individual activity. Writing a paper can also be a group project, from communal brainstorming to group revision of successive drafts.

Unpacking a suitcase. Maybe *repacking* a suitcase is better. You need to "unpack" what the author of the work you are analyzing has packed into her or his poem, story, essay, or play before you can recombine that writer's stuff with your own and repack it into your own suitcase or paper. It's as though that writer's suitcase is a different size, shape, material (hard vs. soft, leather vs. cloth) with different pockets. You take everything out and lay it on the bed next to your own ideas and start making piles of socks, shirts, pants, skirts, and so on. Then you repack into your own suitcase. You may have to leave out some of both yours and the author's, because there won't be room for all of it. So you have to decide what's essential for your destination, what would make life comfortable but isn't absolutely necessary, what is extra and luxurious but you'll take along anyway just for fun.

THE WRITING PROCESS: AN EXAMPLE

Whatever your method of writing, the process of writing a paper is a definite and discrete, creative and critical, psychological as well as intellectual experience. It has moments of frustration and self-searching and you may have to struggle with a writing block at some point in the process. It also has moments of intense satisfaction and delight—when the words are flowing, when you've produced a particularly good insight

or constructed an elegant sentence and, finally, when you are looking
with relief at the completed paper. The essay that follows is one student's
exploration of her own writing-about-literature process, from initial procrastination to final product. You might try some time, as this student
did, to write your own particular writing process, from the moment you
receive a writing assignment until the time you turn it in. Lauri's paper,
which she chose to write as a series of journal entries, is an unusually
good piece of writing which gives valuable insight into the intellectual
stages of the creative process; its "day to dayness" also emphasizes the
human and subjective aspects of the experience of writing a paper. Writing
is not something that happens outside of you; nor is it separate from who
you are and the life you live.

A JOURNAL RECORD: ONE WEEK IN THE CREATION OF A PAPER

Monday

I had two weeks to write this paper. With seven days left
I've more or less exhausted the possibilities for meaningful
procrastination: I've cleaned the house, baked bread, written
letters, taken a sudden interest in learning Russian, created
emotional crises around myself. (Today I decided I couldn't
survive another day without knowing why Mommy stopped
breastfeeding me when I was three months old.) I finally had
to admit to my roommates that, yes, it's paper time again.
That is why I'm running around as if I have only one week
to live, trying desperately to fit every conceivable activity
into too few working hours. That is why I've forsaken sleep
and arranged to be fed intravenously by the coffee machine.

Often I cannot involve myself wholeheartedly in these
activities of delay. They are a ritual of sorts. I go through
the motions of avoidance before I allow myself to come face
to face with the process of writing. The fact that I have a
paper to write does not for an instant leave my awareness
during this time; I just don't acknowledge it directly. Instead
of greeting the assignment with a handshake and getting
down to business, I flirt with it. I do coy little dances around
it. When it is not looking, I sneak peeks at it. I size it up
and imagine our first encounter. I take its measurements
and make a mental list of how I plan to clothe it.

I have to be thoroughly convinced that the assignment
exists before I can sit down and deal with it. After we have
spent a few days together I begin to believe that it is real.

Tuesday

Today I got myself to sit down in front of the typewriter. It could have been worse. We're old friends. I know so well her features: the automatic return, the margin release. We haven't learned to communicate as well as we could; I failed in my end of the bargain, I know, but a typing course didn't seem like one of my top priorities this semester.

As I sat there, before I could press even one key, I took myself on a journey through some of the best and worst terrain of my self-image:

The surface of my confidence cannot be scratched even by a diamond. My mind is an unbreakable pane of glass. It is a telescope to a great spectrum of ideas, a microscope to every mite of detail, a gold inlaid magnifying glass that scans the pages of the classics. The world is open to me. I can write anything!

And then . . .

Who do I think I am? I can't write. My vocabulary has all the flexibility of a marble column and the visionary range of a burrowed mole. I'm not qualified to sit in the same room as a great piece of literature, let alone try to analyze it. The best of my writings have been like painted Easter eggs: pretty on the surface but easy to crack and empty inside. My ideas are as profound and original as Ronald Reagan's press conferences.

Wednesday

I can be a cruel taskmaster. After that debacle I felt shaky. All right, I bargained with myself, you don't have to start writing today, but you do have to think about the topic. Narrow it down. Work out a rough outline. Get some idea of what you're doing.

This was a visual process. First, I typed out all the possible ideas I could think of related to my topic. There were seventy-nine of them, some redundant, some irrelevant, some worthwhile. But I didn't judge them. I cut out each one with my scissors, and placed them in piles, according to the general theme they fell into. The themes, then, were my possible topics. Some ideas fit into more than one theme. I shuffled and reshuffled. Finally, I chose one theme as my topic, assigned it some choice ideas, and drew up an outline.

Thursday

I'm aware that I have to treat myself with more kindness. I cannot expect my brain to function when I batter my self-confidence with accusations of inadequacy. I cannot expect to be able to relax and write this paper when I place in its grips the right to determine my worth as a human being. That's one thing.

The other thing I'm thinking about is my sense of time and place in this process. In order to write I need to create a gap in my daily life. Writing doesn't get done between taking out the trash and doing the laundry. Every woman who has tried to write knows that. But then, I want what I write to come out of my experience and onto the page; the context of the writing needs to be a part of the writing. How can this be done without letting my life crowd out the very possibility of writing?

The gap that I seek is not a removal. I don't want to leave my experience behind and go to an island to engage in a pure interaction with the text I'm about to analyze. The gap is more in time than in space; it is timelessness. Nothing is left behind, not my history, the history of the text, the worlds we come out of. In order to really see each other, we need to freeze in a moment of time, while remaining aware that time continues to flow all around us.

Friday

Synthesis. It's beginning to work. I put the text through my experience, knowledge, ability to understand, and come up with a new creation. The new creation has pieces of the original text and pieces of me. We have parented this child. The balance of our genes produced a healthy offspring. This is not like the last paper I tried to write, in which the text and I were too close; I could not step back and look critically at it. The child of that endeavor bore the scars of incest. This child has the chance to grow to a healthy adulthood. I see the moment of conception, the period of gestation in my mind, the laborious delivery of concept to paper. I watch my young paragraphs learn to walk, see their structure begin to fill out and mature. In anguish I realize that I cannot control every movement of my child, that at some point she will act according to her own needs and temperament. I offer guidance. More and more internal integration occurs within her. She is almost ready to leave home, to test the harsh world where not everyone loves her as much as I do. My baby.

I have paid attention so far to the context of what I've written. I've monitored the consistency of my argument, the clarity of the connections I make, the truth of what I'm saying. I have given little thought to the form this is taking. I have to confess: This is the part I like best. It's the words that I love. When it comes down to it, I have no ethereal love for ideas. I guess I can never hope to be the third genuine intellectual my English professor has ever met. I live in my body more than in my head, and to me words are the sensual aspect of thought. They feel good rolling off the tongue. Their patterns on the page please the eye. They congregate, like old Southern ladies at church, into sentences and paragraphs. The rise and fall of their cadences is punctuated by exclamations (Yes, Jesus!), and commas (Mmmhmm), and question marks (Ain't it so?). In their silences, their hushed pauses, a quiet hymn as soft as magnolias rises from their lips.

Saturday

I approach revision with more hopefulness than I approached the initial writing task. I have a solid piece of writing here in front of me; I'm not reaching into the air for ideas and methods. But it's hard work, almost as difficult as giving up some of my precious rags to Goodwill, that dreadful process I undergo each spring. "Do I really need this? Do I ever wear it?" I feel sometimes that I am so quiet, that it can be so painful for me to verbalize my thoughts and feelings, that anything I say, any word I produce, is acceptable. Then writing becomes my therapy, and I expect my audience to be a supportive listener, to applaud me for having expressed myself at all. If I get any feedback, I want it to be nonjudgmental. If I am criticized harshly, I feel betrayed. Then I remember that I have a journal for that purpose. When I treat all writing as an extension of my diary, I limit myself to exercises in self-exploration. There are elements of my journal writing that I want to incorporate into my more distanced writing: honesty, personal experience, immediacy, simplicity. I also want to be able to treat my subject with some degree of objectivity, to be able to apply to it a larger framework than the scope of my personal experiences. Maybe that's not possible.

I feel un-American as I revise. I do away with "The more the better," "The bigger the better," the comfortable monotony of predictability. I can no longer collect possessions and display them ostentatiously. This paper doesn't work with all its glaring neon six-syllable words, its sentence structure as uniform as McDonalds, its dozen examples for every insignificant point, its eight pages for what could be said in four.

I am coming to the heart of this artichoke, tossing aside the extraneous outer leaves. I am coming to the soft center, the flesh and flavor of my intentions.

Sunday

I love it! I created it from the stuff of my mind. The words flow like the single stream in a desert. No sentimentality! Every word and idea is as clear and as sharp as the point of an aboriginal arrow. The paragraphs have the perfect order of a stellar formation. The metaphors jump out and envelop the reader in their maternal pouches. Praise will be as proliferative as rabbits. I love it! It's mine.

Later:

I hate it! It's as arid as a desert; there is no oasis. The words are inexact, the ideas are blunted. The paragraphs have no symmetry, no order; they fling themselves about like flaming comets. The metaphors jump around hyperactively. Condemnation is all it deserves. I hate it. I disown it.

Another round of revisions.

Monday

Well, I accept it. It may not sparkle, but it communicates what I want to say. I've done what I can with it, at least for now, in my vacuum of creation and self-criticism.

I feel so good! I have an ulcer, but what does that matter? I also have a paper, a baby, an artichoke, a kangaroo. I feel rich in companionship, and quite relieved.

Ritual procrastination, elation, self-doubt, choosing a topic, finding a focus, giving oneself the time to write, synthesis of the literary text and one's own experience, writing a first draft, elation and self-doubt again, paying attention to the content and the shape of one's argument, spinning the words out of oneself in a pleasurable creative fog, revising and editing, elation, self-doubt, acceptance and letting the paper go: these are all characteristic and necessary parts of the writing process.

REVISING AND EDITING

Revising a paper is not simply a matter of correcting the spelling and strewing commas like chocolate sprinkles over the pages. Revising involves a reengagement with your ideas and words and often with the literary text you are writing about. It may involve substantial rethinking and rewriting. Revising is not only editorial and critical; it continues to be creative. However, you do have a complete text of your own to work with at this stage, which raises interesting possibilities for becoming an engaged reader of your own text. How is your relation to *your* text like and unlike your relation to the text you are writing about? Try writing a one- or two-paragraph response to your own completed first draft.

Let your draft sit for a day or two so that you acquire some distance from it. Or until, to use one of Lauri's metaphors, you have cut the umbilical cord between the paper and yourself so that you can treat it as a separate entity. If you can coax someone you trust to be honest to read your first draft and make constructively critical suggestions, this will aid you in revising. Here is where work in pairs and small groups in class can be very valuable. Experiment with letting someone else read your paper aloud to the group, so that you become a relatively detached audience for your own prose. Along with the other group members, offer constructive suggestions for revising that paper which just happens to be yours. During this exercise, flag any place where a listener's attention wanders; this generally indicates a problem area, either because the prose is clunky and people have turned away in embarrassment or because the writing has become unclear and the audience has lost the thread of the argument. Working in groups on a piece of your writing reminds you that you are not writing to yourself. An essay is a public rather than a private document. That *you* understand what you have written is not enough; your readers need to be able to follow it as well. Here are some questions and suggestions to consider as you revise.

The Whole Paper

1. Think about your audience. Your audience may be your instructor and also the rest of your writing community, the class you are in. What is the *tone* of your paper and the stance you are taking toward your audience? Are you arguing for an interpretation that you think everyone else will disagree with? Do you need to anticipate objections? Are you

aiming for gentle persuasion? Note that you *do* have a tone, and monitor it so that your tone is consistent throughout the paper.

2. How much do you need to put in your paper? How much is obvious and needn't be said? As a general rule, it is better to say too much and risk being obvious than to say too little and risk being obscure. In writing about a literary text, you might imagine that your audience read the work very carefully a year ago; that is, they are not ignorant of the text but they may need to be reminded of the details.

3. What is the main point of your paper? Is it clearly stated? Does your paper say what you want it to say?

4. Does everything in the paper support or in some way clearly connect with your main point? If not, you may have to leave something out, as much as you may like it.

5. Do your ideas and your overall argument or thesis develop from beginning to end? Or do you just keep repeating the same point in different words or, worse yet, in the same words? You may want to make a new outline between first draft and second.

6. Have you used evidence from the literary work to support your assertions? Remember that what you write about a quoted passage ought to aim at being at least as long as the quote itself. There are times when it makes sense to include a substantial quote and say something substantial about it. There are other times when you can incorporate a few quoted words from the text into your own sentences to give the flavor of a writer's style or thinking, without losing your own.

7. Have you considered using figurative language and narrative devices along with abstraction (as Lauri does in her paper) to provide variety and vividness?

8. Does your paper have moments of interest and excitement? Build on these. Try to make the rest of the paper come up to the standards you have set for yourself in your best moments.

9. Does your paper have your voice? Does it sound like you? Think about how a letter you write to a friend sounds like you and nobody else. An essay you write should have that much personality.

10. Title your paper. A good title is interesting in itself, is inviting to a reader, and in some way characterizes the paper as a whole.

11. A mnemonic: the final draft should be clear, comprehensive, concise and convincing.

12. Revise as many times as necessary. Each revision will be easier than the previous one.

Paragraphs

1. Does each paragraph cover one main point, however complex?
2. Does each paragraph have some version of a main or topic sentence?
3. Does each contain (and only contain) sentences that are relevant to the subject of that paragraph? Sentences that don't fit still may be relevant to the paper as a whole; they probably either belong in another paragraph already written or could become the topic sentence or in some way part of a new paragraph yet to be written.

4. You may find paragraphs in your paper which are wonderful but do not belong in this paper. Remove them from this paper and store them in your Brilliant Paragraph Box for use in a future paper.
5. Vary the structure and rhythm of your paragraphs. Don't make them all the same length and format. You will lose your reader to a deep slumber.

Beginnings and Endings

Opening paragraphs should be interesting and compelling and invite the reader into the paper. They should say something substantial about the subject of the paper either directly or indirectly and should be as graceful, powerful and polished as you can manage. If you find yourself with any extra time before the paper is due, you might spend it going over your opening paragraph one more time. But be careful not to hypnotize yourself out of clarity with the beauty of your own prose. However gorgeous it sounds, it still has to mean something. You might try aiming for clean lines and a deceptively simple elegance, like Torvill and Dean ice dancing a waltz.

Below are the effective opening paragraphs of three different short papers on the same assignment: "Is 'The Love Song of J. Alfred Prufrock' really a love song? Pay attention to how Prufrock sees himself and to the world T. S. Eliot has fashioned for Prufrock to walk around in."

1. "The Love Song of J. Alfred Prufrock" is a poem that is far removed from the subject of love. The absence of romance in the world of Prufrock is so ostensive that the poem actually mocks its title. Prufrock is as disillusioned by his tedious life as anyone who has ridden through life in the back seat.

2. "The Love Song of J. Alfred Prufrock" describes the journey of T. S. Eliot's symbol of modern man through the character's personal images of his society. This trip supposedly leads to the "overwhelming question" (l. 10) in everyone's life, but in fact, it only explains why Prufrock is not able to answer this question—at least not out loud. The cause of this suppression of true self which leads to Prufrock's false, unmeaningful, and most importantly, loveless life is his society—or, instead, his impressions of his society.

3. SHOULD I SPIT OUT THE BUTT-ENDS?
Dear J. A.,
You were leading me to an overwhelming question. You told me you were going to sing a love song, and I, unseasoned,

did as you bid and unquestioningly (. . . do not ask, "What is it?", l. 11) followed you, thinking all the while that you were leading me into romance. I know you can tell me that you warned me by quoting Dante, but I didn't understand your use of his epigraph until after we had made our visit.

The first of these three gets right to the main point by directly answering the question the instructor has posed with a firm "no"—this poem is not a love poem. The writer goes on to suggest that the absence of romance is so striking as to suggest irony or satire: "the poem actually mocks its title." The third and last sentence addresses itself to the rest of the topic by beautifully characterizing Prufrock's sense of self and relation to his world in the metaphor of riding through life in the back seat of a car. The vivid metaphor catches a reader's attention, pulling us into the paper in hope of more vivid images. It also embodies an apt and accurate insight about Prufrock. The use of metaphor, the compressed and concise language of poetry, allows this writer to say something significant in a very few words.

The second of these writers chooses to begin with the secondary rather than the main question the instructor has posed, that is, with Prufrock's relation to his world. He characterizes this relation as a journey and, further, asserts that Prufrock stands for all of us and his world for modern society. Though this writer does not create a metaphor like the first, he does quote from the poem ("overwhelming question") and gives us an image of Prufrock's avoidance of this question. The final sentence tells us that Prufrock's life is loveless as well as false and meaningless, and loops back to the opening sentence in his comment that the lack of love in Prufrock's life is tangled up with his vision of the world.

The third writer takes a more daring approach by addressing herself directly to Prufrock, casting her essay in the form of a letter to the protagonist of the poem. Here the title of the paper is an adaptation of a quote from the poem and certainly captures a reader's attention, as does the letter format. Since the poem itself is addressed to an invisible companion, it is reasonable and clever to assume a cloak of invisibility oneself and to enter the world of the poem. She quotes from the poem, she mentions the warning epigraph from Dante's *Inferno* and, though she doesn't come right out and say, as the other two writers do, that this is not a love song, you are pretty sure by the end of the paragraph that she thinks it is not.

All three of these opening paragraphs address themselves to the assigned paper topic. They all mix abstraction and idea with vivid imagery or narration and are interesting and provocative enough to encourage one to read on. There are many ways of beginning a paper about a work of literature; give yourself permission to play with the possibilities.

Closing paragraphs should say something substantial but not introduce new information; and, while they can be quietly powerful, they need not sound like Wagnerian opera. Mainly, they should leave readers with a sense of completion and with confidence in the writer, not hanging in mid air wondering where they are going to fall. Here is the concluding paragraph of a nine-paragraph paper on Alan Sillitoe's "The Loneliness of the Long-Distance Runner" (p. 1208).

> Sillitoe's intent is to demonstrate the hypocrisy of a system that condemns the antisocial behavior of those it excludes. He succeeds in showing that, for some, being an Out-law is the only means to a sense of self-worth.

The paper has been about the tension between the individual protagonist and the society he lives in. This writer's conclusion says something about both protagonist and setting and about how the tension between the two is resolved. He speaks both of the author's intent and of his achievement. He restates his thesis and succinctly summarizes his argument, though you'll have to take that on faith. The tone of this closing paragraph is confident but quiet, comprehensive as well as concise.

Sentences and Words

As you revise, look closely at your sentences. Read them aloud or have someone read them to you. Are they varied in length and complexity? You don't want the same sentence structure over and over. Is there a rhythm to the prose? Look for unnecessary repetitions of phrases or words and edit them out; pare the sentences down to their essentials, even if that means losing part of your count toward the required number of words. Are the main and subordinate clauses connected to each other in a way that makes sense? If you have incorporated quotations into your own sentences, they are now subject to the laws of your grammatical universe; that is, they must syntactically meld into the rest of the sentence they are in. We necessarily become more aware of our own style when we write about literature, since style is part of what we are writing about. Do at least a few of your sentences approach elegance? Pick out your very best sentence and use that as the standard to aim for in this essay.

Mark Twain, in his essay on "Fenimore Cooper's Literary Offenses," offers us a number of practical suggestions. The writer should "say what he is proposing to say, not merely come near it"; "use the right word, not its second cousin"; "eschew surplusage"; "not omit necessary details"; "avoid slovenliness of form"; "use good grammar"; and "employ a simple and straightforward style." Have you selected the word with the exact nuance you want? Think about the word you've chosen. Look it up in a dictionary or a thesaurus. Avoid words whose connotations you don't fully understand. Be economical with words; use one appropriate word instead of six or seven vague ones. Words are the basis, the ground of language, where the potential for power and clarity chiefly resides. This is certainly true in the literature you are writing about and can be increasingly true of your own writing. Each well-written literary work we read and study enriches our vocabulary and our own sense of style.

REVISING AND EDITING: AN EXAMPLE

Here is an example (in its first draft and revised versions) of a two-paragraph section of a student paper—an *explication* of Mary Oliver's short poem, "August."

August

When the blackberries hang
swollen in the woods, in the brambles
nobody owns, I spend

all day among the high
branches, reaching   5
my ripped arms, thinking

of nothing, cramming
the black honey of summer
into my mouth; all day my body

accepts what it is. In the dark   10
creeks that run by there is
this thick paw of my life darting among

the black bells, the leaves; there is
this happy tongue.

First Draft

In the poet's final metamorphosis into a tongue, she becomes another black bell shape among the leaves.

Her use of the color, black, is a consistent jab of hue throughout the poem. "Black" punctuates and gives a pulse in every stanza except the second, where the author is still in the process of becoming, maturing. She becomes as mature and psychically fulfilled as the ripe fruit she ingests and from which she gains nourishment.

Revised Version

In the fifth stanza, in the poet's final metamorphosis into a "tongue," she becomes another black bell shape among the leaves. She becomes as mature and psychically fulfilled as the ripe, black fruit which she ingests and from which she gains nourishment.

Oliver's use of the color black is consistent throughout the poem. "Black" punctuates and adds a pulse to every stanza except the second. She highlights important concepts of the poem with the use of this color in the gathering of blackberries; the oblique reference to a black bear and its fondness for honey, "the black honey of summer"; the changes of life in the "dark creeks"; and her final metamorphosis as part of nature, a black bell, a berry, a black "happy tongue."

Revision happens here in a number of ways. Most obvious, perhaps, is that the writer expands by adding in the second paragraph some significant detail from the poem to support her argument about recurring references to the color black. Second, she rearranges the order of her sentences, moving, for example, the sentence "She becomes as mature . . ." from the end of the second paragraph to the end of the first. She replaces that sentence with her list of references to "black," ending it by three references that loop back to the opening of the first paragraph—"a black bell, a berry, a black 'happy tongue.' " Her repetition of these images and the concept of metamorphosis provide a connective flow between the two paragraphs. And since the title of this paper is "Metamorphosis: An Explication of Mary Oliver's 'August'," the writer here has, by moving sentences around, kept the focus on what the main point of her whole paper is.

Moving the long sentence from paragraph two to paragraph one also makes that first paragraph more substantial. Though it is possible to have one-sentence paragraphs, we usually save those for special occasions. These two sentences do belong together, moreover, because "final metamorphosis" and "mature and psychically fulfilled" are concepts that support each other.

The writer cuts from this passage the reference to "still in the process of becoming, maturing"; it doesn't really belong here, since she deals with the developmental aspects of the persona's experience elsewhere in her paper.

As well as reorganizing and reconceptualizing, the writer has edited and polished her sentences. In the revised version, she begins by locating us precisely in the poem ("in the fifth stanza"), which she had not done in her first draft. In the second paragraph, she cuts out the phrase "jab of hue," which had probably been an attempt to jazz up the abstract quality of her thesis sentence. It isn't needed now that she has added, later in the sentence, much actual vivid detail from the poem. Finally, a small change of verb in the second sentence of the second paragraph: from "gives a pulse" to "adds a pulse." "Adds" is a bit more precise, a bit more vivid, than the all-purpose "gives."

Revision is not necessarily something a writer does once and is done with. Very rarely does a piece of writing come out right the second time or even the third. People who write for a living are well aware of this and revise anywhere from three to thirty or more times. The more complex the project, the more factors and components you are trying to fit into place, the more tinkering may be required before you get it the way you want it. Revising can be as creative and absorbing as the production of a first draft. Revision (re-visioning) is an essential stage in the writing process.

KINDS OF WRITING

Explication. In an explication, you go through the work line by line or sentence by sentence, sometimes word by word, unpacking the meanings of the work piece by piece. An explication of a literary work can easily be longer than the work itself, so this approach is usually confined to fairly short poems or to passages in a work of prose or poetry. In an explication, details are crucial and so is the relation of each detail to other details and to the work as a whole. A good explication depends on extremely close reading and while in itself it may seem of limited interest, it is a valuable exercise in learning how to focus on what is there in the literary text. In any writing about literature, explication is a useful tool.

Response. While explication is primarily text centered, a response is primarily reader centered. For example, did Levertov's poem "Life at War," mentioned earlier in this chapter, make you feel nauseous, angry, and sad about the waste of human potential in war? Write down the specific associations the poem evoked in you. If you responded to Mary Oliver's "August" by feeling sensual, happy, and free, and perhaps by remembering blackberry-picking expeditions of your own, then you are launched into a response piece of writing. Your responses to a work of literature and what in the text evoked them are information for you as a writer about literature and, in a response paper, are the main focus. In a response essay you might discuss as well any personal associations the poem or play pulled from you. Like explication, a response paper can be an enjoyable and useful writing project in itself. As techniques, both explication and response are also likely to provide ideas and material that you can use in other types of writing.

Analysis. To analyze means: (1) to separate something such as an idea into its parts to find out their nature, proportion, function, interrelationship; (2) to examine something in detail to determine its nature or tendencies. An analysis of a literary work usually focuses on a particular aspect of the work that will illuminate for your readers the work as a whole. What you choose to analyze needs to be limited enough that you can fully explore it and significant enough that your analysis will advance our understanding of the poem, story, play, or nonfictional work. You might decide that a good way to approach Meridel LeSueur's essay "Women on the Breadlines" (p. 888) would be to analyze the characteristics of the three representative women she describes and show how they create a composite portrait of the plight of women during the Great Depression. Or you might explore the relation between the first-person speaker of the poem in Adrienne Rich's "The Trees" (p. 1244) with the trees themselves, which disengage from their roots and begin to move.

Comparison/Contrast. This is a specific type of analysis. Here you are working with at least two literary works or at least two aspects of one text. You might compare and contrast the experience of women in the Depression as presented in LeSueur's "Women on the Breadlines" and the experience of men during the Depression as it appears in the selection from Tom Kromer's *Waiting for Nothing* (p. 713). It is generally helpful as an early step in comparison/contrast writing to make lists of similarities and differences and to decide which are most important and which less so. You will need to decide whether you find the similarities or the differences more striking; that will help give you your thesis. You might be asked to compare and/or contrast characters within one literary work, for example the three daughters in *King Lear* (p. 221). In structuring a comparison/contrast paper, you might choose to interpret or characterize each work in turn, then analyze the differences. This approach works best in a short paper. Or you might choose to write a point-by-point analysis, each paragraph taking one aspect of the topic and discussing both works in relation to that topic. For example, one paragraph on LeSueur and Kromer might discuss starving quietly versus begging for one's supper. Another might explore what options for survival are open to LeSueur's characters versus Kromer's, and so on. In this kind of analysis, as in any other, you need to deal with all the relevant evidence. That is, you cannot ignore some aspect of the work simply because it doesn't fit your theory.

Review. If you are writing on a whole book (or play or film), try writing a review. Unlike the usual essay on literature, a review assumes your reader has not yet read the book (or seen the play or film) under consideration. So you need to provide enough information about the plot, characters, or overall structure so that your reader can follow you, but you don't want to say so much that your review turns into pure summary or so that you leave nothing to your reader's imagination. As well as describing a book, a review makes a judgment, an evaluation. Was it good or bad, moving or boring, significant or trivial? Why and how? Further, you might want to tell your readers what is singular or special about this book for *you:* characters, language or style, images, politics, balance or arrangement of elements. Give your readers a sense of the texture of the work by quoting from it, but briefly. You might want to put the particular work into a context such as the writer's other works, similar works by the writer's contemporaries, the literary tradition out of which she or he is writing, or the history of the issue written about. You can praise the book, pan it, or write a response somewhere in between, weighing the pros and cons; your judgment of the work will affect the tone of your review. Whatever your opinion, it needs to be backed up with evidence. Be true to your own response and try to write the complexity of that response (far beyond "I liked it" or "I hated it") into the review itself. A *review article*, usually longer than a simple review, does all the above, pays more attention to matters of context, and, in some cases, covers more than one book.

Research paper. Perhaps you will be asked to write a paper that takes into account more than the literary text, you as reader, and your social context. A research assignment might ask that you find out more about a particular writer's life and times and put the literary work into a context that is biographical, social and historical, philosophical and political, or literary historical. Or a research paper might require you to read what other literary critics and historians have said about a particular play, poem, or story. If you are writing a research paper, try to develop a few ideas and a thesis or main point of your own about the literary work before you begin your research. It is hard not to be overwhelmed by the fully worked-through analyses you will encounter in contrast to your own tentative insights at this stage. If you have a good idea of what you want to say about the text (subject to evolution, of course), then you can engage in dialogue with other literary critics rather than feel squashed by their finished, multiply revised, authoritatively-in-print discussions. You may use or discard, agree or disagree with what others have said about a literary work, but remember that the paper you are writing is your own.

Critical reading journal. It can be extremely useful to keep an ongoing journal of your reading in a literature course. Such a journal can function on a number of levels, either separately or simultaneously: (1) explication and analysis of individual texts; (2) your responses, emotional, intellectual, and political, to works of literature; (3) the connections you make, as the semester and your reading go on, between the literary texts you are reading—comparisons and contrasts between characters, ways of writing, recurring themes, social issues; (4) connections between the literature and your own life; (5) arguments with or further explorations of points brought up in class discussion; and (6) experiments in creative writing of your own, perhaps in the mode of a writer you are studying. Following the last suggestion, you might write an opening paragraph that provides a setting and an atmosphere, or try a character sketch, or write a short poem based on one extended image. If you write two or three pages a week in your journal, you will have a substantial amount of writing and a record of your thinking about the literature by the end of the semester. The journal is also a valuable source for any papers you might be asked to write. The trick here is to keep up with your journal week by week and not fall behind.

The writing in a critical reading journal tends to be less formal than in most essays, but it still needs to be clearly organized with the sentences well constructed. You might explore a topic such as the importance of having a job in three short stories by working-class writers, for a couple of paragraphs, then leave a space and move on to something else, like how Tillie Olsen's "I Stand Here Ironing" (p. 680) made you wonder how your own mother thought about you.

PASSAGES FROM STUDENT CRITICAL READING JOURNALS

Here are several examples of passages from critical reading journals, all of them written in the same course. They exemplify the way a reading journal can include many different types of writing, from explication to response and from analysis to experiments in creative writing. These excerpts also demonstrate the way in which the more relaxed format of the reading journal encourages an authentic, lively, and individual writing voice.

1. A response to Tillie Olsen's short story, "I Stand Here Ironing," in which the student identifies with the character of Emily and remembers her own experience as the oldest child in a working-class family:

> In the story Olsen describes the desperate situation many working class mothers find themselves in when they have young children or babies who need their attention and not enough time or energy to give that attention. The situation of course is an economic one, in which the type of care a mother gives her child is controlled by economic factors. As a woman who has not had children, yet is the oldest of six in a working class family I can identify more with some of Emily's experiences. In a large working-class family early childhood responsibilities often fall to the oldest child, especially if that child is female. As a child of six or seven I was standing on a chair pulled up to the sink in order to

wash dishes, by the age of eleven I was cooking meals for four younger siblings. There were more than a few times when I had been left in charge that every strange sound in a house devoid of adults became sinister and amplified beyond measure. On Friday nights when both our parents were working we had frozen food for supper. As keeper of the peace, it was always my responsibility to count the contents of every box and make sure that each person got their fair share.

Early childhood responsibility is something which I think is typical of most working class families. I had occasion to talk one day with a woman who was 94 years old. As I fed her her breakfast she talked about her childhood. She was one of nine children and she had left school in the seventh grade to work. "If I wanted a pair of new shoes, I had to work for them," she said with a mixture of pride and wistfulness. "Black patent leather shoes with cloth tops and seven buttons. That was real class in those days."

2. An analysis of Alice Walker's "Everyday Use" (p. 733) in which the student disagrees with the class discussion of the story:

It was said in class that Dee wanted certain things from her mother's home only because being aware of one's roots was a fashionable thing to do. The story actually backs up this line of reasoning; after all, Dee wants to use the quilts for wall coverings and the churn top for a centerpiece. She only wants to use them as showpieces, examples of her "heritage." Dee is more interested in how the pieces will make her look more chic than she is about how much the family really depends on those things for survival. As much as the story backs up this opinion there is something in me that tends to disagree with it. I believe (and don't ask me why) that Dee really needs those things almost as much as her family does. She needs them in order to remember her working-class background even though it appears that she despises it. She is caught between a rock and a hard place. As much as she wants to despise her background she cannot deny the existence of it. Using her family's furniture as quaint showpieces is her way of coping with this strange paradox.

I am not completely satisfied with my own explanation of this story and Dee. This uneasiness on my part is probably due to the ambivalence I feel toward the character of Dee. I can't really figure out what I think. I read the story and look at the character one way. Then I read it again and I look at her in another way. I decided I can't figure her out because she can't figure herself out.

3.   An explication of two lines of Judy Grahn's poem about a truck-stop waitress, "Ella, in a square apron, on Highway 80" (p. 785):

In Ella's poem, her message or image came in two lines: "Like some isolated lake, her flat blue eyes take care of their own stark bottoms. / Her hands are nervous, curled, ready to strike." Grahn delivers Ella to me on a few different levels: she is alone and self sufficient, unafraid to take care of herself and ready to strike out at those who try to stand in her way, and yet, at the same time she is not a cruel or malicious person, for she is likened to the beauty of a solemn lake. She is a woman who understands self-preservation and also the price one must pay for it.

4.   An explication/analysis of Carolyn Chute's "Tall Woman Love," which connects that prose piece to a current political issue, gentrification, and also to two short stories read in the class previously, Mary Wilkins Freeman's "A Mistaken Charity" (p. 148) and Alice Walker's "Everyday Use":

Having read it several times, I have come to the conclusion that "Tall Woman Love" is about a middle-class man, March, moving into a working-class neighborhood. As is often the case nowadays when old neighborhoods are sited for reno-vation, middle-class tenants move in at low prices and when the neighborhood is completely renovated, a neat profit is made by the "pioneers." All this happens, of course, at the expense of the lower class who are eventually forced out of their neighborhood because of the rising wealth and even-tually pushed into other, less expensive areas of housing. None of the profits are seen by the original tenants, the working class. Partly I draw this conclusion from the date of the writing, 1985; but partly also because of the obvious conflict, or clash, between March and his neighbors, the Beans.
March is a wealthy engineer. We know he's wealthy be-cause he has a shiny forest-green Lincoln; we know he's educated because he's an engineer and also because he tries to exert his "authority" during his exchange with Mrs. Bean. March, though, is the outsider here; he is the "new neighbor." This is why he is so uncomfortable. Roberta Bean, on the other hand, is portrayed as hickish ("Eyup") and rather slow in intelligence but quick in strength. . . .

Chute portrays her characters not through narrative but through actions. She describes each one's physical details, yes; but she shows us their personalities in the description of their actions. Her writing is compact, concentrated and precise. The amount of information she conveys to her reader in such a few short pages is awesome. I admire this type of writing simply because of its precision. Everything is important. Most important, though, I derived a sense of triumph for Roberta Bean. She comes out seeming more intelligent even than March, who looks rather foolish in spite of his control (which he nearly loses).

Roberta's strength here reminds me of the Shattuck sisters in "A Mistaken Charity." They are all strong women of working-class backgrounds unashamed of their lifestyles. In fact, I can even add Dee's mother from "Everyday Use" to this group of female characters. Roberta's strength, though, doesn't get in the way of her charitable impulse to help a neighbor, which brings a touch of humor to Chute's story.

5.   One student's response to and analysis of a class discussion of Richard Wright's "The Man Who Went to Chicago" (p. 895) followed by another student's reaction to the same episode in Wright's essay:

a) . . . the question which arose in class the other day about whether or not Richard Wright was writing as an angry man seems rhetorical (some of my classmates conjecturing that, indeed, he didn't "sound that angry"—that Wright was surprisingly measured and analytical when discussing his experience as a black man in America in the 1930s and 40s). But all one had to do was to give pause to Wright's allusion to the stair washing incident in order to imagine the incredible rage he must have felt: Hell, I got pissed off just reading about it, never mind experiencing it. To think that people could discount a man's labor to such a degree that they openly mocked his efforts (and they were educated people—part of the medical community) and even sought to vandalize his work is enough to make the reader scream out in angry protest and frustration. So how must Mr. Wright have felt when "a sadistically observant white man would notice that he had tracked dirty water up the steps, and he would look back down at me and smile and say: Boy, we sure keep you busy, don't we? And I would not be able to answer . . ."? Angry? We must be kidding. There are times when I truly believe that if I were a black person in America that I would go out, buy a rifle, and shoot every white person that I saw. I mean, to be black and to be aware of the legacy that America has foisted upon people of color and not want to destroy America—burn it to the ground—takes an incredible amount of self-control, probably unfathomable to most of us who have lived in the favored role, as the Western European descendants of privilege.

And so, again, the point is not whether Wright was angry, but rather it's how was he able to focus this anger in such a way as to illuminate the American experience in his brilliant manner. It is part of his genius that he is able to take the stuff of which rage is made and fashion it into works of both power and intelligence.

b) Why bother washing the stairs if White America keeps walking over it?

The answer is simple, either stop washing the stairs or stop White America from walking over them. Simple, right? Oh, wait a minute, I forgot about discrimination, powerlessness, self-hate, ambiguous feelings about who the enemy really is, and inability to change the system.

6. Two examples of creative writing, one poem and one prose piece, inspired by the literature students were reading that semester:

a)

My other job

Familiar faces every day
Some say "The usual."
I grab their brand of cigarettes
before they ask for it.
Megabucks   5
The Numbers Game
"Gimme 3674 across the board"
I finish punching the numbers.
"Three dollars please."
I know all their names.   10
I can tell you whether they like
Coke or Pepsi.
I know everything
about them. When I go home
I forget they exist.   15

b)

Going Up

I have never lived in a house that had an upstairs. Sure I've walked up the stairs, two flights, eleven steps each, of

gray gritty cement to get to my family's apartment, but I
have never gone upstairs. Many times I've wished that I
could say, "Goodnight, I'm going upstairs." It sounds so
homey, so damn middle class comfortable. My family has
always lived in multiple unit dwellings. First, a three family
my father purchased or, more correctly, mortgaged when he
was fresh out of the Navy, then a six family (the very house
my father's father bought when he was fresh out of the
Army), and then a two family. Never, never a house that
was ours and ours alone. I hate mailboxes that have more
than one name on them. I guess that going up the stairs
instead of upstairs was a symptom, a brand that shouted
obscenely our economic situation. We were poor. Not cabbage
soup poor, not cardboard bottom shoe poor, not even uncle
sam could you spare some change poor. We were ugly day
to day getting by poor.

SAMPLE PAPER: FIRST DRAFT AND REVISION

The assignment was to write a three page (600–800 word) explication
of a poem, concentrating on sound and image patterns. This student chose
to write on Carolyn Forché's prose poem, "The Colonel" (p. 997). Look
again at the suggestions for revision given earlier in this chapter. Specifically, how and where has this writer edited and rethought her paper?
Are there any further revisions you would want to add?

First Draft

Have You Heard What the Colonel Said?

Carolyn Forché's poem "The Colonel" is presented to the
reader in a blank verse prose form. A prose poem is written
in a short block form resembling a paragraph except for the
density of the poem and the lack of indentation. The prose
form allows us to concentrate on the serious subject and
tone of the poem. Using brief yet explicit sentences, Forché
creates the tense act and impression that is repeatedly heard
through her choice of words and form that describes the
situation. The words and sounds are entirely significant to
the poem because they develop and create very sensuous and
concrete images and also include many strong connotations.
They describe the environment, the mood, the characters and
their feelings. Some of the sounds in "The Colonel" are hard
and cacaphonic. There were "daily papers, pet dogs, a pistol

on the cushion beside him." Here Forché is using alliteration of the cacaphonic "p" sound to emphasize the pistol which suddenly upsets the regularity of the image we start to create when we read: ". . . daily papers, pet dogs. . . ." There is a subtle rhythm to the poem, giving it an even tone that reflects the emotional statement of the narrator.

In short successions of sentences the poem builds until it reveals the dreadfullness of the encounter and the revulsion displayed by the colonel's message to his visitors. "What you have heard is true. I was in his house." We are introduced to the narrator as she speaks to her fellow comrades perhaps, recalling the incident involving a dinner at a colonel's home one evening. The narrator goes on to briefly describe the colonel's family. "His wife carried a tray of coffee and sugar. His daughter filed her nails, his son went out for the night." In this brief introduction the narrator declares much about the attitudes of the family. Clearly the ignorance to the violence at hand is displayed through the simple unmoving actions displayed by his family. The syntactical repetition of the pronoun "his" in these two sentences emphasize the powerful image of the colonel in his home.

The narrator describes the exterior of the house in a jagged manner. There is violence, illustrated all around from the impression given. "The moon swung bare on its black cord over the house. On the television was a cop show. It was in English. Broken bottles were embedded in the walls around the house to scoop the kneecaps from a man's legs or cut his hands to lace. On the windows there were gratings like those in a liquor store." From these images I see the moon perceived with a sense of gloom, hanging on a black cord like the execution that takes place during the night. There is the blood of the poor and desperate dried on the walls of the colonel's house and on his living soul. Even the television show is violent.

They dine on. . . . "We had dinner, rack of lamb, good wine. A gold bell was on the table for calling the maid. The maid brought green mangoes, salt, a type of bread." The repetition of the initial consonant sound as in good, gold, and green connects the dinner in a flowing manner. This image seems very civilized and festive, with all the ingredients of a nice well mannered meal so this image adds a twist to the violent scene and heightens the tension of the poem.

Following dinner, the narrator is asked how he enjoyed the country. "There was a brief commercial in Spanish. His wife took everything away. There was some talk about how difficult it had become to govern." Each sentence here is linked together yet separate. While the narrator is asked how she enjoys the country, our attention is suddenly focused on the "brief commercial in Spanish," as if there was nothing she could say truthfully about the situation of the country to this imposing colonel without creating a violent reaction. Then there is "talk" of how difficult it has become to govern. There seems to be no real conversation, just "talk" and I assume from the statement that the colonel is doing all the speaking. The mood is too heavy at the colonel's home for an open discussion of opposing political views.

"The parrot said hello on the terrace. The colonel told him to shut up, and pushed himself from the table. My friend said to me with his eyes: say nothing." At this moment the tension is thick and the turning point is descending upon us. The colonel is obviously about to reveal something of great significance. The colonel comes back carrying a sack. He empties its contents, human ears. He shook an ear in their face and forced them to watch as he soaks the dried ear as if he wanted the dead among the living native people to hear his message "As for the rights of your people tell them to go fuck themselves." Here the brutality of the colonel is fully manifested. Like Forché says, "There is no other way to say this." The simplicity of the statement is intentional, because there is no other way to say this. The gruesome horror exposed through the colonel's actions and statement strikes us in the face with brutal force. The colonel is almost finished with his guest as he said, "Something for your poetry, no? Some of the ears on the floor caught this scrap in his voice. Some of the ears on the floor were pressed to the ground." The last two lines imply that some of the persecuted people knew why they were being executed while others did not. In the last sentence I picture the victims' ears literally being pressed to the ground.

The poetic craft displayed in "The Colonel" is Forché's use of the narratative voice which allows the reader to interact with the poem. The brief yet explicit sentences lead us through the sequences of the evening stating clearly the tone, atmosphere, and meaning of "The Colonel."

Revision

Have You Heard What the Colonel Said?

Carolyn Forché's poem "The Colonel" is presented to the reader in a blank verse prose form. A prose poem is written in a short block form resembling a paragraph except for the density of the poem and lack of indentation. The prose form allows us to concentrate on the serious subject and tone of the poem. Using brief yet explicit sentences, Forché creates the tense act and impression that is repeatedly heard through her choice of words and form that describe the situation. The words and sounds are entirely significant to the poem because they develop and create very sensuous and concrete images and also include many strong connotations. Forché uses alliteration, assonance, consonance and repetition to enhance the poem's meaning and mood. There is a subtle rhythm to the poem, giving it an even tone that reflects the emotional statement of the narrator.

In the sound pattern of "The Colonel", the use of alliteration is smooth and balanced throughout the poem to reveal the horror and accentuate the revulsion of this visit to the colonel's home. For example: "There were daily papers, pet dogs, a pistol on the cushion beside him." Here Forché is using alliteration of the cacophonic plosive sounds to emphasize the pistol which suddenly upsets the regularity of the image we start to create when we read: ". . . daily papers, pet dogs. . . ."

"What you have heard is true. I was in his house." We are introduced to the narrator as she speaks to her fellow comrades perhaps, recalling the incident involving a dinner at the colonel's home one evening. The narrator goes on to briefly describe the colonel's family. "His wife carried a tray of coffee and sugar. His daughter filed her nails, his son went out for the night." The family's tranquil attitude is contrasted to the hardened feelings towards violence displayed by the colonel. This gives the sense that his family is protected by his violent actions. The syntactical repetition of the pronoun "his" in these two sentences emphasizes the powerful image of the colonel in his home.

The narrator describes the house in a frightening manner. The impression of violence that surrounds the house is described in:

The moon swung bare on its black cord over the house. On the television was a cop show. It was in English. Broken bottles were embedded in the walls around the house to scoop the kneecaps from a man's legs or cut his hands to lace. On the windows there were gratings like those in liquor stores.

From these images the moon is cast in a shadow of gloom, hanging on a black cord like the execution that takes place during the night. There is blood of the poor and desperate dried on the walls of the colonel's house and on his living soul. Even the television show is violent. Combining concrete images and serious alliteration, the sound heightens our senses to the imagery of the exterior.

They dine: "We had dinner, rack of lamb, good wine. A gold bell was on the table for calling the maid. The maid brought green mangoes, salt, a type of bread." The repetition of the initial consonant sound, as in good, gold, and green connects the dinner in a flowing manner. Also using commas to enhance the alliteration and build up to a climax, Forché adds a twist to the violent scene by adding civilized festive images to the underlying hostility of this meeting with the colonel.

Following dinner, the narrator is asked how she enjoys the country. "There was a brief commercial in Spanish. His wife took everything away. There was some talk of how difficult it had become to govern." Each sentence here is linked together yet separate. While the narrator is asked how she enjoys the country, our attention is suddenly focused on the brief commercial in Spanish, as if there were nothing she could say truthfully about the situation of the country to this imposing colonel without creating a violent reaction.

The colonel returns to the table carrying a sack. He empties its contents. At this moment the tension is thick and the climax is descending upon us. Human ears of the colonel's victims are spilled on the table in front of his visitors. He shook an ear in their faces and forced them to watch as he soaked the dried ear as if he wanted the dead among the living native people to hear his message: "As for the rights of your people, tell them to go fuck themselves." Here the brutality of the colonel is fully manifested. Like Forché says, "There is no other way to say this." The gruesome horror exposed through the colonel's actions and statement strikes us in the face with brutal force.

Forché uses repetition in these two sentences: "Some of the ears on the floor caught this scrap in his voice. Some of the ears on the floor were pressed to the ground." The repetition of these images reemphasize the persecution of the native people. It seems to me the connotation implied by these two sentences is that some of the people knew why they were being executed while others did not. In the last sentence I picture the victims' ears literally being pressed to the ground by the colonel and his men.

In short successions of sentences the poem builds until it reveals the dreadfulness of the encounter and revulsion displayed by the colonel's message to his visitors. The simple sentence structure and concrete sounds intermingle and produce very real and concrete images. The tone of "The Colonel" is flat and unobtrusive. This sound pattern enhances the sequences of events by letting the sounds and word choices increase the tension. If this poem were written in verse it would make too much of an appeal on our emotions towards the colonel and the subject of the poem. The simple sentences disclose the violence and anger that is felt by the narrator and addressed to the audience. The sound pattern, using alliteration, consonance, assonance and repetition, adds to the development of this prose poem.

MANUSCRIPT FORM

It is not a good idea in general to concern yourself with conventions for quoting passages and documenting sources until near the end of the writing process. It would be a shame to lose your writing momentum, to derail an interesting and productive train of thought, in order to work out the exact form for a footnote or to ponder whether the comma goes before or after the quotation mark in the middle of a sentence. But these matters must be faced eventually and, if you handle them correctly, your paper will be more readable for the effort.

Titles

Only the most abstract criticism could avoid mentioning the title of a work of literature, so it is useful to learn the conventions for handling titles. In general, titles of books, full-length plays, films, and periodicals—works that are published as independent physical entities—are italicized in print or underlined when typed: *Catch-22* or *King Lear*, for example. On the other hand, titles of *parts of* books or periodicals—such as poems, short stories, essays, and one-act plays—are enclosed in quotation marks: "Everyday Use," "Trifles," and so on. (If you read newspapers often, you may find this confusing; since newspapers generally do not use italics, they enclose *all* titles in quotation marks.) For your own title, use neither underlining nor quotation marks. And with any title, capitalize the first word, the last word, and all other words except prepositions, coordinating conjunctions, and articles.

Quotations

Quotations from the work or works of literature you are discussing can often clarify and enrich your writing. Quotations can serve as evidence for points you want to argue and can help you give your readers a feel for the work itself. But you should avoid quoting too often and should only quote a passage at length if you discuss it in some detail. Your own words should provide adequate context and identification for whatever you quote, so that your reader does not get lost.

Generally, quotations of more than four typed lines of prose or more than two lines of poetry should be set off from your own text. Indent each line of these "block" quotations ten spaces from the left margin, and do not use quotation marks (except any in the original), since the indenting itself indicates that you are quoting.

Shorter quotations should simply be integrated into your text, with quotation marks at the beginning and at the end of the quotation:

> The narrator in "A Drop in the Bucket" remembers Cousin Tryphena's "somnolent, respectable, unprofitable life."

Short quotations of poetry that span the break between lines should preserve any capitalization at the beginning of a new line and should use a slash to indicate where each new line begins:

> Death had entered the Garden of Love, for the speaker "saw it was filled with graves, / And tomb-stones where flowers should be."

It is essential to quote your original source accurately, but you may sometimes want to insert or delete words for the sake of clarity, brevity, or smooth integration of the quotation into your own text. An insertion is enclosed in square brackets and a deletion is indicated with an ellipsis (three dots):

> "He [Nelson Reed] was a steady husband . . . and a deacon in the Baptist church," we learn early in the story.

In a block quotation, the deletion of a paragraph or more of prose or a line or more of poetry is indicated by a line of spaced dots:

> We are warned to be especially careful this time of year:
> He knows if you are sleeping.
> . . . .
> He knows if you've been bad or good.

Here, though literally only two lines of poetry are quoted, the block format is preferable because otherwise the combination of ellipsis and line breaks would be awkward.

Punctuating short quotations that are merged with your own text takes some care. Periods and commas go inside (that is, before) closing quotation marks, unless the quotation is followed by page number, line number, or other information about the source of the quotation:

> Owen describes the dying soldier's face as "like a devil's sick of sin."

But:

> "Anger sputters in her brainpan" (line 9), Piercy writes of the housewife.

Punctuation marks other than periods and commas go outside the quotation marks, unless they belong to the quoted material:

> What does the chief engineer mean by "irresponsible victims"?

But:

> Hayden ends with a question that gains force through repetition: "What did I know, what did I know / of love's austere and lonely offices?"

Finally, in short quotations, when the quoted material itself contains quotation marks, they are replaced by *single* quotation marks:

> Her mother, the narrator, says that Maggie "thinks her sister has held life always in the palm of one hand, that 'no' is a word the world never learned to say to her."

Documentation

A source may be classified as either a primary source, that is, a work of literature you are writing about, or a secondary source, a work related to or about the primary source such as a biography, a history, or a work of literary criticism. The mechanics of quoting are the same for secondary sources as they are for primary sources, as previously described. Your writing should indicate what sources you used and how you used them. If you quote from a source, you need to indicate where in that source you quoted from. If you borrow ideas from a secondary source—even if you don't copy the language of that source—you need to document that borrowing as well. Documentation can help an interested reader pursue your ideas further or a skeptical reader check up on you. Documentation can also serve to distinguish your own ideas from those you discovered in secondary sources, a distinction most instructors consider very important.

There are two major systems for documenting sources. Traditionally, a raised number in the text points to a numbered note at the bottom of the page (a footnote) or at the end of an essay (an endnote) which provides bibliographical information about the source. Since 1984, the Modern Language Association, borrowing from the sciences and the social sciences, has recommended a "Works Cited" approach, in which a single alphabetical list at the end of an essay provides bibliographical data about all sources, and brief parenthetical references in the text point to particular items in the list. The footnote/endnote method is probably easier for readers, while the Works Cited method is undoubtedly easier for writers.

Since both methods are still in use, both will be explained here, at least briefly. For a fuller explanation of both methods, see Joseph Gibaldi and Walter S. Achtert's *MLA Handbook for Writers of Research Papers*, 2nd ed. (New York: MLA, 1984).

1. The Works Cited Approach

A list of works cited should come after the end of your text and begin on a new page, headed simply, Works Cited. The list should include all works and only those works explicitly cited in the text. Works should be listed alphabetically, by author's last name or, if the name is unknown, by title. If there are two or more works by one author, they should be listed one after another, arranged in reverse chronological order by publication date; and in entries after the first, the author's name should be replaced by three hyphens. Each entry should begin at the left margin and lines after the first line of an entry should be indented five spaces.

The list below illustrates the form for several common types of Works Cited entries:

A book by one author

Williams, Raymond. *Drama From Ibsen to Brecht*. New York: Oxford UP, 1969.

(Note that periods follow the author's name, the title, and the publication data; a colon follows the place of publication; and a comma follows the publisher's name. "UP" stands for "University Press.")

A book by two authors

Gilbert, Sandra M., and Susan Gubar. *The Madwoman in the Attic: The Woman Writer and the Nineteenth-Century Literary Imagination*. New Haven: Yale UP, 1979.

(Note that the name of the second author is in normal order: first name, then last name.)

A work in an anthology or collection

McKay, Claude. "The White House." *Black Voices: An Anthology of Afro-American Literature*. Ed. Abraham Chapman. New York: New American Library, 1968. 375.

("Ed." means "edited by." The number after the date indicates the page on which the poem appears.)

Multiple works in an anthology or collection

Chapman, Abraham, ed. *Black Voices: An Anthology of Afro-American Literature*. New York: New American Library, 1968.

Wright, Richard. "The Ethics of Living Jim Crow." Chapman 288–98.

(If you are citing more than one work from an anthology, you can either: (1) provide a full citation, like the preceding McKay citation, for each; or, (2) provide one full citation, under the editor's name, for the anthology itself, and then use a shortened citation for each work in the anthology that you want to refer to.)

An introduction, preface, foreword, or afterword

Aaron, Daniel. Introduction. *The Disinherited.* By Jack Conroy. New York: Hill and Wang, 1963. vii–xiv.

A translation

Duras, Marguerite. *The War: A Memoir.* Trans. Barbara Bray. New York: Pantheon, 1986.

A journal article

Herzog, Tobey C. "Writing About Vietnam: A Heavy Heart-of-Darkness Trip." *College English* 41 (1980): 680–95.
(The number immediately after the title of the journal is the volume number. *College English* numbers pages continuously; there are eight monthly issues per volume and each new volume, rather than each new issue, begins with page 1. If, instead, a journal begins each new *issue* with page 1, then the year and page number(s) alone will usually not suffice to point to a unique place in the volume and a more precise date such as "(March 1980)" or "(Spring 1980)" is necessary.)

Parenthetical references in your text will indicate that you have quoted from or used ideas or information from specific sources in the Works Cited list. The items in this list are whole works (books, articles, poems, etc.), but you will usually want to cite particular pages of these works, so your parenthetical citations should indicate page numbers as well as sources. In general, a parenthetical citation should include the minimum information necessary to point to a specific place in a unique work on the list.

If your Works Cited list contains only one work by the author in question, you can simply provide the author's last name and the page number(s) you wish to cite:

She sees "a supernatural weariness in his smile" (Duras 54).

The parenthetical citation here tells us that the quote appears on page 54 of the work by Duras on the list of Works Cited. If your text itself indicates the author you are citing, you can simply supply the page number:

Duras sees "a supernatural weariness in his smile" (54).

If two authors on your list have the same last name, supply the first name as well in parenthetical citations. If the work cited has two authors, use the last name of each: (Gilbert and Gubar 26). If there is no known author, supply the full or a shortened version of the title. If the list contains more than one work by the same author, use the author's name together with a full or shortened version of the title: (Williams, *Drama* 147).

2. The Footnote/Endnote Approach

The traditional method of documenting sources uses raised numbers in the text, each of which corresponds to a numbered footnote at the bottom of the page or endnote at the end of the essay. The 1984 *MLA Handbook* recommends endnotes over footnotes, but footnotes still have their champions. Notes of either kind are numbered consecutively, beginning with "1," and the raised number in the text follows any punctuation except a dash.

Here is the text:

She sees "a supernatural weariness in his smile."[1]

Here is the corresponding note:

[1] Marguerite Duras, *The War: A Memoir*, trans. Barbara Bray (New York: Pantheon, 1986) 54.

This approach differs from the Works Cited approach in several ways. The page number here is provided not in the text, but in the note, along with the rest of the bibliographical information. Since there is no Works Cited list to be alphabetized by last name, the author's name appears in normal order in notes. And the first line of each note is indented five spaces, while any lines that follow begin at the left margin.

Note 1 illustrates the form for a translated book. Following are other examples from the earlier discussion of the Works Cited approach, but recast as notes. Each illustrates the form for a common type of source:

[2] Raymond Williams, *Drama From Ibsen to Brecht* (New York: Oxford UP, 1969) 147.

[3] Sandra M. Gilbert and Susan Gubar, *The Madwoman in the Attic: The Woman Writer and the Nineteenth-Century Literary Imagination* (New Haven: Yale UP, 1979) 36.

[4] Claude McKay, "The White House," *Black Voices: An Anthology of Afro-American Literature*, ed. Abraham Chapman (New York: New American Library, 1968) 375.

[5] Daniel Aaron, introduction, *The Disinherited*, by Jack Conroy (New York: Hill and Wang, 1963) ix.

[6] Tobey C. Herzog, "Writing About Vietnam: A Heavy Heart-of-Darkness Trip," *College English* 41 (1980): 687.

Full documentation need not be provided in references after the first reference to a particular work. Generally, the author's last name and the appropriate page number(s) will suffice, though more information (such as a first name or a shortened title) may sometimes be necessary to avoid ambiguity. A second reference to the article cited in note 6 might use a note like this:

[7] Herzog 690–91.

If the same work is cited many times in succession in the text, as it well may be in an essay about a single literary work, citations after the first may be given parenthetically (simply the page number) rather than in notes. This can reduce the needless clutter of a series of notes that are identical except for page numbers. And if the same work is cited repeatedly, but not successively, the author's last name plus the page number(s) can substitute for a note.

Final Manuscript Preparation

Unless your instructor tells you otherwise, try to follow these general guidelines. If it is at all possible, type your essay; if you cannot type it, write neatly with dark ink. Double space your entire essay, including block quotations, footnotes, and the list of Works Cited, and leave top, bottom, left, and right margins of at least an inch. Use white, 8 ½ × 11-inch paper, avoid onionskin and other thin or erasable paper, and type on one side only. Make sure your typewriter or printer ribbon prints reasonably dark, and if you use a dot matrix printer that has more than one print mode, use the highest quality mode. If you print on fanfold computer paper, tear off the sprocket hole strips on each side and separate the sheets.

Put a title and your name at the top of the first page. Number each page and put your last name before the page number on each page after the first, in case your pages get separated. Proofread your paper carefully and make corrections in pen. Keep a photocopy, carbon, or extra print-out of your paper in case the original is lost. Last, simply paper clip the pages together; avoid binders or staples and save your instructor a headache or a puncture wound trying to undo them.

GROWING UP AND
GROWING OLDER

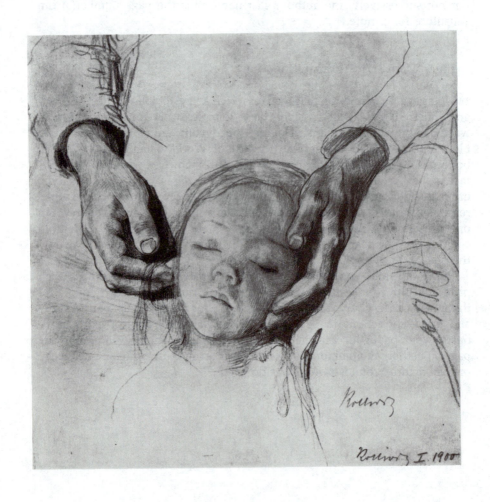

Birth, childhood, puberty, adolescence and adulthood, pregnancy, childbirth and parenting, middle age, aging and old age, death whether it comes early or late: stretching behind us and before us are all the other stages of life, in addition to whichever one we are currently struggling with and enjoying. Writers have celebrated, explored, and puzzled about the entire continuum of human life, sometimes focusing on a moment in the journey between birth and death, sometimes merging events and images from different stages (as when on the brink of adulthood we might look back at a significant moment in our childhood that helps us understand who we are now), sometimes telling in circular or linear fashion the story of an entire life. As readers, our own sense of the variety, complexity, and continuity of human life is enriched by the array of human lives we touch through literature. More often than we might suspect, a life stage is the subject of a work of literature: an insight fueled by a protagonist's or persona's sudden awareness of the slide from middle to old age, for example, or conversely, the arrival at adulthood.

How do people, in life and in literature, construct and maintain an identity as they move through the stages of life, growing up and growing older? What provides continuity? What provokes change? How do people cope with the changes that different life stages bring? Though we might want to think of this as an essentially solitary process, how we as individuals experience the various stages of life is inextricably tied to our social context.

What would the experience of birth and infancy be like if we had all been test-tube babies? In the opening scenes of *Brave New World*, Aldous Huxley shows us an assembly line of bottled babies and their early conditioning, before and after they are "decanted," for the social roles from laborer through technician to ruler that they will be expected to fill as adults. Huxley's "brave new world," his totally planned society, represents an extreme example of social conditioning but, like all dystopian (that is, anti-utopian) writers, he shows us through extrapolation and exaggeration the tendencies and possibilities of our own present world.

We are all conditioned, however subtly, by the social expectations and assumptions of and about our gender, race, social class, and culture, and by the historical period in which we live. We are continually pushed toward our "proper" role; sometimes the conditioning or socialization works and sometimes it doesn't. Jamaica Kincaid's "Girl" captures the voice one young girl from the West Indies hears as she grows up, the admonitions and instructions that encode proper social behavior for a female in her particular culture. The voice in "Girl" may sometimes annoy its recipient, but it is basically loving. In contrast is Ralph Ellison's "Battle Royal," which depicts with savage satiric power the trapped and painful situation of being young, male, and black in a society run by white men who enjoy staging dramas of ritual humiliation to remind black boys, who will grow up to be men, of the powerlessness they will continue to experience as adults.

An important aspect of childhood and adolescence is the relation we have to previous generations—parents, grandparents, and other relatives who are important figures for us in early life. The speaker of Theodore Roethke's poem, "My Papa's Waltz," remembers how, when he was a small child, his father would come home from work and a few drinks at the bar and dance him into bed. There is love in this poem, but also fear, for the dance is as rough as the life his father leads outside the home. The smell of whiskey on his father's breath, his mother's frown, his father beating time on his head—all these details, along with the poem's sense of breathless energy, add up to a poignant but complicated memory. A lyric poem will often capture one intense moment in a life, while the narrative nature of prose lends itself more easily to the gradual unfolding of a substantial portion of a character's life. James Baldwin's short story, "Sonny's Blues," tells us much about the life, from childhood through adulthood, of a young black jazz musician from the point of view of his older brother who loves Sonny, is frustrated by him, and finally comes to understand him through listening to the blues music he plays.

In the late twentieth century, we have fewer rituals marking the passage from one life stage to another than many other times and cultures have had. For example, we do not, as do some cultures, remove young boys from their mother's to their father's house at a prescribed age. We do not send adolescents out into the desert to have a vision and find a name in order to become adults. Though young men and women usually leave home to go to college, get married, go to war or take a job, we rarely mark that change with a recognizable ritual that says to all concerned: one part of your life is over and another is beginning. And what if what is supposed to come next, such as a job, does not? Gwendolyn Brooks's poem, "We Real Cool," captures in eight lines the chilly alienation of a gang of unemployed black youths hanging around outside a pool hall. Another example is Edmund White's *A Boy's Own Story*, which explores one male adolescent's perplexity about his sexual identity. There is an assumption of continuity and conventionality in contemporary Western life that means, perhaps, that when we move into a new stage we are sometimes confused and unprepared, and in order to maintain an equilibrium, we may have to construct our own meaning for the event. The change from childhood to adulthood is particularly confusing in its current lack of ritual.

Female puberty, where the onset of menstruation is a definite marker of the passage from one life stage to another, is the subject of the two prose pieces in this section. "No Name Woman," from Maxine Hong Kingston's *The Woman Warrior*, begins with a cautionary tale from a Chinese-American girl's mother about what can happen to her now that she is able to get pregnant. She, like her nameless aunt in China, her mother tells her, could bear a child in shame, be outcast by her village, and be driven to suicide. "Now that you have started to menstruate, what happened to her could happen to you. Don't humiliate us. You wouldn't like to be forgotten as if you had never been born. The villagers are watchful." Welcome to being a woman! If we are female, we probably remember the warnings we received. And if we are male, we may remember being told to be careful about getting a girl "in trouble," because then we might have to marry her.

What makes Kingston's piece so fascinating is in part its particular cultural context: the young protagonist not only has to cope with growing up female in America; she carries the weight of her Chinese cultural tradition on her back as well. How she handles her mother's cautionary tale, how she rewrites it to her own needs and fits it, in a formally circular way, into the construction of her own identity, is much of the interest of this story. Kingston takes a "universal" situation (puberty), makes it concrete and specific to a particular cultural tradition, and shows how a young girl comes to a strong sense of personal identity in spite of her mother's warnings of female powerlessness and vulnerability. For Audre Lorde, writing out of her Barbadian-American background in *Zami*, puberty is a cause for relief and celebration; it also provides a rare moment of closeness and shared female identity with the protagonist's overworked and often unapproachable mother. Here too, though in a more celebratory way, the young woman's self-image is expressed in terms of her cultural heritage through the lushly sensual description of the mortar and pestle her mother brought with them to the United States.

Brave New World aside, the process of pregnancy and giving birth, like menstruation, is so far an exclusively female experience. Of all the major life stages, this one may be the least written about to date. Why do you suppose that is the case? One work of literature focused entirely on the experience of pregnancy is Sylvia Plath's radio play in verse, "Three Women." The play takes the form of intercut monologues by three women in a maternity ward—one bears her child and keeps it, one has a miscarriage, one has a child and gives it up.

If giving birth is a woman's experience, aging is something we can all anticipate. A number of the poems, stories, and plays in this section are about middle age and old age. They run the gamut of feeling: from the sense of loss and missed opportunity in T. S. Eliot's "The Love Song of J. Alfred Prufrock" and John Updike's "Ex-Basketball Player" to the acceptance of aging in W. B. Yeats's "Sailing to Byzantium" and Doris Lessing's "Our Friend Judith," to an anger over growing old that has serious repercussions on family and society in Shakespeare's *King Lear*, to the comic and pathetic bewilderment of the banana-eating protagonist of *Krapp's Last Tape*, to the celebration of one's middle-aged self in William Carpenter's "Rain" and the redefinition of the concept of "old maid" in Irena Klepfisz's "they did not build wings for them." Concerning death, Dylan Thomas in "Do Not Go Gentle Into That Good Night" and Sylvia Plath in "Edge" provide two starkly contrasting attitudes.

Gender, race, culture, social class, national or regional identity, and the time we live in affect how individuals experience every stage of life from birth to death. These shape the details of our separate biographies, particularize experience, and provide vivid and immediate interest. One last and vividly particular example. The two main characters in Mary E. Wilkins Freeman's "A Mistaken Charity" are not only old; they are female, they are disabled, they are poor, they come from a long line of poor and working-class people, and they are proud. All these particulars affect their response to attempts by the charity minded of their town to put them, "for their own good," into a genteel old ladies home. Though all humanity may share certain aspects of each life stage, finally there is no such thing as a "universal" experience of childhood, of adolescence, of parenting, of aging or of any of the other stages of life. If our experiences were truly universal, life and literature would be excruciatingly boring.

FICTION

ALDOUS HUXLEY (1894–1963)

Grandson of renowned biologist T. H. Huxley, Aldous Huxley was born in Godalming, England and studied at Eton and Oxford. He traveled extensively beginning in the early 1920s and settled in Southern California after World War II. Huxley is by far best known for Brave New World *(1932); his other novels include* Antic Hay *(1923) and* Point Counter Point *(1928).*

FROM **Brave New World** (1932)

A squat grey building of only thirty-four stories. Over the main entrance the words, CENTRAL LONDON HATCHERY AND CONDITIONING CENTRE, and, in a shield, the World State's motto, COMMUNITY, IDENTITY, STABILITY.

The enormous room on the ground floor faced towards the north. Cold for all the summer beyond the panes, for all the tropical heat of the room itself, a harsh thin light glared through the windows, hungrily seeking some draped lay figure, some pallid shape of academic goose-flesh, but finding only the glass and nickel and bleakly shining porcelain of a laboratory. Wintriness responded to wintriness. The overalls of the workers were white, their hands gloved with a pale corpse-coloured rubber. The light was frozen, dead, a ghost. Only from the yellow barrels of the microscopes did it borrow a certain rich and living substance, lying along the polished tubes like butter, streak after luscious streak in long recession down the work tables.

"And this," said the Director opening the door, "is the Fertilizing Room."

Bent over their instruments, three hundred Fertilizers were plunged, as the Director of Hatcheries and Conditioning entered the room, in the scarcely breathing silence, the absent-minded, soliloquizing hum or whistle, of absorbed concentration. A troop of newly arrived students, very young, pink and callow, followed nervously, rather abjectly, at the Director's heels. Each of them carried a notebook, in which, whenever the great man spoke, he desperately scribbled. Straight from the horse's mouth. It was a rare privilege. The D.H.C. for Central London always made a point of personally conducting his new students round the various departments.

"Just to give you a general idea," he would explain to them. For of course some sort of general idea they must have, if they were to do their work intelligently—though as little of one, if they were to be good and happy members of society, as possible. For particulars, as every one knows, make for virtue and happiness; generalities are intellectually necessary evils. Not philosophers but fret-sawyers and stamp collectors compose the backbone of society.

"To-morrow," he would add, smiling at them with a slightly menacing geniality, "you'll be settling down to serious work. You won't have time for generalities. Meanwhile . . ."

Meanwhile, it was a privilege. Straight from the horse's mouth into the notebook. The boys scribbled like mad.

Tall and rather thin but upright, the Director advanced into the room. He had a long chin and big, rather prominent teeth, just covered, when he was not talking, by his full, floridly curved lips. Old, young? Thirty? Fifty? Fifty-five? It was hard to say. And anyhow the question didn't arise; in this year of stability, A.F. 632, it didn't occur to you to ask it.

"I shall begin at the beginning," said the D.H.C. and the more zealous students recorded his intention in their notebooks: *Begin at the beginning.* "These," he waved his hand, "are the incubators." And opening an insulated door he showed them racks upon racks of numbered test-tubes. "The week's supply of ova. Kept," he explained, "at blood heat; whereas the male gametes," and here he opened another door, "they have to be kept at thirty-five instead of thirty-seven.[1] Full blood heat sterilizes." Rams wrapped in theremogene beget no lambs.

Still leaning against the incubators he gave them, while the pencils scurried illegibly across the pages, a brief description of the modern fertilizing process; spoke first, of course, of its surgical introduction—"the operation undergone voluntarily for the good of Society, not to mention the fact that it carries a bonus amounting to six months' salary"; continued with some account of the technique for perserving the excised ovary alive and actively developing; passed on to a consideration of optimum temperature, salinity, viscosity; referred to the liquor in which the detached and ripened eggs were kept; and, leading his charges to the work tables, actually showed them how this liquor was drawn off from the test-tubes; how it was let out drop by drop onto the specially warmed slides of the microscopes; how the eggs which it contained were inspected for abnormalities, counted and transferred to a porous receptacle; how (and he now took them to watch the operation) this receptacle was immersed in a warm bouillon containing free-swimming spermatozoa—at a minimum concentration of one hundred thousand per cubic centimetre, he insisted; and how, after ten minutes, the container was lifted out of the liquor and its contents re-examined; how, if any of the eggs remained unfertilized, it was again immersed, and, if necessary, yet again; how the fertilized ova went back to the incubators; where the Alphas and Betas remained until definitely bottled; while the Gammas, Deltas and Epsilons were brought out again, after only thirty-six hours, to undergo Bokanovsky's Process.

---

[1] 35 and 37 degrees Centigrade are 95 and 98.6 degrees Fahrenheit, respectively.

"Bokanovsky's Process," repeated the Director, and the students under-lined the words in their little notebooks.

One egg, one embryo, one adult—normality. But a bokanovskified egg will bud, will proliferate, will divide. From eight to ninety-six buds, and every bud will grow into a perfectly formed embryo, and every embryo into a full-sized adult. Making ninety-six human beings grow where only one grew before. Progress.

"Essentially," the D.H.C. concluded, "bokanovskification consists of a series of arrests of development. We check the normal growth and, paradoxically enough, the egg responds by budding."

Responds by budding. The pencils were busy.

He pointed. On a very slowly moving band a rack-full of test-tubes was entering a large metal box, another rack-full was emerging. Machinery faintly purred. It took eight minutes for the tubes to go through, he told them. Eight minutes of hard X-rays being about as much as an egg can stand. A few died; of the rest, the least susceptible divided into two; most put out four buds; some eight; all were returned to the incubators, where the buds began to develop; then, after two days, were suddenly chilled, chilled and checked. Two, four, eight, the buds in their turn budded; and having budded were dosed almost to death with alcohol; consequently burgeoned again and having budded—bud out of bud out of bud—were thereafter—further arrest being generally fatal—left to develop in peace. By which time the original egg was in a fair way to becoming anything from eight to ninety-six embryos—a prodigious improvement, you will agree, on nature. Identical twins—but not in piddling twos and threes as in the old viviparous days, when an egg would sometimes accidentally divide; actually by dozens, by scores at a time.

"Scores," the Director repeated and flung out his arms, as though he were distributing largesse. "Scores."

But one of the students was fool enough to ask where the advantage lay.

"My good boy!" The Director wheeled sharply round on him. "Can't you see? Can't you *see?*" He raised a hand; his expression was solemn. "Bokanovsky's Process is one of the major instruments of social stability!"

Major instruments of social stability.

Standard men and women; in uniform batches. The whole of a small factory staffed with the products of a single bokanovskified egg.

"Ninety-six identical twins working ninety-six identical machines!" The voice was almost tremulous with enthusiasm. "You really know where you are. For the first time in history." He quoted the planetary motto. "Community, Identity, Stability." Grand words. "If we could bokanovskify indefinitely the whole problem would be solved."

Solved by standard Gammas, unvarying Deltas, uniform Epsilons. Mil-lions of identical twins. The principle of mass production at last applied to biology.

"But, alas," the Director shook his head, "we *can't* bokanovskify indefinitely."

Ninety-six seemed to be the limit; seventy-two a good average. From the same ovary and with gametes of the same male to manufacture as many batches of identical twins as possible—that was the best (sadly a second best) that they could do. And even that was difficult.

"For in nature it takes thirty years for two hundred eggs to reach maturity. But our business is to stabilize the population at this moment, here and now. Dribbling out twins over a quarter of a century—what would be the use of that?"

Obviously, no use at all. But Podsnap's Technique had immensely accelerated the process of ripening. They could make sure of at least a hundred and fifty mature eggs within two years. Fertilize and bokanovskify—in other words, multiply by seventy-two—and you get an average of nearly eleven thousand brothers and sisters in a hundred and fifty batches of identical twins, all within two years of the same age.

"And in exceptional cases we can make one ovary yield us over fifteen thousand adult individuals."

Beckoning to a fair-haired, ruddy young man who happened to be passing at the moment, "Mr. Foster," he called. The ruddy young man approached. "Can you tell us the record for a single ovary, Mr. Foster?"

"Sixteen thousand and twelve in this Centre," Mr. Foster replied without hesitation. He spoke very quickly, had a vivacious blue eye, and took an evident pleasure in quoting figures. "Sixteen thousand and twelve; in one hundred and eighty-nine batches of identicals. But of course they've done much better," he rattled on, "in some of the tropical Centres. Singapore has often produced over sixteen thousand five hundred; and Mombasa has actually touched the seventeen thousand mark. But then they have unfair advantages. You should see the way a negro ovary responds to pituitary! It's quite astonishing, when you're used to working with European material. Still," he added, with a laugh (but the light of combat was in his eyes and the lift of his chin was challenging), "still, we mean to beat them if we can. I'm working on a wonderful Delta-Minus ovary at this moment. Only just eighteen months old. Over twelve thousand seven hundred children already, either decanted or in embryo. And still going strong. We'll beat them yet."

"That's the spirit I like!" cried the Director, and clapped Mr. Foster on the shoulder. "Come along with us and give these boys the benefit of your expert knowledge."

Mr. Foster smiled modestly. "With pleasure." They went.

In the Bottling Room all was harmonious bustle and ordered activity. Flaps of fresh sow's peritoneum ready cut to the proper size came shooting up in little lifts from the Organ Store in the sub-basement. Whizz and then, click! the lift-hatches flew open; the bottle-liner had only to reach out a hand, take the flap, insert, smooth-down, and before the lined bottle had had time to travel out of reach along the endless band, whizz, click!

another flap of peritoneum had shot up from the depths, ready to be slipped into yet another bottle, the next of that slow interminable procession on the band.

Next to the Liners stood the Matriculators. The procession advanced; one by one the eggs were transferred from their test-tubes to the larger containers; deftly the peritoneal lining was slit, the morula dropped into place, the saline solution poured in . . . and already the bottle had passed, and it was the turn of the labellers. Heredity, date of fertilization, membership of Bokanovsky Group—details were transferred from test-tube to bottle. No longer anonymous, but named, identified, the procession marched slowly on; on through an opening in the wall, slowly on into the Social Predestination Room.

"Eighty-eight cubic metres of card-index," said Mr. Foster with relish, as they entered.

"Containing *all* the relevant information," added the Director.

"Brought up to date every morning."

"And co-ordinated every afternoon."

"On the basis of which they make their calculations."

"So many individuals, of such and such quality," said Mr. Foster.

"Distributed in such and such quantities."

"The optimum Decanting Rate at any given moment."

"Unforeseen wastages promptly made good."

"Promptly," repeated Mr. Foster. "If you knew the amount of overtime I had to put in after the last Japanese earthquake!" He laughed good-humouredly and shook his head.

"The Predestinators send in their figures to the Fertilizers."

"Who give them the embryos they ask for."

"And the bottles come in here to be predestinated in detail."

"After which they are sent down to the Embryo Store."

"Where we now proceed ourselves."

And opening a door Mr. Foster led the way down a staircase into the basement.

The temperature was still tropical. They descended into a thickening twilight. Two doors and a passage with a double turn insured the cellar against any possible infiltration of the day.

"Embryos are like photograph film," said Mr. Foster waggishly, as he pushed open the second door. "They can only stand red light."

And in effect the sultry darkness into which the students now followed him was visible and crimson, like the darkness of closed eyes on a summer's afternoon. The bulging flanks of row on receding row and tier above tier of bottles glinted with innumerable rubies, and among the rubies moved the dim red spectres of men and women with purple eyes and all the symptoms of lupus. The hum and rattle of machinery faintly stirred the air.

"Give them a few figures, Mr. Foster," said the Director, who was tired of talking.

Mr. Foster was only too happy to give them a few figures.

Two hundred and twenty metres long, two hundred wide, ten high. He pointed upwards. Like chickens drinking, the students lifted their eyes towards the distant ceiling.

Three tiers of racks: ground floor level, first gallery, second gallery.

The spidery steel-work of gallery above gallery faded away in all directions into the dark. Near them three red ghosts were busily unloading demijohns from a moving staircase.

The escalator from the Social Predestination Room.

Each bottle could be placed on one of fifteen racks, each rack, though you couldn't see it, was a conveyor travelling at the rate of thirty-three and a third centimetres an hour. Two hundred and sixty-seven days at eight metres a day. Two thousand one hundred and thirty-six metres in all. One circuit of the cellar at ground level, one on the first gallery, half on the second, and on the two hundred and sixty-seventh morning, daylight in the Decanting Room. Independent existence—so called.

"But in the interval," Mr. Foster concluded, "we've managed to do a lot to them. Oh, a very great deal." His laugh was knowing and triumphant.

"That's the spirit I like," said the Director once more. "Let's walk round. You tell them everything, Mr. Foster."

Mr. Foster duly told them.

Told them of the growing embryo on its bed of peritoneum. Made them taste the rich blood surrogate on which it fed. Explained why it had to be stimulated with placentin and thyroxin. Told them of the *corpus luteum* extract. Showed them the jets through which at every twelfth metre from zero to 2040 it was automatically injected. Spoke of those gradually increasing doses of pituitary administered during the final ninety-six metres of their course. Described the artificial maternal circulation installed on every bottle at Metre 112; showed them the reservoir of blood-surrogate, the centrifugal pump that kept the liquid moving over the placenta and drove it through the synthetic lung and waste-product filter. Referred to the embryo's troublesome tendency to anæmia, to the massive doses of hog's stomach extract and foetal foal's liver with which, in consequence, it had to be supplied.

Showed them the simple mechanism by means of which, during the last two metres out of every eight, all the embryos were simultaneously shaken into familiarity with movement. Hinted at the gravity of the so-called "trauma of decanting," and enumerated the precautions taken to minimize, by a suitable training of the bottled embryo, that dangerous shock. Told them of the tests for sex carried out in the neighbourhood of metre 200. Explained the system of labelling—a T for the males, a circle for the females and for those who were destined to become free-martins a question mark, black on a white ground.

"For of course," said Mr. Foster, "in the vast majority of cases, fertility is merely a nuisance. One fertile ovary in twelve hundred—that would really be quite sufficient for our purposes. But we want to have a good choice. And of course one must always leave an enormous margin of safety. So we allow as many as thirty per cent. of the female embryos to develop normally. The others get a dose of male sex-hormone every twenty-four metres for the rest of the course. Result: they're decanted as freemartins—structurally quite normal (except," he had to admit, "that they *do* have just the slightest tendency to grow beards), but sterile. Guaranteed sterile. Which brings us at last," continued Mr. Foster, "out of the realm of mere slavish imitation of nature into the much more interesting world of human invention."

He rubbed his hands. For of course, they didn't content themselves with merely hatching out embryos: any cow could do that.

"We also predestine and condition. We decant our babies as socialized human beings, as Alphas or Epsilons, as future sewage workers or future . . ." He was going to say "future World controllers," but correcting himself, said "future Directors of Hatcheries," instead.

The D.H.C. acknowledged the compliment with a smile.

They were passing Metre 320 on rack II. A young Beta-Minus mechanic was busy with screwdriver and spanner on the blood-surrogate pump of a passing bottle. The hum of the electric motor deepened by fractions of a tone as he turned the nuts. Down, down . . . A final twist, a glance at the revolution counter, and he was done. He moved two paces down the line and began the same process on the next pump.

"Reducing the number of revolutions per minute," Mr. Foster explained. "The surrogate goes round slower; therefore passes through the lung at longer intervals; therefore gives the embryo less oxygen. Nothing like oxygen-shortage for keeping an embryo below par." Again he rubbed his hands.

"But why do you want to keep the embryo below par?" asked an ingenuous student.

"Ass!" said the Director, breaking a long silence. "Hasn't it occurred to you that an Epsilon embryo must have an Epsilon environment as well as an Epsilon heredity?"

It evidently hadn't occurred to him. He was covered with confusion.

"The lower the caste," said Mr. Foster, "the shorter the oxygen." The first organ affected was the brain. After that the skeleton. At seventy per cent. of normal oxygen you got dwarfs. At less than seventy eyeless monsters.

"Who are no use at all," concluded Mr. Foster.

Whereas (his voice became confidential and eager), if they could discover a technique for shortening the period of maturation what a triumph, what a benefaction to Society!

"Consider the horse."

They considered it.

Mature at six; the elephant at ten. While at thirteen a man is not yet sexually mature; and is only full-grown at twenty. Hence, of course, that fruit of delayed development, the human intelligence.

"But in Epsilons," said Mr. Foster very justly, "we don't need human intelligence."

Didn't need and didn't get it. But though the Epsilon mind was mature at ten, the Epsilon body was not fit to work till eighteen. Long years of superfluous and wasted immaturity. If the physical development could be speeded up till it was as quick, say, as a cow's, what an enormous saving to the Community!

"Enormous!" murmured the students. Mr. Foster's enthusiasm was infectious.

He became rather technical; spoke of the abnormal endocrine co-ordination which made men grow so slowly; postulated a germinal mutation to account for it. Could the effects of this germinal mutation be undone? Could the individual Epsilon embryo be made a revert, by a suitable technique, to the normality of dogs and cows? That was the problem. And it was all but solved.

Pilkington, at Mombasa, had produced individuals who were sexually mature at four and full-grown at six and a half. A scientific triumph. But socially useless. Six-year-old men and women were too stupid to do even Epsilon work. And the process was an all-or-nothing one; either you failed to modify at all, or else you modified the whole way. They were still trying to find the ideal compromise between adults of twenty and adults of six. So far without success. Mr. Foster sighed and shook his head.

Their wanderings through the crimson twilight had brought them to the neighbourhood of Metre 170 on Rack 9. From this point onwards Rack 9 was enclosed and the bottles performed the remainder of their journey in a kind of tunnel, interrupted here and there by openings two or three metres wide.

"Heat conditioning," said Mr. Foster.

Hot tunnels alternated with cool tunnels. Coolness was wedded to discomfort in the form of hard X-rays. By the time they were decanted the embryos had a horror of cold. They were predestined to emigrate to the tropics, to be miners and acetate silk spinners and steel workers. Later on their minds would be made to endorse the judgment of their bodies. "We condition them to thrive on heat," concluded Mr. Foster. "Our colleagues upstairs will teach them to love it."

"And that," put in the Director sententiously, "that is the secret of happiness and virtue—liking what you've *got* to do. All conditioning aims at that: making people like their unescapable social destiny."

In a gap between two tunnels, a nurse was delicately probing with a long fine syringe into the gelatinous contents of a passing bottle. The students and their guides stood watching her for a few moments in silence.

"Well, Lenina," said Mr. Foster, when at last she withdrew the syringe and straightened herself up.

The girl turned with a start. One could see that, for all the lupus and the purple eyes, she was uncommonly pretty.

"Henry!" Her smile flashed redly at him—a row of coral teeth.

"Charming, charming," murmured the Director and, giving her two or three little pats, received in exchange a rather deferential smile for himself.

"What are you giving them?" asked Mr. Foster, making his tone very professional.

"Oh, the usual typhoid and sleeping sickness."

"Tropical workers start being inoculated at Metre 150," Mr. Foster explained to the students. "The embryos still have gills. We immunize the fish against the future man's diseases." Then, turning back to Lenina, "Ten to five on the roof this afternoon," he said, "as usual."

"Charming," said the Director once more, and, with a final pat, moved away after the others.

On Rack 10 rows of next generation's chemical workers were being trained in the toleration of lead, caustic soda, tar, chlorine. The first of a batch of two hundred and fifty embryonic rocket-plane engineers was just passing the eleven hundred metre mark on Rack 3. A special mechanism kept their containers in constant rotation. "To improve their sense of balance," Mr. Foster explained. "Doing repairs on the outside of a rocket in mid-air is a ticklish job. We slacken off the circulation when they're right way up, so that they're half starved, and double the flow of surrogate when they're upside down. They learn to associate topsy-turvydom with well-being; in fact, they're only truly happy when they're standing on their heads.

"And now," Mr. Foster went on, "I'd like to show you some very interesting conditioning for Alpha Plus Intellectuals. We have a big batch of them on Rack 5. First Gallery level," he called to two boys who had started to go down to the ground floor.

"They're round about Metre 900," he explained. "You can't really do any useful intellectual conditioning till the foetuses have lost their tails. Follow me."

But the Director had looked at his watch. "Ten to three," he said. "No time for the intellectual embryos, I'm afraid. We must go up to the Nurseries before the children have finished their afternoon sleep."

Mr. Foster was disappointed. "At least one glance at the Decanting Room," he pleaded.

"Very well then." The Director smiled indulgently. "Just one glance."

II

Mr. Foster was left in the Decanting Room. The D.H.C. and his students stepped into the nearest lift and were carried up to the fifth floor.

INFANT NURSERIES. NEO-PAVLOVIAN CONDITIONING ROOMS, announced the notice board.

The Director opened a door. They were in a large bare room, very bright and sunny; for the whole of the southern wall was a single window. Half a dozen nurses, trousered and jacketed in the regulation white viscose-linen uniform, their hair aseptically hidden under white caps, were engaged in setting out bowls of roses in a long row across the floor. Big bowls, packed tight with blossom. Thousands of petals, ripe-blown and silkily smooth, like the cheeks of innumerable little cherubs, but of cherubs, in that bright light, not exclusively pink and Aryan, but also luminously Chinese, also Mexican, also apoplectic with too much blowing of celestial trumpets, also pale as death, pale with the posthumous whiteness of marble.

The nurses stiffened to attention as the D.H.C. came in.

"Set out the books," he said curtly.

In silence the nurses obeyed his command. Between the rose bowls the books were duly set out—a row of nursery quartos opened invitingly each at some gaily coloured image of beast or fish or bird.

"Now bring in the children."

They hurried out of the room and returned in a minute or two, each pushing a kind of tall dumbwaiter laden, on all its four wire-netted shelves, with eight-month-old babies, all exactly alike (a Bokanovsky Group, it was evident) and all (since their caste was Delta) dressed in khaki.

"Put them down on the floor."

The infants were unloaded.

"Now turn them so that they can see the flowers and books."

Turned, the babies at once fell silent, then began to crawl towards those clusters of sleek colours, those shapes so gay and brilliant on the white pages. As they approached, the sun came out of a momentary eclipse behind a cloud. The roses flamed up as though with a sudden passion from within; a new and profound significance seemed to suffuse the shining pages of the books. From the ranks of the crawling babies came little squeals of excitement, gurgles and twitterings of pleasure.

The Director rubbed his hands. "Excellent!" he said. "It might almost have been done on purpose."

The swiftest crawlers were already at their goal. Small hands reached out uncertainly, touched, grasped, unpetaling the transfigured roses, crumpling the illuminated pages of the books. The Director waited until all were happily busy. Then, "Watch carefully," he said. And, lifting his hand, he gave the signal.

The Head Nurse, who was standing by a switchboard at the other end of the room, pressed down a little lever.

There was a violent explosion. Shriller and ever shriller, a siren shrieked. Alarm bells maddeningly sounded.

The children started, screamed; their faces were distorted with terror.

"And now," the Director shouted (for the noise was deafening), "now we proceed to rub in the lesson with a mild electric shock."

He waved his hand again, and the Head Nurse pressed a second lever. The screaming of the babies suddenly changed its tone. There was something desperate, almost insane, about the sharp spasmodic yelps to which they now gave utterance. Their little bodies twitched and stiffened; their limbs moved jerkily as if to the tug of unseen wires.

"We can electrify that whole strip of floor," bawled the Director in explanation. "But that's enough," he signalled to the nurse.

The explosions ceased, the bells stopped ringing, the shriek of the siren died down from tone to tone into silence. The stiffly twitching bodies relaxed, and what had become the sob and yelp of infant maniacs broadened out once more into a normal howl of ordinary terror.

"Offer them the flowers and the books again."

The nurses obeyed; but at the approach of the roses, at the mere sight of those gaily-coloured images of pussy and cock-a-doodle-doo and baa-baa black sheep, the infants shrank away in horror; the volume of their howling suddenly increased.

"Observe," said the Director triumphantly, "observe."

Books and loud noises, flowers and electric shocks—already in the infant mind these couples were compromisingly linked; and after two hundred repetitions of the same or a similar lesson would be wedded indissolubly. What man has joined, nature is powerless to put asunder.

"They'll grow up with what the psychologists used to call an 'instinctive' hatred of books and flowers. Reflexes unalterably conditioned. They'll be safe from books and botany all their lives." The Director turned to his nurses. "Take them away again."

Still yelling, the khaki babies were loaded on to their dumb-waiters and wheeled out, leaving behind them the smell of sour milk and a most welcome silence.

One of the students held up his hand; and though he could see quite well why you couldn't have lower-caste people wasting the Community's time over books, and that there was always the risk of their reading something which might undesirably decondition one of their reflexes, yet . . . well, he couldn't understand about the flowers. Why go to the trouble of making it psychologically impossible for Deltas to like flowers?

Patiently the D.H.C. explained. If the children were made to scream at the sight of a rose, that was on grounds of high economic policy. Not so very long ago (a century or thereabouts), Gammas, Deltas, even Epsilons, had been conditioned to like flowers—flowers in particular and wild nature in general. The idea was to make them want to be going out into the country at every available opportunity, and so compel them to consume transport.

"And didn't they consume transport?" asked the student.

"Quite a lot," the D.H.C. replied. "But nothing else."

Primroses and landscapes, he pointed out, have one grave defect: they are gratuitous. A love of nature keeps no factories busy. It was decided to abolish the love of nature, at any rate among the lower classes; to abolish the love of nature, but *not* the tendency to consume transport. For of course it was essential that they should keep on going to the country, even though they hated it. The problem was to find an economically sounder reason for consuming transport than a mere affection for primroses and landscapes. It was duly found.

"We condition the masses to hate the country," concluded the Director. "But simultaneously we condition them to love all country sports. At the same time, we see to it that all country sports shall entail the use of elaborate apparatus. So that they consume manufactured articles as well as transport. Hence those electric shocks."

"I see," said the student, and was silent, lost in admiration.

There was a silence; then, clearing his throat, "Once upon a time," the Director began, "while our Ford was still on earth, there was a little boy called Reuben Rabinovitch. Reuben was the child of Polish-speaking parents." The Director interrupted himself. "You know what Polish is, I suppose?"

"A dead language."

"Like French and German," added another student, officiously showing off his learning.

"And 'parent'?" questioned the D.H.C.

There was an uneasy silence. Several of the boys blushed. They had not yet learned to draw the significant but often very fine distinction between smut and pure science. One, at last, had the courage to raise a hand.

"Human beings used to be . . ." he hesitated; the blood rushed to his cheeks. "Well, they used to be viviparous."

"Quite right." The Director nodded approvingly.

"And when the babies were decanted . . ."

" 'Born'," came the correction.

"Well, then they were the parents—I mean, not the babies, of course; the other ones." The poor boy was overwhelmed with confusion.

"In brief," the Director summed up, "the parents were the father and the mother." The smut that was really science fell with a crash into the boys' eye-avoiding silence. "Mother," he repeated loudly rubbing in the science; and, leaning back in his chair, "These," he said gravely, "are unpleasant facts; I know it. But then most historical facts *are* unpleasant."

He returned to Little Reuben—to Little Reuben, in whose room, one evening, by an oversight, his father and mother (crash, crash!) happened to leave the radio turned on.

("For you must remember that in those days of gross viviparous reproduction, children were always brought up by their parents and not in State Conditioning Centres.")

While the child was asleep, a broadcast programme from London suddenly started to come through; and the next morning, to the astonishment of his crash and crash (the more daring of the boys ventured to grin at one another), Little Reuben woke up repeating word for word a long lecture by that curious old writer ("one of the very few whose works have been permitted to come down to us"), George Bernard Shaw,[2] who

---

[2] (1856–1950), British playwright.

was speaking, according to a well-authenticated tradition, about his own genius. To Little Reuben's wink and snigger, this lecture was, of course, perfectly incomprehensible and, imagining that their child had suddenly gone mad, they sent for a doctor. He, fortunately, understood English, recognized the discourse as that which Shaw had broadcasted the previous evening, realized the significance of what had happened, and sent a letter to the medical press about it.

"The principle of sleep-teaching, or hypnopædia, had been discovered." The D.H.C. made an impressive pause.

The principle had been discovered; but many, many years were to elapse before that principle was usefully applied.

"The case of Little Reuben occurred only twenty-three years after Our Ford's first T-Model was put on the market." (Here the Director made a sign of the T on his stomach and all the students reverently followed suit.) "And yet . . ."

Furiously the students scribbled. *"Hypnopædia, first used officially in A.F. 214. Why not before? Two reasons. (a) . . ."*

"These early experimenters," the D.H.C. was saying, "were on the wrong track. They thought that hypnopædia could be made an instrument of intellectual education . . ."

(A small boy asleep on his right side, the right arm stuck out, the right hand hanging limp over the edge of the bed. Through a round grating in the side of a box a voice speaks softly.

"The Nile is the longest river in Africa and the second in length of all the rivers of the globe. Although falling short of the length of the Mississippi-Missouri, the Nile is at the head of all rivers as regards the length of its basin, which extends through 35 degrees of latitude . . ."

At breakfast the next morning, "Tommy," some one says, "do you know which is the longest river in Africa?" A shaking of the head. "But don't you remember something that begins: The Nile is the . . ."

"The-Nile-is-the-longest-river-in-Africa-and-the-second-in-length-of-all-the-rivers-of-the-globe . . ." The words come rushing out. "Although-falling-short-of . . ."

"Well now, which is the longest river in Africa?"

The eyes are blank. "I don't know."

"But the Nile, Tommy."

"The-Nile-is-the-longest-river-in-Africa-and-second . . ."

"Then which river is the longest, Tommy?"

Tommy bursts into tears. "I don't know," he howls.)

That howl, the Director made it plain, discouraged the earliest investigators. The experiments were abandoned. No further attempt was made to teach children the length of the Nile in their sleep. Quite rightly. You can't learn a science unless you know what it's all about.

"Whereas, if they'd only started on *moral* education," said the Director, leading the way towards the door. The students followed him, desperately scribbling as they walked and all the way up in the lift. "Moral education, which ought never, in any circumstances, to be rational."

"Silence, silence," whispered a loud speaker as they stepped out at the fourteenth floor, and "Silence, silence," the trumpet mouths indefatigably repeated at intervals down every corridor. The students and even the Director himself rose automatically to the tips of their toes. They were Alphas, of course; but even Alphas have been well conditioned. "Silence, silence." All the air of the fourteenth floor was sibilant with the categorical imperative.

Fifty yards of tiptoeing brought them to a door which the Director cautiously opened. They stepped over the threshold into the twilight of a shuttered dormitory. Eighty cots stood in a row against the wall. There was a sound of light regular breathing and a continuous murmur, as of very faint voices remotely whispering.

A nurse rose as they entered and came to attention before the Director.

"What's the lesson this afternoon?" he asked.

"We had Elementary Sex for the first forty minutes," she answered. "But now it's switched over to Elementary Class Consciousness."

The Director walked slowly down the long line of cots. Rosy and relaxed with sleep, eighty little boys and girls lay softly breathing. There was a whisper under every pillow. The D.H.C. halted and, bending over one of the little beds, listened attentively.

"Elementary Class Consciousness, did you say? Let's have it repeated a little louder by the trumpet."

At the end of the room a loud speaker projected from the wall. The Director walked up to it and pressed a switch.

". . . all wear green," said a soft but very distinct voice, beginning in the middle of a sentence, "and Delta Children wear khaki. Oh no, I don't want to play with Delta children. And Epsilons are still worse. They're too stupid to be able to read or write. Besides they wear black, which is such a beastly colour. I'm *so* glad I'm a Beta."

There was a pause; then the voice began again.

"Alpha children wear grey. They work much harder than we do, because they're so frightfully clever. I'm really awfully glad I'm a Beta, because I don't work so hard. And then we are much better than the Gammas and Deltas. Gammas are stupid. They all wear green, and Delta children wear khaki. Oh no, I *don't* want to play with Delta children. And Epsilons are still worse. They're too stupid to be able . . ."

The Director pushed back the switch. The voice was silent. Only its thin ghost continued to mutter from beneath the eighty pillows.

"They'll have that repeated forty or fifty times more before they wake; then again on Thursday, and again on Saturday. A hundred and twenty times three times a week for thirty months. After which they go on to a more advanced lesson."

Roses and electric shocks, the khaki of Deltas and a whiff of asafœtida— wedded indissolubly before the child can speak. But wordless conditioning is crude and wholesale; cannot bring home the finer distinctions, cannot inculcate the more complex courses of behaviour. For that there must be words, but words without reason. In brief, hypnopædia.

"The greatest moralizing and socializing force of all time."

The students took it down in their little books. Straight from the horse's mouth.

Once more the Director touched the switch.

". . . so frightfully clever," the soft, insinuating, indefatigable voice was saying. "I'm really awfully glad I'm a Beta, because . . ."

Not so much like drops of water, though water, it is true, can wear holes in the hardest granite; rather, drops of liquid sealing-wax, drops that adhere, incrust, incorporate themselves with what they fall on, till finally the rock is all one scarlet blob.

"Till at last the child's mind *is* these suggestions, and the sum of the suggestions *is* the child's mind. And not the child's mind only. The adult's mind too—all his life long. The mind that judges and desires and decides—made up of these suggestions. But all these suggestions are *our* suggestions!" The Director almost shouted in his triumph. "Suggestions from the State." He banged the nearest table. "It therefore follows . . ."

A noise made him turn around.

"Oh, Ford!" he said in another tone, "I've gone and woken the children."

Study and Discussion Questions

1. Why, in the world of *Brave New World,* are babies manufactured rather than born? Why are they conditioned so thoroughly once they've been made?

2. Who is "Our Ford" and why is the present year called "A.F. 632"? Why does the Director (when he is explaining the discovery of hypnopaedia) make "a sign of the T on his stomach" when he mentions "Our Ford"?

3. Why does Huxley repeatedly emphasize the diligence with which the students copy down the Director's every word?

4. What are some of the ways Huxley shapes our attitude towards the society he describes? Begin by looking at the imagery in the second paragraph.

5. What can we infer, from these first two chapters, about the political and economic structure of the society depicted in *Brave New World?*

Writing Exercises

1. Critics often discuss science fiction and utopian or dystopian literature in terms of "extrapolation," that is, a projection of current social trends into a distant future. What aspects of twentieth-century society are illuminated (and satirized) in this extrapolation?

2. The society of *Brave New World,* we learn later, provides its inhabitants with material abundance, unlimited physical pleasure, and freedom from unhappiness. Then what exactly is wrong with this society?
3. Is social conditioning always bad? What criteria could you suggest for deciding when it is good and when it is not? And how it should be accomplished?

RALPH ELLISON (b. 1914)

Ralph Waldo Ellison was born in Oklahoma City and studied music at Tuskegee Institute, but had to leave school for lack of money. He moved to New York City, worked at a variety of jobs, played and composed music, and eventually turned to writing, supported in part by the WPA Federal Writer's Project. Ellison published a number of stories and then, in 1952, Invisible Man. *(The story "Battle Royal" became its first chapter.) This, his only novel, established his reputation as one of the major postwar American writers.* Shadow and Act *(1964) is a collection of his essays.*

Battle Royal   (1947)

It goes a long way back, some twenty years. All my life I had been looking for something, and everywhere I turned someone tried to tell me what it was. I accepted their answers too, though they were often in contradiction and even self-contradictory. I was naïve. I was looking for myself and asking everyone except myself questions which I, and only I, could answer. It took me a long time and much painful boomeranging of my expectations to achieve a realization everyone else appears to have been born with: That I am nobody but myself. But first I had to discover that I am an invisible man!

And yet I am no freak of nature, nor of history. I was in the cards, other things having been equal (or unequal) eighty-five years ago. I am not ashamed of my grandparents for having been slaves. I am only ashamed of myself for having at one time been ashamed. About eighty-five years ago they were told that they were free, united with others of our country in everything pertaining to the common good, and, in everything social, separate like the fingers of the hand. And they believed it. They exulted in it. They stayed in their place, worked hard, and brought up my father to do the same. But my grandfather is the one. He was an odd old guy, my grandfather, and I am told I take after him. It was he who caused the trouble. On his deathbed he called my father to him and said, "Son, after I'm gone I want you to keep up the good fight. I never told you, but our life is a war and I have been a traitor all my born days, a spy in the enemy's country ever since I give up my gun back in the Reconstruction. Live with your head in the lion's mouth. I want you to overcome 'em with yeses, undermine 'em with grins, agree 'em to death and destruction, let 'em swoller you till they vomit or bust wide open." They thought the old man had gone out of his mind. He had been the meekest of men. The younger children were rushed from the room, the shades drawn and the flame of the lamp turned so low that it sputtered on the wick like the old man's breathing. "Learn it to the younguns," he whispered fiercely; then he died.

But my folks were more alarmed over his last words than over his dying. It was as though he had not died at all, his words caused so much anxiety. I was warned emphatically to forget what he had said and, indeed, this is the first time it has been mentioned outside the family circle. It had a tremendous effect upon me, however. I could never be sure of what he meant. Grandfather had been a quiet old man who never made any trouble, yet on his deathbed he had called himself a traitor and a spy, and he had spoken of his meekness as a dangerous activity. It became a constant puzzle which lay unanswered in the back of my mind. And whenever things went well for me I remembered my grandfather and felt guilty and uncomfortable. It was as though I was carrying out his advice in spite of myself. And to make it worse, everyone loved me for it. I was praised by the most lily-white men of the town. I was considered an example of desirable conduct—just as my grandfather had been. And what puzzled me was that the old man had defined it as *treachery*. When I was praised for my conduct I felt a guilt that in some way I was doing something that was really against the wishes of the white folks, that if they had understood they would have desired me to act just the opposite, that I should have been sulky and mean, and that that really would have been what they wanted, even though they were fooled and thought they wanted me to act as I did. It made me afraid that some day they would look upon me as a traitor and I would be lost. Still I was more afraid to act any other way because they didn't like that at all. The old man's words were like a curse. On my graduation day I delivered an oration in which I showed that humility was the secret, indeed, the very essence of progress. (Not that I believed this—how could I, remembering my grandfather?—I only believed that it worked.) It was a great success. Everyone praised me and I was invited to give the speech at a gathering of the town's leading white citizens. It was a triumph for our whole community.

It was in the main ballroom of the leading hotel. When I got there I discovered that it was on the occasion of a smoker, and I was told that since I was to be there anyway I might as well take part in the battle royal to be fought by some of my schoolmates as part of the entertainment. The battle royal came first.

All of the town's big shots were there in their tuxedoes, wolfing down the buffet foods, drinking beer and whiskey and smoking black cigars. It was a large room with a high ceiling. Chairs were arranged in neat rows around three sides of a portable boxing ring. The fourth side was clear, revealing a gleaming space of polished floor. I had some misgivings over the battle royal, by the way. Not from a distaste for fighting, but because I didn't care too much for the other fellows who were to take part. They were tough guys who seemed to have no grandfather's curse worrying their minds. No one could mistake their toughness. And besides, I suspected that fighting a battle royal might detract from the dignity of my speech. In those pre-invisible days I visualized myself as a potential Booker T. Washington. But the other fellows didn't care too much for me either, and there were nine of them. I felt superior to them in my way, and I didn't like the manner in which we were all crowded together into the servants' elevator. Nor did they like my being there. In fact, as the warmly lighted floors flashed past the elevator we had words over the fact that I, by taking part in the fight, had knocked one of their friends out of a night's work.

We were led out of the elevator through a rococo hall into an anteroom and told to get into our fighting togs. Each of us was issued a pair of boxing gloves and ushered out into the big mirrored hall, which we entered looking cautiously about us and whispering, lest we might accidentally be heard above the noise of the room. It was foggy with cigar smoke. And already the whiskey was taking effect. I was shocked to see some of the most important men of the town quite tipsy. They were all there—bankers, lawyers, judges, doctors, fire chiefs, teachers, merchants. Even one of the more fashionable pastors. Something we could not see was going on up front. A clarinet was vibrating sensuously and the men were standing up and moving eagerly forward. We were a small tight group, clustered together, our bare upper bodies touching and shining with anticipatory sweat; while up front the big shots were becoming increasingly excited over something we still could not see. Suddenly I heard the school superintendent, who had told me to come, yell, "Bring up the shines, gentlemen! Bring up the little shines!"

We were rushed up to the front of the ballroom, where it smelled even more strongly of tobacco and whiskey. Then we were pushed into place. I almost wet my pants. A sea of faces, some hostile, some amused, ringed around us, and in the center, facing us, stood a magnificent blonde—stark naked. There was dead silence. I felt a blast of cold air chill me. I tried to back away, but they were behind me and around me. Some of the boys stood with lowered heads, trembling. I felt a wave of irrational guilt and fear. My teeth chattered, my skin turned to goose flesh, my knees knocked. Yet I was strongly attracted and looked in spite of myself. Had the price of looking been blindness, I would have looked. The hair was yellow like that of a circus kewpie doll, the face heavily powdered and rouged, as though to form an abstract mask, the eyes hollow and smeared a cool blue, the color of a baboon's butt. I felt a desire to spit upon her as my eyes brushed slowly over her body. Her breasts were firm and round as the domes of East Indian temples, and I stood so close as to see the fine skin texture and beads of pearly perspiration glistening like dew around the pink and erected buds of her nipples. I wanted at one and the same time to run from the room, to sink through the floor, or go to her and cover her from my eyes and the eyes of the others with my body; to feel the soft thighs, to caress her and destroy her, to love her and murder her, to hide from her, and yet to stroke where below the small American flag tattooed upon her belly her thighs formed a capital V. I had a notion that of all in the room she saw only me with her impersonal eyes.

And then she began to dance, a slow sensuous movement; the smoke of a hundred cigars clinging to her like the thinnest of veils. She seemed like a fair bird-girl girdled in veils calling to me from the angry surface of some gray and threatening sea. I was transported. Then I became aware of the clarinet playing and the big shots yelling at us. Some threatened us if we looked and others if we did not. On my right I saw one boy faint. And now a man grabbed a silver pitcher from a table and stepped close as he dashed ice water upon him and stood him up and forced two of us to support him as his head hung and moans issued from his thick bluish lips. Another boy began to plead to go home. He was the largest of the group, wearing dark red fighting trunks much too small to conceal the erection which projected from him as though in answer to the insinuating low-registered moaning of the clarinet. He tried to hide himself with his boxing gloves.

And all the while the blonde continued dancing, smiling faintly at the big shots who watched her with fascination, and faintly smiling at our fear. I noticed a certain merchant who followed her hungrily, his lips loose and drooling. He was a large man who wore diamond studs in a shirtfront which swelled with the ample paunch underneath, and each time the blonde swayed her undulating hips he ran his hand through the thin hair of his bald head and, with his arms upheld, his posture clumsy like that of an intoxicated panda, wound his belly in a slow and obscene grind. This creature was completely hypnotized. The music had quickened. As the dancer flung herself about with a detached expression on her face, the men began reaching out to touch her. I could see their beefy fingers sink into the soft flesh. Some of the others tried to stop them and she began to move around the floor in graceful circles, as they gave chase, slipping and sliding over the polished floor. It was mad. Chairs went crashing, drinks were spilt, as they ran laughing and howling after her. They caught her just as she reached a door, raised her from the floor, and tossed her as college boys are tossed at a hazing, and above her red, fixed-smiling lips I saw the terror and disgust in her eyes, almost like my own terror and that which I saw in some of the other boys. As I watched, they tossed her twice and her soft breasts seemed to flatten against the air and her legs flung wildly as she spun. Some of the more sober ones helped her to escape. And I started off the floor, heading for the anteroom with the rest of the boys.

Some were still crying and in hysteria. But as we tried to leave we were stopped and ordered to get into the ring. There was nothing to do but what we were told. All ten of us climbed under the ropes and allowed ourselves to be blindfolded with broad bands of white cloth. One of the men seemed to feel a bit sympathetic and tried to cheer us up as we stood with our backs against the ropes. Some of us tried to grin. "See that boy over there?" one of the men said. "I want you to run across at the bell and give it to him right in the belly. If you don't get him, I'm going to get you. I don't like his looks." Each of us was told the same. The blindfolds were put on. Yet even then I had been going over my speech. In my mind each word was as bright as flame. I felt the cloth pressed into place, and frowned so that it would be loosened when I relaxed.

But now I felt a sudden fit of blind terror. I was unused to darkness. It was as though I had suddenly found myself in a dark room filled with poisonous cottonmouths. I could hear the bleary voices yelling insistently for the battle royal to begin.

"Get going in there!"

"Let me at that big nigger!"

I strained to pick up the school superintendent's voice, as though to squeeze some security out of that slightly more familiar sound.

"Let me at those black sonsabitches!" someone yelled.

"No, Jackson, no!" another voice yelled. "Here, somebody, help me hold Jack."

"I want to get at that ginger-colored nigger. Tear him limb from limb," the first voice yelled.

I stood against the ropes trembling. For in those days I was what they called ginger-colored, and he sounded as though he might crunch me between his teeth like a crisp ginger cookie.

Quite a struggle was going on. Chairs were being kicked about and I could hear voices grunting as with a terrific effort. I wanted to see, to see more desperately than ever before. But the blindfold was tight as a thick skin-puckering scab and when I raised my gloved hands to push the layers of white aside a voice yelled, "Oh, no you don't, black bastard! Leave that alone!"

"Ring the bell before Jackson kills him a coon!" someone boomed in the sudden silence. And I heard the bell clang and the sound of the feet scuffling forward.

A glove smacked against my head. I pivoted, striking out stiffly as someone went past, and felt the jar ripple along the length of my arm to my shoulder. Then it seemed as though all nine of the boys had turned upon me at once. Blows pounded me from all sides while I struck out as best I could. So many blows landed upon me that I wondered if I were not the only blindfolded fighter in the ring, or if the man called Jackson hadn't succeeded in getting me after all.

Blindfolded, I could no longer control my motions. I had no dignity. I stumbled about like a baby or a drunken man. The smoke had become thicker and with each new blow it seemed to sear and further restrict my lungs. My saliva became like hot bitter glue. A glove connected with my head, filling my mouth with warm blood. It was everywhere. I could not tell if the moisture I felt upon my body was sweat or blood. A blow landed hard against the nape of my neck. I felt myself going over, my head hitting the floor. Streaks of blue light filled the black world behind the blindfold. I lay prone, pretending that I was knocked out, but felt myself seized by hands and yanked to my feet. "Get going, black boy! Mix it up!" My arms were like lead, my head smarting from blows. I managed to feel my way to the ropes and held on, trying to catch my breath. A glove landed in my mid-section and I went over again, feeling as though the smoke had become a knife jabbed into my guts. Pushed this way and that by the legs milling around me, I finally pulled erect and discovered that I could see the black, sweat-washed forms weaving in the smoky-blue atmosphere like drunken dancers weaving to the rapid drum-like thuds of blows.

Everyone fought hysterically. It was complete anarchy. Everybody fought everybody else. No group fought together for long. Two, three, four, fought one, then turned to fight each other, were themselves attacked. Blows landed below the belt and in the kidney, with the gloves open as well as closed, and with my eye partly opened now there was not so much terror. I moved carefully, avoiding blows, although not too many to attract attention, fighting from group to group. The boys groped about like blind, cautious crabs crouching to protect their mid-sections, their heads pulled in short against their shoulders, their arms stretched nervously before them, with their fists testing the smoke-filled air like the knobbed feelers of hypersensitive snails. In one corner I glimpsed a boy violently punching the air and heard him scream in pain as he smashed his hand against a ring post. For a second I saw him bent over holding his hand, then going down as a blow caught his unprotected head. I played one group against the other, slipping in and throwing a punch then stepping out of range while pushing the others into the melee to take the blows blindly aimed at me. The smoke was agonizing and there were no rounds, no bells at three minute intervals to relieve our exhaustion. The room spun round me, a swirl of lights, smoke, sweating bodies surrounded by tense white faces. I bled from both nose and mouth, the blood spattering upon my chest.

The men kept yelling, "Slug him, black boy! Knock his guts out!"

"Uppercut him! Kill him! Kill that big boy!"

Taking a fake fall, I saw a boy going down heavily beside me as though we were felled by a single blow, saw a sneaker-clad foot shoot into his groin as the two who had knocked him down stumbled upon him. I rolled out of range, feeling a twinge of nausea.

The harder we fought the more threatening the men became. And yet, I had begun to worry about my speech again. How would it go? Would they recognize my ability? What would they give me?

I was fighting automatically when suddenly I noticed that one after another of the boys was leaving the ring. I was surprised, filled with panic, as though I had been left alone with an unknown danger. Then I understood. The boys had arranged it among themselves. It was the custom for the two men left in the ring to slug it out for the winner's prize. I discovered this too late. When the bell sounded two men in tuxedoes leaped into the ring and removed the blindfold. I found myself facing Tatlock, the biggest of the gang. I felt sick at my stomach. Hardly had the bell stopped ringing in my ears than it clanged again and I saw him moving swiftly toward me. Thinking of nothing else to do I hit him smash on the nose. He kept coming, bringing the rank sharp violence of stale sweat. His face was a black blank of a face, only his eyes alive— with hate of me and aglow with a feverish terror from what had happened to us all. I became anxious. I wanted to deliver my speech and he came at me as though he meant to beat it out of me. I smashed him again and again, taking his blows as they came. Then on a sudden impulse I struck him lightly and as we clinched, I whispered, "Fake like I knocked you out, you can have the prize."

"I'll break your behind," he whispered hoarsely.

"For *them?*"

"For *me*, sonofabitch!"

They were yelling for us to break it up and Tatlock spun me half around with a blow, and as a joggled camera sweeps in a reeling scene, I saw the howling red faces crouching tense beneath the cloud of blue-gray smoke. For a moment the world wavered, unraveled, flowed, then my head cleared and Tatlock bounced before me. That fluttering shadow before my eyes was his jabbing left hand. Then falling forward, my head against his damp shoulder, I whispered,

"I'll make it five dollars more."

"Go to hell!"

But his muscles relaxed a trifle beneath my pressure and I breathed, "Seven?"

"Give it to your ma," he said, ripping me beneath the heart.

And while I still held him I butted him and moved away. I felt myself bombarded with punches. I fought back with hopeless desperation. I wanted to deliver my speech more than anything else in the world, because I felt that only these men could judge truly my ability, and now this stupid clown was ruining my chances. I began fighting carefully now, moving in to punch him and out again with my greater speed. A lucky blow to his chin and I had him going too—until I heard a loud voice yell, "I got my money on the big boy."

Hearing this, I almost dropped my guard. I was confused: Should I try to win against the voice out there? Would not this go against my speech, and was not this a moment for humility, for nonresistance? A blow to my head as I danced about sent my right eye popping like a jack-in-the-box and settled my dilemma. The room went red as I fell. It was a dream fall, my body languid and fastidious as to where to land, until the floor became impatient and smashed up to meet me. A moment later I came to. An hypnotic voice said FIVE emphatically. And I lay there, hazily watching a dark red spot of my own blood shaping itself into a butterfly, glistening and soaking into the soiled gray world of the canvas.

When the voice drawled TEN I was lifted up and dragged to a chair. I sat dazed. My eye pained and swelled with each throb of my pounding heart and I wondered if now I would be allowed to speak. I was wringing wet, my mouth still bleeding. We were grouped along the wall now. The other boys ignored me as they congratulated Tatlock and speculated as to how much they would be paid. One boy whimpered over his smashed hand. Looking up front, I saw attendants in white jackets rolling the portable ring away and placing a small square rug in the vacant space surrounded by chairs. Perhaps, I thought, I will stand on the rug to deliver my speech.

Then the M.C. called to us, "Come on up here boys and get your money."

We ran forward to where the men laughed and talked in their chairs, waiting. Everyone seemed friendly now.

"There it is on the rug," the man said. I saw the rug covered with coins of all dimensions and a few crumpled bills. But what excited me, scattered here and there, were the gold pieces.

"Boys, it's all yours," the man said. "You get all you grab."

"That's right, Sambo," a blond man said, winking at me confidentially.

I trembled with excitement, forgetting my pain. I would get the gold and the bills, I thought. I would use both hands. I would throw my body against the boys nearest me to block them from the gold.

"Get down around the rug now," the man commanded, "and don't anyone touch it until I give the signal."

"This ought to be good," I heard.

As told, we got around the square rug on our knees. Slowly the man raised his freckled hand as we followed it upward with our eyes.

I heard, "These niggers look like they're about to pray!"

Then, "Ready," the man said. "Go!"

I lunged for a yellow coin lying on the blue design of the carpet, touching it and sending a surprised shriek to join those rising around me. I tried frantically to remove my hand but could not let go. A hot, violent force tore through my body, shaking me like a wet rat. The rug was electrified. The hair bristled up on my head as I shook myself free. My muscles jumped, my nerves jangled, writhed. But I saw that this was not stopping the other boys. Laughing in fear and embarrassment, some were holding back and scooping up the coins knocked off by the painful contortions of the others. The men roared above us as we struggled.

"Pick it up, goddamnit, pick it up!" someone called like a bass-voiced parrot. "Go on, get it!"

I crawled rapidly around the floor, picking up the coins, trying to avoid the coppers and to get greenbacks and the gold. Ignoring the shock by laughing, as I brushed the coins off quickly, I discovered that I could contain the electricity—a contradiction, but it works. Then the men began to push us onto the rug. Laughing embarrassedly, we struggled out of their hands and kept after the coins. We were all wet and slippery and hard to hold. Suddenly I saw a boy lifted into the air, glistening with sweat like a circus seal, and dropped, his wet back landing flush upon the charged rug, heard him yell and saw him literally dance upon his back, his elbows beating a frenzied tattoo upon the floor, his muscles twitching like the flesh of a horse stung by many flies. When he finally rolled off, his face was gray and no one stopped him when he ran from the floor amid booming laughter.

"Get the money," the M.C. called. "That's good hard American cash!"

And we snatched and grabbed, snatched and grabbed. I was careful not to come too close to the rug now, and when I felt the hot whiskey breath descend upon me like a cloud of foul air I reached out and grabbed the leg of a chair. It was occupied and I held on desperately.

"Leggo, nigger! Leggo!"

The huge face wavered down to mine as he tried to push me free. But my body was slippery and he was too drunk. It was Mr. Colcord, who owned a chain of movie houses and "entertainment palaces." Each time he grabbed me I slipped out of his hands. It became a real struggle. I feared the rug more than I did the drunk, so I held on, surprising myself for a moment by trying to topple *him* upon the rug. It was such an enormous idea that I found myself actually carrying it out. I tried not to be obvious, yet when I grabbed his leg, trying to tumble him out of the chair, he raised up roaring with laughter, and, looking at me with soberness dead in the eye, kicked me viciously in the chest. The chair leg flew out of my hand and I felt myself going and rolled. It was as though I had rolled through a bed of hot coals. It seemed a whole century would pass before I would roll free, a century in which I was seared through the deepest levels of my body to the fearful breath within me and the breath seared and heated to the point of explosion. It'll all be over in a flash, I thought as I rolled clear. It'll all be over in a flash.

But not yet, the men on the other side were waiting, red faces swollen as though from apoplexy as they bent forward in their chairs. Seeing their fingers coming toward me I rolled away as a fumbled football rolls off the receiver's fingertips, back into the coals. That time I luckily sent the rug sliding out of place and heard the coins ringing against the floor and the boys scuffling to pick them up and the M.C. calling, "All right, boys, that's all. Go get dressed and get your money."

I was limp as a dish rag. My back felt as though it had been beaten with wires.

When we had dressed the M.C. came in and gave us each five dollars, except Tatlock, who got ten for being last in the ring. Then he told us to leave. I was not to get a chance to deliver my speech, I thought. I was going out into the dim alley in despair when I was stopped and told to go back. I returned to the ballroom, where the men were pushing back their chairs and gathering in groups to talk.

The M.C. knocked on a table for quiet. "Gentlemen," he said, "we almost forgot an important part of the program. A most serious part, gentlemen. This boy was brought here to deliver a speech which he made at his graduation yesterday . . ."

"Bravo!"

"I'm told that he is the smartest boy we've got out there in Greenwood. I'm told that he knows more big words than a pocket-sized dictionary."

Much applause and laughter.

"So now, gentlemen, I want you to give him your attention."

There was still laughter as I faced them, my mouth dry, my eye throbbing. I began slowly, but evidently my throat was tense, because they began shouting, "Louder! Louder!"

"We of the younger generation extol the wisdom of that great leader and educator," I shouted, "who first spoke these flaming words of wisdom: 'A ship lost at sea for many days suddenly sighted a friendly vessel. From the mast of the unfortunate vessel was seen a signal: "Water, water; we die of thirst!" The answer from the friendly vessel came back: "Cast down your bucket where you are." The captain of the distressed vessel, at last heeding the injunction, cast down his bucket, and it came up full of fresh sparkling water from the mouth of the Amazon River.' And like him I say, and in his words, 'To those of my race who depend upon bettering their condition in a foreign land, or who underestimate the importance of cultivating friendly relations with the Southern white man, who is his next-door neighbor, I would say: "Cast down your bucket where you are"—cast it down in making friends in every manly way of the people of all races by whom we are surrounded . . .' "

I spoke automatically and with such fervor that I did not realize that the men were still talking and laughing until my dry mouth, filling up with blood from the cut, almost strangled me. I coughed, wanting to stop and go to one of the tall brass, sand-filled spittoons to relieve myself, but a few of the men, especially the superintendent, were listening and I was afraid. So I gulped it down, blood, saliva and all, and continued. (What powers of endurance I had during those days! What enthusiasm! What a belief in the rightness of things!) I spoke even louder in spite of the pain. But still they talked and still they laughed, as though deaf with cotton in dirty ears. So I spoke with greater emotional emphasis. I closed my ears and swallowed blood until I was nauseated. The speech seemed a hundred times as long as before, but I could not leave out a single word. All had to be said, each memorized nuance considered, rendered. Nor was that all. Whenever I uttered a word of three or more syllables a group of voices would yell for me to repeat it. I used the phrase "social responsibility" and they yelled:

"What's that word you say, boy?"

"Social responsibility," I said.

"What?"

"Social . . ."

"Louder."

". . . responsibility."

"More!"

"Respon—"

"Repeat!"

"—sibility."

The room filled with the uproar of laughter until, no doubt, distracted by having to gulp down my blood, I made a mistake and yelled a phrase I had often seen denounced in newspaper editorials, heard debated in private.

"Social . . ."

"What?" they yelled.

". . . equality—"

The laughter hung smokelike in the sudden stillness. I opened my eyes, puzzled. Sounds of displeasure filled the room. The M.C. rushed forward. They shouted hostile phrases at me. But I did not understand.

A small dry mustached man in the front row blared out, "Say that slowly, son!"

"What, sir?"

"What you just said!"

"Social responsibility, sir," I said.

"You weren't being smart, were you, boy?" he said, not unkindly.

"No, sir!"

"You sure that about 'equality' was a mistake?"

"Oh, yes, sir," I said. "I was swallowing blood."

"Well, you had better speak more slowly so we can understand. We mean to do right by you, but you've got to know your place at all times. All right, now, go on with your speech."

I was afraid. I wanted to leave but I wanted also to speak and I was afraid they'd snatch me down.

"Thank you, sir," I said, beginning where I had left off, and having them ignore me as before.

Yet when I finished there was a thunderous applause. I was surprised to see the superintendent come forth with a package wrapped in white tissue paper, and, gesturing for quiet, address the men.

"Gentlemen, you see that I did not overpraise this boy. He makes a good speech and some day he'll lead his people in the proper paths. And I don't have to tell you that that is important in these days and times. This is a good, smart boy, and so to encourage him in the right direction, in the name of the Board of Education I wish to present him a prize in the form of this . . ."

He paused, removing the tissue paper and revealing a gleaming calfskin brief case.

". . . in the form of this first-class article from Shad Whitmore's shop."

"Boy," he said, addressing me, "take this prize and keep it well. Consider it a badge of office. Prize it. Keep developing as you are and some day it will be filled with important papers that will help shape the destiny of your people."

I was so moved that I could hardly express my thanks. A rope of bloody saliva forming a shape like an undiscovered continent drooled upon the leather and I wiped it quickly away. I felt an importance that I had never dreamed.

"Open it and see what's inside," I was told.

My fingers a-tremble, I complied, smelling the fresh leather and finding an official-looking document inside. It was a scholarship to the state college for Negroes. My eyes filled with tears and I ran awkwardly off the floor.

I was overjoyed; I did not even mind when I discovered that the gold pieces I had scrambled for were brass pocket tokens advertising a certain make of automobile.

When I reached home everyone was excited. Next day the neighbors came to congratulate me. I even felt safe from grandfather, whose deathbed curse usually spoiled my triumphs. I stood beneath his photograph with my brief case in hand and smiled triumphantly into his stolid black peasant's face. It was a face that fascinated me. The eyes seemed to follow everywhere I went.

That night I dreamed I was at a circus with him and that he refused to laugh at the clowns no matter what they did. Then later he told me to open my brief case and read what was inside and I did, finding an official envelope stamped with the state seal; and inside the envelope I found another and another, endlessly, and I thought I would fall of weariness. "Them's years," he said. "Now open that one." And I did and in it I found an engraved document containing a short message in letters of gold. "Read it," my grandfather said. "Out loud!"

"To Whom It May Concern," I intoned. "Keep This Nigger-Boy Running."

I awoke with the old man's laughter ringing in my ears.

Study and Discussion Questions

1. What is the narrator's attitude toward his former self?
2. In what way is the narrator, as a young man, "an invisible man"?
3. Explain the reactions of the narrator and the other young black men to the naked woman. What do they have in common with her? What does she represent?

4. Discuss the symbolic significance of the battle royal itself, and of the electrified rug.
5. Why do the white men do what they do? What does the whole event—the blond woman's performance, the battle royal, the electrified rug, the narrator's speech—do for them? What does it do *to* the narrator and the other young black men?
6. Considering the abuse the white men inflict on the narrator and the contempt for him it clearly indicates, why do they give him a scholarship?

Writing Exercises

1. What is the narrator's grandfather's deathbed advice to him? In roughly what year is it given? What do you think of this advice? Does it make more sense or less sense today?
2. "I wanted to deliver my speech more than anything else in the world, because I felt that only these men could judge truly my ability." This statement comes not at the beginning of the story, but when the narrator is already bloodied from the battle royal. Discuss this and some of the other striking ironies in the story.

JAMAICA KINCAID (b. 1949)

Jamaica Kincaid was born in St. John's, Antigua and educated there in government schools. In 1966 she moved to the United States and in 1976 became a staff writer for The New Yorker *magazine, in which many of her stories, including "Girl," first appeared. Kincaid has published two collections,* At the Bottom of the River *(1983) and* Annie John *(1985).*

Girl   (1983)

Wash the white clothes on Monday and put them on the stone heap; wash the color clothes on Tuesday and put them on the clothesline to dry; don't walk barehead in the hot sun; cook pumpkin fritters in very hot sweet oil; soak your little cloths right after you take them off; when buying cotton to make yourself a nice blouse, be sure that it doesn't have gum on it, because that way it won't hold up well after a wash; soak salt fish overnight before you cook it; is it true that you sing benna[1] in Sunday school?; always eat your food in such a way that it won't turn someone else's stomach; on Sundays try to walk like a lady and not like the slut you are so bent on becoming; don't sing benna in Sunday school;

---

[1] Calypso or rock and roll.

you mustn't speak to wharf-rat boys, not even to give directions; don't eat fruits on the street—flies will follow you; *but I don't sing benna on Sundays at all and never in Sunday school;* this is how to sew on a button; this is how to make a buttonhole for the button you have just sewed on; this is how to hem a dress when you see the hem coming down and so to prevent yourself from looking like the slut I know you are so bent on becoming; this is how you iron your father's khaki shirt so that it doesn't have a crease; this is how you iron your father's khaki pants so that they don't have a crease; this is how you grow okra—far from the house, because okra tree harbors red ants; when you are growing dasheen, make sure it gets plenty of water or else it makes your throat itch when you are eating it; this is how you sweep a corner; this is how you sweep a whole house; this is how you sweep a yard; this is how you smile to someone you don't like too much; this is how you smile to someone you don't like at all; this is how you smile to someone you like completely; this is how you set a table for tea; this is how you set a table for dinner; this is how you set a table for dinner with an important guest; this is how you set a table for lunch; this is how you set a table for breakfast; this is how to behave in the presence of men who don't know you very well, and this way they won't recognize immediately the slut I have warned you against becoming; be sure to wash every day, even if it is with your own spit; don't squat down to play marbles—you are not a boy, you know; don't pick people's flowers—you might catch something; don't throw stones at blackbirds, because it might not be a blackbird at all; this is how to make a bread pudding; this is how to make doukona; this is how to make pepper pot; this is how to make a good medicine for a cold; this is how to make a good medicine to throw away a child before it even becomes a child; this is how to catch a fish; this is how to throw back a fish you don't like, and that way something bad won't fall on you; this is how to bully a man; this is how a man bullies you; this is how to love a man, and if this doesn't work there are other ways, and if they don't work don't feel too bad about giving up; this is how to spit up in the air if you feel like it, and this is how to move quick so that it doesn't fall on you; this is how to make ends meet; always squeeze bread to make sure it's fresh; *but what if the baker won't let me feel the bread?;* you mean to say that after all you are really going to be the kind of woman who the baker won't let near the bread?

Study and Discussion Questions

1. Who is speaking? To whom? How old do you think the girl being addressed is?
2. Categorize and characterize the advice given.
3. What seems to be the speaker's main concern? What evidence is there that she has it in mind even when she's not talking about it directly?

4. Analyze the impact of the narrator's stringing so many words of advice together. What else makes the story funny?

Writing Exercises

1. What would the girl grow up to be like if she followed all the advice given? Discuss the story as a comment on women's roles in society.
2. Choose someone—a parent, older sibling, employer, teacher—who gives or has given you too much advice and write a short piece modeled on "Girl."

EDMUND WHITE   (b. 1940)

Edmund White was born in Cincinnati, Ohio, attended the University of Michigan, and has worked as an editor of the Saturday Review *and as a creative writing instructor at several universities. Among his other works, besides* A Boy's Own Story, *are* States of Desire: Travels in Gay America *(1980) and the novels* Forgetting Elena *(1973),* Nocturnes for the King of Naples *(1978), and* Caracole *(1985).*

FROM A Boy's Own Story   (1982)

If my sister was happy with other girls in the summer, in the winter she sat home night after night waiting for boys to ask her out on dates she dreaded. Our mother had moved us into a large apartment and furnished it luxuriously—but no one came to visit. By now my sister was certain I was the one who'd been hurting her chances. With a brother so weird, who was in no way athletic or cool or neat, no wonder she had a reputation for being out of it.

Since my sister was only four years older than I, she knew precisely what would appeal to my classmates—what sort of penny loafers, which red-and-white-checked short-sleeved shirt, what style of jeans, what manner of low-key joshing. She helped me buy the right clothes and she showed me how to wear them ("You've got to roll up the sleeves exactly three times—the folds should be tight, see?—and no more than an inch wide"). She taught me to say hi to as many people as possible in the school corridors, to notice with care who responded and to brave each blank stare with a glittery smile.

I kept a phone list of the people I thought I knew well enough to call in the afternoon and evening, and I'd work my way down systematically through all the names. Soon the list was so long, a good thirty names, that I needed three days to complete a full cycle. "Hi, it's me. What are you doing? Yeah, I mean right now—what'd you think I meant, stupid? Geez . . . chewing gum? You call that doing something? Naw . . . I'm staying in. My mom's on my back about the old homework. 'Sides, there's that weird new sci-fi thing on TV—yeah, that's the one. You? Janey coming over to study? I like that blue sweater she had on, but the black loafers looked sort of hoody. I *know* she's not a hood—just see you two on a motorcycle, vrmm, vrmm—can you picture it? You are there: vrmm, vrmm."

And so on for hours, pure ventriloquism, nausea of small talk, a discipline nearly Oriental in its exclusion of content and its focus on empty locutions, the chatter of social fear confused with yearning, for I not only feared my friends, I also wanted to make them love me.

Until now, until this great conversion, friendship for me had been more a minor pleasure than a science. Friends had been people to sit with in the cafeteria, people who had the same hobbies or the same study hall, boys equally hopeless in gym class or girls in assembly whose last names started with the same letter as mine. I hadn't courted those acquaintances. I made no effort to draw them out, to elicit or reflect on their confidences, or to advise them. I required almost nothing of them, for if I wasn't attentive neither was I demanding. Practically anyone could be my friend. For me friendship was an innocent, unconscious habit that didn't confer prestige on anyone, that led nowhere, that scarcely bore thinking about, unremarkable as breath.

When my sister taught me ways to be popular she was teaching me something I hadn't known about. She filled a need the instant she created it. Or perhaps I should say she taught me that the loneliness I felt like a bad burn could be soothed. I most certainly had been lonely. I had ached and writhed with loneliness, twisting around and smearing it on me as though it were a tissue of shame pouring out of my body: shameful, familiar, the feel of shame. And yet the company I longed for, the radiant face smiling down into mine, the arm around my shoulders (an arm so lean every vein could be read through it, as light can be seen between marks on vellum)—in my daydreams this company came to me unbidden. The notion that I might have been able to court friends, win attention, conjure it, would have spoiled it for me. Unbidden love was what I wanted. Under my sister's tutelage I learned that love or at least friendship must be coaxed, that there are skills (listening, smiling, remembering, flattering) that lure it closer. Sometimes, as I learned, a friend is no more than someone to kill time with, a voice chattering into the receiver a litany of questions, all those lumpy sandbags—individually light but cumulatively heavy—that hang from the girdle around the balloon's suspended car to slow its ascent into cold, unbreathable solitude. But the very act of enticing friendship, of managing and conducting it, the whole politics of sentiment—well, I didn't despise it, for how could I despise what I needed so much?

While I was growing up I had never glimpsed the underbrush of kid society that lay just behind the topiary of the classroom. Dumb me—I'd just assumed the kids knew only whoever happened to be in their home room. Nor did I suspect some kids saw each other every day after school, saw and saw each other strolling under a shifting leaf spray of social lights and sexual shadows, imprints of illumination that had nothing to do with the grid of adult arrangements. A popular boy named Butch was the son of a bone surgeon; his girl was the daughter of a delivery man.

They made love every afternoon in the basement of her house. By the time they were fifteen they'd already been lovers for three years and their friends regarded them as older and wiser mentors—parents, really—to whom they could turn for advice. We'd all drop by her house around four-thirty or five. She and he would be coming up out of the basement, smiling, flushed, his fingers on his fly buttons, hers tugging her tartan skirt a quarter-circle around so that the giant safety pin would be on the right side. Then she'd bake chocolate chip cookies while he horsed around outside with a football. Our own parents had only to say a word to us to inject scalding resentment into our veins, but these lesser, better parents, matured not by years but by passion and its induction into sadness, seemed to be mild guardians, he with his chipped tooth and froth of sweat curls above his neck, she with the childhood scar that drew a silky white stitch through one eyebrow and with the melancholy smile. Even the suppers we sat down to of cold milk and hot cookies pocked with runny chocolate were wonderfully unhealthy parodies of nursery meals.

At first I didn't know how to become really popular. The other kids had grown up together and they just more or less accepted one another. Of course, some of them worked at being popular, but others preferred watching TV alone in the afternoons while drinking beer and some had special interests (sewing, dramatics, yearbook, world affairs) that drew them off into tight little groups too peripheral to count. Still others, by virtue of a sudden blossoming into physical beauty or athletic prowess, became leaders without worrying about it. But that left the whole middle ground of those of us with no strange little niche and no inherent distinction (except brains, possibly, or money, neither of which carried much weight), and for us the only way to win popularity was through "personality." Girls, of course, had personality more than boys, but some boys had personality, too, as a jester has jokes or a seducer sherry. Something bogus, that is, something shameful.

I set my sights on the most popular boy in the whole school. I figured that if I could hoodwink him into being my friend, people would have to accept me. I think my strategy, on the whole, was sound. Since I wasn't athletic, I had nothing to offer other people beside the flattering mirror of my attention, a service that suited my sweet, devious nature.

I can't really remember how I met Tommy. I recollect him first as a smooth cloche of shiny light brown hair sporting the slender plume of a cowlick, a head bent over a book in study hall belonging to someone I'd heard was captain of the tennis team, leader of the Crowd and Sally's steady; then, without transition, he was my friend and he was struggling to explain to me his theory about Sartre's *Nausea* as we kicked our way through autumn leaves. "Uh . . . uh . . ." he was crying out on a loud, high note, a sustained nasal sound, as he stopped walking and held a finger up. Then his small blue eyes, straining to see an idea in the distance, blinked, glanced smoothly up and down. The glitter of prophecy faded. He shrugged: "Lost it." He exposed his palms and then pocketed his hands in his trousers. I held my breath and counted ten before I offered my soft, apologetic suggestion: "But aren't you really saying that Sartre thinks man is . . ." and I filled in the blank with the closest approximation I could invent, not of Sartre's thought, but of Tommy's dubious interpretation of it.

"That's it! That's it!" Tommy shouted, and again he excitedly waded out into the philosophical murk. I, who thought only of survival, had no interest in philosophical questions. The proximate ones were enough to obsess me, not as things I chose to contemplate, but as decisions rushing up at me as out of oncoming traffic. These were the things I thought about: Am I boring Tommy? Will he mind if I rest my elbow on his shoulder? Should I powder my white bucks or keep the scuff marks? How low should I let my jeans ride?

If the ultimate questions—the meaning of life, time, being—interested me now, it was only because they interested Tommy. To the extent the other kids thought of me at all they considered me to be something of a brain; certainly in their eyes Tom was a jock. Ironic, then, that he was the one who did all the thinking, who had the taste for philosophy— ironic but predictable, since his sovereignty gave him the ease to wonder about what it all meant, whereas I had to concentrate on means, not meaning. The meaning seemed quite clear: to survive and then to become popular. The game of monarch I'd played in the snow or sand or in cloud castles now became real. The princess, asleep for so many years, awakes to the taste of the prince's lips, a slightly sour taste; she stares up into a face visored in shadow.

In that old, comfortable suburb even the biggest mansions hunkered democratically down on the curb and sat right next to other dwellings. No concealing hedges or isolating parks could be seen anywhere. Even quite massive houses of many rooms and wings engulfed their plots down to the sidewalk. This conspiciousness declared a pride and innocence: we have nothing to hide, and we want to show you what we've got. Tom's house was a Mediterranean villa with six bedrooms and servants' quarters over a double garage, but its gleaming leaded panes and the front door (thick oak gouged into griffins) loomed up just ten paces from the street.

Once inside that door, however, I felt transported into another society that had ways I could never quite master. The Wellingtons were nice but not charming. The Wellingtons gave thought to everything they did. The staircase was lined with expensive, ugly paintings done from photographs of their four children. Their kids' teeth were bound in costly wires, their whims for sailboats or skis or guitars were lavishly but silently honored, they were all paraded in a stupor past the monuments of Europe, their vacations down rapids and over glaciers or up mountains were well funded—but silence reigned. No one said a word.

Dinner there was torture. A student from the university served. Mr. Wellington carved. Mrs. Wellington, a woman with a girlish spirit trapped inside a large, swollen body, made stabs at conversation, but she was so shy she could speak only in comical accents. She'd grunt in a bass voice like a bear or squeak like a mouse or imitate Donald Duck—anything rather than say a simple declarative sentence in her own fragile, mortified voice. The father terrified us all with his manners (the long white hands wielding the fork and knife and expertly slicing the joint). He radiated disapproval. His disapproval was not the martyr's blackmail but a sort of murderous mildness: if he weren't so fastidious he'd murder you. We watched him carve. We were wordless, hypnotized by the candle flames, the neat incisions and deep, bloody invasions, the sound of the metal knife scraping against the tines of the fork, the sickening softness of each red slice laid to the side and the trickle down silver channels ramifying back into a bole of blood.

The odd thing is that the father's spirit did not contaminate the house. His lair, the library, was even the sunniest, most relaxed room of all as the two little dogs, Welsh corgies, trotted from couch to front door at every disturbance, their small, shaggy feet clicking on the polished red tiles. The dogs, the children, his wife—all seemed to prosper in spite of his punitive reserve, his tight eyes, the way he sniffed with contempt at the end of every sentence someone else said. "Oh, yes," he said to me, examining his overly manicured hand, "I know of your mother . . . by reputation," and my heart sank.

In this house the parents maintained a silence except for the father's dreaded little comments, the sugar substitute of his sweetness, and the whole chirping menagerie of the mother's comical voices. No one hovered over the kids. They came and went as they chose, they stayed home and studied or they went out, they ate dinner in or at the last moment they accepted the hospitality of other tables. But under this superficial ease of manner ran their dread of their father and their fear of offending him in some new way. He was a man far milder, far more (shall I say) ladylike than any other father I'd known, and yet his soft way of curling up on a couch and tucking his silk dressing gown modestly around his thin white shanks terrified everyone, as did his way of looking over the tops of his glasses and mouthing without sound the name of his son: "Tommy"—the lips compressed on the double *m* and making a meal out of his swallowed, sorrowing disappointment. He was homely, tall, snowy-haired, hardworking, in bad health. He seemed to me the absolute standard of respectability, and by that standard I failed. My sister had coached me in some sort of charm, but no degree of charm, whether counterfeit or genuine, made an impression on Mr. Wellington. He was charm-proof. He disapproved of me. I was a fraud, a charlatan. His disapproval started with my mother and her "reputation," whatever that might refer to (her divorce? her dates? the fact she worked?). He didn't like me and he didn't want his son to associate with me. When I entered his study I'd stand behind Tom. Only now does it occur to me that Tommy may have liked me precisely because his father didn't. Was Tom's friendship with me one more way in which he was unobtrusively but firmly disappointing his father?

Once we closed Tom's bedroom door we were immersed again in the happy shabbiness of our friendship. For he was my friend—my best friend! Until now other boys my age had frightened me. We might grab each other in the leaves and play Squirrel; Ralph might have hypnotized me, but those painful stabs at pleasure had left me shaken and swollen with yearning—I wanted someone to love me. Someone adult. Someone under my power. I had prayed I'd grow up as fast as possible.

No longer. For the first time I found it exhilarating to be young and with someone young. I loved him, and the love was all the more powerful because I had to hide it. We slept in twin beds only two feet apart. We sat around for hours in our underpants and talked about Sartre and tennis and Sally and all the other kids at school and love and God and the afterlife and infinity. Tom's mother never came to his door, as mine would have, to order us to sleep. The big dark house creaked around us as we lay on our separate beds in zany positions and talked and talked our way into the inner recesses of the night, those dim lands so tender to the couple.

And we talked of friendship, of our friendship, of how it was as intense as love, better than love, a kind of love. I told Tom my father had said friendships don't last, they wear out and must be replaced every decade as we grow older—but I reported this heresy (which I'd invented; my poor father had no friends to discard) only so that Tom and I might denounce it and pledge to each other our eternal fidelity. "Jesus," Tom said, "those guys are so damn *cynical!* Jeez . . ." He was lying on his stomach staring into the pillow; his voice was muffled. Now he propped himself up on one elbow. His forehead was red where he'd been leaning on it. His face was loose from sleepiness. His smile, too, was loose, rubbery, his gaze genial, bleary. "I mean, God! How can they go on if they think that way?" He laughed a laugh on a high brass note, a toot of amazement at the sheer gall of grown-up cynicism.

"Maybe," I said suavely, "because we're not religious, we've made friendship into our religion." I loved ringing these changes on our theme, which was ourselves, our love; to keep the subject going I could relate it to our atheism, which we'd just discovered, or to dozens of other favorite themes.

"Yeah," Tom said. He seemed intrigued by this possibility. "Hold on. Don't forget where we were." He hurried into the adjoining bathroom.

As I listened through the open door to the jet of water falling into the toilet I imagined standing beside him, our streams of urine crossing, dribbling dry, then our hands continuing to shake a final glistening drop of something stickier than water from this new disturbance, this desire our lifting, meeting eyes had to confess.

No sooner would such a temptation present itself than I would smother it. The effect was of snuffing out a candle, two candles, a row of twenty, until the lens pulled back to reveal an entire votive stand exhaling a hundred thin lines of smoke as a terraced offering before the shrine. In this religion hidden lights had been declared superior to those that glared. Somewhere I was storing up merit, accumulating the credit I'd need to buy, one day, the salvation I longed for. Until then (and it was a reckoning that could be forestalled indefinitely, that I preferred putting off) I'd live in that happiest of all conditions: the long but seemingly prosperous courtship. It was a series of tests, ever more arduous, even perverse. For instance, I was required to deny my love in order to prove it.

"You know," Tom said one day, "you can stay over any time you like. Harold"—the minister's son, my old partner at Squirrel—"warned me you'd jump me in my sleep. You gotta forgive me. It's just I don't go in for that weird stuff."

I swallowed painfully and whispered, "Nor—" I cleared my throat and said too primly, "Nor do I."

The medical smell, that Lysol smell of homosexuality, was staining the air again as the rubber-wheeled metal cart of drugs and disinfectants rolled silently by. I longed to open the window, to go away for an hour and come back to a room free of that odor, the smell of shame.

I never doubted that homosexuality was a sickness; in fact, I took it as a measure of how unsparingly objective I was that I could contemplate this very sickness. But in some other part of my mind I couldn't believe that the Lysol smell must bathe me, too, that its smell of stale coal fumes must penetrate my love for Tom. Perhaps I became so vague, so exhilarated with vagueness, precisely in order to forestall a recognition of the final term of the syllogism that begins: If one man loves another he is a homosexual; I love a man . . .

I'd heard that boys passed through a stage of homosexuality, that this stage was normal, nearly universal—then that must be what was happening to me. A stage. A prolonged stage. Soon enough this stage would revolve, and after Tom's bedroom vanished, on would trundle white organdy, blue ribbons, a smiling girl opening her arms . . . But that would come later. As for now, I could continue to look as long as I liked into Tom's eyes the color of faded lapis beneath brows so blond they were visible only at the roots just to each side of his nose—a faint smudge turning gold as it thinned and sped out toward the temples.

He was a ratty boy. He hated to shave and would let his peach fuzz go for a week or even two at a time; it grew in in clumps, full on the chin, sparse along the jaw, patchy beside the deep wicks of his mouth.

His chamois-cloth shirts were all missing buttons. The gaps they left were filled in with glimpses of dingy undershirt. His jockey shorts had holes in them. Around one leg a broken elastic had popped out of the cotton seam and dangled against his thigh like a gray noodle. Since he wore a single pair of shorts for days on end the front pouch would soon be stained with yellow. He got up too late to shower before school; he'd run a hand through his fine hair but could never tame that high spume of a cowlick that tossed and bobbed above him, absurdly, gallantly.

His rattiness wore a jaunty air that redeemed everything. Faded, baggy jeans, Indian moccasins he'd owned so long the soft leather tops had taken on the shape of his toes, sunglasses repaired with Band-Aids, an ancient purple shirt bleached and aged to a dusty plum, a letter jacket with white leather sleeves and on the back white lettering against a dark blue field—these were the accoutrements of a princely pauper, a paupered prince.

We walked beside the lake at night, a spring night. As we walked we rolled gently into each other, so that our shoulders touched with every other step. A coolness scudded in off the lake and we kept our hands in our pockets. Now Tom had leaped up onto the narrow top of a retaining wall and was scampering along it in his moccasins. Although heights terrified me I followed him. The ground on both sides fell away as we crossed a canal flowing into the lake, but I put one foot in front of the other and looked not down but at Tom's back. I prayed to a God I didn't believe in to preserve me. Soon enough I was beside Tom again and my pulse subsided; that dangerous crossing was a sacrifice I'd made to him. Our shoulders touched. As usual he was talking too loud and in his characteristic way, a sustained tenor *uh* as he collected his thoughts, then a chuckle and a rapid, throw-away sentence that came almost as an anticlimax. Since Tom was the most popular boy at school, many guys had imitated his halting, then rushing way of talking (as well as his grungy clothes and haphazard grooming). But I never wanted to be Tom. I wanted Tom to be Tom for me. I wanted him to hold his reedy, sinewy, scruffy maleness in trust for us both.

We were heading toward a concrete pier wide enough for a truck to run down. At the far end people were fishing for smelt, illegal lanterns drawing silver schools into nets. We ambled out and watched the lights play over that dripping, squirming ore being extracted from the lake's mines. A net was dumped at my feet and I saw that cold life arc, panic, die. Tommy knew one of the old guys, who gave us a couple dozen fish, which we took back to the Wellingtons' place.

At midnight everyone was in bed, but Tom decided we were hungry and had to fry up our smelt right now. The odor of burning butter and bitter young fish drew Mrs. Wellington down from her little sitting room where she dozed, watched television and paged through books about gardening and thoroughbred dogs. She came blinking and padding down to the kitchen, lured by the smell of frying fish, the smell of a pleasure forbidden because it comes from a kingdom we dare not enter for long. I was certain she would be gruff—she was frowning, though only against the neon brightness of the kitchen. "What's going on here?" she asked in what must have been at last the sound of her true voice, the poor, flat intonations of the prairies where she'd grown up. Soon she was pouring out tall glasses of milk and setting places for us. She was a good sport in an unselfconscious way I'd never seen in a grown-up before, as though she and we were all part of the same society of hungry, browsing creatures instead of members of two tribes, one spontaneous and the other repressive. She seemed to bend naturally to the will of her son, and this compliance suggested an unspoken respect for the primacy of even such a young and scruffy man. My own mother paid lip service to the notion of male supremacy, but she had had to make her own way in the world too long to stay constant to such a purely decorative belief.

After the midnight supper Tommy started to play the guitar and sing. He and I had trekked more than once downtown to the Folk Center to hear a barefoot hillbilly woman in a long, faded skirt intone Elizabethan songs and pluck at a dulcimer or to listen, frightened and transported, to a big black Lesbian with a crew cut moan her basso way through the blues. The People—those brawny, smiling farmers, those plump, wholesome teens bursting out of bib overalls, those toothless ex-cons, those white-eyed dust bowl victims—the People, half-glimpsed in old photos, films and WPA murals, were about to reemerge, we trusted, into history and our lives.

All this aspiration, this promise of fellowship and equality, informed Tom's songs. We worried a bit (just a bit) that we might be suburban twerps unworthy of the People. We already knew to sneer at certain folk singers for their "commercial" arrangements, their "slickness," their betrayal of the heartrending plainness of real working folks. Although we strove in our daily lives to be as agreeable and popular as possible, to conform exactly to reigning fads, we simultaneously abhorred whatever was ingratiating. We were drawn to a club where a big, scarred Negro with lots of gold jewelry and liverish eyes ruminated over a half-improvised ballad under a spotlight before a breathless, thrilled audience of sheltered white teens (overheard on the way out from the newly elected president of our United Nations Club: "It makes you feel so damn phony. It even makes you Question Your Values").

Of course, the best thing about folk music was that it gave me a chance to stare at Tommy while he sang. After endless false starts, after tunings and retunings and trial runs of newly or imperfectly learned strums, he'd finally accompany himself through one great ballad after another. His voice was harsh and high, his hands grubby, and soon enough his exertions would make the faded blue workshirt cling to his back and chest in dark blue patches. Whereas when he spoke he was evasive or philosophical, certainly jokey in a tepid way, when he sang he was eloquent with passion, with the simple statement of passion. And I was, for once, allowed to stare and stare at him.

Sometimes, after he fell asleep at night, I'd study the composition of grays poised on the pale lozenge of his pillow, those grays that constituted a face, and I'd dream he was awakening, rising to kiss me, the grays blushing with fire and warmth—but then he'd move and I'd realize that what I'd taken to be his face was in fact a fold in the sheet. I'd listen for his breath to quicken, I'd look for his sealed eyes to glint, I'd wait for his hot, strong hand to reach across the chasm between the beds to grab me—but none of that happened. There was no passion displayed between us and I never saw him show any feeling at all beyond a narrow range of teasing and joking.

Except when he sang. Then he was free, that is, constrained by the ceremony of performance, the fiction that the entertainer is alone, that he is expressing grief or joy to himself alone. Tom would close his eyes and tip his head back. Squint lines would stream away from his eyes, his forehead would wrinkle, the veins would stand out along his throat and when he held a high note his whole body would tremble. One time he proudly showed me the calluses he'd earned by playing the guitar; he let me feel them. Sometimes he didn't play at all but just sounded notes as he worked something out. He had forgotten me. He thought he was alone. He'd drop the slightly foolish smile he usually wore to disarm adolescent envy or adult expectation and he looked angry and much older: I took this to be his true face. As a folk singer Tom was permitted to wail and shout and moan and as his audience I was permitted to look at him.

His father invited me to go sailing. I accepted, although I warned him I was familiar only with powerboats and had had no experience as a crew member. Everything about dressing the ship—unshrouding and raising the sails, lowering the keel, installing the rudder, untangling the sheets—confused me. I knew I was in the way and I stood, one hand on the boom, trying to inhale myself into nonexistence. I heard Mr. Wellington's quick sharp breaths as reproaches.

The day was beautiful, a cold, constant spring wind swept past us, high towers of clouds were rolling steadily closer like medieval war machines breaching the blue fortress of sky. Light spilled down out of the clouds onto the choppy lake, gray and cold and faceted, in constant motion but going nowhere. Hundreds of boats were already out, their sails pivoting and flashing in the shifting beams of sunlight. A gull's wings dropped like the slowly closing legs of a draftsman's compass.

At last we were under way. Mr. Wellington, unlike my father, was a smooth, competent sailor. He pulled the boat around so that the wind was behind us and he asked me to attach the spinnaker pole to the jib sail, but I became frightened when I had to lean out over the coursing water and Tommy filled in for me, not vexed at me but, I suspect, worried about what his father would think. And what was I afraid of? Falling in?

But I could swim, a rope could be tossed my way. That wasn't it. Even my vertigo I had overcome on the seawall for Tom's sake. It was, I'm sure, Mr. Wellington's disapproval I feared and invited, that disapproval which, so persistent, had ended by becoming a manner, a way of being, like someone's way of holding his head to one side, something familiar, something I would miss if it were absent. Not that he bestowed his disapproval generously on me. No, even that he withheld and dispensed in only the smallest sums.

The wind blew higher and higher and Mr. Wellington, who'd taken in sail, was holding close to it. We gripped the gunwales and leaned back out over the cold, running waves, the water brushing, then soaking the backs of our shirts. The sun solemnly withdrew into its tent of cloud, disappointed with the world. By the slightest turn of my head I could change the moan of the wind into a whistle. There we were, just a father and his teenage son and the son's friend out for a sail, but in my mind, at least, the story was less simple. For I found in this Mr. Wellington a version of myself so transformed by will and practice as to be not easily recognizable, but familiar nonetheless. He had never been handsome, I was certain, and his lack of romantic appeal shaded his responses to his glamorous son, the muted, wary adoration as well as the less than frank envy.

I'd begun to shiver. The day was turning darker and had blown all the birds out of the sky and half the boats back to harbor. I was huddling, hugging myself down in the hull, wet back to the wind. Mr. Wellington was letting out sail—the tock-tock-tock of the winch releasing the mainsheet—and he was looking at me, holding his judgment in reserve. Between us, these two tight minds, flew the great sail and Tom haunting it as he leaned back into it, pushing it, pushing until we came around, he ducked and the boom swung overhead and stopped with a shocking thud. Here was this boy, laughing and blonded by the sun and smooth-skinned, his whole body straining up as he reached to cleat something so that his T-shirt parted company with his dirty, sagging jeans and we—the father and I—could see Tom's muscles like forked lightning on his taut stomach; here was this boy so handsome and free and well liked and here were we flanking him, looking up at him, at the torso flowering out of the humble calyx of his jeans.

It seemed to me then that beauty is the highest good, the one thing we all want to be or have or, failing that, destroy, and that all the world's virtues are nothing but the world's spleen and deceit. The ugly, the old, the rich and the accomplished speak of invisible virtues—of character and wisdom and power and skill—because they lack the visible ones, that ridiculous down under the lower lip that can't decide to be a beard, those prehensile bare feet racing down the sleek deck, big hands too heavy for slender arms, the sweep of lashes over faded lapis-lazuli eyes, lips deep red, the windblown hair intricate as Velázquez's rendering of lace.

That summer I spent with my father; I worked the Addressograph machine and I hired a hustler, who was as blond as Tommy. When I returned home to my mother I was a bit smug—but also frightened by the tenacity of my homosexual yearnings.

One fall evening Tom called me to ask me if I'd like to go out on a double date. He'd be with Sally, of course, and I'd be with Helen Paper. Just a movie. Maybe a burger afterward. Not too late. School tomorrow. Her regular date had come down with a cold.

I said sure.

I dashed down the hall to tell my mother, who in a rare domestic moment had a sewing basket on her lap. Her glasses had slid down to the tip of her nose and her voice came out slow and without inflection as she tried to thread a needle.

"Guess what!" I shouted.

"What, dear?" She licked the thread and tried again.

"That was Tom and he arranged a date for me with Helen Paper, who's the most beautiful and sophisticated girl in the whole school."

"Sophisticated?" There, the thread had gone through.

"Yes, yes"—I could hear my voice rising higher and higher; somehow I had to convey the excitement of my prospects—"she's only a freshman but she goes out with college boys and everything and she's been to Europe and she's—well, the other girls say top-heavy but only from sour grapes. And she's the leader of the Crowd or could be if she cared and didn't have such a reputation."

My mother was intent upon her sewing. She was dressed to go out and this, yes, it must be a rip in the seam of her raincoat; once she'd fixed it she'd be on her way. "Wonderful, dear."

"But isn't it exciting?" I insisted.

"Well, yes, but I hope she's not too fast."

"For me?"

"For anyone. In general. There, now." My mother bit the thread off, her eyes suddenly as wide and empty and intelligent as a cat's. She stood, examined her handiwork, put the coat on, moved to the door, backtracked, lifted her cheek toward me to peck. "I hope you have fun. You seem terribly nervous. Just look at your hands. You're wringing them—never saw anyone literally wring his hands before."

"Well, it's terribly exciting," I said in wild despair.

My sister wasn't home, so I was alone once my mother had gone—alone to take my second bath of the day in the mean, withholding afternoon light permeating the frosted glass window and to listen to the listless hum of traffic outside, in such contrast to my heart's anticipation. It was as though the very intensity of my feeling had drained the surroundings of significance. I was the unique center of consciousness, its toxic concentration.

I was going out on a date with Helen Paper and I had to calm myself by then because the evening would surely be quicksilver small talk and ten different kinds of smile and there would be hands linking and parting as in a square dance you had to be very subtle to hear called, subtle and calm. I wanted so badly to be popular, to have the others look back as I ran to catch up, then to walk with my left hand around his waist, the right around hers, her long hair blown back on my shoulder, pooling there for a moment in festive intimacy, a sort of gold epaulet of the secret order of joy.

I had spent so much of my childhood sunk into a cross-eyed, nose-picking turpitude of shame and self-loathing, scrunched up in the corner of a sweating leather chair on a hot summer day, the heat having silenced the birds, even the construction workers on the site next door, and delivering me up to the admonishing black head of the fan on the floor slowly shaking from left to right, right to left to signal its tedious repetition of no, no, no, and to exhale the faintly irritating vacillations of its breath. No, no, no—those were the words I repeated to myself, not with force but as a Jesus prayer of listless grief. Energy in itself is a sort of redemption. No wonder we admire Satan. But if the Devil were listless, if he were a pale man in his underwear who watched television by day behind closed venetian blinds—oh, if that were the Devil I would fear him.

That's what Being Popular seemed to promise, a deliverance from the humiliation of daily life, its geological torpor, the dailiness that rusts the blade of resolve and rots the stage curtain, that fades all colors and returns all fields to pasture. Being popular was equivalent to becoming a character, perhaps even a person, since if to be is to be perceived, then to be perceived by many eyes and with envy, interest, respect or affection is to exist more densely, more articulately, every last detail minutely observed and thereby richly rendered. I knew that my sister wasn't popular, at least not at school. She sat at home night after night and no matter how she styled her hair or wore her skirts she looked unliked, dowdy with dislike.

Our mother told us she'd been popular as a girl, but she had grown up on a farm where families did everything together. How could I explain to her how much things had changed, that we kids scarcely admitted we had parents, that to us parents were as uninteresting as the rich in novels about backstairs life; they were large naïve personages who ask irrelevant questions from time to time and from whom the truth must always be kept. In particular the logical or at least consistent standards of adults, their admiration of money, of substance, of homely virtue, were valuable to us kids precisely as rules to flout, for our preferences in clothes, music, people were rigorously whimsical.

As long as I remained unpopular I belonged wholly to my mother. I might fight with her, insult her, sneer at her, ignore her, but I was still hers. She knew that. She even had a way of swaggering around me. There was a coarseness in the speculations she made about me to my face, the way an owner might talk about a horse in its stall. At times she insisted that I had a great future ahead of me, by which she meant a job and a salary, but just as often she'd look at me and ask, "Do you think you're really bright?" Quick smile. "Of course you are. You're very very bright." Pause. "But I wonder. *We* think you are. But shouldn't we have a second opinion? One that's more objective?"

She subjected herself to the same doubts—I was so completely hers that I had to eat what she ate, even her self-hatred, as a fetus must live off its host's blood. The great event of our household had been that my father had left us for someone else. Afterward, how could we like each other all that much, since we were all equally guilty of having driven him away? At least, we'd failed to keep him. Nor was our shared fate black as good ink or crisp as a crow's wing on snow; we hadn't been assigned clear, tragic roles we could play with any sort of despairing joy. Instead, we'd been shamed and we'd become vacant, neglected, shabby with neglect. I don't mean to say that we exhibited interesting symptoms or made trouble for anyone. But we were shadows, like the dead after Orpheus passes them on his way through the Underworld, after this living man vanishes and the last sound of his music is lost to the incoming silence. All my life I've made friends and lost lovers and talked about these two activities as though they were very different, opposed; but in truth love is the direct and therefore hopeless method of calling Orpheus back, whereas friendship is the equally hopeless because irrelevant attempt to find warmth in other shades. Odd that in the story Orpheus is lonely, too.

Helen Paper had a wide, regal forehead, straight dark hair pulled back from her face, curiously narrow hips and strong, thin legs. She was famous for the great globes of her breasts, as evident as her smile and almost as easy to acknowledge and so heavy that her shoulders had become very strong. How her breasts hung naturally I had no way of knowing, since in her surgically sturdy brassiere her form had been idealized into—well, two uncannily symmetrical globes, at once proud, inviting and (by virtue of their symmetry) respectable.

But to describe her without mentioning her face would be absurd, since everyone was dazzled by those fine blue eyes, harder or perhaps less informative than one would have anticipated, and by that nose, so straight and classical, joined to the forehead without a bump or transition of any sort, the nose a prayer ascending above the altar of lips so rich and sweet that one could understand how men had once regarded women as spoils in wars worth fighting. She was a woman (for she surely seemed a woman despite her youth) supremely confident of her own appeal, her status as someone desirable in the abstract, that is, attractive and practicable to anyone under any conditions at any time, rather than in the concrete, to me now as mine. She wasn't shy or passive, but to the extent she was a vessel she was full to the brim with the knowledge that she represented a prize. She was the custodian of her own beauty.

She acted as though she were royalty and being beautiful a sort of Trooping the Colours. At any rate, I once watched her through a window (she didn't know I was there) and she was acting very differently. She was with just one other person, a girl from school, and they were on the floor in front of the television with beers and a big bowl of popcorn. It was a summer night and it must have been very late and they were laughing and laughing. Helen Paper, wearing just shorts and halter, was sprawled on the floor sick with laughter, in a squalor of laughter. She kept saying, "Stop or you'll make me pee."

Our date was quick, unremarkable (it's the particular curse of adolescence that its events are never adequate to the feelings they inspire, that no unadorned retelling of those events can suggest the feelings). Tommy's mother collected us all in her car (we were still too young to drive) and deposited us at the theater. Green spotlights buried in fake ferns in the lobby played on a marble fountain that had long since been drained. The basin was filled with candy wrappers and paper napkins. Inside, behind padded doors each pierced by a grimy porthole, soared the dark splendors of the theater brushed here and there by the ushers' traveling red flashlights or feebly, briefly dispelled by the glow of a match held to a forbidden cigarette. The ceiling had been designed to resemble the night sky, the stars were minute bulbs, the moon a yellow crescent. To either side of the screen was a windswept version of a royal box, a gilt throne on a small carpeted dais under a great blown-back stucco curtain topped by a papier-mâché coronet. When I finally held Helen Paper's hand after sitting beside her for half an hour in the dark, I said to myself, "This hand could be insured for a million dollars."

She surrendered her hand to me, but was I really a likely candidate for it? Was this the way guys became popular? Did certain girls have the guts to tell everyone else, "Look, be nice to this guy. He's not a nerd. He's worth it. He's special"? Or was this date merely some extraordinary favor wangled for me by Tommy, something that would not be repeated? Could it be (and I knew it could) that the Star Chamber of popularity was sealed and that no one would be admitted to it—no one except some casual new prince who belonged there?

Tommy was a prince. He had a knack for demanding attention; even when he called the telephone operator for a number, he'd hold her in conversation. Once he even talked her into meeting him after work. The receptionists in offices downtown, salesladies in stores, the mothers of friends—all of them he sized up, mentally undressed, and though this appraisal might seem to be rude, in fact most women liked it. An efficient woman would be sailing past him. He'd grab her wrist. He'd apologize for the intrusion, but he'd also stand very close to her and his smile wouldn't apologize for a thing. And she, at exactly the moment I would have expected outrage, would flush, her eyes would flutter, not in an experienced way but meltingly, since he'd touched a nerve, since he'd found a way to subvert the social into the sexual—and then she'd smile and rephrase what she was saying in a voice charmingly without conviction.

After the movie we went somewhere for a snack and then I walked Helen home. Her beauty stood between us like an enemy, some sort of hereditary enemy I was supposed to fear, but I liked her well enough. Even the fiercest lovers must like each other at least once in a while. The trees arching above the deserted suburban streets tracked slowly past overhead, their crowns dark against a hazy white night sky, clouds lit up like internal organs dyed for examination, for augury . . . I spoke quietly, deliberately, to Helen Paper and I snatched glances of her famous smile rising to greet my words. Our attention wasn't given over to words but to the formal charting of that night street that we were executing. I mean we, or rather our bodies, the animal sense in us, some orienting device— we were discovering each other, and for one moment I felt exultantly worthy of her. For she did have the power to make me seem interesting, at least to myself. I found myself talking faster and with more confidence as we approached the wide, dimly lit porch of her house. Some late roses perfumed the night. A sprinkler someone had left on by mistake played back and forth over the grass. A sudden breeze snatched up the spray and flung it on the walkway ahead, a momentary darkening of the white pavement. Inside, upstairs, a room was just barely lit behind a drawn curtain. Crickets took the night's pulse.

Although I said something right out of dancing school to Helen—"Good night, it's been great to spend some time with you"—an unexpected understanding had fallen on us. Of course her allure—the sudden rise and fall of her wonderful soft breasts, the dilation of her perfume on the cool night air, the smile of a saint who points, salaciously, toward heaven— this allure had seduced me entirely. I loved her. I didn't know what to do with her. I suspected another, more normal boy would have known how to tease her, make her laugh, would have treated her more as a friend and less as an idol. Had I been expected to do something I would have fled, but now, tonight, I did love her, as one might love a painting one admired but didn't, couldn't, wouldn't own. She was completely relaxed when she took my hand and looked in my eyes, as she thanked me and bobbed a curtsy in a little-girl manner other men, I'm sure, liked better than I; sensing my resistance to anything fetching, she doubled back and intensified her gravity. By which I'm not suggesting she was playing a part. In fact, I don't know what she was doing. Because I loved her she was opaque to me, and her sincerity I doubted not at all until I doubted it completely.

I thanked her and I said I hoped I'd see her soon. For a moment it seemed as though it would be the most natural thing to kiss her on those full, soft lips (had I not seen her a moment ago covertly pop some scented thing into her mouth to prepare for just such an inevitability?). Her eyes were veiled with her awareness of her own beauty. I suppose I suddenly liked myself and I could see a light in which I'd be plausible to others.

My love for Tommy was shameful, something I was also proud of but tried to hide. This moment with Helen—our tallness on the moon-lashed porch, the cool winds that sent black clouds (lit by gold from within) caravelling past a pirate moon, a coolness that glided through opening fingers that now touched, linked, squeezed, slowly drew apart—this moment made me happy, hopeful. An oppression had been lifted. A long apprenticeship to danger had abruptly ended.

After I left her I raced home through the deserted streets laughing and leaping. I sang show tunes and danced and felt as fully alive as someone in a movie (since it was precisely life that was grainy and sepia-tinted, whereas the movies had the audible ping, the habitable color, the embraceable presence of reality). I was more than ready to give up my attraction to men for this marriage to Helen Paper. At last the homosexual phase of my adolescence had drawn to a close. To be sure, I'd continue to love Tommy but as he loved me: fraternally. In my dream the stowaway in the single bunk with me, whom I was trying to keep hidden under a blanket, had miraculously transformed himself into my glorious bride, as the kissed leper in the legend becomes Christ Pantocrator.

When I got home my mother was in bed with the lights out. "Honey?"

"Yes?"

"Come in and talk to me."

"Okay," I said.

"Rub my back, okay?"

"Okay," I said. I sat beside her on the bed. She smelled of bourbon.

"How was your date?"

"Terrific! I never had such a good time."

"How nice. Is she a nice girl?"

"Better than that. She's charming and sophisticated and intelligent."

"You're home earlier than I expected. Not so hard. Rub gently. You bruiser. I'm going to call you that: Bruiser. Is she playful? Is she like me? Does she say cute things?"

"No, thank God."

"Why do you say that? Is she some sort of egghead?"

"Not an egghead. But she's dignified. She's straightforward. She says what she means."

"I think girls should be playful. That doesn't mean dishonest. I'm playful."

"_____"

"Well, I am. Do you think she likes you?"

"How can I tell? It was just a first date." My fingers lightly stroked her neck to either side of her spine. "I doubt if she'll want to see me again. Why should she?"

"But why not? You're handsome and intelligent."

"Handsome! With these big nostrils!"

"Oh that's just your sister. She's so frustrated she has to pick on you. There's nothing wrong with your nostrils. At least I don't see anything wrong. Of course, I know you too well. If you like, we could consult a nose doctor." A long pause. "Nostrils . . . Do people generally dwell on them? I mean, do people think about them a lot?" Small, high voice: "Are mine okay?"

A hopeless silence.

At last she began to snore delicately and I hurried to my own room. My sister's door, next to mine, was closed but her light was burning resentfully.

And I gave myself over to my reverie. I had a record player I'd paid for myself by working as a caddy and records I exchanged each week at the library, the music an outpost of my father's influence in this unmusical female territory.

I slipped out of my clothes as quickly as possible, though I tried to do everything beautifully, as in a movie of my life with Helen. In some way I felt it was already being filmed—not that I looked for hidden cameras but I simplified and smoothed out my movements for the lens. There were those, my mother and sister, who suffered too much and were too graceless to be film-worthy, but there were those others I aspired to join who suffered briefly, consolably and always handsomely, whose remarks were terse and for whom the mechanics of leaving a party or paying a bill had been stylized nearly out of existence in favor of highly emotional exchanges in which eyes said more than lips. Every detail of my room asked me to be solicitous. When the dresser drawer stuck I winced—this sequence would have to be reshot. I turned my sheets down as though she, Helen, were at my side. I rushed to snap off the lights.

She and I lay side by side in the narrow boat and floated downstream. The stars moved not at all and only the occasional fluttering of a branch overhead or the sound of a scraping rock below suggested our passage. The moon was the wound in the night's side from which magic blood flowed; we bathed in it. By dawn I'd made love to Helen four times. The first time was so ceremonial I had a problem molding the mist into arms and legs; all that kept flickering up at me was her smile. The second time was more passionate. I was finally able to free her breasts from their binding. By the third time we'd become gently fraternal; we smiled with tired kindness at each other. We were very intimate. At dawn she began to disintegrate. The certainty of day pulsed into being and all my exertions were able to keep her at my side only a few more moments. At last she fled.

I stumbled from class to class in a numb haze. Strangely enough, I was afraid I'd run into Helen. I didn't feel up to her. I was too tired. In home room I yawned, rested my head on my desk and longed for the privacy of my bed and the saving grace of night. I wanted to be alone with my wraith. In my confusion the real Helen Paper seemed irrelevant, even intrusive.

That night I wrote her a letter. I chose a special yellow parchment, a spidery pen point and black ink. In gym class as I'd stumbled through calisthenics and in study hall as I'd half dozed behind a stack of books, phrases for the letter had dropped into my mind. Now I sat down with great formality at my desk and composed the missive, first in pencil on scratch paper. If I reproduced it (I still have the pencil draft) you'd laugh at me or we would laugh together at the prissy diction and the high-flown sentiment. What would be harder to convey is how much it meant to me, how it read to me back then. I offered her my love and allegiance while admitting I knew how unworthy of her I was. And yet I had half a notion that though I might be worthless as a date (not handsome enough) I might be of some value as a husband (intelligent, slated for success). In marriage merits outweighed appeal, and I could imagine nothing less eternal than marriage with Helen. Naturally I didn't mention marriage in the letter.

A week went by before I received her answer. Twice I saw her in the halls. The first time she came over to me and looked me in the eye and smiled her sweet, intense smile. She was wearing a powder-blue cashmere sweater and her breasts rose and fell monumentally as she asked me in her soft drawl how I was doing. Nothing in her smile or voice suggested a verdict either for or against me. I felt there was something improper about seeing her at all before I got her letter. I mumbled, "Fine," blushed and slinked off. I felt tall and dirty. I was avoiding Tommy as well. Soon enough I would have to tell him about my proposal to Helen, which I suspected he'd disapprove of.

Then one afternoon, a Friday after school, there was her letter to me in the mailbox. Even before I opened it I was mildly grateful she had at least answered me.

The apartment was empty. I went to the sun-room and looked across the street at the lake churning like old machinery in a deserted amusement park, rides without riders. My mind kept two separate sets of books. In one I was fortunate she'd taken the time to write me even this rejection, more than a creep like me deserved. In the other she said, "You're not the person I would have chosen for a date, nor for a summer or semester, but yes, I will marry you. Nor do I want anything less from you. Romance is an expectation of an ideal life to come, and in that sense my feelings for you are romantic."

If someone had made me guess which reply I'd find inside the envelope, I would have chosen the rejection, since pessimism is always accurate, but acceptance would not have shocked me, since I also believed in the miraculous.

I poured myself a glass of milk in the kitchen and returned to the sun-room. Her handwriting was well formed and rounded, the dots over the *i*'s circles, the letters fatter than tall, the lines so straight I suspected she had placed the thin paper over a ruled-off grid. The schoolgirl ordinariness of her hand frightened me—I didn't feel safe in such an ordinary hand. "I like you very much as a friend," she wrote. "I was pleased and surprised to receive your lovely letter. It was one of the sweetest tributes to me I have ever had from anyone. I know this will hurt, but I am forced to say it if I am to prevent you from further pain. I do not love you and I never have. Our friendship has been a matter of mutual and rewarding liking, not loving. I know this is very cruel, but I must say it. Try not to hate me. I think it would be best if we did not see each other for a while. I certainly hope we can continue to be friends. I consider you to be one of my very best friends. Please, please forgive me. Try to understand why I have to be this way. Sincerely, Helen."

Well, her phrasing was less childish than her hand, I thought, as though the letter were a composition in class that concerned me in no way. Even as this attitude broke over me but before I was drawn into another, more troubling one, I had time to notice she said I was one of her very best friends, an honor I'd been unaware of until now, as who had not: I registered the social gain before the romantic loss. Unless (and here I could taste something bitter on the back of my tongue)—unless the "mature" advice ("I think it would be best if we did not see each other for a while") was actually a denial of the consolation prize, a way of keeping me out of her circle at the very moment she was pretending to invite me into it. Could it be that the entire exercise, its assured tone, the concision and familiar ring of the phrasing, figured as nothing more than a "tribute" (her word) she had piled up before the altar of her own beauty? How many people had she shown my letter to?

But then all this mental chatter stopped and I surrendered to something else, something less active, more abiding, something that had been waiting politely all this time but that now stepped forward, diffident yet impersonal: my grief.

For the next few months I grieved. I would stay up all night crying and playing records and writing sonnets to Helen. What was I crying for? I cried during gym class when someone got mad at me for dropping the basketball. In the past I would have hidden my pain but now I just slowly walked off the court, the tears spurting out of my face. I took a shower, still crying, and dressed forlornly and walked the empty halls even though to do so during class time was forbidden. I no longer cared about rules. I let my hair grow, I stopped combing it, I forgot to change my shirt from one week to the next. With a disabused eye I watched other kids striving to succeed, to become popular. I became a sort of vagabond of grief or, as I'd rather put it, I entered grief's vagabondage, which better suggests a simultaneous freedom and slavery. Freedom from the now meaningless pursuit of grades, friends, smiles; slavery to a hopeless love.

Every afternoon I'd stumble home exhausted to my room, but once there my real work would begin, which was to imagine Helen in my arms, Helen beside me laughing, Helen looking up at me through the lace suspended from the orange-blossom chaplet, Helen with other boys, kissing them, unzipping her shorts and stepping out of them, pushing her hair back out of her serious, avid eyes. She was a puppet I could place in one playlet after another, but once I'd invoked her she became independent, tortured me, smiled right through me at another boy, her approaching lover. Her exertions with other men fascinated me, and the longer I suffered, the more outrageous were the humiliations I had other men inflict on her.

I became ill with mononucleosis, ironically the "kissing disease" that afflicted so many teenagers in those days. I was kept out of school for several months. Most of the time I slept, feverish and content: exempted. Just to cross the room required all my energy. Whether or not to drink another glass of ginger ale could absorb my attention for an hour. That my grief had been superceded by illness relieved me; I was no longer willfully self-destructive. I was simply ill. Love was forbidden—my doctor had told me I mustn't kiss anyone. Tommy called me from time to time but I felt he and I had nothing in common now—after all, he was just a boy, whereas I'd become a very old man.

Study and Discussion Questions

1. What does it mean, according to this story, to be "popular"? What does the narrator have to learn to do in order to be popular?
2. What is the difference between popularity and friendship in this story?
3. What is the difference here between love and romance?
4. What are the narrator's concerns about his sexuality?
5. Why does the narrator see his "life with Helen" as a movie?
6. What is the narrator's tone when he describes his experience being a "vagabond of grief"?

Writing Exercises

1. Compare/contrast the narrator's relationship with Tommy and his relationship with Helen.
2. List several qualities or behaviors that you have found aid one's popularity, several others that hinder one's popularity, and a few on the border line. What's your opinion of the data you've just gathered?
3. Pick an incident in the story (sailing with Tommy's father, the date with Helen, Tommy playing the guitar, perhaps) and discuss how it illuminates the narrator's search for identity.

JAMES BALDWIN (1924–1987)

Son of a Harlem preacher, Baldwin himself began preaching at age fourteen, but soon after turned full time to writing. He is known both for his essays, collected in Notes of a Native Son *(1955),* Nobody Knows My Name *(1961), and* The Fire Next Time *(1963), and for his fiction, including* Go Tell It on the Mountain *(1953), a novel about growing up in Harlem;* Giovanni's Room *(1956), a novel about gay male life in Paris; and* Going to Meet the Man *(1965), a collection of stories. After living in Europe for almost a decade, Baldwin returned to the United States in 1957 and soon became a major spokesperson for black civil rights.*

Sonny's Blues   (1957)

I read about it in the paper, in the subway, on my way to work. I read it, and I couldn't believe it, and I read it again. Then perhaps I just stared at it, at the newsprint spelling out his name, spelling out the story. I stared at it in the swinging lights of the subway car, and in the faces and bodies of the people, and in my own face, trapped in the darkness which roared outside.

It was not to be believed and I kept telling myself that, as I walked from the subway station to the high school. And at the same time I couldn't doubt it. I was scared, scared for Sonny. He became real to me again. A great block of ice got settled in my belly and kept melting there slowly all day long, while I taught my classes algebra. It was a special kind of ice. It kept melting, sending trickles of ice water all up and down my veins, but it never got less. Sometimes it hardened and seemed to expand until I felt my guts were going to come spilling out or that I was going to choke or scream. This would always be at a moment when I was remembering some specific thing Sonny had once said or done.

When he was about as old as the boys in my classes his face had been bright and open, there was a lot of copper in it; and he'd had wonderfully direct brown eyes, and great gentleness and privacy. I wondered what he looked like now. He had been picked up, the evening before, in a raid on an apartment downtown, for peddling and using heroin.

I couldn't believe it: but what I mean by that is that I couldn't find any room for it anywhere inside me. I had kept it outside me for a long time. I hadn't wanted to know. I had had suspicions, but I didn't name them, I kept putting them away. I told myself that Sonny was wild, but he wasn't crazy. And he'd always been a good boy, he hadn't ever turned hard or evil or disrespectful, the way kids can, so quick, so quick, especially in Harlem. I didn't want to believe that I'd ever see my brother going down, coming to nothing, all that light in his face gone out, in the condition I'd already seen so many others. Yet it had happened and here I was, talking about algebra to a lot of boys who might, every one of them for all I knew, be popping off needles every time they went to the head. Maybe it did more for them than algebra could.

I was sure that the first time Sonny had ever had horse, he couldn't have been much older than these boys were now. These boys, now, were living as we'd been living then, they were growing up with a rush and their heads bumped abruptly against the low ceiling of their actual possibilities. They were filled with rage. All they really knew were two darknesses, the darkness of their lives, which was now closing in on them, and the darkness of the movies, which had blinded them to that other darkness, and in which they now, vindictively, dreamed, at once more together than they were at any other time, and more alone.

When the last bell rang, the last class ended, I let out my breath. It seemed I'd been holding it for all that time. My clothes were wet—I may have looked as though I'd been sitting in a steam bath, all dressed up, all afternoon. I sat alone in the classroom a long time. I listened to the boys outside, downstairs, shouting and cursing and laughing. Their laughter struck me for perhaps the first time. It was not the joyous laughter which—God knows why—one associates with children. It was mocking and insular, its intent was to denigrate. It was disenchanted, and in this, also, lay the authority of their curses. Perhaps I was listening to them because I was thinking about my brother and in them I heard my brother. And myself.

One boy was whistling a tune, at once very complicated and very simple, it seemed to be pouring out of him as though he were a bird, and it sounded very cool and moving through all that harsh, bright air, only just holding its own through all those other sounds.

I stood up and walked over to the window and looked down into the courtyard. It was the beginning of the spring and the sap was rising in the boys. A teacher passed through them every now and again, quickly, as though he or she couldn't wait to get out of that courtyard, to get those boys out of their sight and off their minds. I started collecting my stuff. I thought I'd better get home and talk to Isabel.

The courtyard was almost deserted by the time I got downstairs. I saw this boy standing in the shadow of a doorway, looking just like Sonny. I almost called his name. Then I saw that it wasn't Sonny, but somebody we used to know, a boy from around our block. He'd been Sonny's friend. He'd never been mine, having been too young for me, and, anyway, I'd never liked him. And now, even though he was a grown-up man, he still hung around that block, still spent hours on the street corners, was always high and raggy. I used to run into him from time to time and he'd often work around to asking me for a quarter or fifty cents. He always had some real good excuse, too, and I always gave it to him, I don't know why.

But now, abruptly, I hated him. I couldn't stand the way he looked at me, partly like a dog, partly like a cunning child. I wanted to ask him what the hell he was doing in the school courtyard.

He sort of shuffled over to me, and he said, "I see you got the papers. So you already know about it."

"You mean about Sonny? Yes, I already know about it. How come they didn't get you?"

He grinned. It made him repulsive and it also brought to mind what he'd looked like as a kid. "I wasn't there. I stay away from them people."

"Good for you." I offered him a cigarette and I watched him through the smoke. "You come all the way down here just to tell me about Sonny?"

"That's right." He was sort of shaking his head and his eyes looked strange, as though they were about to cross. The bright sun deadened his damp dark brown skin and it made his eyes look yellow and showed up the dirt in his kinked hair. He smelled funky. I moved a little away from him and I said, "Well, thanks. But I already know about it and I got to get home."

"I'll walk you a little ways," he said. We started walking. There were a couple of kids still loitering in the courtyard and one of them said goodnight to me and looked strangely at the boy beside me.

"What're you going to do?" he asked me. "I mean, about Sonny?"

"Look. I haven't seen Sonny for over a year, I'm not sure I'm going to do anything. Anyway, what the hell *can* I do?"

"That's right," he said quickly, "ain't nothing you can do. Can't much help old Sonny no more, I guess."

It was what I was thinking and so it seemed to me he had no right to say it.

"I'm surprised at Sonny, though," he went on—he had a funny way of talking, he looked straight ahead as though he were talking to himself—"I thought Sonny was a smart boy, I thought he was too smart to get hung."

"I guess he thought so too," I said sharply, "and that's how he got hung. And now about you? You're pretty goddamn smart, I bet."

Then he looked directly at me, just for a minute. "I ain't smart," he said. "If I was smart, I'd have reached for a pistol a long time ago."

"Look. Don't tell *me* your sad story, if it was up to me, I'd give you one." Then I felt guilty—guilty, probably, for never having supposed that the poor bastard *had* a story of his own, much less a sad one, and I asked, quickly, "What's going to happen to him now?"

He didn't answer this. He was off by himself some place. "Funny thing," he said, and from his tone we might have been discussing the quickest way to get to Brooklyn, "when I saw the papers this morning, the first thing I asked myself was if I had anything to do with it. I felt sort of responsible."

I began to listen more carefully. The subway station was on the corner, just before us, and I stopped. He stopped, too. We were in front of a bar and he ducked slightly, peering in, but whoever he was looking for didn't seem to be there. The juke box was blasting away with something black and bouncy and I half watched the barmaid as she danced her way from the juke box to her place behind the bar. And I watched her face as she laughingly responded to something someone said to her, still keeping time to the music. When she smiled one saw the little girl, one sensed the doomed, still-struggling woman beneath the battered face of the semi-whore.

"I never *give* Sonny nothing," the boy said finally, "but a long time ago I come to school high and Sonny asked me how it felt." He paused, I couldn't bear to watch him, I watched the barmaid, and I listened to the music which seemed to be causing the pavement to shake. "I told him it felt great." The music stopped, the barmaid paused and watched the juke box until the music began again. "It did."

All this was carrying me some place I didn't want to go. I certainly didn't want to know how it felt. It filled everything, the people, the houses, the music, the dark, quicksilver barmaid, with menace; and this menace was their reality.

"What's going to happen to him now?" I asked again.

"They'll send him away some place and they'll try to cure him." He shook his head. "Maybe he'll even think he's kicked the habit. Then they'll let him loose"—he gestured, throwing his cigarette into the gutter. "That's all."

"What do you mean, that's *all?*"

But I knew what he meant.

"I *mean*, that's *all*." He turned his head and looked at me, pulling down the corners of his mouth. "Don't you know what I mean?" he asked, softly.

"How the hell *would* I know what you mean?" I almost whispered it, I don't know why.

"That's right," he said to the air, "how would *he* know what I mean?" He turned toward me again, patient and calm, and yet I somehow felt him shaking, shaking as though he were going to fall apart. I felt that ice in my guts again, the dread I'd felt all afternoon; and again I watched the barmaid, moving about the bar, washing glasses, and singing. "Listen. They'll let him out and then it'll just start all over again. That's what I mean."

"You mean—they'll let him out. And then he'll just start working his way back in again. You mean he'll never kick the habit. Is that what you mean?"

"That's right," he said, cheerfully. "*You* see what I mean."

"Tell me," I said it last, "why does he want to die? He must want to die, he's killing himself, why does he want to die?"

He looked at me in surprise. He licked his lips. "He don't want to die. He wants to live. Don't nobody want to die, ever."

Then I wanted to ask him—too many things. He could not have answered, or if he had, I could not have borne the answers. I started walking. "Well, I guess it's none of my business."

"It's going to be rough on old Sonny," he said. We reached the subway station. "This is your station?" he asked. I nodded. I took one step down. "Damn!" he said, suddenly. I looked up at him. He grinned again. "Damn it if I didn't leave all my money home. You ain't got a dollar on you, have you? Just for a couple of days, is all."

All at once something inside gave and threatened to come pouring out of me. I didn't hate him any more. I felt that in another moment I'd start crying like a child.

"Sure," I said. "Don't sweat." I looked in my wallet and didn't have a dollar, I only had a five. "Here," I said. "That hold you?"

He didn't look at it—he didn't want to look at it. A terrible, closed look came over his face, as though he were keeping the number on the bill a secret from him and me. "Thanks," he said, and now he was dying to see me go. "Don't worry about Sonny. Maybe I'll write him or something."

"Sure," I said. "You do that. So long."

"Be seeing you," he said. I went on down the steps.

And I didn't write Sonny or send him anything for a long time. When I finally did, it was just after my little girl died, he wrote me back a letter which made me feel like a bastard.

Here's what he said:

Dear brother,

You don't know how much I needed to hear from you. I wanted to write you many a time but I dug how much I must have hurt you and so I didn't write. But now I feel like a man who's been trying to climb up out of some deep, real deep and funky hole and just saw the sun up there, outside. I got to get outside.

I can't tell you much about how I got here. I mean I don't know how to tell you. I guess I was afraid of something or I was trying to escape from something and you know I have never been very strong in the head (smile). I'm glad Mama and Daddy are dead and can't see what's happened to their son and I swear if I'd known what I was doing I would never have hurt you so, you and a lot of other fine people who were nice to me and who believed in me.

I don't want you to think it had anything to do with me being a musician. It's more than that. Or maybe less than that. I can't get anything straight in my head down here and I try not to think about what's going to happen to me when I get outside again. Sometime I think I'm going to flip and *never* get outside and sometime I think I'll come straight back. I tell you one thing, though, I'd rather blow my brains out than go through this again. But that's what they all say, so they tell me. If I tell you when I'm coming to New York and if you could meet me, I sure would appreciate it. Give my love to Isabel and the kids and I was sure sorry to hear about little Gracie. I wish I could be like Mama and say the Lord's will be done, but I don't know it seems to me that trouble is the one thing that never does get stopped and I don't know what good it does to blame it on the Lord. But maybe it does some good if you believe it.

Your brother,
Sonny

Then I kept in constant touch with him and I sent him whatever I could and I went to meet him when he came back to New York. When I saw him many things I thought I had forgotten came flooding back to me. This was because I had begun, finally, to wonder about Sonny, about the life that Sonny lived inside. This life, whatever it was, had made him older and thinner and it had deepened the distant stillness in which he had always moved. He looked very unlike my baby brother. Yet, when he smiled, when we shook hands, the baby brother I'd never known looked out from the depths of his private life, like an animal waiting to be coaxed into the light.

"How you been keeping?" he asked me.

"All right. And you?"

"Just fine." He was smiling all over his face. "It's good to see you again."

"It's good to see you."

The seven years' difference in our ages lay between us like a chasm: I wondered if these years would ever operate between us as a bridge. I was remembering, and it made it hard to catch my breath, that I had been there when he was born; and I had heard the first words he had ever spoken. When he started to walk, he walked from our mother straight to me. I caught him just before he fell when he took the first steps he ever took in this world.

"How's Isabel?"

"Just fine. She's dying to see you."

"And the boys?"

"They're fine, too. They're anxious to see their uncle."

"Oh, come on. You know they don't remember me."

"Are you kidding? Of course they remember you."

He grinned again. We got into a taxi. We had a lot to say to each other, far too much to know how to begin.

As the taxi began to move, I asked, "You still want to go to India?"

He laughed. "You still remember that. Hell, no. This place is Indian enough for me."

"It used to belong to them," I said.

And he laughed again. "They damn sure knew what they were doing when they got rid of it."

Years ago, when he was around fourteen, he'd been all hipped on the idea of going to India. He read books about people sitting on rocks, naked, in all kinds of weather, but mostly bad, naturally, and walking barefoot through hot coals and arriving at wisdom. I used to say that it sounded to me as though they were getting away from wisdom as fast as they could. I think he sort of looked down on me for that.

"Do you mind," he asked, "if we have the driver drive alongside the park? On the west side—I haven't seen the city in so long."

"Of course not," I said. I was afraid that I might sound as though I were humoring him, but I hoped he wouldn't take it that way.

So we drove along, between the green of the park and the stony, lifeless elegance of hotels and apartment buildings, toward the vivid, killing streets of our childhood. These streets hadn't changed, though housing projects jutted up out of them now like rocks in the middle of a boiling sea. Most of the houses in which we had grown up had vanished, as had the stores from which we had stolen, the basements in which we had first tried sex, the rooftops from which we had hurled tin cans and bricks. But houses exactly like the houses of our past yet dominated the landscape, boys exactly like the boys we once had been found themselves smothering in these houses, came down into the streets for light and air and found themselves encircled by disaster. Some escaped the trap, most didn't. Those who got out always left something of themselves behind, as some animals amputate a leg and leave it in the trap. It might be said, perhaps, that I had escaped, after all, I was a school teacher; or that Sonny had, he hadn't lived in Harlem for years. Yet, as the cab moved uptown through streets which seemed, with a rush, to darken with dark people, and as I covertly studied Sonny's face, it came to me that what we both were seeking through our separate cab windows was that part of ourselves which had been left behind. It's always at the hour of trouble and confrontation that the missing member aches.

We hit 110th Street and started rolling up Lenox Avenue. And I'd known this avenue all my life, but it seemed to me again, as it had seemed on the day I'd first heard about Sonny's trouble, filled with a hidden menace which was its very breath of life.

"We almost there," said Sonny.

"Almost." We were both too nervous to say anything more.

We live in a housing project. It hasn't been up long. A few days after it was up it seemed uninhabitably new, now, of course, it's already rundown. It looks like a parody of the good, clean, faceless life—God knows the people who live in it do their best to make it a parody. The beat-looking grass lying around isn't enough to make their lives green, the hedges will never hold out the streets, and they know it. The big windows fool no one, they aren't big enough to make space out of no space. They don't bother with the windows, they watch the TV screen instead. The playground is most popular with the children who don't play at jacks, or skip rope, or roller skate, or swing, and they can be found in it after dark. We moved in partly because it's not too far from where I teach, and partly for the kids; but it's really just like the houses in which Sonny and I grew up. The same things happen, they'll have the same things to remember. The moment Sonny and I started into the house

I had the feeling that I was simply bringing him back into the danger he had almost died trying to escape.

Sonny has never been talkative. So I don't know why I was sure he'd be dying to talk to me when supper was over the first night. Everything went fine, the oldest boy remembered him, and the youngest boy liked him, and Sonny had remembered to bring something for each of them; and Isabel, who is really much nicer than I am, more open and giving, had gone to a lot of trouble about dinner and was genuinely glad to see him. And she's always been able to tease Sonny in a way that I haven't. It was nice to see her face so vivid again and to hear her laugh and watch her make Sonny laugh. She wasn't, or, anyway, she didn't seem to be, at all uneasy or embarrassed. She chatted as though there were no subject which had to be avoided and she got Sonny past his first, faint stiffness. And thank God she was there, for I was filled with that icy dread again. Everything I did seemed awkward to me, and everything I said sounded freighted with hidden meaning. I was trying to remember everything I'd heard about dope addiction and I couldn't help watching Sonny for signs. I wasn't doing it out of malice. I was trying to find out something about my brother. I was dying to hear him tell me he was safe.

"Safe!" my father grunted, whenever Mama suggested trying to move to a neighborhood which might be safer for children. "Safe, hell! Ain't no place safe for kids, nor nobody."

He always went on like this, but he wasn't, ever, really as bad as he sounded, not even on weekends, when he got drunk. As a matter of fact, he was always on the lookout for "something a little better," but he died before he found it. He died suddenly, during a drunken weekend in the middle of the war, when Sonny was fifteen. He and Sonny hadn't ever got on too well. And this was partly because Sonny was the apple of his father's eye. It was because he loved Sonny so much and was frightened for him, that he was always fighting with him. It doesn't do any good to fight with Sonny. Sonny just moves back, inside himself, where he can't be reached. But the principal reason that they never hit it off is that they were so much alike. Daddy was big and rough and loud-talking, just the opposite of Sonny, but they both had—that same privacy.

Mama tried to tell me something about this, just after Daddy died. I was home on leave from the army.

This was the last time I ever saw my mother alive. Just the same, this picture gets all mixed up in my mind with pictures I had of her when she was younger. The way I always see her is the way she used to be on a Sunday afternoon, say, when the old folks were talking after the big Sunday dinner. I always see her wearing pale blue. She'd be sitting on the sofa. And my father would be sitting in the easy chair, not far from her. And the living room would be full of church folks and relatives. There they sit, in chairs all around the living room, and the night is creeping up outside, but nobody knows it yet. You can see the darkness growing against the windowpanes and you hear the street noises every now and again, or maybe the jangling beat of a tambourine from one of the churches close by, but it's real quiet in the room. For a moment nobody's talking, but every face looks darkening, like the sky outside. And my mother rocks a little from the waist, and my father's eyes are closed. Everyone is looking at something a child can't see. For a minute they've forgotten the children. Maybe a kid is lying on the rug, half asleep. Maybe somebody's got a kid in his lap and is absent-mindedly stroking the kid's head. Maybe there's a kid, quiet and big-eyed, curled up in a big chair in the corner. The silence, the darkness coming, and the darkness in the faces frightens the child obscurely. He hopes that the hand which strokes his forehead will never stop—will never die. He hopes that there will never come a time when the old folks won't be sitting around the living room, talking about where they've come from, and what they've seen, and what's happened to them and their kinfolk.

But something deep and watchful in the child knows that this is bound to end, is already ending. In a moment someone will get up and turn on the light. Then the old folks will remember the children and they won't talk any more that day. And when light fills the room, the child is filled with darkness. He knows that every time this happens he's moved just a little closer to that darkness outside. The darkness outside is what the old folks have been talking about. It's what they've come from. It's what they endure. The child knows that they won't talk any more because if he knows too much about what's happened to *them*, he'll know too much too soon, about what's going to happen to *him*.

The last time I talked to my mother, I remember I was restless. I wanted to get out and see Isabel. We weren't married then and we had a lot to straighten out between us.

There Mama sat, in black, by the window. She was humming an old church song, *Lord, you brought me from a long ways off.* Sonny was out somewhere. Mama kept watching the streets.

"I don't know," she said, "if I'll ever see you again, after you go off from here. But I hope you'll remember the things I tried to teach you."

"Don't talk like that," I said, and smiled. "You'll be here a long time yet."

She smiled, too, but she said nothing. She was quiet for a long time. And I said, "Mama, don't you worry about nothing. I'll be writing all the time, and you be getting the checks. . . ."

"I want to talk to you about your brother," she said, suddenly. "If anything happens to me he ain't going to have nobody to look out for him."

"Mama," I said, "ain't nothing going to happen to you *or* Sonny. Sonny's all right. He's a good boy and he's got good sense."

"It ain't a question of his being a good boy," Mama said, "nor of his having good sense. It ain't only the bad ones, nor yet the dumb ones that gets sucked under." She stopped, looking at me. "Your Daddy once had a brother," she said, and she smiled in a way that made me feel she was in pain. "You didn't never know that, did you?"

"No," I said, "I never knew that," and I watched her face.

"Oh, yes," she said, "your Daddy had a brother." She looked out of the window again. "I know you never saw your Daddy cry. But *I* did— many a time, through all these years."

I asked her, "What happened to his brother? How come nobody's ever talked about him?"

This was the first time I ever saw my mother look old.

"His brother got killed," she said, "when he was just a little younger than you are now. I knew him. He was a fine boy. He was maybe a little full of the devil, but he didn't mean nobody no harm."

Then she stopped and the room was silent, exactly as it had sometimes been on those Sunday afternoons. Mama kept looking out into the streets.

"He used to have a job in the mill," she said, "and, like all young folks, he just liked to perform on Saturday nights. Saturday nights, him and your father would drift around to different place, go to dances and things like that, or just sit around with people they knew, and your father's brother would sing, he had a fine voice, and play along with himself on his guitar. Well, this particular Saturday night, him and your father was coming home from some place, and they were both a little drunk and there was a moon that night, it was bright like day. Your father's brother was feeling kind of good, and he was whistling to himself, and he had his guitar slung over his shoulder. They was coming down a hill and beneath them was a road that turned off from the highway. Well, your father's brother, being always kind of frisky, decided to run down this hill, and he did, with that guitar banging and clanging behind him, and he ran across the road, and he was making water behind a tree. And your father was sort of amused at him and he was still coming down the hill, kind of slow. Then he heard a car motor and that same minute his brother stepped from behind the tree, into the road, in the moonlight. And he started to cross the road. And your father started to run down the hill, he says he don't know why. This car was full of white men. They was all drunk, and when they seen your father's brother they let out a great whoop and holler and they aimed the car straight at him. They was having fun, they just wanted to scare him, the way they do sometimes, you know. But they was drunk. And I guess the boy, being drunk, too, and scared, kind of lost his head. By the time he jumped it was too late. Your father says he heard his brother scream when the car rolled over him, and he heard the wood of that guitar when it give, and he heard them strings go flying, and he heard them white men shouting, and the car kept on a-going and it ain't stopped till this day. And, time your father got down the hill, his brother weren't nothing but blood and pulp."

Tears were gleaming on my mother's face. There wasn't anything I could say.

"He never mentioned it," she said, "because I never let him mention it before you children. Your Daddy was like a crazy man that night and for many a night thereafter. He says he never in his life seen anything as dark as that road after the lights of that car had gone away. Weren't nothing, weren't nobody on that road, just your Daddy and his brother and that busted guitar. Oh, yes. Your Daddy never did really get right again. Till the day he died he weren't sure but that every white man he saw was the man that killed his brother."

She stopped and took out her handkerchief and dried her eyes and looked at me.

"I ain't telling you all this," she said, "to make you scared or bitter or to make you hate nobody. I'm telling you this because you got a brother. And the world ain't changed."

I guess I didn't want to believe this. I guess she saw this in my face. She turned away from me, toward the window again, searching those streets.

"But I praise my Redeemer," she said at last, "that He called your Daddy home before me. I ain't saying it to throw no flowers at myself, but, I declare, it keeps me from feeling too cast down to know I helped your father get safely through this world. Your father always acted like he was the roughest, strongest man on earth. And everybody took him to be like that. But if he hadn't had *me* there—to see his tears!"

She was crying again. Still, I couldn't move. I said, "Lord, Lord, Mama, I didn't know it was like that."

"Oh, honey," she said, "there's a lot that you don't know. But you are going to find it out." She stood up from the window and came over to me. "You got to hold on to your brother," she said, "and don't let him fall, no matter what it looks like is happening to him and no matter how evil you gets with him. You going to be evil with him many a time. But don't you forget what I told you, you hear?"

"I won't forget," I said. "Don't you worry, I won't forget. I won't let nothing happen to Sonny."

My mother smiled as though she were amused at something she saw in my face. Then, "You may not be able to stop nothing from happening. But you got to let him know you's *there*."

Two days later I was married, and then I was gone. And I had a lot of things on my mind and I pretty well forgot my promise to Mama until I got shipped home on a special furlough for her funeral.

And, after the funeral, with just Sonny and me alone in the empty kitchen, I tried to find out something about him.

"What do you want to do?" I asked him.

"I'm going to be a musician," he said.

For he had graduated, in the time I had been away, from dancing to the juke box to finding out who was playing what, and what they were doing with it, and he had bought himself a set of drums.

"You mean, you want to be a drummer?" I somehow had the feeling that being a drummer might be all right for other people but not for my brother Sonny.

"I don't think," he said, looking at me very gravely, "that I'll ever be a good drummer. But I think I can play a piano."

I frowned. I'd never played the role of the older brother quite so seriously before, had scarcely ever, in fact, *asked* Sonny a damn thing. I sensed myself in the presence of something I didn't really know how to handle, didn't understand. So I made my frown a little deeper as I asked: "What kind of musician do you want to be?"

He grinned, "How many kinds do you think there are?"

"Be *serious*," I said.

He laughed, throwing his head back, and then looked at me. "I *am* serious."

"Well, then, for Christ's sake, stop kidding around and answer a serious question. I mean, do you want to be a concert pianist, you want to play classical music and all that, or—or what?" Long before I finished he was laughing again. "For Christ's *sake*, Sonny!"

He sobered, but with difficulty. "I'm sorry, But you sound so—*scared*!" and he was off again.

"Well, you may think it's funny now, baby, but it's not going to be so funny when you have to make your living at it, let me tell you *that*." I was furious because I knew he was laughing at me and I didn't know why.

"No," he said, very sober now, and afraid, perhaps, that he'd hurt me, "I don't want to be a classical pianist. That isn't what interests me. I mean"—he paused, looking hard at me, as though his eyes would help me to understand, and then gestured helplessly, as though perhaps his hand would help—"I mean, I'll have a lot of studying to do, and I'll have to study *everything*, but, I mean, I want to play *with*—jazz musicians." He stopped. "I want to play jazz," he said.

Well, the word had never before sounded as heavy, as real, as it sounded that afternoon in Sonny's mouth. I just looked at him and I was probably frowning a real frown by this time. I simply couldn't see why on earth he'd want to spend his time hanging around nightclubs, clowning around on bandstands, while people pushed each other around a dance floor. It seemed—beneath him, somehow. I had never thought about it before, had never been forced to, but I suppose I had always put jazz musicians in a class with what Daddy called "good-time people."

"Are you *serious*?"

"Hell, *yes*, I'm serious."

He looked more helpless than ever, and annoyed, and deeply hurt.

I suggested, helpfully: "You mean—like Louis Armstrong?"

His face closed as though I'd struck him. "No. I'm not talking about none of that old-time, down home crap."

"Well, look, Sonny, I'm sorry, don't get mad. I just don't altogether get it, that's all. Name somebody—you know, a jazz musician you admire."

"Bird."

"Who?"

"Bird! Charlie Parker! Don't they teach you nothing in the goddamn army?"

I lit a cigarette. I was surprised and then a little amused to discover that I was trembling. "I've been out of touch," I said. "You'll have to be patient with me. Now. Who's this Parker character?"

"He's just one of the greatest jazz musicians alive," said Sonny, sullenly, his hands in his pockets, his back to me. "Maybe *the* greatest," he added, bitterly, "that's probably why *you* never heard of him."

"All right," I said, "I'm ignorant. I'm sorry. I'll go out and buy all the cat's records right away, all right?"

"It don't," said Sonny, with dignity, "make any difference to me. I don't care what you listen to. Don't do me no favors."

I was beginning to realize that I'd never seen him so upset before. With another part of my mind I was thinking that this would probably turn out to be one of those things kids go through and that I shouldn't make it seem important by pushing it too hard. Still, I didn't think it would do any harm to ask: "Doesn't all this take a lot of time? Can you make a living at it?"

He turned back to me and half leaned, half sat, on the kitchen table. "Everything takes time," he said, "and—well, yes, sure, I can make a living at it. But what I don't seem to be able to make you understand is that it's the only thing I want to do."

"Well, Sonny," I said, gently, "you know people can't always do exactly what they *want* to do—"

"*No*, I don't know that," said Sonny, surprising me. "I think people *ought* to do what they want to do, what else are they alive for?"

"You getting to be a big boy," I said desperately, "it's time you started thinking about your future."

"I'm thinking about my future," said Sonny, grimly. "I think about it all the time."

I gave up. I decided, if he didn't change his mind, that we could always talk about it later. "In the meantime," I said, "you got to finish school." We had already decided that he'd have to move in with Isabel and her folks. I knew this wasn't the ideal arrangement because Isabel's folks are inclined to be dicty[1] and they hadn't especially wanted Isabel to marry me. But I didn't know what else to do. "And we have to get you fixed up at Isabel's."

There was a long silence. He moved from the kitchen table to the window. "That's a terrible idea. You know it yourself."

"Do you have a *better* idea?"

---

[1] Having upper-class pretensions.

He just walked up and down the kitchen for a minute. He was as tall as I was. He had started to shave. I suddenly had the feeling that I didn't know him at all.

He stopped at the kitchen table and picked up my cigarettes. Looking at me with a kind of mocking, amused defiance, he put one between his lips. "You mind?"

"You smoking already?"

He lit the cigarette and nodded, watching me through the smoke. "I just wanted to see if I'd have the courage to smoke in front of you." He grinned and blew a great cloud of smoke to the ceiling. "It was easy." He looked at my face. "Come on, now. I bet you was smoking at my age, tell the truth."

I didn't say anything but the truth was on my face, and he laughed. But now there was something very strained in his laugh. "Sure. And I bet that ain't all you was doing."

He was frightening me a little. "Cut the crap," I said. "We already decided that you was going to go and live at Isabel's. Now what's got into you all of a sudden?"

"*You* decided it," he pointed out. "*I* didn't decide nothing." He stopped in front of me, leaning against the stove, arms loosely folded. "Look, brother. I don't want to stay in Harlem no more, I really don't." He was very earnest. He looked at me, then over toward the kitchen window. There was something in his eyes I'd never seen before, some thoughtfulness, some worry all his own. He rubbed the muscle of one arm. "It's time I was getting out of here."

"Where do you want to *go*, Sonny?"

"I want to join the army. Or the navy, I don't care. If I say I'm old enough, they'll believe me."

Then I got mad. It was because I was so scared. "You must be crazy. You goddamn fool, what the hell do you want to go and join the *army* for?"

"I just told you. To get out of Harlem."

"Sonny, you haven't even finished *school*. And if you really want to be a musician, how do you expect to study if you're in the *army*?"

He looked at me, trapped, and in anguish. "There's ways. I might be able to work out some kind of deal. Anyway, I'll have the G.I. Bill when I come out."

"*If* you come out." We stared at each other. "Sonny, please. Be reasonable. I know the setup is far from perfect. But we got to do the best we can."

"I ain't learning nothing in school," he said. "Even when I go." He turned away from me and opened the window and threw his cigarette out into the narrow alley. I watched his back. "At least, I ain't learning nothing you'd want me to learn." He slammed the window so hard I thought the glass would fly out, and turned back to me. "And I'm sick of the stink of these garbage cans!"

"Sonny," I said, "I know how you feel. But if you don't finish school now, you're going to be sorry later that you didn't." I grabbed him by the shoulders. "And you only got another year. It ain't so bad. And I'll come back and I swear I'll help you do *whatever* you want to do. Just try to put up with it till I come back. Will you please do that? For me?"

He didn't answer and he wouldn't look at me.

"Sonny. You hear me?"

He pulled away. "I hear you. But you never hear anything *I* say."

I didn't know what to say to that. He looked out of the window and then back at me. "OK," he said, and sighed. "I'll try."

Then I said, trying to cheer him up a little, "They got a piano at Isabel's. You can practice on it."

And as a matter of fact, it did cheer him up for a minute. "That's right," he said to himself. "I forgot that." His face relaxed a little. But the worry, the thoughtfulness, played on it still, the way shadows play on a face which is staring into the fire.

But I thought I'd never hear the end of that piano. At first, Isabel, would write me, saying how nice it was that Sonny was so serious about his music and how, as soon as he came in from school, or wherever he had been when he was supposed to be at school, he went straight to that piano and stayed there until suppertime. And, after supper, he went back to that piano and stayed there until everybody went to bed. He was at the piano all day Saturday and all day Sunday. Then he bought a record player and started playing records. He'd play one record over and over again, all day long sometimes, and he'd improvise along with it on the piano. Or he'd play one section of the record, one chord, one change, one progression, then he'd do it on the piano. Then back to the record. Then back to the piano.

Well, I really don't know how they stood it. Isabel finally confessed that it wasn't like living with a person at all, it was like living with sound. And the sound didn't make any sense to her, didn't make any sense to any of them—naturally. They began, in a way, to be afflicted by this presence that was living in their home. It was as though Sonny were some sort of god, or monster. He moved in an atmosphere which wasn't like theirs at all. They fed him and he ate, he washed himself, he walked in and out of their door; he certainly wasn't nasty or unpleasant or rude, Sonny isn't any of those things; but it was as though he were all wrapped up in some cloud, some fire, some vision all his own; and there wasn't any way to reach him.

At the same time, he wasn't really a man yet, he was still a child, and they had to watch out for him in all kinds of ways. They certainly couldn't throw him out. Neither did they dare to make a great scene about that piano because even they dimly sensed, as I sensed, from so many thousands of miles away, that Sonny was at that piano playing for his life.

But he hadn't been going to school. One day a letter came from the school board and Isabel's mother got it—there had, apparently, been other letters but Sonny had torn them up. This day, when Sonny came in, Isabel's mother showed him the letter and asked where he'd been spending his time. And she finally got it out of him that he'd been down in Greenwich Village, with musicians and other characters, in a white girl's apartment. And this scared her and she started to scream at him and what came up, once she began—though she denies it to this day—was what sacrifices they were making to give Sonny a decent home and how little he appreciated it.

Sonny didn't play the piano that day. By evening, Isabel's mother had calmed down but then there was the old man to deal with, and Isabel herself. Isabel says she did her best to be calm but she broken down and started crying. She says she just watched Sonny's face. She could tell, by watching him, what was happening with him. And what was happening was that they penetrated his cloud, they had reached him. Even if their fingers had been a thousand times more gentle than human fingers ever are, he could hardly help feeling that they had stripped him naked and were spitting on that nakedness. For he also had to see that his presence, that music, which was life or death to him, had been torture for them and that they had endured it, not at all for his sake, but only for mine. And Sonny couldn't take that. He can take it a little better today than he could then but he's still not very good at it and, frankly, I don't know anybody who is.

The silence of the next few days must have been louder than the sound of all the music ever played since time began. One morning, before she went to work, Isabel was in his room for something and she suddenly realized that all of his records were gone. And she knew for certain that he was gone. And he was. He went as far as the navy would carry him. He finally sent me a postcard from some place in Greece and that was the first I knew that Sonny was still alive. I didn't see him any more until we were both back in New York and the war had long been over.

He was a man by then, of course, but I wasn't willing to see it. He came by the house from time to time, but we fought almost every time we met. I didn't like the way he carried himself, loose and dreamlike all the time, and I didn't like his friends, and his music seemed to be merely an excuse for the life he led. It sounded just that weird and disordered.

Then we had a fight, a pretty awful fight, and I didn't see him for months. By and by I looked him up, where he was living, in a furnished room in the Village, and I tried to make it up. But there were lots of other people in the room and Sonny just lay on his bed, and he wouldn't come downstairs with me, and he treated these other people as though they were his family and I weren't. So I got mad and then he got mad, and then I told him that he might just as well be dead as live the way he was living. Then he stood up and he told me not to worry about him any more in life, that he *was* dead as far as I was concerned. Then he pushed me to the door and the other people looked on as though nothing were happening, and he slammed the door behind me. I stood in the hallway, staring at the door. I heard somebody laugh in the room and then the tears came to my eyes. I started down the steps, whistling to keep from crying. I kept whistling to myself, *You going to need me, baby, one of these cold, rainy days.*

I read about Sonny's trouble in the spring. Little Grace died in the fall. She was a beautiful little girl. But she only lived a little over two years. She died of polio and she suffered. She had a slight fever for a couple of days, but it didn't seem like anything and we just kept her in bed. And we would certainly have called the doctor, but the fever dropped, she seemed to be all right. So we thought it had just been a cold. Then, one day, she was up, playing, Isabel was in the kitchen fixing lunch for the two boys when they'd come in from school, and she heard Grace fall down in the living room. When you have a lot of children you don't always start running when one of them falls, unless they start screaming or something. And, this time, Grace was quiet. Yet, Isabel says that when she heard that *thump* and then that silence, something happened in her to make her afraid. And she ran to the living room and there was little Grace on the floor, all twisted up, and the reason she hadn't screamed was that she couldn't get her breath. And when she did scream, it was the worst sound, Isabel says, that she'd ever heard in all her life, and she still hears it sometimes in her dreams. Isabel will sometimes wake me up with a low, moaning, strangled sound and I have to be quick to awaken her and hold her to me and where Isabel is weeping against me seems a mortal wound.

I think I may have written Sonny the very day that little Grace was buried. I was sitting in the living room in the dark, by myself, and I suddenly thought of Sonny. My trouble made his real.

One Saturday afternoon, when Sonny had been living with us, or, anyway, been in our house, for nearly two weeks, I found myself wandering aimlessly about the living room, drinking from a can of beer, and trying to work up the courage to search Sonny's room. He was out, he was usually out whenever I was home, and Isabel had taken the children to see their grandparents. Suddenly I was standing still in front of the living room window, watching Seventh Avenue. The idea of searching Sonny's room made me still. I scarcely dared to admit to myself what I'd be searching for. I didn't know what I'd do if I found it. Or if I didn't.

On the sidewalk across from me, near the entrance to a barbecue joint, some people were holding an old-fashioned revival meeting. The barbecue cook, wearing a dirty white apron, his conked[2] hair reddish and metallic in the pale sun, and a cigarette between his lips, stood in the doorway, watching them. Kids and older people paused in their errands and stood

---

[2] Straightened.

there, along with some older men and a couple of very tough-looking women who watched everything that happened on the avenue, as though they owned it, or were maybe owned by it. Well, they were watching this, too. The revival was being carried on by three sisters in black, and a brother. All they had were their voices and their Bibles and a tambourine. The brother was testifying and while he testified two of the sisters stood together, seeming to say, amen, and the third sister walked around with the tambourine outstretched and a couple of people dropped coins into it. Then the brother's testimony ended and the sister who had been taking up the collection dumped the coins into her palm and transferred them to the pocket of her long black robe. Then she raised both hands, striking the tambourine against the air, and then against one hand, and she started to sing. And the two other sisters and the brother joined in.

It was strange, suddenly, to watch, though I had been seeing these street meetings all my life. So, of course, had everybody else down there. Yet, they paused and watched and listened and I stood still at the window. "Tis the old ship of Zion," they sang, and the sister with the tambourine kept a steady, jangling beat, "it has rescued many a thousand!" Not a soul under the sound of their voices was hearing this song for the first time, not one of them had been rescued. Nor had they seen much in the way of rescue work being done around them. Neither did they especially believe in the holiness of the three sisters and the brother, they knew too much about them, knew where they lived, and how. The woman with the tambourine, whose voice dominated the air, whose face was bright with joy, was divided by very little from the woman who stood watching her, a cigarette between her heavy, chapped lips, her hair a cuckoo's nest, her face scarred and swollen from many beatings, and her black eyes glittering like coal. Perhaps they both knew this, which was why, when, as rarely, they addressed each other, they addressed each other as Sister. As the singing filled the air the watching, listening faces underwent a change, the eyes focusing on something within; the music seemed to soothe a poison out of them; and time seemed, nearly, to fall away from the sullen, belligerent, battered faces, as though they were fleeing back to their first condition, while dreaming of their last. The barbecue cook half shook his head and smiled, and dropped his cigarette and disappeared into his joint. A man fumbled in his pockets for change and stood holding it in his hand impatiently, as though he had just remembered a pressing appointment further up the avenue. He looked furious. Then I saw Sonny, standing on the edge of the crowd. He was carrying a wide, flat notebook with a green cover, and it made him look, from where I was standing, almost like a schoolboy. The coppery sun brought out the copper in his skin, he was very faintly smiling, standing very still. Then the singing stopped, the tambourine turned into a collection plate again. The furious man dropped in his coins and vanished, so did a couple of the women, and Sonny dropped some change in the plate, looking directly at the woman with a little smile. He started across the avenue, toward the house. He has a slow, loping walk, something like the way Harlem hipsters walk, only he's imposed on this his own half-beat. I had never really noticed it before.

I stayed at the window, both relieved and apprehensive. As Sonny disappeared from my sight, they began singing again. And they were still singing when his key turned in the lock.

"Hey," he said.

"Hey, yourself. You want some beer?"

"No. Well, maybe." But he came up to the window and stood beside me, looking out. "What a warm voice," he said.

They were singing *If I could only hear my mother pray again!*

"Yes," I said, "and she can sure beat that tambourine."

"But what a terrible song," he said, and laughed. He dropped his notebook on the sofa and disappeared into the kitchen. "Where's Isabel and the kids?"

"I think they went to see their grandparents. You hungry?"

"No." He came back into the living room with his can of beer. "You want to come some place with me tonight?"

I sensed, I don't know how, that I couldn't possibly say no. "Sure. Where?"

He sat down on the sofa and picked up his notebook and started leafing through it. "I'm going to sit in with some fellows in a joint in the Village."

"You mean, you're going to play, tonight?"

"That's right." He took a swallow of his beer and moved back to the window. He gave me a sidelong look. "If you can stand it."

"I'll try," I said.

He smiled to himself and we both watched as the meeting across the way broke up. The three sisters and the brother, heads bowed, were singing *God be with you till we meet again*. The faces around them were very quiet. Then the song ended. The small crowd dispersed. We watched the three women and the lone man walk slowly up the avenue.

"When she was singing before," said Sonny, abruptly, "her voice reminded me for a minute of what heroin feels like sometimes—when it's in your veins. It makes you feel sort of warm and cool at the same time. And distant. And—and sure." He sipped his beer, very deliberately not looking at me. I watched his face. "It makes you feel—in control. Sometimes you've got to have that feeling."

"Do you?" I sat down slowly in the easy chair.

"Sometimes." He went to the sofa and picked up his notebook again. "Some people do."

"In order," I asked, "to play?" And my voice was very ugly, full of contempt and anger.

"Well"—he looked at me with great, troubled eyes, as though, in fact, he hoped his eyes would tell me things he could never otherwise say— "they *think* so. And *if* they think so—!"

"And what do *you* think?" I asked.

He sat on the sofa and put his can of beer on the floor. "I don't know," he said, and I couldn't be sure if he were answering my question or pursuing his thoughts. His face didn't tell me. "It's not so much to *play*. It's to *stand* it, to be able to make it at all. On any level." He frowned and smiled: "In order to keep from shaking to pieces."

"But these friends of yours," I said, "they seem to shake themselves to pieces pretty goddamn fast."

"Maybe." He played with the notebook. And something told me that I should curb my tongue, that Sonny was doing his best to talk, that I should listen. "But of course you only know the ones that've gone to pieces. Some don't—or at least they haven't *yet* and that's just about all *any* of us can say." He paused. "And then there are some who just live, really, in hell, and they know it and they see what's happening and they go right on. I don't know." He sighed, dropped the notebook, folded his arms. "Some guys, you can tell from the way they play, they on something *all* the time. And you can see that, well, it makes something real for them. But of course," he picked up his beer from the floor and sipped it and put the can down again, "they *want* to, too, you've got to see that. Even some of them that say they don't—*some*, not all."

"And what about you?" I asked—I couldn't help it. "What about you? Do *you* want to?"

He stood up and walked to the window and remained silent for a long time. Then he sighed. "Me," he said. Then: "While I was downstairs before, on my way here, listening to that woman sing, it struck me all of a sudden how much suffering she must have had to go through—to sing like that. It's *repulsive* to think you have to suffer that much."

I said: "But there's no way not to suffer—is there, Sonny?"

"I believe not," he said and smiled, "but that's never stopped anyone from trying." He looked at me. "Has it?" I realized, with this mocking look, that there stood between us, forever, beyond the power of time or forgiveness, the fact that I had held silence—so long!—when he had needed human speech to help him. He turned back to the window. "No, there's no way not to suffer. But you try all kinds of ways to keep from drowning in it, to keep on top of it, and to make it seem—well, like *you*. Like you did something, all right, and now you're suffering for it. You know?" I said nothing. "Well you know," he said, impatiently, "why *do* people suffer? Maybe it's better to do something to give it a reason, *any* reason."

"But we just agreed," I said, "that there's no way not to suffer. Isn't it better, then, just to—take it?"

"But nobody just takes it," Sonny cried, "that's what I'm telling you! *Everybody* tries not to. You're just hung up on the *way* some people try—it's not *your* way!"

The hair on my face began to itch, my face felt wet. "That's not true," I said, "that's not true. I don't give a damn what other people do, I don't even care how they suffer. I just care how *you* suffer." And he looked at me. "Please believe me," I said, "I don't want to see you—die—trying not to suffer."

"I won't," he said, flatly, "die trying not to suffer. At least, not any faster than anybody else."

"But there's no need," I said, trying to laugh, "is there? in killing yourself."

I wanted to say more, but I couldn't. I wanted to talk about will power and how life could be—well, beautiful. I wanted to say that it was all within; but was it? or, rather, wasn't that exactly the trouble? And I wanted to promise that I would never fail him again. But it would all have sounded—empty words and lies.

So I made the promise to myself and prayed that I would keep it.

"It's terrible sometimes, inside," he said, "that's what's the trouble. You walk these streets, black and funky and cold, and there's not really a living ass to talk to, and there's nothing shaking, and there's no way of getting it out—that storm inside. You can't talk it and you can't make love with it, and when you finally try to get with it and play it, you realize *nobody's* listening. So *you've* got to listen. You got to find a way to listen."

And then he walked away from the window and sat on the sofa again, as though all the wind had suddenly been knocked out of him. "Sometimes you'll do *anything* to play, even cut your mother's throat." He laughed and looked at me. "Or your brother's." Then he sobered. "Or your own." Then: "Don't worry. I'm all right now and I think I'll *be* all right. But I can't forget—where I've been. I don't mean just the physical place I've been, I mean where I've *been*. And *what* I've been."

"What have you been, Sonny?" I asked.

He smiled—but sat sideways on the sofa, his elbow resting on the back, his fingers playing with his mouth and chin, not looking at me. "I've been something I didn't recognize, didn't know I could be. Didn't know anybody could be." He stopped, looking inward, looking helplessly young, looking old. "I'm not talking about it now because I feel *guilty* or anything like that—maybe it would be better if I did, I don't know. Anyway, I can't really talk about it. Not to you, not to anybody," and now he turned and faced me. "Sometimes, you know, and it was actually when I was most *out* of the world, I felt that I was in it, that I was *with* it, really, and I could play or I didn't really have to *play*, it just came out of me, it was there. And I don't know how I played, thinking about it now, but I know I did awful things, those times, sometimes, to people. Or it wasn't that I *did* anything to them—it was that they weren't real." He picked up the beer can; it was empty; he rolled it between his palms: "And other times—well, I needed a fix, I needed to find a place to lean, I needed to clear a space to *listen*—and I couldn't find it, and I—went crazy, I did terrible things to *me*, I was terrible *for* me." He began pressing the beer can between his hands, I watched the metal begin to give. It glittered, as he played with it, like a knife, and I was afraid he would cut himself, but I said nothing. "Oh well. I can never tell you. I was all by myself at the bottom of something, stinking and sweating and crying and shaking, and I smelled it, you know? *my* stink, and I thought I'd die if I couldn't get away from it and yet, all the same, I knew that everything I was doing was just locking me in with it. And I didn't know," he paused, still flattening the beer can, "I didn't know, I still *don't* know, something kept telling me that maybe it was good to smell your own stink, but I didn't think that *that* was what I'd been trying to do—and—who can stand it?" and he abruptly dropped the ruined beer can, looking at me with a small, still smile, and then rose, walking to the window as though it were the lodestone rock. I watched his face, he watched the avenue. "I couldn't tell you when Mama died—but the reason I wanted to leave Harlem so bad was to get away from drugs. And then, when I ran away, that's what I was running from—really. When I came back, nothing had changed, *I* hadn't changed, I was just—older." And he stopped, drumming with his fingers on the windowpane. The sun had vanished, soon darkness would fall. I watched his face. "It can come again," he said, almost as though speaking to himself. Then he turned to me. "It can come again," he repeated. "I just want you to know that."

"All right," I said, at last. "So it can come again, All right."

He smiled, but the smile was sorrowful. "I had to try to tell you," he said.

"Yes," I said. "I understand that."

"You're my brother," he said, looking straight at me, and not smiling at all.

"Yes," I repeated, "yes. I understand that."

He turned back to the window, looking out. "All that hatred down there," he said, "all that hatred and misery and love. It's a wonder it doesn't blow the avenue apart."

We went to the only nightclub on a short, dark street, downtown. We squeezed through the narrow, chattering, jampacked bar to the entrance of the big room, where the bandstand was. And we stood there for a moment, for the lights were very dim in this room and we couldn't see. Then, "Hello, boy," said a voice and an enormous black man, much older than Sonny or myself, erupted out of all that atmospheric lighting and put an arm around Sonny's shoulder. "I been sitting right here," he said, "waiting for you."

He had a big voice, too, and heads in the darkness turned toward us.

Sonny grinned and pulled a little away, and said, "Creole, this is my brother. I told you about him."

Creole shook my hand. "I'm glad to meet you, son," he said, and it was clear that he was glad to meet me *there*, for Sonny's sake. And he smiled, "You got a real musician in *your* family," and he took his arm from Sonny's shoulder and slapped him, lightly, affectionately, with the back of his hand.

"Well. Now I've heard it all," said a voice behind us. This was another musician, and a friend of Sonny's, a coal-black, cheerful-looking man, built close to the ground. He immediately began confiding to me, at the top of his lungs, the most terrible things about Sonny, his teeth gleaming like a lighthouse and his laugh coming up out of him like the beginning of an earthquake. And it turned out that everyone at the bar knew Sonny, or almost everyone; some were musicians, working there, or nearby, or not working, some were simply hangers-on, and some were there to hear Sonny play. I was introduced to all of them and they were all very polite to me. Yet, it was clear that, for them, I was only Sonny's brother. Here, I was in Sonny's world. Or, rather: his kingdom. Here, it was not even a question that his veins bore royal blood.

They were going to play soon and Creole installed me, by myself, at a table in a dark corner. Then I watched them, Creole, and the little black man, and Sonny, and the others, while they horsed around, standing just below the bandstand. The light from the bandstand spilled just a little short of them and, watching them laughing and gesturing and moving about, I had the feeling that they, nevertheless, were being most careful not to step into that circle of light too suddenly: that if they moved into the light too suddenly, without thinking, they would perish in flame. Then, while I watched, one of them, the small, black man, moved into the light and crossed the bandstand and started fooling around with his drums. Then—being funny and being, also, extremely ceremonious—Creole took Sonny by the arm and led him to the piano. A woman's voice called Sonny's name and a few hands started clapping. And Sonny, also being funny and being ceremonious, and so touched, I think, that he could have cried, but neither hiding it nor showing it, riding it like a man, grinned, and put both hands to his heart and bowed from the waist.

Creole then went to the bass fiddle and a lean, very bright-skinned brown man jumped up on the bandstand and picked up his horn. So there they were, and the atmosphere on the bandstand and in the room began to change and tighten. Someone stepped up to the microphone and announced them. Then there were all kinds of murmurs. Some people at the bar shushed others. The waitress ran around, frantically getting in the last orders, guys and chicks got closer to each other, and the lights on the bandstand, on the quartet, turned to a kind of indigo. Then they all looked different there. Creole looked about him for the last time, as though he were making certain that all his chickens were in the coop, and then he—jumped and struck the fiddle. And there they were.

All I know about music is that not many people ever really hear it. And even then, on the rare occasions when something opens within, and the music enters, what we mainly hear, or hear corroborated, are personal, private, vanishing evocations. But the man who creates the music is hearing something else, is dealing with the roar rising from the void and imposing order on it as it hits the air. What is evoked in him, then, is of another order, more terrible because it has no words, and triumphant, too, for that same reason. And his triumph, when he triumphs, is ours. I just watched Sonny's face. His face was troubled, he was working hard, but he wasn't with it. And I had the feeling that, in a way, everyone on the bandstand was waiting for him, both waiting for him and pushing him along. But as I began to watch Creole, I realized that it was Creole who held them all back. He had them on a short rein. Up there, keeping the beat with his whole body, wailing on the fiddle, with his eyes half closed, he was listening to everything, but he was listening to Sonny. He was having a dialogue with Sonny. He wanted Sonny to leave the shoreline and strike out for the deep water. He was Sonny's witness that deep water and drowning were not the same thing—he had been there, and he knew. And he wanted Sonny to know. He was waiting for Sonny to do the things on the keys which would let Creole know that Sonny was in the water.

And, while Creole listened, Sonny moved, deep within, exactly like someone in torment. I had never before thought of how awful the relationship must be between the musician and his instrument. He has to fill it, this instrument, with the breath of life, his own. He has to make it do what he wants it to do. And a piano is just a piano. It's made out of so much wood and wires and little hammers and big ones, and ivory. While there's only so much you can do with it, the only way to find this out is to try; to try and make it do everything.

And Sonny hadn't been near a piano for over a year. And he wasn't on much better terms with his life, not the life that stretched before him now. He and the piano stammered, started one way, got scared, stopped; started another way, panicked, marked time, started again; then seemed to have found a direction, panicked again, got stuck. And the face I saw on Sonny I'd never seen before. Everything had been burned out of it, and, at the same time, things usually hidden were being burned in, by the fire and fury of the battle which was occurring in him up there.

Yet, watching Creole's face as they neared the end of the first set, I had the feeling that something had happened, something I hadn't heard. Then they finished, there was scattered applause, and then, without an instant's warning, Creole started into something else, it was almost sardonic, it was *Am I Blue*. And, as though he commanded, Sonny began to play. Something began to happen. And Creole let out the reins. The dry, low, black man said something awful on the drums, Creole answered, and the drums talked back. Then the horn insisted, sweet and high, slightly detached perhaps, and Creole listened, commenting now and then, dry, and driving, beautiful and calm and old. Then they all came together again, and Sonny was part of the family again. I could tell this from his face. He seemed to have found, right there beneath his fingers, a damn brand-new piano. It seemed that he couldn't get over it. Then, for awhile, just being happy with Sonny, they seemed to be agreeing with him that brand-new pianos certainly were a gas.

*deep 420
no issue
as morning*

Then Creole stepped forward to remind them that what they were playing was the blues. He hit something in all of them, he hit something in me, myself, and the music tightened and deepened, apprehension began to beat the air. Creole began to tell us what the blues were all about. They were not about anything very new. He and his boys up there were keeping it new, at the risk of ruin, destruction, madness, and death, in order to find new ways to make us listen. For, while the tale of how we suffer, and how we are delighted, and how we may triumph is never new, it always must be heard. There isn't any other tale to tell, it's the only light we've got in all this darkness.

And this tale, according to that face, that body, those strong hands on those strings, has another aspect in every country, and a new depth in every generation. Listen, Creole seemed to be saying, listen. Now these are Sonny's blues. He made the little black man on the drums know it, and the bright, brown man on the horn. Creole wasn't trying any longer to get Sonny in the water. He was wishing him Godspeed. Then he stepped back, very slowly, filling the air with the immense suggestion that Sonny speak for himself.

Then they all gathered around Sonny and Sonny played. Every now and again one of them seemed to say, amen. Sonny's fingers filled the air with life, his life. But that life contained so many others. And Sonny went all the way back, he really began with the spare, flat statement of the opening phrase of the song. Then he began to make it his. It was very beautiful because it wasn't hurried and it was no longer a lament. I seemed to hear with what burning he had made it his, with what burning we had yet to make it ours, how we could cease lamenting. Freedom lurked around us and I understood, at last, that he could help us to be free if we would listen, that he would never be free until we did. Yet, there was no battle in his face now. I heard what he had gone through, and would continue to go through until he came to rest in earth. He had made it his: that long line, of which we knew only Mama and Daddy. And he was giving it back, as everything must be given back, so that, passing through death, it can live forever. I saw my mother's face again, and felt, for the first time, how the stones of the road she had walked on must have bruised her feet. I saw the moonlit road where my father's brother died. And it brought something else back to me, and carried me past it, I saw my little girl again and felt Isabel's tears again, and I felt my own tears begin to rise. And I was yet aware that this was only a moment, that the world waited outside, as hungry as a tiger, and that trouble stretched above us, longer than the sky.

Then it was over. Creole and Sonny let out their breath, both soaking wet, and grinning. There was a lot of applause and some of it was real. In the dark, the girl came by and I asked her to take drinks to the bandstand. There was a long pause, while they talked up there in the indigo light and after awhile I saw the girl put a Scotch and milk on top of the piano for Sonny. He didn't seem to notice it, but just before they started playing again, he sipped from it and looked toward me, and nodded. Then he put it back on top of the piano. For me, then, as they began to play again, it glowed and shook above my brother's head like the very cup of trembling.

Study and Discussion Questions

1. In what ways are Sonny and his brother different? How, for example, do their relationships to the Harlem community differ? What might account for these differences?
2. Why does Baldwin begin the story with the narrator reading about Sonny in the newspaper? Why does the narrator have so little interest in his brother at first? What is he afraid of? Why does he feel guilty?
3. How were the narrator and Sonny able to grow up together and yet remain such strangers?
4. What experiences bring the narrator closer to Sonny and help him understand his brother better?
5. Why does Sonny use heroin? Why does his music mean so much to him? Why the blues?
6. What has the narrator learned by the end of the story?
7. Events in the story are narrated out of chronological order. What is the effect of the story's structure?

Writing Exercises

1. What do you think Sonny's future might be? Write a brief narrative of the next five or ten years.
2. Listen to some instrumental music and try to put into words what is going on in it, in the way Baldwin does at the end of the story.
3. Imagine that, at the end of Sonny's performance, the narrator were, for some reason, swept off to another country, never to see or talk to his brother again. Write the letter he might have written, telling Sonny how he now feels about him.

NATHANIEL HAWTHORNE (1804–1864)

Nathaniel Hawthorne was born in Salem, Massachusetts, into an established Puritan family. He graduated from Bowdoin College in 1825 and then returned to Salem and began writing stories, which appeared in Twice-Told Tales *(1837) and* Mosses from an Old Manse *(1846). Hawthorne participated briefly in the experimental utopian community at Brook Farm, developed a friendship with Herman Melville, served several years as consul in Liverpool, England, lived in Italy, and then, in 1860, returned to Massachusetts. Among his novels are* The Scarlet Letter *(1850),* The House of Seven Gables *(1851),* The Blithedale Romance *(1852), and* The Marble Faun *(1860).*

Young Goodman Brown   (1846)

Young Goodman[1] Brown came forth at sunset into the street at Salem village; but put his head back, after crossing the threshold, to exchange a parting kiss with his young wife. And Faith, as the wife was aptly named, thrust her own pretty head into the street, letting the wind play with the pink ribbons of her cap while she called to Goodman Brown.

"Dearest heart," whispered she, softly and rather sadly, when her lips were close to his ear, "prithee put off your journey until sunrise and sleep in your own bed to-night. A lone woman is troubled with such dreams and such thoughts that she's afeard of herself sometimes. Pray tarry with me this night, dear husband, of all nights in the year."

"My love and my Faith," replied young Goodman Brown, "of all nights in the year, this one night must I tarry away from thee. My journey, as thou callest it, forth and back again, must needs be done 'twixt now and sunrise. What, my sweet, pretty wife, dost thou doubt me already, and we but three months married?"

"Then God bless you!" said Faith, with the pink ribbons; "and may you find all well when you come back."

"Amen!" cried Goodman Brown. "Say thy prayers, dear Faith, and go to bed at dusk, and no harm will come to thee."

So they parted; and the young man pursued his way until, being about to turn the corner by the meeting-house, he looked back and saw the head of Faith still peeping after him with a melancholy air, in spite of her pink ribbons.

"Poor little Faith!" thought he, for his heart smote him. "What a wretch am I to leave her on such an errand! She talks of dreams, too. Methought as she spoke there was trouble in her face, as if a dream had warned her what work is to be done to-night. But no, no; 'twould kill her to think it. Well, she's a blessed angel on earth; and after this one night I'll cling to her skirts and follow her to heaven."

With this excellent resolve for the future, Goodman Brown felt himself justified in making more haste on his present evil purpose. He had taken a dreary road, darkened by all the gloomiest trees of the forest, which barely stood aside to let the narrow path creep through, and closed immediately behind. It was all as lonely as could be; and there is this peculiarity in such a solitude, that the traveller knows not who may be concealed by the innumerable trunks and the thick boughs overhead; so

---

[1] Goodman and Goody (used later) were respectful terms of address for men and women not of the upper classes.

that with lonely footsteps he may yet be passing through an unseen multitude.

"There may be a devilish Indian behind every tree," said Goodman Brown to himself; and he glanced fearfully behind him as he added, "What if the devil himself should be at my very elbow!"

His head being turned back, he passed a crook of the road, and, looking forward again, beheld the figure of a man, in grave and decent attire, seated at the foot of an old tree. He arose at Goodman Brown's approach and walked onward side by side with him.

"You are late, Goodman Brown," said he. "The clock of the Old South was striking as I came through Boston, and that is full fifteen minutes agone."

"Faith kept me back a while," replied the young man, with a tremor in his voice, caused by the sudden appearance of his companion, though not wholly unexpected.

It was now deep dusk in the forest, and deepest in that part of it where these two were journeying. As nearly as could be discerned, the second traveller was about fifty years old, apparently in the same rank of life as Goodman Brown, and bearing a considerable resemblance to him, though perhaps more in expression than features. Still they might have been taken for father and son. And yet, though the elder person was as simply clad as the younger, and as simple in manner too, he had an indescribable air of one who knew the world, and who would not have felt abashed at the governor's dinner table or in King William's court, were it possible that his affairs should call him thither. But the only thing about him that could be fixed upon as remarkable was his staff, which bore the likeness of a great black snake, so curiously wrought that it might almost be seen to twist and wriggle itself like a living serpent. This, of course, must have been an ocular deception, assisted by the uncertain light.

"Come, Goodman Brown," cried his fellow-traveller, "this is a dull pace for the beginning of a journey. Take my staff, if you are so soon weary."

"Friend," said the other, exchanging his slow pace for a full stop, "having kept covenant by meeting thee here, it is my purpose now to return whence I came. I have scruples touching the matter thou wot'st of."

"Sayest thou so?" replied he of the serpent, smiling apart. "Let us walk on, nevertheless, reasoning as we go; and if I convince thee not thou shalt turn back. We are but a little way in the forest yet."

"Too far! too far!" exclaimed the goodman, unconsciously resuming his walk. "My father never went into the woods on such an errand, nor his father before him. We have been a race of honest men and good Christians since the days of the martyrs; and shall I be the first of the name of Brown that ever took this path and kept"—

"Such company, thou wouldst say," observed the elder person, interpreting his pause. "Well said, Goodman Brown! I have been as well
acquainted with your family as with ever a one among the Puritans; and
that's no trifle to say. I helped your grandfather, the constable, when he
lashed the Quaker woman so smartly through the streets of Salem; and
it was I that brought your father a pitch-pine knot, kindled at my own
hearth, to set fire to an Indian village, in King Philip's war.[2] They were
my good friends, both; and many a pleasant walk have we had along
this path, and returned merrily after midnight. I would fain be friends
with you for their sake."

"If it be as thou sayest," replied Goodman Brown, "I marvel they never
spoke of these matters; or, verily, I marvel not, seeing that the least rumor
of the sort would have driven them from New England. We are a people
of prayer, and good works to boot, and abide no such wickedness."

"Wickedness or not," said the traveller with the twisted staff, "I have
a very general acquaintance here in New England. The deacons of many
a church have drunk the communion wine with me; the selectmen of
divers towns make me their chairman; and a majority of the Great and
General Court are firm supporters of my interest. The governor and I,
too—But these are state secrets."

"Can this be so?" cried Goodman Brown, with a stare of amazement
at his undisturbed companion. "Howbeit, I have nothing to do with the
governor and council; they have their own ways, and are no rule for a
simple husbandman like me. But, were I to go on with thee, how should
I meet the eye of that good old man, our minister, at Salem village? Oh,
his voice would make me tremble both Sabbath day and lecture day."

Thus far the elder traveller had listened with due gravity; but now
burst into a fit of irrepressible mirth, shaking himself so violently that his
snake-like staff actually seemed to wriggle in sympathy.

"Ha! ha! ha!" shouted he again and again; then composing himself,
"Well, go on, Goodman Brown, go on; but, prithee, don't kill me with
laughing."

"Well, then, to end the matter at once," said Goodman Brown, considerably nettled, "there is my wife, Faith. It would break her dear little
heart; and I'd rather break my own."

"Nay, if that be the case," answered the other, "e'en go thy ways,
Goodman Brown. I would not for twenty old women like the one hobbling
before us that Faith should come to any harm."

As he spoke he pointed his staff at a female figure on the path, in
whom Goodman Brown recognized a very pious and exemplary dame,
who had taught him his catechism in youth, and was still his moral and
spiritual adviser, jointly with the minister and Deacon Gookin.

"A marvel, truly, that Goody Cloyse should be so far in the wilderness
at nightfall," said he. "But with your leave, friend, I shall take a cut

---

[2] War between Indians and New England colonists, 1675–1676.

through the woods until we have left this Christian woman behind. Being a stranger to you, she might ask whom I was consorting with and whither I was going."

"Be it so," said his fellow-traveller. "Betake you the woods, and let me keep the path."

Accordingly the young man turned aside, but took care to watch his companion, who advanced softly along the road until he had come within a staff's length of the old dame. She, meanwhile, was making the best of her way, with singular speed for so aged a woman, and mumbling some indistinct words—a prayer, doubtless—as she went. The traveller put forth his staff and touched her withered neck with what seemed the serpent's tail.

"The devil!" screamed the pious old lady.

"Then Goody Cloyse knows her old friend?" observed the traveller, confronting her and leaning on his writhing stick.

"Ah, forsooth, and is it your worship indeed?" cried the good dame. "Yea, truly is it, and in the very image of my old gossip, Goodman Brown, the grandfather of the silly fellow that now is. But—would your worship believe it?—my broomstick hath strangely disappeared, stolen, as I suspect, by that unhanged witch, Goody Cory, and that, too, when I was all anointed with the juice of smallage, and cinquefoil, and wolf's bane"—

"Mingled with fine wheat and the fat of a new-born babe," said the shape of old Goodman Brown.

"Ah, your worship knows the recipe," cried the old lady, cackling aloud. "So, as I was saying, being all ready for the meeting, and no horse to ride on, I made up my mind to foot it; for they tell me there is a nice young man to be taken into communion to-night. But now your good worship will lend me your arm, and we shall be there in a twinkling."

"That can hardly be," answered her friend. "I may not spare you my arm, Goody Cloyse; but here is my staff, if you will."

So saying, he threw it down at her feet, where, perhaps, it assumed life, being one of the rods which its owner had formerly lent to the Egyptian magi. Of this fact, however, Goodman Brown could not take cognizance. He had cast up his eyes in astonishment, and, looking down again, beheld neither Goody Cloyse nor the serpentine staff, but this fellow-traveller alone, who waited for him as calmly as if nothing had happened.

"That old woman taught me my catechism," said the young man; and there was a world of meaning in this simple comment.

They continued to walk onward, while the elder traveller exhorted his companion to make good speed and persevere in the path, discoursing so aptly that his arguments seemed rather to spring up in the bosom of his auditor than to be suggested by himself. As they went, he plucked a branch of maple to serve for a walking stick, and began to strip it of the twigs and little boughs, which were wet with evening dew. The moment his fingers touched them they became strangely withered and dried up as with a week's sunshine. Thus the pair proceeded, at a good free pace, until suddenly, in a gloomy hollow of the road, Goodman Brown sat himself down on the stump of a tree and refused to go any farther.

"Friend," said he, stubbornly, "my mind is made up. Not another step will I budge on this errand. What if a wretched old woman do choose to go to the devil when I thought she was going to heaven: is that any reason why I should quit my dear Faith and go after her?"

"You will think better of this by and by," said his acquaintance, composedly. "Sit here and rest yourself a while; and when you feel like moving again, there is my staff to help you along."

Without more words, he threw his companion the maple stick, and was as speedily out of sight as if he had vanished into the deepening gloom. The young man sat a few moments by the roadside, applauding himself greatly, and thinking with how clear a conscience he should meet the minister in his morning walk, nor shrink from the eye of good old Deacon Gookin. And what calm sleep would be his that very night, which was to have been spent so wickedly, but so purely and sweetly now, in the arms of Faith! Amidst these pleasant and praiseworthy meditations, Goodman Brown heard the tramp of horses along the road, and deemed it advisable to conceal himself within the verge of the forest, conscious of the guilty purpose that had brought him thither, though now so happily turned from it.

On came the hoof tramps and the voices of the riders, two grave old voices, conversing soberly as they drew near. These mingled sounds appeared to pass along the road, within a few yards of the young man's hiding-place; but, owing doubtless to the depth of the gloom at that particular spot, neither the travellers nor their steeds were visible. Though their figures brushed the small boughs by the wayside, it could not be seen that they intercepted, even for a moment, the faint gleam from the strip of bright sky athwart which they must have passed. Goodman Brown alternately crouched and stood on tiptoe, pulling aside the branches and thrusting forth his head as far as he durst without discerning so much as a shadow. It vexed him the more, because he could have sworn, were such a thing possible, that he recognized the voices of the minister and Deacon Gookin, jogging along quietly, as they were wont to do, when bound to some ordination or ecclesiastical council. While yet within hearing, one of the riders stopped to pluck a switch.

"Of the two, reverend sir," said the voice like the deacon's, "I had rather miss an ordination dinner than to-night's meeting. They tell me that some of our community are to be here from Falmouth and beyond, and others from Connecticut and Rhode Island, besides several of the Indian powwows, who, after their fashion, know almost as much deviltry as the best of us. Moreover, there is a goodly young woman to be taken into communion."

"Mighty well, Deacon Gookin!" replied the solemn old tones of the minister. "Spur up, or we shall be late. Nothing can be done, you know, until I get on the ground."

The hoofs clattered again; and the voices, talking so strangely in the empty air, passed on through the forest, where no church had ever been gathered or solitary Christian prayed. Whither, then, could these holy men be journeying so deep into the heathen wilderness? Young Goodman Brown caught hold of a tree for support, being ready to sink down on the ground, faint and overburdened with the heavy sickness of his heart. He looked up to the sky, doubting whether there really was a heaven above him. Yet there was the blue arch, and the stars brightening in it.

"With heaven above and Faith below, I will yet stand firm against the devil!" cried Goodman Brown.

While he still gazed upward into the deep arch of the firmament and had lifted his hands to pray, a cloud, though no wind was stirring, hurried across the zenith and hid the brightening stars. The blue sky was still visible, except directly overhead, where this black mass of cloud was sweeping swiftly northward. Aloft in the air, as if from the depths of the cloud, came a confused and doubtful sound of voices. Once the listener fancied that he could distinguish the accents of towns-people of his own, men and women, both pious and ungodly, many of whom he had met at the communion table, and had seen others rioting at the tavern. The next moment, so indistinct were the sounds, he doubted whether he had heard aught but the murmur of the old forest, whispering without a wind. Then came a stronger swell of those familiar tones, heard daily in the sunshine at Salem village, but never until now from a cloud of night. There was one voice, of a young woman, uttering lamentations, yet with an uncertain sorrow, and entreating for some favor, which, perhaps, it would grieve her to obtain; and all the unseen multitude, both saints and sinners, seemed to encourage her onward.

"Faith!" shouted Goodman Brown, in a voice of agony and desperation; and the echoes of the forest mocked him, crying, "Faith! Faith!" as if bewildered wretches were seeking her all through the wilderness.

The cry of grief, rage, and terror was yet piercing the night, when the unhappy husband held his breath for a response. There was a scream, drowned immediately in a louder murmur of voices, fading into far-off laughter, as the dark cloud swept away, leaving the clear and silent sky above Goodman Brown. But something fluttered lightly down through the air and caught on the branch of a tree. The young man seized it, and beheld a pink ribbon.

"My Faith is gone!" cried he, after one stupefied moment. "There is no good on earth; and sin is but a name. Come, devil; for to thee is this world given."

And, maddened with despair, so that he laughed loud and long, did Goodman Brown grasp his staff and set forth again, at such a rate that he seemed to fly along the forest path rather than to walk or run. The road grew wilder and drearier and more faintly traced, and vanished at length, leaving him in the heart of the dark wilderness, still rushing onward with the instinct that guides mortal man to evil. The whole forest was peopled with frightful sounds—the creaking of the trees, the howling of wild beasts, and the yell of Indians; while sometimes the wind tolled like a distant church bell, and sometimes gave a broad roar around the traveller, as if all Nature were laughing him to scorn. But he was himself the chief horror of the scene, and shrank not from its other horrors.

"Ha! ha! ha!" roared Goodman Brown when the wind laughed at him. "Let us hear which will laugh loudest. Think not to frighten me with your deviltry. Come witch, come wizard, come Indian powwow, come devil himself, and here comes Goodman Brown. You may as well fear him as he fear you."

In truth, all through the haunted forest there could be nothing more frightful than the figure of Goodman Brown. On he flew among the black pines, brandishing his staff with frenzied gestures, now giving vent to an inspiration of horrid blasphemy, and now shouting forth such laughter as set all the echoes of the forest laughing like demons around him. The fiend in his own shape is less hideous than when he rages in the breast of man. Thus sped the demoniac on his course, until, quivering among the trees, he saw a red light before him, as when the felled trunks and branches of a clearing have been set on fire, and throw up their lurid blaze against the sky, at the hour of midnight. He paused, in a lull of the tempest that had driven him onward, and heard the swell of what seemed a hymn, rolling solemnly from a distance with the weight of many voices. He knew the tune; it was a familiar one in the choir of the village meeting-house. The verse died heavily away, and was lengthened by a chorus, not of human voices, but of all the sounds of the benighted wilderness pealing in awful harmony together. Goodman Brown cried out, and his cry was lost to his own ear by its unison with the cry of the desert.

In the interval of silence he stole forward until the light glared full upon his eyes. At one extremity of an open space, hemmed in by the dark wall of the forest, arose a rock, bearing some rude, natural resemblance either to an altar or a pulpit, and surrounded by four blazing pines, their tops aflame, their stems untouched, like candles at an evening meeting. The mass of foliage that had overgrown the summit of the rock was all on fire, blazing high into the night and fitfully illuminating the whole field. Each pendent twig and leafy festoon was in a blaze. As the red light arose and fell, a numerous congregation alternately shone forth, then disappeared in shadow, and again grew, as it were, out of the darkness, peopling the heart of the solitary woods at once.

"A grave and dark-clad company," quoth Goodman Brown.

In truth they were such. Among them, quivering to and fro between gloom and splendor, appeared faces that would be seen next day at the council board of the province, and others which, Sabbath after Sabbath, looked devoutly heavenward, and benignantly over the crowded pews, from the holiest pulpits in the land. Some affirm that the lady of the governor was there. At least there were high dames well known to her,

and wives of honored husbands, and widows, a great multitude, and
ancient maidens, all of excellent repute, and fair young girls, who trembled
lest their mothers should espy them. Either the sudden gleams of light
flashing over the obscure field bedazzled Goodman Brown, or he recognized a score of the church members of Salem village famous for their
especial sanctity. Good old Deacon Gookin had arrived, and waited at
the skirts of that venerable saint, his revered pastor. But, irreverently
consorting with these grave, reputable, and pious people, these elders of
the church, these chaste dames and dewy virgins, there were men of
dissolute lives and women of spotted fame, wretches given over to all
mean and filthy vice, and suspected even of horrid crimes. It was strange
to see that the good shrank not from the wicked, nor were the sinners
abashed by the saints. Scattered also among their pale-faced enemies were
the Indian priests, or powwows, who had often scared their native forest
with more hideous incantations than any known to English witchcraft.

"But where is Faith?" thought Goodman Brown; and as hope came
into his heart, he trembled.

Another verse of the hymn arose, a slow and mournful strain, such as
the pious love, but joined to words which expressed all that our nature
can conceive of sin, and darkly hinted at far more. Unfathomable to mere
mortals is the lore of fiends. Verse after verse was sung; and still the
chorus of the desert swelled between like the deepest tone of a mighty
organ; and with the final peal of that dreadful anthem there came a
sound, as if the roaring wind, the rushing streams, the howling beasts,
and every other voice of the unconcerted wilderness were mingling and
according with the voice of guilty man in homage to the prince of all.
The four blazing pines threw up a loftier flame, and obscurely discovered
shapes and visages of horror on the smoke wreaths above the impious
assembly. At the same moment the fire on the rock shot redly forth and
formed a glowing arch above its base, where now appeared a figure. With
reverence be it spoken, the figure bore no slight similitude, both in garb
and manner, to some grave divine of the New England churches.

"Bring forth the converts!" cried a voice that echoed through the field
and rolled into the forest.

At the word, Goodman Brown stepped forth from the shadow of the
trees and approached the congregation, with whom he felt a loathful
brotherhood by the sympathy of all that was wicked in his heart. He
could have well-nigh sworn that the shape of his own dead father beckoned
him to advance, looking downward from a smoke wreath, while a woman,
with dim features of despair, threw out her hand to warn him back. Was
it his mother? But he had no power to retreat one step, nor to resist,
even in thought, when the minister and good old Deacon Gookin seized
his arms and led him to the blazing rock. Thither came also the slender
form of a veiled female, led between Goody Cloyse, that pious teacher
of the catechism, and Martha Carrier, who had received the devil's promise

to be queen of hell. A rampant hag was she. And there stood the proselytes beneath the canopy of fire.

"Welcome, my children," said the dark figure, "to the communion of your race. Ye have found thus young your nature and your destiny. My children, look behind you!"

They turned; and flashing forth, as it were, in a sheet of flame, the fiend worshippers were seen; the smile of welcome gleamed darkly on every visage.

"There," resumed the sable form, "are all whom ye have reverenced from youth. Ye deemed them holier than yourselves, and shrank from your own sin, contrasting it with their lives of righteousness and prayerful aspirations heavenward. Yet here are they all in my worshipping assembly. This night it shall be granted you to know their secret deeds: how hoary-bearded elders of the church have whispered wanton words to the young maids of their households; how many a woman, eager for widows' weeds, has given her husband a drink at bedtime and let him sleep his last sleep in her bosom; how beardless youths have made haste to inherit their fathers' wealth; and how fair damsels—blush not, sweet ones—have dug little graves in the garden, and bidden me, the sole guest, to an infant's funeral. By the sympathy of your human hearts for sin ye shall scent out all the places—whether in church, bed-chamber, street, field, or forest—where crime has been committed, and shall exult to behold the whole earth one stain of guilt, one mighty blood spot. Far more than this. It shall be yours to penetrate, in every bosom, the deep mystery of sin, the fountain of all wicked arts, and which inexhaustibly supplies more evil impulses than human power—than my power at its utmost—can make manifest in deeds. And now, my children, look upon each other."

They did so; and, by the blaze of the hell-kindled torches, the wretched man beheld his Faith, and the wife her husband, trembling before that unhallowed altar.

"Lo, there ye stand, my children," said the figure, in a deep and solemn tone, almost sad with its despairing awfulness, as if his once angelic nature could yet mourn for our miserable race. "Depending upon one another's hearts, ye had still hoped that virtue were not all a dream. Now are ye undeceived. Evil is the nature of mankind. Evil must be your only happiness. Welcome again, my children, to the communion of your race."

"Welcome," repeated the fiend worshippers, in one cry of despair and triumph.

And there they stood, the only pair, as it seemed, who were yet hesitating on the verge of wickedness in this dark world. A basin was hollowed, naturally, in the rock. Did it contain water, reddened by the lurid light? or was it blood? or, perchance, a liquid flame? Herein did the shape of evil dip his hand and prepare to lay the mark of baptism upon their foreheads, that they might be partakers of the mystery of sin, more conscious of the secret guilt of others, both in deed and thought, than they could now be of their own. The husband cast one look at his pale wife, and Faith at him. What polluted wretches would the next glance show them to each other, shuddering alike at what they disclosed and what they saw.

"Faith! Faith!" cried the husband, "look up to heaven, and resist the wicked one."

Whether Faith obeyed he knew not. Hardly had he spoken when he found himself amid calm night and solitude, listening to a roar of the wind which died heavily away through the forest. He staggered against the rock, and felt it chill and damp; while a hanging twig, that had been all on fire, besprinkled his cheek with the coldest dew.

The next morning young Goodman Brown came slowly into the street of Salem village, staring around him like a bewildered man. The good old minister was taking a walk along the graveyard to get an appetite for breakfast and meditate his sermon, and bestowed a blessing, as he passed, on Goodman Brown. He shrank from the venerable saint as if to avoid an anathema. Old Deacon Gookin was at domestic worship, and the holy words of his prayer were heard through the open window. "What God doth the wizard pray to?" quoth Goodman Brown. Goody Cloyse, that excellent old Christian, stood in the early sunshine at her own lattice, catechizing a little girl who had brought her a pint of morning's milk. Goodman Brown snatched away the child as from the grasp of the fiend himself. Turning the corner by the meeting-house, he spied the head of Faith, with the pink ribbons, gazing anxiously forth, and bursting into such joy at sight of him that she skipped along the street and almost kissed her husband before the whole village. But Goodman Brown looked sternly and sadly into her face, and passed on without a greeting.

Had Goodman Brown fallen asleep in the forest and only dreamed a wild dream of a witch-meeting?

Be it so if you will; but, alas! it was a dream of evil omen for young Goodman Brown. A stern, a sad, a darkly meditative, a distrustful, if not a desperate man did he become from the night of that fearful dream. On the Sabbath day, when the congregation were singing a holy psalm, he could not listen because an anthem of sin rushed loudly upon his ear and drowned all the blessed strain. When the minister spoke from the pulpit with power and fervid eloquence, and, with his hand on the open Bible, of the sacred truths of our religion, and of saint-like lives and triumphant deaths, and of future bliss or misery unutterable, then did Goodman Brown turn pale, dreading lest the roof should thunder down upon the gray blasphemer and his hearers. Often, awaking suddenly at midnight, he shrank from the bosom of Faith; and at morning or eventide, when the family knelt down at prayer, he scowled and muttered to himself, and gazed sternly at his wife, and turned away. And when he had lived long, and was borne to his grave a hoary corpse, followed by Faith, an aged woman, and children and grandchildren, a goodly procession, besides neighbors not a few, they carved no hopeful verse upon his tombstone, for his dying hour was gloom.

Study and Discussion Questions

1. Think about the names of the characters. What is the significance of these names?
2. Who is the person young Goodman Brown meets in the forest? Why does Hawthorne mention that the two resemble each other?
3. What is young Goodman Brown's errand this night? Why doesn't he tell his wife what it is?
4. What are the travelling companion's means of persuasion?
5. What finally causes Goodman Brown to go on with his journey?
6. Who is at the meeting in the woods? In what ways does that community differ from the one Goodman Brown (a) comes from and (b) expected to find there?
7. What does this story suggest is the "real" nature of human beings?

Writing Exercises

1. Write about a time you discovered something (or thought you discovered something) that caused a major shift in the way you saw the world.
2. How would the story and your response to it have been changed if Hawthorne had left out the suggestion that all this might have been a dream?

DORIS LESSING (b. 1919)

Doris Lessing was born in Kermanshah, Persia, and moved with her family to a large farm in Southern Rhodesia when she was six. She attended a Roman Catholic convent school but left at fourteen, to work as a secretary. In 1949 she moved to England. Among Lessing's novels are the five autobiographical volumes of Children of Violence *(1950–1969),* The Golden Notebook *(1962),* Briefing for a Descent into Hell *(1971), and* Shikasta *(1979).*

Our Friend Judith (1963)

I stopped inviting Judith to meet people when a Canadian woman remarked, with the satisfied fervour of one who has at last pinned a label on a rare specimen: "She is, of course, one of your typical English spinsters."

This was a few weeks after an American sociologist, having elicited from Judith the facts that she was fortyish, unmarried, and living alone, had enquired of me: "I suppose she has given up?" "Given up what?" I asked; and the subsequent discussion was unrewarding.

Judith did not easily come to parties. She would come after pressure, not so much—one felt—to do one a favour, but in order to correct what she believed to be a defect in her character. "I really ought to enjoy meeting new people more than I do," she said once. We reverted to an earlier pattern of our friendship: odd evenings together, an occasional visit to the cinema, or she would telephone to say: "I'm on my way past you to the British Museum. Would you care for a cup of coffee with me? I have twenty minutes to spare."

It is characteristic of Judith that the word "spinster," used of her, provoked fascinated speculation about other people. There are my aunts, for instance: aged seventy-odd, both unmarried, one an ex-missionary from China, one a retired matron of a famous London hospital. These two old ladies live together under the shadow of the cathedral in a country town. They devote much time to the Church, to good causes, to letter writing with friends all over the world, to the grandchildren and the great-grandchildren of relatives. It would be a mistake, however, on entering a house in which nothing has been moved for fifty years, to diagnose a condition of fossilised late-Victorian integrity. They read every book reviewed in the *Observer* or the *Times*, so that I recently got a letter from Aunt Rose enquiring whether I did not think that the author of *On the Road*[1] was not—perhaps?—exaggerating his difficulties. They know a good deal about music, and write letters of encouragement to young composers they feel are being neglected—"You must understand that anything new and original takes time to be understood." Well-informed and critical Tories, they are as likely to despatch telegrams of protest to the Home Secretary as letters of support. These ladies, my aunts Emily and Rose, are surely what is meant by the phrase "English spinster." And yet, once the connection has been pointed out, there is no doubt that Judith and they are spiritual cousins, if not sisters. Therefore it follows that one's pitying admiration for women who have supported manless and uncomforted lives needs a certain modification?

One will, of course, never know; and I feel now that it is entirely my fault that I shall never know. I had been Judith's friend for upwards of five years before the incident occurred which I involuntarily thought of— stupidly enough—as the first time Judith's mask slipped.

A mutual friend, Betty, had been given a cast-off Dior dress. She was too short for it. Also she said: "It's not a dress for a married woman with three children and a talent for cooking. I don't know why not, but it isn't." Judith was the right build. Therefore one evening the three of us met by appointment in Judith's bedroom, with the dress. Neither Betty nor I was surprised at the renewed discovery that Judith was beautiful. We had both often caught each other, and ourselves, in moments of envy

---

[1] Jack Kerouac (1922–1969), American novelist.

when Judith's calm and severe face, her undemonstratively perfect body, succeeded in making everyone else in a room or a street look cheap.

Judith is tall, small-breasted, slender. Her light brown hair is parted in the centre and cut straight around her neck. A high straight forehead, straight nose, a full grave mouth are setting for her eyes, which are green, large and prominent. Her lids are very white, fringed with gold, and moulded close over the eyeball, so that in profile she has the look of a staring gilded mask. The dress was of dark green glistening stuff, cut straight, with a sort of loose tunic. It opened simply at the throat. In it Judith could of course evoke nothing but classical images. Diana, perhaps, back from the hunt, in a relaxed moment? A rather intellectual wood nymph who had opted for an afternoon in the British Museum Reading Room? Something like that. Neither Betty nor I said a word, since Judith was examining herself in a long mirror, and must know she looked magnificent.

Slowly she drew off the dress and laid it aside. Slowly she put on the old cord skirt and woollen blouse she had taken off. She must have surprised a resigned glance between us, for she then remarked, with the smallest of mocking smiles: "One surely ought to stay in character, wouldn't you say?" She added, reading the words out of some invisible book, written not by her, since it was a very vulgar book, but perhaps by one of us: "It does everything *for* me, I must admit."

"After seeing you in it," Betty cried out, defying her, "I can't bear for anyone else to have it. I shall simply put it away." Judith shrugged, rather irritated. In the shapeless skirt and blouse, and without makeup, she stood smiling at us, a woman at whom forty-nine out of fifty people would not look twice.

A second revelatory incident occurred soon after. Betty telephoned me to say that Judith had a kitten. Did I know that Judith adored cats? "No, but of course she would," I said.

Betty lived in the same street as Judith and saw more of her than I did. I was kept posted about the growth and habits of the cat and its effect on Judith's life. She remarked for instance that she felt it was good for her to have a tie and some responsibility. But no sooner was the cat out of kittenhood than all the neighbours complained. It was a tomcat, ungelded, and making every night hideous. Finally the landlord said that either the cat or Judith must go, unless she was prepared to have the cat "fixed." Judith wore herself out trying to find some person, anywhere in Britain, who would be prepared to take the cat. This person would, however, have to sign a written statement not to have the cat "fixed." When Judith took the cat to the vet to be killed, Betty told me she cried for twenty-four hours.

"She didn't think of compromising? After all, perhaps the cat might have preferred to live, if given the choice?"

"Is it likely I'd have the nerve to say anything so sloppy to Judith? It's the nature of a male cat to rampage lustfully about, and therefore it would be morally wrong for Judith to have the cat fixed, simply to suit her own convenience."

"She said that?"

"She wouldn't have to *say* it, surely?"

A third incident was when she allowed a visiting young American, living in Paris, the friend of a friend and scarcely known to her, to use her flat while she visited her parents over Christmas. The young man and his friends lived it up for ten days of alcohol and sex and marijuana, and when Judith came back it took a week to get the place clean again and the furniture mended. She telephoned twice to Paris, the first time to say that he was a disgusting young thug and if he knew what was good for him he would keep out of her way in the future; the second time to apologise for losing her temper. "I had a choice either to let someone use my flat, or to leave it empty. But having chosen that you should have it, it was clearly an unwarrantable infringement of your liberty to make any conditions at all. I do most sincerely ask your pardon." The moral aspects of the matter having been made clear, she was irritated rather than not to receive letters of apology from him—fulsome, embarrassed, but above all, baffled.

It was the note of curiosity in the letters—he even suggested coming over to get to know her better—that irritated her most. "What do you suppose he means?" she said to me. "He lived in my flat for ten days. One would have thought that should be enough, wouldn't you?"

The facts about Judith, then, are all in the open, unconcealed, and plain to anyone who cares to study them; or, as it became plain she feels, to anyone with the intelligence to interpret them.

She has lived for the last twenty years in a small two-roomed flat high over a busy West London street. The flat is shabby and badly heated. The furniture is old, was never anything but ugly, is now frankly rickety and fraying. She has an income of two hundred pounds a year from a dead uncle. She lives on this and what she earns from her poetry, and from lecturing on poetry to night classes and extramural university classes.

She does not smoke or drink, and eats very little, from preference, not self-discipline.

She studied poetry and biology at Oxford, with distinction.

She is a Castlewell. That is, she is a member of one of the academic upper-middleclass families, which have been producing for centuries a steady supply of brilliant but sound men and women who are the backbone of the arts and sciences in Britain. She is on cool good terms with her family, who respect her and leave her alone.

She goes on long walking tours, by herself, in such places as Exmoor or West Scotland.

Every three or four years she publishes a volume of poems.

The walls of her flat are completely lined with books. They are scientific, classical and historical; there is a great deal of poetry and some drama. There is not one novel. When Judith says: "Of course I don't read novels," this does not mean that novels have no place, or a small place, in literature; or that people should not read novels; but that it must be obvious she can't be expected to read novels.

I had been visiting her flat for years before I noticed two long shelves of books, under a window, each shelf filled with the works of a single writer. The two writers are not, to put it at the mildest, the kind one would associate with Judith. They are mild, reminiscent, vague and whimsical. Typical English *belleslettres*, in fact, and by definition abhorrent to her. Not one of the books in the two shelves has been read; some of the pages are still uncut. Yet each book is inscribed or dedicated to her: gratefully, admiringly, sentimentally and, more than once, amorously. In short, it is open to anyone who cares to examine these two shelves, and to work out dates, to conclude that Judith from the age of fifteen to twenty-five had been the beloved young companion of one elderly literary gentleman, and from twenty-five to thirty-five the inspiration of another.

During all that time she had produced her own poetry, and the sort of poetry, it is quite safe to deduce, not at all likely to be admired by her two admirers. Her poems are always cool and intellectual; that is their form, which is contradicted or supported by a gravely sensuous texture. They are poems to read often; one has to, to understand them.

I did not ask Judith a direct question about these two eminent but rather fusty lovers. Not because she would not have answered, or because she would have found the question impertinent, but because such questions are clearly unnecessary. Having those two shelves of books where they are, and books she could not conceivably care for, for their own sake, is publicly giving credit where credit is due. I can imagine her thinking the thing over, and deciding it was only fair, or perhaps honest, to place the books there; and this despite the fact that she would not care at all for the same attention to be paid to her. There is something almost contemptuous in it. For she certainly despises people who feel they need attention.

For instance, more than once a new emerging wave of "modern" young poets have discovered her as the only "modern" poet among their despised and well-credited elders. This is because, since she began writing at fifteen, her poems have been full of scientific, mechanical and chemical imagery. This is how she thinks, or feels.

More than once has a young poet hastened to her flat, to claim her as an ally, only to find her totally and by instinct unmoved by words like "modern," "new," "contemporary." He has been outraged and wounded by her principle, so deeply rooted as to be unconscious, and to need no expression but a contemptuous shrug of the shoulders, that publicity seeking or to want critical attention is despicable. It goes without saying that there is perhaps one critic in the world she has any time for. He has sulked off, leaving her on her shelf, which she takes it for granted is her proper place, to be read by an appreciative minority.

Meanwhile she gives her lectures, walks alone through London, writes her poems, and is seen sometimes at a concert or a play with a middleaged professor of Greek, who has a wife and two children.

Betty and I had speculated about this professor, with such remarks as: Surely she must sometimes be lonely? Hasn't she ever wanted to marry? What about that awful moment when one comes in from somewhere at night to an empty flat?

It happened recently that Betty's husband was on a business trip, her children visiting, and she was unable to stand the empty house. She asked Judith for a refuge until her own home filled again.

Afterwards Betty rang me up to report: "Four of the five nights Professor Adams came in about ten or so."

"Was Judith embarrassed?"

"Would you expect her to be?"

"Well, if not embarrassed, at least conscious there was a situation?"

"No, not at all. But I must say I don't think he's good enough for her. He can't possibly understand her. He calls her Judy."

"Good God."

"Yes. But I was wondering. Suppose the other two called her Judy— 'little Judy'—imagine it! Isn't it awful? But it does rather throw a light on Judith?"

"It's rather touching."

"I suppose it's touching. But I was embarassed—oh, not because of the situation. Because of how she was, with him. 'Judy, is there another cup of tea in that pot?' And she, rather daughterly and demure, pouring him one."

"Well yes, I can see how you felt."

"Three of the nights he went to her bedroom with her—very casual about it, because she was being. But he was not there in the mornings. So I asked her. You know how it is when you ask her a question. As if you've been having long conversations on that very subject for years and years, and she is merely continuing where you left off last. So when she says something surprising, one feels such a fool to be surprised?"

"Yes, And then?"

"I asked her if she was sorry not to have children. She said yes, but one couldn't have everything."

"One can't have everything, she said?"

"Quite clearly feeling she has nearly everything. She said she thought it was a pity, because she would have brought up children very well."

"When you come to think of it, she would, too."

"I asked about marriage, but she said on the whole the role of a mistress suited her better."

"She used the word 'mistress'?"

"You must admit it's the accurate word."

"I suppose so."

"And then she said that while she liked intimacy and sex and everything, she enjoyed waking up in the morning alone and *her own person.*"

"Yes, *of course.*"

"Of course. But now she's bothered because the professor would like to marry her. Or he feels he ought. At least, he's getting all guilty and obsessive about it. She says she doesn't see the point of divorce, and anyway, surely it would be very hard on his poor old wife after all these years, particularly after bringing up two children so satisfactorily. She talks about his wife as if she's a kind of nice old charwoman, and it wouldn't be *fair* to sack her, you know. Anyway. What with one thing and another. Judith's going off to Italy soon in order to *collect herself.*"

"But how's she going to pay for it?"

"Luckily the Third Programme's[2] commissioning her to do some arty programmes. They offered her a choice of The Cid—El Thid, you know—and the Borgias. Well, the Borghese, then. And Judith settled for the Borgias."

"The Borgias," I said, "*Judith?*"

"Yes, quite. I said that too, in that tone of voice. She saw my point. She says the epic is right up her street, whereas the Renaissance has never been on her wave length. Obviously it couldn't be, all the magnificence and cruelty and *dirt.* But of course chivalry and a high moral code and all those idiotically noble goings-on are right on her wave length."

"Is the money the same?"

"Yes. But is it likely Judith would let money decide? No, she said that one should always choose something new, that isn't up one's street. Well, because it's better for her character, and so on, to get herself unsettled by the Renaissance. She didn't say *that,* of course."

"Of course not."

Judith went to Florence; and for some months postcards informed us tersely of her doings. Then Betty decided she must go by herself for a holiday. She had been appalled by the discovery that if her husband was away for a night she couldn't sleep; and when he went to Australia for three weeks, she stopped living until he came back. She had discussed this with him, and he had agreed that if she really felt the situation to be serious, he would despatch her by air, to Italy, in order to recover her self-respect. As she put it.

I got this letter from her: "It's no use, I'm coming home. I might have known. Better face it, once you're really married you're not fit for man nor beast. And if you remember what I used to be like! *Well!* I moped around Milan. I sunbathed in Venice, then I thought my tan was surely worth something, so I was on the point of starting an affair with another lonely soul, but I lost heart, and went to Florence to see Judith. She wasn't there. She'd gone to the Italian Riviera. I had nothing better to

[2] British public radio.

do, so I followed her. When I saw the place I wanted to laugh, it's so much not Judith, you know, all those palms and umbrellas and gaiety at all costs and ever such an ornamental blue sea. Judith is in an enormous stone room up on the hillside above the sea, with grape vines all over the place. You should see her, she's got beautiful. It seems for the last fifteen years she's been going to Soho every Saturday morning to buy food at an Italian shop. I must have looked surprised, because she explained she liked Soho. I suppose because all that dreary vice and nudes and prostitutes and everything prove how right she is to be as she is? She told the people in the shop she was going to Italy, and the *signora* said, what a coincidence, she was going back to Italy too, and she did hope an old friend like Miss Castlewell would visit her there. Judith said to me: 'I felt lacking, when she used the word friend. Our relations have always been formal. Can you understand it?' she said to me. 'For fifteen years,' I said to her. She said: 'I think I must feel it's a kind of imposition, don't you know, expecting people to feel friendship for one.' *Well.* I said: 'You ought to understand it, because you're like that yourself.' 'Am I?' she said. 'Well, think about it,' I said. But I could see she didn't want to think about it. Anyway, she's here, and I've spent a week with her. The widow Maria Rineiri inherited her mother's house, so she came home, from Soho. On the ground floor is a tatty little *rosticceria*[3] patronised by the neighbours. They are all working people. This isn't tourist country, up on the hill. The widow lives above the shop with her little boy, a nasty little brat of about ten. Say what you like, the English are the only people who know how to bring up children, I don't care if that's insular. Judith's room is at the back, with a balcony. Underneath her room is the barber's shop, and the barber is Luigi Rineiri, the widow's younger brother. Yes, I was keeping him until the last. He is about forty, tall dark handsome, a great *bull*, but rather a sweet fatherly bull. He has cut Judith's hair and made it lighter. Now it looks like a sort of gold helmet. Judith is all brown. The widow Rineiri has made her a white dress and a green dress. They fit, for a change. When Judith walks down the street to the lower town, all the Italian males take one look at the golden girl and melt in their own oil like ice cream. Judith takes all this in her stride. She sort of acknowledges the homage. Then she strolls into the sea and vanishes into the foam. She swims five miles every day. *Naturally.* I haven't asked Judith whether she has collected herself, because you can see she hasn't. The widow Rineiri is matchmaking. When I noticed this I wanted to laugh, but luckily I didn't because Judith asked me, really wanting to know: 'Can you see me married to an Italian barber?' (Not being snobbish, but stating the position, so to speak.) 'Well yes,' I said, 'you're the only woman I know who I can see married to an Italian barber.' Because it wouldn't matter who she married, she'd always be her *own person.* 'At any rate, for a time,' I said. At which she said, asperously:[4] 'You can use

---

[3] Grill.

[4] Harshly.

phrases like for a time in England but not in Italy.' Did you ever see England, at least London, as the home of license, liberty and free love? No, neither did I, but of course she's right. Married to Luigi it would be the family, the neighbours, the church and the *bambini*.[5] All the same she's thinking about it, believe it or not. Here she's quite different, all relaxed and free. She's melting in the attention she gets. The widow mothers her and makes her coffee all the time, and listens to a lot of good advice about how to bring up that nasty brat of hers. Unluckily she doesn't take it. Luigi is crazy for her. At mealtimes she goes to the *trattoria*[6] in the upper square and all the workmen treat her like a goddess. Well, a film star then. I said to her, you're mad to come home. For one thing her rent is ten bob a week, and you eat *pasta* and drink red wine till you bust for about one and sixpence. No, she said, it would be nothing but self-indulgence to stay. Why? I said. She said, she's got nothing to stay for. (Ho ho.) And besides, she's done her research on the Borghese, though so far she can't see her way to an honest presentation of the facts. What made these people tick? She wants to know. And so she's only staying because of the cat. I forgot to mention the cat. This is a town of cats. The Italians here love their cats. I wanted to feed a stray cat at the table, but the waiter said no; and after lunch, all the waiters came with trays crammed with leftover food and stray cats came from everywhere to eat. And at dark when the tourists go in to feed and the beach is empty—you know how empty and forlorn a beach is at dusk?—well cats appear from everywhere. The beach seems to move, then you see it's cats. They go stalking along the thin inch of grey water at the edge of the sea, shaking their paws crossly at each step, snatching at the dead little fish, and throwing them with their mouths up on to the dry sand. Then they scamper after them. You've never seen such a snarling and fighting. At dawn when the fishing boats come in to the empty beach, the cats are there in dozens. The fishermen throw them bits of fish. The cats snarl and fight over it. Judith gets up early and goes down to watch. Sometimes Luigi goes too, being tolerant. Because what he really likes is to join the evening promenade with Judith on his arm around and around the square of the upper town. Showing her off. Can you *see* Judith? But she does it. Being tolerant. But she smiles and enjoys the attention she gets, there's no doubt of it.

"She has a cat in her room. It's a kitten really, but it's pregnant. Judith says she can't leave until the kittens are born. The cat is too young to have kittens. Imagine Judith. She sits on her bed in that great stone room, with her bare feet on the stone floor, and watches the cat, and tries to work out why a healthy uninhibited Italian cat always fed on the best from the *rosticceria* should be neurotic. Because it is. When it sees Judith watching it gets nervous and starts licking at the roots of its tail. But

---

[5] Babies.

[6] Restaurant.

Judith goes on watching, and says about Italy that the reason why the English love the Italians is because the Italians make the English feel superior. They have no discipline. And that's a despicable reason for one nation to love another. Then she talks about Luigi and says he has no sense of guilt, but a sense of sin; whereas she has no sense of sin but she has guilt. I haven't asked her if this has been an insuperable barrier, because judging from how she looks, it hasn't. She says she would rather have a sense of sin, because sin can be atoned for, and if she understood sin, perhaps she would be more at home with the Renaissance. Luigi is very healthy, she says, and not neurotic. He is a Catholic of course. He doesn't mind that she's an atheist. His mother has explained to him that the English are all pagans, but good people at heart. I suppose he thinks a few smart sessions with the local priest would set Judith on the right path for good and all. Meanwhile the cat walks nervously around the room, stopping to lick, and when it can't stand Judith watching it another second, it rolls over on the floor, with its paws tucked up, and rolls up its eyes, and Judith scratches its lumpy pregnant stomach and tells it to relax. It makes *me* nervous to see her, it's not like her, I don't know why. Then Luigi shouts up from the barber's shop, then he comes up and stands at the door laughing, and Judith laughs, and the widow says: Children, enjoy yourselves. And off they go, walking down to the town eating ice cream. The cat follows them. It won't let Judith out of its sight, like a dog. When she swims miles out to sea, the cat hides under a beach hut until she comes back. Then she carries it back up the hill, because that nasty little boy chases it. *Well.* I'm coming home tomorrow thank God, to my dear old Billy, I was mad ever to leave him. There is something about Judith and Italy that has upset me, I don't know what. The point is, what on earth can Judith and Luigi *talk* about? Nothing. How can they? And of course it doesn't matter. So I turn out to be a prude as well. See you next week."

It was my turn for a dose of the sun, so I didn't see Betty. On my way back from Rome I stopped off in Judith's resort and walked up through narrow streets to the upper town, where, in the square with the vine-covered *trattoria* at the corner, was a house with ROSTICCERIA written in black paint on a cracked wooden board over a low door. There was a door curtain of red beads, and flies settled on the beads. I opened the beads with my hands and looked into a small dark room with a stone counter. Loops of salami hung from metal hooks. A glass bell covered some plates of cooked meats. There were flies on the salami and on the glass bell. A few tins on the wooden shelves, a couple of pale loaves, some wine casks and an open case of sticky pale green grapes covered with fruit flies seemed to be the only stock. A single wooden table with two chairs stood in a corner, and two workmen sat there, eating lumps of sausage and bread. Through another bead curtain at the back came a short, smoothly fat, slender-limbed woman with greying hair. I asked for Miss Castlewell, and her face changed. She said in an offended, offhand way: "Miss Castlewell left last week." She took a white cloth from under the counter, and flicked at the flies on the glass bell. "I'm a friend of hers," I said, and she said: "*Si*,"[7] and put her hands palm down on the counter and looked at me, expressionless. The workmen got up, gulped down the last of their wine, nodded and went. She *ciao*'d them;[8] and looked back at me. Then, since I didn't go, she called: "Luigi!" A shout came from the back room, there was a rattle of beads, and in came first a wiry sharp-faced boy, and then Luigi. He was tall, heavy-shouldered, and his black rough hair was like a cap, pulled low over his brows. He looked good-natured, but at the moment uneasy. His sister said something, and he stood beside her, an ally, and confirmed: "Miss Castlewell went away." I was on the point of giving up, when through the bead curtain that screened off a dazzling light eased a thin tabby cat. It was ugly and it walked uncomfortably, with its back quarters bunched up. The child suddenly let out a "Sssssss" through his teeth, and the cat froze. Luigi said something sharp to the child, and something encouraging to the cat, which sat down, looked straight in front of it, then began frantically licking at its flanks. "Miss Castlewell was offended with us," said Mrs. Rineiri suddenly, and with dignity. "She left early one morning. We did not expect her to go." I said: "Perhaps she had to go home and finish some work."

Mrs. Rineiri shrugged, then sighed. Then she exchanged a hard look with her brother. Clearly the subject had been discussed, and closed forever.

"I've known Judith a long time," I said, trying to find the right note. "She's a remarkable woman. She's a poet." But there was no response to this at all. Meanwhile the child, with a fixed bared-teeth grin, was staring at the cat, narrowing his eyes. Suddenly he let out another "Ssssssss" and added a short high yelp. The cat shot backwards, hit the wall, tried desperately to claw its way up the wall, came to its senses and again sat down and began its urgent, undirected licking at its fur. This time Luigi cuffed the child, who yelped in earnest, and then ran out into the street past the cat. Now that the way was clear the cat shot across the floor, up onto the counter, and bounded past Luigi's shoulder and straight through the bead curtain into the barber's shop, where it landed with a thud.

"Judith was sorry when she left us," said Mrs. Rineiri uncertainly. "She was crying."

"I'm sure she was."

"And so," said Mrs. Rineiri, with finality, laying her hands down again, and looking past me at the bead curtain. That was the end. Luigi nodded brusquely at me, and went into the back. I said goodbye to Mrs. Rineiri and walked back to the lower town. In the square I saw the child, sitting

---

[7] Yes.

[8] Said good-bye to them.

on the running board of a lorry parked outside the *trattoria*, drawing in the dust with his bare toes, and directing in front of him a blank, unhappy stare.

I had to go through Florence, so I went to the address Judith had been at. No, Miss Castlewell had not been back. Her papers and books were still here. Would I take them back with me to England? I made a great parcel and brought them back to England.

I telephoned Judith and she said she had already written for the papers to be sent, but it was kind of me to bring them. There had seemed to be no point, she said, in returning to Florence.

"Shall I bring them over?"

"I would be very grateful, of course."

Judith's flat was chilly, and she wore a bunchy sage-green woollen dress. Her hair was still a soft gold helmet, but she looked pale and rather pinched. She stood with her back to a single bar of electric fire—lit because I demanded it—with her legs apart and her arms folded. She contemplated me.

"I went to the Rineiris' house."

"Oh. Did you?"

"They seemed to miss you."

She said nothing.

"I saw the cat too."

"Oh. Oh, I suppose you and Betty discussed it?" This was with a small unfriendly smile.

"Well, Judith, you must see we were likely to?"

She gave this her consideration and said: "I don't understand why people discuss other people. Oh—I'm not criticising you. But I don't see why you are so interested. I don't understand human behavior and I'm not particularly interested."

"I think you should write to the Rineiris."

"I wrote and thanked them, of course."

"I don't mean that."

"You and Betty have worked it out?"

"Yes, we talked about it. We thought we should talk to you, so you should write to the Rineiris."

"Why?"

"For one thing, they are both very fond of you."

"Fond," she said smiling.

"Judith, I've never in my life felt such an atmosphere of being let down."

Judith considered this. "When something happens that shows one there is really a complete gulf in understanding, what is there to say?"

"It could scarcely have been a complete gulf in understanding. I suppose you are going to say we are being interfering?"

Judith showed distaste. "That is a very stupid word. And it's a stupid idea. No one can interfere with me if I don't let them. No, it's that I don't understand people. I don't understand why you or Betty should care. Or why the Rineiris should, for that matter," she added with the small tight smile.

"Judith!"

"If you've behaved stupidly, there's no point in going on. You put an end to it."

"What happened? Was it the cat?"

"Yes, I suppose so. But it's not important." She looked at me, saw my ironical face, and said: "The cat was too young to have kittens. That is all there was to it."

"Have it your way. But that is obviously not all there is to it."

"What upsets me is that I don't understand at all why I was so upset then."

"What happened? Or don't you want to talk about it?"

"I don't give a damn whether I talk about it or not. You really do say the most extraordinary things, you and Betty. If you want to know, I'll tell you. What does it matter?"

"I would like to know, of course."

"*Of course!*" she said. "In your place I wouldn't care. Well, I think the essence of the thing was that I must have had the wrong attitude to that cat. Cats are supposed to be independent. They are supposed to go off by themselves to have their kittens. This one didn't. It was climbing up on to my bed all one night and crying for attention. I don't like cats on my bed. In the morning I saw she was in pain. I stayed with her all that day. Then Luigi—he's the brother, you know."

"Yes."

"Did Betty mention him? Luigi came up to say it was time I went for a swim. He said the cat should look after itself. I blame myself very much. That's what happens when you submerge yourself in somebody else."

Her look at me was now defiant; and her body showed both defensiveness and aggression. "Yes. It's true. I've always been afraid of it. And in the last few weeks I've behaved badly. It's because I let it happen."

"Well, go on."

"I left the cat and swam. It was late, so it was only for a few minutes. When I came out of the sea the cat had followed me and had had a kitten on the beach. That little beast Michele—the son, you know?—well, he always teased the poor thing, and now he had frightened her off the kitten. It was dead, though. He held it up by the tail and waved it at me as I came out of the sea. I told him to bury it. He scooped two inches of sand away and pushed the kitten in—on the beach, where people are all day. So I buried it properly. He had run off. He was chasing the poor cat. She was terrified and running up the town. I ran too. I caught Michele and I was so angry I hit him. I don't believe in hitting children. I've been feeling beastly about it ever since."

"You were angry."

"It's no excuse. I would never have believed myself capable of hitting a child. I hit him very hard. He went off, crying. The poor cat had got under a big lorry parked in the square. Then she screamed. And then a most remarkable thing happened. She screamed just once, and all at once cats just materialised. One minute there was just one cat, lying under a lorry, and the next, dozens of cats. They sat in a big circle around the lorry, all quite still, and watched my poor cat."

"Rather moving," I said.

"Why?"

"There is no evidence one way or the other," I said in inverted commas, "that the cats were there out of concern for a friend in trouble."

"No," she said energetically. "There isn't. It might have been curiosity. Or anything. How do we know? However, I crawled under the lorry. There were two paws sticking out of the cat's back end. The kitten was the wrong way round. It was stuck. I held the cat down with one hand and I pulled the kitten out with the other." She held out her long white hands. They were still covered with fading scars and scratches. "She bit and yelled, but the kitten was alive. She left the kitten and crawled across the square into the house. Then all the cats got up and walked away. It was the most extraordinary thing I've ever seen. They vanished again. One minute they were all there, and then they had vanished. I went after the cat, with the kitten. Poor little thing, it was covered with dust—being wet, don't you know. The cat was on my bed. There was another kitten coming, but it got stuck too. So when she screamed and screamed I just pulled it out. The kittens began to suck. One kitten was very big. It was a nice fat black kitten. It must have hurt her. But she suddenly bit out—snapped, don't you know, like a reflex action, at the back of the kitten's head. It died, just like that. Extraordinary, isn't it?" she said, blinking hard, her lips quivering. "She was its mother, but she killed it. Then she ran off the bed and went downstairs into the shop under the counter. I called to Luigi. You know, he's Mrs. Rineiri's brother."

"Yes, I know."

"He said she was too young, and she was badly frightened and very hurt. He took the alive kitten to her but she got up and walked away. She didn't want it. Then Luigi told me not to look. But I followed him. He held the kitten by the tail and he banged it against the wall twice. Then he dropped it into the rubbish heap. He moved aside some rubbish with his toe, and put the kitten there and pushed rubbish over it. Then Luigi said the cat should be destroyed. He said she was badly hurt and it would always hurt her to have kittens."

"He hasn't destroyed her. She's still alive. But it looks to me as if he were right."

"Yes, I expect he was."

"What upset you—that he killed the kitten?"

"Oh no, I expect the cat would if he hadn't. But that isn't the point, is it?"

"What is the point?"

"I don't think I really know." She had been speaking breathlessly, and fast. Now she said slowly: "It's not a question of right or wrong, is it? Why should it be? It's a question of what one is. That night Luigi wanted to go promenading with me. For him, that was *that*. Something had to be done, and he'd done it. But I felt ill. He was very nice to me. He's a very good person," she said, defiantly.

"Yes, he looks it."

"That night I couldn't sleep. I was blaming myself. I should never have left the cat to go swimming. Well, and then I decided to leave the next day. And I did. And that's all. The whole thing was a mistake, from start to finish."

"Going to Italy at all?"

"Oh, to go for a holiday would have been all right."

"You've done all that work for nothing? You mean you aren't going to make use of all that research?"

"No. It was a mistake."

"Why don't you leave it a few weeks and see how things are then?"

"Why?"

"You might feel differently about it."

"What an extraordinary thing to say. Why should I? Oh, you mean, time passing, healing wounds—that sort of thing? What an extraordinary idea. It's always seemed to me an extraordinary idea. No, right from the beginning I've felt ill at ease with the whole business, not myself at all."

"Rather irrationally, I should have said."

Judith considered this, very seriously. She frowned while she thought it over. Then she said: "But if one cannot rely on what one feels, what can one rely on?"

"On what one thinks, I should have expected you to say."

"Should you? Why? Really, you people are all very strange. I don't understand you." She turned off the electric fire, and her face closed up. She smiled, friendly and distant, and said: "I don't really see any point at all in discussing it."

Study and Discussion Questions

1. Who is the "our" referred to in the title?
2. What work does Judith do?
3. What does the incident in which Judith rejects the dress reveal about her as a person? How about the trouble-making tomcat? The young American she lets use her apartment?
4. Why would Judith rather be a "mistress" than a wife?
5. Why is Judith attracted to Italy? To the barber Luigi Rineiri and his way of life?
6. What are the function and significance of the cats in the section of the story set in Italy?

7. What is the narrator's attitude toward Judith? Does that attitude change?
8. How important is being "her own person" to Judith and how does she accomplish this?

Writing Exercises

1. What is a spinster? What is the dictionary definition and what associations and images does the word raise for you? What social assumptions about women and women's roles are contained in that word? How does Lessing's "Our Friend Judith" consider and redefine the term *spinster*?
2. Write a one-paragraph character sketch of Judith.
3. Write a one-paragraph character sketch of the narrator.

MARY E. WILKINS FREEMAN (1852–1930)

Mary Eleanor Wilkins was born and lived much of her life in Randolph, Massachusetts. After high school, she spent a year at Mount Holyoke Female Seminary and soon after began earning a living writing. She married Dr. Charles Freeman in 1902, when she was almost fifty, and moved with him to New Jersey, but their marriage fell apart due to his growing alcoholism. Freeman's work was widely read during her life, began to disappear from sight after her death, and was rediscovered in recent decades. Her two best-known story collections are A Humble Romance *(1887) and* A New England Nun *(1891).*

A Mistaken Charity   (1887)

There were in a green field a little, low, weather-stained cottage, with a foot-path leading to it from the highway several rods distant, and two old women—one with a tin pan and old knife searching for dandelion greens among the short young grass, and the other sitting on the door-step watching her, or, rather, having the appearance of watching her.

"Air there enough for a mess, Harriét?" asked the old woman on the door-step. She accented oddly the last syllable of the Harriet, and there was a curious quality in her feeble, cracked old voice. Besides the question denoted by the arrangement of her words and the rising inflection, there was another, broader and subtler, the very essence of all questioning, in the tone of her voice itself; the cracked, quavering notes that she used reached out of themselves, and asked, and groped like fingers in the dark. One would have known by the voice that the old woman was blind.

The old woman on her knees in the grass searching for dandelions did not reply; she evidently had not heard the question. So the old woman on the door-step, after waiting a few minutes with her head turned expectantly, asked again, varying her question slightly, and speaking louder:

"Air there enough for a mess, do ye s'pose, Harriét?"

The old woman in the grass heard this time. She rose slowly and laboriously; the effort of straightening out the rheumatic old muscles was evidently a painful one; then she eyed the greens heaped up in the tin pan, and pressed them down with her hand.

"Wa'al, I don't know, Charlotte," she replied, hoarsely. "There's plenty on 'em here, but I 'ain't got near enough for a mess; they do bile down so when you get 'em in the pot; an' it's all I can do to bend my j'ints enough to dig 'em."

"I'd give consider'ble to help ye, Harriét," said the old woman on the door-step.

But the other did not hear her; she was down on her knees in the grass again, anxiously spying out the dandelions.

So the old woman on the door-step crossed her little shrivelled hands over her calico knees, and sat quite still, with the soft spring wind blowing over her.

The old wooden door-step was sunk low down among the grasses, and the whole house to which it belonged had an air of settling down and mouldering into the grass as into its own grave.

When Harriet Shattuck grew deaf and rheumatic, and had to give up her work as tailoress, and Charlotte Shattuck lost her eyesight, and was unable to do any more sewing for her livelihood, it was a small and trifling charity for the rich man who held a mortgage on the little house in which they had been born and lived all their lives to give them the use of it, rent and interest free. He might as well have taken credit to himself for not charging a squirrel for his tenement in some old decaying tree in his woods.

So ancient was the little habitation, so wavering and mouldering, the hands that had fashioned it had lain still so long in their graves, that it almost seemed to have fallen below its distinctive rank as a house. Rain and snow had filtered through its roof, mosses had grown over it, worms had eaten it, and birds built their nests under its eaves; nature had almost completely overrun and obliterated the work of man, and taken her own to herself again, till the house seemed as much a natural ruin as an old treestump.

The Shattucks had always been poor people and common people; no especial grace and refinement or fine ambition had ever characterized any of them; they had always been poor and coarse and common. The father and his father before him had simply lived in the poor little house, grubbed for their living, and then unquestioningly died. The mother had been of no rarer stamp, and the two daughters were cast in the same mould.

After their parents' death Harriet and Charlotte had lived along in the old place from youth to old age, with the one hope of ability to keep a roof over their heads, covering on their backs, and victuals in their mouths—an all-sufficient one with them.

Neither of them had ever had a lover; they had always seemed to repel rather than attract the opposite sex. It was not merely because they were poor, ordinary, and homely; there were plenty of men in the place who would have matched them well in that respect; the fault lay deeper—in their characters. Harriet, even in her girlhood, had a blunt, defiant manner that almost amounted to surliness, and was well calculated to alarm timid adorers, and Charlotte had always had the reputation of not being any too strong in her mind.

Harriet had gone about from house to house doing tailorwork after the primitive country fashion, and Charlotte had done plain sewing and mending for the neighbors. They had been, in the main, except when pressed by some temporary anxiety about their work or the payment thereof, happy and contented, with that negative kind of happiness and contentment which comes not from gratified ambition, but a lack of ambition itself. All that they cared for they had had in tolerable abundance, for Harriet at least had been swift and capable about her work. The patched, mossy old roof had been kept over their heads, the coarse, hearty food that they loved had been set on their table, and their cheap clothes had been warm and strong.

After Charlotte's eyes failed her, and Harriet had the rheumatic fever, and the little hoard of earnings went to the doctors, times were harder with them, though still it could not be said that they actually suffered.

When they could not pay the interest on the mortgage they were allowed to keep the place interest free; there was as much fitness in a mortgage on the little house, anyway, as there would have been on a rotten old apple-tree; and the people about, who were mostly farmers, and good friendly folk, helped them out with their living. One would donate a barrel of apples from his abundant harvest to the two poor old women, one a barrel of potatoes, another a load of wood for the winter fuel, and many a farmer's wife had bustled up the narrow foot-path with a pound of butter, or a dozen fresh eggs, or a nice bit of pork. Besides all this, there was a tiny garden patch behind the house, with a straggling row of currant bushes in it, and one of gooseberries, where Harriet contrived every year to raise a few pumpkins, which were the pride of her life. On the right of the garden were two old apple-trees, a Baldwin and a Porter, both yet in a tolerably good fruit-bearing state.

The delight which the two poor old souls took in their own pumpkins, their apples and currants, was indescribable. It was not merely that they contributed largely towards their living; they were their own, their private share of the great wealth of nature, the little taste set apart for them alone out of her bounty, and worth more to them on that account, though they were not conscious of it, than all the richer fruits which they received from their neighbors' gardens.

This morning the two apple-trees were brave with flowers, the currant bushes looked alive, and the pumpkin seeds were in the ground. Harriet cast complacent glances in their direction from time to time, and she painfully dug her dandelion greens. She was a short, stoutly built old woman, with a large face coarsely wrinkled, with a suspicion of a stubble of beard on the square chin.

When her tin pan was filled to her satisfaction with the sprawling, spidery greens, and she was hobbling stiffly towards her sister on the door-step, she saw another woman standing before her with a basket in her hand.

"Good-morning, Harriet," she said, in a loud, strident voice, as she drew near. "I've been frying some doughnuts, and I brought you over some warm."

"I've been tellin' her it was real good in her," piped Charlotte from the door-step, with an anxious turn of her sightless face towards the sound of her sister's footstep.

Harriet said nothing but a hoarse "Good-mornin', Mis' Simonds." Then she took the basket in her hand, lifted the towel off the top, selected a doughnut, and deliberately tasted it.

"Tough," said she. "I s'posed so. If there is anything I 'spise on this airth it's a tough doughnut."

"Oh, Harriét!" said Charlotte, with a frightened look.

"They air tough," said Harriet, with hoarse defiance, "and if there is anything I 'spise on this airth it's a tough doughnut."

The woman whose benevolence and cookery were being thus ungratefully received only laughed. She was quite fleshy, and had a round, rosy, determined face.

"Well, Harriet," said she, "I am sorry they are tough, but perhaps you had better take them out on a plate, and give me my basket. You may be able to eat two or three of them if they are tough."

"They air tough—turrible tough," said Harriet, stubbornly; but she took the basket into the house and emptied it of its contents nevertheless.

"I suppose your roof leaked as bad as ever in that heavy rain day before yesterday?" said the visitor to Harriet, with an inquiring squint towards the mossy shingles, as she was about to leave with her empty basket.

"It was turrible," replied Harriet, with crusty acquiescence—"turrible. We had to set pails an' pans everywheres, an' move the bed out."

"Mr. Upton ought to fix it."

"There ain't any fix to it; the old ruff ain't fit to nail new shingles on to; the hammerin' would bring the whole thing down on our heads," said Harriet, grimly.

"Well, I don't know as it can be fixed, it's so old. I suppose the wind comes in bad around the windows and doors too?"

"It's like livin' with a piece of paper, or mebbe a sieve, 'twixt you an' the wind an' the rain," quoth Harriet, with a jerk of her head.

"You ought to have a more comfortable home in your old age," said the visitor, thoughtfully.

"Oh, it's well enough," cried Harriet, in quick alarm, and with a complete change of tone; the woman's remark had brought an old dread over her. "The old house'll last as long as Charlotte an' me do. The rain ain't so bad, nuther is the wind; there's room enough for us in the dry places, an' out of the way of the doors an' windows. It's enough sight better than goin' on the town." Her square, defiant old face actually looked pale as she uttered the last words and stared apprehensively at the woman.

"Oh, I did not think of your doing that," she said, hastily and kindly. "We all know how you feel about that, Harriet, and not one of us neighbors will see you and Charlotte go to the poorhouse while we've got a crust of bread to share with you."

Harriet's face brightened. "Thank ye, Mis' Simonds," she said, with reluctant courtesy. "I'm much obleeged to you an' the neighbors. I think mebbe we'll be able to eat some of them doughnuts if they air tough," she added, mollifyingly, as her caller turned down the foot-path.

"My, Harriét," said Charlotte, lifting up a weakly, wondering, peaked old face, "what did you tell her them doughnuts was tough fur?"

"Charlotte, do you want everybody to look down on us, an' think we ain't no account at all, just like any beggars, 'cause they bring us in vittles?" said Harriet, with a grim glance at her sister's meek, unconscious face.

"No, Harriét," she whispered.

"Do you want *to go to the poor-house?*"

"No, Harriét." The poor little old woman on the door-step fairly cowered before her aggressive old sister.

"Then don't hender me agin when I tell folks their doughnuts is tough an' their pertaters is poor. If I don't kinder keep up an' show some sperrit, I sha'n't think nothing of myself, an' other folks won't nuther, and fust thing we know they'll kerry us to the poorhouse. You'd 'a been there before now if it hadn't been for me, Charlotte."

Charlotte looked meekly convinced, and her sister sat down on a chair in the doorway to scrape her dandelions.

"Did you git a good mess, Harriét?" asked Charlotte, in a humble tone. "Toler'ble."

"They'll be proper relishin' with that piece of pork Mis' Mann brought in yesterday. O Lord, Harriét, it's a chink!"

Harriet sniffed.

Her sister caught with her sensitive ear the little contemptuous sound. "I guess," she said, querulously, and with more pertinacity than she had shown in the matter of the doughnuts, "that if you was in the dark, as

I am, Harriét, you wouldn't make fun an' turn up your nose at chinks. If you had seen the light streamin' in all of a sudden through some little hole that you hadn't known of before when you set down on the doorstep this mornin', and the wind with the smell of the apple blows in it came in your face, an' when Mis' Simonds brought them hot doughnuts, an' when I thought of the pork an' greens jest now—O Lord, how it did shine in! An' it does now. If you was me, Harriét, you would know there was chinks."

Tears began starting from the sightless eyes, and streaming pitifully down the pale old cheeks.

Harriet looked at her sister, and her grim face softened.

"Why, Charlotte, hev it that thar *is* chinks if you want to. Who cares?"

"Thar *is* chinks, Harriét."

"Wa'al, thar *is* chinks, then. If I don't hurry, I sha'n't get these greens in in time for dinner."

When the two old women sat down complacently to their meal of pork and dandelion greens in their little kitchen they did not dream how destiny slowly and surely was introducing some new colors into their web of life, even when it was almost completed, and that this was one of the last meals they would eat in their old home for many a day. In about a week from that day they were established in the "Old Ladies' Home" in a neighboring city. It came about in this wise: Mrs. Simonds, the woman who had brought the gift of hot doughnuts, was a smart, energetic person, bent on doing good, and she did a great deal. To be sure, she always did it in her own way. If she chose to give hot doughnuts, she gave hot doughnuts; it made not the slightest difference to her if the recipients of her charity would infinitely have preferred ginger cookies. Still, a great many would like hot doughnuts, and she did unquestionably a great deal of good.

She had a worthy coadjutor in the person of a rich and childless elderly widow in the place. They had fairly entered into a partnership in good works, with about an equal capital on both sides, the widow furnishing the money, and Mrs. Simonds, who had much the better head of the two, furnishing the active schemes of benevolence.

The afternoon after the doughnut episode she had gone to the widow with a new project, and the result was that entrance fees had been paid, and old Harriet and Charlotte made sure of a comfortable home for the rest of their lives. The widow was hand in glove with officers of missionary boards and trustees of charitable institutions. There had been an unusual mortality among the inmates of the "Home" this spring, there were several vacancies, and the matter of the admission of Harriet and Charlotte was very quickly and easily arranged. But the matter which would have seemed the least difficult—inducing the two old women to accept the bounty which Providence, the widow, and Mrs. Simonds were ready to bestow on them—proved the most so. The struggle to persuade them to abandon their tottering old home for a better was a terrible one. The widow had pleaded with mild surprise, and Mrs. Simonds with benevolent determination; the counsel and reverend eloquence of the minister had been called in; and when they yielded at last it was with a sad grace for the recipients of a worthy charity.

It had been hard to convince them that the "Home" was not an almshouse under another name, and their yielding at length to anything short of actual force was only due probably to the plea, which was advanced most eloquently to Harriet, that Charlotte would be so much more comfortable.

The morning they came away, Charlotte cried pitifully, and trembled all over her little shrivelled body. Harriet did not cry. But when her sister had passed out the low, sagging door she turned the key in the lock, then took it out and thrust it slyly into her pocket, shaking her head to herself with an air of fierce determination.

Mrs. Simonds's husband, who was to take them to the depot, said to himself, with disloyal defiance of his wife's active charity, that it was a shame, as he helped the two distressed old souls into his light wagon, and put the poor little box, with their homely clothes in it, in behind.

Mrs. Simonds, the widow, the minister, and the gentleman from the "Home" who was to take charge of them, were all at the depot, their faces beaming with the delight of successful benevolence. But the two poor old women looked like two forlorn prisoners in their midst. It was an impressive illustration of the truth of the saying "that it is more blessed to give than to receive."

Well, Harriet and Charlotte Shattuck went to the "Old Ladies' Home" with reluctance and distress. They stayed two months, and then—they ran away.

The "Home" was comfortable, and in some respects even luxurious; but nothing suited those two unhappy, unreasonable old women.

The fare was of a finer, more delicately served variety than they had been accustomed to; those finely flavored nourishing soups for which the "Home" took great credit to itself failed to please palates used to common, coarser food.

"O Lord, Harriét, when I set down to the table here there ain't no chinks," Charlotte used to say. "If we could hev some cabbage, or some pork an' greens, how the light would stream in!"

Then they had to be more particular about their dress. They had always been tidy enough, but now it had to be something more; the widow, in the kindness of her heart, had made it possible, and the good folks in charge of the "Home," in the kindness of their hearts, tried to carry out the widow's designs.

But nothing could transform these two unpolished old women into two nice old ladies. They did not take kindly to white lace caps and delicate neckerchiefs. They liked their new black cashmere dresses well enough, but they felt as if they broke a commandment when they put them on every afternoon. They had always worn calico with long aprons at home, and they wanted to now; and they wanted to twist up their scanty gray locks into little knots at the back of their heads, and go without caps, just as they always had done.

Charlotte in a dainty white cap was pitiful, but Harriet was both pitiful and comical. They were totally at variance with their surroundings, and they felt it keenly, as people of their stamp always do. No amount of kindness and attention—and they had enough of both—sufficed to reconcile them to their new abode. Charlotte pleaded continually with her sister to go back to their old home.

"O Lord, Harriét," she would exclaim (by the way, Charlotte's "O Lord," which, as she used it, was innocent enough, had been heard with much disfavor in the "Home," and she, not knowing at all why, had been remonstrated with concerning it), "let us go home. I can't stay here no ways in this world. I don't like their vittles, an' I don't like to wear a cap; I want to go home and do different. The currants will be ripe, Harriét. O Lord, thar was almost a chink, thinking about 'em. I want some of 'em; an' the Porter apples will be gettin' ripe, an' we could have some apple-pie. This here ain't good; I want merlasses fur sweeting. Can't we get back no ways, Harriét? It ain't far, an' we could walk, an' they don't lock us in, nor nothin'. I don't want to die here; it ain't so straight up to heaven from here. O Lord, I've felt as if I was slantendicular from heaven ever since I've been here, an' it's been so awful dark. I ain't had any chinks. I want to go home, Harriét."

"We'll go to-morrow mornin'," said Harriet, finally; "we'll pack up our things an' go; we'll put on our old dresses, an' we'll do up the new ones in bundles, an' we'll jest shy out the back way to-morrow mornin'; an' we'll go. I kin find the way, an' I reckon we kin git thar, if it is fourteen mile. Mebbe somebody will give us a lift."

And they went. With a grim humor Harriet hung the new white lace caps with which she and Charlotte had been so pestered, one on each post at the head of the bedstead, so they would meet the eyes of the first person who opened the door. Then they took their bundles, stole slyly out, and were soon on the high-road, hobbling along, holding each other's hands, as jubilant as two children, and chuckling to themselves over their escape, and the probable astonishment there would be in the "Home" over it.

"O Lord, Harriét, what do you s'pose they will say to them caps?" cried Charlotte, with a gleeful cackle.

"I guess they'll see as folks ain't goin' to be made to wear caps agin their will in a free kentry," returned Harriet, with an echoing cackle, as they sped feebly and bravely along.

The "Home" stood on the very outskirts of the city, luckily for them. They would have found it a difficult undertaking to traverse the crowded streets. As it was, a short walk brought them into the free country road— free comparatively, for even here at ten o'clock in the morning there was considerable traveling to and from the city on business or pleasure.

People whom they met on the road did not stare at them as curiously as might have been expected. Harriet held her bristling chin high in air, and hobbled along with an appearance of being well aware of what she was about, that led folks to doubt their own first opinion that there was something unusual about the two old women.

Still their evident feebleness now and then occasioned from one and another more particular scrutiny. When they had been on the road a half-hour or so, a man in a covered wagon drove up behind them. After he had passed them, he poked his head around the front of the vehicle and looked back. Finally he stopped, and waited for them to come up to him.

"Like a ride, ma'am?" said he, looking at once bewildered and compassionate.

"Thankee," said Harriet, "we'd be much obleeged."

After the man had lifted the old women into the wagon, and established them on the back seat, he turned around, as he drove slowly along, and gazed at them curiously.

"Seems to me you look pretty feeble to be walking far," said he. "Where were you going?"

Harriet told him with an air of defiance.

"Why," he exclaimed, "it is fourteen miles out. You could never walk it in the world. Well, I am going within three miles of there, and I can go on a little farther as well as not. But I don't see—Have you been in the city?"

"I have been visitin' my married darter in the city," said Harriet, calmly.

Charlotte started, and swallowed convulsively.

Harriet had never told a deliberate falsehood before in her life, but this seemed to her one of the tremendous exigencies of life which justify a lie. She felt desperate. If she could not contrive to deceive him in some way, the man might turn directly around and carry Charlotte and her back to the "Home" and the white caps.

"I should not have thought your daughter would have let you start for such a walk as that," said the man. "Is this lady your sister? She is blind, isn't she? She does not look fit to walk a mile."

"Yes, she's my sister," replied Harriet, stubbornly: "an' she's blind; an' my darter didn't want us to walk. She felt reel bad about it. But she couldn't help it. She's poor, and her husband's dead, an' she's got four leetle children."

Harriet recounted the hardships of her imaginary daughter with a glibness that was astonishing. Charlotte swallowed again.

"Well," said the man, "I am glad I overtook you, for I don't think you would ever have reached home alive."

About six miles from the city an open buggy passed them swiftly. In it were seated the matron and one of the gentlemen in charge of the "Home." They never thought of looking into the covered wagon—and indeed one can travel in one of those vehicles, so popular in some parts of New England, with as much privacy as he could in his tomb. The two in the buggy were seriously alarmed, and anxious for the safety of the old women, who were chuckling maliciously in the wagon they soon left far behind. Harriet had watched them breathlessly until they disappeared on a curve of the road; then she whispered to Charlotte.

A little after noon the two old women crept slowly up the foot-path across the field to their old home.

"The clover is up to our knees," said Harriet; "an' the sorrel and the white-weed; an' there's lots of yaller butterflies."

"O Lord, Harriét, thar's a chink, an' I do believe I saw one of them yaller butterflies go past it," cried Charlotte, trembling all over, and nodding her gray head violently.

Harriet stood on the old sunken door-step and fitted the key, which she drew triumphantly from her pocket, in the lock, while Charlotte stood waiting and shaking behind her.

Then they went in. Everything was there just as they had left it. Charlotte sank down on a chair and began to cry. Harriet hurried across to the window that looked out on the garden.

"The currants air ripe," said she; "*an'* them pumpkins hev run all over everything."

"O Lord, Harriét," sobbed Charlotte, "thar is so many chinks that they air all runnin' together!"

Study and Discussion Questions

1. Look at the paragraphs that describe the Shattuck sisters' house and yard. How does the setting of this story mirror the characters?
2. What are the "chinks" referred to in the story? Why does Charlotte say at the end: "thar is so many chinks that they air all runnin' together"?
3. List the different kinds of charity in the story. Which ones are "mistaken" and which are not?
4. Why are Charlotte and Harriet uncomfortable in the Old Ladies' Home?
5. Describe the relationship between the two sisters.
6. What do you think is the author's attitude toward the Shattuck sisters?
7. Why does Harriet tell Mrs. Simonds that her doughnuts are "turrible tough"?
8. "It is more blessed to give than to receive." Is there any irony in Freeman's use of this maxim?

Writing Exercises

1. This story was published in 1888. What are some of the issues it raises that are still very much with us today?

2. Have you ever been either a recipient or a giver of charity? (Being taken to the movies by a friend when you couldn't afford it, and volunteering your time and labor to help someone in need are examples.) Describe the situation and how you felt in it.

3. Define *charity*. Give some examples from your own experience or knowledge. Which of these are "mistaken" and which are not? Why?

POETRY

WALT WHITMAN   (1819–1892)

Walt Whitman was born in West Hills, New York, and moved with his family to Brooklyn, where he attended school until, at age twelve, he was apprenticed to a printer. Raised as a Quaker, he taught school, worked as a journalist and newspaper editor, and, during the Civil War, gave care to the wounded in Army hospitals. Outspokenly homosexual in his writing, Whitman lost a job as a government clerk in Washington for the alleged obscenity of his verse, but found other government work until he suffered a paralytic stroke in 1873. He lived the last two decades of his life in Camden, New Jersey. Almost all of Whitman's poetry appeared in the volume Leaves of Grass, *which he first published in 1855 and continued to revise, expand, and republish throughout his life. Whitman also wrote prose, most notably* Democratic Vistas *(1871).*

We Two Boys Together Clinging   (1860)

We two boys together clinging,
One the other never leaving,
Up and down the roads going, North and South excursions making,
Power enjoying, elbows stretching, fingers clutching,
Arm'd and fearless, eating, drinking, sleeping, loving,   5
No law less than ourselves owning, sailing, soldiering, thieving,
      threatening,
Misers, menials, priests alarming, air breathing, water drinking, on the
      turf or the sea-beach dancing,
Cities wrenching, ease scorning, statutes mocking, feebleness chasing,
Fulfilling our foray.

Study and Discussion Questions

1. What is the mood of the poem? Why does Whitman bother to include "air breathing, water drinking"?
2. What is the boys' attitude toward society?
3. What does the last line mean?
4. What is the poem's grammatical structure? How does this help create its meaning?

Writing Exercises

1. How old are these two boys? Describe their relationship.
2. Copying the poem's grammatical structure, try writing a poem of your own about a youthful enthusiasm.

AUDRE LORDE   (b. 1934)

Audre Lorde was born in Harlem, studied at Hunter College and Columbia University, worked as a librarian for several years, and has taught at a number of colleges. She writes directly out of and about her identity as a black lesbian feminist, and her work includes the poetry From a Land Where Other People Live *(1973),* New York Headshop and Museum *(1974), and* The Black Unicorn *(1978), the autobiographical works,* The Cancer Journals *(1980) and* Zami: A New Spelling of My Name *(1982), and a collection of essays and speeches,* Sister Outsider *(1984).*

From the House of Yemanjá[1]   (1978)

My mother had two faces and a frying pot
where she cooked up her daughters
into girls
before she fixed our dinner.
My mother had two faces   5
and a broken pot
where she hid out a perfect daughter
who was not me
I am the sun and moon and forever hungry
for her eyes.   10

I bear two women upon my back
one dark and rich and hidden
in the ivory hungers of the other
mother
pale as a witch   15
yet steady and familiar

---

[1] "Mother of the other *Orisha* [Yoruban deities], Yemanjá is also the goddess of oceans. Rivers are said to flow from her breasts. One legend has it that a son tried to rape her. She fled until she collapsed, and from her breasts, the rivers flowed. Another legend says that a husband insulted Yemanjá's long breasts, and when she fled with her pots he knocked her down. From her breasts flowed the rivers, and from her body then sprang forth all the other *Orisha*. River-smooth stones are Yemanjá's symbol, and the sea is sacred to her followers. Those who please her are blessed with many children" [Lorde's note].

brings me bread and terror
in my sleep
her breasts are huge exciting anchors
in the midnight storm.   20

All this has been
before
in my mother's bed
time has no sense
I have no brothers   25
and my sisters are cruel.

Mother I need
mother I need
mother I need your blackness now
as the august earth needs rain.   30
I am
the sun and moon and forever hungry
the sharpened edge
where day and night shall meet
and not be   35
one.

[handwritten margin note: need for cultural stability]

Study and Discussion Questions

1. List the characteristics of the two faces, the two women, that the speaker's mother is (or at least appears to her daughter to be).
2. What does the speaker need from her mother now? What did she need from her mother earlier?
3. Why is she "forever hungry"?
4. What does it imply to describe yourself as "a sharpened edge"?

Writing Exercise

1. The speaker of the poem says her mother "cooked up her daughters / into girls." Come up with one or more images for your own upbringing.

ROBERT HAYDEN   (1913–1980)

Robert Hayden was born in Detroit, educated at Wayne State University and the University of Michigan, taught for twenty-three years at Fisk Uni-

versity, a primarily black institution, and then returned to teach at Michigan until his death. His poetry includes A Ballad of Remembrance *(1962),* Words in Mourning Time *(1970),* The Night-Blooming Cereus *(1972), and* Angle of Ascent *(1975).*

Those Winter Sundays   (1962)

Sundays too my father got up early
and put his clothes on in the blueblack cold,
then with cracked hands that ached
from labor in the weekday weather made
banked fires blaze. No one ever thanked him.   5

I'd wake and hear the cold splintering, breaking.
When the rooms were warm, he'd call,
and slowly I would rise and dress,
fearing the chronic angers of that house,

Speaking indifferently to him,   10
who had driven out the cold
and polished my good shoes as well.
What did I know, what did I know
of love's austere and lonely offices?

Study and Discussion Questions

1. Is the contrast in the poem between coldness and warmth only physical?
2. What is the significance of "and polished my good shoes as well"?
3. What, besides simply growing up, seems to have happened to change the speaker's attitude towards his father?
4. What does the last word of the poem mean? Why does Hayden use that word? Explain the last two lines.

Writing Exercise

1. Given the subject of the poem, how does Hayden avoid sentimentality?

The Whipping   (1962)

The old woman across the way
is whipping the boy again

and shouting to the neighborhood
　　her goodness and his wrongs.

Wildly he crashes through elephant ears,   5
　　pleads in dusty zinnias,
while she in spite of crippling fat
　　pursues and corners him.

She strikes and strikes the shrilly circling
　　boy till the stick breaks   10
in her hand. His tears are rainy weather
　　to woundlike memories:

My head gripped in bony vise
　　of knees, the writhing struggle
to wrench free, the blows, the fear   15
　　worse than blows that hateful

Words could bring, the face that I
　　no longer knew or loved. . . .
Well, it is over now, it is over,
　　and the boy sobs in his room,   20

And the woman leans muttering against
　　a tree, exhausted, purged—
avenged in part for lifelong hidings
　　she has had to bear.

Study and Discussion Questions

　1. How old do you think the speaker is?
　2. What is ironic about the position the speaker assumed, as a boy, when
　　he was beaten?
　3. What does the speaker understand that the young boy does not?

Writing Exercises

　1. Discuss how Hayden shifts the poem's focus of attention and our
　　sympathies to make his point.
　2. How is this poem like and unlike "Those Winter Sundays"?

JOHN UPDIKE (b. 1932)

John Updike was born in Shillington, Pennsylvania, graduated from Harvard, studied art for a year at Oxford, and returned to the United States to work for The New Yorker *magazine, which began publishing his stories. Though he has written poetry and numerous literary essays, Updike is best known for his fiction, including the novels* Rabbit, Run *(1960),* Couples *(1968),* Rabbit Redux *(1971),* Rabbit Is Rich *(1981), and* The Witches of Eastwick *(1984).*

Ex-Basketball Player (1957)

Pearl Avenue runs past the high-school lot,
Bends with the trolley tracks, and stops, cut off
Before it has a chance to go two blocks,
At Colonel McComsky Plaza. Berth's Garage
Is on the corner facing west, and there, 5
Most days, you'll find Flick Webb, who helps Berth out.

Flick stands tall among the idiot pumps—
Five on a side, the old bubble-head style,
Their rubber elbows hanging loose and low.
One's nostrils are two S's, and his eyes 10
An E and O. And one is squat, without
A head at all—more of a football type.

Once Flick played for the high-school team, the Wizards.
He was good: in fact, the best. In '46
He bucketed three hundred ninety points, 15
A county record still. The ball loved Flick.
I saw him rack up thirty-eight or forty
In one home game. His hands were like wild birds.

He never learned a trade, he just sells gas,
Checks oil, and changes flats. Once in a while, 20
As a gag, he dribbles an inner tube,
But most of us remember anyway.
His hands are fine and nervous on the lug wrench.
It makes no difference to the lug wrench, though.

Off work, he hangs around Mae's luncheonette. 25
Grease-gray and kind of coiled, he plays pinball,
Smokes those thin cigars, nurses lemon phosphates.
Flick seldom says a word to Mae, just nods

Beyond her face toward bright applauding tiers
Of Necco Wafers, Nibs, and Juju Beads.   30

Study and Discussion Questions

1. What are the various indications that Flick is diminished in the present?
2. What is the significance of the first four lines?
3. Analyze the imagery of the second stanza.
4. What is the meaning of the last line of the fourth stanza?

Writing Exercises

1. Is Flick unhappy now?
2. Describe someone you knew in high school who you think is or soon will be somehow less than he or she then was. Is social class a factor?

T. S. ELIOT   (1888–1965)

Thomas Stearns Eliot was born in St. Louis into a distinguished family with roots in New England; he was educated at Harvard, the Sorbonne, and Oxford. He moved to England in 1915 and in 1927 became a British subject and a member of the Anglican Church. His major work, The Waste Land *(1922), is considered one of the most important poems of the century. Other major volumes of poetry are* Prufrock and Other Observations *(1917) and* Four Quartets *(1943). Eliot's early, influential critical essays are collected in* The Sacred Wood *(1920) and he wrote several plays, including* Murder in the Cathedral *(1935) and* The Cocktail Party *(1949). In 1948 he received the Nobel Prize for literature.*

The Love Song of J. Alfred Prufrock   (1917)

S'io credesse che mia risposta fosse
A persona che mai tornasse al mondo,
Questa fiamma staria senza piu scosse.
Ma perciocche giammai di questo fondo
Non torno vivo alcun, s'i'odo il vero,
Senza tema d'infamia ti rispondo.[1]

---

[1] From Dante's *Inferno*, spoken to Dante by Guido da Montelfeltro, who is wrapped in flame: "If I thought that my reply were to someone who could ever return to the world, this flame would shake no more. But since no one has ever returned alive from this place, if what I hear is true, without fear of infamy I answer you."

Let us go then, you and I,
When the evening is spread out against the sky
Like a patient etherised upon a table;
Let us go, through certain half-deserted streets,
The muttering retreats   5
Of restless nights in one-night cheap hotels
And sawdust restaurants with oyster-shells:
Streets that follow like a tedious argument
Of insidious intent
To lead you to an overwhelming question . . .   10
Oh, do not ask, "What is it?"
Let us go and make our visit.

   In the room the women come and go
Talking of Michelangelo.

   The yellow fog that rubs its back upon the window-panes,   15
The yellow smoke that rubs its muzzle on the window-panes
Licked its tongue into the corners of the evening,
Lingered upon the pools that stand in drains,
Let fall upon its back the soot that falls from chimneys,
Slipped by the terrace, made a sudden leap,   20
And seeing that it was a soft October night,
Curled once about the house, and fell asleep.

   And indeed there will be time
For the yellow smoke that slides along the street,
Rubbing its back upon the window-panes;   25
There will be time, there will be time
To prepare a face to meet the faces that you meet;
There will be time to murder and create,
And time for all the works and days of hands
That lift and drop a question on your plate;   30
Time for you and time for me,
And time yet for a hundred indecisions,
And for a hundred visions and revisions,
Before the taking of a toast and tea.

   In the room the women come and go   35
Talking of Michelangelo.

   And indeed there will be time
To wonder, "Do I dare?" and, "Do I dare?"

Time to turn back and descend the stair,
With a bald spot in the middle of my hair— 40
[They will say: "How his hair is growing thin!"]
My morning coat, my collar mounting firmly to the chin,
My necktie rich and modest, but asserted by a simple pin—
[They will say: "But how his arms and legs are thin!"]
Do I dare 45
Disturb the universe?
In a minute there is time
For decisions and revisions which a minute will reverse.

For I have known them all already, known them all:—
Have known the evenings, mornings, afternoons, 50
I have measured out my life with coffee spoons;
I know the voices dying with a dying fall
Beneath the music from a farther room.
So how should I presume?

And I have known the eyes already, known them all— 55
The eyes that fix you in a formulated phrase,
And when I am formulated, sprawling on a pin,
When I am pinned and wriggling on the wall,
Then how should I begin
To spit out all the butt-ends of my days and ways? 60
And how should I presume?

And I have known the arms already, known them all—
Arms that are braceleted and white and bare
[But in the lamplight, downed with light brown hair!]
Is it perfume from a dress 65
That makes me so digress?
Arms that lie along a table, or wrap about a shawl.
And should I then presume?
And how should I begin?

. . . . .

Shall I say, I have gone at dusk through narrow streets 70
And watched the smoke that rises from the pipes
Of lonely men in shirt-sleeves, leaning out of windows? . . .

I should have been a pair of ragged claws
Scuttling across the floors of silent seas.

. . . . .

And the afternoon, the evening, sleeps so peacefully!   75
Smoothed by long fingers,
Asleep . . . tired . . . or it malingers,
Stretched on the floor, here beside you and me.
Should I, after tea and cakes and ices,
Have the strength to force the moment to its crisis?   80
But though I have wept and fasted, wept and prayed,
Though I have seen my head [grown slightly bald] brought in
     upon a platter,
I am no prophet—and here's no great matter;
I have seen the moment of my greatness flicker,   85
And I have seen the eternal Footman hold my coat, and snicker,
And in short, I was afraid.

    And would it have been worth it, after all,
After the cups, the marmalade, the tea,
Among the porcelain, among some talk of you and me,   90
Would it have been worth while,
To have bitten off the matter with a smile,
To have squeezed the universe into a ball
To roll it toward some overwhelming question,
To say: "I am Lazarus, come from the dead,   95
Come back to tell you all, I shall tell you all"—
If one, settling a pillow by her head,
    Should say: "That is not what I meant at all.
    That is not it, at all."

    And would it have been worth it, after all,   100
Would it have been worth while,
After the sunsets and the dooryards and the sprinkled streets,
After the novels, after the teacups, after the skirts that trail
     along the floor—
And this, and so much more?—   105
It is impossible to say just what I mean!
But as if a magic lantern threw the nerves in patterns on a screen:
Would it have been worth while
If one, settling a pillow or throwing off a shawl,
And turning toward the window, should say: 110
    "That is not it at all,
    That is not what I meant, at all."

        . . . . .

No! I am not Prince Hamlet, nor was meant to be;
Am an attendant lord, one that will do
To swell a progress, start a scene or two,   115

Advise the prince; no doubt, an easy tool,
Deferential, glad to be of use,
Politic, cautious, and meticulous;
Full of high sentence, but a bit obtuse;
At times, indeed, almost ridiculous—   120
Almost, at times, the Fool.

I grow old . . . I grow old . . .
I shall wear the bottoms of my trousers rolled.

Shall I part my hair behind? Do I dare to eat a peach?
I shall wear white flannel trousers, and walk upon the beach.   125
I have heard the mermaids singing, each to each.

I do not think that they will sing to me.

I have seen them riding seaward on the waves
Combing the white hair of the waves blown back
When the wind blows the water white and black.   130

We have lingered in the chambers of the sea
By sea-girls wreathed with seaweed red and brown
Till human voices wake us, and we drown.

Study and Discussion Questions

1. Who are the "you and I" in line 1? What are they doing?
2. How does what Prufrock comments on in the first 69 lines reveal his state of mind? What different emotions do you see him feeling throughout the poem?
3. Characterize Prufrock. What is his self-image? What are his fears?
4. What kind of world does Prufrock live in? Describe the setting(s) of Prufrock's journey.
5. Prufrock is concerned with the past and future. He says, "For I have known them all already" and, though he says he is no prophet, he does look into the future and speculate about what will happen to him. How does what Prufrock sees in the past and fears in the future affect his present behavior?
6. Is this poem about love?
7. How does the allusion to Dante's *Inferno* help in understanding the poem? The allusion to John the Baptist? to Lazarus? to Hamlet?
8. How does Eliot use repetition in the poem? Note slight changes in some of the repeated phrases.

Writing Exercises

1. List every question Prufrock asks in the poem. Do they have anything in common?
2. Choose one image from the poem and explain what it adds to your knowledge of Prufrock.
3. What advice would you give Prufrock?

FRANCIS E. W. HARPER   (1825–1911)

Daughter of free blacks, Francis Ellen Watkins Harper was born in Baltimore, attended a school run by her uncle, and worked as a seamstress and as a teacher. In the 1850s, she began traveling and lecturing for abolitionist societies. Harper's writing includes the poetry Poems on Miscellaneous Subjects *(1854) and* Sketches of Southern Life *(1872) and the novel* Iola Leroy *(1892).*

Learning to Read   (1872)

Very soon the Yankee teachers
  Came down and set up school;
But, oh! how the Rebs did hate it,—
  It was agin' their rule.

Our masters always tried to hide   5
  Book learning from our eyes;
Knowledge didn't agree with slavery—
  'Twould make us all too wise.

But some of us would try to steal
  A little from the book,   10
And put the words together,
  And learn by hook or crook.

I remember Uncle Caldwell,
  Who took pot liquor[1] fat
And greased the pages of his book,   15
  And hid it in his hat

And had his master ever seen
  The leaves upon his head,

---

[1] Broth in which meat and/or vegetables have cooked.

He'd have thought them greasy papers,
  But nothing to be read.   20

And there was Mr. Turner's Ben,
  Who heard the children spell,
And picked the words right up by heart,
  And learned to read 'em well.

Well, the Northern folks kept sending   25
  The Yankee teachers down;
And they stood right up and helped us,
  Though Rebs did sneer and frown.

And, I longed to read my Bible,
  For precious words it said;   30
But when I begun to learn it,
  Folks just shook their heads,

And said there is no use trying,
  Oh! Chloe, you're too late;
But as I was rising sixty,   35
  I had no time to wait.

So I got a pair of glasses,
  And straight to work I went,
And never stopped till I could read
  The hymns and Testament.   40

Then I got a little cabin
  A place to call my own—
And I felt as independent
  As the queen upon her throne.

Study and Discussion Questions

1. Explain the lines: "Knowledge didn't agree with slavery—/ 'Twould make us all too wise." Why do you think reading was a danger to the slave system?
2. What examples does Harper give of slaves learning to read despite their masters?
3. Why do people tell Chloe she can't learn to read?
4. How does learning how to read make her feel?

Writing Exercise

1. The last stanza of the poem doesn't appear to have anything to do with reading. Discuss the importance of what Chloe says here to the rest of the poem.

WILLIAM BUTLER YEATS   (1865–1939)

William Butler Yeats was born in Dublin, Ireland, studied art for several years, and then turned to writing. He was active in Irish nationalist causes, helped found an Irish national theater, and served as a senator of the new Irish Free State from 1922 to 1926. Yeats's long, unrequited love for Irish revolutionary Maud Gonne had an important impact on his writing, as did his marriage, in 1917, to Georgie Hyde-Lees, whose "automatic writing" helped him codify his mystical ideas. He carefully shaped his many volumes of poetry into his Collected Poems, *which first appeared in 1933. In 1923 he received the Nobel Prize for literature.*

Sailing to Byzantium[1]   (1927)

I

That is no country for old men. The young
In one another's arms, birds in the trees
—Those dying generations—at their song,
The salmon-falls, the mackerel-crowded seas,
Fish, flesh, or fowl, commend all summer long   5
Whatever is begotten, born, and dies.
Caught in that sensual music all neglect
Monuments of unageing intellect.

II

An aged man is but a paltry thing,
A tattered coat upon a stick, unless   10
Soul clap its hands and sing, and louder sing
For every tatter in its mortal dress,
Nor is there singing school but studying
Monuments of its own magnificence;
And therefore I have sailed the seas and come   15
To the holy city of Byzantium.

---

[1] Now called Istanbul, Byzantium was the capital and cultural center of the Byzantine Empire.

III

O sages standing in God's holy fire
As in the gold mosaic of a wall,
Come from the holy fire, perne in a gyre,[2]
And be the singing-masters of my soul. 20
Consume my heart away; sick with desire
And fastened to a dying animal
It knows not what it is; and gather me
Into the artifice of eternity.

IV

Once out of nature I shall never take 25
My bodily form from any natural thing,
But such a form as Grecian goldsmiths make
Of hammered gold and gold enamelling
To keep a drowsy Emperor awake;
Or set upon a golden bough to sing 30
To lords and ladies of Byzantium
Of what is past, or passing, or to come.

Study and Discussion Questions

1. *What* is "no country for old men"? Why?
2. What about Byzantium appeals to the speaker?
3. How does the speaker of the poem feel about aging?
4. How do people spend their time in the country of the young? How do they spend their time in Byzantium?
5. What constitutes immortality in this poem? What does the speaker mean when he asks to be gathered "into the artifice of eternity"?
6. Why, having left the world, will he sing "of what is past, or passing, or to come"?

Writing Exercises

1. Contrast Byzantium and the world the speaker of the poem has left in terms of the images used to describe each.
2. Write a sentence stating the main point of each stanza.

---

[2] Unwind down a spiral.

WILLIAM SHAKESPEARE (1564–1616)

Born in Stratford-on-Avon in England, William Shakespeare attended the free grammar school there, married Anne Hathaway when he was eighteen, and eventually ended up in London. He began working as an actor and playwright in the early 1590s. The troupe with which he worked built the Globe Theater in 1599 and Shakespeare continued writing plays for them. In 1611, he moved with his family back to Stratford. Shakespeare wrote 154 sonnets, several long poems, and 37 plays, among the latter A Midsummer Night's Dream, The Merchant of Venice, *and* As You Like It *in the 1590s, and* Twelfth Night, Hamlet, Othello, *and* King Lear *in the following decade.*

That time of year thou mayst in me behold   (1609)

LXXIII

That time of year thou mayst in me behold
When yellow leaves, or none, or few, do hang
Upon those boughs which shake against the cold,
Bare ruined choirs where late the sweet birds sang:
In me thou see'st the twilight of such day   5
As after sunset fadeth in the west,
Which by and by black night doth take away,
Death's second self that seals up all in rest:
In me thou see'st the glowing of such fire
That on the ashes of his youth doth lie   10
As the death-bed whereon it must expire,
Consumed with that which it was nourished by:
    This thou perceivest, which makes thy love more strong
    To love that well which thou must leave ere long.

Study and Discussion Questions

1. Who is speaking, and to whom? What are the relative ages of the two?
2. Explain line 12.
3. Explain in detail each of the three metaphors for growing old. How are they similar and how do they differ? What is the meaning of the order in which they appear?
4. How confident does the speaker seem in the assertion the final couplet makes?

Writing Exercises

1. Write a prose paragraph or two describing the speaker's attitude towards growing older.
2. What other metaphors might one use to describe aging? What are the associations and implications of each?

IRENA KLEPFISZ (b. 1941)

Irena Klepfisz was born in Warsaw, Poland, and came to the United States in 1949. She was educated at the City College of New York and the University of Chicago and has worked as a secretary, copy editor, proofreader, and teacher of English, Yiddish, and Women's Studies. Her poetry includes Periods of Stress *(1975) and* Different Enclosures *(1985).*

they did not build wings for them (1974)

they did not build wings for them
the unmarried aunts;   instead they
crammed them into old maids' rooms
or placed them as nannies with
the younger children;   mostly they   5
ate in the kitchen, but sometimes
were permitted to dine with the family
for which they were grateful and
smiled graciously as the food was passed.
they would eat slowly never filling   10
their plates and their hearts would
sink at the evening's end when it was
time to retreat into an upstairs corner.

but there were some who did not smile
who never wished to be grafted on   15
the bursting houses.   these few remained
indifferent to the family gatherings
preferring the aloneness of their small rooms
which they decorated with odd objects
found on long walks.   they collected   20
bird feathers and skulls unafraid to clean
them to whiteness;   stones which resembled
humped bears or the more common tiger and
wolf;   dried leaves whose brilliant colors
never faded;   pieces of wood still covered   25

with fresh moss and earth which retained
their moisture and continued flourishing.
these they placed by their dresser mirrors
in arrangements reminiscent of secret rites
or hung over delicate watercolors of unruly   30
trees whose branches were about to snap
with the wind.

it happened sometimes that among these
one would venture even further.   periodically
would be heard vague tales of a woman   35
withdrawn and inaccessible suddenly disappearing
one autumn night leaving her room bare
of herself.   women gossiped about a man.
but eventually word would come back
she had moved north to the ocean and lived   40
alone.   she was still collecting
but now her house was filled with crab
and lobster shells; discolored claws
which looked like grinning south american
parrots trapped in fish nets decorated   45
the walls; skulls of unidentifiable
creatures were arranged in geometric patterns
and soft reeds in tall green bottles
lined the window sills.   one room
in the back with totally bare walls   50
was a workshop.   here she sorted colored
shells and pasted them on wooden boards
in the shape of common flowers.   these she sold
without sentiment.

such a one might also disappear inland.   55
rumor would claim she had travelled in
men's clothing.   two years later it would
be reported she had settled in the woods
on some cleared land.   she ran a small farm
mainly for supplying herself with food   60
and wore strangely patched dresses and shawls
of oddly matched materials.   but aloneness
was her real distinction.   the house was neat
and the pantry full.   seascapes and pastoral
scenes hung on the walls.   the garden was   65
well kept and the flower beds clearly defined
by color: red   yellow   blue.   in the woods
five miles from the house she had an orchard.

here she secretly grafted and crossed varieties
creating singular fruit of shades and scents   70
never thought possible.   her experiments rarely
failed and each spring she waited eagerly to see
what new forms would hang from the trees.
here the world was a passionate place and she
would visit it at night baring her breasts   75
to the moon.

Study and Discussion Questions

1. How are the "unmarried aunts" treated by their families?
2. Klepfisz uses the word *grafted* twice. What is she doing with the word in each instance?
3. Why are we told in the third stanza that the woman sells what she makes "without sentiment"?
4. What do all the women in stanzas two, three and four have in common?
5. How does the second stanza of the poem function as a transition between the first stanza and the last two stanzas?

Writing Exercise

1. Write a new definition of *old maid* or *spinster* based on this poem. (You might decide to come up with a new word as well as a new definition.)

WILLIAM SHAKESPEARE   (1564–1616)

Like as the waves make towards the pebbled shore   (1609)

LX

Like as the waves make towards the pebbled shore,
So do our minutes hasten to their end;
Each changing place with that which goes before,
In sequent toil all forwards do contend.
Nativity, once in the main of light,   5
Crawls to maturity, wherewith being crowned,
Crooked eclipses 'gainst his glory fight,
And Time that gave doth now his gift confound.
Time doth transfix the flourish set on youth
And delves the parallels in beauty's brow,   10
Feeds on the rarities of nature's truth,

And nothing stands but for his scythe to mow:
  And yet to times in hope my verse shall stand,
  Praising thy worth, despite his cruel hand.

CHARLOTTE SMITH   (1749–1806)

Thirty-Eight   (1786)

ADDRESSED TO MRS. H____Y.

In early youth's unclouded scene,
The brilliant morning of eighteen,
With health and sprightly joy elate
  We gazed on life's enchanting spring,
  Nor thought how quickly time would bring   5
The mournful period—Thirty-eight.

Then the starch maid, or matron sage,
Already of that sober age,
We view'd with mingled scorn and hate;
  In whose sharp words, or sharper face,   10
  With thoughtless mirth we loved to trace
The sad effects of—Thirty-eight.

Till saddening, sickening at the view,
We learn'd to dread what Time might do;
And then preferr'd[1] a prayer to Fate   15
  To end our days ere that arrived;
  When (power and pleasure long survived)
We met neglect and—Thirty-eight.

But Time, in spite of wishes flies,
And Fate our simple prayer denies,   20
And bids us Death's own hour await:
  The auburn locks are mix'd with grey,
  The transient roses fade away,
But Reason comes at—Thirty-eight.

Her voice the anguish contradicts   25
That dying vanity inflicts;
Her hand new pleasures can create,

---

[1] Proffered.

For us she opens to the view
  Prospects less bright—but far more true,
And bids us smile at—Thirty-eight 30

No more shall *Scandal's* breath destroy
The social converse we enjoy
With bard or critic tête à tête;—
  O'er Youth's bright blooms her blights shall pour,
  But spare the improving friendly hour 35
That Science gives to—Thirty-eight.

Stripp'd of their gaudy hues by Truth,
We view the glitt'ring toys of youth,
And blush to think how poor the bait
  For which to public scenes we ran 40
  And scorn'd of sober Sense the plan
Which gives content at—Thirty-eight.

Tho' Time's inexorable sway
Has torn the myrtle bands away,
For other wreaths 'tis not too late, 45
  The amaranth's purple glow survives,
  And still Minerva's olive lives
On the calm brow of—Thirty-eight.

With eye more steady we engage
To contemplate approaching age, 50
And life more justly estimate;
With firmer souls, and stronger powers,
  With reason, faith, and friendship ours,
  We'll not regret the stealing hours
That lead from Thirty—even to Forty-eight. 55

WILLIAM WORDSWORTH (1770–1850)

Ode (1807)

INTIMATIONS OF IMMORTALITY FROM RECOLLECTIONS OF EARLY CHILDHOOD

The Child is father of the Man;
And I could wish my days to be
Bound each to each by natural piety.

I

There was a time when meadow, grove, and stream,
The earth, and every common sight,
    To me did seem
    Apparelled in celestial light,
The glory and the freshness of a dream.   5
It is not now as it hath been of yore;—
    Turn wheresoe'er I may,
    By night or day,
The things which I have seen I now can see no more.

II

    The Rainbow comes and goes,   10
    And lovely is the Rose,
    The Moon doth with delight
Look round her when the heavens are bare;
    Waters on a starry night
    Are beautiful and fair;   15
  The sunshine is a glorious birth;
  But yet I know, where'er I go,
That there hath past away a glory from the earth.

III

Now, while the birds thus sing a joyous song,
    And while the young lambs bound   20
    As to the tabor's sound,
To me alone there came a thought of grief:
A timely utterance gave that thought relief,
    And I again am strong:
The cataracts blow their trumpets from the steep;   25
No more shall grief of mine the season wrong;
I hear the Echoes through the mountains throng,
The Winds come to me from the fields of sleep,
    And all the earth is gay;
      Land and sea   30
    Give themselves up to jollity,
    And with the heart of May
    Doth every Beast keep holiday;—
    Thou Child of Joy,
Shout round me, let me hear thy shouts, thou happy Shepherd-boy! 35

IV

Ye blessèd Creatures, I have heard the call
  Ye to each other make; I see

The heavens laugh with you in your jubilee;
  My heart is at your festival,
    My head hath its coronal,   40
The fulness of your bliss, I feel—I feel it all.
    Oh evil day! if I were sullen
    While Earth herself is adorning,
     This sweet May-morning,
    And the Children are culling   45
     On every side,
    In a thousand valleys far and wide,
    Fresh flowers; while the sun shines warm,
And the Babe leaps up on his Mother's arm:—
    I hear, I hear, with joy I hear!   50
    —But there's a Tree, of many, one,
A single Field which I have looked upon,
Both of them speak of something that is gone:
    The Pansy at my feet
    Doth the same tale repeat: 55
Whither is fled the visionary gleam?
Where is it now, the glory and the dream?

    V
Our birth is but a sleep and a forgetting:
The Soul that rises with us, our life's Star,
    Hath had elsewhere its setting,   60
     And cometh from afar:
    Not in entire forgetfulness,
    And not in utter nakedness,
But trailing clouds of glory do we come
    From God, who is our home: 65
Heaven lies about us in our infancy!
Shades of the prison-house begin to close
    Upon the growing Boy,
      But He
Beholds the light, and whence it flows,
    He sees it in his joy;   70
The Youth, who daily farther from the east
    Must travel, still in Nature's Priest,
    And by the vision splendid
    Is on his way attended;   75
At length the Man perceives it die away,
And fade into the light of common day.

    VI
Earth fills her lap with pleasures of her own;
Yearnings she hath in her own natural kind,

And, even with something of a Mother's mind,   80
    And no unworthy aim,
    The homely Nurse doth all she can
To make her Foster-child, her Inmate Man,
    Forget the glories he hath known,
And that imperial palace whence he came.   85

    VII

Behold the Child among his new-born blisses,
A six years' Darling of a pigmy size!
See, where 'mid work of his own hand he lies,
Fretted by sallies of his mother's kisses,
With light upon him from his father's eyes!   90
See, at his feet, some little plan or chart,
Some fragment from his dream of human life,
Shaped by himself with newly-learned art;
    A wedding or a festival,
    A mourning or a funeral;   95
      And this hath now his heart,
      And unto this he frames his song:
      Then will he fit his tongue
To dialogues of business, love, or strife;
      But it will not be long   100
      Ere this be thrown aside,
      And with new joy and pride
The little Actor cons another part;
Filling from time to time his "humorous[1] stage"
With all the Persons, down to palsied Age,   105
That Life brings with her in her equipage;
      As if his whole vocation
      Were endless imitation.

    VIII

Thou, whose exterior semblance doth belie
    Thy Soul's immensity;   110
Thou best Philosopher, who yet dost keep
Thy heritage, thou Eye among the blind,
That, deaf and silent, read'st the eternal deep,
Haunted for ever by the eternal mind,—
    Mighty Prophet! Seer blest!   115

---

[1] Reference to comedy of humours, in which a character is often dominated by one trait, such as greed or jealousy.

On whom those truths do rest,
Which we are toiling all our lives to find,
In darkness lost, the darkness of the grave;
Thou, over whom thy Immortality
Broods like the Day, a Master o'er a Slave,   120
A Presence which is not to be put by;
Thou little Child, yet glorious in the might
Of heaven-born freedom on thy being's height,
Why with such earnest pains dost thou provoke
The years to bring the inevitable yoke,   125
Thus blindly with thy blessedness at strife?
Full soon thy Soul shall have her earthly freight,
And custom lie upon thee with a weight,
Heavy as frost, and deep almost as life!

IX

O joy! that in our embers   130
Is something that doth live,
That nature yet remembers
What was so fugitive!
The thought of our past years in me doth breed
Perpetual benediction: not indeed   135
For that which is most worthy to be blest;
Delight and liberty, the simple creed
Of Childhood, whether busy or at rest,
With new-fledged hope still fluttering in his breast:—
Not for these I raise   140
The song of thanks and praise;
But for those obstinate questionings
Of sense and outward things,
Fallings from us, vanishings;
Blank misgivings of a Creature   145
Moving about in worlds not realised,
High instincts before which our mortal Nature
Did tremble like a guilty Thing surprised:
But for those first affections,
Those shadowy recollections,   150
Which, be they what they may,
Are yet the fountain light of all our day,
Are yet a master light of all our seeing;
Uphold us, cherish, and have power to make
Our noisy years seem moments in the being   155
Of the eternal Silence: truths that wake,
To perish never;

Which neither listlessness, nor mad endeavour,
    Nor Man nor Boy,
Nor all that is at enmity with joy,   160
Can utterly abolish or destroy!
    Hence in a season of calm weather
    Though inland far we be,
Our Souls have sight of that immortal sea
    Which brought us hither,   165
  Can in a moment travel thither,
And see the Children sport upon the shore,
And hear the mighty waters rolling evermore.

    X
Then sing, ye Birds, sing, sing a joyous song!
    And let the young Lambs bound   170
    As to the tabor's sound!
We in thought will join your throng,
    Ye that pipe and ye that play,
    Ye that through your hearts to-day
    Feel the gladness of the May!   175
What though the radiance which was once so bright
Be now for ever taken from my sight,
    Though nothing can bring back the hour
Of splendour in the grass, of glory in the flower;
    We will grieve not, rather find   180
    Strength in what remains behind;
    In the primal sympathy
    Which having been must ever be;
    In the soothing thoughts that spring
    Out of human suffering;   185
    In the faith that looks through death,
In years that bring the philosophic mind.

    XI
And O, ye Fountains, Meadows, Hills, and Groves,
Forebode not any severing of our loves!
Yet in my heart of hearts I feel your might;   190
I only have relinquished one delight
To live beneath your more habitual sway.
I love the Brooks which down their channels fret,
Even more than when I tripped lightly as they;
The innocent brightness of a new-born Day   195
      Is lovely yet;
The Clouds that gather round the setting sun
Do take a sober colouring from an eye

That hath kept watch o'er man's mortality;
Another race hath been, and other palms are won.   200
Thanks to the human heart by which we live,
Thanks to its tenderness, its joys, and fears,
To me the meanest flower that blows can give
Thoughts that do often lie too deep for tears.

GEORGE GORDON, LORD BYRON   (1788–1824)

So We'll Go No More A-Roving   (1817)

I

So we'll go no more a-roving
  So late into the night,
Though the heart be still as loving,
  And the moon be still as bright.

II

For the sword outwears its sheath,   5
  And the soul wears out the breast,
And the heart must pause to breathe,
  And Love itself have rest.

III

Though the night was made for loving,
  And the day returns too soon,   10
Yet we'll go no more a-roving
  By the light of the moon.

JOHN KEATS   (1795–1821)

When I Have Fears   (1818)

When I have fears that I may cease to be
  Before my pen has glean'd my teeming brain,

Before high-piled books, in charact'ry,[1]
　　Hold like rich garners the full-ripen'd grain;
When I behold, upon the night's starr'd face,　　　　　　　　5
　　Huge cloudy symbols of a high romance,
And think that I may never live to trace
　　Their shadows, with the magic hand of chance;
And when I feel, fair creature of an hour!
　　That I shall never look upon thee more,　　　　　　　　10
Never have relish in the faery[2] power
　　Of unreflecting love!—then on the shore
Of the wide world I stand alone, and think
　　Till Love and Fame to nothingness do sink.

EMILY DICKINSON　　　　　　　　　　　(1830–1886)

I'm ceded—I've stopped being Their's—　　(1862)

I'm ceded—I've stopped being Their's—
The name They dropped upon my face

With water, in the country church
Is finished using, now,
And They can put it with my Dolls,　　　　　　　　　　　5
My childhood, and the string of spools,
I've finished threading—too—

Baptized, before, without the choice,
But this time, consciously, of Grace—
Unto supremest name—　　　　　　　　　　　　　　　10
Called to my Full—The Crescent dropped—
Existence's whole Arc, filled up,
With one small Diadem.

My second Rank—too small the first—
Crowned—Crowing—on my Father's breast—　　　　　　15
A half unconscious Queen—
But this time—Adequate—Erect,

---

[1] Printed characters expressing thought.
[2] Magical.

With Will to choose, or to reject,
And I choose, just a Crown—

EMILY DICKINSON   (1830–1886)

Death is the Supple Suitor   (1878)

Death is the supple Suitor
That wins at last—
It is a stealthy Wooing
Conducted first
By pallid innuendoes   5
And dim approach
But brave at last with Bugles
And a bisected Coach
It bears away in triumph
To Troth unknown   10
And Kinsmen as divulgeless
As throngs of Down—

GERARD MANLEY HOPKINS   (1844–1889)

Spring and Fall   (1880)

TO A YOUNG CHILD
Márgarét, áre you gríeving
Over Goldengrove unleaving?
Leáves, líke the things of man, you
With your fresh thoughts care for, can you?
Áh! ás the heart grows older   5
It will come to such sights colder
By and by, nor spare a sigh
Though worlds of wanwood leafmeal lie;[1]
And yet you *will* weep and know why.
Now no matter, child, the name: 10

---

[1] Pale woods; like "piecemeal," in pieces.

Sórrow's springs áre the same.
Nor mouth had, no nor mind, expressed
What heart heard of, ghost[2] guessed:
It ís the blight man was born for,
It is Margaret you mourn for.   15

WILLIAM BUTLER YEATS   **(1865–1939)**

When You Are Old   (1892)

When you are old and grey and full of sleep,
And nodding by the fire, take down this book,
And slowly read, and dream of the soft look
Your eyes had once, and of their shadows deep;

How many loved your moments of glad grace,   5
And loved your beauty with love false or true,
But one man loved the pilgrim soul in you,
And loved the sorrows of your changing face;

And bending down beside the glowing bars,
Murmur, a little sadly, how Love fled   10
And paced upon the mountains overhead
And hid his face amid a crowd of stars.

RENÉE VIVIEN   **(1877–1909)**

Whitehaired Women[1]   (1904)

> You who talk little, whitehaired
> women, you, flowers of old age
> on earth.

Whitehaired women, winter caressed,
You who rejoice in the intimacy of the fire

---

[2] Soul.
[1] Translated by Catharine Kroger.

And of the dusk, oh flowers of old age,
    You who speak little,

You have the candid peace of many years,   5
You are the chorus of living memories:
Soft, you twine the faded garlands
    Of old dreams.

You linger, as before, on porches
Where Phoebus bleached the moss and the lichen,   10
And smiling you light the red torches
    Of hymens.

You love the brown-eyed autumn and the clatter
Of doors where the wind leaves a salty taste:
You spin, by the song of your humble wheel,   15
    The snowy flax.

The virgin respects and fears your wisdom,
And your greetings are slow like a good-bye,
Whitehaired women, flowers of old age,
    You who speak little. . . .   20

EDNA ST. VINCENT MILLAY   **(1892–1950)**

Grown-up   (1920)

Was it for this I uttered prayers,
And sobbed and cursed and kicked the stairs,
That now, domestic as a plate,
I should retire at half-past eight?

EDNA ST. VINCENT MILLAY   **(1892–1950)**

What Lips My Lips Have Kissed   (1923)

What lips my lips have kissed, and where, and why,
I have forgotten, and what arms have lain

Under my head till morning; but the rain
Is full of ghosts tonight, that tap and sigh
Upon the glass and listen for reply,   5
And in my heart there stirs a quiet pain
For unremembered lads that not again
Will turn to me at midnight with a cry.
Thus in the winter stands the lonely tree,
Nor knows what birds have vanished one by one,   10
Yet knows its boughs more silent than before:
I cannot say what loves have come and gone,
I only know that summer sang in me
A little while, that in me sings no more.

ELINOR WYLIE   **(1885–1928)**

Let No Charitable Hope   **(1923)**

Now let no charitable hope
Confuse my mind with images
Of eagle and of antelope:
I am in nature none of these.

I was, being human, born alone;   5
I am, being woman, hard beset;
I live by squeezing from a stone
The little nourishment I get.

In masks outrageous and austere
The years go by in single file;   10
But none has merited my fear,
And none has quite escaped my smile.

E. E. CUMMINGS   **(1894–1962)**

in Just—   **(1923)**

in Just—
spring   when the world is mud—

luscious the little
lame balloonman

whistles   far   and wee   5

and eddieandbill come
running from marbles and
piracies and it's
spring

when the world is puddle-wonderful   10

the queer
old balloonman whistles
far   and   wee
and bettyandisbel come dancing

from hop-scotch and jump-rope and   15

it's
spring
and
     the

          goat-footed   20

balloonMan   whistles
far
and
wee

SARA TEASDALE   (1884–1933)

The Solitary   (1926)

My heart has grown rich with the passing of years,
  I have less need now than when I was young

To share myself with every comer
  Or shape my thoughts into words with my tongue.

It is one to me that they come or go   5
  If I have myself and the drive of my will,
And strength to climb on a summer night
  And watch the stars swarm over the hill.

Let them think I love them more than I do,
  Let them think I care, though I go alone;   10
If it lifts their pride, what is it to me
  Who am self-complete as a flower or a stone.

MARGARET WALKER   (b. 1915)

Lineage   (1942)

My grandmothers were strong.
They followed plows and bent to toil.
They moved through fields sowing seed.
They touched earth and grain grew.
They were full of sturdiness and singing.   5
My grandmothers were strong.

My grandmothers are full of memories
Smelling of soap and onions and wet clay
With veins rolling roughly over quick hands
They have many clean words to say.   10
My grandmothers were strong.
Why am I not as they?

GWENDOLYN BROOKS   (b. 1917)

a song in the front yard   (1945)

I've stayed in the front yard all my life.
I want a peek at the back

Where it's rough and untended and hungry weed grows.
A girl gets sick of a rose.

I want to go in the back yard now   5
And maybe down the alley,
To where the charity children play.
I want a good time today.

They do some wonderful things.
They have some wonderful fun.   10
My mother sneers, but I say it's fine
How they don't have to go in at quarter to nine.
My mother, she tells me that Johnnie Mae
Will grow up to be a bad woman.
That George'll be taken to Jail soon or late   15
(On account of last winter he sold our back gate.)

But I say it's fine. Honest, I do.
And I'd like to be a bad woman, too,
And wear the brave stockings of night-black lace
And strut down the streets with paint on my face.   20

THEODORE ROETHKE   (1908–1963)

My Papa's Waltz   (1948)

The whiskey on your breath
Could make a small boy dizzy;
But I hung on like death:
Such waltzing was not easy.

We romped until the pans   5
Slid from the kitchen shelf;
My mother's countenance
Could not unfrown itself.

The hand that held my wrist
Was battered on one knuckle;   10

At every step you missed
My right ear scraped a buckle.

You beat time on my head
With a palm caked hard by dirt,
Then waltzed me off to bed   15
Still clinging to your shirt.

DYLAN THOMAS   **(1914–1953)**

Do Not Go Gentle Into That Good Night   (1952)

Do not go gentle into that good night,
Old age should burn and rave at close of day;
Rage, rage against the dying of the light.

Though wise men at their end know dark is right,
Because their words had forked no lightning they   5
Do not go gentle into that good night.

Good men, the last wave by, crying how bright
Their frail deeds might have danced in a green bay,
Rage, rage against the dying of the light.

Wild men who caught and sang the sun in flight   10
And learn, too late, they grieved it on its way,
Do not go gentle into that good night.

Grave men, near death, who see with blinding sight
Blind eyes could blaze like meteors and be gay,
Rage, rage against the dying of the light.   15

And you, my father, there on the sad height,
Curse, bless, me now with your fierce tears, I pray.
Do not go gentle into that good night.
Rage, rage against the dying of the light.

GWENDOLYN BROOKS   (b. 1917)

_____

We Real Cool   (1960)

        THE POOL PLAYERS.
        SEVEN AT THE GOLDEN SHOVEL.

We real cool. We
Left school. We

Lurk late. We
Strike straight. We

Sing sin. We   5
Thin gin. We

Jazz June. We
Die soon.

AMIRI BARAKA   (b. 1934)

_____

Preface to a Twenty Volume Suicide Note   (1961)

(For Kellie Jones, born 16 May 1959)

Lately, I've become accustomed to the way
The ground opens up and envelops me
Each time I go out to walk the dog.
Or the broad edged silly music the wind
Makes when I run for a bus. . .   5

Things have come to that.

And now, each night I count the stars,
And each night I get the same number.
And when they will not come to be counted.
I count the holes they leave.   10

Nobody sings anymore.

And then last night, I tiptoed up
To my daughter's room and heard her
Talking to someone, and when I opened
The door, there was no one there. . .   15
Only she on her knees, peeking into

Her own clasped hands.

SYLVIA PLATH   (1932–1963)

Edge   (1963)

The woman is perfected.
Her dead

Body wears the smile of accomplishment,
The illusion of a Greek necessity

Flows in the scrolls of her toga,   5
Her bare

Feet seem to be saying:
We have come so far, it is over.

Each dead child coiled, a white serpent,
One at each little   10

Pitcher of milk, now empty.
She has folded

Them back into her body as petals
Of a rose close when the garden

Stiffens and odors bleed   15
From the sweet, deep throats of the night flower.

The moon has nothing to be sad about,
Staring from her hood of bone.

She is used to this sort of thing.
Her blacks crackle and drag. 20

NIKKI GIOVANNI (b. 1943)

Woman Poem (1969)

you see, my whole life
is tied up
to unhappiness
it's father cooking breakfast
and me getting fat as a hog 5
or having no food
at all and father proving
his incompetence
again
i wish i knew how it would feel 10
to be free

it's having a job
they won't let you work
or no work at all
castrating me 15
(yes it happens to women too)

it's a sex object if you're pretty
and no love
or love and no sex if you're fat
get back fat black woman be a mother 20
grandmother strong thing but not woman
gameswoman romantic woman love needer
man seeker dick eater sweat getter
fuck needing love seeking woman

it's a hole in your shoe 25
and buying lil' sis a dress

and her saying you shouldn't
when you know
all too well—that you shouldn't

but smiles are only something we give   30
to properly dressed social workers
not each other
only smiles of i know
your game sister
which isn't really   35
a smile

joy is finding a pregnant roach
and squashing it
not finding someone to hold
let go get off get back don't turn   40
me on you black dog
how dare you care
about me
you ain't got no good sense
cause i ain't shit you must be lower   45
than that to care

it's a filthy house
with yesterday's watermelon
and monday's tears
cause true ladies don't   50
know how to clean

it's intellectual devastation
of everybody
to avoid emotional commitment
"yeah honey i would've married   55
him but he didn't have no degree"

its knock-kneed mini-skirted
wig wearing died blond mamma's scar
born dead my scorn your whore
rough heeled broken nailed powdered   60
face me
whose whole life is tied
up to unhappiness
cause it's the only

for real thing   65
i
know

ANNE SEXTON   (1928-1974)

___

Briar Rose
(Sleeping Beauty)   (1971)

Consider
a girl who keeps slipping off,
arms limp as old carrots,
into the hypnotist's trance,
into a spirit world   5
speaking with the gift of tongues.
She is stuck in the time machine,
suddenly two years old sucking her thumb,
as inward as a snail,
learning to talk again.   10
She's on a voyage.
She is swimming further and further back,
up like a salmon,
struggling into her mother's pocketbook.
Little doll child,   15
come here to Papa.
Sit on my knee.
I have kisses for the back of your neck.
A penny for your thoughts, Princess.
I will hunt them like an emerald.   20
Come be my snooky
and I will give you a root.
   That kind of voyage,
   rank as honeysuckle.

Once   25
a king had a christening
for his daughter Briar Rose
and because he had only twelve gold plates
he asked only twelve fairies
to the grand event.   30

The thirteenth fairy,
her fingers as long and thin as straws,
her eyes burnt by cigarettes,
her uterus an empty teacup,
arrived with an evil gift.   35
She made this prophecy:
The princess shall prick herself
on a spinning wheel in her fifteenth year
and then fall down dead.
Kaputt!   40
The court fell silent.
The king looked like Munch's *Scream*.[1]
Fairies' prophecies,
in times like those,
held water.   45
However the twelfth fairy
had a certain kind of eraser
and thus she mitigated the curse
changing that death
into a hundred-year sleep.   50

The king ordered every spinning wheel
exterminated and exorcized.
Briar Rose grew to be a goddess
and each night the king
bit the hem of her gown   55
to keep her safe.
He fastened the moon up
with a safety pin
to give her perpetual light
He forced every male in the court   60
to scour his tongue with Bab-o
lest they poison the air she dwelt in.
Thus she dwelt in his odor.
Rank as honeysuckle.

On her fifteenth birthday   65
she pricked her finger
on a charred spinning wheel
and the clocks stopped.
Yes indeed. She went to sleep.
The king and queen went to sleep,   70
the courtiers, the flies on the wall.

---

[1] Woodcut by Norwegian artist, Edvard Munch (1863–1944).

The fire in the hearth grew still
and the roast meat stopped crackling.
The trees turned into metal
and the dog became china.   75
They all lay in a trance,
each a catatonic
stuck in the time machine.
Even the frogs were zombies.

Only a bunch of briar roses grew   80
forming a great wall of tacks
around the castle.
Many princes
tried to get through the brambles
for they had heard much of Briar Rose   85
but they had not scoured their tongues
so they were held by the thorns
and thus were crucified.
In due time
a hundred years passed   90
and a prince got through.
The briars parted as if for Moses
and the prince found the tableau intact.
He kissed Briar Rose
and she woke up crying: 95
Daddy! Daddy!
Presto! She's out of prison!
She married the prince
and all went well
except for the fear—   100
the fear of sleep.

Briar Rose
was an insomniac. . .
She could not nap
or lie in sleep   105
without the court chemist
mixing her some knock-out drops
and never in the prince's presence.
If it is to come, she said,
sleep must take me unawares   110
while I am laughing or dancing
so that I do not know that brutal place
where I lie down with cattle prods,
the hole in my cheek open.

Further, I must not dream   115
for when I do I see the table set
and a faltering crone at my place,
her eyes burnt by cigarettes
as she eats betrayal like a slice of meat.

I must not sleep   120
for while asleep I'm ninety
and think I'm dying.
Death rattles in my throat
like a marble.
I wear tubes like earrings.   125
I lie as still as a bar of iron.
You can stick a needle
through my kneecap and I won't flinch.
I'm all shot up with Novocain.
This trance girl   130
is yours to do with.
You could lay her in a grave,
an awful package,
and shovel dirt on her face
and she'd never call back: Hello there!   135
But if you kissed her on the mouth
her eyes would spring open
and she'd call out: Daddy! Daddy!
Presto!
She's out of prison.   140

There was a theft.
That much I am told.
I was abandoned.
That much I know.
I was forced backward.   145
I was forced forward.
I was passed hand to hand
like a bowl of fruit.
Each night I am nailed into place
and I forget who I am.   150
Daddy?
That's another kind of prison.
It's not the prince at all,
but my father
drunkenly bent over my bed,   155

circling the abyss like a shark,
my father thick upon me
like some sleeping jellyfish.

What voyage this, little girl?
This coming out of prison?   160
God help—
this life after death?

RAMONA WILSON   (b. 1945)

Keeping Hair   (1973)

My grandmother had braids
at the thickest, pencil wide
held with bright wool
cut from her bed shawl.
No teeth left but white hair   5
combed and wet carefully
early each morning.
The small wild plants found among stones
on the windy and brown plateaus
revealed their secrets to her hand   10
and yielded to her cooking pots.
She made a sweet amber water
from willows,
boiling the life out
to pour onto her old head.   15
"It will keep your hair."
She bathed my head once
rain water not sweeter.
The thought that once
when I was so very young   20
her work-bent hands
very gently and smoothly
washed my hair in willows
may also keep my heart.

CASEY MOTSISI   (1931–1977)

The Efficacy of Prayer   (1973)

They called him Dan the Drunk.
The old people refuse to say how old he was,
Nobody knows where he came from—but they all
Called him Dan the Drunk.
He was a drunk, but perhaps his name was not really Dan.   5
Who knows, he might have been Sam.
But why bother, he's dead, poor Dan.
Gave him a pauper's funeral, they did.
Just dumped him into a hole to rest in eternal drunkenness.
Somehow the old people are glad that Dan the Drunk is dead.   10
Ghastly!
They say he was a bad influence on the children.
But the kids are sad that Dan the Drunk is no more.
No more will the kids frolic to the music that used to flow out
    of his battered concertina. Or listen to the tales he used to tell.   15
All followed him into that pauper's hole.
How the kids used to worship Dan the Drunk!
He was just one of them grown older too soon.
'I'm going to be just like Dan the Drunk,' a little girl said to
    her parents of a night cold while they crowded around a   20
    sleepy brazier
The parents looked at each other and their eyes prayed.
'God Almighty, save our little Sally.'
God heard their prayer.
He saved their Sally.   25
Prayer. It can work miracles.
Sally grew up to become a nanny. . . .

MURIEL RUKEYSER   (1913–1980)

Rondel[1]   (1973)

Now that I am fifty-six
Come and celebrate with me—

---

[1] Lyrical French verse form.

What happens to song and sex
Now that I am fifty-six?

They dance, but differently,   5
Death and distance in the mix;
Now that I'm fifty-six
Come and celebrate with me.

AUDRE LORDE   (b. 1934)

To My Daughter the Junkie on a Train   (1974)

Children we have not borne
bedevil us by becoming
themselves
painfully sharp and unavoidable
like a needle in our flesh.   5

Coming home on the subway from a PTA meeting
of minds committed like murder
or suicide
to their own private struggle
a long-legged girl with a horse in her brain   10
slumps down beside me
begging to be ridden asleep
for the price of a midnight train
free from desire.
Little girl on the nod   15
if we are measured by the dreams we avoid
then you are the nightmare
of all sleeping mothers
rocking back and forth
the dead weight of your arms   20
locked about our necks
heavier than our habit
of looking for reasons.

My corrupt concern will not replace
what you once needed   25
but I am locked into my own addictions
and offer you my help, one eye
out

for my own station.
Roused and deprived   30
your costly dream explodes
into a terrible technicoloured laughter
at my failure
up and down across the aisle
women avert their eyes   35
as the other mothers who became useless
curse their children who became junk.

C. D. WRIGHT   (b. 1949)

Falling Beasts   (1982)

Girls marry young
In towns in the mountains.
They're sent to the garden
For beets. They come to the table
With their hair gleaming,   5
Their breath missing.
In my book love is darker
Than cola. It can burn
A hole clean through you.
When the first satellite   10
Flew over, men stood
On their property, warm
Even in undershirts,
Longing to shoot something.   15
The mule looks down
The barrel of the gun,
Another long row to plow.
Bills pile up in fall
Like letters from a son
In the army. An explosion   20
Kills a quiet man.
Another sits beside a brass lamp
In a white shirt
And cancels his pay.
A thousand dulcimers are carved   25
By the one called Double Thumb.
Winter cuts us down
Like a coach. Spits snow.
Horses flinch

Against the cold spurs in the sky.   30
We look for the oak
Who loves our company
More than other oaks.
The loveliest beds
Are left undone.   35
Hope is a pillow
Hold on.

WILLIAM CARPENTER   (b. 1940)

Rain   (1985)

A man stood in the rain outside his house.
Pretty soon, the rain soaked through
his jacket and shirt. He might have
gone in, but he wanted to be wet, to be
really wet, so that it finally got through   5
his skin and began raining on the rooftops
of the small city that the man always carried
inside him, a city where it hadn't rained
for thirty years, only now the sky darkened
and tremendous drops fell in the thick dust   10
of the streets. The man's wife knocked
on the window, trying to call him in.
She twirled one finger around her ear
to sign that he was crazy, that he'd
get sick again, standing in street clothes   15
in a downpour. She put the finger in her mouth
like a thermometer. She formed the word *idiot*
with her lips, and, always, when she said that
he would give in. But now he stood there.
His whole life he'd wanted to give something,   20
to sacrifice. At times he'd felt like coming up
to people on the street, offering his blood.
Here, you look like you need blood. Take mine.
Now he could feel the people of his city
waking as if from a long drought. He could feel   25
them leaving their houses and jobs, standing
with their heads up and their mouths open,
and the little kids taking their clothes off
and lying on their bellies in the streams
and puddles formed by the new rain that the man   30

made himself, not by doing anything, but standing
there while the rain soaked through his clothes.
He could see his wife and his own kids
staring from the window, the younger kid
laughing at his crazy father, the older one   35
sad, almost in tears, and the dog, Ossian—
but the man wanted to drown the city in rain.
He wanted the small crowded apartments
and the sleazy taverns to empty their people
into the streets. He wanted a single man with   40
an umbrella to break out dancing the same way
Gene Kelly danced in *Singing in the Rain*,[1]
then another man, and more, until the whole
city was doing turns and pirouettes with their
canes or umbrellas, first alone, then taking   45
each other by the arm and waist, forming a larger
and larger circle in the square, and not
to any music but to the percussion of the rain
on the roof of his own house. And if there were
a woman among the dancers, a woman in a flowery   50
print skirt, a woman wetter and happier and more
beautiful than the rest, may this man be
forgiven for falling in love on a spring
morning in the democracy of the rain, may
he be forgiven for letting his family think   55
this is just what to expect from someone who
is every day older and more eccentric, may he
be forgiven for evading his responsibilities,
for growing simple in the middle of his life, for
ruining his best pants and his one decent tie.   60

---

[1] 1952 movie musical.

DRAMA

SYLVIA PLATH (1932–1963)

Sylvia Plath was born in Boston. Her first poem was published when she was eight; by the time she was seventeen, she was regularly sending poems and stories out to magazines. After graduating from Smith College, Plath went to England to study at Cambridge and there married poet Ted Hughes; they had two children. Plath tried college teaching but found that it left no time for writing. Three Women *was first broadcast on BBC radio in London in September 1963. Plath committed suicide five months later. Among her writings are the poetry collection* The Colossus *(1960), the autobiographical novel* The Bell Jar *(1963), and a number of books published posthumously: a story and nonfiction collection,* Johnny Panic and the Bible of Dreams, The Journals of Sylvia Plath, *and three volumes of poetry,* Ariel, Crossing the Water, *and* Winter Trees, *now included in* The Collected Poems.

Three Women
A Poem for Three Voices   (1962)

Setting: A Maternity Ward and round about

First Voice.
I am slow as the world. I am very patient,
Turning through my time, the suns and stars
Regarding me with attention.
The moon's concern is more personal:
She passes and repasses, luminous as a nurse.   5
Is she sorry for what will happen? I do not think so.
She is simply astonished at fertility.

When I walk out, I am a great event.
I do not have to think, or even rehearse.
What happens in me will happen without attention.   10
The pheasant stands on the hill;
He is arranging his brown feathers.

I cannot help smiling at what it is I know.
Leaves and petals attend me. I am ready.

Second Voice.
When I first saw it, the small red seep, I did not believe it.   15
I watched the men walk about me in the office. They were so flat!
There was something about them like cardboard, and now I had caught
     it,
That flat, flat, flatness from which ideas, destructions,
Bulldozers, guillotines, white chambers of shrieks proceed,   20
Endlessly proceed—and the cold angels, the abstractions.
I sat at my desk in my stockings, my high heels,

And the man I work for laughed: 'Have you seen something awful?
You are so white, suddenly.' And I said nothing.
I saw death in the bare trees, a deprivation.   25
I could not believe it. Is it so difficult
For the spirit to conceive a face, a mouth?
The letters proceed from these black keys, and these black keys proceed
From my alphabetical fingers, ordering parts,

Parts, bits, cogs, the shining multiples.   30
I am dying as I sit. I lose a dimension.
Trains roar in my ears, departures, departures!
The silver track of time empties into the distance,
The white sky empties of its promise, like a cup.
These are my feet, these mechanical echoes.   35
Tap, tap, tap, steel pegs. I am found wanting.

This is a disease I carry home, this is a death.
Again, this is a death. Is it the air,
The particles of destruction I suck up? Am I a pulse
That wanes and wanes, facing the cold angel?   40
Is this my lover then? This death, this death?
As a child I loved a lichen-bitten name.
Is this the one sin then, this old dead love of death?

Third Voice.
I remember the minute when I knew for sure.
The willows were chilling,   45
The face in the pool was beautiful, but not mine—
It had a consequential look, like everything else,
And all I could see was dangers: doves and words,
Stars and showers of gold—conceptions, conceptions!
I remember a white, cold wing   50

And the great swan, with its terrible look,
Coming at me, like a castle, from the top of the river.
There is a snake in swans.
He glided by; his eye had a black meaning.
I saw the world in it—small, mean and black,   55
Every little word hooked to every little word, and act to act.
A hot blue day had budded into something.

I wasn't ready. The white clouds rearing
Aside were dragging me in four directions.
I wasn't ready.   60
I had no reverence.
I thought I could deny the consequence—
But it was too late for that. It was too late, and the face
Went on shaping itself with love, as if I was ready.

Second Voice.
It is a world of snow now. I am not at home.   65
How white these sheets are. The faces have no features.
They are bald and impossible, like the faces of my children,
Those little sick ones that elude my arms.
Other children do not touch me: they are terrible.
They have too many colors, too much life. They are not quiet,   70
Quiet, like the little emptinesses I carry.

I have had my chances. I have tried and tried.
I have stitched life into me like a rare organ,
And walked carefully, precariously, like something rare.
I have tried not to think too hard. I have tried to be natural. 75
I have tried to be blind in love, like other women,
Blind in my bed, with my dear blind sweet one,
Not looking, through the thick dark, for the face of another.

I did not look. But still the face was there,
The face of the unborn one that loved its perfections,   80
The face of the dead one that could only be perfect
In its easy peace, could only keep holy so.
And then there were other faces. The faces of nations,
Governments, parliaments, societies,
The faceless faces of important men.   85

It is these men I mind:
They are so jealous of anything that is not flat! They are jealous gods

That would have the whole world flat because they are.
I see the Father conversing with the Son.
Such flatness cannot but be holy.   90
'Let us make a heaven,' they say.
'Let us flatten and launder the grossness from these souls.'

First Voice.

I am calm. I am calm. It is the calm before something awful:
The yellow minute before the wind walks, when the leaves
Turn up their hands, their pallors. It is so quiet here.   95
The sheets, the faces, are white and stopped, like clocks.
Voices stand back and flatten. Their visible hieroglyphs
Flatten to parchment screens to keep the wind off.
They paint such secrets in Arabic, Chinese!

I am dumb and brown. I am a seed about to break.   100
The browness is my dead self, and it is sullen:
It does not wish to be more, or different.
Dusk hoods me in blue now, like a Mary.
O color of distance and forgetfulness!—
When will it be, the second when Time breaks   105
And eternity engulfs it, and I drown utterly?

I talk to myself, myself only, set apart—
Swabbed and lurid with disinfectants, sacrificial.
Waiting lies heavy on my lids. It lies like sleep,
Like a big sea. Far off, far off, I feel the first wave tug   110
Its cargo of agony toward me, inescapable, tidal.
And I, a shell, echoing on this white beach
Face the voices that overwhelm, the terrible element.

Third Voice.

I am a mountain now, among mountainy women.
The doctors move among us as if our bigness   115
Frightened the mind. They smile like fools.
They are to blame for what I am, and they know it.
They hug their flatness like a kind of health.
And what if they found themselves surprised, as I did?
They would go mad with it.   120

And what if two lives leaked between my thighs?
I have seen the white clean chamber with its instruments.
It is a place of shrieks. It is not happy.

'This is where you will come when you are ready.'
The night lights are flat red moons. They are dull with blood.   125
I am not ready for anything to happen.
I should have murdered this, that murders me.

First Voice.

There is no miracle more cruel than this.
I am dragged by the horses, the iron hooves.
I last. I last it out. I accomplish a work.   130
Dark tunnel, through which hurtle the visitations,
The visitations, the manifestations, the startled faces.
I am the center of an atrocity.
What pains, what sorrows must I be mothering?

Can such innocence kill and kill? It milks my life.   135
The trees wither in the street. The rain is corrosive.
I taste it on my tongue, and the workable horrors,
The horrors that stand and idle, the slighted godmothers
With their hearts that tick and tick, with their satchels of instruments.
I shall be a wall and a roof, protecting.   140
I shall be a sky and a hill of good: O let me be!

A power is growing on me, an old tenacity.
I am breaking apart like the world. There is this blackness,
This ram of blackness. I fold my hands on a mountain.
The air is thick. It is thick with this working.   145
I am used. I am drummed into use.
My eyes are squeezed by this blackness.
I see nothing.

Second Voice.

I am accused. I dream of massacres.
I am a garden of black and red agonies. I drink them,   150
Hating myself, hating and fearing. And now the world conceives
Its end and runs toward it, arms held out in love.
It is a love of death that sickens everything.
A dead sun stains the newsprint. It is red.
I lose life after life. The dark earth drinks them.   155

She is the vampire of us all. So she supports us,
Fattens us, is kind. Her mouth is red.
I know her. I know her intimately—
Old winter-face, old barren one, old time bomb.

Men have used her meanly. She will eat them.   160
Eat them, eat them, eat them in the end.
The sun is down. I die. I make a death.

First Voice.

Who is he, this blue, furious boy,
Shiny and strange, as if he had hurtled from a star?
He is looking so angrily!   165
He flew into the room, a shriek at his heel.
The blue color pales. He is human after all.
A red lotus opens in its bowl of blood;
They are stitching me up with silk, as if I were a material.

What did my fingers do before they held him?   170
What did my heart do, with its love?
I have never seen a thing so clear.
His lids are like the lilac-flower
And soft as a moth, his breath.
I shall not let go.   175
There is no guile or warp in him. May he keep so.

Second Voice.

There is the moon in the high window. It is over.
How winter fills my soul! And that chalk light
Laying its scales on the windows, the windows of empty offices,
Empty schoolrooms, empty churches. O so much emptiness!   180
There is this cessation. This terrible cessation of everything.
These bodies mounded around me now, these polar sleepers—
What blue, moony ray ices their dreams?

I feel it enter me, cold, alien, like an instrument.
And that mad, hard face at the end of it, that O-mouth   190
Open in its gape of perpetual grieving.
It is she that drags the blood-black sea around
Month after month, with its voices of failure.
I am helpless as the sea at the end of her string.
I am restless. Restless and useless. I, too, create corpses.   195

I shall move north. I shall move into a long blackness.
I see myself as a shadow, neither man nor woman,
Neither a woman, happy to be like a man, nor a man
Blunt and flat enough to feel no lack. I feel a lack.
I hold my fingers up, ten white pickets.   200

See, the darkness is leaking from the cracks.
I cannot contain it. I cannot contain my life.

I shall be a heroine of the peripheral.
I shall not be accused by isolate buttons,
Holes in the heels of socks, the white mute faces   205
Of unanswered letters, coffined in a letter case.
I shall not be accused, I shall not be accused.
The clock shall not find me wanting, nor these stars
That rivet in place abyss after abyss.

Third Voice.
I see her in my sleep, my red, terrible girl.   210
She is crying through the glass that separates us.
She is crying, and she is furious.
Her cries are hooks that catch and grate like cats.
It is by these hooks she climbs to my notice.
She is crying at the dark, or at the stars   215
That at such a distance from us shine and whirl.

I think her little head is carved in wood,
A red, hard wood, eyes shut and mouth wide open.
And from the open mouth issue sharp cries
Scratching at my sleep like arrows,   220
Scratching at my sleep, and entering my side.
My daughter has no teeth. Her mouth is wide.
It utters such dark sounds it cannot be good.

First Voice.
What is it that flings these innocent souls at us?
Look, they are so exhausted, they are all flat out   225
In their canvas-sided cots, names tied to their wrists,
The little silver trophies they've come so far for.
There are some with thick black hair, there are some bald.
Their skin tints are pink or sallow, brown or red;
They are beginning to remember their differences.   230

I think they are made of water; they have no expression.
Their features are sleeping, like light on quiet water.
They are the real monks and nuns in their identical garments.
I see them showering like stars on to the world—
On India, Africa, America, these miraculous ones,   235

These pure, small images. They smell of milk.
Their footsoles are untouched. They are walkers of air.

Can nothingness be so prodigal?
Here is my son.
His wide eye is that general, flat blue.   240
He is turning to me like a little, blind, bright plant.
One cry. It is the hook I hang on.
And I am a river of milk.
I am a warm hill.

Second Voice.
I am not ugly. I am even beautiful.   245
The mirror gives back a woman without deformity.
The nurses give back my clothes, and an identity.
It is usual, they say, for such a thing to happen.
It is usual in my life, and the lives of others.
I am one in five, something like that. I am not hopeless.   250
I am beautiful as a statistic. Here is my lipstick.

I draw on the old mouth.
The red mouth I put by with my identity
A day ago, two days, three days ago. It was a Friday.
I do not even need a holiday; I can go to work today.   255
I can love my husband, who will understand.
Who will love me through the blur of my deformity
As if I had lost an eye, a leg, a tongue.

And so I stand, a little sightless. So I walk
Away on wheels, instead of legs, they serve as well.   260
And learn to speak with fingers, not a tongue.
The body is resourceful.
The body of a starfish can grow back its arms
And newts are prodigal in legs. And may I be
As prodigal in what lacks me.   265

Third Voice.
She is a small island, asleep and peaceful,
And I am a white ship hooting: Goodbye, goodbye.
The day is blazing. It is very mournful.
The flowers in this room are red and tropical.
They have lived behind glass all their lives, they have been   270
    cared for tenderly.

Now they face a winter of white sheets, white faces.
There is very little to go into my suitcase.

There are the clothes of a fat woman I do not know.
There is my comb and brush. There is an emptiness.   275
I am so vulnerable suddenly.
I am a wound walking out of hospital.
I am a wound that they are letting go.
I leave my health behind. I leave someone
Who would adhere to me: I undo her fingers like bandages: I go.   280

Second Voice.
I am myself again. There are no loose ends.
I am bled white as wax, I have no attachments.
I am flat and virginal, which means nothing has happened,
Nothing that cannot be erased, ripped up and scrapped, begun again.
These little black twigs do not think to bud,   285
Nor do these dry, dry gutters dream of rain.
This woman who meets me in windows—she is neat.

So neat she is transparent, like a spirit.
How shyly she superimposes her neat self
On the inferno of African oranges, the heel-hung pigs.   290
She is deferring to reality.
It is I. It is I—
Tasting the bitterness between my teeth.
The incalculable malice of the everyday.

First Voice.
How long can I be a wall, keeping the wind off?   295
How long can I be
Gentling the sun with the shade of my hand,
Intercepting the blue bolts of a cold moon?
The voices of loneliness, the voices of sorrow
Lap at my back ineluctably.   300
How shall it soften them, this little lullaby?

How long can I be a wall around my green property?
How long can my hands
Be a bandage to his hurt, and my words
Bright birds in the sky, consoling, consoling?   305
It is a terrible thing

To be so open: it is as if my heart
Put on a face and walked into the world.

Third Voice.
Today the colleges are drunk with spring.
My black gown is a little funeral: 310
It shows I am serious.
The books I carry wedge into my side.
I had an old wound once, but it is healing.
I had a dream of an island, red with cries.
It was a dream, and did not mean a thing.   315

First Voice.
Dawn flowers in the great elm outside the house.
The swifts are back. They are shrieking like paper rockets.
I hear the sound of the hours
Widen and die in the hedgerows. I hear the moo of cows.
The colors replenish themselves, and the wet   320
Thatch smokes in the sun.
The narcissi open white faces in the orchard.

I am reassured. I am reassured.
These are the clear bright colors of the nursery,
The talking ducks, the happy lambs.   325
I am simple again. I believe in miracles.
I do not believe in those terrible children
Who injure my sleep with their white eyes, their fingerless hands.
They are not mine. They do not belong to me.

I shall meditate upon normality.   330
I shall meditate upon my little son.
He does not walk. He does not speak a word.
He is still swaddled in white bands.
But he is pink and perfect. He smiles so frequently.
I have papered his room with big roses,   335
I have painted little hearts on everything.

I do not will him to be exceptional.
It is the exception that interests the devil.
It is the exception that climbs the sorrowful hill
Or sits in the desert and hurts his mother's heart.   340
I will him to be common,

To love me as I love him,
And to marry what he wants and where he will.

Third Voice.
Hot noon in the meadows. The buttercups
Swelter and melt, and the lovers   345
Pass by, pass by.
They are black and flat as shadows.
It is so beautiful to have no attachments!
I am solitary as grass. What is it I miss?
Shall I ever find it, whatever it is?   350

The swans are gone. Still the river
Remembers how white they were.
It strives after them with its lights.
It finds their shapes in a cloud.
What is that bird that cries   355
With such sorrow in its voice?
I am young as ever, it says. What is it I miss?

Second Voice.
I am at home in the lamplight. The evenings are lengthening.
I am mending a silk slip: my husband is reading.
How beautifully the light includes these things.   360
There is a kind of smoke in the spring air,
A smoke that takes the parks, the little statues
With pinkness, as if a tenderness awoke,
A tenderness that did not tire, something healing.

I wait and ache. I think I have been healing.   365
There is a great deal else to do. My hands
Can stitch lace neatly on to this material. My husband
Can turn and turn the pages of a book.
And so we are at home together, after hours.
It is only time that weighs upon our hands.   370
It is only time, and that is not material.

The streets may turn to paper suddenly, but I recover
From the long fall, and find myself in bed,
Safe on the mattress, hands braced, as for a fall.
I find myself again. I am no shadow   375
Though there is a shadow starting from my feet. I am a wife.

The city waits and aches. The little grasses
Crack through stone, and they are green with life.

Study and Discussion Questions

1. Why are each of these three women in the hospital? What is the situation of each in regard to her pregnancy?
2. How does each of the three women women feel about herself? About her pregnancy?
3. What is the setting each of these women will return to?
4. How and why does the second voice compare herself to an office machine?
5. The first voice says "I am ready." What does the third speaker say about her readiness?
6. What colors characterize each voice?
7. Who or what does the second speaker consider responsible for her situation?
8. How and why are the first and third voices alike and unlike in their descriptions of their babies?
9. How does each of these women describe the actual experience of giving birth (or, in one case, death)?
10. How does each of the three women feel afterward?

Writing Exercises

1. Write a paragraph about the life of one (or all three) of these women a year later.
2. What images does each woman use to describe herself? How do these help add to your sense of who that character is and how she feels about herself?
3. Why do you suppose Plath intercuts the three monologues? If you were to read through everything the first voice says, then the second, then the third, how would this change your experience of the play?
4. The writer has arranged it so that, though we hear all three women, they do not speak to or hear each other. Why?

WILLIAM SHAKESPEARE   (1564–1616)*

The Tragedy of King Lear**   (1606)

DRAMATIS PERSONAE

Lear, King of Britain
King of France
Duke of Burgundy
Duke of Cornwall, husband to Regan
Duke of Albany, husband to Goneril
Earl of Kent
Earl of Gloucester
Edgar, son to Gloucester
Edmund, bastard son to Gloucester
Curan, a courtier
Oswald, steward to Goneril
Old Man, tenant to Gloucester
Doctor
Lear's Fool
A Captain, subordinate to Edmund
Gentlemen, attending on Cordelia
A Herald
Servants to Cornwall
Goneril
Regan   daughters to Lear
Cordelia
Knights attending on Lear, Officers,
    Messengers, Soldiers, Attendants

Scene: Britain

---

*A brief biography of William Shakespeare appears on page 174.
**Edition and notes by Russell Fraser.

ACT I

Scene I. [*King Lear's palace.*]

Enter Kent, Gloucester, and Edmund.

Kent. I thought the King had more affected[1] the Duke of Albany[2] than Cornwall.

Gloucester. It did always seem so to us; but now, in the division of the kingdom, it appears not which of the dukes he values most,   5 for equalities are so weighed that curiosity in neither can make choice of either's moiety.[3]

Kent. Is not this your son, my lord?

Gloucester. His breeding,[4] sir, hath been at my charge. I have so often blushed to acknowledge him that now I am brazed[5] to't.   10

Kent. I cannot conceive[6] you.

Gloucester. Sir, this young fellow's mother could; whereupon she grew round-wombed, and had indeed, sir, a son for her cradle   15 ere she had a husband for her bed. Do you smell a fault?

Kent. I cannot wish the fault undone, the issue[7] of it being so proper.[8]

Gloucester. But I have a son, sir, by order of law, some year elder than this, who yet is no dearer in my account:[9] though this knave[10]   20 came something saucily[11] to the world before he was sent for, yet was his mother fair, there was good sport at his making, and the whoreson[12] must be acknowledged. Do you know this noble   25 gentleman, Edmund?

Edmund. No, my lord.

---

[1] *affected* loved.

[2] *Albany* Albanacte, whose domain extended "from the river Humber to the point of Caithness" (Holinshed).

[3] *equalities . . . moiety* i.e., shares are so balanced against one another that careful examination by neither can make him wish the other's portion.

[4] *breeding* upbringing.

[5] *brazed* made brazen, hardened.

[6] *conceive* understand (pun follows).

[7] *issue* result (child).

[8] *proper* handsome.

[9] *account* estimation.

[10] *knave* fellow (without disapproval).

[11] *saucily* (1) insolently (2) lasciviously.

[12] *whoreson* fellow (lit., son of a whore).

Gloucester. My Lord of Kent. Remember him hereafter as my honorable friend.

30 **Edmund.** My services to your lordship.

Kent. I must love you, and sue[13] to know you better.

Edmund. Sir, I shall study deserving.

Gloucester. He hath been out[14] nine years, and away he shall again. The King is coming.

Sound a sennet.[15] Enter one bearing a coronet,[16] then King Lear, then the Dukes of Cornwall and Albany, next Goneril, Regan, Cordelia, and Attendants.

35 **Lear.** Attend the lords of France and Burgundy, Gloucester.

Gloucester. I shall, my lord.   *Exit [with Edmund].*

Lear. Meantime we shall express our darker purpose.[17]
Give me the map there. Know that we have divided
40 In three our kingdom; and 'tis our fast[18] intent
To shake all cares and business from our age,
Conferring them on younger strengths, while we
Unburthened crawl toward death. Our son of Cornwall,
And you our no less loving son of Albany,
45 We have this hour a constant will to publish[19]
Our daughters' several[20] dowers, that future strife
May be prevented[21] now. The Princes, France and Burgundy,
Great rivals in our youngest daughter's love,
Long in our court have made their amorous sojourn,
50 And here are to be answered. Tell me, my daughters
(Since now we will divest us both of rule,
Interest[22] of territory, cares of state),
Which of you shall we say doth love us most,
That we our largest bounty may extend

---

[13] *sue* entreat.

[14] *out* away, abroad.

[15] s.d. *sennet* set of notes played on a trumpet, signalizing the entrance or departure of a procession.

[16] s.d. *coronet* small crown, intended for Cordelia.

[17] *darker purpose* hidden intention.

[18] *fast* fixed.

[19] *constant will to publish* fixed intention to proclaim.

[20] *several* separate.

[21] *prevented* forestalled.

[22] *Interest* legal right.

Where nature doth with merit challenge.[23] Goneril,   55
Our eldest-born, speak first.

Goneril.   Sir, I love you more than word can wield[24] the matter;
Dearer than eyesight, space[25] and liberty;
Beyond what can be valued, rich or rare;
No less than life, with grace, health, beauty, honor;   60
As much as child e'er loved, or father found;
A love that makes breath[26] poor, and speech unable:[27]
Beyond all manner of so much[28] I love you.

Cordelia.   [*Aside*] What shall Cordelia speak? Love, and be silent.

Lear.   Of all these bounds, even from this line to this,   65
With shadowy forests, and with champains riched,[29]
With plenteous rivers, and wide-skirted meads,[30]
We make thee lady. To thine and Albany's issues[31]
Be this perpetual.[32] What says our second daughter,
Our dearest Regan, wife of Cornwall? Speak.   70

Regan.   I am made of that self mettle[33] as my sister,
And prize me at her worth.[34] In my true heart
I find she names my very deed of love;[35]
Only she comes too short, that[36] I profess
Myself an enemy to all other joys   75
Which the most precious square of sense professes,[37]
And find I am alone felicitate[38]
In your dear Highness' love.

Cordelia.   [*Aside*] Then poor Cordelia!
And yet not so, since I am sure my love's

---

[23] *nature . . . challenge* i.e., natural affection contends with desert for (or lays claim to) bounty.

[24] *wield* handle.

[25] *space* scope.

[26] *breath* language.

[27] *unable* impotent.

[28] *Beyond . . . much* beyond all these comparisons.

[29] *champains riched* enriched plains.

[30] *wide-skirted meads* extensive grasslands.

[31] *issues* descendants.

[32] *perpetual* in perpetuity.

[33] *self mettle* same material or temperament.

[34] *prize . . . worth* value me the same (imperative).

[35] *my . . . love* what my love really is (a legalism).

[36] *that* in that.

[37] *Which . . . professes* which the choicest estimate of sense avows.

[38] *felicitate* made happy.

80 More ponderous[39] than my tongue.

Lear. To thee and thine hereditary ever
Remain this ample third of our fair kingdom,
No less in space, validity,[40] and pleasure
Than that conferred on Goneril. Now, our joy,
85 Although our last and least;[41] to whose young love
The vines of France and milk[42] of Burgundy
Strive to be interest;[43] what can you say to draw
A third more opulent than your sisters? Speak.

Cordelia. Nothing, my lord.

90 **Lear.** Nothing?

Cordelia. Nothing.

Lear. Nothing will come of nothing. Speak again.

Cordelia. Unhappy that I am, I cannot heave
My heart into my mouth. I love your Majesty
95 According to my bond,[44] no more nor less.

Lear. How, how, Cordelia? Mend your speech a little,
Lest you may mar your fortunes.

Cordelia. Good my lord,
You have begot me, bred me, loved me, I
Return those duties back as are right fit,[45]
100 Obey you, love you, and most honor you.
Why have my sisters husbands, if they say
They love you all? Haply,[46] when I shall wed,
That lord whose hand must take my plight[47] shall carry
Half my love with him, half my care and duty.
105 Sure I shall never marry like my sisters,
To love my father all.

Lear. But goes thy heart with this?

Cordelia. Ay, my good lord.

Lear. So young, and so untender?

---

[39] *ponderous* weighty.

[40] *validity* value.

[41] *least* youngest, smallest.

[42] *milk* i.e., pastures.

[43] *interest* closely connected, as interested parties.

[44] *bond* i.e., filial obligation.

[45] *Return . . . fit* i.e., am correspondingly dutiful.

[46] *Haply* perhaps.

[47] *plight* troth plight.

Cordelia. So young, my lord, and true.

Lear. Let it be so, thy truth then be thy dower!   110
For, by the sacred radiance of the sun,
The mysteries of Hecate[48] and the night,
By all the operation of the orbs[49]
From whom we do exist and cease to be,
Here I disclaim all my paternal care,   115
Propinquity and property of blood,[50]
And as a stranger to my heart and me
Hold thee from this for ever. The barbarous Scythian,[51]
Or he that makes his generation messes[52]
To gorge his appetite, shall to my bosom   120
Be as well neighbored, pitied, and relieved,
As thou my sometime[53] daughter.

Kent.   Good my liege—

Lear. Peace, Kent!
Come not between the Dragon[54] and his wrath.
I loved her most, and thought to set my rest[55]   125
On her kind nursery.[56] Hence and avoid my sight!
So be my grave my peace, as here I give
Her father's heart from her! Call France. Who stirs?
Call Burgundy. Cornwall and Albany,
With my two daughters' dowers digest[57] the third;   130
Let pride, which she calls plainness, marry her.[58]
I do invest you jointly with my power,
Pre-eminence, and all the large effects
That troop with majesty.[59] Ourself,[60] by monthly course,
With reservation[61] of an hundred knights,   135
By you to be sustained, shall our abode

---

[48] *mysteries of Hecate* secret rites of Hecate (goddess of the infernal world, and of witchcraft).

[49] *operation of the orbs* astrological influence.

[50] *Propinquity and property of blood* relationship and common blood.

[51] *Scythian* (type of the savage).

[52] *makes his generation messes* eats his own offspring.

[53] *sometime* former.

[54] *Dragon* (1) heraldic device of Britain (2) emblem of ferocity.

[55] *set my rest* (1) stake my all (a term from the card game of primero) (2) find my rest.

[56] *nursery* care, nursing.

[57] *digest* absorb.

[58] *Let . . . her* i.e., let her pride be her dowry and gain her a husband.

[59] *effects/That troop with majesty* accompaniments that go with kingship.

[60] *Ourself* (the royal "we").

[61] *reservation* the action of reserving a privilege (a legalism).

Make with you by due turn. Only we shall retain
The name, and all th' addition[62] to a king. The sway,
Revènue, execution of the rest,
140 Belovèd sons, be yours; which to confirm,
This coronet[63] part between you.

Kent.   Royal Lear,
Whom I have ever honored as my king,
Loved as my father, as my master followed,
As my great patron thought on in my prayers—

145 **Lear.** The bow is bent and drawn; make from the shaft.[64]

Kent. Let it fall[65] rather, though the fork[66] invade
The region of my heart. Be Kent unmannerly
When Lear is mad. What wouldst thou do, old man?
Think'st thou that duty shall have dread to speak
150 When power to flattery bows? To plainness honor's bound
When majesty falls to folly. Reserve thy state,[67]
And in thy best consideration[68] check
This hideous rashness. Answer my life my judgment,[69]
Thy youngest daughter does not love thee least,
155 Nor are those empty-hearted whose low sounds
Reverb[70] no hollowness.[71]

Lear.   Kent, on thy life, no more!

Kent. My life I never held but as a pawn[72]
To wage[73] against thine enemies; nor fear to lose it,
Thy safety being motive.[74]

Lear.   Out of my sight!

160 **Kent.** See better, Lear, and let me still[75] remain
The true blank[76] of thine eye.

---

[62] *addition* titles and honors.

[63] *coronet* (the crown which was to have been Cordelia's).

[64] *make from the shaft* avoid the arrow.

[65] *fall* strike.

[66] *fork* forked head of the arrow.

[67] *Reserve thy state* retain your kingly authority.

[68] *best consideration* most careful reflection.

[69] *Answer . . . judgment* I will stake my life on my opinion.

[70] *Reverb* reverberate.

[71] *hollowness* (1) emptiness (2) insincerity.

[72] *pawn* stake in a wager.

[73] *wage* (1) wager (2) carry on war.

[74] *motive* moving cause.

[75] *still* always.

[76] *blank* the white spot in the center of the target (at which Lear should aim).

Lear. Now by Apollo—

Kent.   Now by Apollo, King,
Thou swear'st thy gods in vain.

Lear.   O vassal! Miscreant![77]
                    [Laying his hand on his sword.]

Albany, Cornwall. Dear sir, forbear!

Kent. Kill thy physician, and the fee bestow   165
Upon the foul disease. Revoke thy gift,
Or, whilst I can vent clamor[78] from my throat,
I'll tell thee thou dost evil.

Lear.   Hear me, recreant![79]
On thine allegiance,[80] hear me!
That thou hast sought to make us break our vows,   170
Which we durst never yet, and with strained[81] pride
To come betwixt our sentence[82] and our power,
Which nor our nature nor our place can bear,
Our potency made good,[83] take thy reward.
Five days we do allot thee for provision[84]   175
To shield thee from diseases[85] of the world,
And on the sixth to turn thy hated back
Upon our kingdom. If, on the tenth day following,
Thy banished trunk[86] be found in our dominions,
The moment is thy death. Away! By Jupiter,   180
This shall not be revoked.

Kent. Fare thee well, King. Sith[87] thus thou wilt appear,
Freedom lives hence, and banishment is here.
[To Cordelia] The gods to their dear shelter take thee, maid,
That justly think'st, and hast most rightly said.   185
[To Regan and Goneril] And your large speeches may your deeds
    approve,[88]

---

[77] *vassal! Miscreant!* base wretch! Misbeliever!.

[78] *vent clamor* utter a cry.

[79] *recreant* traitor.

[80] *On thine allegiance* (to forswear, which is to commit high treason).

[81] *strained* forced (and so excessive).

[82] *sentence* judgment, decree.

[83] *Our potency made good* my royal authority being now asserted.

[84] *for provision* for making preparation.

[85] *diseases* troubles.

[86] *trunk* body.

[87] *Sith* since.

[88] *approve* prove true.

That good effects[89] may spring from words of love.
Thus Kent, O Princes, bids you all adieu;
He'll shape his old course[90] in a country new.

Exit.

Flourish.[91] Enter Gloucester, with France and Burgundy; Attendants.

190 **Gloucester.**   Here's France and Burgundy, my noble lord.

Lear.   My Lord of Burgundy,
We first address toward you, who with this king
Hath rivaled for our daughter. What in the least
Will you require in present[92] dower with her,
Or cease your quest of love?

195 **Burgundy.**   Most royal Majesty,
I crave no more than hath your Highness offered,
Nor will you tender[93] less.

Lear.   Right noble Burgundy,
When she was dear[94] to us, we did hold her so;
But now her price is fallen. Sir, there she stands.
200 If aught within that little seeming substance,[95]
Or all of it, with our displeasure pieced,[96]
And nothing more, may fitly like[97] your Grace,
She's there, and she is yours.

Burgundy.   I know no answer.

Lear.   Will you, with those infirmities she owes,[98]
205 Unfriended, new adopted to our hate,
Dow'red with our curse, and strangered[99] with our oath,
Take her, or leave her?

Burgundy.   Pardon me, royal sir.
Election makes not up[100] on such conditions.

Lear.   Then leave her, sir; for, by the pow'r that made me,

---

[89] *effects* results.
[90] *shape . . . course* pursue his customary way.
[91] s.d. *Flourish* trumpet fanfare.
[92] *present* immediate.
[93] *tender* offer.
[94] *dear* (1) beloved (2) valued at a high price.
[95] *little seeming substance* person who is (1) inconsiderable (2) outspoken.
[96] *pieced* added to it.
[97] *fitly like* please by its fitness.
[98] *owes* possesses.
[99] *strangered* made a stranger.
[100] *Election makes not up* no one can choose.

I tell you all her wealth. *[To France.]* For you, great King, 210
I would not from your love make such a stray
To[101] match you where I hate; therefore beseech[102] you
T' avert your liking a more worthier way[103]
Than on a wretch whom nature is ashamed
Almost t' acknowledge hers.

France.   This is most strange, 215
That she whom even but now was your best object,[104]
The argument[105] of your praise, balm of your age,
The best, the dearest, should in this trice of time
Commit a thing so monstrous to dismantle[106]
So many folds of favor. Sure her offense 220
Must be of such unnatural degree
That monsters it,[107] or your fore-vouched[108] affection
Fall into taint;[109] which to believe of her
Must be a faith that reason without miracle
Should never plant in me.[110]

Cordelia.   I yet beseech your Majesty, 225
If for[111] I want that glib and oily art
To speak and purpose not,[112] since what I well intend
I'll do't before I speak, that you make known
It is no vicious blot, murder, or foulness,
No unchaste actionor dishonored step, 230
That hath deprived me of your grace and favor;
But even for want of that for which I am richer,
A still-soliciting[113] eye, and such a tongue
That I am glad I have not, though not to have it
Hath lost[114] me in your liking.

---

[101] *make such a stray/To* stray so far as to.

[102] *beseech* I beseech.

[103] *avert . . . way* turn your affections from her and bestow them on a better person.

[104] *best object* i.e., the one you loved most.

[105] *argument* subject.

[106] *dismantle* strip off.

[107] *That monsters it* as makes it monstrous, unnatural.

[108] *forevouched* previously sworn.

[109] *Fall into taint* must be taken as having been unjustified all along i.e., Cordelia was unworthy of your love from the first.

[110] *reason . . . me* my reason would have to be supported by a miracle to make me believe.

[111] *for* because.

[112] *purpose not* not mean to do what I promise.

[113] *still-soliciting* always begging.

[114] *lost* ruined.

235 **Lear.** Better thou
Hadst not been born than not t' have pleased me better.

France. Is it but this? A tardiness in nature[115]
Which often leaves the history unspoke[116]
That it intends to do. My Lord of Burgundy,
240 What say you[117] to the lady? Love's not love
When it is mingled with regards[118] that stands
Aloof from th' entire point.[119] Will you have her?
She is herself a dowry.

Burgundy. Royal King,
Give but that portion which yourself proposed,
245 And here I take Cordelia by the hand,
Duchess of Burgundy.

Lear. Nothing. I have sworn. I am firm.

Burgundy. I am sorry then you have so lost a father
That you must lose a husband.

Cordelia. Peace be with Burgundy.
250 Since that respects of fortune[120] are his love,
I shall not be his wife.

France. Fairest Cordelia, that art most rich being poor,
Most choice forsaken, and most loved despised,
Thee and thy virtues here I seize upon.
255 Be it lawful I take up what's cast away.
Gods, gods! 'Tis strange that from their cold'st neglect
My love should kindle to inflamed respect.[121]
Thy dow'rless daughter, King, thrown to my chance,[122]
Is Queen of us, of ours, and our fair France.
260 Not all the dukes of wat'rish[123] Burgundy
Can buy this unprized precious[124] maid of me.
Bid them farewell, Cordelia, though unkind.
Thou losest here, a better where[125] to find.

---

[115] *tardiness in nature* natural reticence.
[116] *leaves the history unspoke* does not announce the action.
[117] *What say you* i.e., will you have.
[118] *regards* considerations (the dowry).
[119] *stands . . . point* have nothing to do with the essential question (love).
[120] *respects of fortune* mercenary considerations.
[121] *inflamed respect* more ardent affection.
[122] *chance* lot.
[123] *wat'rish* (1) with many rivers (2) weak, diluted.
[124] *unprized precious* unappreciated by others, and yet precious.
[125] *here . . . where* in this place, in another place.

Lear. Thou hast her, France; let her be thine, for we
Have no such daughter, nor shall ever see   265
That face of hers again. Therefore be gone,
Without our grace, our love, our benison[126]
Come, noble Burgundy.

Flourish. Exeunt [Lear, Burgundy, Cornwall, Albany, Gloucester, and
Attendants].

France. Bid farewell to your sisters.

Cordelia. The jewels of our father,[127] with washed[128] eyes   270
Cordelia leaves you. I know you what you are,
And, like a sister,[129] am most loath to call
Your faults as they are named.[130] Love well our father.
To your professèd[131] bosoms I commit him.
But yet, alas, stood I within his grace,   275
I would prefer[132] him to a better place.
So farewell to you both.

Regan. Prescribe not us our duty.

Goneril.   Let your study
Be to content your lord, who hath received you
At Fortune's alms.[133] You have obedience scanted,[134]   280
And well are worth the want that you have wanted.[135]

Cordelia. Time shall unfold what plighted[136] cunning hides,
Who covers faults, at last shame them derides.[137]
Well may you prosper.

France.   Come, my fair Cordelia.

Exit France and Cordelia.

Goneril. Sister, it is not little I have to say of what most nearly   285
appertains to us both. I think our father will hence tonight.

---

126 *benison* blessing.

127 *The jewels of our father* you creatures prized by our father.

128 *washed* (1) weeping (2) clear-sighted.

129 *like a sister* because I am a sister i.e., loyal, affectionate.

130 *as they are named* i.e., by their right and ugly names.

131 *professed* pretending to love.

132 *prefer* recommend.

133 *At Fortune's alms* as a charitable bequ6et from Fortune (and so, by extension,
as one beggared or cast down by Fortune).

134 *scanted* stinted.

135 *worth . . . wanted* deserve to be denied, even as you have denied.

136 *plighted* pleated, enfolded.

137 *Who . . . derides* those who hide their evil are finally exposed and shamed ("He
that hideth his sins, shall not prosper").

Regan. That's most certain, and with you; next month with us.

290 **Goneril.** You see how full of changes his age is. The observation we have made of it hath not been little. He always loved our sister most, and with what poor judgment he hath now cast her off appears too grossly.[138]

295 **Regan.** 'Tis the infirmity of his age; yet he hath ever but slenderly known himself.

Goneril. The best and soundest of his time[139] hath been but rash; then must we look from his age to receive not alone the imper-
300 fections of long-ingrafted[140] condition,[141] but therewithal[142] the unruly waywardness that infirm and choleric years bring with them.

Regan. Such unconstant starts[143] are we like to have from him as this of Kent's banishment.

305 **Goneril.** There is further compliment[144] of leave-taking between France and him. Pray you, let's hit[145] together; if our father carry authority with such disposition as he bears,[146] this last surrender[147] of his will but offend[148] us.

310 **Regan.** We shall further think of it.

Goneril. We must do something, and i' th' heat.[149]

Exeunt.

Scene II. [*The Earl of Gloucester's castle.*]

Enter Edmund [with a letter].

---

[138] *grossly* obviously.
[139] *of his time* period of his life up to now.
[140] *long-ingrafted* implanted for a long time.
[141] *condition* disposition.
[142] *therewithal* with them.
[143] *unconstant starts* impulsive whims.
[144] *compliment* formal courtesy.
[145] *hit* agree.
[146] *carry . . . bears* continues, and in such frame of mind, to wield the sovereign power.
[147] *last surrender* recent abdication.
[148] *offend* vex.
[149] *i' th' heat* while the iron is hot.

Edmund. Thou, Nature,[150] art my goddess; to thy law
My services are bound. Wherefore should I
Stand in the plague of custom,[151] and permit
The curiosity[152] of nations to deprive me,
For that[153] I am some twelve or fourteen moonshines[154]   5
Lag of[155] a brother? Why bastard? Wherefore base?
When my dimensions are as well compact,[156]
My mind as generous,[157] and my shape as true,
As honest[158] madam's issue? Why brand they us
With base? With baseness? Bastardy? Base? Base?   10
Who, in the lusty stealth of nature, take
More composition[159] and fierce[160] quality
Than doth, within a dull, stale, tired bed,
Go to th' creating a whole tribe of fops[161]
Got[162] 'tween asleep and wake? Well then,   15
Legitimate Edgar, I must have your land.
Our father's love is to the bastard Edmund
As to th' legitimate. Fine word, "legitimate."
Well, my legitimate, if this letter speed,[163]
And my invention[164] thrive, Edmund the base   20
Shall top th' legitimate. I grow, I prosper.
Now, gods, stand up for bastards.

Enter Gloucester.

Gloucester. Kent banished thus? and France in choler parted?
And the King gone tonight? prescribed[165] his pow'r?
Confined to exhibition?[166] All this done   25
Upon the gad?[167] Edmund, how now? What news?

---

[150] *Nature* (Edmund's conception of Nature accords with our description of a bastard as a natural child).

[151] *Stand . . . custom* respect hateful convention.

[152] *curiosity* nice distinctions.

[153] *For that* because.

[154] *moonshines* months.

[155] *Lag of* short of being (in age).

[156] *compact* framed.

[157] *generous* gallant.

[158] *honest* chaste.

[159] *composition* completeness.

[160] *fierce* energetic.

[161] *fops* fools.

[162] *Got* begot.

[163] *speed* prosper.

[164] *invention* plan.

[165] *prescribed* limited.

[166] *exhibition* an allowance or pension.

[167] *Upon the gad* on the spur of the moment (as if pricked by a gad or goad).

Edmund. So please your lordship, none.

Gloucester. Why so earnestly seek you to put up[168] that letter?

30 **Edmund.** I know no news, my lord.

Gloucester. What paper were you reading?

Edmund. Nothing, my lord.

Gloucester. No? What needed then that terrible dispatch[169] of it
35   into your pocket? The quality of nothing hath not such need to
hide itself. Let's see. Come, if it be nothing, I shall not need
spectacles.

Edmund. I beseech you, sir, pardon me. It is a letter from my
brother that I have not all o'er-read; and for so much as I have
40   perused, I find it not fit for your o'erlooking.[170]

Gloucester. Give me the letter, sir.

Edmund. I shall offend, either to detain or give it. The contents,
as in part I understand them, are to blame.[171]

45 **Gloucester.** Let's see, let's see.

Edmund. I hope, for my brother's justification, he wrote this but
as an essay or taste[172] of my virtue.

Gloucester. *(Reads)* "This policy and reverence[173] of age makes the
50   world bitter to the best of our times;[174] keeps our fortunes from
us till our oldness cannot relish[175] them. I begin to find an idle
and fond[176] bondage in the oppression of aged tyranny, who
sways, not as it hath power, but as it is suffered.[177] Come to me,
55   that of this I may speak more. If our father would sleep
till I waked him, you should enjoy half his revenue[178] for
ever, and live the beloved of your brother,   EDGAR."
Hum! Conspiracy? "Sleep till I waked him, you should enjoy half
his revenue." My son Edgar! Had he a hand to write this? A heart

---

[168] *put up* put away, conceal.

[169] *terrible dispatch* hasty putting away.

[170] *o'erlooking* inspection.

[171] *to blame* blameworthy.

[172] *essay or taste* test.

[173] *policy and reverence* policy of reverencing (hendiadys).

[174] *best of our times* best years of our lives (i.e., our youth).

[175] *relish* enjoy.

[176] *idle and fond* foolish.

[177] *who . . . suffered* which rules, not from its own strength, but from our allowance.

[178] *revenue* income.

and brain to breed it in? When came you to this? Who brought   60
it?

Edmund.   It was not brought me, my lord; there's the cunning of
it. I found it thrown in at the casement of my closet.[179]   65

Gloucester.   You know the character[180] to be your brother's?

Edmund.   If the matter were good, my lord, I durst swear it were
his; but in respect of that,[181] I would fain[182] think it were not.   70

Gloucester.   It is his.

Edmund.   It is his hand, my lord; but I hope his heart is not in
the contents.

Gloucester.   Has he never before sounded[183] you in this business?   75

Edmund.   Never, my lord. But I have heard him oft maintain it to
be fit that, sons at perfect[184] age, and fathers declined, the father
should be as ward to the son, and the son manage his revenue.

Gloucester.   O villain, villain! His very opinion in the letter. Abhorred   80
villain, unnatural, detested,[185] brutish villain; worse than brutish!
Go, sirrah,[186] seek him. I'll apprehend him. Abominable villain!
Where is he?

Edmund.   I do not well know, my lord. If it shall please you to   85
suspend your indignation against my brother till you can derive
from him better testimony of his intent, you should run a certain
course;[187] where, if you violently proceedst him, mistaking his   90
purpose, it would make a great gap[188] in your own honor and
shake in pieces the heart of his obedience. I dare pawn down[189]
my life for him that he hath writ this to feel[190] my affection to
your honor, and to no other pretense of danger.[191]   95

Gloucester.   Think you so?

---

[179] *casement of my closet* window of my room.
[180] *character* handwriting.
[181] *in respect of that* in view of what it is.
[182] *fain* prefer to.
[183] *sounded* sounded you out.
[184] *perfect* mature.
[185] *detested* detestable.
[186] *sirrah* sir (familiar form of address).
[187] *run a certain course* i.e., proceed safely, know where you are going.
[188] *gap* breach.
[189] *pawn down* stake.
[190] *feel* test.
[191] *pretense of danger* dangerous purpose.

Edmund. If your honor judge it meet,[192] I will place you where
you shall hear us confer of this, and by an auricular assurance[193]
100 have your satisfaction, and that without any further delay than
this very evening.

Gloucester. He cannot be such a monster.

Edmund. Nor is not, sure.

Gloucester. To his father, that so tenderly and entirely loves him.
105 Heaven and earth! Edmund, seek him out; wind me into him,[194]
I pray you; frame[195] the business after your own wisdom. I would
unstate myself to be in a due resolution.[196]

110 **Edmund.** I will seek him, sir, presently;[197] convey[198] the business
as I shall find means, and acquaint you withal.[199]

Gloucester. These late[200] eclipses in the sun and moon portend no
good to us. Though the wisdom of Nature[201] can reason[202] it thus
115 and thus, yet Nature finds itself scourged by the sequent effects.[203]
Love cools, frienship falls off,[204] brothers divide. In cities, mutinies;[205] in countries, discord; in palaces, treason; and the bond
cracked 'twixt son and father. This villain of mine comes under
120 the prediction,[206] there's son against father; the King falls from
bias of nature,[207] there's father against child. We have seen the
best of our time.[208] Machinations, hollowness,[209] treachery, and
all ruinous disorders follow us disquietly[210] to our graves. Find
125 out this villain, Edmund; it shall lose thee nothing.[211] Do it

---

[192] *meet* fit.

[193] *auricular assurance* proof heard with your own ears.

[194] *wind me into him* insinuate yourself into his confidence for me.

[195] *frame* manage.

[196] *unstate . . . resolution* forfeit my earldom to know the truth.

[197] *presently* at once.

[198] *convey* manage.

[199] *withal* with it.

[200] *late* recent.

[201] *wisdom of Nature* scientific learning.

[202] *reason* explain.

[203] *yet . . . effects* nonetheless our world is punished with subsequent disasters.

[204] *falls off* revolts.

[205] *mutinies* riots.

[206] *This . . . prediction* i.e., my son's villainous behavior is included in these portents, and bears them out.

[207] *bias of nature* natural inclination (the metaphor is from the game of bowls).

[208] *best of our time* our best days.

[209] *hollowness* insincerity.

[210] *disquietly* unquietly.

[211] *it . . . nothing* you will not lose by it.

carefully. And the noble and true-hearted Kent banished; his offense, honesty. 'Tis strange.

Exit.

Edmund. This is the excellent foppery[212] of the world, that when we are sick in fortune, often the surfeits of our own behavior,[213]   130 we make guilty of our disasters the sun, the moon, and stars; as if we were villains on[214] necessity; fools by heavenly compulsion; knaves, thieves, and treachers by spherical predominance;[215] drunkards, liars, and adulterers by an enforced obedience of planetary   135 influence;[216] and all that we are evil in, by a divine thrusting on.[217] An admirable evasion of whoremaster[218] man, to lay his goatish[219] disposition on the charge of a star. My father compounded[220] with my mother under the Dragon's Tail,[221] and my   140 nativity[222] was under Ursa Major,[223] so that it follows I am rough and lecherous. Fut![224] I should have been that[225] I am, had the maidenliest star in the firmament twinkled on my bastardizing. Edgar—

Enter Edgar.

and pat he comes, like the catastrophe[226] of the old comedy. My   145 cue is villainous melancholy, with a sigh like Tom o' Bedlam.[227]— O, these eclipses do portend these divisions. Fa, sol, la, mi.[228]

Edgar. How now, brother Edmund; what serious contemplation are   150 you in?

Edmund. I am thinking, brother, of a prediction I read this other day, what should follow these eclipses.

---

[212] *foppery* folly.

[213] *often . . . behavior* often caused by our own excesses.

[214] *on* of.

[215] *treachers . . . predominance* traitors because of the ascendancy of a particular star at our birth.

[216] *by . . . influence* because we had to submit to the influence of our star.

[217] *divine thrusting on* supernatural compulsion.

[218] *whoremaster* lecherous.

[219] *goatish* lascivious.

[220] *compounded* (1) made terms (2) formed (a child).

[221] *Dragon's Tail* the constellation Draco.

[222] *nativity* birthday.

[223] *Ursa Major* the Great Bear.

[224] *Fut!* 's foot (an impatient oath).

[225] *that* what.

[226] *catastrophe* conclusion.

[227] *My . . . Bedlam* I must be doleful, like a lunatic beggar out of Bethlehem (Bedlam) Hospital, the London madhouse.

[228] *Fa, sol, la, mi* (Edmund's humming of the musical notes is perhaps prompted by his use of the word "division," which describes a musical variation).

Edgar. Do you busy yourself with that?

155 **Edmund.** I promise you, the effects he writes of succeed[229] unhappily: as of unnaturalness[230] between the child and the parent, death, dearth, dissolutions of ancient amities,[231] divisions in state, menaces and maledictions against King and nobles, needless diffidences,[232] banishment of friends, dissipation of cohorts,[233] nuptial breaches, and I know not what.

160

Edgar. How long have you been a sectary astronomical?[234]

Edmund. Come, come, when saw you my father last?

165 **Edgar.** Why, the night gone by.

Edmund. Spake you with him?

Edgar. Ay, two hours together.

Edmund. Parted you in good terms? Found you no displeasure in him by word nor countenance?[235]

170 **Edgar.** None at all.

Edmund. Bethink yourself wherein you may have offended him; and at my entreaty forbear his presence[236] until some little time hath qualified[237] the heat of his displeasure, which at this instant so rageth in him that with the mischief of your person it would scarcely allay.[238]

175

Edgar. Some villain hath done me wrong.

Edmund. That's my fear, brother I pray you have a continent forbearance[239] till the speed of his rage goes slower; and, as I say, retire with me to my lodging, from whence I will fitly[240] bring you to hear my lord speak. Pray ye, go; there's my key. If you do stir abroad, go armed.

180

Edgar. Armed, brother?

---

[229] *succeed* follow.
[230] *unnaturalness* unkindness.
[231] *amities* friendships.
[232] *diffidences* distrusts.
[233] *dissipation of cohorts* falling away of supporters.
[234] *sectary astronomical* believer in astrology.
[235] *countenance* expression.
[236] *forbear his presence* keep away from him.
[237] *qualified* lessened.
[238] *with . . . allay* even an injury to you would not appease his anger.
[239] *have a continent forbearance* be restrained and keep yourself withdrawn.
[240] *fitly* at a fit time.

Edmund. Brother, I advise you to the best. Go armed. I am no 185
honest man if there be any good meaning toward you. I have
told you what I have seen and heard; but faintly, nothing like
the image and horror[241] of it. Pray you, away.

Edgar. Shall I hear from you anon?[242]   190

Edmund. I do serve you in this business.

Exit Edgar.

A credulous father, and a brother noble,
Whose nature is so far from doing harms
That he suspects none; on whose foolish honesty
My practices[243] ride easy. I see the business.   195
Let me, if not by birth, have lands by wit.
All with me's meet[244] that I can fashion fit.[245]

Exit.

Scene III. [*The Duke of Albany's palace.*]

Enter Goneril, and [Oswald, her] Steward.

Goneril. Did my father strike my gentleman for chiding of his
Fool?[246]

Oswald. Ay, madam.

Goneril. By day and night he wrongs me. Every hour
He flashes into one gross crime[247] or other   5
That sets us all at odds. I'll not endure it.
His knights grow riotous,[248] and himself upbraids us
On every trifle. When he returns from hunting,
I will not speak with him. Say I am sick,
If you come slack of former services,[249]   10
You shall do well; the fault of it I'll answer.[250]

---

241 *image and horror* true horrible picture.
242 *anon* in a little while.
243 *practices* plots.
244 *meet* proper.
245 *fashion fit* shape to my purpose.
246 *Fool* court jester.
247 *crime* offense.
248 *riotous* dissolute.
249 *come . . . services* are less serviceable to him than formerly.
250 *answer* answer for.

[Horns within.]

Oswald. He's coming, madam; I hear him.

Goneril. Put on what weary negligence you please,
You and your fellows. I'd have it come to question.[251]
15 If he distaste[252] it, let him to my sister,
Whose mind and mine I know in that are one,
Not to be overruled. Idle[253] old man,
That still would manage those authorities
That he hath given away. Now, by my life,
20 Old fools are babes again, and must be used
With checks as flatteries, when they are seen abused.[254]
Remember what I have said.

Oswald. Well, madam.

Goneril. And let his knights have colder looks among you.
What grows of it, no matter; advise your fellows so.
25 I would breed from hence occasions, and I shall,
That I may speak.[255] I'll write straight[256] to my sister
To hold my course. Go, prepare for dinner.

Exeunt.

Scene IV. *[A hall in the same.]*

Enter Kent [disguised].

Kent. If but as well I other accents borrow
That can my speech defuse,[257] my good intent
May carry through itself to that full issue[258]
For which I razed my likeness.[259] Now, banished Kent,
5 If thou canst serve where thou dost stand condemned,
So may it come,[260] thy master whom thou lov'st

---

[251] *come to question* be discussed openly.

[252] *distaste* dislike.

[253] *Idle* foolish.

[254] *With . . . abused* with restraints as well as soothing words when they are misguided.

[255] *breed . . . speak* find in this opportunities for speaking out.

[256] *straight* at once.

[257] *defuse* disguise.

[258] *full issue* perfect result.

[259] *razed my likeness* shaved off, disguised my natural appearance.

[260] *So may it come* so may it fall out.

Shall find thee full of labors.

Horns within.[261] *Enter Lear, [Knights] and Attendants.*

Lear. Let me not stay[262] a jot for dinner; go, get it ready. *[Exit an Attendant.]* How now, what art thou?   10

Kent. A man, sir.

Lear. What dost thou profess?[263] What wouldst thou with us?

Kent. I do profess[264] to be no less than I seem, to serve him truly that will put me in trust, to love him that is honest, to converse   15 with him that is wise and says little, to fear judgment,[265] to fight when I cannot choose, and to eat no fish.[266]

Lear. What art thou?

Kent. A very honest-hearted fellow, and as poor as the King.   20

Lear. If thou be'st as poor for a subject as he's for a king, thou art poor enough. What wouldst thou?

Kent. Service.

Lear. Who wouldst thou serve?   25

Kent. You.

Lear. Dost thou know me, fellow?

Kent. No, sir, but you have that in your countenance[267] which I would fain[268] call master.

Lear. What's that?   30

Kent. Authority.

Lear. What services canst thou do?

Kent. I can keep honest counsel,[269] ride, run, mar a curious tale in telling it,[270] and deliver a plain message bluntly. That which   35

---

[261] s.d. *within* offstage.

[262] *stay* wait.

[263] *What dost thou profess* what do you do.

[264] *profess* claim.

[265] *judgment* (by a heavenly or earthly judge).

[266] *eat no fish* i.e., (1) I am no Catholic, but a loyal Protestant (2) I am no weakling (3) I use no prostitutes.

[267] *countenance* bearing.

[268] *fain* like to.

[269] *honest counsel* honorable secrets.

[270] *mar . . . it* i.e., I cannot speak like an affected courtier ("curious" = "elaborate," as against "plain").

ordinary men are fit for, I am qualified in, and the best of me is
diligence.

Lear. How old art thou?

40 **Kent.** Not so young, sir, to love a woman for singing, nor so old
to dote on her for anything. I have years on my back forty-eight.

Lear. Follow me; thou shalt serve me. If I like thee no worse after
dinner, I will not part from thee yet. Dinner, ho, dinner! Where's
my knave?[271] my Fool? Go you and call my Fool hither.

[Exit an Attendant.]
Enter Oswald.

45 You, you, sirrah, where's my daughter?

Oswald. So please you—

Exit.

Lear. What says the fellow there? Call the clotpoll[272] back. *[Exit a
Knight.]* Where's my Fool? Ho, I think the world's asleep.

[Re-enter Knight.]

50 How now? Where's that mongrel?

Knight. He says, my lord, your daughter is not well.

Lear. Why came not the slave back to me when I called him?

55 **Knight.** Sir, he answered me in the roundest[273] manner, he would
not.

Lear. He would not?

Knight. My lord, I know not what the matter is; but to my judgment
your Highness is not entertained[274] with that ceremonious affection
60 as you were wont. There's a great abatement of kindness appears
as well in the general dependants[275] as in the Duke himself also
and your daughter.

Lear. Ha? Say'st thou so?

65 **Knight.** I beseech you pardon me, my lord, if I be mistaken; for
my duty cannot be silent when I think your Highness wronged.

---

[271] *knave* boy.
[272] *clotpoll* clodpoll, blockhead.
[273] *roundest* rudest.
[274] *entertained* treated.
[275] *dependants* servants.

Lear. Thou but rememb'rest[276] me of mine own conception.[277] I have perceived a most faint neglect[278] of late, which I have rather blamed as mine own jealous curiosity[279] than as a very pretense[280]   70
and purpose of unkindness. I will look further into't. But where's my Fool? I have not seen him this two days.

Knight. Since my young lady's going into France, sir, the Fool hath   75
much pined away.

Lear. No more of that; I have noted it well. Go you and tell my daughter I would speak with her. Go you, call hither my Fool.

[Exit an Attendant.]
Enter Oswald.

O, you, sir, you! Come you hither, sir. Who am I, sir?   80

Oswald. My lady's father.

Lear. "My lady's father"? My lord's knave, you whoreson dog, you slave, you cur!

Oswald. I am none of these, my lord; I beseech your pardon.   85

Lear. Do you bandy[281] looks with me, you rascal?
                                        [Striking him.]

Oswald. I'll not be strucken,[282] my lord.

Kent. Nor tripped neither, you base football[283] player.
                                    [Tripping up his heels.]

Lear. I thank thee, fellow. Thou serv'st me, and I'll love thee.   90

Kent. Come, sir, arise, away. I'll teach you differences.[284] Away, away. If you will measure your lubber's[285] length again, tarry; but away. Go to![286] Have you wisdom?[287] So.[288]
                                        [Pushes Oswald out.]

---

[276] *rememb'rest* remindest.

[277] *conception* idea.

[278] *faint neglect* i.e., "weary negligence" (I.iii.13).

[279] *mine own jealous curiosity* suspicious concern for my own dignity.

[280] *very pretense* actual intention.

[281] *bandy* exchange insolently (metaphor from tennis).

[282] *strucken* struck.

[283] *football* (a low game played by idle boys to the scandal of sensible men).

[284] *differences* (of rank).

[285] *lubber's* lout's.

[286] *Go to* (expression of derisive incredulity).

[287] *Have you wisdom* i.e., do you know what's good for you.

[288] *So* good.

95 **Lear.** Now, my friendly knave, I thank thee. There's earnest[289]of
    thy service.

    [Giving Kent money.]

Enter Fool.

Fool. Let me hire him too. Here's my coxcomb.[290]

    [Offering Kent his cap.]

Lear. How now, my pretty knave? How dost thou?

Fool. Sirrah, you were best[291] take my coxcomb.

100 **Kent.** Why, Fool?

Fool. Why? For taking one's part that's out of favor. Nay, an[292]
    thou canst not smile as the wind sits,[293] thou'lt catch cold shortly.
    There, take my coxcomb. Why, this fellow has banished[294] two
105 on's daughters, and did the third a blessing against his will. If
    thou follow him, thou must needs wear my coxcomb.—How now,
    Nuncle?[295] Would I had two coxcombs and two daughters.

Lear. Why, my boy?

110 **Fool.** If I gave them all my living,[296] I'd keep my coxcombs myself.
    There's mine; beg another of thy daughters.

Lear. Take heed, sirrah—the whip.

115 **Fool.** Truth's a dog must to kennel; he must be whipped out, when
    Lady the Brach[297] may stand by th' fire and stink.

Lear. A pestilent gall[298] to me.

Fool. Sirrah, I'll teach thee a speech.

Lear. Do.

120 **Fool.** Mark it, Nuncle.
    Have more than thou showest,
    Speak less than thou knowest,

---

[289] *earnest* money for services rendered.
[290] *coxcomb* professional fool's cap, shaped like a coxcomb.
[291] *you were best* you had better.
[292] *an* if.
[293] *smile . . . sits* ingratiate yourself with those in power.
[294] *banished* alienated (by making them independent).
[295] *Nuncle* (contraction of "mine uncle").
[296] *living* property.
[297] *Brach* bitch.
[298] *gall* sore.

Lend less than thou owest,[299]
Ride more than thou goest,[300]
Learn more than thou trowest,[301]   125
Set less than thou throwest;[302]
Leave thy drink and thy whore,
And keep in-a-door,
And thou shalt have more
Than two tens to a score.[303]   130

Kent. This is nothing, Fool.

Fool. Then 'tis like the breath of an unfeed[304] lawyer—you gave me nothing for't. Can you make no use of nothing, Nuncle?

Lear. Why, no, boy. Nothing can be made out of nothing.   135

Fool. [*To Kent*] Prithee tell him, so much the rent of his land comes to; he will not believe a Fool.

Lear. A bitter[305] Fool.   140

Fool. Dost thou know the difference, my boy, between a bitter Fool and a sweet one?

Lear. No, lad; teach me.

Fool.   That lord that counseled thee
      To give away thy land,   145
    Come place him here by me,
      Do thou for him stand.
    The sweet and bitter fool
      Will presently appear;
    The one in motley[306] here,   150
    The other found out[307] there.[308]

Lear. Dost thou call me fool, boy?

Fool. All thy other titles thou hast given away; that thou wast born with.

---

[299] *owest* ownest.

[300] *goest* walkest.

[301] *trowest* knowest.

[302] *Set . . . throwest* bet less than you play for (get odds from your opponent).

[303] *have . . . score* i.e., come away with more than you had (two tens, or twenty shillings, make a score, or one pound).

[304] *unfeed* unpaid for.

[305] *bitter* satirical.

[306] *motley* the drab costume of the professional jester.

[307] *found out* revealed.

[308] *there* (the Fool points at Lear, as a fool in the grain).

155 **Kent.** This is not altogether fool, my lord.

Fool. No, faith; lords and great men will not let me.[309] If I had a monopoly[310] out, they would have part on't. And ladies too, they will not let me have all the fool to myself; they'll be snatching.
160   Nuncle, give me an egg, and I'll give thee two crowns.

Lear. What two crowns shall they be?

Fool. Why, after I have cut the egg i' th' middle and eat up the meat, the two crowns of the egg. When thou clovest thy crown
165   i' th' middle and gav'st away both parts, thou bor'st thine ass on thy back o'er the dirt.[311] Thou hadst little wit in thy bald crown when thou gav'st thy golden one away. If I speak like myself[312] in this, let him be whipped[313] that first finds it so.
170   [*Singing*] Fools had ne'er less grace in a year,
        For wise men are grown foppish,
        And know not how their wits to wear,
        Their manners are so apish.[314]

175 **Lear.** When were you wont to be so full of songs, sirrah?

Fool. I have used[315] it, Nuncle, e'er since thou mad'st thy daughters thy mothers; for when thou gav'st them the rod, and put'st down thine own breeches,
    [*Singing*] Then they for sudden joy did weep,
180   And I for sorrow sung,
        That such a king should play bo-peep[316]
        And go the fools among.
    Prithee, Nuncle, keep a schoolmaster that can teach thy Fool to lie. I would fain learn to lie.

185 **Lear.** And[317] you lie, sirrah, we'll have you whipped.

Fool. I marvel what kin thou and thy daughters are. They'll have me whipped for speaking true; thou'lt have me whipped for lying; and sometimes I am whipped for holding my peace. I had rather

---

[309] *let me* (have all the folly to myself).

[310] *monopoly* (James I gave great scandal by granting to his "snatching" courtiers royal patents to deal exclusively in some commodity).

[311] *bor'st . . . dirt* (like the foolish and unnatural countryman in Aesop's fable).

[312] *like myself* like a Fool.

[313] *let him be whipped* i.e., let the man be whipped for a Fool who thinks my true saying to be foolish.

[314] *Fools . . . apish* i.e., fools were never in less favor than now, and the reason is that wise men, turning foolish, and not knowing how to use their intelligence, imitate the professional fools and so make them unnecessary.

[315] *used* practiced.

[316] *play bo-peep* (1) act like a child (2) blind himself.

[317] *And* if.

be any kind o' thing than a Fool, and yet I would not be thee, 190
Nuncle: thou hast pared thy wit o' both sides and left nothing i'
th' middle. Here comes one o' the parings.

Enter Goneril.

Lear. How now, daughter? What makes that frontlet[318] on? Methinks
you are too much of late i' th' frown. 195

Fool. Thou wast a pretty fellow when thou hadst no need to care
for her frowning. Now thou art an O without a figure.[319] I am
better than thou art now: I am a Fool, thou art nothing. [*To* 200
Goneril.] Yes, forsooth, I will hold my tongue. So your face bids
me, though you say nothing. Mum, mum,
    He that keeps nor crust nor crum,[320]
    Weary of all, shall want[321] some.
[*Pointing to Lear*] That's a shealed peascod.[322] 205

Goneril. Not only, sir, this your all-licensed[323] Fool,
But other[324] of your insolent retinue
Do hourly carp and quarrel, breaking forth
In rank[325] and not-to-be-endurèd riots. Sir,
I had thought by making this well known unto you 210
To have found a safe[326] redress, but now grow fearful,
By what yourself too late[327] have spoke and done,
That you protect this course, and put it on
By your allowance;[328] which if you should, the fault
Would not 'scape censure, nor the redresses sleep,[329] 215
Which, in the tender of[330] a wholesome weal,[331]
Might in their working do you that offense,
Which else were shame, that then necessity
Will call discreet proceeding.[332]

---

[318] *frontlet* frown (lit., ornamental band).
[319] *figure* digit, to give value to the cipher (Lear is a nought).
[320] *crum* soft bread inside the loaf.
[321] *want* lack.
[322] *shealed peascod* empty pea pod.
[323] *all-licensed* privileged to take any liberties.
[324] *other* others.
[325] *rank* gross.
[326] *safe* sure.
[327] *too late* lately.
[328] *put . . . allowance* promote it by your approval (*allowance* = approval).
[329] *redresses sleep* correction fail to follow.
[330] *tender of* desire for.
[331] *weal* state.
[332] *Might . . . proceeding* as I apply it, the correction might humiliate you; but the
need to take action cancels what would otherwise be unfilial conduct in me.

220 **Fool.** For you know, Nuncle,
The hedge-sparrow fed the cuckoo[333] so long
That it had it head bit off by it[334] young.
So out went the candle, and we were left darkling.[335]

Lear. Are you our daughter?

225 **Goneril.** Come, sir,
I would you would make use of your good wisdom
Whereof I know you are fraught[336] and put away
These dispositions[337] which of late transport you
From what you rightly are.

230 **Fool.** May not an ass know when the cart draws the horse? Whoop,
Jug,[338] I love thee!

Lear. Does any here know me? This is not Lear.
Does Lear walk thus? Speak thus? Where are his eyes?
Either his notion[339] weakens, or his discernings[340]
235 Are lethargied[341]—Ha! Waking? 'Tis not so.
Who is it that can tell me who I am?

Fool. Lear's shadow.

Lear. I would learn that; for, by the marks of sovereignty,[342] knowl-
240 edge, and reason, I should be false[343] persuaded I had daughters.

Fool. Which[344] they will make an obedient father.

Lear. Your name, fair gentlewoman?

Goneril. This admiration,[345] sir, is much o' th' savor[346]
Of other your[347] new pranks. I do beseech you
245 To understand my purposes aright.
As you are old and reverend, should be wise.

---

[333] *cuckoo* (who lays its eggs in the nests of other birds).
[334] *it* its.
[335] *darkling* in the dark.
[336] *fraught* endowed.
[337] *dispositions* moods.
[338] *Jug* Joan (? a quotation from a popular song).
[339] *notion* understanding.
[340] *discernings* faculties.
[341] *lethargied* paralyzed.
[342] *marks of sovereignty* i.e., tokens that Lear is king, and hence father to his daughters.
[343] *false* falsely.
[344] *Which* whom (Lear).
[345] *admiration* (affected) wonderment.
[346] *is much o' th' savor* smacks much.
[347] *other your* others of your.

Here do you keep a hundred knights and squires,
Men so disordered, so deboshed,[348] and bold,
That this our court, infected with their manners,
Shows[349] like a riotous inn. Epicurism[350] and lust   250
Makes it more like a tavern or a brothel
Than a graced[351] palace. The shame itself doth speak
For instant remedy. Be then desired[352]
By her, that else will take the thing she begs,   255
A little to disquantity your train,[353]
And the remainders[354] that shall still depend,[355]
To be such men as may besort[356] your age,
Which know themselves, and you.

Lear.   Darkness and devils!
Saddle my horses; call my train together.
Degenerate[357] bastard, I'll not trouble thee: 260
Yet have I left a daughter.

Goneril.   You strike my people, and your disordered rabble
Make servants of their betters.

Enter Albany.

Lear.   Woe, that too late repents. O, sir, are you come?
Is it your will? Speak, sir. Prepare my horses.   265
Ingratitude! thou marble-hearted fiend,
More hideous when thou show'st thee in a child
Than the sea-monster.

Albany.   Pray, sir, be patient

Lear.   Detested kite,[358] thou liest.
My train are men of choice and rarest parts,[359]   270
That all particulars of duty know,
And, in the most exact regard,[360] support

---

[348] *deboshed* debauched.

[349] *Shows* appears.

[350] *Epicurism* riotous living.

[351] *graced* dignified.

[352] *desired* requested.

[353] *disquantity your train* reduce the number of your dependents.

[354] *remainders* those who remain.

[355] *depend* attend on you.

[356] *besort* befit.

[357] *Degenerate* unnatural.

[358] *kite* scavenging bird of prey.

[359] *parts* accomplishments.

[360] *exact regard* strict attention to detail.

The worships[361] of their name. O most small fault,
How ugly didst thou in Cordelia show!
275 Which, like an engine,[362] wrenched my frame of nature
From the fixed place;[363] drew from my heart all love,
And added to the gall.[364] O Lear, Lear, Lear!
Beat at this gate that let thy folly in [*Striking his head.*]
And thy dear judgment out. Go, go, my people.

280 **Albany.**   My lord, I am guiltless, as I am ignorant
Of what hath moved you.

Lear.   It may be so, my lord.
Hear, Nature, hear; dear Goddess, hear:
Suspend thy purpose if thou didst intend
To make this creature fruitful.
285 Into her womb convey sterility,
Dry up in her the organs of increase,[365]
And from her derogate[366] body never spring
A babe to honor her. If she must teem,[367]
Create her child of spleen,[368] that it may live
290 And be a thwart disnatured[369] torment to her.
Let it stamp wrinkles in her brow of youth,
With cadent[370] tears fret[371] channels in her cheeks,
Turn all her mother's pains and benefits[372]
To laughter and contempt, that she may feel
295 How sharper than a serpent's tooth it is
To have a thankless child. Away, away!

                                                          Exit.

Albany.   Now, gods that we adore, whereof comes this?

Goneril.   Never afflict yourself to know the cause,
But let his disposition[373] have that scope
300 As[374] dotage gives it.

---

[361] *worships* honor.

[362] *engine* destructive contrivance.

[363] *wrenched . . . place* i.e., disordered my natural self.

[364] *gall* bitterness.

[365] *increase* childbearing.

[366] *derogate* degraded.

[367] *teem* conceive.

[368] *spleen* ill humor.

[369] *thwart disnatured* perverse unnatural.

[370] *cadent* falling.

[371] *fret* wear.

[372] *benefits* the mother's beneficent care of her child.

[373] *disposition* mood.

[374] *As* that.

Enter Lear.

Lear. What, fifty of my followers at a clap?[375]
Within a fortnight?

Albany.   What's the matter, sir?

Lear. I'll tell thee. [*To Goneril*] Life and death, I am ashamed
That thou hast power to shake my manhood[376] thus!
That these hot tears, which break from me perforce,[377]   305
Should make thee worth them. Blasts and fogs upon thee!
Th' untented woundings[378] of a father's curse
Pierce every sense about thee! Old fond[379] eyes,
Beweep[380] this cause again, I'll pluck ye out
And cast you, with the waters that you loose,[381]   310
To temper[382] clay. Yea, is it come to this?
Ha! Let it be so. I have another daughter,
Who I am sure is kind and comfortable.[383]
When she shall hear this of thee, with her nails
She'll flay thy wolvish visage. Thou shalt find   315
That I'll resume the shape[384] which thou dost think
I have cast off for ever.

Exit [Lear with Kent and Attendants].

Goneril.   Do you mark that?

Albany. I cannot be so partial, Goneril,
To the great love I bear you[385]—

Goneril. Pray you, content. What, Oswald, ho!   320
[*To the Fool*] You, sir, more knave than fool, after your master!

Fool. Nuncle Lear, Nuncle Lear, tarry. Take the Fool[386] with thee.
       A fox, when one has caught her,
       And such a daughter,
       Should sure to the slaughter,   325

---

[375] *at a clap* at one stroke.

[376] *shake my manhood* i.e., with tears.

[377] *perforce* involuntarily, against my will.

[378] *untented woundings* wounds too deep to be probed with a tent (a roll of lint).

[379] *fond* foolish.

[380] *Beweep* if you weep over.

[381] *loose* (1) let loose (2) lose, as of no avail.

[382] *temper* mix with and soften.

[383] *comfortable* ready to comfort.

[384] *shape* i.e., kingly role.

[385] *I cannot . . . you* i.e., even though my love inclines me to you, I must protest.

[386] *Fool* (1) the Fool himself (2) the epithet or character of "fool".

If my cap would buy a halter.[387]
So the Fool follows after.[388]

                                      Exit.

Goneril. This man hath had good counsel. A hundred knights!
330 'Tis politic[389] and safe to let him keep
At point[390] a hundred knights: yes, that on every   dream,
Each buzz,[391] each fancy, each complaint, dislike,
He may enguard[392] his dotage with their pow'rs
And hold our lives in mercy.[393] Oswald, I say!

Albany. Well, you may fear too far.

335 **Goneril.**   Safer than trust too far.
Let me still take away the harms I fear,
Not fear still to be taken.[394] I know his heart.
What he hath uttered I have writ my sister.
If she sustain him and his hundred knights,
When I have showed th' unfitness—

Enter Oswald.

340   How now, Oswald?
What, have you writ that letter to my sister?

Oswald. Ay, madam.

Goneril. Take you some company,[395] and away to horse.
Inform her full of my particular[396] fear,
345 And thereto add such reasons of your own
As may compact[397] it more. Get you gone,
And hasten your return. [*Exit Oswald.*] No, no, my lord,
This milky gentleness and course[398] of yours,
Though I condemn not,[399] yet under pardon,
350 You are much more attasked[400] for want of wisdom
Than praised for harmful mildness.[401]

[387-388] *halter, after* pronounced "hauter," "auter".
[389] *politic* good policy.
[390] *At point* armed.
[391] *buzz* rumor.
[392] *enguard* protect.
[393] *in mercy* at his mercy.
[394] *Not . . . taken* rather than remain fearful of being overtaken by them.
[395] *company* escort.
[396] *particular* own.
[397] *compact* strengthen.
[398] *milky . . . course* mild and gentle way (hendiadys).
[399] *condemn not* condemn it not.
[400] *attasked* taken to task, blamed.
[401] *harmful mildness* dangerous indulgence.

Albany. How far your eyes may pierce I cannot tell;
Striving to better, oft we mar what's well.

Goneril. Nay then—

Albany. Well, well, th' event.[402]   355

Exeunt.

Scene V. [*Court before the same.*]

Enter Lear, Kent, and Fool.

Lear. Go you before to Gloucester with these letters. Acquaint my
daughter no further with anything you know than comes from
her demand out of the letter.[403] If your diligence be not speedy,
I shall be there afore you.   5

Kent. I will not sleep, my lord, till I have delivered your letter.

Exit.

Fool. If a man's brains were in's heels, were't[404] not in danger of
kibes?[405]

Lear. Ay, boy.   10

Fool. Then I prithee be merry. Thy wit shall not go slipshod.[406]

Lear. Ha, ha, ha.

Fool. Shalt[407] see thy other daughter will use thee kindly;[408] for   15
though she's as like this as a crab's[409] like an apple, yet I can tell
what I can tell.

Lear. Why, what canst thou tell, my boy?

Fool. She will taste as like this as a crab does to a crab. Thou canst
tell why one's nose stands i' th' middle on's[410] face?   20

Lear. No.

---

[402] *th' event* i.e., we'll see what happens.

[403] *than . . . letter* than her reading of the letter brings her to ask.

[404] *were't* i.e., the brains.

[405] *kibes* chilblains.

[406] *Thy . . . slipshod* your brains shall not go in slippers (because you have no
brains to be protected from chilblains).

[407] *Shalt* thou shalt.

[408] *kindly* (1) affectionately (2) after her kind of nature.

[409] *crab* crab apple.

[410] *on's* of his.

Fool. Why, to keep one's eyes of[411] either side's nose, that what a man cannot smell out, he may spy into.

25 **Lear.** I did her wrong.

Fool. Canst tell how an oyster makes his shell?

Lear. No.

Fool. Nor I neither; but I can tell why a snail has a house.

30 **Lear.** Why?

Fool. Why, to put 's head in; not to give it away to his daughters, and leave his horns[412] without a case.

Lear. I will forget my nature.[413] So kind a father! Be my horses ready?

35 **Fool.** Thy asses are gone about 'em. The reason why the seven stars[414] are no moe[415] than seven is a pretty[416] reason.

Lear. Because they are not eight.

Fool. Yes indeed. Thou wouldst make a good Fool.

40 **Lear.** To take't again perforce![417] Monster ingratitude!

Fool. If thou wert my Fool, Nuncle, I'd have thee beaten for being old before thy time.

Lear. How's that?

45 **Fool.** Thou shouldst not have been old till thou hadst been wise.

Lear. O, let me not be mad, not mad, sweet heaven!
Keep me in temper;[418] I would not be mad!

[Enter Gentleman.]

How now, are the horses ready?

Gentleman. Ready, my lord.

50 **Lear.** Come, boy.

Fool. She that's a maid now, and laughs at my departure,

---

[411] *of* on.

[412] *horns* (1) snail's horns (2) cuckold's horns.

[413] *nature* paternal instincts.

[414] *seven stars* the Pleiades.

[415] *moe* more.

[416] *pretty* apt.

[417] *To . . . perforce* (1) of Goneril, who has forcibly taken away Lear's privileges; or (2) of Lear, who meditates a forcible resumption of authority.

[418] *in temper* sane.

Shall not be a maid long, unless things be cut shorter.[419]

Exeunt.

ACT II

Scene I. [*The Earl of Gloucester's castle.*]

Enter Edmund and Curan, severally.[420]

Edmund. Save[421] thee, Curan.

Curan. And you, sir. I have been with your father, and given him
notice that the Duke of Cornwall and Regan his duchess will be
here with him this night.   5

Edmund. How comes that?

Curan. Nay, I know not. You have heard of the news abroad? I
mean the whispered ones, for they are yet but ear-kissing arguments.[422]

Edmund. Not I. Pray you, what are they?   10

Curan. Have you heard of no likely;[423] wars toward,[424] 'twixt the
Dukes of Cornwall and Albany?

Edmund. Not a word.

Curan. You may do, then, in time. Fare you well, sir.   15

                                                            Exit.

Edmund. The Duke be here tonight? The better![425] best!
This weaves itself perforce[426] into my business.
My father hath set guard to take my brother,
And I have one thing of a queasy question[427]
Which I must act. Briefness[428] and Fortune, work!   20
Brother, a word; descend. Brother, I say!

---

[419] *She . . . shorter* the maid who laughs, missing the tragic implications of this
quarrel, will not have sense enough to preserve her virginity ("things" = penises).

[420] s.d. *severally* separatEly (from different entrances on stage).

[421] *Save* God save.

[422] *ear-kissing arguments* subjects whispered in the ear.

[423] *likely* probable.

[424] *toward* impending.

[425] *The better* so much the better.

[426] *perforce* necessarily.

[427] *of a queasy question* that requires delicate handling (to be "queasy" is to be on
the point of vomiting).

[428] *Briefness* speed.

Enter Edgar.

My father watches. O sir, fly this place.
Intelligence[429] is given where you are hid.
You have now the good advantage of the night.
25 Have you not spoken 'gainst the Duke of Cornwall?
He's coming hither, now i' th' night, i' th' haste,[430]
And Regan with him. Have you nothing said
Upon his party[431] 'gainst the Duke of Albany?
Advise yourself.[432]

Edgar.   I am sure on't,[433] not a word.

30 **Edmund.** I hear my father coming. Pardon me:
In cunning[434] I must draw my sword upon you.
Draw, seem to defend yourself; now quit you[435] well.
Yield! Come before my father! Light ho, here!
Fly, brother. Torches, torches!—So farewell.

Exit Edgar.

35 Some blood drawn on me would beget opinion[436]

[Wounds his arm]

Of my more fierce endeavor. I have seen drunkards
Do more than this in sport. Father, father!
Stop, stop! No help?

Enter Gloucester, and Servants with torches.

Gloucester. Now, Edmund, where's the villain?

40 **Edmund.** Here stood he in the dark, his sharp sword out,
Mumbling of wicked charms, conjuring the moon
To stand auspicious mistress.

Gloucester.   But where is he?

Edmund. Look, sir, I bleed.

Gloucester.   Where is the villain, Edmund?

Edmund. Fled this way, sir, when by no means he could—

---

[429] *Intelligence* information.
[430] *i' th' haste* in great haste.
[431] *Upon his party* censuring his enmity.
[432] *Advise yourself* reflect.
[433] *on't* of it.
[434] *In cunning* as a pretense.
[435] *quit you* acquit yourself.
[436] *beget opinion* create the impression.

Gloucester. Pursue him, ho! Go after.

[Exeunt some Servants.]

By no means what?   45

Edmund. Persuade me to the murder of your lordship;
But that I told him the revenging gods
'Gainst parricides did all the thunder bend;[437]
Spoke with how manifold and strong a bond
The child was bound to th' father. Sir, in fine,[438]   50
Seeing how loathly opposite[439] I stood
To his unnatural purpose, in fell[440] motion[441]
With his preparèd sword he charges home
My unprovided[442] body, latched[443] mine arm;
But when he saw my best alarumed[444] spirits   55
Bold in the quarrel's right,[445] roused to th' encounter,
Or whether gasted[446] by the noise I made,
Full suddenly he fled.

Gloucester.   Let him fly far.
Not in this land shall he remain uncaught;
And found—dispatch.[447] The noble Duke my master,   60
My worthy arch[448] and patron, comes tonight.
By his authority I will proclaim it,
That he which finds him shall deserve our thanks,
Bringing the murderous coward to the stake.
He that conceals him, death.[449]   65

Edmund. When I dissuaded him from his intent,
And found him pight[450] to do it, with curst[451] speech
I threatened to discover[452] him. He replied,

---

[437] *bend* aim.

[438] *in fine* finally.

[439] *loathly opposite* bitterly opposed.

[440] *fell* deadly.

[441] *motion* thrust (a term from fencing).

[442] *unprovided* unprotected.

[443] *latched* wounded (lanced).

[444] *best alarumed* wholly aroused.

[445] *Bold . . . right* confident in the rightness of my cause.

[446] *gasted* struck aghast.

[447] *dispatch* i.e., he will be killed.

[448] *arch* chief.

[449] *death* (the same elliptical form that characterizes "dispatch," 1.60).

[450] *pight* determined.

[451] *curst* angry.

[452] *discover* expose.

"Thou unpossessing[453] bastard, dost thou think,
70 If I would stand against thee, would the reposal[454]
Of any trust, virtue, or worth in thee
Make thy words faithed?[455] No. What I should deny—
As this I would, ay, though thou didst produce
My very character[456]—I'd turn it all
75 To thy suggestion,[457] plot, and damnèd practice.[458]
And thou must make a dullard of the world,[459]
If they not thought[460] the profits of my death
Were very pregnant[461] and potential spirits[462]
To make thee seek it."

Gloucester.   O strange and fastened[463] villain!
80 Would he deny his letter, said he? I never got[464] him.

Tucket[465] within.

Hark, the Duke's trumpets. I know not why he comes.
All ports[466] I'll bar; the villain shall not 'scape;
The Duke must grant me that. Besides, his picture
I will send far and near, that all the kingdom
85 May have due note of him; and of my land,
Loyal and natural[467] boy, I'll work the means
To make thee capable.[468]

Enter Cornwall, Regan, and Attendants.

Cornwall. How now, my noble friend! Since I came hither,
Which I can call but now, I have heard strange news.

90 **Regan.** If it be true, all vengeance comes too short
Which can pursue th' offender. How dost, my lord?

Gloucester. O madam, my old heart is cracked, it's cracked.

---

[453] *unpossessing* beggarly (landless).
[454] *reposal* placing.
[455] *faithed* believed.
[456] *character* handwriting.
[457] *suggestion* instigation.
[458] *practice* device.
[459] *make . . . world* think everyone stupid.
[460] *not thought* did not think.
[461] *pregnant* teeming with incitement.
[462] *potential spirits* powerful evil spirits.
[463] *fastened* hardened.
[464] *got* begot.
[465] s.d. *Tucket* (Cornwall's special trumpet call).
[466] *ports* exits, of whatever sort.
[467] *natural* (1) kind (filial) (2) illegitimate.
[468] *capable* able to inherit.

Regan. What, did my father's godson seek your life?
He whom my father named, your Edgar?

Gloucester. O lady, lady, shame would have it hid.   95

Regan. Was he not companion with the riotous knights
That tended upon my father?

Gloucester. I know not, madam. 'Tis too bad, too bad.

Edmund. Yes, madam, he was of that consort.[469]

Regan. No marvel then, though he were ill affected.[470]   100
'Tis they have put[471] him on the old man's death,
To have th' expense and waste[472] of his revenues.
I have this present evening from my sister
Been well informed of them, and with such cautions
That, if they come to sojourn at my house,   105
I'll not be there.

Cornwall.   Nor I, assure thee, Regan.
Edmund, I hear that you have shown your father
A childlike[473] office.

Edmund. It was my duty, sir.

Gloucester. He did bewray his practice,[474] and received   110
This hurt you see, striving to apprehend him.

Cornwall. Is he pursued?

Gloucester.   Ay, my good lord.

Cornwall. If he be taken, he shall never more
Be feared of doing[475] harm. Make your own purpose,
How in my strength you please.[476] For you, Edmund,   115
Whose virtue and obedience[477] doth this instant
So much commend itself, you shall be ours.
Natures of such deep trust we shall much need;
You we first seize on.

---

[469] *consort* company.

[470] *ill affected* disposed to evil.

[471] *put* set.

[472] *expense and waste* squandering.

[473] *childlike* filial.

[474] *bewray his practice* disclose his plot.

[475] *of doing* because he might do.

[476] *Make . . . please* use my power freely, in carrying out your plans for his capture.

[477] *virtue and obedience* virtuous obedience.

Edmund.   I shall serve you, sir.
Truly, however else.

120 **Gloucester.**   For him I thank your Grace.

Cornwall. You know not why we came to visit you?

Regan. Thus out of season, threading dark-eyed night.
Occasions, noble Gloucester, of some prize,[478]
Wherein we must have use of your advise.
125 Our father he hath writ, so hath our sister,
Of differences,[479] which[480] I best thought it fit
To answer from[481] our home. The several messengers
From hence attend dispatch.[482] Our good old friend,
Lay comforts to your bosom,[483] and bestow
130 Your needful[484] counsel to our businesses,
Which craves the instant use.[485]

Gloucester.   I serve you, madam.
Your Graces are right welcome.

Exeunt. Flourish.

Scene II. [*Before Gloucester's castle.*]

Enter Kent and Oswald, severally.

Oswald. Good dawning[486] to thee, friend. Art of this house?[487]

Kent. Ay.

Oswald. Where may we set our horses?

5 **Kent.** I' th' mire.

Oswald. Prithee, if thou lov'st me, tell me.

Kent. I love thee not.

---

[478] *prize* importance.
[479] *differences* quarrels.
[480] *which* (referring not to "differences," but to the letter Lear has written).
[481] *from* away from.
[482] *attend dispatch* are waiting to be sent off.
[483] *Lay . . . bosom* console yourself (about Edgar's supposed treason).
[484] *needful* needed.
[485] *craves the instant use* demands immediate transaction.
[486] *dawning* (dawn is impending, but not yet arrived).
[487] *Art of this house* i.e., do you live here.

Oswald. Why then, I care not for thee.

Kent. If I had thee in Lipsbury Pinfold,[488] I would make thee care   10
for me.

Oswald. Why dost thou use me thus? I know thee not.

Kent. Fellow, I know thee.

Oswald. What dost thou know me for?

Kent. A knave, a rascal, an eater of broken meats;[489] a base, proud,
shallow, beggarly, three-suited[490] hundred-pound,[491] filthy wor-   15
sted-stocking[492] knave; a lily-livered, action-taking,[493] whoreson,
glass-gazing,[494] superserviceable,[495] finical[496] rogue; one-trunk-inheriting[497] slave; one that wouldst be a bawd in way of good   20
service,[498] and art nothing but the composition[499] of a knave,
beggar, coward, pander, and the son and heir of a mongrel bitch;
one whom I will beat into clamorous whining if thou deniest the
least syllable of thy addition.[500]

Oswald. Why, what a monstrous fellow art thou, thus to rail on   25
one that is neither known of thee nor knows thee!

Kent. What a brazen-faced varlet art thou to deny thou knowest
me! Is it two days since I tripped up thy heels and beat thee   30
before the King? [*Drawing his sword*] Draw, you rogue, for though
it be night, yet the moon shines. I'll make a sop o' th' moonshine[501]
of you. You whoreson cullionly barbermonger,[502] draw!

Oswald. Away, I have nothing to do with thee.   35

---

[488] *Lipsbury Pinfold* a pound or pen in which strayed animals are enclosed ("Lipsbury" may denote a particular place, or may be slang for "between my teeth").

[489] *broken meats* scraps of food.

[490] *three-suited* (the wardrobe permitted to a servant or "knave").

[491] *hundred-pound* (the extent of Oswald's wealth, and thus a sneer at his aspiring
to gentility).

[492] *worsted-stocking* (worn by servants).

[493] *action-taking* one who refuses a fight and goes to law instead.

[494] *glass-gazing* conceited.

[495] *superserviceable* sycophantic, serving without principle.

[496] *finical* overfastidious.

[497] *one-trunk-inheriting* possessing only a trunkful of goods.

[498] *bawd . . . service* pimp, to please his master.

[499] *composition* compound.

[500] *addition* titles.

[501] *sop o' th' moonshine* i.e., Oswald will admit the moonlight, and so sop it up,
through the open wounds Kent is preparing to give him.

[502] *cullionly barbermonger* base patron of hairdressers (effeminate man).

Kent. Draw, you rascal. You come with letters against the King, and take Vanity the puppet's[503] part against the royalty of her father. Draw, you rogue, or I'll so carbonado[504] your shanks. Draw,
40   you rascal. your ways![505]

Oswald. Help, ho! Murder! Help!

Kent. Strike, you slave! Stand, rogue! Stand, you neat[506] slave! Strike!
[*Beating him*]

Oswald. Help, ho! Murder, murder!

Enter Edmund, with his rapier drawn, Cornwall, Regan, Gloucester, Servants.

45 **Edmund.** How now? What's the matter? Part!

Kent. With you,[507] goodman boy,[508] if you please! Come, I'll flesh[509] ye, come on, young master.

Gloucester. Weapons? Arms? What's the matter here?

50 **Cornwall.** Keep peace, upon your lives. He dies that strikes again. What is the matter?

Regan. The messengers from our sister and the King.

Cornwall. What is your difference?[510] Speak.

Oswald. I am scarce in breath, my lord.

55 **Kent.** No marvel, you have so bestirred[511] your valor. You cowardly rascal, nature disclaims in thee.[512] A tailor made thee.[513]

Cornwall. Thou art a strange fellow. A tailor make a man?

60 **Kent.** A tailor, sir. A stonecutter or a painter could not have made him so ill, though they had been but two years o' th' trade.

Cornwall. Speak yet, how grew your quarrel?

---

[503] *Vanity the puppet's* Goneril, here identified with one of the personified characters in the morality plays, which were sometimes put on as puppet shows.

[504] *carbonado* cut across, like a piece of meat before cooking.

[505] *Come your ways* get along.

[506] *neat* (1) foppish (2) unmixed, as in "neat wine."

[507] *With you* i.e., the quarrel is with you.

[508] *goodman boy* young man (peasants are "goodmen"; "boy" is a term of contempt).

[509] *flesh* introduce to blood (term from hunting).

[510] *difference* quarrel.

[511] *bestirred* exercised.

[512] *nature disclaims in thee* nature renounces any part in you.

[513] *A tailor made thee* (from the proverb "The tailor makes the man").

Oswald. This ancient ruffian, sir, whose life I have spared at suit
of[514] his gray beard—

Kent. Thou whoreson zed,[515] thou unnecessary letter! My lord, if   65
you will give me leave, I will tread this unbolted[516] villain into
mortar and daub the wall of a jakes[517] with him. Spare my gray
beard, you wagtail![518]

Cornwall. Peace, sirrah!   70
You beastly[519] knave, know you no reverence?

Kent. Yes, sir, but anger hath a privilege.

Cornwall. Why art thou angry?

Kent. That such a slave as this should wear a sword,
Who wears no honesty. Such smiling rogues as these,   75
Like rats, oft bite the holy cords[520] atwain
Which are too intrince[521] t' unloose; smooth[522] every passion
That in the natures of their lords rebel,
Being oil to fire, snow to the colder moods;
Renege,[523] affirm, and turn their halcyon beaks[524]   80
With every gale and vary[525] of their masters,
Knowing naught, like dogs, but following.
A plague upon your epileptic[526] visage!
Smile you[527] my speeches, as I were a fool?
Goose, if I had you upon Sarum Plain,[528]   85
I'd drive ye cackling home to Camelot.[529]

Cornwall. What, art thou mad, old fellow?

---

[514] *at suit of* out of pity for.

[515] *zed* the letter Z, generally omitted in contemporary dictionaries.

[516] *unbolted* unsifted, i.e., altogether a villain.

[517] *jakes* privy.

[518] *wagtail* a bird that bobs its tail up and down, and thus suggests obsequiousness.

[519] *beastly* irrational.

[520] *holy cords* sacred bonds of affection (as between husbands and wives, parents and children).

[521] *intrince* entangled, intricate.

[522] *smooth* appease.

[523] *Renege* deny.

[524] *halcyon beaks* (the halcyon or kingfisher serves here as a type of the opportunist because, when hung up by the tail or neck, it was supposed to turn with the wind, like a weathervane.)

[525] *gale and vary* varying gale (hendiadys).

[526] *epileptic* distorted by grinning.

[527] *Smile you* do you smile at.

[528] *Sarum Plain* Salisbury Plain.

[529] *Camelot* the residence of King Arthur (presumably a particular point, now lost, is intended here).

Gloucester. How fell you out? Say that.

Kent. No contraries[530] hold more antipathy
90 Than I and such a knave.

Cornwall. Why dost thou call him knave? What is his fault?

Kent. His countenance likes[531] me not.

Cornwall. No more perchance does mine, nor his, nor hers.

Kent. Sir, 'tis my occupation to be plain:
95 I have seen better faces in my time
Than stands on any shoulder that I see
Before me at this instant.

Cornwall.   This is some fellow
Who, having been praised for bluntness, doth affect
A saucy roughness, and constrains the garb
100 Quite from his nature.[532] He cannot flatter, he;
An honest mind and plain, he must speak truth.
And[533] they will take it, so; if not, he's plain.
These kind of knaves I know, which in this plainness
Harbor more craft and more corrupter ends
105 Than twenty silly-ducking observants[534]
That stretch their duties nicely.[535]

Kent. Sir, in good faith, in sincere verity,
Under th' allowance[536] of your great aspect,[537]
Whose influence,[538] like the wreath of radiant fire
On flick'ring Phoebus' front[539]—

110 **Cornwall.**   What mean'st by this?

Kent. To go out of my dialect,[540] which you discommend so much.
I know, sir, I am no flatterer. He[541] that beguiled you in a plain

---

[530] *contraries* opposites.

[531] *likes* pleases.

[532] *constrains . . . nature* forces the manner of candid speech to be a cloak, not for candor but for craft.

[533] *And* if.

[534] *silly-ducking observants* ridiculously obsequious attendants.

[535] *nicely* punctiliously.

[536] *allowance* approval.

[537] *aspect* (1) appearance (2) position of the heavenly bodies.

[538] *influence* astrological power.

[539] *Phoebus' front* forehead of the sun.

[540] *dialect* customary manner of speaking.

[541] *He* i.e., the sort of candid-crafty man Cornwall has been describing.

accent was a plain knave, which, for my part, I will not be, though
I should win your displeasure to entreat me to't.[542]   115

Cornwall. What was th' offense you gave him?

Oswald. I never gave him any.
It pleased the King his master very late[543]
To strike at me, upon his misconstruction;[544]
When he, compact,[545] and flattering his displeasure,   120
Tripped me behind; being down, insulted, railed,
And put upon him such a deal of man[546]
That worthied him,[547] got praises of the King
For him attempting who was self-subdued;[548]
And, in the fleshment[549] of this dread exploit,   125
Drew on me here again.

Kent.   None of these rogues and cowards
But Ajax is their fool.[550]

Cornwall.   Fetch forth the stocks!
You stubborn[551] ancient knave, you reverent[552] braggart,
We'll teach you.

Kent.   Sir, I am too old to learn.
Call not your stocks for me, I serve the King,   130
On whose employment I was sent to you.
You shall do small respect, show too bold malice
Against the grace and person[553] of my master,
Stocking his messenger.

Cornwall. Fetch forth the stocks. As I have life and honor,   135
There shall he sit till noon.

Regan. Till noon? Till night, my lord, and all night too.

---

[542] *though . . . to't* even if I were to succeed in bringing your graceless person
("displeasure" personified, and in lieu of the expected form, "your grace") to beg me
to be a plain knave.

[543] *very late* recently.

[544] *misconstruction* misunderstanding.

[545] *compact* in league with the king.

[546] *put . . . man* pretended such manly behavior.

[547] *worthied him* made him seem heroic.

[548] *For . . . self-subdued* for attacking a man (Oswald) who offered no resistance.

[549] *fleshment* the bloodthirstiness excited by his first success or "fleshing."

[550] *None . . . fool* i.e., cowardly rogues like Oswald always impose on fools like
Cornwall (who is likened to Ajax: [1] the braggart Greek warrior [2] a jakes or privy).

[551] *stubborn* rude.

[552] *reverent* old.

[553] *grace and person* i.e., Lear as sovereign and in his personal character.

Kent. Why, madam, if I were your father's dog,
You should not use me so.

Regan. Sir, being his knave, I will.

140 **Cornwall.** This is a fellow of the selfsame color[554]
Our sister speaks of. Come, bring away[555] the stocks.

Stocks brought out.

Gloucester. Let me beseech your Grace not to do so.
His fault is much, and the good King his master
Will check[556] him for't. Your purposed[557] low correction
145 Is such as basest and contemnèd'st[558] wretches
For pilf'rings and most common trespasses
Are punished with.
The King his master needs must take it ill
That he, so slightly valued in[559] his messenger,
Should have him thus restrained.

150 **Cornwall.** I'll answer[560] that.

Regan. My sister may receive it much more worse,
To have her gentleman abused, assaulted,
For following her affairs. Put in his legs.

[Kent is put in the stocks.]

Come, my good lord, away!

[Exeunt all but Gloucester and Kent.]

155 **Gloucester.** I am sorry for thee, friend. 'Tis the Duke's pleasure,
Whose disposition[561] all the world well knows
Will not be rubbed[562] nor stopped. I'll entreat for thee.

Kent. Pray do not, sir. I have watched[563] and traveled hard.
Some time I shall sleep out, the rest I'll whistle.
160 A good man's fortune may grow out at heels.[564]
Give[565] you good morrow.

---

554 *color* kind.
555 *away* out.
556 *check* correct.
557 *purposed* intended.
558 *contemnèd'st* most despised.
559 *slightly valued in* little honored in the person of.
560 *answer* answer for.
561 *disposition* inclination.
562 *rubbed* diverted (metaphor from the game of bowls).
563 *watched* gone without sleep.
564 *A . . . heels* even a good man may have bad fortune.
565 *Give* God give.

Gloucester.   The Duke's to blame in this. 'Twill be ill taken.[566]
Exit.

Kent.   Good King, that must approve[567] the common saw,[568]
Thou out of Heaven's benediction com'st
To the warm sun.[569]   165
Approach, thou beacon to this under globe,[570]
That by thy comfortable[571] beams I may
Peruse this letter. Nothing almost sees miracles
But misery.[572] I know 'tis from Cordelia,
Who hath most fortunately been informed   170
Of my obscurèd[573] course. And shall find time
From this enormous state, seeking to give
Losses their remedies.[574] All weary and o'erwatched,
Take vantage,[575] heavy eyes, not to behold
This shameful lodging. Fortune, good night;   175
Smile once more, turn thy wheel.[576]

                                         Sleeps.

Scene III. [*A wood.*]

Enter Edgar.

Edgar.   I heard myself proclaimed,
And by the happy[577] hollow of a tree
Escaped the hunt. No port is free, no place
That guard and most unusual vigilance
Does not attend my taking.[578] Whiles I may 'scape,   5
I will preserve myself; and am bethought[579]

---

[566] *taken* received.

[567] *approve* confirm.

[568] *saw* proverb.

[569] *Thou . . . sun* i.e., Lear goes from better to worse, from Heaven's blessing or shelter to lack of shelter.

[570] *beacon . . . globe* i.e., the sun, whose rising Kent anticipates.

[571] *comfortable* comforting.

[572] *Nothing . . . misery* i.e., true perception belongs only to the wretched.

[573] *obscurèd* disguised.

[574] *shall . . . remedies* (a possible reading: Cordelia, away from this monstrous state of things, will find occasion to right the wrongs we suffer).

[575] *vantage* advantage (of sleep).

[576] *turn thy wheel* i.e., so that Kent, who is at the bottom, may climb upward.

[577] *happy* lucky.

[578] *attend my taking* watch to capture me.

[579] *am bethought* have decided.

To take the basest and most poorest shape
That ever penury, in contempt of man,
Brought near to beast;[580] my face I'll grime with filth,
10 Blanket[581] my loins, elf[582] all my hairs in knots,
And with presented[583] nakedness outface[584]
The winds and persecutions of the sky.
The country gives me proof[585] and precedent
Of Bedlam[586] beggars, who, with roaring voices,
15 Strike[587] in their numbed and mortified[588] bare arms
Pins, wooden pricks,[589] nails, sprigs of rosemary;
And with this horrible object,[590] from low[591] farms,
Poor pelting[592] villages, sheepcotes, and mills,
Sometimes with lunatic bans,[593] sometime with prayers.
20 Enforce their charity. Poor Turlygod, Poor Tom,[594]
That's something yet: Edgar I nothing am.[595]

Exit.

Scene IV. [*Before Gloucester's castle. Kent in the stocks.*]

Enter Lear, Fool, and Gentleman.

Lear. 'Tis strange that they should so depart from home,
And not send back my messenger.

Gentleman.   As I learned,
The night before there was no purpose[596] in them

---

[580] *penury . . . beast* poverty, to show how contemptible man is, reduced to the level of a beast.

[581] *Blanket* cover only with a blanket.

[582] *elf* tangle (into "elflocks," supposed to be caused by elves).

[583] *presented* the show of.

[584] *outface* brave.

[585] *proof* example.

[586] *Bedlam* (see I.ii, note 227).

[587] *strike* stick.

[588] *mortified* not alive to pain.

[589] *pricks* skewers.

[590] *object* spectacle.

[591] *low* humble.

[592] *pelting* paltry.

[593] *bans* curses.

[594] *Poor . . . Tom* (Edgar recites the names a Bedlam beggar gives himself).

[595] *That's . . . am* there's a chance for me in that I am no longer known for myself.

[596] *purpose* intention.

Of this remove.[597]

Kent.   Hail to thee, noble master.

Lear. Ha!   5
Mak'st thou this shame thy pastime?[598]

Kent.   No, my lord.

Fool. Ha, ha, he wears cruel[599] garters. Horses are tied by the heads,
dogs and bears by th' neck, monkeys by th' loins, and men by   10
th' legs. When a man's overlusty at legs,[600] then he wears wooden
netherstocks.[601]

Lear. What's he that hath so much thy place mistook
To set thee here?

Kent.   It is both he and she,
Your son and daughter.

Lear. No.

Kent. Yes.   15

Lear. No, I say.

Kent. I say yea.

Lear. No, no, they would not.

Kent. Yes, they have.

Lear. By Jupiter, I swear no!   20

Kent. By Juno, I swear ay!

Lear.   They durst not do't;
They could not, would not do't. 'Tis worse than murder
To do upon respect[602] such violent outrage.
Resolve[603] me with all modest[604] haste which way
Thou mightst deserve or they impose this usage,   25
Coming from us.

Kent.   My lord, when at their home

---

[597] *remove* removal.

[598] *Mak'st . . . pastime* i.e., are you doing this to amuse yourself.

[599] *cruel* (1) painful (2) "crewel," a worsted yarn used in garters.

[600] *overlusty at legs* (1) a vagabond (2) ? sexually promiscuous.

[601] *netherstocks* stockings (as opposed to knee breeches or upperstocks).

[602] *upon respect* (1) on the respect due to the King (2) deliberately.

[603] *Resolve* inform.

[604] *modest* becoming.

I did commend[605] your Highness' letters to them,
Ere I was risen from the place that showed
My duty kneeling, came there a reeking post,[606]
30 Stewed[607] in his haste, half breathless, panting forth
From Goneril his mistress salutations,
Delivered letters, spite of intermission,[608]
Which presently[609] they read; on[610] whose contents
They summoned up their meiny,[611] straight took horse,
35 Commanded me to follow and attend
The leisure of their answer, gave me cold looks,
And meeting here the other messenger,
Whose welcome I perceived had poisoned mine,
Being the very fellow which of late
40 Displayed[612] so saucily against your Highness,
Having more man than wit[613] about me, drew;
He raised[614] the house, with loud and coward cries.
Your son and daughter found this trespass worth[615]
The shame which here it suffers.

45 **Fool.**   Winter's not gone yet, if the wild geese fly that way.[616]
              Fathers that wear rags
                  Do make their children blind,[617]
              But fathers that bear bags[618]
                  Shall see their children kind.
50   Fortune, that arrant whore,
                  Ne'er turns the key[619] to th' poor.
         But for all this, thou shalt have as many dolors[620]
         For thy daughters as thou canst tell[621] in a year.

---

[605] *commend* deliver.

[606] *reeking post* sweating messenger.

[607] *stewed* steaming.

[608] *spite of intermission* in spite of the interrupting of my business.

[609] *presently* at once.

[610] *on* on the strength of.

[611] *meiny* retinue.

[612] *Displayed* showed off.

[613] *more man than wit* more manhood than sense.

[614] *raised* aroused.

[615] *worth* deserving.

[616] *Winter's . . . way* i.e., more trouble is to come, since Cornwall and Regan act so ("geese" is used contemptuously, as in Kent's quarrel with Oswald, II.ii. 85-6).

[617] *blind* i.e., indifferent.

[618] *bags* moneybags.

[619] *turns the key* i.e., opens the door.

[620] *dolors* (1) sorrows (2) dollars (English name for Spanish and German coins).

[621] *tell* (1) tell about (2) count.

Lear. O, how this mother[622] swells up toward my heart!   55
Hysterica passio,[623] down, thou climbing sorrow,
Thy element's[624] below. Where is this daughter?

Kent. With the Earl, sir, here within.

Lear.   Follow me not;
Stay here.   *Exit.*

Gentleman. Made you no more offense but what you speak of?   60

Kent. None.
How chance[625] the King comes with so small a number?

Fool. And[626] thou hadst been set i' th' stocks for that question,
thou'dst well deserved it.

Kent. Why, Fool?   65

Fool. We'll set thee to school to an ant, to teach thee there's no
laboring i' th' winter.[627] All that follow their noses are led by
their eyes but blind men, and there's not a nose among twenty
but can smell him that's stinking.[628] Let go thy hold when a great   70
wheel runs down a hill, lest it break thy neck with following. But
the great one that goes upward, let him draw thee after. When
a wise man gives thee better counsel, give me mine again. I would
have none but knaves follow it since a Fool gives it.   75
   That sir, which serves and seeks for gain,
      And follows but for form,[629]
   Will pack,[630] when it begins to rain,
      And leave thee in the storm.   80
   But I will tarry; the Fool will stay,
      And let the wise man fly.
   The knave turns Fool that runs away,
      The Fool no knave,[631] perdy.[632]

Kent. Where learned you this, Fool?   85

[622-623] *mother . . . Hysterica passio* hysteria, causing suffocation or choking.

[624] *element* proper place.

[625] *How chance* how does it happen that.

[626] *And* if.

[627] *We'll . . . winter* (in the popular fable the ant, unlike the improvident grasshopper, anticipates the winter when none can labor by laying up provisions in the summer. Lear, trusting foolishly to summer days, finds himself unprovided for, and unable to provide, now that "winter" has come).

[628] *All . . . stinking* i.e., all can smell out the decay of Lear's fortunes.

[629] *form* show.

[630] *pack* be off.

[631] *The . . . knave* i.e., the faithless man is the true fool, for wisdom requires fidelity. Lear's Fool, who remains faithful, is at least no knave.

[632] *perdy* by God (Fr. *par Dieu*).

Fool. Not i' th' stocks, fool.

Enter Lear and Gloucester.

Lear. Deny[633] to speak with me? They are sick, they are weary,
They have traveled all the night? Mere fetches,[634]
The images[635] of revolt and flying off![636]
Fetch me a better answer.

90 **Gloucester.** My dear lord,
You know the fiery quality[637] of the Duke,
How unremovable and fixed he is
In his own course.

Lear. Vengeance, plague, death, confusion!
Fiery? What quality? Why, Gloucester, Gloucester,
95 I'd speak with the Duke of Cornwall and his wife.

Gloucester. Well, my good lord, I have informed them so.

Lear. Informed them? Dost thou understand me, man?

Gloucester. Ay, my good lord.

Lear. The King would speak with Cornwall. The dear father
100 Would with his daughter speak, commands—tends[638]—service.
Are they informed of this? My breath and blood!
Fiery? The fiery Duke, tell the hot Duke that—
No, but not yet. May be he is not well.
Infirmity doth still neglect all office
105 Whereto our health is bound.[639] We are not ourselves
When nature, being oppressed, commands the mind
To suffer with the body. I'll forbear;
And am fallen out[640] with my more headier will[641]
To take the indisposed and sickly fit
110 For the sound man. [*Looking on Kent*] Death on my state![642] Wherefore
Should he sit here? This act persuades me
That this remotion[643] of the Duke and her

---

[633] *Deny* refuse.

[634] *fetches* subterfuges, acts of tacking (nautical metaphor).

[635] *images* exact likeness.

[636] *flying off* desertion.

[637] *quality* temperament.

[638] *tends* attends (i.e., awaits); with, possibly, an ironic second meaning, "tenders," or "offers."

[639] *Whereto . . . bound* duties which we are required to perform, when in health.

[640] *fallen out* angry.

[641] *headier will* headlong inclination.

[642] *state* royal condition.

[643] *remotion* (1) removal (2) remaining aloof.

Is practice⁶⁴⁴ only. Give me my servant forth.⁶⁴⁵
Go tell the Duke and's wife I'd speak with them!
Now, presently!⁶⁴⁶ Bid them come forth and hear me,   115
Or at their chamber door I'll beat the drum
Till it cry sleep to death.⁶⁴⁷

Gloucester. I would have all well betwixt you.

Exit.

Lear. O me, my heart, my rising heart! But down!

Fool. Cry to it, Nuncle, as the cockney⁶⁴⁸ did to the eels when she   120
put 'em i' th' paste⁶⁴⁹ alive. She knapped⁶⁵⁰ 'em o' th' coxcombs⁶⁵¹
with a stick and cried, "Down, wantons,⁶⁵² down!" 'Twas her
brother that, in pure kindness to his horse, buttered his hay.⁶⁵³   125

Enter Cornwall, Regan, Gloucester, Servants.

Lear. Good morrow to you both.

Cornwall.   Hail to your Grace.

Kent here set at liberty.

Regan. I am glad to see your Highness.

Lear. Regan, I think you are. I know what reason
I have to think so. If thou shouldst not be glad,
I would divorce me from thy mother's tomb,   130
Sepulchring an adultress.⁶⁵⁴ *[To Kent]* O, are you free?
Some other time for that. Beloved Regan,
Thy sister's naught.⁶⁵⁵ O Regan, she hath tied
Sharp-toothed unkindness, like a vulture, here.

[Points to his heart.]

---

⁶⁴⁴ *practice* pretense.

⁶⁴⁵ *forth* i.e., out of the stocks.

⁶⁴⁶ *presently* at once.

⁶⁴⁷ *cry . . . death* follow sleep, like a cry or pack of hounds, until it kills it.

⁶⁴⁸ *cockney* Londoner (ignorant city dweller).

⁶⁴⁹ *paste* pastry pie.

⁶⁵⁰ *knapped* rapped.

⁶⁵¹ *coxcombs* heads.

⁶⁵² *wantons* i.e., playful things (with a sexual implication).

⁶⁵³ *buttered his hay* i.e., the city dweller does from ignorance what the dishonest
ostler does from craft: greases the hay the traveler has paid for, so that the horse
will not eat.

⁶⁵⁴ *divorce . . . adultress* i.e., repudiate your dead mother as having conceived you
by another man.

⁶⁵⁵ *naught* wicked.

135 I can scarce speak to thee. Thou'lt not believe
With how depraved a quality[656]—O Regan!

Regan. I pray you, sir, take patience. I have hope
You less know how to value her desert
Than she to scant her duty.[657]

Lear.   Say? how is that?

140 **Regan.** I cannot think my sister in the least
Would fail her obligation. If, sir, perchance
She have restrained the riots of your followers,
'Tis on such ground, and to such wholesome end,
As clears her from all blame.

Lear. My curses on her!

145 **Regan.**   O, sir, you are old,
Nature in you stands on the very verge
Of his confine.[658] You should be ruled, and led
By some discretion that discerns your state
Better than you yourself.[659] Therefore I pray you
150 That to our sister you do make return,
Say you have wronged her.

Lear.   Ask her forgiveness?
Do you but mark how this becomes the house:[660]
"Dear daughter, I confess that I am old.

[Kneeling.]

Age is unnecessary. On my knees I beg
155 That you'll vouchsafe me raiment, bed, and food."

Regan. Good sir, no more. These are unsightly tricks.
Return you to my sister.

Lear.   *[Rising]* Never, Regan.
She hath abated[661] me of half my train,
Looked black upon me, struck me with her tongue,
160 Most serpentlike, upon the very heart.
All the stored vengeances of heaven fall

---

[656] *quality* nature.

[657] *I . . . duty* (despite the double negative, the passage means, "I believe that you fail to give Goneril her due, rather than that she fails to fulfill her duty").

[658] *Nature . . . confine* i.e., you are nearing the end of your life.

[659] *some . . . yourself* some discreet person who understands your condition more than you do.

[660] *becomes the house* suits my royal and paternal position.

[661] *abated* curtailed.

On her ingrateful top![662] Strike her young bones,[663]
You taking[664] airs, with lameness.

Cornwall.   Fie, sir, fie!

Lear. You nimble lightnings, dart your blinding flames
Into her scornful eyes! Infect her beauty,   165
You fen-sucked[665] fogs, drawn by the pow'rful sun,
To fall and blister[666] her pride.

Regan.   O the blest gods!
So will you wish on me when the rash mood is on.

Lear. No, Regan, thou shalt never have my curse.
Thy tender-hefted[667] nature shall not give   170
Thee o'er to harshness. Her eyes are fierce, but thine
Do comfort, and not burn. 'Tis not in thee
To grudge my pleasures, to cut off my train,
To bandy[668] hasty words, to scant my sizes,[669]
And, in conclusion, to oppose the bolt[670]   175
Against my coming in. Thou better know'st
The offices of nature, bond of childhood,[671]
Effects[672] of courtesy, dues of gratitude.
Thy half o' th' kingdom hast thou not forgot,
Wherein I thee endowed.

Regan.   Good sir, to th' purpose.[673] 180

Tucket within.

Lear. Who put my man i' th' stocks?

Cornwall.   What trumpet's that?

Regan. I know't—my sister's. This approves[674] her letter,
That she would soon be here.

---

[662] *top* head.

[663] *young bones* (the reference may be to unborn children, rather than to Goneril
herself).

[664] *taking* infecting.

[665] *fen-sucked* drawn up from swamps by the sun.

[666] *fall and blister* fall upon and raise blisters.

[667] *tender-hefted* gently framed.

[668] *bandy* volley (metaphor from tennis).

[669] *scant my sizes* reduce my allowances.

[670] *oppose the bolt* i.e., bar the door.

[671] *offices . . . childhood* natural duties, a child's duty to its parent.

[672] *Effects* manifestations.

[673] *to th' purpose* come to the point.

[674] *approves* confirms.

Enter Oswald.

                                              Is your lady come?

Lear. This is a slave, whose easy borrowed[675] pride
185 Dwells in the fickle grace[676] of her he follows.
Out, varlet,[677] from my sight.

Cornwall.   What means your Grace?

Lear. Who stocked my servant? Regan, I have good hope
Thou didst not know on't.

Enter Goneril.

                              Who comes here? O heavens!
If you do love old men, if your sweet sway
190 Allow[678] obedience, if you yourselves are old,
Make it[679] your cause. Send down, and take my part.
[To Goneril] Art not ashamed to look upon this beard?
O Regan, will you take her by the hand?

Goneril. Why not by th' hand, sir? How have I offended?
195 All's not offense that indiscretion finds[680]
And dotage terms so.

Lear.   O sides,[681] you are too tough!
Will you yet hold? How came my man i' th' stocks?

Cornwall. I set him there, sir; but his own disorders[682]
Deserved much less advancement.[683]

Lear.   You? Did you?

200 **Regan.** I pray you, father, being weak, seem so.[684]
If till the expiration of your month
You will return and sojourn with my sister,
Dismissing half your train, come then to me.
I am now from home, and out of that provision
205 Which shall be needful for your entertainment.[685]

---

[675] *easy borrowed* (1) facile and taken from another (2) acquired without anything
to back it up (like money borrowed without security).

[676] *grace* favor.

[677] *varlet* base fellow.

[678] *Allow* approve of.

[679] *it* i.e., my cause.

[680] *finds* judges.

[681] *sides* breast.

[782] *disorders* misconduct.

[683] *advancement* promotion.

[684] *seem so* i.e., act weak.

[685] *entertainment* maintenance.

Lear. Return to her, and fifty men dismissed?
No, rather I abjure all roofs, and choose
To wage[686] against the enmity o' th' air,
To be a comrade with the wolf and owl,
Necessity's sharp pinch.[687] Return with her?   210
Why, the hot-blooded[688] France, that dowerless took
Our youngest born, I could as well be brought
To knee[689] his throne, and, squirelike,[690] pension beg
To keep base life afoot. Return with her?
Persuade me rather to be slave and sumpter[691]   215
To this detested groom.

                                        [Pointing at Oswald.]

Goneril.   At your choice, sir.

Lear. I prithee, daughter, do not make me mad.
I will not trouble thee, my child; farewell.
We'll no more meet, no more see one another.
But yet thou art my flesh, my blood, my daughter,   220
Or rather a disease that's in my flesh,
Which I must needs call mine. Thou art a boil,
A plague-sore, or embossèd carbuncle[692]
In my corrupted blood. But I'll not chide thee.
Let shame come when it will, I do not call it.   225
I do not bid the Thunder-bearer[693] shoot,
Nor tell tales of thee to high-judging[694] Jove.
Mend when thou canst, be better at thy leisure,
I can be patient, I can stay with Regan,
I and my hundred knights.

Regan.   Not altogether so. 230
I looked not for you yet, nor am provided
For your fit welcome. Give ear, sir, to my sister,
For those that mingle reason with your passion[695]
Must be content to think you old, and so—
But she knows what she does.

Lear.   Is this well spoken? 235

---

[686] *wage* fight.

[687] *Necessity's sharp pinch* (a summing up of the hard choice he has just announced).

[688] *hot-blooded* passionate.

[689] *knee* kneel before.

[690] *squirelike* like a retainer.

[691] *sumpter* pack horse.

[692] *embossèd carbuncle* swollen boil.

[693] *Thunder-bearer* i.e., Jupiter.

[694] *high-judging* (1) supreme (2) judging from heaven.

[695] *mingle . . . passion* i.e., consider your turbulent behavior coolly and reasonably.

Regan. I dare avouch[696] it, sir. What, fifty followers?
Is it not well? What should you need of more?
Yea, or so many, sith that[697] both charge[698] and danger
Speak 'gainst so great a number? How in one house
240 Should many people, under two commands,
Hold[699] amity? 'Tis hard, almost impossible.

Goneril. Why might not you, my lord, receive attendance
From those that she calls servants, or from mine?

Regan. Why not, my lord? If then they chanced to slack[700] ye,
245 We could control them. If you will come to me
(For now I spy a danger), I entreat you
To bring but five-and-twenty. To no more
Will I give place or notice.[701]

Lear. I gave you all.

Regan.   And in good time you gave it.

250 **Lear.** Made you my guardians, my depositaries,[702]
But kept a reservation[703] to be followed
With such a number. What, must I come to you
With five-and-twenty? Regan, said you so?

Regan. And speak't again, my lord. No more with me.

255 **Lear.** Those wicked creatures yet do look well-favored[704]
When others are more wicked; not being the worst
Stands in some rank of praise.[705] *[To Goneril]* I'll go with thee.
Thy fifty yet doth double five-and-twenty,
And thou art twice her love.[706]

Goneril.   Hear me, my lord.
260 What need you five-and-twenty? ten? or five?
To follow[707] in a house where twice so many
Have a command to tend you?

---

[696] *avouch* swear by.

[697] *sith that* since.

[698] *charge* expense.

[699] *hold* preserve.

[700] *slack* neglect.

[701] *notice* recognition.

[702] *depositaries* trustees.

[703] *reservation* condition.

[704] *well-favored* handsome.

[705] *not . . . praise* i.e., that Goneril is not so bad as Regan is one thing in her favor.

[706] *her love* i.e., as loving as she.

[707] *follow* attend on you.

Regan.   What need one?

Lear.   O reason[708] not the need! Our basest beggars
Are in the poorest thing superfluous.[709]
Allow not nature more than nature needs,[710]   265
Man's life is cheap as beast's. Thou art a lady:
If only to go warm were gorgeous,
Why, nature needs not what thou gorgeous wear'st,
Which scarcely keeps thee warm.[711] But, for true need—
You heavens, give me that patience, patience I need.   270
You see me here, you gods, a poor old man,
As full of grief as age, wretched in both.
If it be you that stirs these daughters' hearts
Against their father, fool[712] me not so much
To bear[713] it tamely; touch me with noble anger,   275
And let not women's weapons, water drops,
Stain my man's cheeks. No, you unnatural hags!
I will have such revenges on you both
That all the world shall—I will do such things—
What they are, yet I know not; but they shall be   280
The terrors of the earth. You think I'll weep.
No, I'll not weep.

Storm and tempest.

I have full cause of weeping, but this heart
Shall break into a hundred thousand flaws[714]
Or ere[715] I'll weep. O Fool, I shall go mad!   285

Exeunt Lear, Gloucester, Kent, and Fool.

Cornwall.   Let us withdraw, 'twill be a storm.

Regan.   This house is little; the old man and's people
Cannot be well bestowed.[716]

Goneril.   'Tis his own blame; hath[717] put himself from rest[718]

---

[708] *reason* scrutinize.

[709] *Are . . . superfluous* i.e., have some trifle not absolutely necessary.

[710] *needs* i.e., to sustain life.

[711] *If . . . warm* i.e., if to satisfy the need for warmth were to be gorgeous, you would not need the clothing you wear, which is worn more for beauty than warmth.

[712] *fool* humiliate.

[713] *To bear* as to make me bear.

[714] *flaws* (1) pieces (2) cracks (3) gusts of passion.

[715] *Or ere* before.

[716] *bestowed* lodged.

[717] *hath* he hath.

[718] *rest* (1) place of residence (2) repose of mind.

290 And must needs taste his folly.

Regan. For his particular,[719] I'll receive him gladly,
But not one follower.

Goneril.   So am I purposed.[720]
Where is my Lord of Gloucester?

Cornwall. Followed the old man forth.

Enter Gloucester.

                                    He is returned.

Gloucester. The King is in high rage.

295 **Cornwall.**   Whither is he going?

Gloucester. He calls to horse, but will I know not whither.

Cornwall. 'Tis best to give him way, he leads himself.[721]

Goneril. My lord, entreat him by no means to stay.

Gloucester. Alack, the night comes on, and the high winds
300 Do sorely ruffle.[722] For many miles about
There's scarce a bush.

Regan.   O, sir, to willful men
The injuries that they themselves procure
Must be their schoolmasters. Shut up your doors.
He is attended with a desperate train,
305 And what they may incense[723] him to, being apt
To have his ear abused,[724] wisdom bids fear.

Cornwall. Shut up your doors, my lord; 'tis a wild night.
My Regan counsels well. Come out o' th' storm.

Exeunt.

ACT III

Scene I. [*A heath.*]

Storm still.[725] Enter Kent and a Gentleman severally.

---

[719] *his particular* himself personally.
[720] *purposed* determined.
[721] *give . . . himself* let him go; he insists on his own way.
[722] *ruffle* rage.
[723] *incense* incite.
[724] *being . . . abused* he being inclined to harken to bad counsel.
[725] *still* continually.

Kent. Who's there besides foul weather?

Gentleman. One minded like the weather most unquietly.[726]

Kent. I know you. Where's the King?

Gentleman. Contending with the fretful elements;
Bids the wind blow the earth into the sea,   5
Or swell the curlèd waters 'bove the main,[727]
That things might change,[728] or cease; tears his white hair,
Which the impetuous blasts, with eyeless[729] rage,
Catch in their fury, and make nothing of;
Strives in his little world of man[730] to outscorn   10
The to-and-fro-conflicting wind and rain.
This night, wherein the cub-drawn[731] bear would couch,[732]
The lion, and the belly-pinchèd[733] wolf
Keep their fur dry, unbonneted[734] he runs,
And bids what will take all.[735]

Kent.   But who is with him?   15

Gentleman. None but the Fool, who labors to outjest
His heart-struck injuries.

Kent.   Sir, I do know you,
And dare upon the warrant of my note[736]
Commend a dear thing[737] to you. There is division,
Although as yet the face of it is covered   20
With mutual cunning, 'twixt Albany and Cornwall;
Who have—as who have not, that[738] their great stars
Thronèd[739] and set high?—servants, who seem no less,[740]
Which are to France the spies and speculations

---

[726] *minded . . . unquietly* disturbed in mind, like the weather.

[727] *main* land.

[728] *change* (1) be destroyed (2) be exchanged (i.e., turned upside down) (3) change for the better.

[729] *eyeless* (1) blind (2) invisible.

[730] *little world of man* (the microcosm, as opposed to the universe or macrocosm, which it copies in little).

[731] *cub-drawn* sucked dry by her cubs, and so ravenously hungry.

[732] *couch* take shelter in its lair.

[733] *belly-pinchèd* starved.

[734] *unbonneted* hatless.

[735] *take all* (like the reckless gambler, staking all he has left).

[736] *warrant of my note* strength of what I have taken note (of you).

[737] *Commend . . . thing* entrust important business.

[738] *that* whom.

[739] *stars/Thronèd* destinies have throned.

[740] *seem no less* seem to be so.

25   Intelligent[741] of our state. What hath been seen,
      Either in snuffs and packings[742] of the Dukes,
      Or the hard rein which both of them hath borne[743]
      Against the old kind King, or something deeper,
      Whereof, perchance, these are but furnishings[744]—
30   But, true it is, from France there comes a power[745]
      Into this scattered[746] kingdom, who already,
      Wise in our negligence, have secret feet
      In some of our best ports, and are at point[747]
      To show their open banner. Now to you:
35   If on my credit you dare build[748] so far
      To[749] make your speed to Dover, you shall find
      Some that will thank you, making[750]just[751] report
      Of how unnatural and bemadding[752] sorrow
      The King hath cause to plain.[753]
40   I am a gentleman of blood and breeding,[754]
      And from some knowledge and assurance[755] offer
      This office[756] to you.

Gentleman.   I will talk further with you.

Kent.   No, do not.
      For confirmation that I am much more
45   Than my out-wall,[757] open this purse and take
      What it contains. If you shall see Cordelia,
      As fear not but you shall, show her this ring,
      And she will tell you who that fellow[758] is
      That yet you do not know. Fie on this storm!
50   I will go seek the King.

---

[741] *speculations/Intelligent* giving intelligence.
[742] *snuffs and packings* quarrels and plots.
[743] *hard . . . borne* close and cruel control they have exercised.
[744] *furnishings* excuses.
[745] *power* army.
[746] *scattered* disunited.
[747] *at point* ready.
[748] *If . . . build* if you can trust me, proceed.
[749] *To* as to.
[750] *making* for making.
[751] *just* accurate.
[752] *bemadding* maddening.
[753] *plain* complain of.
[754] *blood and breeding* noble family.
[755] *knowledge and assurance* sure and trustworthy information.
[756] *office* service (i.e., the trip to Dover).
[757] *out-wall* superficial appearance.
[758] *fellow* companion.

Gentleman.   Give me your hand. Have you no more to say?

Kent.   Few words, but, to effect,[759] more than all yet:
That when we have found the King—in which your pain[760]
That way, I'll this—he that first lights on him,
Holla the other.   5

Exeunt [severally].

Scene II. [*Another part of the heath.*]

Storm still.

Enter Lear and Fool.

Lear.   Blow, winds, and crack your cheeks. Rage, blow!
You cataracts and hurricanoes,[761] spout
Till you have drenched our steeples, drowned the cocks.[762]
You sulph'rous and thought-executing[763] fires,
Vaunt-couriers[764] of oak-cleaving thunderbolts,   10
Singe my white head. And thou, all-shaking thunder,
Strike flat the thick rotundity[765] o' th' world,
Crack Nature's molds,[766] all germains spill[767] at once,
That makes ingrateful[768] man.

Fool.   O Nuncle, court holy-water[769] in a dry house is better than   15
this rain water out o' door. Good Nuncle, in; ask thy daughters
blessing. Here's a night pities neither wise man nor fools.

Lear.   Rumble thy bellyful. Spit, fire. Spout, rain!
Nor rain, wind, thunder, fire are my daughters.   20
I tax[770] not you, you elements, with unkindness.

---

[759] *to effect* in their importance.

[760] *pain* labor.

[761] *hurricanoes* waterspouts.

[762] *cocks* weathercocks.

[763] *thought-executing* (1) doing execution as quick as thought (2) executing or carrying
out the thought of him who hurls the lightning.

[764] *Vaunt-couriers* heralds, scouts who range before the main body of the army.

[765] *rotundity* i.e., not only the sphere of the globe, but the roundness of gestation
(Delius).

[766] *Nature's molds* the molds or forms in which men are made.

[767] *all germains spill* destroy the basic seeds of life.

[768] *ingrateful* ungrateful.

[769] *court holy-water* flattery.

[770] *tax* accuse.

I never gave you kingdom, called you children,
You owe me no subscription.[771] Then let fall
Your horrible pleasure.[772] Here I stand your slave,
25 A poor, infirm, weak, and despised old man.
But yet I call you servile ministers,[773]
That will with two pernicious daughters join
Your high-engendered battles[774] 'gainst a head
So old and white as this. O, ho! 'tis foul.

30 **Fool.** He that has a house to put's head in has a good headpiece.[775]
         The codpiece[776] that will house
           Before the head has any,
         The head and he[777] shall louse:
35   So beggars marry many.[778]
         The man that makes his toe
           What he his heart should make
         Shall of a corn cry woe,
         And turn his sleep to wake.[779]
40 For there was never yet fair woman but she made mouths in a
      glass.[780]

Enter Kent.

Lear. No, I will be the pattern of all patience, I will say nothing.

Kent. Who's there?

45 **Fool.** Marry,[781] here's grace and a codpiece; that's a wise man and
      a fool.[782]

Kent. Alas, sir, are you here? Things that love night
Love not such nights as these. The wrathful skies

---

[771] *subscription* allegiance, submission.

[772] *pleasure* will.

[773] *ministers* agents.

[774] *high-engendered battles* armies formed in the heavens.

[775] *headpiece* (1) helmet (2) brain.

[776] *codpiece* penis (lit., padding worn at the crotch of a man's hose).

[777] *he* it.

[778] *many* i.e., lice; *The . . . many* i.e., the man who gratifies his sexual appetites before he has a roof over his head will end up a lousy beggar.

[779] *The . . . wake* i.e., the man who, ignoring the fit order of things, elevates what is base above what is noble, will suffer for it as Lear has, in banishing Cordelia and enriching her sisters.

[780] *made mouths in a glass* posed before a mirror (irrelevant nonsense, except that it calls to mind the general theme of vanity and folly).

[781] *Marry* by the Virgin Mary.

[782] *here's . . . fool* (Kent's question is answered: The King ("grace") is here, and the Fool—who customarily wears an exaggerated codpiece. But which is left ambiguous, since Lear has previously been called a codpiece).

Gallow[783] the very wanderers of the dark
And make them keep[784] their caves. Since I was man,   50
Such sheets of fire, such bursts of horrid[785] thunder,
Such groans of roaring wind and rain, I never
Remember to have heard. Man's nature cannot carry[786]
Th' affliction nor the fear.

Lear.   Let the great gods
That keep this dreadful pudder[787] o'er our heads   55
Find out their enemies now.[788] Tremble, thou wretch,
That hast within thee undivulgèd crimes
Unwhipped of justice. Hide thee, thou bloody hand,
Thou perjured,[789] and thou simular[790] of virtue
That art incestuous. Caitiff,[791] to pieces shake,   60
That under covert and convenient seeming[792]
Has practiced on[793] man's life. Close[794] pent-up guilts,
Rive[795] your concealing continents[796] and cry
These dreadful summoners grace.[797] I am a man
More sinned against than sinning.

Kent.   Alack, bareheaded?   65
Gracious my lord,[798] hard by here is a hovel;
Some friendship will it lend you 'gainst the tempest.
Repose you there, while I do this hard house
(More harder than the stones whereof 'tis raised,
Which even but now, demanding after[799] you,   70
Denied me to come in) return, and force
Their scanted[800] courtesy.

---

[783] *Gallow* frighten.

[784] *keep* remain inside.

[785] *horrid* horrible.

[786] *carry* endure.

[787] *pudder* turmoil.

[788] *Find . . . now* i.e., discover sinners by the terror they reveal.

[789] *perjured* perjurer.

[790] *simular* counterfeiter.

[791] *Caitiff* wretch.

[792] *seeming* hypocrisy.

[793] *practiced on* plotted against.

[794] *Close* hidden.

[795] *Rive* split open.

[796] *continents* containers.

[797] *cry . . . grace* beg mercy from the vengeful gods (here figured as officers who summoned a man charged with immorality before the ecclesiastical court).

[798] *Gracious my lord* my gracious lord.

[799] *demanding after* asking for.

[800] *scanted* stinted.

Lear.   My wits begin to turn.
Come on, my boy. How dost, my boy? Art cold?
I am cold myself. Where is this straw, my fellow?
75 The art[801] of our necessities is strange,
That can make vile things precious. Come, your hovel.
Poor Fool and knave, I have one part in my heart
That's sorry yet for thee.

Fool. *[Singing]*
He that has and a little tiny wit,
80   With heigh-ho, the wind and the rain,
Must make content with his fortunes fit,[802]
Though the rain it raineth every day.

Lear. True, my good boy. Come, bring us to this hovel.

Exit [with Kent].

85 **Fool.** This is a brave[803] night to cool a courtesan. I'll speak a
prophecy ere I go:
When priests are more in word than matter;
When brewers mar their malt with water;
When nobles are their tailors' tutors,
No heretics burned, but wenches' suitors;[804]
90   When every case in law is right,
No squire in debt nor no poor knight;
When slanders do not live in tongues;
Nor cutpurses come not to throngs;
When usurers tell their gold i' th' field,[805]
95   And bawds and whores do churches build,[806]
Then shall the realm of Albion[807]
Come to great confusion.
Then comes the time, who lives to see't,
That going shall be used with feet.[808]

---

[801] *art* magic powers of the alchemists, who sought to transmute base metals into
precious.

[802] *Must . . . fit* must be satisfied with a fortune as tiny as his wit.

[803] *brave* fine.

[804] *When . . . suitors* (the first four prophecies are fulfilled already, and hence
"confusion" has come to England. The priest does not suit his action to his words.
The brewer adulterates his beer. The nobleman is subservient to his tailor [i.e., cares
only for fashion]. Religious heretics escape, and only those burn [i.e., suffer] who are
afflicted with venereal disease).

[805] *tell . . . field* count their money in the open.

[806] *When . . . build* (the last six prophecies, as they are Utopian, are meant ironically.
They will never be fulfilled).

[807] *Albion* England.

[808] *going . . . feet* people will walk on their feet.

This prophecy Merlin[809] shall make, for I live before his time.   5

Exit.

Scene III. [*Gloucester's castle.*]

Enter Gloucester and Edmund.

Gloucester.   Alack, alack, Edmund, I like not this unnatural dealing. When I desired their leave that I might pity[810] him, they took from me the use of mine own house, charged me on pain of perpetual displeasure neither to speak of him, entreat for him, or   10 any way sustain[811] him.

Edmund.   Most savage and unnatural.

Gloucester.   Go to; say you nothing. There is division[812] between the Dukes, and a worse[813] matter than that. I have received a   15 letter this night—'tis dangerous to be spoken[814]—I have locked the letter in my closet.[815] These injuries the King now bears will be revenged home;[816] there is part of a power[817] already footed;[818] we must incline to[819] the King. I will look[820] him and privily[821]   20 relieve him. Go you and maintain talk with the Duke, that my charity be not of[822] him perceived. If he ask for me, I am ill and gone to bed. If I die for it, as no less is threatened me, the King my old master must be relieved. There is strange things toward,[823]   25 Edmund; pray you be careful.

Exit.

Edmund.   This courtesy forbid[824] thee shall the Duke

---

[809] *Merlin* King Arthur's great magician who, according to Holinshed's *Chronicles,* lived later than Lear.

[810] *pity* show pity to.

[811] *sustain* care for.

[812] *division* falling out.

[813] *worse* more serious (i.e., the French invasion).

[814] *spoken* spoken of.

[815] *closet* room.

[816] *home* to the utmost.

[817] *power* army.

[818] *footed* landed.

[819] *incline to* take the side of.

[820] *look* search for.

[821] *privily* secretly.

[822] *of* by.

[823] *toward* impending.

[824] *courtesy forbid* kindness forbidden (i.e., to Lear).

Instantly know, and of that letter too.
This seems a fair deserving,[825] and must draw me
5 That which my father loses—no less than all.
The younger rises when the old doth fall.

Exit.

Scene IV. [*The heath. Before a hovel.*]

Enter Lear, Kent, and Fool.

Kent. Here is the place, my lord. Good my lord, enter.
The tyranny of the open night's too rough
For nature to endure.

Storm still.

Lear.   Let me alone.

Kent. Good my lord, enter here.

Lear.   Wilt break my heart?[826]

10 **Kent.** I had rather break mine own. Good my lord, enter.

Lear. Thou think'st 'tis much that this contentious storm
Invades us to the skin: so 'tis to thee;
But where the greater malady is fixed,[827]
The lesser is scarce felt. Thou'dst shun a bear;
15 But if thy flight lay toward the roaring sea,
Thou'dst meet the bear i' th' mouth.[828] When the mind's free,[829]
The body's delicate. The tempest in my mind
Doth from my senses take all feeling else,
Save what beats there. Filial ingratitude,
20 Is it not as[830] this mouth should tear this hand
For lifting food to't? But I will punish home.[831]
No, I will weep no more. In such a night
To shut me out! Pour on, I will endure.
In such a night as this! O Regan, Goneril,
25 Your old kind father, whose frank[832] heart gave all—

---

[825] *fair deserving* an action deserving reward.
[826] *break my heart* i.e., by shutting out the storm which distracts me from thinking.
[827] *fixed* lodged (in the mind).
[828] *i' th' mouth* in the teeth.
[829] *free* i.e., from care.
[830] *as* as if.
[831] *home* to the utmost.
[832] *frank* liberal (magnanimous).

O, that way madness lies; let me shun that.
No more of that.

Kent.   Good my lord, enter here.

Lear. Prithee go in thyself; seek thine own ease.
This tempest will not give me leave to ponder
On things would hurt me more, but I'll go in.   30
[To the Fool] In, boy; go first. You houseless poverty[833]—
Nay, get thee in. I'll pray, and then I'll sleep.

Exit [Fool]

Poor naked wretches, wheresoe'er you are,
That bide[834] the pelting of this pitiless storm,
How shall your houseless heads and unfed sides,   35
Your looped and windowed[835] raggedness, defend you
From seasons such as these? O, I have ta'en
Too little care of this! Take physic, pomp;[836]
Expose thyself to feel what wretches feel,
That thou mayst shake the superflux[837] to them,   40
And show the heavens more just.

Edgar. [Within] Fathom and half, fathom and half![838]
Poor Tom!

Enter Fool.

Fool. Come not in here, Nuncle, here's a spirit. Help me, help me!   45

Kent. Give me thy hand. Who's there?

Fool. A spirit, a spirit. He says his name's Poor Tom.

Kent. What art thou that dost grumble there i' th' straw?
Come forth.

Enter Edgar [disguised as a madman].

Edgar. Away! the foul fiend follows me. Through the sharp haw-   50
thorn blows the cold wind.[839] Humh! Go to thy cold bed, and
warm thee.[840]

---

[833] *houseless poverty* (the unsheltered poor, abstracted).
[834] *bide* endure.
[835] *looped and windowed* full of holes.
[836] *Take physic, pomp* take medicine to cure yourselves, you great men.
[837] *superflux* superfluity.
[838] *Fathom and half* (Edgar, because of the downpour, pretends to take soundings).
[839] *Through . . . wind* (a line from the ballad of "The Friar of Orders Gray").
[840] *go . . . thee* (a reminiscence of *The Taming of the Shrew*, Induction, 1.10).

Lear. Didst thou give all to thy daughters? And art thou come to this?

55 **Edgar.** Who gives anything to Poor Tom? Whom the foul fiend hath led through fire and through flame, through ford and whirlpool, o'er bog and quagmire; that hath laid knives under his pillow and halters in his pew,[841] set ratsbane[842] by his porridge,[843] made
60 him proud of heart, to ride on a bay trotting horse over fourinched bridges,[844] to course[845] his own shadow for[846] a traitor. Bless thy five wits,[847] Tom's a-cold. O, do, de, do, de, do, de. Bless thee from whirlwinds, star-blasting,[848] and taking.[849] Do Poor
65 Tom some charity, whom the foul fiend vexes. There could I have him now—and there—and there again—and there.

Storm still.

Lear. What, has his daughters brought him to this pass?[850] Couldst thou save nothing? Wouldst thou give 'em all?

70 **Fool.** Nay, he reserved a blanket,[851] else we had been all shamed.

Lear. Now all the plagues that in the pendulous[852] air Hang fated o'er[853] men's faults light on thy daughters!

Kent. He hath no daughters, sir.

75 **Lear.** Death, traitor; nothing could have subdued[854] nature
To such a lowness but his unkind daughters.
Is it the fashion that discarded fathers
Should have thus little mercy on[855] their flesh?
Judicious punishment—'twas this flesh begot
80 Those pelican[856] daughters.

---

[841] *pew* gallery or balcony outside a window.
[842] *knives . . . halters . . . ratsbane* (the fiend tempts Poor Tom to suicide).
[843] *porridge* broth.
[844] *ride . . . bridges* i.e., risk his life.
[845] *course* chase.
[846] *for* as.
[847] *five wits* i.e., common wit, imagination, fantasy, estimation, memory.
[848] *star-blasting* the evil caused by malignant stars.
[849] *taking* pernicious influences.
[850] *pass* wretched condition.
[851] *blanket* i.e., to cover his nakedness.
[852] *pendulous* overhanging.
[853] *fated o'er* destined to punish.
[854] *subdued* reduced.
[855] *on* i.e., shown to.
[856] *pelican* (supposed to feed on its parent's blood).

Edgar. Pillicock sat on Pillicock Hill.[857] Alow, alow, loo, loo![858]

Fool. This cold night will turn us all to fools and madmen.

Edgar. Take heed o' th' foul fiend; obey thy parents; keep thy   85
word's justice;[859] swear not; commit not[860] with man's sworn
spouse; set not thy sweet heart on proud array. Tom's a-cold.

Lear. What hast thou been?

Edgar. A servingman, proud in heart and mind; that curled my   90
hair, wore gloves in my cap;[861] served the lust of my mistress'
heart, and did the act of darkness with her; swore as many oaths
as I spake words, and broke them in the sweet face of heaven.   95
One that slept in the contriving of lust, and waked to do it. Wine
loved I deeply, dice dearly; and in woman out-paramoured the
Turk.[862] False of heart, light of ear,[863] bloody of hand; hog in
sloth, fox in stealth, wolf in greediness, dog in madness, lion in
prey.[864] Let not the creaking[865] of shoes nor the rustling of silks   100
betray thy poor heart to woman. Keep thy foot out of brothels,
thy hand out of plackets,[866] thy pen from lenders' books,[867] and
defy the foul fiend. Still through the hawthorn blows the cold
wind; says suum, mun, nonny.[868] Dolphin[869] my boy, boy, sessa![870]   105
let him trot by.

Storm still

Lear. Thou wert better in a grave than to answer[871] with thy
uncovered body this extremity[872] of the skies. Is man no more
than this? Consider him well. Thou ow'st[873] the worm no silk,   110

---

[857] *Pillicock . . . Hill* (probably quoted from a nursery rhyme, and suggested by
"pelican." *Pillicock* is a term of endearment and the phallus).

[858] *Alow . . . loo* (? a hunting call, or the refrain of the song).

[859] *keep . . . justice* i.e., do not break thy word.

[860] *commit not* i.e., adultery.

[861] *gloves in my cap* i.e., as a pledge from his mistress.

[862] *out-paramoured the Turk* had more concubines than the Sultan.

[863] *light of ear* ready to hear flattery and slander.

[864] *prey* preying.

[865] *creaking* (deliberately cultivated, as fashionable).

[866] *plackets* openings in skirts.

[867] *pen . . . books* i.e., do not enter your name in the moneylender's account book.

[868] *suum, mun, nonny* the noise of the wind.

[869] *Dolphin* the French Dauphin (identified by the English with the devil. Poor
Tom is presumably quoting from a ballad).

[870] *sessa* an interjection: "Go on!"

[871] *answer* confront, bear the brunt of.

[872] *extremity* extreme severity.

[873] *ow'st* have taken from.

the beast no hide, the sheep no wool, the cat[874] no perfume. Ha!
here's three on's[875] are sophisticated.[876] Thou are the thing itself;
115   unaccommodated[877] man is no more but such a poor, bare, forked[878]
animal as thou art. Off, off, you lendings![879] Come, unbutton here.
[Tearing off his clothes.]

Fool.   Prithee, Nuncle, be contented, 'tis a naughty[880] night to swim
in. Now a little fire in a wild[881] field were like an old lecher's
120   heart—a small spark, all the rest on's body, cold. Look, here comes
a walking fire.

Enter Gloucester, with a torch.

Edgar.   This is the foul fiend Flibbertigibbet.[882] He begins at curfew,[883] and walks till the first cock.[884] He gives the web and the
125   pin,[885] squints[886] the eye, and makes the harelip; mildews the
white[887] wheat, and hurts the poor creature of earth.
Swithold footed thrice the old;[888]
He met the nightmare,[889] and her nine fold;[890]
Bid her alight[891]
130   And her troth plight,[892]
And aroint[893] thee, witch, aroint thee!

Kent.   How fares your Grace?

Lear.   What's he?

Kent.   Who's there? What is't you seek?

---

[874] *cat* civet cat, whose glands yield perfume.

[875] *on's* of us.

[876] *sophisticated* adulterated, made artificial.

[877] *unaccommodated* uncivilized.

[878] *forked* i.e., two-legged.

[879] *lendings* borrowed garments.

[880] *naughty* wicked.

[881] *wild* barren.

[882] *Flibbertigibbet* (a figure from Elizabethan demonology).

[883] *curfew* 9 P.M.

[884] *first cock* midnight.

[885] *web and the pin* cataract.

[886] *squints* crosses.

[887] *white* ripening.

[888] *Swithold . . . old* Withold (an Anglo-Saxon saint who subdued demons) walked
three times across the open country.

[889] *nightmare* demon.

[890] *fold* offspring.

[891] *alight* i.e., from the horse she had possessed.

[892] *her troth plight* pledge her word.

[893] *aroint* be gone.

Gloucester. What are you there? Your names?   135

Edgar. Poor Tom, that eats the swimming frog, the toad, the todpole, the wall-newt and the water;[894] that in the fury of his heart, when the foul fiend rages, eats cow-dung for sallets,[895] swallows the old rat and the ditch-dog,[896] drinks the green mantle[897] of the standing[898] 140 pool; who is whipped from tithing[899] to tithing, and stocked, punished, and imprisoned; who hath had three suits to his back, six shirts to his body,

> Horse to ride, and weapon to wear,   145
> But mice and rats, and such small deer[900]
> Have been Tom's food for seven long year.[901]

Beware my follower![902] Peace, Smulkin,[903] peace, thou fiend!

Gloucester. What, hath your Grace no better company?   150

Edgar. The Prince of Darkness is a gentleman. Modo he's called, and Mahu.[904]

Gloucester. Our flesh and blood, my Lord, is grown so vile
That it doth hate what gets[905] it.

Edgar. Poor Tom's a-cold.   155

Gloucester. Go in with me. My duty cannot suffer[906]
T' obey in all your daughters' hard commands.
Though their injunction be to bar my doors
And let this tyrannous night take hold upon you,
Yet have I ventured to come seek you out   160
And bring you where both fire and food is ready.

Lear. First let me talk with this philosopher.
What is the cause of thunder?

Kent. Good my lord, take his offer; go into th' house.

---

[894] *todpole . . . water* tadpole, wall lizard, water newt.

[895] *sallets* salads.

[896] *ditch-dog* dead dog in a ditch.

[897] *mantle* scum.

[898] *standing* stagnant.

[899] *tithing* a district comprising ten families.

[900] *deer* game.

[901] *But . . . year* (adapted from a popular romance, "Bevis of Hampton").

[902] *follower* familiar.

[903-904] *Smulkin, Modo, Mahu* (Elizabethan devils, from Samuel Harsnett's *Declaration* of 1603).

[905] *gets* begets.

[906] *suffer* permit me.

165   **Lear.**   I'll talk a word with this same learnèd Theban.[907]
What is your study?[908]

Edgar.   How to prevent[909] the fiend, and to kill vermin.

Lear.   Let me ask you one word in private.

Kent.   Importune him once more to go, my lord.
His wits begin t' unsettle.

170   **Gloucester.**   Canst thou blame him?

Storm still.

His daughters seek his death. Ah, that good Kent,
He said it would be thus, poor banished man!
Thou say'st the King grows mad—I'll tell thee, friend,
I am almost mad myself. I had a son,
175   Now outlawed from my blood;[910] he sought my life
But lately, very late,[911] I loved him, friend,
No father his son dearer. True to tell thee,
The grief hath crazed my wits. What a night's this!
I do beseech your Grace—

Lear.   O, cry you mercy,[912] sir.
180   Noble philosopher, your company.

Edgar.   Tom's a-cold.

Gloucester.   In, fellow, there, into th' hovel; keep thee warm.

Lear.   Come, let's in all.

Kent.   This way, my lord.

Lear.   With him!
I will keep still with my philosopher.

185   **Kent.**   Good my lord, soothe[913] him; let him take the fellow.

Gloucester.   Take him you on.[914]

Kent.   Sirrah, come on; go along with us.

---

[907] *Theban* i.e., Greek philosopher.

[908] *study* particular scientific study.

[909] *prevent* balk.

[910] *outlawed from my blood* disowned and tainted, like a carbuncle in the corrupted blood.

[911] *late* recently.

[912] *cry you mercy* I beg your pardon.

[913] *soothe* humor.

[914] *you on* with you.

Lear. Come, good Athenian.[915]

Gloucester. No words, no words! Hush.

Edgar. Child Rowland to the dark tower came;[916]   5
His word was still,[917] "Fie, foh, and fum,
I smell the blood of a British man."[918]

Exeunt.

Scene V. [*Gloucester's castle.*]

Enter Cornwall and Edmund.

Cornwall. I will have my revenge ere I depart his house.

Edmund. How, my lord, I may be censured,[919] that nature thus
gives way to loyalty, something fears[920] me to think of.   10

Cornwall. I now perceive it was not altogether your brother's evil
disposition made him seek his death; but a provoking merit, set
a-work by a reprovable badness in himself.[921]

Edmund. How malicious is my fortune that I must repent to be   15
just! This is the letter which he spoke of, which approves[922] him
an intelligent party[923] to the advantages[924] of France. O heavens,
that his treason were not! or not I the detector!

Cornwall. Go with me to the Duchess.   20

Edmund. If the matter of this paper be certain, you have mighty
business in hand.

Cornwall. True or false, it hath made thee Earl of Gloucester. Seek
out where thy father is, that he may be ready for our appre-   25
hension.[925]

---

[915] *Athenian* i.e., philosopher (like "Theban").

[916] *Child . . . came* (? from a lost ballad; "child"—a candidate for knighthood;
Rowland was Charlemagne's nephew, the hero of *The Song of Roland*).

[917] *His . . . still* his motto was always.

[918] *Fie . . . man* (a deliberately absurd linking of the chivalric hero with the nursery
tale of Jack the Giant-Killer).

[919] *censured* judged.

[920] *something fears* somewhat frightens.

[921] *a provoking . . . himself* a stimulating goodness in Edgar, brought into play by
a blamable badness in Gloucester.

[922] *approves* proves.

[923] *intelligent party* (1) spy (2) well-informed person.

[924] *to the advantages* on behalf of.

[925] *apprehension* arrest.

Edmund. [Aside] If I find him comforting[926] the King, it will stuff his suspicion more fully.—I will persever[927] in my course of loyalty, though the conflict be sore between that and my blood.[928]

5 **Cornwall.** I will lay trust upon[929] thee, and thou shalt find a dearer father in my love.

Exeunt.

Scene VI. [*A chamber in a farmhouse adjoining the castle.*]

Enter Kent and Gloucester.

Gloucester. Here is better than the open air; take it thankfully. I will piece out the comfort with what addition I can. I will not be long from you.

10 **Kent.** All the power of his wits have given way to his impatience.[930] The gods reward your kindness.

Exit [Gloucester].
Enter Lear, Edgar, and Fool.

Edgar. Frateretto[931] calls me, and tells me Nero[932] is an angler in the lake of darkness. Pray, innocent,[933] and beware the foul fiend.

15 **Fool.** Prithee, Nuncle, tell me whether a madman be a gentleman or a yeoman.[934]

Lear. A king, a king.

Fool. No, he's a yeoman that has a gentleman to his son; for he's a mad yeoman that sees his son a gentleman before him.

20 **Lear.** To have a thousand with red burning spits
Come hizzing[935] in upon 'em—

---

[926] *comforting* supporting (a legalism).

[927] *persever* persevere.

[928] *blood* natural feelings.

[929] *lay trust upon* (1) trust (2) advance.

[930] *impatience* raging.

[931] *Frateretto* Elizabethan devil, from Harsnett's *Declaration*.

[932] *Nero* (who is mentioned by Harsnett, and whose angling is reported by Chaucer in "The Monk's Tale").

[933] *innocent* fool.

[934] *yeoman* farmer (just below a gentleman in rank. The Fool asks what class of man has most indulged his children, and thus been driven mad).

[935] *hizzing* hissing.

Edgar. The foul fiend bites my back.

Fool. He's mad that trusts in the tameness of a wolf, a horse's health, a boy's love, or a whore's oath.

Lear. It shall be done; I will arraign[936] them straight.[937]   25
[To Edgar] Come, sit thou here, most learned justice.[938]
[To the Fool] Thou, sapient[939] sir, sit here. Now, you she-foxes—

Edgar. Look, where he[940] stands and glares. Want'st thou eyes at trial, madam?[941]
Come o'er the bourn,[942] Bessy, to me.   30

Fool.   Her boat hath a leak,
    And she must not speak
    Why she dares not come over to thee.[943]

Edgar. The foul fiend haunts Poor Tom in the voice of a night-   35
ingale,[944] Hoppedance[945] cries in Tom's belly for two white herring.[946] Croak[947] not, black angel; I have no food for thee.

Kent. How do you, sir? Stand you not so amazed.[948]
Will you lie down and rest upon the cushions?

Lear. I'll see their trial first. Bring in their evidence.[949]   40
[To Edgar] Thou, robèd man of justice, take thy place.
[To the Fool] And thou, his yokefellow of equity,[950]
Bench[951] by his side. *[To Kent]* You are o' th' commission;[952]
Sit you too.

Edgar. Let us deal justly.   45
    Sleepest or wakest thou, jolly shepherd?

---

[936] *arraign* bring to trial.
[937] *straight* straightaway.
[938] *justice* justicer, judge.
[939] *sapient* wise.
[940] *he* i.e., a fiend.
[941] *Want'st . . . madam* (to Goneril) i.e., do you want eyes to look at you during your trial? The fiend serves that purpose.
[942] *bourn* brook (Edgar quotes from a popular ballad).
[943] *Her . . . thee* (the Fool parodies the ballad).
[944] *nightingale* i.e., the Fool's singing.
[945] *Hoppedance* Hoberdidance (another devil from Harsnett's *Declaration*).
[946] *white herring* unsmoked (? as against the black and sulfurous devil).
[947] *Croak* rumble (because his belly is empty).
[948] *amazed* astonished.
[949] *evidence* the evidence of witnesses against them.
[950] *yokefellow of equity* partner in justice.
[951] *Bench* sit on the bench.
[952] *commission* those commissioned as king's justices.

Thy sheep be in the corn;[953]
And for one blast of thy minikin[954] mouth
Thy sheep shall take no harm.[955]
50 Purr, the cat is gray.[956]

Lear. Arraign her first. 'Tis Goneril, I here take my oath before this honorable assembly, she kicked the poor King her father.

Fool. Come hither, mistress. Is your name Goneril?

55 **Lear.** She cannot deny it.

Fool. Cry you mercy, I took you for a joint stool.[957]

Lear. And here's another, whose warped looks proclaim
What store[958] her heart is made on. Stop her there!
Arms, arms, sword, fire! Corruption in the place![959]
60 False justicer, why hast thou let her 'scape?

Edgar. Bless thy five wits!

Kent. O pity! Sir, where is the patience now
That you so oft have boasted to retain?

Edgar. *[Aside]* My tears begin to take his part so much
65 They mar my counterfeiting.[960]

Lear. The little dogs and all,
Tray, Blanch, and Sweetheart—see, they bark at me.

Edgar. Tom will throw his head at them. Avaunt, you curs.
Be thy mouth or black or[961] white,
Tooth that poisons if it bite;
Mastiff, greyhound, mongrel grim,
Hound or spaniel, brach[962] or lym,[963]

---

[953] *corn* wheat.

[954] *minikin* shrill.

[955] *Sleepest . . . harm* (probably quoted or adapted form an Elizabethan song).

[956] *gray* (devils were thought to assume the shape of a gray cat).

[957] *Cry . . . joint stool* (proverbial and deliberately impudent apology for overlooking a person. A joint stool was a low stool made by a joiner, perhaps here a stage property to represent Goneril and in line 52, Regan. "Joint stool" can also suggest the judicial bench; hence Goneril may be identified by the Fool, ironically, with those in power, who judge).

[958] *store* stuff.

[959] *Corruption . . . place* bribery in the court.

[960] *counterfeiting* i.e., feigned madness.

[961] *or . . . or* either . . . or.

[962] *brach* bitch.

[963] *lym* bloodhound (from the liam or leash with which he was led).

    Or bobtail tike, or trundle-tail[964]—
    Tom will make him weep and wail;
    For, with throwing[965] thus my head,   70
    Dogs leaped the hatch,[966] and all are fled.
Do, de, de, de. Sessa![967] Come, march to wakes[968] and fairs and
market towns. Poor Tom, thy horn[969] is dry.

Lear. Then let them anatomize Regan. See what breeds about her   75
heart.[970] Is there any cause in nature that make[971] these hard
hearts? *[To Edgar]* You, sir, I entertain[972] for one of my hundred;[973]
only I do not like the fashion of your garments. You will say
they are Persian;[974] but let them be changed.   80

Kent. Now, good my lord, lie here and rest awhile.

Lear. Make no noise, make no noise; draw the curtains.[975]
So, so. We'll go to supper i' th' morning.

Fool. And I'll go to bed at noon.[976]

Enter Gloucester.

Gloucester. Come hither, friend. Where is the King my master?   85

Kent. Here, sir, but trouble him not; his wits are gone.

Gloucester. Good friend, I prithee take him in thy arms.
I have o'erheard a plot of death upon him.
There is a litter ready; lay him in't
And drive toward Dover, friend, where thou shalt meet   90
Both welcome and protection. Take up thy master.
If thou shouldst dally half an hour, his life,
With thine and all that offer to defend him,
Stand in assurèd loss. Take up, take up,

---

[964] *bobtail . . . trundle-tail* short-tailed or long-tailed cur.

[965] *throwing* jerking (as a hound lifts its head from the ground, the scent having been lost).

[966] *leaped the hatch* leaped over the lower half of a divided door (i.e., left in a hurry).

[967] *Sessa* be off.

[968] *wakes* feasts attending the dedication of a church.

[969] *horn* horn bottle which the Bedlam used in begging a drink (Edgar is suggesting that he is unable to play his role any longer).

[970] *Then . . . heart* i.e., if the Bedlam's horn is dry, let Regan, whose heart has become as hard as horn, be dissected.

[971] *make* (subjunctive).

[972] *entertain* engage.

[973] *hundred* i.e., Lear's hundred knights.

[974] *Persian* gorgeous (ironically of Edgar's rags).

[975] *curtains* (Lear imagines himself in bed).

[976] *And . . . noon* (the Fool's last words).

95   And follow me, that will to some provision⁹⁷⁷
        Give thee quick conduct⁹⁷⁸

Kent.   Oppressèd nature sleeps.
This rest might yet have balmed thy broken sinews,⁹⁷⁹
Which, if convenience⁹⁸⁰ will not allow,
Stand in hard cure.⁹⁸¹ [To the Fool] Come, help to bear thy master.
Thou must not stay behind.

100 **Gloucester.** Come, come, away!

Exeunt [all but Edgar].

Edgar. When we our betters see bearing our woes,
We scarcely think our miseries our foes.⁹⁸²
Who alone suffers suffers most i' th' mind,
Leaving free⁹⁸³ things and happy shows⁹⁸⁴ behind;
105 But then the mind much sufferance⁹⁸⁵ doth o'erskip
When grief hath mates, and bearing fellowship.⁹⁸⁶
How light and portable⁹⁸⁷ my pain seems now,
When that which makes me bend makes the King bow.
He childed as I fathered. Tom, away.
110 Mark the high noises,⁹⁸⁸ and thyself bewray⁹⁸⁹
When false opinion, whose wrong thoughts⁹⁹⁰ defile thee,
In thy just proof repeals and reconciles thee.⁹⁹¹
What will hap more⁹⁹² tonight, safe 'scape the King!
Lurk,⁹⁹³ lurk.   [Exit.]

Scene VII. [*Gloucester's castle.*]

Enter Cornwall, Regan, Goneril, Edmund, and Servants.

---

⁹⁷⁷ *provision* maintenance.

⁹⁷⁸ *conduct* direction.

⁹⁷⁹ *balmed thy broken sinews* soothed thy racked nerves.

⁹⁸⁰ *convenience* fortunate occasion.

⁹⁸¹ *Stand . . . cure* will be hard to cure.

⁹⁸² *our foes* enemies peculiar to ourselves.

⁹⁸³ *free* carefree.

⁹⁸⁴ *shows* scenes.

⁹⁸⁵ *sufferance* suffering.

⁹⁸⁶ *bearing fellowship* suffering has company.

⁹⁸⁷ *portable* able to be supported or endured.

⁹⁸⁸ *Mark the high noises* observe the rumors of strife among those in power.

⁹⁸⁹ *bewray* reveal.

⁹⁹⁰ *wrong thoughts* misconceptions.

⁹⁹¹ *In . . . thee* on the manifesting of your innocence recalls you from outlawry and restores amity between you and your father.

⁹⁹² *What . . . more* whatever else happens.

⁹⁹³ *Lurk* hide.

Cornwall. *[To Goneril]* Post speedily to my Lord your husband; show him this letter. The army of France is landed. *[To Servants]* Seek out the traitor Gloucester.

[Exeunt some of the Servants.]

Regan. Hang him instantly.   5

Goneril. Pluck out his eyes.

Cornwall. Leave him to my displeasure. Edmund, keep you our sister company. The revenges we are bound[994] to take upon your traitorous father are not fit for your beholding. Advise the Duke   10 where you are going, to a most festinate[995] preparation. We are bound to the like. Our posts[996] shall be swift and intelligent[997] betwixt us. Farewell, dear sister; farewell, my Lord of Gloucester.[998]

Enter Oswald.

How now? Where's the King?   15

Oswald. My Lord of Gloucester hath conveyed him hence.
Some five or six and thirty of his knights,
Hot questrists[999] after him, met him at gate;
Who, with some other of the lords dependants,[1000]
Are gone with him toward Dover, where they boast   20
To have well-armèd friends.

Cornwall.   Get horses for your mistress.

[Exit Oswald.]

Goneril. Farewell, sweet lord, and sister.

Cornwall. Edmund, farewell.

[Exeunt Goneril and Edmund.]

                                         Go seek the traitor Gloucester,
Pinion him like a thief, bring him before us.

[Exeunt other Servants.]

---

[994] *bound* (1) forced (2) purposing to.
[995] *festinate* speedy.
[996] *posts* messengers.
[997] *intelligent* full of information.
[998] *Lord of Gloucester* i.e., Edmund, **now** elevated to the title.
[999] *questrists* searchers.
[1000] *lords dependants* attendant lords (members of Lear's retinue).

25 Though well we may not pass upon[1001] his life
Without the form of justice, yet our power
Shall do a court'sy to[1002] our wrath, which men
May blame, but not control.

Enter Gloucester, brought in by two or three.

Who's there, the traitor?

Regan. Ingrateful fox, 'tis he.

30 **Cornwall.** Bind fast his corky[1003] arms.

Gloucester. What means your Graces? Good my friends, consider
You are my guests. Do me no foul play, friends.

Cornwall. Bind him, I say.

[Servants bind him.]

Regan.   Hard, hard! O filthy traitor.

Gloucester. Unmerciful lady as you are, I'm none.

35 **Cornwall.** To this chair bind him. Villain, thou shalt find—

[Regan plucks his beard.[1004]]

Gloucester. By the kind gods, 'tis mostly ignobly done
To pluck me by the beard.

Regan. So white, and such a traitor?

Gloucester.   Naughty[1005] lady,
These hairs which thou dost ravish from my chin
40 Will quicken[1006] and accuse thee. I am your host.
With robber's hands my hospitable favors[1007]
You should not ruffle[1008] thus. What will you do?

Cornwall. Come, sir, what letters had you late[1009] from France?

Regan. Be simple-answered,[1010] for we know the truth.

45 **Cornwall.** And what confederacy have you with the traitors

----

1001 *pass upon* pass judgment on.
1002 *do a court'sy to* indulge.
1003 *corky* sapless (because old).
1004 s.d. *plucks his beard* (a deadly insult).
1005 *Naughty* wicked.
1006 *quicken* come to life.
1007 *hospitable favors* face of your host.
1008 *ruffle* tear at violently.
1009 *late* recently.
1010 *simple-answered* straightforward in answering.

Late footed in the kingdom?

Regan. To whose hands you have sent the lunatic King:
Speak.

Gloucester. I have a letter guessingly[1011] set down,
Which came from one that's of a neutral heart,
And not from one opposed.

Cornwall.   Cunning.

Regan.   And false. 50

Cornwall. Where hast thou sent the king?

Gloucester. To Dover.

Regan. Wherefore to Dover? Wast thou not charged at peril[1012]—

Cornwall. Wherefore to Dover? Let him answer that.

Gloucester. I am tied to th' stake, and I must stand the course.[1013] 55

Regan. Wherefore to Dover?

Gloucester. Because I would not see thy cruel nails
Pluck out his poor old eyes; nor thy fierce sister
In his anointed[1014] flesh rash[1015] boarish fangs.
The sea, with such a storm as his bare head   60
In hell-black night endured, would have buoyed[1016] up
And quenched the stellèd[1017] fires.
Yet, poor old heart, he holp[1018] the heavens to rain.
If wolves had at thy gate howled that dearn[1019] time,
Thou shouldst have said, "Good porter, turn the key."[1020]   65
All cruels else subscribe.[1021] But I shall see
The wingèd[1022] vengeance overtake such children.

Cornwall. See't shalt thou never. Fellows, hold the chair.
Upon these eyes of thine I'll set my foot.

[1011] *guessingly* without certain knowledge.

[1012] *charged at peril* ordered under penalty.

[1013] *course* coursing (in which a relay of dogs baits a bull or bear tied in the pit).

[1014] *anointed* holy (because king).

[1015] *rash* strike with the tusk, like a boar.

[1016] *buoyed* risen.

[1017] *stellèd* (1) fixed (as opposed to the planets or wandering stars) (2) starry.

[1018] *holp* helped.

[1019] *dearn* dread.

[1020] *turn the key* i.e., unlock the gate.

[1021] *All cruels else subscribe* all cruel creatures but man are compassionate.

[1022] *wingèd* (1) heavenly (2) swift.

70 **Gloucester.** He that will think[1023] to live till he be old,
Give me some help.—O cruel! O you gods!

Regan. One side will mock[1024] another. Th' other too.

Cornwall. If you see vengeance—

First Servant.   Hold your hand, my lord!
I have served you ever since I was a child;
75 But better service have I never done you
Than now to bid you hold.

Regan.   How now, you dog?

First Servant. If you did wear a beard upon your chin,
I'd shake it[1025] on this quarrel. What do you mean![1026]

Cornwall. My villain![1027]

Draw and fight.

80 **First Servant.** Nay, then, come on, and take the chance of anger.

Regan. Give me thy sword. A peasant stand up thus?

She takes a sword and runs at him behind, kills him.

First Servant. O, I am slain! my lord, you have one eye left
To see some mischief[1028] on him. O!

Cornwall. Lest it see more, prevent it. Out, vile jelly.
85 Where is thy luster now?

Gloucester. All dark and comfortless. Where's my son Edmund?
Edmund, enkindle all the sparks of nature[1029]
To quit[1030] this horrid act.

Regan.   Out, treacherous villain,
Thou call'st on him that hates thee. It was he
90 That made the overture[1031] of thy treasons to us;
Who is too good to pity thee.

Gloucester. O my follies! Then Edgar was abused.[1032]

1023 *will think* expects.
1024 *mock* make ridiculous (because of the contrast).
1025 *shake it* (an insult comparable to Regan's plucking of Gloucester's beard).
1026 *What . . . mean* i.e., what terrible thing are you doing.
1027 *villain* serf (with a suggestion of the modern meaning).
1028 *mischief* injury.
1029 *enkindle . . . nature* fan your natural feeling into flame.
1030 *quit* requite.
1031 *overture* disclosure.
1032 *abused* wronged.

Kind gods, forgive me that, and prosper him.

Regan.   Go thrust him out at gates, and let him smell
His way to Dover.

Exit [one] with Gloucester.

                              How is't, my lord? How look you?[1033]   95

Cornwall.   I have received a hurt. Follow me, lady.
Turn out that eyeless villain. Throw this slave
Upon the dunghill. Regan, I bleed apace.
Untimely comes this hurt. Give me your arm.

Exeunt.

Second Servant.   I'll never care what wickedness I do,   100
If this man come to good.

Third Servant.   If she live long,
And in the end meet the old course of death,[1034]
Women will all turn monsters.

Second Servant.   Let's follow the old Earl, and get the Bedlam
To lead him where he would. His roguish madness   105
Allows itself to anything.[1035]

Third Servant.   Go thou. I'll fetch some flax and whites of eggs
To apply to his bleeding face. Now heaven help him.

[Exeunt severally.]

ACT IV

Scene I. [*The heath.*]

Enter Edgar.

Edgar.   Yet better thus, and known to be contemned,[1036]
Than still contemned and flattered. To be worst,
The lowest and most dejected[1037] thing of fortune,
Stands still in esperance,[1038] lives not in fear:
The lamentable change is from the best,   5

[1033] *How look you* how are you.
[1034] *meet . . . death* die the customary death of old age.
[1035] *His . . . anything* his lack of all self-control leaves him open to any suggestion.
[1036] *known to be contemned* conscious of being despised.
[1037] *dejected* abased.
[1038] *esperance* hope.

The worst returns to laughter.[1039] Welcome then,
Thou unsubstantial air that I embrace!
The wretch that thou hast blown unto the worst
Owes[1040] nothing to thy blasts.

Enter Gloucester, led by an Old Man.

But who comes here?

10 My father, poorly led?[1041] World, world, O world!
But that thy strange mutations make us hate thee,
Life would not yield to age.[1042]

Old Man. O, my good lord, I have been your tenant, and your
father's tenant, these fourscore years.

15 **Gloucester.** Away, get thee away; good friend, be gone:
Thy comforts[1043] can do me no good at all;
Thee they may hurt.[1044]

Old Man.   You cannot see your way.

Gloucester. I have no way and therefore want[1045] no eyes;
I stumbled when I saw. Full oft 'tis seen,
20 Our means secure us, and our mere defects
Prove our commodities.[1046] Oh, dear son Edgar,
The food[1047] of thy abusèd[1048] father's wrath!
Might I but live to see thee in[1049] my touch,
I'd say I had eyes again!

Old Man.   How now! Who's there?

25 **Edgar.** *[Aside]* O gods! Who is 't can say "I am at the worst"?
I am worse than e'er I was.

Old Man.   'Tis poor mad Tom.

Edgar. *[Aside]* And worse I may be yet: the worst is not

[1039] *returns to laughter* changes for the better.

[1040] *Owes* is in debt for.

[1041] *poorly led* (1) led like a poor man, with only one attendant (2) led by a poor
man.

[1042] *But . . . age* we should not agree to grow old and hence die, except for the
hateful mutability of life.

[1043] *comforts* ministrations.

[1044] *hurt* injure.

[1045] *want* require.

[1046] *Our . . . commodities* our resources make us overconfident, while our afflictions
make for our advantage.

[1047] *food* i.e., the object on which Gloucester's anger fed.

[1048] *abusèd* deceived.

[1049] *in* i.e., with, by means of.

So long as we can say "This is the worst."[1050]

Old Man.   Fellow, where goest?

Gloucester.   Is it a beggar-man?

Old Man.   Madman and beggar too.   30

Gloucester.   He has some reason,[1051] else he could not beg.
I' th' last night's storm I such a fellow saw,
Which made me think a man a worm. My son
Came then into my mind, and yet my mind
Was then scarce friends with him. I have heard   35
more since.
As flies to wanton[1052] boys, are we to th' gods,
They kill us for their sport.

Edgar.   *[Aside]* How should this be?[1053]
Bad is the trade that must play fool to sorrow,
Ang'ring[1054] itself and others. Bless thee, master!

Gloucester.   Is that the naked fellow?

Old Man.   Ay, my lord.   40

Gloucester.   Then, prithee, get thee gone: if for my sake
Thou wilt o'ertake us hence a mile or twain
I' th' way toward Dover, do it for ancient[1055] love,
And bring some covering for this naked soul,
Which I'll entreat to lead me.

Old Man.   Alack, sir, he is mad.   45

Gloucester.   'Tis the times' plague,[1056] when madmen lead the blind.
Do as I bid thee, or rather do thy pleasure;[1057]
Above the rest,[1058] be gone.

Old Man.   I'll bring him the best 'parel[1059] that I have,
Come on 't what will.   *Exit.*   50

[1050] *the . . . worst* so long as a man continues to suffer (i.e., is still alive), even greater suffering may await him.

[1051] *reason* faculty of reasoning.

[1052] *wanton* (1) playful (2) reckless.

[1053] *How should this be* i.e., how can this horror be?

[1054] *Ang'ring* offending.

[1055] *ancient* (1) the love the Old Man feels, by virtue of his long tenancy (2) the love that formerly obtained between master and man.

[1056] *times' plague* characteristic disorder of this time.

[1057] *thy pleasure* as you like.

[1058] *the rest* all.

[1059] *'parel* apparel.

Gloucester. Sirrah, naked fellow—

Edgar. Poor Tom's a-cold. *[Aside]* I cannot daub it[1060] further.

Gloucester. Come hither, fellow.

55 **Edgar.** *[Aside]* And yet I must.—Bless thy sweet eyes, they bleed.

Gloucester. Know'st thou the way to Dover?

Edgar. Both stile and gate, horse-way and footpath. Poor Tom hath
been scared out of his good wits. Bless thee, good man's son,
60 from the foul fiend! Five fiends have been in Poor Tom at once;
of lust, as Obidicut;[1061] Hobbididence, prince of dumbness;[1062]
Mahu, of stealing; Modo, of murder; Flibbertigibbet, of mopping
and mowing;[1063] who since possesses chambermaids and waiting-
65 women. So, bless thee, master!

Gloucester. Here, take this purse, thou whom the heavens' plagues
Have humbled to all strokes:[1064] that I am wretched
Makes thee the happier. Heavens, deal so still!
Let the superfluous[1065] and lust-dieted[1066] man,
70 That slaves[1067] your ordinance,[1068] that will not see
Because he does not feel, feel your pow'r quickly;
So distribution should undo excess,[1069]
And each man have enough. Dost thou know Dover?

Edgar. Ay, master.

75 **Gloucester.** There is a cliff whose high and bending[1070] head
Looks fearfully[1071] in the confinèd deep:[1072]
Bring me but to the very brim of it,
And I'll repair the misery thou dost bear
With something rich about me: from that place
I shall no leading need.

[1060] *daub it* lay it on (figure from plastering mortar).

[1061] *Obidicut* Hoberdicut, a devil (like the four that follow, from Harsnett's *Declaration*).

[1062] *dumbness* muteness (like the crimes and afflictions in the next lines, the result of diabolic possession).

[1063] *mopping and mowing* grimacing and making faces.

[1064] *humbled to all strokes* brought so low as to bear anything humbly.

[1065] *superfluous* possessed of superfluities.

[1066] *lust-dieted* whose lust is gratified (like Gloucester's).

[1067] *slaves* (1) tramples, spurns like a slave (2) ? tears, rends (Old English *slaefan*).

[1068] *ordinance* law.

[1069] *So . . . excess* then the man with too much wealth would distribute it among those with too little.

[1070] *bending* overhanging.

[1071] *fearfully* occasioning fear.

[1072] *confinèd deep* the sea, hemmed in below.

Edgar.   Give me thy arm: 80
Poor Tom shall lead thee.

Exeunt.

Scene II. [*Before the Duke of Albany's palace.*]

Enter Goneril and Edmund.

Goneril. Welcome, my lord: I marvel our mild husband
Not met[1073] us on the way.

Enter Oswald.

                                  Now, where's your master?

Oswald. Madam, within; but never man so changed.
I told him of the army that was landed:
He smiled at it. I told him you were coming;   5
His answer was, "The worse." Of Gloucester's treachery,
And of the loyal service of his son
When I informed him, then he called me sot,[1074]
And told me I had turned the wrong side out:
What most he should dislike seems pleasant to him;   10
What like,[1075] offensive.

Goneril. [*To Edmund*] Then shall you go no further.
It is the cowish[1076] terror of his spirit,
That dares not undertake:[1077] he'll not feel wrongs,
Which tie him to an answer.[1078] Our wishes on the way
May prove effects.[1079] Back, Edmund, to my brother;   15
Hasten his musters[1080] and conduct his pow'rs.[1081]
I must change names[1082] at home and give the distaff[1083]
Into my husband's hands. This trusty servant

1073 *Not met* did not meet.
1074 *sot* fool.
1075 *What like* what he should like.
1076 *cowish* cowardly.
1077 *undertake* venture.
1078 *tie him to an answer* oblige him to retaliate.
1079 *Our . . . effects* our desires (that you might be my husband), as we journeyed here, may be fulfilled.
1080 *musters* collecting of troops.
1081 *conduct his pow'rs* lead his army.
1082 *change names* i.e., exchange the name of "mistress" for that of "master."
1083 *distaff* spinning stick (wifely symbol).

Shall pass between us: ere long you are like to hear,
20 If you dare venture in your own behalf,
A mistress's[1084] command. Wear this; spare speech;

[Giving a favor]

Decline your head.[1085] This kiss, if it durst speak,
Would stretch thy spirits up into the air:
Conceive,[1086] and fare thee well.

25 **Edmund.**   Yours in the ranks of death.

Goneril.   My most dear Gloucester!

Exit [Edmund].

O, the difference of man and man!
To thee a woman's services are due:
My fool usurps my body.[1087]

Oswald.   Madam, here comes my lord.
                                                         Exit.

Enter Albany.

Goneril.   I have been worth the whistle.[1088]

Albany.   O Goneril!
30 You are not worth the dust which the rude wind
Blows in your face. I fear your disposition:[1089]
That nature which contemns[1090] its origin
Cannot be bordered certain in itself;[1091]
She that herself will sliver and disbranch[1092]
35 From her material sap,[1093] perforce must wither
And come to deadly use.[1094]

Goneril.   No more; the text[1095] is foolish.

[1084] *mistress's* lover's (and also, Albany having been disposed of, lady's or wife's).

[1085] *Decline your head* i.e., that Goneril may kiss him.

[1086] *Conceive* understand (with a sexual implication, that includes "stretch thy spirits," 1.23; and "death," 1.25: "to die," meaning "to experience sexual intercourse").

[1087] *My fool usurps body* my husband wrongfully enjoys me.

[1088] *I . . . whistle* i.e., once you valued me (the proverb is implied, "It is a poor dog that is not worth the whistling").

[1089] *disposition* nature.

[1090] *contemns* despises.

[1091] *bordered . . . itself* kept within its normal bounds.

[1092] *sliver and disbranch* cut off.

[1093] *material sap* essential and life-giving sustenance.

[1094] *come to deadly use* i.e., be as a dead branch for the burning.

[1095] *text* i.e., on which your sermon is based.

Albany. Wisdom and goodness to the vile seem vile:
Filths savor but themselves.[1096] What have you done?
Tigers, not daughters, what have you performed?   40
A father, and a gracious agèd man,
Whose reverence even the head-lugged bear[1097] would lick,
Most barbarous, most degenerate, have you madded.[1098]
Could my good brother suffer you to do it?
A man, a prince, by him so benefited!   45
If that the heavens do not their visible spirits[1099]
Send quickly down to tame these vile offenses,
It will come,
Humanity must perforce prey on itself,
Like monsters of the deep.

Goneril.   Milk-livered[1100] man!   50
That bear'st a cheek for blows, a head for wrongs;
Who hast not in thy brows an eye discerning
Thine honor from thy suffering;[1101] that not know'st
Fools do those villains pity who are punished
Ere they have done their mischief.[1102] Where's thy drum?   55
France spreads his banners in our noiseless[1103] land,
With plumèd helm[1104] thy state begins to threat,[1105]
Whilst thou, a moral[1106] fool, sits still and cries
"Alack, why does he so?"

Albany.   See thyself, devil!
Proper[1107] deformity seems not in the fiend   60
So horrid as in woman.

Goneril.   O vain fool!

Albany. Thou changèd and self-covered[1108] thing,

[1096] *Filths savor but themselves* the filthy relish only the taste of filth.

[1097] *head-lugged bear* bear-baited by the dogs, and hence enraged.

[1098] *madded* made mad.

[1099] *visible spirits* avenging spirits in material form.

[1100] *Milk-livered* lily-livered (hence cowardly, the liver being regarded as the seat of courage).

[1101] *discerning . . . suffering* able to distinguish between insults that ought to be resented, and ordinary pain that is to be borne.

[1102] *Fools . . . mischief* only fools are sorry for criminals whose intended criminality is prevented by punishment.

[1103] *noiseless* i.e., the drum, signifying preparation for war, is silent.

[1104] *helm* helmet.

[1105] *thy . . . threat* France begins to threaten Albany's realm.

[1106] *moral* moralizing; but also with the implication that morality and folly are one.

[1107] *Proper* (1) natural (to a fiend) (2) fair-appearing.

[1108] *changèd and self-covered* i.e., transformed, by the contorting of her woman's face, on which appears the fiendish behavior she has allowed herself. (Goneril has disguised nature by wickedness).

for shame,
Be-monster not thy feature.[1109] Were't my fitness[1110]
To let these hands obey my blood,[1111]
65 They are apt enough to dislocate and tear
Thy flesh and bones: howe'er[1112] thou art a fiend,
A woman's shape doth shield thee.

Goneril. Marry,[1113] your manhood mew[1114]—

Enter a Messenger.

Albany. What news?

70 **Messenger.** O, my good lord, the Duke of Cornwall's dead,
Slain by his servant, going to[1115] put out
The other eye of Gloucester.

Albany.   Gloucester's eyes!

Messenger. A servant that he bred,[1116] thrilled with remorse,[1117]
Opposed against the act, bending his sword
75 To his great master, who thereat enraged
Flew on him, and amongst them felled[1118] him dead,
But not without that harmful stroke which since
Hath plucked him after.[1119]

Albany.   This shows you are above,
You justicers,[1120] that these our nether[1121] crimes
80 So speedily can venge.[1122] But, O poor Gloucester!
Lost he his other eye?

Messenger.   Both, both, my lord.
This letter, madam, craves[1123] a speedy answer;
'Tis from your sister.

[1109] *Bemonster not thy feature* do not change your appearance into a fiend's.

[1110] *my fitness* appropriate for me.

[1111] *blood* passion.

[1112] *howe'er* but even if.

[1113] *Marry* by the Virgin Mary.

[1114] *your manhood mew* (1) coop up or confine your (pretended) manhood (2) molt or shed it, if that is what is supposed to "shield" me from you.

[1115] *going to* as he was about to.

[1116] *bred* reared.

[1117] *thrilled with remorse* pierced by compassion.

[1118] *amongst them felled* others assisting, they felled.

[1119] *plucked him after* i.e., brought Cornwall to death with his servant.

[1120] *justicers* judges.

[1121] *nether* committed below (on earth).

[1122] *venge* avenge.

[1123] *craves* demands.

Goneril.   *[Aside]* One way I like this well;
But being widow, and my Gloucester with her,
May all the building in my fancy pluck   85
Upon my hateful life.[1124] Another way,[1125]
The news is not so tart.[1126]—I'll read, and answer.

                                                                    Exit.

Albany.   Where was his son when they did take his eyes?

Messenger.   Come with my lady hither.

Albany.   He is not here.

Messenger.   No, my good lord; I met him back[1127] again.   90

Albany.   Knows he the wickedness?

Messenger.   Ay, my good lord; 'twas he informed against him,
And quit the house on purpose, that their punishment
Might have the freer course.

Albany.   Gloucester, I live
To thank thee for the love thou showed'st the King,   95
And to revenge thine eyes. Come hither, friend:
Tell me what more thou know'st.

Exeunt.

Scene III. *[The French camp near Dover.]*

Enter Kent and a Gentleman.

Kent.   Why the King of France is so suddenly gone back, know you
    no reason?

Gentleman.   Something he left imperfect in the state,[1128] which since
    his coming forth is thought of, which imports[1129] to the kingdom   5
    so much fear and danger that his personal return was most required
    and necessary.

Kent.   Who hath he left behind him general?

[1124] *May . . . life* these things (1.84) may send my future hopes, my castles in air,
crashing down upon the hateful (married) life I lead now.

[1125] *Another way* looked at another way.

[1126] *tart* sour.

[1127] *back* going back.

[1128] *imperfect in the state* unsettled in his own kingdom.

[1129] *imports* portends.

Gentleman.   The Marshal of France, Monsieur La Far.

10 **Kent.**   Did your letters pierce[1130] the queen to any demonstration
      of grief?

Gentleman.   Ay, sir; she took them, read them in my presence,
And now and then an ample tear trilled[1131] down
Her delicate cheek: it seemed she was a queen
15 Over her passion, who most rebel-like
Sought to be king o'er her.

Kent.   O, then it moved her.

Gentleman.   Not to a rage: patience and sorrow strove
Who should express her goodliest.[1132] You have seen
Sunshine and rain at once: her smiles and tears
20 Were like a better way:[1133] those happy smilets[1134]
That played on her ripe lip seemed not to know
What guests were in her eyes, which parted thence
As pearls from diamonds dropped. In brief,
Sorrow would be a rarity most belovèd,
If all could so become it.[1135]

25 **Kent.**   Made she no verbal question?

Gentleman.   Faith, once or twice she heaved[1136] the name of "father"
Pantingly forth, as if it pressed her heart;
Cried "Sisters! Sisters! Shame of ladies! Sisters!
Kent! Father! Sisters! What, i' th' storm? i' th' night?
30 Let pity not be believed!"[1137] There she shook
The holy water from her heavenly eyes,
And clamor moistened:[1138] then away she started
To deal with grief alone.

Kent.   It is the stars,
The stars above us, govern our conditions;[1139]
35 Else one self mate and make could not beget

[1130] *pierce* impel.

[1131] *trilled* trickled.

[1132] *Who . . . goodliest* which should give her the most becoming expression.

[1133] *Were like a better way* i.e., improved on that spectacle.

[1134] *smilets* little smiles.

[1135] *Sorrow . . . it* sorrow would be a coveted jewel if it became others as it does her.

[1136] *heaved* expressed with difficulty.

[1137] *Let pity not be believed* let it not be believed for pity.

[1138] *clamor moistened* moistened clamor, i.e., mixed (and perhaps assuaged) her outcries with tears.

[1139] *govern our conditions* determine what we are.

Such different issues.[1140] You spoke not with her since?

Gentleman. No.

Kent. Was this before the King returned?

Gentleman.   No, since.

Kent. Well, sir, the poor distressèd Lear's i' th' town;
Who sometime in his better tune[1141] remembers   40
What we are come about, and by no means
Will yield to see his daughter.

Gentleman.   Why, good sir?

Kent. A sovereign[1142] shame so elbows[1143] him: his own unkindness
That stripped her from his benediction, turned her
To foreign casualties,[1144] gave her dear rights   45
To his dog-hearted daughters: these things sting
His mind so venomously that burning shame
Detains him from Cordelia.

Gentleman.   Alack, poor gentleman!

Kent. Of Albany's and Cornwall's powers you heard not?

Gentleman. 'Tis so;[1145] they are afoot.   50

Kent. Well, sir, I'll bring you to our master Lear,
And leave you to attend him: some dear cause[1146]
Will in concealment wrap me up awhile;
When I am known aright, you shall not grieve
Lending me this acquaintance. I pray you, go   55
Along with me.

[*Exeunt.*]

Scene IV. [*The same. A tent.*]

Enter, with drum and colors, Cordelia, Doctor, and Soldiers.

[1140] *Else . . . issues* otherwise the same husband and wife could not produce such different children.

[1141] *better tune* composed, less jangled intervals.

[1142] *sovereign* overpowering.

[1143] *elbows* jogs his elbow i.e., reminds him.

[1144] *casualties* chances.

[1145] *'Tis so* i.e., I have heard of them.

[1146] *dear cause* important reason.

Cordelia.   Alack, 'tis he: why, he was met even now
As mad as the vexed sea; singing aloud;
Crowned with rank femiter and furrow-weeds,
With hardocks, hemlock, nettles, cuckoo-flow'rs,
5 Darnel,[1147] and all the idle weeds that grow
In our sustaining corn.[1148] A century[1149] send forth;
Search every acre in the high-grown field,
And bring him to our eye *[Exit an Officer.]* What can man's wisdom[1150]
In the restoring his bereavèd[1151] sense?
10 He that helps him take all my outward[1152] worth.

Doctor.   There is means, madam:
Our foster-nurse[1153] of nature is repose,
The which he lacks: that to provoke[1154] in him,
Are many simples operative,[1155] whose power
Will close the eye of anguish.

15 **Cordelia.**   All blest secrets,
All you unpublished virtues[1156] of the earth,
Spring with my tears! be aidant and remediate[1157]
In the good man's distress! Seek, seek for him,
Lest his ungoverned rage dissolve the life
That wants the means to lead it.[1158]

Enter Messenger.

20 **Messenger.**   News, madam;
The British pow'rs are marching hitherward.

Cordelia.   'Tis known before. Our preparation stands
In expectation of them. O dear father,
It is thy business that I go about;
25 Therefore[1159] great France

[1147] *femiter . . . Darnel: femiter* fumitory, whose leaves and juice are bitter; *furrow-weeds* weeds that grow in the furrow; or plowed land; *hardocks* ? hoar or white docks, burdocks, harlocks; *hemlock* a poison; *nettles* plants which sting and burn; *cuckoo-flow'rs* identified with a plant employed to remedy diseases of the brain; *Darnel* tares, noisome weeds.

[1148] *sustaining corn* life-maintaining wheat.

[1149] *century* ? sentry; troop of a hundred soldiers.

[1150] *What can man's wisdom* what can science accomplish.

[1151] *bereavèd* impaired.

[1152] *outward* material

[1153] *foster-nurse* fostering nurse.

[1154] *provoke* induce.

[1155] *simples operative* efficacious medicinal herbs.

[1156] *unpublished virtues* i.e., secret remedial herbs.

[1157] *remediate* remedial.

[1158] *wants . . . it* i.e., lacks the reason to control the rage.

[1159] *Therefore* because of that.

My mourning and importuned[1160] tears hath pitied.
No blown[1161] ambition doth our arms incite,
But love, dear love, and our aged father's right:
Soon may I hear and see him!

Exeunt.

Scene V. [*Gloucester's castle.*]

Enter Regan and Oswald.

Regan.   But are my brother's pow'rs set forth?

Oswald.   Ay, madam.

Regan.   Himself in person there?

Oswald.   Madam, with much ado:[1162]
Your sister is the better soldier.

Regan.   Lord Edmund spake not with your lord at home?

Oswald.   No, madam.   5

Regan.   What might import[1163] my sister's letter to him?

Oswald.   I know not, lady.

Regan.   Faith, he is posted[1164] hence on serious matter.
It was great ignorance,[1165] Gloucester's eyes being out,
To let him live. Where he arrives he moves   10
All hearts against us: Edmund, I think, is gone,
In pity of his misery, to dispatch
His nighted[1166] life; moreover, to descry
The strength o' th' enemy.

Oswald.   I must needs after him, madam, with my letter.   15

Regan.   Our troops set forth tomorrow: stay with us;
The ways are dangerous.

Oswald.   I may not, madam:

[1160] *importuned* importunate.
[1161] *blown* puffed up.
[1162] *ado* bother and persuasion.
[1163] *import* purport, carry as its message.
[1164] *is posted* has ridden speedily.
[1165] *ignorance* folly.
[1166] *nighted* (1) darkened, because blinded (2) benighted.

My lady charged my duty[1167] in this business.

Regan. Why should she write to Edmund? Might not you
20 Transport her purposes[1168] by word? Belike,[1169]
Some things I know not what. I'll love thee much,
Let me unseal the letter.

Oswald.   Madam, I had rather—

Regan. I know your lady does not love her husband;
I am sure of that: and at her late[1170] being here
25 She gave strange eliads[1171] and most speaking looks
To noble Edmund. I know you are of her bosom.[1172]

Oswald. I, madam?

Regan. I speak in understanding: y'are; I know 't:
Therefore I do advise you, take this note:[1173]
30 My lord is dead; Edmund and I have talked;
And more convenient[1174] is he for my hand
Than for your lady's: you may gather more.[1175]
If you do find him, pray you, give him this;[1176]
And when your mistress hears thus much from you,
35 I pray, desire her call[1177] her wisdom to her.
So, fare you well.
If you do chance to hear of that blind traitor,
Preferment[1178] falls on him that cuts him off.

Oswald. Would I could meet him, madam! I should show
What party I do follow.

40 **Regan.**   Fare thee well.

Exeunt.

Scene VI. [*Fields near Dover.*]

Enter Gloucester and Edgar.

[1167] *charged my duty* ordered me as a solemn duty
[1168] *Transport her purposes* convey her intentions.
[1169] *Belike* probably.
[1170] *late* recently.
[1171] *eliads* amorous looks.
[1172] *of her bosom* in her confidence.
[1173] *take this note* take note of this.
[1174] *convenient* fitting.
[1175] *gather more* surmise more yourself.
[1176] *this* this advice.
[1177] *call* recall.
[1178] *Preferment* promotion.

Gloucester. When shall I come to th' top of that same hill?

Edgar. You do climb up it now. Look, how we labor.

Gloucester. Methinks the ground is even.

Edgar.   Horrible steep.
Hark, do you hear the sea?

Gloucester.   No, truly.   5

Edgar. Why then your other senses grow imperfect
By your eyes' anguish.[1179]

Gloucester.   So may it be indeed.
Methinks thy voice is altered, and thou speak'st
In better phrase and matter than thou didst.

Edgar. Y'are much deceived: in nothing am I changed
But in my garments.

Gloucester.   Methinks y'are better spoken.   10

Edgar. Come on, sir; here's the place: stand still. How fearful
And dizzy 'tis to cast one's eyes so low!
The crows and choughs[1180] that wing the midway air[1181]
Show scarce so gross[1182] as beetles. Half way down
Hangs one that gathers sampire,[1183] dreadful trade!   15
Methinks he seems no bigger than his head.
The fishermen that walk upon the beach
Appear like mice; and yond tall anchoring[1184] bark
Diminished to her cock;[1185] her cock, a buoy
Almost too small for sight. The murmuring surge   20
That on th' unnumb'red idle pebble[1186] chafes
Cannot be heard so high. I'll look no more,
Lest my brain turn and the deficient sight
Topple[1187] down headlong.

Gloucester.   Set me where you stand.

[1179] *anguish* pain.

[1180] *choughs* a kind of crow.

[1181] *midway air* i.e., halfway down the cliff.

[1182] *gross* large.

[1183] *sampire* samphire, an aromatic herb associated with Dover Cliffs.

[1184] *anchoring* anchored.

[1185] *cock* cockboat, a small boat usually towed behind the ship.

[1186] *unnumb'red idle pebble* innumerable pebbles, moved to and fro by the waves to no purpose.

[1187] *the deficient sight/Topple* my failing sight topple me.

25 **Edgar.**   Give me your hand: you are now within a foot
Of th' extreme verge: for all beneath the moon
Would I not leap upright.[1188]

Gloucester.   Let go my hand.
Here, friend, 's another purse; in it a jewel
Well worth a poor man's taking. Fairies[1189] and gods
30 Prosper it with thee! Go thou further off;
Bid me farewell, and let me hear thee going.

Edgar.   Now fare ye well, good sir.

Gloucester.   With all my heart.

Edgar.   *[Aside]* Why I do trifle thus with his despair
Is done to cure it.[1190]

Gloucester.   O you mighty gods!

He kneels.

35 This world I do renounce, and in your sights
Shake patiently my great affliction off:
If I could bear it longer and not fall
To quarrel[1191] with your great opposeless[1192] wills,
My snuff[1193] and loathèd part of nature should
40 Burn itself out. If Edgar live, O bless him!
Now, fellow, fare thee well.

                                                     He falls.

Edgar.   Gone, sir, farewell.
And yet I know not how[1194] conceit[1195] may rob
The treasury of life, when life itself
Yields to[1196] the theft. Had he been where he thought,
45 By this had thought been past. Alive or dead?
Ho, you sir! friend! Hear you, sir! speak!
Thus might he pass[1197] indeed: yet he revives.
What are you, sir?

Gloucester.   Away, and let me die.

[1188] *upright* i.e., even up in the air, to say nothing of forward, over the cliff.
[1189] *Fairies* (who are supposed to guard and multiply hidden treasure).
[1190] *Why . . . it* I play on his despair in order to cure it.
[1191] *fall/To quarrel with* rebel against.
[1192] *opposeless* not to be, and not capable of being, opposed.
[1193] *snuff* the guttering (and stinking) wick of a burnt-out candle.
[1194] *how* but what.
[1195] *conceit* imagination.
[1196] *Yields to* allows.
[1197] *pass* die.

Edgar. Hadst thou been aught but gossamer, feathers, air,
So many fathom down precipitating,[1198]   50
Thou'dst shivered like an egg: but thou dost breathe;
Hast heavy substance; bleed'st not; speak'st; art sound.
Ten masts at each[1199] make not the altitude
Which thou hast perpendicularly fell:
Thy life's[1200] a miracle. Speak yet again.   55

Gloucester. But have I fall'n, or no?

Edgar. From the dread summit of this chalky bourn.[1201]
Look up a-height;[1202] the shrill-gorged[1203] lark so far
Cannot be seen or heard: do but look up.

Gloucester. Alack, I have no eyes.   60
Is wretchedness deprived that benefit,
To end itself by death? 'Twas yet some comfort,
When misery could beguile[1204] the tyrant's rage
And frustrate his proud will.

Edgar.   Give me your arm.
Up, so. How is't? Feel you[1205] your legs? You stand.   65

Gloucester. Too well, too well.

Edgar.   This is above all strangeness.
Upon the crown o' th' cliff, what thing was that
Which parted from you?

Gloucester.   A poor unfortunate beggar.

Edgar. As I stood here below, methought his eyes
Were two full moons; he had a thousand noses,   70
Horns whelked[1206] and waved like the enridgèd[1207] sea:
It was some fiend; therefore, thou happy father,[1208]
Think that the clearest[1209] gods, who make them honors
Of men's impossibilities,[1210] have preserved thee.

[1198] *precipitating* falling.

[1199] *at each* one on top of the other.

[1200] *life's* survival.

[1201] *bourn* boundary.

[1202] *a-height* on high.

[1203] *gorged* throated, voiced.

[1204] *beguile* cheat (i.e., by suicide).

[1205] *Feel you* have you any feeling in.

[1206] *whelked* twisted.

[1207] *enridgèd* i.e., furrowed into waves.

[1208] *happy father* fortunate old man.

[1209] *clearest* purest.

[1210] *who . . . impossibilities* who cause themselves to be honored and revered by performing miracles of which men are incapable.

75 **Gloucester.** I do remember now: henceforth I'll bear
Affliction till it do cry out itself
"Enough, enough," and die. That thing you speak of,
I took it for a man; often 'twould say
"The fiend, the fiend"—he led me to that place.

Edgar. Bear free[1211] and patient thoughts.

Enter Lear [fantastically dressed with wild flowers].

80   But who comes here?
The safer[1212] sense will ne'er accommodate[1213]
His master thus.

Lear. No, they cannot touch me for coining;[1214] I am the King
himself.

85 **Edgar.** O thou side-piercing sight!

Lear. Nature's above art in that respect.[1215] There's your press-
money.[1216] That fellow handles his bow like a crow-keeper;[1217]
draw me a clothier's yard.[1218] Look, look, a mouse! Peace, peace;
90   this piece of toasted cheese will do 't. There's my gauntlet;[1219] I'll
prove it on[1220] a giant. Bring up the brown bills.[1221] O, well
flown,[1222] bird! i' th' clout, i' th' clout:[1223] hewgh![1224] Give the
word.[1225]

Edgar. Sweet marjoram.[1226]

95 **Lear.** Pass.

Gloucester. I know that voice.

[1211] *free* i.e., emancipated from grief and despair, which fetter the soul.

[1212] *safer* sounder, saner.

[1213] *accommodate* dress, adorn.

[1214] *touch me for coining* arrest me for minting coins (the king's prerogative).

[1215] *Nature's . . . respect* i.e., a born king is superior to legal (and hence artificial) inhibition. There is also a glance here at the popular Renaissance debate, concerning the relative importance of nature (inspiration) and art (training).

[1216] *press-money* (paid to conscripted soldiers).

[1217] *crow-keeper* a farmer scaring away crows.

[1218] *clothier's yard* (the standard English arrow was a cloth-yard long. Here the injunction is to draw the arrow back, like a powerful archer, a full yard to the ear).

[1219] *gauntlet* armored glove, thrown down as a challenge.

[1220] *prove it on* maintain my challenge even against.

[1221] *brown bills* halberds varnished to prevent rust (here the reference is to the soldiers who carry them).

[1222] *well flown* (falconer's cry; and perhaps a reference to the flight of the arrow).

[1223] *clout* the target shot at.

[1224] *hewgh* ? imitating the whizzing of the arrow.

[1225] *word* password.

[1226] *Sweet marjoram* herb, used as a remedy for brain disease.

Lear. Ha! Goneril, with a white beard! They flattered me like a
dog,[1227] and told me I had white hairs in my beard ere the black
ones were there.[1228] To say "ay" and "no" to everything that I   100
said! "Ay" and "no" too was no good divinity.[1229] When the rain
came to wet me once and the wind to make me chatter; when
the thunder would not peace at my bidding; there I found 'em,
there I smelt 'em out. Go to, they are not men o' their words: 105
they told me I was everything; 'tis a lie, I am not ague-proof.[1230]

Gloucester. The trick[1231] of that voice I do well remember: Is't not
the king?

Lear.   Ay, every inch a king.
When I do stare, see how the subject quakes.   110
I pardon that man's life. What was thy cause?[1232]
Adultery?
Thou shalt not die: die for adultery! No:
The wren goes to 't, and the small gilded fly
Does lecher[1233] in my sight.   115
Let copulation thrive; for Gloucester's bastard son
Was kinder to his father than my daughters
Got[1234] 'tween the lawful sheets.
To 't, luxury,[1235] pell-mell! for I lack soldiers.[1236]
Behold yond simp'ring dame,   120
Whose face between her forks presages snow,[1237]
That minces[1238] virtue and does shake the head
To hear of pleasure's name.[1239]
The fitchew,[1240] nor the soilèd[1241] horse, goes to 't

[1227] *like a dog* as a dog flatters.

[1228] *I . . . there* I was wise before I had even grown a beard.

[1229] *no good divinity* (bad theology, because contrary to the Biblical saying [II Corinthians 1:18], "Our word toward you was not yea and nay." See also James 5:12 "But let your yea be yea, and your nay, nay; lest ye fall into condemnation"; and Matthew 5:36-37).

[1230] *ague-proof* secure against fever.

[1231] *trick* intonation.

[1232] *cause* offense.

[1233] *lecher* copulate.

[1234] *Got* begot.

[1235] *luxury* lechery.

[1236] *for . . . soldiers* i.e., ? (1) whom copulation will supply (2) and am therefore powerless.

[1237] *Whose . . . snow* whose cold demeanor seems to promise chaste behavior ("forks": legs).

[1238] *minces* squeamishly pretends to.

[1239] *pleasure's name* the very name of sexual pleasure.

[1240] *fitchew* polecat (and slang for "prostitute").

[1241] *soilèd* put to pasture, and hence wanton with feeding.

125 With a more riotous appetite.
Down from the waist they are Centaurs,[1242]
Though women all above:
But to the girdle[1243] do the gods inherit,[1244]
Beneath is all the fiend's.

130 There's hell, there's darkness, there is the sulphurous pit,
Burning, scalding, stench, consumption; fie, fie, fie!
pah, pah! Give me an ounce of civet;[1245] good apothecary, sweeten
my imagination: there's money for thee.

Gloucester. O, let me kiss that hand!

135 **Lear.** Let me wipe it first; it smells of mortality.[1246]

Gloucester. O ruined piece of nature! This great world
Shall so wear out to nought.[1247] Dost thou know me?

Lear. I remember thine eyes well enough. Dost thou squiny[1248] at
140 me? No, do thy worst, blind Cupid;[1249] I'll not love. Read thou
this challenge;[1250] mark but the penning of it.

Gloucester. Were all thy letters suns, I could not see.

Edgar. I would not take[1251] this from report: it is,
And my heart breaks at it.

145 **Lear.** Read.

Gloucester. What, with the case[1252] of eyes?

Lear. O, ho, are you there with me?[1253] No eyes in your head, nor
no money in your purse? Your eyes are in a heavy case,[1254] your
150 purse in a light,[1255] yet you see how this world goes.

Gloucester. I see it feelingly.[1256]

[1242] *Centaurs* lustful creatures, half man and half horse.
[1243] *girdle* waist.
[1244] *inherit* possess.
[1245] *civet* perfume.
[1246] *mortality* (1) death (2) existence.
[1247] *This . . . nought* i.e., the universe (macrocosm) will decay to nothing in the same way as the little world of man (microcosm).
[1248] *squiny* squint, look sideways, like a prostitute.
[1249] *blind Cupid* the sign hung before a brothel.
[1250] *challenge* a reminiscence of ll. 89-90.
[1251] *take* believe.
[1252] *case* empty sockets.
[1253] *are . . . me* is that what you tell me.
[1254] *heavy case* sad plight (pun on l. 146).
[1255] *light* i.e., empty.
[1256] *feelingly* (1) by touch (2) by feeling pain (3) with emotion.

Lear. What, art mad? A man may see how this world goes with
no eyes. Look with thine ears: see how yond justice rails upon   155
yond simple[1257] thief. Hark, in thine ear: change places, and, handy-
dandy,[1258] which is the justice, which is the thief? Thou hast seen
a farmer's dog bark at a beggar?

Gloucester. Ay, sir.

Lear. And the creature run from the cur? There thou mightst behold
the great image of authority:[1259] a dog's obeyed in office.[1260]   160
Thou rascal beadle,[1261] hold thy bloody hand!
Why dost thou lash that whore? Strip thy own back;
Thou hotly lusts to use her in that kind[1262]
For which thou whip'st her. The usurer hangs the cozener.[1263]   165
Through tattered clothes small vices do appear;
Robes and furred gowns[1264] hide all. Plate sin with gold,
And the strong lance of justice hurtless[1265] breaks;
Arm it in rags, a pygmy's straw does pierce it.
None does offend, none, I say, none; I'll able[1266] 'em: 170
Take that[1267] of me, my friend, who have the power
To seal th' accuser's lips. Get thee glass eyes,[1268]
And, like a scurvy politician,[1269] seem
To see the things thou dost not. Now, now, now, now.
Pull off my boots: harder, harder: so.   175

Edgar. O, matter and impertinency[1270] mixed!
Reason in madness!

Lear. If thou wilt weep my fortunes, take my eyes.
I know thee well enough; thy name is Gloucester:
Thou must be patient; we came crying hither: 180
Thou know'st, the first time that we smell the air

[1257] *simple* common, of low estate.

[1258] *handy-dandy* i.e., choose, guess (after the children's game—"Handy-dandy,
prickly prandy"—of choosing the right hand).

[1259] *image of authority* symbol revealing the true meaning of authority.

[1260] *a . . . office* i.e., whoever has power is obeyed.

[1261] *beadle* parish constable.

[1262] *kind* i.e., sexual act.

[1263] *The usurer . . . cozener* i.e., the powerful moneylender, in his role as judge,
puts to death the petty cheat.

[1264] *Robes and furred gowns* (worn by a judge).

[1265] *hurtless* i.e., without hurting the sinner.

[1266] *able* vouch for.

[1267] *that* (the immunity just conferred) (l. 170).

[1268] *glass eyes* spectacles.

[1269] *scurvy politician* vile politic man.

[1270] *matter and impertinency* sense and nonsense.

We wawl and cry. I will preach to thee: mark.

Gloucester. Alack, alack the day!

Lear. When we are born, we cry that we are come
185 To this great stage of fools. This'[1271] a good block.[1272]
It were a delicate[1273] stratagem, to shoe
A troop of horse with felt: I'll put 't in proof;[1274]
And when I have stol'n upon these son-in-laws,
Then, kill, kill, kill, kill, kill, kill!

Enter a Gentleman [with Attendants].

190 **Gentleman.** O, here he is: lay hand upon him. Sir,
Your most dear daughter—

Lear. No rescue? What, a prisoner? I am even
The natural fool[1275] of fortune. Use me well;
You shall have ransom. Let me have surgeons;
I am cut[1276] to th' brains.

195 **Gentleman.** You shall have anything.

Lear. No seconds?[1277] all myself?
Why, this would make a man a man of salt,[1278]
To use his eyes for garden water-pots,
Ay, and laying autumn's dust.

200 **Gentleman.** Good sir—

Lear. I will die bravely,[1279] like a smug[1280] bridegroom.[1281] What!
I will be jovial: come, come; I am a king;
Masters, know you that?

[1271] *This'* this is.

[1272] *block* (various meanings have been suggested, for example, the stump of a tree, on which Lear is supposed to climb; a mounting block, which suggests "horse" l. 187; a hat [which Lear or another must be made to wear], from the block on which a felt hat is molded, and which would suggest a "felt" l. 187. The proposal here is that "block" be taken to denote the quintain, whose function is to bear blows, "a mere lifeless block" [*As You Like It,* I.ii.263], an object shaped like a man and used for tilting practice. See also *Much Ado,* II.i.246-7, "she misused me past the endurance of a block!" and, in the same passage, the associated reference, "I stood like a man at a mark [target]" [l. 253]).

[1273] *delicate* subtle.

[1274] *put't in proof* test it.

[1275] *natural fool* born sport (with pun on "natural": "imbecile").

[1276] *cut* wounded.

[1277] *seconds* supporters.

[1278] *man of salt* i.e., all (salt) tears.

[1279] *bravely* (1) smartly attired (2) courageously.

[1280] *smug* spick and span.

[1281] *bridegroom* whose "brave" sexual feats are picked up in the pun on "die".

Gentleman.   You are a royal one, and we obey you.

Lear.   Then there's life in 't.[1282] Come, and you get it, you shall get   205
it by running. Sa, sa, sa, sa.[1283]

Exit [running; Attendants follow].

Gentleman.   A sight most pitiful in the meanest wretch,
Past speaking of in a king! Thou has one daughter
Who redeems nature from the general curse
Which twain have brought her to.[1284]   210

Edgar.   Hail, gentle[1285] sir.

Gentleman.   Sir, speed[1286] you: what's your will?

Edgar.   Do you hear aught, sir, of a battle toward?[1287]

Gentleman.   Most sure and vulgar:[1288] every one hears that,
Which can distinguish sound.

Edgar.   But, by your favor,
How near's the other army?   215

Gentleman.   Near and on speedy foot; the main descry
Stands on the hourly thought.[1289]

Edgar.   I thank you, sir: that's all.

Gentleman.   Though that the Queen on special cause is here,
Her army is moved on.

Edgar.   I thank you, sir.

Exit [Gentleman].

Gloucester.   You ever-gentle gods, take my breath from me;   220
Let not my worser spirit[1290] tempt me again
To die before you please.

Edgar.   Well pray you, father.

Gloucester.   Now, good sir, what are you?

[1282] *there's life in 't* there's still hope.

[1283] *Sa . . . sa* hunting and rallying cry; also an interjection of defiance.

[1284] *general . . . to* (1) universal condemnation which Goneril and Regan have made
for (2) damnation incurred by the original sin of Adam and Eve.

[1285] *gentle* noble.

[1286] *speed* God speed.

[1287] *toward* impending.

[1288] *vulgar* common knowledge.

[1289] *the . . . thought* we expect to see the main body of the army any hour.

[1290] *worser spirit* bad angel, evil side of my nature.

Edgar. A most poor man, made tame[1291] to fortune's blows;
225 Who, by the art of known and feeling sorrows,[1292]
Am pregnant[1293] to good pity. Give me your hand,
I'll lead you to some biding.[1294]

Gloucester. Hearty thanks;
The bounty and the benison[1295] of heaven
To boot, and boot.[1296]

Enter Oswald.

Oswald. A proclaimed prize![1297] Most happy![1298]
230 That eyeless head of thine was first framed[1299] flesh
To raise my fortunes. Thou old unhappy traitor,
Briefly thyself remember:[1300] the sword is out
That must destroy thee.

Gloucester. Now let thy friendly[1301] hand
Put strength enough to 't.

[Edgar interposes.]

Oswald. Wherefore, bold peasant,
235 Dar'st thou support a published[1302] traitor? Hence!
Lest that th' infection of his fortune take
Like hold on thee. Let go his arm.

Edgar. Chill[1303] not let go, zir, without vurther 'casion.[1304]

Oswald. Let go, slave, or thou diest!

240 **Edgar.** Good gentleman, go your gait,[1305] and let poor volk[1306] pass.
And chud ha' bin zwaggered[1307] out of my life, 'twould not ha'
bin zo long as 'tis by a vortnight. Nay, come not near th' old

---

[1291] *tame* submissive.

[1292] *art . . . sorrows* instructions of sorrows painfully experienced.

[1293] *pregnant* disposed.

[1294] *biding* place of refuge.

[1295] *benison* blessing.

[1296] *To boot, and boot* also, and in the highest degree.

[1297] *proclaimed prize* i.e., one with a price on his head.

[1298] *happy* fortunate (for Oswald).

[1299] *framed* created.

[1300] *thyself remember* i.e., pray, think of your sins.

[1301] *friendly* i.e., because it offers the death Gloucester covets.

[1302] *published* proclaimed.

[1303] *Chill . . .* Edgar speaks in rustic dialect *Chill* I will.

[1304] *vurther 'casion* further occasion.

[1305] *gait* way.

[1306] *volk* folk.

[1307] *And chud ha' bin zwaggered* if I could have been swaggered.

man; keep out, che vor' ye,[1308] or I'se[1309] try whether your costard[1310] or my ballow[1311] be the harder: chill be plain with you. 245

Oswald. Out, dunghill!

They fight.

Edgar. Chill pick your teeth,[1312] zir: come; no matter vor your
foins.[1313]

[Oswald falls.]

Oswald. Slave, thou hast slain me. Villain, take my purse: 250
If ever thou wilt thrive, bury my body,
And give the letters which thou find'st about[1314] me
To Edmund Earl of Gloucester; seek him out
Upon the English party.[1315] O, untimely death!
Death! 255

              He dies.

Edgar. I know thee well. A serviceable[1316] villain,
As duteous[1317] to the vices of thy mistress
As badness would desire.

Gloucester.   What, is he dead?

Edgar. Sit you down, father; rest you.
Let's see these pockets: the letters that he speaks of 260
May be my friends. He's dead; I am only sorry
He had no other deathsman.[1318] Let us see:
Leave,[1319] gentle wax;[1320] and, manners, blame us not:
To know our enemies' minds, we rip their hearts;
Their papers[1321] is more lawful. 265

Reads the letter.

[1308] *Che vor' ye* I warrant you.
[1309] *I'se* I shall.
[1310] *costard* head (literally, "apple").
[1311] *ballow* cudgel.
[1312] *Chill pick your teeth* I will knock your teeth out.
[1313] *foins* thrusts.
[1314] *about* upon.
[1315] *party* side.
[1316] *serviceable* ready to be used.
[1317] *duteous* obedient.
[1318] *deathsman* executioner.
[1319] *Leave* by your leave.
[1320] *wax* (with which the letter is sealed).
[1321] *Their papers* i.e., to rip their papers.

"Let our reciprocal vows be remembered. You have many opportunities to cut him off: if your will want not,[1322] time and place
will be fruitfully offered. There is nothing done, if he return the
270 conqueror: then am I the prisoner, and his bed my jail; from the
loathed warmth whereof deliver me, and supply the place for your
labor.

"Your—wife, so I would[1323] say—affectionate servant, and for
you her own for venture,[1324]
275   'Goneril.' "

O indistinguished space of woman's will![1325]
A plot upon her virtuous husband's life;
And the exchange[1326] my brother! Here in the sands
Thee I'll rake up,[1327] the post unsanctified[1328]
280 Of murderous lechers; and in the mature[1329] time,
With this ungracious paper[1330] strike[1331] the sight
Of the death-practiced[1332] Duke: for him 'tis well
That of thy death and business I can tell.

Gloucester.   The King is mad: how stiff[1333] is my vile sense,[1334]
285 That I stand up, and have ingenious[1335] feeling
Of my huge sorrows! Better I were distract:[1336]
So should my thoughts be severed from my griefs,
And woes by wrong imaginations[1337] lose
The knowledge of themselves.

Drum afar off.

Edgar.   Give me your hand:
290 Far off, methinks, I hear the beaten drum.

[1322] *if . . . not* if your desire (and lust) be not lacking.

[1323] *would* would like to.

[1324] *and . . . venture* i.e., and one who holds you her own for venturing (Edmund
had earlier been promised union by Goneril, "If you dare venture in your own behalf,"
IV.ii.20).

[1325] *indistinguished . . . will* unlimited range of woman's lust.

[1326] *exchange* substitute.

[1327] *rake up* cover up, bury.

[1328] *post unsanctified* unholy messenger.

[1329] *mature* ripe.

[1330] *ungracious paper* wicked letter.

[1331] *strike* blast.

[1332] *death-practiced* whose death is plotted.

[1333] *stiff* unbending.

[1334] *vile sense* hateful capacity for feeling.

[1335] *ingenious* conscious.

[1336] *distract* distracted, mad.

[1337] *wrong imaginations* delusions.

Come, father, I'll bestow[1338] you with a friend.

Exeunt.

Scene VII. [*A tent in the French camp.*]

Enter Cordelia, Kent, Doctor, and Gentleman.

Cordelia.　O thou good Kent, how shall I live and work,
To match thy goodness? My life will be too short,
And every measure fail me.

Kent.　To be acknowledged, madam, is o'erpaid.
All my reports go[1339] with the modest truth,　　　　　　　　　　5
Nor more nor clipped,[1340] but so.

Cordelia.　　　　　　　　　　　　　Be better suited:[1341]
These weeds[1342] are memories[1343] of those worser hours:
I prithee, put them off.

Kent.　　　　　　　　　　　　Pardon, dear madam;
Yet to be known shortens my made intent:[1344]
My boon I make it,[1345] that you know me not　　　　　　　　　10
Till time and I think meet.[1346]

Cordelia.　Then be 't so, my good lord. [*To the Doctor.*] How does
the King?

Doctor.　Madam, sleeps still.

Cordelia.　O you kind gods!
Cure this great breach in his abusèd[1347] nature.　　　　　　　　15
Th' untuned and jarring senses, O, wind up[1348]
Of this child-changèd[1349] father.

[1338] *bestow* lodge.

[1339] *go* conform.

[1340] *clipped* curtailed.

[1341] *suited* attired.

[1342] *weeds* clothes.

[1343] *memories* reminders.

[1344] *Yet . . . intent* to reveal myself just yet interferes with the plan I have made.

[1345] *My boon I make it* I ask this reward.

[1346] *meet* fitting.

[1347] *abusèd* disturbed.

[1348] *wind up* tune.

[1349] *child-changèd* changed, deranged (and also, reduced to a child) by the cruelty of his children.

Doctor. So please your Majesty
That we may wake the King: he hath slept long.

Cordelia. Be governed by your knowledge, and proceed
20 I' th' sway of[1350] your own will. Is he arrayed?

Enter Lear in a chair carried by Servants.

Gentleman. Ay, madam; in the heaviness of sleep
We put fresh garments on him.

Doctor. Be by, good madam, when we do awake him;
I doubt not of his temperance.[1351]

Cordelia. Very well.

25 **Doctor.** Please you, draw near. Louder the music there!

Cordelia. O my dear father, restoration hang
Thy medicine on my lips, and let this kiss
Repair those violent harms that my two sisters
Have in thy reverence[1352] made.

Kent. Kind and dear Princess.

30 **Cordelia.** Had you not been their father, these white flakes[1353]
Did challenge[1354] pity of them. Was this a face
To be opposed against the warring winds?
To stand against the deep dread-bolted[1355] thunder?
In the most terrible and nimble stroke
35 Of quick, cross[1356] lightning to watch—poor perdu![1357]—
With this thin helm?[1358] Mine enemy's dog,
Though he had bit me, should have stood that night
Against my fire; and wast thou fain,[1359] poor father,
To hovel thee with swine and rogues[1360] forlorn,
40 In short[1361] and musty straw? Alack, alack!

[1350] *I' th' sway of* according to.

[1351] *temperance* sanity.

[1352] *reverence* revered person.

[1353] *flakes* hairs (in long strands).

[1354] *challenge* claim.

[1355] *deep dread-bolted* deep-voiced and furnished with the dreadful thunderbolt.

[1356] *cross* zigzag.

[1357] *perdu* (1) sentry in a forlorn position (2) lost one.

[1358] *helm* helmet (his scanty hair).

[1359] *fain* pleased.

[1360] *rogues* vagabonds.

[1361] *short* (when straw is freshly cut, it is long, and suitable for bedding, given its flexibility and crispness. As it is used, it becomes musty, shreds into pieces, is "short." In contemporary Maine usage, "short manure" refers to dung mixed with straw that has been broken up; "long manure" to dung mixed with coarse new straw).

'Tis wonder that thy life and wits at once
Had not concluded all.[1362] He wakes; speak to him.

Doctor. Madam, do you; 'tis fittest.

Cordelia. How does my royal lord? How fares your Majesty?

Lear. You do me wrong to take me out o' th' grave: 45
Thou art a soul in bliss; but I am bound
Upon a wheel of fire,[1363] that mine own tears
Do scald like molten lead.

Cordelia.   Sir, do you know me?

Lear. You are a spirit, I know. Where did you die?

Cordelia. Still, still, far wide.[1364]   50

Doctor. He's scarce awake: let him alone awhile.

Lear. Where have I been? Where am I? Fair daylight?
I am mightily abused.[1365] I should ev'n die with pity,
To see another thus. I know not what to say.
I will not swear these are my hands: let's see;   55
I feel this pin prick. Would I were assured
Of my condition.

Cordelia.   O, look upon me, sir,
And hold your hand in benediction o'er me.
You must not kneel.

Lear.   Pray, do not mock me:
I am a very foolish fond[1366] old man,   60
Fourscore and upward, not an hour more nor less;
And, to deal plainly,
I fear I am not in my perfect mind.
Methinks I should know you and know this man,
Yet I am doubtful; for I am mainly[1367] ignorant   65
What place this is, and all the skill I have
Remembers not these garments, nor I know not
Where I did lodge last night. Do not laugh at me,
For, as I am a man, I think this lady
To be my child Cordelia.

[1362] *concluded all* come to a complete end.

[1353] *wheel of fire* (torment associated by the Middle Ages with Hell, where Lear thinks he is).

[1364] *wide* i.e., of the mark (of sanity).

[1365] *abused* deluded.

[1366] *fond* in dotage.

[1367] *mainly* entirely.

70 **Cordelia.**   And so I am, I am.

Lear. Be your tears wet? Yes, faith. I pray, weep not.
If you have poison for me, I will drink it.
I know you do not love me; for your sisters
Have, as I do remember, done me wrong.
You have some cause, they have not.

75 **Cordelia.**   No cause, no cause.

Lear. Am I in France?

Kent.   In your own kingdom, sir.

Lear. Do not abuse[1368] me.

Doctor. Be comforted, good madam: the great rage,[1369]
You see, is killed in him: and yet it is danger
80 To make him even o'er[1370] the time he has lost.
Desire him to go in; trouble him no more
Till further settling.[1371]

Cordelia. Will 't please your Highness walk?[1372]

85 **Lear.** You must bear with me. Pray you now, forget and forgive.
I am old and foolish.

Exeunt. Mane[n]t[1373] Kent and Gentleman.

Gentleman. Holds it true, sir, that the Duke of Cornwall was so
slain?

Kent. Most certain, sir.

Gentleman. Who is conductor of his people?

90 **Kent.** As 'tis said, the bastard son of Gloucester.

Gentleman. They say Edgar, his banished son, is with the Earl of
Kent in Germany.

Kent. Report is changeable.[1374] 'Tis time to look about; the powers[1375] of the kingdom approach apace.

[1368] *abuse* deceive.
[1369] *rage* frenzy.
[1370] *even o'er* smooth over by filling in; and hence, "recollect".
[1371] *settling* calming.
[1372] *walk* (perhaps in the sense of "withdraw").
[1373] s.d. *Mane[n]t* remain.
[1374] *Report is changeable* rumors are unreliable.
[1375] *powers* armies.

Gentleman. The arbitrement[1376] is like to be bloody.   95
Fare you well, sir.

[Exit.]

Kent. My point and period will be throughly wrought,[1377]
Or well or ill, as this day's battle's fought.

Exit.

ACT V

Scene I. [*The British camp near Dover.*]

Enter, with drum and colors, Edmund, Regan, Gentlemen, and Soldiers.

Edmund. Know[1378] of the Duke if his last purpose hold,[1379]
Or whether since he is advised[1380] by aught
To change the course: he's full of alteration
And self-reproving: bring his constant pleasure.[1381]

[To a Gentleman, who goes out.]

Regan. Our sister's man is certainly miscarried.[1382]   5

Edmund. 'Tis to be doubted,[1383] madam.

Regan.   Now, sweet lord,
You know the goodness I intend upon you:
Tell me, but truly, but then speak the truth,
Do you not love my sister?

Edmund.   In honored[1384] love.

Regan. But have you never found my brother's way   10
To the forfended[1385] place?

Edmund.   That thought abuses[1386] you.

[1376] *arbitrement* deciding encounter.

[1377] *My . . . wrought* the aim and end, the close of my life will be completely
worked out.

[1378] *Know* learn.

[1379] *last purpose hold* most recent intention (to fight) be maintained.

[1380] *advised* induced.

[1381] *constant pleasure* fixed (final) decision.

[1382] *miscarried* come to grief.

[1383] *doubted* feared.

[1384] *honored* honorable.

[1385] *forfended* forbidden.

[1386] *abuses* (1) deceives (2) demeans, is unworthy of.

Regan. I am doubtful that you have been conjunct
And bosomed with her, as far as we call hers.[1387]

Edmund. No, by mine honor, madam.

15 **Regan.** I shall never endure her: dear my lord,
Be not familiar with her.

Edmund.   Fear[1388] me not.—
She and the Duke her husband!

Enter, with drum and colors, Albany, Goneril [and] Soldiers.

Goneril. *[Aside]* I had rather lose the battle than that sister
Should loosen[1389] him and me.

20 **Albany.** Our very loving sister, well be-met.[1390]
Sir, this I heard, the King is come to his daughter,
With others whom the rigor of our state[1391]
Forced to cry out. Where I could not be honest,[1392]
I never yet was valiant: for this business,
25 It touches us, as[1393] France invades our land,
Not bolds the King, with others, whom, I fear,
Most just and heavy causes make oppose.[1394]

Edmund. Sir, you speak nobly.

Regan.   Why is this reasoned?[1395]

Goneril. Combine together 'gainst the enemy;
30 For these domestic and particular broils[1396]
Are not the question[1397] here.

Albany.   Let's then determine
With th' ancient of war[1398] on our proceeding.

Edmund. I shall attend you presently at your tent.

[1387] *I . . . hers* I fear that you have united with her intimately, in the fullest possible way.

[1388] *Fear* distrust.

[1389] *loosen* separate.

[1390] *be-met* met.

[1391] *rigor . . . state* tyranny of our government.

[1392] *honest* honorable.

[1393] *touches us, as* concerns me, only in that.

[1394] *Not . . . oppose* and not in that France emboldens the King and others, who have been led, by real and serious grievances, to take up arms against us.

[1395] *reasoned* argued.

[1396] *particular broils* private quarrels.

[1397] *question* issue.

[1398] *th' ancient of war* experienced commanders.

Regan. Sister, you'll go with us?[1399]

Goneril. No.   35

Regan. 'Tis most convenient;[1400] pray you, go with us.

Goneril. *[Aside]* O, ho, I know the riddle.[1401]—I will go.

Exeunt both the Armies. Enter Edgar [disguised].

Edgar. If e'er your Grace had speech with man so poor,
Hear me one word.

Albany. *[To those going out]* I'll overtake you. *[To Edgar]* Speak.

Exeunt [all but Albany and Edgar].

Edgar. Before you fight the battle, ope this letter.   40
If you have victory, let the trumpet sound
For[1402] him that brought it: wretched though I seem,
I can produce a champion that will prove[1403]
What is avouchèd[1404] there. If you miscarry,
Your business of[1405] the world hath so an end,   45
And machination[1406] ceases. Fortune love you.

Albany. Stay till I have read the letter.

Edgar.   I was forbid it.
When time shall serve, let but the herald cry,
And I'll appear again.

Albany. Why, fare thee well: I will o'erlook[1407] thy paper.   50

Exit [Edgar].

Enter Edmund.

Edmund. The enemy's in view: draw up your powers.
Here is the guess[1408] of their true strength and forces
By diligent discovery;[1409] but your haste
Is now urged on you.

[1399] *us* me (rather than Edmund).

[1400] *convenient* fitting, desirable.

[1401] *riddle* real reason (for Regan's curious request).

[1402]*sound/For* summon.

[1403] *prove* i.e., by trial of combat.

[1404] *avouchèd* maintained.

[1405] *of* in.

[1406] *machination* plotting.

[1407] *o'erlook* read over.

[1408] *guess* estimate.

[1409] *By diligent discovery* obtained by careful reconnoitering.

Albany.   We will greet[1410] the time.

Exit.

55 **Edmund.**   To both these sisters have I sworn my love;
Each jealous[1411] of the other, as the stung
Are of the adder. Which of them shall I take?
Both? One? Or neither? Neither can be enjoyed,
If both remain alive: to take the widow
60 Exasperates, makes mad her sister Goneril;
And hardly[1412] shall I carry out my side,[1413]
Her husband being alive. Now then, we'll use
His countenance[1414] for the battle; which being done,
Let her who would be rid of him devise
65 His speedy taking off. As for the mercy
Which he intends to Lear and to Cordelia,
The battle done, and they within our power,
Shall never see his pardon; for my state
Stands on me to defend, not to debate.[1415]

Exit.

Scene II. [*A field between the two camps.*]

*Alarum[1416] within. Enter, with drum and colors, Lear, Cordelia, and
Soldiers, over the stage; and exeunt.
Enter Edgar and Gloucester.*

Edgar.   Here, father,[1417] take the shadow of this tree
For your good host; pray that the right may thrive.
If ever I return to you again,
I'll bring you comfort.

Gloucester.   Grace go with you, sir

Exit [Edgar.].

Alarum and retreat[1418] within. [Re-]enter Edgar.

[1410] *greet* i.e., meet the demands of.

[1411] *jealous* suspicious.

[1412] *hardly* with difficulty.

[1413] *carry . . . side* (1) satisfy my ambition (2) fulfill my bargain (with Goneril).

[1414] *countenance* authority.

[1415] *for . . . debate* my position requires me to act, not to reason about right and wrong.

[1416] *Alarum* a trumpet call to battle.

[1417] *father* i.e., venerable old man (Edgar has not yet revealed his identity).

[1418] *retreat* (signaled by a trumpet).

Edgar. Away, old man; give me thy hand; away!   5
King Lear hath lost, he and his daughter ta'en:[1419]
Give me thy hand; come on.

Gloucester. No further, sir; a man may rot even here.

Edgar. What, in ill thoughts again? Men must endure
Their going hence, even as their coming hither: 10
Ripeness[1420] is all. Come on.

Gloucester.   And that's true too.

Exeunt.

Scene III. [*The British camp near Dover.*]

Enter, in conquest, with drum and colors, Edmund; Lear and Cordelia,
    as prisoners; Soldiers, Captain.

Edmund. Some officers take them away: good guard,[1421]
Until their greater pleasures[1422] first be known
That are to censure[1423] them.

Cordelia.   We are not the first
Who with best meaning[1424] have incurred the worst.
For thee, oppressèd King, I am cast down;   5
Myself could else out-frown false fortune's frown.
Shall we not see these daughters and these sisters?

Lear. No, no, no, no! Come, let's away to prison:
We two alone will sing like birds i' th' cage:
When thou dost ask me blessing, I'll kneel down   10
And ask of thee forgiveness: so we'll live,
And pray, and sing, and tell old tales, and laugh
At gilded butterflies,[1425] and hear poor rogues
Talk of court news; and we'll talk with them too,
Who loses and who wins, who's in, who's out;   15
And take upon's the mystery of things,

[1419] *ta'en* captured.

[1420] *Ripeness* maturity, as of fruit that is ready to fall.

[1421] *good guard* let there be good guard.

[1422] *their greater pleasures* the will of those in command, the great ones.

[1423] *censure* pass judgment.

[1424] *meaning* intentions.

[1425] *gilded butterflies* i.e., gorgeously attired courtiers, fluttering after nothing.

As if we were God's spies:[1426] and we'll wear out,[1427]
In a walled prison, packs and sects of great ones
That ebb and flow by th' moon.[1428]

Edmund.   Take them away.

20 **Lear.** Upon such sacrifices, my Cordelia,
The gods themselves throw incense.[1429] Have I caught thee?
He that parts us shall bring a brand from heaven,
And fire us hence like foxes.[1430] Wipe thine eyes;
The good years[1431] shall devour them,[1432] flesh and fell,[1433]
25 Ere they shall make us weep. We'll see 'em starved first.
Come.

[Exeunt Lear and Cordelia, guarded.]

Edmund. Come hither, captain; hark.
Take thou this note: go follow them to prison:
One step I have advanced thee; if thou dost
30 As this instructs thee, thou dost make thy way
To noble fortunes: know thou this, that men
Are as the time is:[1434] to be tender-minded
Does not become a sword:[1435] thy great employment
Will not bear question;[1436] either say thou'lt do 't,
Or thrive by other means.

35 **Captain.**   I'll do 't, my lord.

Edmund. About it; and write happy[1437] when th' hast done.
Mark; I say, instantly, and carry it so[1438]
As I have set it down.

Captain. I cannot draw a cart, nor eat dried oats;

[1426] *take . . . spies* profess to read the riddle of existence, as if endowed with divine omniscience.

[1427] *wear out* outlast.

[1428] *packs . . . moon* intriguing and partisan cliques of those in high station, whose fortunes change every month.

[1429] *Upon . . . incense* i.e., the gods approve our renunciation of the world.

[1430] *He . . . foxes* no human agency can separate us, but only divine interposition, as of a heavenly torch parting us like foxes who are driven from their place of refuge by fire and smoke.

[1431] *good years* plague and pestilence ("undefined malefic power or agency," *N.E.D.*).

[1432] *them* i.e., the enemies of Lear and Cordelia.

[1433] *fell* skin.

[1434] *as the time is* i.e., absolutely determined by the exigencies of the moment.

[1435] *become a sword* befit a soldier.

[1436] *bear question* admit of discussion.

[1437] *write happy* style yourself fortunate.

[1438] *carry it so* manage the affair in exactly that manner (as if Cordelia had taken her own life).

If it be man's work, I'll do 't.   40
                                              Exit Captain.
Flourish. Enter Albany, Goneril, Regan [another Captain, and] Soldiers.

Albany. Sir, you have showed today your valiant strain,[1439]
And fortune led you well: you have the captives
Who were the opposites of[1440] this day's strife:
I do require them of you, so to use them
As we shall find their merits[1441] and our safety   45
May equally determine.

Edmund.   Sir, I thought it fit
To send the old and miserable King
To some retention and appointed guard;[1442]
Whose[1443] age had charms in it, whose title more,
To pluck the common bosom on his side[1444]   50
And turn our impressed lances in our eyes[1445]
Which do command them. With him I sent the Queen:
My reason all the same; and they are ready
Tomorrow, or at further space,[1446] t' appear
Where you shall hold your session.[1447] At this time   55
We sweat and bleed: the friend hath lost his friend;
And the best quarrels, in the heat, are cursed
By those that feel their sharpness.[1448]
The question of Cordelia and her father
Requires a fitter place.

Albany.   Sir, by your patience,   60
I hold you but a subject of[1449] this war,
Not as a brother.

Regan.   That's as we list to grace[1450] him.
Methinks our pleasure might have been demanded,
Ere you had spoke so far. He led our powers,
Bore the commission of my place and person;   65

[1439] *strain* (1) stock (2) character.

[1440] *opposites of* opponents in.

[1441] *merits* deserts.

[1442] *retention . . . guard* confinement under duly appointed guard.

[1443] *Whose* i.e., Lear's.

[1444] *pluck . . . side* win the sympathy of the people to himself.

[1445] *turn . . . eyes* turn our conscripted lancers against us.

[1446] *further space* a later time.

[1447] *session* trial.

[1448] *the . . . sharpness* the worthiest causes may be judged badly by those who have been affected painfully by them, and whose passion has not yet cooled.

[1449] *subject of* subordinate in.

[1450] *list to grace* wish to honor.

The which immediacy may well stand up
And call itself your brother.[1451]

Goneril.   Not so hot:
In his own grace he doth exalt himself
More than in your addition.[1452]

Regan.   In my rights,
70 By me invested, he compeers[1453] the best.

Goneril.   That were the most,[1454] if he should husband you.[1455]

Regan.   Jesters do oft prove prophets.

Goneril.   Holla, holla!
That eye that told you so looked but a-squint.[1456]

Regan.   Lady, I am not well; else I should answer
75 From a full-flowing stomach.[1457] General,
Take thou my soldiers, prisoners, patrimony;[1458]
Dispose of them, of me; the walls is thine:[1459]
Witness the world, that I create thee here
My lord, and master.

Goneril.   Mean you to enjoy him?

80 **Albany.**   The let-alone[1460] lies not in your good will.

Edmund.   Nor in thine, lord.

Albany.   Half-blooded[1461] fellow, yes.

Regan.   [To Edmund] Let the drum strike, and prove my title thine.[1462]

Albany.   Stay yet; hear reason. Edmund, I arrest thee
On capital treason; and in thy attaint[1463]
85 This gilded serpent [pointing to Goneril]. For your claim, fair sister,
I bar it in the interest of my wife.

[1451] Bore . . . brother was authorized, as my deputy, to take command; his present
status, as my immediate representative, entitles him to be considered your equal.

[1452] your addition honors you have bestowed on him.

[1453] compeers equals.

[1454] most most complete investing in your rights.

[1455] husband you become your husband.

[1456] a-squint cross-eyes.

[1457] From . . . stomach angrily.

[1458] patrimony inheritance.

[1459] walls is thine i.e., Regan's person, which Edmund has stormed and won.

[1460] let-alone power to prevent.

[1461] half-blooded bastard, and so only half noble.

[1462] prove . . . thine prove by combat your entitlement to my rights.

[1463] in thy attaint as a sharer in the treason for which you are impeached.

'Tis she is subcontracted[1464] to this lord,
And I, her husband, contradict your banes.[1465]
If you will marry, make your loves[1466] to me;
My Lady is bespoke.[1467]

Goneril.　　　　　　　　　　　　　　　　An interlude![1468]　　90

Albany.　Thou art armed, Gloucester: let the trumpet sound:
If none appear to prove upon thy person
Thy heinous, manifest, and many treasons,
There is my pledge[1469] *[throwing down a glove]:*
I'll make[1470] it on thy heart,
Ere I taste bread, thou art in nothing less　　　　　　　　95
Than I have here proclaimed thee.

Regan.　　　　　　　　　　　　　　　　　Sick, O, sick!

Goneril.　*[Aside]* If not, I'll ne'er trust medicine.[1471]

Edmund.　*[Throwing down a glove]* There's my exchange:[1472] what
　in the world he is
That names me traitor, villain-like he lies:[1473]
Call by the trumpet:[1474] he that dares approach,　　　　　100
On him, on you—who not?—I will maintain
My truth and honor firmly.

Albany.　A herald, ho!

Edmund.　　　　　　　　　　　　A herald, ho, a herald!

Albany.　Trust to thy single virtue;[1475] for thy soldiers,
All levied in my name, have in my name　　　　　　　105
Took their discharge.

Regan.　　　　　　　　　　　My sickness grows upon me.

[1464] *subcontracted* pledged by a contract which is called into question by the existence of a previous contract (Goneril's marriage).

[1465] *contradict your banes* forbid your announced intention to marry (by citing the precontract).

[1466] *loves* love-suits.

[1467] *bespoke* already pledged.

[1468] *interlude* play.

[1469] *pledge* gage.

[1470] *make* prove.

[1471] *medicine* poison.

[1472] *exchange* (technical term, denoting the glove Edmund throws down).

[1473] *villain-like he lies* (the lie direct, a challenge to mortal combat).

[1474] *trumpet* trumpeter.

[1475] *single virtue* unaided valor.

Albany. She is not well; convey her to my tent.

[Exit Regan, led.]
Enter a Herald.

Come hither, herald. Let the trumpet sound—
And read out this.

110 **Captain.** Sound, trumpet!

A trumpet sounds.

Herald. *(Reads.)* "If any man of quality or degree[1476] within the
lists[1477] of the army will maintain upon Edmund, supposed Earl
of Gloucester, that he is a manifold traitor, let him appear by the
115   third sound of the trumpet: he is bold in his defense."

Edmund. Sound!

First trumpet.

Herald. Again!

Second trumpet.

Herald. Again!

Third trumpet.
Trumpet answers within. Enter Edgar, at the third sound, armed, a
trumpet before him.[1478]

Albany. Ask him his purposes, why he appears
Upon this call o' th' trumpet.

120 **Herald.**   What are you?
Your name, your quality,[1479] and why you answer
This present summons?

Edgar.   Know, my name is lost;
By treason's tooth bare-gnawn and canker-bit:[1480]
Yet am I noble as the adversary
I come to cope.[1481]

125 **Albany.**   Which is that adversary?

Edgar. What's he that speaks for Edmund, Earl of Gloucester?

[1476] *quality or degree* rank or position.
[1477] *lists* rolls.
[1478] *s.d. trumpet before him* trumpeter preceding him.
[1479] *quality* rank.
[1480] *canker-bit* eaten by the caterpillar.
[1481] *cope* encounter.

Edmund.   Himself: what say'st thou to him?

Edgar.   Draw thy sword,
That if my speech offend a noble heart,
Thy arm may do thee justice: here is mine.
Behold it is my privilege,   130
The privilege of mine honors,
My oath, and my profession.[1482] I protest,
Maugre[1483] thy strength, place, youth, and eminence,
Despite thy victor sword and fire-new[1484] fortune,
Thy valor and thy heart,[1485] thou art a traitor,   135
False to thy gods, thy brother, and thy father,
Conspirant[1486] 'gainst this high illustrious prince,
And from th' extremest upward[1487] of thy head
To the descent and dust below thy foot,[1488]
A most toad-spotted traitor.[1489] Say thou "No,"   140
This sword, this arm and my best spirits are bent[1490]
To prove upon thy heart, whereto I speak,[1491]
Thou liest.

Edmund.   In wisdom[1492] I should ask thy name,
But since thy outside looks so fair and warlike,
And that thy tongue some say[1493] of breeding breathes,   145
What safe and nicely[1494] I might well delay[1495]
By rule of knighthood, I disdain and spurn:
Back do I toss these treasons[1496] to thy head;
With the hell-hated[1497] lie o'erwhelm thy heart;
Which for they yet glance by and scarcely bruise,   150

[1482] *it . . . profession* my knighthood entitles me to challenge you, and to have my challenge accepted.

[1483] *Maugre* despite.

[1484] *fire-new* fresh from the forge or mint.

[1485] *heart* courage.

[1486] *Conspirant* conspiring, a conspirator.

[1487] *extremest upward* the very top.

[1488] *the . . . foot* your lowest part (sole) and the dust beneath it.

[1489] *toad-spotted traitor* spotted with treason (and hence venomous, as the toad is allegedly marked with spots that exude venom).

[1490] *bent* directed.

[1491] *whereto I speak* (Edgar speaks from the heart, and speaks to the heart of Edmund).

[1492] *wisdom* prudence (since he is not obliged to fight with one of lesser rank).

[1493] *say* essay (i.e., touch, sign).

[1494] *safe and nicely* cautiously and punctiliously.

[1495] *delay* i.e., avoid.

[1496] *treasons* accusations of treason.

[1497] *hell-hated* hated like hell.

This sword of mine shall give them instant way,
Where they shall rest for ever.[1498] Trumpets, speak!

Alarums. [They] fight. [Edmund falls.]

Albany. Save[1499] him, save him!

Goneril. This is practice,[1500] Gloucester:
By th' law of war thou wast not bound to answer
155 An unknown opposite;[1501] thou art not vanquished,
But cozened and beguiled.

Albany. Shut your mouth, dame,
Or with this paper shall I stop it. Hold, sir;[1502]
Thou[1503] worse than any name, read thine own evil.
No tearing, lady; I perceive you know it.

160 **Goneril.** Say, if I do, the laws are mine, not thine:
Who can arraign me for 't?

Albany. Most monstrous! O!
Know'st thou this paper?

Goneril. Ask me not what I know.
Exit.

Albany. Go after her; she's desperate; govern[1504] her.

Edmund. What you have charged me with, that have I done;
165 And more, much more; the time will bring it out.
'Tis past, and so am I. But what art thou
That hast this fortune on[1505] me? If thou 'rt noble,
I do forgive thee.

Edgar. Let's exchange charity.[1506]
I am no less in blood[1507] than thou art, Edmund;
170 If more,[1508] the more th' hast wronged me.
My name is Edgar, and thy father's son.

[1498] *Which . . . ever* which accusations of treason, since as yet they do no harm, even though I have hurled them back, I now thrust upon you still more forcibly, with my sword, so that they may remain with you permanently.

[1499] *Save* spare.

[1500] *practice* trickery.

[1501] *opposite* opponent.

[1502] *Hold, sir* (to Edmund: "Just a moment!").

[1503] *Thou* (probably Goneril).

[1504] *govern* control.

[1505] *fortune on* victory over.

[1506] *charity* forgiveness and love.

[1507] *blood* lineage.

[1508] *If more* if I am more noble (since legitimate).

The gods are just, and of our pleasant[1509] vices
Make instruments to plague us:
The dark and vicious place[1510] where thee he got[1511]
Cost him his eyes.

Edmund.   Th' hast spoken right, 'tis true;   175
The wheel is come full circle; I am here.[1512]

Albany. Methought thy very gait did prophesy[1513]
A royal nobleness: I must embrace thee:
Let sorrow split my heart, if ever I
Did hate thee or thy father!

Edgar.   Worthy[1514] Prince, I know 't.   180

Albany. Where have you hid yourself?
How have you known the miseries of your father?

Edgar. By nursing them, my lord. List a brief tale;
And when 'tis told, O, that my heart would burst!
The bloody proclamation to escape[1515]   185
That followed me so near—O, our lives' sweetness,
That we the pain of death would hourly die
Rather than die at once![1516]—taught me to shift
Into a madman's rags, t' assume a semblance
That very dogs disdained: and in this habit[1517]   190
Met I my father with his bleeding rings,[1518]
Their precious stones new lost; became his guide,
Led him, begged for him, saved him from despair;
Never—O fault!—revealed myself unto him,
Until some half-hour past, when I was armed,   195
Not sure, though hoping, of this good success,
I asked his blessing, and from first to last
Told him our pilgrimage.[1519] But his flawed[1520] heart—
Alack, too weak the conflict to support—

[1509] *of our pleasant* out of our pleasurable.

[1510] *place* i.e., the adulterous bed.

[1511] *got* begot.

[1512] *Wheel . . . here* i.e., Fortune's wheel, on which Edmund ascended, has now, in its downward turning, deposited him at the bottom, whence he began.

[1513] *gait did prophesy* carriage did promise.

[1514] *Worthy* honorable.

[1515] *to escape* (my wish) to escape the sentence of death.

[1516] *O . . . once* how sweet is life, that we choose to suffer death every hour rather than make an end at once.

[1517] *habit* attire.

[1518] *rings* sockets.

[1519] *our pilgrimage* of our (purgatorial) journey.

[1520] *flawed* cracked.

200 'Twixt two extremes of passion, joy and grief,
Burst smilingly.

Edmund.   This speech of yours hath moved me,
And shall perchance do good: but speak you on;
You look as you had something more to say.

Albany. If there be more, more woeful, hold it in;
205 For I am almost ready to dissolve,[1521]
Hearing of this.

Edgar.   This would have seemed a period[1522]
To such as love not sorrow; but another,
To amplify too much, would make much more,
And top extremity.[1523]
210 Whilst I was big in clamor,[1524] came there in a man,
Who, having seen me in my worst estate,[1525]
Shunned my abhorred[1526] society; but then, finding
Who 'twas that so endured, with his strong arms
He fastened on my neck, and bellowed out
215 As he'd burst heaven; threw him on my father;
Told the most piteous tale of Lear and him
That ever ear received: which in recounting
His grief grew puissant,[1527] and the strings of life
Began to crack: twice then the trumpets sounded,
And there I left him tranced.[1528]

220 **Albany.**   But who was this?

Edgar. Kent, sir, the banished Kent; who in disguise
Followed his enemy[1529] king, and did him service
Improper for a slave.

Enter a Gentleman, with a bloody knife.

Gentleman. Help, help, O, help!

Edgar.   What kind of help?

Albany.   Speak, man.

[1521] *dissolve* i.e., into tears.

[1522] *period* limit.

[1523] *but . . . extremity* just one woe more, described too fully, would go beyond
the extreme limit.

[1524] *big in clamor* loud in lamentation.

[1525] *estate* condition.

[1526] *abhorred* abhorrent.

[1527] *puissant* overmastering.

[1528] *tranced* insensible.

[1529] *enemy* hostile.

Edgar. What means this bloody knife?

Gentleman.   'Tis hot, it smokes;[1530] 225
It came even from the heart of—O, she's dead!

Albany. Who dead? Speak, man.

Gentleman. Your lady, sir, your lady: and her sister
By her is poisoned; she confesses it.

Edmund. I was contracted[1531] to them both: all three   230
Now marry[1532] in an instant.

Edgar. Here comes Kent.

Albany. Produce the bodies, be they alive or dead.

[Exit Gentleman.]

This judgment of the heavens, that makes us tremble,
Touches us not with pity.

Enter Kent.

                                  O, is this he?
The time will not allow the compliment[1533]   235
Which very manners[1534] urges.

Kent.   I am come
To bid my king and master aye[1535] good night:
Is he not here?

Albany.   Great thing of[1536] us forgot!
Speak, Edmund, where's the King? and where's Cordelia?
Seest thou this object,[1537] Kent?   240

The bodies of Goneril and Regan are brought in.

Kent. Alack, why thus?

Edmund.   Yet[1538] Edmund was beloved:
The one the other poisoned for my sake,
And after slew herself.

[1530] *smokes* steams.
[1531] *contracted* betrothed.
[1532] *marry* i.e., unite in death.
[1533] *compliment* ceremony.
[1534] *very manners* ordinary civility.
[1535] *aye* forever.
[1536] *thing of* matter by.
[1537] *object* sight (the bodies of Goneril and Regan).
[1538] *Yet* in spite of all.

Albany. Even so. Cover their faces.

245 **Edmund.** I pant for life:[1539] some good I mean to do,
Despite of mine own nature. Quickly send,
Be brief in it, to th' castle; for my writ[1540]
Is on the life of Lear and on Cordelia:
Nay, send in time.

Albany.   Run, run, O, run!

250 **Edgar.** To who, my lord? Who has the office?[1541] Send Thy token
of reprieve.[1542]

Edmund. Well thought on: take my sword,
Give it the captain.

Edgar.   Haste thee, for thy life.

[Exit Messenger.]

Edmund. He hath commission from thy wife and me
255 To hang Cordelia in the prison, and
To lay the blame upon her own despair,
That she fordid[1543] herself.

Albany. The gods defend her! Bear him hence awhile.

[Edmund is borne off.]
Enter Lear, with Cordelia in his arms [Gentleman, and others following].

Lear. Howl, howl, howl, howl! O, you are men of stones:
260 Had I your tongues and eyes, I'd use them so
That heaven's vault should crack. She's gone for ever.
I know when one is dead and when one lives;
She's dead as earth. Lend me a looking glass;
If that her breath will mist or stain the stone,[1544]
Why, then she lives.

265 **Kent.**   Is this the promised end?[1545]

Edgar. Or image[1546] of that horror?

Albany.   Fall and cease.[1547]

[1539] *pant for life* gasp for breath.
[1540] *writ* command (ordering the execution).
[1541] *office* commission.
[1542] *token of reprieve* sign that they are reprieved.
[1543] *fordid* destroyed.
[1544] *stone* i.e., the surface of the crystal looking glass.
[1545] *promised end* Doomsday.
[1546] *image* exact likeness.
[1547] *Fall and cease* i.e., let the heavens fall, and all things finish.

Lear. This feather stirs; she lives. If it be so,
It is a chance which does redeem[1548] all sorrows
That ever I have felt.

Kent.   O my good master.

Lear. Prithee, away.

Edgar.   'Tis noble Kent, your friend.   270

Lear. A plague upon you, murderers, traitors all!
I might have saved her; now she's gone for ever.
Cordelia, Cordelia, stay a little. Ha,
What is 't thou say'st? Her voice was ever soft,
Gentle and low, an excellent thing in woman.   275
I killed the slave that was a-hanging thee.

Gentleman. 'Tis true, my lords, he did.

Lear.   Did I not, fellow?
I have seen the day, with my good biting falchion[1549]
I would have made them skip: I am old now,
And these same crosses[1550] spoil me.[1551] Who are you?   280
Mine eyes are not o' th' best: I'll tell you straight.[1552]

Kent. If Fortune brag of two[1553] she loved and hated,
One of them we behold.

Lear. This is a dull sight.[1554] Are you not Kent?

Kent.   The same,
Your servant Kent. Where is your servant Caius?[1555]   285

Lear. He's a good fellow, I can tell you that;
He'll strike, and quickly too: he's dead and rotten.

Kent. No, my good lord; I am the very man.

Lear. I'll see that straight.[1556]

Kent. That from your first of difference and decay[1557]   290

[1548] *redeem* make good.

[1549] *falchion* small curved sword.

[1550] *crosses* troubles.

[1551] *spoil me* i.e., my prowess as a swordsman.

[1552] *tell you straight* recognize you straightway.

[1553] *two* i.e., Lear, and some hypothetical second, who is also a prime example of Fortune's inconstancy ("loved and hated").

[1554] *dull sight* (1) melancholy spectacle (2) faulty eyesight (Lear's own, clouded by weeping).

[1555] *Caius* (Kent's name, in disguise).

[1556] *see that straight* attend to that in a moment.

[1557] *your . . . decay* beginning of your decline in fortune.

Have followed your sad steps.

Lear.   You are welcome hither.

Kent. Nor no man else:[1558] all's cheerless, dark and deadly.
Your eldest daughters have fordone[1559] themselves,
And desperately[1560] are dead.

Lear.   Ay, so I think.

295 **Albany.** He knows not what he says, and vain is it
That we present us to him.

Edgar.   Very bootless.[1561]

Enter a Messenger.

Messenger. Edmund is dead, my lord.

Albany.   That's but a trifle here.
You lords and noble friends, know our intent.
What comfort to this great decay may come[1562]
300 Shall be applied. For us, we[1563] will resign,
During the life of this old majesty,
To him our absolute power: *[To Edgar and Kent]* you, to your rights;
With boot,[1564] and such addition[1565] as your honors
Have more than merited. All friends shall taste
305 The wages of their virtue, and all foes
The cup of their deservings. O, see, see!

Lear. And my poor fool[1566] is hanged: no, no, no life?
Why should a dog, a horse, a rat, have life,
And thou no breath at all? Thou'lt come no more,
310 Never, never, never, never, never.
Pray you, undo this button.[1567] Thank you, sir.
Do you see this? Look on her. Look, her lips,
Look there, look there.

                                                                He dies.

Edgar.   He faints. My lord, my lord!

[1558] *Nor no man else* no, I am not welcome, nor is anyone else.

[1559] *fordone* destroyed.

[1560] *desperately* in despair.

[1561] *bootless* fruitless.

[1562] *What . . . come* Whatever aid may present itself to this great ruined man.

[1563] *us, we* (the royal "we").

[1564] *boot* good measure.

[1565] *addition* additional titles and rights.

[1566] *fool* Cordelia ("fool" being a term of endearment. But it is perfectly possible to take the word as referring also to the Fool).

[1567] *undo this button* i.e., to ease the suffocation Lear feels.

Kent. Break, heart; I prithee, break.

Edgar.   Look up, my lord.

Kent. Vex not his ghost:[1568] O, let him pass! He hates him   315
That would upon the rack[1569] of this tough world
stretch him out longer.[1570]

Edgar.   He is gone indeed.

Kent. The wonder is he hath endured so long:
He but usurped[1571] his life.

Albany. Bear them from hence. Our present business   320
Is general woe. *[To Kent and Edgar]* Friends of my soul, you twain,
Rule in this realm and the gored state sustain.

Kent. I have a journey, sir, shortly to go;
My master calls me, I must not say no.

Edgar. The weight of this sad time we must obey,[1572]   325
Speak what we feel, not what we ought to say.
The oldest hath borne most: we that are young.
Shall never see so much, nor live so long.

Exeunt, with a dead march.

FINIS

Study and Discussion Questions

1. How do each of Lear's daughters answer his question about how much she loves him? Why do they answer in the way they do?
2. Is Cordelia "proud," as Lear accuses? How would *you* characterize her?
3. When do Lear's problems begin, and what does this have to do with the power he has as a king? What is the irony in his intention "to shake all cares and business from our age"?
4. What is the arrangement Lear makes with Albany and Cornwall concerning his own position in the kingdom? What happens to the agreement?
5. Make a list of words to characterize: Lear, Cordelia, Goneril and Regan, Edmund, Edgar, the Fool.
6. What is the Fool's analysis in Act I, scene iv, of Lear's decision to give away his kingdom?

[1568] *Vex . . . ghost* do not trouble his departing spirit.

[1569] *rack* instrument of torture, stretching the victim's joints to dislocation.

[1570] *longer* (1) in time (2) in bodily length.

[1571] *usurped* possessed beyond the allotted term.

[1572] *obey* submit to.

7. What do you think causes both Lear and Gloucester to have such bad judgment about their children?
8. Why are Kent and Edgar in disguise during most of the play? What is the significance of their disguises?
9. Why does Lear want to stay out in the storm?
10. Lear says in the midst of the storm (Act III, scene ii), "I am a man more sinned against than sinning." Do you agree or not?
11. Discuss Albany's change of heart. When does it begin?
12. How are Albany's final words a comment on the play as a whole?
13. What has been the fate of each of these characters—Lear, Cordelia, Gloucester, Edmund, Edgar, Goneril, Regan, Kent, Cornwall and Albany—by the end of the play?
14. How do sight, eyes, and blindness function as symbols in *King Lear?*

Writing Exercises

1. Kent says (Act II, scene ii), "but anger hath a privelege." Write a brief essay about how anger gets various people in trouble in this play. Give examples.
2. Discuss the connections between age, weakness, and wisdom. What do various characters have to say about this cluster?
3. Is Lear mad? If so, does he become mad or was he always mad? At what point does Lear step over the line into madness? Discuss the stages of his madness or the way he moves in and out of madness. Is he mad still at the end of the play?
4. What does the *Tragedy of King Lear* suggest about responsibility?
5. Discuss the theme of honesty in the play.
6. Name some of the power struggles going on in this play.
7. Trace the stages of Goneril's and Regan's moral decline, or the revelation of their real characters, depending on which view you take.
8. Discuss the portrayal of women characters in this play. What is suggested about the status of women in Shakespeare's time?
9. Sketch a modern version of *King Lear.*

Samuel Beckett. (b. 1906)

Samuel Beckett was born in Dublin, Ireland, studied there at Trinity College, and then moved to France, where he has lived since the 1930s and where he served in the anti-Nazi resistance during World War II. His early experimental fiction and poetry were greatly influenced by his friend, novelist James Joyce. Beckett wrote most of his plays in French and later translated them into English. His play, Waiting for Godot *(1953), was a major event in the development of the Theater of the Absurd. Among his other plays are* Endgame *(1957),* How It is *(1961), and* Happy Days *(1961). Beckett has also written several novels, including* Molloy *(1951),* Malone Dies *(1951),* Watt *(1953),* and The Unnamable *(1953). In 1969 he won the Nobel Prize for literature.*

Krapp's Last Tape   (1958)

A late evening in the future.

Krapp's den.

Front centre a small table, the two drawers of which open towards audience.

Sitting at the table, facing front, i.e. across from the drawers, a wearish old man: Krapp.

Rusty black narrow trousers too short for him. Rusty black sleeveless waistcoat, four capacious pockets. Heavy silver watch and chain. Grimy white shirt open at neck, no collar. Surprising pair of dirty white boots, size ten at least, very narrow and pointed.

White face. Purple nose. Disordered grey hair. Unshaven.

Very near-sighted (but unspectacled). Hard of hearing.

Cracked voice. Distinctive intonation.

Laborious walk.

On the table a tape-recorder with microphone and a number of cardboard boxes containing reels of recorded tapes.

Table and immediately adjacent area in strong white light. Rest of stage in darkness.

Krapp remains a moment motionless, heaves a great sigh, looks at his watch, fumbles in his pockets, takes out an envelope, puts it back, fumbles, takes out a small bunch of keys, raises it to his eyes, chooses a key, gets up and moves to front of table. He stoops, unlocks first drawer, peers into it, feels about inside it, takes out a reel of tape, peers at it, puts it back, locks drawer, unlocks second drawer, peers into it, feels about inside it, takes out a large banana, peers at it, locks drawer, puts keys back in his pocket. He turns, advances to edge of stage, halts, strokes banana, peels it, drops skin at his feet, puts end of banana in his mouth and remains motionless, staring vacuously before him. Finally he bites off the end, turns aside and begins pacing to and fro at edge of stage, in the light, i.e. not more than four or five paces either way, meditatively eating banana. He treads on skin, slips, nearly falls, recovers himself, stoops and peers at skin and finally pushes it, still stooping, with his foot over the edge of stage into pit. He resumes his pacing, finishes banana, returns to table, sits down, remains a moment motionless, heaves a great sigh, takes keys from his pockets, raises them to his eyes, chooses key, gets up and moves to front of table, unlocks second drawer, takes out a second large banana, peers at it, locks drawer, puts back keys in his pocket, turns, advances to edge of stage, halts, strokes banana, peels it, tosses skin into pit, puts end of banana in his mouth and remains motionless, staring vacuously before him. Finally he has an idea, puts banana in his waistcoat pocket, the end emerging, and goes with all the speed he can muster backstage into darkness. Ten seconds. Loud pop of cork. Fifteen seconds. He comes back into light carrying an old ledger and sits down at table. He lays ledger on table, wipes his mouth, wipes his hands on the front of his waistcoat, brings them smartly together and rubs them.

Krapp. *(briskly).* Ah! *(He bends over ledger, turns the pages, finds the entry he wants, reads.)* Box . . . thrree . . . spool . . . five. *(He raises his head and stares front. With relish.)* Spool! *(Pause.)* Spooool! *(Happy smile. Pause. He bends over table, starts peering and poking at the boxes.)* Box . . . thrree . . . thrree . . . four . . . two . . . *(with surprise)* nine! good God! . . . seven . . . ah! the little rascal! *(He takes up box, peers at it.)* Box thrree. *(He lays it on table, opens it and peers at spools inside.)* Spool . . . *(he peers at ledger)* . . . five . . . *(he peers at spools)* . . . five . . . five . . . ah! the little scoundrel! *(He takes out a spool, peers at it.)* Spool five. *(He lays it on table, closes box three, puts it back with the others, takes up the spool.)* Box thrree, spool five. *(He bends over the machine, looks up. With relish.)* Spooool! *(Happy smile. He bends, loads spool on machine, rubs his hands.)* Ah! *(He peers at ledger, reads entry at foot of page.)* Mother at rest at last . . . Hm . . . The black ball . . . *(He raises his head, stares blankly front. Puzzled.)* Black ball? . . . *(He peers again at ledger, reads.)* The dark nurse . . . *(He raises his head, broods, peers again at ledger, reads.)* Slight improvement in bowel condition . . . Hm . . . Memorable . . . what? *(He peers closer.)* Equinox, memorable equinox. *(He raises his head, stares blankly front. Puzzled.)* Memorable equinox? . . . *(Pause. He shrugs his shoulders, peers again at ledger, reads.)* Farewell to—*(he turns the page)*—love.

He raises his head, broods, bends over machine, switches on and assumes listening posture, i.e. leaning forward, elbows on table, hand cupping ear towards machine, face front.

Tape. *(strong voice, rather pompous, clearly Krapp's at a much earlier time.)* Thirty-nine today, sound as a—*(Settling himself more comfortably he knocks one of the boxes off the table, curses, switches off, sweeps boxes* *and ledger violently to the ground, winds tape back to beginning, switches on, resumes posture.)* Thirty-nine today, sound as a bell, apart from my old weakness, and intellectually I have now every reason to suspect at the . . . *(hesitates)* . . . crest of the wave—or thereabouts. Celebrated the awful occasion, as in recent years, quietly at the Winehouse. Not a soul. Sat before the fire with closed eyes, separating the grain from the husks. Jotted down a few notes, on the back of an envelope. Good to be back in my den, in my old rags. Have just eaten I regret to say three bananas and only with difficulty refrained from a fourth. Fatal things for a man with my condition. *(Vehemently.)* Cut 'em out! *(Pause.)* The new light above my table is a great improvement. With all this darkness round me I feel less alone. *(Pause.)* In a way. *(Pause.)* I love to get up and move about in it, then back here to . . . *(hesitates)* . . . me. *(Pause.)* Krapp.   *Pause*

The grain, now what I wonder do I mean by that, I mean . . . *(hesitates)* . . . I suppose I mean those things worth having when all the dust has—when all *my* dust has settled. I close my eyes and try and imagine them.   *Pause. Krapp closes his eyes briefly.*

Extraordinary silence this evening, I strain my ears and do not hear a sound. Old Miss McGlome always sings at this hour. But not tonight. Songs of her girlhood, she says. Hard to think of her as a girl. Wonderful woman though. Connaught, I fancy. *(Pause.)* Shall I sing when I am her age, if I ever am? No. *(Pause.)* Did I sing as a boy? No. *(Pause.)* Did I ever sing? No.   *Pause.*

Just been listening to an old year, passages at random. I did not check in the book, but it must be at least ten or twelve years ago. At that time I think I was still living on and off with Bianca in Kedar Street. Well out of that, Jesus yes! Hopeless business. *(Pause.)* Not much about her, apart from a tribute to her eyes. Very warm. I suddenly saw them again. *(Pause.)* Incomparable! *(Pause.)* Ah well . . . *(Pause.)* These old P.M.s are gruesome, but I often find them—*(Krapp switches off, broods, switches on)*—a help before embarking on a new . . . *(hesitates)* . . . retrospect. Hard to believe I was ever that young whelp. The voice! Jesus! And the aspirations! *(Brief laugh in which Krapp joins.)* And the resolutions! *(Brief laugh in which Krapp joins.)* To drink less, in particular. *(Brief laugh of Krapp alone.)* Statistics. Seventeen hundred hours, out of the preceding eight thousand odd, consumed on licensed premises alone. More than 20%, say 40% of his waking life. *(Pause.)* Plans for a less . . . *(hesitates)* . . . engrossing sexual life. Last illness of his father. Flagging pursuit of happiness. Unattainable laxation. Sneers at what he calls his youth and thanks to God that it's over. *(Pause.)* False ring there. *(Pause.)* Shadows of the opus . . . magnum. Closing with a— *(brief laugh)*—yelp to Providence. *(Prolonged laugh in which Krapp joins.)*

What remains of all that misery? A girl in a shabby green coat, on a
railway-station platform? No?   *Pause.*   When I look—

*Krapp switches off, broods, looks at his watch, gets up, goes backstage into
darkness. Ten seconds. Pop of cork. Ten seconds. Second cork. Ten seconds.
Third cork. Ten seconds. Brief burst of quavering song.*

Krapp. *(sings).*

> Now the day is over,
> Night is drawing nigh-igh,
> Shadows—

*Fit of coughing. He comes back into light, sits down, wipes his mouth, switches
on, resumes his listening posture.*

Tape.   —back on the year that is gone, with what I hope is perhaps a
glint of the old eye to come, there is of course the house on the canal
where mother lay a-dying, in the late autumn, after her long viduity
(Krapp gives a start), and the—*(Krapp switches off, winds back tape a
little, bends his ear closer to machine, switches on)* —a-dying, after her
long viduity, and the—

*Krapp switches off, raises his head, stares blankly before him. His lips move
in the syllables of "viduity." No sound. He gets up, goes backstage into
darkness, comes back with an enormous dictionary, lays it on table, sits
down and looks up the word.*

Krapp. *(reading from dictionary).* State—or condition of being—or remaining—a widow—or widower. *(Looks up. Puzzled.)* Being—or remaining? . . . *(Pause. He peers again at dictionary. Reading.)* "Deep weeds
of viduity" . . . Also of an animal, especially a bird . . . the vidua or
weaver-bird . . . Black plumage of male . . . *(He looks up. With relish.)*
The vidua-bird!

Pause. He closes dictionary, switches on, resumes listening posture.

Tape.   —bench by the weir from where I could see her window. There
I sat, in the biting wind, wishing she were gone. *(Pause.)* Hardly a soul,
just a few regulars, nursemaids, infants, old men, dogs. I got to know
them quite well—oh by appearance of course I mean! One dark young
beauty I recollect particularly, all white and starch, incomparable bosom,
with a big black hooded perambulator, most funereal thing. Whenever
I looked in her direction she had her eyes on me. And yet when I
was bold enough to speak to her—not having been introduced—she
threatened to call a policeman. As if I had designs on her virtue! *(Laugh.
Pause.)* The face she had! The eyes! Like . . .*(hesitates)* . . . chrysolite!

(Pause.) Ah well . . . *(Pause.)* I was there when—*(Krapp switches off, broods, switches on again)*—the blind went down, one of those dirty brown roller affairs, throwing a ball for a little white dog, as chance would have it. I happened to look up and there it was. All over and done with, at last. I sat on for a few moments with the ball in my hand and the dog yelping and pawing at me. *(Pause.)* Moments. Her moments, my moments. *(Pause.)* The dog's moments. *(Pause.)* In the end I held it out to him and he took it in his mouth, gently, gently. A small, old, black, hard, solid rubber ball. *(Pause.)* I shall feel it, in my hand, until my dying day. *(Pause.)* I might have kept it. *(Pause.)* But I gave it to the dog.   *Pause.*   Ah well . . .   *Pause.*

Spiritually a year of profound gloom and indigence until that memorable night in March, at the end of the jetty, in the howling wind, never to be forgotten, when suddenly I saw the whole thing. The vision, at last. This I fancy is what I have chiefly to record this evening, against the day when my work will be done and perhaps no place left in my memory, warm or cold, for the miracle that . . . *(hesitates)* . . . for the fire that set it alight. What I suddenly saw then was this, that the belief I had been going on all my life, namely—*(Krapp switches off impatiently, winds tape forward, switches on again)*—great granite rocks the foam flying up in the light of the lighthouse and the wind-gauge spinning like a propellor, clear to me at last that the dark I have always struggled to keep under is in reality my most—*(Krapp curses, switches off, winds tape forward, switches on again)*—unshatterable association until my dissolution of storm and night with the light of the understanding and the fire—*(Krapp curses louder, switches off, winds tape forward, switches on again)*—my face in her breasts and my hand on her. We lay there without moving. But under us all moved, and moved us, gently, up and down, and from side to side.   *Pause.*

Past midnight. Never knew such silence. The earth might be uninhabited.   *Pause.*
      Here I end—

Krapp switches off, winds tape back, switches on again.

—upper lake, with the punt, bathed off the bank, then pushed out into the stream and drifted. She lay stretched out on the floorboards with her hands under her head and her eyes closed. Sun blazing down, bit of a breeze, water nice and lively. I noticed a scratch on her thigh and asked her how she came by it. Picking gooseberries, she said. I said again I thought it was hopeless and no good going on, and she agreed, without opening her eyes. *(Pause.)* I asked her to look at me and after a few moments—*(pause)*—after a few moments she did, but the eyes just slits, because of the glare. I bent over her to get them in the

shadow and they opened. *(Pause. Low.)* Let me in. *(Pause.)* We drifted in among the flags and stuck. The way they went down, sighing, before the stem! *(Pause.)* I lay down across her with my face in her breasts and my hand on her. We lay there without moving. But under us all moved, and moved us, gently, up and down, and from side to side.
Pause.   Past midnight. Never knew—

Krapp switches off, broods. Finally he fumbles in his pockets, encounters the banana, takes it out, peers at it, puts it back, fumbles, brings out the envelope, fumbles, puts back envelope, looks at his watch, gets up and goes backstage into darkness. Ten seconds. Sound of bottle against glass, then brief siphon. Ten seconds. Bottle against glass alone. Ten seconds. He comes back a little unsteadily into light, goes to front of table, takes out keys, raises them to his eyes, chooses key. Unlocks first drawer, peers into it, feels about inside, takes out reel, peers at it, locks drawer, puts keys back in his pocket, goes and sits down, takes reel off machine, lays it on dictionary, loads virgin reel on machine, takes envelope from his pocket, consults back of it, lays it on table, switches on, clears his throat and begins to record.

Krapp. Just been listening to that stupid bastard I took myself for thirty years ago, hard to believe I was ever as bad as that. Thank God that's all done with anyway. *(Pause.)* The eyes she had! *(Broods, realizes he is recording silence, switches off, broods. Finally.)* Everything there, everything, all the—*(Realizes this is not being recorded, switches on.)* Everything there, everything on this old muckball, all the light and dark and famine and feasting of . . . *(hesitates)* . . . the ages! *(In a shout.)* Yes! *(Pause.)* Let that go! Jesus! Take his mind off his homework! Jesus! *(Pause. Weary.)* Ah well, maybe he was right. *(Pause.)* Maybe he was right. *(Broods. Realizes. Switches off. Consults envelope.)* Pah! *(Crumples it and throws it away. Broods. Switches on.)* Nothing to say, not a squeak. What's a year now? The sour cud and the iron stool. *(Pause.)* Revelled in the word spool. *(With relish.)* Spooool! Happiest moment of the past half million. *(Pause.)* Seventeen copies sold, of which eleven at trade price to free circulating libraries beyond the seas. Getting known. *(Pause.)* One pound six and something, eight I have little doubt. *(Pause.)* Crawled out once or twice, before the summer was cold. Sat shivering in the park, drowned in dreams and burning to be gone. Not a soul. *(Pause.)* Last fancies. *(Vehemently.)* Keep 'em under! *(Pause.)* Scalded the eyes out of me reading *Effie* again, a page a day, with tears again. Effie . . . *(Pause.)* Could have been happy with her, up there on the Baltic, and the pines, and the dunes. *(Pause.)* Could I? *(Pause.)* And she? *(Pause.)* Pah! *(Pause.)* Fanny came in a couple of times. Bony old ghost of a whore. Couldn't do much, but I suppose better than a kick in the crutch. The last time wasn't so bad. How do you manage it, she said, at your age? I told her I'd been saving up for her all my life. *(Pause.)* Went to Vespers once, like when I was in short trousers. *(Pause. Sings.)*

> Now the day is over,
> Night is drawing nigh-igh,
> Shadows—(*coughing, then almost*
>   *inaudible*)—of the evening
> Steal across the sky.

(*Gasping.*) Went to sleep and fell off the pew. (*Pause.*) Sometimes wondered in the night if a last effort mightn't—(*Pause.*) Ah finish your booze now and get to your bed. Go on with this drivel in the morning. Or leave it at that. (*Pause.*) Leave it at that. (*Pause.*) Lie propped up in the dark— and wander. Be again in the dingle on a Christmas Eve, gathering holly, the red-berried. (*Pause.*) Be again on Croghan on a Sunday morning, in the haze, with the bitch, stop and listen to the bells. (*Pause.*) And so on. (*Pause.*) Be again, be again. (*Pause.*) All that old misery. (*Pause.*) Once wasn't enough for you. (*Pause.*) Lie down across her.

Long pause. He suddenly bends over machine, switches off, wrenches off tape, throws it away, puts on the other, winds it forward to the passage he wants, switches on, listens staring front.

Tape. —gooseberries, she said. I said again I thought it was hopeless and no good going on, and she agreed, without opening her eyes. (*Pause.*) I asked her to look at me and after a few moments—(*pause*)— after a few moments she did, but the eyes just slits, because of the glare. I bent over her to get them in the shadow and they opened. (*Pause. Low.*) Let me in. (*Pause.*) We drifted in among the flags and stuck. The way they went down, sighing, before the stem! (*Pause.*) I lay down across her with my face in her breasts and my hand on her. We lay there without moving. But under us all moved, and moved us, gently, up and down, and from side to side.

Pause. Krapp's lips move. No sound.

Past midnight. Never knew such silence. The earth might be uninhabited.   *Pause.*

Here I end this reel. Box—(*pause*)—three, spool—(*pause*)—five. (*Pause.*) Perhaps my best years are gone. When there was a chance of happiness. But I wouldn't want them back. Not with the fire in me now. No, I wouldn't want them back.

Krapp motionless staring before him. The tape runs on in silence.

CURTAIN

Study and Discussion Questions

1. About how old is Krapp now? How old is he in the tape he listens to? On tape, he talks of listening to himself on an earlier tape. How old is he on that tape?
2. What was Krapp's life like in earlier years? What is it like now?
3. Why did Krapp end his relationship with the woman in the punt? How does he feel about her now?
4. Discuss the staging and lighting of the play. How do they help shape the play's meaning?
5. Why is Krapp having so much trouble recording this year's tape? Why might this be Krapp's last tape?
6. What is the significance of Krapp's ignorance of the meaning of "viduity," a word he hears on his tape?
7. Krapp, we learn, is a writer. What is the importance of this?
8. What is the significance of all those bananas Krapp eats?
9. Explain the significance of Krapp's last words in the play, when he says, of his earlier years, "No, I wouldn't want them back."

Writing Exercises

1. Describe the younger Krapp from the point of view of the woman in the punt.
2. What do you think Krapp's book was like? Write a brief review of it.
3. What (besides the existence of tape recorders) makes this a modern, twentieth-century play?
4. If you once kept a journal or diary, read through it and describe how you feel about your earlier self.

NONFICTION

MAXINE HONG KINGSTON   (b. 1940)

Maxine Hong Kingston was born in Stockton, California, where her Chinese immigrant parents ran a laundry. She studied at the University of California at Berkeley and has taught at California and Hawaii high schools and at the University of Hawaii. Kingston's work includes two collections that seem to blend fiction and nonfiction, The Woman Warrior: Memoirs of a Girlhood Among Ghosts *(1976) and* China Men *(1980). "No Name Woman" is the first section of* The Woman Warrior.

No Name Woman   (1976)

"You must not tell anyone," my mother said, "what I am about to tell you. In China your father had a sister who killed herself. She jumped into the family well. We say that your father has all brothers because it is as if she had never been born.

"In 1924 just a few days after our village celebrated seventeen hurry-up weddings—to make sure that every young man who went 'out on the road' would responsibly come home—your father and his brothers and your grandfather and his brothers and your aunt's new husband sailed for America, the Gold Mountain. It was your grandfather's last trip. Those lucky enough to get contracts waved goodbye from the decks. They fed and guarded the stowaways and helped them off in Cuba, New York, Bali, Hawaii. 'We'll meet in California next year,' they said. All of them sent money home.

"I remember looking at your aunt one day when she and I were dressing; I had not noticed before that she had such a protruding melon of a stomach. But I did not think, 'She's pregnant,' until she began to look like other pregnant women, her shirt pulling and the white tops of her black pants showing. She could not have been pregnant, you see, because her husband had been gone for years. No one said anything. We did not discuss it. In early summer she was ready to have the child, long after the time when it could have been possible.

"The village had also been counting. On the night the baby was to be born the villagers raided our house. Some were crying. Like a great saw, teeth strung with lights, files of people walked zigzag across our land, tearing the rice. Their lanterns doubled in the disturbed black water, which drained away through the broken bunds. As the villagers closed in, we could see that some of them, probably men and women we knew well, wore white masks. The people with long hair hung it over their faces. Women with short hair made it stand up on end. Some had tied white bands around their foreheads, arms, and legs.

"At first they threw mud and rocks at the house. Then they threw eggs and began slaughtering our stock. We could hear the animals scream their deaths—the roosters, the pigs, a last great roar from the ox. Familiar wild heads flared in our night windows; the villagers encircled us. Some of the faces stopped to peer at us, their eyes rushing like searchlights. The hands flattened against the panes, framed heads, and left red prints.

"The villagers broke in the front and the back doors at the same time, even though we had not locked the doors against them. Their knives dripped with the blood of our animals. They smeared blood on the doors and walls. One woman swung a chicken, whose throat she had slit, splattering blood in red arcs about her. We stood together in the middle of our house, in the family hall with the pictures and tables of the ancestors around us, and looked straight ahead.

"At that time the house had only two wings. When the men came back, we would build two more to enclose our courtyard and a third one to begin a second courtyard. The villagers pushed through both wings, even your grandparents' rooms, to find your aunt's, which was also mine until the men returned. From this room a new wing for one of the younger families would grow. They ripped up her clothes and shoes and broke her combs, grinding them underfoot. They tore her work from the loom. They scattered the cooking fire and rolled the new weaving in it. We could hear them in the kitchen breaking our bowls and banging the pots. They overturned the great waist-high earthenware jugs; duck eggs, pickled fruits, vegetables burst out and mixed in acrid torrents. The old woman from the next field swept a broom through the air and loosed the spirits-of-the-broom over our heads. 'Pig.' 'Ghost.' 'Pig,' they sobbed and scolded while they ruined our house.

"When they left, they took sugar and oranges to bless themselves. They cut pieces from the dead animals. Some of them took bowls that were not broken and clothes that were not torn. Afterward we swept up the rice and sewed it back up into sacks. But the smells from the spilled preserves lasted. Your aunt gave birth in the pigsty that night. The next morning when I went for the water, I found her and the baby plugging up the family well.

"Don't let your father know what I told you. He denies her. Now that you have started to menstruate, what happened to her could happen to you. Don't humiliate us. You wouldn't like to be forgotten as if you had never been born. The villagers are watchful."

Whenever she had to warn us about life, my mother told stories that ran like this one, a story to grow up on. She tested our strength to establish realities. Those in the emigrant generations who could not reassert brute survival died young and far from home. Those of us in the first

American generations have had to figure out how the invisible world the emigrants built around our childhoods fit in solid America.

The emigrants confused the gods by diverting their curses, misleading them with crooked streets and false names. They must try to confuse their offspring as well, who, I suppose, threaten them in similar ways— always trying to get things straight, always trying to name the unspeakable. The Chinese I know hide their names; sojourners take new names when their lives change and guard their real names with silence.

Chinese-Americans, when you try to understand what things in you are Chinese, how do you separate what is peculiar to childhood, to poverty, insanities, one family, your mother who marked your growing with stories, from what is Chinese? What is Chinese tradition and what is the movies?

If I want to learn what clothes my aunt wore, whether flashy or ordinary, I would have to begin, "Remember Father's drowned-in-the-well sister?" I cannot ask that. My mother has told me once and for all the useful parts. She will add nothing unless powered by Necessity, a riverbank that guides her life. She plants vegetable gardens rather than lawns; she carries the odd-shaped tomatoes home from the fields and eats food left for the gods.

Whenever we did frivolous things, we used up energy; we flew high kites. We children came up off the ground over the melting cones our parents brought home from work and the American movie on New Year's Day—*Oh, You Beautiful Doll* with Betty Grable one year, and *She Wore a Yellow Ribbon* with John Wayne another year. After the one carnival ride each, we paid in guilt; our tired father counted his change on the dark walk home.

Adultery is extravagance. Could people who hatch their own chicks and eat the embryos and the heads for delicacies and boil the feet in vinegar for party food, leaving only the gravel, eating even the gizzard lining—could such people engender a prodigal aunt? To be a woman, to have a daughter in starvation time was a waste enough. My aunt could not have been the lone romantic who gave up everything for sex. Women in the old China did not choose. Some man had commanded her to lie with him and be his secret evil. I wonder whether he masked himself when he joined the raid on her family.

Perhaps she encountered him in the fields or on the mountain where the daughters-in-law collected fuel. Or perhaps he first noticed her in the marketplace. He was not a stranger because the village housed no strangers. She had to have dealings with him other than sex. Perhaps he worked an adjoining field, or he sold her the cloth for the dress she sewed and wore. His demand must have surprised, then terrified her. She obeyed him; she always did as she was told.

When the family found a young man in the next village to be her husband, she stood tractably beside the best rooster, his proxy, and promised before they met that she would be his forever. She was lucky that he was her age and she would be the first wife, an advantage secure now. The night she first saw him, he had sex with her. Then he left for America. She had almost forgotten what he looked like. When she tried to envision him, she only saw the black and white face in the group photograph the men had had taken before leaving.

The other man was not, after all, much different from her husband. They both gave orders: she followed. "If you tell your family, I'll beat you. I'll kill you. Be here again next week." No one talked sex, ever. And she might have separated the rapes from the rest of living if only she did not have to buy her oil from him or gather wood in the same forest. I want her fear to have lasted just as long as rape lasted so that the fear could have been contained. No drawn-out fear. But women at sex hazarded birth and hence lifetimes. The fear did not stop but permeated everywhere. She told the man, "I think I'm pregnant." He organized the raid against her.

On nights when my mother and father talked about their life back home, sometimes they mentioned an "outcast table" whose business they still seemed to be settling, their voices tight. In a commensal tradition, where food is precious, the powerful older people made wrongdoers eat alone. Instead of letting them start separate new lives like the Japanese, who could become samurais and geishas, the Chinese family, faces averted but eyes glowering sideways, hung on to the offenders and fed them leftovers. My aunt must have lived in the same house as my parents and eaten at an outcast table. My mother spoke about the raid as if she had seen it, when she and my aunt, a daughter-in-law to a different household, should not have been living together at all. Daughters-in-law lived with their husbands' parents, not their own; a synonym for marriage in Chinese is "taking a daughter-in-law." Her husband's parents could have sold her, mortgaged her, stoned her. But they had sent her back to her own mother and father, a mysterious act hinting at disgraces not told me. Perhaps they had thrown her out to deflect the avengers.

She was the only daughter; her four brothers went with her father, husband, and uncles "out on the road" and for some years became western men. When the goods were divided among the family, three of the brothers took land, and the youngest, my father, chose an education. After my grandparents gave their daughter away to her husband's family, they had dispensed all the adventure and all the property. They expected her alone to keep the traditional ways, which her brothers, now among the barbarians, could fumble without detection. The heavy, deep-rooted women were to maintain the past against the flood, safe for returning. But the rare urge west had fixed upon our family, and so my aunt crossed boundaries not delineated in space.

The work of preservation demands that the feelings playing about in one's guts not be turned into action. Just watch their passing like cherry blossoms. But perhaps my aunt, my forerunner, caught in a slow life, let dreams grow and fade and after some months or years went toward what persisted. Fear at the enormities of the forbidden kept her desires delicate, wire and bone. She looked at a man because she liked the way the hair was tucked behind his ears, or she liked the question-mark line of a long torso curving at the shoulder and straight at the hip. For warm eyes or a soft voice or a slow walk—that's all—a few hairs, a line, a brightness, a sound, a pace, she gave up family. She offered us up for a charm that vanished with tiredness, a pigtail that didn't toss when the wind died. Why, the wrong lighting could erase the dearest thing about him.

It could very well have been, however, that my aunt did not take subtle enjoyment of her friend, but, a wild woman, kept rollicking company. Imagining her free with sex doesn't fit, though. I don't know any women like that, or men either. Unless I see her life branching into mine, she gives me no ancestral help.

To sustain her being in love, she often worked at herself in the mirror, guessing at the colors and shapes that would interest him, changing them frequently in order to hit on the right combination. She wanted him to look back.

On a farm near the sea, a woman who tended her appearance reaped a reputation for eccentricity. All the married women blunt-cut their hair in flaps about their ears or pulled it back in tight buns. No nonsense. Neither style blew easily into heart-catching tangles. And at their weddings they displayed themselves in their long hair for the last time. "It brushed the backs of my knees," my mother tells me. "It was braided, and even so, it brushed the backs of my knees."

At the mirror my aunt combed individuality into her bob. A bun could have been contrived to escape into black streamers blowing in the wind or in quiet wisps about her face, but only the older women in our picture album wear buns. She brushed her hair back from her forehead, tucking the flaps behind her ears. She looped a piece of thread, knotted into a circle between her index fingers and thumbs, and ran the double strand across her forehead. When she closed her fingers as if she were making a pair of shadow geese bite, the string twisted together catching the little hairs. Then she pulled the thread away from her skin, ripping the hairs out neatly, her eyes watering from the needles of pain. Opening her fingers, she cleaned the thread, then rolled it along her hairline and the tops of her eyebrows. My mother did the same to me and my sisters and herself. I used to believe that the expression "caught by the short hairs" meant a captive held with a depilatory string. It especially hurt at the temples, but my mother said we were lucky we didn't have to have our feet bound when we were seven. Sisters used to sit on their beds and cry together, she said, as their mothers or their slaves removed the bandages for a few minutes each night and let the blood gush back into their veins. I hope that the man my aunt loved appreciated a smooth brow, that he wasn't just a tits-and-ass man.

Once my aunt found a freckle on her chin, at a spot that the almanac said predestined her for unhappiness. She dug it out with a hot needle and washed the wound with peroxide.

More attention to her looks than these pullings of hairs and pickings at spots would have caused gossip among the villagers. They owned work clothes and good clothes, and they wore good clothes for feasting the new seasons. But since a woman combing her hair hexes beginnings, my aunt rarely found an occasion to look her best. Women looked like great sea snails—the corded wood, babies, and laundry they carried were the whorls on their backs. The Chinese did not admire a bent back; goddesses and warriors stood straight. Still there must have been a marvelous freeing of beauty when a worker laid down her burden and stretched and arched.

Such commonplace loveliness, however, was not enough for my aunt. She dreamed of a lover for the fifteen days of New Year's, the time for families to exchange visits, money, and food. She plied her secret comb. And sure enough she cursed the year, the family, the village, and herself.

Even as her hair lured her imminent lover, many other men looked at her. Uncles, cousins, nephews, brothers would have looked, too, had they been home between journeys. Perhaps they had already been restraining their curiosity, and they left, fearful that their glances, like a field of nesting birds, might be startled and caught. Poverty hurt, and that was their first reason for leaving. But another, final reason for leaving the crowded house was the never-said.

She may have been unusually beloved, the precious only daughter, spoiled and mirror gazing because of the affection the family lavished on her. When her husband left, they welcomed the chance to take her back from the in-laws; she could live like the little daughter for just a while longer. There are stories that my grandfather was different from other people, "crazy ever since the little Jap bayoneted him in the head." He used to put his naked penis on the dinner table, laughing. And one day he brought home a baby girl, wrapped up inside his brown western-style greatcoat. He had traded one of his sons, probably my father, the youngest, for her. My grandmother made him trade back. When he finally got a daughter of his own, he doted on her. They must have all loved her, except perhaps my father, the only brother who never went back to China, having once been traded for a girl.

Brothers and sisters, newly men and women, had to efface their sexual color and present plain miens. Disturbing hair and eyes, a smile like no other threatened the ideal of five generations living under one roof. To focus blurs, people shouted face to face and yelled from room to room. The immigrants I know have loud voices, unmodulated to American tones even after years away from the village where they called their friendships out across the fields. I have not been able to stop my mother's screams in public libraries or over telephones. Walking erect (knees straight, toes pointed forward, not pigeon-toed, which is Chinese-feminine) and speaking in an inaudible voice, I have tried to turn myself American-feminine. Chinese communication was loud, public. Only sick people had to whisper. But at the dinner table, where the family members came nearest one another, no one could talk, not the outcasts nor any eaters. Every word that falls from the mouth is a coin lost. Silently they gave and accepted food with both hands. A preoccupied child who took his bowl with one hand got a sideways glare. A complete moment of total attention is due everyone alike. Children and lovers have no singularity here, but my aunt used a secret voice, a separate attentiveness.

She kept the man's name to herself throughout her labor and dying; she did not accuse him that he be punished with her. To save her inseminator's name she gave silent birth.

He may have been somebody in her own household, but intercourse with a man outside the family would have been no less abhorrent. All the village were kinsmen, and the titles shouted in loud country voices never let kinship be forgotten. Any man within visiting distance would have been neutralized as a lover—"brother," "younger brother," "older brother"—one hundred and fifteen relationship titles. Parents researched birth charts probably not so much to assure good fortune as to circumvent incest in a population that has but one hundred surnames. Everybody has eight million relatives. How useless then sexual mannerisms, how dangerous.

As if it came from an atavism deeper than fear, I used to add "brother" silently to boys' names. It hexed the boys, who would or would not ask me to dance, and made them less scary and as familiar and deserving of benevolence as girls.

But, of course, I hexed myself also—no dates. I should have stood up, both arms waving, and shouted out across libraries, "Hey, you! Love me back." I had no idea, though, how to make attraction selective, how to control its direction and magnitude. If I made myself American-pretty so that the five or six Chinese boys in the class fell in love with me, everyone else—the Caucasian, Negro, and Japanese boys—would too. Sisterliness, dignified and honorable, made much more sense.

Attraction eludes control so stubbornly that whole societies designed to organize relationships among people cannot keep order, not even when they bind people to one another from childhood and raise them together. Among the very poor and the wealthy, brothers married their adopted sisters, like doves. Our family allowed some romance, paying adult brides' prices and providing dowries so that their sons and daughters could marry strangers. Marriage promises to turn strangers into friendly relatives—a nation of siblings.

In the village structure, spirits shimmered among the live creatures, balanced and held in equilibrium by time and land. But one human being flaring up into violence could open up a black hole, a maelstrom that pulled in the sky. The frightened villagers, who depended on one another to maintain the real, went to my aunt to show her a personal, physical representation of the break she had made in the "roundness." Misallying couples snapped off the future, which was to be embodied in true offspring. The villagers punished her for acting as if she could have a private life, secret and apart from them.

If my aunt had betrayed the family at a time of large grain yields and peace, when many boys were born, and wings were being built on many houses, perhaps she might have escaped such severe punishment. But the men—hungry, greedy, tired of planting in dry soil, cuckolded—had had to leave the village in order to send food-money home. There were ghost plagues, bandit plagues, wars with the Japanese, floods. My Chinese brother and sister had died of an unknown sickness. Adultery, perhaps only a mistake during good times, became a crime when the village needed food.

The round moon cakes and round doorways, the round tables of graduated size that fit one roundness inside another, round windows and rice bowls—these talismens had lost their power to warn this family of the law: a family must be whole, faithfully keeping the descent line by having sons to feed the old and the dead, who in turn look after the family. The villagers came to show my aunt and her lover-in-hiding a broken house. The villagers were speeding up the circling of events because she was too shortsighted to see that her infidelity had already harmed the village, that waves of consequences would return unpredictably, sometimes in disguise, as now, to hurt her. This roundness had to be made coin-sized so that she would see its circumference: punish her at the birth of her baby. Awaken her to the inexorable. People who refused fatalism because they could invent small resources insisted on culpability. Deny accidents and wrest fault from the stars.

After the villagers left, their lanterns now scattering in various directions toward home, the family broke their silence and cursed her. "Aiaa, we're going to die. Death is coming. Death is coming. Look what you've done. You've killed us. Ghost! Dead ghost! Ghost! You've never been born." She ran out into the fields, far enough from the house so that she could no longer hear their voices, and pressed herself against the earth, her own land no more. When she felt the birth coming, she thought that she had been hurt. Her body seized together. "They've hurt me too much," she thought. "This is gall, and it will kill me." Her forehead and knees against the earth, her body convulsed and then released her onto her back. The black well of sky and stars went out and out and out forever; her body and her complexity seemed to disappear. She was one of the stars, a bright dot in blackness, without home, without a companion, in eternal cold and silence. An agoraphobia rose in her, speeding higher and higher, bigger and bigger; she would not be able to contain it; there would be no end to fear.

Flayed, unprotected against space, she felt pain return, focusing her body. This pain chilled her—a cold, steady kind of surface pain. Inside, spasmodically, the other pain, the pain of the child, heated her. For hours she lay on the ground, alternately body and space. Sometimes a vision of normal comfort obliterated reality: she saw the family in the evening gambling at the dinner table, the young people massaging their elders' backs. She saw them congratulating one another, high joy on the mornings the rice shoots came up. When these pictures burst, the stars drew yet further apart. Black space opened.

She got to her feet to fight better and remembered that old-fashioned women gave birth in their pigsties to fool the jealous, pain-dealing gods, who do not snatch piglets. Before the next spasms could stop her, she ran to the pigsty, each step a rushing out into emptiness. She climbed over the fence and knelt in the dirt. It was good to have a fence enclosing her, a tribal person alone.

Laboring, this woman who had carried her child as a foreign growth that sickened her every day, expelled it at last. She reached down to touch the hot, wet, moving mass, surely smaller than anything human, and could feel that it was human after all—fingers, toes, nails, nose. She pulled it up on to her belly, and it lay curled there, butt in the air, feet precisely tucked one under the other. She opened her loose shirt and buttoned the child inside. After resting, it squirmed and thrashed and she pushed it up to her breast. It turned its head this way and that until it found her nipple. There, it made little snuffling noises. She clenched her teeth at its preciousness, lovely as a young calf, a piglet, a little dog.

She may have gone to the pigsty as a last act of responsibility: she would protect this child as she had protected its father. It would look after her soul, leaving supplies on her grave. But how would this tiny child without family find her grave when there would be no marker for her anywhere, neither in the earth nor the family hall? No one would give her a family hall name. She had taken the child with her into the wastes. At its birth the two of them had felt the same raw pain of separation, a wound that only the family pressing tight could close. A child with no descent line would not soften her life but only trail after her, ghostlike, begging her to give it purpose. At dawn the villagers on their way to the fields would stand around the fence and look.

Full of milk, the little ghost slept. When it awoke, she hardened her breasts against the milk that crying loosens. Toward morning she picked up the baby and walked to the well.

Carrying the baby to the well shows loving. Otherwise abandon it. Turn its face into the mud. Mothers who love their children take them along. It was probably a girl; there is some hope of forgiveness for boys.

"Don't tell anyone you had an aunt. Your father does not want to hear her name. She has never been born." I have believed that sex was unspeakable and words so strong and fathers so frail that "aunt" would do my father mysterious harm. I have thought that my family, having settled among immigrants who had also been their neighbors in the ancestral land, needed to clean their name, and a wrong word would incite the kinspeople even here. But there is more to this silence: they want me to participate in her punishment. And I have.

In the twenty years since I heard this story I have not asked for details nor said my aunt's name; I do not know it. People who can comfort the dead can also chase after them to hurt them further—a reverse ancestor worship. The real punishment was not the raid swiftly inflicted by the villagers, but the family's deliberately forgetting her. Her betrayal so maddened them, they saw to it that she would suffer forever, even after death. Always hungry, always needing, she would have to beg food from other ghosts, snatch and steal it from those whose living descendants give them gifts. She would have to fight the ghosts massed at crossroads for the buns a few thoughtful citizens leave to decoy her away from village and home so that the ancestral spirits could feast unharassed. At peace, they could act like gods, not ghosts, their descent lines providing them with paper suits and dresses, spirit money, paper houses, paper automobiles, chicken, meat, and rice into eternity—essences delivered up in smoke and flames, steam and incense rising from each rice bowl. In an attempt to make the Chinese care for people outside the family, Chairman Mao encourages us now to give our paper replicas to the spirits of outstanding soldiers and workers, no matter whose ancestors they may be. My aunt remains forever hungry. Goods are not distributed evenly among the dead.

My aunt haunts me—her ghost drawn to me because now, after fifty years of neglect, I alone devote pages of paper to her, though not origamied into houses and clothes. I do not think she always means me well. I am telling on her, and she was a spite suicide, drowning herself in the drinking water. The Chinese are always very frightened of the drowned one, whose weeping ghost, wet hair hanging and skin bloated, waits silently by the water to pull down a substitute.

Study and Discussion Questions

1. What is the occasion on which the narrator's mother tells her the story? What is her reason for doing so?
2. What does the title of this piece signify?
3. Why do the villagers raid the house? What were they trying to accomplish at the time? What were they afraid of? What does the narrator say was the "real punishment" they inflicted on her aunt?
4. What are the different stories the narrator makes up to account for her aunt's pregnancy?
5. How does Kingston characterize Chinese immigrants to America?
6. How does the narrator say she has contributed to her aunt's punishment?
7. What does Kingston say about ghosts? What function do they play in the lives of the Chinese villagers?
8. What are the ghosts in the narrator's own life?

Writing Exercises

1. What stories were you told, what warnings were you given, at the beginning of puberty?

2. Why does the narrator refuse any longer to participate in her aunt's punishment? How does she act out this refusal?

3. What do we learn from "No Name Woman" about the position of women in prerevolutionary Chinese village society? What do we learn about the position of women today?

AUDRE LORDE (b. 1934)*

FROM Zami: A New Spelling of My Name (1982)

When I was growing up in my mother's house, there were spices you grated and spices you pounded, and whenever you pounded spice and garlic or other herbs, you used a mortar. Every West Indian woman worth her salt had her own mortar. Now if you lost or broke your mortar, you could, of course, buy another one in the market over on Park Avenue, under the bridge, but those were usually Puerto Rican mortars, and even though they were made out of wood and worked exactly the same way, somehow they were never really as good as West Indian mortars. Now where the best mortars came from I was never really sure, but I knew it must be in the vicinity of that amorphous and mystically perfect place called "home." And whatever came from "home" was bound to be special.

My mother's mortar was an elaborate affair, quite at variance with most of her other possessions, and certainly with her projected public view of herself. It stood, solid and elegant, on a shelf in the kitchen cabinet for as long as I can remember, and I loved it dearly.

The mortar was of a foreign fragrant wood, too dark for cherry and too red for walnut. To my child eyes, the outside was carved in an intricate and most enticing manner. There were rounded plums and oval indeterminate fruit, some long and fluted like a banana, others ovular and end-swollen like a ripe alligator pear. In between these were smaller rounded shapes like cherries, lying in batches against and around each other.

I loved to finger the hard roundness of the carved fruit, and the always surprising termination of the shapes as the carvings stopped at the rim and the bowl sloped abruptly downward, smoothly oval but suddenly businesslike. The heavy sturdiness of this useful wooden object always made me feel secure and somehow full; as if it conjured up from all the many different flavors pounded into the inside wall, visions of delicious feasts both once enjoyed and still to come.

---

* A brief biography of Audre Lorde appears on page 160.

The pestle was long and tapering, fashioned from the same mysterious rose-deep wood, and fitted into the hand almost casually, familiarly. The actual shape reminded me of a summer crook-necked squash uncurled and slightly twisted. It could also have been an avocado, with the neck of the alligator pear elongated and the whole made efficient for pounding, without ever losing the apparent soft firmness and the character of the fruit which the wood suggested. It was slightly bigger at the grinding end than most pestles, and the widened curved end fitted into the bowl of the mortar easily. Long use and years of impact and grinding within the bowl's worn hollow had softened the very surface of the wooden pestle, until a thin layer of split fibers coated the rounded end like a layer of velvet. A layer of the same velvety mashed wood lined the bottom inside the sloping bowl.

My mother did not particularly like to pound spice, and she looked upon the advent of powdered everything as a cook's boon. But there were some certain dishes that called for a particular savory blending of garlic, raw onion, and pepper, and souse was one of them.

For our mother's souse, it didn't matter what kind of meat was used. You could have hearts, or beefends, or even chicken backs and gizzards when we were really poor. It was the pounded-up saucy blend of herb and spice rubbed into the meat before it was left to stand so for a few hours before cooking that made that dish so special and unforgettable. But my mother had some very firm ideas about what she liked best to cook and about which were her favorite dishes, and souse was definitely not one of either.

On the very infrequent occasions that my mother would allow one of us three girls to choose a meal—as opposed to helping to prepare it, which was a daily routine—on those occasions my sisters would usually choose one of those proscribed dishes so dear to our hearts remembered from our relatives' tables, contraband, and so very rare in our house. They might ask for hot dogs, perhaps, smothered in ketchup sauce, or with crusty Boston-baked beans; or american chicken, breaded first and fried crispy the way the southern people did it; or creamed something-or-other that one of my sisters had tasted at school; what-have-you croquettes or anything fritters; or once even a daring outrageous request for slices of fresh watermelon, hawked from the back of a rickety wooden pickup truck with the southern road-dust still on her slatted sides, from which a young bony Black man with a turned-around baseball cap on his head would hang and half-yell, half-yodel—"Wahr—deeeeeee-mayyyyyyy-lawnnnnnnnn."

There were many american dishes I longed for too, but on the one or two occasions a year that I got to choose a meal, I would always ask for souse. That way, I knew that I would get to use my mother's mortar, and this in itself was more treat for me than any of the forbidden foods. Besides, if I really wanted hot dogs or anything croquettes badly enough,

I could steal some money from my father's pocket and buy them in the school lunch.

"Mother, let's have souse," I'd say, and never even stop to think about it. The anticipated taste of the soft spicy meat had become inseparable in my mind from the tactile pleasures of using my mother's mortar.

"But what makes you think anybody can find time to mash up all that stuff?" My mother would cut her hawk-grey eyes at me from beneath their heavy black brows. "Among-you children never stop to think," and she'd turn back to whatever it was she had been doing. If she had just come from the office with my father, she might be checking the day's receipts, or she might be washing the endless piles of dirty linen that always seemed to issue from rooming-houses.

"Oh, I'll pound the garlic, Mommy!" would be my next line in the script written by some ancient and secret hand, and off I'd go to the cabinet to get down the heavy wooden mortar and pestle.

I took a head of garlic out from the garlic bottle in the icebox, and breaking off ten or twelve cloves from the head, I carefully peeled away the tissue lavender skin, slicing each stripped peg in half lengthwise. I dropped them piece by piece into the capacious waiting bowl of the mortar. Taking a slice from a small onion, I put the rest aside to be used later over the meat, and cutting the slice into quarters, I tossed it into the mortar also. Next came the coarsely ground fresh black pepper, and then a lavish blanketing cover of salt over the whole. Last, if we had any, a few leaves from the top of a head of celery. My mother sometimes added a slice of green pepper, but I did not like the texture of the pepper-skin under the pestle, and preferred to add it along with the sliced onion later on, leaving it all to sit over the seasoned and resting meat.

After all the ingredients were in the bowl of the mortar, I fetched the pestle and placing it into the bowl, slowly rotated the shaft a few times, working it gently down through all the ingredients to mix them. Only then would I lift the pestle, and with one hand firmly pressed around the carved side of the mortar caressing the wooden fruit with my aromatic fingers, I thrust sharply downward, feeling the shifting salt and the hard little pellets of garlic right up through the shaft of the wooden pestle. Up again, down, around, and up—so the rhythm began.

The *thud push rub rotate up* repeated over and over. The muted thump of the pestle on the bed of grinding spice as the salt and pepper absorbed the slowly yielding juices of the garlic and celery leaves.

Thud push rub rotate up. The mingling fragrances rising from the bowl of the mortar.

Thud push rub rotate up. The feeling of the pestle held between my curving fingers, and the mortar's outside rounding like fruit into my palm as I steadied it against my body.

All these transported me into a world of scent and rhythm and movement and sound that grew more and more exciting as the ingredients liquefied.

Sometimes my mother would look over at me with that amused annoyance which passed for tenderness.

"What you think you making there, garlic soup? Enough, go get the meat now." And I would fetch the lamb hearts, for instance, from the icebox and begin to prepare them. Cutting away the hardened veins at the top of the smooth firm muscles, I divided each oval heart into four wedge-shaped pieces, and taking a bit of the spicy mash from the mortar with my fingertips, I rubbed each piece with the savory mix, the pungent smell of garlic and onion and celery enveloping the kitchen.

The last day I ever pounded seasoning for souse was in the summer of my fifteenth year. It had been a fairly unpleasant summer for me. I had just finished my first year in high school. Instead of being able to visit my newly found friends, all of whom lived in other parts of the city, I had had to accompany my mother on a round of doctors with whom she would have long whispered conversations. Only a matter of utmost importance could have kept her away from the office for so many mornings in a row. But my mother was concerned because I was fourteen and a half years old and had not yet menstruated. I had breasts but no period, and she was afraid there was something "wrong" with me. Yet, since she had never discussed this mysterious business of menstruation with me, I was certainly not supposed to know what all this whispering was about, even though it concerned my own body.

Of course, I knew as much as I could have possibly found out in those days from the hard-to-get books on the "closed shelf" behind the librarian's desk at the public library, where I had brought a forged note from home in order to be allowed to read them, sitting under the watchful eye of the librarian at a special desk reserved for that purpose.

Although not terribly informative, they were fascinating books, and used words like *menses* and *ovulation* and *vagina*.

But four years before, I had had to find out if I was going to become pregnant, because a boy from school much bigger than me had invited me up to the roof on my way home from the library and then threatened to break my glasses if I didn't let him stick his "thing" between my legs. And at that time I knew only that being pregnant had something to do with sex, and sex had something to do with that thin pencil-like "thing" and was in general nasty and not to be talked about by nice people, and I was afraid my mother might find out and what would she do to me then? I was not supposed to be looking at the mailboxes in the hallway of that house anyway, even though Doris was a girl in my class at St. Mark's who lived in that house and I was always so lonely in the summer, particularly that summer when I was ten.

So after I got home I washed myself up and lied about why I was late getting home from the library and got a whipping for being late. That must have been a hard summer for my parents at the office too, because that was the summer that I got a whipping for something or other almost every day between the Fourth of July and Labor Day.

When I wasn't getting whippings, I hid out at the library on 135th Street, and forged notes from my mother to get books from the "closed shelf," and read about sex and having babies, and waited to become pregnant. None of the books were very clear to me about the relationship between having your period and having a baby, but they were all very clear about the relationship between penises and getting pregnant. Or maybe the confusion was all in my own mind, because I had always been a very fast but not a very careful reader.

So four years later, in my fifteenth year, I was a very scared little girl, still half-afraid that one of that endless stream of doctors would look up into my body and discover my four-year-old shame and say to my mother, "Aha! So that's what's wrong! Your daughter is about to become pregnant!"

On the other hand, if I let Mother know that I knew what was happening and what these medical safaris were all about, I would have to answer her questions about how and wherefore I knew, since she hadn't told me, divulging in the process the whole horrible and self-incriminating story of forbidden books and forged library notes and rooftops and stairwell conversations.

It was a year after the rooftop incident, when we had moved farther uptown. The kids at St. Catherine's seemed to know a lot more about sex than at St. Mark's. In the eighth grade, I had stolen money and bought my classmate Adeline a pack of cigarettes and she had confirmed my bookish suspicions about how babies were made. My response to her graphic descriptions had been to think to myself, *there obviously must be another way that Adeline doesn't know about, because my parents have children and I know they never did anything like that!* But the basic principles were all there, and sure enough they were the same as I had gathered from *The Young People's Family Book.*

So in my fifteenth summer, on examining table after examining table, I kept my legs open and my mouth shut, and when I saw blood on my pants one hot July afternoon, I rinsed them out secretly in the bathroom and put them back on wet because I didn't know how to break the news to my mother that both her worries and mine were finally over. (All this time I had at least understood that having your period was a sign you were not pregnant.)

What then happened felt like a piece of an old and elaborate dance between my mother and me. She discovers finally, through a stain on the toilet seat left there on purpose by me as a mute announcement, what has taken place; she scolds, "Why didn't you tell me about all of this, now? It's nothing to get upset over, you are a woman, not a child anymore. Now you go over to the drugstore and ask the man for . . ."

I was just relieved the whole damn thing was over with. It's difficult to talk about double messages without having a twin tongue. Nightmarish evocations and restrictions were being verbalized by my mother:

"This means from now on you better watch your step and not be so friendly with every Tom, Dick, and Harry . . ." (which must have meant my staying late after school to talk with my girlfriends, because I did not even know any boys); and, "Now remember, too, after you wrap up your soiled napkins in newspaper, don't leave them hanging around on the bathroom floor where your father has to see them, not that it's anything shameful but all the same, remember . . ."

Along with all of these admonitions, there was something else coming from my mother that I could not define. It was the lurking of that amused/annoyed brow-furrowed half-smile of hers that made me feel—all her nagging words to the contrary—that something very good and satisfactory and pleasing to her had just happened, and that we were both pretending otherwise for some very wise and secret reasons. I would come to understand these reasons later, as a reward, if I handled myself properly. Then, at the end of it all, my mother thrust the box of Kotex at me (I had fetched it in its plain wrapper back from the drugstore, along with a sanitary belt), saying to me,

"But look now what time it is already, I wonder what we're going to eat for supper tonight?" She waited. At first I didn't understand, but I quickly picked up the cue. I had seen the beefends in the icebox that morning.

"Mommy, please let's have some souse—I'll pound the garlic." I dropped the box onto a kitchen chair and started to wash my hands in anticipation.

"Well, go put your business away first. What did I tell you about leaving that lying around?" She wiped her hands from the washtub where she had been working and handed the plain wrapped box of Kotex back to me.

"I have to go out, I forgot to pick up tea at the store. Now make sure you rub the meat good."

When I came back into the kitchen, my mother had left. I moved toward the kitchen cabinet to fetch down the mortar and pestle. My body felt new and special and unfamiliar and suspect all at the same time.

I could feel bands of tension sweeping across my body back and forth, like lunar winds across the moon's face. I felt the slight rubbing bulge of the cotton pad between my legs, and I smelled the delicate breadfruit smell rising up from the front of my print blouse that was my own womansmell, warm, shameful, but secretly utterly delicious.

Years afterward when I was grown, whenever I thought about the way I smelled that day, I would have a fantasy of my mother, her hands wiped dry from the washing, and her apron untied and laid neatly away, looking down upon me lying on the couch, and then slowly, thoroughly, our touching and caressing each other's most secret places.

I took the mortar down, and smashed the cloves of garlic with the edge of its underside, to loosen the thin papery skins in a hurry. I sliced them and flung them into the mortar's bowl along with some black pepper and celery leaves. The white salt poured in, covering the garlic and black pepper and pale chartreuse celery fronds like a snowfall. I tossed in the onion and some bits of green pepper and reached for the pestle.

It slipped through my fingers and clattered to the floor, rolling around in a semicircle back and forth, until I bent to retrieve it. I grabbed the head of the wooden stick and straightened up, my ears ringing faintly. Without even wiping it, I plunged the pestle into the bowl, feeling the blanket of salt give way, and the broken cloves of garlic just beneath. The downward thrust of the wooden pestle slowed upon contact, rotated back and forth slowly, and then gently altered its rhythm to include an up and down beat. Back and forth, round, up and down, back, forth, round, round, up and down. . . . There was a heavy fullness at the root of me that was exciting and dangerous.

As I continued to pound the spice, a vital connection seemed to establish itself between the muscles of my fingers curved tightly around the smooth pestle in its insistent downward motion, and the molten core of my body whose source emanated from a new ripe fullness just beneath the pit of my stomach. That invisible thread, taut and sensitive as a clitoris exposed, stretched through my curled fingers up my round brown arm into the moist reality of my armpits, whose warm sharp odor with a strange new overlay mixed with the ripe garlic smells from the mortar and the general sweat-heavy aromas of high summer.

The thread ran over my ribs and along my spine, tingling and singing, into a basin that was poised between my hips, now pressed against the low kitchen counter before which I stood, pounding spice. And within that basin was a tiding ocean of blood beginning to be made real and available to me for strength and information.

The jarring shocks of the velvet-lined pestle, striking the bed of spice, traveled up an invisible pathway along the thread into the center of me, and the harshness of the repeated impacts became increasingly more unbearable. The tidal basin suspended between my hips shuddered at each repetition of the strokes which now felt like assaults. Without my volition my downward thrusts of the pestle grew gentler and gentler, until its velvety surface seemed almost to caress the liquefying mash at the bottom of the mortar.

The whole rhythm of my movements softened and elongated, until, dreamlike, I stood, one hand tightly curved around the carved mortar, steadying it against the middle of my body; while my other hand, around the pestle, rubbed and pressed the moistening spice into readiness with a sweeping circular movement.

I hummed tunelessly to myself as I worked in the warm kitchen, thinking with relief about how simple my life would be now that I had become a woman. The catalogue of dire menstruation-warnings from my mother passed out of my head. My body felt strong and full and open, yet captivated by the gentle motions of the pestle, and the rich smells filling the kitchen, and the fullness of the young summer heat.

I heard my mother's key in the lock.

She swept into the kitchen briskly, like a ship under full sail. There were tiny beads of sweat over her upper lip, and vertical creases between her brows.

"You mean to tell me no meat is ready?" My mother dropped her parcel of tea onto the table, and looking over my shoulder, sucked her teeth loudly in weary disgust. "What do you call yourself doing, now? You have all night to stand up there playing with the food? I go all the way to the store and back already and still you can't mash up a few pieces of garlic to season some meat? But you know how to do the thing better than this! Why you vex me so?"

She took the mortar and pestle out of my hands and started to grind vigorously. And there were still bits of garlic left at the bottom of the bowl.

"Now you do, so!" She brought the pestle down inside the bowl of the mortar with dispatch, crushing the last of the garlic. I heard the thump of wood brought down heavily upon wood, and I felt the harsh impact throughout my body, as if something had broken inside of me. Thump, thump, went the pestle, purposefully, up and down in the old familiar way.

"It was getting mashed, Mother," I dared to protest, turning away to the icebox. "I'll fetch the meat." I was surprised at my own brazenness in answering back.

But something in my voice interrupted my mother's efficient motions. She ignored my implied contradiction, itself an act of rebellion strictly forbidden in our house. The thumping stopped.

"What's wrong with you, now? Are you sick? You want to go to your bed?"

"No, I'm all right, Mother."

But I felt her strong fingers on my upper arm, turning me around, her other hand under my chin as she peered into my face. Her voice softened.

"Is it your period making you so slow-down today?" She gave my chin a little shake, as I looked up into her hooded grey eyes, now becoming almost gentle. The kitchen felt suddenly oppressively hot and still, and I felt myself beginning to shake all over.

Tears I did not understand started from my eyes, as I realized that my old enjoyment of the bone-jarring way I had been taught to pound spice would feel different to me from now on, and also that in my mother's kitchen there was only one right way to do anything. Perhaps my life had not become so simple, after all.

My mother stepped away from the counter and put her heavy arm around my shoulders. I could smell the warm herness rising from between her arm and her body, mixed with the smell of glycerine and rosewater, and the scent of her thick bun of hair.

"I'll finish up the food for supper." She smiled at me, and there was a tenderness in her voice and an absence of annoyance that was welcome, although unfamiliar.

"You come inside now and lie down on the couch and I'll make you a hot cup of tea."

Her arm across my shoulders was warm and slightly damp. I rested my head upon her shoulder, and realized with a shock of pleasure and surprise that I was almost as tall as my mother, as she led me into the cool darkened parlor.

Study and Discussion Questions

1. What words in Lorde's description of the mortar evoke a sensual response? Group the words under the various senses: taste, touch, smell, sight, sound.
2. Do the same with the first description of pounding the spice.
3. Make a list of words to characterize the narrator's mother.
4. Why are both the narrator and her mother silent with each other on the subject of menstruation?
5. How and to what extent does her mother's behavior toward the narrator change when she begins menstruating?
6. How does the narrator feel when her mother takes over the mortar and pestle?
7. What does the narrator say she has learned about herself?

Writing Exercises

1. Describe an object or an activity important to you, using sensual detail as Lorde does in her description of the mortar or in her description of pounding the spice.
2. Describe the process of making a favorite meal in that same kind of vivid detail.
3. Compare/contrast the two scenes Lorde gives us of using the mortar. How do they differ? What is the tone of each one? What do you think the writer's purpose was in including two such scenes? What is the effect on you of the repetition?

GROWING UP AND GROWING OLDER: PAPER TOPICS

1. Contrast a narrator you consider trustworthy with one you do not. (Suggestions: Lessing, "Our Friend Judith"; Ellison, "Battle Royal")
2. Compare two works that deal with birth and its social context. (Suggestions: Huxley, *Brave New World*; Plath, *Three Women*)
3. Discuss the socialization of young people into gender roles in one or more works. (Suggestions: Kingston, "No Name Woman"; Kincaid, "Girl")

4. Discuss the portrayal of growing up in terms of the closing off of possibilities in one or more works. (Suggestions: Huxley, *Brave New World*; C. D. Wright, "Falling Beasts"; Baldwin, "Sonny's Blues")

5. Discuss the portrayal of growing *older* in terms of the closing off of possibilities in one or more works. (Suggestions: Updike, "Ex-Basketball Player"; Beckett, *Krapp's Last Tape*)

6. Discuss the difficult nature of the relationship between children and parents in one or more works. (Suggestions: Shakespeare, *King Lear*; Sexton, "Briar Rose")

7. Discuss one or more works as explorations of what it means to be an adult. (Suggestions: Hawthorne, "Young Goodman Brown"; Lorde, "From the House of Yemanjá")

8. Compare the treatment of their subject in two works by the same author. (Suggestions: Yeats, Lorde, Hayden)

9. Discuss one or more works that explore the experience of middle age. (Suggestions: Eliot, "The Love Song of J. Alfred Prufrock"; Lessing, "Our Friend Judith"; Carpenter, "Rain")

10. Discuss how social factors such as gender and class affect the way one experiences aging. (Suggestions: Freeman, "A Mistaken Charity"; Shakespeare, *King Lear*)

11. Discuss the poet's use of sound and imagery to express his or her feelings about death in one or more works. (Suggestions: Thomas, "Do Not Go Gentle Into That Good Night"; Plath, "Edge")

12. Discuss growing up as a search for identity in one or more works. (Suggestions: White, *A Boy's Own Story*; Kingston, "No Name Woman"; Brooks, "We Real Cool")

WOMEN AND MEN

From the anonymous author of "The Song of Solomon" to ntozake shange and Adrienne Rich, the politics of sexuality has been a major subject of literature. Different cultures and historical eras have written into their drama, fiction, poetry, and nonfictional prose their sexual/social codes: what it means to be a woman, what it means to be a man, what behavior is appropriate and permissible for each gender, how men and women are expected to meet and marry or not, and how women and men form bonds with members of their own sex. Gender and sexuality are political, in the larger sense of that term, since they justify and exemplify the distribution and management of power.

Karl Shapiro's "Buick," a love poem to a car, makes us think of other instances in which men have assigned female gender to objects they control and direct. In the short story "The White Stocking," D. H. Lawrence explores the power relations of marriage. Looking at her husband, the young wife thinks:

> It was as if his fine, clear-cut temples and steady eyes were degraded by the lower, rather brutal part of his face. But she loved it. . . . He was such a man. . . . He was so sure, so permanent, he had her so utterly in his power. It gave her a delightful, mischievous sense of liberty. Within his grasp, she could dart about excitingly.

We see a further example of sexual politics as power relations in Adrienne Rich's poem "Trying to Talk with a Man," which shows the connections between male/female relations and national politics. The man and woman in the poem have gone into the desert to protest the testing of atomic bombs but, once there, the female speaker of the poem realizes that they are testing themselves as well. "Out here," she says, "I feel more helpless / with you than without you."

The different ways women and men perceive the world and the conflict, trouble, tragedy, and sometimes comedy that result have been the subject of much literature. From Shakespearian drama to television sitcoms, misunderstandings that arise when women and men look at the same event and interpret it in widely divergent ways have been a source of laughter and of anger, of tragedy and of comedy. The way men and women see and judge each other's behavior is central to many of the works included in this section. Muriel Rukeyser's poem "Waiting for Icarus" retells with sardonic humor the Greek myth of the man who stole his father's wings and flew too high. Rukeyser provides us the perspective of the woman who waits for Icarus, increasingly annoyed as the day wears on. Ntozake shange's *for colored girls who have considered suicide when the rainbow is enuf* presents an array of female perspectives on such subjects as love, infidelity, abortion, self-love, spirituality, and men. The play holds a mirror up to the way men behave around women, providing comic and often uncomfortable reflections. Woman as the embodiment of mysterious and inexplicable yearnings of the puzzled male consciousness is central to Jean Toomer's "Fern," an attempt by the northern black male narrator to come to terms with the pain and beauty of the South. Gloria Naylor's portrait of "Etta Mae Johnson" weighs the ephemeral romance and the blues of male/female relationships against the solid comfort of a long-term friendship with another woman.

The roles women and men are trained to assume can be comfortable or entrapping. A number of the selections included in this section explore the meaning of gender identity. Ernest Hemingway's story, "The Short Happy Life of Francis Macomber" and John Updike's "A & P" deal with what it means "to be a man" and with the associated social concepts of "honor" and "bravery." Though one of the stories is set in Africa and the other takes place in an American supermarket, the authors' twentieth-century American notions about "right action" and "grace under pressure" are quite similar. But given such a schema, what is woman's place? How are women defined? Judy Grahn's story "Boys at the Rodeo" looks at one example of twentieth-century ritualized machismo, an afternoon at the rodeo, from a radical feminist perspective. The narrator's point of view, both inside and outside the system she observes, is crucial to the story's meaning and power. Judy Syfers's satiric essay, "Why I Want a Wife," defines the nurturing, support, and mirroring functions of the role of wife in terms which are simultaneously comic and infuriating. Escaped slave Sojourner Truth's speech, "Ain't I a Woman," reminds readers that gender roles have a racial (and by implication, class and ethnic) component. Her speech challenges the definition of "woman" as white and middle class. "I could work as much and eat as much as a man—when I could get it—and bear the lash as well! And ain't I a woman?" Wakako Yamauchi's story, "And the Soul Shall Dance," written from a Japanese-American perspective, explores the "strangeness" of a female character who doesn't act like a Japanese woman is supposed to act.

Some of the selections included focus on women characters testing the limits of their socially defined roles. Virginia Woolf's sketch of Shakespeare's hypothetical sister, Judith, shows what might have happened in the Elizabethan Age to a young woman rebelling against social convention. Marge Piercy's "The woman in the ordinary" describes a woman on the verge of breaking out of her socially defined limitations: "in you bottled up is a woman peppery as curry." Kate Rushin's "The Tired Poem: Last Letter from a Typical Unemployed Black Professional Woman" deals with the double trouble of being black and female. It is useful to compare these two poems from the second wave of feminism (roughly 1967 to the present) with an example from an earlier era of feminist writing (roughly 1875 to 1919), Charlotte Perkins Gilman's 1892 short story, "The Yellow Wallpaper," which chronicles an ambiguous breakthrough which is also a breakdown, and which raises important questions about social conventions and the social definition of madness.

Beyond the sexual politics of gender (which we consider from other perspectives in "Growing Up and Growing Older," "Varieties of Protest," and other thematic sections), the most common crisis we encounter in the realm of sexual politics begins when we fall in love. The meaning and the experience of love have traditionally been subjects of lyric poetry: from Shakespeare's sonnets to Adrienne Rich's *Twenty-One Love Poems*, from Robert Frost's view of a disrupted encounter in "The Subverted Flower" to Jack Gilbert's sad and funny "Love Poem" about an aging immigrant couple on a bus, from Edna St. Vincent Millay's "Love is not all: it is not meat nor drink" to Elizabeth Barrett Browning's "How Do I Love Thee," from John Donne's comic "The Flea" to Langston Hughes's brief and chilling "Mellow," from Amy Lowell's satisfied "A Decade" to Olga Broumas's poem about a missed opportunity, "Song for Sanna." These poems present a variety of relations between lovers—ritualized equality or inequality, conflict and hostility, romance and reverence—and they include realistic as well as idealistic explorations of human relations in the realm of love. In each case, the images which the poet uses to express or describe love are a clue to the sexual politics of the poem. Not all writing about love, of course, is in the form of poetry. Aristophanes' speech from Plato's *Symposium* is both an origin myth and a parable about the nature of love. Henrik Ibsen's 1879 play, *A Doll's House*, dramatizes one woman's experience of falling out of the doll house of love and marriage and into the possibility of discovering herself.

The poems, plays, short stories, and essays included in this section offer a wide range of attitudes, expressed both in content and through form, about gender, sexuality, friendship, and love, about the limitations and the possibilities for human growth. In a successful literary work, what we think of as form is not separable from meaning. Formal elements—including character, image, setting, plot structure, and point of view—are where the assumptions, "meaning," and resonance of a work reside. That Hemingway's omniscient narrator in "The Short Happy Life of Francis Macomber" virtually avoids the point of view of the major female character is not peripheral but central to the story's meaning. In Tess Slesinger's story, "Mother to Dinner," the thunderstorm in the background reflects and charts the progress of the narrator's conflicting loyalties to her mother and to her new husband. The title image of Diane Wakoski's poem "Slicing Oranges for Jeremiah" comes to stand for all the ways in which women's nurturing keeps men alive. The female speaker of that poem wishes that there were someone to give her that kind of nurturing. The "colored girls" of shange's choreopoem move, through an exploration of their difficult and vibrant lives, from a despairing definition of themselves primarily in relation to men to a discovery of their own strength and potential. Collectively they conclude: "I found God in myself / & i loved her / i loved her fiercely." Sexual politics is an arena where women and men struggle with other issues of identity, spirituality, power, autonomy, need, and the limiting or the realization of our freedom and potential.

FICTION

CHARLOTTE PERKINS GILMAN   (1860–1935)

Soon after Charlotte Perkins Gilman's birth in Hartford, Connecticut, her father abandoned his wife and two children to sudden poverty. Charlotte worked as a teacher and commercial artist, married at twenty-four, and became deeply depressed after the birth of her first child. A famous neurologist ordered complete bed rest, which made matters worse. Eventually, Gilman left her husband, moved to California, and began writing and speaking on economics and feminism. She edited a monthly journal, The Forerunner, *from 1909 until 1916. Among Gilman's writings are* Women and Economics *(1898);* Herland *(1915), a satirical utopian novel; and* The Living of Charlotte Perkins Gilman *(1935), her autobiography.*

The Yellow Wallpaper   (1892)

It is very seldom that mere ordinary people like John and myself secure ancestral halls for the summer.

A colonial mansion, a hereditary estate, I would say a haunted house and reach the height of romantic felicity—but that would be asking too much of fate!

Still I will proudly declare that there is something queer about it.

Else, why should it be let so cheaply? And why have stood so long untenanted?

John laughs at me, of course, but one expects that.

John is practical in the extreme. He has no patience with faith, an intense horror of superstition, and he scoffs openly at any talk of things not to be felt and seen and put down in figures.

John is a physician, and *perhaps*—(I would not say it to a living soul, of course, but this is dead paper and a great relief to my mind)—*perhaps* that is one reason I do not get well faster.

You see, he does not believe I am sick! And what can one do?

If a physician of high standing, and one's own husband, assures friends and relatives that there is really nothing the matter with one but temporary nervous depression—a slight hysterical tendency—what is one to do?

My brother is also a physician, and also of high standing, and he says the same thing.

So I take phosphates or phosphites—whichever it is—and tonics, and air and exercise, and journeys, and am absolutely forbidden to "work" until I am well again.

Personally, I disagree with their ideas.

Personally, I believe that congenial work, with excitement and change, would do me good.

But what is one to do?

I did write for a while in spite of them; but it *does* exhaust me a good deal—having to be so sly about it, or else meet with heavy opposition.

I sometimes fancy that in my condition, if I had less opposition and more society and stimulus—but John says the very worst thing I can do is to think about my condition, and I confess it always makes me feel bad.

So I will let it alone and talk about the house.

The most beautiful place! It is quite alone, standing well back from the road, quite three miles from the village. It makes me think of English places that you read about, for there are hedges and walls and gates that lock, and lots of separate little houses for the gardeners and people.

There is a *delicious* garden! I never saw such a garden—large and shady, full of box-bordered paths, and lined with long grape-covered arbors with seats under them.

There were greenhouses, but they are all broken now.

There was some legal trouble, I believe, something about the heirs and co-heirs; anyhow, the place has been empty for years.

That spoils my ghostliness, I am afraid, but I don't care—there is something strange about the house—I can feel it.

I even said so to John one moonlight evening, but he said what I felt was a draught, and shut the window.

I get unreasonably angry with John sometimes. I'm sure I never used to be so sensitive. I think it is due to this nervous condition.

But John says if I feel so I shall neglect proper self-control; so I take pains to control myself—before him, at least, and that makes me very tired.

I don't like our room a bit. I wanted one downstairs that opened onto the piazza and had roses all over the window, and such pretty old-fashioned chintz hangings! But John would not hear of it.

He said there was only one window and not room for two beds, and no near room for him if he took another.

He is very careful and loving, and hardly lets me stir without special direction.

I have a schedule prescription for each hour in the day; he takes all care from me, and so I feel basely ungrateful not to value it more.

He said he came here solely on my account, that I was to have perfect rest and all the air I could get. "Your exercise depends on your strength, my dear," said he, "and your food somewhat on your appetite; but air you can absorb all the time." So we took the nursery at the top of the house.

It is a big, airy room, the whole floor nearly, with windows that look all ways, and air and sunshine galore. It was nursery first, and then playroom and gymnasium, I should judge, for the windows are barred for little children, and there are rings and things in the walls.

The paint and paper look as if a boys' school had used it. It is stripped off—the paper—in great patches all around the head of my bed, about as far as I can reach, and in a great place on the other side of the room low down. I never saw a worse paper in my life. One of those sprawling, flamboyant patterns committing every artistic sin.

It is dull enough to confuse the eye in following, pronounced enough constantly to irritate and provoke study, and when you follow the lame uncertain curves for a little distance they suddenly commit suicide—plunge off at outrageous angles, destroy themselves in unheard-of contradictions.

The color is repellent, almost revolting: a smouldering unclean yellow, strangely faded by the slow-turning sunlight. It is a dull yet lurid orange in some places, a sickly sulphur tint in others.

No wonder the children hated it! I should hate it myself if I had to live in this room long.

There comes John, and I must put this away—he hates to have me write a word.

We have been here two weeks, and I haven't felt like writing before, since that first day.

I am sitting by the window now, up in this atrocious nursery, and there is nothing to hinder my writing as much as I please, save lack of strength.

John is away all day, and even some nights when his cases are serious.

I am glad my case is not serious!

But these nervous troubles are dreadfully depressing.

John does not know how much I really suffer. He knows there is no reason to suffer, and that satisfies him.

Of course it is only nervousness. It does weigh on me so not to do my duty in any way!

I meant to be such a help to John, such a real rest and comfort, and here I am a comparative burden already!

Nobody would believe what an effort it is to do what little I am able— to dress and entertain, and order things.

It is fortunate Mary is so good with the baby. Such a dear baby!

And yet I *cannot* be with him, it makes me so nervous.

I suppose John never was nervous in his life. He laughs at me so about this wallpaper!

At first he meant to repaper the room, but afterward he said that I was letting it get the better of me, and that nothing was worse for a nervous patient than to give way to such fancies.

He said that after the wallpaper was changed it would be the heavy bedstead, and then the barred windows, and then that gate at the head of the stairs, and so on.

"You know the place is doing you good," he said, "and really, dear, I don't care to renovate the house just for a three months' rental."

"Then do let us go downstairs," I said. "There are such pretty rooms there."

Then he took me in his arms and called me a blessed little goose, and said he would go down cellar, if I wished, and have it whitewashed into the bargain.

But he is right enough about the beds and windows and things.

It is as airy and comfortable a room as anyone need wish, and, of course, I would not be so silly as to make him uncomfortable just for a whim.

I'm really getting quite fond of the big room, all but that horrid paper.

Out of one window I can see the garden—those mysterious deep-shaded arbors, the riotous old-fashioned flowers, and bushes and gnarly trees.

Out of another I get a lovely view of the bay and a little private wharf belonging to the estate. There is a beautiful shaded lane that runs down there from the house. I always fancy I see people walking in these numerous paths and arbors, but John has cautioned me not to give way to fancy in the least. He says that with my imaginative power and habit of story-making, a nervous weakness like mine is sure to lead to all manner of excited fancies, and that I ought to use my will and good sense to check the tendency. So I try.

I think sometimes that if I were only well enough to write a little it would relieve the press of ideas and rest me.

But I find I get pretty tired when I try.

It is so discouraging not to have any advice and companionship about my work. When I get really well, John says we will ask Cousin Henry and Julia down for a long visit; but he says he would as soon put fireworks in my pillow-case as to let me have those stimulating people about now.

I wish I could get well faster.

But I must not think about that. This paper looks to me as if it *knew* what a vicious influence it had!

There is a recurrent spot where the pattern lolls like a broken neck and two bulbous eyes stare at you upside down.

I get positively angry with the impertinence of it and the everlastingness. Up and down and sideways they crawl, and those absurd unblinking eyes are everywhere. There is one place where two breadths didn't match, and the eyes go all up and down the line, one a little higher than the other.

I never saw so much expression in an inanimate thing before, and we all know how much expression they have! I used to lie awake as a child and get more entertainment and terror out of blank walls and plain furniture than most children could find in a toy-store.

I remember what a kindly wink the knobs of our big old bureau used to have, and there was one chair that always seemed like a strong friend.

I used to feel that if any of the other things looked too fierce I could always hop into that chair and be safe.

The furniture in this room is no worse than inharmonious, however, for we had to bring it all from downstairs. I suppose when this was used as a playroom they had to take the nursery things out, and no wonder! I never saw such ravages as the children have made here.

The wallpaper, as I said before, is torn off in spots, and it sticketh closer than a brother—they must have had perseverance as well as hatred.

Then the floor is scratched and gouged and splintered, the plaster itself is dug out here and there, and this great heavy bed, which is all we found in the room, looks as if it had been through the wars.

But I don't mind it a bit—only the paper.

There comes John's sister. Such a dear girl as she is, and so careful of me! I must not let her find me writing.

She is a perfect and enthusiastic housekeeper, and hopes for no better profession. I verily believe she thinks it is the writing which made me sick!

But I can write when she is out, and see her a long way off from these windows.

There is one that commands the road, a lovely shaded winding road, and one that just looks off over the country. A lovely country, too, full of great elms and velvet meadows.

This wallpaper has a kind of sub-pattern in a different shade, a particularly irritating one, for you can only see it in certain lights, and not clearly then.

But in the places where it isn't faded and where the sun is just so— I can see a strange, provoking, formless sort of figure that seems to skulk about behind that silly and conspicuous front design.

There's sister on the stairs!

Well, the Fourth of July is over! The people are all gone, and I am tired out. John thought it might do me good to see a little company, so we just had Mother and Nellie and the children down for a week.

Of course I didn't do a thing. Jennie sees to everything now.

But it tired me all the same.

John says if I don't pick up faster he shall send me to Weir Mitchell[1] in the fall.

But I don't want to go there at all. I had a friend who was in his hands once, and she says he is just like John and my brother, only more so!

Besides, it is such an undertaking to go so far.

I don't feel as if it was worthwhile to turn my hand over for anything, and I'm getting dreadfully fretful and querulous.

---

[1] American neurologist who treated Gilman.

I cry at nothing, and cry most of the time.

Of course I don't when John is here, or anybody else, but when I am alone.

And I am alone a good deal just now. John is kept in town very often by serious cases, and Jennie is good and lets me alone when I want her to.

So I walk a little in the garden or down that lovely lane, sit on the porch under the roses, and lie down up here a good deal.

I'm getting really fond of the room in spite of the wallpaper. Perhaps *because* of the wallpaper.

It dwells in my mind so!

I lie here on this great immovable bed—it is nailed down, I believe—and follow that pattern about by the hour. It is as good as gymnastics, I assure you. I start, we'll say, at the bottom, down in the corner over there where it has not been touched, and I determine for the thousandth time that I *will* follow that pointless pattern to some sort of a conclusion.

I know a little of the principle of design, and I know this thing was not arranged on any laws of radiation, or alternation, or repetition, or symmetry, or anything else that I ever heard of.

It is repeated, of course, by the breadths, but not otherwise.

Looked at in one way, each breadth stands alone; the bloated curves and flourishes—a kind of "debased Romanesque" with delirium tremens—go waddling up and down in isolated columns of fatuity.

But, on the other hand, they connect diagonally, and the sprawling outlines run off in great slanting waves of optic horror, like a lot of wallowing sea-weeds in full chase.

The whole thing goes horizontally, too, at least it seems so, and I exhaust myself trying to distinguish the order of its going in that direction.

They have used a horizontal breadth for a frieze, and that adds wonderfully to the confusion.

There is one end of the room where it is almost intact, and there, when the crosslights fade and the low sun shines directly upon it, I can almost fancy radiation after all—the interminable grotesque seems to form around a common center and rush off in headlong plunges of equal distraction.

It makes me tired to follow it. I will take a nap, I guess.

I don't know why I should write this.

I don't want to.

I don't feel able.

And I know John would think it absurd. But I *must* say what I feel and think in some way—it is such a relief!

But the effort is getting to be greater than the relief.

Half the time now I am awfully lazy, and lie down ever so much. John says I mustn't lose my strength, and has me take cod liver oil and lots of tonics and things, to say nothing of ale and wine and rare meat.

Dear John! He loves me very dearly, and hates to have me sick. I tried to have a real earnest reasonable talk with him the other day, and tell him how I wish he would let me go and make a visit to Cousin Henry and Julia.

But he said I wasn't able to go, nor able to stand it after I got there; and I did not make out a very good case for myself, for I was crying before I had finished.

It is getting to be a great effort for me to think straight. Just this nervous weakness, I suppose.

And dear John gathered me up in his arms, and just carried me upstairs and laid me on the bed, and sat by me and read to me till it tired my head.

He said I was his darling and his comfort and all he had, and that I must take care of myself for his sake, and keep well.

He says no one but myself can help me out of it, that I must use my will and self-control and not let any silly fancies run away with me.

There's one comfort—the baby is well and happy, and does not have to occupy this nursery with the horrid wallpaper.

If we had not used it, that blessed child would have! What a fortunate escape! Why, I wouldn't have a child of mine, an impressionable little thing, live in such a room for worlds.

I never thought of it before, but it is lucky that John kept me here after all; I can stand it so much easier than a baby, you see.

Of course I never mention it to them any more—I am too wise—but I keep watch for it all the same.

There are things in that wallpaper that nobody knows about but me, or ever will.

Behind that outside pattern the dim shapes get clearer every day.

It is always the same shape, only very numerous.

And it is like a woman stooping down and creeping about behind that pattern. I don't like it a bit. I wonder—I begin to think—I wish John would take me away from here!

It is so hard to talk with John about my case, because he is so wise, and because he loves me so.

But I tried it last night.

It was moonlight. The moon shines in all around just as the sun does.

I hate to see it sometimes, it creeps so slowly, and always comes in by one window or another.

John was asleep and I hated to waken him, so I kept still and watched the moonlight on that undulating wallpaper till I felt creepy.

The faint figure behind seemed to shake the pattern, just as if she wanted to get out.

I got up softly and went to feel and see if the paper *did* move, and when I came back John was awake.

"What is it, little girl?" he said. "Don't go walking about like that—you'll get cold."

I thought it was a good time to talk, so I told him that I really was not gaining here, and that I wished he would take me away.

"Why, darling!" said he. "Our lease will be up in three weeks, and I can't see how to leave before.

"The repairs are not done at home, and I cannot possibly leave town just now. Of course, if you were in any danger, I could and would, but you really are better, dear, whether you can see it or not. I am a doctor, dear, and I know. You are gaining flesh and color, your appetite is better, I feel really much easier about you."

"I don't weigh a bit more," said I, "nor as much; and my appetite may be better in the evening when you are here but it is worse in the morning when you are away!"

"Bless her little heart!" said he with a big hug. "She shall be as sick as she pleases! But now let's improve the shining hours by going to sleep, and talk about it in the morning!"

"And you won't go away?" I asked gloomily.

"Why, how can I, dear? It is only three weeks more and then we will take a nice little trip of a few days while Jennie is getting the house ready. Really, dear, you are better!"

"Better in body perhaps—" I began, and stopped short, for he sat up straight and looked at me with such a stern, reproachful look that I could not say another word.

"My darling," said he, "I beg of you, for my sake and for our child's sake, as well as for your own, that you will never for one instant let that idea enter your mind! There is nothing so dangerous, so fascinating, to a temperament like yours. It is a false and foolish fancy. Can you not trust me as a physician when I tell you so?"

So of course I said no more on that score, and we went to sleep before long. He thought I was asleep first, but I wasn't, and lay there for hours trying to decide whether that front pattern and the back pattern really did move together or separately.

On a pattern like this, by daylight, there is a lack of sequence, a defiance of law, that is a constant irritant to a normal mind.

The color is hideous enough, and unreliable enough, and infuriating enough, but the pattern is torturing.

You think you have mastered it, but just as you get well under way in following, it turns a back-somersault and there you are. It slaps you in the face, knocks you down, and tramples upon you. It is like a bad dream.

The outside pattern is a florid arabesque, reminding one of a fungus. If you can imagine a toadstool in joints, an interminable string of toadstools, budding and sprouting in endless convolutions—why, that is something like it.

That is, sometimes!

There is one marked peculiarity about this paper, a thing nobody seems to notice but myself, and that is that it changes as the light changes.

When the sun shoots in through the east window—I always watch for that first long, straight ray—it changes so quickly that I never can quite believe it.

That is why I watch it always.

By moonlight—the moon shines in all night when there is a moon— I wouldn't know it was the same paper.

At night in any kind of light, in twilight, candlelight, lamplight, and worst of all by moonlight, it becomes bars! The outside pattern, I mean, and the woman behind it is as plain as can be.

I didn't realize for a long time what the thing was that showed behind, that dim sub-pattern, but now I am quite sure it is a woman.

By daylight she is subdued, quiet. I fancy it is the pattern that keeps her so still. It is so puzzling. It keeps me quiet by the hour.

I lie down ever so much now. John says it is good for me, and to sleep all I can.

Indeed he started the habit by making me lie down for an hour after each meal.

It is a very bad habit, I am convinced, for you see, I don't sleep.

And that cultivates deceit, for I don't tell them I'm awake—oh, no!

The fact is I am getting a little afraid of John.

He seems very queer sometimes, and even Jennie has an inexplicable look.

It strikes me occasionally, just as a scientific hypothesis, that perhaps it is the paper!

I have watched John when he did not know I was looking, and come into the room suddenly on the most innocent excuses, and I've caught him several times *looking at the paper!* And Jennie too. I caught Jennie with her hand on it once.

She didn't know I was in the room, and when I asked her in a quiet, a very quiet voice, with the most restrained manner possible, what she was doing with the paper, she turned around as if she had been caught stealing, and looked quite angry—asked me why I should frighten her so!

Then she said that the paper stained everything it touched, that she had found yellow smooches on all my clothes and John's and she wished we would be more careful!

Did not that sound innocent? But I know she was studying that pattern, and I am determined that nobody shall find it out but myself!

Life is very much more exciting now than it used to be. You see, I have something more to expect, to look forward to, to watch. I really do eat better, and am more quiet than I was.

John is so pleased to see me improve! He laughed a little the other day, and said I seemed to be flourishing in spite of my wallpaper.

I turned it off with a laugh. I had no intention of telling him it was *because* of the wallpaper—he would make fun of me. He might even want to take me away.

I don't want to leave now until I have found it out. There is a week more, and I think that will be enough.

I'm feeling so much better!

I don't sleep much at night, for it is so interesting to watch developments; but I sleep a good deal during the daytime.

In the daytime it is tiresome and perplexing.

There are always new shoots on the fungus, and new shades of yellow all over it. I cannot keep count of them, though I have tried conscientiously.

It is the strangest yellow, that wallpaper! It makes me think of all the yellow things I ever saw—not beautiful ones like buttercups, but old, foul, bad yellow things.

But there is something else about that paper—the smell! I noticed it the moment we came into the room, but with so much air and sun it was not bad. Now we have had a week of fog and rain, and whether the windows are open or not, the smell is here.

It creeps all over the house.

I find it hovering in the dining-room, skulking in the parlor, hiding in the hall, lying in wait for me on the stairs.

It gets into my hair.

Even when I go to ride, if I turn my head suddenly and surprise it—there is that smell!

Such a peculiar odor, too! I have spent hours in trying to analyze it, to find what it smelled like.

It is not bad—at first—and very gentle, but quite the subtlest, most enduring odor I ever met.

In this damp weather it is awful. I wake up in the night and find it hanging over me.

It used to disturb me at first. I thought seriously of burning the house—to reach the smell.

But now I am used to it. The only thing I can think of that it is like is the *color* of the paper! A yellow smell.

There is a very funny mark on this wall, low down, near the mopboard. A streak that runs round the room. It goes behind every piece of furniture, except the bed, a long, straight, even *smooch*, as if it had been rubbed over and over.

I wonder how it was done and who did it, and what they did it for. Round and round and round—round and round and round—it makes me dizzy!

I really have discovered something at last.

Through watching so much at night, when it changes so, I have finally found out.

The front pattern *does* move—and no wonder! The woman behind shakes it!

Sometimes I think there are a great many women behind, and sometimes only one, and she crawls around fast, and her crawling shakes it all over.

Then in the very bright spots she keeps still, and in the very shady spots she just takes hold of the bars and shakes them hard.

And she is all the time trying to climb through. But nobody could climb through that pattern—it strangles so; I think that is why it has so many heads.

They get through, and then the pattern strangles them off and turns them upside down, and makes their eyes white!

If those heads were covered or taken off it would not be half so bad.

I think that woman gets out in the daytime!

And I'll tell you why—privately—I've seen her!

I can see her out of every one of my windows!

It is the same woman, I know, for she is always creeping, and most women do not creep by daylight.

I see her in that long shaded lane, creeping up and down. I see her in those dark grape arbors, creeping all around the garden.

I see her on that long road under the trees, creeping along, and when a carriage comes she hides under the blackberry vines.

I don't blame her a bit. It must be very humiliating to be caught creeping by daylight!

I always lock the door when I creep by daylight. I can't do it at night, for I know John would suspect something at once.

And John is so queer now that I don't want to irritate him. I wish he would take another room! Besides, I don't want anybody to get that woman out at night but myself.

I often wonder if I could see her out of all the windows at once.

But, turn as fast as I can, I can only see out of one at one time.

And though I always see her, she *may* be able to creep faster than I can turn! I have watched her sometimes away off in the open country, creeping as fast as a cloud shadow in a wind.

If only that top pattern could be gotten off from the under one! I mean to try it, little by little.

I have found out another funny thing, but I shan't tell it this time! It does not do to trust people too much.

There are only two more days to get this paper off, and I believe John is beginning to notice. I don't like the look in his eyes.

And I heard him ask Jennie a lot of professional questions about me. She had a very good report to give.

She said I slept a good deal in the daytime.

John knows I don't sleep very well at night, for all I'm so quiet!

He asked me all sorts of questions, too, and pretended to be very loving and kind.

As if I couldn't see through him!

Still, I don't wonder he acts so, sleeping under this paper for three months.

It only interests me, but I feel sure John and Jennie are affected by it.

Hurrah! This is the last day, but it is enough. John is to stay in town over night, and won't be out until this evening.

Jennie wanted to sleep with me—the sly thing; but I told her I should undoubtedly rest better for a night all alone.

That was clever, for really I wasn't alone a bit! As soon as it was moonlight and that poor thing began to crawl and shake the pattern, I got up and ran to help her.

I pulled and she shook. I shook and she pulled, and before morning we had peeled off yards of that paper.

A strip about as high as my head and half around the room.

And then when the sun came and that awful pattern began to laugh at me, I declared I would finish it today!

We go away tomorrow, and they are moving all my furniture down again to leave things as they were before.

Jennie looked at the wall in amazement, but I told her merrily that I did it out of pure spite at the vicious thing.

She laughed and said she wouldn't mind doing it herself, but I must not get tired.

How she betrayed herself that time!

But I am here, and no person touches this paper but Me—not *alive!*

She tried to get me out of the room—it was too patent! But I said it was so quiet and empty and clean now that I believed I would lie down again and sleep all I could, and not to wake me even for dinner—I would call when I woke.

So now she is gone, and the servants are gone, and the things are gone, and there is nothing left but that great bedstead nailed down, with the canvas mattress we found on it.

We shall sleep downstairs tonight, and take the boat home tomorrow.

I quite enjoy the room, now it is bare again.

How those children did tear about here!

This bedstead is fairly gnawed!

But I must get to work.

I have locked the door and thrown the key down into the front path.

I don't want to go out, and I don't want to have anybody come in, till John comes.

I want to astonish him.

I've got a rope up here that even Jennie did not find. If that woman does get out, and tries to get away, I can tie her!

But I forgot I could not reach far without anything to stand on!

This bed will *not* move!

I tried to lift and push it until I was lame, and then I got so angry I bit off a little piece at one corner—but it hurt my teeth.

Then I peeled off all the paper I could reach standing on the floor. It sticks horribly and the pattern just enjoys it! All those strangled heads and bulbous eyes and waddling fungus growths just shriek with derision!

I am getting angry enough to do something desperate. To jump out of the window would be admirable exercise, but the bars are too strong even to try.

Besides I wouldn't do it. Of course not. I know well enough that a step like that is improper and might be misconstrued.

I don't like to *look* out of the windows even—there are so many of those creeping women, and they creep so fast.

I wonder if they all come out of that wallpaper as I did?

But I am securely fastened now by my well-hidden rope—you don't get *me* out in the road there!

I suppose I shall have to get back behind the pattern when it comes night, and that is hard!

It is so pleasant to be out in this great room and creep around as I please!

I don't want to go outside. I won't, even if Jennie asks me to.

For outside you have to creep on the ground, and everything is green instead of yellow.

But here I can creep smoothly on the floor, and my shoulder just fits in that long smooch around the wall, so I cannot lose my way.

Why, there's John at the door!

It is no use, young man, you can't open it!

How he does call and pound!

Now he's crying to Jennie for an axe.

It would be a shame to break down that beautiful door!

"John, dear!" said I in the gentlest voice. "The key is down by the front steps, under a plantain leaf!"

That silenced him for a few moments.

Then he said, very quietly indeed, "Open the door, my darling!"

"I can't," said I. "The key is down by the front door under a plantain leaf!" And then I said it again, several times, very gently and slowly, and said it so often that he had to go and see, and he got it of course, and came in. He stopped short by the door.

"What is the matter?" he cried. "For God's sake, what are you doing!"

I kept on creeping just the same, but I looked at him over my shoulder.

"I've got out at last," said I, "in spite of you and Jane. And I've pulled off most of the paper, so you can't put me back!"

Now why should that man have fainted? But he did, and right across my path by the wall, so that I had to creep over him every time!

Study and Discussion Questions

1. What do the narrator and the woman in the wallpaper have in common?
2. Is the narrator right to be suspicious of her husband or is her suspicion simply a manifestation of her nervous ailment?
3. Why is the narrator so tired?

4. What kind of person does John want his wife to be? How does he try to maneuver her into being that?
5. What is the significance of the fact that the narrator's room was originally a nursery?
6. "There comes John, and I must put this away—he hates to have me write a word." Why doesn't John want her to write? Why does she disagree with him?
7. How does the way the narrator sees and feels about the yellow wallpaper change during the story?

Writing Exercises

1. Who is John? List the words that describe him. Write a brief character sketch.
2. Gilman wrote this story in 1890 as a warning about a treatment for nervous depression fashionable then. Gilman herself was told to "live as domestic a life as possible," to "have but two hours' intellectual life a day" and "never to touch pen, brush, or pencil again." Discuss the way in which the treatment which is supposed to cure the narrator worsens her condition, and speculate about the reasons.
3. What is wrong with this marriage?

D. H. LAWRENCE   (1885–1930)

David Herbert Lawrence was born in Nottinghamshire, England, his father a coal miner, his mother a schoolteacher. He attended University College at Nottingham, taught school for four years, and then ran off to Italy with Frieda von Richthoven Weekly, wife of one of his professors. He began writing full time, and he and Frieda continued to travel until his death. Lawrence is known for his poetry, his criticism, and especially his fiction, which includes the novels Sons and Lovers *(1913),* The Rainbow *(1915),* Women in Love *(1920), and* Lady Chatterley's Lover *(1928).*

The White Stocking   (1914)

I

"I'm getting up, Teddilinks," said Mrs. Whiston, and she sprang out of bed briskly.

"What the Hanover's got you?" asked Whiston.

"Nothing. Can't I get up?" she replied animatedly.

It was about seven o'clock, scarcely light yet in the cold bedroom. Whiston lay still and looked at his wife. She was a pretty little thing, with her fleecy, short black hair all tousled. He watched her as she dressed quickly, flicking her small, delightful limbs, throwing her clothes about her. Her slovenliness and untidiness did not trouble him. When she picked up the edge of her petticoat, ripped off a torn string of white lace, and flung it on the dressing-table, her careless abandon made his spirit glow. She stood before the mirror and roughly scrambled together her profuse little mane of hair. He watched the quickness and softness of her young shoulders, calmly, like a husband, and appreciatively.

"Rise up," she cried, turning to him with a quick wave of her arm—"and shine forth."

They had been married two years. But still, when she had gone out of the room, he felt as if all his light and warmth were taken away, he became aware of the raw, cold morning. So he rose himself, wondering casually what had roused her so early. Usually she lay in bed as late as she could.

Whiston fastened a belt round his loins and went downstairs in shirt and trousers. He heard her singing in her snatchy fashion. The stairs creaked under his weight. He passed down the narrow little passage, which she called a hall, of the seven and sixpenny house which was his first home.

He was a shapely young fellow of about twenty-eight, sleepy now and easy with well-being. He heard the water drumming into the kettle, and she began to whistle. He loved the quick way she dodged the supper cups under the tap to wash them for breakfast. She looked an untidy minx, but she was quick and handy enough.

"Teddilinks," she cried.

"What?"

"Light a fire, quick."

She wore an old, sack-like dressing-jacket of black silk pinned across her breast. But one of the sleeves, coming unfastened, showed some delightful pink upper-arm.

"Why don't you sew your sleeve up?" he said, suffering from the sight of the exposed soft flesh.

"Where?" she cried, peering round. "Nuisance," she said, seeing the gap, then with light fingers went on drying the cups.

The kitchen was of fair size, but gloomy. Whiston poked out the dead ashes.

Suddenly a thud was heard at the door down the passage.

"I'll go," cried Mrs. Whiston, and she was gone down the hall.

The postman was a ruddy-faced man who had been a soldier. He smiled broadly, handing her some packages.

"They've not forgot you," he said impudently.

"No—lucky for them," she said, with a toss of the head. But she was interested only in her envelopes this morning. The postman waited inquisitively, smiling in an ingratiating fashion. She slowly, abstractedly, as if she did not know anyone was there, closed the door in his face, continuing to look at the addresses on her letters.

She tore open the thin envelope. There was a long, hideous, cartoon valentine. She smiled briefly and dropped it on the floor. Struggling with the string of a packet, she opened a white cardboard box, and there lay a white silk handkerchief packed neatly under the paper lace of the box, and her initial, worked in heliotrope, fully displayed. She smiled pleasantly, and gently put the box aside. The third envelope contained another white packet—apparently a cotton handkerchief neatly folded. She shook it out. It was a long white stocking, but there was a little weight in the toe. Quickly, she thrust down her arm, wriggling her fingers into the toe of the stocking, and brought out a small box. She peeped inside the box, then hastily opened a door on her left hand, and went into the little cold sitting-room. She had her lower lip caught earnestly between her teeth.

With a little flash of triumph, she lifted a pair of pearl earrings from the small box, and she went to the mirror. There, earnestly, she began to hook them through her ears, looking at herself sideways in the glass. Curiously concentrated and intent she seemed as she fingered the lobes of her ears, her head bent on one side.

Then the pearl ear-rings dangled under her rosy, small ears. She shook her head sharply, to see the swing of the drops. They went chill against her neck, in little, sharp touches. Then she stood still to look at herself, bridling her head in the dignified fashion. Then she simpered at herself. Catching her own eye, she could not help winking at herself and laughing.

She turned to look at the box. There was a scrap of paper with this posy:

"Pearls may be fair, but thou art fairer.
Wear these for me, and I'll love the wearer."

She made a grimace and a grin. But she was drawn to the mirror again, to look at her ear-rings.

Whiston had made the fire burn, so he came to look for her. When she heard him, she started round quickly, guiltily. She was watching him with intent blue eyes when he appeared.

He did not see much, in his morning-drowsy warmth. He gave her, as ever, a feeling of warmth and slowness. His eyes were very blue, very kind, his manner simple.

"What ha' you got?" he asked.

"Valentines," she said briskly, ostentatiously turning to show him the silk handkerchief. She thrust it under his nose. "Smell how good," she said.

"Who's that from?" he replied, without smelling.

"It's a valentine," she cried. "How do I know who it's from?"

"I'll bet you know," he said.

"Ted!—I don't!" she cried, beginning to shake her head, then stopping because of the ear-rings.

He stood still a moment, displeased.

"They've no right to send you valentines now," he said.

"Ted!—Why not? You're not jealous, are you? I haven't the least idea who it's from. Look—there's my initial"—she pointed with an emphatic finger at the heliotrope embroidery—

"E for Elsie,
Nice little gelsie,"[1]

she sang.

"Get out," he said. "You know who it's from."

"Truth, I don't," she cried.

He looked round, and saw the white stocking lying on a chair.

"Is this another?" he said.

"No, that's a sample," she said. "There's only a comic." And she fetched in the long cartoon.

He stretched it out and looked at it solemnly.

"Fools!" he said, and went out of the room.

She flew upstairs and took off the ear-rings. When she returned, he was crouched before the fire blowing the coals. The skin of his face was flushed, and slightly pitted, as if he had had small-pox. But his neck was white and smooth and goodly. She hung her arms round his neck as he crouched there, and clung to him. He balanced on his toes.

"This fire's a slow-coach," he said.

"And who else is a slow-coach?" she said.

"One of us two, I know," he said, and he rose carefully. She remained clinging round his neck, so that she was lifted off her feet.

"Ha!—swing me," she cried.

He lowered his head, and she hung in the air, swinging from his neck, laughing. Then she slipped off.

"The kettle is singing," she sang, flying for the teapot. He bent down again to blow the fire. The veins in his neck stood out, his shirt collar seemed too tight.

"Doctor Wyer,
Blow the fire,
Puff! puff! puff!"

she sang, laughing.

He smiled at her.

She was so glad because of her pearl ear-rings.

---

[1] Perhaps gelsemium, a fragrant flowering plant.

Over the breakfast she grew serious. He did not notice. She became portentous in her gravity. Almost it penetrated through his steady good-humour to irritate him.

"Teddy!" she said at last.

"What?" he asked.

"I told you a lie," she said, humbly tragic.

His soul stirred uneasily.

"Oh aye?" he said casually.

She was not satisfied. He ought to be more moved.

"Yes," she said.

He cut a piece of bread.

"Was it a good one?" he asked.

She was piqued. Then she considered—*was* it a good one? Then she laughed.

"No," she said, "it wasn't up to much."

"Ah!" he said easily, but with a steady strength of fondness for her in his tone. "Get it out then."

It became a little more difficult.

"You know that white stocking," she said earnestly. "I told you a lie. It wasn't a sample. It was a valentine."

A little frown came on his brow.

"Then what did you invent it as a sample for?" he said. But he knew this weakness of hers. The touch of anger in his voice frightened her.

"I was afraid you'd be cross," she said pathetically.

"I'll bet you were vastly afraid," he said.

"I *was*, Teddy."

There was a pause. He was resolving one or two things in his mind.

"And who sent it?" he asked.

"I can guess," she said, "though there wasn't a word with it—except—"

She ran to the sitting-room and returned with a slip of paper.

"Pearls may be fair, but thou art fairer.
Wear these for me, and I'll love the wearer."

He read it twice, then a dull red flush came on his face.

"And *who* do you guess it is?" he asked, with a ringing of anger in his voice.

"I suspect it's Sam Adams," she said, with a little virtuous indignation.

Whiston was silent for a moment.

"Fool!" he said. "An' what's it got to do with pearls?—and how can he say 'wear these for me' when there's only one? He hasn't got the brain to invent a proper verse."

He screwed the slip of paper into a ball and flung it into the fire.

"I suppose he thinks it'll make a pair with the one last year," she said.

"Why, did he send one then?"

"Yes. I thought you'd be wild if you knew."

His jaw set rather sullenly.

Presently he rose, and went to wash himself, rolling back his sleeves and pulling open his shirt at the breast. It was as if his fine, clear-cut temples and steady eyes were degraded by the lower, rather brutal part of his face. But she loved it. As she whisked about, clearing the table, she loved the way in which he stood washing himself. He was such a man. She liked to see his neck glistening with water as he swilled it. It amused her and pleased her and thrilled her. He was so sure, so permanent, he had her so utterly in his power. It gave her a delightful, mischievous sense of liberty. Within his grasp, she could dart about excitingly.

He turned round to her, his face red from the cold water, his eyes fresh and very blue.

"You haven't been seeing anything of him, have you?" he asked roughly.

"Yes," she answered, after a moment, as if caught guilty. "He got into the tram with me, and he asked me to drink a coffee and a Benedictine in the Royal."

"You've got it off fine and glib," he said sullenly. "And did you?"

"Yes," she replied, with the air of a traitor before the rack.

The blood came up into his neck and face, he stood motionless, dangerous.

"It was cold, and it was such fun to go into the Royal," she said.

"You'd go off with a nigger for a packet of chocolate," he said, in anger and contempt, and some bitterness. Queer how he drew away from her, cut her off from him.

"Ted—how beastly!" she cried. "You know quite well—" She caught her lip, flushed, and the tears came to her eyes.

He turned away, to put on his neck-tie. She went about her work, making a queer pathetic little mouth, down which occasionally dripped a tear.

He was ready to go. With his hat jammed down on his head, and his overcoat buttoned up to his chin, he came to kiss her. He would be miserable all the day if he went without. She allowed herself to be kissed. Her cheek was wet under his lip, and his heart burned. She hurt him so deeply. And she felt aggrieved, and did not quite forgive him.

In a moment she went upstairs to her ear-rings. Sweet they looked nestling in the little drawer—sweet! She examined them with voluptuous pleasure, she threaded them in her ears, she looked at herself, she posed and postured and smiled and looked sad and tragic and winning and appealing, all in turn before the mirror. And she was happy, and very pretty.

She wore her ear-rings all morning, in the house. She was self-conscious, and quite brilliantly winsome, when the baker came, wondering if he would notice. All the tradesmen left her door with a glow in them, feeling elated, and unconsciously favouring the delightful little creature, though there had been nothing to notice in her behaviour.

She was stimulated all the day. She did not think about her husband. He was the permanent basis from which she took these giddly little flights into nowhere. At night, like chickens and curses, she would come home to him, to roost.

Meanwhile Whiston, a traveller and confidential support of a small firm, hastened about his work, his heart all the while anxious for her, yearning for surety, and kept tense by not getting it.

II

She had been a warehouse girl in Adams's lace factory before she was married. Sam Adams was her employer. He was a bachelor of forty, growing stout, a man well dressed and florid, with a large brown moustache and thin hair. From the rest of his well-groomed, showy appearance, it was evident his baldness was a chagrin to him. He had a good presence, and some Irish blood in his veins.

His fondness for the girls, or the fondness of the girls for him, was notorious. And Elsie, quick, pretty, almost witty little thing—she *seemed* witty, although, when her sayings were repeated, they were entirely trivial—she had a great attraction for him. He would come into the warehouse dressed in a rather sporting reefer coat, of fawn colour, and trousers of fine black-and-white check, a cap with a big peak and scarlet carnation in his button-hole, to impress her. She was only half impressed. He was too loud for her good taste. Instinctively perceiving this, he sobered down to navy blue. Then a well-built man, florid, with large brown whiskers, smart navy blue suit, fashionable boots, and manly hat, he was the irreproachable. Elsie was impressed.

But meanwhile Whiston was courting her, and she made splendid little gestures, before her bedroom mirror, of the constant-and-true sort.

"True, true till death—"

That was her song. Whiston was made that way, so there was no need to take thought for him.

Every Christmas Sam Adams gave a party at his house, to which he invited his superior work-people—not factory hands and labourers, but those above. He was a generous man in his way, with a real warm feeling for giving pleasure.

Two years ago Elsie had attended this Christmas-party for the last time. Whiston had accompanied her. At that time he worked for Sam Adams.

She had been very proud of herself, in her close-fitting, full-skirted dress of blue silk. Whiston called for her. Then she tripped beside him, holding her large cashmere shawl across her breast. He strode with long strides, his trousers handsomely strapped under his boots, and her silk shoes bulging the pocket of his full-skirted overcoat.

They passed through the park gates, and her spirits rose. Above them the Castle Rock loomed grandly in the night, the naked trees stood still and dark in the frost, along the boulevard.

They were rather late. Agitated with anticipation, in the cloak-room she gave up her shawl, donned her silk shoes, and looked at herself in the mirror. The loose bunches of curls on either side her face danced prettily, her mouth smiled.

She hung a moment in the door of the brilliantly lighted room. Many people were moving within the blaze of lamps, under the crystal chandeliers, the full skirts of the women balancing and floating, the side-whiskers and white cravats of the men bowing above. Then she entered the light.

In an instant Sam Adams was coming forward, lifting both his arms in boisterous welcome. There was a constant red laugh on his face.

"Come late, would you," he shouted, "like royalty."

He seized her hands and led her forward. He opened his mouth wide when he spoke, and the effect of the warm, dark opening behind the brown whiskers was disturbing. But she was floating into the throng on his arm. He was very gallant.

"Now then," he said, taking her card to write down the dances, "I've got *carte blanche*, haven't I?"

"Mr. Whiston doesn't dance," she said.

"I am a lucky man!" he said, scribbling his initials. "I was born with an *amourette*[2] in my mouth."

He wrote on, quietly. She blushed and laughed, not knowing what it meant.

"Why, what is that?" she said.

"It's you, even littler than you are, dressed in little wings," he said.

"I should have to be pretty small to get in your mouth," she said.

"You think you're too big, do you!" he said easily.

He handed her her card, with a bow.

"Now I'm set up, my darling, for this evening," he said.

Then, quick, always at his ease, he looked over the room. She waited in front of him. He was ready. Catching the eye of the band, he nodded. In a moment, the music began. He seemed to relax, giving himself up.

"Now then, Elsie," he said, with a curious caress in his voice that seemed to lap the outside of her body in a warm glow, delicious. She gave herself to it. She liked it.

He was an excellent dancer. He seemed to draw her close in to him by some male warmth of attraction, so that she became all soft and pliant to him, flowing to his form, whilst he united her with him and they lapsed along in one movement. She was just carried in a kind of strong, warm flood, her feet moved of themselves, and only the music threw her away from him, threw her back to him, to his clasp, in his strong form moving against her, rhythmically, deliciously.

---

[2] A little cupid.

When it was over, he was pleased and his eyes had a curious gleam which thrilled her and yet had nothing to do with her. Yet it held her. He did not speak to her. He only looked straight into her eyes with a curious, gleaming look that disturbed her fearfully and deliciously. But also there was in his look some of the automatic irony of the *roué*. It left her partly cold. She was not carried away.

She went, driven by an opposite, heavier impulse, to Whiston. He stood looking gloomy, trying to admit that she had a perfect right to enjoy herself apart from him. He received her with rather grudging kindliness.

"Aren't you going to play whist?" she asked.

"Aye," he said. "Directly."

"I do wish you could dance."

"Well, I can't," he said. "So you enjoy yourself."

"But I should enjoy it better if I could dance with you."

"Nay, you're all right," he said. "I'm not made that way."

"Then you ought to be!" she cried.

"Well, it's my fault, not yours. You enjoy yourself," he bade her. Which she proceeded to do, a little bit irked.

She went with anticipation to the arms of Sam Adams, when the time came to dance with him. It *was* so gratifying, irrespective of the man. And she felt a little grudge against Whiston, soon forgotten when her host was holding her near to him, in a delicious embrace. And she watched his eyes, to meet the gleam in them, which gratified her.

She was getting warmed right through, the glow was penetrating into her, driving away everything else. Only in her heart was a little tightness, like conscience.

When she got a chance, she escaped from the dancing-room to the card-room. There, in a cloud of smoke, she found Whiston playing cribbage. Radiant, roused, animated, she came up to him and greeted him. She was too strong, too vibrant a note in the quiet room. He lifted his head, and a frown knitted his gloomy forehead.

"Are you playing cribbage? Is it exciting? How are you getting on?" she chattered.

He looked at her. None of these questions needed answering, and he did not feel in touch with her. She turned to the cribbage-board.

"Are you white or red?" she asked.

"He's red," replied the partner.

"Then you're losing," she said, still to Whiston. And she lifted the red peg from the board. "One—two—three—four—five—six—seven—eight— Right up there you ought to jump—"

"Now put it back in its right place," said Whiston.

"Where was it?" she asked gaily, knowing her transgression. He took the little red peg away from her and stuck it in its hole.

The cards were shuffled.

"What a shame you're losing," said Elsie.

"You'd better cut for him," said the partner.

She did so hastily. The cards were dealt. She put her hand on his shoulder, looking at his cards.

"It's good," she cried, "isn't it?"

He did not answer, but threw down two cards. It moved him more strongly than was comfortable, to have her hand on his shoulder, her curls dangling and touching his ears, whilst she was roused to another man. It made the blood flame over him.

At that moment Sam Adams appeared, florid and boisterous, intoxicated more with himself, with the dancing, than with wine. In his eye the curious, impersonal light gleamed.

"I thought I should find you here, Elsie," he cried boisterously, a disturbing, high note in his voice.

"What made you think so?" she replied, the mischief rousing in her.

The florid, well-built man narrowed his eyes to a smile.

"I should never look for you among the ladies," he said, with a kind of intimate, animal call to her. He laughed, bowed, and offered her his arm.

"Madam, the music waits."

She went almost helplessly, carried along with him, unwilling, yet delighted.

That dance was an intoxication to her. After the first few steps, she felt herself slipping away from herself. She almost knew she was going, she did not even want to go. Yet she must have chosen to go. She lay in the arm of the steady, close man with whom she was dancing, and she seemed to swim away out of contact with the room, into him. She had passed into another, denser element of him, an essential privacy. The room was all vague around her, like an atmosphere, like under sea, with a flow of ghostly, dumb movements. But she herself was held real against her partner, and it seemed she was connected with him, as if the movements of his body and limbs were her own movements, yet not her own movements—and oh, delicious! He also was given up, oblivious, concentrated, into the dance. His eye was unseeing. Only his large, voluptuous body gave off a subtle activity. His fingers seemed to search into her flesh. Every moment, and every moment, she felt she would give way utterly, and sink molten: the fusion point was coming when she would fuse down into perfect unconsciousness at his feet and knees. But he bore her round the room in the dance, and he seemed to sustain all her body with his limbs, his body, and his warmth seemed to come closer into her, nearer, till it would fuse right through her, and she would be as liquid to him as an intoxication only.

It was exquisite. When it was over, she was dazed, and was scarcely breathing. She stood with him in the middle of the room as if she were alone in a remote place. He bent over her. She expected his lips on her bare shoulder, and waited. Yet they were not alone, they were not alone. It was cruel.

" 'Twas good, wasn't it, my darling?" he said to her, low and delighted. There was a strange impersonality about his low, exultant call that appealed to her irresistibly. Yet why was she aware of some part shut off in her? She pressed his arm, and he led her towards the door.

She was not aware of what she was doing, only a little grain of resistant trouble was in her. The man, possessed, yet with a superficial presence of mind, made way to the dining-room, as if to give her refreshment, cunningly working to his own escape with her. He was molten hot, filmed over with presence of mind, and bottomed with cold disbelief. In the dining-room was Whiston, carrying coffee to the plain, neglected ladies. Elsie saw him, but felt as if he could not see her. She was beyond his reach and ken. A sort of fusion existed between her and the large man at her side. She ate her custard, but an incomplete fusion all the while sustained and contained within the being of her employer.

But she was growing cooler. Whiston came up. She looked at him, and saw him with different eyes. She saw his slim, young man's figure real and enduring before her. That was he. But she was in the spell with the other man, fused with him, and she could not be taken away.

"Have you finished your cribbage?" she asked, with hasty evasion of him.

"Yes," he replied. "Aren't you getting tired of dancing?"

"Not a bit," she said.

"Not she," said Adams heartily. "No girl with any spirit gets tired of dancing. Have something else, Elsie. Come—sherry. Have a glass of sherry with us, Whiston."

Whilst they sipped the wine, Adams watched Whiston almost cunningly, to find his advantage.

"We'd better be getting back—there's the music," he said. "See the women get something to eat, Whiston, will you, there's a good chap."

And he began to draw away. Elsie was drifting helplessly with him. But Whiston put himself beside them, and went along with them. In silence they passed through to the dancing-room. There Adams hesitated, and looked round the room. It was as if he could not see.

A man came hurrying forward, claiming Elsie, and Adams went to his other partner. Whiston stood watching during the dance. She was conscious of him standing there observant of her, like a ghost, or a judgment, or a guardian angel. She was also conscious, much more intimately and impersonally, of the body of the other man moving somewhere in the room. She still belonged to him, but a feeling of distraction possessed her, and helplessness. Adams danced on, adhering to Elsie, waiting his time, with the persistence of cynicism.

The dance was over. Adams was detained. Elsie found herself beside Whiston. There was something shapely about him as he sat, about his knees and his distinct figure, that she clung to. It was as if he had enduring form. She put her hand on his knee.

"Are you enjoying yourself?" he asked.

"*Ever* so," she replied, with a fervent, yet detached tone.

"It's going on for one o'clock," he said.

"Is it?" she answered. It meant nothing to her.

"Should we be going?" he said.

She was silent. For the first time for an hour or more an inkling of her normal consciousness returned. She resented it.

"What for?" she said.

"I thought you might have had enough," he said.

A slight soberness came over her, an irritation at being frustrated of her illusion.

"Why?" she said.

"We've been here since nine," he said.

That was no answer, no reason. It conveyed nothing to her. She sat detached from him. Across the room Sam Adams glanced at her. She sat there exposed for him.

"You don't want to be too free with Sam Adams," said Whiston cautiously, suffering. "You know what he is."

"How, free?" she asked.

"Why—you don't want to have too much to do with him."

She sat silent. He was forcing her into consciousness of her position. But he could not get hold of her feelings, to change them. She had a curious, perverse desire that he should not.

"I like him," she said.

"What do you find to like in him?" he said, with a hot heart.

"I don't know—but I like him," she said.

She was immutable. He sat feeling heavy and dulled with rage. He was not clear as to what he felt. He sat there unliving whilst she danced. And she, distracted, lost to herself between the opposing forces of the two men, drifted. Between the dances, Whiston kept near to her. She was scarcely conscious. She glanced repeatedly at her card, to see when she would dance again with Adams, half in desire, half in dread. Sometimes she met his steady, glaucous eye as she passed him in the dance. Sometimes she saw the steadiness of his flank as he danced. And it was always as if she rested on his arm, were borne along, up-borne by him, away from herself. And always there was present the other's antagonism. She was divided.

The time came for her to dance with Adams. Oh, the delicious closing of contact with him, of his limbs touching her limbs, his arm supporting her. She seemed to resolve. Whiston had not made himself real to her. He was only a heavy place in her consciousness.

But she breathed heavily, beginning to suffer from the closeness of strain. She was nervous. Adams also was constrained. A tightness, a tension was coming over them all. And he was exasperated, feeling something counteracting physical magnetism, feeling a will stronger with her than his own, intervening in what was becoming a vital necessity to him.

Elsie was almost lost to her own control. As she went forward with
him to take her place at the dance, she stooped for her pocket handkerchief.
The music sounded for quadrilles. Everybody was ready. Adams stood
with his body near her, exerting his attraction over her. He was tense
and fighting. She stooped for her pocket handkerchief, and shook it as
she rose. It shook out and fell from her hand. With agony, she saw she
had taken a white stocking instead of a handkerchief. For a second it lay
on the floor, a twist of white stocking. Then, in an instant, Adams picked
it up, with a little, surprised laugh of triumph.

"That'll do for me," he whispered—seeming to take possession of her.
And he stuffed the stocking in his trousers pocket, and quickly offered
her his handkerchief.

The dance began. She felt weak and faint, as if her will were turned
to water. A heavy sense of loss came over her. She could not help herself
any more. But it was peace.

When the dance was over, Adams yielded her up. Whiston came to
her.

"What was it as you dropped?" Whiston asked.

"I thought it was my handkerchief—I'd taken a stocking by mistake,"
she said, detached and muted.

"And he's got it?"

"Yes."

"What does he mean by that?"

She lifted her shoulders.

"Are you going to let him keep it?" he asked.

"I don't let him."

There was a long pause.

"Am I to go and have it out with him?" he asked, his face flushed,
his blue eyes going hard with opposition.

"No," she said, pale.

"Why?"

"No—I don't want you to say anything about it."

He sat exasperated and nonplussed.

"You'll let him keep it, then?" he asked.

She sat silent and made no form of answer.

"What do you mean by it?" he said, dark with fury. And he started
up.

"No!" she cried. "Ted!" And she caught hold of him, sharply detaining
him.

It made him black with rage.

"Why?" he said.

The something about her mouth was pitiful to him. He did not understand, but he felt she must have her reasons.

"Then I'm not stopping here," he said. "Are you coming with me?"

She rose mutely, and they went out of the room. Adams had not
noticed.

In a few moments they were in the street.

"What the hell do you mean?" he said, in a black fury.

She went at his side, in silence, neutral.

"That great hog, an' all," he added.

Then they went a long time in silence through the frozen, deserted darkness of the town. She felt she could not go indoors. They were drawing near her house.

"I don't want to go home," she suddenly cried in distress and anguish. "I don't want to go home."

He looked at her.

"Why don't you?" he said.

"I don't want to go home," was all she could sob.

He heard somebody coming.

"Well, we can walk a bit farther," he said.

She was silent again. They passed out of the town into the fields. He held her by the arm—they could not speak.

"What's a-matter?" he asked at length, puzzled.

She began to cry again.

At last he took her in his arms, to soothe her. She sobbed by herself, almost unaware of him.

"Tell me what's a-matter, Elsie," he said. "Tell me what's a-matter— my dear—tell me, then—"

He kissed her wet face, and caressed her. She made no response. He was puzzled and tender and miserable.

At length she became quiet. Then he kissed her, and she put her arms round him, and clung to him very tight, as if for fear and anguish. He held her in his arms, wondering.

"Ted!" she whispered, frantic. "Ted!"

"What, my love?" he answered, becoming also afraid.

"Be good to me," she cried. "Don't be cruel to me."

"No, my pet," he said, amazed and grieved. "Why?"

"Oh, be good to me," she sobbed.

And he held her very safe, and his heart was white-hot with love for her. His mind was amazed. He could only hold her against his chest that was white-hot with love and belief in her. So she was restored at last.

III

She refused to go to her work at Adams's any more. Her father had to submit and she sent in her notice—she was not well. Sam Adams was ironical. But he had a curious patience. He did not fight.

In a few weeks, she and Whiston were married. She loved him with passion and worship, a fierce little abandon of love that moved him to the depths of his being, and gave him a permanent surety and sense of realness in himself. He did not trouble about himself any more: he felt he was fulfilled and now he had only the many things in the world to busy himself about. Whatever troubled him, at the bottom was surety. He had found himself in this love.

They spoke once or twice of the white stocking.

"Ah!" Whiston exclaimed. "What does it matter?"

He was impatient and angry, and could not bear to consider the matter. So it was left unresolved.

She was quite happy at first, carried away by her adoration of her husband. Then gradually she got used to him. He always was the ground of her happiness, but she got used to him, as to the air she breathed. He never got used to her in the same way.

Inside of marriage she found her liberty. She was rid of the responsibility of herself. Her husband must look after that. She was free to get what she could out of her time.

So that, when, after some months, she met Sam Adams, she was not quite as unkind to him as she might have been. With a young wife's new and exciting knowledge of men, she perceived he was in love with her, she knew he had always kept an unsatisfied desire for her. And, sportive, she could not help playing a little with this, though she cared not one jot for the man himself.

When Valentine's day came, which was near the first anniversary of her wedding day, there arrived a white stocking with a little amethyst brooch. Luckily Whiston did not see it, so she said nothing of it to him. She had not the faintest intention of having anything to do with Sam Adams, but once a little brooch was in her possession, it was hers, and she did not trouble her head for a moment how she had come by it. She kept it.

Now she had the pearl ear-rings. They were a more valuable and a more conspicuous present. She would have to ask her mother to give them to her, to explain their presence. She made a little plan in her head. And she was extraordinarily pleased. As for Sam Adams, even if he saw her wearing them, he would not give her away. What fun, if he saw her wearing his ear-rings! She would pretend she had inherited them from her grandmother, her mother's mother. She laughed to herself as she went down-town in the afternoon, the pretty drops dangling in front of her curls. But she saw no one of importance.

Whiston came home tired and depressed. All day the male in him had been uneasy, and this had fatigued him. She was curiously against him, inclined, as she sometimes was nowadays, to make mock of him and jeer at him and cut him off. He did not understand this, and it angered him deeply. She was uneasy before him.

She knew he was in a state of suppressed irritation. The veins stood out on the backs of his hands, his brow was drawn stiffly. Yet she could not help goading him.

"What did you do wi' that white stocking?" he asked, out of a gloomy silence, his voice strong and brutal.

"I put it in a drawer—why?" she replied flippantly.

"Why didn't you put it on the fire-back?" he said harshly. "What are you hoarding it up for?"

"I'm not hoarding it up," she said. "I've got a pair."

He relapsed into gloomy silence. She, unable to move him, ran away upstairs, leaving him smoking by the fire. Again she tried on the earrings. Then another little inspiration came to her. She drew on the white stockings, both of them.

Presently she came down in them. Her husband still sat immovable and glowering by the fire.

"Look!" she said. "They'll do beautifully."

And she picked up her skirts to her knees, and twisted round, looking at her pretty legs in the neat stockings.

He filled with unreasonable rage, and took the pipe from his mouth.

"Don't they look nice?" she said. "One from last year and one from this, they just do. Save you buying a pair."

And she looked over her shoulders at her pretty calves, and at the dangling frills of her knickers.

"Put your skirts down and don't make a fool of yourself," he said.

"Why a fool of myself?" she asked.

And she began to dance slowly round the room, kicking up her feet half reckless, half jeering, in ballet-dancer's fashion. Almost fearful, yet in defiance, she kicked up her legs at him, singing as she did so. She resented him.

"You little fool, ha' done with it," he said. "And you'll backfire them stockings, I'm telling you." He was angry. His face flushed dark, he kept his head bent. She ceased to dance.

"I shan't," she said. "They'll come in very useful."

He lifted his head and watched her, with lighted, dangerous eyes.

"You'll put 'em on the fire-back, I tell you," he said.

It was a war now. She bent forward, in a ballet-dancer's fashion, and put her tongue between her teeth.

"I shan't back-fire them stockings," she sang, repeating his words, "I shan't, I shan't, I shan't."

And she danced round the room doing a high kick to the tune of her words. There was a real biting indifference in her behaviour.

"We'll see whether you will or not," he said, "trollops! You'd like Sam Adams to know you was wearing 'em, wouldn't you? That's what would please you."

"Yes, I'd like him to see how nicely they fit me, he might give me some more then."

And she looked down at her pretty legs.

He knew somehow that she *would* like Sam Adams to see how pretty her legs looked in the white stockings. It made his anger go deep, almost to hatred.

"Yer nasty trolley," he cried. "Put yer petticoats down, and stop being so foul-minded."

"I'm not foul-minded," she said. "My legs are my own. And why shouldn't Sam Adams think they're nice?"

There was a pause. He watched her with eyes glittering to a point.

"Have you been havin' owt to do with him?" he asked.

"I've just spoken to him when I've seen him," she said. "He's not as bad as you would make out."

"Isn't he?" he cried, a certain wakefulness in his voice. "Them who has anything to do wi' him is too bad for me, I tell you."

"Why, what are you frightened of him for?" she mocked.

She was rousing all his uncontrollable anger. He sat glowering. Every one of her sentences stirred him up like a red-hot iron. Soon it would be too much. And she was afraid herself; but she was neither conquered nor convinced.

A curious little grin of hate came on his face. He had a long score against her.

"What am I frightened of him for?" he repeated automatically. "What am I frightened of him for? Why, for you, you stray-running little bitch."

She flushed. The insult went deep into her, right home.

"Well, if you're so dull—" she said, lowering her eyelids, and speaking coldly, haughtily.

"If I'm so dull I'll break your neck the first word you speak to him," he said, tense.

"Pf!" she sneered. "Do you think I'm frightened of you?" She spoke coldly, detached.

She was frightened, for all that, white round the mouth.

His heart was getting hotter.

"You *will* be frightened of me, the next time you have anything to do with him," he said.

"Do you think *you'd* ever be told—ha!"

Her jeering scorn made him go white-hot, molten. He knew he was incoherent, scarcely responsible for what he might do. Slowly, unseeing, he rose and went out of doors, stifled, moved to kill her.

He stood leaning against the garden fence, unable either to see or hear. Below him, far off, fumed the lights of the town. He stood still, unconscious with a black storm of rage, his face lifted to the night.

Presently, still unconscious of what he was doing, he went indoors again. She stood, a small, stubborn figure with tight-pressed lips and big, sullen, childish eyes, watching him, white with fear. He went heavily across the floor and dropped into his chair.

There was a silence.

"*You're* not going to tell me everything I shall do, and everything I shan't," she broke out at last.

He lifted his head.

"I tell you *this*," he said, low and intense. "Have anything to do with Sam Adams, and I'll break your neck."

She laughed, shrill and false.

"How I hate your word 'break your neck'," she said, with a grimace of the mouth. "It sounds so common and beastly. Can't you say something else—"

There was a dead silence.

"And besides," she said, with a queer chirrup of mocking laughter. "what do you know about anything? He sent me an amethyst brooch and a pair of pearl ear-rings."

"He what?" said Whiston, in a suddenly normal voice. His eyes were fixed on her.

"Sent me a pair of pearl ear-rings, and an amethyst brooch," she repeated, mechanically, pale to the lips.

And her big, black, childish eyes watched him, fascinated, held in her spell.

He seemed to thrust his face and his eyes forward at her, as he rose slowly and came to her. She watched transfixed in terror. Her throat made a small sound, as she tried to scream.

Then, quick as lightning, the back of his hand struck her with a crash across the mouth, and she was flung black blinded against the wall. The shock shook a queer sound out of her. And then she saw him still coming on, his eyes holding her, his fist drawn back, advancing slowly. At any instant the blow might crash into her.

Mad with terror, she raised her hands with a queer clawing movement to cover her eyes and her temples, opening her mouth in a dumb shriek. There was no sound. But the sight of her slowly arrested him. He hung before her, looking at her fixedly, as she stood crouched against the wall with open, bleeding mouth, and wide-staring eyes, and two hands clawing over her temples. And his lust to see her bleed, to break her and destroy her, rose from an old source against her. It carried him. He wanted satisfaction.

But he had seen her standing there, a piteous, horrified thing, and he turned his face aside in shame and nausea. He went and sat heavily in his chair, and a curious ease, almost like sleep, came over his brain.

She walked away from the wall towards the fire, dizzy, white to the lips, mechanically wiping her small, bleeding mouth. He sat motionless. Then, gradually, her breath began to hiss, she shook, and was sobbing silently, in grief for herself. Without looking, he saw. It made his mad desire to destroy her come back.

At length he lifted his head. His eyes were glowing again, fixed on her.

"And what did he give them you for?" he asked, in a steady, unyielding voice.

Her crying dried up in a second. She also was tense.

"They came as valentines," she replied, still not subjugated, even if beaten.

"When, to-day?"

"The pearl ear-rings to-day—the amethyst brooch last year."

"You've had it a year?"

"Yes."

She felt that now nothing would prevent him if he rose to kill her. She could not prevent him any more. She was yielded up to him. They both trembled in the balance, unconscious.

"What have you had to do with him?" he asked, in a barren voice.

"I've not had anything to do with him," she quavered.

"You just kept 'em because they were jewellery?" he said.

A weariness came over him. What was the worth of speaking any more of it? He did not care any more. He was dreary and sick.

She began to cry again, but he took no notice. She kept wiping her mouth on her handkerchief. He could see it, the blood-mark. It made him only more sick and tired of the responsibility of it, the violence, the shame.

When she began to move about again, he raised his head once more from his dead, motionless position.

"Where are the things?" he said.

"They are upstairs," she quavered. She knew the passion had gone down in him.

"Bring them down," he said.

"I won't," she wept, with rage. "You're not going to bully me and hit me like that on the mouth."

And she sobbed again. He looked at her in contempt and compassion and in rising anger.

"Where are they?" he said.

"They're in the little drawer under the looking-glass," she sobbed.

He went slowly upstairs, struck a match, and found the trinkets. He brought them downstairs in his hand.

"These?" he said, looking at them as they lay in his palm.

She looked at them without answering. She was not interested in them any more.

He looked at the little jewels. They were pretty.

"It's none of their fault," he said to himself.

And he searched round slowly, persistently, for a box. He tied the things up and addressed them to Sam Adams. Then he went out in his slippers to post the little package.

When he came back she was still sitting crying.

"You'd better go to bed," he said.

She paid no attention. He sat by the fire. She still cried.

"I'm sleeping down here," he said. "Go you to bed."

In a few moments she lifted her tear-stained, swollen face and looked at him with eyes all forlorn and pathetic. A great flash of anguish went over his body. He went over, slowly, and very gently took her in his hands. She let herself be taken. Then as she lay against his shoulder, she sobbed aloud:

"I never meant—"

"My love—my little love—" he cried, in anguish of spirit, holding her in his arms.

Study and Discussion Questions

1. How does Elsie view her marriage? What does she want from it? How does Ted view the marriage, and what does he want from it?
2. What are the sources of Elsie's power in their relationship? Of Ted's?
3. What is the appeal of Sam Adams for Elsie? Why does she keep the jewelry he sends and why does she keep it a secret from Ted?
4. Discuss the structure of the story, in particular its division into three parts.
5. What is the meaning of the ending?

Writing Exercises

1. What is "The White Stocking" saying about relationships between men and women? What do you think of what it is saying?
2. How convincingly does Lawrence, a man, write about a female character's sexual feelings, especially in Part II? Might a woman have written differently? If so, how?

ERNEST HEMINGWAY   (1899–1961)

Ernest Hemingway was born in Oak Park, Illinois and as a boy went on frequent hunting and fishing trips in northern Michigan with his father, a doctor. He boxed and played football in high school and, after graduating, worked as a newspaper reporter. Near the end of World War I, Hemingway was a volunteer ambulance driver and then a soldier in Italy, where he was wounded. He spent much of the 1920s in Paris and the 1930s in Key West, Florida. He was an active supporter of the Republican cause in the Spanish Civil War and a war correspondent during World War II. Hemingway committed suicide in 1961. His writings include the novels The Sun Also Rises *(1926),* A Farewell to Arms *(1929),* For Whom the Bells Tolls *(1940), and* The Old Man and the Sea *(1952), and the collections* In Our Time *(1925) and* The Fifth Column and the First Forty-Nine Stories *(1938). In 1954, he received the Nobel Prize for literature.*

The Short Happy Life
of Francis Macomber (1936)

It was now lunch time and they were all sitting under the double green fly of the dining tent pretending that nothing had happened.

"Will you have lime juice or lemon squash?" Macomber asked.

"I'll have a gimlet," Robert Wilson told him.

"I'll have a gimlet too. I need something," Macomber's wife said.

"I suppose it's the thing to do," Macomber agreed. "Tell him to make three gimlets."

The mess boy had started them already, lifting the bottles out of the canvas cooling bags that sweated wet in the wind that blew through the trees that shaded the tents.

"What had I ought to give them?" Macomber asked.

"A quid would be plenty," Wilson told him. "You don't want to spoil them."

"Will the headman distribute it?"

"Absolutely."

Francis Macomber had, half an hour before, been carried to his tent from the edge of the camp in triumph on the arms and shoulders of the cook, the personal boys, the skinner and the porters. The gun-bearers had taken no part in the demonstration. When the native boys put him down at the door of his tent, he had shaken all their hands, received their congratulations, and then gone into the tent and sat on the bed until his wife came in. She did not speak to him when she came in and he left the tent at once to wash his face and hands in the portable wash basin outside and go over to the dining tent to sit in a comfortable canvas chair in the breeze and the shade.

"You've got your lion," Robert Wilson said to him, "and a damned fine one too."

Mrs. Macomber looked at Wilson quickly. She was an extremely handsome and well-kept woman of the beauty and social position which had, five years before, commanded five thousand dollars as the price of endorsing, with photographs, a beauty product which she had never used. She had been married to Francis Macomber for eleven years.

"He is a good lion, isn't he?" Macomber said. His wife looked at him now. She looked at both these men as though she had never seen them before.

One, Wilson, the white hunter, she knew she had never truly seen before. He was about middle height with sandy hair, a stubby mustache, a very red face and extremely cold blue eyes with faint white wrinkles at the corners that grooved merrily when he smiled. He smiled at her now and she looked away from his face at the way his shoulders sloped in the loose tunic he wore with the four big cartridges held in loops where the left breast pocket should have been, at his big brown hands, his old slacks, his very dirty boots and back to his red face again. She noticed where the baked red of his face stopped in a white line that marked the circle left by his Stetson hat that hung now from one of the pegs of the tent pole.

"Well, here's to the lion," Robert Wilson said. He smiled at her again and, not smiling, she looked curiously at her husband.

Francis Macomber was very tall, very well built if you did not mind that length of bone, dark, his hair cropped like an oarsman, rather thin-lipped, and was considered handsome. He was dressed in the same sort of safari clothes that Wilson wore except that his were new, he was thirty-five years old, kept himself very fit, was good at court games, had a number of big-game fishing records, and had just shown himself, very publicly, to be a coward.

"Here's to the lion," he said. "I can't ever thank you for what you did."

Margaret, his wife, looked away from him and back to Wilson.

"Let's not talk about the lion," she said.

Wilson looked over at her without smiling and now she smiled at him.

"It's been a very strange day," she said. "Hadn't you ought to put your hat on even under the canvas at noon? You told me that, you know."

"Might put it on," said Wilson.

"You know you have a very red face, Mr. Wilson," she told him and smiled again.

"Drink," said Wilson.

"I don't think so," she said. "Francis drinks a great deal, but his face is never red."

"It's red today," Macomber tried a joke.

"No," said Margaret. "It's mine that's red today. But Mr. Wilson's is always red."

"Must be racial," said Wilson. "I say, you wouldn't like to drop my beauty as a topic, would you?"

"I've just started on it."

"Let's chuck it," said Wilson.

"Conversation is going to be so difficult," Margaret said.

"Don't be silly, Margot," her husband said.

"No difficulty," Wilson said. "Got a damn fine lion."

Margot looked at them both and they both saw that she was going to cry. Wilson had seen it coming for a long time and he dreaded it. Macomber was past dreading it.

"I wish it hadn't happened. Oh, I wish it hadn't happened," she said and started for her tent. She made no noise of crying but they could see that her shoulders were shaking under the rose-colored, sun-proofed shirt she wore.

"Women upset," said Wilson to the tall man. "Amounts to nothing. Strain on the nerves and one thing'n another."

"No," said Macomber. "I suppose that I rate that for the rest of my life now."

"Nonsense. Let's have a spot of the giant killer," said Wilson. "Forget the whole thing. Nothing to it anyway."

"We might try," said Macomber. "I won't forget what you did for me though."

"Nothing," said Wilson. "All nonsense."

So they sat there in the shade where the camp was pitched under some wide-topped acacia trees with a boulder-strewn cliff behind them, and a stretch of grass that ran to the bank of a boulder-filled stream in front with forest beyond it, and drank their just-cool lime drinks and avoided one another's eyes while the boys set the table for lunch. Wilson could tell that the boys all knew about it now and when he saw Macomber's personal boy looking curiously at his master while he was putting dishes on the table he snapped at him in Swahili. The boy turned away with his face blank.

"What were you telling him?" Macomber asked.

"Nothing. Told him to look alive or I'd see he got about fifteen of the best."

"What's that? Lashes?"

"It's quite illegal," Wilson said. "You're supposed to fine them."

"Do you still have them whipped?"

"Oh, yes. They could raise a row if they chose to complain. But they don't. They prefer it to the fines."

"How strange!" said Macomber.

"Not strange, really," Wilson said. "Which would you rather do? Take a good birching or lose your pay?"

Then he felt embarrassed at asking it and before Macomber could answer he went on, "We all take a beating every day, you know, one way or another."

This was no better. "Good God," he thought. "I am a diplomat, aren't I?"

"Yes, we take a beating," said Macomber, still not looking at him. "I'm awfully sorry about that lion business. It doesn't have to go any further, does it? I mean no one will hear about it, will they?"

"You mean will I tell it at the Mathaiga Club?" Wilson looked at him now coldly. He had not expected this. So he's a bloody four-letter man as well as a bloody coward, he thought. I rather liked him too until today. But how is one to know about an American?

"No," said Wilson. "I'm a professional hunter. We never talk about our clients. You can be quite easy on that. It's supposed to be bad form to ask us not to talk though."

He had decided now that to break would be much easier. He would eat, then, by himself and could read a book with his meals. They would eat by themselves. He would see them through the safari on a very formal basis—what was it the French called it? Distinguished consideration—and

it would be a damn sight easier than having to go through this emotional
trash. He'd insult him and make a good clean break. Then he could read
a book with his meals and he'd still be drinking their whisky. That was
the phrase for it when a safari went bad. You ran into another white
hunter and you asked, "How is everything going?" and he answered,
"Oh, I'm still drinking their whisky," and you knew everything had gone
to pot.

"I'm sorry," Macomber said and looked at him with his American face
that would stay adolescent until it became middle-aged, and Wilson noted
his crew-cropped hair, fine eyes only faintly shifty, good nose, thin lips
and handsome jaw. "I'm sorry I didn't realize that. There are lots of
things I don't know."

So what could he do, Wilson thought. He was all ready to break it off
quickly and neatly and here the beggar was apologizing after he had just
insulted him. He made one more attempt. "Don't worry about me talking,"
he said. "I have a living to make. You know in Africa no woman ever
misses her lion and no white man ever bolts."

"I bolted like a rabbit," Macomber said.

Now what in hell were you going to do about a man who talked like
that, Wilson wondered.

Wilson looked at Macomber with his flat, blue, machine-gunner's eyes
and the other smiled back at him. He had a pleasant smile if you did
not notice how his eyes showed when he was hurt.

"Maybe I can fix it up on buffalo," he said. "We're after them next,
aren't we?"

"In the morning if you like," Wilson told him. Perhaps he had been
wrong. This was certainly the way to take it. You most certainly could
not tell a damned thing about an American. He was all for Macomber
again. If you could forget the morning. But, of course, you couldn't. The
morning had been about as bad as they come.

"Here comes the Memsahib," he said. She was walking over from her
tent looking refreshed and cheerful and quite lovely. She had a very
perfect oval face, so perfect that you expected her to be stupid. But she
wasn't stupid, Wilson thought, no, not stupid.

"How is the beautiful red-faced Mr. Wilson? Are you feeling better,
Francis, my pearl?"

"Oh, much," said Macomber.

"I've dropped the whole thing," she said, sitting down at the table.
"What importance is there to whether Francis is any good at killing lions?
That's not his trade. That's Mr. Wilson's trade. Mr. Wilson is really very
impressive killing anything. You do kill anything, don't you?"

"Oh, anything," said Wilson. "Simply anything." They are, he thought,
the hardest in the world; the hardest, the cruelest, the most predatory
and the most attractive and their men have softened or gone to pieces
nervously as they have hardened. Or is it that they pick men they can
handle? They can't know that much at the age they marry, he thought.

He was grateful that he had gone through his education on American women before now because this was a very attractive one.

"We're going after buff in the morning," he told her.

"I'm coming," she said.

"No, you're not."

"Oh, yes, I am. Mayn't I, Francis?"

"Why not stay in camp?"

"Not for anything," she said. "I wouldn't miss something like today for anything."

When she left, Wilson was thinking, when she went off to cry, she seemed a hell of a fine woman. She seemed to understand, to realize, to be hurt for him and for herself and to know how things really stood. She is away for twenty minutes and now she is back, simply enamelled in that American female cruelty. They are the damnedest women. Really the damnedest.

"We'll put on another show for you tomorrow," Francis Macomber said.

"You're not coming," Wilson said.

"You're very mistaken," she told him. "And I want *so* to see you perform again. You were lovely this morning. That is if blowing things' heads off is lovely."

"Here's the lunch," said Wilson. "You're very merry, aren't you?"

"Why not? I didn't come out here to be dull."

"Well, it hasn't been dull," Wilson said. He could see the boulders in the river and the high bank beyond with the trees and he remembered the morning.

"Oh, no," she said. "It's been charming. And tomorrow. You don't know how I look forward to tomorrow."

"That's eland he's offering you," Wilson said.

"They're the big cowy things that jump like hares, aren't they?"

"I suppose that describes them," Wilson said.

"It's very good meat," Macomber said.

"Did you shoot it, Francis?" she asked.

"Yes."

"They're not dangerous, are they?"

"Only if they fall on you," Wilson told her.

"I'm so glad."

"Why not let up on the bitchery just a little, Margot," Macomber said, cutting the eland steak and putting some mashed potato, gravy and carrot on the down-turned fork that tined through the piece of meat.

"I suppose I could," she said, "since you put it so prettily."

"Tonight we'll have champagne for the lion," Wilson said. "It's a bit too hot at noon."

"Oh, the lion," Margot said. "I'd forgotten the lion!"

So, Robert Wilson thought to himself, she *is* giving him a ride, isn't she? Or do you suppose that's her idea of putting up a good show? How should a woman act when she discovers her husband is a bloody coward? She's damn cruel but they're all cruel. They govern, of course, and to govern one has to be cruel sometimes. Still, I've seen enough of their damn terrorism.

"Have some more eland," he said to her politely.

That afternoon, late, Wilson and Macomber went out in the motor car with the native driver and the two gun-bearers. Mrs. Macomber stayed in the camp. It was too hot to go out, she said, and she was going with them in the early morning. As they drove off Wilson saw her standing under the big tree, looking pretty rather than beautiful in her faintly rosy khaki, her dark hair drawn back off her forehead and gathered in a knot low on her neck, her face as fresh, he thought, as though she were in England. She waved to them as the car went off through the swale of high grass and curved around through the trees into the small hills of orchard bush.

In the orchard bush they found a herd of impala, and leaving the car they stalked one old ram with long, wide-spread horns and Macomber killed it with a very creditable shot that knocked the buck down at a good two hundred yards and sent the herd off bounding wildly and leaping over one another's backs in long, leg-drawn-up leaps as unbelievable and as floating as those one makes sometimes in dreams.

"That was a good shot," Wilson said. "They're a small target."

"Is it a worth-while head?" Macomber asked.

"It's excellent," Wilson told him. "You shoot like that and you'll have no trouble."

"Do you think we'll find buffalo tomorrow?"

"There's a good chance of it. They feed out early in the morning and with luck we may catch them in the open."

"I'd like to clear away that lion business," Macomber said. "It's not very pleasant to have your wife see you do something like that."

I should think it would be even more unpleasant to do it, Wilson thought, wife or no wife, or to talk about it having done it. But he said, "I wouldn't think about that any more. Any one could be upset by his first lion. That's all over."

But that night after dinner and a whisky and soda by the fire before going to bed, as Francis Macomber lay on his cot with the mosquito bar over him and listened to the night noises it was not all over. It was neither all over nor was it beginning. It was there exactly as it happened with some parts of it indelibly emphasized and he was miserably ashamed at it. But more than shame he felt cold, hollow fear in him. The fear was still there like a cold, hollow fear in him. The fear was still there like a cold slimy hollow in all the emptiness where once his confidence had been and it made him feel sick. It was still there with him now.

It had started the night before when he had wakened and heard the lion roaring somewhere up along the river. It was a deep sound and at the end there were sort of coughing grunts that made him seem just outside the tent, and when Francis Macomber woke in the night to hear it he was afraid. He could hear his wife breathing quietly, asleep. There was no one to tell he was afraid, nor to be afraid with him, and, lying alone, he did not know the Somali proverb that says a brave man is always frightened three times by a lion; when he first sees his track, when he first hears him roar and when he first confronts him. Then while they were eating breakfast by lantern light out in the dining tent, before the sun was up, the lion roared again and Francis thought he was just at the edge of camp.

"Sounds like an old-timer," Robert Wilson said, looking up from his kippers and coffee. "Listen to him cough."

"Is he very close?"

"A mile or so up the stream."

"Will we see him?"

"We'll have a look."

"Does his roaring carry that far? It sounds as though he were right in camp."

"Carries a hell of a long way," said Robert Wilson. "It's strange the way it carries. Hope he's a shootable cat. The boys said there was a very big one about here."

"If I get a shot, where should I hit him," Macomber asked, "to stop him?"

"In the shoulders," Wilson said. "In the neck if you can make it. Shoot for bone. Break him down."

"I hope I can place it properly," Macomber said.

"You shoot very well," Wilson told him. "Take your time. Make sure of him. The first one in is the one that counts."

"What range will it be?"

"Can't tell. Lion has something to say about that. Won't shoot unless it's close enough so you can make sure."

"At under a hundred yards?" Macomber asked.

Wilson looked at him quickly.

"Hundred's about right. Might have to take him a bit under. Shouldn't chance a shot at much over that. A hundred's a decent range. You can hit him wherever you want at that. Here comes the Memsahib."

"Good morning," she said. "Are we going after that lion?"

"As soon as you deal with your breakfast," Wilson said. "How are you feeling?"

"Marvellous," she said. "I'm very excited."

"I'll just go and see that everything is ready," Wilson went off. As he left the lion roared again.

"Noisy beggar," Wilson said. "We'll put a stop to that."

"What's the matter, Francis?" his wife asked him.

"Nothing," Macomber said.

"Yes, there is," she said. "What are you upset about?"

"Nothing," he said.

"Tell me," she looked at him. "Don't you feel well?"

"It's that damned roaring," he said. "It's been going on all night, you know."

"Why didn't you wake me," she said. "I'd love to have heard it."

"I've got to kill the damned thing," Macomber said, miserably.

"Well, that's what you're out here for, isn't it?"

"Yes. But I'm nervous. Hearing the thing roar gets on my nerves."

"Well then, as Wilson said, kill him and stop his roaring."

"Yes, darling," said Francis Macomber. "It sounds easy, doesn't it?"

"You're not afraid, are you?"

"Of course not. But I'm nervous from hearing him roar all night."

"You'll kill him marvellously," she said. "I know you will. I'm awfully anxious to see it."

"Finish your breakfast and we'll be starting."

"It's not light yet," she said. "This is a ridiculous hour."

Just then the lion roared in a deep-chested moaning, suddenly guttural, ascending vibration that seemed to shake the air and ended in a sigh and a heavy, deep-chested grunt.

"He sounds almost here," Macomber's wife said.

"My God," said Macomber. "I hate that damned noise."

"It's very impressive."

"Impressive. It's frightful."

Robert Wilson came up then carrying his short, ugly, shockingly big-bored .505 Gibbs and grinning.

"Come on," he said. "Your gun-bearer has your Springfield and the big gun. Everything's in the car. Have you solids?"

"Yes."

"I'm ready," Mrs. Macomber said.

"Must make him stop that racket," Wilson said. "You get in front. The Memsahib can sit back here with me."

They climbed into the motor car and, in the gray first daylight, moved off up the river through the trees. Macomber opened the breech of his rifle and saw he had metal-cased bullets, shut the bolt and put the rifle on safety. He saw his hand was trembling. He felt in his pocket for more cartridges and moved his fingers over the cartridges in the loops of his tunic front. He turned back to where Wilson sat in the rear seat of the doorless, box-bodied motor car beside his wife, them both grinning with excitement, and Wilson leaned forward and whispered,

"See the birds dropping. Means the old boy has left his kill."

On the far bank of the stream Macomber could see, above the trees, vultures circling and plummeting down.

"Chances are he'll come to drink along here," Wilson whispered. "Before he goes to lay up. Keep an eye out."

They were driving slowly along the high bank of the stream which here cut deeply to its boulder-filled bed, and they wound in and out through big trees as they drove. Macomber was watching the opposite bank when he felt Wilson take hold of his arm. The car stopped.

"There he is," he heard the whisper. "Ahead and to the right. Get out and take him. He's a marvellous lion."

Macomber saw the lion now. He was standing almost broadside, his great head up and turned toward them. The early morning breeze that blew toward them was just stirring his dark mane, and the lion looked huge, silhouetted on the rise of bank in the gray morning light, his shoulders heavy, his barrel of a body bulking smoothly.

"How far is he?" asked Macomber, raising his rifle.

"About seventy-five. Get out and take him."

"Why not shoot from where I am?"

"You don't shoot them from cars," he heard Wilson saying in his ear. "Get out. He's not going to stay there all day."

Macomber stepped out of the curved opening at the side of the front seat, onto the step and down onto the ground. The lion still stood looking majestically and coolly toward this object that his eyes only showed in silhouette, bulking like some super-rhino. There was no man smell carried toward him and he watched the object, moving his great head a little from side to side. Then watching the object, not afraid, but hesitating before going down the bank to drink with such a thing opposite him, he saw a man figure detach itself from it and he turned his heavy head and swung away toward the cover of the trees as he heard a cracking crash and felt the slam of a .30-06 220-grain solid bullet that bit his flank and ripped in sudden hot scalding nausea through his stomach. He trotted, heavy, bigfooted, swinging wounded full-bellied, through the trees toward the tall grass and cover, and the crash came again to go past him ripping the air apart. Then it crashed again and he felt the blow as it hit his lower ribs and ripped on through, blood sudden hot and frothy in his mouth, and he galloped toward the high grass where he could crouch and not be seen and make them bring the crashing thing close enough so he could make a rush and get the man that held it.

Macomber had not thought how the lion felt as he got out of the car. He only knew his hands were shaking and as he walked away from the car it was almost impossible for him to make his legs move. They were stiff in the thighs, but he could feel the muscles fluttering. He raised the rifle, sighted on the junction of the lion's head and shoulders and pulled the trigger. Nothing happened though he pulled until he thought his finger would break. Then he knew he had the safety on and as he lowered the rifle to move the safety over he moved another frozen pace forward, and the lion seeing his silhouette now clear of the silhouette of the car, turned and started off at a trot, and, as Macomber fired, he heard a whunk that meant that the bullet was home; but the lion kept on going. Macomber shot again and every one saw the bullet throw a spout of dirt beyond the trotting lion. He shot again, remembering to lower his aim, and they all heard the bullet hit, and the lion went into a gallop and was in the tall grass before he had the bolt pushed forward.

Macomber stood there feeling sick at his stomach, his hands that held the Springfield still cocked, shaking, and his wife and Robert Wilson were standing by him. Beside him too were the two gun-bearers chattering in Wakamba.

"I hit him," Macomber said. "I hit him twice."

"You gut-shot him and you hit him somewhere forward," Wilson said without enthusiasm. The gun-bearers looked very grave. They were silent now.

"You may have killed him," Wilson went on. "We'll have to wait a while before we go in to find out."

"What do you mean?"

"Let him get sick before we follow him up."

"Oh," said Macomber.

"He's a hell of a fine lion," Wilson said cheerfully. "He's gotten into a bad place though."

"Why is it bad?"

"Can't see him until you're on him."

"Oh," said Macomber.

"Come on," said Wilson. "The Memsahib can stay here in the car. We'll go to have a look at the blood spoor."

"Stay here, Margot," Macomber said to his wife. His mouth was very dry and it was hard for him to talk.

"Why?" she asked.

"Wilson says to."

"We're going to have a look," Wilson said. "You stay here. You can see even better from here."

"All right."

Wilson spoke in Swahili to the driver. He nodded and said, "Yes, Bwana."

Then they went down the steep bank and across the stream, climbing over and around the boulders and up the other bank, pulling up by some projecting roots, and along it until they found where the lion had been trotting when Macomber first shot. There was dark blood on the short grass that the gun-bearers pointed out with grass stems, and that ran away behind the river bank trees.

"What do we do?" asked Macomber.

"Not much choice," said Wilson. "We can't bring the car over. Bank's too steep. We'll let him stiffen up a bit and then you and I'll go in and have a look for him."

"Can't we set the grass on fire?" Macomber asked.

"Too green."

"Can't we send beaters?"

Wilson looked at him appraisingly. "Of course we can," he said. "But it's just a touch murderous. You see we know the lion's wounded. You can drive an unwounded lion—he'll move on ahead of a noise—but a wounded lion's going to charge. You can't see him until you're right on him. He'll make himself perfectly flat in cover you wouldn't think would hide a hare. You can't very well send boys in there to that sort of a show. Somebody bound to get mauled."

"What about the gun-bearers?"

"Oh, they'll go with us. It's their *shauri*. You see, they signed on for it. They don't look too happy though, do they?"

"I don't want to go in there," said Macomber. It was out before he knew he'd said it.

"Neither do I," said Wilson very cheerily. "Really no choice though." Then, as an afterthought, he glanced at Macomber and saw suddenly how he was trembling and the pitiful look on his face.

"You don't have to go in, of course," he said. "That's what I'm hired for, you know. That's why I'm so expensive."

"You mean you'd go in by yourself? Why not leave him there?"

Robert Wilson, whose entire occupation had been with the lion and the problem he presented, and who had not been thinking about Macomber except to note that he was rather windy, suddenly felt as though he had opened the wrong door in a hotel and seen something shameful.

"What do you mean?"

"Why not just leave him?"

"You mean pretend to ourselves he hasn't been hit?"

"No. Just drop it."

"It isn't done."

"Why not?"

"For one thing, he's certain to be suffering. For another, some one else might run onto him."

"I see."

"But you don't have to have anything to do with it."

"I'd like to," Macomber said. "I'm just scared, you know."

"I'll go ahead when we go in," Wilson said, "with Kongoni tracking. You keep behind me and a little to one side. Chances are we'll hear him growl. If we see him we'll both shoot. Don't worry about anything. I'll keep you backed up. As a matter of fact, you know, perhaps you'd better not go. It might be much better. Why don't you go over and join the Memsahib while I just get it over with?"

"No, I want to go."

"All right," said Wilson. "But don't go in if you don't want to. This is my *shauri* now, you know."

"I want to go," said Macomber.

They sat under a tree and smoked.

"Want to go back and speak to the Memsahib while we're waiting?" Wilson asked.

"No."

"I'll just step back and tell her to be patient."

"Good," said Macomber. He sat there, sweating under his arms, his mouth dry, his stomach hollow feeling, wanting to find courage to tell Wilson to go on and finish off the lion without him. He could not know that Wilson was furious because he had not noticed the state he was in earlier and sent him back to his wife. While he sat there Wilson came up. "I have your big gun," he said. "Take it. We've given him time, I think. Come on."

Macomber took the big gun and Wilson said:

"Keep behind me and about five yards to the right and do exactly as I tell you." Then he spoke in Swahili to the two gun-bearers who looked the picture of gloom.

"Let's go," he said.

"Could I have a drink of water?" Macomber asked. Wilson spoke to the older gun-bearer, who wore a canteen on his belt, and the man unbuckled it, unscrewed the top and handed it to Macomber, who took it noticing how heavy it seemed and how hairy and shoddy the felt covering was in his hand. He raised it to drink and looked ahead at the high grass with the flattopped trees behind it. A breeze was blowing toward them and the grass rippled gently in the wind. He looked at the gun-bearer and he could see the gun-bearer was suffering too with fear.

Thirty-five yards into the grass the big lion lay flattened out along the ground. His ears were back and his only movement was a slight twitching up and down of his long, blacktufted tail. He had turned at bay as soon as he had reached this cover and he was sick with the wound through his full belly, and weakening with the wound through his lungs that brought a thin foamy red to his mouth each time he breathed. His flanks were wet and hot and flies were on the little openings the solid bullets had made in his tawny hide, and his big yellow eyes, narrowed with hate, looked straight ahead, only blinking when the pain came as he breathed, and his claws dug in the soft baked earth. All of him, pain, sickness, hatred and all of his remaining strength, was tightening into an absolute concentration for a rush. He could hear the men talking and he waited, gathering all of himself into this preparation for a charge as soon as the men would come into the grass. As he heard their voices his tail stiffened to twitch up and down, and, as they came into the edge of the grass, he made a coughing grunt and charged.

Kongoni, the old gun-bearer, in the lead watching the blood spoor, Wilson watching the grass for any movement, his big gun ready, the second gun-bearer looking ahead and listening, Macomber close to Wilson, his rifle cocked, they had just moved into the grass when Macomber heard the blood-choked coughing grunt, and saw the swishing rush in the grass. The next thing he knew he was running; running wildly, in panic in the open, running toward the stream.

He heard the *ca-ra-wong!* of Wilson's big rifle, and again in a second crashing *carawong!* and turning saw the lion, horrible-looking now, with half his head seeming to be gone, crawling toward Wilson in the edge of the tall grass while the red-faced man worked the bolt on the short ugly rifle and aimed carefully as another blasting *carawong!* came from the muzzle, and the crawling, heavy, yellow bulk of the lion stiffened and the huge, mutilated head slid forward and Macomber, standing by himself in the clearing where he had run, holding a loaded rifle, while two black men and a white man looked back at him in contempt, knew the lion was dead. He came toward Wilson, his tallness all seeming a naked reproach, and Wilson looked at him and said:

"Want to take pictures?"

"No," he said.

That was all any one had said until they reached the motor car. Then Wilson had said:

"Hell of a fine lion. Boys will skin him out. We might as well stay here in the shade."

Macomber's wife had not looked at him nor he at her and he had sat by her in the back seat with Wilson sitting in the front seat. Once he had reached over and taken his wife's hand without looking at her and she had removed her hand from his. Looking across the stream to where the gun-bearers were skinning out the lion he could see that she had been able to see the whole thing. While they sat there his wife had reached forward and put her hand on Wilson's shoulder. He turned and she had leaned forward over the low seat and kissed him on the mouth.

"Oh, I say," said Wilson, going redder than his natural baked color.

"Mr. Robert Wilson," she said. "The beautiful red-faced Mr. Robert Wilson."

Then she sat down beside Macomber again and looked away across the stream to where the lion lay, with uplifted, white-muscled, tendon-marked naked forearms, and white bloating belly, as the black men fleshed away the skin. Finally the gun-bearers brought the skin over, wet and heavy, and climbed in behind with it, rolling it up before they got in, and the motor car started. No one had said anything more until they were back in camp.

That was the story of the lion. Macomber did not know how the lion had felt before he started his rush, nor during it when the unbelievable smash of the .505 with a muzzle velocity of two tons had hit him in the mouth, nor what kept him coming after that, when the second ripping crash had smashed his hind quarters and he had come crawling on toward the crashing, blasting thing that had destroyed him. Wilson knew something about it and only expressed it by saying, "Damned fine lion," but Macomber did not know how Wilson felt about things either. He did not know how his wife felt except that she was through with him.

His wife had been through with him before but it never lasted. He was very wealthy, and would be much wealthier, and he knew she would not leave him ever now. That was one of the few things that he really knew. He knew about that, about motor cycles—that was earliest—about motor cars, about duck-shooting, about fishing, trout, salmon and big-sea, about sex in books, many books, too many books, about all court games, about dogs, not much about horses, about hanging on to his money, about most of the other things his world dealt in, and about his wife not leaving him. His wife had been a great beauty and she was still a great beauty in Africa, but she was not a great enough beauty any more at home to be able to leave him and better herself and she knew it and he knew it. She had missed the chance to leave him and he knew it. If he had been better with women she would probably have started to worry about him getting another new, beautiful wife; but she knew too much about him to worry about him either. Also, he had always had a great tolerance which seemed the nicest thing about him if it were not the most sinister.

All in all they were known as a comparatively happily married couple, one of those whose disruption is often rumored but never occurs, and as the society columnist put it, they were adding more than a spice of *adventure* to their much envied and ever-enduring *Romance* by a *Safari* in what was known as *Darkest Africa* until the Martin Johnsons lighted it on so many silver screens where they were pursuing *Old Simba* the lion, the buffalo, *Tembo* the elephant and as well collecting specimens for the Museum of Natural History. This same columnist had reported them *on the verge* as least three times in the past and they had been. But they always made it up. They had a sound basis of union. Margot was too beautiful for Macomber to divorce her and Macomber had too much money for Margot ever to leave him.

It was now about three o'clock in the morning and Francis Macomber, who had been asleep a little while after he had stopped thinking about the lion, wakened and then slept again, woke suddenly, frightened in a dream of the bloody-headed lion standing over him, and listening while his heart pounded, he realized that his wife was not in the other cot in the tent. He lay awake with that knowledge for two hours.

At the end of that time his wife came into the tent, lifted her mosquito bar and crawled cozily into bed.

"Where have you been?" Macomber asked in the darkness.

"Hello," she said. "Are you awake?"

"Where have you been?"

"I just went out to get a breath of air."

"You did, like hell."

"What do you want me to say, darling?"

"Where have you been?"

"Out to get a breath of air."

"That's a new name for it. You *are* a bitch."

"Well, you're a coward."

"All right," he said. "What of it?"

"Nothing as far as I'm concerned. But please let's not talk, darling, because I'm very sleepy."

"You think that I'll take anything."

"I know you will, sweet."

"Well, I won't."

"Please, darling, let's not talk. I'm so very sleepy."

"There wasn't going to be any of that. You promised there wouldn't be."

"Well, there is now," she said sweetly.

"You said if we made this trip that there would be none of that. You promised."

"Yes, darling. That's the way I meant it to be. But the trip was spoiled yesterday. We don't have to talk about it, do we?"

"You don't wait long when you have an advantage, do you?"

"Please let's not talk. I'm so sleepy, darling."

"I'm going to talk."

"Don't mind me then, because I'm going to sleep." And she did.

At breakfast they were all three at the table before daylight and Francis Macomber found that, of all the many men that he had hated, he hated Robert Wilson the most.

"Sleep well?" Wilson asked in his throaty voice, filling a pipe.

"Did you?"

"Topping," the white hunter told him.

You bastard, thought Macomber, you insolent bastard.

So she woke him when she came in, Wilson thought, looking at them both with his flat, cold eyes. Well, why doesn't he keep his wife where she belongs? What does he think I am, a bloody plaster saint? Let him keep her where she belongs. It's his own fault.

"Do you think we'll find buffalo?" Margot asked, pushing away a dish of apricots.

"Chance of it," Wilson said and smiled at her. "Why don't you stay in camp?"

"Not for anything," she told him.

"Why not order her to stay in camp?" Wilson said to Macomber.

"You order her," said Macomber coldly.

"Let's not have any ordering, nor," turning to Macomber, "any silliness, Francis," Margot said quite pleasantly.

"Are you ready to start?" Macomber asked.

"Any time," Wilson told him. "Do you want the Memsahib to go?"

"Does it make any difference whether I do or not?"

The hell with it, thought Robert Wilson. The utter complete hell with it. So this is what it's going to be like. Well, this is what it's going to be like, then.

"Makes no difference," he said.

"You're sure you wouldn't like to stay in camp with her yourself and let me go out and hunt the buffalo?" Macomber asked.

"Can't do that," said Wilson. "Wouldn't talk rot if I were you."

"I'm not talking rot. I'm disgusted."

"Bad word, disgusted."

"Francis, will you please try to speak sensibly!" his wife said.

"I speak too damned sensibly," Macomber said. "Did you ever eat such filthy food?"

"Something wrong with the food?" asked Wiilson quietly.

"No more than with everything else."

"I'd pull yourself together, laddybuck," Wilison said very quiety. "There's a boy waits at table that understands a little English."

"The hell with him."

Wilson stood up and puffing on his pipe strolled away, speaking a few words in Swahili to one of the gun-bearers who was standing waiting for him. Macomber and his wife sat on at the table. He was staring at his coffee cup.

"If you make a scene I'll leave you, darling," Margot said quietly.

"No, you won't."

"You can try it and see."

"You won't leave me."

"No," she said. "I won't leave you and you'll behave yourself."

"Behave myself? That's a way to talk. Behave myself."

"Yes. Behave yourself."

"Why don't *you* try behaving?"

"I've tried it so long. So very long."

"I hate that red-faced swine," Macomber said. "I loathe the sight of him."

"He's really *very* nice."

"Oh, *shut up*," Macomber almost shouted. Just then the car came up and stopped in front of the dining tent and the driver and the two gun-bearers got out. Wilson walked over and looked at the husband and wife sitting there at the table.

"Going shooting?" he asked.

"Yes," said Macomber, standing up. "Yes."

"Better bring a woolly. It will be cool in the car," Wilson said.

"I'll get my leather jacket," Margot said.

"The boy has it," Wilson told her. He climbed into the front with the driver and Francis Macomber and his wife sat, not speaking, in the back seat.

Hope the silly beggar doesn't take a notion to blow the back of my head off, Wilson thought to himself. Women *are* a nuisance on safari.

The car was grinding down to cross the river at a pebbly ford in the gray daylight and then climbed, angling up the steep bank, where Wilson had ordered a way shovelled out the day before so they could reach the parklike wooded rolling country on the far side.

It was a good morning, Wilson thought. There was a heavy dew and as the wheels went through the grass and low bushes he could smell the odor of the crushed fronds. It was an odor like verbena and he liked this early morning smell of the dew, the crushed bracken and the look of the tree trunks showing black through the early morning mist, as the car made its way through the untracked, parklike country. He had put the two in the back seat out of his mind now and was thinking about buffalo. The buffalo that he was after stayed in the daytime in a thick swamp where it was impossible to get a shot, but in the night they fed out into an open stretch of country and if he could come between them and their swamp with the car, Macomber would have a good chance at them in the open. He did not want to hunt buff with Macomber in thick cover. He did not want to hunt buff or anything else with Macomber at all, but he was a professional hunter and he had hunted with some rare ones in his time. If they got buff today there would only be rhino to come and the poor man would have gone through his dangerous game and things might pick up. He'd have nothing more to do with the woman and Macomber would get over that too. He must have gone through plenty of that before by the look of things. Poor beggar. He must have a way of getting over it. Well, it was the poor sod's own bloody fault.

He, Robert Wilson, carried a double size cot on safari to accommodate any windfalls he might receive. He had hunted for a certain clientele, the international, fast, sporting set, where the women did not feel they were getting their money's worth unless they had shared that cot with the white hunter. He despised them when he was away from them although he liked some of them well enough at the time, but he made his living by them; and their standards were his standards as long as they were hiring him.

They were his standards in all except the shooting. He had his own standards about the killing and they could live up to them or get some one else to hunt them. He knew, too, that they all respected him for this. This Macomber was an odd one though. Damned if he wasn't. Now the wife. Well, the wife. Yes, the wife. Hm, the wife. Well he'd dropped all that. He looked around at them. Macomber sat grim and furious. Margot smiled at him. She looked younger today, more innocent and fresher and not so professionally beautiful. What's in her heart God knows, Wilson thought. She hadn't talked much last night. At that it was a pleasure to see her.

The motor car climbed up a slight rise and went on through the trees and then out into a grassy prairie-like opening and kept in the shelter of the trees along the edge, the driver going slowly and Wilson looking carefully out across the prairie and all along its far side. He stopped the car and studied the opening with his field glasses. Then he motioned to the driver to go on and the car moved slowly along, the driver avoiding wart-hog holes and driving around the mud castles ants had built. Then, looking across the opening, Wilson suddenly turned and said,

"By God, there they are!"

And looking where he pointed, while the car jumped forward and Wilson spoke in rapid Swahili to the driver, Macomber saw three huge, black animals looking almost cylindrical in their long heaviness, like big black tank cars, moving at a gallop across the far edge of the open prairie. They moved at a stiff-necked, stiff bodied gallop and he could see the upswept wide black horns on their heads as they galloped heads out; the heads not moving.

"They're three old bulls," Wilson said. "We'll cut them off before they get to the swamp."

The car was going a wild forty-five miles an hour across the open and as Macomber watched, the buffalo got bigger and bigger until he could see the gray, hairless, scabby look of one huge bull and how his neck was a part of his shoulders and the shiny black of his horns as he galloped a little behind the others that were strung out in that steady plunging gait; and then, the car swaying as though it had just jumped a road, they drew up close and he could see the plunging hugeness of the bull, and the dust in his sparsely haired hide, the wide boss of horn and his outstretched, wide-nostrilled muzzle, and he was raising his rifle when Wilson shouted, "Not from the car, you fool!" and he had no fear, only hatred of Wilson, while the brakes clamped on and the car skidded, plowing sideways to an almost stop and Wilson was out on one side and he on the other, stumbling as his feet hit the still speeding-by of the earth, and then he was shooting at the bull as he moved away, hearing the bullets whunk into him, emptying his rifle at him as he moved steadily away, finally remembering to get his shots forward into the shoulder, and as he fumbled to re-load, he saw the bull was down. Down on his knees, his big head tossing, and seeing the other two still galloping he shot at the leader and hit him. He shot again and missed and he heard the *carawonging* roar as Wilson shot and saw the leading bull slide forward onto his nose.

"Get that other," Wilson said. "Now you're shooting!"

But the other bull was moving steadily at the same gallop and he missed, throwing a spout of dirt, and Wilson missed and the dust rose in a cloud and Wilson shouted, "Come on. He's too far!" and grabbed his arm and they were in the car again, Macomber and Wilson hanging on the sides and rocketing swayingly over the uneven ground, drawing up on the steady, plunging, heavy-necked, straight-moving gallop of the bull.

They were behind him and Macomber was filling his rifle, dropping shells onto the ground, jamming it, clearing the jam, then they were almost up with the bull when Wilson yelled "Stop," and the car skidded so that it almost swung over and Macomber fell forward onto his feet, slammed his bolt forward and fired as far forward as he could aim into the galloping, rounded black back, aimed and shot again, then again, then again, and the bullets, all of them hitting, had no effect on the buffalo that he could see. Then Wilson shot, the roar deafening him, and he could see the bull stagger. Macomber shot again, aiming carefully, and down he came, onto his knees.

"All right," Wilson said. "Nice work. That's the three."

Macomber felt a drunken elation.

"How many times did you shoot?" he asked.

"Just three," Wilson said. "You killed the first bull. The biggest one. I helped you finish the other two. Afraid they might have got into cover. You had them killed. I was just mopping up a little. You shot damn well."

"Let's go to the car," said Macomber. "I want a drink."

"Got to finish off that buff first," Wilson told him. The buffalo was on his knees and he jerked his head furiously and bellowed in pig-eyed, roaring rage as they came toward him.

"Watch he doesn't get up," Wilson said. Then, "Get a little broadside and take him in the neck just behind the ear."

Macomber aimed carefully at the center of the huge, jerking, rage-driven neck and shot. At the shot the head dropped forward.

"That does it," said Wilson. "Got the spine. They're a hell of a looking thing, aren't they?"

"Let's get the drink," said Macomber. In his life he had never felt so good.

In the car Macomber's wife sat very white faced. "You were marvellous, darling," she said to Macomber. "What a ride."

"Was it rough?" Wilson asked.

"It was frightful. I've never been more frightened in my life."

"Let's all have a drink," Macomber said.

"By all means," said Wilson. "Give it to the Memsahib." She drank the neat whisky from the flask and shuddered a little when she swallowed. She handed the flask to Macomber who handed it to Wilson.

"It was frightfully exciting," she said. "It's given me a dreadful headache. I didn't know you were allowed to shoot them from cars though."

"No one shot from cars," said Wilson coldly.

"I mean chase them from cars."

"Wouldn't ordinarily," Wilson said. "Seemed sporting enough to me though while we were doing it. Taking more chance driving that way across the plain full of holes and one thing and another than hunting on foot. Buffalo could have charged us each time we shot if he liked. Gave him every chance. Wouldn't mention it to any one though. It's illegal if that's what you mean."

"It seemed very unfair to me," Margot said, "chasing those big helpless things in a motor car."

"Did it?" said Wilson.

"What would happen if they heard about it in Nairobi?"

"I'd lose my licence for one thing. Other unpleasantnesses," Wilson said, taking a drink from the flask. "I'd be out of business."

"Really?"

"Yes, really."

"Well," said Macomber, and he smiled for the first time all day. "Now she has something on you."

"You have such a pretty way of putting things, Francis," Margot Macomber said. Wilson looked at them both. If a four-letter man marries a five-letter women, he was thinking, what number of letters would their children be? What he said was, "We lost a gun-bearer. Did you notice it?"

"My God, no," Macomber said.

"Here he comes," Wilson said. "He's all right. He must have fallen off when we left the first bull."

Approaching them was the middle-aged gun-bearer, limping along in his knitted cap, khaki tunic, shorts and rubber sandals, gloomy-faced and disgusted looking. As he came up he called out to Wilson in Swahili and they all saw the change in the white hunter's face.

"What does he say?" asked Margot.

"He says the first bull got up and went into the bush," Wilson said with no expression in his voice.

"Oh," said Macomber blankly.

"Then it's going to be just like the lion," said Margot, full of anticipation.

"It's not going to be a damned bit like the lion," Wilson told her. "Did you want another drink, Macomber?"

"Thanks, yes," Macomber said. He expected the feeling he had had about the lion to come back but it did not. For the first time in his life he really felt wholly without fear. Instead of fear he had a feeling of definite elation.

"We'll go and have a look at the second bull," Wilson said. "I'll tell the driver to put the car in the shade."

"What are you going to do?" asked Margaret Macomber.

"Take a look at the buff," Wilson said.

"I'll come."

"Come along."

The three of them walked over to where the second buffalo bulked blackly in the open, head forward on the grass, the massive horns swung wide.

"He's a very good head," Wilson said. "That's close to a fifty-inch spread."

Macomber was looking at him with delight.

"He's hateful looking," said Margot. "Can't we go into the shade?"

"Of course," Wilson said. "Look," he said to Macomber, and pointed. "See that patch of bush?"

"Yes."

"That's where the first bull went in. The gun-bearer said when he fell off the bull was down. He was watching us helling along and the other two buff galloping. When he looked up there was the bull up and looking at him. Gun-bearer ran like hell and the bull went off slowly into that bush."

"Can we go in after him now?" asked Macomber eagerly.

Wilson looked at him appraisingly. Damned if this isn't a strange one, he thought. Yesterday he's scared sick and today he's a ruddy fire eater.

"No, we'll give him a while."

"Let's please go into the shade," Margot said. Her face was white and she looked ill.

They made their way to the car where it stood under a single, wide-spreading tree and all climbed in.

"Chances are he's dead in there," Wilson remarked. "After a little we'll have a look."

Macomber felt a wild unreasonable happiness that he had never known before.

"By God, that was a chase," he said. "I've never felt any such feeling. Wasn't it marvellous, Margot?"

"I hated it."

"Why?"

"I hated it," she said bitterly. "I loathed it."

"You know I don't think I'd ever be afraid of anything again," Macomber said to Wilson. "Something happened in me after we first saw the buff and started after him. Like a dam bursting. It was pure excitement."

"Cleans out your liver," said Wilson. "Damn funny things happen to people."

Macomber's face was shining. "You know something did happen to me," he said. "I feel absolutely different."

His wife said nothing and eyed him strangely. She was sitting far back in the seat and Macomber was sitting forward talking to Wilson who turned sideways talking over the back of the front seat.

"You know, I'd like to try another lion," Macomber said. "I'm really not afraid of them now. After all, what can they do to you?"

"That's it," said Wilson. "Worst one can do is kill you. How does it go? Shakespeare. Damned good. See if I can remember. Oh, damned good. Used to quote it to myself at one time. Let's see. 'By my troth, I care not; a man can die but once; we owe God a death and let it go which way it will he that dies this year is quit for the next.'[1] Damned fine, eh?"

He was very embarrassed, having brought out this thing he had lived by, but he had seen men come of age before and it always moved him. It was not a matter of their twenty-first birthday.

It had taken a strange chance of hunting, a sudden precipitation into action without opportunity for worrying beforehand, to bring this about with Macomber, but regardless of how it had happened it had most certainly happened. Look at the beggar now, Wilson thought. It's that some of them stay little boys so long, Wilson thought. Sometimes all their lives. Their figures stay boyish when they're fifty. The great American boy-men. Damned strange people. But he liked this Macomber now. Damned strange fellow. Probably meant the end of cuckoldry too. Well, that would be a damned good thing. Damned good thing. Beggar had probably been afraid all his life. Don't know what started it. But over

---

[1] *Henry IV, Part 2*, III, ii, 250–55.

now. Hadn't had time to be afraid with the buff. That and being angry too. Motor car too. Motor cars made it familiar. Be a damn fire eater now. He'd seen it in the war work the same way. More of a change than any loss of virginity. Fear gone like an operation. Something else grew in its place. Main thing a man had. Made him into a man. Women knew it too. No bloody fear.

From the far corner of the seat Margaret Macomber looked at the two of them. There was no change in Wilson. She saw Wilson as she had seen him the day before when she had first realized what his great talent was. But she saw the change in Francis Macomber now.

"Do you have that feeling of happiness about what's going to happen?" Macomber asked, still exploring his new wealth.

"You're not supposed to mention it," Wilson said, looking in the other's face. "Much more fashionable to say you're scared. Mind you, you'll be scared too, plenty of times."

"But you *have* a feeling of happiness about action to come?"

"Yes," said Wilson. "There's that. Doesn't do to talk too much about all this. Talk the whole thing away. No pleasure in anything if you mouth it up too much."

"You're both talking rot," said Margot. "Just because you've chased some helpless animals in a motor car you talk like heroes."

"Sorry," said Wilson. "I have been gassing too much." She's worried about it already, he thought.

"If you don't know what we're talking about why not keep out of it?" Macomber asked his wife.

"You've gotten awfully brave, awfully suddenly," his wife said contemptuously, but her contempt was not secure. She was very afraid of something.

Macomber laughed, a very natural hearty laugh. "You know I *have*," he said. "I really have."

"Isn't it sort of late?" Margot said bitterly. Because she had done the best she could for many years back and the way they were together now was no one person's fault.

"Not for me," said Macomber.

Margot said nothing but sat back in the corner of the seat.

"Do you think we've given him time enough?" Macomber asked Wilson cheerfully.

"We might have a look," Wilson said. "Have you any solids left?"

"The gun-bearer has some."

Wilson called in Swahili and the older gun-bearer, who was skinning out one of the heads, straightened up, pulled a box of solids out of his pocket and brought them over to Macomber, who filled his magazine and put the remaining shells in his pocket.

"You might as well shoot the Springfield," Wilson said. "You're used to it. We'll leave the Mannlicher in the car with the Memsahib. Your gun-bearer can carry your heavy gun. I've this damned cannon. Now let me tell you about them." He had saved this until the last because he did not want to worry Macomber. "When a buff comes he comes with his head high and thrust straight out. The boss of the horns covers any sort of a brain shot. The only shot is straight into the nose. The only other shot is into his chest or, if you're to one side, into the neck or the shoulders. After they've been hit once they take a hell of a lot of killing. Don't try anything fancy. Take the easiest shot there is. They've finished skinning out that head now. Should we get started?"

He called to the gun-bearers, who came up wiping their hands, and the older one got into the back.

"I'll only take Kongoni," Wilson said. "The other can watch to keep the birds away."

As the car moved slowly across the open space toward the island of brushy trees that ran in a tongue of foliage along a dry water course that cut the open swale, Macomber felt his heart pounding and his mouth was dry again, but it was excitement, not fear.

"Here's where he went in," Wilson said. Then to the gun-bearer in Swahili, "Take the blood spoor."

The car was parallel to the patch of bush. Macomber, Wilson and the gun-bearer got down. Macomber, looking back, saw his wife, with the rifle by her side, looking at him. He waved to her and she did not wave back.

The brush was very thick ahead and the ground was dry. The middle-aged gun-bearer was sweating heavily and Wilson had his hat down over his eyes and his red neck showed just ahead of Macomber. Suddenly the gun-bearer said something in Swahili to Wilson and ran forward.

"He's dead in there," Wilson said. "Good work," and he turned to grip Macomber's hand and as they shook hands, grinning at each other, the gun-bearer shouted wildly and they saw him coming out of the bush sideways, fast as a crab, and the bull coming, nose out, mouth tight closed, blood dripping, massive head straight out, coming in a charge, his little pig eyes bloodshot as he looked at them. Wilson, who was ahead was kneeling shooting, and Macomber, as he fired, unhearing his shot in the roaring of Wilson's gun, saw fragments like slate burst from the huge boss of the horns, and the head jerked, he shot again at the wide nostrils and saw the horns jolt again and fragments fly, and he did not see Wilson now and, aiming carefully, shot again with the buffalo's huge bulk almost on him and his rifle almost level with the on-coming head, nose out, and he could see the little wicked eyes and the head started to lower and he felt a sudden white-hot, blinding flash explode inside his head and that was all he ever felt.

Wilson had ducked to one side to get in a shoulder shot. Macomber had stood solid and shot for the nose, shooting a touch high each time and hitting the heavy horns, splintering and chipping them like hitting a slate roof, and Mrs. Macomber, in the car, had shot at the buffalo with the 6.5 Mannlicher as it seemed about to gore Macomber and had hit her husband about two inches up and a little to one side of the base of his skull.

Francis Macomber lay now, face down, not two yards from where the buffalo lay on his side and his wife knelt over him with Wilson beside her.

"I wouldn't turn him over," Wilson said.

The woman was crying hysterically.

"I'd get back in the car," Wilson said. "Where's the rifle?"

She shook her head, her face contorted. The gun-bearer picked up the rifle.

"Leave it as it is," said Wilson. Then, "Go get Abdulla so that he may witness the manner of the accident."

He knelt down, took a handkerchief from his pocket, and spread it over Francis Macomber's crew-cropped head where it lay. The blood sank into the dry, loose earth.

Wilson stood up and saw the buffalo on his side, his legs out, his thinly-haired belly crawling with ticks. "Hell of a good bull," his brain registered automatically. "A good fifty inches, or better. Better." He called to the driver and told him to spread a blanket over the body and stay by it. Then he walked over to the motor car where the woman sat crying in the corner.

"That was a pretty thing to do," he said in a toneless voice. "He *would* have left you too."

"Stop it," she said.

"Of course it's an accident," he said. "I know that."

"Stop it," she said.

"Don't worry," he said. "There will be a certain amount of unpleasantness but I will have some photographs taken that will be very useful at the inquest. There's the testimony of the gun-bearers and the driver too. You're perfectly all right."

"Stop it," she said.

"There's a hell of a lot to be done," he said. "And I'll have to send a truck off to the lake to wireless for a plane to take the three of us into Nairobi. Why didn't you poison him? That's what they do in England."

"Stop it. Stop it. Stop it," the woman cried.

Wilson looked at her with his flat blue eyes.

"I'm through now," he said. "I was a little angry. I'd begun to like your husband."

"Oh, please stop it," she said. "Please, please stop it."

"That's better," Wilson said. "Please is much better. Now I'll stop."

Study and Discussion Questions

1. What kind of person is Robert Wilson? What does he value? What about Francis Macomber? And Margot Macomber?

2. Why does it matter so much whether Francis is a good hunter? Why does he feel so bad after he runs away from a lion and so good after he kills buffalo? What is the significance of the story's title?

3. What is Francis and Margot's marriage like? What kind of power does each have in the relationship? What is the source of their problems?

4. What evidence can you find that the death of Francis is not accidental? Besides opportunity, what leads Margot to shoot her husband when she does?

5. From whose point of view is the story told most often? Least often? What is the significance of this?

6. What do Wilson, Francis, and Margot each think it means to be a real man? What would you guess Hemingway thinks?

7. What is the story saying about what women are like, and should be like?

8. Hemingway does not narrate the story chronologically, but starts in the middle, flashes back to an earlier scene, and then moves on to his conclusion. How does this structure shape the meaning of the story?

Writing Exercises

1. Robert Wilson does not like talk. "No pleasure in anything," he advises Francis, "if you mouth it up too much." How does this fit in with his other views on what men should be like?

2. The story suggests the relationship between men and women is a power struggle, a war. Do you agree?

3. What would have happened to the Macombers if Margot had not killed her husband? Where would their marriage have gone?

4. Pick a point in the story—right after Francis has run away from the lion, for example—and imagine you are Margot. Write a journal or diary entry.

JOHN UPDIKE (b. 1932)*

A & P (1962)

In walks these three girls in nothing but bathing suits. I'm in the third checkout slot, with my back to the door, so I don't see them until they're over by the bread. The one that caught my eye first was the one in the plaid green two-piece. She was a chunky kid, with a good tan and a sweet broad soft-looking can with those two crescents of white just under

---

* A brief biography of John Updike appears on page 164.

it, where the sun never seems to hit, at the top of the backs of her legs. I stood there with my hand on a box of HiHo crackers trying to remember if I rang it up or not. I ring it up again and the customer starts giving me hell. She's one of these cash-register-watchers, a witch about fifty with rouge on her cheekbones and no eyebrows, and I know it made her day to trip me up. She'd been watching cash registers for fifty years and probably never seen a mistake before.

By the time I got her feathers smoothed and her goodies into a bag—she gives me a little snort in passing, if she'd been born at the right time they would have burned her over in Salem—by the time I get her on her way the girls had circled around the bread and were coming back, without a pushcart, back my way along the counters, in the aisle between the checkouts and the Special bins. They didn't even have shoes on. There was this chunky one, with the two-piece—it was bright green and the seams on the bra were still sharp and her belly was still pretty pale so I guessed she just got it (the suit)—there was this one, with one of those chubby berry-faces, the lips all bunched together under her nose, this one, and a tall one, with black hair that hadn't quite frizzed right, and one of these sunburns right across under the eyes, and a chin that was too long—you know, the kind of girl other girls think is very "striking" and "attractive" but never quite makes it, as they very well know, which is why they like her so much—and then the third one, that wasn't quite so tall. She was the queen. She kind of led them, the other two peeking around and making their shoulders round. She didn't look around, not this queen, she just walked straight on slowly, on these long white prima-donna legs. She came down a little hard on her heels, as if she didn't walk in her bare feet that much, putting down her heels and then letting the weight move along to her toes as if she was testing the floor with every step, putting a little deliberate extra action into it. You never know for sure how girls' minds work (do you really think it's a mind in there or just a little buzz like a bee in a glass jar?) but you got the idea she had talked the other two into coming in here with her, and now she was showing them how to do it, walk slow and hold yourself straight.

She had on a kind of dirty-pink—beige maybe, I don't know—bathing suit with a little nubble all over it and, what got me, the straps were down. They were off her shoulders looped loose around the cool tops of her arms, and I guess as a result the suit had slipped a little on her, so all around the top of the cloth there was this shining rim. If it hadn't been there you wouldn't have known there could have been anything whiter than those shoulders. With the straps pushed off, there was nothing between the top of the suit and the top of her head except just *her*, this clean bare plane of the top of her chest down from the shoulder bones like a dented sheet of metal tilted in the light. I mean, it was more than pretty.

She had sort of oaky hair that the sun and salt had bleached, done up in a bun that was unravelling, and a kind of prim face. Walking into the A & P with your straps down, I suppose it's the only kind of face you *can* have. She held her head so high her neck, coming up out of those white shoulders, looked kind of stretched, but I didn't mind. The longer her neck was, the more of her there was.

She must have felt in the corner of her eye me and over my shoulder Stokesie in the second slot watching, but she didn't tip. Not this queen. She kept her eyes moving across the racks, and stopped, and turned so slow it made my stomach rub the inside of my apron, and buzzed to the other two, who kind of huddled against her for relief, and then they all three of them went up the cat-and-dog-food-breakfast-cereal-macaroni-rice-raisins-seasonings-spreads-spaghetti-soft-drinks-crackers-and-cookies aisle. From the third slot I look straight up this aisle to the meat counter, and I watched them all the way. The fat one with the tan sort of fumbled with the cookies, but on second thought she put the package back. The sheep pushing their carts down the aisle—the girls were walking against the usual traffic (not that we have one-way signs or anything)—were pretty hilarious. You could see them, when Queenie's white shoulders dawned on them, kind of jerk, or hop, or hiccup, but their eyes snapped back to their own baskets and on they pushed. I bet you could set off dynamite in an A & P and the people would by and large keep reaching and checking oatmeal off their lists and muttering "Let me see, there was a third thing, began with A, asparagus, no, ah, yes, applesauce!" or whatever it is they do mutter. But there was no doubt, this jiggled them. A few houseslaves in pin curlers even looked around after pushing their carts past to make sure what they had seen was correct.

You know, it's one thing to have a girl in a bathing suit down on the beach, where what with the glare nobody can look at each other much anyway, and another thing in the cool of the A & P, under the fluorescent lights, against all those stacked packages, with her feet paddling along naked over our checkerboard green-and-cream rubber-tile floor.

"Oh Daddy," Stokesie said beside me. "I feel so faint."

"Darling," I said. "Hold me tight." Stokesie's married, with two babies chalked up on his fuselage already, but as far as I can tell that's the only difference. He's twenty-two, and I was nineteen this April.

"Is it done?" he asks, the responsible married man finding his voice. I forgot to say he thinks he's going to be manager some sunny day, maybe in 1990 when it's called the Great Alexandrov and Petrooshki Tea Company or something.

What he meant was, our town is five miles from a beach, with a big summer colony out on the Point, but we're right in the middle of town, and the women generally put on a shirt or shorts or something before they get out of the car into the street. And anyway these are usually women with six children and varicose veins mapping their legs and nobody, including them, could care less. As I say, we're right in the middle of town, and if you stand at our front doors you can see two banks and the Congregational church and the newspaper store and three real-estate offices and about twenty-seven old freeloaders tearing up Central Street because the sewer broke again. It's not as if we're on the Cape; we're north of Boston and there's people in this town haven't seen the ocean for twenty years.

The girls had reached the meat counter and were asking McMahon something. He pointed, they pointed, and they shuffled out of sight behind a pyramid of Diet Delight peaches. All that was left for us to see was old McMahon patting his mouth and looking after them sizing up their joints. Poor kids, I began to feel sorry for them, they couldn't help it.

Now here comes the sad part of the story, at least my family says it's sad, but I don't think it's so sad myself. The store's pretty empty, it being Thursday afternoon, so there was nothing much to do except lean on the register and wait for the girls to show up again. The whole store was like a pinball machine and I didn't know which tunnel they'd come out of. After a while they come around out of the far aisle, around the light bulbs, records at discount of the Caribbean Six or Tony Martin Sings or some such gunk you wonder they waste the wax on, sixpacks of candy bars, and plastic toys done up in cellophane that fall apart when a kid looks at them anyway. Around they come, Queenie still leading the way, and holding a little gray jar in her hands. Slots Three through Seven are unmanned and I could see her wondering between Stokes and me, but Stokesie with his usual luck draws an old party in baggy gray pants who stumbles up with four giant cans of pineapple juice (what do these bums *do* with all that pineapple juice? I've often asked myself) so the girls come to me. Queenie puts down the jar and I take it into my fingers icy cold. Kingfish Fancy Herring Snacks in Pure Sour Cream: 49¢. Now her hands are empty, not a ring or a bracelet, bare as God made them, and I wonder where the money's coming from. Still with that prim look she lifts a folded dollar bill out of the hollow at the center of her nubbled pink top. The jar went heavy in my hand. Really, I thought that was so cute.

Then everybody's luck begins to run out. Lengel comes in from haggling with a truck full of cabbages on the lot and is about to scuttle into that door marked MANAGER behind which he hides all day when the girls touch his eye. Lengel's pretty dreary, teaches Sunday school and the rest, but he doesn't miss that much. He comes over and says, "Girls, this isn't the beach."

Queenie blushes, though maybe it's just a brush of sunburn I was noticing for the first time, now that she was so close. "My mother asked me to pick up a jar of herring snacks." Her voice kind of startled me, the way voices do when you see the people first, coming out so flat and dumb yet kind of tony, too, the way it ticked over "pick up" and "snacks." All of a sudden I slid right down her voice into her living room. Her father and the other men were standing around in icecream coats and bow ties and the women were in sandals picking up herring snacks on toothpicks off a big glass plate and they were all holding drinks the color of water with olives and sprigs of mint in them. When my parents have somebody over they get lemonade and if it's a real racy affair Schlitz in tall glasses with "They'll Do It Every Time" cartoons stenciled on.

"That's all right," Lengel said. "But this isn't the beach." His repeating this struck me as funny, as if it had just occurred to him, and he had been thinking all these years the A & P was a great big dune and he was the head lifeguard. He didn't like my smiling—as I say he doesn't miss much—but he concentrates on giving the girls that sad Sunday-school-superintendent stare.

Queenie's blush is no sunburn now, and the plump one in plaid, that I liked better from the back—a really sweet can—pipes up. "We weren't doing any shopping. We just came in for the one thing."

"That makes no difference," Lengel tells her, and I could see from the way his eyes went that he hadn't noticed she was wearing a two-piece before. "We want you decently dressed when you come in here."

"We *are* decent," Queenie says suddenly, her lower lip pushing, getting sore now that she remembers her place, a place from which the crowd that runs the A & P must look pretty crummy. Fancy Herring Snacks flashed in her very blue eyes.

"Girls, I don't want to argue with you. After this come in here with your shoulders covered. It's our policy." He turns his back. That's policy for you. Policy is what the kingpins want. What the others want is juvenile delinquency.

All this while, the customers had been showing up with their carts but, you know, sheep, seeing a scene, they had all bunched up on Stokesie, who shook open a paper bag as gently as peeling a peach, not wanting to miss a word. I could feel in the silence everybody getting nervous, most of all Lengel, who asks me, "Sammy, have you rung up their purchase?"

I thought and said "No" but it wasn't about that I was thinking. I go through the punches, 4, 9, GROC, TOT—it's more complicated than you think, and after you do it often enough, it begins to make a little song, that you hear words to, in my case "Hello (*bing*) there, you (*gung*) happy *pee*-pul (*splat*)!"—the *splat* being the drawer flying out. I uncrease the bill, tenderly as you may imagine, it just having come from between the two smoothest scoops of vanilla I had ever known were there, and pass a half and a penny into her narrow pink palm, and nestle the herrings in a bag and twist its neck and hand it over, all the time thinking.

The girls, and who'd blame them, are in a hurry to get out, so I say "I quit" to Lengel quick enough for them to hear, hoping they'll stop and watch me, their unsuspected hero. They keep right on going, into the electric eye; the door flies open and they flicker across the lot to their car, Queenie and Plaid and Big Tall Goony-Goony (not that as raw material she was so bad), leaving me with Lengel and a kink in his eyebrow.

"Did you say something, Sammy?"

"I said I quit."

"I thought you did."

"You didn't have to embarrass them."

"It was they who were embarrassing us."

I started to say something that came out "Fiddle-de-doo." It's a saying of my grandmother's, and I know she would have been pleased.

"I don't think you know what you're saying," Lengel said.

"I know you don't," I said. "But I do." I pull the bow at the back of my apron and start shrugging it off my shoulders. A couple customers that had been heading for my slot begin to knock against each other, like scared pigs in a chute.

Lengel sighs and begins to look very patient and old and gray. He's been a friend of my parents for years. "Sammy, you don't want to do this to your Mom and Dad," he tells me. It's true, I don't. But it seems to me that once you begin a gesture it's fatal not to go through with it. I fold the apron, "Sammy" stitched in red on the pocket, and put it on the counter, and drop the bow tie on top of it. The bow tie is theirs, if you've ever wondered. "You'll feel this for the rest of your life," Lengel says, and I know that's true, too, but remembering how he made that pretty girl blush makes me so scrunchy inside I punch the No Sale tab and the machine whirs "pee-pul" and the drawer splats out. One advantage to this scene taking place in summer, I can follow this up with a clean exit, there's no fumbling around getting your coat and galoshes, I just saunter into the electric eye in my white shirt that my mother ironed the night before, and the door heaves itself open, and outside the sunshine is skating around on the asphalt.

I look around for my girls, but they're gone, of course. There wasn't anybody but some young married screaming with her children about some candy they didn't get by the door of a powder-blue Falcon station wagon. Looking back in the big windows, over the bags of peat moss and aluminum lawn furniture stacked on the pavement, I could see Lengel in my place in the slot, checking the sheep through. His face was dark gray and his back stiff, as if he'd just had an injection of iron, and my stomach kind of fell as I felt how hard the world was going to be to me hereafter.

Study and Discussion Questions

1. What does the story gain from being narrated by Sammy rather than, say, by Stokesie, or even by an omniscient narrator?

2. Characterize Sammy's attitude towards "girls" and towards women? Does the way he views Queenie change?

3. What evidence is there of a difference in social class between Sammy and the three young women? Does this difference in any way help explain his quitting?

4. Aside from his desire to impress Queenie and her friends, why does Sammy quit? Explain the significance of his last words in the story: "I felt how hard the world was going to be to me hereafter."

Writing Exercises

1. Briefly retell of the story from Queenie's point of view.
2. "A & P" was published in 1962 and, presumably, takes place around then, before the women's liberation movement that began in the late 1960s. What, if anything, would likely be different if the story took place today?

JUDY GRAHN (b. 1940)

Judy Grahn grew up in New Mexico and has worked as a waitress, typist, sandwich maker, and meat wrapper. She has lived in California for many years and was a cofounder of Diana Press. Her writings include The Work of a Common Women *(1978) and* The Queen of Wands *(1982), poetry; and* Another Mother Tongue: Gay Words, Gay Worlds *(1984), nonfiction. She edited two volumes of* True to Life Adventure Stories *(1978, 1980).*

Boys at the Rodeo   (1978)

A lot of people have spent time on some women's farm this summer of 1972 and one day six of us decide to go to the rodeo. We are all mature and mostly in our early thirties. We wear levis and shirts and short hair. Susan has shaved her head.

The man at the gate, who looks like a cousin of the sheriff, is certain we are trying to get in for free. It must have been something in the way we are walking. He stares into Susan's face. "I know you're at least fourteen," he says. He slaps her shoulder, in that comradely way men have with each other. That's when we know he thinks we are boys.

"You're over thirteen," he says to Wendy.

"You're over thirteen," he says to me. He examines each of us closely, and sees only that we have been outdoors, are muscled, and look him directly in the eye. Since we are too short to be men, we must be boys. Everyone else at the rodeo are girls.

We decide to play it straight, so to speak. We make up boys' names for each other. Since Wendy has missed the episode with Susan at the gate, I slap her on the shoulder to demonstrate. "This is what he did." Slam. She never missed a step. It didn't feel bad to me at all. We laugh uneasily. We have achieved the status of fourteen year old boys, what a disguise for travelling through the world. I split into two pieces for the rest of the evening, and have never decided if it is worse to be 31 years old and called a boy or to be 31 years old and called a girl.

Irregardless, we are starved so we decide to eat, and here we have the status of boys for real. It seems to us that all the men and all the women attached to the men and most of the children are eating steak dinner plates; and we are the only women not attached to men. We eat hot dogs, which cost one tenth as much. A man who has taken a woman to the rodeo on this particular day has to have at least $12.00 to spend. So he has charge of all of her money and some of our money too, for we average $3.00 apiece and have taken each other to the rodeo.

Hot dogs in hand we escort ourselves to the wooden stands, and first is the standing up ceremony. We are pledging allegiance for the way of life—the competition, the supposed masculinity and pretty girls. I stand up, cursing, pretending I'm in some other country. One which has not been rediscovered. The loudspeaker plays Anchors Aweigh, that's what I like about rodeos, always something unexpected. At the last one I attended in another state the men on horses threw candy and nuts to the kids, chipping their teeth and breaking their noses. Who is it, I wonder, that has put these guys in charge. Even quiet mothers raged over that episode.

Now it is time for the rodeo queen contest, and a display of four very young women on horses. They are judged for queen 30% on their horsemanship and 70% on the number of queen tickets which people bought on their behalf to 'elect' them. Talk about stuffed ballot boxes. I notice the winner as usual is the one on the registered thoroughbred whose daddy owns tracts and tracts of something—lumber, minerals, animals. His family name is all over the county.

The last loser sits well on a scrubby little pony and lives with her aunt and uncle. I pick her for the dyke even though it is speculation without clues. I can't help it, it's a pleasant habit. I wish I could give her a ribbon. Not for being a dyke, but for sitting on her horse well. For believing there ever was a contest, for not being the daughter of anyone who owns thousands of acres of anything.

Now the loudspeaker announces the girls' barrel races, which is the only grown women's event. It goes first because it is not really a part of the rodeo, but more like a mildly athletic variation of a parade by women to introduce the real thing. Like us boys in the stand, the girls are simply bearing witness to someone else's act.

The voice is booming that barrel racing is a new, modern event, that these young women are the wives and daughters of cowboys, and barrel racing is a way for them to participate in their own right. How generous of these northern cowboys to have resurrected barrel racing for women and to have forgotten the hard roping and riding which women always used to do in rodeos when I was younger. Even though I was a town child, I heard thrilling rumors of the all-women's rodeo in Texas, including that the finest brahma bull rider in all of Texas was a forty year old woman who weighed a hundred pounds.

Indeed, my first lover's first lover was a big heavy woman who was normally slow as a cold python, but she was just hell when she got up on a horse. She could rope and tie a calf faster than any cowboy within 500 miles of Sweetwater, Texas. That's what the West Texas dykes said, and they never lied about anything as important to them as calf roping, or the differences between women and men. And what about that news story I had heard recently on the radio, about a bull rider who was eight months pregnant? The newsman just had apoplectic fits over her, but not me. I was proud of her. She makes me think of all of us who have had our insides so overly protected from jarring we cannot possibly get through childbirth without an anesthetic.

While I have been grumbling these thoughts to myself, three barrels have been set up in a big triangle on the field, and the women one by one have raced their horses around each one and back to start. The trick is to turn your horse as sharply as possible without overthrowing the barrel.

After this moderate display, the main bulk of the rodeo begins, with calf roping, bronco riding, bull riding. It's a very male show during which the men demonstrate their various abilities at immobilizing, cornering, maneuvering and conquering cattle of every age.

A rodeo is an interminable number of roped and tied calves, ridden and unridden broncoes. The repetition is broken by a few antics from the agile, necessary clown. His long legs nearly envelope the little jackass he is riding for the satire of it.

After a number of hours they produce an event I have never seen before—goat tying. This is for the girls eleven and twelve. They use one goat for fourteen participants. The goat is supposed to be held in place on a rope by a large man on horseback. Each girl rushes out in a long run half way across the field, grabs the animal, knocks it down, ties its legs together. Sometimes the man lets his horse drift so the goat pulls six or eight feet away from her, something no one would allow to happen in a male event. Many of the girls take over a full minute just to do their tying, and the fact that only one goat has been used makes everybody say, 'poor goat, poor goat,' and start laughing. This has become the real comedy event of the evening, and the purpose clearly is to show how badly girls do in the rodeo.

Only one has broken through this purpose to the other side. One small girl is not disheartened by the years of bad training, the ridiculous cross-field run, the laughing superior man on his horse, or the shape-shifting goat. She downs it in a beautiful flying tackle. This makes me whisper, as usual, 'that's the dyke', but for the rest of it we watch the girls look ludicrous, awkward, outclassed and totally dominated by the large handsome man on horse. In the stands we six boys drink beer in disgust, groan and hug our breasts, hold our heads and twist our faces at each other in embarrassment.

As the calf roping starts up again, we decide to use our disguises to walk around the grounds. Making our way around to the cowboy side of the arena, we pass the intricate mazes of rail where the stock is stored, to the chutes where they are loading the bull riders onto the bulls.

I wish to report that although we pass by dozens of men, and although we have pressed against wild horses and have climbed on rails overlooking thousands of pounds of angry animalflesh, though we touch ropes and halters, we are never once warned away, never told that this is not the proper place for us, that we had better get back for our own good, are not safe, etc., none of the dozens of warnings and threats we would have gotten if we had been recognized as thirty one year old girls instead of fourteen year old boys. It is a most interesting way to wander around the world for the day.

We examine everything closely. The brahma bulls are in the chutes, ready to be released into the ring. They are bulky, kindly looking creatures with rolling eyes; they resemble overgrown pigs. One of us whispers, "Aren't those the same kind of cattle that walk around all over the streets in India and never hurt anybody?"

Here in the chutes made exactly their size, they are converted into wild antagonistic beasts by means of a nasty belt around their loins, squeezed tight to mash their most tender testicles just before they are released into the ring. This torture is supplemented by a jolt of electricity from an electric cattle prod to make sure they come out bucking. So much for the rodeo as a great drama between man and nature.

A pale, nervous cowboy sits on the bull's back with one hand in a glove hooked under a strap around the bull's midsection. He gains points by using his spurs during the ride. He has to remain on top until the timing buzzer buzzes a few seconds after he and the bull plunge out of the gate. I had always considered it the most exciting event.

Around the fence sit many eager young men watching, helping, and getting in the way. We are easily accepted among them. How depressing this can be.

Out in the arena a dismounted cowboy reaches over and slaps his horse fiercely on the mouth because it has turned its head the wrong way.

I squat down peering through the rails where I see the neat, tight-fitting pants of two young men standing provocatively chest to chest.

"Don't you think Henry's a queer," one says with contempt.

"Hell, I *know* he's a queer," the other says. They hold an informal spitting contest for the punctuation. Meantime their eyes have brightened and their fronts are moving toward each other in their clean, smooth shirts. I realize they are flirting with each other, using Henry to bring up the dangerous subject of themselves. I am remembering all the gay cowboys I ever knew. This is one of the things I like about cowboys. They don't wear those beautiful pearl button shirts and tight levis for nothing.

As the events inside the arena subside, we walk down to a roped off pavillion where there is a dance. The band consists of one portly, bouncing enthusiastic man of middle age who is singing with great spirit into the microphone. The rest of the band are three grim, lean young men over fourteen. The drummer drums angrily, while jerking his head behind himself as though searching the air for someone who is already two hours late and had seriously promised to take him away from here. The two guitar players are sleepwalking from the feet up with their eyes so glassy you could read by them.

A redhaired man appears, surrounded by redhaired children who ask, "Are you drunk, Daddy?"

"No, I am not drunk," Daddy says.

"Can we have some money?"

"No," Daddy says, "I am not drunk enough to give you any money."

During a break in the music the redhaired man asks the bandleader where he got his band.

"Where did I get this band?" the bandleader puffs up, "I raised this band myself. These are all my sons—I raised this band myself." The redhaired man is so very impressed he is nearly bowing and kissing the hand of the bandleader, as they repeat this conversation two or three times. "This is *my* band," the bandleader says, and the two guitar players exchange grim and glassy looks.

Next the bandleader has announced "Okie From Muskogee", a song intended to portray the white country morality of cowboys. The crowd does not respond but he sings enthusiastically anyway. Two of his more alert sons drag themselves to the microphone to wail that they don't smoke marijuana in Muskogee—as those hippies down in San Francisco do, and they certainly don't. From the look of it they shoot hard drugs and pop pills.

In the middle of the song a very drunk thirteen year old boy has staggered up to Wendy, pounding her on the shoulder and exclaiming, "Can you dig it, brother?" Later she tells me she has never been called brother before, and she likes it. Her first real identification as one of the brothers, in the brotherhood of man.

We boys begin to walk back to our truck, past a cowboy vomiting on his own pretty boots, past another lying completely under a car. Near our truck, a young man has calf-roped a young woman. She shrieks for him to stop, hopping weakly along behind him. This is the first bid for public attention I have seen from any woman here since the barrel race. I understand that this little scene is a re-enactment of the true meaning of the rodeo, and of the conquest of the west. And oh how much I do not want to be her; I do not want to be the conquest of the west.

I am remembering how the clown always seems to be tall and riding on an ass, that must be a way of poking fun at the small and usually dark people who tried to raise sheep or goats or were sod farmers and rode burros instead of tall handsome blond horses, and who were driven under by the beef raisers. And so today we went to a display of cattle handling instead of a sheep shearing or a goat milking contest—or to go into even older ghost territory, a corn dance, or acorn gathering. . . .

As we reach the truck, the tall man passes with the rodeo queen, who must surely be his niece, or something. All this non-contest, if it is for anyone, must certainly be for him. As a boy, I look at him. He is his own spitting image, of what is manly and white and masterly, so tall in his high heels, so *well horsed*. His manner portrays his theory of life as the survival of the fittest against wild beasts, and all the mythical rest of us who are too female or dark, not straight, or much too native to the earth to now be trusted as more than witnesses, flags, cheerleaders and unwilling stock.

As he passes, we step out of the way and I am glad we are in our disguise. I hate to step out of his way as a full grown woman, one who hasn't enough class status to warrant his thinly polite chivalry. He has knocked me off the sidewalk of too many towns, too often.

Yet somewhere in me I know I have always wanted to be manly, what I mean is having that expression of courage, control, coordination, ability I associate with men. To *provide.*

But here I am in this truck, not a man at all, a fourteen year old boy only. Tomorrow is my thirty second birthday. We six snuggle together in the bed of this rickety truck which is our world for the time being. We are headed back to the bold and shakey adventures of our all-women's farm, our all-women's households and companies, our expanding minds, ambitions and bodies, we who are neither male nor female at this moment in the pageant world, who are not the rancher's wife, mother earth, Virgin Mary or the rodeo queen—we who are really the one who took her self seriously, who once took an all out dive at the goat believing that the odds were square and that she was truly in the contest.

And now that we know it is not a contest, just a play—we have run off with the goat ourselves to try another way of life.

Because I certainly do not want to be a 32 year old girl, or calf either, and I certainly also do always remember Gertrude Stein's[1] beautiful dykely voice saying, what is the use of being a boy if you grow up to be a man.

Study and Discussion Questions

1. Why does the man at the gate decide the women are boys?
2. What kind of freedom does being seen as 14-year-old boys give to these women in their thirties?
3. By providing a narrator who is an outsider to the scene, Grahn is able to penetrate the mystique of the rodeo. Discuss how this works in the section on the brahma bull riding.
4. Is Grahn only talking about the rodeo in this story or are there larger implications?

---

[1] (1874–1946), American experimental writer.

5. Why does the narrator award the word *dyke* to one of the losers of the queen contest and to the one girl who takes the goat-tying event seriously?
6. What is the tone of "Boys at the Rodeo"?

Writing Exercises

1. What does Grahn suggest about the rodeo as a male ritual?
2. If these six women had been seen as "girls," what would their day at the rodeo have been like?
3. Discuss the depiction of the goat-tying event as an example of social criticism.

TESS SLESINGER   (1905–1945)

Tess Slesinger was born in New York City and educated at the Ethical Culture Society School, Swarthmore College, and Columbia University. She worked for a while in her twenties with a group of leftist Jewish intellectuals that published the Menorah Journal *and in 1935 she went to Hollywood to work as a screenwriter. With her husband, Frank Davis, she worked on* The Good Earth *(1937),* Dance, Girl, Dance *(1940),* A Tree Grows in Brooklyn *(1945), and other films, and she was active in the Screen Writers Guild. Slesinger published a novel,* The Unpossessed, *in 1934 and a collection of stories,* Time: The Present, *in 1935.*

Mother to Dinner   (1929)

Katherine Benjamin, who had been Katherine Jastrow for something less than a year, said Goodafternoon to the groceryman and, stooping to the counter, gathered two large and unwieldy packages close to her body, balancing one elbow on her hip so that the hand, crawling to the top, could hold sternly separate the bottle of milk from the package of Best Eggs. The thin, one-eyed errand boy who sprawled on an empty packing-box near the door leaped to his feet and opened it with a flourish and a "hot, isn't it?" And sliding past him, curving her body to make a nest for the projecting bundle, she heard the screen door swing lightly closed behind her, flutter against the wood frame in a series of gently diminishing taps.

Why did one say Goodafternoon instead of Goodbye to tradesmen and teachers, she wondered, following her packages as they bobbed evenly down the street before her, recalling (as she adjusted her gait to her

burden) countless times when she had waited, in middies and broad sailor
hats, for her mother's comforting "Good*morning*, Mr Schmidt," and Mr
Schmidt's answering "*Good*morning, Mrs Benjamin, *good*morning I'm sure."
And now Katherine, no longer in middies or accompanied by her mother
but modestly wearing a ring on her left hand, heard herself kindly bidding
Mr Papenmeyer Goodafternoon, and feeling, as she said it, very close to
her mother, feeling almost, as she nodded firmly to him, that she was
her mother. (Gerald predicted with scorn that it would not be long before
Katherine would speak of Mr Papenmeyer as "my Mr Papenmeyer" and
he suspected that she would even add, in time, "he never disappoints";
but she was not to suppose, he said, that he would glance benignly over
his *Saturday Evening Post* as her father did, and listen.)

Katherine hugged her packages like babies; in them lay, wrapped in
glossy wax paper, in brown paper bags, in patent boxes, the dinner to
which Katherine's mother and father were coming as guests . . . The
dinner over which Katherine would frown at Gerald politely insulting Mrs
Benjamin; over which Mr Benjamin would cough and insist on the worst
cuts of everything . . . She hoped nervously that Gerald would not be
insolent and argumentative, that her mother would not be stupid. . . .
She must protect them both . . . And she began to dread the strangeness
which always oppressed her on beholding her mother in a house which
was her home and not her mother's. . . . Ridiculous, she said brightly,
I'm not going to let *that* happen again . . .

The spire of the church on the corner raised itself in the form of a
huge salt-shaker against the mild, colorless sky. The sun, a blurred yellow
lamp, glimmered palely behind veils of soiled cloud; it might rain, for
the air was sodden, the leaves on the tree before the church hovered on
the air with a peculiar waiting indifference, like dead fish turned over on
their backs and floating in still water.

And for years to come she, "Mrs Gerald Jastrow," would walk, heavily
laden with her thoughts and her packages, in Fall, in Winter, and in
Spring, from Mr Papenmeyer's meat-and-grocery store through these same
streets, past the church with its salt-shaker spire, past the row of low
brick houses, past the tall india-rubber apartment with the liveried doorman
shuffling his feet under the awning, stretched like a hollow wrinkled
caterpillar to the curb, to her own home, which she shared with Gerald,
of whom she had never heard two years before . . .

Katherine's fingers, tapping the sagging bundles, reviewed their contents.
Meat—Mr Papenmeyer's recommended cut for four—bread, milk, corn,
tomatoes—without her asking, the clerk had passionately assured her they
were firm—two large packages it amounted to, one small slippery one
under her elbow, and her purse. By a minute flexing of her left hand she
could feel the key tucked neatly in her glove to save her trouble when
she reached her door. An absurd ritual, that, said Gerald; one which in
the sum total could not save her much trouble. You've picked up all these

damn habits, he said, from your mother: they're a waste of time, they take more time to remember than simply to leave out; be careful, Katherine, before you know it you will be keeping a platinum-framed marketlist. But these little rituals made doing the things fun, Katherine argued; when she remembered, at the grocer's before picking up her packages, to tuck the key in her glove, a horde of vague recollections, almost recollections of recollections, unravelled pleasantly in her mind. They gave meaning to what would otherwise be just marketing; they formed a link not only with yesterday and tomorrow, but with other women squinting at scales and selecting dinners for strange men to whom they found themselves married; with, if you like, her mother, who had been doing these things every day for thirty years. You may say pooh Gerald, she said, but there are many things which you, who are after all a man, cannot be expected to know; why two years ago you didn't even know *me* . . .

Were the flat faces she had left haggling over green peas and punching cantaloupes aware of the waiting uncertainties, the uprooting, the transplanting, the bleeding, involved in their calmly leaving their homes to go to live with strangers? Strangers—husbands—Gerald A. Jastrow—I met a boy named Gerald A. Jastrow at a party, he asked to take me home—I am sorry, I am seeing a boy named Gerald Jastrow, he has a cowlick which trembles when he argues—but mother I am seeing Gerald tonight—Gerald says, Gerald thinks—I am going to be married—his name? (*whose* name?—oh, the Stranger's)—his name is Jastrow, Gerald Jastrow—I've been married for eleven months—my husband's name is Gerald Jastrow, no I don't know him, he's a Stranger to me, but I put away his male-smelling underwear. . . . Katherine reached the sidewalk just in time to avoid a cab which sped down the street in front of her house.

She smiled brightly at the elevator man, an expert, busy, kindly smile; she felt again like her mother. "Wouldn't be surprised if a storm blew up," Albert said to her shrewdly, resting his hand in a friendly way on the lever. (A storm, she didn't want a storm, Katherine thought, suddenly frightened; Gerald might say what he liked about the risk of motoring being greater than that of flying, and the chance of being murdered in sleep greater than that of being struck by lightning: she *wouldn't* fly, and she cowered before thunder and lightning.) "Oh do you think so?" said Mrs Gerald Jastrow, and she looked in awe at the elevator man, as if it was all in his hands whether a storm came or not. "Oh I hope not," she pleaded. The elevator stopped on a level with her floor, her door was before her, familiar, with its arty streaks, its brass knob and keyhole, the number 21 in black painted letters. Albert, slamming the door of his cage, determined to go the whole hog. "Well I wouldn't be surprised," he said, and dropped suddenly out of sight.

Katherine could not bear to drop a single one of her burdens, now that she had come so far; she made a series of supreme efforts, balancing, juggling, squirming, forcing her key out of her glove with fractional, inchworm motions, still carefully separating the bottle of milk from the package of Best Eggs, evoking a new muscle to keep the small package from slipping.

And then she was in, in her own house, with the door shut behind her, and the yellow curtains dancing on the window panes, the stove standing, homely and patient, in the small kitchen, the chairs sitting in friendly fashion, as if themselves guests at a tea-party, just as she had left them . . .

Suddenly she was overcome by a swift engulfing depression. She stood at the door of the yellow room and was unable to put down the packages in her arms. The air in the room stood hot and heavy, waiting, like Albert, with melancholy assurance, for storm; the curtains flapped treacherously.

What nonsense, she said crisply, amazingly comforted by a slant of faint sunlight which quivered through the gloom. Look, she said, it is my own house . . . Reassured, she dropped her packages on the kitchen table. But someone should be there to greet her, she felt, to rise from one of those friendly chairs and say to her: What did you buy? How was Mr Papenmeyer the butcher? Was the one-eyed errand boy there today? Come in, take off your hat and gloves, I am glad you are home . . . A year ago she would have stood at the door and shouted *Moth-er*, where *are* you? And if Mrs Benjamin had not come in haste at her call, a white-aproned German maid (Mrs Benjamin chaperoned their love-affairs so successfully that they generally stayed with her for years, like obedient nuns) would have come and said, Oh Miss Katy, your mother said to tell you she went over to your Aunt Sarah, your uncle's not feeling just right.

But she would call *up* her mother, she thought gleefully, running to the telephone: He*llo*, mother, what do you think I bought for supper? The butcher said . . . Do you think there will be a storm, mother? . . . As she lifted the receiver from its hook she thought she heard faint steps behind her; Gerald, she thought in a flash, and slid the receiver back to its place. Of course it wasn't Gerald, at four o'clock in the afternoon, of course it wasn't anybody; but suppose he had come upon her telephoning her mother: she could hear him say, as he had said last Sunday, catching her at the telephone (and of course one thought of one's mother on a long Sunday), Oh for God's sake, Katherine, like a two-year-old baby you are always running home to mother . . . Cut off from her mother. Yet Gerald was right, she mustn't, she mustn't.

Loneliness surrounded Katherine like a high black fence. Then why not call up Gerald, why not rush to the telephone and call Gerald at his office (where she could never visualize him); if only she could call him up and say to him: I have just come home to our house. It is pleasant and cool, the curtains are still yellow. I shall take off my dress and read. Then I shall cook dinner, for you, for me, for my father and mother— you haven't forgotten they are coming? you'll come early?—*Gerald, what are you doing?* But she knew his firm "Jastrow speaking," and she could guess, if she dared to go beyond it, at his business-like: "What do you *want*, dear?" Well, what *did* she want, she wondered impatiently, and strained to discover whether that was thunder or furniture moving.

Probably Gerald was right, she thought wearily—for he was so often "right" in a logical, meaningless way—that thinking about every small thing, attaching significances to every moment, wishing to communicate every small thought, was, besides being sentimental, "an imbecilic waste of time." Gerald railed against sentimentality, and, charmingly, disarmingly, gave way to it at moments. When the moment passed Gerald shed it like a wet bathing suit, and emerged cool and casual, forgetful and untouched. But with her mother, these moments grew into comfortable hours, never forgotten, linking one with another, remaining always, a steady undercurrent, ready to rise and fill them at the lightest touch.

And sliding the bread into the shining modern breadbox she felt a strong nostalgia for the wornout tin that had stood for years on her mother's shelf. This cold affair of shelves and sliding doors, glittering knobs and antiseptic lettering suggested too much newness, too little use and familiarity; her mother's loomed in contrast, a symbol of security, almost a refuge from storm. And yet Mrs Benjamin, with the vision of that old, battered, loyal thing in the back of her mind, had come with Katherine graciously, gayly even, to buy this tawdry substitute. (My little girl, she had said to the clerk, smiling ironically at him and drawing him into her sympathy, would like that Modern Breadbox. It was as if she had said, My little girl has tired of her old mother, she wants the latest thing in young men, one that can scientifically explain away the fear of lightning.) Feeling warmly bound to her mother, she caught herself opening and slamming the little door a second, unnecessary time, an old nervous habit of her mother's. For a moment she felt purified, intensely loyal, as if by this gesture she had renounced the new for the old. She walked from the kitchen with her mother's tired, elastic step, the step of a stout woman who has shopped all day, whose weary body will neither submit to rest nor ignore the stern orders of fashion. It was a step singularly unsuited to Katherine's slimness, but it was comfortable now, familiar; she slid gratefully into it, like one falling into a cushioned rocker which is too large for the body but provides, nevertheless, a warm and comfortable harbor. And so she bent her body back from the waist and became her mother, balancing her stout body, carrying the heaviest part bravely before her. (Your mother navigates like a boat, Gerald had said to her once. Katherine, ruefully succumbing to the justice of the description, had come starkly awake on the edge of falling asleep that night, and cried bitterly, not because Gerald, whom she hated for sleeping soundly beside her, had said it, but because she had laughed.)

Oh of course Gerald was "right," she told herself. And yet, this coming home eagerly, her arms aching with pleasant weights, delighting in facing those yellow curtains again, with no one to greet her, and unable to telephone because what she had to say to her husband was irrelevant— her mother wouldn't like it, she felt. But between two people who lived together, why should anything be irrelevant? nothing she could ever say, she knew, would be irrelevant to her mother: how eagerly Mrs Benjamin had awaited reports of adventures no more important than a shopping expedition, a subway jam, a lunch engagement. (Oh but that had been stupid, stupid—inadequate. You told your mother insignificant things because you knew she wouldn't understand the important ones. Gerald's words: but true, true.) But Gerald himself had so *little* concern for the small things she did all day that she refrained from telling him anecdotes which she passionately feared might bore him, but which, nevertheless, she collected like bouquets of precious flowers to lay before him if she dared. Looking about the empty room, Gerald's desk standing solidly in one corner reproved her; she became irritated that her mind flew so often to thoughts of her mother. . . .

Like a human shuttle she wove her way between these two, between Gerald and her mother, the two opposites who supported her web. (Why couldn't they both leave her alone?) When she was with her mother she could not rest, for she thought continually of the beacon of Gerald's intelligence, which must be protected from her mother's sullying incomprehension. And when she was with Gerald her heart ached for her deserted mother, she longed for her large enveloping sympathy in which to hide away from Gerald's too-clear gaze. From sheer hopelessness and irritation, tears filled her eyes. . . .

She was glad to escape from the kitchen, for she had begun to hate Mr Papenmeyer's excellent foods, which would merge artfully and serve as the camouflage of a family battle. As long as the dinner lasted, she knew the conversation could be kept meager and on a safely mediocre level. But Katherine, sitting between her mother and father, and eyeing her husband with apprehension, would know that around her own table, consuming food she herself had prepared, a victim would be fattened for slaughter, a victor strengthened for battle. And whoever won, Katherine lost . . . Oh come, she told herself, exasperated, this isn't the Last Supper . . .

But that wasn't furniture moving, she told herself grimly, crouching on the window-sill and regarding the street which was lying quietly in its place before her house—not twice, she said, that's Albert's thunder. It rumbled from a great distance, as though it were in hiding.

Certainly, she thought, her mind returning, like a dog worrying a bone, she lived with Gerald on a higher plane—if her misery was sometimes more acute, her pleasure, in proportion, was more poignant. While they had felt nothing deeply, Katherine and her mother, as they had built up, over teatables, simple patterns of thought, simplified ways of looking at things. What if Katherine had had to stoop her mind so that they might stay together? at least they could talk, at least they kept each other company. (Gerald said their talk was no more than gossip; he said that Katherine and her mother had shut themselves up in a hot-house, talking and comforting each other for griefs that could never come to them while they remained in their lethargic half-life.) But in a world like this, thought Katherine, where thunder-storms can creep on one ruthlessly, why shouldn't two people who love each other hide away and give one another comfort?

Thunder rumbled more constantly now. Katherine, suspicious of it, in spite of its distance, detected in its muffled rolling a growing concentration, as if it were slowly gathering its strength, as if it were winding itself up for a tremendous spring. Should she telephone Gerald?—*no.*

The thought of Gerald frightened her. He led such a curious existence apart from her every day from nine till six. Katherine and her mother had always known exactly what the other was doing, at almost every hour in the day. It was a comfort to stop suddenly, look at one's watch, and think "Mother's at the dentist's now" or "I should think mother would be on the way home now." But there were times when Gerald was in the room with her, sitting beside her, lying beside her in bed, when she didn't know exactly where he was. . . .

Gerald said—and with some justice, she admitted to herself—that she and her mother had lived like two spoiled wives in a harem kept by a simple old gentleman who demanded nothing of them beyond their presence and the privilege of supporting them. But because of his docility one could not take seriously a possible injustice to him. Beside his work downtown, Mr Benjamin mailed their letters, called for their purchases, or did any of the little errands which they had spent the day in pleasantly avoiding. If he entered the room where Katherine and her mother were talking, it had seemed quite natural for Mrs Benjamin to say, "Dear, we are talking"; it seemed natural because of the peaceful expression with which Mr Benjamin picked up his *Saturday Evening Post* on the way out of the room. All Katherine's uncles were disposed of in the same way by her aunts.

Gerald referred to the Benjamin men as "poor devils," as "emasculated boobs". You resent me, he said to Katherine, because you have a pre-conceived idea of the role to which all husbands are relegated by their wives; you'd like to laugh me out of any important existence. (Indeed, it was only at moments when he was away and when she was performing, in his absence, some intimate service for him, that she could look upon Gerald as her mother looked upon her father; with ease, with possession, with a maternal tolerance touched by affectionate irony. Here were things of which she could be certain: that he rolled his underwear into a ball and dropped it on the floor, that he left his shoes to lie where they fell, that he draped yesterday's tie around the back of a chair. But she could never achieve this intimacy in his presence: when Gerald was with her, when she *thought* about Gerald, it faded; there was more strangeness.) Gerald again! She was aware of a wish to sink Gerald into the bottom of her mind: she was too much aware of him; when she read, when she visited, when she noticed things, it was always with the desire to report back to Gerald: nothing was complete until Gerald had been told.

She and her mother had discussed and reported everything. But she could no longer be alone with her mother, for it seemed as though Gerald sat in taunting effigy between them, forcing Katherine for her mother's sake to deprecate him, for his sake to protect him, from obscurity, from misrepresentation, from neglect . . .

His presence, even now, while she was alone, sat heavily, reproachfully, in the empty rooms, forbidding her to call him up, forbidding her to recall comfortably past days she had spent with her mother. This was not living, Gerald said, to spend one's hours in introspective analysis, to brood over the past. Katherine's flights he called "a worthless luxury, like the visits of the rich to Palm Beach or Paris." But it was living, Katherine knew unhappily; she was living most acutely.

The room darkened suddenly. Something of the tension which would be upon her later, as it always was when her mother and Gerald were in the same room, came upon her now, as she sat straining for the sound of thunder, watching shades of gloom silently lay themselves in the hot room. Katherine held her breath waiting for thunder, for rain, anything. Voices of children floated reassuringly up from the street, and in a moment the sunlight reappeared, tentative, tempting one to believe in it for all its faintness. The thunder sounded like the chopping of wood in a far-off field. Katherine longed for her mother. She wished she were not so near the heart of the storm.

She hated herself for thinking of her mother. But not to think of her demanded a complete uprooting, demanded a final shoving off from a safe dock into unknown waters. Besides, she felt guilty toward her mother, she brooded over her as one does over a victim, pitying him, resenting him and utterly unable to forget him.

For against her mother Katherine felt that she had committed a crime. She had abandoned that elderly lady for a young man who, from her mother's point of view, had been merely one of several who had taken her to dances, to dinner, who had kissed her in the parlor, with whom finally, inexplicably, she had come to have more dates than with any other. She had abandoned her mother, left her sitting at home with no more evening gowns to "take in", no one to sit up for, no young men to laugh about in the bathroom at four o'clock in the morning when Katherine came home. She had left her to sit opposite an old man at dinner every evening, she had imposed upon her the tragedy of being a guest in her own daughter's house; she had reduced her to a stranger.

But a little bit her mother had the advantage. She had seen Gerald, after all, in the absurd rig of tuxedo and stiff shirt, calling upon her daughter with flowers, with books, leaping to his feet when she (Mrs Benjamin) entered the room. She had watched Gerald for a year politely talking parlor politics with Katherine's father, posturing ridiculously when he held Katherine's coat, becoming perforce friendly with the elevator boys in the Benjamin apartment, slinking shamefacedly before a doorman who had seen him too often. Nothing, Katherine reflected, could be more unreal, more unconvincing, than a young man in the act of courting. She could never forgive Gerald for having let her mother observe him in that role. (Equally she could never forgive her mother, blameless as she was, for having seen him.) Her mother could never take seriously, surely, a marriage which had grown from love-making in taxi-cabs which had been reported to her with amusement by Katherine, brushing her teeth in the bathroom. She had not shared with her mother the tortuous transition which had left her no longer an amused observer, but a helpless, suffering participant. All the indication Mrs Benjamin had had of Katherine's growing need of Gerald was a burst of hysteria and a state of nervous irritability which had succeeded the usual calm of Katherine's disposition—before suddenly one evening, preparing her charity report in a black lace dress, she was confronted by two embarrassed young people who declared their ridiculous intention to marry.

This, Katherine felt, she should have spared her mother. She should not have caused her, so heartbreakingly, to drop her charity report on the marble table and to look suddenly at her daughter with reproachful eyes, saying, half-humorously, What, daughter, tired of your old mother already?

She had left her parents for no reason, they had given her no cause to leave them, she had left them for no better reason than that when Gerald said to her that he would never again ask her to marry him, she had been seized with panic lest he meant it.

Gerald, who two years before had not existed. Whereas her father and mother had fed her porridge, given her blackboards, measured her growth against a door, for a long period of twenty years during which Gerald had never heard of her. She was unsafe, she cried internally. She was living with a stranger in a strange land where storms evolved closely about one. She was living with a stranger who had no knowledge of the first twenty years of her life, the major portion of her life. She was living in a strange land where her childhood had no existence. It was unreal, it was unsafe, it was terrifying. Gerald liked to hear her tell stories of her childhood; but it was as if, when she told him little things she remembered, she and he were together contemplating the childhood of a stranger. She held tightly to the arms of her chair, but the slippery wood was repelling. Suddenly everything was reduced to an absurdity. It was, to Gerald, as though she had not begun to exist until he had noticed her two years before, at a party, and asked to take her home; but suppose she had not come to the party—she had come only out of boredom; or suppose, to make it more ridiculous, she had not worn the particular blue dress which had caught Gerald's eye? and he hadn't asked to take her home? Their life together seemed no more than the result of a series of insignificant accidents. Could it be real? Could she share the rest of her life with a stranger whose eye had casually fallen on a blue dress? With someone who had known her for only two years out of her twenty-two?

Katherine felt herself to be struggling somewhere in the middle, between two harbors, unable to decide whether to swim backward or forward, tempted almost to close her eyes and quietly drown where she was. Shuttle, shuttle, she murmured to herself, miserably, exasperated at her weakness, her helplessness.

Smoking in the yellow room, she waited with unhappy certainty for Albert's storm which would surely come now. The air was oppressive, sullenly pregnant. It was as if an evil thing crouched in the room, waiting for birth. Dark was gathering in shades, permitting still a faint yellowish gloom. Wind was dead. Katherine, fearing and hating the coming storm, nevertheless feared and hated the moments of waiting even more. A clock on the mantel slowly ticked off the moments she would have to wait; it was in league with the coming storm. Her body was chill in the midst of heat.

She was weary already with the nervous effort she would make to bring Gerald and her mother close to each other, with her own struggle to remain equally close to both of them, simultaneous with her desperate attempt to conceal from each the affection she felt for the other. Gerald and her mother sitting and eating in this room, which now was the home of the storm, would be a cat and mouse, quietly stalking each other under cover. (Was this true? or did their struggle for supremacy take place merely in her own mind? Because she must know, she must know.) Katherine would twist herself this way and that to keep the evening characterless and blessedly dull, rather than immerse them all in the horror of an argument, in which their superficial sides would represent symbolically their eternal, fundamental resentment. Katherine must take no sides, Katherine must flit nervously from one side to the other, breaching gaps with hysterical giggles, throwing herself into outbursts of hysterical affection, making a clown of herself in order to distract these two who fought silently for her. She was loathsome to herself.

Her mind struggled with a remote memory. Something—perhaps the slumbering quality of the air which sheltered the coming storm so that its pent-up evil would suddenly roll forth and smother the world—reminded her of a thing which seemed to have happened when she was a child. Frowning, she gazed into herself to recall. And it came back to her. She had cried one day for her mother and they had told her that Mrs Benjamin had gone to Atlantic City for two days and that this young lady would take care of Katherine while her mother was away. Katherine kicked and screamed, but Miss Anna proved so entertaining—she showed her how to make a whole family of paper dolls live through a day's work and play—that she forgot her mother and was surprised to hear the next day that she would be home in an hour. Suddenly she hated Miss Anna, and when Mrs Benjamin came home she found her daughter crying angrily, Miss Anna bewildered, murmuring, But she seemed so happy, she seemed perfectly happy. . . I was not happy for a minute, Katherine screamed, I was waiting the whole time for my mother to come back.

Enraged with herself, she wondered whether she retained somewhere the idea that because her life had begun with her mother, it would end with her, whether some childish part of her could not accept their parting as final and looked upon her life with Gerald as no more than an interlude. Oh Gerald, Gerald, she sobbed, I am worse than unfaithful to you . . . I hate my mother, she is a venomous old woman who tries to keep me from you. . . . The injustice to her mother overwhelmed her. She hated herself. She felt like the child of divorced parents, driven from one to the other and unable with either to make a home.

I have been married during every month except June, she thought, lifting her head and quietly looking, as if to remember, about the room. She was comforted by Gerald's desk, which had been with her during eleven months. Thunder, blasting the earth in a distant place, filled the room. She had been married for eleven months and had never told her mother anything but housekeeping troubles. Why? A second roll of thunder sounded.

She was surrounded, she could not escape. She was suspended, she could take refuge with neither Gerald nor her mother, she was caught fairly by the thunder . . .

Deception had begun with her engagement. One had to keep one's eyes constantly glowing, however terrifiedly they looked at the approaching cliff, one's words constantly gay and effervescent, lest one's mother look searchingly at the prospective bride and say, But are you sure, Darling, absolutely *sure*? Of course one was not sure. One was suspended, even as now, with thunders rolling in from all sides. (I ought to start the dinner, I ought to start the dinner: I *can't*, I can't.)

During a wedding trip one was awakened to innumerable things, most of them delightful, all of them terrifying. A longing had filled Katherine intermittently to be back from this trip of surprises: she pictured herself talking to her mother all day for many days, sharing with her, not details, but the contemplation, of intimacies. It seemed to her the most delicious part of the trip, that she would return and talk about it to her mother. Gerald's jealous allusions to her mother she had accepted with a tolerant smile; his analyses—for it was then that he had violently expounded his harem theory—meant nothing to her, they seemed to have no connection with reality. "Dearest mother," she had written, "all the things I have to tell you! I can hardly wait to see you . . . So many things have happened. And of course, Gerald being a man . . ." (Was that lightning, or was it the mere lifting of the curtain by the wind? The dinner, the dinner was waiting to be cooked: I won't *touch* it.)

The awful farce at the station, where Mr and Mrs Benjamin had come to meet them, came to her vividly now. Mr Benjamin, having screwed his courage to the point of making Katherine remember his presence long enough to kiss him, retiring to help Gerald, competently wasting time with the luggage in the background, mother and daughter swaying in a series of embraces—Katherine was suddenly lost, locked, imprisoned, in the body of a stout, fashionable stranger. Why doesn't she look at me? she thought, all she wants is to hold me, to squeeze me, to choke me to death, it never occurs to her to look in my face. Sweeping her daughter to one side, Mrs Benjamin sprang forth to smother Gerald. She had no right to, cried Katherine wildly to herself, as she turned from her father's vague embrace, and all the things which Gerald had said of her mother came back to her and they seemed true. And at the same time she felt passionately that Mrs Benjamin must not expose herself to Gerald's unsympathetic eye; horrible embarrassment arose in her, when, thank God, she saw that Mrs Benjamin in her eagerness had missed her aim; her kiss floated on past Gerald's clean indifferent cheek—he at least was unsullied, and at the same time her mother was protected from nakedness. Mrs Benjamin, discarding Gerald, threw her arms around Katherine once more, with force and meaning, and kissed her in great wet gulps. "Katherine, Katherine," she sobbed, rocking her great body from side to side, "I've got you again, darling. Let's leave all these men and go off together, darling." Katherine felt fastidious, she drew her body back delicately from the impact of her mother's.

Mrs Benjamin shook off the two men, she carried Katherine off to a tea-room—their old favorite tea-room—for lunch, a confidential lunch it was supposed to be, but Katherine had grown to hate tea-rooms, a month with Gerald had taught her to hate shrimp salad . . . Mrs Benjamin, suddenly squeezing her hand under the candle-lit table, looked into her eyes, her own eyes fatuous, confident, worried and questioning, "Katherine, darling Katherine, now tell me the 'many things' you wrote about." Katherine, looking into her mother's avid eyes, knew that she could never tell her anything again.

How horribly she must have hurt her, thought Katherine, gravely hurt herself at the recollection. In bed beside Gerald that night she had lain, trying to make the night go faster, so that she might see her mother and change what she had done. She thought of her mother lying sleepless, even as she was, beside a sleeping husband, thinking, bitterly thinking, of the thing that had happened between them. But Katherine could never undo the thing that was between them, for it was Gerald who stood between her mother and herself, just as her mother stood between herself and Gerald.

Well, *was* Albert's storm coming or wasn't it, she thought impatiently, and beat out her cigarette on the window-sill, dropped the dead stub and watched it hurtle past awnings and window-boxes and land haphazardly in the gutter. (And what about the dinner?)

A clap of thunder brought her trembling to her feet. It had traveled with treacherous silence from a great distance to burst like a shell in her ear. And now lightning quivered across the pewter sky in a blinding streak. Katherine, trembling, holding to the mantel, felt all the elements of storm gathering closely about her. The intense heat and stillness in the room vibrated with suppressed force. She had a sense of something evil, something unhealthy, waiting beneath the table to be born. The room was alive, awake, crouching before the storm, waiting in every sense for its approach.

She laughed aloud, nervously, when the thunder sounded next, meek and far-off; it rumbled for a few seconds, then it rolled toward her with increasing force until something cut it off sharply in the height of its passion. The storm was playing with her; it was here, but it played at hiding, it retreated and advanced so that she could never be sure of it.

What was she to do, what was she to do? Should she, could she telephone?—*no.*

Thunder shook the house. Malicious streaks of lightning drew themselves across the sky, lighting up the gloom until the day shone for a second like steel. Suddenly night came. Winds came alive and tore drunkenly down the street. Another long reverberating crash of thunder, incredibly near and ear-splitting. There was a moment of suspension, while only the wind moved. And then the sky retched and large cold drops of rain like stones pelted the windowpanes . . .

Panic seized Katherine. She rushed to the window to escape. She was afraid of the room. It rocked with unhappy speculation. She stood at the window facing in, and saw how the storm was fed from within her room. The lightning lit it like quick fire, the thunder sounded in it long after it had died outside.

The thunder bounced about the room, striking at corners, rolling over furniture, shaking the walls, groveling derisively at her feet.

It seemed to her that before the next clap of thunder she must have reached a decision or she would die. But what decision, she cried, striking her fist against the window? What decision? about what? The problem was obscure. (She imagined her mother struck by lightning, her stout body collapsing with dignity under a tree, she heard herself telling Gerald with triumph as an overtone to her grief, My mother is dead, I have only you now.) And if the problem was obscure, how much more obscure the solution. (She imagined Gerald struck by lightning, a look of hurt surprise in his eyes as he fell beneath a tree, murmuring something about scientific chance, she heard herself telling her mother, strange relief mingling with her sorrow, Gerald is gone, mother, I shall have to come back to you.) And the next thunder rolled down a hill, louder and louder, faster and nearer, and fell to the bottom, bursting into cannon balls, exploding with insane crashes, and in a thousand voices splitting the earth in its center. Katherine burst into passionate tears.

Now everything was the storm. The storm, which had circled about the room, wished for closer nucleus, and entered her body. The lightning pierced her stomach, the thunder shook her limbs, and retreated, growling, to its home in her bowels. There was no escape for her; she was no longer imprisoned in the storm: the storm was imprisoned in her.

She stood in a shaking lethargy, she had no will, no feeling. She was frozen; she was a shell in which storm raged without her will. All the world had entered the room . . .

It came to her slowly that there was a new sound in the air, a sharp metallic ring that repeated itself at intervals. She had no idea how long she might have been hearing it in the back of her head before she took notice of it. Now it rang again, sharply, there seemed to be fright in it, or anger, she could not tell which. On stiff legs she ran down the hall toward the door, by reflex knowing that it was the doorbell which had sounded. But with her hand on the knob something held her back. She could not force herself to turn the knob, to move her hand, even to call out, Wait, wait . . .

Was it her mother, or was it Gerald? Which, in the midst of storm, did she want it to be? It seemed to her that she could not open the door until she knew. A great ball of thunder followed her out of the room she had left, hurtled down the hall and broke beside her, and in the midst of it the terrified bell rang repeatedly, in small staccato notes, shrilling through the depth of the thunder, prodding . . .

She did not know. She knew only, as she closed her eyes and slowly turned the handle of the door, and drew it in toward herself, that she wished that one of them, Gerald or her mother, were dead.

Study and Discussion Questions

1. Why does Katherine miss her mother so much? Why does she take such pleasure in small rituals (like tucking her house key in her glove) that she learned from her mother? Why does Katherine's husband Gerald find these rituals so annoying?

2. What does Gerald expect of a wife? Why does Katherine have so much trouble filling this role? Why does she refer to him as "Gerald, of whom she had never heard two years before"? Why does she feel most intimate with him "in his absence"?

3. From whose point of view does Slesinger tell Katherine's story? How does this choice strengthen and how does it limit our understanding of Katherine's predicament?

4. As Katherine began walking home from the grocer's, she "hugged her packages like babies"; later, while she was thinking about Gerald and her mother, the leaves on a tree seemed to her like "dead fish turned over on their backs and floating in still water." What do these images reveal about Katherine's state of mind? Can you find other significant images in the story?

5. Why does Slesinger introduce a thunderstorm into the story? What is its function? Is it effective?

Writing Exercises

1. Who is most to blame for Katherine's troubles? Her mother? Her husband? Her weak father? Katherine herself?

2. How would Gerald react if he read this story, this record of his wife's thoughts? Try expressing in writing the flow of *his* thoughts, as Slesinger does with Katherine's.

3. Is Katherine's problem just a personal problem? Is she simply married to the wrong person? Does she suffer from arrested development, from a neurotic attachment to her mother and an inability to develop a healthy relationship with her husband?

4. Katherine, at one point, describes women who marry as "leaving their homes to go live with strangers." To what extent do you agree with this description? Is it equally true for men who marry?

5. Katherine comes from a wealthy family and seems to have married quite comfortably. How would her predicament be different if financially she were less well off?

6. "Mother to Dinner" was written in 1929. How true does it seem today? Are men's and women's worlds so different now as they seem then?

7. Imagine you are Katherine. Write a letter to Gerald, explaining why you have left him.

WAKAKO YAMAUCHI (b. 1924)

Wakako Yamauchi was born in Westmoreland, California, where her parents, Japanese immigrants, worked as farmers. During World War II, along with over 100,000 other Japanese-Americans, she and her family were sent to an internment camp. Since then, Yamauchi has worked as a free-lance writer, and her stories have appeared in a number of anthologies. Her adaption as a play of "And the Soul Shall Dance" has been performed on public television.

And the Soul Shall Dance   (1974)

It's all right to talk about it now. Most of the principals are dead, except, of course, me and my younger brother, and possibly Kiyoko Oka, who might be near forty-five now, because, yes, I'm sure of it, she was fourteen then. I was nine, and my brother about four, so he hardly counts at all. Kiyoko's mother is dead, my father is dead, my mother is dead, and her father could not have lasted all these years with his tremendous appetite for alcohol and pickled chilies—those little yellow ones, so hot they could make your mouth hurt; he'd eat them like peanuts and tears would surge from his bulging thyroid eyes in great waves and stream down the dark coarse terrain of his face.

My father farmed then in the desert basin resolutely named Imperial Valley, in the township called Westmoreland; twenty acres of tomatoes, ten of summer squash, or vice versa, and the Okas lived maybe a mile, mile and a half, across an alkaline road, a stretch of greasewood, tumbleweed and white sand, to the south of us. We didn't hobnob much with them, because you see, they were a childless couple and we were a family: father, mother, daughter, and son, and we went to the Buddhist church on Sundays where my mother taught Japanese, and the Okas kept pretty much to themselves. I don't mean they were unfriendly; Mr. Oka would sometimes walk over (he rarely drove) on rainy days, all dripping wet, short and squat under a soggy newspaper, pretending to need a plow-blade or a file, and he would spend the afternoon in our kitchen drinking sake and eating chilies with my father. As he got progressively drunker, his large mouth would draw down and with the stream of tears, he looked like a kindly weeping bullfrog.

Not only were they childless, impractical in an area where large families were looked upon as labor potentials, but there was a certain strangeness about them. I became aware of it the summer our bathhouse burned down, and my father didn't get right down to building another, and a Japanese without a bathhouse . . . well, Mr. Oka offered us the use of his. So every night that summer we drove to the Okas for our bath, and we came in frequent contact with Mrs. Oka, and this is where I found the strangeness.

Mrs. Oka was small and spare. Her clothes hung on her like loose skin and when she walked, the skirt about her legs gave her a sort of webbed look. She was pretty in spite of the boniness and the dull calico and the barren look; I know now she couldn't have been over thirty. Her eyes were large and a little vacant, although once I saw them fill with tears; the time I insisted we take the old Victrola over and we played our Japanese records for her. Some of the songs were sad, and I imagined the nostalgia she felt, but my mother said the tears were probably from yawning or from the smoke of her cigarettes. I thought my mother resented her for not being more hospitable; indeed, never a cup of tea appeared before us, and between them the conversation of women was totally absent: the rise and fall of gentle voices, the arched eyebrows, the croon of polite surprise. But more than this, Mrs. Oka was *different*.

Obviously she was shy, but some nights she disappeared altogether. She would see us drive into her yard and then lurch from sight. She was gone all evening. Where could she have hidden in that two-roomed house—where in that silent desert? Some nights she would wait out our visit with enormous forbearance, quietly pushing wisps of stray hair behind her ears and waving gnats away from her great moist eyes, and some nights she moved about with nervous agitation, her khaki canvas shoes slapping loudly as she walked. And sometimes there appeared to be welts and bruises on her usually smooth brown face, and she would sit solemnly, hands on lap, eyes large and intent on us. My mother hurried us home then: "Hurry, Masako, no need to wash well; hurry."

You see, being so poky, I was always last to bathe. I think the Okas bathed after we left because my mother often reminded me to keep the water clean. The routine was to lather outside the tub (there were buckets and pans and a small wooden stool), rinse off the soil and soap, and then soak in the tub of hot hot water and contemplate. Rivulets of perspiration would run down the scalp.

When my mother pushed me like this, I dispensed with ritual, rushed a bar of soap around me and splashed about a pan of water. So hastily toweled, my wet skin trapped the clothes to me, impeding my already clumsy progress. Outside, my mother would be murmuring her many apologies and my father, I knew, would be carrying my brother whose feet were already sandy. We would hurry home.

I thought Mrs. Oka might be insane and I asked my mother about it, but she shook her head and smiled with her mouth drawn down and said that Mrs. Oka loved her sake. This was unusual, yes, but there were other unusual women we knew. Mrs. Nagai was bought by her husband from a geisha house; Mrs. Tani was a militant Christian Scientist; Mrs. Abe, the midwife, was occult. My mother's statement explained much: sometimes Mrs. Oka was drunk and sometimes not. Her taste for liquor and cigarettes was a step in the realm of men; unusual for a Japanese wife, but at that time, in that place, and to me, Mrs. Oka loved her sake in the way my father loved his, in the way of Mr. Oka, the way I loved my candy. That her psychology may have demanded this anesthetic, that she lived with something unendurable, did not occur to me. Nor did I perceive the violence of emotions that the purple welts indicated—or the masochism that permitted her to display these wounds to us.

In spite of her masculine habits, Mrs. Oka was never less than a woman. She was no lady in the area of social amenities; but the feminine in her was innate and never left her. Even in her disgrace, she was a small broken sparrow, slightly floppy, too slowly enunciating her few words, too carefully rolling her Bull Durham, cocking her small head and moistening the ocher tissue. Her aberration was a protest of the life assigned her; it was obstinate, but unobserved, alas, unheeded. "Strange" was the only concession we granted her.

Toward the end of summer, my mother said we couldn't continue bathing at the Okas'; when winter set in we'd all catch our death from the commuting and she'd always felt dreadful about our imposition on Mrs. Oka. So my father took the corrugated tin sheets he'd found on the highway and had been saving for some other use and built up our bathhouse again. Mr. Oka came to help.

While they raised the quivering tin walls, Mr. Oka began to talk. His voice was sharp and clear above the low thunder of the metal sheets.

He told my father he had been married in Japan previously to the present Mrs. Oka's older sister. He had a child by the marriage, Kiyoko, a girl. He had left the two to come to America intending to send for them soon, but shortly after his departure, his wife passed away from an obscure stomach ailment. At the time, the present Mrs. Oka was young and had foolishly become involved with a man of poor reputation. The family was anxious to part the lovers and conveniently arranged a marriage by proxy and sent him his dead wife's sister. Well that was all right, after all, they were kin, and it would be good for the child when she came to join them. But things didn't work out that way; year after year he postoned calling for his daughter, couldn't get the price of fare together, and the wife—ahhh, the wife, Mr. Oka's groan was lost in the rumble of his hammering.

He cleared his throat. The girl was now fourteen, he said, and begged to come to America to be with her own real family. Those relatives had forgotten the favor he'd done in accepting a slightly used bride, and now tormented his daughter for being forsaken. True, he'd not sent much money, but if they knew, if they only knew how it was here.

"Well," he signed, "who could be blamed? It's only right she be with me anyway."

"That's right," my father said.

"Well, I sold the horse and some other things and managed to buy a third-class ticket on the Taiyo-Maru. Kiyoko will get here the first week of September." Mr. Oka glanced toward my father, but my father was peering into a bag of nails. "I'd be much obliged to you if your wife and little girl," he rolled his eyes toward me, "would take kindly to her. She'll be lonely."

Kiyoko-san came in September. I was surprised to see so very nearly a woman; short, robust, buxom: the female counterpart of her father; thyroid eyes and protruding teeth, straight black hair banded impudently into two bristly shucks, Cuban heels and white socks. Mr. Oka brought her proudly to us.

"Little Masako here," for the first time to my recollection, he touched me; he put his rough fat hand on the top of my head, "is very smart in school. She will help you with your school work, Kiyoko," he said.

I had so looked forward to Kiyoko-san's arrival. She would be my soul mate; in my mind I had conjured a girl of my own proportions: thin and tall, but with the refinement and beauty I didn't yet possess that would surely someday come to the fore. My disappointment was keen and apparent. Kiyoko-san stepped forward shyly, then retreated with a short bow and small giggle, her fingers pressed to her mouth.

My mother took her away. They talked for a long time—about Japan, about enrollment in American school, the clothes Kiyoko-san would need, and where to look for the best values. As I watched them, it occurred to me that I had been deceived: this was not a child, this was a woman. The smile pressed behind her fingers, the way of her nod, so brief, like my mother when father scolded her: the face was inscrutable, but something—maybe spirit—shrank visibly, like a piece of silk in water. I was disappointed; Kiyoko-san's soul was barricaded in her unenchanting appearance and the smile she fenced behind her fingers.

She started school from third grade, one below me, and as it turned out, she quickly passed me by. There wasn't much I could help her with except to drill her on pronunciation—the "L" and "R" sounds. Every morning walking to our rural school: land, leg, library, loan, lot; every afternoon returning home: ran, rabbit, rim, rinse, roll. That was the extent of our communication; friendly but uninteresting.

One particularly cold November night—the wind outside was icy; I was sitting on my bed, my brother's and mine, oiling the cracks in my chapped hands by lamplight—someone rapped urgently at our door. It was Kiyoko-san; she was hysterical, she wore no wrap, her teeth were chattering, and except for the thin straw zori, her feet were bare. My mother led her to the kitchen, started a pot of tea, and gestured to my brother and me to retire. I lay very still but because of my brother's restless tossing and my father's snoring, was unable to hear much. I was aware, though, that drunken and savage brawling had brought Kiyoko-san to us. Presently they came to the bedroom. I feigned sleep. My mother gave Kiyoko-san a gown and pushed me over to make room for her. My mother spoke firmly: "Tomorrow you will return to them; you must not leave them again. They are your people." I could almost feel Kiyoko-san's short nod.

All night long I lay cramped and still, afraid to intrude into her hulking back. Two or three times her icy feet jabbed into mine and quickly retreated. In the morning I found my mother's gown neatly folded on the spare pillow. Kiyoko-san's place in bed was cold.

She never came to weep at our house again but I know she cried: her eyes were often swollen and red. She stopped much of her giggling and routinely pressed her fingers to her mouth. Our daily pronunciation drill petered off from lack of interest. She walked silently with her shoulders hunched, grasping her books with both arms, and when I spoke to her in my halting Japanese, she absently corrected my prepositions.

Spring comes early in the Valley; in February the skies are clear though the air is still cold. By March, winds are vigorous and warm and wild flowers dot the desert floor, cockleburs are green and not yet tenacious, the sand is crusty underfoot, everywhere there is the smell of things growing and the first tomatoes are showing green and bald.

As the weather changed, Kiyoko-san became noticeably more cheerful. Mr. Oka who hated so to drive could often be seen steering his dusty old Ford over the road that passes our house, and Kiyoko-san sitting in front would sometimes wave gaily to us. Mrs. Oka was never with them. I thought of these trips as the westernizing of Kiyoko-san: with a permanent wave, her straight black hair became tangles of tiny frantic curls; between her textbooks she carried copies of *Modern Screen* and *Photoplay*, her clothes were gay with print and piping, and she bought a pair of brown suede shoes with alligator trim. I can see her now picking her way gingerly over the deceptive white peaks of alkaline crust.

At first my mother watched their coming and going with vicarious pleasure. "Probably off to a picture show; the stores are all closed at this hour," she might say. Later her eyes would get distant and she would muse, "They've left her home again; Mrs. Oka is alone again, the poor woman."

Now when Kiyoko-san passed by or came in with me on her way home, my mother would ask about Mrs. Oka—how is she, how does she occupy herself these rainy days, or these windy or warm or cool days. Often the answers were polite: "Thank you, we are fine," but sometimes Kiyoko-san's upper lip would pull over her teeth, and her voice would become very soft and she would say, "Drink, always drinking and fighting." At those times my mother would invariably say, "Endure, soon you will be marrying and going away."

Once a young truck driver delivered crates at the Oka farm and he dropped back to our place to tell my father that Mrs. Oka had lurched behind his truck while we was backing up, and very nearly let him kill her. Only the daughter pulling her away saved her, he said. Thoroughly unnerved, he stopped by to rest himself and talk about it. Never, never, he said in wide-eyed wonder, had he seen a drunken Japanese woman. My father nodded gravely, "Yes, it's unusual," he said and drummed his knee with his fingers.

Evenings were longer now, and when my mother's migraines drove me from the house in unbearable self-pity, I would take walks in the desert. One night with the warm wind against me, the dune primrose and yellow poppies closed and fluttering, the greasewood swaying in languid orbit, I lay on the white sand beneath a shrub and tried to disappear.

A voice sweet and clear cut through the half-dark of the evening:

> Red lips press against a glass
> Drink the purple wine
> And the soul shall dance

Mrs. Oka appeared to be gathering flowers. Bending, plucking, standing, searching, she added to a small bouquet she clasped. She held them away; looked at them slyly, lids lowered, demure, then in a sudden and sinuous movement, she broke into a stately dance. She stopped, gathered more flowers, and breathed deeply into them. Tossing her head, she laughed— softly, beautifully, from her dark throat. The picture of her imagined grandeur was lost to me, but the delusion that transformed the bouquet of tattered petals and sandy leaves, and the aloneness of a desert twilight into a fantasy that brought such joy and abandon made me stir with discomfort. The sound broke Mrs. Oka's dance. Her eyes grew large and her neck tense—like a cat on the prowl. She spied me in the bushes. A peculiar chill ran through me. Then abruptly and with childlike delight, she scattered the flowers around her and walked away singing:

Falling, falling, petals on a wind . . .

That was the last time I saw Mrs. Oka. She died before the spring harvest. It was pneumonia. I didn't attend the funeral, but my mother said it was sad. Mrs. Oka looked peaceful, and the minister expressed the irony of the long separation of Mother and Child and the short-lived reunion; hardly a year together, she said. We went to help Kiyoko-san address and stamp those black-bordered acknowledgements.

When harvest was over, Mr. Oka and Kiyoko-san moved out of the Valley. We never heard from them or saw them again and I suppose in a large city, Mr. Oka found some sort of work, perhaps as a janitor or a dishwasher and Kiyoko-san grew up and found someone to marry.

Study and Discussion Questions

1. Why does the narrator feel she has to wait until "most of the principals are dead" before she can tell her story?
2 What is the "strangeness" or difference in Mrs. Oka that the narrator refers to?
3. At the time the events in the story take place, the narrator is a preadolescent girl. What role models does she have for becoming a woman?
4. What is the setting of this story? How does the setting help shape what happens?

Writing Exercises

1. Discuss some of the tensions the women in this story encounter being Japanese and living in the United States.
2. Analyze the scene toward the end of the story of Mrs. Oka's singing and dancing. Why does this make the narrator "stir with discomfort"?

JEAN TOOMER (1894–1967)

Jean Toomer grew up in Washington, DC, attended a number of colleges, including the University of Wisconsin, and worked briefly as the headmaster of a black school in Georgia. Cane (1923), his collection of poems, stories, and brief sketches, made him an important figure in the Harlem Renaissance in the 1920s, but he disappeared from the literary scene soon after its publication.

Fern   (1923)

Face flowed into her eyes. Flowed in soft cream foam and plaintive ripples, in such a way that wherever your glance may momentarily have rested, it immediately thereafter wavered in the direction of her eyes. The soft suggestion of down slightly darkened, like the shadow of a bird's wing might, the creamy brown color of her upper lip. Why, after noticing it, you sought her eyes, I cannot tell you. Her nose was aquiline, Semitic. If you have heard a Jewish cantor sing, if he has touched you and made your own sorrow seem trivial when compared with his, you will know my feeling when I follow the curves of her profile, like mobile rivers, to their common delta. They were strange eyes. In this, that they sought nothing—that is, nothing that was obvious and tangible and that one could see, and they gave the impression that nothing was to be denied. When a woman seeks, you will have observed, her eyes deny. Fern's eyes desired nothing that you could give her; there was no reason why they should withhold. Men saw her eyes and fooled themselves. Fern's eyes said to them that she was easy. When she was young, a few men took her, but got no joy from it. And then, once done, they felt bound to her (quite unlike their hit and run with other girls), felt as though it would take them a lifetime to fulfill an obligation which they could find no name for. They became attached to her, and hungered after finding the barest trace of what she might desire. As she grew up, new men who came to town felt as almost everyone did who ever saw her: that they would not be denied. Men were everlastingly bringing her their bodies. Something inside of her got tired of them, I guess, for I am certain that for the life of her she could not tell why or how she began to turn them off. A man in fever is no trifling thing to send away. They began to leave her, baffled and ashamed, yet vowing to themselves that some day they would do some fine thing for her: send her candy every week and not let her know whom it came from, watch out for her wedding-day and give her a magnificent something with no name on it, buy a house and deed it to her, rescue her from some unworthy fellow who had tricked her into marrying him. As you know, men are apt to idolize or fear that which they cannot understand, especially if it be a woman. She did not deny them, yet the fact was that they were denied. A sort of superstition crept into their consciousness of her being somehow above them. Being above them meant that she was not to be approached by anyone. She became a virgin. Now a virgin in a small southern town is by no means the usual thing, if you will believe me. That the sexes were made to mate is the practice of the South. Particularly, black folks were made to mate. And it is black folks whom I have been talking about thus far. What white men thought of Fern I can arrive at only by analogy. They let her alone.

Anyone, of course, could see her, could see her eyes. If you walked up the Dixie Pike most any time of day, you'd be most like to see her resting listless-like on the railing of her porch, back propped against a post, head tilted a little forward because there was a nail in the porch post just where her head came which for some reason or other she never took the trouble to pull out. Her eyes, if it were sunset, rested idly where the sun, molten and glorious, was pouring down between the fringe of pines. Or maybe they gazed at the gray cabin on the knoll from which an evening folk-song was coming. Perhaps they followed a cow that had been turned loose to roam and feed on cotton-stalks and corn leaves. Like as not they'd settle on some vague spot above the horizon, though hardly a trace of wistfulness would come to them. If it were dusk, then they'd wait for the search-light of the evening train which you could see miles up the track before it flared across the Dixie Pike, close to her home. Wherever they looked, you'd follow them and then waver back. Like her face, the whole countryside seemed to flow into her eyes. Flowed into them with the soft listless cadence of Georgia's South. A young Negro, once, was looking at her, spellbound, from the road. A white man passing in a buggy had to flick him with his whip if he was to get by without running him over. I first saw her on her porch. I was passing with a fellow whose crusty numbness (I was from the North and suspected of being prejudiced and stuck-up) was melting as he found me warm. I asked him who she was. "That's Fern," was all that I could get from him. Some folks already thought that I was given to nosing around; I let it go at that, so far as questions were concerned. But at first sight of her I felt as if I heard a Jewish cantor sing. As if his singing rose above the unheard chorus of a folk-song. And I felt bound to her. I too had my dreams: something I would do for her. I have knocked about from town to town too much not to know the futility of mere change of place. Besides, picture if you can, this cream-colored solitary girl sitting at a tenement window looking down on the indifferent throngs of Harlem. Better that she listen to folk-songs-at dusk in Georgia, you would say, and so would I. Or, suppose she came up North and married. Even a doctor or a lawyer, say, one who would be sure to get along—that is, make money. You and I know, who have had experience in such things, that love is not a thing like prejudice which can be bettered by changes of town. Could men in Washington, Chicago, or New York, more than the men of Georgia, bring her something left vacant by the bestowal of their bodies? You and I who know men in these cities will have to say, they could not. See her out and out a prostitute along State Street in Chicago. See her move into a southern town where white men are more aggressive. See her become a white man's concubine. . . . Something I must do for her. There was myself. What could I do for her? Talk, of course. Push back the fringe of pines upon new horizons. To what purpose? and what for? Her? Myself? Men in her case seem to lose their selfishness. I lost mine before I touched her. I ask you, friend (it makes no difference if you sit in the Pullman or the Jim Crow as the train crosses her road), what thoughts would come to you—that is, after you'd finished with the thoughts that leap into men's minds at the sight of a pretty woman who will not deny them; what thoughts would come to you, had you seen her in a quick flash, keen and intuitively, as she sat there on her porch when your train thundered by? Would you have got off at the next station and come back for her to take her where? Would you have completely forgotten her as soon as you reached Macon, Atlanta, Augusta, Pasadena, Madison, Chicago, Boston, or New Orleans? Would you tell your wife or sweetheart about a girl you saw? Your thoughts can help me, and I would like to know. Something I would do for her . . .

One evening I walked up the Pike on purpose, and stopped to say hello. Some of her family were about, but they moved away to make room for me. Damn if I knew how to begin. Would you? Mr. and Miss So-and-So, people, the weather, the crops, the new preacher, the frolic, the church benefit, rabbit and possum hunting, the new soft drink they had at old Pap's store, the schedule of the trains, what kind of town Macon was, Negro's migration north, bollweevils, syrup, the Bible—to all these things she gave a yassur or nassur, without further comment. I began to wonder if perhaps my own emotional sensibility had played one of its tricks on me. "Lets take a walk," I at last ventured. The suggestion, coming after so long an isolation, was novel enough, I guess, to surprise. But it wasn't that. Something told me that men before me had said just that as a prelude to the offering of their bodies. I tried to tell her with my eyes. I think she understood. The thing from her that made my throat catch, vanished. Its passing left her visible in a way I'd thought, but never seen. We walked down the Pike with people on all the porches gaping at us. "Doesn't it make you mad?" She meant the row of petty gossiping people. She meant the world. Through a canebrake that was ripe for cutting, the branch was reached. Under a sweet-gum tree, and where reddish leaves had dammed the creek a little, we sat down. Dusk, suggesting the almost imperceptible procession of giant trees, settled with a purple haze about the cane. I felt strange, as I always do in Georgia, particularly at dusk. I felt that things unseen to men were tangibly immediate. It would not have surprised me had I had vision. People have them in Georgia more often than you would suppose. A black woman once saw the mother of Christ and drew her in charcoal on the courthouse wall . . . When one is on the soil of one's ancestors, most anything can come to one . . . From force of habit, I suppose, I held Fern in my arms—that is, without at first noticing it. Then my mind came back to her. Her eyes, unusually weird and open, held me. Held God. He flowed in as I've seen the countryside flow in. Seen men. I must have done something—what, I don't know, in the confusion of my emotion. She sprang up. Rushed some distance from me. Fell to her knees, and began swaying, swaying. Her body was tortured with something it could not let out. Like boiling sap it flooded arms and fingers till she shook them as if they burned her. It found her throat, and spattered inarticulately in plaintive, convulsive sounds, mingled with calls to Christ Jesus. And then she sang, brokenly. A Jewish cantor singing with a broken voice. A child's voice, uncertain, or an old man's. Dusk hid her; I could hear only her song. It seemed to me as though she were pounding her head in anguish upon the ground. I rushed to her. She fainted in my arms.

There was talk about her fainting with me in the canefield. And I got one or two ugly looks from town men who'd set themselves up to protect her. In fact, there was talk of making me leave town. But they never did. They kept a watch-out for me, though. Shortly after, I came back North. From the train window I saw her as I crossed her road. Saw her on her porch, head tilted a little forward where the nail was, eyes vaguely focused on the sunset. Saw her face flow into them, the countryside and something that I call God, flowing into them . . . Nothing ever really happened. Nothing ever came to Fern, not even I. Something I would do for her. Some fine unnamed thing . . . And, friend, you? She is still living, I have reason to know. Her name, against the chance that you might happen down that way, is Fernie May Rosen.

Study and Discussion Questions

1. What is it about Fern's eyes?
2. What is the history of Fern's relationships with men? How do men feel about her?
3. How does the narrator, who is an outsider to Fern's community, see her? Is his view any different than that of the men who live there?
4. Who is the audience the narrator is imagining when he says "you and I"?
5. How is Fern's southern setting important to the narrator's sense of her?
6. List examples of imagery in this story. What mood do they evoke?

Writing Exercises

1. Discuss the power of point of view in this story.
2. Write a paragraph from Fern's point of view.
3. What does Fern represent or symbolize to the narrator?

GLORIA NAYLOR   (b. 1950)

Gloria Naylor was born in New York City and studied English at Brooklyn College and Afro-American Studies at Yale University. She has worked for the Jehovah's Witnesses and as a telephone operator for hotels in New York. Naylor's fiction includes The Women of Brewster Place: A Novel in Seven Stories *(1982) and* Linden Hills *(1985).*

Etta Mae Johnson   (1982)

*The unpainted walls of the long rectangular room were soaked with the
smell of greasy chicken and warm, headless beer. The brown and pink faces
floated above the trails of used cigarette smoke like bodiless carnival balloons.
The plump yellow woman with white gardenias pinned to the side of her
head stood with her back pressed against the peeling sides of the baby grand
and tried to pierce the bloated hum in the room with her thin scratchy voice.
Undisturbed that she remained for the most part ignored, she motioned for
the piano player to begin.*

*It wasn't the music or the words or the woman that took that room by its
throat until it gasped for air—it was the pain. There was a young southern
girl, Etta Johnson, pushed up in a corner table, and she never forgot. The
music, the woman, the words.*

I love my man
I'm a lie if I say I don't
I love my man
I'm a lie if I say I don't
But I'll quit my man
I'm a lie if I say I won't

My man wouldn't give me no breakfast
Wouldn't give me no dinner
Squawked about my supper
Then he put me out of doors

Had the nerve to lay
A matchbox to my clothes
I didn't have so many
But I had a long, long, way to go

Children bloomed on Brewster Place during July and August with their
colorful shorts and tops plastered against gold, ebony, and nut-brown legs
and arms; they decorated the street, rivaling the geraniums and ivy found
on the manicured boulevard downtown. The summer heat seemed to
draw the people from their cramped apartments onto the stoops, as it
drew the tiny drops of perspiration from their foreheads and backs.

The apple-green Cadillac with the white vinyl roof and Florida plates
turned into Brewster like a greased cobra. Since Etta had stopped at a
Mobil station three blocks away to wash off the evidence of a hot, dusty

1200-mile odyssey home, the chrome caught the rays of the high afternoon sun and flung them back into its face. She had chosen her time well.

The children, free from the conditioned restraints of their older counterparts, ran along the sidewalks flanking this curious, slow-moving addition to their world. Every eye on the block, either openly or covertly, was on the door of the car when it opened. They were rewarded by the appearance of a pair of white leather sandals attached to narrow ankles and slightly bowed, shapely legs. The willow-green sundress, only ten minutes old on the short chestnut woman, clung to a body that had finished a close second in its race with time. Large two-toned sunglasses hid the weariness that had defied the freshly applied mascara and burnt-ivory shadow. After taking twice the time needed to stretch herself, she reached into the back seat of the car and pulled out her plastic clothes bag and Billie Holiday[1] albums.

The children's curiosity reached the end of its short life span, and they drifted back to their various games. The adults sucked their teeth in disappointment, and the more envious felt self-righteousness twist the corners of their mouths. It was only Etta. Looked like she'd done all right by herself—this time around.

Slowly she carried herself across the street—head high and eyes fixed unwaveringly on her destination. The half-dozen albums were clutched in front of her chest like cardboard armor.

> There ain't nothing I ever do
> Or nothing I ever say
> That folks don't criticize me
> But I'm going to do
> Just what I want to, anyway
> And don't care just what people say
> If I should take a notion
> To jump into the ocean
> Ain't nobody's business if I do . . .

Any who bothered to greet her never used her first name. No one called Etta Mae "Etta," except in their minds; and when they spoke to each other about her, it was Etta Johnson; but when they addressed her directly, it was always Miss Johnson. This baffled her because she knew what they thought about her, and she'd always call them by their first names and invited them to do the same with her. But after a few awkward attempts, they'd fall back into the pattern they were somehow comfortable with. Etta didn't know if this was to keep the distance on her side or theirs, but it was there. And she had learned to tread through these alien

---

[1] American jazz singer (1915–1959).

undercurrents so well that to a casual observer she had mastered the ancient secret of walking on water.

Mattie sat in her frayed brocade armchair, pushed up to the front window, and watched her friend's brave approach through the dusty screen. Still toting around them oversized records, she thought. That woman is a puzzlement.

Mattie rose to open the door so Etta wouldn't have to struggle to knock with her arms full. "Lord, child, thank you," she gushed, out of breath. "The younger I get, the higher those steps seem to stretch."

She dumped her load on the sofa and swept off her sunglasses. She breathed deeply of the freedom she found in Mattie's presence. Here she had no choice but to be herself. The carefully erected decoys she was constantly shuffling and changing to fit the situation were of no use here. Etta and Mattie went way back, a singular term that claimed co-knowledge of all the important events in their lives and almost all of the unimportant ones. And by rights of this possession, it tolerated no secrets.

"Sit on down and take a breather. Must have been a hard trip. When you first said you were coming, I didn't expect you to be driving."

"To tell the truth, I didn't expect it myself, Mattie. But Simeon got very ornery when I said I was heading home, and he refused to give me the money he'd promised for my plane fare. So I said, just give me half and I'll take the train. Well, he wasn't gonna even do that. And Mattie, you know I'll be damned if I was coming into this city on a raggedy old Greyhound. So one night he was by my place all drunk up and snoring, and as kindly as you please, I took the car keys and registration and so here I am."

"My God, woman! You stole the man's car?"

"Stole—nothing. He owes me that and then some."

"Yeah, but the police don't wanna hear that. It's a wonder the highway patrol ain't stopped you before now."

"They ain't stopped me because Simeon didn't report it."

"How you know that?"

"His wife's daddy is the sheriff of that county." Laughter hung dangerously on the edge of the two women's eyes and lips.

"Yeah, but he could say you picked his pockets."

Etta went to her clothes bag and pulled out a pair of pink and red monogrammed shorts. "I'd have to be a damned good pickpocket to get away with all this." The laughter lost its weak hold on their mouths and went bouncing crazily against the walls of the living room.

> Them that's got, shall get
> Them that's not, shall lose
> So the Bible says
> And it still is news

Each time the laughter would try to lie still, the two women would look at each other and send it hurling between them, once again.

> Mama may have
> Papa may have
> But God bless the child
> That's got his own
> That's got his own

"Lord, Tut, you're a caution." Mattie wiped the tears off her cheeks with the back of a huge dark hand.

Etta was unable to count the years that had passed since she had heard someone call her that. Look a' that baby gal strutting around here like a bantam. You think she'd be the wife of King Tut.[2] The name had stayed because she never lost the walk. The washed-out grime and red mud of backwoods Rock Vale, Tennessee, might wrap itself around her bare feet and coat the back of her strong fleshy legs, but Etta always had her shoulders flung behind her collarbone and her chin thrust toward the horizon that came to mean everything Rock Vale did not.

Etta spent her teenage years in constant trouble. Rock Vale had no place for a black woman who was not only unwilling to play by the rules, but whose spirit challenged the very right of the game to exist. The whites in Rock Vale were painfully reminded of this rebellion when she looked them straight in the face while putting in her father's order at the dry goods store, when she reserved her sirs and mams for those she thought deserving, and when she smiled only if pleased, regardless of whose presence she was in. That Johnson gal wasn't being an uppity nigger, as talk had it; she was just being herself.

> Southern trees bear strange fruit
> Blood on the leaves and blood at the root
> Black bodies swinging
> In the southern breeze
> Strange fruit hanging
> From the poplar trees

But Rutherford County wasn't ready for Etta's blooming independence, and so she left one rainy summer night about three hours ahead of dawn and Johnny Brick's furious pursuing relatives. Mattie wrote and told her they had waited in ambush for two days on the county line, and then had returned and burned down her father's barn. The sheriff told Mr. Johnson that he had gotten off mighty light—considering. Mr. Johnson

---

[2] Tutankhamen, ancient Egyptian king.

thought so, too. After reading Mattie's letter, Etta was sorry she hadn't killed the horny white bastard when she had the chance.

Rock Vale had followed her to Memphis, Detroit, Chicago, and even to New York. Etta soon found out that America wasn't ready for her yet—not in 1937. And so along with the countless other disillusioned, restless children of Ham with so much to give and nowhere to give it, she took her talents to the street. And she learned to get over, to hook herself to any promising rising black star, and when he burnt out, she found another.

Her youth had ebbed away quickly under the steady pressure of the changing times, but she was existing as she always had. Even if someone had bothered to stop and tell her that the universe had expanded for her, just an inch, she wouldn't have known how to shine alone.

Etta and Mattie had taken totally different roads that with all of their deceptive winding had both ended up on Brewster Place. Their laughter now drew them into a conspiratorial circle against all the Simeons outside of that dead-end street, and it didn't stop until they were both weak from the tears that flowed down their faces.

"So," Mattie said, blowing her nose on a large cotton handkerchief, "trusting you stay out of jail, what you plan on doing now?"

"Child, I couldn't tell you." Etta dropped back down on the couch. "I should be able to get a coupla thousand for the car to tide me over till another business opportunity comes along."

Mattie raised one eyebrow just a whisper of an inch. "Ain't it time you got yourself a regular job? These last few years them *business opportunities* been fewer and farther between."

Etta sucked her small white teeth. "A job doing what? Come on, Mattie, what kind of experience I got? Six months here, three there. I oughta find me a good man and settle down to live quiet in my old age." She combed her fingers confidently through the thick sandy hair that only needed slight tinting at the roots and mentally gave herself another fifteen years before she had to worry about this ultimate fate.

Mattie, watching the creeping tiredness in her eyes, gave her five. "You done met a few promising ones along the way, Etta."

"No, honey, it just seemed so. Let's face it, Mattie. All the good men are either dead or waiting to be born."

"Why don't you come to meeting with me tonight. There's a few settle-minded men in our church, some widowers and such. And a little prayer wouldn't hurt your soul one bit."

"I'll thank you to leave my soul well alone, Mattie Michael. And if your church is so full of upright Christian men, why you ain't snagged one yet?"

"Etta, I done banked them fires a long time ago, but seeing that you still keeping up steam . . ." Her eyes were full of playful kindness.

"Just barely, Mattie, just barely."

And laughter rolled inside of 2E, once again.

"Etta, Etta Mae!" Mattie banged on the bathroom door. "Come on out now. You making me late for the meeting."

"Just another second, Mattie. The church ain't gonna walk away."

"Lord," Mattie grumbled, "she ain't bigger than a minute, so it shouldn't take more than that to get ready."

Etta came out of the bathroom in an exaggerated rush. "My, my, you the most impatient Christian I know."

"Probably, the only Christian you know." Mattie refused to be humored as she bent to gather up her sweater and purse. She turned and was stunned with a barrage of colors. A huge white straw hat reigned over layers of gold and pearl beads draped over too much bosom and too little dress. "You plan on dazzling the Lord, Etta?"

"Well, honey," Etta said, looking down the back of her stocking leg to double-check for runs, "last I heard, He wasn't available. You got more recent news?"

"Um, um, um." Mattie pressed her lips together and shook her head slowly to swallow down the laughter she felt crawling up her throat. Realizing she wasn't going to succeed, she quickly turned her face from Etta and headed toward the door. "Just bring your blasphemin' self on downstairs. I done already missed morning services waiting on you today."

Canaan Baptist Church, a brooding, ashen giant, sat in the middle of a block of rundown private homes. Its multi-colored, dome-shaped eyes glowered into the darkness. Fierce clapping and thunderous organ chords came barreling out of its mouth. Evening services had begun.

Canaan's congregation, the poor who lived in a thirty-block area around Brewster Place, still worshiped God loudly. They could not afford the refined, muted benediction of the more prosperous blacks who went to Sinai Baptist on the northern end of the city, and because each of their requests for comfort was so pressing, they took no chances that He did not hear them.

> When Israel was in Egypt's land
> Let my people go
> Oppressed so hard, they could not stand
> Let my people go

The words were as ancient as the origin of their misery, but the tempo had picked up threefold in its evolution from the cotton fields. They were now sung with the frantic determination of a people who realized that the world was swiftly changing but for some mystic, complex reason their burden had not.

> God said to go down
> Go down

Brother Moses
Brother Moses
To the shore of the great Nile River

The choir clapped and stomped each syllable into a devastating reality,
and just as it did, the congregation reached up, grabbed the phrase, and
tried to clap and stomp it back into oblivion.

Go to Egypt
Go to Egypt
Tell Pharaoh
Tell Pharaoh
Let my people go

Etta entered the back of the church like a reluctant prodigal, prepared
at best to be amused. The alien pounding and the heat and the dark
glistening bodies dragged her back, back past the cold ashes of her
innocence to a time when pain could be castrated on the sharp edges of
iron-studded faith. The blood rushed to her temples and began to throb
in unison with the musical pleas around her.

Yes, my God is a mighty God
Lord, deliver
And he set old Israel free
Swallowed that Egyptian army
Lord, deliver
With the waves of the great Red Sea

Etta glanced at Mattie, who was swaying and humming, and she saw
that the lines in her face had almost totally vanished. She had left Etta
in just that moment for a place where she was free. Sadly, Etta looked
at her, at them all, and was very envious. Unaccustomed to the irritating
texture of doubt, she felt tears as its abrasiveness grated over the fragile
skin of her life. Could there have been another way?

The song ended with a huge expulsion of air, and the congregation
sat down as one body.

"Come on, let's get us a seat." Mattie tugged her by the arm.

The grizzled church deacon with his suit hanging loosely off his stooped
shoulders went up to the pulpit to read the church business.

"That's one of the widowers I was telling you about," Mattie whispered,
and poked Etta.

"Unmm." The pressure on her arm brought Etta back onto the uncomfortable wooden pew. But she didn't want to stay there, so she climbed

back out the window, through the glass eyes of the seven-foot Good Shepherd, and started again the futile weaving of invisible ifs and slippery mights into an equally unattainable past.

The scenes of her life reeled out before her with the same aging script; but now hindsight sat as the omniscient director and had the young star of her epic recite different brilliant lines and make the sort of stunning decisions that propelled her into the cushioned front pews on the right of the minister's podium. There she sat with the deacons' wives, officers of the Ladies' Auxiliary, and head usherettes. And like them, she would wear on her back a hundred pairs of respectful eyes earned the hard way, and not the way she had earned the red sundress, which she now self-consciously tugged up in the front. Was it too late?

The official business completed, the treasurer pulled at his frayed lapels, cleared his throat, and announced the guest speaker for the night.

The man was magnificent.

He glided to the podium with the effortlessness of a well-oiled machine and stood still for an interminable long moment. He eyed the congregation confidently. He only needed their attention for that split second because once he got it, he was going to wrap his voice around their souls and squeeze until they screamed to be relieved. They knew it was coming and waited expectantly, breathing in unison as one body. First he played with them and threw out fine silken threads that stroked their heart muscles ever so gently. They trembled ecstatically at the touch and invited more. The threads multiplied and entwined themselves solidly around the one pulsating organ they had become and tightened slightly, testing them for a reaction.

The "Amen, brothers" and "Yes, Jesus" were his permission to take that short hop from the heart to the soul and lay all pretense of gentleness aside. Now he would have to push and pound with clenched fists in order to be felt, and he dared not stop the fierce rhythm of his voice until their replies had reached that fevered pitch of satisfaction. Yes, Lord—grind out the unheated tenements! Merciful Jesus—shove aside the low-paying boss man. Perfect Father—fill me, fill me till there's no room, no room for nothing else, not even that great big world out there that exacts such a strange penalty for my being born black.

It was hard work. There was so much in them that had to be replaced. The minister's chest was heaving in long spasms, and the sweat was pouring down his gray temples and rolling under his chin. His rich voice was now hoarse, and his legs and raised arms trembled on the edge of collapse. And as always they were satisfied a half-breath before he reached the end of his endurance. They sat back, limp and spent, but momentarily at peace. There was no price too high for this service. At that instant they would have followed him to do battle with the emperor of the world, and all he was going to ask of them was money for the "Lord's work." And they would willingly give over half of their little to keep this man in comfort.

Etta had not been listening to the message; she was watching the man. His body moved with the air of one who had not known recent deprivation. The tone of his skin and the fullness around his jawline told her that he was well-off, even before she got close enough to see the manicured hands and diamond pinkie ring.

The techniques he had used to brand himself on the minds of the congregation were not new to her. She'd encountered talent like that in poolrooms, nightclubs, grimy second-floor insurance offices, numbers dens, and on a dozen street corners. But here was a different sort of power. The jungle-sharpened instincts of a man like that could move her up to the front of the church, ahead of the deacons' wives and Ladies' Auxiliary, off of Brewster Place for good. She would find not only luxury but a place that complemented the type of woman she had fought all these years to become.

"Mattie, is that your regular minister?" she whispered.

"Who, Reverend Woods? No, he just visits on occasion, but he sure can preach, can't he?"

"What you know about him, he married?"

Mattie cut her eyes at Etta. "I should have figured it wasn't the sermon that moved you. At least wait till after the prayer before you jump all into the man's business."

During the closing song and prayer Etta was planning how she was going to maneuver Mattie to the front of the church and into introducing her to Reverend Woods. It wasn't going to be as difficult as she thought. Moreland T. Woods had noticed Etta from the moment she'd entered the church. She stood out like a bright red bird among the drab morality that dried up the breasts and formed rolls around the stomachs of the other church sisters. This woman was still dripping with the juices of a full-fleshed life—the kind of life he was soon to get up and damn into hell for the rest of the congregation—but how it fitted her well. He had to swallow to remove the excess fluid from his mouth before he got up to preach.

Now the problem was to make his way to the back of the church before she left without seeming to be in a particular hurry. A half-dozen back slaps, handshakes, and thank-you sisters only found him about ten feet up the aisle, and he was growing impatient. However, he didn't dare to turn his neck and look in the direction where he'd last seen her. He felt a hand on his upper arm and turned to see a grim-faced Mattie flanked by the woman in the scarlet dress.

"Reverend Woods, I really enjoyed your sermon," Mattie said.

"Why, thank you, sister—sister?"

"Sister Michael, Mattie Michael." While he was addressing his words to her, the smile he sent over her shoulder to Etta was undeniable.

"Especially the part," Mattie raised her voice a little, "About throwing away temptation to preserve the soul. That was a mighty fine point."

"The Lord moves me and I speak, Sister Michael. I'm just a humble instrument for his voice."

The direction and intent of his smile was not lost to Etta. She inched her way in front of Mattie. "I enjoyed it, too, Reverend Woods. It's been a long time since I heard preaching like that." She increased the pressure of her fingers on Mattie's arm.

"Oh, excuse my manners. Reverend Woods, this is an old friend of mine, Etta Mae Johnson. Etta Mae, Reverend Woods." She intoned the words as if she were reciting a eulogy.

"Please to meet you, Sister Johnson." He beamed down on the small woman and purposely held her hand a fraction longer than usual. "You must be a new member—I don't recall seeing you the times I've been here before."

"Well, no, Reverend, I'm not a member of the congregation, but I was raised up in the church. You know how it is, as you get older sometimes you stray away. But after your sermon, I'm truly thinking of coming back."

Mattie tensed, hoping that the lightning that God was surely going to strike Etta with wouldn't hit her by mistake.

"Well, you know what the Bible says, sister. The angels rejoice more over one sinner who turns around than over ninety-nine righteous ones."

"Yes, indeed, and I'm sure a shepherd like you has helped to turn many back to the fold." She looked up and gave him the full benefit of her round dark eyes, grateful she hadn't put on that third coat of mascara.

"I try, Sister Johnson, I try."

"It's a shame Mrs. Woods wasn't here tonight to hear you. I'm sure she must be mighty proud of your work."

"My wife has gone to her glory, Sister Johnson. I think of myself now as a man alone—rest her soul."

"Yes, rest her soul," Etta sighed.

"Please, Lord, yes." Mattie muttered, giving out the only sincere request among the three. The intensity of her appeal startled them, and they turned to look at her. "Only knows how hard this life is, she's better in the arms of Jesus."

"Yes"—Etta narrowed her eyes at Mattie and then turned back to the minister—"I can testify to that. Being a woman alone, it seems all the more hard. Sometimes you don't know where to turn."

Moreland Woods knew Etta was the type of woman who not only knew which way to turn, but, more often than not, had built her own roads when nothing else was accessible. But he was enjoying this game immensely—almost as much as the growing heat creeping into his groin.

"Well, if I can be of any assistance, Sister Johnson, don't hesitate to ask. I couldn't sleep knowing one of the Lord's sheep is troubled. As a matter of fact, if you have anything you would like to discuss with me this evening, I'd be glad to escort you home."

"I don't have my own place. You see, I'm just up from out of state and staying with my friend Mattie here."

"Well, perhaps we could all go out for coffee."

"Thank you, but I'll have to decline, Reverend," Mattie volunteered before Etta did it for her. "The services have me all tired out, but if Etta wants to, she's welcome."

"That'll be just fine," Etta said.

"Good, good." And now it was his turn to give her the benefit of a mouth full of strong gold-capped teeth. "Just let me say good-bye to a few folks here, and I'll meet you outside."

"Girl, you oughta patent that speed and sell it to the airplane companies," Mattie said outside. " 'After that sermon, Reverend, I'm thinking of coming back'—indeed!"

"Aw, hush your fussing."

"I declare if you had batted them lashes just a little faster, we'd of had a dust storm in there."

"You said you wanted me to meet some nice men. Well, I met one."

"Etta, I meant a man who'd be serious about settling down with you." Mattie was exasperated. "Why, you're going on like a schoolgirl. Can't you see what he's got in mind?"

Etta turned an indignant face toward Mattie. "The only thing I see is that you're telling me I'm not good enough for a man like that. Oh, no, not Etta Johnson. No upstanding decent man could ever see anything in her but a quick good time. Well, I'll tell you something, Mattie Michael. I've always traveled first class, maybe not in the way you'd approve with all your fine Christian principles, but it's done all right by me. And I'm gonna keep going top drawer till I leave this earth. Don't you think I got a mirror? Each year there's a new line to cover. I lay down with this body and get up with it every morning, and each morning it cries for just a little more rest than it did the day before. Well, I'm finally gonna get that rest, and it's going to be with a man like Reverend Woods. And you and the rest of those slack-mouthed gossips on Brewster be damned!" Tears frosted the edges of her last words. "They'll be humming a different tune when I show up there the wife of a big preacher. I've always known what they say about me behind my back, but I never thought you were right in there with them."

Mattie was stunned by Etta's tirade. How could Etta have so totally misunderstood her words? What had happened back there to stuff up her senses to the point that she had missed the obvious? Surely she could not believe that the vibrations coming from that unholy game of charades in the church aisle would lead to something as permanent as marriage? Why, it had been nothing but the opening gestures to a mating dance. Mattie had gone through the same motions at least once in her life, and Etta must have known a dozen variations to it that were a mystery to her. And yet, somehow, back there it had been played to a music that had totally distorted the steps for her friend. Mattie suddenly felt the helplessness of a person who is forced to explain that for which there are no words.

She quietly turned her back and started down the steps. There was no need to defend herself against Etta's accusations. They shared at least a hundred memories that could belie those cruel words. Let them speak for her.

Sometimes being a friend means mastering the art of timing. There is a time for silence. A time to let go and allow people to hurl themselves into their own destiny. And a time to prepare to pick up the pieces when it's all over. Mattie realized that this moment called for all three.

"I'll see ya when you get home, Etta," she threw gently over her shoulder.

Etta watched the bulky figure become slowly enveloped by the shadows. Her angry words had formed a thick mucus in her throat, and she couldn't swallow them down. She started to run into the darkness where she'd seen Mattie disappear, but at that instant Moreland Woods came out of the lighted church, beaming.

He took her arm and helped her into the front seat of his car. Her back sank into the deep upholstered leather, and the smell of the freshly vacuumed carpet was mellow in her nostrils. All of the natural night sounds of the city were blocked by the thick tinted windows and the hum of the air conditioner, but they trailed persistently behind the polished back of the vehicle as it turned and headed down the long gray boulevard.

> Smooth road
> Clear day
> But why am I the only one
> Traveling this way
> How strange the road to love
> Can be so easy
> Can there be a detour ahead?

Moreland Woods was captivated by the beautiful woman at his side. Her firm brown flesh and bright eyes carried the essence of nectar from some untamed exotic flower, and the fragrance was causing a pleasant disturbance at the pit of his stomach. He marveled at how excellently she played the game. A less alert observer might have been taken in, but his survival depended upon knowing people, knowing exactly how much to give and how little to take. It was this razor-thin instinct that had catapulted him to the head of his profession and that would keep him there.

And although she cut her cards with a reckless confidence, pushed her chips into the middle of the table as though the supply was unlimited, and could sit out the game until dawn, he knew. Oh, yes. Let her win a few, and then he would win just a few more, and she would be bankrupt long before the sun was up. And then there would be only one thing left to place on the table—and she would, because the stakes they were playing for were very high. But she was going to lose that last deal. She would lose because when she first sat down in that car she had everything riding on the fact that he didn't know the game existed.

And so it went. All evening Etta had been in another world, weaving his tailored suit and the smell of his expensive cologne into a custom-made future for herself. It took his last floundering thrusts into her body to bring her back to reality. She arrived in enough time to feel him beating against her like a dying walrus, until he shuddered and was still.

She kept her eyes closed because she knew when she opened them there would be the old familiar sights around her. To her right would be the plastic-coated nightstand that matched the cheaply carved headboard of the bed she lay in. She felt the bleached coarseness of the sheet under her sweaty back and predicted the roughness of the worn carpet path that led from the bed to the white-tiled bathroom with bright fluorescent lights, sterilized towels, and tissue-wrapped water glasses. There would be two or three small thin rectangles of soap wrapped in bright waxy covers that bore the name of the hotel.

She didn't try to visualize what the name would be. It didn't matter. They were all the same, all meshed together into one lump that rested like an iron ball on her chest. And the expression on the face of this breathing mass to her left would be the same as all the others. She could turn now and go through the rituals that would tie up the evening for them both, but she wanted just one more second of this soothing darkness before she had to face the echoes of the locking doors she knew would be in his eyes.

Etta got out of the car unassisted and didn't bother to turn and watch the taillights as it pulled off down the deserted avenue adjacent to Brewster Place. She had asked him to leave her at the corner because there was no point in his having to make a U-turn in the dead-end street, and it was less than a hundred yards to her door. Moreland was relieved that she had made it easy for him, because it had been a long day and he was anxious to get home and go to sleep. But then, the whole business had gone pretty smoothly after they left the hotel. He hadn't even been called upon to use any of the excuses he had prepared for why it would be a while before he'd see her again. A slight frown crossed his forehead as he realized that she had seemed as eager to get away from him as he had been to leave. Well, he shrugged his shoulders and placated his dented ego, that's the nice part about these worldly women. They understand the temporary weakness of the flesh and don't make it out to be something bigger than it is. They can have a good time without pawing and hanging all onto a man. Maybe I should drop around sometime. He glanced into his rearview mirror and saw that Etta was still standing on the corner, looking straight ahead into Brewster. There was something about the slumped profile of her body, silhouetted against the dim street light, that caused him to press down on the accelerator.

Etta stood looking at the wall that closed off Brewster from the avenues farther north and found it hard to believe that it had been just this afternoon when she had seen it. It had looked so different then, with the August sun highlighting the browns and reds of the bricks and the young children bouncing their rubber balls against its side. Now it crouched there in the thin predawn light, like a pulsating mouth awaiting her arrival. She shook her head sharply to rid herself of the illusion, but an uncanny fear gripped her, and her legs felt like lead. If I walk into this street, she thought, I'll never come back. I'll never get out. Oh, dear God, I am so tired—so very tired.

Etta removed her hat and massaged her tight forehead. Then, giving a resigned sigh, she started slowly down the street. Had her neighbors been out on their front stoops, she could have passed through their milling clusters as anonymously as the night wind. They had seen her come down that street once in a broken Chevy that had about five hundred dollars' worth of contraband liquor in its trunk, and there was even the time she'd come home with a broken nose she'd gotten in some hair-raising escapade in St. Louis, but never had she walked among them with a broken spirit. This middle-aged woman in the wrinkled dress and wilted straw hat would have been a stranger to them.

When Etta got to the stoop, she noticed there was a light under the shade at Mattie's window, and she strained to hear what actually sounded like music coming from behind the screen. Mattie was playing her records! Etta stood very still, trying to decipher the broken air waves into intelligible sound, but she couldn't make out the words. She stopped straining when it suddenly came to her that it wasn't important what song it was— someone was waiting up for her. Someone who would deny fiercely that there had been any concern—just a little indigestion from them fried onions that kept me from sleeping. Thought I'd pass the time by figuring out what you see in all this loose-life music.

Etta laughed softly to herself as she climbed the steps toward the light and the love and the comfort that awaited her.

Study and Discussion Questions

1. How are Etta and Mattie similar and how are they different? Describe their relationship.
2. Why is Etta, experienced as she is, so blind about Reverend Woods? Besides his personal charm, what is the source of his power over her?
3. Look carefully at the first three paragraphs describing Woods at the podium. What is Naylor saying?
4. What light does the description of Etta's earlier years shed on her present situation?

5. What is the significance of the last sentence? What is the story saying about relationships between men and women and between women and other women?

Writing Exercises

1. Discuss the function of the song lyrics that run through the story.
2. Soon after Etta gets into Woods's car, Naylor introduces an extended poker-game metaphor. What is this saying about relations between men and women? What do you think of what it is saying?
3. Select a short section of the story (other than one of those already mentioned) and analyze Naylor's use of language.
4. Describe the photograph, painting, or drawing that you think would best accompany the story if it were printed in a literary magazine.

POETRY

JOHN DONNE (1572–1631)

John Donne was born in London into a prominent Roman Catholic family. Because of his religion, he was prevented from taking a degree at Oxford; he became an Anglican convert soon after. He participated in naval expeditions and upon return to England studied law and was appointed secretary to Sir Thomas Egerton. But his secret marriage to Egerton's niece cost him his position and led to brief imprisonment. Donne struggled to earn a living for a number of years, but eventually found a patron to support his writing. In 1615, he was ordained an Anglican priest and his sermons became immensely popular. Only after his death did he gain a reputation as the leading "metaphysical" poet. His Poems *were published by his son in 1633.*

The Flea   (1633)

Mark but this flea, and mark in this,
How little that which thou deny'st me is;
Me it sucked first, and now sucks thee,
And in this flea, our two bloods mingled be;
Confess it, this cannot be said   5
A sin, or shame, or loss of maidenhead,
   Yet this enjoys before it woo,
   And pampered swells with one blood made of two,
   And this, alas, is more than we would do.

Oh stay, three lives in one flea spare,   10
Where we almost, nay more than married are.
This flea is you and I, and this
Our marriage bed, and marriage temple is;
Though parents grudge, and you, we are met,
And cloistered in these living walls of jet.   15
   Though use make you apt to kill me,
   Let not to this, self murder added be,
   And sacrilege, three sins in killing three.

Cruel and sudden, hast thou since
Purpled thy nail, in blood of innocence?   20
In what could this flea guilty be,
Except in that drop which it sucked from thee?

Yet thou triumph'st, and say'st that thou
Find'st not thyself, nor me the weaker now;
  'Tis true, then learn how false, fears be;   25
  Just so much honour, when thou yield'st to me,
  Will waste, as this flea's death took life from thee.

Study and Discussion Questions

1. To whom is the poem addressed?
2. "The Flea" is an example of a *conceit*, an ingenious metaphor. What does the speaker of the poem mean when he says: "This flea is you and I, and this/ Our marriage bed, and marriage temple is"?
3. What literally is happening in this poem?
4. What is the tone of the poem?

Writing Exercises

1. Write a description of how you imagine the setting and characters in this poem.
2. What is happening in each stanza of "The Flea"? That is, what are the stages of the speaker's argument?
3. Write an answer to the speaker of the poem from the point of view of the person the poem is addressed to.

WILLIAM BLAKE   (1757–1827)

William Blake was born in London. He had no formal education, was apprenticed at a young age to an engraver, and earned his living engraving the rest of his life. Blake published his own poems, often surrounding the verse with his own illustrations; he engraved the plates himself and, with his wife, colored the printed pages by hand. His visionary poetry was little appreciated in his time, but he is now considered one of the most important poets in English. His major works include Songs of Innocence *(1789),* The Marriage of Heaven and Hell *(1790), and* Songs of Experience *(1794).*

The Garden of Love   (1794)

I went to the Garden of Love,
And saw what I never had seen:
A Chapel was built in the midst,
Where I used to play on the green.

And the gates of this Chapel were shut,   5
And "Thou shalt not" writ over the door;
So I turn'd to the Garden of Love
That so many sweet flowers bore;

And I saw it was filled with graves,
And tomb-stones where flowers should be;   10
And Priests in black gowns were walking their rounds,
And binding with briars my joys & desires.

Study and Discussion Questions

1. What contrast runs through the poem?
2. What does "Thou shalt not" allude to?
3. Why a *garden* of love?
4. Why are the gates of the chapel shut?
5. Discuss the importance of the rhythm and internal rhymes of the last two lines.

Writing Exercise

1. What is the poem saying about organized religion? What do you think of what it is saying?

EDNA ST. VINCENT MILLAY   (1892–1950)

Edna St. Vincent Millay was born in Rockland, Maine and educated at Vassar. After graduation, she moved to Greenwich Village, continued writing poetry, prose, and drama, and acted with the Provincetown Players and other groups. In 1923, she married and moved to a farm in New York. Millay is best known for her poetry, which includes Renascence *(1917),* A Few Figs From Thistles *(1920), and* The Harp-Weaver *(1923).*

Love is not all: it is not meat nor drink   (1931)

Love is not all: it is not meat nor drink
Nor slumber nor a roof against the rain;
Nor yet a floating spar to men that sink
And rise and sink and rise and sink again;
Love can not fill the thickened lung with breath,   5
Nor clean the blood, nor set the fractured bone;

Yet many a man is making friends with death
Even as I speak, for lack of love alone.
It well may be that in a difficult hour,
Pinned down by pain and moaning for release, 10
Or nagged by want past resolution's power,
I might be driven to sell your love for peace,
Or trade the memory of this night for food.
It well may be. I do not think I would.

Study and Discussion Questions

1. Given the rhyme scheme of this poem and the number of lines, what kind of poem is it?
2. The first quatrain (four lines) lists a number of things love is not. What are they? What observation do the next four lines make?
3. In the last six lines of the poem, the speaker moves from the general to her own case. What does she say might cause her to deny her love? What is her tone in these lines?
4. Read lines three and four aloud. How do rhythm and repetition replicate the image in these lines?

Writing Exercises

1. What might you add to Millay's list of what love is not?
2. Would you call this a love poem? Why or why not?

ANNE SEXTON   (1928–1974)

Anne Sexton was born in Newton, Massachusetts, attended Garland Junior College for a year, and married at twenty. After one of the first of the many nervous breakdowns she was to suffer throughout her life, a psychiatrist urged her to try writing, which she did with immediate success. Sexton's poetry includes To Bedlam and Part Way Back *(1960),* Live or Die *(1966), which won a Pulitzer Prize,* Love Poems *(1969),* Transformations *(1971), and* The Death Notebooks *(1974). At the age of forty-five, she took her own life.*

For My Lover, Returning to His Wife   (1967)

She is all there.
She was melted carefully down for you

and cast up from your childhood,
cast up from your one hundred favorite aggies.[1]

She has always been there, my darling.   5
She is, in fact, exquisite.
Fireworks in the dull middle of February
and as real as a cast-iron pot.

Let's face it, I have been momentary.
A luxury. A bright red sloop in the harbor.   10
My hair rising like smoke from the car window.
Littleneck clams out of season.

She is more than that. She is your have to have,
has grown you your practical your tropical growth.
This is not an experiment. She is all harmony.   15
She sees to oars and oarlocks for the dinghy,

has placed wild flowers at the window at breakfast,
sat by the potter's wheel at midday,
set forth three children under the moon,
three cherubs drawn by Michelangelo,   20

done this with her legs spread out
in the terrible months in the chapel.
If you glance up, the children are there
like delicate balloons resting on the ceiling.

She has also carried each one down the hall   25
after supper, their heads privately bent,
two legs protesting, person to person,
her face flushed with a song and their little sleep.

I give you back your heart.
I give you permission——   30

for the fuse inside her, throbbing
angrily in the dirt, for the bitch in her
and the burying of her wound——
for the burying of her small red wound alive——

---

[1] Colorful playing marbles.

for the pale flickering flare under her ribs,   35
for the drunken sailor who waits in her left pulse,
for the mother's knee, for the stockings,
for the garter belt, for the call——

the curious call
when you will burrow in arms and breasts   40
and tug at the orange ribbon in her hair
and answer the call, the curious call.

She is so naked and singular.
She is the sum of yourself and your dream.
Climb her like a monument, step after step.   45
She is solid.

As for me, I am a watercolor.
I wash off.

Study and Discussion Questions

1. What kind of imagery does the speaker use to describe herself? To describe the wife?
2. What does the first stanza mean?
3. "If you glance up, the children are there/ like delicate balloons resting on the ceiling." What is the speaker saying about her lover and his children?
4. What is the speaker's assessment of her lover as a husband? What does she think of the role of husband?
5. Characterize the speaker's tone.

Writing Exercises

1. Would the speaker want to change places with the wife?
2. How would a poem with a male *persona*, entitled "For My Lover, Returning to Her Husband," have to be different?

GENNY LIM (b. 1946)

Genny Lim has published poetry in a variety of journals and has been a contributing editor to a national Asian-American quarterly, Bridge. *Her play* Paper Angels *was produced in 1980 by the Asian American Theater Company in San Francisco. Lim is coauthor of* Island: Poetry and History of Chinese Immigrants on Angel Island, 1910–1940 *(1980).*

Wonder Woman (1981)

Sometimes I see reflections on bits of glass on sidewalks
I catch the glimmer of empty bottles floating out to sea
Sometimes I stretch my arms way above my head and wonder if
There are women along the Mekong[1] doing the same

Sometimes I stare longingly at women who I will never know   5
Generous, laughing women with wrinkled cheeks and white teeth
Dragging along chubby, rosy-cheeked babies on fat, wobbly legs
Sometimes I stare at Chinese grandmothers
Getting on the 30 Stockton with shopping bags
Japanese women tourists in European hats   10
Middle-aged mothers with laundry carts
Young wives holding hands with their husbands
Lesbian women holding hands in coffee-houses
Smiling debutantes with bouquets of yellow daffodils
Silver-haired matrons with silver rhinestoned poodles   15
Painted prostitutes posing along MacArthur Boulevard
Giddy teenage girls snapping gum in fast cars
Widows clutching bibles, crucifixes

I look at them and wonder if
They are a part of me   20
I look in their eyes and wonder if
They share my dreams

I wonder if the woman in mink is content
If the stockbroker's wife is afraid of growing old   25
If the professor's wife is an alcoholic
If the woman in prison is me

There are copper-tanned women in Hyannis Port playing tennis
Women who eat with finger bowls
There are women in factories punching time clocks   30
Women tired every waking hour of the day

---

[1] River in Southeast Asia, scene of much fighting during the Vietnam War.

I wonder why there are women born with silver spoons in their mouths
Women who have never known a day of hunger
Women who have never changed their own bed linen
And I wonder why there are women who must work   35
Women who must clean other women's houses
Women who must shell shrimps for pennies a day
Women who must sew other women's clothes
Who must cook
Who must die   40
In childbirth
In dreams

Why must woman stand divided?
Building the walls that tear them down?
Jill-of-all-trades   45
Lover, mother, housewife, friend, breadwinner
Heart and spade
A woman is a ritual
A house that must accommodate
A house that must endure   50
Generation after generation
Of wind and torment, of fire and rain
A house with echoing rooms
Closets with hidden cries
Walls with stretchmarks   55
Windows with eyes

Short, tall, skinny, fat
Pregnant, married, white, yellow, black, brown, red
Professional, working-class, aristocrat
Women cooking over coals in sampans   60
Women shining tiffany spoons in glass houses
Women stretching their arms way above the clouds
In Samarkand, in San Francisco
Along the Mekong

Study and Discussion Questions

1. What does the speaker mean when she says, "I wonder . . . If the woman in prison is me"?
2. Explain the second line in the seventh stanza: "Building the walls that tear them down?"
3. What is the significance of the "house" metaphor in that same stanza?
4. Why does Lim end the poem, "Along the Mekong"?

Writing Exercises

1. I "wonder if / They share my dreams," the third stanza ends. What dreams might "painted prostitutes" and "silver-haired matrons with silver rhinestoned poodles" share with the speaker?
2. State explicitly the argument that the poem is making.

ROBERT FROST (1874–1963)

Robert Frost was born in San Francisco but moved with his family to rural New England when he was ten. After high school in Lawrence, Massachusetts, he spent a semester at Dartmouth College, worked odd jobs while he wrote, and then went to Harvard. His grandfather gave him a farm in New Hampshire, which he worked for ten years. Then, after teaching school, Frost went to England in 1912, where he published his first book of poems, A Boy's Will, *in 1913. He returned to the United States in 1915 and settled on another New Hampshire farm. Frost's poetry includes* North of Boston *(1914),* Mountain Interval *(1916),* New Hampshire *(1923),* West-Running Brook *(1928),* A Further Range *(1936), and* A Witness Tree *(1942).*

The Subverted Flower   (1942)

She drew back; he was calm:
"It is this that had the power."
And he lashed his open palm
With the tender-headed flower.
He smiled for her to smile,   5
But she was either blind
Or willfully unkind.
He eyed her for a while
For a woman and a puzzle.
He flicked and flung the flower,   10
And another sort of smile
Caught up like fingertips
The corners of his lips
And cracked his ragged muzzle.
She was standing to the waist   15
In goldenrod and brake,
Her shining hair displaced.
He stretched her either arm
As if she made it ache
To clasp her—not to harm;   20
As if he could not spare

To touch her neck and hair.
"If this has come to us
And not to me alone—"
So she thought she heard him say;   25
Though with every word he spoke
His lips were sucked and blown
And the effort made him choke
Like a tiger at a bone.
She had to lean away.   30
She dared not stir a foot,
Lest movement should provoke
The demon of pursuit
That slumbers in a brute.
It was then her mother's call   35
From inside the garden wall
Made her steal a look of fear
To see if he could hear
And would pounce to end it all
Before her mother came.   40
She looked and saw the shame:
A hand hung like a paw,
An arm worked like a saw
As if to be persuasive,
An ingratiating laugh   45
That cut the snout in half,
An eye become evasive.
A girl could only see
That a flower had marred a man,
But what she could not see   50
Was that the flower might be
Other than base and fetid:
That the flower had done but part,
And what the flower began
Her own too meager heart   55
Had terribly completed.
She looked and saw the worst.
And the dog or what it was,
Obeying bestial laws,
A coward save at night,   60
Turned from the place and ran.
She heard him stumble first
And use his hands in flight.
She heard him bark outright.
And oh, for one so young   65
The bitter words she spit
Like some tenacious bit

That will not leave the tongue.
She plucked her lips for it,
And still the horror clung. 70
Her mother wiped the foam
From her chin, picked up her comb,
And drew her backward home.

Study and Discussion Questions

1. Think about the title of the poem. How is the flower "subverted"?
2. What words in the poem indicate the young woman's perception of the man? What does she compare him to?
3. How do you think the poet feels about the young woman in this poem? Whose side is he on? Where does Frost seem to be speaking to us directly?
4. The third "character" in this poem is the young woman's mother. When does she enter the poem, and what does her entrance precipitate?
5. Characterize the young woman's relationship with her mother.

Writing Exercises

1. What emotion or emotions do you think the young woman is feeling? What about the man's emotions? Provide evidence from the poem.
2. "And he lashed his open palm/ With the tender-headed flower." Discuss these lines in relation to the encounter the poem is about.
3. Retell "The Subverted Flower" as a contemporary boy-meets-girl story.

AMIRI BARAKA   (b. 1934)

LeRoi Jones was born in Newark, New Jersey and went to school there and to Rutgers, Howard, and Columbia Universities. After three years in the Air Force, he moved to New York's bohemian Lower East Side. In the 1960s, he became increasingly involved with black nationalist politics and changed his name to Amiri Baraka. He has taught at a number of colleges and universities and has published poetry, including Preface to a Twenty Volume Suicide Note *(1961),* The Dead Lecturer *(1964), and* Black Magic *(1969); drama, including* Dutchman *(1964) and* The Slave *(1964); and nonfiction, most notably* Blues People *(1963).*

Beautiful Black Women . . .   (1969)

Beautiful black women, fail, they act. Stop them, raining.
They are so beautiful, we want them with us. Stop them, raining.

Beautiful, stop raining, they fail. We fail them and their lips
stick out perpetually, at our weakness. Raining. Stop them. Black
queens. Ruby Dee[1] weeps at the window, raining, being lost in her   5
life, being what we all will be, sentimental bitter frustrated
deprived of her fullest light. Beautiful black women, it is
still raining in this terrible land. We need you. We flex our
muscles, turn to stare at our tormentor, we need you. Raining.
We need you, reigning, black queen. This/terrible black ladies   10
wander, Ruby Dee weeps, the window, raining, she calls, and her voice
is left to hurt us slowly. It hangs against the same wet glass, her
sadness and age, and the trip, and the lost heat, and the gray cold
buildings of our entrapment. Ladies. Women. We need you. We are still
trapped and weak, but we build and grow heavy with our knowledge.
     Women.   15
Come to us. Help us get back what was always ours. Help us. women.
     Where
are you, women, where, and who, and where, and who, and will you
     help
us, will you open your bodysouls, will you lift me up mother, will you
let me help you, daughter, wife/lover, will you

Study and Discussion Questions

1. Line 2 reads, in part, "we want them with us." Who does "we" refer
   to? And where are the black women, if not "with us"?
2. Who is "our tormentor"? Does "our" refer to the same group of people
   as "we"? If so, what does this suggest about the speaker?
3. Why does Baraka repeat "raining" so often?
4. "Help us get back what was always ours." What does this mean?

Writing Exercises

1. What does the speaker want black women to be and do?
2. How might a black woman reply to this poem?

KARL SHAPIRO   (b. 1913)

*Karl Shapiro was born in Baltimore, Maryland and educated at the University
of Virginia and Johns Hopkins University. While a soldier in the South Pacific
during World War II, he wrote* V-Letter and Other Poems *(1944), which won*

---

[1] American actress (b.1924).

him a Pulitzer Prize, and he returned from the war a well-known poet. Shapiro has taught at a number of universities and served as editor of Poetry *magazine. His other poetry includes* Essays on Rime *(1945),* Poems 1940–1953 *(1953),* Poems of a Jew *(1958), and* Adult Bookstore *(1976).*

Buick   (1953)

As a sloop with a sweep of immaculate wing on her delicate spine
And a keel as steel as a root that holds in the sea as she leans,
Leaning and laughing, my warm-hearted beauty, you ride, you ride,
You tack on the curves with parabola speed and a kiss of goodbye,
Like a thoroughbred sloop, my new high-spirited spirit, my kiss.   5

As my foot suggests that you leap in the air with your hips of a girl,
My finger that praises your wheel and announces your voices of song,
Flouncing your skirts, you blueness of joy, you flirt of politeness,
You leap, you intelligence, essence of wheelness with silvery nose,
And your platinum clocks of excitement stir like the hairs of a fern.   10

But how alien you are from the booming belts of your birth and the
      smoke
Where you turned on the stinging lathes of Detroit and Lansing at night
And shrieked at the torch in your secret parts and the amorous tests,
But now with your eyes that enter the future of roads you forget;
You are all instinct with your phosphorous glow and your streaking
      hair.   15

And now when we stop it is not as the bird from the shell that I leave
Or the leathery pilot who steps from his bird with a sneer of delight,
And not as the ignorant beast do you squat and watch me depart,
But with exquisite breathing you smile, with satisfaction of love,
And I touch you again as you tick in the silence and settle in sleep. 20

Study and Discussion Questions

1. Who is speaking in the poem? Why can you assume the speaker is male? What else can you say about him?
2. Go through the poem and list the ways in which the speaker compares his car to a woman. The poem is ostensibly about the speaker's feelings for his car. But what does it suggest about how he perceives women?
3. How do sound and rhythm in the first stanza help convey the speaker's experience as he drives? How and why is the first line of the third

stanza different from what comes before? What new emotion does the
third stanza reveal?

4. What is the function of the negative comparisons ("it is not as . . . ")
   in the last stanza? How is the speaker feeling at the end of the poem?
5. What is the poet's attitude toward the speaker, towards the *persona* he
   has created? How can you tell?

Writing Exercises

1. To what extent is "Buick" an accurate portrayal of male feelings rather
   than just a parody of them?
2. Why are cars in our culture usually seen as female? What other kinds
   of objects or machines are viewed in gendered terms? Why are they
   so often seen as female?
3. Which line or phrase from the poem stands out most in your mind?
   Try to explain why.
4. Try writing a poem or prose passage in which the speaker dramatizes
   his or her intense emotional relationship with an object other than an
   automobile. Think carefully before ascribing a gender to this object.

TED HUGHES   (b. 1930)

*Ted Hughes was born in Mytholmroyd, Yorkshire, England, served in the
Royal Air Force, and was educated at Cambridge. In 1956, he married American
poet Sylvia Plath; they separated shortly before her suicide in 1963. He has
written radio plays and short stories, but is best known for his poetry, which
includes* The Hawk in the Rain *(1957),* Crow *(1970), and* Moortown *(1979).
Hughes is the Poet Laureate of England.*

The Lovepet   (1971)

Was it an animal was it a bird?
She stroked it. He spoke to it softly.
She made her voice its happy forest.
He brought it out with sugarlump smiles.
Soon it was licking their kisses.   5

She gave it the strings of her voice which it swallowed
He gave it the blood of his face it grew eager
She gave it the liquorice of her mouth it began to thrive
He opened the aniseed of his future
And it bit and gulped, grew vicious, snatched   10
The focus of his eyes

She gave it the steadiness of her hand
He gave it the strength of his spine it ate everything

It began to cry what could they give it
They gave it their calendars it bolted their diaries   15
They gave it their sleep it gobbled their dreams
Even while they slept
It ate their bodyskin and the muscle beneath
They gave it vows its teeth clashed its starvation
Through every word they uttered   20

It found snakes under the floor it ate them
It found a spider horror
In their palms and ate it.

They gave it double smiles and blank silence
It chewed holes in their carpets   25
They gave it logic
It ate the colour of their hair
They gave it every argument that would come
They gave it shouting and yelling they meant it
It ate the faces of their children   30
They gave it their photograph albums they gave it their records
It ate the colour of the sun
They gave it a thousand letters they gave it money
It ate their future complete it waited for them
Staring and starving   35
They gave it screams it had gone too far
It ate into their brains
It ate the roof
It ate lonely stone it ate wind crying famine   40
It went furiously off

They wept they called it back it could have everything
It stripped out their nerves chewed chewed flavourless
It bit at their numb bodies they did not resist
It bit into their blank brains they hardly knew

It moved bellowing   45
Through a ruin of starlight and crockery

It drew slowly off they could not move

It went far away they could not speak

Study and Discussion Questions

1. What are the stages this marriage, or love relationship, goes through?
2. Classify the types of "food" the lovepet eats.
3. "They wept they called it back." Why?
4. Discuss Hughes's use of repetition of sounds, words, and phrases in "The Lovepet."

Writing Exercises

1. Why is the lovepet so hungry?
2. Choose or invent an animal or plant that represents a relationship in your life (it could be family or work as easily as love). Describe its qualities.

OLGA BROUMAS   (b. 1949)

Olga Broumas was born in Greece and moved to the United States at age ten. She was educated at the University of Oregon and has taught at Goddard College. Her poetry includes Beginning with O *(1977) and* Soie Sauvage *(1980).*

Cinderella   (1977)

> *. . . the joy that isn't shared*
> *I heard, dies young.*
> Anne Sexton, 1928–1974

Apart from my sisters, estranged
from my mother, I am a woman alone
in a house of men
who secretly
call themselves princes, alone   5
with me usually, under cover of dark. I am the one allowed in

to the royal chambers, whose small foot conveniently
fills the slipper of glass. The woman writer, the lady

umpire, the madam chairman, anyone's wife.
I know what I know. 10
And I once was glad

of the chance to use it, even alone
in a strange castle, doing overtime on my own, cracking
the royal code. The princes spoke
in their fathers' language, were eager to praise me 15
my nimble tongue. I am a woman in a state of siege, alone

as one piece of laundry, strung on a windy clothesline a
mile long. A woman co-opted by promises: the lure
of a job, the ruse of a choice, a woman forced
to bear witness, falsely 20
against my kind, as each
other sister was judged inadequate, bitchy, incompetent,
jealous, too thin, too fat. I know what I know.
What sweet bread I make

for myself in this prosperous house 25
is dirty, what good soup I boil turns
in my mouth to mud. Give
me my ashes. A cold stove, a cinder-block pillow, wet
canvas shoes in my sisters', my sisters' hut. Or I swear

I'll die young 30
like those favored before me, hand-picked each one
for her joyful heart.

Study and Discussion Questions

1. What price has the speaker of the poem had to pay for success?
2. List specific images of loneliness in the poem.
3. What is the speaker's relation to other women? What is her relation to men?

Writing Exercise

1. How has Broumas rewritten the Cinderella fairy tale for modern readers? What changes has she made in the story? (Remember, there is more than one version of the fairy tale.) How do the changes serve her purpose?

CHRISTOPHER MARLOWE   (1564–1593)

The Passionate Shepherd to His Love   (1600)

Come live with me and be my love,
And we will all the pleasures prove[1]
That valleys, groves, hills, and fields,
Woods, or steepy mountain yields.

And we will sit upon the rocks,   5
Seeing the shepherds feed their flocks,
By shallow rivers to whose falls
Melodious birds sing madrigals.

And I will make thee beds of roses
And a thousand fragrant posies,   10
A cap of flowers, and a kirtle[2]
Embroidered all with leaves of myrtle;

A gown made of the finest wool
Which from our pretty lambs we pull;
Fair lined slippers for the cold,   15
With buckles of the purest gold;

A belt of straw and ivy buds,
With coral clasps and amber studs:
And if these pleasures may thee move,
Come live with me, and be my love.   20

The shepherds' swains shall dance and sing
For thy delight each May morning:
If these delights thy mind may move,
Then live with me and be my love.

---

[1] Try out.
[2] Dress.

WILLIAM SHAKESPEARE   (1564–1616)

When my love swears that she is made of truth   (1609)

CXXXVIII

When my love swears that she is made of truth,
I do believe her, though I know she lies,
That she might think me some untutor'd youth,
Unlearned in the world's false subtleties.
Thus vainly thinking that she thinks me young,   5
Although she knows my days are past the best,
Simply I credit her false-speaking tongue:
On both sides thus is simple truth supprest.
But wherefore says she not she is unjust?
And wherefore say not I that I am old?   10
O! love's best habit is in seeming trust,
And age in love loves not to have years told:
   Therefore I lie with her, and she with me,
   And in our faults by lies we flatter'd be.

ANONYMOUS

The Song of Solomon[1]

Behold, thou *art* fair, my love; behold, thou *art* fair; thou *hast* doves' eyes within thy locks: thy hair *is* as a flock of goats, that appear from mount Gĭl'ē-ăd.

2 Thy teeth *are* are like a flock *of sheep that are even* shorn, which came up from the washing; whereof every one bear twins, and none *is* barren among them.

3 Thy lips *are* like a thread of scarlet, and thy speech *is* comely: thy temples *are* like a piece of a pomegranate within thy locks.

4 Thy neck *is* like the tower of David builded for an armory, whereon there hang a thousand bucklers, all shields of mighty men.

5 Thy two breasts *are* like two young roes that are twins, which feed among the lilies.

---

[1] *King James Bible* (1611).

6 Until the day break, and the shadows flee away, I will get me to the mountain of myrrh, and to the hill of frankincense.

7 Thou *art* all fair, my love; *there is* no spot in thee.

8 ¶ Come with me from Lebanon, *my* spouse, with me from Lebanon: look from the top of Ăm'å-nå, from the top of Shē'nir and Hermon, from the lions' dens, from the mountains of the leopards.

9 Thou hast ravished my heart, my sister, *my* spouse; thou hast ravished my heart with one of thine eyes, with one chain of thy neck.

10 How fair is thy love, my sister, *my* spouse! how much better is thy love than wine! and the smell of thine ointments than all spices!

11 Thy lips, O *my* spouse, drop *as* the honeycomb: honey and milk *are* under thy tongue; and the smell of thy garments *is* like the smell of Lebanon.

12 A garden inclosed *is* my sister, *my* spouse; a spring shut up, a fountain sealed.

13 Thy plants *are* an orchard of pomegranates, with pleasant fruits; camphire, with spikenard,

14 Spikenard and saffron; calamus and cinnamon, with all trees of frankincense; myrrh and aloes, with all the chief spices:

15 A fountain of gardens, a well of living waters, and streams from Lebanon.

16 ¶ Awake, O north wind; and come, thou south; blow upon my garden, *that* the spices thereof may flow out. Let my beloved come into his garden, and eat his pleasant fruits.

JOHN DONNE   (1572–1631)

The Sun Rising   (1633)

Busy old fool, unruly sun,
   Why dost thou thus,
Through windows, and through curtains call on us?
Must to thy motions lovers' seasons run?
   Saucy pedantic wretch, go chide   5
    Late school-boys, and sour prentices,
  Go tell court-huntsmen, that the King will ride,
   Call country ants[1] to harvest offices;
Love, all alike, no season knows, nor clime,
Nor hours, days, months, which are the rags of time.   10

---

[1] Rural workers.

Thy beams, so reverend, and strong
   Why shouldst thou think?
I could eclipse and cloud them with a wink,
But that I would not lose her sight so long:
   If her eyes have not blinded thine,   15
   Look, and tomorrow late, tell me,
  Whether both the Indias[2] of spice and mine
  Be where thou left'st them, or lie here with me.
Ask for those kings whom thou saw'st yesterday,
And thou shalt hear, All here in one bed lay.   20

She is all states, and all princes, I,
   Nothing else is.
Princes do but play us; compared to this,
All honour's mimic; all wealth alchemy.
   Thou sun art half as happy as we,   25
   In that the world's contracted thus;
  Thine age asks ease, and since thy duties be
  To warm the world, that's done in warming us.
Shine here to us, and thou art everywhere;
This bed thy centre[3] is, these walls, thy sphere.   30

JOHN DONNE   **(1572–1631)**

The Canonization   **(1633)**

For God's sake hold your tongue, and let me love,
   Or chide my palsy, or my gout,
My five grey hairs, or ruined fortune flout,
   With wealth your state, your mind with arts improve,
     Take you a course, get you a place   5
     Observe his Honour, or his Grace,
Or the King's real, or his stamped face
   Contemplate; what you will, approve,[1]
   So you will let me love.

---

[2] The East and West Indies.
[3] Orbital center.
[1] Try.

Alas, alas, who's injured by my love? 10
   What merchant's ships have my sighs drowned?
Who says my tears have overflowed his ground?
   When did my colds a forward spring remove?
      When did the heats which my veins fill
      Add one more to the plaguy bill?[2] 15
Soldiers find wars, and lawyers find out still
   Litigious men, which quarrels move,
   Though she and I do love.

Call us what you will, we are made such by love;
   Call her one, me another fly, 20
We are tapers too, and at our own cost die,[3]
   And we in us find the Eagle and the Dove.
      The Phoenix riddle hath more wit
      By us; we two being one, are it.
So to one neutral thing both sexes fit, 25
   We die and rise the same, and prove
   Mysterious by this love.

We can die by it, if not live by love,
   And if unfit for tombs and hearse
Our legend be, it will be fit for verse; 30
   And if no piece of chronicle we prove,
      We'll build in sonnets pretty rooms;
      As well a well-wrought urn becomes
The greatest ashes, as half-acre tombs,
   And by these hymns, all shall approve 35
   Us canonized for love:

And thus invoke us; 'You whom reverend love
   Made one another's hermitage;
You, to whom love was peace, that now is rage;
   Who did the whole world's soul contract, and drove 40
      Into the glasses of your eyes
      (So made such mirrors, and such spies,
That they did all to you epitomize),
   Countries, towns, courts: beg from above
   A pattern of your love!' 45

---

[2] List of victims of the plague.
[3] Climax sexually.

ANDREW MARVELL   (1621–1678)

To His Coy Mistress   (1681)

  Had we but world enough, and time,
This coyness, Lady, were no crime.
We would sit down, and think which way
To walk, and pass our long love's day.
Thou by the Indian Ganges' side   5
Shouldst rubies find; I by the tide
Of Humber would complain. I would
Love you ten years before the Flood,
And you should, if you please, refuse
Till the Conversion of the Jews.   10
My vegetable[1] love should grow
Vaster than empires and more slow;
An hundred years should go to praise
Thine eyes, and on thy forehead gaze;
Two hundred to adore each breast,   15
But thirty thousand to the rest;
An age at least to every part,
And the last age should show your heart.
For, Lady, you deserve this state,
Nor would I love at lower rate.   20
  But at my back I always hear
Time's wingèd chariot hurrying near;
And yonder all before us lie
Deserts of vast eternity.
Thy beauty shall no more be found,   25
Nor, in thy marble vault, shall sound
My echoing song; then worms shall try
That long-preserved virginity,
And your quaint honour turn to dust,
And into ashes all my lust: 30
The grave's a fine and private place,
But none, I think, do there embrace.
  Now therefore, while the youthful hue
Sits on thy skin like morning dew,
And while thy willing soul transpires   35
At every pore with instant fires,
Now let us sport us while we may,
And now, like amorous birds of prey,

---

[1] Growing on its own.

Rather at once our time devour
Than languish in his slow chapt[2] power.   40
Let us roll all our strength and all
Our sweetness up into one ball,
And tear our pleasures with rough strife
Thorough[3] the iron gates of life;
Thus, though we cannot make our sun   45
Stand still, yet we will make him run.

JOHN KEATS   (1795–1821)

FROM **The Eve of St. Agnes**[4]   (1819)

> ### XXX
> And still she slept an azure-lidded sleep,
> In blanched linen, smooth, and lavender'd,
> While he from forth the closet brought a heap
> Of candied apple, quince, and plum, and gourd;
> With jellies soother than the creamy curd,   5
> And lucent syrops, tinct with cinnamon;
> Manna and dates, in argosy transferr'd
> From Fez;[5] and spiced dainties, every one,
> From silken Samarcand[6] to cedar'd Lebanon.
>
> ### XXXI
> These delicates he heap'd with glowing hand   10
> On golden dishes and in baskets bright
> Of wreathed silver: sumptuous they stand
> In the retired quiet of the night,
> Filling the chilly room with perfume light.——
> 'And now, my love, my seraph fair, awake!   15
> 'Thou art my heaven, and I thine eremite:[7]

---

[2] Slow-jawed.

[3] Through.

[4] On January 20, St. Agnes's Eve, it was believed, maidens would dream a vision of their future husbands. In the poem, Madeline has gone to sleep expecting such a vision, and Porphyro has stolen into her room.

[5] City in Morocco.

[6] City now in the Soviet Union.

[7] Hermit, usually religious.

'Open thine eyes, for meek St. Agnes' sake,
'Or I shall drowse beside thee, so my soul doth ache.'

ELIZABETH BARRETT BROWNING   (1806–1861)

How Do I Love Thee?   (1850)

How do I love thee? Let me count the ways.
I love thee to the depth and breadth and height
My soul can reach, when feeling out of sight
For the ends of Being and ideal Grace.
I love thee to the level of everyday's   5
Most quiet need, by sun and candle-light.
I love thee freely, as men strive for Right;
I love thee purely, as they turn from Praise.
I love thee with the passion put to use
In my old griefs, and with my childhood's faith.   10
I love thee with a love I seemed to lose
With my lost saints,—I love thee with the breath,
Smiles, tears, of all my life!—and, if God choose,
I shall but love thee better after death.

WALT WHITMAN   (1819–1892)

To a Stranger   (1860)

Passing stranger! you do not know how longingly I look upon you,
You must be he I was seeking, or she I was seeking (it comes to me
       as of a dream,)
I have somewhere surely lived a life of joy with you,
All is recall'd as we flit by each other, fluid, affectionate, chaste,   5
       matured,
You grew up with me, were a boy with me or a girl with me,
I ate with you and slept with you, your body has become not yours
       only nor left my body mine only,
You give me the pleasure of your eyes, face, flesh, as we pass, you
       take of my beard, breast, hands, in return,   10

I am not to speak to you, I am to think of you when I sit alone or
 wake at night alone,
I am to wait, I do not doubt I am to meet you again,
I am to see to it that I do not lose you.

WALT WHITMAN   (1819–1892)

I Saw in Louisiana a Live-Oak Growing (1860)

I saw in Louisiana a live-oak growing,
All alone stood it and the moss hung down from the branches,
Without any companion it grew there uttering joyous leaves of dark
 green,
And its look, rude, unbending, lusty, made me think of myself, 5
But I wonder'd how it could utter joyous leaves standing alone there
 without its friend near, for I knew I could not,
And I broke off a twig with a certain number of leaves upon it, and
 twined around it a little moss,
And brought it away, and I have placed it in sight in my room, 10
It is not needed to remind me as of my own dear friends,
(For I believe lately I think of little else than of them,)
Yet it remains to me a curious token, it makes me think of manly love;
For all that, and though the live-oak glistens there in Louisiana solitary
 in a wide flat space, 15
Uttering joyous leaves all its life without a friend a lover near,
I know very well I could not.

CHRISTINA ROSSETTI   (1830–1894)

A Birthday (1862)

My heart is like a singing bird
 Whose nest is in a watered shoot;
My heart is like an apple-tree
 Whose boughs are bent with thickset fruit;
My heart is like a rainbow shell 5
 That paddles in a halcyon sea;

My heart is gladder than all these
  Because my love is come to me.

Raise me a dais of silk and down;
  Hang it with vair and purple dyes;   10
Carve it in doves and pomegranates,
  And peacocks with a hundred eyes;
Work it in gold and silver grapes,
  In leaves and silver fleurs-de-lys;
Because the birthday of my life   15
  Is come, my love is come to me.

EMILY DICKINSON   (1830–1886)

My Life had stood—a Loaded Gun   (1863)

My Life had stood—a Loaded Gun—
In Corners—till a Day
The Owner passed—identified—
And carried Me away—

And now We roam in Sovreign Woods—   5
And now We hunt the Doe—
And every time I speak for Him—
The Mountains straight reply—

And do I smile, such cordial light
Upon the Valley glow—   10
It is as a Vesuvian face
Had let it's pleasure through—

And when at Night—Our good Day done—
I guard My Master's Head—
'Tis better than the Eider-Duck's   15
Deep Pillow—to have shared—

To foe of His—I'm deadly foe—
None stir the second time—

On whom I lay a Yellow Eye—
Or an emphatic Thumb—   20

Though I than He—may longer live
He longer must—than I—
For I have but the power to kill,
Without—the power to die—

AMY LOWELL   (1874–1925)

A Decade   (1919)

When you came, you were like red wine
    and honey,
And the taste of you burnt my mouth
    with its sweetness.
Now you are like morning bread,   5
Smooth and pleasant.
I hardly taste you at all for I know your
    savour,
But I am completely nourished.

ALBERTA HUNTER/   (1895–1984)
LOVIE AUSTIN   (1887–1972)

SONG: **Down Hearted Blues**   (1922)

Gee, but it's hard to love someone, when that someone don't love you.
I'm so digusted, heartbroken too. I've got the downhearted blues.
Once I was crazy about a man. He mistreated me all the time.
The next man I get, he's got to promise to be mine, all mine.

'Cause you mistreated me, and you drove me from your door.
You mistreated me, and you drove me from your door.
But the Good Book says, "You've got to reap just what you sow."

Trouble, trouble, seems like I've had it all my days.
Trouble, trouble, seems like I've had it all my days.
Sometime I think trouble is gonna follow me to my grave.

I ain't never loved but three men in my life.
Lord, I ain't never loved but three men in my life.
One's my father, and my brother, and the man that wrecked my life.

Now it may be a week, and it may be a month or two.
I said, it may be a week, and it may be a month or two.
All the dirt you're doing to me is, honey, coming back home to you.

I've got the world in a jug and the stopper in my hand.
I've got the world in a jug and the stopper in my hand.
And if you want me, pretty papa, you've got to come under my command.

CLAUDE MCKAY   (1890–1948)

The Harlem Dancer   (1922)

Applauding youths laughed with young prostitutes
And watched her perfect, half-clothed body sway;
Her voice was like the sound of blended flutes
Blown by black players upon a picnic day.
She sang and danced on gracefully and calm,   5
The light gauze hanging loose about her form;
To me she seemed a proudly-swaying palm
Grown lovelier for passing through a storm.
Upon her swarthy neck black shiny curls
Luxuriant fell; and tossing coins in praise,   10
The wine-flushed, bold-eyed boys, and even the girls,
Devoured her shape with eager, passionate gaze;
But looking at her falsely-smiling face,
I knew her self was not in that strange place.

WILLIAM BUTLER YEATS (1865–1939)

Leda and the Swan[1] (1923)

A sudden blow: the great wings beating still
Above the staggering girl, her thighs caressed
By the dark webs, her nape caught in his bill,
He holds her helpless breast upon his breast.

How can those terrified vague fingers push 5
The feathered glory from her loosening thighs?
And how can body, laid in that white rush,
But feel the strange heart beating where it lies?

A shudder in the loins engenders there
The broken wall, the burning roof and tower 10
And Agamemnon dead.
     Being so caught up,
So mastered by the brute blood of the air,
Did she put on his knowledge with his power
Before the indifferent beak could let her drop? 15

LOUISE BOGAN (1897–1970)

Women (1923)

Women have no wilderness in them,
They are provident instead,
Content in the tight hot cell of their hearts
To eat dusty bread.

They do not see cattle cropping red winter grass, 5
They do not hear
Snow water going down under culverts
Shallow and clear.

---

[1] Greek god Zeus, in the form of a swan, raped Leda, who bore Helen of Troy (whose abduction led to the Trojan War) and Clytemnestra (who murdered her husband Agamemnon upon his return from that war).

They wait, when they should turn to journeys,
They stiffen, when they should bend.   10
They use against themselves that benevolence
To which no man is friend.

They cannot think of so many crops to a field
Or of clean wood cleft by an axe.
Their love is an eager meaninglessness   15
Too tense, or too lax.

They hear in every whisper that speaks to them
A shout and a cry.
As like as not, when they take life over their door-sills
They should let it go by.   20

GLADYS BENTLEY

SONG: **How Much Can I Stand?**   **(1928)**

I've heard about your lovers
Your pinks and browns
I've heard about your sheiks
And hand me downs

I've got a man   5
I've loved all the while
But now he treats me
Like a darn bad child

One time he said my sugar
Was so sweet   10
But now for his dessert
He goes across the street
How much of that dog can I stand?

My man's love
Has got so cold and dead   15
That now he has to wear

An overcoat to bed
How much of that dog can I **stand?**

Women selling snakeskins
And alligator tails   20
Tryin to get money
To get my man out of jail
How much of that dog can I **stand?**

Said I was an angel
He was born to treat me right   25
Who in the devil ever heard of angels
That get beat up every night
How much of that dog can I **stand?**

Went down to the drug store
Asked the clerk for a dose   30
But when I received the poison
I eyed it very close
Lord, how much of this dog can I **stand?**

Come home from work
Feelin' tired and sore   35
He makes me shove my money
Underneath my front door
How much of that dog can I **stand?**

The next man I get
Must be guaranteed   40
When I walk down the aisle
You're gonna hear me scream
How much of this dog can I **stand?**

ANDRÉ BRETON   (1896–1966)

Freedom of Love[1]   (1931)

My wife with the hair of a wood fire
With the thoughts of heat lightning

---

[1] Translated by Edouard Roditi.

With the waist of an hourglass
With the waist of an otter in the teeth of a tiger
My wife with the lips of a cockade and of a bunch of stars of the   5
           last magnitude
With the teeth of tracks of white mice on the white earth
With the tongue of rubbed amber and glass
My wife with the tongue of a stabbed host
With the tongue of a doll that opens and closes its eyes
With the tongue of an unbelievable stone   10
My wife with the eyelashes of strokes of a child's writing
With brows of the edge of a swallow's nest
My wife with the brow of slates of a hothouse roof
And of steam on the panes
My wife with shoulders of champagne   15
And of a fountain with dolphin-heads beneath the ice
My wife with wrists of matches
My wife with fingers of luck and ace of hearts
With fingers of mown hay
My wife with armpits of marten and of beechnut   20
And of Midsummer Night
Of privet and of an angelfish nest
With arms of seafoam and of riverlocks
And of a mingling of the wheat and the mill
My wife with legs of flares   25
With the movements of clockwork and despair
My wife with calves of eldertree pith
My wife with feet of initials
With feet of rings of keys and Java sparrows drinking
My wife with a neck of unpearled barley   30
My wife with a throat of the valley of gold
Of a tryst in the very bed of the torrent
With breasts of night
My wife with breasts of a marine molehill
My wife with breasts of the ruby's crucible   35
With breasts of the rose's spectre beneath the dew
My wife with the belly of an unfolding of the fan of days
With the belly of a gigantic claw
My wife with the back of a bird fleeing vertically
With a back of quicksilver   40
With a back of light
With a nape of rolled stone and wet chalk
And of the drop of a glass where one has just been drinking
My wife with hips of a skiff
With hips of a chandelier and of arrow-feathers   45
And of shafts of white peacock plumes
Of an insensible pendulum

My wife with buttocks of sandstone and asbestos
My wife with buttocks of swans' backs
My wife with buttocks of spring   50
With the sex of an iris
My wife with the sex of a mining-placer and of a platypus
My wife with a sex of seaweeed and ancient sweetmeat
My wife with a sex of mirror
My wife with eyes full of tears   55
With eyes of purple panoply and of a magnetic needle
My wife with savanna eyes
My wife with eyes of water to be drunk in prison
My wife with eyes of wood always under the axe
My wife with eyes of water-level of level of air earth and fire   60

GWENDOLYN BROOKS   (b. 1917)

---

when you have forgotten Sunday:
the love story   (1945)

———And when you have forgotten the bright bedclothes
    on a Wednesday and a Saturday,
And most especially when you have forgotten Sunday—
When you have forgotten Sunday halves in bed,
Or me sitting on the front-room radiator in the limping   5
    afternoon
Looking off down the long street
To nowhere,
Hugged by my plain old wrapper of no-expectation
And nothing-I-have-to-do and I'm-happy-why?   10
And if-Monday-never-had-to-come—
When you have forgotten that, I say,
And how you swore, if somebody beeped the bell,
And how my heart played hopscotch if the telephone
    rang;   15
And how we finally went in to Sunday dinner,
That is to say, went across the front room floor to the
    ink-spotted table in the southwest corner
To Sunday dinner, which was always chicken and
    noodles   20
Or chicken and rice
And salad and rye bread and tea

And chocolate chip cookies—
I say, when you have forgotten that,
When you have forgotten my little presentiment 25
That the war would be over before they got to you;
And how we finally undressed and whipped out the
    light and flowed into bed,
And lay loose-limbed for a moment in the week-end
Bright bedclothes, 30
Then gently folded into each other—
When you have, I say, forgotten all that,
Then you may tell,
Then I may believe
You have forgotten me well. 35

OWEN DODSON   (b. 1914)

Drunken Lover   (1946)

This is the stagnant hour:
The dead communion between mouth and mouth,
The drunken kiss lingered,
The dreadful equator south.

This is the hour of impotence 5
When the unfulfilled is unfulfilled.
Only the stale breath is anxious
And warm. All else is stilled.

Why did I come to this reek,
This numb time, this level? 10
Only for you, my love, only for you
Could I endure this devil.

I dreamed when I was
A pimply and urgent adolescent
Of these hours when love would be fire 15
And you the steep descent.

My mouth's inside is like cotton,
Your arm is dead on my arm.
What I pictured so lovely and spring
Is August and fungus calm.   20

O lover, draw away, grow small, go magic,
O lover, disappear into the tick of this bed;
Open all the windows to the north
For the wind to cool my head.

LÉOPOLD SÉDAR SENGHOR   (b. 1906)

You Held the Black Face[1]
(for Khalam)   **(1949)**

You held the black face of the warrior between your hands
Which seemed with fateful twilight luminous.
From the hill I watched the sunset in the bays of your eyes.
When shall I see my land again, the pure horizon of your face?
When shall I sit at the table of your dark breasts?   5
The nest of sweet decisions lies in the shade.
I shall see different skies and different eyes,
And shall drink from the sources of other lips, fresher than lemons,
I shall sleep under the roofs of other hair, protected from storms.
But every year, when the rum of spring kindles the veins afresh,   10
I shall mourn anew my home, and the rain of your eyes over the
   thirsty savannah.

LANGSTON HUGHES   (1902–1967)

Mellow   **(1951)**

Into the laps
of black celebrities

---

[1] Translated by Gerald Moore and Ulli Beier.

white girls fall
like pale plums from a tree
beyond a high tension wall   5
wired for killing
which makes it
more thrilling.

GREGORY CORSO   (b. 1930)

Marriage   (1960)

Should I get married? Should I be good?
Astound the girl next door
with my velvet suit and faustus hood?
Don't take her to movies but to cemeteries
tell all about werewolf bathtubs and forked clarinets   5
then desire her and kiss her and all the preliminaries
and she going just so far and I understanding why
not getting angry saying You must feel! It's beautiful to feel!
Instead take her in my arms
lean against an old crooked tombstone   10
and woo her the entire night the constellations in the sky—

When she introduces me to her parents
back straightened, hair finally combed, strangled by a tie,
should I sit knees together on their 3rd degree sofa
and not ask Where's the bathroom?   15
How else to feel other than I am,
often thinking Flash Gordon[1] soap—
O how terrible it must be for a young man
seated before a family and the family thinking
We never saw him before! He wants our Mary Lou!   20
After tea and homemade cookies they ask
What do you do for a living?
Should I tell them? Would they like me then?
Say All right get married, we're not losing a daughter
we're gaining a son—   25
And should I then ask Where's the bathroom?

---

[1] Science fiction hero of comic strip and film.

O God, and the wedding! All her family and her friends
and only a handful of mine all scroungy and bearded
just wait to get at the drinks and food—
And the priest! he looking at me as if I masturbated   30
asking me Do you take this woman
for your lawful wedded wife!
And I trembling what to say say Pie Glue!
I kiss the bride all those corny men slapping me on the back
She's all yours, boy! Ha-ha-ha!   35
And in their eyes you could see
some obscene honeymoon going on—
Then all that absurd rice and clanky cans and shoes
Niagara Falls! Hordes of us!
Husbands! Wives! Flowers! Chocolates!   40
All streaming into cosy hotels
All going to do the same thing tonight
The indifferent clerk he knowing what was going to happen
The lobby zombies they knowing what
The whistling elevator man he knowing   45
The winking bellboy knowing
Everybody knowing!
I'd be almost inclined not to do anything!
Stay up all night! Stare that hotel clerk in the eye!
Screaming: I deny honeymoon! I deny honeymoon!   50
running rampant into those almost climactic suites
yelling Radio belly! Cat shovel!
O I'd live in Niagara forever! in a dark cave beneath the Falls
I'd sit there the Mad Honeymooner
devising ways to break marriages, a scourge of bigamy   55
a saint of divorce—

But I should get married I should be good
How nice it'd be to come home to her
and sit by the fireplace and she in the kitchen
aproned young and lovely wanting my baby   60
and so happy about me she burns the roast beef
and comes crying to me and I get up from my big papa chair
saying Christmas teeth! Radiant brains! Apple deaf!
God what a husband I'd make! Yes, I should get married!
So much to do! like sneaking into Mr Jones' house late at night   65
and cover his golf clubs with 1920 Norwegian books
Like hanging a picture of Rimbaud on the lawnmower
Like pasting Tannu Tuva[2] postage stamps

---

[2] Region of Soviet Union in Asia.

all over the picket fence
Like when Mrs Kindhead comes to collect 70
for the Community Chest
grab her and tell her There are unfavourable omens in the sky!
And when the mayor comes to get my vote tell him
When are you going to stop people killing whales!
And when the milkman comes leave him a note in the bottle 75
Penguin dust, bring me penguin dust, I want penguin dust—

Yet if I should get married and it's Connecticut and snow
and she gives birth to a child and I am sleepless, worn,
up for nights, head bowed against a quiet window
the past behind me, 80
finding myself in the most common of situations
a trembling man knowledged with responsibility
not twig-smear nor Roman coin soup—
O what would that be like!
Surely I'd give it for a nipple a rubber Tacitus 85
For a rattle a bag of broken Bach records
Tack Della Francesca all over its crib
Sew the Greek alphabet on its bib
And build for its playpen a roofless Parthenon

No, I doubt I'd be that kind of father 90
not rural not snow no quiet window
but hot smelly tight New York City
seven flights up, roaches and rats in the walls
a fat Reichian[3] wife screeching over potatoes Get a job!
And five nose running brats in love with Batman[4] 95
And the neighbours all toothless and dry haired
like those hag masses of the 18th century
all wanting to come in and watch TV
The landlord wants his rent
Grocery store Blue Cross Gas & Electric Knights of Columbus 100
Impossible to lie back and dream
Telephone snow, ghost parking—
No! I should not get married I should never get married!
But—imagine if I were married
to a beautiful sophisticated woman 105
tall and pale wearing an elegant black dress
and long black gloves
holding a cigarettte holder in one hand

---

[3] Wilhelm Reich (1897–1957), psychoanalyst.
[4] Comic book and TV hero.

and a highball in the other
and we lived high up in a penthouse with a huge window   110
from which we could see all of New York
and even farther on clearer days
No, can't imagine myself married to that pleasant prison
    dream—

O but what about love? I forget love   115
not that I am incapable of love
it's just that I see love as odd as wearing shoes—
I never wanted to marry a girl who was like my mother
And Ingrid Bergman[5] was always impossible
And there's maybe a girl now but she's already married   120
And I don't like men and—
but there's got to be somebody!
Because what if I'm 60 years old and not married,
all alone in a furnished room with pee stains on my underwear
and everybody else is married!   125
All the universe married but me!

Ah, yet well I know that were a woman possible as I am possible
then marriage would be possible—
Like SHE[6] in her lonely alien gaud waiting her Egyptian lover
so I wait—bereft of 2,000 years and the bath of life.   130

DIANE WAKOSKI   (b. 1937)

Slicing Oranges for Jeremiah   (1968)

as the juice ran out on the wooden board
    the third orange you had cut for this son of yours
    opened
    and he grabbed the slices like a little raccoon running to
    prepare them,   5
    carrying his bowl to the table where he ate,
his instinct trying to make up for something not in his throat
or his fingers,
trying to make up for the thyroid gland he was born without

---

[5] Movie actress (b. 1915).
[6] Novel and movie heroine; SHE possesses eternal life.

he would eat a dozen oranges if you would let him   10
rosy Jeremiah, with long eyelashes

what does it mean
if a child cannot talk when he is six,
if he shits in the toilet one day; in his pants the next?
what does it mean   15
if a man drinks and can't earn enough money?
and what if he tells his wife he'd like another woman
but wouldn't have one,
and what does it mean
if he tells his wife she's unpleasant or dull   20
and what
does
it mean
if his wife takes sleeping pills or walks
in front of a car?   25
and what
does it mean,
if Jeremiah takes the sun
and slices it up
like the oranges and eats a little fire   30
thirsty for the juice?

When you take the knife in your hand
to slice an orange first into quarters, then into eighths,
each slice shining—
        as orange jelly, a goldfish,   35
        lights on the water at night,
and you cut, competently, efficiently, a housewife
who knows how to divide,
when you take your instrument and use it
making pools of orange juice, letting the peel spray into 40
your nostrils,
what does it mean?
        And your son,
eating orange after orange,
until I felt the juice in my own mouth,   45
just watching,
and the sweetness,
and I wondered what was missing,
or why,
and where his thyroid went   50
or why there was no gland there,
and how even this baby animal,

your son,
must know that it was you who kept him alive,
remembering his pill each day,   55
and taking him places where people would respect him
and letting him make drawings
and build garbage structures:
and how his father knew too
it was you who kept him, your husband, alive,   60
giving him whatever artificial gland it was you did each day,
and how they both resented it,
depending on it as they did,
the men needing the woman more than any man could admit.

And what does it mean,   65
this strength you have?
It keeps you hovering towards death.
It keeps you near the pill bottles and close to the wheels of cars.
It keeps you sad and compassionate,
willing to understand the miseries of others.   70
It isn't weakness that points us towards death, but strength,
men dying earlier than women,
trying to show their strength,
women taking their own lives with gas, in ovens with their
gold-clock babies under their aprons,   75
with sleeping pills glistening like amber necklaces poured into
the stomach's cave,
stepping quietly under car wheels,
as they lie with their men at night,
not murmuring,   80
enduring
until the breath is pushed out.

Slicing oranges for your son,
you cannot see what I see,
the oranges growing outside my own back door when I was five,   85
the dusty dark citrus leaves making black smudges
against my sweater.
There is a gypsy in me
who wants to run
with all these oranges in a bag   90
and trade them for the sun
or find someone who will cut them for me
the way you slice them for Jeremiah.
That care;
that efficiency.   95

Instead of some gland, I might have
an orange tree
growing just behind my throat
straining to stay alive, to endure,
waiting for the efficient hand to reach inside   100
and slice the oranges
as you do,
as I saw you
slice oranges for Jeremiah,   105
slice the oranges for your son
who could eat a dozen you said
if you'd let him

NAYO (BARBARA MALCOLM)

First Time I Was Sweet Sixteen   (1969)

First time I was sweet sixteen
    marriage license, zircon ring—all legit
    he was captain of the football team
            and hero of all the chicks
    and I was hot stuff cause I caught him   5
then after graduation
    the military, stockade, dishonorable discharge
    job after job and all that
    he was still captain of the football team
            and hero of all the chicks   10
    and I got tired of being the football
so, picked up my two babies and split

But I was scared, you see, insecure
    I needed a cat to pay the bills
    and along come this big shouldered honey   15
    told me his shoulders were big enough—
    swept me right into his "protective" arms.
Never saw a cat work 40 hours a week
plus overtime and never have a cent
Never saw so many cut-off and   20
shut-off men in my life
Everything got mighty quiet
the radio wouldn't sizzle (electricity cut off)

meat wouldn't sizzle (gas was off)
babies wouldn't cry (they were too sick)   25
not even a drip from the water faucet
and him—he didn't have a word to say
too quiet for me—so I up and split
five babies by now

Welfare check was better than that   30
   didn't need no no-good man no how
   I'd make it on my own
   be independent
   cept it's hard to sleep in a cold bed
   and ain't no sedative for lonliness   35
so when this beau-ti-ful cat comes rapping
   tongue like it was pure silk
   I was gone again—nose wide open—
   and oops—knocked up again
   Haven't seen him for a couple of weeks   40
   not since I happened to be
   where he happened to be
   'cept he wasn't alone.
Maybe he'll come home after while
I hope so—I won't hit him with the frying pan.   45

Anyway meanwhile I was just sitting here—
   thinking—rocking—and getting big—
   I'm really a good woman—
        fit to be loved.

MARGE PIERCY   **(b. 1936)**

The woman in the ordinary   (1970)

The woman in the ordinary pudgy downcast girl
is crouching with eyes and muscles clenched.
Round and pebble smooth she effaces herself
under ripples of conversation and debate.
The woman in the block of ivory soap   5
has massive thighs that neigh,
great breasts that blare and strong arms that trumpet.

The woman of the golden fleece
laughs uproariously from the belly
inside the girl who imitates   10
a Christmas card virgin with glued hands,
who fishes for herself in other's eyes,
who stoops and creeps to make herself smaller.
In her bottled up is a woman peppery as curry,
a yam of a woman of butter and brass,   15
compounded of acid and sweet like a pineapple,
like a handgrenade set to explode,
like goldenrod ready to bloom.

SONIA SANCHEZ   (b. 1934)

a poem for my father   (1970)

how sad it must be
to love so many women
to need so many black
perfumed bodies weeping
underneath you.   5
                    when i remember all those nights
i filled my mind with
long wars between short
sighted trojans & greeks
while you slapped some   10
wide hips about in
your pvt dungeon,
when i remember your
deformity   i want to
do something about your   15
makeshift manhood.
i guess
          that is why
on meeting your sixth
wife, i cross myself   20
with her confessionals.

ADRIENNE RICH   (b. 1929)

Trying to Talk with a Man   (1971)

Out in this desert we are testing bombs,

that's why we came here.

Sometimes I feel an underground river
forcing its way between deformed cliffs
an acute angle of understanding   5
moving itself like a locus of the sun
into this condemned scenery.

What we've had to give up to get here—
whole LP collections, films we starred in
playing in the neighborhoods, bakery windows   10
full of dry, chocolate-filled Jewish cookies,
the language of love-letters, of suicide notes,
afternoons on the riverbank
pretending to be children

Coming out to this desert   15
we meant to change the face of
driving among dull green succulents
walking at noon in the ghost town
surrounded by a silence

that sounds like the silence of the place   20
except that it came with us
and is familiar
and everything we were saying until now
was an effort to blot it out—
Coming out here we are up against it   25

Out here I feel more helpless
with you than without you
You mention the danger
and list the equipment
we talk of people caring for each other   30
in emergencies—laceration, thirst—
but you look at me like an emergency

Your dry heat feels like power
your eyes are stars of a different magnitude
they reflect lights that spell out: EXIT   35
when you get up and pace the floor

talking of the danger
as if it were not ourselves
as if we were testing anything else.

ADRIENNE RICH   (b. 1929)

Diving into the Wreck   (1972)

First having read the book of myths,
and loaded the camera,
and checked the edge of the knife-blade,
I put on
the body-armor of black rubber   5
the absurd flippers
the grave and awkward mask.
I am having to do this
not like Cousteau with his
assiduous team   10
aboard the sun-flooded schooner
but here alone.

There is a ladder.
The ladder is always there
hanging innocently   15
close to the side of the schooner.
We know what it is for,
we who have used it.
Otherwise
it's a piece of maritime floss   20
some sundry equipment.

I go down.
Rung after rung and still
the oxygen immerses me
the blue light   25
the clear atoms
of our human air.
I go down.
My flippers cripple me,
I crawl like an insect down the ladder   30

and there is no one
to tell me when the ocean
will begin.

First the air is blue and then
it is bluer and then green and then   35
black I am blacking out and yet
my mask is powerful
it pumps my blood with power
the sea is another story
the sea is not a question of power   40
I have to learn alone
to turn my body without force
in the deep element.

And now: it is easy to forget
what I came for   45
among so many who have always
lived here
swaying their crenellated[1] fans
between the reefs
and besides   50
you breathe differently down here.

I came to explore the wreck.
The words are purposes.
The words are maps.
I came to see the damage that was done   55
and the treasures that prevail.
I stroke the beam of my lamp
slowly along the flank
of something more permanent
than fish or weed   60

the thing I came for:
the wreck and not the story of the wreck
the thing itself and not the myth
the drowned face always staring
toward the sun   65
the evidence of damage
worn by salt and sway into this threadbare beauty
the ribs of the disaster

---

[1] Notched.

curving their assertion
among the tentative haunters.   70

This is the place.
And I am here, the mermaid whose dark hair
streams black, the merman in his armored body
We circle silently
about the wreck   75
we dive into the hold.
I am she: I am he

whose drowned face sleeps with open eyes
whose breasts still bear the stress
whose silver, copper, vermeil cargo lies   80
obscurely inside barrels
half-wedged and left to rot
we are the half-destroyed instruments
that once held to a course
the water-eaten log   85
the fouled compass

We are, I am, you are
by cowardice or courage
the one who find our way   90
back to this scene
carrying a knife, a camera
a book of myths
in which
our names do not appear.

MURIEL RUKEYSER   **(1913–1980)**

Looking at Each Other   **(1973)**

Yes, we were looking at each other
Yes, we knew each other very well
Yes, we had made love with each other many times
Yes, we had heard music together
Yes, we had gone to the sea together   5
Yes, we had cooked and eaten together

Yes, we had laughed often day and night
Yes, we fought violence and knew violence
Yes, we hated the inner and outer oppression   10
Yes, that day we were looking at each other
Yes, we saw the sunlight pouring down
Yes, the corner of the table was between us
Yes, bread and flowers were on the table
Yes, our eyes saw each other's eyes
Yes, our mouths saw each other's mouth   15
Yes, our breasts saw each other's breasts
Yes, our bodies entire saw each other
Yes, it was beginning in each
Yes, it threw waves across our lives
Yes, the pulses were becoming very strong   20
Yes, the beating became very delicate
Yes, the calling   the arousal
Yes, the arriving   the coming
Yes, there it was for both entire
Yes, we were looking at each other   25

MURIEL RUKEYSER   **(1913–1980)**

Waiting For Icarus[1]   **(1973)**

He said he would be back and we'd drink wine together
He said that everything would be better than before
He said we were on the edge of a new relation
He said he would never again cringe before his father
He said that he was going to invent full-time   5
He said he loved me that going into me
He said was going into the world and the sky
He said all the buckles were very firm
He said the wax was the best wax
He said Wait for me here on the beach   10
He said Just don't cry

I remember the gulls and the waves
I remember the islands going dark on the sea

---

[1] In Greek myth, the son of Daedalus; he tried to escape Crete on wings his father made, but flew too close to the sun, and the wax that held the wings on melted, plunging him into the sea.

I remember the girls laughing
I remember they said he only wanted to get away from me   15
I remember mother saying: Inventors are like poets,
                              a trashy lot
I remember she told me those who try out inventions are
   worse
I remember she added: Women who love such are the worst   20
   of all

I have been waiting all day, or perhaps longer.
I would have liked to try those wings myself.
It would have been better than this.

OLGA BROUMAS   (b. 1949)

Song / for Sanna   (1977)

> . . . in this way the future enters
> into us, in order to transform itself
> in us before it happens.
>   R. M. Rilke

What hasn't happened
intrudes, so much
hasn't yet happened. In the steamy

kitchens we meet in, kettles
are always boiling, water for tea, the steep   5
infusions we occupy
hands and mouth with, steam
filming our breath, a convenient

subterfuge, a disguise
for the now   10
sharp intake, the measured
outlet of air, the sigh, the gutting
loneliness

of the present where
what hasn't happened will   15

not be ignored, intrudes, separates
from the conversation like milk
from cream, desire

rising between the cups, brimming
over our saucers, clouding the minty   20
air, its own
aroma a pungent
stress, once again, you will get
up, put on your coat, go

home to the safer passions, moisture   25
clinging still to your spoon, as the afternoon
wears on, and I miss, I
miss you.

JACK ANDERSON   (b. 1935)

A Lecture on Avant-Garde Art   (1977)

Look in the Salon des Refusés[1] of most periods
and there will hang the homosexuals,
labeled by critics
"contrary to nature."

Now, to use a familiar set of distinctions, what   5
exists but is not nature must be art;
yet art is also an imitation
of some process of nature: so art, too, is natural,
whatever its manner.

Art may evolve through accretions of tradition   10
or leap ahead into the unknown.
This form of expression, the gay life
so maddening and unimaginable to some,
necessarily involves a leap into the unknown,
for its traditions, such as they are, are shadowy.   15

---

[1] An 1863 protest exhibition organized by artists whose works were rejected for the annual Salon exhibition in Paris.

Note how, on every side, images proclaim
and sustain the straight life. In parks and town squares
one may behold the monumental figures of, say,
Cohibere guarding his family from the Amplecti,
of Scruta and Amentia denouncing the barbarians,   20
or of the marriage of Turpa and Insulsus[2] on the battlefield.

Images of the gay life, in contrast, are obscure, are
curiosities kept locked from the public in cabinets: in consequence,
gay lives must style themselves with craft,
with daring. Many fail. Even so,   25
some grow amazing and beautiful.

And since such triumphs are typically achieved
amidst general bewilderment and in defiance
of academic theory, the gay life
deserves to be ranked among   30
the significant examples of art, past and present.
And because it has disordered whatever may be
the accustomed ways of seeing in its time,
it is therefore avant-garde,
naturally avant-garde.   35

ANITA ENDREZZE   (b. 1952)

Making Adjustments   (1977)

Marry the man your parents want for a son.
Go to bed with him like clockwork.
Keep your poems in the stove,
your hands away from knives.

Sleep around with quick, ugly men.   5
Talk to yourself and let them answer for you.
Adjust your body to thieving hands;
count the times they come and subtract
them like years from your life.

---

[2] Cohibere, the Amplecti, Scruta, Amentia, Turpa, Insulsus are made-up names.

When you've got it all swallowed,   10
when you've turned your bones into nothing
but someone else's sexual hardness,
men will damn you Medusa
and you'll long to burn their genitals
in your ritual fires. You'll want   15
to sit on your haunches devouring
your scabby skin, each lesion
a portrait of a lover, each howl
a memory of your last adjustment.

But you will wipe their feet   20
with your hair, light
their pipes with your burning,
betray your betrayal with the arch
of your back. You will need
no further announcement   25
of your death.

ADRIENNE RICH   (b. 1929)

FROM **Twenty-one Love Poems**   **(1978)**

XI
Every peak is a crater. This is the law of volcanoes,
making them eternally and visibly female.
No height without depth, without a burning core,
though our straw soles shred on the hardened lava.
I want to travel with you to every sacred mountain   5
smoking within like the sibyl stooped over her tripod,
I want to reach for your hand as we scale the path,
to feel your arteries glowing in my clasp,
never failing to note the small, jewel-like flower
unfamiliar to us, nameless till we rename her,   10
that clings to the slowly altering rock—
that detail outside ourselves that brings us to ourselves,
was here before us, knew we would come, and sees beyond us.

MARGE PIERCY   (b. 1936)

Right to Life   (1979)

A woman is not a pear tree
thrusting her fruit in mindless fecundity
into the world. Even pear trees bear
heavily one year and rest and grow the next.
An orchard gone wild drops few warm rotting   5
fruit in the grass but the trees stretch
high and wiry gifting the birds forty
feet up among inch long thorns
broken atavistically from the smooth wood.

A woman is not a basket you place   10
your buns in to keep them warm. Not a brood
hen you can slip duck eggs under.
Not a purse holding the coins of your
descendants till you spend them in wars.
Not a bank where your genes gather interest   15
and interesting mutations in the tainted
rain, any more than you are.

You plant corn and you harvest
it to eat or sell. You put the lamb
in the pasture to fatten and haul it in   20
to butcher for chops. You slice
the mountain in two for a road and gouge
the high plains for coal and the waters
run muddy for miles and years.
Fish die but you do not call them yours   25
unless you wished to eat them.

Now you legislate mineral rights in a woman.
You lay claim to her pastures for grazing,
fields for growing babies like iceberg
lettuce. You value children so dearly   30
that none ever go hungry, none weep
with no one to tend them when mothers
work, none lack fresh fruit,
none chew lead or cough to death and your
orphanages are empty. Every noon the best   35
restaurants serve poor children steaks.

At this moment at nine o'clock a *partera*[1]
is performing a table top abortion on an
unwed mother in Texas who can't get Medicaid
any longer. In five days she will die   40
of tetanus and her little daughter will cry
and be taken away. Next door a husband
and wife are sticking pins in the son
they did not want. They will explain
for hours how wicked he is,   45
how he wants discipline.

We are all born of woman, in the rose
of the womb we suckled our mother's blood
and every baby born has a right to love
like a seedling to sun. Every baby born   50
unloved, unwanted is a bill that will come
due in twenty years with interest, an anger
that must find a target, a pain that will
beget pain. A decade downstream a child
screams, a woman falls, a synagogue is torched,   55
a firing squad is summoned, a button
is pushed and the world burns.

I will choose what enters me, what becomes
flesh of my flesh. Without choice, no politics,
no ethics lives. I am not your cornfield,   60
not your uranium mine, not your calf
for fattening, not your cow for milking.
You may not use me as your factory.
Priests and legislators do not hold
shares in my womb or my mind.   65
This is my body. If I give it to you
I want it back. My life
is a non-negotiable demand.

KATE RUSHIN   **(b. 1951)**

The Tired Poem: Last Letter From a Typical Unemployed Black Professional Woman   (1979)

So it's a gorgeous afternoon in the park
It's so nice you forget your Attitude

---
[1] Midwife (Spanish).

The one your mama taught you
The one that says Don't-Mess-With-Me
You forget until you hear all this   5
Whistling and lip-smacking
You whip around and say
I ain't no damn dog
It's a young guy
His mouth drops open   10
Excuse me Sister
How you doing
You lie and smile and say
I'm doing good
Everything's cool Brother   15

Then five minutes later
Hey you Sweet Devil
Hey girl come here
You tense sigh calculate
You know the lean boys and bearded men   20
Are only cousins and lovers and friends
Sometimes when you say hey
You get a beautiful surprised smile
Or a good talk
And you've listened to your uncle when he was drunk   25
Talking about how he has to scuffle to get by and

How he'd wanted to be an engineer
And you talk to Joko who wants to be a singer and
Buy some clothes and get a house for his mother
The Soc and Psych books say you're domineering   30
And you've been to enough
Sisters-Are-Not-Taking-Care-Of-Business discussions
To know where you went wrong
It's decided it had to be the day you decided to go to school
Still you remember the last time you said hey   35
So you keep on walking
What you too good to speak
Don't nobody want you no way Ho'

You go home sit on the front steps and listen to
Your neighbor's son brag about   40
How many girls he has pregnant
You ask him if he's going to take care of the babies
What if he gets taken to court
And what are the girls going to do

He has pictures of them all   45
This real cute one was supposed to go to college
Dumb broad knew she could get pregnant
I'll just say it's not mine
On the back of this picture of a girl in a cap and gown
It says something like   50
I love you in my own strange way
Thank you

Then you go in the house
Flip through a magazine and there is
An Ode-To-My-Black-Queen poem   55
The kind where the Brother
Thanks all of the Sisters who Endured
Way back when he didn't have his Shit Together
And you wonder where they are now
And you know what happens when you try to resist   60
All of this Enduring
And you think how this
Thank-you poem is really
No consolation at all
Unless you believe   65
What the man you met on the train told you
The Black man who worked for the State Department
And had lived in 5 countries
He said
Dear you were born to suffer   70
Why don't you give me your address
And I'll come visit

So you try to talk to your friend
About the train and the park and everything
And how it all seems somehow connected   75
And he says
You're just a Typical Black Professional Woman
Some sisters know how to deal
Right about here
Your end of the conversation phases out   80
He goes on to say how
Black Professional Women have always had the advantage
You have to stop and think about that one
Maybe you are supposed to be grateful for those sweaty
Beefy-faced white businessmen who try to pick you up at

lunchtime

And you wonder how many times your friend has had pennies
                                                    thrown at him
How many times he's been felt up in the subway
How many times he's been cussed out on the street   90
You wonder how many times he's been offered $10 for a piece
                                                    of himself
$10 for a piece
So you're waiting for the bus
And you look at this young Black man   95
Asking if you want to make some money
You look at him for a long time
You imagine the little dingy room at the Y
It would only take 20 minutes or less
You think about how you only get $15 for spending all day
                                                    with 30 kids
And how nobody is offering you
Any cash for your poems
You remember again how you have the advantage
How you're not taking care of business   105
How this man is somebody's kid brother or cousin and could be
                                                    your own
So you try to explain how $10 wouldn't pay for what you'd
                                                    have to give up
He pushes a handful of sticky crumpled dollars into your face
                                                    and says
Why not
You think I can't pay
Look at that roll
Don't tell me you don't need the money   115
Cause I know you do
I'll give you 15

You maintain your sense of humor
You remember a joke you heard
Well no matter what   120
A Black Woman never has to starve
Just as long as there are
Dirty toilets and. . .
Somehow it isn't funny
Then you wonder if he would at least   125
Give you the money
And not beat you up
But you're very cool and say
No thanks
You tell him he should spend his time   130
Looking for someone he cares about
Who cares about him

He waves you off
Get outta my face
I don't have time for that bullshit   135
You blew it Bitch

Then
(Is it suddenly)
Your voice gets loud
And fills the night street   140
Your voice gets louder and louder
Your bus comes
The second shift people file on
The watchmen and nurse's aides
Look at you like you're crazy   145

Get on the damn bus
And remember
You blew it
He turns away
Your bus pulls off   150
There is no one on the street but you

And then
It is
Very
Quiet   155

JACK GILBERT   (b. 1925?)

Love Poem   (1982)

The couple on the San Francisco bus looked Russian,
and spoke what sounded like it. He was already an old man
at fifty. She could have been his wife or daughter.
At first I thought she was retarded. She was probably drunk
and maybe stupid. He had on a grey suit and was always angry.   5
Whatever she did made him glare and tug at her sleeve.
She fought back dutifully, but without conviction.

Knowing her role was to be wrong. She was wrong. She had
the whole bus watching. It was hard to quarrel properly,
also because everything pleased her so much.   10
She craned to read the advertisements
or twisted around to see out the other window
or stared with her mouth open at the people who got on.
When there was a seat they could sit in together,
she messed it up. He went to the rear.   15
She kept whispering, and signaling who would get off next.
He sat proud and closed on a seat that ran the wrong way,
getting thrown about. She wore a cheap babushka
and a foolish old coat and white socks.
Even stopping for red lights pleased her.   20
Finally a place was empty and she plunged into it,
crying to him and making great scooping gestures.
He pretended not to hear. But she just got louder in her delight,
until she was standing, guarding the seat, and calling
the length of the bus. He had no choice.   25
She settled in as happy as anyone I ever saw,
pointing out the ads for him all over again.

KITTY TSUI   (b. 1952)

It's In The Name   (1983)

i've been called sway
      sue
      suey
      suzy
      tissue   5
      ha-chiew.

my father pronounced it choy
so i grew up saying choy,
always careful to add: t-s-u-i.

the first name is kit fan,   10
fragrant purity.
but can also mean
marriage.

in chinese, choy
can also mean hurry, fast, *faidee*.   15

i am constantly
chased by the chant
hurry to get married. . .

if it's not bad enough
it's in the name   20
it's also in the face.

one day a woman instructor
insisted i had been
one of her guest speakers
in a class.   25

she was so sure of herself
she had me convinced
it was during my alcohol days
when memory was gone.

genny lim[1] was the speaker.   30

it happens all the time.
orientals so hard to tell apart.

the same day
a woman stopped
to wish me a good opening.   35

i was not in a play or an art show.

zand gee, nancy hom and stephanie lowe
had a three-woman show.

that's not all.
i've been called   40
willyce kim,

---
[1] See poem "Wonder Woman," p. 503

canyon sam,
louise low.

it happens all the time.

a newspaper woman thought   45
i was willyce kim for months.
willyce kim gets called susan kwong.
nellie wong is made nellie kim
or not mentioned by name at all.
merle woo is called merle wong   50
or smeared as yellow woman
in a gay male publication.

it happens all the time.
it's in the name.
it's in the face.   55

orientals so hard to tell apart.

our faces,
strong, brown,
different as
the bumps   60
on the skin of
bittermelon.
our tongues,
sharp and fragrant
as ginger,   65

telling our history,
our experiences
as asian american women,
workers and poets,
cutting the ropes   70
that bind us,
breaking from
the silence of centuries

to write
our dreams into action,   75
give voice to our visions

and tongues
to our foreparents,
those who entered
at chinese hospital   80
or the paper sons
who came by way of
angel island,
forced to take
false names.   85

the sewing shop worker,
the secretary,
the doctor,
the *deem sum*[2] girl,
the lesbian,   90
the bike messenger,
the typesetter,
the boxer,
the student.

each with a name.   95
each with a face,

blood, bone, breath.

MARTHA COLLINS   (b. 1940)

Several Things   (1985)

Several things could happen in this poem.
Plums could appear, on a pewter plate.
A dead red hare, hung by one foot.
A vase of flowers. Three shallots.

A man could sing, in a burgundy robe   5
with a gold belt tied in a square knot.

---

[2] Dumplings.

Someone could untie the knot.
A woman could toss a gold coin.

A stranger could say the next line,
I have been waiting for this,   10
and offer a basket piled with apples
picked this morning, before the rain.

It could rain in this poem,
but if it rained, the man would continue
to sing as the burgundy silk fell   15
to the polished parquet floor.

It could snow in this poem:
remember how the hunter stamped his feet
before he leaned his gun in the corner
and hung his cap on the brass hook?   20

Perhaps the woman should open the ebony bench
and find the song her mother used to sing.
Listen: the woman is playing the song.
The man is singing the words.

Meanwhile the hunter is taking a warm bath   25
in the clean white tub with clawed legs.
Or has the hunter left? Are his boots
making tracks in the fallen snow?

When does the woman straighten the flowers?
Is that before the hunter observes   30
the tiny pattern on the vase?
Before the man begins to peel the shallots?

Now it is time for the woman
to slice the apples into a blue bowl.
A child could be watching the unbroken peel   35
spiral below the knife.

Last but not least, you could appear.
You could be the red-cheeked child,
the hunter, or the stranger.
You could stay for a late meal.   40

A Provençal recipe.
A bright red hare, shot at dawn.
Shallots. Brandy. Pepper, salt.
An apple in the pan.

DRAMA

HENRIK IBSEN   (1828–1906)

Henrik Ibsen was born in Skien, Norway into a family that had fallen into poverty. He worked as an apothecary's apprentice, attended but never completed university, and took jobs as a playwright, as a stage manager, and later as a theater director. Dissatisfied with the political and cultural climate of his native country, Ibsen left in 1864 and lived thereafter in Rome, Dresden, and Munich until 1891 when he returned to Norway. His "problem plays," as his works of social criticism were called, angered many but also won him an international reputation. They include A Doll's House *(1879),* Ghosts *(1881),* An Enemy of the People *(1882),* The Wild Duck *(1884), and* Hedda Gabbler *(1890).*

A DOLL'S HOUSE[1]   (1879)

CHARACTERS

Torvald Helmer.
Nora, *his wife.*
Doctor Rank.
Mrs. Linden.
Nils Krogstad.
The Helmers' Three Children.
Anna, *their nurse.*
A Maid-servant (Ellen).
A Porter.

The action passes in Helmer's house (a flat) in Christiania.

ACT I

A room, comfortably and tastefully, but not expensively, furnished. In the back, on the right, a door leads to the hall; on the left another door leads to Helmer's study. Between the two doors a pianoforte. In the middle of the left wall a door, and nearer the front a window. Near the window a round table with armchairs and a small sofa. In the right wall, somewhat to the back, a door, and against the same wall, further forward, a porcelain

---

[1] Translated by William Archer.

*stove; in front of it a couple of arm-chairs and a rocking-chair. Between
the stove and the side-door a small table. Engravings on the walls. A what-
not with china and bric-à-brac. A small bookcase filled with handsomely
bound books. Carpet. A fire in the stove. It is a winter day.*

*A bell rings in the hall outside. Presently the outer door of the flat is heard
to open. Then* Nora *enters, humming gaily. She is in outdoor dress, and
carries several parcels, which she lays on the right-hand table. She leaves
the door into the hall open, and a* Porter *is seen outside, carrying a
Christmas-tree and a basket, which he gives to the* Maid-servant *who has
opened the door.*

Nora. Hide the Christmas-tree carefully, Ellen; the children must on no
account see it before this evening, when it's lighted up. *[To the* Porter,
taking out her purse.] How much?
Porter. Fifty öre.
Nora. There is a crown. No, keep the change.

[The Porter *thanks her and goes.* Nora *shuts the door. She continues smiling
in quiet glee as she takes off her outdoor things. Taking from her pocket
a bag of macaroons, she eats one or two. Then she goes on tip-toe to her
husband's door and listens.*

Nora. Yes; he is at home.

[She begins humming again, crossing to the table on the right.

Helmer. *[In his room.]* Is that my lark twittering there?
Nora. *[Busy opening some of her parcels.]* Yes, it is.
Helmer. Is it the squirrel frisking around?
Nora. Yes!
Helmer. When did the squirrel get home?
Nora. Just this minute. *[Hides the bag of macaroons in her pocket and
wipes her mouth.]* Come here, Torvald, and see what I've been buying.
Helmer. Don't interrupt me. *[A little later he opens the door and looks in,
pen in hand.]* Buying, did you say? What! All that? Has my little
spendthrift been making the money fly again?
Nora. Why, Torvald, surely we can afford to launch out a little now.
It's the first Christmas we haven't had to pinch.
Helmer. Come come; we can't afford to squander money.
Nora. Oh yes, Torvald, do let us squander a little, now—just the least
little bit! You know you'll soon be earning heaps of money.
Helmer. Yes, from New Year's Day. But there's a whole quarter before
my first salary is due.

Nora. Never mind; we can borrow in the meantime.

Helmer. Nora! *[He goes up to her and takes her playfully by the ear.]* Still my little featherbrain! Supposing I borrowed a thousand crowns to-day, and you made ducks and drakes of them during Christmas week, and then on New Year's Eve a tile blew off the roof and knocked my brains out—

Nora. *[Laying her hand on his mouth.]* Hush! How can you talk so horridly?

Helmer. But supposing it were to happen—what then?

Nora. If anything so dreadful happened, it would be all the same to me whether I was in debt or not.

Helmer. But what about the creditors?

Nora. They! Who cares for them? They're only strangers.

Helmer. Nora, Nora! What a woman you are! But seriously, Nora, you know my principles on these points. No debts! No borrowing! Home life ceases to be free and beautiful as soon as it is founded on borrowing and debt. We two have held out bravely till now, and we are not going to give in at the last.

Nora. *[Going to the fireplace.]* Very well—as you please, Torvald.

Helmer. *[Following her.]* Come come; my little lark mustn't droop her wings like that. What? Is my squirrel in the sulks? *[Takes out his purse.]* Nora, what do you think I have here?

Nora. *[Turning round quickly.]* Money!

Helmer. There! *[Gives her some notes.]* Of course I know all sorts of things are wanted at Christmas.

Nora. *[Counting.]* Ten, twenty, thirty, forty. Oh, thank you, thank you, Torvald! This will go a long way.

Helmer. I should hope so.

Nora. Yes, indeed; a long way! But come here, and let me show you all I've been buying. And so cheap! Look, here's a new suit for Ivar, and a little sword. Here are a horse and a trumpet for Bob. And here are a doll and a cradle for Emmy. They're only common; but they're good enough for her to pull to pieces. And dress-stuffs and kerchiefs for the servants. I ought to have got something better for old Anna.

Helmer. And what's in that other parcel?

Nora. *[Crying out.]* No, Torvald, you're not to see that until this evening.

Helmer. Oh! Ah! But now tell me, you little spendthrift, have you thought of anything for yourself?

Nora. For myself! Oh, I don't want anything.

Helmer. Nonsense! Just tell me something sensible you would like to have.

Nora. No, really I don't know of anything—Well, listen, Torvald——

Helmer. Well?

Nora. *[Playing with his coat-buttons, without looking him in the face.]* If you really want to give me something, you might, you know—you might—

Helmer. Well? Out with it!

Nora. *[Quickly.]* You might give me money, Torvald. Only just what you think you can spare; then I can buy something with it later on.

Helmer. But, Nora—

Nora. Oh, please do, dear Torvald, please do! I should hang the money in lovely gilt paper on the Christmas-tree. Wouldn't that be fun?

Helmer. What do they call the birds that are always making the money fly?

Nora. Yes, I know—spendthrifts, of course. But please do as I ask you, Torvald. Then I shall have time to think what I want most. Isn't that very sensible, now?

Helmer. *[Smiling.]* Certainly; that is to say, if you really kept the money I gave you, and really spent it on something for yourself. But it all goes in housekeeping, and for all manner of useless things, and then I have to pay up again.

Nora. But, Torvald—

Helmer. Can you deny it, Nora dear? *[He puts his arm round her.]* It's a sweet little lark, but it gets through a lot of money. No one would believe how much it costs a man to keep such a little bird as you.

Nora. For shame! How can you say so? Why, I save as much as ever I can.

Helmer. *[Laughing.]* Very true—as much as you can—but that's precisely nothing.

Nora. *[Hums and smiles with covert glee.]* H'm! If you only knew, Torvald, what expenses we larks and squirrels have.

Helmer. You're a strange little being! Just like your father—always on the look-out for all the money you can lay your hands on; but the moment you have it, it seems to slip through your fingers; you never know what becomes of it. Well, one must take you as you are. It's in the blood. Yes, Nora, that sort of thing is hereditary.

Nora. I wish I had inherited many of papa's qualities.

Helmer. And I don't wish you anything but just what you are—my own, sweet little song-bird. But I say—it strikes me you look so—so—what shall I call it?—so suspicious to-day—

Nora. Do I?

Helmer. You do, indeed. Look me full in the face.

Nora. *[Looking at him.]* Well?

Helmer. *[Threatening with his finger.]* Hasn't the little sweet-tooth been playing pranks to-day?

Nora. No; how can you think such a thing!

Helmer. Didn't she just look in at the confectioner's?

Nora. No, Torvald; really—

Helmer. Not to sip a little jelly?

Nora. No; certainly not.

Helmer. Hasn't she even nibbled a macaroon or two?

Nora. No, Torvald, indeed, indeed!

Helmer. Well, well, well; of course I'm only joking.

Nora. [*Goes to the table on the right.*] I shouldn't think of doing what you disapprove of.

Helmer. No, I'm sure of that; and, besides, you've given me your word—
[*Going towards her.*] Well, keep your little Christmas secrets to yourself, Nora darling. The Christmas-tree will bring them all to light, I daresay.

Nora. Have you remembered to invite Doctor Rank?

Helmer. No. But it's not necessary; he'll come as a matter of course. Besides, I shall ask him when he looks in to-day. I've ordered some capital wine. Nora, you can't think how I look forward to this evening.

Nora. And I too. How the children will enjoy themselves, Torvald!

Helmer. Ah, it's glorious to feel that one has an assured position and ample means. Isn't it delightful to think of?

Nora. Oh, it's wonderful!

Helmer. Do you remember last Christmas? For three whole weeks beforehand you shut yourself up every evening till long past midnight to make flowers for the Christmas-tree, and all sorts of other marvels that were to have astonished us. I was never so bored in my life.

Nora. I didn't bore myself at all.

Helmer. [*Smiling.*] But it came to little enough in the end, Nora.

Nora. Oh, are you going to tease me about that again? How could I help the cat getting in and pulling it all to pieces?

Helmer. To be sure you couldn't, my poor little Nora. You did your best to give us all pleasure, and that's the main point. But, all the same, it's a good thing the hard times are over.

Nora. Oh, isn't it wonderful?

Helmer. Now I needn't sit here boring myself all alone; and you needn't tire your blessed eyes and your delicate little fingers—

Nora. [*Clapping her hands.*] No, I needn't, need I, Torvald? Oh, how wonderful it is to think of? [*Takes his arm.*] And now I'll tell you how I think we ought to manage, Torvald. As soon as Christmas is over—
[*The hall-door bell rings.*] Oh, there's a ring! [*Arranging the room.*] That's somebody come to call. How tiresome!

Helmer. I'm "not at home" to callers; remember that.

Ellen. [*In the doorway.*] A lady to see you, ma'am.

Nora. Show her in.

Ellen. [*To Helmer.*] And the doctor has just come, sir.

Helmer. Has he gone into my study?

Ellen. Yes, sir.

[*Helmer goes into his study. Ellen ushers in Mrs. Linden, in travelling costume, and goes out, closing the door.*

Mrs. Linden. [*Embarrassed and hesitating.*] How do you do, Nora?

Nora. [*Doubtfully.*] How do you do?

Mrs. Linden. I see you don't recognise me!

Nora. No, I don't think—oh yes!—I believe—*[Suddenly brightening.]* What, Christina! Is it really you?

Mrs. Linden. Yes; really I!

Nora. Christina! And to think I didn't know you! But how could I— *[More softly.]* How changed you are, Christina!

Mrs. Linden. Yes, no doubt. In nine or ten years—

Nora. Is it really so long since we met? Yes, so it is. Oh, the last eight years have been a happy time, I can tell you. And now you have come to town? All that long journey in mid-winter! How brave of you!

Mrs. Linden. I arrived by this morning's steamer.

Nora. To have a merry Christmas, of course. Oh, how delightful! Yes, we will have a merry Christmas. Do take your things off. Aren't you frozen? *[Helping her.]* There; now we'll sit cosily by the fire. No, you take the arm-chair; I shall sit in this rocking-chair. *[Seizes her hands.]* Yes, now I can see the dear old face again. It was only at the first glance—But you're a little paler, Christina—and perhaps a little thinner.

Mrs. Linden And much, much older, Nora.

Nora. Yes, perhaps a little older—not much—ever so little. *[She suddenly checks herself; seriously.]* Oh, what a thoughtless wretch I am! Here I sit chattering on, and—Dear, dear Christina, can you forgive me!

Mrs. Linden. What do you mean, Nora?

Nora. *[Softly.]* Poor Christina! I forgot: you are a widow.

Mrs. Linden. Yes, my husband died three years ago.

Nora. I know, I know; I saw it in the papers. Oh, believe me, Christina, I did mean to write to you; but I kept putting it off, and something always came in the way.

Mrs. Linden. I can quite understand that, Nora dear.

Nora. No, Christina; it was horrid of me. Oh, you poor darling! how much you must have gone through!—And he left you nothing?

Mrs. Linden. Nothing.

Nora. And no children?

Mrs. Linden. None.

Nora. Nothing, nothing at all?

Mrs. Linden. Not even a sorrow or a longing to dwell upon.

Nora. *[Looking at her incredulously.]* My dear Christina, how is that possible?

Mrs. Linden. *[Smiling sadly and stroking her hair.]* Oh, it happens so sometimes, Nora.

Nora. So utterly alone! How dreadful that must be! I have three of the loveliest children. I can't show them to you just now; they're out with their nurse. But now you must tell me everything.

Mrs. Linden. No, no; I want you to tell me—

Nora. No, you must begin; I won't be egotistical to-day. To-day I'll think only of you. Oh! but I must tell you one thing—perhaps you've heard of our great stroke of fortune?

Mrs. Linden. No. What is it?

Nora. Only think! my husband has been made manager of the Joint Stock Bank.

Mrs. Linden. Your husband! Oh, how fortunate!

Nora. Yes; isn't it? A lawyer's position is so uncertain, you see, especially when he won't touch any business that's the least bit—shady, as of course Torvald never would; and there I quite agree with him. Oh! you can imagine how glad we are. He is to enter on his new position at the New Year, and then he'll have a large salary, and percentages. In future we shall be able to live quite differently—just as we please, in fact. Oh, Christina, I feel so lighthearted and happy! It's delightful to have lots of money, and no need to worry about things, isn't it?

Mrs. Linden. Yes; at any rate it must be delightful to have what you need.

Nora. No, not only what you need, but heaps of money—heaps!

Mrs. Linden. *[Smiling.]* Nora, Nora, haven't you learnt reason yet? In our schooldays you were a shocking little spendthrift.

Nora. *[Quietly smiling.]* Yes; that's what Torvald says I am still. *[Holding up her forefinger.]* But "Nora, Nora" is not so silly as you all think. Oh! I haven't had the chance to be much of a spendthrift. We have both had to work.

Mrs. Linden. You too?

Nora. Yes, light fancy work: crochet, and embroidery, and things of that sort; *[Carelessly]* and other work too. You know, of course, that Torvald left the Government service when we were married. He had little chance of promotion, and of course he required to make more money. But in the first year after our marriage he overworked himself terribly. He had to undertake all sorts of extra work, you know, and to slave early and late. He couldn't stand it, and fell dangerously ill. Then the doctors declared he must go to the South.

Mrs. Linden. You spent a whole year in Italy, didn't you?

Nora. Yes, we did. It wasn't easy to manage, I can tell you. It was just after Ivar's birth. But of course we had to go. Oh, it was a wonderful, delicious journey! And it saved Torvald's life. But it cost a frightful lot of money, Christina.

Mrs. Linden. So I should think.

Nora. Twelve hundred dollars! Four thousand eight hundred crowns! Isn't that a lot of money?

Mrs. Linden. How lucky you had the money to spend!

Nora. We got it from father, you must know.

Mrs. Linden. Ah, I see. He died just about that time, didn't he?

Nora. Yes, Christina, just then. And only think! I couldn't go and nurse him! I was expecting little Ivar's birth daily; and then I had my poor sick Torvald to attend to. Dear, kind old father! I never saw him again, Christina. Oh! that's the hardest thing I have had to bear since my marriage.

Mrs. Linden. I know how fond you were of him. But then you went to Italy?

Nora. Yes; you see, we had the money, and the doctors said we must lose no time. We started a month later.

Mrs. Linden. And your husband came back completely cured.

Nora. Sound as a bell.

Mrs. Linden. But—the doctor?

Nora. What do you mean?

Mrs. Linden. I thought as I came in your servant announced the doctor—

Nora. Oh, yes; Doctor Rank. But he doesn't come professionally. He is our best friend, and never lets a day pass without looking in. No, Torvald hasn't had an hour's illness since that time. And the children are so healthy and well, and so am I. *[Jumps up and claps her hands.]* Oh, Christina, Christina, what a wonderful thing it is to live and to be happy!—Oh, but it's really too horrid of me! Here am I talking about nothing but my own concerns. *[Seats herself upon a footstool close to* Christina, *and lays her arms on her friend's lap.]* Oh, don't be angry with me! Now tell me, is it really true that you didn't love your husband? What made you marry him, then?

Mrs. Linden. My mother was still alive, you see, bedridden and helpless; and then I had my two younger brothers to think of. I didn't think it would be right for me to refuse him.

Nora. Perhaps it wouldn't have been. I suppose he was rich then?

Mrs. Linden. Very well off, I believe. But his business was uncertain. It fell to pieces at his death, and there was nothing left.

Nora. And then—?

Mrs. Linden. Then I had to fight my way by keeping a shop, a little school, anything I could turn my hand to. The last three years have been one long struggle for me. But now it is over, Nora. My poor mother no longer needs me; she is at rest. And the boys are in business, and can look after themselves.

Nora. How free your life must feel!

Mrs. Linden. No, Nora; only inexpressibly empty. No one to live for! *[Stands up restlessly.]* That's why I could not bear to stay any longer in that out-of-the-way corner. Here it must be easier to find something to take one up—to occupy one's thoughts. If I could only get some settled employment—some office work.

Nora. But, Christina, that's such drudgery, and you look worn out already. It would be ever so much better for you to go to some watering-place and rest.

Mrs. Linden. *[Going to the window.]* I have no father to give me the money, Nora.

Nora. *[Rising.]* Oh, don't be vexed with me.

Mrs. Linden. *[Going to her.]* My dear Nora, don't you be vexed with me. The worst of a position like mine is that it makes one so bitter. You have no one to work for, yet you have to be always on the strain.

You must live; and so you become selfish. When I heard of the happy change in your fortunes—can you believe it?—I was glad for my own sake more than for yours.

Nora. How do you mean? Ah, I see! You think Torvald can perhaps do something for you.

Mrs. Linden. Yes; I thought so.

Nora. And so he shall, Christina. Just you leave it all to me. I shall lead up to it beautifully!—I shall think of some delightful plan to put him in a good humour! Oh, I should so love to help you.

Mrs. Linden. How good of you, Nora, to stand by me so warmly! Doubly good in you, who knows so little of the troubles and burdens of life.

Nora. I? I know so little of?—

Mrs. Linden. *[Smiling.]* Oh, well—a little fancy-work, and so forth.— You're a child, Nora.

Nora. *[Tosses her head and paces the room.]* Oh, come, you mustn't be so patronising!

Mrs. Linden. No?

Nora. You're like the rest. You all think I'm fit for nothing really serious—

Mrs. Linden. Well, well—

Nora. You think I've had no troubles in this weary world.

Mrs. Linden. My dear Nora, you've just told me all your troubles.

Nora. Pooh—those trifles! *[Softly.]* I haven't told you the great thing.

Mrs. Linden. The great thing? What do you mean?

Nora. I know you look down upon me, Christina; but you have no right to. You are proud of having worked so hard and so long for your mother.

Mrs. Linden. I am sure I don't look down upon any one; but it's true I am both proud and glad when I remember that I was able to keep my mother's last days free from care.

Nora. And you're proud to think of what you have done for your brothers, too.

Mrs. Linden. Have I not the right to be?

Nora. Yes indeed. But now let me tell you, Christina—I, too, have something to be proud and glad of.

Mrs. Linden. I don't doubt it. But what do you mean?

Nora. Hush! Not so loud. Only think, if Torvald were to hear! He mustn't—not for worlds! No one must know about it, Christina—no one but you.

Mrs. Linden. Why, what can it be?

Nora. Come over here. *[Draws her down beside her on the sofa.]* Yes, Christina—I, too, have something to be proud and glad of. I saved Torvald's life.

Mrs. Linden. Saved his life? How?

Nora. I told you about our going to Italy. Torvald would have died but for that.

Mrs. Linden. Well—and your father gave you the money.

Nora. *[Smiling.]* Yes, so Torvald and every one believes; but—

Mrs. Linden. But—?

Nora. Papa didn't give us one penny. It was *I* that found the money.

Mrs. Linden. You? All that money?

Nora. Twelve hundred dollars. Four thousand eight hundred crowns. What do you say to that?

Mrs. Linden. My dear Nora, how did you manage it? Did you win it in the lottery?

Nora. *[Contemptuously.]* In the lottery? Pooh! Any one could have done that!

Mrs. Linden. Then wherever did you get it from?

Nora. *[Hums and smiles mysteriously.]* H'm; tra-la-la-la!

Mrs. Linden. Of course you couldn't borrow it.

Nora. No? Why not?

Mrs. Linden. Why, a wife can't borrow without her husband's consent.

Nora. *[Tossing her head.]* Oh! when the wife has some idea of business, and knows how to set about things—

Mrs. Linden. But, Nora, I don't understand—

Nora. Well, you needn't. I never said I borrowed the money. There are many ways I may have got it. *[Throws herself back on the sofa.]* I may have got it from some admirer. When one is so—attractive as I am—

Mrs. Linden. You're too silly, Nora.

Nora. Now I'm sure you're dying of curiosity, Christina—

Mrs. Linden. Listen to me, Nora dear: haven't you been a little rash?

Nora. *[Sitting upright again.]* Is it rash to save one's husband's life?

Mrs. Linden. I think it was rash of you, without his knowledge—

Nora. But it would have been fatal for him to know! Can't you understand that? He wasn't even to suspect how ill he was. The doctors came to me privately and told me his life was in danger—that nothing could save him but a winter in the South. Do you think I didn't try diplomacy first? I told him how I longed to have a trip abroad, like other young wives; I wept and prayed; I said he ought to think of my condition, and not to thwart me; and then I hinted that he could borrow the money. But then, Christina, he got almost angry. He said I was frivolous, and that it was his duty as a husband not to yield to my whims and fancies—so he called them. Very well, thought I, but saved you must be; and then I found the way to do it.

Mrs. Linden. And did your husband never learn from your father that the money was not from him?

Nora. No; never. Papa died at that very time. I meant to have told him all about it, and begged him to say nothing. But he was so ill— unhappily, it wasn't necessary.

Mrs. Linden. And you have never confessed to your husband?

Nora. Good heavens! What can you be thinking of? Tell him, when he has such a loathing of debt! And besides—how painful and humiliating it would be for Torvald, with his manly self-respect, to know that he owed anything to me! It would utterly upset the relation between us; our beautiful, happy home would never again be what it is.

Mrs. Linden. Will you never tell him?

Nora. *[Thoughtfully, half-smiling.]* Yes, some time perhaps—many, many years hence, when I'm—not so pretty. You mustn't laugh at me! Of course I mean when Torvald is not so much in love with me as he is now; when it doesn't amuse him any longer to see me dancing about, and dressing up and acting. Then it might be well to have something in reserve. *[Breaking off.]* Nonsense! nonsense! That time will never come. Now, what do you say to my grand secret, Christina? Am I fit for nothing now? You may believe it has cost me a lot of anxiety. It has been no joke to meet my engagements punctually. You must know, Christina, that in business there are things called instalments, and quarterly interest, that are terribly hard to provide for. So I've had to pinch a little here and there, wherever I could. I couldn't save much out of the housekeeping, for of course Torvald had to live well. And I couldn't let the children go about badly dressed; all I got for them, I spent on them, the blessed darlings!

Mrs. Linden. Poor Nora! So it had to come out of your own pocket-money.

Nora. Yes, of course. After all, the whole thing was my doing. When Torvald gave me money for clothes, and so on, I never spent more than half of it; I always bought the simplest and cheapest things. It's a mercy that everything suits me so well—Torvald never had any suspicions. But it was often very hard, Christina dear. For it's nice to be beautifully dressed—now, isn't it?

Mrs. Linden. Indeed it is.

Nora. Well, and besides that, I made money in other ways. Last winter I was so lucky—I got a heap of copying to do. I shut myself up every evening and wrote far into the night. Oh, sometimes I was so tired, so tired. And yet it was splendid to work in that way and earn money. I almost felt as if I was a man.

Mrs. Linden. Then how much have you been able to pay off?

Nora. Well, I can't precisely say. It's difficult to keep that sort of business clear. I only know that I've paid everything I could scrape together. Sometimes I really didn't know where to turn. *[Smiles.]* Then I used to sit here and pretend that a rich old gentleman was in love with me—

Mrs. Linden. What! What gentleman?

Nora. Oh, nobody!—that he was dead now, and that when his will was opened, there stood in large letters: "Pay over at once everything of which I die possessed to that charming person, Mrs. Nora Helmer."

Mrs. Linden. But, my dear Nora—what gentleman do you mean?

Nora. Oh dear, can't you understand? There wasn't any old gentleman: it was only what I used to dream and dream when I was at my wits' end for money. But it doesn't matter now—the tiresome old creature may stay where he is for me. I care nothing for him or his will; for now my troubles are over. *[Springing up.]* Oh, Christina, how glorious it is to think of! Free from all anxiety! Free, quite free. To be able to play and romp about with the children; to have things tasteful and pretty in the house, exactly as Torvald likes it! And then the spring will soon be here, with the great blue sky. Perhaps then we shall have a little holiday. Perhaps I shall see the sea again. Oh, what a wonderful thing it is to live and to be happy!

[The hall-door bell rings.]

Mrs. Linden. *[Rising.]* There's a ring. Perhaps I had better go.
Nora. No; do stay. No one will come here. It's sure to be some one for Torvald.
Ellen. *[In the doorway.]* If you please, ma'am, there's a gentleman to speak to Mr. Helmer.
Nora. Who is the gentleman?
Krogstad. *[In the doorway.]* It is I, Mrs. Helmer.

[Mrs. Linden starts and turns away to the window.]

Nora. *[Goes a step towards him, anxiously, speaking low.]* You? What is it? What do you want with my husband?
Krogstad. Bank business—in a way. I hold a small post in the Joint Stock Bank, and your husband is to be our new chief, I hear.
Nora. Then it is—?
Krogstad. Only tiresome business, Mrs. Helmer; nothing more.
Nora. Then will you please go to his study.

[Krogstad goes. She bows indifferently while she closes the door into the hall. Then she goes to the stove and looks to the fire.]

Mrs. Linden. Nora—who was that man?
Nora. A Mr. Krogstad—a lawyer.
Mrs. Linden. Then it was really he?
Nora. Do you know him?
Mrs. Linden. I used to know him—many years ago. He was in a lawyer's office in our town.
Nora. Yes, so he was.
Mrs. Linden. How he has changed!
Nora. I believe his marriage was unhappy.
Mrs. Linden. And he is a widower now?
Nora. With a lot of children. There! Now it will burn up.

[She closes the stove, and pushes the rocking-chair a little aside.]

Mrs. Linden. His business is not of the most creditable, they say?

Nora. Isn't it? I daresay not. I don't know. But don't let us think of business—it's so tiresome.

Dr. Rank *comes out of* Helmer's *room.*

Rank. *[Still in the doorway.]* No, no; I'm in your way. I shall go and have a chat with your wife. *[Shuts the door and sees* Mrs. Linden.*]* Oh, I beg your pardon. I'm in the way here too.

Nora. No, not in the least. *[Introduces them.]* Doctor Rank—Mrs. Linden.

Rank. Oh, indeed; I've often heard Mrs. Linden's name; I think I passed you on the stairs as I came up.

Mrs. Linden. Yes; I go so very slowly. Stairs try me so much.

Rank. Ah—you are not very strong?

Mrs. Linden. Only overworked.

Rank. Nothing more? Then no doubt you've come to town to find rest in a round of dissipation?

Mrs. Linden. I have come to look for employment.

Rank. Is that an approved remedy for overwork?

Mrs. Linden. One must live, Doctor Rank.

Rank. Yes, that seems to be the general opinion.

Nora. Come, Doctor Rank—you want to live yourself.

Rank. To be sure I do. However wretched I may be, I want to drag on as long as possible. All my patients, too, have the same mania. And it's the same with people whose complaint is moral. At this very moment Helmer is talking to just such a moral incurable—

Mrs. Linden. *[Softly.]* Ah!

Nora. Whom do you mean?

Rank. Oh, a fellow named Krogstad, a man you know nothing about— corrupt to the very core of his character. But even he began by announcing, as a matter of vast importance, that he must live.

Nora. Indeed? And what did he want with Torvald?

Rank. I haven't an idea; I only gathered that it was some bank business.

Nora. I didn't know that Krog—that this Mr. Krogstad had anything to do with the Bank?

Rank. Yes. He has got some sort of place there. *[To* Mrs. Linden.*]* I don't know whether in your part of the country, you have people who go grubbing and sniffing around in search of moral rottenness—and then, when they have found a "case," don't rest till they have got their man into some good position, where they can keep a watch upon him. Men with a clean bill of health they leave out in the cold.

Mrs. Linden. Well, I suppose the—delicate characters require most care.

Rank. *[Shrugs his shoulders.]* There we have it! It's that notion that makes society a hospital.

[Nora, *deep in her own thoughts, breaks into half-stifled laughter and claps her hands.]*

Rank. Why do you laugh at that? Have you any idea what "society" is?

Nora. What do I care for your tiresome society? I was laughing at something else—something excessively amusing. Tell me, Doctor Rank, are all the employees at the Bank dependent on Torvald now?

Rank. Is that what strikes you as excessively amusing?

Nora. *[Smiles and hums.]* Never mind, never mind! *[Walks about the room.]* Yes, it is funny to think that we—that Torvald has such power over so many people. *[Takes the bag from her pocket.]* Doctor Rank, will you have a macaroon?

Rank. What!—macaroons! I thought they were contraband here.

Nora. Yes; but Christina brought me these.

Mrs. Linden. What! I?—

Nora., Oh, well! Don't be frightened. You couldn't possibly know that Torvald had forbidden them. The fact is, he's afraid of me spoiling my teeth. But, oh bother, just for once!—That's for you, Doctor Rank! *[Puts a macaroon into his mouth.]* And you too, Christina. And I'll have one while we're about it—only a tiny one, or at most two. *[Walks about again.]* Oh dear, I am happy! There's only one thing in the world I really want.

Rank. Well; what's that?

Nora. There's something I should so like to say—in Torvald's hearing.

Rank. Then why don't you say it?

Nora. Because I daren't, it's so ugly.

Mrs. Linden. Ugly!

Rank. In that case you'd better not. But to us you might—What is it you would so like to say in Helmer's hearing?

Nora. I should so love to say "Damn it all!"

Rank. Are you out of your mind?

Mrs. Linden. Good gracious, Nora—!

Rank. Say it—there he is!

Nora. *[Hides the macaroons.]* Hush—sh—sh!

Helmer *comes out of his room, hat in hand, with his overcoat on his arm.*

Nora. *[Going to him.]* Well, Torvald dear, have you got rid of him?

Helmer. Yes; he has just gone.

Nora. Let me introduce you—this is Christina, who has come to town—

Helmer. Christina? Pardon me, I don't know—

Nora. Mrs. Linden, Torvald dear—Christina Linden.

Helmer. *[To* Mrs. Linden.*]* Indeed! A school-friend of my wife's, no doubt?

Mrs. Linden. Yes; we knew each other as girls.

Nora. And only think! she has taken this long journey on purpose to speak to you.

Helmer. To speak to me!

Mrs. Linden. Well, not quite—

Nora. You see, Christina is tremendously clever at office-work, and she's so anxious to work under a first-rate man of business in order to learn still more—

Helmer. *[To* Mrs. Linden.*]* Very sensible indeed.

Nora. And when she heard you were appointed manager—it was telegraphed, you know—she started off at once, and—Torvald, dear, for my sake, you must do something for Christina. Now can't you?

Helmer. It's not impossible. I presume Mrs. Linden is a widow?

Mrs. Linden. Yes.

Helmer. And you have already had some experience of business?

Mrs. Linden. A good deal.

Helmer. Well, then, it's very likely I may be able to find a place for you.

Nora. *[Clapping her hands.]* There now! There now!

Helmer. You have come at a fortunate moment, Mrs. Linden.

Mrs. Linden. Oh, how can I thank you?—

Helmer. *[Smiling.]* There is no occasion. *[Puts on his overcoat.]* But for the present you must excuse me—

Rank. Wait; I am going with you.

[Fetches his fur coat from the hall and warms it at the fire.]

Nora. Don't be long, Torvald dear.

Helmer. Only an hour; not more.

Nora. Are you going too, Christina?

Mrs. Linden. *[Putting on her walking things.]* Yes; I must set about looking for lodgings.

Helmer. Then perhaps we can go together?

Nora. *[Helping her.]* What a pity we haven't a spare room for you; but it's impossible—

Mrs. Linden. I shouldn't think of troubling you. Good-bye, dear Nora, and thank you for all your kindness.

Nora. Good-bye for the present. Of course you'll come back this evening. And you, too, Doctor Rank. What! If you're well enough? Of course you'll be well enough. Only wrap up warmly. *[They go out, talking, into the hall. Outside on the stairs are heard children's voices.]* There they are! There they are! *[She runs to the outer door and opens it. The nurse, Anna, enters the hall with the children.]* Come in! Come in! *[Stoops down and kisses the children.]* Oh, my sweet darlings! Do you see them, Christina? Aren't they lovely?

Rank. Don't let us stand here chattering in the draught.

Helmer. Come, Mrs. Linden; only mothers can stand such a temperature.

[Dr. Rank, Helmer, and Mrs. Linden go down the stairs; Anna enters the room with the children; Nora also, shutting the door.]

Nora. How fresh and bright you look! And what red cheeks you've got! Like apples and roses. *[The children chatter to her during what follows.]* Have you had great fun? That's splendid! Oh, really! You've been giving Emmy and Bob a ride on your sledge!—both at once, only think! Why, you're quite a man, Ivar. Oh, give her to me a little, Anna. My sweet little dolly! *[Takes the smallest from the nurse and dances with her.]* Yes, yes; mother will dance with Bob too. What! Did you have a game of snowballs? Oh, I wish I'd been there. No; leave them, Anna; I'll take their things off. Oh, yes, let me do it; it's such fun. Go to the nursery; you look frozen. You'll find some hot coffee on the stove. *[The Nurse goes into the room on the left. Nora takes off the children's things and throws them down anywhere, while the children talk all together.]* Really! A big dog ran after you? But he didn't bite you? No; dogs don't bite dear little dolly children. Don't peep into those parcels, Ivar. What is it? Wouldn't you like to know? Take care—it'll bite! What? Shall we have a game? What shall we play at? Hide-and-seek? Yes, let's play hide-and-seek. Bob shall hide first. Am I to? Yes, let me hide first.

[She and the children play, with laughter and shouting, in the room and the adjacent one to the right. At last Nora hides under the table; the children come rushing in, look for her, but cannot find her, hear her half-choked laughter, rush to the table, lift up the cover and see her. Loud shouts. She creeps out, as though to frighten them. Fresh shouts. Meanwhile there has been a knock at the door leading into the hall. No one has heard it. Now the door is half opened and Krogstad appears. He waits a little; the game is renewed.]

Krogstad. I beg your pardon, Mrs. Helmer—

Nora. *[With a suppressed cry, turns round and half jumps up.]* Ah! What do you want?

Krogstad. Excuse me; the outer door was ajar—somebody must have forgotten to shut it—

Nora. *[Standing up.]* My husband is not at home, Mr. Krogstad.

Krogstad. I know it.

Nora. Then what do you want here?

Krogstad. To say a few words to you.

Nora. To me? *[To the children, softly.]* Go in to Anna. What? No, the strange man won't hurt mamma. When he's gone we'll go on playing. *[She leads the children into the left-hand room, and shuts the door behind them. Uneasy, in suspense.]* It is to me you wish to speak?

Krogstad. Yes, to you.

Nora. To-day? But it's not the first yet—

Krogstad. No, to-day is Christmas Eve. It will depend upon yourself whether you have a merry Christmas.

Nora. What do you want? I'm not ready to-day—

Krogstad. Never mind that just now. I have come about another matter. You have a minute to spare?

Nora. Oh, yes I suppose so; although—

Krogstad. Good. I was sitting in the restaurant opposite, and I saw your husband go down the street—

Nora. Well?

Krogstad. —with a lady.

Nora. What then?

Krogstad. May I ask if the lady was a Mrs. Linden?

Nora. Yes.

Krogstad. Who has just come to town?

Nora. Yes. To-day.

Krogstad. I believe she is an intimate friend of yours.

Nora. Certainly. But I don't understand—

Krogstad. I used to know her too.

Nora. I know you did.

Krogstad. Ah! You know all about it. I thought as much. Now, frankly, is Mrs. Linden to have a place in the Bank?

Nora. How dare you catechise me in this way, Mr. Krogstad—you, a subordinate of my husband's? But since you ask, you shall know. Yes, Mrs. Linden is to be employed. And it is I who recommended her, Mr. Krogstad. Now you know.

Krogstad. Then my guess was right.

Nora. *[Walking up and down.]* You see one has a wee bit of influence, after all. It doesn't follow because one's only a woman—When people are in a subordinate position, Mr. Krogstad, they ought really to be careful how they offend anybody who—h'm—

Krogstad. —who has influence?

Nora. Exactly.

Krogstad. *[Taking another tone.]* Mrs. Helmer, will you have the kindness to employ your influence on my behalf?

Nora. What? How do you mean?

Krogstad. Will you be so good as to see that I retain my subordinate position in the Bank?

Nora. What do you mean? Who wants to take it from you?

Krogstad. Oh, you needn't pretend ignorance. I can very well understand that it cannot be pleasant for your friend to meet me; and I can also understand now for whose sake I am to be hounded out.

Nora. But I assure you—

Krogstad. Come come now, once for all: there is time yet, and I advise you to use your influence to prevent it.

Nora. But, Mr. Krogstad, I have no influence—absolutely none.

Krogstad. None? I thought you said a moment ago—

Nora. Of course not in that sense. I! How can you imagine that I should have any such influence over my husband?

Krogstad. Oh, I know your husband from our college days. I don't think he is any more inflexible than other husbands.

Nora. If you talk disrespectfully of my husband, I must request you to leave the house.

Krogstad. You are bold, madam.

Nora. I am afraid of you no longer. When New Year's Day is over, I shall soon be out of the whole business.

Krogstad. *[Controlling himself.]* Listen to me, Mrs. Helmer. If need be, I shall fight as though for my life to keep my little place in the Bank.

Nora. Yes, so it seems.

Krogstad. It's not only for the salary: that is what I care least about. It's someting else—Well, I had better make a clean breast of it. Of course you know, like every one else, that some years ago I—got into trouble.

Nora. I think I've heard something of the sort.

Krogstad. The matter never came into court; but from that moment all paths were barred to me. Then I took up the business you know about. I had to turn my hand to something; and I don't think I've been one of the worst. But now I must get clear of it all. My sons are growing up; for their sake I must try to recover my character as well as I can. This place in the Bank was the first step; and now your husband wants to kick me off the ladder, back into the mire.

Nora. But I assure you, Mr. Krogstad, I haven't the least power to help you.

Krogstad. That is because you have not the will; but I can compel you.

Nora. You won't tell my husband that I owe you money?

Krogstad. H'm; suppose I were to?

Nora. It would be shameful of you. *[With tears in her voice.]* The secret that is my joy and my pride—that he should learn it in such an ugly, coarse way—and from you. It would involve me in all sorts of unpleasantness—

Krogstad. Only unpleasantness?

Nora. *[Hotly.]* But just do it. It's you that will come off worst, for then my husband will see what a bad man you are, and then you certainly won't keep your place.

Krogstad. I asked whether it was only domestic unpleasantness you feared?

Nora. If my husband gets to know about it, he will of course pay you off at once, and then we shall have nothing more to do with you.

Krogstad. *[Coming a pace nearer.]* Listen, Mrs. Helmer: either your memory is defective, or you don't know much about business. I must make the position a little clearer to you.

Nora. How so?

Krogstad. When your husband was ill, you came to me to borrow twelve hundred dollars.

Nora. I knew of nobody else.

Krogstad. I promised to find you the money—

Nora. And you did find it.

Krogstad. I promised to find you the money, on certain conditions. You were so much taken up at the time about your husband's illness, and so eager to have the wherewithal for your journey, that you probably did not give much thought to the details. Allow me to remind you of them. I promised to find you the amount in exchange for a note of hand, which I drew up.

Nora. Yes, and I signed it.

Krogstad. Quite right. But then I added a few lines, making your father security for the debt. Your father was to sign this.

Nora. Was to—? He did sign it!

Krogstad. I had left the date blank. That is to say, your father was himself to date his signature. Do you recollect that?

Nora. Yes, I believe—

Krogstad. Then I gave you the paper to send to your father, by post. Is not that so?

Nora. Yes.

Krogstad. And of course you did so at once; for within five or six days you brought me back the document with your father's signature; and I handed you the money.

Nora. Well? Have I not made my payments punctually?

Krogstad. Fairly—yes. But to return to the point: You were in great trouble at the time, Mrs. Helmer.

Nora. I was indeed!

Krogstad. Your father was very ill, I believe?

Nora. He was on his death-bed.

Krogstad. And died soon after?

Nora. Yes.

Krogstad. Tell me, Mrs. Helmer: do you happen to recollect the day of his death? The day of the month, I mean?

Nora. Father died on the 29th of September.

Krogstad. Quite correct. I have made inquiries. And here comes in the remarkable point—*[Produces a paper.]* which I cannot explain.

Nora. What remarkable point? I don't know—

Krogstad. The remarkable point, madam, that your father signed this paper three days after his death!

Nora. What! I don't understand—

Krogstand. Your father died on the 29th of September. But look here: he has dated his signature October 2nd! Is not that remarkable, Mrs. Helmer? [*Nora is silent.*] Can you explain it? [*Nora continues silent.*] It is noteworthy, too, that the words "October 2nd" and the year are not in your father's handwriting, but in one which I believe I know. Well, this may be explained; your father may have forgotten to date his signature, and somebody may have added the date at random, before the fact of your father's death was known. There is nothing wrong in that. Everything depends on the signature. Of course it is genuine, Mrs. Helmer? It was really your father himself who wrote his name here?

Nora. [*After a short silence, throws her head back and looks defiantly at him.*] No, it was not. *I* wrote father's name.

Krogstad. Ah!—Are you aware, madam, that that is a dangerous admission?

Nora. How so? You will soon get your money.

Krogstad. May I ask you one more question? Why did you not send the paper to your father?

Nora. It was impossible. Father was ill. If I had asked him for his signature, I should have had to tell him why I wanted the money; but he was so ill I really could not tell him that my husband's life was in danger. It was impossible.

Krogstad. Then it would have been better to have given up your tour.

Nora. No, I couldn't do that; my husband's life depended on that journey. I couldn't give it up.

Krogstad. And did it never occur to you that you were playing me false?

Nora. That was nothing to me. I didn't care in the least about you. I couldn't endure you for all the cruel difficulties you made, although you knew how ill my husband was.

Krogstad. Mrs. Helmer, you evidently do not realise what you have been guilty of. But I can assure you it was nothing more and nothing worse that made me an outcast from society.

Nora. You! You want me to believe that you did a brave thing to save your wife's life?

Krogstad. The law takes no account of motives.

Nora. Then it must be a very bad law.

Krogstad. Bad or not, if I produce this document in court, you will be condemned according to law.

Nora. I don't believe that. Do you mean to tell me that a daughter has no right to spare her dying father trouble and anxiety?—that a wife has no right to save her husband's life? I don't know much about the law, but I'm sure you'll find, somewhere or another, that that is allowed. And you don't know that—you, a lawyer! You must be a bad one, Mr. Krogstad.

Krogstad. Possibly. But business—such business as ours—I do understand. You believe that? Very well; now do as you please. But this I may tell you, that if I am flung into the gutter a second time, you shall keep me company. *[Bows and goes out through hall.]*

Nora. *[Stands a while thinking, then tosses her head.]* Oh nonsense! He wants to frighten me. I'm not so foolish as that. *[Begins folding the children's clothes. Pauses.]* But—? No, it's impossible! Why, I did it for love!

Children. *[At the door, left.]* Mamma, the strange man has gone now.

Nora. Yes, yes, I know. But don't tell any one about the strange man. Do you hear? Not even papa!

Children. No, mamma; and now will you play with us again?

Nora. No, no; not now.

Children. Oh, do, mamma; you know you promised.

Nora. Yes, but I can't just now. Run to the nursery; I have so much to do. Run along, run along, and be good, my darlings! *[She pushes them gently into the inner room, and closes the door behind them. Sits on the sofa, embroiders a few stitches, but soon pauses.]* No! *[Throws down the work, rises, goes to the hall door and calls out.]* Ellen, bring in the Christmas-tree! *[Goes to table, left, and opens the drawer; again pauses.]* No, it's quite impossible!

Ellen. *[With Christmas-tree.]* Where shall I stand it, ma'am?

Nora. There, in the middle of the room.

Ellen. Shall I bring in anything else?

Nora. No, thank you, I have all I want.

[Ellen, having put down the tree, goes out.]

Nora. *[Busy dressing the tree.]* There must be a candle here—and flowers there.—That horrible man! Nonsense, nonsense! there's nothing to be afraid of. The Christmas-tree shall be beautiful. I'll do everything to please you, Torvald; I'll sing and dance, and—

Enter Helmer by the hall door, with a bundle of documents.

Nora. Oh! You're back already?

Helmer. Yes. Has anybody been here?

Nora. Here? No.

Helmer. That's odd. I saw Krogstad come out of the house.

Nora. Did you? Oh, yes, by-the-bye, he was here for a minute.

Helmer. Nora, I can see by your manner that he has been begging you to put in a good word for him.

Nora. Yes.

Helmer. And you were to do it as if of your own accord? You were to say nothing to me of his having been here. Didn't he suggest that too?

Nora. Yes, Torvald; but—

Helmer. Nora, Nora! And you could condescend to that! To speak to such a man, to make him a promise! And then to tell me an untruth about it!

Nora. An untruth!

Helmer. Didn't you say that nobody had been here? *[Threatens with his finger.]* My little bird must never do that again! A song-bird must sing clear and true; no false notes. *[Puts his arm around her.]* That's so, isn't it? Yes, I was sure of it. *[Lets her go.]* And now we'll say no more about it. *[Sits down before the fire.]* Oh, how cozy and quiet it is here! *[Glances into his documents.]*

Nora. *[Busy with the tree, after a short silence.]* Torvald!

Helmer. Yes.

Nora. I'm looking forward so much to the Stenborgs' fancy ball the day after to-morrow.

Helmer. And I'm on tenterhooks to see what surprise you have in store for me.

Nora. Oh, it's too tiresome!

Helmer. What is?

Nora. I can't think of anything good. Everything seems so foolish and meaningless.

Helmer. Has little Nora made that discovery?

Nora. *[Behind his chair, with her arms on the back.]* Are you very busy, Torvald?

Helmer. Well—

Nora. What papers are those?

Helmer. Bank business.

Nora. Already!

Helmer. I have got the retiring manager to let me make some necessary changes in the staff and the organization. I can do this during Christmas week. I want to have everything straight by the New Year.

Nora. Then that's why that poor Krogstad—

Helmer. H'm.

Nora. *[Still leaning over the chair-back and slowly stroking his hair.]* If you hadn't been so very busy, I should have asked you a great, great favour, Torvald.

Helmer. What can it be? Out with it.

Nora. Nobody has such perfect taste as you; and I should so love to look well at the fancy ball. Torvald, dear, couldn't you take me in hand, and settle what I'm to be, and arrange my costume for me?

Helmer. Aha! So my wilful little woman is at a loss, and making signals of distress.

Nora. Yes, please, Torvald. I can't get on without your help.

Helmer. Well, well, I'll think it over, and we'll soon hit upon something.

Nora. Oh, how good that is of you! *[Goes to the tree again; pause.]* How well the red flowers show.—Tell me, was it anything so very dreadful this Krogstad got into trouble about?

Helmer. Forgery, that's all. Don't you know what that means?

Nora. Mayn't he have been driven to it by need?

Helmer. Yes; or, like so many others, he may have done it in pure heedlessness. I am not so hard-hearted as to condemn a man absolutely for a single fault.

Nora. No, surely not, Torvald!

Helmer. Many a man can retrieve his character, if he owns his crime and takes the punishment.

Nora. Punishment—?

Helmer. But Krogstad didn't do that. He evaded the law by means of tricks and subterfuges; and that is what has morally ruined him.

Nora. Do you think that—?

Helmer. Just think how a man with a thing of that sort on his conscience must be always lying and canting and shamming. Think of the mask he must wear even towards those who stand nearest him—towards his own wife and children. The effect on the children—that's the most terrible part of it, Nora.

Nora. Why?

Helmer. Because in such an atmosphere of lies home life is poisoned and contaminated in every fibre. Every breath the children draw contains some germ of evil.

Nora. *[Closer behind him.]* Are you sure of that?

Helmer. As a lawyer, my dear, I have seen it often enough. Nearly all cases of early corruption may be traced to lying mothers.

Nora. Why—mothers?

Helmer. It generally comes from the mother's side; but of course the father's influence may act in the same way. Every lawyer knows it too well. And here has this Krogstad been poisoning his own children for years past by a life of lies and hypocrisy—that is why I call him morally ruined. *[Holds out both hands to her.]* So my sweet little Nora must promise not to plead his cause. Shake hands upon it. Come, come, what's this? Give me your hand. That's right. Then it's a bargain. I assure you it would have been impossible for me to work with him. It gives me a positive sense of physical discomfort to come in contact with such people.

[Nora draws her hand away, and moves to the other side of the Christmas-tree.]

Nora. How warm it is here. And I have so much to do.

Helmer. *[Rises and gathers up his papers.]* Yes, and I must try to get some of these papers looked through before dinner. And I shall think over your costume too. Perhaps I may even find something to hang in gilt paper on the Christmas-tree. *[Lays his hand on her head.]* My precious little song-bird!

[He goes into his room and shuts the door.]

Nora. *[Softly, after a pause.]* It can't be. It's impossible. It must be impossible!

Anna. *[At the door, left.]* The little ones are begging so prettily to come to mamma.

Nora. No, no, no; don't let them come to me! Keep them with you, Anna.

Anna. Very well, ma'am. *[Shuts the door.]*

Nora. *[Pale with terror.]* Corrupt my children!—Poison my home! *[Short pause. She throws back her head.]* It's not true! It can never, never be true!

ACT II

The same room. In the corner, beside the piano, stands the Christmas-tree, stripped, and with the candles burnt out. Nora's outdoor things lie on the sofa.

Nora, *alone, is walking about restlessly. At last she stops by the sofa, and takes up her cloak.*

Nora. *[Dropping the cloak.]* There's somebody coming! *[Goes to the hall door and listens.]* Nobody; of course nobody will come to-day, Christmas-day; nor to-morrow either. But perhaps—*[Opens the door and looks out.]*—No, nothing in the letter box; quite empty. *[Comes forward.]* Stuff and nonsense! Of course he won't really do anything. Such a thing couldn't happen. It's impossible! Why, I have three little children.

[Anna enters from the left, with a large cardboard box.]

Anna. I've found the box with the fancy dress at last.

Nora. Thanks; put it down on the table.

Anna. *[Does so.]* But I'm afraid it's very much out of order.

Nora. Oh, I wish I could tear it into a hundred thousand pieces!

Anna. Oh, no. It can easily be put to rights—just a little patience.

Nora. I shall go and get Mrs. Linden to help me.

Anna. Going out again? In such weather as this! You'll catch cold, ma'am, and be ill.

Nora. Worse things might happen.—What are the children doing?

Anna. They're playing with their Christmas presents, poor little dears; but—

Nora. Do they often ask for me?

Anna. You see they've been so used to having their mamma with them.

Nora. Yes; but, Anna, I can't have them so much with me in future.

Anna. Well, little children get used to anything.

Nora. Do you think they do? Do you believe they would forget their mother if she went quite away?

Anna. Gracious me! Quite away?

Nora. Tell me, Anna—I've so often wondered about it—how could you bring yourself to give your child up to strangers?

Anna. I had to when I came to nurse my little Miss Nora.

Nora. But how could you make up your mind to it?

Anna. When I had the chance of such a good place? A poor girl who's been in trouble must take what comes. That wicked man did nothing for me.

Nora. But your daughter must have forgotten you.

Anna. Oh, no, ma'am, that she hasn't. She wrote to me both when she was confirmed and when she was married.

Nora. [Embracing her.] Dear old Anna—you were a good mother to me when I was little.

Anna. My poor little Nora had no mother but me.

Nora. And if my little ones had nobody else, I'm sure you would— Nonsense, nonsense! [Opens the box.] Go in to the children. Now I must—You'll see how lovely I shall be to-morrow.

Anna. I'm sure there will be no one at the ball so lovely as my Miss Nora. [She goes into the room on the left.]

Nora. [Takes the costume out of the box, but soon throws it down again.] Oh, if I dared go out. If only nobody would come. If only nothing would happen here in the meantime. Rubbish; nobody is coming. Only not to think. What a delicious muff! Beautiful gloves, beautiful gloves! To forget—to forget! One, two, three, four, five, six—[With a scream] Ah, there they come. [Goes towards the door, then stands irresolute.]

[Mrs. Linden *enters from the hall, where she has taken off her things.*]

Nora. Oh, it's you, Christina. There's nobody else there? I'm so glad you have come.

Mrs. Linden. I hear you called at my lodgings.

Nora. Yes, I was just passing. There's something you must help me with. Let us sit here on the sofa—so. To-morrow evening there's to be a fancy ball at Consul Stenborg's overhead, and Torvald wants me to appear as a Neapolitan fisher-girl, and dance the tarantella; I learned it at Capri.

Mrs. Linden. I see—quite a performance.

Nora. Yes, Torvald wishes it. Look, this is the costume; Torvald had it made for me in Italy. But now it's all so torn, I don't know—

Mrs. Linden. Oh, we shall soon set that to rights. It's only the trimming that has come loose here and there. Have you a needle and thread? Ah, here's the very thing.

Nora. Oh, how kind of you.

Mrs. Linden. *[Sewing.]* So you're to be in costume to-morrow, Nora? I'll tell you what—I shall come in for a moment to see you in all your glory. But I've quite forgotten to thank you for the pleasant evening yesterday.

Nora. *[Rises and walks across the room.]* Oh, yesterday, it didn't seem so pleasant as usual.—You should have come to town a little sooner, Christina.—Torvald has certainly the art of making home bright and beautiful.

Mrs. Linden. You too, I should think, or you wouldn't be your father's daughter. But tell me—is Doctor Rank always so depressed as he was last evening?

Nora. No, yesterday it was particularly noticeable. You see, he suffers from a dreadful illness. He has spinal consumption, poor fellow. They say his father was a horrible man, who kept mistresses and all sorts of things—so the son has been sickly from his childhood, you understand.

Mrs. Linden. *[Lets her sewing fall into her lap.]* Why, my darling Nora, how do you come to know such things?

Nora. *[Moving about the room.]* Oh, when one has three children, one sometimes has visits from women who are half—half doctors—and they talk of one thing and another.

Mrs. Linden. *[Goes on sewing; a short pause.]* Does Doctor Rank come here every day?

Nora. Every day of his life. He has been Torvald's most intimate friend from boyhood, and he's a good friend of mine too. Doctor Rank is quite one of the family.

Mrs. Linden. But tell me—is he quite sincere? I mean, isn't he rather given to flattering people?

Nora. No, quite the contrary. Why should you think so?

Mrs. Linden. When you introduced us yesterday he said he had often heard my name; but I noticed afterwards that your husband had no notion who I was. How could Doctor Rank—?

Nora. He was quite right, Christina. You see, Torvald loves me so indescribably, he wants to have me all to himself, as he says. When we were first married he was almost jealous if I even mentioned any of my old friends at home; so naturally I gave up doing it. But I often talk of the old times to Doctor Rank, for he likes to hear about them.

Mrs. Linden. Listen to me, Nora! You are still a child in many ways. I am older than you, and have had more experience. I'll tell you something? You ought to get clear of all this with Dr. Rank.

Nora. Get clear of what?

Mrs. Linden. The whole affair, I should say. You were talking yesterday of a rich admirer who was to find you money—

Nora. Yes, one who never existed, worse luck. What then?

Mrs. Linden. Has Doctor Rank money?

Nora. Yes, he has.

Mrs. Linden. And nobody to provide for?

Nora. Nobody. But—?

Mrs. Linden. And he comes here every day?

Nora. Yes, I told you so.

Mrs. Linden. I should have thought he would have had better taste.

Nora. I don't understand you a bit.

Mrs. Linden. Don't pretend, Nora. Do you suppose I can't guess who lent you the twelve hundred dollars?

Nora. Are you out of your senses? How can you think such a thing? A friend who comes here every day! Why, the position would be unbearable!

Mrs. Linden. Then it really is not he?

Nora. No, I assure you. It never for a moment occurred to me—Besides, at that time he had nothing to lend; he came into his property afterwards.

Mrs. Linden. Well, I believe that was lucky for you, Nora dear.

Nora. No, really, it would never have struck me to ask Dr. Rank—And yet, I'm certain that if I did—

Mrs. Linden. But of course you never would.

Nora. Of course not. It's unconceivable that it should ever be necessary. But I'm quite sure that if I spoke to Doctor Rank—

Mrs. Linden. Behind your husband's back?

Nora. I must get clear of the other thing; that's behind his back too. I must get clear of that.

Mrs. Linden. Yes, yes, I told you so yesterday; but—

Nora. [Walking up and down] A man can manage these things much better than a woman.

Mrs. Linden. One's own husband, yes.

Nora. Nonsense. [Stands still.] When everything is paid, one gets back the paper.

Mrs. Linden. Of course.

Nora. And can tear it into a hundred thousand pieces, and burn it up, the nasty, filthy thing!

Mrs. Linden. [Looks at her fixedly, lays down her work, and rises slowly.] Nora, you are hiding something from me.

Nora. Can you see it in my face?

Mrs. Linden. Something has happened since yesterday morning. Nora, what is it?

Nora. [Going towards her.] Christina—! [Listens.] Hush! There's Torvald coming home. Do you mind going into the nursery for the present? Torvald can't bear to see dressmaking going on. Get Anna to help you.

Mrs. Linden. *[Gathers some of the things together.]* Very well; but I shan't go away until you have told me all about it.

[She goes out to the left, as Helmer enters from the hall.]

Nora. *[Runs to meet him.]* Oh, how I've been longing for you to come, Torvald dear!
Helmer. Was that the dressmaker—?
Nora. No, Christina. She's helping me with my costume. You'll see how nice I shall look.
Helmer. Yes, wasn't that a happy thought of mine?
Nora. Splendid! But isn't it good of me, too, to have given in to you about the tarantella?
Helmer. *[Takes her under the chin.]* Good of you! To give in to your own husband? Well well, you little madcap, I know you don't mean it. But I won't disturb you. I daresay you want to be "trying on."
Nora. And you are going to work, I suppose?
Helmer. Yes. *[Shows her a bundle of papers.]* Look here. I've just come from the Bank—

[Goes towards his room.]

Nora. Torvald.
Helmer. *[Stopping.]* Yes?
Nora. If your little squirrel were to beg you for something so prettily—
Helmer. Well?
Nora. Would you do it?
Helmer. I must know first what it is.
Nora. The squirrel would skip about and play all sorts of tricks if you would only be nice and kind.
Helmer. Come, then, out with it.
Nora. Your lark would twitter from morning till night—
Helmer. Oh, that she does in any case.
Nora. I'll be an elf and dance in the moonlight for you, Torvald.
Helmer. Nora—you can't mean what you were hinting at this morning?
Nora. *[Coming nearer.]* Yes, Torvald, I beg and implore you!
Helmer. Have you really the courage to begin that again?
Nora. Yes, yes; for my sake, you must let Krogstad keep his place in the Bank.
Helmer. My dear Nora, it's his place I intend for Mrs. Linden.
Nora. Yes, that's so good of you. But instead of Krogstad, you could dismiss some other clerk.
Helmer. Why, this is incredible obstinacy! Because you have thoughtlessly promised to put in a word for him, I am to—!

Nora. It's not that, Torvald. It's for your own sake. This man writes for the most scurrilous newspapers; you said so yourself. He can do you no end of harm. I'm so terribly afraid of him—

Helmer. Ah, I understand; it's old recollections that are frightening you.

Nora. What do you mean?

Helmer. Of course you're thinking of your father.

Nora. Yes—yes, of course. Only think of the shameful slanders wicked people used to write about father. I believe they would have got him dismissed if you hadn't been sent to look into the thing, and been kind to him, and helped him.

Helmer. My little Nora, between your father and me there is all the difference in the world. Your father was not altogether unimpeachable. I am; and I hope to remain so.

Nora. Oh, no one knows what wicked men may hit upon. We could live so quietly and happily now, in our cosy, peaceful home, you and I and the children, Torvald! That's why I beg and implore you—

Helmer. And it is just by pleading his cause that you make it impossible for me to keep him. It's already known at the Bank that I intend to dismiss Krogstad. If it were now reported that the new manager let himself be turned round his wife's little finger—

Nora. What then?

Helmer. Oh, nothing, so long as a wilful woman can have her way—! I am to make myself a laughing-stock to the whole staff, and set people saying that I am open to all sorts of outside influence? Take my word for it, I should soon feel the consequences. And besides—there is one thing that makes Krogstad impossible for me to work with—

Nora. What thing?

Helmer. I could perhaps have overlooked his moral failings at a pinch—

Nora. Yes, couldn't you, Torvald?

Helmer. And I hear he is good at his work. But the fact is, he was a college chum of mine—there was one of those rash friendships between us that one so often repents of later. I may as well confess it at once— he calls me by my Christian name; and he is tactless enough to do it even when others are present. He delights in putting on airs of familiarity—Torvald here. Torvald there! I assure you it's most painful to me. He would make my position at the Bank perfectly unendurable.

Nora. Torvald, surely you're not serious?

Helmer. No? Why not?

Nora. That's such a petty reason.

Helmer. What! Petty! Do you consider me petty!

Nora. No, on the contrary, Torvald dear; and that's just why—

Helmer. Never mind; you call my motives petty; then I must be petty too. Petty! Very well!—Now we'll put an end to this, once and for all. [Goes to the door into the hall and calls.] Ellen!

Nora. What do you want?

Helmer. *[Searching among his papers.]* To settle the thing. *[Ellen enters.]* Here; take this letter; give it to a messenger. See that he takes it at once. The address is on it. Here's the money.

Ellen. Very well, sir. *[Goes with the letter.]*

Helmer. *[Putting his papers together.]* There, Madam Obstinacy.

Nora. *[Breathless]* Torvald—what was in the letter?

Helmer. Krogstad's dismissal.

Nora. Call it back again, Torvald! There's still time. Oh, Torvald, call it back again! For my sake, for your own, for the children's sake! Do you hear, Torvald? Do it! You don't know what that letter may bring upon us all.

Helmer. Too late.

Nora. Yes, too late.

Helmer. My dear Nora, I forgive your anxiety, though it's anything but flattering to me. Why should you suppose that *I* would be afraid of a wretched scribbler's spite? But I forgive you all the same, for it's a proof of your great love for me. *[Takes her in his arms.]* That's as it should be, my own dear Nora. Let what will happen—when it comes to the pinch, I shall have strength and courage enough. You shall see: my shoulders are broad enough to bear the whole burden.

Nora. *[Terror-struck.]* What do you mean by that?

Helmer. The whole burden, I say—

Nora. *[With decision.]* That you shall never, never do!

Helmer. Very well; then we'll share it, Nora, as man and wife. That is how it should be. *[Petting her.]* Are you satisfied now? Come, come, come, don't look like a scared dove. It's all nothing—foolish fancies.— Now you ought to play the tarantella through and practice with the tambourine. I shall sit in my inner room and shut both doors, so that I shall hear nothing. You can make as much noise as you please. *[Turns round in doorway.]* And when Rank comes, just tell him where I'm to be found.

[He nods to her, and goes with his papers into his room, closing the door.]

Nora. *[Bewildered with terror, stands as though rooted to the ground, and whispers.]* He would do it. Yes, he would do it. He would do it, in spite of all the world.—No, never that, never, never! Anything rather than that! Oh, for some way of escape! What shall I do—! *[Hall bell rings.]* Doctor Rank—!—Anything, anything, rather than—!

[Nora draws her hands over her face, pulls herself together, goes to the door and opens it. Rank stands outside hanging up his fur coat. During what follows it begins to grow dark.]

Nora. Good afternoon, Doctor Rank, I knew you by your ring. But you mustn't go to Torvald now. I believe he's busy.

Rank. And you?

[Enters and closes the door.]

Nora. Oh, you know very well, I have always time for you.

Rank. Thank you. I shall avail myself of your kindness as long as I can.

Nora. What do you mean? As long as you can?

Rank. Yes. Does that frighten you?

Nora. I think it's an odd expression. Do you expect anything to happen?

Rank. Something I have long been prepared for; but I didn't think it would come so soon.

Nora. *[Catching his arm.]* What have you discovered? Doctor Rank, you must tell me!

Rank. *[Sitting down by the stove.]* I am running down hill. There's no help for it.

Nora. *[Draws a long breath of relief.]* It's you—?

Rank. Who else should it be?—Why lie to one's self? I am the most wretched of all my patients, Mrs. Helmer. In these last days I have been auditing my life-account—bankrupt! Perhaps before a month is over, I shall lie rotting in the church-yard.

Nora. Oh! What an ugly way to talk.

Rank. The thing itself is so confoundedly ugly, you see. But the worst of it is, so many other ugly things have to be gone through first. There is only one last investigation to be made, and when that is over I shall know pretty certainly when the break-up will begin. There's one thing I want to say to you: Helmer's delicate nature shrinks so from all that is horrible: I will not have him in my sick-room—

Nora. But, Doctor Rank—

Rank. I won't have him, I say—not on any account! I shall lock my door against him.—As soon as I am quite certain of the worst, I shall send you my visiting-card with a black cross on it; and then you will know that the final horror has begun.

Nora. Why, you're perfectly unreasonable to-day; and I did so want you to be in a really good humour.

Rank. With death staring me in the face?—And to suffer thus for another's sin! Where's the justice of it? And in one way or another you can trace in every family some such inexorable retribution—

Nora. *[Stopping her ears.]* Nonsense, nonsense! Now cheer up!

Rank. Well, after all, the whole thing's only worth laughing at. My poor innocent spine must do penance for my father's wild oats.

Nora. *[At table, left.]* I suppose he was too fond of asparagus and Strasbourg pâté, wasn't he?

Rank. Yes; and truffles.

Nora. Yes, truffles, to be sure. And oysters, I believe?

Rank. Yes, oysters; oysters, of course.

Nora. And then all the port and champagne! It's sad that all these good things should attack the spine.

Rank. Especially when the luckless spine attacked never had any good of them.

Nora. Ah, yes, that's the worst of it.

Rank. [Looks at her searchingly.] H'm—

Nora. [A moment later.] Why did you smile?

Rank. No; it was you that laughed.

Nora. No; it was you that smiled, Doctor Rank.

Rank. [Standing up.] I see you're deeper than I thought.

Nora. I'm in such a crazy mood to-day.

Rank. So it seems.

Nora. [With her hands on his shoulders.] Dear, dear Doctor Rank, death shall not take you away from Torvald and me.

Rank. Oh, you'll easily get over the loss. The absent are soon forgotten.

Nora. [Looks at him anxiously.] Do you think so?

Rank. People make fresh ties, and then—

Nora. Who make fresh ties?

Rank. You and Helmer will, when I am gone. You yourself are taking time by the forelock, it seems to me. What was that Mrs. Linden doing here yesterday?

Nora. Oh!—you're surely not jealous of poor Christina?

Rank. Yes, I am. She will be my successor in this house. When I am out of the way, this woman will perhaps—

Nora. Hush! Not so loud! She's in there.

Rank. To-day as well? You see!

Nora. Only to put my costume in order—dear me, how unreasonable you are! [Sits on sofa.] Now do be good, Doctor Rank! To-morrow you shall see how beautifully I shall dance; and then you may fancy that I'm doing it all to please you—and of course Torvald as well. [Takes various things out of box.] Doctor Rank, sit down here, and I'll show you something.

Rank. [Sitting.] What is it?

Nora. Look here. Look!

Rank. Silk stockings.

Nora. Flesh-coloured. Aren't they lovely? It's so dark here now; but to-morrow—No, no, no; you must only look at the feet. Oh, well, I suppose you may look at the rest too.

Rank. H'm—

Nora. What are you looking so critical about? Do you think they won't fit me?

Rank. I can't possibly give any competent opinion on that point.

Nora. [Looking at him a moment.] For shame! [Hits him lightly on the ear with the stockings.] Take that.

[Rolls them up again.]

Rank. And what other wonders am I to see?

Nora. You sha'n't see anything more; for you don't behave nicely. *[She hums a little and searches among the things.]*

Rank. *[After a short silence.]* When I sit here gossiping with you, I can't imagine—I simply cannot conceive—what would have become of me if I had never entered this house.

Nora. *[Smiling.]* Yes, I think you do feel at home with us.

Rank. *[More softly—looking straight before him.]* And now to have to leave it all—

Nora. Nonsense. You sha'n't leave us.

Rank. *[In the same tone.]* And not to be able to leave behind the slightest token of gratitude; scarcely even a passing regret—nothing but an empty place, that can be filled by the first comer.

Nora. And if I were to ask you for—? No—

Rank. For what?

Nora. For a great proof of your friendship.

Rank. Yes—yes?

Nora. I mean—for a very, very great service—

Rank. Would you really, for once, make me so happy?

Nora. Oh, you don't know what it is.

Rank. Then tell me.

Nora. No, I really can't, Doctor Rank. It's far, far too much—not only a service, but help and advice besides—

Rank. So much the better. I can't think what you can mean. But go on. Don't you trust me?

Nora. As I trust no one else. I know you are my best and truest friend. So I will tell you. Well then, Doctor Rank, there is something you must help me to prevent. You know how deeply, how wonderfully Torvald loves me; he wouldn't hesitate a moment to give his very life for my sake.

Rank. *[Bending towards her.]* Nora—do you think he is the only one who—?

Nora. *[With a slight start.]* Who—?

Rank. Who would gladly give his life for you?

Nora. *[Sadly.]* Oh!

Rank. I have sworn that you shall know it before I—go. I shall never find a better opportunity.—Yes, Nora, now I have told you; and now you know that you can trust me as you can no one else.

Nora. *[Standing up; simply and calmly.]* Let me pass, please.

Rank. *[Makes way for her, but remains sitting.]* Nora—

Nora. *[In the doorway.]* Ellen, bring the lamp. *[Crosses to the stove.]* Oh dear, Doctor Rank, that was too bad of you.

Rank. *[Rising.]* That I have loved you as deeply as—any one else? Was that too bad of me?

Nora. No, but that you should have told me so. It was so unneccessary—

Rank. What do you mean? Did you know—? [*Ellen enters with the lamp; sets it on the table and goes out again.*]

Rank. Nora—Mrs. Helmer—I ask you, did you know?

Nora. Oh, how can I tell what I knew or didn't know? I really can't say—How could you be so clumsy, Doctor Rank? It was all so nice!

Rank. Well, at any rate, you know now that I am at your service, body and soul. And now, go on.

Nora. [*Looking at him.*] Go on—now?

Rank. I beg you to tell me what you want.

Nora. I can tell you nothing now.

Rank. Yes, yes! You mustn't punish me in that way. Let me do for you whatever a man can.

Nora. You can do nothing for me now.—Besides, I really want no help. You shall see it was only my fancy. Yes, it must be so. Of course! [*Sits in the rockingchair, looks at him and smiles.*] You are a nice person, Doctor Rank! Aren't you ashamed of yourself, now that the lamp is on the table?

Rank. No; not exactly. But perhaps I ought to go—for ever.

Nora. No, indeed you mustn't. Of course you must come and go as you've always done. You know very well, that Torvald can't do without you.

Rank. Yes, but you?

Nora. Oh, you know I always like to have you here.

Rank. That is just what led me astray. You are a riddle to me. It has often seemed to me as if you liked being with me almost as much as being with Helmer.

Nora. Yes; don't you see? There are people one loves, and others one likes to talk to.

Rank. Yes—there's something in that.

Nora. When I was a girl, of course I loved papa best. But it always delighted me to steal into the servants' room. In the first place they never lectured me, and in the second it was such fun to hear them talk.

Rank. Ah, I see; then it's their place I have taken?

Nora. [*Jumps up and hurries towards him.*] Oh, my dear Doctor Rank, I don't mean that. But you understand, with Torvald it's the same as with papa—

[*Ellen enters from the hall.*]

Ellen. Please ma'am—[*Whispers to Nora, and gives her a card.*]

Nora. [*Glancing at card.*] Ah! [*Puts it in her pocket.*]

Rank. Anything wrong?

Nora. No, no, not in the least. It's only—it's my new costume—

Rank. Your costume! Why, it's there.

Nora. Oh, that one, yes. But this is another that—I have ordered it—Torvald mustn't know—

Rank. Aha! So that's the great secret.

Nora. Yes, of course. Please go to him; he's in the inner room. Do keep him while I—

Rank. Don't be alarmed; he sha'n't escape.

[Goes into Helmer's room.]

Nora. *[To Ellen.]* Is he waiting in the kitchen?

Ellen. Yes, he came up the back stair—

Nora. Didn't you tell him I was engaged?

Ellen. Yes, but it was no use.

Nora. He won't go away?

Ellen. No, ma'am, not until he has spoken to you.

Nora. Then let him come in; but quietly. And, Ellen—say nothing about it; it's a surprise for my husband.

Ellen. Oh, yes, ma'am, I understand. *[She goes out.]*

Nora. It is coming! The dreadful thing is coming, after all. No, no, no, it can never be; it shall not!

[She goes to Helmer's *door and slips the bolt.* Ellen *opens the hall door for* Krogstad, *and shuts it after him. He wears a travelling-coat, high boots, and a fur cap.]*

Nora. *[Goes towards him.]* Speak softly; my husband is at home.

Krogstad. All right. That's nothing to me.

Nora. What do you want?

Krogstad. A little information.

Nora. Be quick, then. What is it?

Krogstad. You know I have got my dismissal.

Nora. I couldn't prevent it, Mr. Krogstad. I fought for you to the last, but it was of no use.

Krogstad. Does your husband care for you so little? He knows what I can bring upon you, and yet he dares—

Nora. How could you think I should tell him?

Krogstad. Well, as a matter of fact, I didn't think it. It wasn't like my friend Torvald Helmer to show so much courage—

Nora. Mr. Krogstad, be good enough to speak respectfully of my husband.

Krogstad. Certainly, with all due respect. But since you are so anxious to keep the matter secret, I suppose you are a little clearer than yesterday as to what you have done.

Nora. Clearer than you could ever make me.

Krogstad. Yes, such a bad lawyer as I—

Nora. What is it you want?

Krogstad. Only to see how you are getting on, Mrs. Helmer. I've been thinking about you all day. Even a mere money-lender, a gutter-journalist, a—in short, a creature like me—has a little bit of what people call feeling.

Nora. Then show it; think of my little children.

Krogstad. Did you and your husband think of mine? But enough of that. I only wanted to tell you that you needn't take this matter too seriously. I shall not lodge any information, for the present.

Nora. No, surely not. I knew you wouldn't.

Krogstad. The whole thing can be settled quite amicably. Nobody need know. It can remain among us three.

Nora. My husband must never know.

Krogstad. How can you prevent it? Can you pay off the balance?

Nora. No, not at once.

Krogstad. Or have you any means of raising the money in the next few days?

Nora. None—that I will make use of.

Krogstad. And if you had, it would not help you now. If you offered me ever so much money down, you should not get back your I.O.U.

Nora. Tell me what you want to do with it.

Krogstad. I only want to keep it—to have it in my possession. No outsider shall hear anything of it. So, if you have any desperate scheme in your head—

Nora. What if I have?

Krogstad. If you should think of leaving your husband and children—

Nora. What if I do?

Krogstad. Or if you should think of—something worse—

Nora. How do you know that?

Krogstad. Put all that out of your head.

Nora. How did you know what I had in my mind?

Krogstad. Most of us think of that at first. I thought of it, too; but I hadn't the courage—

Nora. *[Tonelessly.]* Nor I.

Krogstad. *[Relieved.]* No, one hasn't. You haven't the courage either, have you?

Nora. I haven't, I haven't.

Krogstad. Besides, it would be very foolish.—Just one domestic storm, and it's all over. I have a letter in my pocket for your husband—

Nora. Telling him everything?

Krogstad. Sparing you as much as possible.

Nora. *[Quickly.]* He must never read that letter. Tear it up. I will manage to get the money somehow—

Krogstad. Pardon me, Mrs. Helmer, but I believe I told you—

Nora. Oh, I'm not talking about the money I owe you. Tell me how much you demand from my husband—I will get it.

Krogstad. I demand no money from your husband.

Nora. What do you demand then?

Krogstad. I will tell you. I want to regain my footing in the world. I want to rise; and your husband shall help me to do it. For the last eighteen months my record has been spotless; I have been in bitter need all the time; but I was content to fight my way up, step by step. Now, I've been thrust down again, and I will not be satisfied with merely being reinstated as a matter of grace. I want to rise, I tell you. I must get into the Bank again, in a higher position than before. Your husband shall create a place on purpose for me—

Nora. He will never do that!

Krogstad. He will do it; I know him—he won't dare to show fight! And when he and I are together there, you shall soon see! Before a year is out I shall be the manager's right hand. It won't be Torvald Helmer, but Nils Krogstad, that manages the Joint Stock Bank.

Nora. That shall never be.

Krogstad. Perhaps you will—?

Nora. Now I have the courage for it.

Krogstad. Oh, you don't frighten me! A sensitive, petted creature like you—

Nora. You shall see, you shall see!

Krogstad. Under the ice, perhaps? Down into the cold, black water? And next spring to come up again, ugly, hairless, unrecognisable—

Nora. You can't terrify me.

Krogstad. Nor you me. People don't do that sort of thing, Mrs. Helmer. And, after all, what would be the use of it? I have your husband in my pocket, all the same.

Nora. Afterwards? When I am no longer—?

Krogstad. You forget, your reputation remains in my hands! [*Nora stands speechless and looks at him.*] Do nothing foolish. As soon as Helmer has received my letter, I shall expect to hear from him. And remember that it is your husband himself who has forced me back again into such paths. That I will never forgive him. Good-bye, Mrs. Helmer.

[*Goes out through the hall. Nora hurries to the door, opens it a little, and listens.*]

Nora. He's going. He's not putting the letter into the box. No, no, it would be impossible! [*Opens the door further and further.*] What's that. He's standing still; not going down stairs. Has he changed his mind? Is he—? [*A letter falls into the box. Krogstad's footsteps are heard gradually receding down the stair. Nora utters a suppressed shriek, and rushes forward towards the sofa-table; pause.*] In the letter-box! [*Slips shrinkingly up to the hall door.*] There it lies.—Torvald, Torvald—now we are lost!

[Mrs. Linden *enters from the left with the costume.*]

Mrs. Linden.   There, I think it's all right now. Shall we just try it on?
Nora.   [*Hoarsely and softly.*] Christina, come here.
Mrs. Linden   [*Throws down the dress on the sofa.*] What's the matter? You look quite distracted.
Nora.   Come here. Do you see that letter? There, see—through the glass of the letter-box.
Mrs. Linden.   Yes, yes, I see it.
Nora.   That letter is from Krogstad—
Mrs. Linden.   Nora—it was Krogstad who lent you the money?
Nora.   Yes; and now Torvald will know everything.
Mrs. Linden.   Believe me, Nora, it's the best thing for both of you.
Nora.   You don't know all yet. I have forged a name—
Mrs. Linden.   Good heavens!
Nora.   Now, listen to me, Christina; you shall bear me witness—
Mrs. Linden.   How "witness"? What am I to—?
Nora.   If I should go out of my mind—it might easily happen—
Mrs. Linden.   Nora!
Nora.   Or if anything else should happen to me—so that I couldn't be here—!
Mrs. Linden.   Nora, Nora, you're quite beside yourself!
Nora.   In case any one wanted to take it all upon himself—the whole blame—you understand—
Mrs. Linden.   Yes, yes; but how can you think—?
Nora.   You shall bear witness that it's not true, Christina. I'm not out of my mind at all; I know quite well what I'm saying; and I tell you nobody else knew anything about it; I did the whole thing, I myself. Remember that.
Mrs. Linden.   I shall remember. But I don't understand what you mean—
Nora.   Oh, how should you? It's the miracle coming to pass.
Mrs. Linden.   The miracle?
Nora.   Yes, the miracle. But it's so terrible, Christina; it mustn't happen for all the world.
Mrs. Linden.   I shall go straight to Krogstad and talk to him.
Nora.   Don't; he'll do you some harm.
Mrs. Linden.   Once he would have done anything for me.
Nora.   He?
Mrs. Linden.   Where does he live?
Nora.   Oh, how can I tell—? Yes—[*Feels in her pocket.*] Here's his card. But the letter, the letter—!
Helmer.   [*Knocking outside.*] Nora!
Nora.   [*Shrieks in terror.*] Oh, what is it? What do you want?
Helmer.   Well, well, don't be frightened. We're not coming in; you've bolted the door. Are you trying on your dress?

Nora. Yes, yes, I'm trying it on. It suits me so well, Torvald.

Mrs. Linden. [*Who has read the card.*] Why, he lives close by here.

Nora. Yes, but it's no use now. We are lost. The letter is there in the box.

Mrs. Linden. And your husband has the key?

Nora. Always.

Mrs. Linden. Krogstad must demand his letter back, unread. He must find some pretext—

Nora. But this is the very time when Torvald generally—

Mrs. Linden. Prevent him. Keep him occupied. I shall come back as quickly as I can.

[*She goes out hastily by the hall door.*]

Nora. [*Opens* Helmer's *door and peeps in.*] Torvald!

Helmer. Well, may one come into one's own room again at last? Come, Rank, we'll have a look—[*In the doorway.*] But how's this?

Nora. What, Torvald dear?

Helmer. Rank led me to expect a grand transformation.

Rank. [*In the doorway.*] So I understood. I suppose I was mistaken.

Nora. No, no one shall see me in my glory till to-morrow evening.

Helmer. Why, Nora dear, you look so tired. Have you been practising too hard?

Nora. No, I haven't practised at all yet.

Helmer. But you'll have to—

Nora. Oh yes, I must, I must! But, Torvald, I can't get on at all without your help. I've forgotten everything.

Helmer. Oh, we shall soon freshen it up again.

Nora. Yes, do help me, Torvald. You must promise me—Oh, I'm so nervous about it. Before so many people—This evening you must give yourself up entirely to me. You mustn't do a stroke of work; you mustn't even touch a pen. Do promise, Torvald dear!

Helmer. I promise. All this evening I shall be your slave. Little helpless thing—! But, by-the-bye, I must just—

[*Going to hall door*]

Nora. What do you want there?

Helmer. Only to see if there are any letters.

Nora. No, no, don't do that, Torvald.

Helmer. Why not?

Nora. Torvald, I beg you not to. There are none there.

Helmer. Let me just see. [*Is going.*]

[Nora, *at the piano, plays the first bars of the tarantella.*]

Helmer. *[At the door, stops.]* Aha!

Nora. I can't dance to-morrow if I don't rehearse with you first.

Helmer. *[Going to her.]* Are you really so nervous, dear Nora?

Nora. Yes, dreadfully! Let me rehearse at once. We have time before dinner. Oh, do sit down and play for me, Torvald dear; direct me and put me right, as you used to do.

Helmer. With all the pleasure in life, since you wish it. *[Sits at piano.]*

[Nora *snatches the tambourine out of the box, and hurriedly drapes herself in a long parti-coloured shawl; then, with a bound, stands in the middle of the floor.*]

Nora. Now play for me! Now I'll dance!

[Helmer *plays and* Nora *dances.* Rank *stands at the piano behind* Helmer *and looks on.*]

Helmer. *[Playing.]* Slower! Slower!

Nora. Can't do it slower!

Helmer. Not so violently, Nora.

Nora. I must! I must!

Helmer. *[Stops.]* No, no, Nora—that will never do.

Nora. *[Laughs and swings her tambourine.]* Didn't I tell you so!

Rank. Let me play for her.

Helmer. *[Rising.]* Yes, do—then I can direct her better.

[Rank *sits down to the piano and plays;* Nora *dances more and more wildly.* Helmer *stands by the stove and addresses frequent corrections to her; she seems not to hear. Her hair breaks loose, and falls over her shoulders. She does not notice it, but goes on dancing.* Mrs. Linden *enters and stands spellbound in the doorway.*]

Mrs. Linden. Ah—!

Nora. *[Dancing.]* We're having such fun here, Christina!

Helmer. Why, Nora dear, you're dancing as if it were a matter of life and death.

Nora. So it is.

Helmer. Rank, stop! This is the merest madness. Stop, I say!

[Rank *stops playing, and* Nora *comes to a sudden standstill.*]

Helmer. *[Going towards her.]* I couldn't have believed it. You've positively forgotten all I taught you.

Nora. *[Throws the tambourine away.]* You see for yourself.

Helmer. You really do want teaching.

Nora. Yes, you see how much I need it. You must practise with me up to the last moment. Will you promise me, Torvald?

Helmer. Certainly, certainly.

Nora. Neither to-day nor to-morrow must you think of anything but me. You mustn't open a single letter—mustn't look at the letter-box.

Helmer. Ah, you're still afraid of that man—

Nora. Oh yes, yes, I am.

Helmer. Nora, I can see it in your face—there's a letter from him in the box.

Nora. I don't know, I believe so. But you're not to read anything now; nothing ugly must come between us until all is over.

Rank. *[Softly, to* Helmer.*]* You mustn't contradict her.

Helmer. *[Putting his arm around her.]* The child shall have her own way. But to-morrow night, when the dance is over—

Nora. Then you shall be free.

*[*Ellen *appears in the doorway, right.]*

Ellen. Dinner is on the table, ma'am.

Nora. We'll have some champagne, Ellen.

Ellen. Yes, ma'am. *[Goes out.]*

Helmer. Dear me! Quite a banquet.

Nora. Yes, and we'll keep it up till morning. *[Calling out.]* And macaroons, Ellen—plenty—just this once.

Helmer. *[Seizing her hand.]* Come, come, don't let us have this wild excitement! Be my own little lark again.

Nora. Oh yes, I will. But now go into the dining-room; and you too, Doctor Rank. Christina, you must help me to do up my hair.

Rank. *[Softly, as they go.]* There's nothing in the wind? Nothing—I mean—?

Helmer. Oh no, nothing of the kind. It's merely this babyish anxiety I was telling you about.

[They go out to the right.]

Nora. Well?

Mrs. Linden. He's gone out of town.

Nora. I saw it in your face.

Mrs. Linden. He comes back to-morrow evening. I left a note for him.

Nora.   You shouldn't have done that. Things must take their course. After all, there's something glorious in waiting for the miracle.
Mrs. Linden.   What is it you're waiting for?
Nora.   Oh, you can't understand. Go to them in the dining-room; I shall come in a moment.

[Mrs. Linden *goes into the dining-room.* Nora *stands for a moment as though collecting her thoughts; then looks at her watch.*]

Nora.   Five. Seven hours till midnight. Then twenty-four hours till the next midnight. Then the tarantella will be over. Twenty-four and seven? Thirty-one hours to live.

[Helmer *appears at the door, right.*]

Helmer.   What has become of my little lark?
Nora.   [*Runs to him with open arms.*] Here she is!

ACT III

The same room. The table, with the chairs around it, in the middle. A lighted lamp on the table. The door to the hall stands open. Dance music is heard from the floor above.
Mrs. Linden *sits by the table and absently turns the pages of a book. She tries to read, but seems unable to fix her attention; she frequently listens and looks anxiously towards the hall door.*

Mrs. Linden.   [*Looks at her watch.*] Not here yet; and the time is nearly up. If only he hasn't—[*Listens again.*] Ah, there he is. [*She goes into the hall and cautiously opens the outer door; soft footsteps are heard on the stairs; she whispers.*] Come in; there is no one here.
Krogstad.   [*In the doorway.*] I found a note from you at my house. What does it mean?
Mrs. Linden.   I must speak to you.
Krogstad.   Indeed? And in this house?
Mrs. Linden.   I could not see you at my rooms. They have no separate entrance. Come in; we are quite alone. The servants are asleep, and the Helmers are at the ball upstairs.
Krogstad.   [*Coming into the room.*] Ah! So the Helmers are dancing this evening? Really?
Mrs. Linden.   Yes. Why not?
Krogstad.   Quite right. Why not?

Mrs. Linden. And now let us talk a little.

Krogstad. Have we two anything to say to each other?

Mrs. Linden. A great deal.

Krogstad. I should not have thought so.

Mrs. Linden. Because you have never really understood me.

Krogstad. What was there to understand? The most natural thing in the world—a heartless woman throws a man over when a better match offers.

Mrs. Linden. Do you really think me so heartless? Do you think I broke with you lightly?

Krogstad. Did you not?

Mrs. Linden. Do you really think so?

Krogstad. If not, why did you write me that letter?

Mrs. Linden. Was it not best? Since I had to break with you, was it not right that I should try to put an end to all that you felt for me?

Krogstad. *[Clenching his hands together.]* So that was it? And all this—for the sake of money!

Mrs. Linden. You ought not to forget that I had a helpless mother and two little brothers. We could not wait for you, Nils, as your prospects then stood.

Krogstad. Perhaps not; but you had no right to cast me off for the sake of others, whoever the others might be.

Mrs. Linden. I don't know. I have often asked myself whether I had the right.

Krogstad. *[More softly.]* When I had lost you, I seemed to have no firm ground left under my feet. Look at me now. I am a shipwrecked man clinging to a spar.

Mrs. Linden. Rescue may be at hand.

Krogstad. It was at hand; but then you came and stood in the way.

Mrs. Linden. Without my knowledge, Nils. I did not know till to-day that it was you I was to replace in the Bank.

Krogstad. Well, I take your word for it. But now that you do know, do you mean to give way?

Mrs. Linden. No, for that would not help you in the least.

Krogstad. Oh, help, help—! I should do it whether or no.

Mrs. Linden. I have learnt prudence. Life and bitter necessity have schooled me.

Krogstad. And life has taught me not to trust fine speeches.

Mrs. Linden. Then life has taught you a very sensible thing. But deeds you will trust?

Krogstad. What do you mean?

Mrs. Linden. You said you were a shipwrecked man, clinging to a spar.

Krogstad. I have good reason to say so.

Mrs. Linden. I too am shipwrecked, and clinging to a spar. I have no one to mourn for, no one to care for.

Krogstad. You made your own choice.

Mrs. Linden. No choice was left me.

Krogstad. Well, what then?

Mrs. Linden. Nils, how if we two shipwrecked people could join hands?

Krogstad. What!

Mrs. Linden. Two on a raft have a better chance than if each clings to a separate spar.

Krogstad. Christina!

Mrs. Linden. What do you think brought me to town?

Krogstad. Had you any thought of me?

Mrs. Linden. I must have work or I can't bear to live. All my life, as long as I can remember, I have worked; work has been my one great joy. Now I stand quite alone in the world, aimless and forlorn. There is no happiness in working for one's self. Nils, give me somebody and something to work for.

Krogstad. I cannot believe in all this. It is simply a woman's romantic craving for self-sacrifice.

Mrs. Linden. Have you ever found me romantic?

Krogstad. Would you really—? Tell me: do you know all my past?

Mrs. Linden. Yes.

Krogstad. And do you know what people say of me?

Mrs. Linden. Did you not say just now that with me you could have been another man?

Krogstad. I am sure of it.

Mrs. Linden. Is it too late?

Krogstad. Christina, do you know what you are doing? Yes, you do; I see it in your face. Have you the courage then—?

Mrs. Linden. I need some one to be a mother to, and your children need a mother. You need me, and I—I need you. Nils, I believe in your better self. With you I fear nothing.

Krogstad. [Seizing her hands.] Thank you—thank you, Christina. Now I shall make others see me as you do.—Ah, I forgot—

Mrs. Linden. [Listening.] Hush! The tarantella! Go! go!

Krogstad. Why? What is it?

Mrs. Linden. Don't you hear the dancing overhead? As soon as that is over they will be here.

Krogstad. Oh yes, I shall go. Nothing will come of this, after all. Of course, you don't know the step I have taken against the Helmers.

Mrs. Linden. Yes, Nils, I do know.

Krogstad. And yet you have the courage to—?

Mrs. Linden. I know to what lengths despair can drive a man.

Krogstad. Oh, if I could only undo it!

Mrs. Linden. You could. Your letter is still in the box.

Krogstad. Are you sure?

Mrs. Linden. Yes; but—

Krogstad. [Looking to her searchingly.] Is that what it all means? You want to save your friend at any price. Say it out—is that your idea?

Mrs. Linden. Nils, a woman who has once sold herself for the sake of others, does not do so again.

Krogstad. I shall demand my letter back again.

Mrs. Linden. No, no.

Krogstad. Yes, of course. I shall wait till Helmer comes; I shall tell him to give it back to me—that it's only about my dismissal—that I don't want it read—

Mrs. Linden. No, Nils, you must not recall the letter.

Krogstad. But tell me, wasn't that just why you got me to come here?

Mrs. Linden. Yes, in my first alarm. But a day has passed since then, and in that day I have seen incredible things in this house. Helmer must know everything; there must be an end to this unhappy secret. These two must come to a full understanding. They must have done with all these shifts and subterfuges.

Krogstad. Very well, if you like to risk it. But one thing I can do, and at once—

Mrs. Linden. [Listening.] Make haste! Go, go! The dance is over; we're not safe another moment.

Krogstad. I shall wait for you in the street.

Mrs. Linden. Yes, do; you must see me home.

Krogstad. I never was so happy in all my life!

[Krogstad goes out by the outer door. The door between the room and the hall remains open.]

Mrs. Linden. [Arranging the room and getting her outdoor things together.] What a change! What a change! To have some one to work for, to live for; a home to make happy! Well, it shall not be my fault if I fail.— I wish they would come.—[Listens.] Ah, here they are! I must get my things on.

[Takes bonnet and cloak. Helmer's and Nora's voices are heard outside, a key is turned in the lock, and Helmer drags Nora almost by force into the hall. She wears the Italian costume with a large black shawl over it. He is in evening dress and wears a black domino, open.]

Nora. [Struggling with him in the doorway.] No, no, no! I won't go in! I want to go upstairs again; I don't want to leave so early!

Helmer. But, my dearest girl—!

Nora. Oh, please, please, Torvald, I beseech you—only one hour more!

Helmer. Not one minute more, Nora dear; you know what we agreed. Come, come in; you're catching cold here.

[He leads her gently into the room in spite of her resistance.]

Mrs. Linden. Good-evening.

Nora. Christina!

Helmer. What, Mrs. Linden! You here so late?

Mrs. Linden. Yes, I ought to apologise. I did so want to see Nora in her costume.

Nora. Have you been sitting here waiting for me?

Mrs. Linden. Yes; unfortunately I came too late. You had gone upstairs already, and I felt I couldn't go away without seeing you.

Helmer. *[Taking Nora's shawl off.]* Well then, just look at her! I assure you she's worth it. Isn't she lovely, Mrs. Linden?

Mrs. Linden. Yes, I must say—

Helmer. Isn't she exquisite? Every one said so. But she's dreadfully obstinate, dear little creature. What's to be done with her? Just think, I had almost to force her away.

Nora. Oh, Torvald, you'll be sorry some day that you didn't let me stay, if only for one half-hour more.

Helmer. There! You hear her, Mrs. Linden? She dances her tarantella with wild applause, and well she deserved it, I must say—though there was, perhaps, a little too much nature in her rendering of the idea— more than was, strictly speaking, artistic. But never mind—the point is, she made a great success, a tremendous success. Was I to let her remain after that—to weaken the impression? Not if I know it. I took my sweet little Capri girl—my capricious little Capri girl, I might say— under my arm; a rapid turn round the room, a curtsey to all sides, and—as they say in novels—the lovely apparition vanished! An exit should always be effective, Mrs. Linden; but I can't get Nora to see it. By Jove! it's warm here. *[Throws his domino on a chair and opens the door to his room.]* What! No light there? Oh, of course. Excuse me— *[Goes in and lights candles.]*

Nora. *[Whispers breathlessly.]* Well?

Mrs. Linden. *[Softly.]* I've spoken to him.

Nora. And—?

Mrs. Linden. Nora—you must tell your husband everything—

Nora. *[Tonelessly.]* I knew it!

Mrs. Linden. You have nothing to fear from Krogstad; but you must speak out.

Nora. I shall not speak!

Mrs. Linden. Then the letter will.

Nora. Thank you, Christina. Now I know what I have to do. Hush—!

Helmer. *[Coming back.]* Well, Mrs. Linden, have you admired her?

Mrs. Linden. Yes; and now I must say good-night.

Helmer. What, already? Does this knitting belong to you?

Mrs. Linden. *[Takes it.]* Yes, thanks; I was nearly forgetting it.

Helmer. Then you do knit?

Mrs. Linden. Yes.

Helmer. Do you know, you ought to embroider instead?

Mrs. Linden. Indeed! Why?

Helmer. Because it's so much prettier. Look now! You hold the embroidery in the left hand, so, and then work the needle with the right hand, in a long, graceful curve—don't you?

Mrs. Linden. Yes, I suppose so.

Helmer. But knitting is always ugly. Just look—your arms close to your sides, and the needles going up and down—there's something Chinese about it.—They really gave us splendid champagne to-night.

Mrs. Linden. Well, good-night, Nora, and don't be obstinate any more.

Helmer. Well said, Mrs. Linden!

Mrs. Linden. Good-night, Mr. Helmer.

Helmer. *[Accompanying her to the door.]* Good-night, good-night; I hope you'll get safely home. I should be glad to—but you have such a short way to go. Good-night, good-night. *[She goes; Helmer shuts the door after her and comes forward again.]* At last we've got rid of her: she's a terrible bore.

Nora. Aren't you very tired, Torvald?

Helmer. No, not in the least.

Nora. Nor sleepy?

Helmer. Not a bit. I feel particularly lively. But you? You do look tired and sleepy.

Nora. Yes, very tired. I shall soon sleep now.

Helmer. There, you see. I was right after all not to let you stay longer.

Nora. Oh, everything you do is right.

Helmer. *[Kissing her forehead.]* Now my lark is speaking like a reasonable being. Did you notice how jolly Rank was this evening?

Nora. Indeed? Was he? I had no chance of speaking to him.

Helmer. Nor I, much; but I haven't seen him in such good spirits for a long time. *[Looks at Nora a little, then comes nearer her.]* It's splendid to be back in our own home, to be quite alone together!—Oh, you enchanting creature!

Nora. Don't look at me in that way, Torvald.

Helmer. I am not to look at my dearest treasure?—at all the loveliness that is mine, mine only, wholly and entirely mine?

Nora. *[Goes to the other side of the table.]* You mustn't say these things to me this evening.

Helmer. *[Following.]* I see you have the tarantella still in your blood—and that makes you all the more enticing. Listen! the other people are going now. *[More softly.]* Nora—soon the whole house will be still.

Nora. Yes, I hope so.

Helmer. Yes, don't you, Nora darling? When we are among strangers, do you know why I speak so little to you, and keep so far away, and only steal a glance at you now and then—do you know why I do it?

Because I am fancying that we love each other in secret, that I am secretly betrothed to you, and that no one dreams that there is anything between us.

Nora. Yes, yes, yes. I know all your thoughts are with me.

Helmer. And then, when the time comes to go, and I put the shawl about your smooth, soft shoulders, and this glorious neck of yours, I imagine you are my bride, that our marriage is just over, that I am bringing you for the first time to my home—that I am alone with you for the first time—quite alone with you, in your trembling loveliness! All this evening I have been longing for you, and you only. When I watched you swaying and whirling in the tarantella—my blood boiled— I could endure it no longer; and that's why I made you come home with me so early—

Nora. Go now, Torvald! Go away from me. I won't have all this.

Helmer. What do you mean? Ah, I see you're teasing me, little Nora! Won't—won't! Am I not your husband—? *[A knock at the outer door.]*

Nora. *[Starts.]* Did you hear—?

Helmer. *[Going towards the hall.]* Who's there?

Rank. *[Outside.]* It is I; may I come in for a moment?

Helmer. *[In a low tone, annoyed.]* Oh, what can he want just now? *[Aloud.]* Wait a moment. *[Opens door.]* Come, it's nice of you to look in.

Rank. I thought I heard your voice, and that put it into my head. *[Looks round]* Ah, this dear old place! How cosy you two are here!

Helmer. You seemed to find it pleasant enough upstairs, too.

Rank. Exceedingly. Why not? Why shouldn't one take one's share of everything in this world? All one can, at least, and as long as one can. The wine was splendid—

Helmer. Especially the champagne.

Rank. Did you notice it? It's incredible the quantity I contrived to get down.

Nora. Torvald drank plenty of champagne, too.

Rank. Did he?

Nora. Yes, and it always puts him in such spirits.

Rank. Well, why shouldn't one have a jolly evening after a well-spent day?

Helmer. Well-spent! Well, I haven't much to boast of in that respect.

Rank. *[Slapping him on the shoulder.]* But I have, don't you see?

Nora. I suppose you have been engaged in a scientific investigation, Doctor Rank?

Rank. Quite right.

Helmer. Bless me! Little Nora talking about scientific investigations!

Nora. Am I to congratulate you on the result?

Rank. By all means.

Nora. It was good then?

Rank. The best possible, both for doctor and patient—certainty.

Nora. *[Quickly and searchingly.]* Certainty?

Rank. Absolute certainty. Wasn't I right to enjoy myself after that?

Nora. Yes, quite right, Doctor Rank.

Helmer. And so say I, provided you don't have to pay for it to-morrow.

Rank. Well, in this life nothing is to be had for nothing.

Nora. Doctor Rank—I'm sure you are very fond of masquerades?

Rank. Yes, when there are plenty of amusing disguises—

Nora. Tell me, what shall we two be at our next masquerade?

Helmer. Little featherbrain! Thinking of your next already!

Rank. We two? I'll tell you. You must go as a good fairy.

Helmer. Ah, but what costume would indicate that?

Rank. She has simply to wear her everyday dress.

Helmer. Capital! But don't you know what you will be yourself?

Rank. Yes, my dear friend, I am perfectly clear upon that point.

Helmer. Well?

Rank. At the next masquerade I shall be invisible.

Helmer. What a comical idea!

Rank. There's a big black hat—haven't you heard of the invisible hat? It comes down all over you, and then no one can see you.

Helmer. *[With a suppressed smile.]* No, you're right there.

Rank. But I'm quite forgetting what I came for. Helmer, give me a cigar— one of the dark Havanas.

Helmer. With the greatest pleasure. *[Hands cigar-case.]*

Rank. *[Takes one and cuts the end off.]* Thank you.

Nora. *[Striking a wax match.]* Let me give you a light.

Rank. A thousand thanks.

[She holds the match. He lights his cigar at it.]

Rank. And now, good-bye!

Helmer. Good-bye, good-bye, my dear fellow.

Nora. Sleep well, Doctor Rank.

Rank. Thanks for the wish.

Nora. Wish me the same.

Rank. You? Very well, since you ask me—Sleep well. And thanks for the light. *[He nods to them both and goes out.]*

Helmer. *[In an undertone.]* He's been drinking a good deal.

Nora. *[Absently.]* I daresay. [Helmer *takes his bunch of keys from his pocket and goes into the hall.]* Torvald, what are you doing there?

Helmer. I must empty the letter-box; it's quite full; there will be no room for the newspapers to-morrow morning.

Nora. Are you going to work to-night?

Helmer. You know very well I am not.—Why, how is this? Some one has been at the lock.

Nora. The lock—?

Helmer. I'm sure of it. What does it mean? I can't think that the servants—? Here's a broken hair-pin. Nora, it's one of yours.

Nora. [*Quickly.*] It must have been the children—

Helmer. Then you must break them of such tricks.—There! At last I've got it open. [*Takes contents out and calls into the kitchen.*] Ellen!—Ellen, just put the hall door lamp out.

[*He returns with letters in his hand, and shuts the inner door.*]

Helmer. Just see how they've accumulated. [*Turning them over.*] Why, what's this?

Nora. [*At the window.*] The letter! Oh no, no, Torvald!

Helmer. Two visiting-cards—from Rank.

Nora. From Doctor Rank?

Helmer. [*Looking at them.*] Doctor Rank. They were on the top. He must just have put them in.

Nora. Is there anything on them?

Helmer. There's a black cross over the name. Look at it. What an unpleasant idea! It looks just as if he were announcing his own death.

Nora. So he is.

Helmer. What! Do you know anything? Has he told you anything?

Nora. Yes. These cards mean that he has taken his last leave of us. He is going to shut himself up and die.

Helmer. Poor fellow! Of course I knew we couldn't hope to keep him long. But so soon—! And to go and creep into his lair like a wounded animal—

Nora. When we must go, it is best to go silently. Don't you think so, Torvald?

Helmer. [*Walking up and down.*] He had so grown into our lives, I can't realise that he is gone. He and his sufferings and his loneliness formed a sort of cloudy background to the sunshine of our happiness.—Well, perhaps it's best as it is—at any rate for him. [*Stands still.*] And perhaps for us too, Nora. Now we two are thrown entirely upon each other. [*Takes her in his arms.*] My darling wife! I feel as if I could never hold you close enough. Do you know, Nora, I often wish some danger might threaten you, that I might risk body and soul, and everything, everything, for your dear sake.

Nora. [*Tears herself from him and says firmly.*] Now you shall read your letters, Torvald.

Helmer. No, no; not to-night. I want to be with you, my sweet wife.

Nora. With the thought of your dying friend—?

Helmer. You are right. This has shaken us both. Unloveliness has come between us—thoughts of death and decay. We must seek to cast them off. Till then—we will remain apart.

Nora. [*Her arms round his neck.*] Torvald! Good-night! good-night!

Helmer. *[Kissing her forehead.]* Good-night, my little songbird. Sleep well, Nora. Now I shall go and read my letters.

[He goes with the letters in his hand into his room and shuts the door.

Nora. *[With wild eyes, gropes about her, seizes* Helmer's *domino, throws it round her, and whispers quickly, hoarsely, and brokenly.]* Never to see him again. Never, never, never. *[Throws her shawl over her head.]* Never to see the children again. Never, never.—Oh that black, icy water! Oh that bottomless—! If it were only over! Now he has it; he's reading it. Oh, no, no, no, not yet. Torvald, good-bye—! Good-bye, my little ones—!

[She is rushing out by the hall; at the same moment Helmer *flings his door open, and stands there with an open letter in his hand.]*

Helmer. Nora!
Nora. *[Shrieks.]* Ah—!
Helmer. What is this? Do you know what is in this letter?
Nora. Yes, I know. Let me go! Let me pass!
Helmer. *[Holds her back.]* Where do you want to go?
Nora. *[Tries to break away from him.]* You shall not save me, Torvald.
Helmer. *[Falling back.]* True! Is what he writes true? No, no, it is impossible that this can be true.
Nora. It is true. I have loved you beyond all else in the world.
Helmer. Pshaw—no silly evasions!
Nora. *[A step nearer him.]* Torvald—!
Helmer. Wretched woman—what have you done!
Nora. Let me go—you shall not save me! You shall not take my guilt upon yourself!
Helmer. I don't want any melodramatic airs. *[Locks the outer door.]* Here you shall stay and give an account of yourself. Do you understand what you have done? Answer! Do you understand it?
Nora. *[Looks at him fixedly, and says with a stiffening expression.]* Yes; now I begin fully to understand it.
Helmer. *[Walking up and down.]* Oh! what an awful awakening! During all these eight years—she who was my pride and my joy—a hypocrite, a liar—worse, worse—a criminal. Oh, the unfathomable hideousness of it all! Ugh! Ugh!

[Nora says nothing, and continues to look fixedly at him.]

Helmer. I ought to have known how it would be. I ought to have foreseen it. All your father's want of principle—be silent!—all your father's want of principle you have inherited—no religion, no morality, no sense of duty. How I am punished for screening him! I did it for your sake; and you reward me like this.

Nora. Yes—like this.

Helmer. You have destroyed my whole happiness. You have ruined my future. Oh, it's frightful to think of! I am in the power of a scoundrel; he can do whatever he pleases with me, demand whatever he chooses; he can domineer over me as much as he likes, and I must submit. And all this disaster and ruin is brought upon me by an unprincipled woman!

Nora. When I am out of the world, you will be free.

Helmer. Oh, no fine phrases. Your father, too, was always ready with them. What good would it do me, if you were "out of the world," as you say? No good whatever! He can publish the story all the same; I might even be suspected of collusion. People will think I was at the bottom of it all and egged you on. And for all this I have you to thank—you whom I have done nothing but pet and spoil during our whole married life. Do you understand now what you have done to me?

Nora. [With cold calmness.] Yes.

Helmer. The thing is so incredible, I can't grasp it. But we must come to an understanding. Take that shawl off. Take it off, I say! I must try to pacify him in one way or another—the matter must be hushed up, cost what it may.—As for you and me, we must make no outward change in our way of life—no outward change, you understand. Of course, you will continue to live here. But the children cannot be left in your care. I dare not trust them to you.—Oh, to have to say this to one I have loved so tenderly—whom I still—! But that must be a thing of the past. Henceforward there can be no question of happiness, but merely of saving the ruins, the shreds, the show—[A ring; Helmer starts.] What's that? So late! Can it be the worst? Can he—? Hide yourself, Nora; say you are ill.

[Nora *stands motionless.* Helmer *goes to the door and opens it.*]

Ellen. [Half dressed, in the hall.] Here is a letter for you, ma'am.

Helmer. Give it to me. [Seizes the letter and shuts the door.] Yes, from him. You shall not have it. I shall read it.

Nora. Read it!

Helmer. [By the lamp.] I have hardly the courage to. We may both be lost, both you and I. Ah! I must know. [Hastily tears the letter open; reads a few lines, looks at an enclosure; with a cry of joy.] Nora!

[Nora *looks inquiringly at him.*]

Helmer. Nora!—Oh! I must read it again.—Yes, yes, it is so. I am saved! Nora, I am saved!

Nora. And I?

Helmer. You too, of course; we are both saved, both of us. Look here— he sends you back your promissory note. He writes that he regrets and apologises, that a happy turn in his life—Oh, what matter what he writes. We are saved, Nora! No one can harm you. Oh, Nora, Nora— but first to get rid of this hateful thing. I'll just see—*[Glances at the I.O.U.]* No, I will not look at it; the whole thing shall be nothing but a dream to me. *[Tears the I.O.U. and both letters in pieces. Throws them into the fire and watches them burn.]* There! it's gone!—He said that ever since Christmas Eve—Oh, Nora, they must have been three terrible days for you!

Nora. I have fought a hard fight for the last three days.

Helmer. And in your agony you saw no other outlet but—No; we won't think of that horror. We will only rejoice and repeat—it's over, all over! Don't you hear, Nora? You don't seem able to grasp it. Yes, it's over. What is this set look on your face? Oh, my poor Nora, I understand; you cannot believe that I have forgiven you. But I have, Nora; I swear it. I have forgiven everything. I know that what you did was all for love of me.

Nora. That is true.

Helmer. You loved me as a wife should love her husband. It was only the means that, in your inexperience, you misjudged. But do you think I love you the less because you cannot do without guidance? No, no. Only lean on me; I will counsel you, and guide you. I should be no true man if this very womanly helplessness did not make you doubly dear in my eyes. You mustn't dwell upon the hard things I said in my first moment of terror, when the world seemed to be tumbling about my ears. I have forgiven you, Nora—I swear I have forgiven you.

Nora. I thank you for your forgiveness.

[Goes out, to the right.]

Helmer. No, stay—! *[Looking through the doorway.]* What are you going to do?

Nora. *[Inside.]* To take off my masquerade dress.

Helmer. *[In the doorway.]* Yes, do, dear. Try to calm down, and recover your balance, my scared little song-bird. You may rest secure. I have broad wings to shield you. *[Walking up and down near the door.]* Oh, how lovely—how cosy our home is, Nora! Here you are safe; here I can shelter you like a hunted dove whom I have saved from the claws of the hawk. I shall soon bring your poor beating heart to rest; believe me, Nora, very soon. To-morrow all this will seem quite different— everything will be as before. I shall not need to tell you again that I forgive you; you will feel for yourself that it is true. How could you think I could find it in my heart to drive you away, or even so much as to reproach you? Oh, you don't know a true man's heart, Nora. There is something indescribably sweet and soothing to a man in having forgiven his wife—honestly forgiven her, from the bottom of his heart. She becomes his property in a double sense. She is as though born again; she has become, so to speak, at once his wife and his child. That is what you shall henceforth be to me, my bewildered, helpless darling. Don't be troubled about anything, Nora; only open your heart to me, and I will be both will and conscience to you. [Nora *enters in everyday dress.*] Why, what's this? Not gone to bed? You have changed your dress?

Nora. Yes, Torvald; now I have changed my dress.

Helmer. But why now, so late—?

Nora. I shall not sleep to-night.

Helmer. But, Nora dear—

Nora. [*Looking at her watch.*] It's not so late yet. Sit down, Torvald; you and I have much to say to each other.

[*She sits at one side of the table.*]

Helmer. Nora—what does this mean? Your cold, set face—

Nora. Sit down. It will take some time. I have much to talk over with you.

[Helmer *sits at the other side of the table.*]

Helmer. You alarm me, Nora. I don't understand you.

Nora. No, that is just it. You don't understand me; and I have never understood you—till to-night. No, don't interrupt. Only listen to what I say.—We must come to a final settlement, Torvald.

Helmer. How do you mean?

Nora. [*After a short silence.*] Does not one thing strike you as we sit here?

Helmer. What should strike me?

Nora. We have been married eight years. Does it not strike you that this is the first time we two, you and I, man and wife, have talked together seriously?

Helmer. Seriously! What do you call seriously?

Nora. During eight whole years, and more—ever since the day we first met—we have never exchanged one serious word about serious things.

Helmer. Was I always to trouble you with the cares you could not help me to bear?

Nora. I am not talking of cares. I say that we have never yet set ourselves seriously to get to the bottom of anything.

Helmer. Why, my dearest Nora, what have you to do with serious things?

Nora. There we have it! You have never understood me.—I have had great injustice done me, Torvald; first by father, and then by you.

Helmer. What! By your father and me?—By us, who have loved you more than all the world?

Nora. [Shaking her head.] You have never loved me. You only thought it amusing to be in love with me.

Helmer. Why, Nora, what a thing to say!

Nora. Yes, it is so, Torvald. While I was at home with father, he used to tell me all his opinions, and I held the same opinions. If I had others I said nothing about them, because he wouldn't have liked it. He used to call me his doll-child, and played with me as I played with my dolls. Then I came to live in your house—

Helmer. What an expression to use about our marriage!

Nora. [Undisturbed.] I mean I passed from father's hands into yours. You arranged everything according to your taste; and I got the same tastes as you; or I pretended to—I don't know which—both ways, perhaps; sometimes one and sometimes the other. When I look back on it now, I seem to have been living here like a beggar, from hand to mouth. I lived by performing tricks for you, Torvald. But you would have it so. You and father have done me a great wrong. It is your fault that my life has come to nothing.

Helmer. Why, Nora, how unreasonable and ungrateful you are! Have you not been happy here?

Nora. No, never. I thought I was; but I never was.

Helmer. Not—not happy!

Nora. No; only merry. And you have always been so kind to me. But our house has been nothing but a play-room. Here I have been your doll-wife, just as at home I used to be papa's doll-child. And the children, in their turn, have been my dolls. I thought it fun when you played with me, just as the children did when I played with them. That has been our marriage, Torvald.

Helmer. There is some truth in what you say, exaggerated and over-strained though it be. But henceforth it shall be different. Play-time is over; now comes the time for education.

Nora. Whose education? Mine, or the children's?

Helmer. Both, my dear Nora.

Nora. Oh, Torvald, you are not the man to teach me to be a fit wife for you.

Helmer. And you can say that?

Nora. And I—how have I prepared myself to educate the children?

Helmer. Nora!

Nora. Did you not say yourself, a few minutes ago, you dared not trust them to me?

Helmer. In the excitement of the moment! Why should you dwell upon that?

Nora. No—you were perfectly right. That problem is beyond me. There is another to be solved first—I must try to educate myself. You are not the man to help me in that. I must set about it alone. And that is why I am leaving you.

Helmer. *[Jumping up.]* What—do you mean to say—?

Nora. I must stand quite alone if I am ever to know myself and my surroundings; so I cannot stay with you.

Helmer. Nora! Nora!

Nora. I am going at once. I daresay Christina will take me in for to-night—

Helmer. You are mad! I shall not allow it! I forbid it!

Nora. It is of no use your forbidding me anything now. I shall take with me what belongs to me. From you I will accept nothing, either now or afterwards.

Helmer. What madness this is!

Nora. To-morrow I shall go home—I mean to what was my home. It will be easier for me to find some opening there.

Helmer. Oh, in your blind inexperience—

Nora. I must try to gain experience, Torvald.

Helmer. To forsake your home, your husband, and your children! And you don't consider what the world will say.

Nora. I can pay no heed to that. I only know that I must do it.

Helmer. This is monstrous! Can you forsake your holiest duties in this way?

Nora. What do you consider my holiest duties?

Helmer. Do I need to tell you that? Your duties to your husband and your children.

Nora. I have other duties equally sacred.

Helmer. Impossible! What duties do you mean?

Nora. My duties towards myself.

Helmer. Before all else you are a wife and a mother.

Nora. That I no longer believe. I believe that before all else I am a human being, just as much as you are—or at least that I should try to become one. I know that most people agree with you, Torvald, and that they say so in books. But henceforth I can't be satisfied with what most people say, and what is in books. I must think things out for myself, and try to get clear about them.

Helmer. Are you not clear about your place in your own home? Have you not an infallible guide in questions like these? Have you not religion?

Nora. Oh, Torvald, I don't really know what religion is.

Helmer. What do you mean?

Nora. I know nothing but what Pastor Hansen told me when I was confirmed. He explained that religion was this and that. When I get away from all this and stand alone, I will look into that matter too. I will see whether what he taught me is right, or, at any rate, whether it is right for me.

Helmer. Oh, this is unheard of! And from so young a woman! But if religion cannot keep you right, let me appeal to your conscience—for I suppose you have some moral feeling? Or, answer me: perhaps you have none?

Nora. Well, Torvald, it's not easy to say. I really don't know—I am all at sea about these things. I only know that I think quite differently from you about them. I hear, too, that the laws are different from what I thought; but I can't believe that they can be right. It appears that a woman has no right to spare her dying father, or to save her husband's life! I don't believe that.

Helmer. You talk like a child. You don't understand the society in which you live.

Nora. No, I do not. But now I shall try to learn. I must make up my mind which is right—society or I.

Helmer. Nora, you are ill; you are feverish; I almost think you are out of your senses.

Nora. I have never felt so much clearness and certainty as to-night.

Helmer. You are clear and certain enough to forsake husband and children?

Nora. Yes, I am.

Helmer. Then there is only one explanation possible.

Nora. What is that?

Helmer. You no longer love me.

Nora. No; that is just it.

Helmer. Nora!—Can you say so!

Nora. Oh, I'm so sorry, Torvald; for you've always been so kind to me. But I can't help it. I do not love you any longer.

Helmer. [Mastering himself with difficulty.] Are you clear and certain on this point too?

Nora. Yes, quite. That is why I will not stay here any longer.

Helmer. And can you also make clear to me how I have forfeited your love?

Nora. Yes, I can. It was this evening, when the miracle did not happen; for then I saw you were not the man I had imagined.

Helmer. Explain yourself more clearly; I don't understand.

Nora. I have waited so patiently all these eight years; for of course I saw clearly enough that miracles don't happen every day. When this crushing blow threatened me, I said to myself so confidently, "Now comes the miracle!" When Krogstad's letter lay in the box, it never for a moment occurred to me that you would think of submitting to that man's conditions. I was convinced that you would say to him, "Make it known to all the world"; and that then—

Helmer. Well? When I had given my own wife's name up to disgrace and shame—?

Nora. Then I firmly believed that you would come forward, take everything upon yourself, and say, "I am the guilty one."

Helmer. Nora—!

Nora. You mean I would never have accepted such a sacrifice? No, certainly not. But what would my assertions have been worth in opposition to yours?—That was the miracle that I hoped for and dreaded. And it was to hinder that that I wanted to die.

Helmer. I would gladly work for you day and night, Nora—bear sorrow and want for your sake. But no man sacrifices his honour, even for one he loves.

Nora. Millions of women have done so.

Helmer. Oh, you think and talk like a silly child.

Nora. Very likely. But you neither think nor talk like the man I can share my life with. When your terror was over—not for what threatened me, but for yourself—when there was nothing more to fear—then it seemed to you as though nothing had happened. I was your lark again, your doll, just as before—whom you would take twice as much care of in future, because she was so weak and fragile. *[Stands up.]* Torvald—in that moment it burst upon me that I had been living here these eight years with a strange man, and had borne him three children.—Oh, I can't bear to think of it! I could tear myself to pieces!

Helmer. *[Sadly.]* I see it, I see it; an abyss has opened between us.—But, Nora, can it never be filled up?

Nora. As I now am, I am no wife for you.

Helmer. I have strength to become another man.

Nora. Perhaps—when your doll is taken away from you.

Helmer. To part—to part from you! No, Nora, no; I can't grasp the thought.

Nora. *[Going into room on the right.]* The more reason for the thing to happen.

[She comes back with out-door things and a small travelling-bag, which she places on a chair.]

Helmer. Nora, Nora, not now! Wait till to-morrow.

Nora. *[Putting on cloak.]* I can't spend the night in a strange man's house.

Helmer. But can we not live here, as brother and sister—?

Nora. *[Fastening her hat.]* You know very well that wouldn't last long. *[Puts on the shawl.]* Good-bye, Torvald. No, I won't go to the children. I know they are in better hands than mine. As I now am, I can be nothing to them.

Helmer. But some time, Nora—some time—?

Nora. How can I tell? I have no idea what will become of me.

Helmer. But you are my wife, now and always!

Nora. Listen, Torvald—when a wife leaves her husband's house, as I am doing, I have heard that in the eyes of the law he is free from all duties towards her. At any rate, I release you from all duties. You must not feel yourself bound, any more than I shall. There must be perfect freedom on both sides. There, I give you back your ring. Give me mine.

Helmer. That too?

Nora. That too.

Helmer. Here it is.

Nora. Very well. Now it is all over. I lay the keys here. The servants know about everything in the house—better than I do. To-morrow, when I have started, Christina will come to pack up the things I brought with me from home. I will have them sent after me.

Helmer. All over! all over! Nora, will you never think of me again?

Nora. Oh, I shall often think of you, and the children, and this house.

Helmer. May I write to you, Nora?

Nora. No—never. You must not.

Helmer. But I must send you—

Nora. Nothing, nothing.

Helmer. I must help you if you need it.

Nora. No, I say. I take nothing from strangers.

Helmer. Nora—can I never be more than a stranger to you?

Nora. *[Taking her travelling-bag.]* Oh, Torvald, then the miracle of miracles would have to happen—

Helmer. What is the miracle of miracles?

Nora. Both of us would have to change so that—Oh, Torvald, I no longer believe in miracles.

Helmer. But *I* will believe. Tell me! We must so change that—?

Nora. That communion between us shall be a marriage. Good-bye. *[She goes out by the hall door.]*

Helmer. *[Sinks into a chair by the door with his face in his hands.]* Nora! Nora! *[He looks round and rises.]* Empty. She is gone. *[A hope springs up in him.]* Ah! The miracle of miracles—?!

[From below is heard the reverberation of a heavy door closing.]

The End.

Study and Discussion Questions

1. Describe Torvald's attitude towards his wife Nora. How does he view her? How does he treat her? Does his attitude change?

2. Who has more power in this relationship and why? Discuss the sources of Torvald's power and of Nora's.
3. Describe Nora's attitude towards Torvald. Trace how it changes and why. What finally leads to her decision to leave?
4. Why does Ibsen give Torvald the last line and then end the play with the slam of a door?
5. What is the role of Dr. Rank in the play? What would the play lack without him?
6. Discuss the significance of Nora's wild dancing of the tarantella. Are there other important symbols in the play?
7. Compare the relationship between Mrs. Linden and Nils Krogstad with that between Nora and Torvald. How does this first relationship help shape what the play is saying about marriage?
8. Nora, Mrs. Linden, and Anna, the Helmers' nurse, have all been in difficult situations for lack of money. How are their experiences similar and how are they different? What is the play saying about social class and about money?
9. In what other ways does the play extend its social criticism beyond criticism of relations between men and women and of the institution of marriage?

Writing Exercises

1. Speculate on what happens to Nora after she slams the door. Outline the next ten years of her life.
2. Suppose you were casting for this play. What would you want each character to look like? Write a physical description of each.
3. Some critics have complained that Nora's clear and impassioned declarations in the last quarter of Act III as well as her bold decision to leave her husband and children seem improbable coming from the character we've seen up until then. Do you agree or disagree?
4. A Doll's House was extremely controversial, and one famous actress in Germany refused to play Nora unless the ending were changed. Since Ibsen had no control over how the play was performed in Germany, he wrote an alternate ending himself, in which Torvald makes Nora take a last look at their children before leaving and, seeing them, she loses her will to go. Ibsen called this new ending a "barbaric outrage," but critic Otto Reinert suggests that the German version might be "a stronger indictment of male society" than the original. Discuss what he might mean and whether you agree.
5. What is and is not dated about this 1879 play? What might need to be different in a similar play written today?

NTOZAKE SHANGE (b. 1948)

Paulette Williams was born in Trenton, New Jersey and educated at Barnard College and the University of Southern California. In 1971, she took the name ntozake, which in Zulu means "she who comes with her own things," and shange, "she who walks like a lion." Shange has performed as a dancer, given many poetry recitals, and taught at several colleges. Among her works are the poetry collections Nappy Edges *(1978) and* A Daughter's Geography *(1983), the novels* Sassafrass *(1976) and* Betsey Brown *(1985), and the plays* For Colored Girls Who Have Considered Suicide When the Rainbow is Enuf *(1976),* Spell No. 7 *(1979), and* Boogie Woogie Landscapes *(1980).*

for colored girls who have considered suicide/ when the rainbow is enuf

a choreopoem   (1977)

The stage is in darkness. Harsh music is heard as dim blue lights come up. One after another, seven women run onto the stage from each of the exits. They all freeze in postures of distress. The follow spot picks up the lady in brown. She comes to life and looks around at the other ladies. All of the others are still. She walks over to the lady in red and calls to her. The lady in red makes no response.

lady in brown
dark phrases of womanhood
of never havin been a girl
half-notes scattered
without rhythm/ no tune
distraught laughter fallin
over a black girl's shoulder
it's funny/ it's hysterical
the melody-less-ness of her dance
don't tell nobody don't tell a soul
she's dancin on beer cans & shingles

this must be the spook house
another song with no singers
lyrics/ no voices
& interrupted solos
unseen performances

are we ghouls?
children of horror?
the joke?

don't tell nobody don't tell a soul
are we animals? have we gone crazy?

i can't hear anythin
but maddening screams
& the soft strains of death
& you promised me
you promised me . . .
somebody/ anybody
sing a black girl's song
bring her out
to know herself
to know you
but sing her rhythms
carin/ struggle/ hard times
sing her song of life
she's been dead so long
closed in silence so long
she doesn't know the sound
of her own voice
her infinite beauty

she's half-notes scattered
without rhythm/ no tune
sing her sighs
sing the song of her possibilities
sing a righteous gospel
let her be born
let her be born
& handled warmly.

    lady in brown.
i'm outside chicago

    lady in yellow.
i'm outside detroit

lady in purple.
i'm outside houston

lady in red.
i'm outside baltimore

lady in green.
i'm outside san francisco

lady in blue.
i'm outside manhattan

lady in orange.
i'm outside st. louis

lady in brown.
& this is for colored girls who have considered suicide
but moved to the ends of their own rainbows.

everyone.
mama's little baby likes shortnin, shortnin,
mama's little baby likes shortnin bread
mama's little baby likes shortnin, shortnin,
mama's little baby likes shortnin bread

little sally walker, sittin in a saucer
rise, sally, rise, wipe your weepin eyes
an put your hands on your hips
an let your backbone slip
o, shake it to the east
o, shake it to the west
shake it to the one
that you like the best

lady in purple.
you're it

*As the lady in brown tags each of
the other ladies they freeze. When
each one has been tagged the lady in
brown freezes. Immediately "Dancing
in the Streets" by Martha and the
Vandellas is heard. All of the ladies
start to dance. The lady in green, the
lady in blue, and the lady in yellow
do the pony, the big boss line, the*

> *swim, and the nose dive. The other*
> *ladies dance in place.*

lady in yellow.

it was graduation nite & i waz the only virgin in the crowd
bobby mills martin jerome & sammy yates eddie jones & randi
all cousins
all the prettiest niggers in this factory town
carried me out wit em
in a deep black buick
smellin of thunderbird & ladies in heat
we rambled from camden to mount holly
laughin at the afternoon's speeches
& danglin our tassles from the rear view mirror
climbin different sorta project stairs
movin toward snappin beer cans &
GET IT GET IT THAT'S THE WAY TO DO IT MAMA
all mercer county graduated the same nite
        cosmetology secretarial pre-college autoshop & business
all us movin from mama to what ever waz out there

that nite we raced a big ol truck from the barbeque stand
trying to tell him bout the party at jacqui's
where folks graduated last year waz waitin to hit it wid us

i got drunk & cdnt figure out
whose hand waz on my thigh/ but it didn't matter
cuz these cousins martin eddie sammy jerome & bobby
waz my sweethearts alternately since the seventh grade
& everybody knew i always started cryin if somebody actually
tried to take advantage of me
                at jacqui's
ulinda mason was stickin her mouth all out
while we tumbled out the buick
eddie jones waz her lickin stick
but i knew how to dance
                it got soo hot
vincent ramos puked all in the punch
& harly jumped all in tico's face
cuz he was leavin for the navy in the mornin
hadda kick ass so we'd all remember how bad he waz
seems like sheila & marguerite waz fraid
to get their hair turnin back
so they laid up against the wall
lookin almost sexy

didnt wanna sweat
but me & my fellas   we waz dancin

since 1963 i'd won all kinda contests
wid the cousins at the POLICE ATHLETIC LEAGUE DANCES
all mercer county knew
any kin to martin yates cd turn somersaults
fore smokey robinson cd get a woman excited

The Dells singing "Stay" is heard

we danced   doin nasty ol tricks

*The lady in yellow sings along with
the Dells for a moment. The lady in
orange and the lady in blue jump up
and parody the lady in yellow and
the Dells. The lady in yellow stares
at them. They sit down.*

doin nasty ol tricks i'd been thinkin since may
cuz graduation nite had to be hot
& i waz the only virgin
so i hadda make like my hips waz inta some business
that way everybody thot whoever was gettin it
was a older man cdnt run the streets wit youngsters
martin slipped his leg round my thigh
the dells bumped "stay"
up & down—up & down the new carver homes
WE WAZ GROWN   WE WAZ FINALLY GROWN

ulinda alla sudden went crazy
went over to eddie cursin & carryin on
tearin his skin wid her nails
the cousins tried to talk sense to her
tried to hold her arms
lissin bitch sammy went on

bobby whispered i shd go wit him
fore they go ta cuttin
fore the police arrived
we teetered silently thru the parkin lot
no un uhuh
we didn't know nothin bout no party
bobby started lookin at me
yeah

he started looking at me real strange
like i waz a woman or somethin/
started talkin real soft
in the backseat of that ol buick
WOW
by daybreak
i just cdnt stop grinnin.

*The Dells singing "Stay" comes in
and all of the ladies except the lady
in blue join in and sing along.*

lady in blue.
you gave it up in a buick?

lady in yellow.
yeh, and honey, it was wonderful.

lady in green.
we used to do it all up in the dark
in the corners . . .

lady in blue.
some niggah sweating all over you.

lady in red.
it was good!

lady in blue.
i never did like to grind

lady in yellow.
what other kind of dances are there?

lady in blue.
mambo, bomba, merengue

when i waz sixteen i ran off to the south bronx
cuz i waz gonna meet up wit willie colon
& dance all the time
        mamba bomba merengue

lady in yellow.
do you speak spanish?

lady in blue.

olà
my papa thot he was puerto rican & we wda been
cept we waz just reglar niggahs wit hints of spanish
so off i made it to this 36 hour marathon dance
con salsa con ricardo
'sugggggggggggar' ray on southern blvd
next door to this fotografi place
jammed wit burial weddin & communion relics
next door to la real ideal genuine spanish barber
        up up up up up stairs & stairs & lotsa hallway
wit my colored new jersey self
didn't know what anybody waz saying
cept if dancin waz proof of origin
        i was jibarita[1] herself that nite
& the next day
i kept smilin & right on steppin
if he cd lead i waz ready to dance
if he cdnt lead
i caught this attitude
        i'd seen rosa do
& wd not be bothered
i waz twirlin hippin givin much quik feet
& bein a mute cute colored puerto rican
til saturday afternoon when the disc-jockey say
'SORRY FOLKS WILLIE COLON[2] AINT GONNA MAKE IT TODAY'
& alla my niggah temper came outta control
& i wdnt dance wit nobody
& i talked english loud
& i love you more than i waz mad
uh huh uh huh
more than more than
when i discovered archie shepp & subtle blues
doncha know i wore out the magic of juju
heroically resistin being possessed

ooooooooooooooh the sounds
sneakin in under age to slug's
to stare ata real 'artiste'
& every word outta imamu's[3] mouth waz gospel
& if jesus cdnt play a horn like shepp
waznt no need for colored folks to bear no cross at all

---

[1] Little girl from the hills (Spanish).

[2] Salsa musician.

[3] Leader, in Arabic.

& poem is my thank-you for music
& i love you more than poem
more than aureliano buendia loved macondo
more than hector lavoe loved himself
more than the lady loved gardenias
more than celia loves cuba or graciela loves el son
more than the flamingoes shoo-do-n-doo-wah love bein pretty

oyè négro
te amo mas que[4]   te amo mas que
when you play
yr flute

    everyone *(very softly)*.
te amo mas que   te amo mas que

    lady in red.
without any assistance or guidance from you
i have loved you assiduously for 8 months 2 wks & a day
i have been stood up four times
i've left 7 packages on yr doorstep

forty poems 2 plants & 3 handmade notecards i left
town so i cd send to you have been no help to me
on my job
you call at 3:00 in the mornin on weekdays
so i cd drive 27½ miles cross the bay before i go to work
charmin charmin
but you are of no assistance
i want you to know
this waz an experiment
to see how selfish i cd be
if i wd really carry on to snare a possible lover
if i waz capable of debasin my self for the love of another
if i cd stand not being wanted
when i wanted to be wanted
& i cannot
so
with no further assistance & no guidance from you
i am endin this affair

this note is attached to a plant
i've been waterin since the day i met you

---

[4] Look, black man. I love you more than . . .

you may water it
yr damn self

lady in orange.
i dont wanna write
in english or spanish
i wanna sing   make you dance
like the bata   dance   scream

twitch hips wit me cuz
i done forgot all abt words
aint got no definitions
i wanna whirl
            with you

> *Music starts, "Che Che Cole" by*
> *Willie Colon. Everyone starts to*
> *dance.*

our whole body
wrapped like a ripe mango
ramblin whippin thru space
on the corner in the park
where the rug useta be
let willie colon take you out
swing your head
push your leg to the moon with me

i'm on the lower east side
in new york city
and i can't   i can't
talk witchu no more

lady in yellow.
we gotta dance to keep from cryin

lady in brown
we gotta dance to keep from dyin

lady in red.
so come on

lady in brown.
come on

lady in purple.
come on

lady in orange.
hold yr head like it was ruby sapphire
i'm a poet
who writes in english
come to share the worlds witchu

everyone.
come to share our worlds witchu
come here to be dancin
        to be dancin
      to be dancin
      baya

*There is a sudden light change, all of
the ladies react as if they had been
struck in the face. The lady in green
and the lady in yellow run out up
left, the lady in orange runs out the
left volm, the lady in brown runs out
up right.*

lady in blue.
a friend is hard to press charges against

lady in red.
if you know him
you must have wanted it

lady in purple.
a misunderstanding

lady in red.
you know
these things happen

lady in blue.
are you sure
you didnt suggest

lady in purple.
had you been drinkin

lady in red.
a rapist is always to be a stranger
to be legitimate
someone you never saw
a man wit obvious problems

lady in purple.
pin-ups attached to the insides of his lapels

lady in blue.
ticket stubs from porno flicks in his pocket

lady in purple.
a lil dick

lady in red.
or a strong mother

lady in blue.
or just a brutal virgin

lady in red.
but if you've been seen in public wit him
danced one dance
kissed him good-bye lightly

lady in purple.
wit closed mouth

lady in blue.
pressin charges will be as hard
as keepin yr legs closed
while five fools try to run a train on you

lady in red.
these men friends of ours
who smile nice
stay employed
and take us out to dinner

lady in purple.
lock the door behind you

lady in blue.
wit fist in face
to fuck

lady in red.
who make elaborate mediterranean dinners
& let the art ensemble carry all ethical burdens
while they invite a coupla friends over to have you
are sufferin from latent rapist bravado
& we are left wit the scars

lady in blue.
bein betrayed by men who know us

lady in purple.
& expect
like the stranger
we always thot waz comin

lady in blue.
that we will submit

lady in purple.
we must have known

lady in red.
women relinquish all personal rights
in the presence of a man
who apparently cd be considered a rapist

lady in purple.
especially if he has been considered a friend

lady in blue.
& is no less worthy of bein beat witin an inch of his life
bein publicly ridiculed
havin two fists shoved up his ass

lady in red.
than the stranger
we always thot it wd be

lady in blue.
who never showed up

lady in red.
cuz it turns out the nature of rape has changed

lady in blue.
we can now meet them in circles we frequent for companionship

lady in purple.
we see them at the coffeehouse

lady in blue.
wit someone else we know

lady in red.
we cd even have em over for dinner
& get raped in our own houses
by invitation
a friend

> *The lights change, and the ladies are*
> *all hit by an imaginary slap, the lady*
> *in red runs off up left.*

lady in blue.
eyes

lady in purple.
mice

lady in blue.
womb

lady in blue & lady in purple.
nobody

> *The lady in purple exits up right.*

lady in blue.
tubes tables white washed windows
grime from age wiped over once
legs spread
anxious
eyes crawling up on me
eyes rollin in my thighs
metal horses gnawin my womb
dead mice fall from my mouth
i really didnt mean to
i really didnt think i cd
just one day off . . .
get offa me alla this blood
bones shattered like soft ice-cream cones

i cdnt have people
lookin at me
pregnant
i cdnt have my friends see this
dyin danglin tween my legs
& i didnt say a thing
not a sigh
or a fast scream
to get
those eyes offa me
get them steel rods outta me
this hurts
this hurts me

& nobody came
cuz nobody knew
once i waz pregnant & shamed of myself.

> *The lady in blue exits stage left*
> *volm.*
>
> *Soft deep music is heard, voices*
> *calling "Sechita" come from the wings*
> *and volms. The lady in purple enters*
> *from up right.*

lady in purple.
once there were quadroon balls/ elegance in st. louis/ laced
mulattoes/ gamblin down the mississippi/ to memphis/ new
orleans n okra crepes near the bayou/ where the poor white trash
wd sing/ moanin/ strange/ liquid tones/ thru the swamps/

> *The lady in green enters from the*
> *right volm; she is Sechita and for the*
> *rest of the poem dances out Sechita's*
> *life.*

sechita had heard these things/ she moved
as if she'd known them/ the silver n high-toned laughin/
the violins n marble floors/ sechita pushed the clingin
delta dust wit painted toes/ the patch-work tent waz
poka-dotted/ stale lights snatched at the shadows/ creole
carnival waz playin natchez in ten minutes/ her splendid
red garters/ gin-stained n itchy on her thigh/ blk-diamond
stockings darned wit yellow threads/ an ol starched taffeta
can-can fell abundantly orange/ from her waist round the

splinterin chair/ sechita/ egyptian/ goddess of creativity/
2nd millennium/ threw her heavy hair in a coil over her neck/
sechita/ goddess/ the recordin of history/ spread crimson oil
on her cheeks/ waxed her eyebrows/ n unconsciously slugged
the last hard whiskey in the glass/ the broken mirror she
used to decorate her face/ made her forehead tilt backwards/
her cheeks appear sunken/ her sassy chin only large enuf/
to keep her full lower lip/ from growin into her neck/ sechita/
had learned to make allowances for the distortions/
but the heavy dust of the delta/ left a tinge of grit n
darkness/ on every one of her dresses/ on her arms & her
shoulders/ sechita/ waz anxious to get back to st. louis/
the dirt there didnt crawl from the earth into yr soul/
at least/ in st. louis/ the grime waz store bought
second-hand/ here in natchez/ god seemed to be wipin his
feet in her face/

one of the wrestlers had finally won
tonite/ the mulatto/ raul/ was sposed to hold the boomin
half-caste/ searin eagle/ in a bear hug/ 8 counts/ get
thrown unawares/ fall out the ring/ n then do searin eagle
in for good/ sechita/ cd hear redneck whoops n slappin on
the back/ she gathered her sparsely sequined skirts/ tugged
the waist cincher from under her greyin slips/ n made her face
immobile/ she made her face like nefertiti/ approachin her
own tomb/ she suddenly threw/ her leg full-force/ thru the
canvas curtain/ a deceptive glass stone/ sparkled/ malignant
on her ankle/ her calf waz tauntin in the brazen carnie
lights/ the full moon/ sechita/ goddess/ of love/ egypt/
2nd millennium/ performin the rites/ the conjurin of men/
conjurin the spirit/ in natchez/ the mississippi spewed
a heavy fume of barely movin waters/ sechita's legs slashed
furiously thru the cracker nite/ & gold pieces hittin the
makeshift stage/ her thighs/ they were aimin coins tween her
thighs/ sechita/ egypt/ goddess/ harmony/ kicked viciously
thru the nite/ catchin stars tween her toes.

> *The lady in green exits into the stage
> left volm, the lady in purple exits
> into up stage left.*

> *The lady in brown enters from up
> stage right.*

lady in brown.
de library waz right down from de trolly tracks

cross from de laundry-mat
thru de big shinin floors & granite pillars
ol st. louis is famous for
i found toussaint
but not til after months uv
cajun katie/ pippi longstockin
christopher robin/ eddie heyward & a pooh bear
in the children's room
only pioneer girls & magic rabbits
& big city white boys
i knew i waznt sposedta
but i ran inta the ADULT READING ROOM
              & came across

TOUSSAINT

            my first blk man
(i never counted george washington carver
cuz i didnt like peanuts)
                still
TOUSSAINT waz a blk man a negro like my mama say
who refused to be a slave
& he spoke french
& didnt low no white man to tell him nothin
             not napolean
             not maximillien
             not robespierre

TOUSSAINT L'OUVERTURE
waz the beginnin uv reality for me
in the summer contest for
who colored child can read
15 books in three weeks
i won & raved abt TOUSSAINT L'OUVERTURE
at the afternoon ceremony

waz disqualified
            cuz Toussaint
                belonged in the ADULT READING ROOM
                  & i cried
& carried dead Toussaint home in the book
he waz dead & livin to me
cuz TOUSSAINT & them
they held the citadel gainst the french
wid the spirits of ol dead africans from outta the ground
TOUSSAINT led they army of zombies

walkin cannon ball shootin spirits to free Haiti
& they waznt slaves no more

TOUSSAINT L'OUVERTURE

became my secret lover at the age of 8
i entertained him in my bedroom
widda flashlight under my covers
way inta the night/ we discussed strategies
how to remove white girls from my hopscotch games
& etc.
TOUSSAINT
waz layin in bed wit me next to raggedy ann
the night i decided to run away from my
              integrated home
                  integrated street
                    integrated school
1955 waz not a good year for lil blk girls

Toussaint said 'lets go to haiti'
i said 'awright'
& packed some very important things in a brown paper bag
so i wdnt haveta come back
then Toussaint & i took the hodiamont streetcar
to the river
last stop
only 15¢
cuz there waznt nobody cd see Toussaint cept me
& we walked all down thru north st. louis
where the french settlers usedta live
in tiny brick houses all huddled together
wit barely missin windows & shingles uneven
wit colored kids playin & women on low porches sippin beer

i cd talk to Toussaint down by the river
like this waz where we waz gonna stow away
on a boat for new orleans
& catch a creole fishin-rig for port-au-prince
then we waz just gonna read & talk all the time
& eat fried bananas
                    we waz just walkin & skippin past ol drunk men
when dis ol young boy jumped out at me sayin
'HEY GIRL YA BETTAH COME OVAH HEAH N TALK TO ME'
well
i turned to TOUSSAINT (who waz furious)
& i shouted
'ya silly ol boy

ya bettah leave me alone
or TOUSSAINT'S gonna get yr ass'
de silly ol boy came round de corner laughin all in my face
'yellah gal
ya sure must be somebody to know my name so quick'
i waz disgusted
& wanted to get on to haiti
widout some tacky ol boy botherin me
still he kept standin there
kickin milk cartons & bits of brick
tryin to get all in my business
                         i mumbled to L'OUVERTURE 'what shd I do'
finally
i asked this silly ol boy
'WELL WHO ARE YOU?'
he say
'MY NAME IS TOUSSAINT JONES'
well
i looked right at him
those skidded out cordoroy pants
a striped teashirt wid holes in both elbows
a new scab over his left eye
& i said
                         'what's yr name again'
he say
'i'm toussaint jones'
'wow
i am on my way to see
TOUSSAINT L'OUVERTURE in HAITI

are ya any kin to him
he dont take no stuff from no white folks
& they gotta country all they own
& there aint no slaves'
that silly ol boy squinted his face all up
'looka heah girl
i am TOUSSAINT JONES
& i'm right heah lookin at ya
& i dont take no stuff from no white folks
ya dont see none round heah do ya?'
& he sorta pushed out his chest
then he say
'come on lets go on down to the docks
& look at the boats'
i waz real puzzled goin down to the docks
wit my paper bag & my books

i felt TOUSSAINT L'OUVERTURE sorta leave me
& i waz sad
til i realized
TOUSSAINT JONES waznt too different
from TOUSSAINT L'OUVERTURE
cept the ol one waz in haiti
& this one wid me speakin english & eatin apples
yeah.
toussaint jones waz awright wit me
no tellin what all spirits we cd move
down by the river
st. louis 1955   hey wait.

> *The lady in brown exits into the*
> *stage right volm.*

> *The lady in red enters from the stage*
> *left volm.*

lady in red.
orange butterflies & aqua sequins
ensconsed tween slight bosoms
silk roses dartin from behind her ears
the passion flower of southwest los angeles
meandered down hoover street
past dark shuttered houses where
women from louisiana shelled peas
round 3:00 & sent their sons
whistlin to the store for fatback & black-eyed peas
she glittered in heat
& seemed to be lookin for rides
when she waznt & absolutely
eyed every man who waznt lame white or noddin out
she let her thigh slip from her skirt
crossin the street
she slowed to be examined
& she never looked back to smile
or acknowledge a sincere 'hey mama'
or to meet the eyes of someone
purposely findin sometin to do in
her direction
   she waz sullen
   & the rhinestones etchin the corners of her mouth
   suggested tears
   fresh kisses that had done no good
she always wore her stomach out

lined with small iridescent feathers
the hairs round her navel seemed to dance
& she didnt let on
she knew
from behind her waist waz aching to be held
the pastel ivy drawn on her shoulders
to be brushed with lips & fingers
smellin of honey & jack daniels

       she waz hot
       a deliberate coquette
       who never did without
       what she wanted
& she wanted to be unforgettable
she wanted to be a memory
a wound   to every man
arragant enough to want her
       she waz the wrath
         of women in windows
            fingerin shades/ ol lace curtains
              camoflagin despair &
                stretch marks
so she glittered honestly
delighted she waz desired
& allowed those especially
schemin/ tactful suitors
to experience her body & spirit
tearin/ so easily blendin with theirs/
& they were so happy
& lay on her lime sheets full & wet
from her tongue   she kissed
them reverently   even ankles
edges of beards . . .

> *The stage goes to darkness except for*
> *a special on the lady in red, who lies*
> *motionless on the floor; as the lights*
> *slowly fade up the lady in red sits*
> *up.*

at 4:30 AM
she rose
movin the arms & legs that trapped her
she sighed affirmin the sculptured man
& made herself a bath
of dark musk oil egyptian crystals
& florida water to remove his smell

to wash away the glitter
to watch the butterflies melt into
suds & the rhinestones fall beneath
her buttocks like smooth pebbles
in a missouri creek
layin in water
she became herself
ordinary
brown braided woman
with big legs & full lips
reglar
seriously intendin to finish her
night's work
she quickly walked to her guest
straddled on her pillows & began
              'you'll have to go now/ i've
              a lot of work to do/ & i cant
              with a man around/ here are yr pants/
              there's coffee on the stove/ its been
              very nice/ but i cant see you again/
              you got what you came for/ didnt you'
& she smiled
he wd either mumble curses bout crazy bitches
or sit dumbfounded
while she repeated
              'i cdnt possibly wake up/ with
              a strange man in my bed/ why
              dont you go home'
she cda been slapped upside the head
or verbally challenged
but she never waz
& the ones who fell prey to the
dazzle of hips painted with
orange blossoms & magnolia scented wrists
had wanted no more
than to lay between her sparklin thighs
& had planned on leavin before dawn
& she had been so divine
devastatingly bizarre the way
her mouth fit round
& now she stood a
reglar colored girl
fulla the same malice
livid indifference as a sistah
worn from supportin a wd be hornplayer
or waitin by the window

                    & they knew
                    & left in a hurry
she wd gather her tinsel &
jewels from the tub
& laugh gayly or vengeful
she stored her silk roses by her bed
& when she finished writin
the account of her exploit in a diary
embroidered with lilies & moonstones
she placed the rose behind her ear
& cried herself to sleep.

                              All the lights fade except for a
                              special on the lady in red; the lady
                              in red exits into the stage left volm.

                              The lady in blue enters from up
                              right.

    lady in blue.
i usedta live in the world
then i moved to HARLEM
& my universe is now six blocks

when i walked in the pacific
i imagined waters ancient from accra/ tunis
cleansin me/ feedin me
now my ankles are coated in grey filth
from the puddle neath the hydrant

my oceans were life
what waters i have here sit stagnant
circlin ol men's bodies
shit & broken lil whiskey bottles
left to make me bleed

i usedta live in the world
now i live in harlem & my universe is six blocks
a tunnel with a train
i can ride anywhere
remaining a stranger

         NO MAN YA CANT GO WIT ME/ I DONT EVEN
         KNOW YOU/ NO/ I DONT WANNA KISS YOU/
         YOU AINT BUT 12 YRS OLD/ NO MAN/ PLEASE
         PLEASE PLEASE LEAVE ME ALONE/ TOMORROW/ YEAH/
         NO/ PLEASE/ I CANT USE IT

i cd stay alone
a woman in the world
then i moved to
HARLEM
i come in at dusk
stay close to the curb

The lady in yellow enters, she's wait-
ing for a bus.

round midnite
praying wont no young man
think i'm pretty in a dark mornin

The lady in purple enters, she's wait-
ing for a bus.

wdnt be good
not good at all
to meet a tall short black brown young man fulla his power
in the dark
in my universe of six blocks
straight up brick walls
women hangin outta windows
like ol silk stockings
cats cryin/ children gigglin/ a tavern wit red curtains
bad smells/ kissin ladies smilin & dirt
sidewalks spittin/ men cursing/ playin

The lady in orange enters, she is
being followed by a man, the lady in
blue becomes that man.

'I SPENT MORE MONEY YESTERDAY
THAN THE DAY BEFORE & ALL THAT'S MORE N YOU
NIGGAH EVER GOTTA HOLD TO
COME OVER HERE BITCH
CANT YA SEE THIS IS $5'

never mind sister
dont pay him no mind
go go go go go go sister
do yr thing
never mind

i usedta live in the world
really be in the world

free & sweet talkin
good mornin & thank-you & nice day
uh huh
i cant now
i cant be nice to nobody
nice is such a rip-off
reglar beauty & a smile in the street
is just a set-up

i usedta be in the world
a woman in the world
i hadda right to the world
then i moved to harlem
for the set-up
a universe
six blocks of cruelty
piled up on itself
a tunnel
closin

*The four ladies on stage freeze, count
4, then the ladies in blue, purple,
yellow and orange move to their
places for the next poem.*

lady in purple.
three of us like a pyramid
three friends
one laugh
one music
one flowered shawl
knotted on each neck

we all saw him at the same time
& he saw us
i felt a quick thump in each one of us
didnt know what to do
we all wanted what waz comin our way
so we split
but he found one
& she loved him

the other two were tickled
& spurned his advances
when the one who loved him waz somewhere else
he wd come to her saying

yr friends love you very much
i have tried
& they keep askin where are you
she smiled
wonderin how long her friends
wd hold out
he waz what they were lookin for
he bided his time
he waited til romance waned
the three of us made up stories
bout usedta & cda been nice
the season waz dry
no men
no quickies
not one dance or eyes unrelentin

one day after another
cept for the one who loved him
he appeared irregularly
expectin graciousness no matter what
she cut fresh strawberries
her friends callt less frequently
went on hunts for passin fancies
she cdnt figure out what waz happenin
then the rose
she left by his pillow
she found on her friends desk
& there waz nothing to say
she said
i wanna tell you
he's been after me
all the time
says he's free & can explain
what's happenin wit you
is nothin to me
& i dont wanna hurt you
but you know i need someone now
& you know
how wonderful he is

her friend cdnt speak or cry
they hugged & went to where he waz
wit another woman
he said good-bye to one
tol the other he wd call
he smiled a lot

she held her head on her lap
the lap of her sisters soakin up tears
each understandin how much love stood between them
how much love between them
love between them
love like sisters

> *Sharp music is heard, each lady*
> *dances as if catching a disease from*
> *the lady next to her, suddenly they*
> *all freeze.*

lady in orange.

ever since i realized there waz someone callt
a colored girl an evil woman a bitch or a nag
i been tryin not to be that & leave bitterness
in somebody else's cup/ come to somebody to love me
without deep & nasty smellin scald from lye or bein
left screamin in a street fulla lunatics/ whisperin
slut bitch bitch niggah/ get outta here wit alla that/
i didnt have any of that for you/ i brought you what joy
i found & i found joy/ honest fingers round my face/ with
dead musicians on 78's from cuba/ or live musicians on five
dollar lp's from chicago/ where i have never been/ & i love
willie colon & arsenio rodriquez[5]/ especially cuz i can make
the music loud enuf/ so there is no me but dance/ & when
i can dance like that/ there's nothin cd hurt me/ but
i get tired & i haveta come offa the floor & then there's
that woman who hurt you/ who you left/ three or four times/
& just went back/ after you put my heart in the bottom of
yr shoe/ you just walked back to where you hurt/ & i didnt
have nothin/ so i went to where somebody had somethin for me/
but he waznt you/ & i waz on the way back from her house
in the bottom of yr shoe/ so this is not a love poem/ cuz there
are only memorial albums available/ & even charlie mingus[6]
wanted desperately to be a pimp/ & i wont be able to see eddie
palmieri for months/ so this is a requium for myself/ cuz i
have died in a real way/ not wid aqua coffins & du-wop cadillacs/
i used to joke abt when i waz messin round/ but a real dead
lovin is here for you now / cuz i dont know anymore/ how
to avoid my own face wet wit my tears/ cuz i had convinced
myself colored girls had no right to sorrow/ & i lived
& loved that way & kept sorrow on the curb/ allegedly

---

[5] Salsa musician.

[6] (b. 1922), jazz musician

for you/ but i know i did it for myself/
i cdnt stand it
i cdnt stand bein sorry & colored at the same time
it's so redundant in the modern world

lady in purple.
i lived wit myths & music waz my ol man & i cd dance
a dance outta time/ a dance wit no partners/ take my
pills & keep right on steppin/ linger in non-english
speakin arms so there waz no possibility of understandin

& you YOU
came sayin i am the niggah/ i am the baddest muthafuckah
out there/
i said yes/ this is who i am waitin for
& to come wit you/ i hadta bring everythin
the dance & the terror
the dead musicians & the hope
& those scars i had hidden wit smiles & good fuckin
lay open
& i dont know i dont know any more tricks
i am really colored & really sad sometimes & you hurt me
more than i ever danced outta/ into oblivion isnt far enuf
to get outta this/ i am ready to die like a lily in the
desert/ & i cdnt let you in on it cuz i didnt know/ here
is what i have/ poems/ big thighs/ lil tits/ &
so much love/ will you take it from me this one time/
please this is for you/ arsenio's tres[7] cleared the way
& makes me pure again/ please please/ this is for you
i want you to love me/ let me love you/ i dont wanna
dance wit ghosts/ snuggle lovers i made up in my drunkenness/
lemme love you just like i am/ a colored girl/ i'm finally bein
real/ no longer symmetrical & impervious to pain

lady in blue.
we deal wit emotion too much
so why dont we go on ahead & be white then/
& make everythin dry & abstract wit no rhythm & no
reelin for sheer sensual pleasure/ yes let's go on
& be white/ we're right in the middle of it/ no use
holdin out/ holdin onto ourselves/ lets think our
way outta feelin/ lets abstract ourselves some families
& maybe maybe tonite/ i'll find a way to make myself
come witout you/ no fingers or other objects just thot

---

[7] three (spanish).

which isnt spiritual evolution cuz its empty & godliness
is plenty is ripe & fertile/ thinkin wont do me a bit of
good tonite/ i need to be loved/ & havent the audacity
to say
where are you/ & dont know who to say it to

lady in yellow.
i've lost it
touch wit reality/ i dont know who's doin it
i thot i waz but i waz so stupid i waz able to be hurt
& that's not real/ not anymore/ i shd be immune/ if i'm
still alive & that's what i waz discussin/ how i am still
alive & my dependency on other livin beins for love
i survive on intimacy & tomorrow/ that's all i've got goin
& the music waz like smack & you knew abt that
& still refused my dance waz not enuf/ & it waz all i had
but bein alive & bein a woman & bein colored is a metaphysical
dilemma/ i havent conquered yet/ do you see the point
my spirit is too ancient to understand the separation of
soul & gender/ my love is too delicate to have thrown
back on my face

*The ladies in red, green, and brown
enter quietly; in the background all of
the ladies except the lady in yellow
are frozen; the lady in yellow looks
at them, walks by them, touches
them; they do not move.*

lady in yellow.
my love is too delicate to have thrown back on my face

*The lady in yellow starts to exit into
the stage right volm. Just as she gets
to the volm, the lady in brown comes
to life.*

lady in brown.
my love is too beautiful to have thrown back on my face

lady in purple.
my love is too sanctified to have thrown back on my face

lady in blue.
my love is too magic to have thrown back on my face

lady in orange.
my love is too saturday nite to have thrown back on my face

lady in red.
my love is too complicated to have thrown back on my face

lady in green.
my love is too music to have thrown back on my face

everyone.
music
music

> *The lady in green then breaks into a*
> *dance, the other ladies follow her*
> *lead and soon they are all dancing*
> *and chanting together.*

lady in green.
yank dankka dank dank

everyone.
music

lady in green.
yank dankka dank dank

everyone.
music

lady in green.
yank dankka dank dank

everyone (*but started by the lady in yellow*).
delicate
delicate
delicate

everyone (*but started by the lady in brown*).
and beautiful
and beautiful
and beautiful

everyone (*but started by the lady in purple*).
oh sanctified

oh sanctified
oh sanctified

everyone *(but started by the lady in blue).*
magic
magic
magic

everyone *(but started by the lady in orange).*
and saturday nite
and saturday nite
and saturday nite

everyone *(but started by the lady in red).*
and complicated
and complicated
and complicated
and complicated
and complicated
and complicated
and complicated
and complicated

*The dance reaches a climax and all
of the ladies fall out tired, but full of
life and togetherness.*

lady in green
somebody almost walked off wid alla my stuff
not my poems or a dance i gave up in the street
but somebody almost walked off wid alla my stuff
like a kleptomaniac workin hard & forgettin while stealin
this is mine/ this aint yr stuff/
now why dont you put me back & let me hang out in my own self
somebody almost walked off wid alla my stuff
& didnt care enuf to send a note home sayin
i waz late for my solo conversation
or two sizes too small for my own tacky skirts
what can anybody do wit somethin of no value on
a open market/ did you getta dime for my things/
hey man/ where are you goin wid alla my stuff/
this is a woman's trip & i need my stuff/
to ohh & ahh abt/ daddy/ i gotta mainline number
from my own shit/ now wontchu put me back / & let
me play this duet/ wit this silver ring in my nose/
honest to god/ somebody almost run off wit alla my stuff/

& i didnt bring anythin but the kick & sway of it
the perfect ass for my man & none of it is theirs
this is mine/ ntozake 'her own things'/ that's my name/
now give me my stuff/ i see ya hidin my laugh/ & how i
sit wif my legs open sometimes/ to give my crotch
some sunlight/ & there goes my love my toes my chewed
up finger nails/ niggah/ wif the curls in yr hair/
mr. louisiana hot link/ i want my stuff back/
my rhythms & my voice/ open my mouth/ & let me talk ya
outta/ throwin my shit in the sewar/ this is some delicate
leg & whimsical kiss/ i gotta have to give to my choice/
without you runnin off wit alla my shit/
now you cant have me less i give me away/ & i waz
doin all that/ til ya run off on a good thing/
who is this you left me wit/ some simple bitch
widda bad attitude/ i wants my things/
i want my arm wit the hot iron scar/ & my leg wit the
flea bite/ i want my calloused feet & quik language back
in my mouth/ fried plantains/ pineapple pear juice/
sun-ra & joseph & jules/ i want my own things/ how i lived them/
& give me my memories/ how i waz when i waz there/
you cant have them or do nothin wit them/
stealin my shit from me/ dont make it yrs/ makes it stolen/
somebody almost run off wit alla my stuff/ & i waz standin
there/ lookin at myself/ the whole time
& it waznt a spirit took my stuff/ waz a man whose
ego walked round like Rodan's[8] shadow/ waz a man faster
n my innocence/ az a lover/ i made too much
room for/ almost run off wit alla my stuff/
& i didnt know i'd give it up so quik/ & the one running wit it/
dont know he got it/ & i'm shoutin this is mine/ & he dont
know he got it/ my stuff is the anonymous ripped off treasure
of the year/ did you know somebody almost got away with me/
me in a plastic bag under their arm/ me
danglin on a string of personal carelessness/ i'm splattered wit
mud & city rain/ & no i didnt get a chance to take a douche/
hey man/ this is not your perogative/ i gotta have me in my
pocket/ to get round like a good woman shd/ & make the poem
in the pot or the chicken in the dance/ what i got to do/
i gotta have my stuff to do it to/
why dont ya find yr own things/ & leave this package
of me for my destiny/ what ya got to get from me/
i'll give it to ya/ yeh/ i'll give it to ya/
round 5:00 in the winter/ when the sky is blue-red/

---

[8] Prehistoric monster in movie of that title.

& Dew City is gettin pressed/ if it's really my stuff/
ya gotta give it to me/ if ya really want it/ i'm
the only one/ can handle it

lady in blue.
that niggah will be back tomorrow, sayin 'i'm sorry'

lady in yellow.
get this, last week my ol man came in sayin, 'i don't know
how she got yr number baby, i'm sorry'

lady in brown.
no this one is it, 'o baby, ya know i waz high, i'm sorry'

lady in purple.
'i'm only human, and inadequacy is what makes us human, &
if we was perfect we wdnt have nothin to strive for, so you
might as well go on and forgive me pretty baby, cause i'm sorry'

lady in green.
'shut up bitch, i told you i waz sorry'

lady in orange.
no this one is it, 'i do ya like i do ya cause i thot
ya could take it, now i'm sorry'

lady in red.
'now i know that ya know i love ya, but i ain't ever gonna
love ya like ya want me to love ya, i'm sorry'

lady in blue.
one thing i dont need
is any more apologies
i got sorry greetin me at my front door
you can keep yrs
i dont know what to do wit em
they dont open doors
or bring the sun back
they dont make me happy
or get a mornin paper
didnt nobody stop usin my tears to wash cars
cuz a sorry

i am simply tired
of collectin
          i didnt know

i was so important toyou'
i'm gonna haveta throw some away
i cant get to the clothes in my closet
for alla the sorries
i'm gonna tack a sign to my door
leave a message by the phone
    'if you called
    to say yr sorry
    call somebody
    else
    i dont use em anymore'
i let sorry/ didnt meanta/ & how cd i know abt that
take a walk down a dark & musty street in brooklyn
i'm gonna do exactly what i want to
& i wont be sorry for none of it
letta sorry soothe yr soul/ i'm gonna soothe mine

you were always inconsistent
doin somethin & then bein sorry
beatin my heart to death
talkin bout you sorry
well
i will not call
i'm not goin to be nice
i will raise my voice
& scream & holler
& break things & race the engine
& tell all yr secrets bout yrself to yr face
& i will list in detail everyone of my wonderful lovers
& their ways
i will play oliver lake
loud
& i wont be sorry for none of it

i loved you on purpose
i was open on purpose
i still crave vulnerability & close talk
& i'm not even sorry bout you bein sorry
you can carry all the guilt & grime ya wanna
just dont give it to me
i cant use another sorry
next time
you should admit
you're mean/ low-down/ triflin/ & no count straight out
steada bein sorry alla the time
enjoy bein yrself

lady in red.
there waz no air/ the sheets made ripples under his
body like crumpled paper napkins in a summer park/ & lil
specks of somethin from tween his toes or the biscuits
from the day before ran in the sweat that tucked the sheet
into his limbs like he waz an ol frozen bundle of chicken/
& he'd get up to make coffee, drink wine, drink water/ he
wished one of his friends who knew where he waz wd come by
with some blow or some shit/ anythin/ there waz no air/
he'd see the spotlights in the alleyways downstairs movin
in the air/ cross his wall over his face/ & get under the
covers & wait for an all clear or til he cd hear traffic
again/

there waznt nothin wrong with him/ there waznt nothin wrong
with him/ he kept tellin crystal/
any niggah wanna kill vietnamese children more n stay home
& raise his own is sicker than a rabid dog/
that's how their thing had been goin since he got back/
crystal just got inta sayin whatta fool niggah beau waz
& always had been/ didnt he go all over uptown sayin the
child waznt his/ waz some no counts bastard/ & any ol city
police cd come & get him if they wanted/ cuz as soon as
the blood type & shit waz together/ everybody wd know that
crystal waz a no good lyin whore/ and this after she'd been
his girl since she waz thirteen/ when he caught her
on the stairway/

he came home crazy as hell/ he tried to get veterans benefits
to go to school & they kept right on puttin him in
remedial classes/ he cdnt read wortha damn/ so beau
cused the teachers of holdin him back & got himself
a gypsy cab to drive/ but his cab kept breakin
down/ & the cops was always messin wit him/ plus not
gettin much bread/

& crystal went & got pregnant again/ beau most beat
her to death when she tol him/ she still gotta scar
under her right tit where he cut her up/ still crystal
went right on & had the baby/ so now beau willie had
two children/ a little girl/ naomi kenya & a boy/ kwame beau
willie brown/ & there waz no air/

how in the hell did he get in this mess anyway/ somebody
went & tol crystal that beau waz spendin alla his money
on the bartendin bitch down at the merry-go-round cafe/

beau sat straight up in the bed/ wrapped up in the sheets
lookin like john the baptist or a huge baby wit stubble
& nuts/ now he hadta get alla that shit outta crystal's
mind/ so she wd let him come home/ crystal had gone &
got a court order saying beau willie brown had no access
to his children/ if he showed his face he waz subject
to arrest/ shit/ she'd been in his ass to marry her
since she waz 14 years old & here when she 22/ she wanna
throw him out cuz he say he'll marry her/ she burst
out laughin/ hollerin whatchu wanna marry me for now/
so i can support yr
ass/ or come sit wit ya when they lock yr behind
up/ cause they gonna come for ya/ ya goddamn lunatic/
they gonna come/ & i'm not gonna have a thing to do
wit it/ o no i wdnt marry yr pitiful black ass for
nothin & she went on to bed/

the next day beau willie came in blasted & got ta swingin
chairs at crystal/ who cdnt figure out what the hell
he waz doin/ til he got ta shoutin bout how she waz gonna
marry him/ & get some more veterans benefits/ & he cd
stop drivin them crazy spics round/ while they tryin
to kill him for $15/ beau waz sweatin terrible/ beatin
on crystal/ & he cdnt do no more with the table n chairs/
so he went to get the high chair/ & lil kwame waz in it/
& beau waz beatin crystal with the high chair & her son/
& some notion got inta him to stop/ and he run out/

crystal most died/ that's why the police wdnt low
beau near where she lived/ & she'd been tellin the kids
their daddy tried to kill her & kwame/ & he just wanted
to marry her/ that's what/ he wanted to marry her/ &
have a family/ but the bitch waz crazy/ beau willie
waz sittin in this hotel in his drawers drinkin
coffee & wine in the heat of the day spillin shit all
over hisself/ laughin/ bout how he waz gonna get crystal
to take him back/ & let him be a man in the house/ & she
wdnt even have to go to work no more/ he got dressed
all up in his ivory shirt & checkered pants to go see
crystal & get this mess all cleared up/
he knocked on the door to crystal's rooms/ & she
didnt answer/ he beat on the door & crystal & naomi
started cryin/ beau gotta shoutin again how he wanted
to marry her/ & waz she always gonna be a whore/ or
did she wanna husband/ & crystal just kept on
screamin for him to leave us alone/ just leave us

alone/ so beau broke the door down/ crystal held
the children in fronta her/ she picked kwame off the
floor/ in her arms/ & she held naomi by her shoulders/
& kept on sayin/ beau willie brown/ get outta here/
the police is gonna come for ya/ ya fool/ get outta here/
do you want the children to see you act the fool again/
you want kwame to brain damage from you throwin him
round/ niggah/ get outta here/ get out & dont show yr
ass again or i'll kill ya/ i swear i'll kill ya/
he reached for naomi/ crystal grabbed the lil girl &
stared at beau willie like he waz a leper or somethin/
dont you touch my children/ muthafucker/ or i'll kill
you/

beau willie jumped back all humble & apologetic/ i'm
sorry/ i dont wanna hurt em/ i just wanna hold em &
get on my way/ i dont wanna cuz you no more trouble/
i wanted to marry you & give ya things
what you gonna give/ a broken jaw/ niggah get outta here/
he ignored crystal's outburst & sat down motionin for
naomi to come to him/ she smiled back at her daddy/

crystal felt naomi givin in & held her tighter/
naomi/ pushed away & ran to her daddy/ cryin/ daddy, daddy
come back daddy/ come back/ but be nice to mommy/
cause mommy loves you/ and ya gotta be nice/
he sat her on his knee/ & played with her ribbons &
they counted fingers & toes/ every so often he
looked over to crystal holdin kwame/ like a statue/
& he'd say/ see crystal/ i can be a good father/
now let me see my son/ & she didnt move/ &
he coaxed her & he coaxed her/ tol her she waz
still a hot lil ol thing & pretty & strong/ didnt
she get right up after that lil ol fight they had
& go back to work/ beau willie oozed kindness &
crystal who had known so lil/ let beau hold kwame/

as soon as crystal let the baby outta her arms/ beau
jumped up a laughin & a gigglin/ a hootin & a hollerin/
awright bitch/ awright bitch/ you gonna marry me/
you gonna marry me . . .
i aint gonna marry ya/ i aint ever gonna marry ya/
for nothin/ you gonna be in the jail/ you gonna be
under the jail for this/ now gimme my kids/ ya give
me back my kids/

he kicked the screen outta the window/ & held the kids
offa the sill/ you gonna marry me/ yeh, i'll marry ya/
anything/ but bring the children back in the house/
he looked from where the kids were hangin from the
fifth story/ at alla the people screamin at him/ &
he started sweatin again/ say to alla the neighbors/
you gonna marry me/

i stood by beau in the window/ with naomi reachin
for me/ & kwame screamin mommy mommy from the fifth
story/ but i cd only whisper/ & he dropped em

lady in red.
i waz missin somethin

lady in purple.
somethin so important

lady in orange.
somethin promised

lady in blue.
a layin on of hands

lady in green.
fingers near my forehead

lady in yellow.
strong

lady in green.
cool

lady in orange.
movin

lady in purple.
makin me whole

lady in orange.
sense

lady in green.
pure

lady in blue.
all the gods comin into me
layin me open to myself

lady in red.
i waz missin somethin

lady in green.
somethin promised

lady in orange.
somethin free

lady in purple.
a layin on of hands

lady in blue.
i know bout/ layin on bodies/ layin outta man
bringin him alla my fleshy self & some of my pleasure
bein taken full eager wet like i get sometimes
i waz missin somethin

lady in purple.
a layin on of hands

lady in blue.
not a man

lady in yellow.
layin on

lady in purple.
not my mama/ holdin me tight/ sayin
i'm always gonna be her girl
not a layin on of bosom & womb
a layin on of hands
the holiness of myself released

lady in red.
i sat up one nite walkin a boardin house

screamin/ cryin/ the ghost of another woman
who waz missin what i waz missin
i wanted to jump up outta my bones
& be done wit myself
leave me alone
& go on in the wind
it waz too much
i fell into a numbness
til the only tree i cd see
took me up in her branches
held me in the breeze
made me dawn dew
that chill at daybreak
the sun wrapped me up swingin rose light everywhere
the sky laid over me like a million men
i waz cold/ i waz burnin up/ a child
& endlessly weavin garments for the moon
wit my tears

i found god in myself
& i loved her/ i loved her fiercely

> *All of the ladies repeat to themselves
> softly the lines 'i found god in myself
> & i loved her.' It soon becomes a
> song of joy, started by the lady in
> blue. The ladies sing first to each
> other, then gradually to the audience.
> After the song peaks the ladies enter
> into a closed tight circle.*

lady in brown.
& this is for colored girls who have considered
suicide/ but are movin to the ends of their own
rainbows

Study and Discussion Questions

1. Why does shange call this a "choreopoem"? Of what mixture of genres does this work consist?
2. Why does shange choose the word "colored"? How many levels of meaning does the word have?
3. Are the Ladies identifiable as separate and consistent individuals; that is, does the Lady in Red have the same characteristics each time she appears?

4. What attitudes do the women express about rape, abortion, men, friendship, infidelity, marriage and children?
5. Why is each woman from a different city?
6. On stage (you can tell this from the stage directions) the poems are danced. Why do the women say "we gotta dance to keep from cryin" and "we gotta dance to keep from dyin"?
7. List a number of comments the women make about love.
8. What does the Lady in Green mean by the phrase "alla my stuff"? What is her stuff? Who's trying to walk away with it?

Writing Exercises

1. Discuss the function of disguise in the poem by the Lady in Red that begins "orange butterflies & aqua sequins."
2. Give yourself an appropriate color and write a poem in shange's mode about yourself.
3. Take a short section of *for colored girls . . .* and rewrite it in "standard" English. What is lost in translation?
4. *for colored girls . . .* began as radical theater, yet became a Broadway success in 1976–77. Speculate on why you think it received acceptance and acclaim from mainstream critics and audiences.
5. Almost the last words of the play are "i found god in myself/ & i loved her/ i loved her fiercely". How are these lines an answer to the play's title? How do the women get from there to here?

NONFICTION

PLATO   (427?–347 B.C.)

Born into the upper classes in Athens, Plato, at about the age of twenty, became a student and friend of the philosopher Socrates. In 399 B.C., after Socrates was executed for heresy, Plato left Athens, but returned a decade or so later and founded the Academy, where he taught philosophy and mathematics until his death. During his life, he wrote many dialogues—dramatic conversations in which Socrates and other characters argue fundamental philosophical issues. Among them are the Apology, Crito, Phaedo, Symposium, *and* Republic.

FROM **The Symposium**[1] (ca. 370 B.C.)

'Well, Eryximachus,' began Aristophanes[2], 'it is quite true that I intend to take a different line from you and Pausanias. Men seem to me to be utterly insensible of the power of Love; otherwise he would have had the largest temples and altars and the largest sacrifices. As it is, he has none of these things, though he deserves them most of all. For of all the gods he is the most friendly to man, and his helper and physician in those diseases whose cure constitutes the greatest happiness of the human race. I shall therefore try to initiate you into the secret of his power, and you in turn shall teach others.

'First of all, you must learn the constitution of man and the modifications which it has undergone, for originally it was different from what it is now. In the first place there were three sexes, not, as with us, two, male and female; the third partook of the nature of both the others and has vanished, though its name survives. The hermaphrodite was a distinct sex in form as well as in name, with the characteristics of both male and female, but now the name alone remains, and that solely as a term of abuse. Secondly, each human being was a rounded whole, with double back and flanks forming a complete circle; it had four hands and an equal number of legs, and two identically similar faces upon a circular neck, with one head common to both the faces, which were turned in opposite directions. It had four ears and two organs of generation and everything

---

[1] Translated by Walter Hamilton.

[2] Aristophanes (448?–385? B.C.), Athenian comic playwright. Eryximachus, Pausanias (following), and Agathon and Socrates (later) are other participants at the banquet, where love is the topic of discussion.

else to correspond. These people could walk upright like us in either direction, backwards or forwards, but when they wanted to run quickly they used all their eight limbs, and turned rapidly over and over in a circle, like tumblers who perform a cart-wheel and return to an upright position. The reason for the existence of three sexes and for their being of such a nature is that originally the male sprang from the sun and the female from the earth, while the sex which was both male and female came from the moon, which partakes of the nature of both sun and earth. Their circular shape and their hoop-like method of progression were both due to the fact that they were like their parents. Their strength and vigour made them very formidable, and their pride was overweening; they attacked the gods, and Homer's story of Ephialtes and Otus attempting to climb up to heaven and set upon the gods is related also of these beings.[3]

'So Zeus and the other gods debated what was to be done with them. For a long time they were at a loss, unable to bring themselves either to kill them by lightning, as they had the giants, and extinguish the race—thus depriving themselves for ever of the honours and sacrifice due from humanity—or to let them go on in their insolence. At last, after much painful thought, Zeus had an idea. "I think," he said, "that I have found a way by which we can allow the human race to continue to exist and also put an end to their wickedness by making them weaker. I will cut each of them in two; in this way they will be weaker, and at the same time more profitable to us by being more numerous. They shall walk upright upon two legs. If there is any sign of wantonness in them after that, and they will not keep quiet, I will bisect them again, and they shall hop on one leg." With these words he cut the members of the human race in half, just like fruit which is to be dried and preserved, or like eggs which are cut with a hair. As he bisected each, he bade Apollo turn round the face and the half-neck attached to it towards the cut side, so that the victim, having the evidence of bisection before his eyes, might behave better in future. He also bade him heal the wounds. So Apollo turned round the faces, and gathering together the skin, like a purse with drawstrings, on to what is now called the belly, he tied it tightly in the middle of the belly round a single aperture which men call the navel. He smoothed out the other wrinkles, which were numerous, and moulded the chest with a tool like those which cobblers use to smooth wrinkles in the leather on their last. But he left a few on the belly itself round the navel, to remind man of the state from which he had fallen.

'Man's original body having been thus cut in two, each half yearned for the half from which it had been severed. When they met they threw their arms round one another and embraced, in their longing to grow together again, and they perished of hunger and general neglect of their concerns, because they would not do anything apart. When one member of a pair died and the other was left, the latter sought after and embraced

---

[3] Giants Ephialtes and Otus tried to climb to heaven by piling mountain upon mountain.

another partner, which might be the half either of a female whole (what is now called a woman) or a male. So they went on perishing till Zeus took pity on them, and hit upon a second plan. He moved their reproductive organs to the front: hitherto they had been placed on the outer side of their bodies, and the processes of begetting and birth had been carried on not by the physical union of the sexes, but by emission on to the ground, as is the case with grasshoppers. By moving their genitals to the front, as they are now, Zeus made it possible for reproduction to take place by the intercourse of the male with the female. His object in making this change was twofold; if male coupled with female, children might be begotten and the race thus continued, but if male coupled with male, at any rate the desire for intercourse would be satisfied, and men set free from it to turn to other activities and to attend to the rest of the business of life. It is from this distant epoch, then, that we may date the innate love which human beings feel for one another, the love which restores us to our ancient state by attempting to weld two beings into one and to heal the wounds which humanity suffered.

'Each of us then is the mere broken tally of a man, the result of a bisection which has reduced us to a condition like that of flat fish, and each of us is perpetually in search of his corresponding tally. Those men who are halves of a being of the common sex, which was called, as I told you, hermaphrodite, are lovers of women, and most adulterers come from this class, as also do women who are mad about men and sexually promiscuous. Women who are halves of a female whole direct their affections towards women and pay little attention to men; Lesbians belong to this category. But those who are halves of a male whole pursue males, and being slices, so to speak, of the male, love men throughout their boyhood, and take pleasure in physical contact with men. Such boys and lads are the best of their generation, because they are the most manly. Some people say that they are shameless, but they are wrong. It is not shamelessness which inspires their behaviour, but high spirit and manliness and virility, which lead them to welcome the society of their own kind. A striking proof of this is that such boys alone, when they reach maturity, engage in public life. When they grow to be men, they become lovers of boys, and it requires the compulsion of convention to overcome their natural disinclination to marriage and procreation; they are quite content to live with one another unwed. In a word, such persons are devoted to lovers in boyhood and themselves lovers of boys in manhood, because they always cleave to what is akin to themselves.

'Whenever the lover of boys—or any other person for that matter— has the good fortune to encounter his own actual other half, affection and kinship and love combined inspire in him an emotion which is quite overwhelming, and such a pair practically refuse ever to be separated even for a moment. It is people like these who form lifelong partnerships, although they would find it difficult to say what they hope to gain from one another's society. No one can suppose that it is mere physical en-

joyment which causes the one to take such intense delight in the company
of the other. It is clear that the soul of each has some other longing
which it cannot express, but can only surmise and obscurely hint at.
Suppose Hephaestus with his tools were to visit them as they lie together,
and stand over them and ask: "What is it, mortals, that you hope to gain
from one another?" Suppose too that when they could not answer he
repeated his question in these terms: "Is the object of your desire to be
always together as much as possible, and never to be separated from one
another day or night? If that is what you want, I am ready to melt and
weld you together, so that, instead of two, you shall be one flesh; as long
as you live you shall live a common life, and when you die, you shall
suffer a common death, and be still one, not two, even in the next world.
Would such a fate as this content you, and satisfy your longings?" We
know what their answer would be; no one would refuse the offer; it
would be plain that this is what everybody wants, and everybody would
regard it as the precise expression of the desire which he had long felt
but had been unable to formulate, that he should melt into his beloved,
and that henceforth they should be one being instead of two. The reason
is that this was our primitive condition when we were wholes, and love
is simply the name of the desire and pursuit of the whole. Originally, as
I say, we were whole beings, before our wickedness caused us to be split
by Zeus, as the Arcadians have been split apart by the Spartans.[4] We
have reason to fear that if we do not behave ourselves in the sight of
heaven, we may be split in two again, like dice which are bisected for
tallies, and go about like the people represented in profile on tombstones,
sawn in two vertically down the line of our noses. That is why we ought
to exhort everyone to conduct himself reverently towards the gods; we
shall thus escape a worse fate, and even win the blessings which Love
has in his power to bestow, if we take him for our guide and captain.
Let no man set himself in opposition to Love—which is the same thing
as incurring the hatred of the gods—for if we are his friends and make
our peace with him, we shall succeed, as few at present succeed, in finding
the person to love who in the strictest sense belongs to us. I know that
Eryximachus is anxious to make fun of my speech, but he is not to suppose
that in saying this I am pointing at Pausanias and Agathon. They may,
no doubt, belong to this class, for they are both unquestionably halves
of male wholes, but I am speaking of men and women in general when
I say that the way to happiness for our race lies in fulfilling the behests
of Love, and in each finding for himself the mate who properly belongs
to him; in a word, in returning to our original condition. If that condition
was the best, it follows that it is best for us to come as near to it as our
present circumstances allow; and the way to do that is to find a sympathetic
and congenial object for our affections.

---

[4] The conquering Spartans forced the residents of the Arcadian city of Mantinea to live
in four separate villages.

'If we are to praise the god who confers this benefit upon us, it is to Love that our praises should be addressed. It is Love who is the author of our well-being in this present life, by leading us towards what is akin to us, and it is Love who gives us a sure hope that, if we conduct ourselves well in the sight of heaven, he will hereafter make us blessed and happy by restoring us to our former state and healing our wounds.

'There is my speech about Love, Eryximachus, and you will see that it is of quite a different type from yours. Remember my request, and don't make fun of it, but let us hear what each of the others has to say. I should have said "each of the other two", for only Agathon and Socrates are left.'

Study and Discussion Questions

1. What were human beings like originally, according to Aristophanes?
2. Why do we have navels?
3. According to Plato's myth, why do human beings fall in love?
4. How does this myth explain homosexuality and heterosexuality?
5. Which of the three types of love relationship does Aristophanes most approve of? Why?
6. What will happen to human beings if we anger the gods again?
7. What is Aristophanes's tone in this speech?

Writing Exercises

1. How does Plato's myth about the origin of human beings compare to the Biblical story of the Garden of Eden?
2. Do you agree or disagree with Aristophanes's theory that we are each looking for our other half, "each finding for himself the mate who properly belongs to him"? Give reasons and evidence for your opinion.

VIRGINIA WOOLF   (1882–1941)

Daughter of man of letters Leslie Stephen, Virginia Woolf was born in London and grew up in an environment of wealth and culture, meeting many of the most distinguished intellectuals of the time. Unlike their brothers, Virginia and her sister were not sent to school or university but educated at home. From her mother's death in 1895 to her father's in 1904, she was responsible for running the household; after that, she moved to London and became the center of the intellectual and artistic Bloomsbury Group. In 1912, she married Leonard Woolf; a decade later, she began a long relationship with the writer Vita Sackville-West. Woolf's experimental fiction helped to define modernism as a literary movement and earned her a reputation as a major

English novelist. Her continuing attacks of depression and her fear of a Nazi invasion of England led to her suicide in 1941. Among her works are the novels Mrs. Dalloway *(1925),* To the Lighthouse *(1927), and* The Waves *(1931), and the nonfiction* A Room of One's Own *(1929) and* Three Guineas *(1938).*

Shakespeare's Sister   (1929)

It would have been impossible, completely and entirely, for any woman to have written the plays of Shakespeare in the age of Shakespeare. Let me imagine, since facts are so hard to come by, what would have happened had Shakespeare had a wonderfully gifted sister, called Judith, let us say. Shakespeare himself went, very probably—his mother was an heiress—to the grammar school, where he may have learnt Latin—Ovid, Virgil and Horace—and the elements of grammar and logic. He was, it is well known, a wild boy who poached rabbits, perhaps shot a deer, and had, rather sooner than he should have done, to marry a woman in the neighbourhood, who bore him a child rather quicker than was right. That escapade sent him to seek his fortune in London. He had, it seemed, a taste for the theatre; he began by holding horses at the stage door. Very soon he got work in the theatre, became a successful actor, and lived at the hub of the universe, meeting everybody, knowing everybody, practising his art on the boards, exercising his wits in the streets, and even getting access to the palace of the queen. Meanwhile his extraordinarily gifted sister, let us suppose, remained at home. She was as adventurous, as imaginative, as agog to see the world as he was. But she was not sent to school. She had no chance of learning grammar and logic, let alone of reading Horace and Virgil. She picked up a book now and then, one of her brother's perhaps, and read a few pages. But then her parents came in and told her to mend the stockings or mind the stew and not moon about with books and papers. They would have spoken sharply but kindly, for they were substantial people who knew the conditions of life for a woman and loved their daughter—indeed, more likely than not she was the apple of her father's eye. Perhaps she scribbled some pages up in an apple loft on the sly, but was careful to hide them or set fire to them. Soon, however, before she was out of her teens, she was to be betrothed to the son of a neighbouring woolstapler. She cried out that marriage was hateful to her, and for that she was severely beaten by her father. Then he ceased to scold her. He begged her instead not to hurt him, not to shame him in this matter of her marriage. He would give her a chain of beads or a fine petticoat, he said; and there were tears in his eyes. How could she disobey him? How could she break his heart? The force of her own gift alone drove her to it. She made up a small parcel of her belongings, let herself down by a rope one summer's night and took the road to London. She was not seventeen. The birds that sang in the hedge were not more musical than she was. She had the quickest fancy, a gift like her brother's, for the tune of words. Like him, she had a taste for the theatre. She stood at the stage door; she wanted to act, she said. Men laughed in her face. The manager—a fat, loose-lipped man—guffawed. He bellowed something about poodles dancing and women acting—no woman, he said, could possibly be an actress. He hinted— you can imagine what. She could get no training in her craft. Could she even seek her dinner in a tavern or roam the streets at midnight? Yet her genius was for fiction and lusted to feed abundantly upon the lives of men and women and the study of their ways. At last—for she was very young, oddly like Shakespeare the poet in her face, with the same grey eyes and rounded brows—at last Nick Greene the actor-manager took pity on her; she found herself with child by that gentleman and so—who shall measure the heat and violence of the poet's heart when caught and tangled in a woman's body?—killed herself one winter's night and lies buried at some cross-roads where the omnibuses now stop outside the Elephant and Castle.[1]

That, more or less, is how the story would run, I think, if a woman in Shakespeare's day had had Shakespeare's genius. But for my part, I agree with the deceased bishop, if such he was—it is unthinkable that any woman in Shakespeare's day should have had Shakespeare's genius. For genius like Shakespeare's is not born among labouring, uneducated, servile people. It was not born in England among the Saxons and the Britons. It is not born today among the working classes. How, then, could it have been born among women whose work began, according to Professor Trevelyan, almost before they were out of the nursery, who were forced to it by their parents and held to it by all the power of law and custom? Yet genius of a sort must have existed among women as it must have existed among the working classes. Now and again an Emily Brontë or a Robert Burns[2] blazes out and proves its presence. But certainly it never got itself on to paper. When, however, one reads of a witch being ducked, of a woman possessed by devils, of a wise woman selling herbs, or even of a very remarkable man who had a mother, then I think we are on the track of a lost novelist, a suppressed poet, of some mute and inglorious Jane Austen, some Emily Brontë who dashed her brains out on the moor or mopped and mowed about the highways crazed with the torture that her gift had put her to. Indeed, I would venture to guess that Anon, who wrote so many poems without signing them, was often a woman.

Study and Discussion Questions

1. What kind of education does Woolf say Shakespeare received? What kind would Judith receive?

---

[1] A tavern.
[2] Brontë (1818–1848), English novelist; Burns (1759–1796), Scottish poet.

2. How do Judith's parents demonstrate their love for her?
3. How does Judith's father try to get her to marry?
4. How do theater people respond to her desire to act and to write?
5. Woolf writes that Judith's "genius was for fiction and lusted to feed abundantly upon the lives of men and women and the study of their ways." What kept her from doing this?

Writing Exercises

1. What are the dangers of challenging the limits of what you are allowed to do—in this sketch? in your own life?
2. Write a paragraph stating Woolf's thesis. Why is creating Judith as a character an effective way of making this argument?
3. Are there any ways in which women today who want to write are barred from certain kinds of experience?

SOJOURNER TRUTH   (1797?–1883)

Isabella (later Isabella Van Wagener) was born a slave in New York state, escaped in 1827, and in 1829 moved to New York City, where she worked as a servant. She developed her speaking talent working with an evangelical preacher. In 1843, she had visions and heard voices that led her to take the name Sojourner Truth and to begin touring the country preaching religion and, soon, the abolition of slavery. Near the end of the Civil War, she helped recruit black troops for the Union army. She was a powerful and a popular speaker, and at an 1851 women's rights convention in Akron, Ohio, she turned the tide in an angry debate between feminists and conservative ministers with the following speech, recorded by a convention participant.

Ain't I a Woman?   (1851)

Well, children, where there is so much racket there must be something out of kilter. I think that 'twixt the negroes of the South and the women at the North, all talking about rights, the white men will be in a fix pretty soon. But what's all this here talking about?

That man over there says that women need to be helped into carriages, and lifted over ditches, and to have the best place everywhere. Nobody ever helps me into carriages, or over mud-puddles, or gives me any best place! And ain't I a woman? Look at me! Look at my arm! I have ploughed and planted, and gathered into barns, and no man could head me! And ain't I a woman? I could work as much and eat as much as a man—

when I could get it—and bear the lash as well! And ain't I a woman? I have borne thirteen children, and seen them most all sold off to slavery, and when I cried out with my mother's grief, none but Jesus heard me! And ain't I a woman?

Then they talk about this thing in the head; what's this they call it? [Intellect, someone whispers.] That's it, honey. What's that got to do with women's rights or negro's rights? If my cup won't hold but a pint, and yours holds a quart, wouldn't you be mean not to let me have my little half-measure full?

Then that little man in black there, he says women can't have as much rights as men, 'cause Christ wasn't a woman! Where did your Christ come from? Where did your Christ come from? From God and a woman! Man had nothing to do with Him.

If the first woman God ever made was strong enough to turn the world upside down all alone, these women together ought to be able to turn it back, and get it right side up again! And now they is asking to do it, the men better let them.

Obliged to you for hearing me, and now old Sojourner ain't got nothing more to say.

Study and Discussion Questions

1. Why is it significant that Sojourner Truth uses the Bible to argue for women's rights?
2. What is ironic about her argument concerning intellect?

Writing Exercise

1. Rewrite her speech as a straightforward argumentative essay. What is lost?

JUDY SYFERS (b. 1937)

Judy Syfers was born in San Francisco and earned a B.F.A. in painting at the University of Iowa. She married in 1960 and raised two children. Now divorced, Syfers lives in San Francisco, where she works as a writer and political activist and earns her living as a secretary.

Why I Want a Wife (1972)

I belong to that classification of people known as wives. I am A Wife. And, not altogether incidentally, I am a mother.

Not too long ago a male friend of mine appeared on the scene fresh from a recent divorce. He had one child, who is, of course, with his ex-wife. He is obviously looking for another wife. As I thought about him while I was ironing one evening, it suddenly occurred to me that I, too, would like to have a wife. Why do I want a wife?

I would like to go back to school so that I can become economically independent, support myself, and, if need be, support those dependent upon me. I want a wife who will work and send me to school. And while I am going to school I want a wife to take care of my children. I want a wife to keep track of the children's doctor and dentist appointments. And to keep track of mine, too. I want a wife to make sure my children eat properly and are kept clean. I want a wife who will wash the children's clothes and keep them mended. I want a wife who is a good nurturant attendant to my children, who arranges for their schooling, makes sure that they have an adequate social life with their peers, takes them to the park, the zoo, etc. I want a wife who takes care of the children when they are sick, a wife who arranges to be around when the children need special care, because, of course, I cannot miss classes at school. My wife must arrange to lose time at work and not lose the job. It may mean a small cut in my wife's income from time to time, but I guess I can tolerate that. Needless to say, my wife will arrange and pay for the care of the children while my wife is working.

I want a wife who will take care of *my* physical needs. I want a wife who will keep my house clean. A wife who will pick up after me. I want a wife who will keep my clothes clean, ironed, mended, replaced when need be, and who will see to it that my personal things are kept in their proper place so that I can find what I need the minute I need it. I want a wife who cooks the meals, a wife who is a *good* cook. I want a wife who will plan the menus, do the necessary grocery shopping, prepare the meals, serve them pleasantly, and then do the cleaning up while I do my studying. I want a wife who will care for me when I am sick and sympathize with my pain and loss of time from school. I want a wife to go along when our family takes a vacation so that someone can continue to care for me and my children when I need a rest and change of scene.

I want a wife who will not bother me with rambling complaints about a wife's duties. But I want a wife who will listen to me when I feel the need to explain a rather difficult point I have come across in my course of studies. And I want a wife who will type my papers for me when I have written them.

I want a wife who will take care of the details of my social life. When my wife and I are invited out by my friends, I want a wife who will take care of the babysitting arrangements. When I meet people at school that I like and want to entertain, I want a wife who will have the house clean, will prepare a special meal, serve it to me and my friends, and not interrupt when I talk about the things that interest me and my friends.

I want a wife who will have arranged that the children are fed and ready for bed before my guests arrive so that the children do not bother us.

And I want a wife who knows that sometimes I need a night out by myself.

I want a wife who is sensitive to my sexual needs, a wife who makes love passionately and eagerly when I feel like it, a wife who makes sure that I am satisfied. And, of course, I want a wife who will not demand sexual attention when I am not in the mood for it. I want a wife who assumes the complete responsibility for birth control, because I do not want more children. I want a wife who will remain sexually faithful to me so that I do not have to clutter up my intellectual life with jealousies. And I want a wife who understands that *my* sexual needs may entail more than strict adherence to monogamy. I must, after all, be able to relate to people as fully as possible.

If, by chance, I find another person more suitable as a wife than the wife I already have, I want the liberty to replace my present wife with another one. Naturally, I will expect a fresh, new life; my wife will take the children and be solely responsible for them so that I am left free.

When I am through with school and have a job, I want my wife to quit working and remain at home so that my wife can more fully and completely take care of a wife's duties.

My god, who *wouldn't* want a wife?

Study and Discussion Questions

1. What is the point of this essay? Is Syfers simply trying to explain how hard a wife works?
2. What does Syfers achieve by making her point indirectly? Why doesn't she simply *tell* us how she feels about being a wife? How does the choice of form—satire—serve the writer's purposes?
3. How does repetition function in the essay? Why do so many sentences begin with "I want . . . "—in fact with "I want a wife who . . ."? What effect does this have on the reader?
4. Syfers names a great many things she wants a wife for. How does she organize them? Is the ordering of the paragraphs in which she lists her wants significant?
5. How does the mention, in the second paragraph, of Syfers's divorced male friend serve her purpose in the essay?

Writing Exercises

1. Would a parallel essay, "Why I Want a Husband," have equal force? Explain.
2. Try writing an essay modeled on this one, but protesting some other social role you think unfair, one that you might be or imagine yourself in—"Why I Want a Secretary," for example.

3. Study a number of television or magazine advertisements that depict housewives. How closely do they correspond to the role of wife as Syfers describes it? What attitudes do they express towards the role or roles they depict?

WOMEN AND MEN: PAPER TOPICS

1. Trace and compare the use of images of entrapment and liberation in two or more poems in this section. (Suggestions: Piercy, "The Woman in the Ordinary"; Yeats, "Leda and the Swan")
2. Analyze the critique or rewriting of myths or fairy tales in one or more poems. (Suggestions: Rukeyser, "Waiting for Icarus"; Broumas, "Cinderella"; Rich, "Diving into the Wreck")
3. Explore the way the author uses a character's strangeness or madness, apparent or real, as social criticism in one or more short stories. (Suggestions: Yamauchi, "And the Soul Shall Dance"; Gilman, "The Yellow Wallpaper")
4. Pick a poem and a short story that explore similar themes and analyze how the choice of genre shapes meaning. Could each be rewritten in the other genre? If so, what consequences would the change of form bring?
5. Analyze how their social class affects the relations between men and women in one or more works. (Suggestions: Lawrence, "The White Stocking"; Naylor, "Etta Mae Johnson")
6. Compare/contrast any two works as comments on the meaning of "masculinity." (Suggestions: Grahn, "Boys at the Rodeo"; Updike, "A & P"; Marvell, "To His Coy Mistress")
7. Discuss the significance of the presence or absence of relationships between women in one or more works. (Suggestions: Naylor, "Etta Mae Johnson"; Broumas, "Song for Sanna"; shange, *for colored girls*)
8. Discuss how one or more stories and/or plays show the problems men and women have understanding each other. (Suggestions: Toomer, "Fern"; Slesinger, "Mother to Dinner"; Ibsen, *A Doll's House*)
9. Using one or more works, discuss how race, class, or ethnic identity shapes the experience of being a woman or being a man. (Suggestions: Baraka, "Beautiful Black Women"; Yamauchi, "And the Soul Shall Dance")
10. Explore the use of humor in one or more works. (Suggestions: Syfers, "Why I Want a Wife"; Corso, "Marriage"; Donne, "The Flea")

MONEY AND WORK

"Work makes life sweet," declares a woman interviewed in *The Life and Times of Rosie the Riveter*, a documentary film about American women workers during World War II. Between 1941 and 1945, many women had for the first time in their lives real, important, and well-paid work outside the home. It gave them independence, dignity, and pride. When the war ended and the men came back, the women were pushed out of their jobs and back into their kitchens, where they continued to work but now at a job which wasn't valued and for which they received no pay. What does this situation suggest about work and about how work and money are interwoven?

We probably all know the satisfaction of a job well done, whether it is a lawn mowed, a souffle that doesn't fall, or an essay finally completed. Further, there is the joy of the work itself, moment by moment, when you are entirely absorbed in what you are doing. We can see an example of this sort of nonalienated work in Barbara Smith's poem "The Bowl," about making bread, or in Robert Frost's "Two Tramps in Mudtime," where the speaker of the poem is enjoying his physical labor and doesn't want to give it up to the tramps who have asked to do it for pay. We see it again in "Tall Woman Love," in Carolyn Chute's description of Roberta's woodchopping. Nonalienated work is satisfying, engages us beyond any considerations of pay, and usually involves doing the job from start to finish—that is, we are able to see the result or product of our labor, have a sense of control and completion, and say, "I accomplished that."

The need for satisfying work is probably as basic and central to what it means to be human as is the urge to love. "Work makes life sweet." Though we might fantasize winning the lottery and never working again, how many of us could actually never work? We might give up our jobs as waitresses or computer technicians, but we would find some other satisfying activity like organic vegetable gardening or writing a book or sailing singlehandedly across the Pacific Ocean or doing some kind of political or community work—because, without work, most of us would go a little nuts. That gardening or writing, or making pottery or playing the piano, are usually seen as hobbies has mostly to do with the fact that people are not generally paid for these activities; but they are work nonetheless. Can you imagine a world in which we all were doing the kind of work we most wanted to do?

Why, then, do we generally put money and work together in the same thought? Work may be a basic human need, but what has that to do with money? Money is certainly a need, too, but it is a social or socialized rather than a purely human need. That is to say, we live in a time and in a society where money is the medium of exchange between work, regardless of our motivation, and everything else which we need. We work, get paid, and use the money to buy what will satisfy other basic needs. History, not human nature, has linked work to money. Visionary and utopian thinkers have repeatedly sought ways to free work from the grip of money.

B. Traven in "Assembly Line" shows us a situation in which one character, a North American investor, attempts to restructure a situation of nonalienated labor in order to maximize profit. The other main character, a Mexican farmer, is an artisan who weaves baskets in his spare time with, as he puts it, "my song in them and with bits of my soul woven into them." The conflict or tension in the story is between work as an expression of human creativity and work as a means of making money. Ultimately, of course, the investor would make most of the money, and the assembly-line process he plans would destroy much of the baskets' beauty and all of their individuality. It would also greatly decrease the artisan's satisfaction in making them. A number of other selections in "Money and Work" take up the theme of unsatisfying or alienated labor. Judy Grahn's poem, "Ella, in a square apron, on Highway 80," gives us a portrait of a tired and angry truck-stop waitress; Theodore Roethke's "Dolor" paints a terrifyingly static and colorless portrait of office work, emblematic of our bureaucratic and paper-choked society. Under certain conditions, though, even alienating work can be empowering. In the essay, "The Silk Workers," Agnes Smedley writes about her visit to a Chinese community whose economy is based on silk making. Because this work is thought to be best done by women, the women are in economic control; because their work is essential to the economic well-being of their community, they have a freedom, dignity, and self-confidence that are quite threatening to the male translator who accompanies Smedley.

Richard Wright in "The Man Who Went to Chicago" surveys bitterly the kind of jobs open to black men in the 1930s and the effect the available work has on their self-esteem. The kinds of work black Americans traditionally have been limited to is also treated in the play *Florence*. Kate Rushin, in her poem "The Black Back-Ups," writes about the unpraised but necessary labor of those people, usually women, singing behind the main vocalist on popular records. Ted Hughes in "Her Husband" delineates the hostility a mine worker feels for the wife he comes home to, as he ignores entirely the fact that she too has been working all day. "Let her suffer as he's suffered," he thinks. Because it is usually a) unpaid and b) woman's work, housework is often ignored or taken for granted.

And what about when there is no work? In an economy based on labor for wages, those who cannot find work fall between the cracks. Meridel LeSueur's essay, "Women on the Breadlines," and the episode from Tom Kromer's novel, *Waiting for Nothing*, are both set in the worst years of the Great Depression, 1932 to 1934. "Women on the Breadlines" treats the plight of unemployed women through character portraits of three representative types—an immigrant woman in her thirties, a young woman of eighteen or so, and a woman in her fifties with a number of children. Tom Kromer, who was himself a stiff or hobo during those same years, recounts in the episode from *Waiting for Nothing* an evening in the life of a penniless man we would now call a homeless or street person, as he searches for something to eat and a place to sleep. What happens when capitalism breaks down, as it did in a big way during the 1930s? In contrast to the realism of LeSueur and Kromer are William Carlos Williams's poem, "The Poor," which romanticizes poverty, and Carl Sandburg's poem "Fish Crier," which compares a street vendor's selling fish to ballerina Pavlova's joy in her dancing.

Money as a force or entity in itself, not in relation to work but to the commodities it can buy, is the subject of Toni Cade Bambara's story, "The Lesson," in which a number of poor black school children are taken on a window shopping expedition. Here they begin to learn of the luxuries that some people can afford, but that they cannot. The story is told from the point of view of one of the children, a young girl, and her resistance to this painful lesson is a central tension in the story. William Faulkner's story, "Spotted Horses," is also about money rather than work. In some parts of the South and West, until fairly recently, "horse trading" was almost synonymous with sharp practice. Making a good trade on a horse was a measure of shrewdness, and getting conned on a horse deal was a humiliation which one might have to live down for the rest of his (usually "his") life. "Spotted Horses" tells how a whole town was conned into giving up their money for a dream of pinto ponies, and asks where the responsibility falls when people spend their money for an illusion. In this story, we have moved very far from the simple exchange of work for money and money for goods.

Woven through this section on money and work is the concept of social class. What does it mean to be working class, middle class, upper class? What does it mean to be comfortably off instead of scrambling for a job? What does it mean to have privilege and choice, and what does it mean to do without? What does it mean to own a bank or a factory or, on the other hand, to have to sell your labor for wages? One angry and potentially revolutionary answer emerges in Bertolt Brecht's "A Worker Reads History," Berton Bailey's "The Worker," and Nazim Hikmet's "About Your Hands and Lies."

One's work and the social status that work confers do have a tendency to affect one's life outside of work. Focused on the subtleties of class relations is Carolyn Chute's "Tall Woman Love," portraying an encounter between a poor Maine farm woman and a male middle-class professional, from his point of view but on her territory. Alice Walker's "Everyday Use" considers class relations within a family when an upwardly mobile daughter comes home for a visit with her mother and sister. Like "Everyday Use," Tillie Olsen's "I Stand Here Ironing" gives us the perspective of a working-class mother thinking about her daughter. Olsen's character tries to account for the gap between the social definition of what it means to be a good mother and the grim necessities of her life as a woman who had to work outside the home, who had to leave her child so they could have a home and food, and who was often tired, irritable, and not available to her daughter. Again, the question of responsibility comes up. And guilt. If our notions of appropriate behavior are based on middle-class privilege, how is a person who struggles to get and keep a job, put food on the table and a roof over her head to judge herself? Arthur Miller's *Death of a Salesman* explores, from a male perspective, similar stresses around money and work and how those affect family life, since Willy Loman has dragged his wife and his sons into his fantasies about making it big. Gwendolyn Brooks's poem, "Bronzeville Woman in a Red Hat," is written by a black woman poet but from the point of view of a white upper middle-class housewife threatened by the power and vitality of the black woman she has just hired as a maid. Reading this poem, we might ask to what extent the *persona* or speaker of the poem is able to come to terms with her class and race prejudices.

In this section, we hear about money and work from the perspective of artisans, waitresses, silk workers, secretaries, prostitutes, housewives, horse traders, farmers, children, mineworkers and people who would like to have a job but don't. Work makes life sweet, but the combination of money and work is more complicated.

FICTION

TILLIE OLSEN (b. 1913)

Tillie Lerner was born in Omaha, Nebraska, quit high school to work, and during the Depression became a labor activist and also a writer. She married Jack Olsen, raised four children while continuing to work at a variety of jobs, and had little time to write until the 1950s. Among her works are the story collection Tell Me a Riddle *(1961); a novel* Yonnondio: From the Thirties *(published in 1974, but begun four decades earlier); and a collection of essays,* Silences *(1978).*

I Stand Here Ironing (1954)

I stand here ironing, and what you asked me moves tormented back and forth with the iron.

"I wish you would manage the time to come in and talk with me about your daughter. I'm sure you can help me understand her. She's a youngster who needs help and whom I'm deeply interested in helping."

"Who needs help." . . . Even if I came, what good would it do? You think because I am her mother I have a key, or that in some way you could use me as a key? She has lived for nineteen years. There is all that life that has happened outside of me, beyond me.

And when is there time to remember, to sift, to weigh, to estimate, to total? I will start and there will be an interruption and I will have to gather it all together again. Or I will become engulfed with all I did or did not do, with what should have been and what cannot be helped.

She was a beautiful baby. The first and only one of our five that was beautiful at birth. You do not guess how new and uneasy her tenancy in her now-loveliness. You did not know her all those years she was thought homely, or see her poring over her baby pictures, making me tell her over and over how beautiful she had been—and would be, I would tell her—and was now, to the seeing eye. But the seeing eyes were few or nonexistent. Including mine.

I nursed her. They feel that's important nowadays. I nursed all the children, but with her, with all the fierce rigidity of first motherhood, I did like the books then said. Though her cries battered me to trembling and my breasts ached with swollenness, I waited till the clock decreed.

Why do I put that first? I do not even know if it matters, or if it explains anything.

She was a beautiful baby. She blew shining bubbles of sound. She loved motion, loved light, loved color and music and textures. She would lie on the floor in her blue overalls patting the surface so hard in ecstasy her hands and feet would blur. She was a miracle to me, but when she was eight months old I had to leave her daytimes with the woman downstairs to whom she was no miracle at all, for I worked or looked for work and for Emily's father, who "could no longer endure" (he wrote in his good-bye note) "sharing want with us."

I was nineteen. It was the pre-relief, pre-WPA world of the depression. I would start running as soon as I got off the streetcar, running up the stairs, the place smelling sour, and awake or asleep to startle awake, when she saw me she would break into a clogged weeping that could not be comforted, a weeping I can hear yet.

After a while I found a job hashing at night so I could be with her days, and it was better. But it came to where I had to bring her to his family and leave her.

It took a long time to raise the money for her fare back. Then she got chicken pox and I had to wait longer. When she finally came, I hardly knew her, walking quick and nervous like her father, looking like her father, thin, and dressed in a shoddy red that yellowed her skin and glared at the pockmarks. All the baby loveliness gone.

She was two. Old enough for nursery school they said, and I did not know then what I know now—the fatigue of the long day, and the lacerations of group life in the kinds of nurseries that are only parking places for children.

Except that it would have made no difference if I had known. It was the only place there was. It was the only way we could be together, the only way I could hold a job.

And even without knowing, I knew. I knew the teacher that was evil because all these years it has curdled into my memory, the little boy hunched in the corner, her rasp, "why aren't you outside, because Alvin hits you? that's no reason, go out, scaredy." I knew Emily hated it even if she did not clutch and implore "don't go Mommy" like the other children, mornings.

She always had a reason why we should stay home. Momma, you look sick. Momma, I feel sick. Momma, the teachers aren't there today, they're sick. Momma, we can't go, there was a fire there last night. Momma, it's a holiday today, no school, they told me.

But never a direct protest, never rebellion. I think of our others in their three-, four-year-oldness—the explosions, the tempers, the denunciations, the demands—and I feel suddenly ill. I put the iron down. What in me demanded that goodness in her? And what was the cost, the cost to her of such goodness?

The old man living in the back once said in his gentle way: "You should smile at Emily more when you look at her." What *was* in my face when I looked at her? I loved her. There were all the acts of love.

It was only with the others I remembered what he said, and it was the face of joy, and not of care or tightness or worry I turned to them— too late for Emily. She does not smile easily, let alone almost always as her brothers and sisters do. Her face is closed and sombre, but when she wants, how fluid. You must have seen it in her pantomimes, you spoke of her rare gift for comedy on the stage that rouses a laughter out of the audience so dear they applaud and applaud and do not want to let her go.

Where does it come from, that comedy? There was none of it in her when she came back to me that second time, after I had had to send her away again. She had a new daddy now to learn to love, and I think perhaps it was a better time.

Except when we left her alone nights, telling ourselves she was old enough.

"Can't you go some other time, Mommy, like tomorrow?" she would ask. "Will it be just a little while you'll be gone? Do you promise?"

The time we came back, the front door open, the clock on the floor in the hall. She rigid awake. "It wasn't just a little while. I didn't cry. Three times I called you, just three times, and then I ran downstairs to open the door so you could come faster. The clock talked loud. I threw it away, it scared me what it talked."

She said the clock talked loud again that night I went to the hospital to have Susan. She was delirious with the fever that comes before red measles, but she was fully conscious all the week I was gone and the week after we were home when she could not come near the new baby or me.

She did not get well. She stayed skeleton thin, not wanting to eat, and night after night she had nightmares. She would call for me, and I would rouse from exhaustion to sleepily call back: "You're all right, darling, go to sleep, it's just a dream," and if she still called, in a sterner voice, "now go to sleep, Emily, there's nothing to hurt you." Twice, only twice, when I had to get up for Susan anyhow, I went in to sit with her.

Now when it is too late (as if she would let me hold and comfort her like I do the others) I get up and go to her at once at her moan or restless stirring. "Are you awake, Emily? Can I get you something?" And the answer is always the same: "No, I'm all right, go back to sleep, Mother."

They persuaded me at the clinic to send her away to a convalescent home in the country where "she can have the kind of food and care you can't manage for her, and you'll be free to concentrate on the new baby." They still send children to that place. I see pictures on the society page of sleek young women planning affairs to raise money for it, or dancing at the affairs, or decorating Easter eggs or filling Christmas stockings for the children.

They never have a picture of the children so I do not know if the girls still wear those gigantic red bows and the ravaged looks on the every other Sunday when parents can come to visit "unless otherwise notified"—as we were notified the first six weeks.

Oh it is a handsome place, green lawns and tall trees and fluted flower beds. High up on the balconies of each cottage the children stand, the girls in their red bows and white dresses, the boys in white suits and giant red ties. The parents stand below shrieking up to be heard and the children shriek down to be heard, and between them the invisible wall "Not To Be Contaminated by Parental Germs or Physical Affection."

There was a tiny girl who always stood hand in hand with Emily. Her parents never came. One visit she was gone. "They moved her to Rose Cottage" Emily shouted in explanation. "They don't like you to love anybody here."

She wrote once a week, the labored writing of a seven-year-old. "I am fine. How is the baby. If I write my leter nicly I will have a star. Love." There never was a star. We wrote every other day, letters she could never hold or keep but only hear read—once. "We simply do not have room for children to keep any personal possessions," they patiently explained when we pieced one Sunday's shrieking together to plead how much it would mean to Emily, who loved so to keep things, to be allowed to keep her letters and cards.

Each visit she looked frailer. "She isn't eating," they told us.

(They had runny eggs for breakfast or mush with lumps, Emily said later, I'd hold it in my mouth and not swallow. Nothing ever tasted good, just when they had chicken.)

It took us eight months to get her released home, and only the fact that she gained back so little of her seven lost pounds convinced the social worker.

I used to try to hold and love her after she came back, but her body would stay stiff, and after a while she'd push away. She ate little. Food sickened her, and I think much of life too. Oh she had physical lightness and brightness, twinkling by on skates, bouncing like a ball up and down up and down over the jump rope, skimming over the hill; but these were momentary.

She fretted about her appearance, thin and dark and foreign-looking at a time when every little girl was supposed to look or thought she should look a chubby blonde replica of Shirley Temple. The doorbell sometimes rang for her, but no one seemed to come and play in the house or be a best friend. Maybe because we moved so much.

There was a boy she loved painfully through two school semesters. Months later she told me how she had taken pennies from my purse to buy him candy. "Licorice was his favorite and I brought him some every day, but he still liked Jennifer better'n me. Why, Mommy?" The kind of question for which there is no answer.

School was a worry to her. She was not glib or quick in a world where glibness and quickness were easily confused with ability to learn. To her overworked and exasperated teachers she was an overconscientious "slow learner" who kept trying to catch up and was absent entirely too often.

I let her be absent, though sometimes the illness was imaginary. How different from my now-strictness about attendance with the others. I wasn't working. We had a new baby, I was home anyhow. Sometimes, after Susan grew old enough, I would keep her home from school, too, to have them all together.

Mostly Emily had asthma, and her breathing, harsh and labored, would fill the house with a curiously tranquil sound. I would bring the two old dresser mirrors and her boxes of collections to her bed. She would select beads and single earrings, bottle tops and shells, dried flowers and pebbles, old postcards and scraps, all sorts of oddments; then she and Susan would play Kingdom, setting up landscapes and furniture, peopling them with action.

Those were the only times of peaceful companionship between her and Susan. I have edged away from it, that poisonous feeling between them, that terrible balancing of hurts and needs I had to do between the two, and did so badly, those earlier years.

Oh there are conflicts between the others too, each one human, needing, demanding, hurting, taking—but only between Emily and Susan, no, Emily toward Susan that corroding resentment. It seems so obvious on the surface, yet it is not obvious. Susan, the second child, Susan, golden- and curly-haired and chubby, quick and articulate and assured, everything in appearance and manner Emily was not; Susan, not able to resist Emily's precious things, losing or sometimes clumsily breaking them; Susan telling jokes and riddles to company for applause while Emily sat silent (to say to me later: that was *my* riddle, Mother, I told it to Susan); Susan, who for all the five years' difference in age was just a year behind Emily in developing physically.

I am glad for that slow physical development that widened the difference between her and her contemporaries, though she suffered over it. She was too vulnerable for that terrible world of youthful competition, of preening and parading, of constant measuring of yourself against every other, of envy, "If I had that copper hair," "If I had that skin. . . ." She tormented herself enough about not looking like the others, there was enough of the unsureness, the having to be conscious of words before you speak, the constant caring—what are they thinking of me? without having it all magnified by the merciless physical drives.

Ronnie is calling. He is wet and I change him. It is rare there is such a cry now. That time of motherhood is almost behind me when the ear is not one's own but must always be racked and listening for the child cry, the child call. We sit for a while and I hold him, looking out over the city spread in charcoal with its soft aisles of light. "*Shoogily*," he breathes and curls closer. I carry him back to bed, asleep. *Shoogily.* A funny word, a family word, inherited from Emily, invented by her to say: *comfort.*

In this and other ways she leaves her seal, I say aloud. And startle at my saying it. What do I mean? What did I start to gather together, to try and make coherent? I was at the terrible, growing years. War years. I do not remember them well. I was working, there were four smaller ones now, there was not time for her. She had to help be a mother, and housekeeper, and shopper. She had to set her seal. Mornings of crisis and near hysteria trying to get lunches packed, hair combed, coats and shoes found, everyone to school or Child Care on time, the baby ready for transportation. And always the paper scribbled on by a smaller one, the book looked at by Susan then mislaid, the homework not done. Running out to that huge school where she was one, she was lost, she was a drop; suffering over the unpreparedness, stammering and unsure in her classes.

There was so little time left at night after the kids were bedded down. She would struggle over books, always eating (it was in those years she developed her enormous appetite that is legendary in our family) and I would be ironing, or preparing food for the next day, or writing V-mail to Bill, or tending the baby. Sometimes, to make me laugh, or out of her despair, she would imitate happenings or types at school.

I think I said once: "Why don't you do something like this in the school amateur show?" One morning she phoned me at work, hardly understandable through the weeping: "Mother, I did it. I won, I won; they gave me first prize; they clapped and clapped and wouldn't let me go."

Now suddenly she was Somebody, and as imprisoned in her difference as she had been in anonymity.

She began to be asked to perform at other high schools, even in colleges, then at city and statewide affairs. The first one we went to, I only recognized her that first moment when thin, shy, she almost drowned herself into the curtains. Then: Was this Emily? The control, the command, the convulsing and deadly clowning, the spell, then the roaring, stamping audience, unwilling to let this rare and precious laughter out of their lives.

Afterwards: You ought to do something about her with a gift like that— but without money or knowing how, what does one do? We have left it all to her, and the gift has as often eddied inside, clogged and clotted, as been used and growing.

She is coming. She runs up the stairs two at a time with her light graceful step, and I know she is happy tonight. Whatever it was that occasioned your call did not happen today.

"Aren't you ever going to finish the ironing, Mother? Whistler painted his mother in a rocker. I'd have to paint mine standing over an ironing board." This is one of her communicative nights and she tells me everything and nothing as she fixes herself a plate of food out of the icebox.

She is so lovely. Why did you want me to come in at all? Why were you concerned? She will find her way.

She starts up the stairs to bed. "Don't get me up with the rest in the morning." "But I thought you were having midterms." "Oh, those," she comes back in, kisses me, and says quite lightly, "in a couple of years when we'll all be atom-dead they won't matter a bit."

She has said it before. She *believes* it. But because I have been dredging the past, and all that compounds a human being is so heavily and meaningful in me, I cannot endure it tonight.

I will never total it all. I will never come in to say: She was a child seldom smiled at. Her father left me before she was a year old. I had to work her first six years when there was work, or I sent her home and to his relatives. There were years she had care she hated. She was dark and thin and foreign-looking in a world where the prestige went to blondeness and curly hair and dimples, she was slow where glibness was prized. She was a child of anxious, not proud, love. We were poor and could not afford for her the soil of easy growth. I was a young mother, I was a distracted mother. There were the other children pushing up, demanding. Her younger sister seemed all that she was not. There were years she did not want me to touch her. She kept too much in herself, her life was such she had to keep too much in herself. My wisdom came too late. She has much to her and probably little will come of it. She is a child of her age, of depression, of war, of fear.

Let her be. So all that is in her will not bloom—but in how many does it? There is still enough left to live by. Only help her to know— help make it so there is cause for her to know—that she is more than this dress on the ironing board, helpless before the iron.

Study and Discussion Questions

1. How does ironing function as a symbol in this story?
2. How does the narrator feel about herself as a mother?
3. What regrets does the mother have about Emily's childhood?
4. "And when is there time . . .," the mother says. How does the paragraph that begins this way anticipate what happens in the story?
5. What forms did the narrator's love for her daughter take?
6. What connections can you make between Emily's gift for comedy and her early life?

Writing Exercises

1. How did economic factors affect the narrator's relationship with her daughter?
2. Who is the narrator's imagined audience, the "you" of the opening sentence? What is the narrator's tone?
3. If Emily were to write an account of these same years, what might she say?

WILLIAM FAULKNER (1897–1962)

William Faulkner grew up in Oxford, Mississippi. His ancestors included a great-grandfather who was a famous Civil War colonel and popular novelist. Little interested in high school, Faulkner dropped out and, because he was too short for the U.S. Army, enlisted in the Canadian Royal Air Force. He studied briefly at the University of Mississippi, held odd jobs in New York City and then back in Oxford, and, in 1924, published a volume of poetry. He then turned to fiction and published the novel Soldier's Pay *in 1926.* Sartoris *(1929) was the first of his many novels set in the fictional Yokna-patawpha County in Mississippi, and* The Sound and the Fury *(1929) and* As I Lay Dying *(1930) followed soon after. Among Faulkner's other major novels are* Sanctuary *(1931),* Light in August *(1932), and* Absalom, Absalom! *(1936). He received the Nobel Prize for literature in 1950.*

Spotted Horses   (1931)

I

Yes, sir. Flem Snopes has filled that whole country full of spotted horses. You can hear folks running them all day and all night, whooping and hollering, and the horses running back and forth across them little wooden bridges ever now and then kind of like thunder. Here I was this morning pretty near half way to town, with the team ambling along and me setting in the buckboard about half asleep, when all of a sudden something come swurging up outen the bushes and jumped the road clean, without touching hoof to it. It flew right over my team, big as a billboard and flying through the air like a hawk. It taken me thirty minutes to stop my team and untangle the harness and the buckboard and hitch them up again.

That Flem Snopes. I be dog if he ain't a case, now. One morning about ten years ago, the boys was just getting settled down on Varner's porch for a little talk and tobacco, when here come Flem out from behind the counter, with his coat off and his hair all parted, like he might have been clerking for Varner for ten years already. Folks all knowed him; it was a big family of them about five miles down the bottom. That year, at least. Share-cropping. They never stayed on any place over a year. Then they would move on to another place, with the chap or maybe the twins of that year's litter. It was a regular nest of them. But Flem. The rest of them stayed tenant farmers, moving ever year, but here come Flem one day, walking out from behind Jody Varner's counter like he owned it. And he wasn't there but a year or two before folks knowed that, if him and Jody was both still in that store in ten years more, it would be Jody clerking for Flem Snopes. Why, that fellow could make a nickel where it wasn't but four cents to begin with. He skun me in two trades, myself, and the fellow that can do that, I just hope he'll get rich before I do; that's all.

All right. So here Flem was, clerking at Varner's, making a nickel here and there and not telling nobody about it. No, sir. Folks never knowed when Flem got the better of somebody lessen the fellow he beat told it. He'd just set there in the store-chair, chewing his tobacco and keeping his own business to hisself, until about a week later we'd find out it was somebody else's business he was keeping to hisself—provided the fellow he trimmed was mad enough to tell it. That's Flem.

We give him ten years to own ever thing Jody Varner had. But he never waited no ten years. I reckon you-all know that gal of Uncle Billy Varner's, the youngest one; Eula. Jody's sister. Ever Sunday ever yellow-wheeled buggy and curried riding horse in that country would be hitched to Bill Varner's fence, and the young bucks setting on the porch, swarming around Eula like bees around a honey pot. One of these here kind of big, soft-looking gals that could giggle richer than plowed new-ground. Wouldn't none of them leave before the others, and so they would set there on the porch until time to go home, with some of them with nine and ten miles to ride and then get up tomorrow and go back to the field. So they would all leave together and they would ride in a clump down to the creek ford and hitch them curried horses and yellow-wheeled buggies and get out and fight one another. Then they would get in the buggies again and go on home.

Well, one day about a year ago, one of them yellow-wheeled buggies and one of them curried saddle-horses quit this country. We heard they was heading for Texas. The next day Uncle Billy and Eula and Flem come in to town in Uncle Bill's surrey, and when they come back, Flem and Eula was married. And on the next day we heard that two more of them yellow-wheeled buggies had left the country. They mought have gone to Texas, too. It's a big place.

Anyway, about a month after the wedding, Flem and Eula went to Texas, too. They was gone pretty near a year. Then one day last month, Eula come back, with a baby. We figured up, and we decided that it was as well-growed a three-months-old baby as we ever see. It can already pull up on a chair. I reckon Texas makes big men quick, being a big place. Anyway, if it keeps on like it started, it'll be chewing tobacco and voting time it's eight years old.

And so last Friday here come Flem himself. He was on a wagon with another fellow. The other fellow had one of these two-gallon hats and a ivory-handled pistol and a box of gingersnaps sticking out of his hind pocket, and tied to the tail-gate of the wagon was about two dozen of them Texas ponies, hitched to one another with barbed wire. They was colored like parrots and they was quiet as doves, and ere a one of them would kill you quick as a rattlesnake. Nere a one of them had two eyes the same color, and nere a one of them had ever see a bridle, I reckon; and when that Texas man got down offen the wagon and walked up to them to show how gentle they was, one of them cut his vest clean offen him, same as with a razor.

Flem had done already disappeared; he had went on to see his wife, I reckon, and to see if that ere baby had done gone on to the field to help Uncle Billy plow maybe. It was the Texas man that taken the horses on to Mrs. Littlejohn's lot. He had a little trouble at first, when they come to the gate, because they hadn't never see a fence before, and when he finally got them in and taken a pair of wire cutters and unhitched them and got them into the barn and poured some shell corn into the trough, they durn nigh tore down the barn. I reckon they thought that shell corn was bugs, maybe. So he left them in the lot and he announced that the auction would begin at sunup to-morrow.

That night we was setting on Mrs. Littlejohn's porch. You-all mind the moon was nigh full that night, and we could watch them spotted varmints swirling along the fence and back and forth across the lot same as minnows in a pond. And then now and then they would all kind of huddle up against the barn and rest themselves by biting and kicking one another. We would hear a squeal, and then a set of hoofs would go Bam! against the barn, like a pistol. It sounded just like a fellow with a pistol, in a nest of cattymounts,[1] taking his time.

II

It wasn't ere a man knowed yet if Flem owned them things or not. They just knowed one thing: that they wasn't never going to know for sho if Flem did or not, or if maybe he didn't just get on that wagon at the edge of town, for the ride or not. Even Eck Snopes didn't know, Flem's own cousin. But wasn't nobody surprised at that. We knowed that Flem would skin Eck quick as he would ere a one of us.

They was there by sunup next morning, some of them come twelve and sixteen miles, with seed-money tied up in tobacco sacks in their overalls, standing along the fence, when the Texas man come out of Mrs. Littlejohn's after breakfast and clumb onto the gate post with that ere white pistol butt sticking outen his hind pocket. He taken a new box of gingersnaps outen his pocket and bit the end offen it like a cigar and spit out the paper, and said the auction was open. And still they was coming up in wagons and a horse- and mule-back and hitching the teams across the road and coming to the fence. Flem wasn't nowhere in sight.

But he couldn't get them started. He begun to work on Eck, because Eck holp him last night to get them into the barn and feed them that shell corn. Eck got out just in time. He come outen that barn like a chip

---

[1] Wildcats.

on the crest of a busted dam of water, and clumb into the wagon just in time.

He was working on Eck when Henry Armstid come up in his wagon. Eck was saying he was skeered to bid on one of them, because he might get it, and the Texas man says, "Them ponies? Them little horses?" He clumb down offen the gate post and went toward the horses. They broke and run, and him following them, kind of chirping to them, with his hand out like he was fixing to catch a fly, until he got three or four of them cornered. Then he jumped into them, and then we couldn't see nothing for a while because of the dust. It was a big cloud of it, and them blare-eyed, spotted things swoaring outen it twenty foot to a jump, in forty directions without counting up. Then the dust settled and there they was, that Texas man and the horse. He had its head twisted clean around like a owl's head. Its legs was braced and it was trembling like a new bride and groaning like a saw mill, and him holding its head wrung clean around on its neck so it was snuffing sky. "Look it over," he says, with his heels dug too and that white pistol sticking outen his pocket and his neck swole up like a spreading adder's until you could just tell what he was saying, cussing the horse and talking to us all at once: "Look him over, the fiddle-headed son of fourteen fathers. Try him, buy him; you will get the best—" Then it was all dust again, and we couldn't see nothing but spotted hide and mane, and that ere Texas man's boot-heels like a couple of walnuts on two strings, and after a while that two-gallon hat come sailing out like a fat old hen crossing a fence.

When the dust settled again, he was just getting outen the far fence corner, brushing himself off. He come and got his hat and brushed it off and come and clumb onto the gate post again. He was breathing hard. He taken the gingersnap box outen his pocket and et one, breathing hard. The hammer-head horse was still running round and round the lot like a merry-go-round at a fair. That was when Henry Armstid come shoving up to the gate in them patched overalls and one of them dangle-armed shirts of hisn. Hadn't nobody noticed him until then. We was all watching the Texas man and the horses. Even Mrs. Littlejohn; she had done come out and built a fire under the wash-pot in her back yard, and she would stand at the fence a while and then go back into the house and come out again with a arm full of wash and stand at the fence again. Well, here come Henry shoving up, and then we see Mrs. Armstid right behind him, in that ere faded wrapper and sunbonnet and them tennis shoes. "Git on back to that wagon," Henry says.

"Henry," she says.

"Here, boys," the Texas man says; "make room for missus to git up and see. Come on, Henry," he says; "here's your chance to buy that saddle-horse missus has been wanting. What about ten dollars, Henry?"

"Henry," Mrs. Armstid says. She put her hand on Henry's arm. Henry knocked her hand down.

"Git on back to that wagon, like I told you," he says.

Mrs. Armstid never moved. She stood behind Henry, with her hands rolled into her dress, not looking at nothing. "He hain't no more despair than to buy one of them things," she says. "And us not five dollars ahead of the pore house, he hain't no more despair." It was the truth, too. They ain't never made more than a bare living offen that place of theirs, and them with four chaps and the very clothes they wears she earns by weaving by the firelight at night while Henry's asleep.

"Shut your mouth and git on back to that wagon," Henry says. "Do you want I taken a wagon stake to you here in the big road?"

Well, that Texas man taken one look at her. Then he begun on Eck again, like Henry wasn't even there. But Eck was skeered. "I can git me a snapping turtle or a water moccasin for nothing. I ain't going to buy none."

So the Texas man said he would give Eck a horse. "To start the auction, and because you holp me last night. If you'll start the bidding on the next horse," he says, "I'll give you that fiddle-head horse."

I wish you could have seen them, standing there with their seed-money in their pockets, watching that Texas man give Eck Snopes a live horse, all fixed to call him a fool if he taken it or not. Finally Eck says he'll take it. "Only I just starts the bidding," he says. "I don't have to buy the next one lessen I ain't overtopped." The Texas man said all right, and Eck bid a dollar on the next one, with Henry Armstid standing there with his mouth already open, watching Eck and the Texas man like a mad-dog or something. "A dollar," Eck says.

The Texas man looked at Eck. His mouth was already open too, like he had started to say something and what he was going to say had up and died on him. "A dollar?" he says. "One dollar? You mean, *one* dollar, Eck?"

"Durn it," Eck says; "two dollars, then."

Well, sir, I wish you could a seen that Texas man. He taken out that gingersnap box and held it up and looked into it, careful, like it might have been a diamond ring in it, or a spider. Then he throwed it away and wiped his face with a bandanna. "Well," he says. "Well, Two dollars. Two dollars. Is your pulse all right, Eck?" he says. "Do you have ager-sweats[2] at night, maybe?" he says. "Well," he says, "I got to take it. But are you boys going to stand there and see Eck get two horses at a dollar a head?"

That done it. I be dog if he wasn't nigh as smart as Flem Snopes. He hadn't no more than got the words outen his mouth before here was Henry Armstid, waving his hand. "Three dollars," Henry says. Mrs. Armstid tried to hold him again. He knocked her hand off, shoving up to the gate post.

"Mister," Mrs. Armstid says, "we got chaps in the house and not corn to feed the stock. We got five dollars I earned my chaps a-weaving after dark, and him snoring in the bed. And he hain't no more despair."

---

[2] Ague, cold sweats.

"Henry bids three dollars," the Texas man says. "Raise him a dollar, Eck, and the horse is yours."

"Henry," Mrs. Armstid says.

"Raise him, Eck," the Texas man says.

"Four dollars," Eck says.

"Five dollars," Henry says, shaking his fist. He shoved up right under the gate post. Mrs. Armstid was looking at the Texas man too.

"Mister," she says, "if you take that five dollars I earned my chaps a-weaving for one of them things, it'll be a curse onto you and yourn during all the time of man."

But it wasn't no stopping Henry. He had shoved up, waving his fist at the Texas man. He opened it; the money was in nickels and quarters, and one dollar bill that looked like a cow's cud. "Five dollars," he says. "And the man that raises it'll have to beat my head off, or I'll beat hisn."

"All right," the Texas man says. "Five dollars is bid. But don't you shake your hand at me."

III

It taken till nigh sundown before the last one was sold. He got them hotted up once and the bidding got up to seven dollars and a quarter, but most of them went around three or four dollars, him setting on the gate post and picking the horses out one at a time by mouth-word, and Mrs. Littlejohn pumping up and down at the tub and stopping and coming to the fence for a while and going back to the tub again. She had done got done too, and the wash was hung on the line in the back yard, and we could smell supper cooking. Finally they was all sold; he swapped the last two and the wagon for a buckboard.

We was all kind of tired, but Henry Armstid looked more like a mad-dog than ever. When he bought, Mrs. Armstid had went back to the wagon, setting in it behind them two rabbit-sized, bone-pore mules, and the wagon itself looking like it would fall all to pieces soon as the mules moved. Henry hadn't even waited to pull it outen the road; it was still in the middle of the road and her setting in it, not looking at nothing, ever since this morning.

Henry was right up against the gate. He went up to the Texas man. "I bought a horse and I paid cash," Henry says. "And yet you expect me to stand around here until they are all sold before I can get my horse. I'm going to take my horse outen that lot."

The Texas man looked at Henry. He talked like he might have been asking for a cup of coffee at the table. "Take your horse," he says.

Then Henry quit looking at the Texas man. He begun to swallow, holding onto the gate. "Ain't you going to help me?" he says.

"It ain't my horse," the Texas man says.

Henry never looked at the Texas man again, he never looked at nobody. "Who'll help me catch my horse?" he says. Never nobody said nothing. "Bring the plowline," Henry says. Mrs. Armstid got outen the wagon and brought the plowline. The Texas man got down offen the post. The woman made to pass him, carrying the rope.

"Don't you go in there, missus," the Texas man says.

Henry opened the gate. He didn't look back. "Come on here," he says.

"Don't you go in there, missus," the Texas man says.

Mrs. Armstid wasn't looking at nobody, neither, with her hands across her middle, holding the rope. "I reckon I better," she says. Her and Henry went into the lot. The horses broke and run. Henry and Mrs. Armstid followed.

"Get him into the corner," Henry says. They got Henry's horse cornered finally, and Henry taken the rope, but Mrs. Armstid let the horse get out. They hemmed it up again, but Mrs. Armstid let it get out again, and Henry turned and hit her with the rope. "Why didn't you head him back?" Henry says. He hit her again. "Why didn't you?" It was about that time I looked around and see Flem Snopes standing there.

It was the Texas man that done something. He moved fast for a big man. He caught the rope before Henry could hit the third time, and Henry whirled and made like he would jump at the Texas man. But he never jumped. The Texas man went and taken Henry's arm and led him outen the lot. Mrs. Armstid come behind them and the Texas man taken some money outen his pocket and he give it into Mrs. Armstid's hand. "Get him into the wagon and take him on home," the Texas man says, like he might have been telling them he enjoyed his supper.

Then here come Flem. "What's that for, Buck?" Flem says.

"Thinks he bought one of them ponies," the Texas man says. "Get him on away, missus."

But Henry wouldn't go. "Give him back that money," he says. "I bought that horse and I aim to have him if I have to shoot him."

And there was Flem, standing there with his hands in his pockets, chewing, like he had just happened to be passing.

"You take your money and I take my horse," Henry says. "Give it back to him," he says to Mrs. Armstid.

"You don't own no horse of mine," the Texas man says. "Get him on home, missus."

Then Henry seen Flem. "You got something to do with these horses," he says. "I bought one. Here's the money for it." He taken the bill outen Mrs. Armstid's hand. He offered it to Flem. "I bought one. Ask him. Here. Here's the money," he says, giving the bill to Flem.

When Flem taken the money, the Texas man dropped the rope he had snatched outen Henry's hand. He had done sent Eck Snopes's boy up to the store for another box of gingersnaps, and he taken the box outen his pocket and looked into it. It was empty and he dropped it on the ground. "Mr. Snopes will have your money for you to-morrow," he says to Mrs.

Armstid. "You can get it from him to-morrow. He don't own no horse. You get him into the wagon and get him on home." Mrs. Armstid went back to the wagon and got in. "Where's that ere buckboard I bought?" the Texas man says. It was after sundown then. And then Mrs. Littlejohn come out on the porch and rung the supper bell.

IV

I come on in and et supper. Mrs. Littlejohn would bring in a pan of bread or something, then she would go out to the porch a minute and come back and tell us. The Texas man had hitched his team to the buckboard he had swapped them last two horses for, and him and Flem had gone, and then she told that the rest of them that never had ropes had went back to the store with I.O. Snopes to get some ropes, and wasn't nobody at the gate but Henry Armstid, and Mrs. Armstid setting in the wagon in the road, and Eck Snopes and that boy of hisn. "I don't care how many of them fool men gets killed by them things," Mrs. Littlejohn says, "but I ain't going to let Eck Snopes take that boy into that lot again." So she went down to the gate, but she come back without the boy or Eck neither.

"It ain't no need to worry about that boy," I says. "He's charmed." He was right behind Eck last night when Eck went to help feed them. The whole drove of them jumped clean over that boy's head and never touched him. It was Eck that touched him. Eck snatched him into the wagon and taken a rope and frailed the tar outen him.

So I had done et and went to my room and was undressing, long as I had a long trip to make next day; I was trying to sell a machine to Mrs. Bundren up past Whiteleaf; when Henry Armstid opened that gate and went in by hisself. They couldn't make him wait for the balance of them to get back with their ropes. Eck Snopes said he tried to make Henry wait, but Henry wouldn't do it. Eck said Henry walked right up to them and that when they broke, they run clean over Henry like a haymow breaking down. Eck said he snatched that boy of hisn out of the way just in time and that them things went through that gate like a creek flood and into the wagons and teams hitched side the road, busting wagon tongues and snapping harness like it was fishing-line, with Mrs. Armstid still setting in their wagon in the middle of it like something carved outen wood. Then they scattered, wild horses and tame mules with pieces of harness and single trees dangling offen them, both ways up and down the road.

"There goes ourn, paw!" Eck says his boy said. "There it goes, into Mrs. Littlejohn's house." Eck says it run right up the steps and into the house like a boarder late for supper. I reckon so. Anyway, I was in my room, in my underclothes, with one sock on and one sock in my hand, leaning out the window when the commotion busted out, when I heard something run into the melodeon in the hall; it sounded like a railroad engine. Then the door to my room come sailing in like when you throw a tin bucket top into the wind and I looked over my shoulder and see something that looked like a fourteen-foot pinwheel a-blaring its eyes at me. It had to blare them fast, because I was already done jumped out the window.

I reckon it was anxious, too. I reckon it hadn't never seen barbed wire or shell corn before, but I know it hadn't never seen underclothes before, or maybe it was a sewing-machine agent it hadn't never seen. Anyway, it swirled and turned to run back up the hall and outen the house, when it met Eck Snopes and that boy just coming in, carrying a rope. It swirled again and run down the hall and out the back door just in time to meet Mrs. Littlejohn. She had just gathered up the clothes she had washed, and she was coming onto the back porch with a armful of washing in one hand and a scrubbing-board in the other, when the horse skidded up to her, trying to stop and swirl again. It never taken Mrs. Littlejohn no time a-tall.

"Git outen here, you son," she says. She hit it across the face with the scrubbing-board; that ere scrubbing-board split as neat as ere a axe could have done it, and when the horse swirled to run back up the hall, she hit it again with what was left of the scrubbing-board, not on the head this time. "And stay out," she says.

Eck and that boy was half-way down the hall by this time. I reckon that horse looked like a pinwheel to Eck too. "Git to hell outen here, Ad!" Eck says. Only there wasn't time. Eck dropped flat on his face, but the boy never moved. The boy was about a yard tall maybe, in overhalls just like Eck's; that horse swoared over his head without touching a hair. I saw that, because I was just coming back up the front steps, still carrying that ere sock and still in my underclothes, when the horse come onto the porch again. It taken one look at me and swirled again and run to the end of the porch and jumped the banisters and the lot fence like a hen-hawk and lit in the lot running and went out the gate again and jumped eight or ten upside-down wagons and went on down the road. It was a full moon then. Mrs. Armstid was still setting in the wagon like she had done been carved outen wood and left there and forgot.

That horse. It ain't never missed a lick. It was going about forty miles a hour when it come to the bridge over the creek. It would have had a clear road, but it so happened that Vernon Tull was already using the bridge when it got there. He was coming back from town; he hadn't heard about the auction; him and his wife and three daughters and Mrs. Tull's aunt, all setting in chairs in the wagon bed, and all asleep, including the mules. They waked up when the horse hit the bridge one time, but Tull said the first he knew was when the mules tried to turn the wagon around in the middle of the bridge and he seen that spotted varmint run right twixt the mules and run up the wagon tongue like a squirrel. He said he just had time to hit it across the face with his whip-stock, because about that time the mules turned the wagon around on that ere one-way bridge and that horse clumb across one of the mules and jumped down onto the bridge again and went on, with Vernon standing up in the wagon and kicking at it.

Tull said the mules turned in the harness and clumb back into the wagon too, with Tull trying to beat them out again, with the reins wrapped around his wrist. After that he says all he seen was overturned chairs and womenfolks' legs and white drawers shining in the moonlight, and his mules and that spotted horse going on up the road like a ghost.

The mules jerked Tull outen the wagon and drug him a spell on the bridge before the reins broke. They thought at first that he was dead, and while they was kneeling around him, picking the bridge splinters outen him, here come Eck and that boy, still carrying the rope. They was running and breathing a little hard. "Where'd he go?" Eck says.

V

I went back and got my pants and shirt and shoes on just in time to go and help get Henry Armstid outen the trash in the lot. I be dog if he didn't look like he was dead, with his head hanging back and his teeth showing in the moonlight, and a little rim of white under his eyelids. We could still hear them horses, here and there; hadn't none of them got more than four-five miles away yet, not knowing the country, I reckon. So we could hear them and folks yelling now and then: "Whooey. Head him!"

We toted Henry into Mrs. Littlejohn's. She was in the hall; she hadn't put down the armful of clothes. She taken one look at us, and she laid down the busted scrubbing-board and taken up the lamp and opened a empty door. "Bring him in here," she says.

We toted him in and laid him on the bed. Mrs. Littlejohn set the lamp on the dresser, still carrying the clothes. "I'll declare, you men," she says. Our shadows was way up the wall, tiptoeing too; we could hear ourselves breathing. "Better get his wife," Mrs. Littlejohn says. She went out, carrying the clothes.

"I reckon we had," Quick says. "Go get her, somebody."

"Whyn't you go?" Winterbottom says.

"Let Ernest git her," Durley says. "He lives neighbors with them."

Ernest went to fetch her. I be dog if Henry didn't look like he was dead. Mrs. Littlejohn come back, with a kettle and some towels. She went to work on Henry, and then Mrs. Armstid and Ernest come in. Mrs. Armstid come to the foot of the bed and stood there, with her hands rolled into her apron, watching what Mrs. Littlejohn was doing, I reckon.

"You men git outen the way," Mrs. Littlejohn says. "Git outside," she says. "See if you can't find something else to play with that will kill some more of you."

"Is he dead?" Winterbottom says.

"It ain't your fault if he ain't," Mrs. Littlejohn says. "Go tell Will Varner to come up here. I reckon a man ain't so different from a mule, come long come short. Except maybe a mule's got more sense."

We went to get Uncle Billy. It was a full moon. We could hear them, now and then, four mile away: "Whooey. Head him." The country was full of them, one on ever wooden bridge in the land, running across it like thunder: "Whooey. There he goes. Head him."

We hadn't got far before Henry begun to scream. I reckon Mrs. Littlejohn's water had brung him to; anyway, he wasn't dead. We went on to Uncle Billy's. The house was dark. We called to him, and after a while the window opened and Uncle Billy put his head out, peart as a peckerwood[3], listening. "Are they still trying to catch them durn rabbits?" he says.

He come down, with his britches on over his night-shirt and his suspenders dangling, carrying his horse-doctoring grip. "Yes, sir," he says, cocking his head like a woodpecker; "They're still a-trying."

We could hear Henry before we reached Mrs. Littlejohn's. He was going Ah-Ah-Ah. We stopped in the yard. Uncle Billy went on in. We could hear Henry. We stood in the yard, hearing them on the bridges, this-a-way and that: "Whooey. Whooey."

"Eck Snopes ought to caught hisn," Ernest says.

"Looks like he ought," Winterbottom said.

Henry was going Ah-Ah-Ah steady in the house; then he begun to scream. "Uncle Billy's started," Quick says. We looked into the hall. We could see the light where the door was. Then Mrs. Littlejohn come out.

"Will needs some help," she says. "You, Ernest. You'll do." Ernest went into the house.

"Hear them?" Quick said. "That one was on Four Mile bridge." We could hear them; it sounded like thunder a long way off; it didn't last long:

"Whooey."

We could hear Henry: "Ah-Ah-Ah-Ah-Ah."

"They are both started now," Winterbottom says. "Ernest too."

That was early in the night. Which was a good thing, because it taken a long night for folks to chase them things right and for Henry to lay there and holler, being as Uncle Billy never had none of this here chloryfoam to set Henry's leg with. So it was considerate of Flem to get them started early. And what do you reckon Flem's com-ment was?

That's right. Nothing. Because he wasn't there. Hadn't nobody see him since that Texas man left.

VI

That was Saturday night. I reckon Mrs. Armstid got home about daylight, to see about the chaps. I don't know where they thought her and Henry

---

[3] Woodpecker.

was. But lucky the oldest one was a gal, about twelve, big enough to take care of the little ones. Which she did for the next two days. Mrs. Armstid would nurse Henry all night and work in the kitchen for hern and Henry's keep, and in the afternoon she would drive home (it was about four miles) to see to the chaps. She would cook up a pot of victuals and leave it on the stove, and the gal would bar the house and keep the little ones quiet. I would hear Mrs. Littlejohn and Mrs. Armstid talking in the kitchen. "How are the chaps making out?" Mrs. Littlejohn says.

"All right," Mrs. Armstid says.

"Don't they git skeered at night?" Mrs. Littlejohn says.

"Ina May bars the door when I leave," Mrs. Armstid says. "She's got the axe in bed with her. I reckon she can make out."

I reckon they did. And I reckon Mrs. Armstid was waiting for Flem to come back to town; hadn't nobody seen him until this morning; to get her money the Texas man said Flem was keeping for her. Sho. I reckon she was.

Anyway, I heard Mrs. Armstid and Mrs. Littlejohn talking in the kitchen this morning while I was eating breakfast. Mrs. Littlejohn had just told Mrs. Armstid that Flem was in town. "You can ask him for that five dollars," Mrs. Littlejohn says.

"You reckon he'll give it to me?" Mrs. Armstid says.

Mrs. Littlejohn was washing dishes, washing them like a man, like they was made out of iron. "No," she says. "But asking him won't do no hurt. It might shame him. I don't reckon it will, but it might."

"If he wouldn't give it back, it ain't no use to ask," Mrs. Armstid says.

"Suit yourself," Mrs. Littlejohn says. "It's your money."

I could hear the dishes.

"Do you reckon he might give it back to me?" Mrs. Armstid says. "That Texas man said he would. He said I could get it from Mr. Snopes later."

"Then go and ask him for it," Mrs. Littlejohn says.

I could hear the dishes.

"He won't give it back to me," Mrs. Armstid says.

"All right," Mrs. Littlejohn says. "Don't ask him for it, then."

I could hear the dishes; Mrs. Armstid was helping. "You don't reckon he would, do you?" she says. Mrs. Littlejohn never said nothing. It sounded like she was throwing the dishes at one another. "Maybe I better go and talk to Henry about it," Mrs. Armstid says.

"I would," Mrs. Littlejohn says. I be dog if it didn't sound like she had two plates in her hands, beating them together. "Then Henry can buy another five-dollar horse with it. Maybe he'll buy one next time that will out and out kill him. If I thought that, I'd give you back the money, myself."

"I reckon I better talk to him first," Mrs. Armstid said. Then it sounded like Mrs. Littlejohn taken up all the dishes and throwed them at the cookstove, and I come away.

That was this morning. I had been up to Bundren's and back, and I thought that things would have kind of settled down. So after breakfast, I went up to the store. And there was Flem, setting in the store-chair and whittling, like he might not have ever moved since he come to clerk for Jody Varner. I. O. was leaning in the door, in his shirt sleeves and with his hair parted too, same as Flem was before he turned the clerking job over to I. O. It's a funny thing about them Snopes: they all looks alike, yet there ain't ere a two of them that claims brothers. They're always just cousins, like Flem and Eck and Flem and I. O. Eck was there too, squatting against the wall, him and that boy, eating cheese and crackers outen a sack; they told me that Eck hadn't been home a-tall. And that Lon Quick hadn't got back to town, even. He followed his horse clean down to Samson's Bridge, with a wagon and a camp outfit. Eck finally caught one of hisn. It run into a blind lane at Freeman's and Eck and the boy taken and tied their rope across the end of the lane, about three foot high. The horse come to the end of the lane and whirled and run back without ever stopping. Eck says it never seen the rope a-tall. He says it looked just like one of these here Christmas pinwheels. "Didn't it try to run again?" I says.

"No," Eck says, eating a bite of cheese offen his knife blade. "Just kicked some."

"Kicked some?" I says.

"It broke its neck," Eck says.

Well, they was squatting there, about six of them, talking, talking at Flem; never nobody knowed yet if Flem had ere a interest in them horses or not. So finally I come right out and asked him. "Flem's done skun all of us so much," I says, "that we're proud of him. Come on, Flem," I says, "how much did you and that Texas man make offen them horses? You can tell us. Ain't nobody here but Eck that bought one of them; the others ain't got back to town yet, and Eck's your own cousin; he'll be proud to hear, too. How much did you-all make?"

They was all whittling, not looking at Flem, making like they was studying. But you could a heard a pin drop. And I. O. He had been rubbing his back up and down on the door, but he stopped now, watching Flem like a pointing dog. Flem finished cutting the sliver offen his stick. He spit across the porch, into the road. " 'Twarn't none of my horses," he says.

I. O. cackled, like a hen, slapping his legs with both hands. "You boys might just as well quit trying to get ahead of Flem," he said.

Well, about that time I see Mrs. Armstid come outen Mrs. Littlejohn's gate, coming up the road. I never said nothing. I says, "Well, if a man can't take care of himself in a trade, he can't blame the man that trims him."

Flem never said nothing, trimming at the stick. He hadn't seen Mrs. Armstid. "Yes, sir," I says. "A fellow like Henry Armstid ain't got nobody but hisself to blame."

"Course he ain't," I. O. says. He ain't seen her, neither. "Henry Armstid's a born fool. Always is been. If Flem hadn't a got his money, somebody else would."

We looked at Flem. He never moved. Mrs. Armstid come on up the road.

"That's right," I says. "But, come to think of it, Henry never bought no horse." We looked at Flem; you could a heard a match drop. "That Texas man told her to get that five dollars back from Flem next day. I reckon Flem's done already taken that money to Mrs. Littlejohn's and give it to Mrs. Armstid."

We watched Flem. I. O. quit rubbing his back against the door again. After a while Flem raised his head and spit across the porch, into the dust. I. O. cackled, just like a hen. "Ain't he a beating fellow, now?" I. O. says.

Mrs. Armstid was getting closer, so I kept on talking, watching to see if Flem would look up and see her. But he never looked up. I went on talking about Tull, about how he was going to sue Flem, and Flem setting there, whittling his stick, not saying nothing else after he said they wasn't none of his horses.

Then I. O. happened to look around. He seen Mrs. Armstid. "Psssst!" he says. Flem looked up. "Here she comes!" I. O. says. "Go out the back. I'll tell her you done went in to town to-day."

But Flem never moved. He just set there, whittling, and we watched Mrs. Armstid come up onto the porch, in that ere faded sunbonnet and wrapper and them tennis shoes that made a kind of hissing noise on the porch. She come onto the porch and stopped, her hands rolled into her dress in front, not looking at nothing.

"He said Saturday," she says, "that he wouldn't sell Henry no horse. He said I could get the money from you."

Flem looked up. The knife never stopped. It went on trimming off a sliver same as if he was watching it. "He taken that money off with him when he left," Flem says.

Mrs. Armstid never looked at nothing. We never looked at her, neither, except that boy of Eck's. He had a half-et cracker in his hand, watching her, chewing.

"He said Henry hadn't bought no horse," Mrs. Armstid says. "He said for me to get the money from you today."

"I reckon he forgot about it," Flem said. "He taken that money off with him Saturday." He whittled again. I. O. kept on rubbing his back, slow. He licked his lips. After a while the woman looked up the road, where it went on up the hill, toward the graveyard. She looked up that way for a while, with that boy of Eck's watching her and I. O. rubbing his back slow against the door. Then she turned back toward the steps.

"I reckon it's time to get dinner started," she says.

"How's Henry this morning, Mrs. Armstid?" Winterbottom says.

She looked at Winterbottom; she almost stopped. "He's resting, I thank you kindly," she says.

Flem got up, outen the chair, putting his knife away. He spit across the porch. "Wait a minute, Mrs. Armstid," he says. She stopped again. She didn't look at him. Flem went on into the store, with I. O. done quit rubbing his back now, with his head craned after Flem, and Mrs. Armstid standing there with her hands rolled into her dress, not looking at nothing. A wagon come up the road and passed; it was Freeman, on the way to town. Then Flem come out again, with I. O. still watching him. Flem had one of these little striped sacks of Jody Varner's candy; I bet he still owes Jody that nickel, too. He put the sack into Mrs. Armstid's hand, like he would have put it into a hollow stump. He spit again across the porch. "A little sweetening for the chaps," he says.

"You're right kind," Mrs. Armstid says. She held the sack of candy in her hand, not looking at nothing. Eck's boy was watching the sack, the half-et cracker in his hand; he wasn't chewing now. He watched Mrs. Armstid roll the sack into her apron. "I reckon I better get on back and help with dinner," she says. She turned and went back across the porch. Flem set down in the chair again and opened his knife. He spit across the porch again, past Mrs. Armstid where she hadn't went down the steps yet. Then she went on, in that ere sunbonnet and wrapper all the same color, back down the road toward Mrs. Littlejohn's. You couldn't see her dress move, like a natural woman walking. She looked like a old snag still standing up and moving along on a high water. We watched her turn in at Mrs. Littlejohn's and go outen sight. Flem was whittling. I. O. begun to rub his back on the door. Then he begun to cackle, just like a durn hen.

"You boys might just as well quit trying," I. O. says. "You can't git ahead of Flem. You can't touch him. Ain't he a sight, now?"

I be dog if he ain't. If I had brung a herd of wild cattymounts into town and sold them to my neighbors and kinfolks, they would have lynched me. Yes, sir.

Study and Discussion Questions

1. List or sum up the characteristics of each of the following characters in the story: the Texan, Flem, Mrs. Littlejohn, Mrs. Armstid, Henry Armstid.
2. Who is the narrator of "Spotted Horses"? What is his relation to the events of the story?
3. Who owns the horses?
4. What words are used to describe the horses? What are the horses compared to?
5. What do Flem and the spotted horses have in common?
6. What is Mrs. Littlejohn's opinion of the situation? Give examples of her expressing her opinion.

Writing Exercises

1. Find a passage that made you smile or laugh and analyze Faulkner's use of humor.
2. Though he is the focus of much of the story, Flem Snopes rarely speaks and is not even present for much of the action. How is it, then, that Flem has so much power? Why is it, as I. O. says, that "you can't touch him"?
3. What do the horses represent or mean to the community? How do they operate as a symbol in the story? That is, what do they come to mean for the reader?
4. Consider Henry Armstid's purchase of a horse and how the Texas man handles that situation. Can you state the unwritten code of ethics out of which the Texas man is acting? What is Flem Snope's relation to that same code of ethics?

B. TRAVEN   (1890?–1969)

The facts of B. Traven's life remain a mystery. He was probably born in Chicago in 1890, but may have been born in Germany in 1882. It seems he had little schooling, worked as a cabin boy and then as a sailor in the early 1920s, and jumped ship in Mexico, where he spent most of the rest of his life. Much of Traven's fiction was published, though perhaps not written, first in German. It includes The Cotton Pickers *(1926),* The Treasure of the Sierra Madre *(1927),* Death Ship *(1934),* The Rebellion of the Hanged *(1936), and* The Night Visitor and Other Stories *(1966).*

Assembly Line   (1966)

Mr. E. L. Winthrop of New York was on vacation in the Republic of Mexico. It wasn't long before he realized that this strange and really wild country had not yet been fully and satisfactorily explored by Rotarians and Lions[1], who are forever conscious of their glorious mission on earth. Therefore, he considered it his duty as a good American citizen to do his part in correcting this oversight.

In search for opportunities to indulge in his new avocation, he left the beaten track and ventured into regions not especially mentioned, and hence not recommended, by travel agents to foreign tourists. So it happened that one day he found himself in a little, quaint Indian village somewhere in the State of Oaxaca.

---

[1] Members of two business organizations.

Walking along the dusty main street of this pueblecito,[2] which knew nothing of pavements, drainage, plumbing, or of any means of artificial light save candles or pine splinters, he met with an Indian squatting on the earthen-floor front porch of a palm hut, a so-called jacalito.

The Indian was busy making little baskets from bast and from all kinds of fibers gathered by him in the immense tropical bush which surrounded the village on all sides. The material used had not only been well prepared for its purpose but was also richly colored with dyes that the basket-maker himself extracted from various native plants, barks, roots and from certain insects by a process known only to him and the members of his family.

His principal business, however, was not producing baskets. He was a peasant who lived on what the small property he possessed—less than fifteen acres of not too fertile soil—would yield, after much sweat and labor and after constantly worrying over the most wanted and best suited distribution of rain, sunshine, and wind and the changing balance of birds and insects beneficial or harmful to his crops. Baskets he made when there was nothing else for him to do in the fields, because he was unable to dawdle. After all, the sale of his baskets, though to a rather limited degree only, added to the small income he received from his little farm.

In spite of being by profession just a plain peasant, it was clearly seen from the small baskets he made that at heart he was an artist, a true and accomplished artist. Each basket looked as if covered all over with the most beautiful sometimes fantastic ornaments, flowers, butterflies, birds, squirrels, antelope, tigers, and a score of other animals of the wilds. Yet, the most amazing thing was that these decorations, all of them symphonies of color, were not painted on the baskets but were instead actually part of the baskets themselves. Bast and fibers dyed in dozens of different colors were so cleverly—one must actually say intrinsically—interwoven that those attractive designs appeared on the inner part of the basket as well as on the outside. Not by painting but by weaving were those highly artistic effects achieved. This performance he accomplished without ever looking at any sketch or pattern. While working on a basket these designs came to light as if by magic, and as long as a basket was not entirely finished one could not perceive what in this case or that the decoration would be like.

People in the market town who bought these baskets would use them for sewing baskets or to decorate tables with or window sills, or to hold little things to keep them from lying around. Women put their jewelry in them or flowers or little dolls. There were in fact a hundred and two ways they might serve certain purposes in a household or in a lady's own room.

Whenever the Indian had finished about twenty of the baskets he took them to town on market day. Sometimes he would already be on his

---

[2] Small village.

way shortly after midnight because he owned only a burro to ride on, and if the burro had gone astray the day before, as happened frequently, he would have to walk the whole way to town and back again.

At the market he had to pay twenty centavos in taxes to sell his wares. Each basket cost him between twenty and thirty hours of constant work, not counting the time spent gathering bast and fibers, preparing them, making dyes and coloring the bast. All this meant extra time and work. The price he asked for each basket was fifty centavos, the equivalent of about four cents. It seldom happened, however, that a buyer paid outright the full fifty centavos asked—or four reales[3] as the Indian called that money. The prospective buyer started bargaining, telling the Indian that he ought to be ashamed to ask such a sinful price. "Why, the whole dirty thing is nothing but ordinary petate straw which you find in heaps wherever you may look for it; the jungle is packed full of it," the buyer would argue. "Such a little basket, what's it good for anyhow? If I paid you, you thief, ten centavitos for it you should be grateful and kiss my hand. Well, it's your lucky day, I'll be generous this time, I'll pay you twenty, yet not one green centavo more. Take it or run along."

So he sold finally for twenty-five centavos, but then the buyer would say, "Now, what do you think of that? I've got only twenty centavos change on me. What can we do about that? If you can change me a twenty-peso bill, all right, you shall have your twenty-five fierros." Of course, the Indian could not change a twenty-peso bill and so the basket went for twenty centavos.

He had little if any knowledge of the outside world or he would have known that what happened to him was happening every hour of every day to every artist all over the world. That knowledge would perhaps have made him very proud, because he would have realized that he belonged to the little army which is the salt of the earth and which keeps culture, urbanity and beauty for their own sake from passing away.

Often it was not possible for him to sell all the baskets he had brought to market, for people here as elsewhere in the world preferred things made by the millions and each so much like the other that you were unable, even with the help of a magnifying glass, to tell which was which and where was the difference between two of the same kind.

Yet he, this craftsman, had in his life made several hundreds of those exquisite baskets, but so far no two of them had he ever turned out alike in design. Each was an individual piece of art and as different from the other as was a Murillo from a Velásquez.[4]

Naturally he did not want to take those baskets which he could not sell at the market place home with him again if he could help it. In such a case he went peddling his products from door to door where he was treated partly as a beggar and partly as a vagrant apparently looking for

---

[3] One hundred centavos make one peso; "four reales" is four U.S. cents.

[4] Spanish painters.

an opportunity to steal, and he frequently had to swallow all sorts of insults and nasty remarks.

Then, after a long run, perhaps a woman would finally stop him, take one of the baskets and offer him ten centavos, which price through talks and talks would perhaps go up to fifteen or even to twenty. Nevertheless, in many instances he would actually get no more than just ten centavos, and the buyer, usually a woman, would grasp that little marvel and right before his eyes throw it carelessly upon the nearest table as if to say, "Well, I take that piece of nonsense only for charity's sake. I know my money is wasted. But then, after all, I'm a Christian and I can't see a poor Indian die of hunger since he has come such a long way from his village." This would remind her of something better and she would hold him and say, "Where are you at home anyway, Indito? What's your pueblo?[5] So, from Huehuetonoc? Now, listen here, Indito, can't you bring me next Saturday two or three turkeys from Huehuetonoc? But they must be heavy and fat and very, very cheap or I won't even touch them. If I wish to pay the regular price I don't need you to bring them. Understand? Hop along, now, Indito."

The Indian squatted on the earthen floor in the portico of his hut, attended to his work and showed no special interest in the curiosity of Mr. Winthrop watching him. He acted almost as if he ignored the presence of the American altogether.

"How much that little basket, friend?" Mr. Winthrop asked when he felt that he at least had to say something as not to appear idiotic.

"Fifty centavitos, patroncito,[6] my good little lordy, four reales," the Indian answered politely.

"All right, sold," Mr. Winthrop blurted out in a tone and with a wide gesture as if he had bought a whole railroad. And examining his buy he added, "I know already who I'll give that pretty little thing to. She'll kiss me for it, sure. Wonder what she'll use it for?"

He had expected to hear a price of three or even four pesos. The moment he realized that he had judged the value six times too high, he saw right away what great business possibilities this miserable Indian village might offer to a dynamic promoter like himself. Without further delay he started exploring those possibilities. "Suppose, my good friend, I buy ten of these little baskets of yours which, as I might as well admit right here and now, have practically no real use whatsoever. Well, as I was saying, if I buy ten, how much would you then charge me apiece?"

The Indian hesitated for a few seconds as if making calculations. Finally he said, "If you buy ten I can let you have them for forty-five centavos each, señorito gentleman."

"All right, amigo. And now, let's suppose I buy from you straight away one hundred of these absolutely useless baskets, how much will cost me each?"

---

[5] Little Indian; village.

[6] Diminutive form of "patron," boss or patron.

The Indian, never fully looking up to the American standing before him and hardly taking his eyes off his work, said politely and without the slightest trace of enthusiasm in his voice, "In such a case I might not be quite unwilling to sell each for forty centavitos."

Mr. Winthrop bought sixteen baskets, which was all the Indian had in stock.

After three weeks' stay in the Republic, Mr. Winthrop was convinced that he knew this country perfectly, that he had seen everything and knew all about the inhabitants, their character and their way of life, and that there was nothing left for him to explore. So he returned to good old Nooyorg and felt happy to be once more in a civilized country, as he expressed it to himself.

One day going out for lunch he passed a confectioner's and, looking at the display in the window, he suddenly remembered the little baskets he had bought in that faraway Indian village.

He hurried home and took all the baskets he still had left to one of the best-known candy-makers in the city.

"I can offer you here," Mr. Winthrop said to the confectioner, "one of the most artistic and at the same time the most original of boxes, if you wish to call them that. These little baskets would be just right for the most expensive chocolates meant for elegant and high-priced gifts. Just have a good look at them, sir, and let me listen."

The confectioner examined the baskets and found them extraordinarily well suited for a certain line in his business. Never before had there been anything like them for originality, prettiness and good taste. He, however, avoided most carefully showing any sign of enthusiasm, for which there would be time enough once he knew the price and whether he could get a whole load exclusively.

He shrugged his shoulders and said, "Well, I don't know. If you asked me I'd say it isn't quite what I'm after. However, we might give it a try. It depends, of course, on the price. In our business the package mustn't cost more than what's in it."

"Do I hear an offer?" Mr. Winthrop asked.

"Why don't you tell me in round figures how much you want for them? I'm not good at guessing."

"Well, I'll tell you, Mr. Kemple: since I'm the smart guy who discovered these baskets and since I'm the only Jack who knows where to lay his hands on more, I'm selling to the highest bidder, on an exclusive basis, of course. I'm positive you can see it my way, Mr. Kemple."

"Quite so, and may the best man win," the confectioner said. "I'll talk the matter over with my partners. See me tomorrow same time, please, and I'll let you know how far we might be willing to go."

Next day when both gentlemen met again Mr. Kemple said: "Now, to be frank with you, I know art on seeing it, no getting around that. And these baskets are little works of art, they surely are. However, we are no art dealers, you realize that of course. We've no other use for these pretty little things except as fancy packing for our French pralines made by us. We can't pay for them what we might pay considering them pieces of art. After all to us they're only wrappings. Fine wrappings, perhaps, but nevertheless wrappings. You'll see it our way I hope, Mr.——oh, yes, Mr. Winthrop. So, here is our offer, take it or leave it: a dollar and a quarter apiece and not one cent more."

Mr. Winthrop made a gesture as if he had been struck over the head.

The confectioner, misunderstanding this involuntary gesture of Mr. Winthrop, added quickly, "All right, all right, no reason to get excited, no reason at all. Perhaps we can do a trifle better. Let's say one-fifty."

"Make it one-seventy-five," Mr. Winthrop snapped, swallowing his breath while wiping his forehead.

"Sold. One-seventy-five apiece free at port of New York. We pay the customs and you pay the shipping. Right?"

"Sold," Mr. Winthrop said also and the deal was closed.

"There is, of course, one condition," the confectioner explained just when Mr. Winthrop was to leave. "One or two hundred won't do for us. It wouldn't pay the trouble and the advertising. I won't consider less than ten thousand, or one thousand dozens if that sounds better in your ears. And they must come in no less than twelve different patterns well assorted. How about that?"

"I can make it sixty different patterns or designs."

"So much the better. And you're sure you can deliver ten thousand let's say early October?"

"Absolutely," Mr. Winthrop avowed and signed the contract.

Practically all the way back to Mexico, Mr. Winthrop had a notebook in his left hand and a pencil in his right and he was writing figures, long rows of them, to find out exactly how much richer he would be when this business had been put through.

"Now, let's sum up the whole goddamn thing," he muttered to himself. "Damn it, where is that cursed pencil again? I had it right between my fingers. Ah, there it is. Ten thousand he ordered. Well, well, there we got a clean-cut profit of fifteen thousand four hundred and forty genuine dollars. Sweet smackers. Fifteen grand right into papa's pocket. Come to think of it, that Republic isn't so backward after all."

"Buenas tardes,[7] mi amigo, how are you?" he greeted the Indian whom he found squatting in the porch of his jacalito as if he had never moved from his place since Mr. Winthrop had left for New York.

The Indian rose, took off his hat, bowed politely and said in his soft voice, "Be welcome, patroncito. Thank you, I feel fine, thank you. Muy buenas tardes.[8] This house and all I have is at your kind disposal." He

---

[7] Good afternoon.

[8] Good afternoon (emphatically).

bowed once more, moved his right hand in a gesture of greeting and sat down again. But he excused himself for doing so by saying, "Perdoneme,[9] patroncito, I have to take advantage of the daylight, soon it will be night."

"I've got big business for you, my friend," Mr. Winthrop began.

"Good to hear that, señor."

Mr. Winthrop said to himself, "Now, he'll jump up and go wild when he learns what I've got for him." And aloud he said: "Do you think you can make me one thousand of these little baskets?"

"Why not, patroncito? If I can make sixteen, I can make one thousand also."

"That's right, my good man. Can you also make five thousand?"

"Of course, señor. I can make five thousand if I can make one thousand."

"Good. Now, if I should ask you to make me ten thousand, what would you say? And what would be the price of each? You can make ten thousand, can't you?"

"Of course, I can, señor. I can make as many as you wish. You see, I am an expert in this sort of work. No one else in the whole state can make them the way I do."

"That's what I thought and that's exactly why I came to you."

"Thank you for the honor, patroncito."

"Suppose I order you to make me ten thousand of these baskets, how much time do you think you would need to deliver them?"

The Indian, without interrupting his work, cocked his head to one side and then to the other as if he were counting the days or weeks it would cost him to make all these baskets.

After a few minutes he said in a slow voice, "It will take a good long time to make so many baskets, patroncito. You see, the bast and the fibers must be very dry before they can be used properly. Then all during the time they are slowly drying, they must be worked and handled in a very special way so that while drying they won't lose their softness and their flexibility and their natural brilliance. Even when dry they must look fresh. They must never lose their natural properties or they will look just as lifeless and dull as straw. Then while they are drying up I got to get the plants and roots and barks and insects from which I brew the dyes. That takes much time also, believe me. The plants must be gathered when the moon is just right or they won't give the right color. The insects I pick from the plants must also be gathered at the right time and under the right conditions or else they produce no rich colors and are just like dust. But, of course, jefecito,[10] I can make as many of these canastitas[11] as you wish, even as many as three dozens if you want them. Only give me time."

"Three dozens? Three dozens?" Mr. Winthrop yelled, and threw up both arms in desperation. "Three dozens!" he repeated as if he had to

---

[9] Excuse me.

[10] Diminutive form of "jefe," chief or boss.

[11] Little baskets.

say it many times in his own voice so as to understand the real meaning of it, because for a while he thought that he was dreaming. He had expected the Indian to go crazy on hearing that he was to sell ten thousand of his baskets without having to peddle them from door to door and be treated like a dog with a skin disease.

So the American took up the question of price again, by which he hoped to activate the Indian's ambition. "You told me that if I take one hundred baskets you will let me have them for forty centavos apiece. Is that right, my friend?"

"Quite right, jefecito."

"Now," Mr. Winthrop took a deep breath, "now, then, if I ask you to make me one thousand, that is, ten times one hundred baskets, how much will they cost me, each basket?"

That figure was too high for the Indian to grasp. He became slightly confused and for the first time since Mr. Winthrop had arrived he interrupted his work and tried to think it out. Several times he shook his head and looked vaguely around as if for help. Finally he said, "Excuse me, jefecito, little chief, that is by far too much for me to count. Tomorrow, if you will do me the honor, come and see me again and I think I shall have my answer ready for you, patroncito."

When on the next morning Mr. Winthrop came to the hut he found the Indian as usual squatting on the floor under the overhanging palm roof working at his baskets.

"Have you got the price for ten thousand?" he asked the Indian the very moment he saw him, without taking the trouble to say "Good Morning!"

"Si, patroncito, I have the price ready. You may believe me when I say it has cost me much labor and worry to find out the exact price, because, you see, I do not wish to cheat you out of your honest money."

"Skip that, amigo. Come out with the salad. What's the price?" Mr. Winthrop asked nervously.

"The price is well calculated now without any mistake on my side. If I got to make one thousand canastitas each will be three pesos. If I must make five thousand, each will cost nine pesos. And if I have to make ten thousand, in such a case I can't make them for less than fifteen pesos each." Immediately he returned to his work as if he were afraid of losing too much time with such idle talk.

Mr. Winthrop thought that perhaps it was his faulty knowledge of this foreign language that had played a trick on him.

"Did I hear you say fifteen pesos each if I eventually would buy ten thousand?"

"That's exactly and without any mistake what I've said, patroncito," the Indian answered in his soft courteous voice.

"But now, see here, my good man, you can't do this to me. I'm your friend and I want to help you get on your feet."

"Yes, patroncito, I know this and I don't doubt any of your words."

"Now, let's be patient and talk this over quietly as man to man. Didn't you tell me that if I would buy one hundred you would sell each for forty centavos?"

"Sí, jefecito, that's what I said. If you buy one hundred you can have them for forty centavos apiece, provided that I have one hundred, which I don't."

"Yes, yes, I see that." Mr. Winthrop felt as if he would go insane any minute now. "Yes, so you said. Only what I can't comprehend is why you cannot sell at the same price if you make me ten thousand. I certainly don't wish to chisel on the price. I am not that kind. Only, well, let's see now, if you can sell for forty centavos at all, be it for twenty or fifty or a hundred, I can't quite get the idea why the price has to jump that high if I buy more than a hundred."

"Bueno, patroncito, what is there so difficult to understand? It's all very simple. One thousand canastitas cost me a hundred times more work than a dozen. Ten thousand cost me so much time and labor that I could never finish them, not even in a hundred years. For a thousand canastitas I need more bast than for a hundred, and I need more little red beetles and more plants and roots and bark for the dyes. It isn't that you just can walk into the bush and pick all the things you need at your heart's desire. One root with the true violet blue may cost me four or five days until I can find one in the jungle. And have you thought how much time it costs and how much hard work to prepare the bast and fibers? What is more, if I must make so many baskets, who then will look after my corn and my beans and my goats and chase for me occasionally a rabbit for meat on Sunday? If I have no corn, then I have no tortillas to eat, and if I grow no beans, where do I get my frijoles[12] from?"

"But since you'll get so much money from me for your baskets you can buy all the corn and beans in the world and more than you need."

"That's what you think, señorito, little lordy. But you see, it is only the corn I grow myself that I am sure of. Of the corn which others may or may not grow, I cannot be sure to feast upon."

"Haven't you got some relatives here in this village who might help you to make baskets for me?" Mr. Winthrop asked hopefully.

"Practically the whole village is related to me somehow or other. Fact is, I got lots of close relatives in this here place."

"Why then can't they cultivate your fields and look after your goats while you make baskets for me? Not only this, they might gather for you the fibers and the colors in the bush and lend you a hand here and there in preparing the material you need for the baskets."

"They might, patroncito, yes, they might. Possible. But then you see who would take care of their fields and cattle if they work for me? And if they help me with the baskets it turns out the same. No one would any longer work his fields properly. In such a case corn and beans would

---

[12] Beans.

get up so high in price that none of us could buy any and we all would starve to death. Besides, as the price of everything would rise and rise higher still how could I make baskets at forty centavos apiece? A pinch of salt or one green chili would set me back more than I'd collect for one single basket. Now you'll understand, highly estimated caballero[13] and jefecito, why I can't make the baskets any cheaper than fifteen pesos each if I got to make that many."

Mr. Winthrop was hard-boiled, no wonder considering the city he came from. He refused to give up the more than fifteen thousand dollars which at that moment seemed to slip through his fingers like nothing. Being really desperate now, he talked and bargained with the Indian for almost two full hours, trying to make him understand how rich he, the Indian, would become if he would take this greatest opportunity of his life.

The Indian never ceased working on his baskets while he explained his points of view.

"You know, my good man," Mr. Winthrop said, "such a wonderful chance might never again knock on your door, do you realize that? Let me explain to you in ice-cold figures what fortune you might miss if you leave me flat on this deal."

He tore out leaf after leaf from his notebook, covered each with figures and still more figures, and while doing so told the peasant he would be the richest man in the whole district.

The Indian without answering watched with a genuine expression of awe as Mr. Winthrop wrote down these long figures, executing complicated multiplications and divisions and subtractions so rapidly that it seemed to him the greatest miracle he had ever seen.

The American, noting this growing interest in the Indian, misjudged the real significance of it. "There you are, my friend," he said. "That's exactly how rich you're going to be. You'll have a bankroll of exactly four thousand pesos. And to show you that I'm a real friend of yours, I'll throw in a bonus. I'll make it a round five thousand pesos, and all in silver."

The Indian, however, had not for one moment thought of four thousand pesos. Such an amount of money had no meaning to him. He had been interested solely in Mr. Winthrop's ability to write figures so rapidly.

"So, what do you say now? Is it a deal or is it? Say yes and you'll get your advance this very minute."

"As I have explained before, patroncito, the price is fifteen pesos each."

"But, my good man," Mr. Winthrop shouted at the poor Indian in utter despair, "where have you been all this time? On the moon or where? You are still at the same price as before."

"Yes, I know that, jefecito, my little chief," the Indian answered, entirely unconcerned. "It must be the same price because I cannot make any other one. Besides, señor, there's still another thing which perhaps you don't

---

[13] Gentleman.

know. You see, my good lordy and caballero, I've to make these canastitas my own way and with my song in them and with bits of my soul woven into them. If I were to make them in great numbers there would no longer be my soul in each, or my songs. Each would look like the other with no difference whatever and such a thing would slowly eat up my heart. Each has to be another song which I hear in the morning when the sun rises and when the birds begin to chirp and the butterflies come and sit down on my baskets so that I may see a new beauty, because, you see, the butterflies like my baskets and the pretty colors on them, that's why they come and sit down, and I can make my canastitas after them. And now, señor jefecito, if you will kindly excuse me, I have wasted much time already, although it was a pleasure and a great honor to hear the talk of such a distinguished caballero like you. But I'm afraid I've to attend to my work now, for day after tomorrow is market day in town and I got to take my baskets there. Thank you, señor, for your visit. Adiós."

And in this way it happened that American garbage cans escaped the fate of being turned into receptacles for empty, torn, and crumpled little multicolored canastitas into which an Indian of Mexico had woven dreams of his soul, throbs of his heart: his unsung poems.

Study and Discussion Questions

1. What is the narrator's tone? Does it change? Is there greater narrative distance from Winthrop or from the Indian?
2. Why does the Indian make baskets? What do they mean to him? To his Mexican customers? To Winthrop? What is the story saying about art and commerce?
3. We witness three kinds of business discussions in the story: between the Indian and other Mexicans, between Winthrop and the candy manufacturer, and between the Indian and Winthrop. What similarities and differences are there?
4. Why does Winthrop think the price per basket should be lower for 10,000 than for a few? What assumptions is he making when he thinks this? What is he blind to?

Writing Exercises

1. What would Winthrop say to the charge that, by buying baskets at less than four cents each and selling them for $1.75 each, he would be exploiting the Indian? How might you reply to him?
2. Summarize the Indian's reasons why the price per basket should be higher for thousands than for a few. Suppose the Indian's life (and

much of the village) were reorganized, as he suggests it would have to be, for mass production for export. What further consequences might there be? What light might this story shed on Third World poverty and its relation to investment from wealthier countries?

3. Consider a creative hobby or craft you enjoy. What would change if you set up for full-time, large-scale production for profit?

TOM KROMER (1906–1969)

Tom Kromer was born to a working-class family in Huntington, West Virginia. His parents died young, leaving him at twenty to care for a brother and three sisters. He managed to finish three years of college, taught for two years and when the Depression came, hopped a freight train to Kansas. Kromer found no work in the wheat fields there, nor anywhere else, and like countless others during the Great Depression roamed the country looking for work. His largely autobiographical novel Waiting for Nothing *(1935) won critical acclaim. Tuberculosis forced Kromer to settle in New Mexico where, with his wife, he put out a small magazine for a few years.*

FROM Waiting for Nothing (1935)

It is night. I am walking along this dark street, when my foot hits a stick. I reach down and pick it up. I finger it. It is a good stick, a heavy stick. One sock from it would lay a man out. It wouldn't kill him, but it would lay him out. I plan. Hit him where the crease is in his hat, hard, I tell myself, but not too hard. I do not want his head to hit the concrete. It might kill him. I do not want to kill him. I will catch him as he falls. I can frisk him in a minute. I will pull him over in the shadows and walk off. I will not run. I will walk.

I turn down a side street. This is a better street. There are fewer houses along this street. There are large trees on both sides of it. I crouch behind one of these. It is dark here. The shadows hide me. I wait. Five, ten minutes, I wait. Then under an arc light a block away a man comes walking. He is a well-dressed man. I can tell even from that distance. I have good eyes. This guy will be in the dough. He walks with his head up and a jaunty step. A stiff does not walk like that. A stiff shuffles with tired feet, his head huddled in his coat collar. This guy is in the dough. I can tell that. I clutch my stick tighter. I notice that I am calm. I am not scared. I am calm. In the crease of his hat, I tell myself. Not too hard. Just hard enough. On he comes. I slink farther back in the shadows. I press closer against this tree. I hear his footsteps thud on the concrete walk. I raise my arm high. I must swing hard. I poise myself. He crosses in front of me. Now is my chance. Bring it down hard, I tell myself, but not too hard. He is under my arm. He is right under my arm, but my stick does not come down. Something has happened to me. I am sick in the stomach. I have lost my nerve. Christ, I have lost my nerve. I am shaking all over. Sweat stands out on my forehead. I can feel the clamminess of it in the cold, damp night. This will not do. This will not do. I've got to get me something to eat. I am starved.

I stagger from the shadows and follow behind this guy. He had a pretty good face. I could tell as he passed beneath my arm. This guy ought to be good for two bits. Maybe he will be good for four bits. I quicken my steps. I will wait until he is under an arc light before I give him my story. I do not have long to wait. He stops under an arc light and fumbles in his pocket for a cigarette. I catch up with him.

"Pardon me, mister, but could you help a hungry man get—"

"You goddam bums give me a pain in the neck. Get the hell away from me before I call a cop."

He jerks his hand into his overcoat pocket. He wants me to think he has a gun. He has not got a gun. He is bluffing.

I hurry down the street. The bastard. The dirty bastard. I could have laid him out cold with the stick. I could have laid him out cold with the stick, and he calls me a goddam bum. I had the stick over his head, and I could not bring it down. I am yellow. I can see that I am yellow. If I am not yellow, why am I shaking like a leaf? I am starved, too, and I ought to starve. A guy without enough guts to get himself a feed ought to starve.

I walk on up the street. I pass people, but I let them pass. I do not ding them. I have lost my nerve. I walk until I am on the main stem. Never have I been so hungry. I have got to get me something to eat. I pass a restaurant. In the window is a roast chicken. It is brown and fat. It squats in a silver platter. The platter is filled with gravy. The gravy is thick and brown. It drips over the side, slow. I stand there and watch it drip. Underneath it the sign says: "All you can eat for fifty cents." I lick my lips. My mouth waters. I sure would like to sit down with that before me. I look inside. It is a classy joint. I can see waitresses in blue and white uniforms. They hurry back and forth. They carry heavy trays. The dishes stick over the edge of the trays. There are good meals still left in these trays. They will throw them in the garbage cans. In the center of the floor a water fountain bubbles. It is made of pink marble. The chairs are red leather, bordered in black. The counter is full of men eating. They are eating, and I am hungry. There are long rows of tables. The cloths on them are whiter than white. The glassware sparkles like diamonds on its whiteness. The knives and forks on the table are silver. I can tell that they are pure silver from where I am standing on the street. They shine so bright. I cannot go in there. It is too classy, and besides there are too many people. They will laugh at my seedy clothes, and my shoes without soles.

I stare in at this couple that eat by the window. I pull my coat collar up around my neck. A man will look hungrier with his coat collar up around his neck. These people are in the dough. They are in evening clothes. This woman is sporting a satin dress. The blackness of it shimmers and glows in the light that comes from the chandelier that hangs from the dome. Her fingers are covered with diamonds. There are diamond bracelets on her wrists. She is beautiful. Never have I seen a more beautiful woman. Her lips are red. They are even redder against the whiteness of her teeth when she laughs. She laughs a lot.

I stare in at the window. Maybe they will know a hungry man when they see him. Maybe this guy will be willing to shell out a couple of nickels to a hungry stiff. It is chicken they are eating. A chicken like the one in the window. Brown and fat. They do not eat. They only nibble. They are nibbling at chicken, and they are not even hungry. I am starved. That chicken was meant for a hungry man. I watch them as they cut it into tiny bits. I watch their forks as they carry them to their mouths. The man is facing me. Twice he glances out of the window. I meet his eyes with mine. I wonder if he can tell the eyes of a hungry man. He has never been hungry himself. I can tell that. This one has always nibbled at chicken. I see him speak to the woman. She turns her head and looks at me through the window. I do not look at her. I look at the chicken on the plate. They can see that I am a hungry man. I will stand here until they come out. When they come out, they will maybe slip me a four-bit piece.

A hand slaps down on my shoulder. It is a heavy hand. It spins me around in my tracks.

"What the hell are you doin' here?" It is a cop.

"Me? Nothing," I say. "Nothing, only watching a guy eat chicken. Can't a guy watch another guy eat chicken?"

"Wise guy," he says. "Well, I know what to do with wise guys."

He slaps me across the face with his hand, hard. I fall back against the building. His hands are on the holster by his side. What can I do? Take it is all I can do. He will plug me if I do anything.

"Put up your hands," he says.

I put up my hands.

"Where's your gat?" he says.

"I have no gat," I say. "I never had a gat in my life."

"That's what they all say," he says.

He pats my pockets. He don't find anything. There is a crowd around here now. Everybody wants to see what is going on. They watch him go through my pockets. They think I am a stick-up guy. A hungry stiff stands and watches a guy eat chicken, and they think he is a stick-up guy. That is a hell of a note.

"All right," he says, "get down the street before I run you in. If I ever catch you stemming this beat, I will sap the living hell out of you. Beat it."

I hurry down the street. I know better than not to hurry. The lousy son of a bitch. I had a feed right in my lap, and he makes me beat it. That guy was all right in there. He was a good guy. That guy could see I was a hungry man. He would have fixed me up right when he came out.

I pass a small café. There are no customers in here. There is only a guy sitting by the cash register. This is my place. I go in and walk up to him. He is a fat guy with a double chin. I can see very well that he hasn't missed many meals in his life.

"Mister," I say, "have you got some kind of work like washing dishes I can do for something to eat? I am damn near starved. I'll do anything."

He looks hard at me. I can see right away that this guy is no good.

"Tell me," he says, "in God's name, why do you stiffs always come in here? You're the fourth guy in the last half-hour. I can't even pay my rent. There ain't been a customer in here for an hour. Go to some of the big joints where they do all the business."

"Could you maybe give me a cup of coffee?" I say. "That would hold me over. I've been turned down at about twenty places already."

"I can't give you nothing. Coffee costs money," he says. "Go to one of the chain stores and bum your coffee. When you've got any money, where do you go to spend it? You go to the chains. I can't do nothing for you."

I walk out. Wouldn't even give a hungry man a cup of coffee. Can you imagine a guy like that? The bastard. I'd like to catch him on a dark street. I'd give him a cup of coffee, and a sock on the snout he wouldn't soon forget. I walk. When I pass a place where there are no customers, I go in. They turn me down flat. No business, they say. Why don't I go to the big places? I am getting sick in the stomach. I feel like vomiting. I have to get me something to eat. What the hell? I will hit me one of these classy joints. Pride! What do I care about pride? Who cares about me? Nobody. The bastards don't care if I live or die.

I pass a joint. A ritzy place. It is all white inside. The tables are full. The counters are full. They are eating, and I am hungry. These guys pay good dough for a feed, and they are not even hungry. When they are through, they will maybe tip the waitress four bits. It is going to be cold tonight. Four bits will buy me a flop that will be warm, and not cold.

I go into this joint and walk up to the middle of the counter. I flop down in a seat. These cash customers gape at me. I am clean, but my front is seedy. They know I don't belong in here. I know I don't belong in here, too. But I am hungry. A hungry man belongs where there is food. Let them gape.

This waiter sticks the menu out to me. I do not take it. What do I want with a menu?

"Buddy," I say, "I am broke and hungry. Could you maybe give me something to eat?"

He shakes his head no, he cannot give me anything to eat.

"Busy. Manager's not in. Sorry."

I can feel my face getting red. They are all gaping at me. They crane their necks to gape at me. I get up out of this seat and walk towards the door. I can't get anything to eat anywhere. God damn them, if I could get my fingers on a gat.

"Say, buddy."

I turn around. A guy in a gray suit is motioning to me. He sits at the middle of the counter. I go back.

"You hungry?"

"I'm damn near starved. I have not eat in two days, and that is the God's truth."

"Down on your luck?" he says.

"Down so far I don't know how far," I say.

"Sit down. I've been down on my luck myself. I know how it is."

I sit down beside him.

"What'll it be?" he says.

"You order it," I say. "Anything you say."

"Order up anything you want. Fill up."

"A ham sandwich and a cup of coffee," I tell this waiter.

He is all smiles now, damn him. He sees where he can make a dime. I bet he owns this joint. He said the manager wasn't in, and I bet he's the manager himself.

"Give him a beef-steak dinner with everything that goes with it," says this guy in the gray suit. "This man is hungry."

This is a good guy. He orders my steak dinner in a loud voice so everyone can see how big-hearted he is, but he is a good guy anyway. Any guy is a good guy when he is going to buy me a steak dinner. Let him show off a little bit. He deserves to show off a little bit. I sit here at this counter, and I feel like pinching myself. This is a funny world. Five minutes ago I was down in the dumps. Here I am now waiting on a steak dinner in a classy joint. Let them gape. What do I care? Didn't they ever see a hungry man before?

This waiter shoves my dinner in front of me. Christ, I've never seen anything look so good. This steak with all the trimmings is a picture for sore eyes. Big and thick and brown, it sits there. Around it, all around it, are tomatoes, sliced. I start in. I do not look up from my plate. They are all gaping at me. Fill up and get out of here, I tell myself.

The guy three seats down gets up and calls for his check. He is a little guy with horn-rimmed glasses. The check is thirty cents. I see it before the waiter turns it upside down. Why do they always have to turn a man's check upside down? Afraid the price will turn his stomach? This guy pulls a dollar out of his pocket and walks over to the cashier. I wonder how it feels to have a buck in your jeans. Four bits will set me on top of the world right now. A good warm flop tonight and breakfast in the morning. That's the way to live. Pay for what you get, and look every copper you pass on the street straight in the eye, and say: "You bastard, I don't owe you a cent."

The cashier hands this guy his change. He walks back and lays it down by my plate.

"Flop for tonight," he says.

He speaks low. He is not trying to show off like this guy in the gray suit. Not that I don't think that this guy in the gray suit is not all right. He is a good guy. He bought me a steak dinner when I was damn near starved. No, he is a good guy, but he likes to show off a little bit. I look up at this guy. He is walking out of the door. I do not thank him. He is too far away, and besides, what can I say? I can't believe it. Thirty cents, the check said. Thirty cents from a dollar. That makes seventy cents. I got seventy cents. A good warm flop tonight, breakfast in the morning, and enough left over for cigarettes. No fishing around in the gutters for snipes for me. I will have me a package of tailor-made cigarettes. I pick up this change and stick it in my pocket. That guy is a mind-reader. I was sitting here wishing I had four bits, and before I know it, I got seventy cents. That guy is all right. I bet that guy has had troubles of his own some time. I bet he knows how it is to be hungry. I hurry up with my dinner. In here I am only a hungry stiff. Outside with seventy cents in my kick, I am as good as the next one. Say, I'd like to meet that guy, and I had a million dollars.

"Do you remember the time you give me seventy cents in a restaurant? You don't? Well, you give me seventy cents in a restaurant one time. I was damn near starved. I was just about ready to bump myself off, and you give me seventy cents."

I hand him a roll of bills. It is a big roll of bills. I walk off. That guy won't have to worry any more about dough. There was plenty in that roll to keep him in wheatcakes the rest of his life.

I finish my pie and get up.

"Thank you, Jack," I say to this guy in the gray suit. "I certainly appreciate what you done for me. I was damn near starved."

"That's all right, buddy," he says. "Glad to help a hungry man."

He speaks loud. They can hear him to the other end of the counter. He is a good guy, though. He bought me a steak dinner.

I walk outside. I put my hand in my pocket and jingle my money. It feels good to have money to jingle. I am not broke or hungry now. I cannot imagine I was broke and hungry an hour ago. No park for me tonight. No lousy mission flop.

I go down the street and walk through the park. I look at these benches with their iron legs and their wooden slats.

"To hell with you," I say. "I have nothing to do with you. I do not know you. You will leave no grooves in my back tonight. Tonight I will have me a good warm flop. I will have me a flop that will be warm, and not cold."

I look at these stiffs sprawled out on the benches. I like to walk to the time of the jingle in my pocket and think how miserable I was last night.

It is getting late, and I am tired. I head down the skid road and stop in front of my four-bit flop. There is no marquee in front to keep the guests from getting wet. There is no doorman dressed like a major in the Imperial Guards. They do not need these things, because all the suites are on the fourth floor. I am puffing when I get to the top of the rickety stairs. At the landing a guy squats on a stool in a wire cage.

"I want a four-bit flop," I say, "a four-bit flop with a clean bed."

This guy is hunched over a desk with his belly sticking out of a dirty green sweater. He rubs his hands together and shows his yellow teeth in a grin. He winks one of his puffy eyes.

"For a little extra, just a little extra," he says, "I can give you a nice room, a very nice room. But it is too big a room for one. You will be lonely. A little company will not go bad, eh? Especially if the company is very young and very pretty?" He licks his puffy lips. "We have a girl, a new girl. Only tonight she came. Because it is you, and she must learn, only a dollar extra, yes?"

I look at him, and I think of the fish-eyed, pot-bellied frogs I used to gig when I was a kid. I imagine myself sticking a sharp gig into his belly and watching him kick and croak.

"A four-bit flop is what I want," I say. "I do not wish to play nursemaid to your virgins. I am broke, and besides, I am sleepy."

"But you should see her," he says, "so tiny, so beautiful. I will get her. You will change your mind when you see her."

"I do not want to see her," I say.

"So high," he says. "Only so high she is, and so beautiful. I will get her. You will see how beautiful she is."

He climbs off his stool.

"Do I get me a flop or do I have to bury my foot in your dirty belly?" I say.

"Some other time, then," he says, "some other time when you have more money. You will see how very beautiful."

He waddles through the dirty hall. I follow him. His legs are swollen with dropsy. His ankles overflow his ragged houseslippers and hang down in folds over the sides. I can imagine I hear the water gurgling as he walks. He opens the door and holds out his hand for the money.

"How many beds in this room?" I say.

"Forty," he says, "but they are good, clean beds."

I walk into this room. It is a big room. It is filled with these beds. They do not look so hot to me. They are only cots. They look lousy. I bet they are lousy, but a stiff has got to sleep, lousy or not. Most of these beds are already full. I can hear the snores of the stiffs as they sleep. I pick me out a flop at the other end of the room. There is no mattress.

Only two dirty blankets. They are smelly. Plenty of stiffs have slept under these blankets.

Four or five stiffs are gathered in a bunch over next to the wall. I watch them. I know very well what they are going to do. They are gas hounds, and they are going to get soused on derail.

"Give me that handkerchief," says this red-headed guy with the wens on his face. "I will squeeze more alky out of a can of heat than any stiff I know."

This little guy with the dirty winged collar examines this can of heat.

"The bastards," he says. "You know what? They're makin' the cans smaller and smaller. This can right here is smaller than they was yestiddy. The dirty crooks. They'd take the bread right out of your mouths, the bastards would."

He jumps up and down as he talks. His red eyes flash. The sweat stands in beads on his forehead. How can a guy get so mad about the size of a can of heat? Well, it does not take much to make you mad when you have been swigging heat for a year.

This red-headed guy takes this can of heat and empties it out in a handkerchief. The handkerchief is filthy, but that don't worry them none. What's a little filth to a gas hound? Pretty soon they will be high and nothing will worry them. Pretty soon they won't have any more troubles. This derail will see to that. They squeeze this stuff out of the handkerchief and let it drip into the glass. They pour water into the glass. The smell of this stuff will turn your stomach, but it don't turn their stomach. They are going to drink it. They take turns about taking a swig. They elbow each other out of the way to get at the glass. When it is all gone, they squeeze out some more. They choke and gag when this stuff goes down, but they drink it. Pretty soon they have guzzled all the heat they have. In a little while they are singing. I do not blame these guys for getting soused on derail. A guy can't always be thinking. If a guy is thinking all the time, pretty soon he will go crazy. A man is bound to land up in the booby-hatch if he stays on the fritz. So these guys make derail and drink it.

This stiff in the bed next to mine turns up his nose at these guys who are soused up on derail.

"I got my opinion of a guy who will drink derail," he says. "A guy who will drink derail is lower down than a skunk."

He pulls a bottle out from under his pillow. It is marked: "Bay Rum." There are directions on the label. It says it will grow new hair. It says it will stop the old from falling out. But this guy does not need this stuff to keep his hair from falling out. This stiff has not had a haircut for a year.

"This is the stuff," he says. "I have been drinkin' this old stuff for a year, and I don't even get a headache afterwards."

He sticks this bottle up to his trap, and he does not take it down until he has emptied it.

"This is good stuff," he says. "It has got derail beat all to a frazzle."

I do not see how it can be such good stuff when he has to gag so much when he downs it. But that is his business. If a guy has been drinking this stuff for a year, he ought to know if it is good stuff or not. Pretty soon this guy is dead to the world. He sprawls out on his bunk and sleeps. He sleeps with his eyes wide open. Christ, he gives me the willies with his eyes wide open like that. He looks like a dead man, but I never see a dead man with his face covered with sweat like his is. It is plenty chilly in this room, but his face is covered with sweat. That is the bay rum coming out of him. A guy that has been drinking this stuff for a year must have plenty inside him. I bet the inside of his gut is covered with hair. That would be a good way to find out if this bay rum is a fake or not. When this stiff croaks from swigging too much bay rum, just cut him open. If his gut is not covered with hair, then this bay rum is a fake.

I watch him. I cannot keep my eyes off him. His legs twitch. He quivers and jerks. He is having a spasm. He almost jumps off the bed. All the time his eyes are wide open, and the sweat pours out of him. But he does not know what it is all about. He is dead to the world. If this is the good stuff, I will take the bad stuff. I will not even put this stuff on my hair. I would be afraid it would sink down into my gut and give me the spasms like this guy has got. The rest of these stiffs do not pay any attention to him. These bay horse fiends are old stuff to them. But they are not old stuff to me. It gets on my nerves. If this guy is going to act like this all night, I am going to walk the streets. It will be cold as hell walking the streets all night, but it will not be as bad as watching this guy jump up and down with his eyes wide open, and him dead to the world.

I cover up my head with this dirty blanket and try not to think about him.

Study and Discussion Questions

1. This selection from *Waiting for Nothing* contains a number of separate episodes. List as many as you can.
2. Characterize the style of Kromer's sentences—their length, verb tense, and so on. How are they unusual?
3. The narrator uses a number of slang words in this story. List them and define them as well as you can from the context.
4. Describe the physical setting, the world the narrator lives in.
5. Discuss the social setting of the story. Can you classify the types of people Kromer encounters?
6. What significance does the title have?
7. The narrator stares into a restaurant window and thinks, "That chicken was meant for a hungry man." What can we infer about his political philosophy from this statement?

8. How does the narrator's attitude change when he has seventy cents in his pocket?
9. What do we learn about the narrator in the flophouse scene?

Writing Exercises

1. How does the narrator view himself? Give evidence. Do you agree with his self-assessment?
2. Does the narrator ever get anything for free? Analyze the scene in the restaurant. How does he "pay" for his meal?
3. Has anyone ever asked you for spare change? How did you react? Narrate such an incident.

TONI CADE BAMBARA (b. 1939)

Toni Cade was born in New York City, attended Queens College and City College there, and has worked as a welfare investigator and as a community organizer. In 1970, she adopted the name "Bambara," from a signature she found in her great-grandmother's trunk. She has edited The Black Woman: An Anthology *(1970) and* Tales and Stories for Black Folks *(1971) and has published two volumes of stories,* Gorilla, My Love *(1972) and* The Sea Birds Are Still Alive *(1977), and a novel,* The Salt Eaters *(1980).*

The Lesson   (1972)

Back in the days when everyone was old and stupid or young and foolish and me and Sugar were the only ones just right, this lady moved on our block with nappy hair and proper speech and no makeup. And quite naturally we laughed at her, laughed the way we did at the junk man who went about his business like he was some big-time president and his sorry-ass horse his secretary. And we kinda hated her too, hated the way we did the winos who cluttered up our parks and pissed on our handball walls and stank up our hallways and stairs so you couldn't halfway play hide-and-seek without a goddamn gas mask. Miss Moore was her name. The only woman on the block with no first name. And she was black as hell, cept for her feet, which were fish-white and spooky. And she was always planning these boring-ass things for us to do, us being my cousin, mostly, who lived on the block cause we all moved North the same time and to the same apartment then spread out gradual to breathe. And our parents would yank our heads into some kinda shape and crisp up our clothes so we'd be presentable for travel with Miss

Moore, who always looked like she was going to church, though she never did. Which is just one of things the grownups talked about when they talked behind her back like a dog. But when she came calling with some sachet she'd sewed up or some gingerbread she'd made or some book, why then they'd all be too embarrassed to turn her down and we'd get handed over all spruced up. She'd been to college and said it was only right that she should take responsibility for the young ones' education, and she not even related by marriage or blood. So they'd go for it. Specially Aunt Gretchen. She was the main gofer in the family. You got some ole dumb shit foolishness you want somebody to go for, you send for Aunt Gretchen. She been screwed into the go-along for so long, it's a blood-deep natural thing with her. Which is how she got saddled with me and Sugar and Junior in the first place while our mothers were in a la-de-da apartment up the block having a good ole time.

So this one day Miss Moore rounds us all up at the mailbox and it's puredee hot and she's knockin herself out about arithmetic. And school suppose to let up in summer I heard, but she don't never let up. And the starch in my pinafore scratching the shit outta me and I'm really hating this nappy-head bitch and her goddamn college degree. I'd much rather go to the pool or to the show where it's cool. So me and Sugar leaning on the mailbox being surly, which is a Miss Moore word. And Flyboy checking out what everybody brought for lunch. And Fat Butt already wasting his peanut-butter-and-jelly sandwich like the pig he is. And Junebug punchin on Q.T.'s arm for potato chips. And Rosie Giraffe shifting from one hip to the other waiting for somebody to step on her foot or ask her if she from Georgia so she can kick ass, preferably Mercedes'. And Miss Moore asking us do we know what money is, like we a bunch of retards. I mean real money, she say, like it's only poker chips or monopoly papers we lay on the grocer. So right away I'm tired of this and say so. And would much rather snatch Sugar and go to the Sunset and terrorize the West Indian kids and take their hair ribbons and their money too. And Miss Moore files that remark away for next week's lesson on brotherhood, I can tell. And finally I say we oughta get to the subway cause it's cooler and besides we might meet some cute boys. Sugar done swiped her mama's lipstick, so we ready.

So we heading down the street and she's boring us silly about what things cost and what our parents make and how much goes for rent and how money ain't divided up right in this country. And then she gets to the part about we all poor and live in the slums, which I don't feature. And I'm ready to speak on that, but she steps out in the street and hails two cabs just like that. Then she hustles half the crew in with her and hands me a five-dollar bill and tells me to calculate 10 percent tip for the driver. And we're off. Me and Sugar and Junebug and Flyboy hangin out the window and hollering to everybody, putting lipstick on each other cause Flyboy a faggot anyway, and making farts with our sweaty armpits. But I'm mostly trying to figure how to spend this money. But they all fascinated with the meter ticking and Junebug starts laying bets as to how much it'll read when Flyboy can't hold his breath no more. Then Sugar lays bets as to how much it'll be when we get there. So I'm stuck. Don't nobody want to go for my plan, which is to jump out at the next light and run off to the first bar-b-que we can find. Then the driver tells us to get the hell out cause we there already. And the meter reads eighty-five cents. And I'm stalling to figure out the tip and Sugar say give him a dime. And I decide he don't need it bad as I do, so later for him. But then he tries to take off with Junebug foot still in the door so we talk about his mama something ferocious. Then we check out that we on Fifth Avenue and everybody dressed up in stockings. One lady in a fur coat, hot as it is. White folks crazy.

"This is the place," Miss Moore say, presenting it to us in the voice she uses at the museum. "Let's look in the windows before we go in."

"Can we steal?" Sugar asks very serious like she's getting the ground rules squared away before she plays. "I beg your pardon," say Miss Moore, and we fall out. So she leads us around the windows of the toy store and me and Sugar screamin, "This is mine, that's mine, I gotta have that, that was made for me, I was born for that," till Big Butt drowns us out.

"Hey, I'm goin to buy that there."

"That there? You don't even know what it is, stupid."

"I do so," he say punchin on Rosie Giraffe. "It's a microscope."

"Whatcha gonna do with a microscope, fool?"

"Look at things."

"Like what, Ronald?" ask Miss Moore. And Big Butt ain't got the first notion. So here go Miss Moore gabbing about the thousands of bacteria in a drop of water and the somethinorother in a speck of blood and the million and one living things in the air around us is invisible to the naked eye. And what she say that for? Junebug go to town on that "naked" and we rolling. Then Miss Moore ask what it cost. So we all jam into the window smudgin it up and the price tag say $300. So then she ask how long'd take for Big Butt and Junebug to save up their allowances. "Too long," I say. "Yeh," adds Sugar, "outgrown it by that time." And Miss Moore say no, you never outgrow learning instruments. "Why, even medical students and interns and," blah, blah, blah. And we ready to choke Big Butt for bringing it up in the first damn place.

"This here costs four hundred eighty dollars," say Rosie Giraffe. So we pile up all over her to see what she pointin out. My eyes tell me it's a chunk of glass cracked with something heavy, and different-color inks dripped into the splits, then the whole thing put into a oven or something. But for $480 it don't make sense.

"That's a paperweight made of semi-precious stones fused together under tremendous pressure," she explains slowly, with her hands doing the mining and all the factory work.

"So what's a paperweight?" asks Rosie Giraffe.

"To weigh paper with, dumbbell," say Flyboy, the wise man from the East.

"Not exactly," say Miss Moore, which is what she say when you warm or way off too. "It's to weigh paper down so it won't scatter and make your desk untidy." So right away me and Sugar curtsy to each other and then to Mercedes who is more the tidy type.

"We don't keep paper on top of the desk in my class," say Junebug, figuring Miss Moore crazy or lyin one.

"At home, then," she say. "Don't you have a calendar and a pencil case and a blotter and a letter-opener on your desk at home where you do your homework?" And she know damn well what our homes look like cause she nosys around in them every chance she gets.

"I don't even have a desk," say Junebug. "Do we?"

"No. And I don't get no homework neither," say Big Butt.

"And I don't even have a home," say Flyboy like he do at school to keep the white folks off his back and sorry for him. Send this poor kid to camp posters, is his specialty.

"I do," says Mercedes. "I have a box of stationery on my desk and a picture of my cat. My godmother bought the stationery and the desk. There's a big rose on each sheet and the envelopes smell like roses."

"Who wants to know about your smelly-ass stationery," say Rosie Giraffe fore I can get my two cents in.

"It's important to have a work area all your own so that . . ."

"Will you look at this sailboat, please," say Flyboy, cuttin her off and pointin to the thing like it was his. So once again we tumble all over each other to gaze at this magnificent thing in the toy store which is just big enough to maybe sail two kittens across the pond if you strap them to the posts tight. We all start reciting the price tag like we in assembly. "Handcrafted sailboat of fiberglass at one thousand one hundred ninety-five dollars."

"Unbelievable," I hear myself say and am really stunned. I read it again for myself just in case the group recitation put me in a trance. Same thing. For some reason this pisses me off. We look at Miss Moore and she lookin at us, waiting for I dunno what.

"Who'd pay all that when you can buy a sailboat set for a quarter at Pop's, a tube of glue for a dime, and a ball of string for eight cents? It must have a motor and a whole lot else besides," I say. "My sailboat cost me about fifty cents."

"But will it take water?" say Mercedes with her smart ass.

"Took mine to Alley Pond Park once," say Flyboy. "String broke, Lost it. Pity."

"Sailed mine in Central Park and it keeled over and sank. Had to ask my father for another dollar."

"And you got the strap," laugh Big Butt. "The jerk didn't even have a string on it. My old man wailed on his behind."

Little Q.T. was staring hard at the sailboat and you could see he wanted it bad. But he too little and somebody'd just take it from him. So what the hell. "This boat for kids, Miss Moore?"

"Parents silly to buy something like that just to get all broke up," say Rosie Giraffe.

"That much money it should last forever," I figure.

"My father'd buy it for me if I wanted it."

"Your father, my ass," say Rosie Giraffe getting a chance to finally push Mercedes.

"Must be rich people shop here," say Q.T.

"You are a very bright boy," say Flyboy. "What was your first clue?" And he rap him on the head with the back of his knuckles, since Q.T. the only one he could get away with. Though Q.T. liable to come up behind you years later and get his licks in when you half expect it.

"What I want to know is," I says to Miss Moore though I never talk to her, I wouldn't give the bitch that satisfaction, "is how much a real boat costs? I figure a thousand'd get you a yacht any day."

"Why don't you check that out," she says, "and report back to the group?" Which really pains my ass. If you gonna mess up a perfectly good swim day least you could do is have some answers. "Let's go in," she say like she got something up her sleeve. Only she don't lead the way. So me and Sugar turn the corner to where the entrance is, but when we get there I kinda hang back. Not that I'm scared, what's there to be afraid of, just a toy store. But I feel funny, shame. But what I got to be shamed about? Got as much right to go in as anybody. But somehow I can't seem to get hold of the door, so I step away for Sugar to lead. But she hangs back too. And I look at her and she looks at me and this is ridiculous. I mean, damn, I have never ever been shy about doing nothing or going nowhere. But then Mercedes steps up and then Rosie Giraffe and Big Butt crowd in behind and shove, and next thing we all stuffed into the doorway with only Mercedes squeezing past us, smoothing out her jumper and walking right down the aisle. Then the rest of us tumble in like a glued-together jigsaw done all wrong. And people lookin at us. And it's like the time me and Sugar crashed into the Catholic church on a dare. But once we got in there and everything so hushed and holy and the candles and the bowin and the handkerchiefs on all the drooping heads, I just couldn't go through with the plan. Which was for me to run up to the altar and do a tap dance while Sugar played the nose flute and messed around in the holy water. And Sugar kept givin me the elbow. Then later teased me so bad I tied her up in the shower and turned it on and locked her in. And she'd be there till this day if Aunt Gretchen hadn't finally figured I was lyin about the boarder takin a shower.

Same thing in the store. We all walkin on tiptoe and hardly touchin the games and puzzles and things. And I watched Miss Moore who is steady watchin us like she waitin for a sign. Like Mama Drewery watches the sky and sniffs the air and takes note of just how much slant is in the bird formation. Then me and Sugar bump smack into each other, so busy gazing at the toys, 'specially the sailboat. But we don't laugh and go into our fat-lady bump-stomach routine. We just stare at that price tag. Then Sugar run a finger over the whole boat. And I'm jealous and want to hit her. Maybe not her, but I sure want to punch somebody in the mouth.

"Watcha bring us here for, Miss Moore?"

"You sound angry, Sylvia. Are you mad about something?" Givin me one of them grins like she tellin a grown-up joke that never turns out to be funny. And she's lookin very closely at me like maybe she plannin to do my portrait from memory. I'm mad, but I won't give her that satisfaction. So I slouch around the store bein very bored and say, "Let's go."

Me and Sugar at the back of the train watchin the tracks whizzin by large then small then gettin gobbled up in the dark. I'm thinkin about this tricky toy I saw in the store. A clown that somersaults on a bar then does chin-ups just cause you yank lightly at his leg. Cost $35. I could see me askin my mother for a $35 birthday clown. "You wanna who that costs what?" she'd say, cocking her head to the side to get a better view of the hole in my head. Thirty-five dollars could buy new bunk beds for Junior and Gretchen's boy. Thirty-five dollars and the whole household could go visit Granddaddy Nelson in the country. Thirty-five dollars would pay for the rent and the piano bill too. Who are these people that spend that much for performing clowns and $1,000 for toy sailboats? What kinda work they do and how they live and how come we ain't in on it? Where we are is who we are, Miss Moore always pointin out. But it don't necessarily have to be that way, she always adds then waits for somebody to say that poor people have to wake up and demand their share of the pie and don't none of us know what kind of pie she talkin about in the first damn place. But she ain't so smart cause I still got her four dollars from the taxi and she sure ain't gettin it. Messin up my day with this shit. Sugar nudges me in my pocket and winks.

Miss Moore lines us up in front of the mailbox where we started from, seem like years ago, and I got a headache for thinkin so hard. And we lean all over each other so we can hold up under the draggy-ass lecture she always finishes us off with at the end before we thank her for borin us to tears. But she just looks at us like she readin tea leaves. Finally she say, "Well, what did you think of F.A.O. Schwartz?"

Rosie Giraffe mumbles, "White folks crazy."

"I'd like to go there again when I get my birthday money," says Mercedes, and we shove her out the pack so she has to lean on the mailbox by herself.

"I'd like a shower. Tiring day," say Flyboy.

Then Sugar surprises me by sayin, "You know, Miss Moore, I don't think all of us here put together eat in a year what that sailboat costs."

And Miss Moore lights up like somebody goosed her. "And?" she say, urging Sugar on. Only I'm standin on her foot so she don't continue.

"Imagine for a minute what kind of society it is in which some people can spend on a toy what it would cost to feed a family of six or seven. What do you think?"

"I think," say Sugar pushing me off her feet like she never done before, cause I whip her ass in a minute, "that this is not much of a democracy if you ask me. Equal chance to pursue happiness means an equal crack at the dough, don't it?" Miss Moore is besides herself and I am disgusted with Sugar's treachery. So I stand on her foot one more time to see if she'll shove me. She shuts up, and Miss Moore looks at me, sorrowfully I'm thinkin. And somethin weird is goin on, I can feel it in my chest.

"Anybody else learn anything today?" lookin dead at me. I walk away and Sugar has to run to catch up and don't even seem to notice when I shrug her arm off my shoulder.

"Well, we got four dollars anyway," she says.

"Uh hunh."

"We could go to Hascombs and get half a chocolate layer and then go to the Sunset and still have plenty money for potato chips and ice-cream sodas."

"Uh hunh."

"Race you to Hascombs," she say.

We start down the block and she gets ahead which is O.K. by me cause I'm goin to the West End and then over to the Drive to think this day through. She can run if she want to and even run faster. But ain't nobody gonna beat me at nuthin.

Study and Discussion Questions

1. What exactly is the lesson Miss Moore is trying to teach? To what extent does the narrator, Sylvia, learn it? What are the sources of her resistance to it?
2. Why does Sylvia feel ashamed entering the toy store? What does this reveal about her?
3. What is the significance of the last sentence of the story?
4. Why does Miss Moore feel the need to teach Sylvia and her friends a lesson now that they would no doubt eventually learn on their own?
5. What does Bambara gain by using Sylvia as a first-person narrator?

Writing Exercises

1. What kind of society is it, Miss Moore asks, "in which some people can spend on a toy what it would cost to feed a family of six or seven"? How would you answer?

2. Describe the first time you can remember being aware of social class differences.

CAROLYN CHUTE   (b. 1947)

Carolyn Chute was born in Cape Elizabeth, Maine, left school at sixteen to get married, and was divorced three years later. While supporting herself and her daughter through potato picking, welfare, and work as a domestic, she earned her high school diploma, took courses at the University of Maine, and began writing. Chute has worked as a journalist and published fiction in a number of periodicals. "Tall Woman Love" is from The Beans of Egypt, Maine *(1985), her first novel.*

Tall Woman Love   (1985)

The door opens and the new neighbor, March Goodspeed, the celebrated highway engineer, hurries down the hot-top path to the hot-top driveway in his pointy dress-up shoes and asphalt-color suit.

Across the road, the tall woman, Roberta Bean, is dressed in a man's ribbed undershirt and green wool pants. She is circling a piece of bare ground with an axe, her babies in yellow raincoats. The babies ornament her ankles, dangle from her pant legs. Thwank! Thwank! Thwank! Her axe beats upon the chopping block.

March Goodspeed picks open the door of his forest-green Lincoln. He lays a folder of papers on the seat. He does not say good morning to Roberta Bean. He quickly dives into his car. The tall woman circles the chopping block, her babies moving as she moves.

Roberta Bean has the smallest head of all Beans, her head being about the size of a fifteen-cent turnip with a blue knit cap stretched over the top of it. The hat has a chrome-yellow cuff. Nowhere does her black black hair show.

March Goodspeed shuts the door of his Lincoln.

Roberta Bean's axe goes Thwank! Thwank! Thwank!

March was to be in Portland by ten . . . a site walk for a new shopping center. It is 10:03. He turns the key. The Lincoln breathes almost like a human being. March pats the folder of papers on the seat. He clicks on the news. He starts to back out of the yard.

The tall woman is so tall she divides March's rearview mirror into two clean halves, white grass to the left, white grass to the right. And everywhere, shuffling and darting, are babies and the tall woman's peach-color hens.

The Lincoln stalls partway into the road. March twists the key.

Out of the openings of the undershirt, Roberta Bean's assiduous, straining, bony neck and scarry long long arms work the axe on the stringy wood. Faster. Faster. Now and then one of her dark eyes turns onto the Lincoln Continental.

The Lincoln whispers, "A-herm hm hm hm" . . . little burps, little giggles. "Start, damn you!" the highway engineer demands.

Some of the peach-color hens have come to his lawn, poke in his short grass. March rubs his eyes.

The tall woman moves all over the Lincoln's rearview mirror as a prizefighter moves around the ring. The white wood is spewed into the pile . . . faster, faster. Her back is to March now. She seems to ignore him.

March checks his watch. 10:09. He twists the key. "Start!" he commands.

The Lincoln only laughs.

The man slumps in his seat, his heart scrambling inside his dress shirt like a pillowcase full of puppies.

The babies seem unconvinced of the possibility of being stepped upon by one of the tall woman's mighty boots. Dazed by their love, they keep in step.

March squints at the mirror.

Roberta puts down her axe. She looks at March Goodspeed.

March can smell gas.

Roberta Bean crosses the road. With her flutters an army of boots and yellow raincoats, a hollow tromp tromp tromp tromp.

"Why is this happening?" March breathes. He picks a ballpoint pen from his breast pocket and snaps it fast. He takes a breath of his Lincoln's rich interior.

Roberta Bean's tiny head is smiling at him through the glass.

March has blond hair, the color of faded newspapers. You'd never know he had been a redhead as a child; you'd never have known he had been a child. His eyes show leadership, are fibrous as salad olives. Green.

Her eyes look tired.

Reluctantly he scratches at the button. The window glass disappears as naturally as a lake thaws.

March says, "It's just flooded. It'll be all right in a few moments."

Roberta Bean redistributes her stature, somewhat to the left, and simultaneously there's the rumble of ten oversized boots, each boot to the left.

Long feelerlike noses sniff up at March. He looks down just in time to see one baby pick up a small piece of broken glass and aim it at his Lincoln. "Make that child behave!" March shouts.

Roberta's dark, close-together eyes move onto the child.

The baby puts the glass in its raincoat pocket.

Another baby spits. The foamy wob slides down the door of the Lincoln.

"You need a jump," the tall woman says. Then her mouth opens for a smile, the teeth like the far-apart teeth of a Doberman, long, fat, yellow, sharp.

March says, "It's flooded. That's all."

Roberta says, "Eyup . . . gas stinks." She puts both hands on the window frame and rocks the Lincoln so that March and the Lincoln move in great waves on the luxurious springs. "Ain't she a dandy!" the tall woman says.

March's eyes rest on the front of her undershirt, its rapt, fat flowers of spilled coffee, and some year-old blood shaped like the paw of a cat.

She says, "You set there, mistah, an' I'll getcha some help."

"No. In a few moments the gas will dry out. You just go back to what you were doing." He is as commanding as a trainer to a huge but humble dog.

"Yes-suh," she sneers, withdrawing her hands. "If it was just flooded. But you cranked on your throttle till she don't hardly turn over . . . does she? . . . You've run your batt'ry down. I'll getcha some help." And she veers away in the horrible scuffing of many boots.

He hangs his head.

One of the peach-color hens steps up and hammers with her beak on her reflection in the Lincoln's hubcap.

On the same side of the road as Roberta Bean's wee blue house is Beans' Variety Store. With sweaty dread, March anticipates four or five of those woolly, squinting Egypt, Maine, men over on the piazza of the store—fluorescent vests, black nails, wagging beards—loping toward him, hailed by Roberta Bean. And they would study him frankly through the tinted windshield, the way visitors to hospitals gape through Plexiglas at newborns.

But no. She returns without them.

Her black truck is parked by the front steps of her wee blue house like you tie a dog out to pee. She and her babies get into this truck, and she backs it out onto the pavement with a clanging like a half-dozen cowbells. The yellow-raincoated shapes of her children bounce around beside her on the seat.

She lines up her hood with his hood.

March closes his eyes, opens them slowly.

He turns in his seat and there's the tall woman, hurrying, helpful, steam rising out of her like what rises on the backs of straining spotted oxen. He squares his shoulders, pats the knot of his asphalt-color necktie.

"Shit!" he cries as his folder of many papers slips to the floor, covering the pedals and his pointy, shiny shoes.

Roberta flings up both hoods and uncoils jumper cables from around her neck and shoulders, cables which she carries there with the exuberance of one who wields pet snakes. He opens his eyes to see her fingers strum the cables' silken skins. And how gracefully she capers between the vehicles, her eyes misting in a joy March cannot fathom.

A half-dozen hens are now pecking at the bright hubcaps.

Meanwhile, the babies storm out of the black fenderless truck, three of them fastening to one of the tall woman's calves, two the other.

March sweeps open the door of his Lincoln, authority written on his face, knotting him up hard.

She is clasping the cables onto the terminals as he drives his own arms through her long long bare ones. "I'll do that now," he says.

But she is done.

The babies glare up at him. One is looking at March's left pointy black shoe.

March's arms are still parallel with the tall woman's bare ones. He is drawing back in slow motion, in disbelief. His heart is just one of the babies' oversized boots . . . tromp tromp tromp tromp. Roberta Bean's smell is in his face, a smell he is convinced is the smell of the inside of her wee blue house. Because of this smell, he sees the long fingers worrying the rubber from a Mason jar of cloudy green beans, boiling them hard, doling out baggy white yeast rolls, everything of a hotness that is injurious to the lips and gums, while this brood with crew cuts and long noses, like a bizarre litter of moles, tries even at the table to get close to her, forever close, madly close.

He backs onto the short grass of his yard. His necktie flounces.

With curling lips, the babies stare at March Goodspeed's pointy black shoes. "YUKK!" one of them says.

A small hen sees her reflection in his heel, jabs at it.

March re-enters his Lincoln.

In a matter of moments he is shifting into reverse, giving the Lincoln the gas. It lurches over the road, backwards. Hens squawk. The babies look up at the tall woman, their eyes wrinkled up with love. The big car lunges up the grade and springs into the sun.

Study and Discussion Questions

1. From whose perspective is this story told? Is there any irony created by this perspective?
2. What evidence is there that March feels uncomfortable? Why do you suppose he is?
3. How is authority depicted in this story? Are there different kinds of authority? What kind does March have? What kind does Roberta have?
4. What is March's relation to his car?
5. What is Roberta's relation to her babies (and what is their relation to her)?
6. Make a list of words that describe or refer to Roberta.
7. How do the babies and the chickens react to March?
8. List examples of competence and incompetence in the story.

Writing Exercises

1. Chart the progress of Roberta's gain in power and authority and March's loss of it through the story.
2. Discuss these two images: "The tall woman is so tall she divides March's rearview mirror into two clean halves . . ." and "the tall woman moves all over the Lincoln's rearview mirror as a prizefighter moves around the ring."
3. What does March wish had happened instead?

ALICE WALKER (b. 1944)

Alice Walker was born in Eatonton, Georgia, where her parents were sharecroppers. She studied at Spelman and Sarah Lawrence Colleges and worked actively in the civil rights movement. Walker has taught at a number of universities, has been a contributing editor of Ms. *magazine, and now works with Wild Trees Press in California. Her writing includes the story collections* In Love and Trouble: Stories of Black Women *(1973) and* You Can't Keep a Good Woman Down *(1981); the novels* Meridian *(1976) and* The Color Purple *(1982); the poetry collection,* Revolutionary Petunias *(1973); and the volume of essays,* In Search of Our Mothers' Gardens: Womanist Prose *(1983).*

Everyday Use (1973)

for your grandmama

I will wait for her in the yard that Maggie and I made so clean and wavy yesterday afternoon. A yard like this is more comfortable than most people know. It is not just a yard. It is like an extended living room. When the hard clay is swept clean as a floor and the fine sand around the edges lined with tiny, irregular grooves, anyone can come and sit and look up into the elm tree and wait for the breezes that never come inside the house.

Maggie will be nervous until after her sister goes: she will stand hopelessly in corners, homely and ashamed of the burn scars down her arms and legs, eying her sister with a mixture of envy and awe. She thinks her sister has held life always in the palm of one hand, that "no" is a word the world never learned to say to her.

You've no doubt seen those TV shows where the child who has "made it" is confronted, as a surprise, by her own mother and father, tottering

in weakly from backstage. (A pleasant surprise, of course: What would
they do if parent and child came on the show only to curse out and
insult each other?) On TV mother and child embrace and smile into each
other's faces. Sometimes the mother and father weep, the child wraps
them in her arms and leans across the table to tell how she would not
have made it without their help. I have seen these programs.

Sometimes I dream a dream in which Dee and I are suddenly brought
together on a TV program of this sort. Out of a dark and soft-seated
limousine I am ushered into a bright room filled with many people. There
I meet a smiling, gray, sporty man like Johnny Carson who shakes my
hand and tells me what a fine girl I have. Then we are on the stage and
Dee is embracing me with tears in her eyes. She pins on my dress a large
orchid, even though she has told me once that she thinks orchids are
tacky flowers.

In real life I am a large, big-boned woman with rough, man-working
hands. In the winter I wear flannel nightgowns to bed and overalls during
the day. I can kill and clean a hog as mercilessly as a man. My fat keeps
me hot in zero weather. I can work outside all day, breaking ice to get
water for washing; I can eat pork liver cooked over the open fire minutes
after it comes steaming from the hog. One winter I knocked a bull calf
straight in the brain between the eyes with a sledge hammer and had
the meat hung up to chill before nightfall. But of course all this does not
show on television. I am the way my daughter would want me to be: a
hundred pounds lighter, my skin like an uncooked barley pancake. My
hair glistens in the hot bright lights. Johnny Carson has much to do to
keep up with my quick and witty tongue.

But that is a mistake. I know even before I wake up. Who ever knew
a Johnson with a quick tongue? Who can even imagine me looking a
strange white man in the eye? It seems to me I have talked to them
always with one foot raised in flight, with my head turned in whichever
way is farthest from them. Dee, though. She would always look anyone
in the eye. Hesitation was no part of her nature.

"How do I look, Mama?" Maggie says, showing just enough of her
thin body enveloped in pink skirt and red blouse for me to know she's
there, almost hidden by the door.

"Come out into the yard," I say.

Have you ever seen a lame animal, perhaps a dog run over by some
careless person rich enough to own a car, sidle up to someone who is
ignorant enough to be kind to him? That is the way my Maggie walks.
She has been like this, chin on chest, eyes on ground, feet in shuffle,
ever since the fire that burned the other house to the ground.

Dee is lighter than Maggie, with nicer hair and a fuller figure. She's a
woman now, though sometimes I forget. How long ago was it that the
other house burned? Ten, twelve years? Sometimes I can still hear the
flames and feel Maggie's arms sticking to me, her hair smoking and her

dress falling off her in little black papery flakes. Her eyes seemed stretched open, blazed open by the flames reflected in them. And Dee. I see her standing off under the sweet gum tree she used to dig gum out of; a look of concentration on her face as she watched the last dingy gray board of the house fall in toward the red-hot brick chimney. Why don't you do a dance around the ashes? I'd wanted to ask her. She had hated the house that much.

I used to think she hated Maggie, too. But that was before we raised the money, the church and me, to send her to Augusta to school. She used to read to us without pity; forcing words, lies, other folks' habits, whole lives upon us two, sitting trapped and ignorant underneath her voice. She washed us in a river of make-believe, burned us with a lot of knowledge we didn't necessarily need to know. Pressed us to her with the serious way she read, to shove us away at just the moment, like dimwits, we seemed about to understand.

Dee wanted nice things. A yellow organdy dress to wear to her graduation from high school; black pumps to match a green suit she'd made from an old suit somebody gave me. She was determined to stare down any disaster in her efforts. Her eyelids would not flicker for minutes at a time. Often I fought off the temptation to shake her. At sixteen she had a style of her own: and knew what style was.

I never had an education myself. After second grade the school was closed down. Don't ask me why: in 1927 colored asked fewer questions than they do now. Sometimes Maggie reads to me. She stumbles along good-naturedly but can't see well. She knows she is not bright. Like good looks and money, quickness passed her by. She will marry John Thomas (who has mossy teeth in an earnest face) and then I'll be free to sit here and I guess just sing church songs to myself. Although I never was a good singer. Never could carry a tune. I was always better at a man's job. I used to love to milk till I was hooked in the side in '49. Cows are soothing and slow and don't bother you, unless you try to milk them the wrong way.

I have deliberately turned my back on the house. It is three rooms, just like the one that burned, except the roof is tin; they don't make shingle roofs any more. There are no real windows, just some holes cut in the sides, like the portholes in a ship, but not round and not square, with rawhide holding the shutters up on the outside. This house is in a pasture, too, like the other one. No doubt when Dee sees it she will want to tear it down. She wrote me once that no matter where we "choose" to live, she will manage to come see us. But she will never bring her friends. Maggie and I thought about this and Maggie asked me, "Mama, when did Dee ever *have* any friends?"

She had a few. Furtive boys in pink shirts hanging about on washday after school. Nervous girls who never laughed. Impressed with her they worshiped the well-turned phrase, the cute shape, the scalding humor that erupted like bubbles in lye. She read to them.

When she was courting Jimmy T she didn't have much time to pay to us, but turned all her faultfinding power on him. He *flew* to marry a cheap city girl from a family of ignorant flashy people. She hardly had time to recompose herself.

When she comes I will meet—but there they are!

Maggie attempts to make a dash for the house; in her shuffling way, but I stay her with my hand. "Come back here," I say. And she stops and tries to dig a well in the sand with her toe.

It is hard to see them clearly through the strong sun. But even the first glimpse of leg out of the car tells me it is Dee. Her feet were always neat-looking, as if God himself had shaped them with a certain style. From the other side of the car comes a short, stocky man. Hair is all over his head a foot long and hanging from his chin like a kinky mule tail. I hear Maggie suck in her breath. "Uhnnnh," is what it sounds like. Like when you see the wriggling end of a snake just in front of your foot on the road. "Uhnnnh."

Dee next. A dress down to the ground, in this hot weather. A dress so loud it hurts my eyes. There are yellows and oranges enough to throw back the light of the sun. I feel my whole face warming from the heat waves it throws out. Earrings gold, too, and hanging down to her shoulders. Bracelets dangling and making noises when she moves her arm up to shake the folds of the dress out of her armpits. The dress is loose and flows, and as she walks closer, I like it. I hear Maggie go "Uhnnnh" again. It is her sister's hair. It stands straight up like the wool on a sheep. It is black as night and around the edges are two long pigtails that rope about like small lizards disappearing behind her ears.

"Wa-su-zo-Tean-o!"[1] she says, coming on in that gliding way the dress makes her move. The short stocky fellow with the hair to his navel is all grinning and he follows up with "Asalamalakim,[2] my mother and sister!" He moves to hug Maggie but she falls back, right up against the back of my chair. I feel her trembling there and when I look up I see the perspiration falling off her chin.

"Don't get up," says Dee. Since I am stout it takes something of a push. You can see me trying to move a second or two before I make it. She turns, showing white heels through her sandals, and goes back to the car. Out she peeks next with a Polaroid. She stoops down quickly and lines up picture after picture of me sitting there in front of the house with Maggie cowering behind me. She never takes a shot without making sure the house is included. When a cow comes nibbling around the edge of the yard she snaps it and me and Maggie *and* the house. Then she

---

[1] Swahili greeting.
[2] Arabic greeting.

puts the Polaroid in the back seat of the car, and comes up and kisses me on the forehead.

Meanwhile Asalamalakim is going through motions with Maggie's hand. Maggie's hand is as limp as a fish, and probably as cold, despite the sweat, and she keeps trying to pull it back. It looks like Asalamalakim wants to shake hands but wants to do it fancy. Or maybe he don't know how people shake hands. Anyhow, he soon gives up on Maggie.

"Well," I say. "Dee."

"No, Mama," she says. "Not 'Dee,' Wangero Leewanika Kemanjo!"

"What happened to 'Dee'?" I wanted to know.

"She's dead," Wangero said. "I couldn't bear it any longer, being named after the people who oppress me."

"You know as well as me you was named after your aunt Dicie," I said. Dicie is my sister. She named Dee. We called her "Big Dee" after Dee was born.

"But who was *she* named after?" asked Wangero.

"I guess after Grandma Dee," I said.

"And who was she named after?" asked Wangero.

"Her mother," I said, and saw Wangero was getting tired. "That's about as far back as I can trace it," I said. Though, in fact, I probably could have carried it back beyond the Civil War through the branches.

"Well," said Asalamalakim, "there you are."

"Uhnnnh," I heard Maggie say.

"There I was not," I said, "before 'Dicie' cropped up in our family, so why should I try to trace it that far back?"

He just stood there grinning, looking down on me like somebody inspecting a Model A car. Every once in a while he and Wangero sent eye signals over my head.

"How do you pronounce this name?" I asked.

"You don't have to call me by it if you don't want to," said Wangero.

"Why shouldn't I?" I asked. "If that's what you want us to call you, we'll call you."

"I know it might sound awkward at first," said Wangero.

"I'll get used to it," I said. "Ream it out again."

Well, soon we got the name out of the way. Asalamalakim had a name twice as long and three times as hard. After I tripped over it two or three times he told me to just call him Hakim-a-barber. I wanted to ask him was he a barber, but I didn't really think he was, so I didn't ask.

"You must belong to those beef-cattle peoples down the road," I said. They said "Asalamalakim" when they met you, too, but they didn't shake hands. Always too busy: feeding the cattle, fixing the fences, putting up salt-lick shelters, throwing down hay. When the white folks poisoned some of the herd the men stayed up all night with rifles in their hands. I walked a mile and a half just to see the sight.

Hakim-a-barber said, "I accept some of their doctrines, but farming and raising cattle is not my style." (They didn't tell me, and I didn't ask, whether Wangero (Dee) had really gone and married him.)

We sat down to eat and right away he said he didn't eat collards and pork was unclean. Wangero, though, went on through the chitlins and corn bread, the greens and everything else. She talked a blue streak over the sweet potatoes. Everything delighted her. Even the fact that we still used the benches her daddy made for the table when we couldn't afford to buy chairs.

"Oh, Mama!" she cried. Then turned to Hakim-a-barber. "I never knew how lovely these benches are. You can feel the rump prints," she said, running her hands underneath her and along the bench. Then she gave a sigh and her hand closed over Grandma Dee's butter dish. "That's it!" she said. "I knew there was something I wanted to ask you if I could have." She jumped up from the table and went over in the corner where the churn stood, the milk in it clabber by now. She looked at the churn and looked at it.

"This churn top is what I need," she said. "Didn't Uncle Buddy whittle it out of a tree you all used to have?"

"Yes," I said.

"Uh huh," she said happily. "And I want the dasher, too."

"Uncle Buddy whittle that, too?" asked the barber.

Dee (Wangero) looked up at me.

"Aunt Dee's first husband whittled the dash," said Maggie so low you almost couldn't hear her. "His name was Henry, but they called him Stash."

"Maggie's brain is like an elephant's," Wangero said, laughing. "I can use the churn top as a centerpiece for the alcove table," she said, sliding a plate over the churn, "and I'll think of something artistic to do with the dasher."

When she finished wrapping the dasher the handle stuck out. I took it for a moment in my hands. You didn't even have to look close to see where hands pushing the dasher up and down to make butter had left a kind of sink in the wood. In fact, there were a lot of small sinks; you could see where thumbs and fingers had sunk into the wood. It was beautiful light yellow wood, from a tree that grew in the yard where Big Dee and Stash had lived.

After dinner Dee (Wangero) went to the trunk at the foot of my bed and started rifling through it. Maggie hung back in the kitchen over the dishpan. Out came Wangero with two quilts. They had been pieced by Grandma Dee and then Big Dee and me had hung them on the quilt frames on the front porch and quilted them. One was in the Lone Star pattern. The other was Walk Around the Mountain. In both of them were scraps of dresses Grandma Dee had worn fifty and more years ago. Bits and pieces of Grandpa Jarrell's Paisley shirts. And one teeny faded blue piece, about the size of a penny matchbox, that was from Great Grandpa Ezra's uniform that he wore in the Civil War.

"Mama," Wangero said sweet as a bird. "Can I have these old quilts?"

I heard something fall in the kitchen, and a minute later the kitchen door slammed.

"Why don't you take one or two of the others?" I asked. "These old things was just done by me and Big Dee from some tops your grandma pieced before she died."

"No," said Wangero. "I don't want those. They are stitched around the borders by machine."

"That'll make them last better," I said.

"That's not the point," said Wangero. "These are all pieces of dresses Grandma used to wear. She did all this stitching by hand. Imagine!" She held the quilts securely in her arms, stroking them.

"Some of the pieces, like those lavender ones, come from old clothes her mother handed down to her," I said, moving up to touch the quilts. Dee (Wangero) moved back just enough so that I couldn't reach the quilts. They already belonged to her.

"Imagine!" she breathed again, clutching them closely to her bosom.

"The truth is," I said, "I promised to give them quilts to Maggie, for when she marries John Thomas."

She gasped like a bee had stung her.

"Maggie can't appreciate these quilts!" she said. "She'd probably be backward enough to put them to everyday use."

"I reckon she would," I said. "God knows I been saving 'em for long enough with nobody using 'em. I hope she will!" I didn't want to bring up how I had offered Dee (Wangero) a quilt when she went away to college. Then she had told me they were old-fashioned, out of style.

"But they're *priceless!*" she was saying now, furiously; for she has a temper. "Maggie would put them on the bed and in five years they'd be in rags. Less than that!"

"She can always make some more," I said. "Maggie knows how to quilt."

Dee (Wangero) looked at me with hatred. "You just will not understand. The point is these quilts, *these* quilts!"

"Well," I said, stumped. "What would *you* do with them?"

"Hang them," she said. As if that was the only thing you *could* do with quilts.

Maggie by now was standing in the door. I could almost hear the sound her feet made as they scraped over each other.

"She can have them, Mama," she said, like somebody used to never winning anything, or having anything reserved for her. "I can 'member Grandma Dee without the quilts."

I looked at her hard. She had filled her bottom lip with checkerberry snuff and it gave her face a kind of dopey, hangdog look. It was Grandma Dee and Big Dee who taught her how to quilt herself. She stood there with her scarred hands hidden in the folds of her skirt. She looked at her sister with something like fear but she wasn't mad at her. This was Maggie's portion. This was the way she knew God to work.

When I looked at her like that something hit me in the top of my head and ran down to the soles of my feet. Just like when I'm in church and the spirit of God touches me and I get happy and shout. I did something I never had done before: hugged Maggie to me, then dragged her on into the room, snatched the quilts out of Miss Wangero's hands and dumped them into Maggie's lap. Maggie just sat there on my bed with her mouth open.

"Take one or two of the others," I said to Dee.

But she turned without a word and went out to Hakim-a-barber.

"You just don't understand," she said, as Maggie and I came out to the car.

"What don't I understand?" I wanted to know.

"Your heritage," she said. And then she turned to Maggie, kissed her, and said, "You ought to try to make something of yourself, too, Maggie. It's really a new day for us. But from the way you and Mama still live you'd never know it."

She put on some sunglasses that hid everything above the tip of her nose and her chin.

Maggie smiled; maybe at the sunglasses. But a real smile, not scared. After we watched the car dust settle I asked Maggie to bring me a dip of snuff. And then the two of us sat there just enjoying, until it was time to go in the house and go to bed.

Study and Discussion Questions

1. Who is the first-person narrator of this story?
2. Why do you think the mother describes herself in terms of the work she does? What are the differences between the real mother and the TV version she sometimes dreams?
3. What are we told about Dee before we ever meet her?
4. What does the house-burning incident tell us about the three characters and their relation to each other?
5. What does the title of the story refer to?
6. How has Dee changed, according to her mother? What have social class and class mobility to do with this?
7. Why does Dee take pictures of the house and want the churn top and the quilts?
8. What does Dee plan to do with the quilts? What will Maggie do with them?

Writing Exercises

1. Contrast Maggie and Dee.
2. Do you have any sympathy for Dee? If so, on what grounds? If not, why not?

3. Discuss the importance in this story of education, what it is, and what one does with it.
4. What is the wealth this family possesses? How do Maggie, Dee, and the mother each see that wealth and themselves in relation to it?
5. What does "Everyday Use" suggest about one's relation to one's past, heritage, and tradition?
6. Discuss the importance of names in the story.
7. Write about an experience you've had going home, either from your own perspective or from the point of view of another family member.

POETRY

BERTOLT BRECHT   (1898–1956)

Bertolt Brecht was born in Augsburg, Germany, studied medicine at Munich University, and worked as an orderly in a military hospital at the end of World War I. He soon became a radical critic of war and nationalism. He wrote poems and stories, but concentrated on drama. In 1929 he married actress Helene Weigel, for whom he wrote many roles. With the rise of Hitler, Brecht left Germany in 1933, eventually coming to California in 1941, where he worked with Charlie Chaplin and others in the film industry. He settled in East Berlin in the late 1940s. Among Brecht's major plays are The Threepenny Opera *(1928), written with Kurt Weill,* The Life of Galileo *(1939),* Mother Courage and Her Children *(1939),* The Good Woman of Setzuan *(1940), and* The Caucasian Chalk Circle *(1945).*

A Worker Reads History[1]   (1936)

Who built the seven gates of Thebes?
The books are filled with names of kings.
Was it kings who hauled the craggy blocks of stone?
And Babylon, so many times destroyed,
Who built the city up each time? In which of Lima's houses,   5
That city glittering with gold, lived those who built it?
In the evening when the Chinese wall was finished
Where did the masons go? Imperial Rome
Is full of arcs of triumph. Who reared them up? Over whom
Did the Caesars triumph? Byzantium lives in song,   10
Were all her dwellings palaces? And even in Atlantis of the legend
The night the sea rushed in,
The drowning men still bellowed for their slaves.

Young Alexander conquered India.
He alone?   15
Caesar beat the Gauls.
Was there not even a cook in his army?
Philip of Spain wept as his fleet
Was sunk and destroyed. Were there no other tears?

---

[1] Translated by H.R. Hays.

Frederick the Great triumphed in the Seven Years War. Who   20
Triumphed with him?

Each page a victory,
At whose expense the victory ball?
Every ten years a great man,   25
Who paid the piper?

So many particulars.
So many questions.

Study and Discussion Questions

1. List the different roles in the poem (invisible in history books) that members of the lower classes have played.
2. Why are so many sentences in the poem questions? Is this only a rhetorical device?
3. What are the meanings and the irony of "Each page a victory"?
4. Explain "Every ten years a great man, / Who paid the piper?"

Writing Exercises

1. Where do women of the lower classes appear in the poem? Why doesn't Brecht mention *their* work?
2. To what extent and how were the lower classes represented in the history you learned in school?
3. Write a poem or paragraph about a woman or a black person or a member of another historically dispossessed group reading history.

JONATHAN SWIFT (1667–1745)

Jonathan Swift was born in Dublin, Ireland and educated at Trinity College there. At various times, he was secretary to essayist and diplomat Sir William Temple, a vicar, a political pamphleteer and journalist, and Dean of St. Patrick's Cathedral in Dublin. By 1720, he had become a passionate critic of British imperial exploitation of Ireland and much of his stinging satiric writing is on behalf of Irish national interests. Swift is best known for his prose writings, including Battle of the Books *(1704),* The Tale of a Tub *(1704),* Gulliver's Travels *(1726), and* A Modest Proposal *(1729).*

A Description of the Morning (1709)

Now hardly here and there a hackney-coach
Appearing, showed the ruddy morn's approach.
Now Betty from her master's bed had flown,
And softly stole to discompose her own;
The slip-shod 'prentice from his master's door 5
Had pared the dirt and sprinkled round the floor.
Now Moll had whirled her mop with dext'rous airs,
Prepared to scrub the entry and the stairs.
The youth with broomy stumps began to trace
The kennel-edge, where wheels had worn the place.[1] 10
The small-coal man was heard with cadence deep,
Till drowned in shriller notes of chimney-sweep:
Duns at his lordship's gate began to meet;
And brickdust Moll had screamed through half the street.
The turnkey now his flock returning sees, 15
Duly let out a-nights to steal for fees:[2]
The watchful bailiffs take their silent stands,
And schoolboys lag with satchels in their hands.

Study and Discussion Questions

1. Spell out what each person described is doing and why.
2. What is the speaker's attitude towards what is described?
3. What comment is the poem making on differences in social class?
4. What is the significance of the juxtaposition in the last two lines?

Writing Exercises

1. There is a long tradition of poems describing the morning's beauty in *pastoral* terms, picturing glorious fields, idle shepherds, and so on. What relation does "A Description of the Morning" have to such poems?
2. Try capturing Swift's tone in a paragraph describing the morning at a place you are familiar with.

THOMAS HARDY (1840–1928)

Thomas Hardy was born near Dorchester, England, and lived there most of his life. He worked as an architect until he was able to support himself

---

[1] The youth is scavenging in the gutter.
[2] To pay their jailer.

*writing novels. He wrote poetry early on and also later in life; it was in part
the scandalized reaction to his novel* Jude the Obscure *which led Hardy to
return to poetry. While he was alive, his reputation rested on his fiction, but
today his poetry is considered equally important. Among Hardy's novels are*
Far from the Madding Crowd *(1874),* Return of the Native *(1878),* The
Mayor of Casterbridge *(1885),* Tess of the d'Urbervilles *(1891), and* Jude
the Obscure *(1895). Between 1898 and 1928 he published seven volumes of
verse and a verse epic-drama,* The Dynasts *(1908).*

The Ruined Maid (1866)

'O 'Melia, my dear, this does everything crown!
Who could have supposed I should meet you in Town?
And whence such fair garments, such prosperi-ty?'—
'O didn't you know I'd been ruined?' said she.

—'You left us in tatters, without shoes or socks,   5
Tired of digging potatoes, and spudding up docks;[1]
And now you've gay bracelets and bright feathers three!'—
'Yes: that's how we dress when we're ruined,' said she.

—'At home in the barton[2] you said "thee" and "thou",
And "thik oon", and "theäs oon", and "t'other"; but now   10
Your talking quite fits 'ee for high compa-ny!'—
'A polish is gained with one's ruin,' said she.

—'Your hands were like paws then, your face blue and bleak,
But now I'm bewitched by your delicate cheek,
And your little gloves fit as on any la-dy!'—   15
'We never do work when we're ruined,' said she.

—'You used to call home-life a hag-ridden dream,
And you'd sigh, and you'd sock[3]; but at present you seem
To know not of megrims[4] or melancho-ly!'—
'True. One's pretty lively when ruined,' said she.   20

—'I wish I had feathers, a fine sweeping gown,
And a delicate face, and could strut about Town!'—

---

[1] Digging weeds.
[2] Farm yard.
[3] Sigh.
[4] Severe headaches.

'My dear—a raw country girl, such as you be,
Cannot quite expect that. You ain't ruined,' said she.

Study and Discussion Questions

1. Who is speaking to 'Melia?
2. Define "ruined." What is the attitude of each of the two young women toward ruin?
3. What do we learn about the other woman from her observations about 'Melia?
4. What is the significance of "ain't" in the last line?

Writing Exercise

1. What attitude towards prostitution does the poem as a whole express? What do you think of this attitude?

JUDY GRAHN   (b. 1940)*

Asking for Ruthie   (1970)

you know her hustle
you know her white legs
flicker among headlights
and her eyes pick up the wind
while the fast hassle of living   5
ticks off her days
you know her ways

you know her hustle
you know her lonely pockets
lined with tricks   10
turned and forgotten
the men like mice hide
under her mind
lumpy, bigeyed
you know her pride   15

---

* A brief biography of Judy Grahn appears on page 451.

you know her blonde arms cut
by broken nickels in
hotelrooms and by razors of
summer lightning on the road
but you know the wizard   20
highway, no resisting so
she moves, she is forever missing

get her a stopping place
before the night slides dirty
fingers under her eyelids and   25
the weight of much bad kissing
breaks that ricepaper face

sun cover her, earth
make love to Ruthie
stake her to hot lunches in the wheat fields   30
make bunches of purple ravens
fly out in formation, over her eyes
and let her newest lovers
be gentle as women   35
and longer lasting

Study and Discussion Questions

1. What kind of work does Ruthie do?
2. What patterns of sound do you notice in this poem? Note uses of phrase repetition, of alliteration, and of rhyme.
3. What does the speaker of the poem wish for Ruthie?

Writing Exercise

1. "Asking for Ruthie" has two parts. What are they and what does each part do?

WENDY ROSE   (b. 1948)

Wendy Rose, of Hopi and Miwok ancestry, was born in Oakland, California. She graduated from the University of California at Berkeley, has taught there, and has been editor of the American Indian Quarterly. *Rose's poetry includes*

Hopi Roadrunner Dancing *(1973)*, Academic Squaw *(1977)*, Lost Copper
(1980), and The Halfbreed Chronicles *(1985)*.

Three Thousand Dollar Death Song   (1980)

> "Nineteen American Indian skeletons from
> Nevada . . . valued at $3000 . . ."—Museum
> invoice, 1975

Is it in cold hard cash? the kind
that dusts the insides of men's pockets
lying silver-polished surface along the cloth.
Or in bills? papering the wallets of they
who thread the night with dark words. Or   5
checks? paper promises weighing the same
as words spoken once on the other side
of the grown grass and dammed rivers
of history. However it goes, it goes.
Through my body it goes   10
assessing each nerve, running its edges
along my arteries, planning ahead
for whose hands will rip me
into pieces of dusty red paper,
whose hands will smooth or smatter me   15
into traces of rubble. Invoiced now,
it's official how our bones are valued
that stretch out pointing to sunrise
or are flexed into one last foetal bend,
that are removed and tossed about,   20
catalogued, numbered with black ink
on newly-white foreheads.
As we were formed to the white soldier's voice,
so we explode under white students' hands.
Death is a long trail of days   25
in our fleshless prison.

From this distant point we watch our bones
auctioned with our careful beadwork,
our quilled medicine bundles, even the bridles
of our shot-down horses.   You: who have   30
priced us, you who have removed us: at what cost?
What price the pits where our bones share
a single bit of memory, how one century
turns our dead into specimens, our history
into dust, our survivors into clowns.   35

Our memory might be catching, you know;
picture the mortars, the arrowheads, the labrets
shaking off their labels like bears
suddenly awake to find the seasons have ended
while they slept. Watch them touch each other,   40
measure reality, march out the museum door!
Watch as they lift their faces
and smell about for us; watch our bones rise
to meet them and mount the horses once again!
The cost, then, will be paid   45
for our sweetgrass-smelling having-been
in clam shell beads and steatite,
dentalia and woodpecker scalp, turquoise
and copper, blood and oil, coal
and uranium, children, a universe   50
of stolen things.

Study and Discussion Questions

1. Who is speaking? To whom does "we" refer?
2. Why does Rose begin the poem with questions? Why those questions?
3. Early on, she writes of "words spoken once on the other side/ of the grown grass and damned rivers/ of history." Explain.
4. Trace the use of the language of money throughout the poem.

Writing Exercise:

1. Explain, as if to someone who simply did not understand, what the poet might find so appalling about the museum invoice.

THEODORE ROETHKE   (1908–1963)

Theodore Roethke was born in Saginaw, Michigan, where his German immigrant grandfather and his father owned greenhouses. Roethke attended the University of Michigan and Harvard and taught for years at the University of Washington. His poetry includes Open House *(1941),* The Lost Son *(1948),* Praise the End! *(1951), and* The Waking *(1953).*

Dolor   (1948)

I have known the inexorable sadness of pencils,
Neat in their boxes, dolor of pad and paper-weight,

All the misery of manilla folders and mucilage,
Desolation in immaculate public places,
Lonely reception room, lavatory, switchboard,   5
The unalterable pathos of basin and pitcher,
Ritual of multigraph, paper-clip, comma,
Endless duplication of lives and objects.
And I have seen dust from the walls of institutions,
Finer than flour, alive, more dangerous than silica,   10
Sift, almost invisible, through long afternoons of tedium,
Dropping a fine film on nails and delicate eyebrows,
Glazing the pale hair, the duplicate grey standard faces.

Study and Discussion Questions

1. Look up *dolor* in the dictionary. How does the poem convey the various aspects of the definition of that word?
2. What does Roethke suggest is the effect of office work on office workers?
3. What specific kinds of office work does Roethke have in mind? It can be said that the boss also works in an office. Do you think Roethke's poem refers to that person?
4. Many of the words in "Dolor," like the title itself, are abstract rather than concrete. List some of those words. How does the extensive use of abstractions add to the effect of the poem?

Writing Exercise

1. Gather the materials to write a comparable poem about some kind of work you have done. What objects would you select? What are their qualities? What is the relation between the workers and those objects? What kind of mood would you want to convey? What would you title your poem?

CARL SANDBURG (1878–1967)

Son of Swedish immigrants, Carl Sandburg was born in Galesburg, Illinois. He left school at thirteen to work at odd jobs and at nineteen began traveling, working as a dishwasher and farm laborer. After military service in Puerto Rico during the Spanish-American War, he enrolled in college in Galesburg, but left in 1902 to continue his travels. Sandburg worked as a journalist, as a political organizer, and as secretary to the socialist mayor of Milwaukee. The controversial Chicago Poems *(1916) brought him much attention as a poet; the volumes that followed included* Cornhuskers *(1918),* Smoke and

Steel *(1920) and* The People Yes *(1936). In 1939, Sandburg completed a six-volume biography of Abraham Lincoln.*

Chicago   (1916)

Hog Butcher for the World,
Tool Maker, Stacker of Wheat,
Player with Railroads and the Nation's Freight
    Handler;
Stormy, husky, brawling,   5
City of the Big Shoulders:

They tell me you are wicked and I believe them, for I
    have seen your painted women under the gas lamps
    luring the farm boys.
And they tell me you are crooked and I answer: Yes, it   10
    is true I have seen the gunman kill and go free to
    kill again.
And they tell me you are brutal and my reply is: On the
    faces of women and children I have seen the marks
    of wanton hunger.   15
And having answered so I turn once more to those who
    sneer at this my city, and I give them back the sneer
    and say to them:
Come and show me another city with lifted head singing
    so proud to be alive and coarse and strong and cun-   20
    ning.
Flinging magnetic curses amid the toil of piling job on
    job, here is a tall bold slugger set vivid against the
    little soft cities;
Fierce as a dog with tongue lapping for action, cunning   25
    as a savage pitted against the wilderness,
        Bareheaded,
        Shoveling,
        Wrecking,
        Planning,   30
        Building, breaking, rebuilding,
Under the smoke, dust all over his mouth, laughing with
    white teeth,
Under the terrible burden of destiny laughing as a young
    man laughs,   35
Laughing even as an ignorant fighter laughs who has
    never lost a battle,
Bragging and laughing that under his wrist is the pulse,

and under his ribs the heart of the people,   40
      Laughing!
Laughing the stormy, husky, brawling laughter of
  Youth, half-naked, sweating, proud to be Hog
  Butcher, Tool Maker, Stacker of Wheat, Player with
  Railroads and Freight Handler to the Nation.

Study and Discussion Questions

1. What criticisms of the city does the speaker accept? What is it about the city that the speaker celebrates nonetheless?
2. How does the style of the poem match the speaker's feelings about Chicago?
3. What do the way the city is personified and the dismissal of "the soft little cities" tell us about the speaker's values?

Writing Exercises

1. What do the treatment of the city's problems and the way physical labor is portrayed in the poem suggest about the social class of the speaker?
2. Write a poem or an image-filled prose piece about the city or town you live in. Like "Chicago," it might be a poem of praise. If you don't like where you live, you might consider writing a parody of Sandburg's style.

LANGSTON HUGHES   (1902–1967)

Langston Hughes was born in Joplin, Missouri, and after attending Columbia University for a year, he traveled on a merchant ship to Africa and Europe. He returned to the United States in 1925, published a volume of poems, Weary Blues, *in 1926 and then became a student again, graduating from Lincoln University in 1929. Hughes was a major figure in the Harlem Renaissance, and among his many writings are the novel* Not Without Laughter *(1930), the story collection* The Ways of White Folks *(1934), the autobiography* The Big Sea *(1940), the poetry sequence* Montage of a Dream Deferred *(1951), a number of plays, and several volumes of sketches centering on his character Jesse B. Simple.*

Passing   (1951)

On sunny summer Sunday afternoons in Harlem
when the air is one interminable ball game

and grandma cannot get her gospel hymns
from the Saints of God in Christ
on account of the Dodgers on the radio,   5
on sunny Sunday afternoons
when the kids look all new
and far too clean to stay that way,
and Harlem has its
washed-and-ironed-and-cleaned-best out,   10
the ones who've crossed the line
to live downtown
miss you,
Harlem of the bitter dream,
since their dream has   15
come true.

Study and Discussion Questions

1. After reading "Passing," what do you think the title of the poem means?
2. Who are "the ones who've crossed the line" and why did they do so?
3. What is "the line"? Is it only geographical?
4. What are the two dreams Hughes refers to?
5. What do "the ones who've crossed the line" miss?

Writing Exercise

1. Write about an experience you have had leaving home (your family, community, region, or the social class you grew up in).

GWENDOLYN BROOKS   (b. 1917)

Gwendolyn Brooks was born in Topeka, Kansas, grew up in Chicago, attended Wilson Junior College, and in the 1930s worked for the NAACP Youth Council. She has taught at a number of colleges and in 1950 won the Pulitzer Prize for her volume of poetry, Annie Allen. *Brooks has published a novel,* Maud Martha *(1953), and a number of other volumes of poems, including* A Street in Bronzeville *(1945),* The Bean Eaters *(1960), and* Riot *(1969).*

Bronzeville¹ Woman in a Red Hat   (1960)

Hires Out to
Mrs. Miles

I

They had never had one in the house before.
    The strangeness of it all. Like unleashing

---

¹ Black ghetto in Chicago.

A lion, really. Poised
To pounce. A puma. A panther. A black
Bear.   5
There it stood in the door,
Under a red hat that was rash, but refreshing—
In a tasteless way, of course—across the dull dare,
The semi-assault of that extraordinary blackness.
The slackness   10
Of that light pink mouth told little. The eyes told of heavy
  care . . .
But that was neither here nor there,
And nothing to a wage-paying mistress as should
Be getting her due whether life had been good   15
For her slave, or bad.
There it stood
In the door. They had never had
One in the house before.

But the Irishwoman had left!   20
A message had come.
Something about a murder at home.
A daughter's husband—"berserk," that was the phrase:
The dear man had "gone berserk"
And short work—   25
With a hammer—had been made
Of this daughter and her nights and days.
The Irishwoman (underpaid,
Mrs. Miles remembered with smiles),
Who was a perfect jewel, a red-faced trump,   30
A good old sort, a baker
Of rum cake, a maker
Of Mustard, would never return.
Mrs. Miles had begged the bewitched woman
To finish, at least, the biscuit blending,   35
To tarry till the curry was done,
To show some concern
For the burning soup, to attend to the tending
Of the tossed salad. "Inhuman,"
Patsy Houlihan had called Mrs. Miles.   40
"Inhuman." And "a fool."
And "a cool
One."

The Alert Agency had leafed through its files—
On short notice could offer   45

Only this dusky duffer
That now made its way to her kitchen and sat on her
    kitchen stool.

    II

Her creamy child kissed by the black maid! square on the
    mouth!   50
World yelled, world writhed, world turned to light and
    rolled
Into her kitchen, nearly knocked her down.

Quotations, of course, from baby books were great
Ready armor; (but her animal distress   55
Wore, too and under, a subtler metal dress,
Inheritance of approximately hate).
Say baby shrieked to see his finger bleed,
Wished human humoring—there was a kind
Of unintimate love, a love more of the mind   60
To order the nebulousness of that need.
—This was the way to put it, this the relief.
This sprayed a honey upon marvelous grime.
This told it possible to postpone the reef.
Fashioned a huggable darling out of crime.   65
Made monster personable in personal sight
By cracking mirrors down the personal night.

Disgust crawled through her as she chased the theme.
She, quite supposing purity despoiled,
Committed to sourness, disordered, soiled,   70
Went in to pry the ordure from the cream.
Cooing, "Come." (Come out of the cannibal wilderness,
Dirt, dark, into the sun and bloomful air.
Return to freshness of your right world, wear
Sweetness again. Be done with beast, duress.)   75

Child with continuing cling issued his No in final fire,
    Kissed back the colored maid,
    Not wise enough to freeze or be afraid.
    Conscious of kindness, easy creature bond.
    Love had been handy and rapid to respond.   80

Heat at the hariline, heat between the bowels,
Examining seeming coarse unnatural scene,

She saw all things except herself serene:
Child, big black woman, pretty kitchen towels.

Study and Discussion Questions

1. Who is the speaker of this poem?
2. How is the Bronzeville woman described in part I? What is she compared to?
3. Why does Mrs. Miles refer to her as "it"?
4. What does the stanza about her previous domestic worker, the Irish woman, tell us about Mrs. Miles?
5. What is the crisis described in part II? Why is it a crisis for Mrs. Miles?

Writing Exercises

1. Gwendolyn Brooks, who is black, has created a white upper middle-class persona, Mrs. Miles, through whose eyes we see the black woman who comes to work for her. How does this situation create intentional irony in the poem?
2. Are there any places where human sympathy and identity begin to break through the wall of Mrs. Miles's racism? What does she do when that happens?
3. What does Mrs. Miles's racism consist of? Give examples.

Robert Burns   (1759–1796)

To a Mouse[1]   (1785)

On Turning Her up in Her Nest with the Plough,
November 1785

I

Wee, sleekit, cowrin, tim'rous beastie,	sleek
O, what a panic's in thy breastie!	
Thou need na start awa sae hasty	
Wi' bickering brattle!	hurrying scamper
I wad be laith to rin an' chase thee,	loth 5
Wi' murdering pattle!	plough-staff

---

[1] Marginal glosses by W. E. Henley and T. F. Henderson.

II

I'm truly sorry man's dominion
Has broken Nature's social union,
An' justifies that ill opinion
          Which makes thee startle   10
At me, thy poor, earth-born companion
          An' fellow mortal!

III

I doubt na, whyles, but thou may thieve;   sometimes
What then? poor beastie, thou maun live!   odd ear;
A daimen icker in a thrave   twenty-four   15
          'S a sma' request;   sheaves
I'll get a blessin wi' the lave,   what's left
          An' never miss't!

IV

Thy wee-bit housie, too, in ruin!
Its silly wa's the win's are strewin!   feeble; winds   20
An' naething, now, to big a new ane,
          O' foggage green!   coarse grass
An' bleak December's win's ensuin,
          Baith snell an' keen!   bitter

V

Thou saw the fields laid bare an' waste,   25
An' weary winter comin fast,
An' cozie here, beneath the blast,
          Thou thought to dwell,
Till crash! the cruel coulter past
          Out thro' thy cell.   30

VI

That wee bit heap o' leaves an' stibble,   stubble
Has cost thee monie a weary nibble!
Now thou's turned out, for a' thy trouble,   Without;
          But house or hald,   holding
To thole the winter's sleety dribble,   endure   35
          An' cranreuch cauld!   hoar-frost

VII

But Mousie, thou art no thy lane,   alone
In proving foresight may be vain:

The best-laid schemes o' mice an' men
　　　　　Gang aft agley,   askew   40
An' lea'e us nought but grief an' pain,
　　　　　For promis'd joy!

VIII

Still thou art blest, compared wi' me!
The present only toucheth thee:
But och! I backward cast my e'e,   45
　　　　　On prospects drear!
An' forward, tho' I canna see,
　　　　　I guess an' fear!

WILLIAM WORDSWORTH   (1770–1850)

The World Is Too Much With Us   (1807)

The world is too much with us; late and soon,
Getting and spending, we lay waste our powers:
Little we see in Nature that is ours;
We have given our hearts away, a sordid boon!
This Sea that bares her bosom to the moon;   5
The winds that will be howling at all hours,
And are up-gathered now like sleeping flowers;
For this, for everything, we are out of tune;
It moves us not.—Great God! I'd rather be
A Pagan suckled in a creed outworn;   10
So might I, standing on this pleasant lea,
Have glimpses that would make me less forlorn;
Have sight of Proteus rising from the sea;
Or hear old Triton blow his wreathèd horn.

ANONYMOUS

SONG: **We raise de wheat**[1]

We raise de wheat,
Dey gib us de corn;

---

[1] Printed in *My Bondage and My Freedom* (1855), by Frederick Douglass.

We bake de bread,
Dey gib us de cruss;
We sif de meal,   5
Dey gib us de huss;
We peal de meat,
Dey gib us de skin,
And dat's de way
Dey takes us in.   10
We skim de pot,
Dey gib us the liquor,
And say dat's good enough for nigger.

    Walk over! walk over!
    Tom butter and de fat;   15
    Poor nigger you can't get over dat;
           Walk over!

EMILY DICKINSON   (1830–1886)

Publication—is the Auction   (1863)

Publication—is the Auction
Of the Mind of Man—
Poverty—be justifying
For so foul a thing

Possibly—but We—would rather   5
From Our Garret go
White—Unto the White Creator—
Than invest—Our Snow—

Thought belong to Him who gave it—
Then—to Him Who bear   10
It's Corporeal illustration—Sell
The Royal Air—

In the Parcel—Be the Merchant
Of the Heavenly Grace—
But reduce no Human Spirit   15
To Disgrace of Price—

MATTHEW ARNOLD (1822–1888)

West London (1867)

Crouch'd on the pavement, close by Belgrave Square,
A tramp I saw, ill, moody, and tongue-tied.
A babe was in her arms, and at her side
A girl; their clothes were rags, their feet were bare.

Some labouring men, whose work lay somewhere there,   5
Pass'd opposite; she touch'd her girl, who hied
Across, and begg'd, and came back satisfied.
The rich she had let pass with frozen stare.

Thought I: 'Above her state this spirit towers;
She will not ask of aliens, but of friends,   10
Of sharers in a common human fate.

'She turns from the cold succour, which attends
The unknown little from the unknowing great,
And points us to a better time than ours.'

CARL SANDBURG (1878–1967)

Fish Crier (1916)

I know a Jew fish crier down on Maxwell Street with a
     voice like a north wind blowing over corn stubble
     in January.
He dangles herring before prospective customers evincing
     a joy identical with that of Pavlowa[1] dancing.   5
His face is that of a man terribly glad to be selling fish,
     terribly glad that God made fish, and customers to
     whom he may call his wares from a pushcart.

---

[1] Anna Pavlova (1885–1931), Russian ballerina.

WILLIAM CARLOS WILLIAMS   (1883–1963)

The Young Housewife   **(1917)**

At ten A.M. the young housewife
moves about in negligee behind
the wooden walls of her husband's house.
I pass solitary in my car.

Then again she comes to the curb   5
to call the ice-man, fish-man, and stands
shy, uncorseted, tucking in
stray ends of hair, and I compare her
to a fallen leaf.

The noiseless wheels of my car   10
rush with a crackling sound over
dried leaves as I bow and pass smiling.

BERTON BRALEY

The Worker   **(1917)**

I have broken my hands on your granite,
I have broken my strength on your steel;
I have sweated through years for your pleasure,
I have worked like a slave for your weal;
And what is the wage you have paid me?   5
You masters and drivers of men—
Enough so I come in my hunger
        To beg for more labor again!

I have given my manhood to serve you,
I have given my gladness and youth,   10
You have used me, and spent me, and crushed me
And thrown me aside without ruth;
You have shut my eyes off from the sunlight—
My lungs from the untainted air,

You have housed me in horrible places   15
   Surrounded by squalor and care.

I have built you the world in its beauty,
I have brought you the glory and spoil;
You have blighted my sons and my daughters,
You have scourged me again to my toil,   20
Yet I suffer it all in my patience,
For, somehow, I dimly have known
That someday the worker will conquer
In a world that was meant for his own.

SARAH CLEGHORN   (1876–1959)

The golf links lie so near the mill   (1917)

The golf links lie so near the mill
   That almost every day
The laboring children can look out
   And see the men at play.

FENTON JOHNSON   (1888–1958)

Tired   (1922)

I am tired of work; I am tired of building up somebody
   else's civilization.
Let us take a rest, M'Lissy Jane.
I will go down to the Last Chance Saloon, drink a gallon
   or two of gin, shoot a game or two of dice and   5
   sleep the rest of the night on one of Mike's barrels.
You will let the old shanty go to rot, the white people's
   clothes turn to dust, and the Calvary Baptist Church
   sink to the bottomless pit.
You will spend your days forgetting you married me and   10
   your nights hunting the warm gin Mike serves the

ladies in the rear of the Last Chance Saloon.
Throw the children into the river; civilization has given
   us too many. It is better to die than it is to grow up
   and find out that you are colored.   15
Pluck the stars out of the heavens. The stars mark our
   destiny. The stars marked my destiny.
I am tired of civilization.

COUNTEE CULLEN   (1903–1946)

For a Lady I Know   (1925)

She even thinks that up in heaven
   Her class lies late and snores,
While poor black cherubs rise at seven
   To celestial chores.

ANONYMOUS[1]

SONG: # Let Them Wear Their Watches Fine   (ca. 1925)

I lived in a town away down south
By the name of Buffalo;
And worked in the mill with the rest of the trash
As we're often called, you know.

You factory folks who sing this rime,   5
Will surely understand
The reason why I love you so
Is I'm a factory hand.

---

[1] Transcribed by Will Geer from singing by a West Virginian woman who said she composed the lyrics.

While standing here between my looms
You know I lose no time   10
To keep my shuttles in a whiz
And write this little rime.

We rise up early in the morn
And work all day real hard;
To buy our little meat and bread   15
And sugar, tea, and lard.

We work from week end to week end
And never lose a day;
And when that awful payday comes
We draw our little pay.   20

We then go home on payday night
And sit down in a chair;
The merchant raps upon the door—
He's come to get his share.

When all our little debts are paid   25
And nothing left behind,
We turn our pocket wrong side out
But not a cent can we find.

We rise up early in the morn
And toil from soon to late;   30
We have no time to primp or fix
And dress right up to date.

Our children they grow up unlearned
No time to go to school;
Almost before they've learned to walk   35
They learn to spin or spool.

The boss man jerks them round and round
And whistles very keen;
I'll tell you what, the factory kids
Are really treated mean.   40

The folks in town who dress so fine
And spend their money free

Will hardly look at a factory hand
Who dresses like you and me.

As we go walking down the street   45
All wrapped in lint and strings,
They call us fools and factory trash
And other low-down things.

Well, let them wear their watches fine,
Their rings and pearly strings;   50
When the day of judgment comes
We'll make them shed their pretty things.

EASY PAPA JOHNSON (ROOSEVELT SYKES)   (1906–1983)

SONG: **Cotton Seed Blues**   **(1930)**

When the sun goes down, mama, lord, the whole
    round world turns red
When the sun goes down, mama, lord, the whole
    round world turns red
Lord, my mind falls on things that my dear old   5
    mother have said

Lord, I ain't gonna make no more cotton, mama, lord,
    I'll tell you the reason that I say so
Lord, I ain't gonna make no more cotton, mama, lord,
    I'll tell you the reason that I say so   10
I don't get nothin' out of my seed and the cotton
    price is so doggone low

The boss man told me go to the commissary, I could
    get anything that I need
The boss man told me go to the commissary, I could   15
    get anything that I need
He said I didn't have to have no money right away,
    lord, he said he would take it out of my seed

Lord make a cotton crop, mama, lord it's just the
    same as shootin' dice   20
Lord make a cotton crop, mama, lord it's just the
    same as shootin' dice
Lord, you work the whole year 'round, and then
    cotton won't be no price

Lord, I plowed all this summer long and the sun would   25
    burn my skin
Lord, I plowed all this summer long and the sun would
    burn my skin
And then the cotton sold for twelve and a half cents,
    you know no way that I could win   30

D. H. LAWRENCE   (1885–1930)

City-Life   (1930)

When I see the great cities—

When I am in a great city, I know that I despair.
I know there is no hope for us, death waits, it is useless to
    care.

For oh the poor people, that are flesh of my flesh,   5
I, that am flesh of their flesh,
when I see the iron hooked into their faces
their poor, their fearful faces
I scream in my soul, for I know I cannot   10
take the iron hook out of their faces, that makes them so
    drawn,
nor cut the invisible wires of steel that pull them
back and forth, to work,
back and forth, to work,   15
like fearful and corpse-like fishes hooked and being played
by some malignant fisherman on an unseen shore
where he does not choose to land them yet, hooked fishes
    of the factory world.

BERTOLT BRECHT (1898–1956)

Song of the Invigorating Effect of Money[1] (1933)

Upon this earth we hear dispraise of money
Yet, without it, earth is very cold
And it can be warm and friendly
Suddenly through the power of gold.
Everything that seemed so hard to bear 5
In a gleaming golden glow is cloaked.
Sun is melting what was frozen.
Every man fulfills his hopes!
Rosy beams light the horizon,
Look on high: the chimney smokes! 10
Yes, all at once this world seems quite a different one.
Higher beats the heart, the glance sweeps wider.
Richer are the meals and clothes are finer.
Man himself becomes another man.

Ah, how very sorely they're mistaken 15
They who think that money doesn't count.
Fruitfulness turns into famine
When the kindly stream gives out.
Each one starts to yell and grabs it where he can.
Even were it not so hard to live 20
He who doesn't hunger yet is fearful.
Every heart is empty now of love.
Father, Mother, Brother—cross and tearful!
See, the chimney smokes no more above!
Thick displeasing fog about us furled, 25
All is filled with hatred now and striving.
None will be the horse, all would be riding
And the world becomes an icy world.

So it goes with all that's great and worthy.
In this world it's quickly spoiled indeed, 30
For when feet are bare and bellies empty
Love of virtue always turns to greed.
Gold, not greatness, is what people need.
Poverty of soul puts out our hopes.

---

[1] Translated by H.R. Hays.

Good plus money, too, is what it takes   35
To keep man virtuous without a slip.
He whom crime's already given breaks
Looks up on high: the chimney smokes!
Faith in the human race again grows bright.
Man is noble, good, so on and so forth.   40
Sentiment awakes. Need dimmed its light.
Faster beats the heart. The glance sweeps wider.
We know who the horse is, who the rider.
And once more it's clear that right is right.

C. DAY LEWIS   (1904–1972)

Come, live with me and be my love   (1935)

Come, live with me and be my love,
And we will all the pleasures prove
Of peace and plenty, bed and board,
That chance employment may afford.

I'll handle dainties on the docks   5
And thou shalt read of summer frocks:
At evening by the sour canals
We'll hope to hear some madrigals.

Care on thy maiden brow shall put
A wreath of wrinkles, and thy foot   10
Be shod with pain: not silken dress
But toil shall tire thy loveliness.

Hunger shall make thy modest zone
And cheat fond death of all but bone—
If these delights thy mind may move,   15
Then live with me and be my love.

ROBERT FROST   **(1874–1963)**

Two Tramps In Mud Time   **(1936)**

Out of the mud two strangers came
And caught me splitting wood in the yard.
And one of them put me off my aim
By hailing cheerily "Hit them hard!"
I knew pretty well why he dropped behind   5
And let the other go on a way.
I knew pretty well what he had in mind:
He wanted to take my job for pay.

Good blocks of oak it was I split,
As large around as the chopping block;   10
And every piece I squarely hit
Fell splinterless as a cloven rock.
The blows that a life of self-control
Spares to strike for the common good,
That day, giving a loose to my soul,   15
I spent on the unimportant wood.

The sun was warm but the wind was chill.
You know how it is with an April day
When the sun is out and the wind is still,
You're one month on in the middle of May.   20
But if you so much as dare to speak,
A cloud comes over the sunlit arch,
A wind comes off a frozen peak,
And you're two months back in the middle of March.

A bluebird comes tenderly up to alight   25
And turns to the wind to unruffle a plume,
His song so pitched as not to excite
A single flower as yet to bloom.
It is snowing a flake: and he half knew
Winter was only playing possum.   30
Except in color he isn't blue,
But he wouldn't advise a thing to blossom.

The water for which we may have to look
In summertime with a witching wand,

In every wheelrut's now a brook,   35
In every print of a hoof a pond.
Be glad of water, but don't forget
The lurking frost in the earth beneath
That will steal forth after the sun is set
And show on the water its crystal teeth.   40

The time when most I loved my task
These two must make me love it more
By coming with what they came to ask.
You'd think I never had felt before
The weight of an ax-head poised aloft,   45
The grip on earth of outspread feet,
The life of muscles rocking soft
And smooth and moist in vernal heat.

Out of the woods two hulking tramps
(From sleeping God knows where last night,   50
But not long since in the lumber camps).
They thought all chopping was theirs of right.
Men of the woods and lumberjacks,
They judged me by their appropriate tool.
Except as a fellow handled an ax   55
They had no way of knowing a fool.

Nothing on either side was said.
They knew they had but to stay their stay
And all their logic would fill my head:
As that I had no right to play   60
With what was another man's work for gain.
My right might be love but theirs was need.
And where the two exist in twain
Theirs was the better right—agreed.

But yield who will to their separation,   65
My object in living is to unite
My avocation and my vocation
As my two eyes make one in sight.
Only where love and need are one,
And the work is play for mortal stakes,   70
Is the deed ever really done
For Heaven and the future's sakes.

WILLIAM CARLOS WILLIAMS   (1883–1963)

The Poor   (1938)

It's the anarchy of poverty
delights me, the old
yellow wooden house indented
among the new brick tenements

Or a cast-iron balcony   5
with panels showing oak branches
in full leaf. It fits
the dress of the children

reflecting every stage and
custom of necessity—   10
Chimneys, roofs, fences of
wood and metal in an unfenced

age and enclosing next to
nothing at all: the old man
in a sweater and soft black   15
hat who sweeps the sidewalk—

his own ten feet of it
in a wind that fitfully
turning his corner has
overwhelmed the entire city   20

MURIEL RUKEYSER   (1913–1980)

Boy with His Hair Cut Short   (1938)

Sunday shuts down on this twentieth-century evening.
The El passes. Twilight and bulb define
the brown room, the overstuffed plum sofa,
the boy, and the girl's thin hands above his head.
A neighbor radio sings stocks, news, serenade.   5

He sits at the table, head down, the young clear neck exposed,
watching the drugstore sign from the tail of his eye;
tattoo, neon, until the eye blears, while his
solicitous tall sister, simple in blue, bending
behind him, cuts his hair with her cheap shears.   10

The arrow's electric red always reaches its mark,
successful neon! He coughs, impressed by that precision.
His child's forehead, forever protected by his cap,
is bleached against the lamplight as he turns head
and steadies to let the snippets drop.   15

Erasing the failure of weeks with level fingers,
she sleeks the fine hair, combing: "You'll look fine tomorrow!
You'll surely find something, they can't keep turning you down;
the finest gentleman's not so trim as you!" Smiling, he raises
the adolescent forehead wrinkling ironic now.   20

He sees his decent suit laid out, new-pressed,
his carfare on the shelf. He lets his head fall, meeting
her earnest hopeless look, seeing the sharp blades splitting,
the darkened room, the impersonal sign, her motion,
the blue vein, bright on her temple, pitifully beating.   25

PHYLLIS McGINLEY   **(b. 1905)**

View from a Suburban Window   (1941)

When I consider how my light is spent,
    Also my sweetness, ditto all my power,
Papering shelves or saving for the rent
    Or prodding grapefruit while the grocers glower,
Or dulcetly persuading to the dentist   5
    The wailing young, or fitting them for shoes,
Beset by menus and my days apprenticed
    Forever to a grinning household muse;

And how I might, in some tall town instead,
  From nine to five be furthering a Career,   10
  Dwelling unfettered in my single flat,
My life my own, likewise my daily bread—
  When I consider this, it's very clear
  I might have done much worse. I might, at that.

NAZIM HIKMET   (1902–1963)

About Your Hands and Lies[1]   (1949)

Your hands grave like all stones,
sad like all songs sung in prison,
clumsy and heavy like all beasts of burden,
your hands that are like the sullen faces of hungry children.
Your hands nimble and light like bees,   5
full like breasts with milk,
brave like nature,
your hands that hide their friendly softness under their rough
                                                          skin.
This world doesn't rest on the horns of a bull,   10
              this world rests on your hands.
People, oh my people,
they feed you with lies.
But you're hungry,
you need to be fed with meat and bread.   15
And never once eating a full meal at a white table,
you leave this world where every branch is loaded with fruit.
Oh my people,
especially those in Asia, Africa,
              the Near East, Middle East, Pacific islands   20
                      and my countrymen—
I mean, more than seventy percent of all people—
you are old and absent-minded like your hands,
you are curious, amazed, and young like your hands.   25
Oh my people,
my European, my American,
you are awake, bold, and forgetful like your hands,

---

[1] Translated by Randy Blasing and Mutlu Konuk.

like your hands you're quick to seduce,
                                    easy to deceive. . .

People, oh my people,   30
if the antennas are lying,
if the presses are lying,
if the books lie,
if the poster on the wall and the ad in the column lie,
if the naked thighs of girls on the white screen lie,   35
if the prayer lies,
if the lullaby lies,
if the dream is lying,
if the violin player at the tavern is lying,
if the moonlight on the nights of hopeless days lies,   40
if the voice lies,
if the word lies,
if everything but your hands,
        if everyone, is lying,
it's so your hands will be obedient like clay,   45
blind like darkness,
stupid like sheep dogs,
        it's so your hands won't rebel.
And it's so that in this mortal, this livable world
        —where we are guests so briefly anyway—   50
        this merchant's empire, this cruelty, won't end.

TED HUGHES   (b. 1930)

Her Husband   (1967)

Comes home dull with coal-dust deliberately
To grime the sink and foul towels and let her
Learn with scrubbing brush and scrubbing board
The stubborn character of money.

And let her learn through what kind of dust   5
He has earned his thirst and the right to quench it
And what sweat he has exchanged for his money
And the blood-weight of money. He'll humble her

With new light on her obligations.
The fried, woody chips, kept warm two hours in the oven,   10
Are only part of her answer.
Hearing the rest, he slams them to the fire back

And is away round the house-end singing
'Come back to Sorrento' in a voice
Of resounding corrugated iron.   15
Her back has bunched into a hump as an insult.

For they will have their rights.
Their jurors are to be assembled
From the little crumbs of soot. Their brief
Goes straight up to heaven and nothing more is heard of it.   20

RUTH PITTER   **(b. 1897)**

Yorkshire Wife's Saga   **(1968)**

War was her life, with wand and the wild air;
Not for life only; she was out to win.
Houses and ground were cheap, out on the bare
Moor, and the land not bad; they could begin,
Now that the seven sons were mostly men.   5

Two acres and a sow, on hard-saved brass;
Men down the mine, and mother did the rest.
Pity, with all those sons, they had no lass;
No help, no talk, no mutual interest,
Made fourteen slaving hours empty at best.   10

Fierce winter mornings, up at three or four;
Men bawl, pigs shriek against the raving beck.
Off go the eight across the mile of moor,
With well-filled dinner-pail and sweat-ragged neck;
But pigs still shriek, and wind blows door off sneck.[1]   15

---

[1] Latch.

Of course they made it; what on earth could stop
People like that? Marrying one by one,
This got a farm, the other got a shop;
Now she was left with but the youngest son,
But she could look about and feel she'd won.   20

Doctor had told her she was clean worn out.
All pulled to bits, and nowt[2] that he could do.
But plenty get that way, or die, without
Having a ruddy ten-quid note to show.
She'd got seven thriving sons all in a row.   25

And grandchildren. She liked going by bus
Or train, to stay a bit in those snug homes.
They were her colonies, fair glorious.
"Sit by the fire, ma, till the dinner comes.
Sit by the fire and cuddle little lass."   30

MARI EVANS

When in Rome   (1970)

Mattie dear
the box is full
take
whatever you like
to eat   5
            (an egg
            or soup
            . . .there ain't no meat)

there's endive there
and   10
cottage cheese
            (whew! if I had some
            black-eyed peas . . .)

---

[2] Naught.

there's sardines
on the shelves   15
and such
but
don't
get my anchovies

                                                                 20
they cost
too much!
       (me get the
       anchovies indeed!
       what she think, she got—
       a bird to feed?)   25
there's plenty in there
to fill you up.
       (yes'm. just the
       sight's
       enough!   30

       Hope I lives till I get
       home
       I'm tired of eatin'
       what they eats in Rome . . .)

DEREK WALCOTT   (b. 1930)

The Virgins   (1971)

Down the dead streets of sun-stoned Frederiksted,[1]
the first free port to die for tourism,
strolling at funeral pace, I am reminded
of life not lost to the American dream;
but my small-islander's simplicities   5
can't better our new empire's civilized
exchange of cameras, watches, perfumes, brandies
for the good life, so cheaply underpriced
that only the crime rate is on the rise
in streets blighted with sun, stone arches   10

---

[1] Port on St. Croix, one of the Virgin Islands.

and plazas blown dry by the hysteria
of rumour. A condominium drowns
in vacancy; its bargains are dusted,
but only a jewelled housefly drones
over the bargains. The roulettes spin   15
rustily to the wind—the vigorous trade
that every morning would begin afresh
by revving up green water round the pierhead
heading for where the banks of silver thresh.

MAFIKA MBULI

The Miners   (1973)

This dungeon
Makes the mind weary
Kneaded with the sight of
A million stones
Passing through my hands   5
I see the flesh sticking like hair
On thorns
Against the grating rocks
Of these hills dug for gold,
And life is bitter here.   10
Crawling through the day
In a sleepwalker's dream,
Frightening the night away with my snores,
I dream of the diminished breath
Of miners planted in the stones—   15
The world is not at ease
But quakes under the march of our boots
Tramping the dust under our feet. . . .
Click, clack, our picks knock for life
Until the eyes are dazed   20
Counting the rubble of scattered stones.

Day and night are one,
but I know each day dawns
And the heated sun licks every shrub dry
While we who burrow the earth   25
Tame the dust with our lungs.

Click, clack we knock with picks
And our minds
Drone with the voices of women
Harassing our loins   30
To force courage into the heart.
Wherefore might we scorn their sacrifice
Made in blood,
Greater that the blood of men
Sacrificed to the earth   35
For its possession!
And so
Clap, scrape
With our hands manacled
With weariness   40
We mine
All our lives
Till the mind is numb
And ceases to ask. . . .

MARGE PIERCY   (b. 1936)

To Be of Use   (1973)

The people I love the best
jump into work head first
without dallying in the shallows
and swim off with sure strokes almost out of sight.
They seem to become natives of that element,   5
the black sleek heads of seals
bouncing like half-submerged balls.

I love people who harness themselves, an ox to a heavy cart,
who pull like water buffalo, with massive patience,
who strain in the mud and the muck to move things forward,   10
who do what has to be done, again and again.

I want to be with people who submerge
in the task, who go into the fields to harvest
and work in a row and pass the bags along,
who are not parlor generals and field deserters   15

but move in a common rhythm
when the food must come in or the fire be put out.

The work of the world is common as mud.
Botched, it smears the hands, crumbles to dust.
But the thing worth doing well done   20
has a shape that satisfies, clean and evident.
Greek amphoras for wine or oil,
Hopi vases that held corn, are put in museums
but you know they were made to be used.
The pitcher cries for water to carry   25
and a person for work that is real.

BARBARA SMITH   (b. 1946)

The Bowl   (1975)

Today
I'm making for my friends
a rich dark dough,
coarse with a million seeds,
a smell as deep as dreaming.   5
What do I have to hold it?

I search and find a
crockery bowl,
leftover from my childhood.

Suddenly work is ritual.   10

This empty bowl,
bright-sky-blue-striped,
is full of pictures,
Everything.
Rolls and cake and sweet potato pie,   15
stuffing, cream,
my mouth and eyes fill up.

My people used this bowl to mix their lives.
It's where I learned   20
a way of giving
caring
with a cake.

I see them mixing now:
Beating,
Stirring,   25
Keeping time.
(My fingers slyly dipping in.)

If women's lives were fables
and kitchen feats adventures,
this bowl would be a talisman,   30
tell tales
and even fly.

But now it is an ordinary bowl.

The place those first women in my world
taught me to shape more   35
than necessary bread
my life.

SUSAN GRIFFIN   **(b. 1943)**

This Is the Story of the Day in the Life   **(1976)**
of a Woman Trying

This is the story of the day in the life of a woman trying
to be a writer and her child got sick. And in the midst of
writing this story someone called her on the telephone.
And, of course, despite her original hostile reaction to the
ring of the telephone, she got interested in the conversation   5
which was about teaching writing in a women's prison,
for no pay of course, and she would have done it if it
weren't for the babysitting and the lack of money for the
plane fare, and then she hung up the phone and looked

at her typewriter, and for an instant swore her original　　　　10
sentence was not there. But after a while she found it. Then
she began again, but in the midst of the second sentence,
a man telephoned wanting to speak to the woman she
shares her house with, who was not available to speak on
the telephone, and by the time she got back to her type-　　　15
writer she began to worry about her sick daughter downstairs. And why hadn't the agency for babysitters called back
and why hadn't the department for health called back
because she was looking for a day sitter and a night sitter,
one so she could teach the next day and one so she could　　　20
read her poetry. And she was hoping that the people who
had asked her to read poetry would pay for the babysitter
since the next evening after that would be a meeting of
teachers whom she wanted to meet and she could not afford
two nights of babysitters let alone one, actually. This was　　　25
the second day her child was sick and the second day she
tried to write (she had been trying to be a writer for years)
but she failed entirely the first day because of going to the
market to buy Vitamin C and to the toy store to buy cutouts
and crayons, and making soup from the chicken carcass that　　　30
had been picked nearly clean to make sandwiches for
lunch, and watering the plants, sending in the mortgage
check and other checks to cover that check to the bank,
and feeling tired, wishing she had a job, talking on the telephone, and putting out newspaper and glue and scissors　　　35
on the kitchen table for her tired, bored child and squinting her eyes at the clock waiting for *Sesame Street*[1] to begin
again. Suddenly, after she went upstairs to her bedroom
with a book, having given up writing as impossible, it was
time to cook dinner. But she woke up on the second day　　　40
with the day before as a lesson in her mind. Then an old
friend called who had come to town whom she was eager
to see and she said, "Yes, I'm home with a sick child," and
they spent the morning talking. She was writing poetry and
teaching she said. He had written four books he　　　45
said. Her daughter showed him her red and blue and
orange colored pictures. She wished he didn't have to leave
so early, she thought but didn't say, and went back to pick
up tissue paper off the floor and fix lunch for her and her
child and begin telephoning for babysitters because she　　　50
knew she had to teach the next day. And the truth was,
if she did not have a sick child to care for, she was
not sure she could write anyway because the kitchen was

---

[1] Television program for children.

still there needing cleaning, the garden there needing   55
weeding and watering, the living room needing curtains,
the couch needing pillows, a stack of mail needing answers
(for instance if she didn't call the woman who had lived
in her house the month before about the phone bill soon,
she would lose a lot of money). All besides, she had
nothing to write. She had had fine thoughts for writing the   60
night before but in the morning they took on a sickly
complexion. And anyway, she had begun to think her life
trivial and so it was, and she was tired writing the same
words, or different words about the same situation, the
situation or situations being that she was tired, tired of try-   65
ing to write, tired of poverty or almost poverty or fear of
poverty, tired of the kitchen being dirty, tired of having
no lover. She was amazed that she had gotten herself
dressed, actually, with thoughts like these, and caught herself saying maybe I should take a trip when she realized she   70
had just come back from a trip and had wanted to be
home so much she came back early. And even in the writing of this she thought I have written all this before and
went downstairs to find her daughter had still not eaten a
peanut butter sandwich and she wondered to herself what   75
keeps that child alive?

LAUREEN MAR   (b. 1953)

My Mother, Who Came From China, Where She Never Saw Snow   (1977)

In the huge, rectangular room, the ceiling
a machinery of pipes and fluorescent lights,
ten rows of women hunch over machines,
their knees pressing against pedals
and hands pushing the shiny fabric thick as tongues   5
through metal and thread.
My mother bends her head to one of these machines.
Her hair is coarse and wiry, black as burnt scrub.
She wears glasses to shield her intense eyes.
A cone of orange thread spins. Around her,   10
talk flutters harshly in Toisan wah.[1]

---

[1] Chinese dialect.

Chemical stings. She pushes cloth
through a pounding needle, under, around, and out,
breaks thread with a snap against fingerbone, tooth.
Sleeve after sleeve, sleeve.   15
It is easy. The same piece.
For eight or nine hours, sixteen bundles maybe,
250 sleeves to ski coats, all the same.
It is easy, only once she's run the needle
through her hand. She earns money   20
by each piece, on a good day,
thirty dollars. Twenty-four years.
It is frightening how fast she works.
She and the women who were taught sewing
terms in English as Second Language.   25
Dull thunder passes through their fingers.

MARGE PIERCY   (b. 1936)

The market economy   (1977)

Suppose some peddler offered
you can have a color TV
but your baby will be
born with a crooked spine;
you can have polyvinyl cups   5
and wash and wear
suits but it will cost
you your left lung
rotted with cancer; suppose
somebody offered you   10
a frozen precooked dinner
every night for ten years
but at the end
your colon dies
and then you do,   15
slowly and with much pain.
You get a house in the suburbs
but you work in a new plastics
factory and die at fifty-one
when your kidneys turn off.   20

But where else will you
work? where else can
you rent but Smog City?
The only houses for sale   25
are under the yellow sky.
You've been out of work for
a year and they're hiring
at the plastics factory.
Don't read the fine   30
print, there isn't any.

JUDY GRAHN   (b. 1936)

Ella, in a square apron, along Highway 80   (1978)

She's a copperheaded waitress,
tired and sharp-worded, she hides
her bad brown tooth behind a wicked
smile, and flicks her ass   5
out of habit, to fend off the pass
that passes for affection.
She keeps her mind the way men
keep a knife—keen to strip the game
down to her size. She has a thin spine,   10
swallows her eggs cold, and tells lies.
She slaps a wet rag at the truck drivers
if they should complain. She understands
the necessity for pain, turns away
the smaller tips, out of pride, and   15
keeps a flask under the counter. Once,
she shot a lover who misused her child.
Before she got out of jail, the courts had pounced
and given the child away. Like some isolated lake,
her flat blue eyes take care of their own stark   20
bottoms. Her hands are nervous, curled, ready
to scrape.
The common woman is as common
as a rattlesnake.

GWEN HAUSER   (b. 1944)

Where Things Come From   (1981)

working at
  the canadadry plant
cleaning out
        cigarette cases
kleenex etc.   5
from the crates
       for pop
  (we even found a make-up compact)
i have dreams
  of putting notes in bottles: 10
    "Help
  i'm being held
a prisoner in
a canada dry factory"

maybe if   15
       we all
did this
people would realize
where things come from.

KATE RUSHIN   (b. 1951)

The Black Back-Ups   (1983)

This is dedicated to Merry Clayton, Cissy Houston, Vonetta
Washington, Dawn, Carrietta McClellen, Rosie Farmer, Marsha
Jenkins and Carolyn Williams. This is for all of the Black
women who sang back-up for Elvis Presley, John Denver, James
Taylor, Lou Reed, Etc. Etc. Etc.   5

I said Hey Babe
Take a Walk on the Wild Side
I said Hey Babe
Take a Walk on the Wild Side

And the colored girls say   10

Do dodo do do dodododo
Do dodo do do dodododo
Do dodo do do dodododo ooooo

This is for my Great Grandmother Esther, my Grandmother
Addie, my Grandmother called Sister, my Great Aunt Rachel,   15
my Aunt Hilda, my Aunt Tine, my Aunt Breda, my Aunt
Gladys, my Aunt Helen, my Aunt Ellie, my Cousin Barbara, my
Cousin Dottie and my Great Great Aunt Vene

This is dedicated to all of the Black women riding on buses
and subways Back and forth to the Main Line, Haddonfield,   20
N.J., Cherry Hill and Chevy Chase. This is for those women who
spend their summers in Rockport, Newport, Cape Cod and
Camden, Maine. This is for the women who open bundles of
dirty laundry sent home from ivy-covered campuses

And the colored girls say   25

Do dodo do do dodododo
Do dodo do do dodododo
Do dodo do do dodododo ooooo

Jane Fox   Jane Fox
Calling Jane Fox   30
Where are you Jane?

My Great Aunt Rachel worked for the Foxes
Ever since I can remember
There was The Boy
Whose name I never knew   35
And there was The Girl
Whose name was Jane

My Aunt Rachel brought Jane's dresses for me to wear
Perfectly Good Clothes
And I should've been glad to get them   40
Perfectly Good Clothes
No matter they didn't fit quite right
Perfectly Good Clothes Jane

Brought home in a brown paper bag with an air of
Accomplishment and excitement   45
Perfectly Good Clothes
Which I hated

It's not that I have anything *personal* against *you* Jane

It's just that I felt guilty
For hating those clothes   50

I mean
Can you get to the irony of it Jane?

And the colored girls say

Do dodo do do dodododo
Do dodo do do dodododo   55
Do dodo do do dodododo ooooo

At school
In Ohio
I swear to Gawd
There was always somebody   60
Telling me that the only person
In their whole house
Who listened and understood them
Despite the money and the lessons
Was the housekeeper   65
And I knew it was true
But what was I supposed to say?

I know it's true
I watch them getting off the train
And moving slowly toward the Country Squire   70
With their uniform in their shopping bag
And the closer they get to the car
The more the two little kids jump and laugh
And even the dog is about to
Turn inside out   75
Because they just can't wait until she gets there
Edna Edna Wonderful Edna

(But Aunt Edna to me, or Gram, or Miz Johnson, or Sister
Johnson on Sundays)

And the colored girls say   80

Do dodo do do dodododo
Do dodo do do dodododo
Do dodo do do dodododo ooooo

This is for Hattie McDaniel, Butterfly McQueen, Ethel Waters[1]
Saphire[2]   85
Saphronia
Ruby Begonia
Aunt Jemima
Aunt Jemima on the Pancake Box
Aunt Jemima on the Pancake Box?   90
AuntJemimaonthepancakebox?
auntjemimaonthepancakebox?
Ainchamamaonthepancakebox?
Ain't chure Mama on the pancake box?

Mama Mama   95
Get offa that damn box
And come home to me

And my Mama leaps offa that box
She swoops down in her nurse's cape
Which she wears on Sunday   100
And on Wednesday night prayer meeting
And she wipes my forehead
And she fans my face for me
And she makes me a cup o' tea
And it don't do a thing for my real pain   105
Except she is my Mama
Mama Mommy Mommy Mammy Mammy
Mam-mee Mam-mee
I'd Walk a mill-yon miles   110
For one o' your smiles

---

[1] The first two are actresses, the third a jazz and blues singer.
[2] Black character on a popular radio and television show.

This is for the Black Back-ups
This is for my mama and your mama
My grandma and your grandma
This is for the thousand thousand Black Back-Ups

And the colored girls say   115

Do dodo do do dodododo
Do   do do   do   do
    Do   do
                                        do
Do   120
              do

JAMES BERRY   (b. 1924)

Fantasy of an African Boy   (1985)

Such a peculiar lot
we are, we people
without money, in daylong
yearlong sunlight, knowing
money is somewhere, somewhere.   5

Everybody says it's a big
bigger brain bother now,
money. Such millions and millions
of us don't manage at all
without it, like war going on.   10

And we can't eat it. Yet
without it our heads alone
stay big, as lots and lots do,
coming from nowhere joyful,
going nowhere happy.   15

We can't drink it up. Yet
without it we shrivel when small
and stop forever

where we stopped,   20
as lots and lots do.

We can't read money for books.
Yet without it we don't
read, don't write numbers,
don't open gates in other countries,
as lots and lots never do.   25

We can't use money to bandage
sores, can't pound it
to powder for sick eyes
and sick bellies. Yet without
it, flesh melts from our bones.   30

Such walled-round gentlemen
overseas minding money! Such
bigtime gentlemen, body guarded
because of too much respect
and too many wishes on them: 35

too many wishes, everywhere,
wanting them to let go
magic of money, and let it fly
away, everywhere, day and night,
just like dropped leaves in wind!   40

JUNE JORDAN   **(b. 1936)**

Des Moines Iowa Rap   **(1985)**

So his wife and his daughters could qualify
Lester Williams told the people he was gonna try suicide:

suicide.
He promised the papers he would definitely try
so his wife and his babies could qualify for welfare   5
in the new year.
Welfare.
In the new year.

I wanna job so bad I can taste it I won't waste it
Wanna job so bad   10

36 years old and home from the Navy
Take my blood, he said, and my bones, he said,
for the meat and the gravy / I'm a vet from the Navy!
Take my meat. Take my bones.
I'm a blood, he said.   15

Tried suicide. Tried suicide.

Lester Williams made the offer and the offer made news
Wasn't all that much to dispute and confuse
Wouldn't hide in no closet and under no bed
Said he'd straightaway shoot himself dead instead   20
Like a man
Like a natural man
Like a natural man wanna job so bad he
can taste it
he can taste it   25

Took the wife in his arms. Held the children in his heart.
Took the gun from his belt. Held the gun to his head.
Like a man.
Like a natural man.
Like a natural man wanna job so bad gotta waste it.   30
Gotta waste it.

Tried Suicide.
Tried Suicide.

DRAMA

ARTHUR MILLER   (b. 1915)

Born and raised in Brooklyn, New York, Arthur Miller worked for two years after high school in an auto parts warehouse, and then attended the University of Michigan where he began writing plays. In 1938 he returned to New York and continued writing while working in the Brooklyn Navy Yard. Miller's career took off with the production on Broadway of All My Sons *(1947) and of the immensely successful* Death of a Salesman *(1949). His 1953 play* The Crucible, *about the seventeenth-century Salem, Massachusetts witch trials, was an attack on the anti-Communist "witch hunts" of the early 1950s and helped lead to Miller's being called before the House Un-American Activities Committee in 1956 and to his blacklisting by Hollywood. Among his other works are* A View from the Bridge *(1955);* The Misfits *(1961), a script for a movie that starred his wife Marilyn Monroe;* After the Fall *(1964); and the autobiographical* Timebends: A Life *(1987).*

Death of a Salesman   (1949)

Certain private conversations
in two acts and a requiem

CHARACTERS

Willy Loman	Uncle Ben
Linda	Howard Wagner
Biff	Jenny
Happy	Stanley
Bernard	Miss Forsythe
The Woman	Letta
Charley	

The action takes place in Willy Loman's house and yard and in various places he visits in the New York and Boston of today.

Throughout the play, in the stage directions, left and right mean stage left and stage right.

ACT I

A melody is heard, played upon a flute. It is small and fine, telling of grass and trees and the horizon. The curtain rises.

Before us is the Salesman's house. We are aware of towering, angular shapes behind it, surrounding it on all sides. Only the blue light of the sky falls upon the house and forestage; the surrounding area shows an angry glow of orange. As more light appears, we see a solid vault of apartment houses around the small, fragile-seeming home. An air of the dream clings to the place, a dream rising out of reality. The kitchen at center seems actual enough, for there is a kitchen table with three chairs, and a refrigerator. But no other fixtures are seen. At the back of the kitchen there is a draped entrance, which leads to the living-room. To the right of the kitchen, on a level raised two feet, is a bedroom furnished only with a brass bedstead and a straight chair. On a shelf over the bed a silver athletic trophy stands. A window opens onto the apartment house at the side.

Behind the kitchen, on a level raised six and a half feet, is the boys' bedroom, at present barely visible. Two beds are dimly seen, and at the back of the room a dormer window. (This bedroom is above the unseen living-room.) At the left a stairway curves up to it from the kitchen.

The entire setting is wholly or, in some places, partially transparent. The roof-line of the house is one-dimensional; under and over it we see the apartment buildings. Before the house lies an apron, curving beyond the forestage into the orchestra. This forward area serves as the back yard as well as the locale of all Willy's imaginings and of his city scenes. Whenever the action is in the present the actors observe the imaginary wall-lines, entering the house only through its door at the left. But in the scenes of the past these boundaries are broken, and characters enter or leave a room by stepping "through" a wall onto the forestage.

From the right, Willy Loman, the Salesman, enters, carrying two large sample cases. The flute plays on. He hears but is not aware of it. He is past sixty years of age, dressed quietly. Even as he crosses the stage to the doorway of the house, his exhaustion is apparent. He unlocks the door, comes into the kitchen, and thankfully lets his burden down, feeling the soreness of his palms. A word-sigh escapes his lips—it might be "Oh, boy, oh, boy." He closes the door, then carries his cases out into the living-room, through the draped kitchen doorway.

Linda, his wife, has stirred in her bed at the right. She gets out and puts on a robe, listening. Most often jovial, she has developed an iron repression of her exceptions to Willy's behavior—she more than loves him, she admires him, as though his mercurial nature, his temper, his massive dreams and little cruelties, served her only as sharp reminders of the turbulent longings within him, longings which she shares but lacks the temperament to utter and follow to their end.

Linda, *hearing Willy outside the bedroom, calls with some trepidation.* Willy!

Willy. It's all right. I came back.

Linda. Why? What happened? *Slight pause.* Did something happen, Willy?

Willy. No, nothing happened.

Linda. You didn't smash the car, did you?

Willy, *with casual irritation.* I said nothing happened. Didn't you hear me?

Linda. Don't you feel well?

Willy. I'm tired to the death. *The flute has faded away. He sits on the bed beside her, a little numb.* I couldn't make it. I just couldn't make it, Linda.

Linda, *very carefully, delicately.* Where were you all day? You look terrible.

Willy. I got as far as a little above Yonkers. I stopped for a cup of coffee. Maybe it was the coffee.

Linda. What?

Willy, *after a pause.* I suddenly couldn't drive any more. The car kept going off onto the shoulder, y'know?

Linda, *helpfully.* Oh. Maybe it was the steering again. I don't think Angelo knows the Studebaker.

Willy. No, it's me, it's me. Suddenly I realize I'm goin' sixty miles an hour and I don't remember the last five minutes. I'm—I can't seem to—keep my mind to it.

Linda. Maybe it's your glasses. You never went for your new glasses.

Willy. No, I see everything. I came back ten miles an hour. It took me nearly four hours from Yonkers.

Linda, *resigned.* Well, you'll just have to take a rest, Willy, you can't continue this way.

Willy. I just got back from Florida.

Linda. But you didn't rest your mind. Your mind is overactive, and the mind is what counts, dear.

Willy. I'll start out in the morning. Maybe I'll feel better in the morning. *She is taking off his shoes.* These goddam arch supports are killing me.

Linda. Take an aspirin. Should I get you an aspirin? It'll soothe you.

Willy, *with wonder.* I was driving along, you understand? And I was fine. I was even observing the scenery. You can imagine, me looking at scenery, on the road every week of my life. But it's so beautiful up there, Linda, the trees are so thick, and the sun is warm. I opened the windshield and just let the warm air bathe over me. And then all of a sudden I'm goin' off the road! I'm tellin' ya, I absolutely forgot I was driving. If I'd've gone the other way over the white line I might've killed somebody. So I went on again—and five minutes later I'm dreamin' again, and I nearly—*He presses two fingers against his eyes.* I have such thoughts, I have such strange thoughts.

Linda. Willy, dear. Talk to them again. There's no reason why you can't work in New York.

Willy. They don't need me in New York. I'm the New England man. I'm vital in New England.

Linda. But you're sixty years old. They can't expect you to keep traveling every week.

Willy. I'll have to send a wire to Portland. I'm supposed to see Brown and Morrison tomorrow morning at ten o'clock to show the line. Goddammit, I could sell them!

He starts putting on his jacket.

Linda, *taking the jacket from him.* Why don't you go down to the place tomorrow and tell Howard you've simply got to work in New York? You're too accommodating, dear.

Willy. If old man Wagner was alive I'd a been in charge of New York now! That man was a prince, he was a masterful man. But that boy of his, that Howard, he don't appreciate. When I went north the first time, the Wagner Company didn't know where New England was!

Linda. Why don't you tell those things to Howard, dear?

Willy, *encouraged.* I will, I definitely will. Is there any cheese?

Linda. I'll make you a sandwich.

Willy. No, go to sleep. I'll take some milk. I'll be up right away. The boys in?

Linda. They're sleeping. Happy took Biff on a date tonight.

Willy, *interested.* That so?

Linda. It was so nice to see them shaving together, one behind the other, in the bathroom. And going out together. You notice? The whole house smells of shaving lotion.

Willy. Figure it out. Work a lifetime to pay off a house. You finally own it, and there's nobody to live in it.

Linda. Well, dear, life is a casting off. It's always that way.

Willy. No, no, some people—some people accomplish something. Did Biff say anything after I went this morning?

Linda. You shouldn't have criticized him, Willy, especially after he just got off the train. You mustn't lose your temper with him.

Willy. When the hell did I lose my temper? I simply asked him if he was making any money. Is that a criticism?

Linda. But, dear, how could he make any money?

Willy, *worried and angered.* There's such an undercurrent in him. He became a moody man. Did he apologize when I left this morning?

Linda. He was crestfallen, Willy. You know how he admires you. I think if he finds himself, then you'll both be happier and not fight any more.

Willy. How can he find himself on a farm? Is that a life? A farmhand? In the beginning, when he was young, I thought, well, a young man, it's good for him to tramp around, take a lot of different jobs. But it's more than ten years now and he has yet to make thirty-five dollars a week!

Linda. He's finding himself, Willy.

Willy. Not finding yourself at the age of thirty-four is a disgrace!

Linda. Shh!

Willy. The trouble is he's lazy, goddammit!

Linda. Willy, please!

Willy. Biff is a lazy bum!

Linda. They're sleeping. Get something to eat. Go on down.

Willy. Why did he come home? I would like to know what brought him home.

Linda. I don't know. I think he's still lost, Willy. I think he's very lost.

Willy. Biff Loman is lost. In the greatest country in the world a young man with such—personal attractiveness, gets lost. And such a hard worker. There's one thing about Biff—he's not lazy.

Linda. Never.

Willy, *with pity and resolve.* I'll see him in the morning; I'll have a nice talk with him. I'll get him a job selling. He could be big in no time. My God! Remember how they used to follow him around in high school? When he smiled at one of them their faces lit up. When he walked down the street . . .

He loses himself in reminiscences.

Linda, *trying to bring him out of it.* Willy, dear, I got a new kind of American-type cheese today. It's whipped.

Willy. Why do you get American when I like Swiss?

Linda. I just thought you'd like a change—

Willy. I don't want a change! I want Swiss cheese. Why am I always being contradicted?

Linda, *with a covering laugh.* I thought it would be a surprise.

Willy. Why don't you open a window in here, for God's sake?

Linda, *with infinite patience.* They're all open, dear.

Willy. The way they boxed us in here. Bricks and windows, windows and bricks.

Linda. We should've bought the land next door.

Willy. The street is lined with cars. There's not a breath of fresh air in the neighborhood. The grass don't grow any more, you can't raise a carrot in the back yard. They should've had a law against apartment houses. Remember those two beautiful elm trees out there? When I and Biff hung the swing between them?

Linda. Yeah, like being a million miles from the city.

Willy. They should've arrested the builder for cutting those down. They massacred the neighborhood. *Lost:* More and more I think of those days, Linda. This time of year it was lilac and wisteria. And then the peonies would come out, and the daffodils. What fragrance in this room!

Linda. Well, after all, people had to move somewhere.

Willy. No, there's more people now.

Linda. I don't think there's more people. I think—

Willy. There's more people! That's what's ruining this country! Population is getting out of control. The competition is maddening! Smell the stink from that apartment house! And another one on the other side . . . How can they whip cheese?

On Willy's last line, Biff and Happy raise themselves up in their beds, listening.

Linda. Go down, try it. And be quiet.

Willy, *turning to Linda, guiltily.* You're not worried about me, are you, sweetheart?

Biff. What's the matter?

Happy. Listen!

Linda. You've got too much on the ball to worry about.

Willy. You're my foundation and my support, Linda.

Linda. Just try to relax, dear. You make mountains out of molehills.

Willy. I won't fight with him any more. If he wants to go back to Texas, let him go.

Linda. He'll find his way.

Willy. Sure. Certain men just don't get started till later in life. Like Thomas Edison, I think. Or B.F. Goodrich. One of them was deaf. *He starts for the bedroom doorway.* I'll put my money on Biff.

Linda. And Willy—if it's warm Sunday we'll drive in the country. And we'll open the windshield, and take lunch.

Willy. No, the windshields don't open on the new cars.

Linda. But you opened it today.

Willy. Me? I didn't. *He stops.* Now isn't that peculiar! Isn't that a remarkable—

He breaks off in amazement and fright as the flute is heard distantly.

Linda. What, darling?

Willy. That is the most remarkable thing.

Linda. What, dear?

Willy. I was thinking of the Chevvy. *Slight pause.* Nineteen twenty-eight . . . when I had that red Chevvy—*Breaks off.* That funny? I coulda sworn I was driving that Chevvy today.

Linda. Well, that's nothing. Something must've reminded you.

Willy. Remarkable. Ts. Remember those days? The way Biff used to simonize that car? The dealer refused to believe there was eighty thousand miles on it. *He shakes his head.* Heh! *To Linda:* Close your eyes, I'll be right up.

He walks out of the bedroom.

Happy, *to Biff.* Jesus, maybe he smashed up the car again! (N ¬T)

Linda, *calling after Willy.* Be careful on the stairs, dear! The cheese is on the middle shelf!

She turns, goes over to the bed, takes his jacket, and goes out of the bedroom.

Light has risen on the boys' room. Unseen, Willy is heard talking to himself, "Eighty thousand miles," and a little laugh. Biff gets out of bed, comes downstage a bit, and stands attentively. Biff is two years older than his brother Happy, well built, but in these days bears a worn air and seems less self-assured. He has succeeded less, and his dreams are stronger and less acceptable than Happy's. Happy is tall, powerfully made. Sexuality is like a visible color on him, or a scent that many women have discovered. He, like his brother, is lost, but in a different way, for he has never allowed himself to turn his face toward defeat and is thus more confused and hard-skinned, although seemingly more content.

Happy, *getting out of bed.* He's going to get his license taken away if he keeps that up. I'm getting nervous about him, y'know, Biff?

Biff. His eyes are going.

Happy. No, I've driven with him. He sees all right. He just doesn't keep his mind on it. I drove into the city with him last week. He stops at a green light and then it turns red and he goes.

He laughs.

Biff. Maybe he's color-blind.

Happy. Pop? Why he's got the finest eye for color in the business. You know that.

Biff, *sitting down on his bed.* I'm going to sleep.

Happy. You're not still sour on Dad, are you, Biff?

Biff. He's all right, I guess.

Willy, *underneath them, in the living-room.* Yes, sir, eighty thousand miles—eighty-two thousand!

Biff. You smoking?

Happy, *holding out a pack of cigarettes.* Want one?

Biff, *taking a cigarette.* I can never sleep when I smell it.

Willy. What a simonizing job, heh!

Happy, *with deep sentiment.* Funny, Biff, y'know? Us sleeping in here again? The old beds. *He pats his bed affectionately.* All the talk that went across those two beds, huh? Our whole lives.

Biff. Yeah. Lotta dreams and plans.

Happy, *with a deep and masculine laugh.* About five hundred women would like to know what was said in this room.

They share a soft laugh.

Biff. Remember that big Betsy something—what the hell was her name—over on Bushwick Avenue?

Happy, *combing his hair.* With the collie dog!

Biff. That's the one. I got you in there, remember?

Happy. Yeah, that was my first time—I think. Boy, there was a pig! *They laugh, almost crudely.* You taught me everything I know about women. Don't forget that.

Biff. I bet you forgot how bashful you used to be. Especially with girls.

Happy. Oh, I still am, Biff.

Biff. Oh, go on.

Happy. I just control it, that's all. I think I got less bashful and you got more so. What happened, Biff? Where's the old humor, the old confidence? *He shakes Biff's knee. Biff gets up and moves restlessly about the room.* What's the matter?

Biff. Why does Dad mock me all the time?

Happy. He's not mocking you, he—

Biff. Everything I say there's a twist of mockery on his face. I can't get near him.

Happy. He just wants you to make good, that's all. I wanted to talk to you about Dad for a long time, Biff. Something's—happening to him. He—talks to himself.

Biff. I noticed that this morning. But he always mumbled.

Happy. But not so noticeable. It got so embarrassing I sent him to Florida. And you know something? Most of the time he's talking to you.

Biff. What's he say about me?

Happy. I can't make it out.

Biff. What's he say about me?

Happy. I think the fact that you're not settled, that you're still kind of up in the air . . .

Biff. There's one or two other things depressing him, Happy.

Happy. What do you mean?

Biff. Never mind. Just don't lay it all to me.

Happy. But I think if you just got started—I mean—is there any future for you out there?

Biff. I tell ya, Hap, I don't know what the future is. I don't know—what I'm supposed to want.

Happy. What do you mean?

Biff. Well, I spent six or seven years after high school trying to work myself up. Shipping clerk, salesman, business of one kind or another. And it's a measly manner of existence. To get on that subway on the hot mornings in summer. To devote your whole life to keeping stock, or making phone calls, or selling or buying. To suffer fifty weeks of the year for the sake of a two-week vacation, when all you really desire is to be outdoors, with your shirt off. And always to have to get ahead of the next fella. And still—that's how you build a future.

Happy. Well, you really enjoy it on a farm? Are you content out there?

Biff, *with rising agitation.* Hap, I've had twenty or thirty different kinds of jobs since I left home before the war, and it always turns out the same. I just realized it lately. In Nebraska when I herded cattle, and the Dakotas, and Arizona, and now in Texas. It's why I came home now, I guess, because I realized it. This farm I work on, it's spring there now, see? And they've got about fifteen new colts. There's nothing more inspiring or—beautiful than the sight of a mare and a new colt. And it's cool there now, see? Texas is cool now, and it's spring. And whenever spring comes to where I am, I suddenly get the feeling, my God, I'm not gettin' anywhere! What the hell am I doing, playing around with horses, twenty-eight dollars a week! I'm thirty-four years old, I oughta be makin' my future. That's when I come running home. And now, I get here, and I don't know what to do with myself. *After a pause:* I've always made a point of not wasting my life, and everytime I come back here I know that all I've done is to waste my life.

Happy. You're a poet, you know that, Biff? You're a—you're an idealist!

Biff. No, I'm mixed up very bad. Maybe I oughta get married. Maybe I oughta get stuck into something. Maybe that's my trouble. I'm like a boy. I'm not married, I'm not in business, I just—I'm like a boy. Are you content, Hap? You're a success, aren't you? Are you content?

Happy. Hell, no!

Biff. Why? You're making money, aren't you?

Happy, *moving about with energy, expressiveness.* All I can do now is wait for the merchandise manager to die. And suppose I get to be merchandise manager? He's a good friend of mine, and he just built a terrific estate on Long Island. And he lived there about two months and sold it, and now he's building another one. He can't enjoy it once it's finished. And I know that's just what I would do. I don't know what the hell I'm workin' for. Sometimes I sit in my apartment—all alone. And I think of the rent I'm paying. And it's crazy. But then, it's what I always wanted. My own apartment, a car, and plenty of women. And still, goddammit, I'm lonely.

Biff, *with enthusiasm.*   Listen, why don't you come out West with me?

Happy.   You and I, heh?

Biff.   Sure, maybe we could buy a ranch. Raise cattle, use our muscles. Men built like we are should be working out in the open.

Happy, *avidly.*   The Loman Brothers, heh?

Biff, *with vast affection.*   Sure, we'd be known all over the counties!

Happy, *entralled.*   That's what I dream about, Biff. Sometimes I want to just rip my clothes off in the middle of the store and outbox that goddam merchandise manager. I mean I can outbox, outrun, and outlift anybody in that store, and I have to take orders from those common, petty sons-of-bitches till I can't stand it any more.

Biff.   I'm tellin' you, kid, if you were with me I'd be happy out there.

Happy, *enthused.*   See, Biff, everybody around me is so false that I'm constantly lowering my ideals . . .

Biff.   Baby, together we'd stand up for one another, we'd have someone to trust.

Happy.   If I were around you—

Biff.   Hap, the trouble is we weren't brought up to grub for money. I don't know how to do it.

Happy.   Neither can I!

Biff.   Then let's go!

Happy.   The only thing is—what can you make out there?

Biff.   But look at your friend. Builds an estate and then hasn't the peace of mind to live in it.

Happy.   Yeah, but when he walks into the store the waves part in front of him. That's fifty-two thousand dollars a year coming through the revolving door, and I got more in my pinky finger than he's got in his head.

Biff.   Yeah, but you just said—

Happy.   I gotta show some of those pompous, self-important executives over there that Hap Loman can make the grade. I want to walk into the store the way he walks in. Then I'll go with you, Biff. We'll be together yet, I swear. But take those two we had tonight. Now weren't they gorgeous creatures?

Biff.   Yeah, yeah, most gorgeous I've had in years.

Happy.   I get that any time I want, Biff. Whenever I feel disgusted. The only trouble is, it gets like bowling or something. I just keep knockin' them over and it doesn't mean anything. You still run around a lot?

Biff.   Naa. I'd like to find a girl—steady, somebody with substance.

Happy.   That's what I long for.

Biff.   Go on! You'd never come home.

Happy.   I would! Somebody with character, with resistance! Like Mom, y'know? You're gonna call me a bastard when I tell you this. That girl Charlotte I was with tonight is engaged to be married in five weeks.

He tries on his new hat.

Biff. No kiddin'!

Happy. Sure, the guy's in line for the vice-presidency of the store. I don't know what gets into me, maybe I just have an overdeveloped sense of competition or something, but I went and ruined her, and furthermore I can't get rid of her. And he's the third executive I've done that to. Isn't that a crummy characteristic? And to top it all, I go to their weddings! *Indignantly, but laughing:* Like I'm not supposed to take bribes. Manufacturers offer me a hundred-dollar bill now and then to throw an order their way. You know how honest I am, but it's like this girl, see. I hate myself for it. Because I don't want the girl, and, still, I take it and—I love it!

Biff. Let's go to sleep.

Happy. I guess we didn't settle anything, heh?

Biff. I just got one idea that I think I'm going to try.

Happy. What's that?

Biff. Remember Bill Oliver?

Happy. Sure, Oliver is very big now. You want to work for him again?

Biff. No, but when I quit he said something to me. He put his arm on my shoulder, and he said, "Biff, if you ever need anything, come to me."

Happy. I remember that. That sounds good.

Biff. I think I'll go to see him. If I could get ten thousand or even seven or eight thousand dollars I could buy a beautiful ranch.

Happy. I bet he'd back you. 'Cause he thought highly of you, Biff. I mean, they all do. You're well liked, Biff. That's why I say to come back here, and we both have the apartment. And I'm tellin' you, Biff, any babe you want . . .

Biff. No, with a ranch I could do the work I like and still be something. I just wonder though. I wonder if Oliver still thinks I stole that carton of basketballs.

Happy. Oh, he probably forgot that long ago. It's almost ten years. You're too sensitive. Anyway, he didn't really fire you.

Biff. Well, I think he was going to. I think that's why I quit. I was never sure whether he knew or not. I know he thought the world of me, though. I was the only one he'd let lock up the place.

Willy, *below.* You gonna wash the engine, Biff?

Happy. Shh!

Biff looks at Happy, who is gazing down, listening. Willy is mumbling in the parlor.

Happy. You hear that?

They listen. Willy laughs warmly.

Biff, *growing angry.*   Doesn't he know Mom can hear that?
Willy. Don't get your sweater dirty, Biff!

A look of pain crosses Biff's face.

Happy. Isn't that terrible? Don't leave again, will you? You'll find a job
   here. You gotta stick around. I don't know what to do about him, it's
   getting embarrassing.
Willy. What a simonizing job!
Biff. Mom's hearing that!
Willy. No kiddin', Biff, you got a date? Wonderful!
Happy. Go on to sleep. But talk to him in the morning, will you?
Biff, *reluctantly getting into bed.*   With her in the house. Brother!
Happy, *getting into bed.*   I wish you'd have a good talk with him.

The light on their room begins to fade.

Biff, *to himself in bed.*   That selfish, stupid . . .
Happy. Sh . . . Sleep, Biff.

*Their light is out. Well before they have finished speaking, Willy's form is
   dimly seen below in the darkened kitchen. He opens the refrigerator, searches
   in there, and takes out a bottle of milk. The apartment houses are fading
   out, and the entire house and surroundings become covered with leaves.
   Music insinuates itself as the leaves appear.*

Willy. Just wanna be careful with those girls, Biff, that's all. Don't make
   any promises. No promises of any kind. Because a girl, y'know, they
   always believe what you tell 'em, and you're very young, Biff, you're
   too young to be talking seriously to girls.

*Light rises on the kitchen. Willy, talking, shuts the refrigerator door and comes
   downstage to the kitchen table. He pours milk into a glass. He is totally
   immersed in himself, smiling faintly.*

Willy. Too young entirely, Biff. You want to watch your schooling first.
   Then when you're all set, there'll be plenty of girls for a boy like you.
   He smiles broadly at a kitchen chair. That so? The girls pay for you? *He
   laughs.* Boy, you must really be makin' a hit.

Willy is gradually addressing—physically—a point offstage, speaking through the wall of the kitchen, and his voice has been rising in volume to that of a normal conversation.

Willy. I been wondering why you polish the car so careful. Ha! Don't leave the hubcaps, boys. Get the chamois to the hubcaps. Happy, use newspaper on the windows, it's the easiest thing. Show him how to do it, Biff! You see, Happy? Pad it up, use it like a pad. That's it, that's it, good work. You're doin' all right, Hap. *He pauses, then nods in approbation for a few seconds, then looks upward.* Biff, first thing we gotta do when we get time is clip that big branch over the house. Afraid it's gonna fall in a storm and hit the roof. Tell you what. We get a rope and sling her around, and then we climb up there with a couple of saws and take her down. Soon as you finish the car, boys, I wanna see ya. I got a surprise for you, boys.

Biff, *offstage.* Whatta ya got, Dad?

Willy. No, you finish first. Never leave a job till you're finished— remember that. *Looking toward the "big trees":* Biff, up in Albany I saw a beautiful hammock. I think I'll buy it next trip, and we'll hang it right between those two elms. Wouldn't that be something? Just swingin' there under those branches. Boy, that would be . . .

Young Biff and Young Happy appear from the direction Willy was addressing. Happy carries rags and a pail of water. Biff, wearing a sweater with a block "S," carries a football.

Biff, *pointing in the direction of the car offstage.* How's that, Pop, professional?

Willy. Terrific. Terrific job, boys. Good work, Biff.

Happy. Where's the surprise, Pop?

Willy. In the back seat of the car.

Happy. Boy! *He runs off.*

Biff. What is it, Dad? Tell me, what'd you buy?

Willy, *laughing, cuffs him.* Never mind, something I want you to have.

Biff, *turns and starts off.* What is it, Hap?

Happy, *offstage.* It's a punching bag!

Biff. Oh, Pop!

Willy. It's got Gene Tunney's[1] signature on it!

Happy runs onstage with a punching bag.

---

[1] Heavy-weight boxing champion.

Biff. Gee, how'd you know we wanted a punching bag?

Willy. Well, it's the finest thing for the timing.

Happy, *lies down on his back and pedals with his feet.* I'm losing weight, you notice, Pop?

Willy, *to Happy.* Jumping rope is good too.

Biff. Did you see the new football I got?

Willy, *examining the ball.* Where'd you get a new ball?

Biff. The coach told me to practice my passing.

Willy. That so? And he gave you the ball, heh?

Biff. Well, I borrowed it from the locker room.

He laughs confidentially.

Willy, *laughing with him at the theft.* I want you to return that.

Happy. I told you he wouldn't like it!

Biff, *angrily.* Well, I'm bringing it back!

Willy, *stopping the incipient argument, to Happy.* Sure, he's gotta practice with a regulation ball, doesn't he? *To Biff:* Coach'll probably congratulate you on your initiative!

Biff. Oh, he keeps congratulating my initiative all the time, Pop.

Willy. That's because he likes you. If somebody else took that ball there'd be an uproar. So what's the report, boys, what's the report?

Biff. Where'd you go this time, Dad? Gee we were lonesome for you.

Willy, *pleased, puts an arm around each boy and they come down to the apron.* Lonesome, heh?

Biff. Missed you every minute.

Willy. Don't say? Tell you a secret, boys. Don't breathe it to a soul. Someday I'll have my own business, and I'll never have to leave home any more.

Happy. Like Uncle Charley, heh?

Willy. Bigger than Uncle Charley! Because Charley is not—liked. He's liked, but he's not—well liked.

Biff. Where'd you go this time, Dad?

Willy. Well, I got on the road, and I went north to Providence. Met the Mayor.

Biff. The Mayor of Providence!

Willy. He was sitting in the hotel lobby.

Biff. What'd he say?

Willy. He said, "Morning!" And I said, "You got a fine city here, Mayor." And then he had coffee with me. And then I went to Waterbury. Waterbury is a fine city. Big clock city, the famous Waterbury clock. Sold a nice bill there. And then Boston—Boston is the cradle of the Revolution. A fine city. And a couple of other towns in Mass., and on to Portland and Bangor and straight home!

Biff. Gee, I'd love to go with you sometime, Dad.

Willy.   Soon as summer comes.

Happy.   Promise?

Willy.   You and Hap and I, and I'll show you all the towns. America is full of beautiful towns and fine, upstanding people. And they know me, boys, they know me up and down New England. The finest people. And when I bring you fellas up, there'll be open sesame for all of us, 'cause one thing, boys: I have friends. I can park my car in any street in New England, and the cops protect it like their own. This summer, heh?

Biff and Happy, *together.*   Yeah! You bet!

Willy.   We'll take our bathing suits.

Happy.   We'll carry your bags, Pop!

Willy.   Oh, won't that be something! Me comin' into the Boston stores with you boys carryin' my bags. What a sensation!

Biff is prancing around, practicing passing the ball.

Willy.   You nervous, Biff, about the game?

Biff.   Not if you're gonna be there.

Willy.   What do they say about you in school, now that they made you captain?

Happy.   There's a crowd of girls behind him every time the classes change.

Biff, *taking Willy's hand.*   This Saturday, Pop, this Saturday—just for you, I'm going to break through for a touchdown.

Happy.   You're supposed to pass.

Biff.   I'm takin' one play for Pop. You watch me, Pop, and when I take off my helmet, that means I'm breakin' out. Then you watch me crash through that line!

Willy, *kisses Biff.*   Oh, wait'll I tell this in Boston!

Bernard enters in knickers. He is younger than Biff, earnest and loyal, a worried boy.

Bernard.   Biff, where are you? You're supposed to study with me today.

Willy.   Hey, looka Bernard. What're you lookin' so anemic about, Bernard?

Bernard.   He's gotta study, Uncle Willy. He's got Regents[2] next week.

Happy, *tauntingly, spinning Bernard around.*   Let's box, Bernard!

Bernard.   Biff! *He gets away from Happy.* Listen, Biff, I heard Mr. Birnbaum say that if you don't start studyin' math he's gonna flunk you, and you won't graduate. I heard him!

Willy.   You better study with him, Biff. Go ahead now.

Bernard.   I heard him!

---

[2] Standardized examinations for high school students in New York state.

Biff. Oh, Pop, you didn't see my sneakers!

He holds up a foot for Willy to look at.

Willy. Hey, that's a beautiful job of printing!

Bernard, *wiping his glasses.* Just because he printed University of Virginia on his sneakers doesn't mean they've got to graduate him, Uncle Willy!

Willy, *angrily.* What're you talking about? With scholarships to three universities they're gonna flunk him?

Bernard. But I heard Mr. Birnbaum say—

Willy. Don't be a pest, Bernard! *To his boys:* What an anemic!

Bernard. Okay, I'm waiting for you in my house, Biff.

Bernard goes off. The Lomans laugh.

Willy. Bernard is not well liked, is he?

Biff. He's liked, but he's not well liked.

Happy. That's right, Pop.

Willy. That's just what I mean. Bernard can get the best marks in school, y'understand, but when he gets out in the business world, y'understand, you are going to be five times ahead of him. That's why I thank Almighty God you're both built like Adonises. Because the man who makes an appearance in the business world, the man who creates personal interest, is the man who gets ahead. Be liked and you will never want. You take me, for instance. I never have to wait in line to see a buyer. "Willy Loman is here!" That's all they have to know, and I go right through.

Biff. Did you knock them dead, Pop?

Willy. Knocked 'em cold in Providence, slaughtered 'em in Boston.

Happy, *on his back, pedaling again.* I'm losing weight, you notice, Pop?

Linda enters, as of old, a ribbon in her hair, carrying a basket of washing.

Linda, *with youthful energy.* Hello, dear!

Willy. Sweetheart!

Linda. How'd the Chevvy run?

Willy. Chevrolet, Linda, is the greatest car ever built. *To the boys:* Since when do you let your mother carry wash up the stairs?

Biff. Grab hold there, boy!

Happy. Where to, Mom?

Linda. Hang them up on the line. And you better go down to your friends, Biff. The cellar is full of boys. They don't know what to do with themselves.

Biff. Ah, when Pop comes home they can wait!

Willy, *laughs appreciatively.* You better go down and tell them what to do, Biff.

Biff. I think I'll have them sweep out the furnace room.

Willy. Good work, Biff.

Biff, *goes through wall-line of kitchen to doorway at back and calls down.* Fellas! Everybody sweep out the furnace room! I'll be right down!

Voices. All right! Okay, Biff.

Biff. George and Sam and Frank, come out back! We're hangin' up the wash! Come on, Hap, on the double!

He and Happy carry out the basket.

Linda. The way they obey him!

Willy. Well, that's training, the training. I'm tellin' you, I was sellin' thousands and thousands, but I had to come home.

Linda. Oh, the whole block'll be at that game. Did you sell anything?

Willy. I did five hundred gross in Providence and seven hundred gross in Boston.

Linda. No! Wait a minute, I've got a pencil. *She pulls pencil and paper out of her apron pocket.* That makes your commission . . . Two hundred— my God! Two hundred and twelve dollars!

Willy. Well, I didn't figure it yet, but . . .

Linda. How much did you do?

Willy. Well, I—I did—about a hundred and eighty gross in Providence. Well, no—it came to—roughly two hundred gross on the whole trip.

Linda, *without hesitation.* Two hundred gross. That's . . .

She figures.

Willy. The trouble was that three of the stores were half closed for inventory in Boston. Otherwise I woulda broke records.

Linda. Well, it makes seventy dollars and some pennies. That's very good.

Willy. What do we owe?

Linda. Well, on the first there's sixteen dollars on the refrigerator—

Willy. Why sixteen?

Linda. Well, the fan belt broke, so it was a dollar eighty.

Willy. But it's brand new.

Linda. Well, the man said that's the way it is. Till they work themselves in, y'know.

They move through the wall-line into the kitchen.

Willy. I hope we didn't get stuck on that machine.
Linda. They got the biggest ads of any of them!
Willy. I know, it's a fine machine. What else?
Linda. Well, there's nine-sixty for the washing machine. And for the
vacuum cleaner there's three and a half due on the fifteenth. Then the
roof, you got twenty-one dollars remaining.
Willy. It don't leak, does it?
Linda. No, they did a wonderful job. Then you owe Frank for the
carburetor.
Willy. I'm not going to pay that man! That goddam Chevrolet, they
ought to prohibit the manufacture of that car!
Linda. Well, you owe him three and a half. And odds and ends, comes
to around a hundred and twenty dollars by the fifteenth.
Willy. A hundred and twenty dollars! My God, if business don't pick
up I don't know what I'm gonna do!
Linda. Well, next week you'll do better.
Willy. Oh, I'll knock 'em dead next week. I'll go to Hartford. I'm very
well liked in Hartford. You know, the trouble is, Linda, people don't
seem to take to me.

They move onto the forestage.

Linda. Oh, don't be foolish.
Willy. I know it when I walk in. They seem to laugh at me.
Linda. Why? Why would they laugh at you? Don't talk that way, Willy.

*Willy moves to the edge of the stage. Linda goes into the kitchen and starts
to darn stockings.*

Willy. I don't know the reason for it, but they just pass me by. I'm not
noticed.
Linda. But you're doing wonderful, dear. You're making seventy to a
hundred dollars a week.
Willy. But I gotta be at it ten, twelve hours a day. Other men—I don't
know—they do it easier. I don't know why—I can't stop myself—I
talk too much. A man oughta come in with a few words. One thing
about Charley. He's a man of few words, and they respect him.
Linda. You don't talk too much, you're just lively.
Willy, *smiling.* Well, I figure, what the hell, life is short, a couple of
jokes. *To himself:* I joke too much! *The smile goes.*
Linda. Why? You're—

Sher

Willy. I'm fat. I'm very—foolish to look at, Linda. I didn't tell you, but Christmas time I happened to be calling on F.H. Stewarts, and a salesman I know, as I was going in to see the buyer I heard him say something about—walrus. And I—I cracked him right across the face. I won't take that. I simply will not take that. But they do laugh at me. I know that.

Linda. Darling . . .

Willy. I gotta overcome it. I know I gotta overcome it. I'm not dressing to advantage, maybe.

Linda. Willy, darling, you're the handsomest man in the world—

Willy. Oh, no, Linda.

Linda. To me you are. *Slight pause.* The handsomest.

From the darkness is heard the laughter of a woman. Willy doesn't turn to it, but it continues through Linda's lines.

Linda. And the boys, Willy. Few men are idolized by their children the way you are.

Music is heard as behind a scrim, to the left of the house, The Woman, dimly seen, is dressing.

Willy, *with great feeling.* You're the best there is, Linda, you're a pal, you know that? On the road—on the road I want to grab you sometimes and just kiss the life outa you.

The laughter is loud now, and he moves into a brightening area at the left, where The Woman has come from behind the scrim and is standing, putting on her hat, looking into a "mirror" and laughing.

Willy. 'Cause I get so lonely—especially when business is bad and there's nobody to talk to. I get the feeling that I'll never sell anything again, that I won't make a living for you, or a business, a business for the boys. *He talks through The Woman's subsiding laughter; The Woman primps at the "mirror."* There's so much I want to make for—

The Woman. Me? You didn't make me, Willy. I picked you.

Willy, *pleased.* You picked me?

The Woman, *who is quite proper-looking, Willy's age.* I did. I've been sitting at that desk watching all the salesmen go by, day in, day out. But you've got such a sense of humor, and we do have such a good time together, don't we?

Willy. Sure, sure. *He takes her in his arms.* Why do you have to go now?

The Woman. It's two o'clock . . .

Willy. No, come on in! *He pulls her.*

The Woman.   . . . my sisters'll be scandalized. When'll you be back?
Willy.   Oh, two weeks about. Will you come up again?
The Woman.   Sure thing. You do make me laugh. It's good for me. *She squeezes his arm, kisses him.* And I think you're a wonderful man.
Willy.   You picked me, heh?
The Woman.   Sure. Because you're so sweet. And such a kidder.
Willy.   Well, I'll see you next time I'm in Boston.
The Woman.   I'll put you right through to the buyers.
Willy, *slapping her bottom.*   Right. Well, bottoms up!
The Woman, *slaps him gently and laughs.*   You just kill me, Willy. *He suddenly grabs her and kisses her roughly.* You kill me. And thanks for the stockings. I love a lot of stockings. Well, good night.
Willy.   Good night. And keep your pores open!
The Woman.   Oh, Willy!

The Woman bursts out laughing, and Linda's laughter blends in. The Woman disappears into the dark. Now the area at the kitchen table brightens. Linda is sitting where she was at the kitchen table, but now is mending a pair of her silk stockings.

Linda.   You are, Willy. The handsomest man. You've got no reason to feel that—
Willy, *coming out of The Woman's dimming area and going over to Linda.*   I'll make it all up to you, Linda, I'll—
Linda.   There's nothing to make up, dear. You're doing fine, better than—
Willy, *noticing her mending.*   What's that?
Linda.   Just mending my stockings. They're so expensive—
Willy, *angrily, taking them from her.*   I won't have you mending stockings in this house! Now throw them out!

Linda puts the stockings in her pocket.

Bernard, *entering on the run.*   Where is he? If he doesn't study!
Willy, *moving to the forestage, with great agitation.*   You'll give him the answers!
Bernard.   I do, but I can't on a Regents! That's a state exam! They're liable to arrest me!
Willy.   Where is he? I'll whip him, I'll whip him!
Linda.   And he'd better give back that football, Willy, it's not nice.
Willy.   Biff! Where is he? Why is he taking everything?
Linda.   He's too rough with the girls, Willy. All the mothers are afraid of him!
Willy.   I'll whip him!
Bernard.   He's driving the car without a license!

The Woman's laugh is heard.

Willy. Shut up!
Linda. All the mothers—
Willy. Shut up!
Bernard, *backing quietly away and out.* Mr. Birnbaum says he's stuck up.
Willy. Get outa here!
Bernard. If he doesn't buckle down he'll flunk math!

He goes off.

Linda. He's right, Willy, you've gotta—
Willy, *exploding at her.* There's nothing the matter with him! You want
  him to be a worm like Bernard? He's got spirit, personality . . .

*As he speaks, Linda, almost in tears, exits into the living-room. Willy is alone
  in the kitchen, wilting and staring. The leaves are gone. It is night again,
  and the apartment houses look down from behind.*

Willy. Loaded with it. Loaded! What is he stealing? He's giving it back,
  isn't he? Why is he stealing? What did I tell him? I never in my life
  told him anything but decent things.

*Happy in pajamas has come down the stairs; Willy suddenly becomes aware
  of Happy's presence.*

Happy. Let's go now, come on.
Willy, *sitting down at the kitchen table.* Huh! Why did she have to wax
  the floors herself? Everytime she waxes the floors she keels over. She
  knows that!
Happy. Shh! Take it easy. What brought you back tonight?
Willy. I got an awful scare. Nearly hit a kid in Yonkers. God! Why
  didn't I go to Alaska with my brother Ben that time! Ben! That man
  was a genius, that man was success incarnate! What a mistake! He
  begged me to go.
Happy. Well, there's no use in—
Willy. You guys! There was a man started with the clothes on his back
  and ended up with diamond mines!
Happy. Boy, someday I'd like to know how he did it.
Willy. What's the mystery? The man knew what he wanted and went
  out and got it! Walked into a jungle, and comes out, the age of twenty-

one, and he's rich! The world is an oyster, but you don't crack it open on a mattress!

Happy. Pop, I told you I'm gonna retire you for life.

Willy. You'll retire me for life on seventy goddam dollars a week? And your women and your car and your apartment, and you'll retire me for life! Christ's sake, I couldn't get past Yonkers today! Where are you guys, where are you? The woods are burning! I can't drive a car!

Charley has appeared in the doorway. He is a large man, slow of speech, laconic, immovable. In all he says, despite what he says, there is pity, and, now, trepidation. He has a robe over pajamas, slippers on his feet. He enters the kitchen.

Charley. Everything all right?

Happy. Yeah, Charley, everything's . . .

Willy. What's the matter?

Charley. I heard some noise. I thought something happened. Can't we do something about the walls? You sneeze in here, and in my house hats blow off.

Happy. Let's go to bed, Dad. Come on.

Charley signals to Happy to go.

Willy. You go ahead, I'm not tired at the moment.

Happy, *to Willy.* Take it easy, huh? *He exits.*

Willy. What're you doin' up?

Charley, *sitting down at the kitchen table opposite Willy.* Couldn't sleep good. I had a heartburn.

Willy. Well, you don't know how to eat.

Charley. I eat with my mouth.

Willy. No, you're ignorant. You gotta know about vitamins and things like that.

Charley. Come on, let's shoot. Tire you out a little.

Willy, *hesitantly.* All right. You got cards?

Charley, *taking a deck from his pocket.* Yeah, I got them. Someplace. What is it with those vitamins?

Willy, *dealing,* They build up your bones. Chemistry.

Charley. Yeah, but there's no bones in a heartburn.

Willy. What are you talkin' about? Do you know the first thing about it?

Charley. Don't get insulted.

Willy. Don't talk about something you don't know anything about.

They are playing. Pause.

Charley. What're you doin' home?

Willy. A little trouble with the car.

Charley. Oh. *Pause.* I'd like to take a trip to California.

Willy. Don't say.

Charley. You want a job?

Willy. I got a job, I told you that. *After a slight pause:* What the hell are you offering me a job for?

Charley. Don't get insulted.

Willy. Don't insult me.

Charley. I don't see no sense in it. You don't have to go on this way.

Willy. I got a good job. *Slight pause.* What do you keep comin' in here for?

Charley. You want me to go?

Willy, *after a pause, withering.* I can't understand it. He's going back to Texas again. What the hell is that?

Charley. Let him go.

Willy. I got nothin' to give him, Charley, I'm clean, I'm clean.

Charley. He won't starve. None a them starve. Forget about him.

Willy. Then what have I got to remember?

Charley. You take it too hard. To hell with it. When a deposit bottle is broken you don't get your nickel back.

Willy. That's easy enough for you to say.

Charley. That ain't easy for me to say.

Willy. Did you see the ceiling I put up in the living-room?

Charley. Yeah, that's a piece of work. To put up a ceiling is a mystery to me. How do you do it?

Willy. What's the difference?

Charley. Well, talk about it.

Willy. You gonna put up a ceiling?

Charley. How could I put up a ceiling?

Willy. Then what the hell are you bothering me for?

Charley. You're insulted again.

Willy. A man who can't handle tools is not a man. You're disgusting.

Charley. Don't call me disgusting, Willy.

Uncle Ben, carrying a valise and an umbrella, enters the forestage from around the right corner of the house. He is a stolid man, in his sixties, with a mustache and an authoritative air. He is utterly certain of his destiny, and there is an aura of far places about him. He enters exactly as Willy speaks.

Willy. I'm getting awfully tired, Ben.

Ben's music is heard. Ben looks around at everything.

Charley. Good, keep playing; you'll sleep better. Did you call me Ben?

Ben looks at his watch.

Willy. That's funny. For a second there you reminded me of my brother Ben.

Ben. I only have a few minutes. *He strolls, inspecting the place. Willy and Charley continue playing.*

Charley. You never heard from him again, heh? Since that time?

Willy. Didn't Linda tell you? Couple of weeks ago we got a letter from his wife in Africa. He died.

Charley. That so.

Ben, *chuckling.* So this is Brooklyn, eh?

Charley. Maybe you're in for some of his money.

Willy. Naa, he had seven sons. There's just one opportunity I had with that man . . .

Ben. I must make a train, William. There are several properties I'm looking at in Alaska.

Willy. Sure, sure! If I'd gone with him to Alaska that time, everything would've been totally different.

Charley. Go on, you'd froze to death up there.

Willy. What're you talking about?

Ben. Opportunity is tremendous in Alaska, William. Surprised you're not up there.

Willy. Sure, tremendous.

Charley. Heh?

Willy. There was the only man I ever met who knew the answers.

Charley. Who?

Ben. How are you all?

Willy, *taking a pot, smiling.* Fine, fine.

Charley. Pretty sharp tonight.

Ben. Is Mother living with you?

Willy. No, she died a long time ago.

Charley. Who?

Ben. That's too bad. Fine specimen of a lady, Mother.

Willy, *to Charley.* Heh?

Ben. I'd hoped to see the old girl.

Charley. Who died?

Ben. Heard anything from Father, have you?

Willy, *unnerved.* What do you mean, who died?

Charley, *taking a pot.* What're you talkin' about?

Ben, *looking at his watch.* William, it's half-past eight!

Willy, *as though to dispel his confusion he angrily stops Charley's hand.* That's my build!

Charley. I put the ace—

Willy. If you don't know how to play the game I'm not gonna throw my money away on you!

Charley, *rising.* It was my ace, for God's sake!

Willy. I'm through, I'm through!

Ben. When did Mother die?

Willy. Long ago. Since the beginning you never knew how to play cards.

Charley, *picks up the cards and goes to the door.* All right! Next time I'll bring a deck with five aces.

Willy. I don't play that kind of game!

Charley, *turning to him.* You ought to be ashamed of yourself!

Willy. Yeah?

Charley. Yeah! *He goes out.*

Willy, *slamming the door after him.* Ignoramus!

Ben, *as Willy comes toward him through the wall-line of the kitchen.* So you're William.

Willy, *shaking Ben's hand.* Ben! I've been waiting for you so long! What's the answer? How did you do it?

Ben. Oh, there's a story in that.

Linda enters the forestage, as of old, carrying the wash basket.

Linda. Is this Ben?

Ben, *gallantly.* How do you do, my dear.

Linda. Where've you been all these years? Willy's always wondered why you—

Willy, *pulling Ben away from her impatiently.* Where is Dad? Didn't you follow him? How did you get started?

Ben. Well, I don't know how much you remember.

Willy. Well, I was just a baby, of course, only three or four years old—

Ben. Three years and eleven months.

Willy. What a memory, Ben!

Ben. I have many enterprises, William, and I have never kept books.

Willy. I remember I was sitting under the wagon in—was it Nebraska?

Ben. It was South Dakota, and I gave you a bunch of wild flowers.

Willy. I remember you walking away down some open road.

Ben, *laughing.* I was going to find Father in Alaska.

Willy. Where is he?

Ben. At that age I had a very faulty view of geography, William. I discovered after a few days that I was heading due south, so instead of Alaska, I ended up in Africa.

Linda. Africa!

Willy. The Gold Coast!

Ben. Principally diamond mines.

Linda. Diamond mines!

Ben. Yes, my dear. But I've only a few minutes—

Willy. No! Boys! Boys! *Young Biff and Happy appear.* Listen to this. This is your Uncle Ben, a great man! Tell my boys, Ben!

Ben. Why, boys, when I was seventeen I walked into the jungle, and when I was twenty-one I walked out. *He laughs.* And by God I was rich.

Willy, *to the boys.* You see what I been talking about? The greatest things can happen!

Ben, *glancing at his watch.* I have an appointment in Ketchikan Tuesday week.

Willy. No, Ben! Please tell about Dad. I want my boys to hear. I want them to know the kind of stock they spring from. All I remember is a man with a big beard, and I was in Mamma's lap, sitting around a fire, and some kind of high music.

Ben. His flute. He played the flute.

Willy. Sure, the flute, that's right!

New music is heard, a high, rollicking tune.

Ben. Father was a very great and a very wild-hearted man. We would start in Boston, and he'd toss the whole family into the wagon, and then he'd drive the team right across the country; through Ohio, and Indiana, Michigan, Illinois, and all the Western states. And we'd stop in the towns and sell the flutes that he'd made on the way. Great inventor, Father. With one gadget he made more in a week than a man like you could make in a lifetime.

Willy. That's just the way I'm bringing them up, Ben—rugged, well liked, all-around.

Ben. Yeah? *To Biff:* Hit that, boy—hard as you can. *He pounds his stomach.*

Biff. Oh, no, sir!

Ben, *taking boxing stance.* Come on, get to me! *He laughs.*

Willy. Go to it, Biff! Go ahead, show him!

Biff. Okay! *He cocks his fists and starts in.*

Linda, *to Willy.* Why must he fight, dear?

Ben, *sparring with Biff.* Good boy! Good boy!

Willy. How's that, Ben, heh?

Happy. Give him the left, Biff!

Linda. Why are you fighting?

Ben. Good boy! *Suddenly comes in, trips Biff, and stands over him, the point of his umbrella poised over Biff's eye.*

Linda. Look out, Biff!

Biff. Gee!

Ben, *patting Biff's knee.* Never fight fair with a stranger, boy. You'll never get out of the jungle that way. *Taking Linda's hand and bowing.* It was an honor and a pleasure to meet you, Linda.

Linda, *withdrawing her hand coldly, frightened.* Have a nice—trip.

Ben, *to Willy.* And good luck with your—what do you do?

Willy. Selling.

Ben. Yes. Well . . . *He raises his hand in farewell to all.*

Willy. No, Ben, I don't want you to think . . . *He takes Ben's arm to show him.* It's Brooklyn, I know, but we hunt too.

Ben. Really, now.

Willy. Oh, sure, there's snakes and rabbits and—that's why I moved out here. Why, Biff can fell any one of these trees in no time! Boys! Go right over to where they're building the apartment house and get some sand. We're gonna rebuild the entire front stoop right now! Watch this, Ben!

Biff. Yes, sir! On the double, Hap!

Happy, *as he and Biff run off.* I lost weight, Pop, you notice?

Charley enters in knickers, even before the boys are gone.

Charley. Listen, if they steal any more from that building the watchman'll put the cops on them!

Linda, *to Willy.* Don't let Biff . . .

Ben laughs lustily.

Willy. You shoulda seen the lumber they brought home last week. At least a dozen six-by-tens worth all kinds a money.

Charley. Listen, if that watchman—

Willy. I gave them hell, understand. But I got a couple of fearless characters there.

Charley. Willy, the jails are full of fearless characters.

Ben, *clapping Willy on the back, with a laugh at Charley.* And the stock exchange, friend!

Willy, *joining in Ben's laughter.* Where are the rest of your pants?

Charley. My wife bought them.

Willy. Now all you need is a golf club and you can go upstairs and go to sleep. *To Ben:* Great athlete! Between him and his son Bernard they can't hammer a nail!

Bernard, *rushing in.* The watchman's chasing Biff!

Willy, *angrily.* Shut up! He's not stealing anything!

Linda, *alarmed, hurrying off left.* Where is he? Biff, dear! *She exits.*

Willy, *moving toward the left, away from Ben.* There's nothing wrong. What's the matter with you?

Ben. Nervy boy. Good!

Willy, *laughing.* Oh, nerves of iron, that Biff!

Charley. Don't know what it is. My New England man comes back and he's bleedin', they murdered him up there.

Willy. It's contacts, Charley, I got important contacts!

Charley, *sarcastically.* Glad to hear it, Willy. Come in later, we'll shoot a little casino. I'll take some of your Portland money. *He laughs at Willy and exists.*

Willy, *turning to Ben.* Business is bad, it's murderous. But not for me, of course.

Ben. I'll stop by on my way back to Africa.

Willy, *longingly.* Can't you stay a few days? You're just what I need, Ben, because I—I have a fine position here, but I—well, Dad left when I was such a baby and I never had a chance to talk to him and I still feel—kind of temporary about myself.

Ben. I'll be late for my train.

They are at opposite ends of the stage.

Willy. Ben, my boys—can't we talk? They'd go into the jaws of hell for me, see, but I—

Ben. William, you're being first-rate with your boys. Outstanding, manly chaps!

Willy, *hanging on to his words.* Oh, Ben, that's good to hear! Because sometimes I'm afraid that I'm not teaching them the right kind of— Ben, how should I teach them?

Ben, *giving great weight to each word, and with a certain vicious audacity.* William, when I walked into the jungle, I was seventeen. When I walked out I was twenty-one. And, by God, I was rich! *He goes off into darkness around the right corner of the house.*

Willy. . . . was rich! That's just the spirit I want to imbue them with! To walk into a jungle! I was right! I was right! I was right!

Ben is gone, but Willy is still speaking to him as Linda, in nightgown and robe, enters the kitchen, glances around for Willy, then goes to the door of the house, looks out and sees him. Comes down to his left. He looks at her.

Linda. Willy, dear? Willy?

Willy. I was right!

Linda. Did you have some cheese? *He can't answer.* It's very late, darling. Come to bed, heh?

Willy, *looking straight up.* Gotta break your neck to see a star in this yard.

Linda. You coming in?

Willy. Whatever happened to that diamond watch fob? Remember? When Ben came from Africa that time? Didn't he give me a watch fob with a diamond in it?

Linda. You pawned it, dear. Twelve, thirteen years ago. For Biff's radio correspondence course.

Willy. Gee, that was a beautiful thing. I'll take a walk.

Linda. But you're in your slippers.

Willy, *starting to go around the house at the left.* I was right! I was! *Half to Linda, as he goes, shaking his head:* What a man! There was a man worth talking to. I was right!

Linda, *calling after Willy.* But in your slippers, Willy!

Willy is almost gone when Biff, in his pajamas, comes down the stairs and enters the kitchen.

Biff. What is he doing out there?

Linda. Sh!

Biff. God Almighty, Mom, how long has he been doing this?

Linda. Don't, he'll hear you.

Biff. What the hell is the matter with him?

Linda. It'll pass by morning.

Biff. Shouldn't we do anything?

Linda. Oh, my dear, you should do a lot of things, but there's nothing to do, so go to sleep.

Happy comes down the stair and sits on the steps.

Happy. I never heard him so loud, Mom.

Linda. Well, come around more often; you'll hear him. *She sits down at the table and mends the lining of Willy's jacket.*

Biff. Why didn't you ever write me about this, Mom?

Linda. How would I write to you? For over three months you had no address.

Biff. I was on the move. But you know I thought of you all the time. You know that, don't you, pal?

Linda. I know, dear, I know. But he likes to have a letter. Just to know that there's still a possibility for better things.

Biff. He's not like this all the time, is he?

Linda. It's when you come home he's always the worst.

Biff. When I come home?

Linda. When you write you're coming, he's all smiles, and talks about the future, and—he's just wonderful. And then the closer you seem to come, the more shaky he gets, and then, by the time you get here, he's arguing, and he seems angry at you. I think it's just that maybe he can't bring himself to—to open up to you. Why are you so hateful to each other? Why is that?

Biff, *evasively.* I'm not hateful, Mom.

Linda. But you no sooner come in the door than you're fighting!

Biff. I don't know why. I mean to change. I'm tryin', Mom, you understand?

Linda. Are you home to stay now?

Biff. I don't know. I want to look around, see what's doin'.

Linda. Biff, you can't look around all your life, can you?

Biff. I just can't take hold, Mom. I can't take hold of some kind of a life.

Linda. Biff, a man is not a bird, to come and go with the springtime.

Biff. Your hair . . . *He touches her hair.* Your hair got so gray.

Linda. Oh, it's been gray since you were in high school. I just stopped dyeing it, that's all.

Biff. Dye it again, will ya? I don't want my pal looking old. *He smiles.*

Linda. You're such a boy! You think you can go away for a year and . . . You've got to get it into your head now that one day you'll knock on this door and there'll be strange people here—

Biff. What are you talking about? You're not even sixty, Mom.

Linda. But what about your father?

Biff, *lamely.* Well, I meant him too.

Happy. He admires Pop.

Linda. Biff, dear, if you don't have any feeling for him, then you can't have any feeling for me.

Biff. Sure I can, Mom.

Linda. No. You can't just come to see me, because I love him. *With a threat, but only a threat, of tears.* He's the dearest man in the world to me, and I won't have anyone making him feel unwanted and low and blue. You've got to make up your mind now, darling, there's no leeway any more. Either he's your father and you pay him that respect, or else you're not to come here. I know he's not easy to get along with—nobody knows that better than me—but . . .

Willy, *from the left, with a laugh.* Hey, hey, Biffo!

Biff, *starting to go out after Willy.* What the hell is the matter with him? *Happy stops him.*

Linda. Don't—don't go near him!

Biff. Stop making excuses for him! He always, always wiped the floor with you. Never had an ounce of respect for you.

Happy. He's always had respect for—

Biff. What the hell do you know about it?

Happy, *surlily.* Just don't call him crazy!

Biff. He's got no character—Charley wouldn't do this. Not in his own house—spewing out that vomit from his mind.

Happy. Charley never had to cope with what he's got to.

Biff. People are worse off than Willy Loman. Believe me, I've seen them!

Linda. Then make Charley your father, Biff. You can't do that, can you? I don't say he's a great man. Willy Loman never made a lot of money. His name was never in the paper. He's not the finest character that ever lived. But he's a human being, and a terrible thing is happening to him. So attention must be paid. He's not to be allowed to fall into his grave like an old dog. Attention, attention must be finally paid to such a person. You called him crazy—

Biff. I didn't mean—

Linda. No, a lot of people think he's lost his—balance. But you don't have to be very smart to know what his trouble is. The man is exhausted.

Happy. Sure!

Linda. A small man can be just as exhausted as a great man. He works for a company thirty-six years this March, opens up unheard-of territories to their trademark, and now in his old age they take his salary away.

Happy, *indignantly.* I didn't know that, Mom.

Linda. You never asked, my dear! Now that you get your spending money someplace else you don't trouble your mind with him.

Happy. But I gave you money last—

Linda. Christmas time, fifty dollars! To fix the hot water it cost ninety-seven fifty! For five weeks he's been on straight commission, like a beginner, an unknown!

Biff. Those ungrateful bastards!

Linda. Are they any worse than his sons? When he brought them business, when he was young, they were glad to see him. But now his old friends, the old buyers that loved him so and always found some order to hand him in a pinch—they're all dead, retired. He used to be able to make six, seven calls a day in Boston. Now he takes his valises out of the car and puts them back and takes them out again and he's exhausted. Instead of walking he talks now. He drives seven hundred miles, and when he gets there no one knows him any more, no one welcomes him. And what goes through a man's mind, driving seven hundred miles home without having earned a cent? Why shouldn't he talk to himself? Why? When he has to go to Charley and borrow fifty dollars a week and pretend to me that it's his pay? How long can that go on? How long? You see what I'm sitting here and waiting for? And you tell me he has no character? The man who never worked a day but for your benefit? When does he get the medal for that? Is this his reward—to turn around at the age of sixty-three and find his sons, who he loved better than his life, one a philandering bum—

Happy. Mom!

Linda. That's all you are, my baby! *To Biff:* And you! What happened to the love you had for him? You were such pals! How you used to talk to him on the phone every night! How lonely he was till he could come home to you!

Biff. All right, Mom. I'll live here in my room, and I'll get a job. I'll keep away from him, that's all.

Linda. No, Biff. You can't stay here and fight all the time.

Biff. He threw me out of this house, remember that.

Linda. Why did he do that? I never knew why.

Biff. Because I know he's a fake and he doesn't like anybody around who knows!

Linda. Why a fake? In what way? What do you mean?

Biff. Just don't lay it all at my feet. It's between me and him—that's all I have to say. I'll chip in from now on. He'll settle for half my pay check. He'll be all right. I'm going to bed. *He starts for the stairs.*

Linda. He won't be all right.

Biff, *turning on the stairs, furiously.* I hate this city and I'll stay here. Now what do you want?

Linda. He's dying, Biff.

Happy turns quickly to her, shocked.

Biff, *after a pause.* Why is he dying?

Linda. He's been trying to kill himself.

Biff, *with great horror.* How?

Linda. I live from day to day.

Biff. What're you talking about?

Linda. Remember I wrote you that he smashed up the car again? In February?

Biff. Well?

Linda. The insurance inspector came. He said that they have evidence. That all these accidents in the last year—weren't—weren't—accidents.

Happy. How can they tell that? That's a lie.

Linda. It seems there's a woman . . . *She takes a breath as*

  { **Biff,** *sharply but contained.* What woman? *foreshadowing*

  { **Linda,** *simultaneously.* . . . and this woman . . .

Linda. What?

Biff. Nothing. Go ahead.

Linda. What did you say?

Biff. Nothing. I just said what woman?

Happy. What about her?

Linda. Well, it seems she was walking down the road and saw his car. She says that he wasn't driving fast at all, and that he didn't skid. She says he came to that little bridge, and then deliberately smashed into the railing, and it was only the shallowness of the water that saved him.

Biff. Oh, no, he probably just fell asleep again.

Linda. I don't think he fell asleep.

Biff. Why not?

Linda. Last month . . . *With great difficulty.* Oh, boys, it's so hard to say a thing like this! He's just a big stupid man to you, but I tell you there's more good in him than in many other people. *She chokes, wipes her eyes.* I was looking for a fuse. The lights blew out, and I went down the cellar. And behind the fuse box—it happened to fall out— was a length of rubber pipe—just short.

Happy. No kidding?

Linda. There's a little attachment on the end of it. I knew right away. And sure enough, on the bottom of the water heater there's a new little nipple on the gas pipe.

Happy, *angrily.* That—jerk.

Biff. Did you have it taken off?

Linda. I'm—I'm ashamed to. How can I mention it to him? Every day I go down and take away that little rubber pipe. But, when he comes home, I put it back where it was. How can I insult him that way? I don't know what to do. I live from day to day, boys. I tell you, I know every thought in his mind. It sounds so old-fashioned and silly, but I tell you he put his whole life into you and you've turned your backs on him. *She is bent over in the chair, weeping, her face in her hands.* Biff, I swear to God! Biff, his life is in your hands!

Happy, *to Biff.* How do you like that damned fool!

Biff, *kissing her.* All right, pal, all right. It's all settled now. I've been remiss. I know that, Mom. But now I'll stay, and I swear to you, I'll apply myself. *Kneeling in front of her, in a fever of self-reproach.* It's just—you see, Mom, I don't fit in business. Not that I won't try. I'll try, and I'll make good.

Happy. Sure you will. The trouble with you in business was you never tried to please people.

Biff. I know, I—

Happy. Like when you worked for Harrison's. Bob Harrison said you were tops, and then you go and do some damn fool thing like whistling whole songs in the elevator like a comedian.

Biff, *against Happy.* So what? I like to whistle sometimes.

Happy. You don't raise a guy to a responsible job who whistles in the elevator!

Linda. Well, don't argue about it now.

Happy. Like when you'd go off and swim in the middle of the day instead of taking the line around.

Biff, *his resentment rising.* Well, don't you run off? You take off sometimes, don't you? On a nice summer day?

Happy. Yeah, but I cover myself!

Linda. Boys!

Happy. If I'm going to take a fade the boss can call any number where I'm supposed to be and they'll swear to him that I just left. I'll tell you something that I hate to say, Biff, but in the business world some of them think you're crazy.

Biff, *angered.* Screw the business world!

Happy. All right, screw it! Great, but cover yourself!

Linda. Hap, Hap!

Biff. I don't care what they think! They've laughed at Dad for years, and you know why? Because we don't belong in this nuthouse of a city! We should be mixing cement on some open plain, or—or carpenters. A carpenter is allowed to whistle!

Willy walks in from the entrance of the house, at left.

Willy. Even your grandfather was better than a carpenter. *Pause. They watch him.* You never grew up. Bernard does not whistle in the elevator, I assure you.

Biff, *as though to laugh Willy out of it.* Yeah, but you do, Pop.

Willy. I never in my life whistled in an elevator! And who in the business world thinks I'm crazy?

Biff. I didn't mean it like that, Pop. Now don't make a whole thing out of it, will ya?

Willy. Go back to the West! Be a carpenter, a cowboy, enjoy yourself!

Linda. Willy, he was just saying—

Willy. I heard what he said!

Happy, *trying to quiet Willy.* Hey, Pop, come on now . . .

Willy, *continuing over Happy's line.* They laugh at me, heh? Go to Filene's, go to the Hub, go to Slattery's, Boston. Call out the name Willy Loman and see what happens! Big shot!

Biff. All right, Pop.

Willy. Big!

Biff. All right!

Willy. Why do you always insult me?

Biff. I didn't say a word. *To Linda:* Did I say a word?

Linda. He didn't say anything, Willy.

Willy, *going to the doorway of the living-room.* All right, good night, good night.

Linda. Willy, dear, he just decided . . .

Willy, *to Biff.* If you get tired hanging around tomorrow, paint the ceiling I put up in the living-room.

Biff. I'm leaving early tomorrow.

Happy. He's going to see Bill Oliver, Pop.

Willy, *interestedly.* Oliver? For what?

Biff, *with reserve, but trying, trying.* He always said he'd stake me. I'd like to go into business, so maybe I can take him up on it.

Linda. Isn't that wonderful?

Willy. Don't interrupt. What's wonderful about it? There's fifty men in the City of New York who'd stake him. *To Biff:* Sporting goods?

Biff. I guess so. I know something about it and—

Willy. He knows something about it! You know sporting goods better than Spalding, for God's sake! How much is he giving you?

Biff. I don't know, I didn't even see him yet, but—

Willy. Then what're you talkin' about?

Biff, *getting angry.* Well, all I said was I'm gonna see him, that's all!

Willy, *turning away.* Ah, you're counting your chickens again.

Biff, *starting left for the stairs.* Oh, Jesus, I'm going to sleep!

Willy, *calling after him.* Don't curse in this house!

Biff, *turning.* Since when did you get so clean?

Happy, *trying to stop them.* Wait a . . .

Willy. Don't use that language to me! I won't have it!

Happy, *grabbing Biff, shouts.* Wait a minute! I got an idea. I got a feasible idea. Come here, Biff, let's talk this over now, let's talk some sense here. When I was down in Florida last time, I thought of a great idea to sell sporting goods. It just came back to me. You and I, Biff—we have a line, the Loman Line. We train a couple of weeks, and put on a couple of exhibitions, see?

Willy. That's an idea!

Happy. Wait! We form two basketball teams, see? Two waterpolo teams. We play each other. It's a million dollars' worth of publicity. Two brothers, see? The Loman Brothers. Displays in the Royal Palms—all the hotels. And banners over the ring and the basketball court: "Loman Brothers." Baby, we could sell sporting goods!

Willy. That is a one-million-dollar idea!

Linda. Marvelous!

Biff. I'm in great shape as far as that's concerned.

Happy. And the beauty of it is, Biff, it wouldn't be like a business. We'd be out playin' ball again . . .

Biff, *enthused.* Yeah, that's . . .

Willy. Million-dollar . . .

Happy. And you wouldn't get fed up with it, Biff. It'd be the family again. There'd be the old honor, and comradeship, and if you wanted to go off for a swim or somethin'—well, you'd do it! Without some smart cooky gettin' up ahead of you!

Willy. Lick the world! You guys together could absolutely lick the civilized world.

Biff. I'll see Oliver tomorrow. Hap, if we could work that out . . .

Linda. Maybe things are beginning to—

Willy, *wildly enthused, to Linda.* Stop interrupting! *To Biff:* But don't wear sport jacket and slacks when you see Oliver.

Biff. No, I'll—

Willy. A business suit, and talk as little as possible, and don't crack any jokes.

Biff. He did like me. Always liked me.

Linda. He loved you!

Willy, *to Linda.* Will you stop! *To Biff:* Walk in very serious. You are not applying for a boy's job. Money is to pass. Be quiet, fine, and serious. Everybody likes a kidder, but nobody lends him money.

Happy. I'll try to get some myself, Biff. I'm sure I can.

Willy. I see great things for you kids, I think your troubles are over. But remember, start big and you'll end big. Ask for fifteen. How much you gonna ask for?

Biff. Gee, I don't know—

Willy. And don't say "Gee." "Gee" is a boy's word. A man walking in for fifteen thousand dollars does not say "Gee!"

Biff. Ten, I think, would be top though.

Willy. Don't be so modest. You always started too low. Walk in with a big laugh. Don't look worried. Start off with a couple of your good stories to lighten things up. It's not what you say, it's how you say it—because personality always wins the day.

Linda. Oliver always thought the highest of him—

Willy. Will you let me talk?

Biff. Don't yell at her, Pop, will ya?

Willy, *angrily.* I was talking, wasn't I?

Biff. I don't like you yelling at her all the time, and I'm tellin' you, that's all.

Willy. What're you, takin' over this house?

Linda. Willy—

Willy, *turning on her.* Don't take his side all the time, goddammit!

Biff, *furiously.* Stop yelling at her!

Willy, *suddenly pulling on his cheek, beaten down, guilt ridden.* Give my best to Bill Oliver—he may remember me. *He exits through the living-room doorway.*

Linda, *her voice subdued.* What'd you have to start that for? *Biff turns away.* You see how sweet he was as soon as you talked hopefully? *She goes over to Biff.* Come up and say good night to him. Don't let him go to bed that way.

Happy. Come on, Biff, let's buck him up.

Linda. Please, dear. Just say good night. It takes so little to make him happy. Come. *She goes through the living-room doorway, calling upstairs from within the living-room:* Your pajamas are hanging in the bathroom, Willy!

Happy, *looking toward where Linda went out.* What a woman! They broke the mold when they made her. You know that, Biff?

Biff. He's off salary. My God, working on commission!

Happy. Well, let's face it: he's no hot-shot selling man. Except that sometimes, you have to admit, he's a sweet personality.

Biff, *deciding.* Lend me ten bucks, will ya? I want to buy some new ties.

Happy. I'll take you to a place I know. Beautiful stuff. Wear one of my striped shirts tomorrow.

Biff. She got gray. Mom got awful old. Gee, I'm gonna go in to Oliver tomorrow and knock him for a—

Happy. Come on up. Tell that to Dad. Let's give him a whirl. Come on.

Biff, *steamed up.* You know, with ten thousand bucks, boy!

Happy, *as they go into the living-room.* That's the talk, Biff, that's the first time I've heard the old confidence out of you! *From within the living-room, fading off:* You're gonna live with me, kid, and any babe you want just say the word . . . *The last lines are hardly heard. They are mounting the stairs to their parents' bedroom.*

Linda, *entering her bedroom and addressing Willy, who is in the bathroom. She is straightening the bed for him.* Can you do anything about the shower? It drips.

Willy, *from the bathroom.* All of a sudden everything falls to pieces! Goddam plumbing, oughta be sued, those people. I hardly finished putting it in and the thing . . . *His words rumble off.*

Linda. I'm just wondering if Oliver will remember him. You think he might?

Willy, *coming out of the bathroom in his pajamas.* Remember him? What's the matter with you, you crazy? If he'd've stayed with Oliver he'd be on top by now! Wait'll Oliver gets a look at him. You don't know the average caliber any more. The average young man today—*he is getting into bed*—is got a caliber of zero. Greatest thing in the world for him was to bum around.

Biff and Happy enter the bedroom. Slight pause.

Willy, *stops short, looking at Biff.* Glad to hear it, boy.

Happy. He wanted to say good night to you, sport.

Willy, *to Biff.* Yeah. Knock him dead, boy. What'd you want to tell me?

Biff. Just take it easy, Pop. Good night. *He turns to go.*

Willy, *unable to resist.* And if anything falls off the desk while you're talking to him—like a package or something—don't you pick it up. They have office boys for that.

Linda. I'll make a big breakfast—

Willy. Will you let me finish? *To Biff:* Tell him you were in the business in the West. Not farm work.

Biff. All right, Dad.

Linda. I think everything—

Willy, *going right through her speech.* And don't undersell yourself. No less than fifteen thousand dollars.

Biff, *unable to bear him.* Okay. Good night, Mom. *He starts moving.*

Willy. Because you got a greatness in you, Biff, remember that. You got all kinds a greatness . . . *He lies back, exhausted. Biff walks out.*

Linda, *calling after Biff.* Sleep well, darling!

Happy. I'm gonna get married, Mom. I wanted to tell you.

Linda. Go to sleep, dear.

Happy, *going.* I just wanted to tell you.

Willy. Keep up the good work. *Happy exits.* God . . . remember that Ebbets Field[3] game? The championship of the city?

Linda. Just rest. Should I sing to you?

Willy. Yeah. Sing to me. *Linda hums a soft lullaby.* When that team came out—he was the tallest, remember?

Linda. Oh, yes. And in gold.

Biff enters the darkened kitchen, takes a cigarette, and leaves the house. He comes downstage into a golden pool of light. He smokes, staring at the night.

Willy. Like a young god. Hercules—something like that. And the sun, the sun all around him. Remember how he waved to me? Right up from the field, with the representatives of three colleges standing by? And the buyers I brought, and the cheers when he came out—Loman, Loman, Loman! God Almighty, he'll be great yet. A star like that, magnificent, can never really fade away!

The light on Willy is fading. The gas heater begins to glow through the kitchen wall, near the stairs, a blue flame beneath red coils.

Linda, *timidly.* Willy dear, what has he got against you?

Willy. I'm so tired. Don't talk any more.

Biff slowly returns to the kitchen. He stops, stares toward the heater.

Linda. Will you ask Howard to let you work in New York?

Willy. First thing in the morning. Everything'll be all right.

Biff reaches behind the heater and draws out a length of rubber tubing. He is horrified and turns his head toward Willy's room, still dimly lit, from which the strains of Linda's desperate but monotonous humming rise.

Willy, *staring through the window into the moonlight.* Gee, look at the moon moving between the buildings!

Biff wraps the tubing around his hand and quickly goes up the stairs.

Curtain

---

[3] Sports stadium in Brooklyn, New York.

ACT II

Music is heard, gay and bright. The curtain rises as the music fades away. Willy, in shirt sleeves, is sitting at the kitchen table, sipping coffee, his hat in his lap. Linda is filling his cup when she can.

Willy. Wonderful coffee. Meal in itself.

Linda. Can I make you some eggs?

Willy. No. Take a breath.

Linda. You look so rested, dear.

Willy. I slept like a dead one. First time in months. Imagine, sleeping till ten on a Tuesday morning. Boys left nice and early, heh?

Linda. They were out of here by eight o'clock.

Willy. Good work!

Linda. It was so thrilling to see them leaving together. I can't get over the shaving lotion in this house!

Willy, *smiling.* Mmm—

Linda. Biff was very changed this morning. His whole attitude seemed to be hopeful. He couldn't wait to get downtown to see Oliver.

Willy. He's heading for a change. There's no question, there simply are certain men that take longer to get—solidified. How did he dress?

Linda. His blue suit. He's so handsome in that suit. He could be a— anything in that suit!

Willy gets up from the table. Linda holds his jacket for him.

Willy. There's no question, no question at all. Gee, on the way home tonight I'd like to buy some seeds.

Linda, *laughing.* That'd be wonderful. But not enough sun gets back there. Nothing'll grow any more.

Willy. You wait, kid, before it's all over we're gonna get a little place out in the country, and I'll raise some vegetables, a couple of chickens . . .

Linda. You'll do it yet, dear.

Willy walks out of his jacket. Linda follows him.

Willy. And they'll get married, and come for a weekend. I'd build a little guest house. 'Cause I got so many fine tools, all I'd need would be a little lumber and some peace of mind.

Linda, *joyfully.* I sewed the lining . . .

Willy. I could build two guest houses, so they'd both come. Did he decide how much he's going to ask Oliver for?

Linda, *getting him into the jacket.* He didn't mention it, but I imagine ten or fifteen thousand. You going to talk to Howard today?

Willy. Yeah. I'll put it to him straight and simple. He'll just have to take me off the road.

Linda. And Willy, don't forget to ask for a little advance, because we've got the insurance premium. It's the grace period now.

Willy. That's a hundred . . . ?

Linda. A hundred and eight, sixty-eight. Because we're a little short again.

Willy. Why are we short?

Linda. Well, you had the motor job on the car . . .

Willy. That goddam Studebaker!

Linda. And you got one more payment on the refrigerator .

Willy. But it just broke again!

Linda. Well, it's old, dear.

Willy. I told you we should've bought a well-advertised machine. Charley bought a General Electric and it's twenty years old and it's still good, that son-of-a-bitch.

Linda. But, Willy—

Willy. Whoever heard of a Hastings refrigerator? Once in my life I would like to own something outright before it's broken! I'm always in a race with the junkyard! I just finished paying for the car and it's on its last legs. The refrigerator consumes belts like a goddam maniac. They time those things. They time them so when you finally paid for them, they're used up.

Linda, *buttoning up his jacket as he unbuttons it.* All told, about two hundred dollars would carry us, dear. But that includes the last payment on the mortgage. After this payment, Willy, the house belongs to us.

Willy. It's twenty-five years!

Linda. Biff was nine years old when we bought it.

Willy. Well, that's a great thing. To weather a twenty-five year mortgage is—

Linda. It's an accomplishment.

Willy. All the cement, the lumber, the reconstruction I put in this house! There ain't a crack to be found in it any more.

Linda. Well, it served its purpose.

Willy. What purpose? Some stranger'll come along, move in, and that's that. If only Biff would take this house, and raise a family . . . *He starts to go.* Good-by, I'm late.

Linda, *suddenly remembering.* Oh, I forgot! You're supposed to meet them for dinner.

Willy. Me?

Linda. At Frank's Chop House on Forty-eighth near Sixth Avenue.

Willy. Is that so! How about you?

Linda. No, just the three of you. They're gonna blow you to a big meal!

Willy. Don't say! Who thought of that?

Linda. Biff came to me this morning, Willy, and he said, "Tell Dad, we want to blow him to a big meal." Be there six o'clock. You and your two boys are going to have dinner.

Willy. Gee whiz! That's really somethin'. I'm gonna knock Howard for a loop, kid. I'll get an advance, and I'll come home with a New York job. Goddammit, now I'm gonna do it!

Linda. Oh, that's the spirit, Willy!

Willy. I will never get behind a wheel the rest of my life!

Linda. It's changing, Willy, I can feel it changing!

Willy. Beyond a question. G'by, I'm late. *He starts to go again.*

Linda, *calling after him as she runs to the kitchen table for a handkerchief.* You got your glasses?

Willy, *feels for them, then comes back in.* Yeah, yeah, got my glasses.

Linda, *giving him the handkerchief.* And a handkerchief.

Willy. Yeah, handkerchief.

Linda. And your saccharine?

Willy. Yeah, my saccharine.

Linda. Be careful on the subway stairs.

She kisses him, and a silk stocking is seen hanging from her hand. Willy notices it.

Willy. Will you stop mending stockings? At least while I'm in the house. It gets me nervous. I can't tell you. Please.

Linda hides the stocking in her hand as she follows Willy across the forestage in front of the house.

Linda. Remember, Frank's Chop House.

Willy, *passing the apron.* Maybe beets would grow out there.

Linda, *laughing.* But you tried so many times.

Willy. Yeah. Well, don't work hard today. *He disappears around the right corner of the house.*

Linda. Be careful!

As Willy vanishes, Linda waves to him. Suddenly the phone rings. She runs across the stage and into the kitchen and lifts it.

Linda. Hello? Oh, Biff! I'm so glad you called, I just . . . Yes, sure, I just told him. Yes, he'll be there for dinner at six o'clock, I didn't forget. Listen, I was just dying to tell you. You know that little rubber pipe I told you about? That he connected to the gas heater? I finally decided to go down the cellar this morning and take it away and destroy it. But it's gone! Imagine? He took it away himself, it isn't there! *She listens.* When? Oh, then you took it. Oh—nothing, it's just that I'd hoped he'd taken it away himself. Oh, I'm not worried, darling, because this morning he left in such high spirits, it was like the old days! I'm not afraid any more. Did Mr. Oliver see you? . . . Well, you wait there then. And make a nice impression on him, darling. Just don't perspire too much before you see him. And have a nice time with Dad. He may have big news too! . . . That's right, a New York job. And be sweet to him tonight, dear. Be loving to him. Because he's only a little boat looking for a harbor. *She is trembling with sorrow and joy.* Oh, that's wonderful, Biff, you'll save his life. Thanks, darling. Just put your arm around him when he comes into the restaurant. Give him a smile. That's the boy . . . Good-by, dear . . . You got your comb? . . . That's fine. Good-by, Biff dear.

In the middle of her speech, Howard Wagner, thirty-six, wheels on a small typewriter table on which is a wire-recording machine and proceeds to plug it in. This is on the left forestage. Light slowly fades on Linda as it rises on Howard. Howard is intent on threading the machine and only glances over his shoulder as Willy appears.

Willy. Pst! Pst!

Howard. Hello, Willy, come in.

Willy. Like to have a little talk with you, Howard.

Howard. Sorry to keep you waiting. I'll be with you in a minute.

Willy. What's that, Howard?

Howard. Didn't you ever see one of these? Wire recorder.

Willy. Oh. Can we talk a minute?

Howard. Records things. Just got delivery yesterday. Been driving me crazy, the most terrific machine I ever saw in my life. I was up all night with it.

Willy. What do you do with it?

Howard. I bought it for dictation, but you can do anything with it. Listen to this. I had it home last night. Listen to what I picked up. The first one is my daughter. Get this. *He flicks the switch and "Roll out the Barrel" is heard being whistled.* Listen to that kid whistle.

Willy. That is lifelike, isn't it?

Howard. Seven years old. Get that tone.

Willy. Ts, ts. Like to ask a little favor if you . . .

The whistling breaks off, and the voice of Howard's daughter is heard.

His Daughter. "Now you, Daddy."
Howard. She's crazy for me! *Again the same song is whistled.* That's me! Ha! *He winks.*
Willy. You're very good!

The whistling breaks off again. The machine runs silent for a moment.

Howard. Sh! Get this now, this is my son.
His Son. "The capital of Alabama is Montgomery; the capital of Arizona is Phoenix; the capital of Arkansas is Little Rock; the capital of California is Sacramento . . . " *and on, and on.*
Howard, *holding up five fingers.* Five years old, Willy!
Willy. He'll make an announcer some day!
His Son, *continuing.* "The capital . . . "
Howard. Get that—alphabetical order! *The machine breaks off suddenly.* Wait a minute. The maid kicked the plug out.
Willy. It certainly is a—
Howard. Sh, for God's sake!
His Son. "It's nine o'clock, Bulova watch time. So I have to go to sleep."
Willy. That really is—
Howard. Wait a minute! The next is my wife.

They wait.

Howard's Voice. "Go on, say something." *Pause.* "Well, you gonna talk?"
His Wife. "I can't think of anything."
Howard's Voice. "Well, talk—it's turning."
His Wife, *shyly, beaten.* "Hello." *Silence.* "Oh, Howard, I can't talk into this . . . "
Howard, *snapping the machine off.* That was my wife.
Willy. That is a wonderful machine. Can we—
Howard. I tell you, Willy, I'm gonna take my camera, and my bandsaw, and all my hobbies, and out they go. This is the most fascinating relaxation I ever found.
Willy. I think I'll get one myself.
Howard. Sure, they're only a hundred and a half. You can't do without it. Supposing you wanna hear Jack Benny,[4] see? But you can't be at home at that hour. So you tell the maid to turn the radio on when Jack Benny comes on, and this automatically goes on with the radio . . .
Willy. And when you come home you . . .

---

[4] (1894–1974), comedian.

Howard. You can come home twelve o'clock, one o'clock, any time you like, and you get yourself a Coke and sit yourself down, throw the switch, and there's Jack Benny's program in the middle of the night!

Willy. I'm definitely going to get one. Because lots of time I'm on the road, and I think to myself, what I must be missing on the radio!

Howard. Don't you have a radio in the car?

Willy. Well, yeah, but who ever thinks of turning it on?

Howard. Say, aren't you supposed to be in Boston?

Willy. That's what I want to talk to you about, Howard. You got a minute? *He draws a chair in from the wing.*

Howard. What happened? What're you doing here?

Willy. Well . . .

Howard. You didn't crack up again, did you?

Willy. Oh, no. No . . .

Howard. Geez, you had me worried there for a minute. What's the trouble?

Willy. Well, tell you the truth, Howard. I've come to the decision that I'd rather not travel any more.

Howard. Not travel! Well, what'll you do?

Willy. Remember, Christmas time, when you had the party here? You said you'd try to think of some spot for me here in town.

Howard. With us?

Willy. Well, sure.

Howard. Oh, yeah, yeah. I remember. Well, I couldn't think of anything for you, Willy.

Willy. I tell ya, Howard. The kids are all grown up, y'know. I don't need much any more. If I could take home—well, sixty-five dollars a week, I could swing it.

Howard. Yeah, but Willy, see I—

Willy. I tell ya why, Howard. Speaking frankly and between the two of us, y'know—I'm just a little tired.

Howard. Oh, I could understand that, Willy. But you're a road man, Willy, and we do a road business. We've only got a half-dozen salesmen on the floor here.

Willy. God knows, Howard, I never asked a favor of any man. But I was with the firm when your father used to carry you in here in his arms.

Howard. I know that, Willy, but—

Willy. Your father came to me the day you were born and asked me what I thought of the name of Howard, may he rest in peace.

Howard. I appreciate that, Willy, but there just is no spot here for you. If I had a spot I'd slam you right in, but I just don't have a single solitary spot.

He looks for his lighter. Willy has picked it up and gives it to him. Pause.

Willy, *with increasing anger.* Howard, all I need to set my table is fifty dollars a week.

Howard. But where am I going to put you, kid?

Willy. Look, it isn't a question of whether I can sell merchandise, is it?

Howard. No, but it's a business, kid, and everybody's gotta pull his own weight.

Willy, *desperately.* Just let me tell you a story, Howard—

Howard. 'Cause you gotta admit, business is business.

Willy, *angrily.* Business is definitely business, but just listen for a minute. You don't understand this. When I was a boy—eighteen, nineteen—I was already on the road. And there was a question in my mind as to whether selling had a future for me. Because in those days I had a yearning to go to Alaska. See, there were three gold strikes in one month in Alaska, and I felt like going out. Just for the ride, you might say.

Howard, *barely interested.* Don't say.

Willy. Oh, yeah, my father lived many years in Alaska. He was an adventurous man. We've got quite a little streak of self-reliance in our family. I thought I'd go out with my older brother and try to locate him, and maybe settle in the North with the old man. And I was almost decided to go, when I met a salesman in the Parker House. His name was Dave Singleman. And he was eighty-four years old, and he'd drummed merchandise in thirty-one states. And old Dave, he'd go up to his room, y'understand, put on his green velvet slippers—I'll never forget—and pick up his phone and call the buyers, and without ever leaving his room, at the age of eighty-four, he made his living. And when I saw that, I realized that selling was the greatest career a man could want. 'Cause what could be more satisfying than to be able to go, at the age of eighty-four, into twenty or thirty different cities, and pick up a phone, and be remembered and loved and helped by so many different people? Do you know? when he died—and by the way he died the death of a salesman, in his green velvet slippers in the smoker of the New York, New Haven and Hartford, going into Boston—when he died, hundreds of salesmen and buyers were at his funeral. Things were sad on a lotta trains for months after that. *He stands up. Howard has not looked at him.* In those days there was personality in it, Howard. There was respect, and comradeship, and gratitude in it. Today, it's all cut and dried, and there's no chance for bringing friendship to bear—or personality. You see what I mean? They don't know me any more.

Howard, *moving away, to the right.* That's just the thing, Willy.

Willy. If I had forty dollars a week—that's all I'd need. Forty dollars, Howard.

Howard. Kid, I can't take blood from a stone, I—

Willy, *desperation is on him now.* Howard, the year Al Smith[5] was nominated, your father came to me and—

---

[5] Democratic candidate for President in 1928.

Howard, *starting to go off.*   I've got to see some people, kid.

Willy, *stopping him.*   I'm talking about your father! There were promises made across this desk! You mustn't tell me you've got people to see— I put thirty-four years into this firm, Howard, and now I can't pay my insurance! You can't eat the orange and throw the peel away—a man is not a piece of fruit! *After a pause:* Now pay attention. Your father— in 1928 I had a big year. I averaged a hundred and seventy dollars a week in commissions.

Howard, *impatiently.*   Now, Willy, you never averaged—

Willy, *banging his hand on the desk.*   I averaged a hundred and seventy dollars a week in the year of 1928! And your father came to me—or rather, I was in the office here—it was right over this desk—and he put his hand on my shoulder—

Howard, *getting up.*   You'll have to excuse me, Willy, I gotta see some people. Pull yourself together. *Going out:* I'll be back in a little while.

On Howard's exit, the light on his chair grows very bright and strange.

Willy.   Pull myself together! What the hell did I say to him? My God, I was yelling at him! How could I! *Willy breaks off, staring at the light, which occupies the chair, animating it. He approaches this chair, standing across the desk from it.* Frank, Frank, don't you remember what you told me that time? How you put your hand on my shoulder, and Frank . . . *He leans on the desk and as he speaks the dead man's name he accidentally switches on the recorder, and instantly*

Howard's Son.   ". . . of New York is Albany. The capital of Ohio is Cincinnati, the capital of Rhode Island is . . ." *The recitation continues.*

Willy, *leaping away with fright, shouting.*   Ha! Howard! Howard! Howard!

Howard, *rushing in.*   What happened?

Willy, *pointing at the machine, which continues nasally, childishly, with the capital cities.*   Shut it off! Shut it off!

Howard, *pulling the plug out.*   Look, Willy . . .

Willy, *pressing his hands to his eyes.*   I gotta get myself some coffee. I'll get some coffee . . .

Willy starts to walk out. Howard stops him.

Howard, *rolling up the cord.*   Willy, look . . .

Willy.   I'll go to Boston.

Howard.   Willy, you can't go to Boston for us.

Willy.   Why can't I go?

Howard.   I don't want you to represent us. I've been meaning to tell you for a long time now.

Willy.   Howard, are you firing me?

Howard. I think you need a good long rest, Willy.

Willy. Howard—

Howard. And when you feel better, come back, and we'll see if we can work something out.

Willy. But I gotta earn money, Howard. I'm in no position to—

Howard. Where are your sons? Why don't your sons give you a hand?

Willy. They're working on a very big deal.

Howard. This is no time for false pride, Willy. You go to your sons and you tell them that you're tired. You've got two great boys, haven't you?

Willy. Oh, no question, no question, but in the meantime . . .

Howard. Then that's that, heh?

Willy. All right, I'll go to Boston tomorrow.

Howard. No, no.

Willy. I can't throw myself on my sons. I'm not a cripple!

Howard. Look, kid, I'm busy this morning.

Willy, *grasping Howard's arm.* Howard, you've got to let me go to Boston!

Howard, *hard, keeping himself under control.* I've got a line of people to see this morning. Sit down, take five minutes, and pull yourself together, and then go home, will ya? I need the office, Willy. *He starts to go, turns, remembering the recorder, starts to push off the table holding the recorder.* Oh, yeah. Whenever you can this week, stop by and drop off the samples. You'll feel better, Willy, and then come back and we'll talk. Pull yourself together, kid, there's people outside.

Howard exits, pushing the table off left. Willy stares into space, exhausted. Now the music is heard—Ben's music—first distantly, then closer, closer. As Willy speaks, Ben enters from the right. He carries valise and umbrella.

Willy. Oh, Ben, how did you do it? What is the answer? Did you wind up the Alaska deal already?

Ben. Doesn't take much time if you know what you're doing. Just a short business trip. Boarding ship in an hour. Wanted to say good-by.

Willy. Ben, I've got to talk to you.

Ben, *glancing at his watch.* Haven't the time, William.

Willy, *crossing the apron to Ben.* Ben, nothing's working out. I don't know what to do.

Ben. Now, look here, William. I've bought timberland in Alaska and I need a man to look after things for me.

Willy. God, timberland! Me and my boys in those grand outdoors!

Ben. You've a new continent at your doorstep, William. Get out of these cities, they're full of talk and time payments and courts of law. Screw on your fists and you can fight for a fortune up there.

Willy. Yes, yes! Linda, Linda!

Linda enters as of old, with the wash.

Linda. Oh, you're back?

Ben. I haven't much time.

Willy. No, wait! Linda, he's got a proposition for me in Alaska.

Linda. But you've got—*To Ben:* He's got a beautiful job here.

Willy. But in Alaska, kid, I could—

Linda. You're doing well enough, Willy!

Ben, *to Linda.* Enough for what, my dear?

Linda, *frightened of Ben and angry at him.* Don't say those things to him! Enough to be happy right here, right now. *To Willy, while Ben laughs:* Why must everybody conquer the world? You're well liked, and the boys love you, and someday—*to Ben* —why, old man Wagner told him just the other day that if he keeps it up he'll be a member of the firm, didn't he, Willy?

Willy. Sure, sure. I am building something with this firm, Ben, and if a man is building something he must be on the right track, mustn't he?

Ben. What are you building? Lay your hand on it. Where is it?

Willy, *hesitantly.* That's true, Linda, there's nothing.

Linda. Why? *To Ben:* There's a man eighty-four years old—

Willy. That's right, Ben, that's right. When I look at that man I say, what is there to worry about?

Ben. Bah!

Willy. It's true, Ben. All he has to do is go into any city, pick up the phone, and he's making his living and you know why?

Ben, *picking up his valise.* I've got to go.

Willy, *holding Ben back.* Look at this boy!

Biff, in his high school sweater, enters carrying suitcase. Happy carries Biff's shoulder guards, gold helmet, and football pants.

Willy. Without a penny to his name, three great universities are begging for him, and from there the sky's the limit, because it's not what you do, Ben. It's who you know and the smile on your face! It's contacts, Ben, contacts! The whole wealth of Alaska passes over the lunch table at the Commodore Hotel, and that's the wonder, the wonder of this country, that a man can end with diamonds here on the basis of being liked! *He turns to Biff.* And that's why when you get out on that field today it's important. Because thousands of people will be rooting for you and loving you. *To Ben, who has again begun to leave:* And Ben! when he walks into a business office his name will sound out like a bell and all the doors will open to him! I've seen it, Ben, I've seen it a thousand times! You can't feel it with your hand like timber, but it's there!

Ben.   Good-by, William.

Willy.   Ben, am I right? Don't you think I'm right? I value your advice.

Ben.   There's a new continent at your doorstep, William. You could walk out rich. Rich! *He is gone.*

Willy.   We'll do it here, Ben! You hear me? We're gonna do it here!

Young Bernard rushes in. The gay music of the Boys is heard.

Bernard.   Oh, gee, I was afraid you left already!

Willy.   Why? What time is it?

Bernard.   It's half-past one!

Willy.   Well, come on, everybody! Ebbets Field next stop! Where's the pennants? *He rushes through the wall-line of the kitchen and out into the living-room.*

Linda, *to Biff.*   Did you pack fresh underwear?

Biff, *who has been limbering up.*   I want to go!

Bernard.   Biff, I'm carrying your helmet, ain't I?

Happy.   No, I'm carrying the helmet.

Bernard.   Oh, Biff, you promised me.

Happy.   I'm carrying the helmet.

Bernard.   How am I going to get in the locker room?

Linda.   Let him carry the shoulder guards. *She puts her coat and hat on in the kitchen.*

Bernard.   Can I, Biff? 'Cause I told everybody I'm going to be in the locker room.

Happy.   In Ebbets Field it's the clubhouse.

Bernard.   I meant the clubhouse. Biff!

Happy.   Biff!

Biff, *grandly, after a slight pause.*   Let him carry the shoulder guards.

Happy, *as he gives Bernard the shoulder guards.*   Stay close to us now.

Willy rushes in with the pennants.

Willy, *handing them out.*   Everybody wave when Biff comes out on the field. *Happy and Bernard run off.* You set now, boy?

The music has died away.

Biff.   Ready to go, Pop. Every muscle is ready.

Willy, *at the edge of the apron.*   You realize what this means?

Biff.   That's right, Pop.

Willy, *feeling Biff's muscles.* You're comin' home this afternoon captain of the All-Scholastic Championship Team of the City of New York.

Biff. I got it, Pop. And remember, pal, when I take off my helmet, that touchdown is for you.

Willy. Let's go! *He is starting out, with his arm around Biff, when Charley enters, as of old, in knickers.* I got no room for you, Charley.

Charley. Room? For what?

Willy. In the car.

Charley. You goin' for a ride? I wanted to shoot some casino.

Willy, *furiously.* Casino! *Incredulously:* Don't you realize what today is?

Linda. Oh, he knows, Willy. He's just kidding you.

Willy. That's nothing to kid about!

Charley. No, Linda, what's goin' on?

Linda. He's playing in Ebbets Field.

Charley. Baseball in this weather?

Willy. Don't talk to him. Come on, come on! *He is pushing them out.*

Charley. Wait a minute, didn't you hear the news?

Willy. What?

Charley. Don't you listen to the radio? Ebbets Field just blew up.

Willy. You go to hell! *Charley laughs. Pushing them out:* Come on, come on! We're late.

Charley, *as they go.* Knock a homer, Biff, knock a homer!

Willy, *the last to leave, turning to Charley.* I don't think that was funny, Charley. This is the greatest day of his life.

Charley. Willy, when are you going to grow up?

Willy. Yeah, heh? When this game is over, Charley, you'll be laughing out of the other side of your face. They'll be calling him another Red Grange.[6] Twenty-five thousand a year.

Charley, *kidding.* Is that so?

Willy. Yeah, that's so.

Charley. Well, then, I'm sorry, Willy. But tell me something.

Willy. What?

Charley. Who is Red Grange?

Willy. Put up your hands. Goddam you, put up your hands!

Charley, chuckling, shakes his head and walks away, around the left corner of the stage. Willy follows him. The music rises to a mocking frenzy.

Willy. Who the hell do you think you are, better than everybody else? You don't know everything, you big, ignorant, stupid. . . . Put up your hands!

---

[6] College, then professional football player.

Light rises, on the right side of the forestage, on a small table in the reception room of Charley's office. Traffic sounds are heard. Bernard, now mature, sits whistling to himself. A pair of tennis rackets and an overnight bag are on the floor beside him.

Willy, *offstage.* What are you walking away for? Don't walk away! If you're going to say something say it to my face! I know you laugh at me behind my back. You'll laugh out of the other side of your goddam face after this game. Touchdown! Touchdown! Eighty thousand people! Touchdown! Right between the goal posts.

Bernard is a quiet, earnest, but self-assured young man. Willy's voice is coming from right upstage now. Bernard lowers his feet off the table and listens. Jenny, his father's secretary, enters.

Jenny, *distressed.* Say, Bernard, will you go out in the hall?

Bernard. What is that noise? Who is it?

Jenny. Mr. Loman. He just got off the elevator.

Bernard, *getting up.* Who's he arguing with?

Jenny. Nobody. There's nobody with him. I can't deal with him any more, and your father gets all upset everytime he comes. I've got a lot of typing to do, and your father's waiting to sign it. Will you see him?

Willy, *entering.* Touchdown! Touch—*He sees Jenny.* Jenny, Jenny, good to see you. How're ya? Workin'? Or still honest?

Jenny. Fine. How've you been feeling?

Willy. Not much any more, Jenny. Ha, ha! *He is surprised to see the rackets.*

Bernard. Hello, Uncle Willy.

Willy, *almost shocked.* Bernard! Well, look who's here! *He comes quickly, guiltily, to Bernard and warmly shakes his hand.*

Bernard. How are you? Good to see you.

Willy. What are you doing here?

Bernard. Oh, just stopped by to see Pop. Get off my feet till my train leaves. I'm going to Washington in a few minutes.

Willy. Is he in?

Bernard. Yes, he's in his office with the accountant. Sit down.

Willy, *sitting down.* What're you going to do in Washington?

Bernard. Oh, just a case I've got there, Willy.

Willy. That so? *Indicating the rackets:* You going to play tennis there?

Bernard. I'm staying with a friend who's got a court.

Willy. Don't say. His own tennis court. Must be fine people, I bet.

Bernard. They are, very nice. Dad tells me Biff's in town.

Willy, *with a big smile.* Yeah, Biff's in. Working on a very big deal, Bernard.

Bernard. What's Biff doing?

Willy. Well, he's been doing very big things in the West. But he decided to establish himself here. Very big. We're having dinner. Did I hear your wife had a boy?

Bernard. That's right. Our second.

Willy. Two boys! What do you know!

Bernard. What kind of a deal has Biff got?

Willy. Well, Bill Oliver—very big sporting-goods man—he wants Biff very badly. Called him in from the West. Long distance, carte blanche, special deliveries. Your friends have their own private tennis court?

Bernard. You still with the old firm, Willy?

Willy, *after a pause.* I'm—I'm overjoyed to see how you made the grade, Bernard, overjoyed. It's an encouraging thing to see a young man really—really—Looks very good for Biff—very—*He breaks off, then:* Bernard—*He is so full of emotion, he breaks off again.*

Bernard. What is it, Willy?

Willy, *small and alone.* What—what's the secret?

Bernard. What secret?

Willy. How—how did you? Why didn't he ever catch on?

Bernard. I wouldn't know that, Willy.

Willy, *confidentially, desperately.* You were his friend, his boyhood friend. There's something I don't understand about it. His life ended after that Ebbets Field game. From the age of seventeen nothing good ever happened to him.

Bernard. He never trained himself for anything.

Willy. But he did, he did. After high school he took so many correspondence courses. Radio mechanics; television; God knows what, and never made the slightest mark.

Bernard, *taking off his glasses.* Willy, do you want to talk candidly?

Willy, *rising, faces Bernard.* I regard you as a very brilliant man, Bernard. I value your advice.

Bernard. Oh, the hell with the advice, Willy. I couldn't advise you. There's just one thing I've always wanted to ask you. When he was supposed to graduate, and the math teacher flunked him—

Willy. Oh, that son-of-a-bitch ruined his life.

Bernard. Yeah, but, Willy, all he had to do was go to summer school and make up that subject.

Willy. That's right, that's right.

Bernard. Did you tell him not to go to summer school?

Willy. Me? I begged him to go. I ordered him to go!

Bernard. Then why wouldn't he go?

Willy. Why? Why! Bernard, that question has been trailing me like a ghost for the last fifteen years. He flunked the subject, and laid down and died like a hammer hit him!

Bernard. Take it easy, kid.

Willy. Let me talk to you—I got nobody to talk to. Bernard, Bernard, was it my fault? Y'see? It keeps going around in my mind, maybe I did something to him. I got nothing to give him.

Bernard. Don't take it so hard.

Willy. Why did he lay down? What is the story there? You were his friend!

Bernard. Willy, I remember, it was June, and our grades came out. And he'd flunked math.

Willy. That son-of-a-bitch!

Bernard. No, it wasn't right then. Biff just got very angry, I remember, and he was ready to enroll in summer school.

Willy, *surprised.* He was?

Bernard. He wasn't beaten by it at all. But then, Willy, he disappeared from the block for almost a month. And I got the idea that he'd gone up to New England to see you. Did he have a talk with you then?

Willy stares in silence.

Bernard. Willy?

Willy, *with a strong edge of resentment in his voice.* Yeah, he came to Boston. What about it?

Bernard. Well, just that when he came back—I'll never forget this, it always mystifies me. Because I'd thought so well of Biff, even though he'd always taken advantage of me. I loved him, Willy, y'know? And he came back after that month and took his sneakers—remember those sneakers with "University of Virginia" printed on them? He was so proud of those, wore them every day. And he took them down in the cellar, and burned them up in the furnace. We had a fist fight. It lasted at least half an hour. Just the two of us, punching each other down the cellar, and crying right through it. I've often thought of how strange it was that I knew he'd given up his life. What happened in Boston, Willy?

Willy looks at him as at an intruder.

Bernard. I just bring it up because you asked me.

Willy, *angrily.* Nothing. What do you mean, "What happened?" What's that got to do with anything?

Bernard. Well, don't get sore.

Willy. What are you trying to do, blame it on me? If a boy lays down is that my fault?

Bernard. Now, Willy, don't get—

Willy. Well, don't—don't talk to me that way! What does that mean, "What happened?"

Charley enters. He is in his vest, and he carries a bottle of bourbon.

Charley. Hey, you're going to miss that train. *He waves the bottle.*

Bernard. Yeah, I'm going. *He takes the bottle.* Thanks, Pop. *He picks up his rackets and bag.* Good-by, Willy, and don't worry about it. You know, "If at first you don't succeed . . ."

Willy. Yes, I believe in that.

Bernard. But sometimes, Willy, it's better for a man just to walk away.

Willy. Walk away?

Bernard. That's right.

Willy. But if you can't walk away?

Bernard, *after a slight pause.* I guess that's when it's tough. *Extending his hand:* Good-by, Willy.

Willy, *shaking Bernard's hand.* Good-by, boy.

Charley, *an arm on Bernard's shoulder.* How do you like this kid? Gonna argue a case in front of the Supreme Court.

Bernard, *protesting.* Pop!

Willy, *genuinely shocked, pained, and happy.* No! The Supreme Court!

Bernard. I gotta run. 'By, Dad!

Charley. Knock 'em dead, Bernard!

Bernard goes off.

Willy, *as Charley takes out his wallet.* The Supreme Court! And he didn't even mention it!

Charley, *counting out money on the desk.* He don't have to—he's gonna do it.

Willy. And you never told him what to do, did you? You never took any interest in him.

Charley. My salvation is that I never took any interest in anything. There's some money—fifty dollars. I got an accountant inside.

Willy. Charley, look . . . *With difficulty:* I got my insurance to pay. If you can manage it—I need a hundred and ten dollars.

Charley doesn't reply for a moment; merely stops moving.

Willy. I'd draw it from my bank but Linda would know, and I . . .

Charley. Sit down, Willy.

Willy, *moving toward the chair.* I'm keeping an account of everything, remember. I'll pay every penny back. *He sits.*

Charley. Now listen to me, Willy.

Willy. I want you to know I appreciate . . .

Charley, *sitting down on the table.* Willy, what're you doin'? What the hell is goin' on in your head?

Willy. Why? I'm simply . . .

Charley. I offered you a job. You can make fifty dollars a week. And I won't send you on the road.

Willy. I've got a job.

Charley. Without pay? What kind of a job is a job without pay? *He rises.* Now, look, kid, enough is enough. I'm no genius but I know when I'm being insulted.

Willy. Insulted!

Charley. Why don't you want to work for me?

Willy. What's the matter with you? I've got a job.

Charley. Then what're you walkin' in here every week for?

Willy, *getting up.* Well, if you don't want me to walk in here—

Charley. I am offering you a job.

Willy. I don't want your goddam job!

Charley. When the hell are you going to grow up?

Willy, *furiously.* You big ignoramus, if you say that to me again I'll rap you one! I don't care how big you are! *He's ready to fight.*

Pause.

Charley, *kindly, going to him.* How much do you need, Willy?

Willy. Charley, I'm strapped. I'm strapped. I don't know what to do. I was just fired.

Charley. Howard fired you?

Willy. That snotnose. Imagine that? I named him. I named him Howard.

Charley. Willy, when're you gonna realize that them things don't mean anything? You named him Howard, but you can't sell that. The only thing you got in this world is what you can sell. And the funny thing is that you're a salesman, and you don't know that.

Willy. I've always tried to think otherwise, I guess. I always felt that if a man was impressive, and well liked, that nothing—

Charley. Why must everybody like you? Who liked J. P. Morgan? Was he impressive? In a Turkish bath he'd look like a butcher. But with his pockets on he was very well liked. Now listen, Willy, I know you don't like me, and nobody can say I'm in love with you, but I'll give you a job because—just for the hell of it, put it that way. Now what do you say?

Willy. I—I just can't work for you, Charley.

Charley. What're you, jealous of me?

Willy. I can't work for you, that's all, don't ask me why.

Charley, *angered, takes out more bills.* You been jealous of me all your life, you damned fool! Here, pay your insurance. *He puts the money in Willy's hand.*

Willy. I'm keeping strict accounts.

Charley. I've got some work to do. Take care of yourself. And pay your insurance. — *foreshadowing*

Willy, *moving to the right.* Funny, y'know? After all the highways, and the trains, and the appointments, and the years, you end up worth more dead than alive.

Charley. Willy, nobody's worth nothin' dead. *After a slight pause:* Did you hear what I said? *foreshadowing*

Willy stands still, dreaming.

Charley. Willy!

Willy. Apologize to Bernard for me when you see him. I didn't mean to argue with him. He's a fine boy. They're all fine boys, and they'll end up big—all of them. Someday they'll all play tennis together. Wish me luck, Charley. He saw Bill Oliver today.

Charley. Good luck.

Willy, *on the verge of tears.* Charley, you're the only friend I got. Isn't that a remarkable thing? *He goes out.*

Charley. Jesus!

Charley stares after him a moment and follows. All light blacks out. Suddenly raucous music is heard, and a red glow rises behind the screen at right. Stanley, a young waiter, appears, carrying a table, followed by Happy, who is carrying two chairs.

Stanley, *putting the table down.* That's all right, Mr. Loman, I can handle it myself. *He turns and takes the chairs from Happy and places them at the table.*

Happy, *glancing around.* Oh, this is better.

Stanley. Sure, in the front there you're in the middle of all kinds a noise. Whenever you got a party, Mr. Loman, you just tell me and I'll put you back here. Y'know, there's a lotta people they don't like it private, because when they go out they like to see a lotta action around them because they're sick and tired to stay in the house by theirself. But I know you, you ain't from Hackensack. You know what I mean?

Happy, *sitting down.* So how's it coming, Stanley?

Stanley. Ah, it's a dog's life. I only wish during the war they'd a took me in the Army. I coulda been dead by now.

Happy. My brother's back, Stanley.

Stanley. Oh, he come back, heh? From the Far West.

Happy. Yeah, big cattle man, my brother, so treat him right. And my father's coming too.

Stanley. Oh, your father too!

Happy. You got a couple of nice lobsters?

Stanley. Hundred per cent, big.

Happy. I want them with the claws.

Stanley. Don't worry, I don't give you no mice. *Happy laughs.* How about some wine? It'll put a head on the meal.

Happy. No. You remember, Stanley, that recipe I brought you from overseas? With the champagne in it?

Stanley. Oh, yeah, sure. I still got it tacked up yet in the kitchen. But that'll have to cost a buck apiece anyways.

Happy. That's all right.

Stanley. What'd you, hit a number or somethin'?

Happy. No, it's a little celebration. My brother is—I think he pulled off a big deal today. I think we're going into business together.

Stanley. Great! That's the best for you. Because a family business, you know what I mean?—that's the best.

Happy. That's what I think.

Stanley. 'Cause what's the difference? Somebody steals? It's in the family. Know what I mean? *Sotto voce:* Like this bartender here. The boss is goin' crazy what kinda leak he's got in the cash register. You put it in but it don't come out.

Happy, *raising his head.* Sh!

Stanley. What?

Happy. You notice I wasn't lookin' right or left, was I?

Stanley. No.

Happy. And my eyes are closed.

Stanley. So what's the—?

Happy. Strudel's comin'.

Stanley, *catching on, looks around.* Ah, no, there's no—

He breaks off as a furred, lavishly dressed girl enters and sits at the next table. Both follow her with their eyes.

Stanley. Geez, how'd ya know?

Happy. I got radar or something. *Staring directly at her profile:* Ooooooooo . . . Stanley.

Stanley. I think that's for you, Mr. Loman.

Happy. Look at that mouth. Oh, God. And the binoculars.

Stanley. Geez, you got a life, Mr. Loman.

Happy. Wait on her.

Stanley, *going to the girl's table.* Would you like a menu, ma'am?

Girl. I'm expecting someone, but I'd like a—

Happy. Why don't you bring her—excuse me, miss, do you mind? I sell champagne, and I'd like you to try my brand. Bring her a champagne, Stanley.

Girl. That's awfully nice of you.

Happy. Don't mention it. It's all company money. *He laughs.*

Girl. That's a charming product to be selling, isn't it?

Happy. Oh, gets to be like everything else. Selling is selling, y'know.

Girl. I suppose.

Happy. You don't happen to sell, do you?

Girl. No, I don't sell.

Happy. Would you object to a compliment from a stranger? You ought
  to be on a magazine cover.

Girl, *looking at him a little archly.* I have been.

Stanley comes in with a glass of champagne.

Happy. What'd I say before, Stanley? You see? She's a cover girl.

Stanley. Oh, I could see, I could see.

Happy, *to the Girl.* What magazine?

Girl. Oh, a lot of them. *She takes the drink.* Thank you.

Happy. You know what they say in France, don't you? "Champagne is
  the drink of the complexion"—Hya, Biff!

Biff has entered and sits with Happy.

Biff. Hello, kid. Sorry I'm late.

Happy. I just got here. Uh, Miss—?

Girl. Forsythe.

Happy. Miss Forsythe, this is my brother.

Biff. Is Dad here?

Happy. His name is Biff. You might've heard of him. Great football
  player.

Girl. Really? What team?

Happy. Are you familiar with football?

Girl. No, I'm afraid I'm not.

Happy. Biff is quarterback with the New York Giants.

Girl. Well, that is nice, isn't it? *She drinks.*

Happy. Good health.

Girl. I'm happy to meet you.

Happy. That's my name. Hap. It's really Harold, but at West Point they
  called me Happy.

Girl, *now really impressed.* Oh, I see. How do you do? *She turns her
  profile.*

Biff. Isn't Dad coming?

Happy. You want her?

Biff. Oh, I could never make that.

Happy. I remember the time that idea would never come into your head.
  Where's the old confidence, Biff?

Biff. I just saw Oliver—

Happy. Wait a minute. I've got to see that old confidence again. Do you want her? She's on call.

Biff. Oh, no. *He turns to look at the Girl.*

Happy. I'm telling you. Watch this. *Turning to the Girl:* Honey? *She turns to him.* Are you busy?

Girl. Well, I am . . . but I could make a phone call.

Happy. Do that, will you, honey? And see if you can get a friend. We'll be here for a while. Biff is one of the greatest football players in the country.

Girl, *standing up.* Well, I'm certainly happy to meet you.

Happy. Come back soon.

Girl. I'll try.

Happy. Don't try, honey, try hard.

The Girl exits. Stanley follows, shaking his head in bewildered admiration.

Happy. Isn't that a shame now? A beautiful girl like that? That's why I can't get married. There's not a good woman in a thousand. New York is loaded with them, kid!

Biff. Hap, look—

Happy. I told you she was on call!

Biff, *strangely unnerved.* Cut it out, will ya? I want to say something to you.

Happy. Did you see Oliver?

Biff. I saw him all right. Now look, I want to tell Dad a couple of things and I want you to help me.

Happy. What? Is he going to back you?

Biff. Are you crazy? You're out of your goddam head, you know that?

Happy. Why? What happened?

Biff, *breathlessly.* I did a terrible thing today, Hap. It's been the strangest day I ever went through. I'm all numb, I swear.

Happy. You mean he wouldn't see you?

Biff. Well, I waited six hours for him, see? All day. Kept sending my name in. Even tried to date his secretary so she'd get me to him, but no soap.

Happy. Because you're not showin' the old confidence, Biff. He remembered you, didn't he?

Biff, *stopping Happy with a gesture.* Finally, about five o'clock, he comes out. Didn't remember who I was or anything. I felt like such an idiot, Hap.

Happy. Did you tell him my Florida idea?

Biff. He walked away. I saw him for one minute. I got so mad I could've torn the walls down! How the hell did I ever get the idea I was a salesman there? I even believed myself that I'd been a salesman for him! And then he gave me one look and—I realized what a ridiculous lie my whole life has been! We've been talking in a dream for fifteen years. I was a shipping clerk.

Happy.　What'd you do?

Biff, *with great tension and wonder.*　Well, he left, see. And the secretary went out. I was all alone in the waiting-room. I don't know what came over me, Hap. The next thing I know I'm in his office—paneled walls, everything. I can't explain it. I—Hap, I took his fountain pen.

Happy.　Geez, did he catch you?

Biff.　I ran out. I ran down all eleven flights. I ran and ran and ran.

Happy.　That was an awful dumb—what'd you do that for?

Biff, *agonized.*　I don't know, I just—wanted to take something, I don't know. You gotta help me, Hap, I'm gonna tell Pop.

Happy.　You crazy? What for?

Biff.　Hap, he's got to understand that I'm not the man somebody lends that kind of money to. He thinks I've been spiting him all these years and it's eating him up.

Happy.　That's just it. You tell him something nice.

Biff.　I can't.

Happy.　Say you got a lunch date with Oliver tomorrow.

Biff.　So what do I do tomorrow?

Happy.　You leave the house tomorrow and come back at night and say Oliver is thinking it over. And he thinks it over for a couple of weeks, and gradually it fades away and nobody's the worse.

Biff.　But it'll go on forever!

Happy.　Dad is never so happy as when he's looking forward to something!

Willy enters.

Happy.　Hello, scout!

Willy.　Gee, I haven't been here in years!

Stanley has followed Willy in and sets a chair for him. Stanley starts off but Happy stops him.

Happy.　Stanley!

Stanley stands by, waiting for an order.

Biff, *going to Willy with guilt, as to an invalid.*　Sit down, Pop. You want a drink?

Willy.　Sure, I don't mind.

Biff. Let's get a load on.

Willy. You look worried.

Biff. N-no. *To Stanley:* Scotch all around. Make it doubles.

Stanley. Doubles, right. *He goes.*

Willy. You had a couple already, didn't you?

Biff. Just a couple, yeah.

Willy. Well, what happened, boy? *Nodding affirmatively, with a smile:* Everything go all right?

Biff, *takes a breath, then reaches out and grasps Willy's hand.* Pal . . . *He is smiling bravely, and Willy is smiling too.* I had an experience today.

Happy. Terrific, Pop.

Willy. That so? What happened?

Biff, *high, slightly alcoholic, above the earth.* I'm going to tell you everything from first to last. It's been a strange day. *Silence. He looks around, composes himself as best he can, but his breath keeps breaking the rhythm of his voice.* I had to wait quite a while for him, and—

Willy. Oliver?

Biff. Yeah, Oliver. All day, as a matter of cold fact. And a lot of— instances—facts, Pop, facts about my life came back to me. Who was it, Pop? Who ever said I was a salesman with Oliver?

Willy. Well, you were.

Biff. No, Dad, I was a shipping clerk.

Willy. But you were practically—

Biff, *with determination.* Dad, I don't know who said it first, but I was never a salesman for Bill Oliver.

Willy. What're you talking about?

Biff. Let's hold on to the facts tonight, Pop. We're not going to get anywhere bullin' around. I was a shipping clerk.

Willy, *angrily.* All right, now listen to me—

Biff. Why don't you let me finish?

Willy. I'm not interested in stories about the past or any crap of that kind because the woods are burning, boys, you understand? There's a big blaze going on all around. I was fired today.

Biff, *shocked.* How could you be?

Willy. I was fired, and I'm looking for a little good news to tell your mother, because the woman has waited and the woman has suffered. The gist of it is that I haven't got a story left in my head, Biff. So don't give me a lecture about facts and aspects. I am not interested. Now what've you got to say to me?

Stanley enters with three drinks. They wait until he leaves.

Willy. Did you see Oliver?

Biff. Jesus, Dad!

Willy. You mean you didn't go up there?

Happy. Sure he went up there.

Biff. I did. I—saw him. How could they fire you?

Willy, *on the edge of his chair.* What kind of a welcome did he give you?

Biff. He won't even let you work on commission?

Willy. I'm out! *Driving:* So tell me, he gave you a warm welcome?

Happy. Sure, Pop, sure!

Biff, *driven.* Well, it was kind of—

Willy. I was wondering if he'd remember you. *To Happy:* Imagine, man doesn't see him for ten, twelve years and gives him that kind of a welcome!

Happy. Damn right!

Biff, *trying to return to the offensive.* Pop, look—

Willy. You know why he remembered you, don't you? Because you impressed him in those days.

Biff. Let's talk quietly and get this down to the facts, huh?

Willy, *as though Biff had been interrupting.* Well, what happened? It's great news, Biff. Did he take you into his office or'd you talk in the waiting-room?

Biff. Well, he came in, see, and—

Willy, *with a big smile.* What'd he say? Betcha he threw his arm around you.

Biff. Well, he kinda—

Willy. He's a fine man. *To Happy:* Very hard man to see, y'know.

Happy, *agreeing.* Oh, I know.

Willy, *to Biff.* Is that where you had the drinks?

Biff. Yeah, he gave me a couple of—no, no!

Happy, *cutting in.* He told him my Florida idea.

Willy. Don't interrupt. *To Biff:* How'd he react to the Florida idea?

Biff. Dad, will you give me a minute to explain?

Willy. I've been waiting for you to explain since I sat down here! What happened? He took you into his office and what?

Biff. Well—I talked. And—and he listened, see.

Willy. Famous for the way he listens, y'know. What was his answer?

Biff. His answer was—*He breaks off, suddenly angry.* Dad, you're not letting me tell you what I want to tell you!

Willy, *accusing, angered.* You didn't see him, did you?

Biff. I did see him!

Willy. What'd you insult him or something? You insulted him, didn't you?

Biff. Listen, will you let me out of it, will you just let me out of it!

Happy. What the hell!

Willy. Tell me what happened!

Biff, *to Happy.* I can't talk to him!

A single trumpet note jars the ear. The light of green leaves stains the house, which holds the air of night and a dream. Young Bernard enters and knocks on the door of the house.

Young Bernard, *frantically.* Mrs. Loman, Mrs. Loman!
Happy. Tell him what happened!
Biff, *to Happy.* Shut up and leave me alone!
Willy. No, no! You had to go and flunk math!
Biff. What math? What're you talking about?
Young Bernard. Mrs. Loman, Mrs. Loman!

Linda appears in the house, as of old.

Willy, *wildly.* Math, math, math!
Biff. Take it easy, Pop!
Young Bernard Mrs. Loman!
Willy, *furiously.* If you hadn't flunked you'd've been set by now!
Biff. Now, look, I'm gonna tell you what happened, and you're going
   to listen to me.
Young Bernard. Mrs. Loman!
Biff. I waited six hours—
Happy. What the hell are you saying?
Biff. I kept sending in my name but he wouldn't see me. So finally he
   . . . *He continues unheard as light fades low on the restaurant.*
Young Bernard. Biff flunked math!
Linda. No!
Young Bernard. Birnbaum flunked him! They won't graduate him!
Linda. But they have to. He's gotta go to the university. Where is he?
   Biff! Biff!
Young Bernard. No, he left. He went to Grand Central.
Linda. Grand—You mean he went to Boston!
Young Bernard. Is Uncle Willy in Boston?
Linda. Oh, maybe Willy can talk to the teacher. Oh, the poor, poor boy!

Light on house area snaps out.

Biff, *at the table, now audible, holding up a gold fountain pen.* . . . so I'm
   washed up with Oliver, you understand? Are you listening to me?
Willy, *at a loss.* Yeah, sure. If you hadn't flunked—
Biff. Flunked what? What're you talking about?
Willy. Don't blame everything on me! I didn't flunk math—you did!
   What pen?
Happy. That was awful dumb, Biff, a pen like that is worth—
Willy, *seeing the pen for the first time.* You took Oliver's pen?
Biff, *weakening.* Dad, I just explained it to you.
Willy. You stole Bill Oliver's fountain pen!
Biff. I didn't exactly steal it! That's just what I've been explaining to
   you!

Happy. He had it in his hand and just then Oliver walked in, so he got nervous and stuck it in his pocket!

Willy. My God, Biff!

Biff. I never intended to do it, Dad!

Operator's Voice. Standish Arms, good evening!

Willy, *shouting.* I'm not in my room!

Biff, *frightened.* Dad, what's the matter? *He and Happy stand up.*

Operator. Ringing Mr. Loman for you!

Willy. I'm not there, stop it!

Biff, *horrified, gets down on one knee before Willy.* Dad, I'll make good, I'll make good. *Willy tries to get to his feet. Biff holds him down.* Sit down now.

Willy. No, you're no good, you're no good for anything.

Biff. I am, Dad, I'll find something else, you understand? Now don't worry about anything. *He holds up Willy's face:* Talk to me, Dad.

Operator. Mr. Loman does not answer. Shall I page him?

Willy, *attempting to stand, as though to rush and silence the Operator.* No, no, no!

Happy. He'll strike something, Pop.

Willy. No, no . . .

Biff, *desperately, standing over Willy.* Pop, listen! Listen to me! I'm telling you something good. Oliver talked to his partner about the Florida idea. You listening? He—he talked to his partner, and he came to me . . . I'm going to be all right, you hear? Dad, listen to me, he said it was just a question of the amount!

Willy. Then you . . . got it?

Happy. He's gonna be terrific, Pop!

Willy, *trying to stand.* Then you got it, haven't you? You got it! You got it!

Biff, *agonized, holds Willy down.* No, no. Look, Pop. I'm supposed to have lunch with them tomorrow. I'm just telling you this so you'll know that I can still make an impression, Pop. And I'll make good somewhere, but I can't go tomorrow, see?

Willy. Why not? You simply—

Biff. But the pen, Pop!

Willy. You give it to him and tell him it was an oversight!

Happy. Sure, have lunch tomorrow!

Biff. I can't say that—

Willy. You were doing a crossword puzzle and accidentally used his pen!

Biff. Listen, kid, I took those balls years ago, now I walk in with his fountain pen? That clinches it, don't you see? I can't face him like that! I'll try elsewhere.

Page's Voice. Paging Mr. Loman!

Willy. Don't you want to be anything?

Biff. Pop, how can I go back?

Willy. You don't want to be anything, is that what's behind it?

Biff, *now angry at Willy for not crediting his sympathy.* Don't take it that way! You think it was easy walking into that office after what I'd done to him? A team of horses couldn't have dragged me back to Bill Oliver!

Willy. They why'd you go?

Biff. Why did I go? Why did I go! Look at you! Look at what's become of you!

Off left, The Woman laughs.

Willy. Biff, you're going to go to that lunch tomorrow, or—

Biff. I can't go. I've got no appointment!

Happy. Biff, for . . .!

Willy. Are you spiting me?

Biff. Don't take it that way! Goddammit!

Willy, *strikes Biff and falters away from the table.* You rotten little louse! Are you spiting me?

The Woman. Someone's at the door, Willy!

Biff. I'm no good, can't you see what I am?

Happy, *separating them.* Hey, you're in a restaurant! Now cut it out, both of you! *The girls enter.* Hello, girls, sit down.

The Woman laughs, off left.

Miss Forsythe. I guess we might as well. This is Letta.

The Woman. Willy, are you going to wake up?

Biff, *ignoring Willy.* How're ya, miss, sit down. What do you drink?

Miss Forsythe. Letta might not be able to stay long.

Letta. I gotta get up very early tomorrow. I got jury duty. I'm so excited! Were you fellows ever on a jury?

Biff. No, but I been in front of them! *The girls laugh.* This is my father.

Letta. Isn't he cute? Sit down with us, Pop.

Happy. Sit him down, Biff!

Biff, *going to him.* Come on, slugger, drink us under the table. To hell with it! Come on, sit down, pal.

On Biff's last insistence, Willy is about to sit.

The Woman, *now urgently.* Willy, are you going to answer the door!

The Woman's call pulls Willy back. He starts right, befuddled.

Biff. Hey, where are you going?
Willy. Open the door.
Biff. The door?
Willy. The washroom . . . the door . . . where's the door?
Biff, *leading Willy to the left.* Just go straight down.

Willy moves left.

The Woman. Willy, Willy, are you going to get up, get up, get up, get up?

Willy exits left.

Letta. I think it's sweet you bring your daddy along.
Miss Forsythe. Oh, he isn't really your father!
Biff, *at left, turning to her resentfully.* Miss Forsythe, you've just seen a prince walk by. A fine, troubled prince. A hardworking, unappreciated prince. A pal, you understand? A good companion. Always for his boys.
Letta. That's so sweet.
Happy. Well, girls, what's the program? We're wasting time. Come on, Biff. Gather round. Where would you like to go?
Biff. Why don't you do something for him?
Happy. Me!
Biff. Don't you give a damn for him, Hap?
Happy. What're you talking about? I'm the one who—
Biff. I sense it, you don't give a good goddam about him. *He takes the rolled-up hose from his pocket and puts it on the table in front of Happy.* Look what I found in the cellar, for Christ's sake. How can you bear to let it go on?
Happy. Me? Who goes away? Who runs off and—
Biff. Yeah, but he doesn't mean anything to you. You could help him— I can't! Don't you understand what I'm talking about? He's going to kill himself, don't you know that?
Happy. Don't I know it! Me!
Biff. Hap, help him! Jesus . . . help him . . . Help me, help me, I can't bear to look at his face! *Ready to weep, he hurries out, up right.*
Happy, *starting after him.* Where are you going?
Miss Forsythe. What's he so mad about?
Happy. Come on, girls, we'll catch up with him.
Miss Forsythe, *as Happy pushes her out.* Say, I don't like that temper of his!
Happy. He's just a little overstrung, he'll be all right!
Willy, *off left, as The Woman laughs.* Don't answer! Don't answer!

Letta. Don't you want to tell your father—

Happy. No, that's not my father. He's just a guy. Come on, we'll catch Biff, and, honey, we're going to paint this town! Stanley, where's the check! Hey, Stanley!

They exit. Stanley looks toward left.

Stanley, *calling to Happy indignantly.* Mr. Loman! Mr. Loman!

Stanley picks up a chair and follows them off. Knocking is heard off left. The Woman enters, laughing. Willy follows her. She is in a black slip; he is buttoning his shirt. Raw, sensuous music accompanies their speech.

Willy. Will you stop laughing? Will you stop?

The Woman. Aren't you going to answer the door? He'll wake the whole hotel.

Willy. I'm not expecting anybody.

The Woman. Whyn't you have another drink, honey, and stop being so damn self-centered?

Willy. I'm so lonely.

The Woman. You know you ruined me, Willy? From now on, whenever you come to the office, I'll see that you go right through to the buyers. No waiting at my desk any more, Willy. You ruined me.

Willy. That's nice of you to say that.

The Woman. Gee, you are self-centered! Why so sad? You are the saddest, self-centeredest soul I ever did see-saw. *She laughs. He kisses her.* Come on inside, drummer boy. It's silly to be dressing in the middle of the night. *As knocking is heard:* Aren't you going to answer the door?

Willy. They're knocking on the wrong door.

The Woman. But I felt the knocking. And he heard us talking in here. Maybe the hotel's on fire!

Willy, *his terror rising.* It's a mistake.

The Woman. Then tell him to go away!

Willy. There's nobody there.

The Woman. It's getting on my nerves, Willy. There's somebody standing out there and it's getting on my nerves!

Willy, *pushing her away from him.* All right, stay in the bathroom here, and don't come out. I think there's a law in Massachusetts about it, so don't come out. It may be that new room clerk. He looked very mean. So don't come out. It's a mistake, there's no fire.

The knocking is heard again. He takes a few steps away from her, and she vanishes into the wing. The light follows him, and now he is facing Young Biff, who carries a suitcase. Biff steps toward him. The music is gone.

Biff. Why didn't you answer?

Willy. Biff! What are you doing in Boston?

Biff. Why didn't you answer? I've been knocking for five minutes, I called you on the phone—

Willy. I just heard you. I was in the bathroom and had the door shut. Did anything happen home?

Biff. Dad—I let you down.

Willy. What do you mean?

Biff. Dad . . .

Willy. Biffo, what's this about? *Putting his arm around Biff:* Come on, let's go downstairs and get you a malted.

Biff. Dad, I flunked math.

Willy. Not for the term?

Biff. The term. I haven't got enough credits to graduate.

Willy. You mean to say Bernard wouldn't give you the answers?

Biff. He did, he tried, but I only got a sixty-one.

Willy. And they wouldn't give you four points?

Biff. Birnbaum refused absolutely. I begged him, Pop, but he won't give me those points. You gotta talk to him before they close the school. Because if he saw the kind of man you are, and you just talked to him in your way, I'm sure he'd come through for me. The class came right before practice, see, and I didn't go enough. Would you talk to him? He'd like you, Pop. You know the way you could talk.

Willy. You're on. We'll drive right back.

Biff. Oh, Dad, good work! I'm sure he'll change it for you!

Willy. Go downstairs and tell the clerk I'm checkin' out. Go right down.

Biff. Yes, sir! See, the reason he hates me, Pop—one day he was late for class so I got up at the blackboard and imitated him. I crossed my eyes and talked with a lithp.

Willy, *laughing.* You did? The kids like it?

Biff. They nearly died laughing!

Willy. Yeah? What'd you do?

Biff. The thquare root of thixthy twee is . . . *Willy bursts out laughing; Biff joins him.* And in the middle of it he walked in!

Willy laughs and The Woman joins in offstage.

Willy, *without hesitation.* Hurry downstairs and—

Biff. Somebody in there?

Willy. No, that was next door.

The Woman laughs offstage.

Biff. Somebody got in your bathroom!

Willy. No, it's the next room, there's a party—

The Woman, *enters, laughing. She lisps this.* Can I come in? There's something in the bathtub, Willy, and it's moving!

Willy looks at Biff, who is staring open-mouthed and horrified at The Woman.

Willy. Ah—you better go back to your room. They must be finished painting by now. They're painting her room so I let her take a shower here. Go back, go back . . . *He pushes her.*

The Woman, *resisting.* But I've got to get dressed, Willy, I can't—

Willy. Get out of here! Go back, go back . . . *Suddenly striving for the ordinary:* This is Miss Francis, Biff, she's a buyer. They're painting her room. Go back, Miss Francis, go back . . .

The Woman. But my clothes, I can't go out naked in the hall!

Willy, *pushing her offstage.* Get outa here! Go back, go back!

Biff slowly sits down on his suitcase as the argument continues offstage.

The Woman. Where's my stockings? You promised me stockings, Willy!

Willy. I have no stockings here!

The Woman. You had two boxes of size nine sheers for me, and I want them!

Willy. Here, for God's sake, will you get outa here!

The Woman, *enters holding a box of stockings.* I just hope there's nobody in the hall. That's all I hope. *To Biff:* Are you football or baseball?

Biff. Football.

The Woman, *angry, humiliated.* That's me too. G'night. *She snatches her clothes from Willy, and walks out.*

Willy, *after a pause.* Well, better get going. I want to get to the school first thing in the morning. Get my suits out of the closet. I'll get my valise. *Biff doesn't move.* What's the matter? *Biff remains motionless, tears falling.* She's a buyer. Buys for J. H. Simmons. She lives down the hall—they're painting. You don't imagine—*He breaks off. After a pause:* Now listen, pal, she's just a buyer. She sees merchandise in her room and they have to keep it looking just so . . . *Pause. Assuming command:* All right, get my suits. *Biff doesn't move.* Now stop crying and do as I say. I gave you an order. Biff, I gave you an order! Is that what you do when I give you an order? How dare you cry! *Putting his arm around Biff:* Now look, Biff, when you grow up you'll understand about these things. You mustn't—you mustn't overemphasize a thing like this. I'll see Birnbaum first thing in the morning.

Biff. Never mind.

Willy, *getting down beside Biff.* Never mind! He's going to give you those points. I'll see to it.

-loss of respect

Biff. He wouldn't listen to you.

Willy. He certainly will listen to me. You need those points for the U. of Virginia.

Biff. I'm not going there.

Willy. Heh? If I can't get him to change that mark you'll make it up in summer school. You've got all summer to—

Biff, *his weeping breaking from him.* Dad . . .

Willy, *infected by it.* Oh, my boy . . .

Biff. Dad . . .

Willy. She's nothing to me, Biff. I was lonely, I was terribly lonely.

Biff. You—you gave her Mama's stockings! *His tears break through and he rises to go.*

Willy, *grabbing for Biff.* I gave you an order!

Biff. Don't touch me, you—liar!

Willy. Apologize for that!

Biff. You fake! You phony little fake! You fake! *Overcome, he turns quickly and weeping fully goes out with his suitcase. Willy is left on the floor on his knees.*

Willy. I gave you an order! Biff, come back here or I'll beat you! Come back here! I'll whip you!

Stanley comes quickly in from the right and stands in front of Willy.

Willy, *shouts at Stanley.* I gave you an order . . .

Stanley. Hey, let's pick it up, pick it up, Mr. Loman. *He helps Willy to his feet.* Your boys left with the chippies. They said they'll see you home.

A second waiter watches some distance away.

Willy. But we were supposed to have dinner together.

Music is heard, Willy's theme.

Stanley. Can you make it?

Willy. I'll—sure, I can make it. *Suddenly concerned about his clothes:* Do I—I look all right?

Stanley. Sure, you look all right. *He flicks a speck off Willy's lapel.*

Willy. Here—here's a dollar.

Stanley. Oh, your son paid me. It's all right.

Willy, *putting it in Stanley's hand.* No, take it. You're a good boy.

Stanley. Oh, no, you don't have to . . .

Willy. Here—here's some more, I don't need it any more. *After a slight pause:* Tell me—is there a seed store in the neighborhood?
Stanley. Seeds? You mean like to plant?

As Willy turns, Stanley slips the money back into his jacket pocket.

Willy. Yes. Carrots, peas . . .
Stanley. Well, there's hardware stores on Sixth Avenue, but it may be too late now.
Willy, *anxiously.* Oh, I'd better hurry. I've got to get some seeds. *He starts off to the right.* I've got to get some seeds, right away. Nothing's planted. I don't have a thing in the ground.

Willy hurries out as the light goes down. Stanley moves over to the right after him, watches him off. The other waiter has been staring at Willy.

Stanley, *to the waiter.* Well, whatta you looking at?

The waiter picks up the chairs and moves off right. Stanley takes the table and follows him. The light fades on this area. There is a long pause, the sound of the flute coming over. The light gradually rises on the kitchen, which is empty. Happy appears at the door of the house, followed by Biff. Happy is carrying a large bunch of long-stemmed roses. He enters the kitchen, looks around for Linda. Not seeing her, he turns to Biff, who is just outside the house door, and makes a gesture with his hands, indicating "Not here, I guess." He looks into the living-room and freezes. Inside, Linda, unseen, is seated, Willy's coat on her lap. She rises ominously and quietly and moves toward Happy, who backs up into the kitchen, afraid.

Happy. Hey, what're you doing up? *Linda says nothing but moves toward him implacably.* Where's Pop? *He keeps backing to the right, and now Linda is in full view in the doorway to the living-room.* Is he sleeping?
Linda. Where were you?
Happy, *trying to laugh it off.* We met two girls, Mom, very fine types. Here, we brought you some flowers. *Offering them to her:* Put them in your room, Ma.

She knocks them to the floor at Biff's feet. He has now come inside and closed the door behind him. She stares at Biff, silent.

Happy. Now what'd you do that for? Mom, I want you to have some flowers—

Linda, *cutting Happy off, violently to Biff.* Don't you care whether he lives or dies?

Happy, *going to the stairs.* Come upstairs, Biff.

Biff, *with a flare of disgust, to Happy.* Go away from me! *To Linda:* What do you mean, lives or dies? Nobody's dying around here, pal.

Linda. Get out of my sight! Get out of here!

Biff. I wanna see the boss.

Linda. You're not going near him!

Biff. Where is he? *He moves into the living-room and Linda follows.*

Linda, *shouting after Biff.* You invite him for dinner. He looks forward to it all day—*Biff appears in his parents' bedroom, looks around, and exits*—and then you desert him there. There's no stranger you'd do that to!

Happy. Why? He had a swell time with us. Listen, when I—*Linda comes back into the kitchen*—desert him I hope I don't outlive the day!

Linda. Get out of here!

Happy. Now look, Mom . . .

Linda. Did you have to go to women tonight? You and your lousy rotten whores!

Biff re-enters the kitchen.

Happy. Mom, all we did was follow Biff around trying to cheer him up! *To Biff:* Boy, what a night you gave me!

Linda. Get out of here, both of you, and don't come back! I don't want you tormenting him any more. Go on now, get your things together! *To Biff:* You can sleep in his apartment. *She starts to pick up the flowers and stops herself.* Pick up this stuff, I'm not your maid any more. Pick it up, you bum, you!

Happy turns his back to her in refusal. Biff slowly moves over and gets down on his knees, picking up the flowers.

Linda. You're a pair of animals! Not one, not another living soul would have had the cruelty to walk out on that man in a restaurant!

Biff, *not looking at her.* Is that what he said?

Linda. He didn't have to say anything. He was so humiliated he nearly limped when he came in.

Happy. But, Mom, he had a great time with us—

Biff, *cutting him off violently.* Shut up!

Without another word, Happy goes upstairs.

Linda. You! You didn't even go in to see if he was all right!

Biff, *still on the floor in front of Linda, the flowers in his hand; with self-loathing.* No. Didn't. Didn't do a damned thing. How do you like that, heh? Left him babbling in a toilet.

Linda. You louse. You . . .

Biff. Now you hit it on the nose! *He gets up, throws the flowers in the wastebasket.* The scum of the earth, and you're looking at him!

Linda. Get out of here!

Biff. I gotta talk to the boss, Mom. Where is he?

Linda. You're not going near him. Get out of this house!

Biff, *with absolute assurance, determination.* No. We're gonna have an abrupt conversation, him and me.

Linda. You're not talking to him!

Hammering is heard from outside the house, off right. Biff turns toward the noise.

Linda, *suddenly pleading.* Will you please leave him alone?

Biff. What's he doing out there?

Linda. He's planting the garden!

Biff, *quietly.* Now? Oh, my God!

Biff moves outside, Linda following. The light dies down on them and comes up on the center of the apron as Willy walks into it. He is carrying a flashlight, a hoe, and a handful of seed packets. He raps the top of the hoe sharply to fix it firmly, and then moves to the left, measuring off the distance with his foot. He holds the flashlight to look at the seed packets, reading off the instructions. He is in the blue of night.

Willy. Carrots . . . quarter-inch apart. Rows . . . one-foot rows. *He measures it off.* One foot. *He puts down a package and measures off.* Beets. *He puts down another package and measures again.* Lettuce. *He reads the package, puts it down.* One foot—*He breaks off as Ben appears at the right and moves slowly down to him.* What a proposition, ts, ts. Terrific, terrific. 'Cause she's suffered, Ben, the woman has suffered. You understand me? A man can't go out the way he came in, Ben, a man has got to add up to something. You can't, you can't—*Ben moves toward him as though to interrupt.* You gotta consider, now. Don't answer so quick. Remember, it's a guaranteed twenty-thousand-dollar proposition. Now look, Ben, I want you to go through the ins and outs of this thing with me. I've got nobody to talk to, Ben, and the woman has suffered, you hear me?

Ben, *standing still, considering.* What's the proposition?

Willy. It's twenty thousand dollars on the barrelhead. Guaranteed, gilt-edged, you understand?

Ben. You don't want to make a fool of yourself. They might not honor the policy.

Willy. How can they dare refuse? Didn't I work like a coolie to meet every premium on the nose? And now they don't pay off? Impossible!

Ben. It's called a cowardly thing, William.

Willy. Why? Does it take more guts to stand here the rest of my life ringing up a zero?

Ben, *yielding.* That's a point, William. *He moves, thinking, turns.* And twenty thousand—that *is* something one can feel with the hand, it is there.

Willy, *now assured, with rising power.* Oh, Ben, that's the whole beauty of it! I see it like a diamond, shining in the dark, hard and rough, that I can pick up and touch in my hand. Not like—like an appointment! This would not be another damned-fool appointment, Ben, and it changes all the aspects. Because he thinks I'm nothing, see, and so he spites me. But the funeral—*Straightening up:* Ben, that funeral will be massive! They'll come from Maine, Massachusetts, Vermont, New Hampshire! All the old-timers with the strange license plates—that boy will be thunder-struck, Ben, because he never realized—I am known! Rhode Island, New York, New Jersey—I am known, Ben, and he'll see it with his eyes once and for all. He'll see what I am, Ben! He's in for a shock, that boy!

Ben, *coming down to the edge of the garden.* He'll call you a coward.

Willy, *suddenly fearful.* No, that would be terrible.

Ben. Yes. And a damned fool.

Willy. No, no, he mustn't, I won't have that! *He is broken and desperate.*

Ben. He'll hate you, William.

The gay music of the Boys is heard.

Willy. Oh, Ben, how do we get back to all the great times? Used to be so full of light, and comradeship, the sleigh-riding in winter, and the ruddiness on his cheeks. And always some kind of good news coming up, always something nice coming up ahead. And never even let me carry the valises in the house, and simonizing, simonizing that little red car! Why, why can't I give him something and not have him hate me?

Ben. Let me think about it. *He glances at his watch.* I still have a little time. Remarkable proposition, but you've got to be sure you're not making a fool of yourself.

Ben drifts off upstage and goes out of sight. Biff comes down from the left.

Willy, *suddenly conscious of Biff, turns and looks up at him, then begins picking up the packages of seeds in confusion.* Where the hell is that seed? *Indignantly:* You can't see nothing out here! They boxed in the whole goddam neighborhood!

Biff. There are people all around here. Don't you realize that?

Willy. I'm busy. Don't bother me.

Biff, *taking the hoe from Willy.* I'm saying good-by to you, Pop. *Willy looks at him, silent, unable to move.* I'm not coming back any more.

Willy. You're not going to see Oliver tomorrow?

Biff. I've got no appointment, Dad.

Willy. He put his arm around you, and you've got no appointment?

Biff. Pop, get this now, will you? Everytime I've left it's been a fight that sent me out of here. Today I realized something about myself and I tried to explain it to you and I—I think I'm just not smart enough to make any sense out of it for you. To hell with whose fault it is or anything like that. *He takes Willy's arm.* Let's just wrap it up, heh? Come on in, we'll tell Mom. *He gently tries to pull Willy to left.*

Willy, *frozen, immobile, with guilt in his voice.* No, I don't want to see her.

Biff. Come on! *He pulls again, and Willy tries to pull away.*

Willy, *highly nervous.* No, no, I don't want to see her.

Biff, *tries to look into Willy's face, as if to find the answer there.* Why don't you want to see her?

Willy, *more harshly now.* Don't bother me, will you?

Biff. What do you mean, you don't want to see her? You don't want them calling you yellow, do you? This isn't your fault; it's me, I'm a bum. Now come inside! *Willy strains to get away.* Did you hear what I said to you?

Willy pulls away and quickly goes by himself into the house. Biff follows.

Linda, *to Willy.* Did you plant, dear?

Biff, *at the door, to Linda.* All right, we had it out. I'm going and I'm not writing any more.

Linda, *going to Willy in the kitchen.* I think that's the best way, dear. 'Cause there's no use drawing it out, you'll just never get along.

Willy doesn't respond.

Biff. People ask where I am and what I'm doing, you don't know, and you don't care. That way it'll be off your mind and you can start brightening up again. All right? That clears it, doesn't it? *Willy is silent, and Biff goes to him.* You gonna wish me luck, scout? *He extends his hand.* What do you say?

Linda. Shake his hand, Willy.

Willy, *turning to her, seething with hurt.* There's no necessity to mention the pen at all, y'know.

Biff, *gently.* I've got no appointment, Dad.

Willy, *erupting fiercely.* He put his arm around . . . ?

Biff. Dad, you're never going to see what I am, so what's the use of arguing? If I strike oil I'll send you a check. Meantime forget I'm alive.

Willy, *to Linda.* Spite, see?

Biff. Shake hands, Dad.

Willy. Not my hand.

Biff. I was hoping not to go this way.

Willy. Well, this is the way you're going. Good-by.

Biff looks at him a moment, then turns sharply and goes to the stairs.

Willy, *stops him with.* May you rot in hell if you leave this house!

Biff, *turning.* Exactly what is it that you want from me?

Willy. I want you to know, on the train, in the mountains, in the valleys, wherever you go, that you cut down your life for spite!

Biff. No, no.

Willy. Spite, spite, is the word of your undoing! And when you're down and out, remember what did it. When you're rotting somewhere beside the railroad tracks, remember, and don't you dare blame it on me!

Biff. I'm not blaming it on you!

Willy. I won't take the rap for this, you hear?

Happy comes down the stairs and stands on the bottom step, watching.

Biff. That's just what I'm telling you!

Willy, *sinking into a chair at the table, with full accusation.* You're trying to put a knife in me—don't think I don't know what you're doing!

Biff. All right, phony! Then let's lay it on the line. *He whips the rubber tube out of his pocket and puts it on the table.*

Happy. You crazy—

Linda. Biff! *She moves to grab the hose, but Biff holds it down with his hand.*

Biff. Leave it there! Don't move it!

Willy, *not looking at it.* What is that?

Biff. You know goddam well what that is.

Willy, *caged, wanting to escape.* I never saw that.

Biff. You saw it. The mice didn't bring it into the cellar! What is this supposed to do, make a hero out of you? This supposed to make me sorry for you?

Willy. Never heard of it.

Biff. There'll be no pity for you, you hear it? No pity!

Willy, *to Linda.* You hear the spite!

Biff. No, you're going to hear the truth—what you are and what I am!

Linda. Stop it!

Willy. Spite!

Happy, *coming down toward Biff.* You cut it now!

Biff, *to Happy.* The man don't know who we are! The man is gonna know! *To Willy:* We never told the truth for ten minutes in this house!

Happy. We always told the truth!

Biff, *turning on him.* You big blow, are you the assistant buyer? You're one of the two assistants to the assistant, aren't you?

Happy. Well, I'm practically—

Biff. You're practically full of it! We all are! And I'm through with it. *To Willy:* Now hear this, Willy, this is me.

Willy. I know you!

Biff. You know why I had no address for three months? I stole a suit in Kansas City and I was in jail. *To Linda, who is sobbing:* Stop crying. I'm through with it.

Linda turns away from them, her hands covering her face.

Willy. I suppose that's my fault!

Biff. I stole myself out of every good job since high school!

Willy. And whose fault is that?

Biff. And I never got anywhere because you blew me so full of hot air I could never stand taking orders from anybody! That's whose fault it is!

Willy. I hear that!

Linda. Don't, Biff!

Biff. It's goddam time you heard that! I had to be boss big shot in two weeks, and I'm through with it!

Willy. Then hang yourself! For spite, hang yourself!

Biff. No! Nobody's hanging himself, Willy! I ran down eleven flights with a pen in my hand today. And suddenly I stopped, you hear me? And in the middle of that office building, do you hear this? I stopped in the middle of that building and I saw—the sky. I saw the things that I love in this world. The work and the food and time to sit and smoke. And I looked at the pen and said to myself, what the hell am I grabbing this for? Why am I trying to become what I don't want to be? What am I doing in an office, making a contemptuous, begging fool of myself, when all I want is out there, waiting for me the minute I say I know who I am! Why can't I say that, Willy? *He tries to make Willy face him, but Willy pulls away and moves to the left.*

Willy, *with hatred, threateningly.* The door of your life is wide open!

Biff. Pop! I'm a dime a dozen, and so are you!

Willy, *turning on him now in an uncontrolled outburst.* I am not a dime a dozen! I am Willy Loman, and you are Biff Loman!

Biff starts for Willy, but is blocked by Happy. In his fury, Biff seems on the verge of attacking his father.

Biff. I am not a leader of men, Willy, and neither are you. You were never anything but a hard-working drummer who landed in the ash can like all the rest of them! I'm one dollar an hour, Willy! I tried seven states and couldn't raise it. A buck an hour! Do you gather my meaning? I'm not bringing home any prizes any more, and you're going to stop waiting for me to bring them home!

Willy, *directly to Biff.* You vengeful, spiteful mut!

Biff breaks from Happy. Willy, in fright, starts up the stairs. Biff grabs him.

Biff, *at the peak of his fury.* Pop, I'm nothing! I'm nothing, Pop. Can't you understand that? There's no spite in it any more. I'm just what I am, that's all.

Biff's fury has spent itself, and he breaks down, sobbing, holding on to Willy, who dumbly fumbles for Biff's face.

Willy, *astonished.* What're you doing? What're you doing? *To Linda:* Why is he crying?

Biff, *crying, broken.* Will you let me go, for Christ's sake? Will you take that phony dream and burn it before something happens? *Struggling to contain himself, he pulls away and moves to the stairs.* I'll go in the morning. Put him—put him to bed. *Exhausted, Biff moves up the stairs to his room.*

Willy, *after a long pause, astonished, elevated.* Isn't that—isn't that remarkable? Biff—he likes me!

Linda. He loves you, Willy!

Happy, *deeply moved.* Always did, Pop.

Willy. Oh, Biff! *Staring wildly:* He cried! Cried to me. *He is choking with his love, and now cries out his promise:* That boy—that boy is going to be magnificent!

Ben appears in the light just outside the kitchen.

Ben. Yes, outstanding, with twenty thousand behind him.

Linda, *sensing the racing of his mind, fearfully, carefully.* Now come to bed, Willy. It's all settled now.

Willy, *finding it difficult not to rush out of the house.* Yes, we'll sleep. Come on. Go to sleep, Hap.

Ben. And it does take a great kind of a man to crack the jungle.

In accents of dread, Ben's idyllic music starts up.

Happy, *his arm around Linda.* I'm getting married, Pop, don't forget it. I'm changing everything. I'm gonna run that department before the year is up. You'll see, Mom. *He kisses her.*

Ben. The jungle is dark but full of diamonds, Willy.

Willy turns, moves, listening to Ben.

Linda. Be good. You're both good boys, just act that way, that's all.

Happy. 'Night, Pop. *He goes upstairs.*

Linda, *to Willy.* Come, dear.

Ben, *with greater force.* One must go in to fetch a diamond out.

Willy, *to Linda, as he moves slowly along the edge of the kitchen, toward the door.* I just want to get settled down, Linda. Let me sit alone for a little.

Linda, *almost uttering her fear.* I want you upstairs.

Willy, *taking her in his arms.* In a few minutes, Linda. I couldn't sleep right now. Go on, you look awful tired. *He kisses her.*

Ben. Not like an appointment at all. A diamond is rough and hard to the touch.

Willy. Go on now. I'll be right up.

Linda. I think this is the only way, Willy.

Willy. Sure, it's the best thing.

Ben. Best thing!

Willy. The only way. Everything is gonna be—go on, kid, get to bed. You look so tired.

Linda. Come right up.

Willy. Two minutes.

Linda goes into the living-room, then reappears in her bedroom. Willy moves just outside the kitchen door.

Willy. Loves me. *Wonderingly:* Always loved me. Isn't that a remarkable thing? Ben, he'll worship me for it!

Ben, *with promise.* It's dark there, but full of diamonds.

Willy. Can you imagine that magnificence with twenty thousand dollars in his pocket?

Linda, *calling from her room.* Willy! Come up!

Willy, *calling into the kitchen.* Yes! Yes. Coming! It's very smart, you realize that, don't you, sweetheart? Even Ben sees it. I gotta go, baby. 'By! 'By! *Going over to Ben, almost dancing:* Imagine? When the mail comes he'll be ahead of Bernard again!

Ben. A perfect proposition all around.

Willy. Did you see how he cried to me? Oh, if I could kiss him, Ben!

Ben. Time, William, time!

Willy. Oh, Ben, I always knew one way or another we were gonna make it, Biff and I!

Ben, *looking at his watch.* The boat. We'll be late. *He moves slowly off into the darkness.*

Willy, *elegiacally, turning to the house.* Now when you kick off, boy, I want a seventy-yard boot, and get right down the field under the ball, and when you hit, hit low and hit hard, because it's important, boy. *He swings around and faces the audience.* There's all kinds of important people in the stands, and the first thing you know . . . *Suddenly realizing he is alone:* Ben! Ben, where do I . . .? *He makes a sudden movement of search.* Ben, how do I . . .?

Linda, *calling.* Willy, you coming up?

Willy, *uttering a gasp of fear, whirling about as if to quiet her.* Sh! *He turns around as if to find his way; sounds, faces, voices, seem to be swarming in upon him and he flicks at them, crying, Sh! Sh! Suddenly music, faint and high, stops him. It rises in intensity, almost to an unbearable scream. He goes up and down on his toes, and rushes off around the house.* Shhh!

Linda. Willy?

There is no answer. Linda waits. Biff gets up off his bed. He is still in his clothes. Happy sits up. Biff stands listening.

Linda, *with real fear.* Willy, answer me! Willy!

There is the sound of a car starting and moving away at full speed.

Linda. No!

Biff, *rushing down the stairs.* Pop!

As the car speeds off, the music crashes down in a frenzy of sound, which becomes the soft pulsation of a single cello string. Biff slowly returns to his bedroom. He and Happy gravely don their jackets. Linda slowly walks out of her room. The music has developed into a dead march. The leaves of day are appearing over everything. Charley and Bernard, somberly dressed, appear and knock on the kitchen door. Biff and Happy slowly descend the stairs to the kitchen as Charley and Bernard enter. All stop a moment when Linda, in clothes of mourning, bearing a little bunch of roses, comes through the draped doorway into the kitchen. She goes to Charley and takes his arm. Now all move toward the audience, through the wall-line of the kitchen. At the limit of the apron, Linda lays down the flowers, kneels, and sits back on her heels. All stare down at the grave.

Requiem

Charley. It's getting dark, Linda.

Linda doesn't react. She stares at the grave.

Biff. How about it, Mom? Better get some rest, heh? They'll be closing the gate soon.

Linda makes no move. Pause.

Happy, *deeply angered.*   He had no right to do that. There was no necessity for it. We would've helped him.
Charley, *grunting.*   Hmmm.
Biff. Come along, Mom.
Linda. Why didn't anybody come?
Charley. It was a very nice funeral.
Linda. But where are all the people he knew? Maybe they blame him.
Charley. Naa. It's a rough world, Linda. They wouldn't blame him.
Linda. I can't understand it. At this time especially. First time in thirty-five years we were just about free and clear. He only needed a little salary. He was even finished with the dentist.
Charley. No man only needs a little salary.
Linda. I can't understand it.
Biff. There were a lot of nice days. When he'd come home from a trip; or on Sundays, making the stoop; finishing the cellar; putting on the new porch; when he built the extra bathroom; and put up the garage. You know something, Charley, there's more of him in that front stoop than in all the sales he ever made.
Charley. Yeah. He was a happy man with a batch of cement.
Linda. He was so wonderful with his hands.
Biff. He had the wrong dreams. All, all, wrong.
Happy, *almost ready to fight Biff.* Don't say that!
Biff. He never knew who he was.

Charley, *stopping Happy's movement and reply. To Biff.* Nobody dast blame this man. You don't understand: Willy was a salesman. And for a salesman, there is no rock bottom to the life. He don't put a bolt to a nut, he don't tell you the law or give you medicine. He's a man way out there in the blue, riding on a smile and a shoeshine. And when they start not smiling back—that's an earthquake. And then you get yourself a couple of spots on your hat, and you're finished. Nobody dast blame this man. A salesman is got to dream, boy. It comes with the territory.

Biff. Charley, the man didn't know who he was.

Happy, *infuriated.* Don't say that!

Biff. Why don't you come with me, Happy?

Happy. I'm not licked that easily. I'm staying right in this city, and I'm gonna beat this racket! *He looks at Biff, his chin set.* The Loman Brothers!

Biff. I know who I am, kid.

Happy. All right, boy. I'm gonna show you and everybody else that Willy Loman did not die in vain. He had a good dream. It's the only dream you can have—to come out number-one man. He fought it out here, and this is where I'm gonna win it for him.

Biff, *with a hopeless glance at Happy, bends toward his mother.* Let's go, Mom.

Linda. I'll be with you in a minute. Go on, Charley. *He hesitates.* I want to, just for a minute. I never had a chance to say good-by.

Charley moves away, followed by Happy. Biff remains a slight distance up and left of Linda. She sits there, summoning herself. The flute begins, not far away, playing behind her speech.

Linda. Forgive me, dear. I can't cry. I don't know what it is, but I can't cry. I don't understand it. Why did you ever do that? Help me, Willy, I can't cry. It seems to me that you're just on another trip. I keep expecting you. Willy, dear, I can't cry. Why did you do it? I search and search and I search, and I can't understand it, Willy. I made the last payment on the house today. Today, dear. And there'll be nobody home. *A sob rises in her throat.* We're free and clear. *Sobbing more fully, released:* We're free. *Biff comes slowly toward her.* We're free . . . We're free . . .

Biff lifts her to her feet and moves out up right with her in his arms. Linda sobs quietly. Bernard and Charley come together and follow them, followed by Happy. Only the music of the flute is left on the darkening stage as over the house the hard towers of the apartment buildings rise into sharp focus, and

The Curtain Falls

Study and Discussion Questions

1. Characterize Happy and Biff. How is each like and unlike his father?
2. What is Linda's relationship to Willy like? How does she help him? Is there any way in which she hurts him? Who suffers more, Linda or Willy?
3. What does Willy feel is the key to getting ahead? Is he right?
4. What is the significance of Ben in the play? Of Charley? Of Bernard?
5. When Willy comes to Howard to ask for a desk job, Howard refuses, saying "business is business." What is Willy trying to say to *him*? What clash of values does this scene dramatize?
6. What is the significance of Willy's occupation? What would be lost if the play were rewritten as, say, *Death of a Plumber?*
7. How does Happy try to compensate for the powerlessness and lack of status he feels at work?
8. What kind of work did Willy's father do? What kind of work does Biff describe so lyrically to Happy early in Act I? How do these kinds of work differ from Willy's? At the funeral, why does Biff say "there's more of him in that front stoop [he built] than in all the sales he ever made"?

Writing Exercises

1. The family is often viewed as a refuge from the harsh reality of the competitive business world. What comment is the play making on that notion?
2. Willy Loman is not an appealing fellow. He is a tiresome blowhard. He is rude and insulting to his wife, his sons, and his very generous friend Charley. He snivels shamelessly before his boss, Howard. Why, then, does he get our sympathy (if he does)?
3. Characterize Linda as fully as possible. How would the play be different if she, rather than Willy, were the central character?
4. Take one section of the play and analyze the logic of Willy's drifting into and out of the past.
5. If the surviving Lomans did get $20,000 from Willy's life insurance, what do you think they would do with it?
6. To a great extent, the plot of the play hinges on the fact, fully revealed only near the end, that Biff found his father with a woman in a hotel room. Some critics have seen this as a weakness, since (a) the incident cannot carry the weight it is meant to in explaining Biff's failure; and (b) it distracts from the social criticism of the play by pointing to Willy himself as the cause of his and Biff's problems. Do you agree or disagree?

ALICE CHILDRESS (b. 1920)

Born in Charleston, South Carolina, Alice Childress grew up in New York City. For over a decade she was a director and actress with the American Negro Theater and she has acted on Broadway and on television. Among the plays she has written are Florence *(1950),* Gold Through the Trees *(1952),* Trouble in Mind *(1955), which won an Obie Award for best off-Broadway play, and* Wine in the Wilderness *(1969). She has also written fiction, including* Like One of the Family: Conversations from a Domestic's Life *(1956) and two books for young adults,* A Hero Ain't Nothin' But a Sandwich *(1973) and* Rainbow Jordan *(1981).*

Florence   (1950)

Place: A very small town in the South.
Time: The present.
Scene: *A railway station waiting room. The room is divided in two sections by a low railing. Upstage center is a double door which serves as an entrance to both sides of the room. Over the doorway stage right is a sign "Colored," over the doorway stage left is another sign "White." Stage right are two doors . . . one marked "Colored men" . . . the other "Colored women." Stage left two other doorways are "White ladies" and "White gentlemen." There are two benches . . . one on each side. The room is drab and empty looking. Through the double doors upstage center can be seen a gray lighting which gives the effect of early evening and open platform.*

At rise of curtain the stage remains empty for about twenty seconds. . . . A middle aged Negro woman enters, looks offstage . . . then crosses to the "Colored" side and sits on the bench. A moment later she is followed by a young Negro woman about twenty-one years old. She is carrying a large new cardboard suitcase and a wrapped shoebox. She is wearing a shoulder strap bag and a newspaper protrudes from the flap. She crosses to the Colored side and rests the suitcase at her feet as she looks at her mother with mild annoyance.

Marge. You didn't have to get here so early mama. Now you got to wait!
Mama. If I'm goin' someplace . . . I like to get there in plenty time. You don't have to stay.
Marge. You shouldn't wait 'round here alone.
Mama. I ain't scared. Ain't a soul going to bother me.
Marge. I got to get back to Ted. He don't like to be in the house by himself. (*She picks up the bag and places it on the bench by* Mama.)
Mama. You'd best go back. (*Smiles*) You know I think he misses Florence.

Marge. He's just a little fellow. He needs his mother. You make her come home! She shouldn't be way up there in Harlem. She ain't got nobody there.

Mama. You know Florence don't like the South.

Marge. It ain't what we like in this world! You tell her that.

Mama. If Mr. Jack ask about the rent. You tell him we gonna be a little late on account of the trip.

Marge. I'll talk with him. Don't worry so about everything. *(Places suitcase on floor.)* What you carryin', mama . . . bricks?

Mama. If Mr. Jack won't wait . . . write to Rudley. He oughta send a little somethin'.

Marge. Mama . . . Rudley ain't got nothin' fo himself. I hate to ask him to give us.

Mama. That's your brother! If push comes to shove, we got to ask.

Marge *(Places box on bench).* Don't forget to eat your lunch . . . and try to get a seat near the window so you can lean on your elbow and get a little rest.

Mama. Hmmmm . . . mmmph. Yes.

Marge. Buy yourself some coffee when the man comes through. You'll need something hot and you can't go to the diner.

Mama. I know that. You talk like I'm a northern greenhorn.

Marge. You got handkerchiefs?

Mama. I got everything, Marge.

Marge *(Wanders upstage to the railing division line).* I know Florence is real bad off or she wouldn't call on us for money. Make her come home. She ain't gonna get rich up there and we can't afford to do for her.

Mama. We talked all of that before.

Marge *(Touches rail).* Well, you got to be strict on her. She got notions a Negro woman don't need.

Mama. But she was in a real play. Didn't she send us twenty-five dollars a week?

Marge. For two weeks.

Mama. Well the play was over.

Marge *(Crosses to Mama and sits beside her).* It's not money, Mama. Sarah wrote us about it. You know what she said Florence was doin'! Sweepin' the stage!

Mama. She was *in* the play!

Marge. Sure she was in it! Sweepin'! Them folks ain't gonna let her be no actress. You tell her to wake up.

Mama. I . . . I . . . think.

Marge. Listen Ma. . . . She won't wanna come. We know that . . . but she gotta!

Mama. Maybe we shoulda told her to expect me. It's kind of mean to just walk in like this.

Marge. I bet she's livin' terrible. What's the matter with her? Don't she know we're keepin' her son?

Mama. Florence don't feel right 'bout down here since Jim got killed.

Marge. Who does? I should be the one goin' to get her. You tell her she ain't gonna feel right no place. Mama, honestly! She must think she's white!

Mama. Florence is brownskin.

Marge. I don't mean that. I'm talkin' about her attitude. Didn't she go into Strumley's down here and ask to be a sales girl? *(Rises)* Now ain't that somethin'? They don't hire no Colored folks.

Mama. Others besides Florence been talkin' about their rights.

Marge. I know it . . . but there's things we can't do cause they ain't gonna let us. *(She wanders over to the "White" side of the stage)* Don't feel a damn bit different over here than it does on our side.

(Silence)

Mama. Maybe we shoulda just sent her the money this time. This one time.

Marge *(Coming back to "Colored" side).* Mama! Don't you let her cash that check for nothin' but to bring her back home.

Mama. I know.

Marge *(Restless . . . fidgets with her hair . . . patting it in place).* I oughta go now.

Mama. You best get back to Ted. He might play with the lamp.

Marge. He better not let me catch him! If you got to go to the ladies' room take your grip.

Mama. I'll be alright. Make Ted get up on time for school.

Marge *(Kisses her quickly and gives her the newspaper).* Here's something to read. So long Mama.

Mama. G'bye, Margie baby.

Marge *(Goes to door . . . stops and turns to her mother).* You got your smelling salts?

Mama. In my pocketbook.

Marge *(Wistfully).* Tell Florence I love her and I miss her too.

Porter *(Can be heard singing in the distance.)*

Mama. Sure.

Marge *(Reluctant to leave).* Pin that check in your bosom, Mama. You might fall asleep and somebody'll rob you.

Mama. I got it pinned to me. *(Feels for the check which is in her blouse)*

Marge *(Almost pathetic).* Bye, Ma.

Mama. *(Sits for a moment looking at her surroundings. She opens the paper and begins to read.)*

Porter *(Offstage).* Hello, Marge. What you doin' down here?

Marge. I came to see Mama off.

Porter. Where's she going?

Marge. She's in there; she'll tell you. I got to get back to Ted.

Porter. Bye now. . . . Say, wait a minute, Marge.

Marge. Yes?

Porter. I told Ted he could have some of my peaches and he brought all them Brandford boys over and they picked 'em all. I wouldn't lay a hand on him but I told him I was gonna tell you.

Marge. I'm gonna give it to him!

Porter (*Enters and crosses to white side of waiting room. He carries a pail of water and a mop. He is about fifty years old. He is obviously tired but not lazy*). Every peach off my tree!

Mama. There wasn't but six peaches on that tree.

Porter (*Smiles . . . glances at* Mama *as he crosses to white side and begins to mop*). How d'ye do, Mrs. Whitney . . . you going on a trip?

Mama. Fine, I thank you. I'm going to New York.

Porter. Wish it was me. You gonna stay?

Mama. No, Mr. Brown. I'm bringing Florence . . . I'm visiting Florence.

Porter. Tell her I said hello. She's a fine girl.

Mama. Thank you.

Porter. My brother Bynum's in Georgia now.

Mama. Well now, that's nice.

Porter. Atlanta.

Mama. He goin' to school?

Porter. Yes'm. He saw Florence in a Colored picture. A moving picture.

Mama. Do tell! She didn't say a word about it.

Porter. They got Colored moving picture theatres in Atlanta.

Mama. Yes. Your brother going to be a doctor?

Porter (*With pride*). No. He writes things.

Mama. Oh.

Porter. My son is goin' back to Howard next year.

Mama. Takes an awful lot of goin' to school to be anything. Lot of money leastways.

Porter (*Thoughtfully*). Yes'm, it sure do.

Mama. That sure was a nice church sociable the other night.

Porter. Yes'm. We raised 87 dollars.

Mama. That's real nice.

Porter. I won your cake at the bazaar.

Mama. The chocolate one?

Porter (*As he wrings mop*). Yes'm . . . was light as a feather. That old train is gonna be late this evenin'. It's number 42.

Mama. I don't mind waitin'.

Porter (*Lifts pail, tucks mop handle under his arm. Looks about in order to make certain no one is around. Leans over and addresses* Mama *in a confidential tone*). Did you buy your ticket from that Mr. Daly?

Mama (*In a low tone*). No. Marge bought it yesterday.

Porter (*Leaning against railing*).   That's good. That man is mean. Especially if he thinks you're goin' north. (*He starts to leave . . . then turns back to* Mama): If you go to the rest room use the Colored men's . . . the other one is out of order.

Mama.   Thank you, sir.

Mrs. Carter (*A white woman . . . well dressed, wearing furs and carrying a small, expensive overnight bag. She breezes in . . . breathless . . . flustered and smiling. She addresses the porter as she almost collides with him*).   Boy! My bags are out there. The taxi driver just dropped them. Will they be safe?

Porter.   Yes, mam. I'll see after them.

Mrs. Carter.   I thought I'd missed the train.

Porter.   It's late, mam.

Mrs. Carter (*Crosses to bench on the White side and rests her bag*).   Fine! You come back here and get me when it comes. There'll be a tip in it for you.

Porter.   Thank you, mam. I'll be here. (*As he leaves*) Miss Whitney, I'll take care of your bag too.

Mama.   Thank you, sir.

Mrs. Carter (*Wheels around . . . notices* Mama).   Oh. . . . Hello there. . . .

Mama.   Howdy, mam. (*She opens her newspaper and begins to read.*)

Mrs. Carter (*Paces up and down rather nervously. She takes a cigarette from her purse, lights it. Takes a deep draw. She looks at her watch. Speaks to* Mama *across the railing*).   Have you any idea how late the train will be?

Mama.   No mam. (*Starts to read again.*)

Mrs. Carter.   I can't leave this place fast enough. Two days of it and I'm bored to tears. Do you live here?

Mama. (*Rests paper on her lap*).   Yes, mam.

Mrs. Carter.   Where are you going?

Mama.   New York City, mam.

Mrs. Carter.   Good for you! You can stop "maming"me. My name is Mrs. Carter. I'm not a southerner really.

Mama.   Yes'm . . . Mrs. Carter.

Mrs. Carter (*Takes handkerchief from her purse and covers her nose for a moment*).   My God! Disinfectant! This is a frightful place. My brother's here writing a book. Wants atmosphere. Well he's got it. I'll never come back here ever.

Mama.   That's too bad, mam . . . Mrs. Carter.

Mrs. Carter.   That's good. I'd die in this place. Really die. Jeff . . . Mr. Wiley . . . my brother. . . . He's tied in knots, a bundle of problems . . . positively knots.

Mama (*Amazed*).   That so, mam?

Mrs. Carter.   You don't have to call me mam. It's so southern. Mrs. Carter! These people are still fighting the Civil War. I'm really a New

Yorker now. Of course I was born here . . . in the South I mean. Memphis. Listen . . . am I annoying you? I've simply got to talk to someone.

Mama (*Places newspaper on bench*). No, Mrs. Carter. It's perfectly alright.

Mrs. Carter. Fine! You see Jeff has ceased writing. Stopped! Just like that! (*Snaps fingers.*)

Mama (*Turns to her*). That so?

Mrs. Carter. Yes. The reviews came out on his last book. Poor fellow.

Mama. I'm sorry, mam . . . Mrs. Carter. They didn't like his book?

Mrs. Carter. Well enough . . . but Jeff's . . . well Mr. Wiley is a genius. He says they missed the point! Lost the whole message! Did you read . . . do you . . . have you heard of *Lost My Lonely Way?*

Mama. No, mam. I can't say I have.

Mrs. Carter. Well it doesn't matter. It's profound. Real . . . you know. (*Stands at railing upstage.*) It's about your people.

Mama. That's nice.

Mrs. Carter. Jeff poured his complete self into it. Really delved into the heart of the problem, pulled no punches! He hardly stopped for his meals. . . . And of course I wasn't here to see that he didn't overdo. He suffers so with his characters.

Mama. I guess he wants to do his best.

Mrs. Carter. Zelma! . . . That's his heroine. . . . Zelma! A perfect character.

Mama (*Interested . . . coming out of her shell eagerly*). She was colored, mam?

Mrs. Carter. Oh yes! . . . But of course you don't know what it's about do you?

Mama. No, miss . . . Would you tell me?

Mrs. Carter (*Leaning on railing*). Well . . . she's almost white, see? Really you can't tell except in small ways. She wants to be a lawyer . . . and . . . well, there she is full of complexes and this deep shame you know.

Mama (*Excitedly but with curiosity*). Do tell! What shame has she got?

Mrs. Carter (*Takes off her fur neckpiece and places it on bench with overnight bag*). It's obvious! This lovely creature . . . intelligent, ambitious, and well . . . she's a Negro!

Mama (*Waiting eagerly*). Yes'm, you said that. . . .

Mrs. Carter. Surely you understand? She's constantly hating herself. Just before she dies she says it! . . . Right on the bridge. . . .

Mama (*Genuinely moved*). How sad. Ain't it a shame she had to die?

Mrs. Carter. It was inevitable . . . couldn't be any other way!

Mama. What did she say on the bridge?

Mrs. Carter. Well . . . just before she jumped. . . .

Mama (*Slowly straightening*). You mean she killed *herself?*

Mrs. Carter. Of course. Close your eyes and picture it!

Mama (*Turns front and closes her eyes tightly with enthusiasm*). Yes'm.

Mrs. Carter (*Center stage of white side*). Now . . . ! She's standing on the bridge in the moonlight. . . . Out of her shabby purse she takes a mirror . . . and by the light of the moon she looks at her reflection in the glass.

Mama (*Clasps her hands together gently*). I can see her just as plain.

Mrs. Carter (*Sincerely*). Tears roll down her cheeks as she says . . . almost! almost white . . . but I'm black! I'm a Negro! and then . . . (*Turns to* Mama) she jumps and drowns herself!

Mama (*Opens her eyes. Speaks quietly*). Why?

Mrs. Carter. She can't face it! Living in a world where she almost belongs but not quite. (*Drifts upstage*) Oh it's so . . . so . . . tragic.

Mama (*Carried away by her convictions . . . not anger . . . she feels challenged. She rises*). That ain't so! Not one bit it ain't!

Mrs. Carter (*Surprised*). But it is!

Mama. (*During the following she works her way around the railing until she crosses about one foot over to the white side and is face to face with* Mrs. Carter). I know it ain't! Don't my friend Essie Kitredge daughter look just like a German or somethin'? She didn't kill herself! She's teachin' the third grade in the colored school right here. Even the bus drivers ask her to sit in the front seats cause they think she's white! . . . an . . . an . . . she just says as clear as you please . . . "I'm sittin' where my people got to sit by law. I'm a Negro woman!"

Mrs. Carter (*Uncomfortable but not knowing why*). . . . But there you have it. The exception makes the rule. That's proof!

Mama. No such a thing! My cousin Hemsly's as white as you! . . . an' . . . an' he never. . . .

Mrs. Carter (*Flushed with anger . . . yet lost . . . because she doesn't know why*). Are you losing your temper? (*Weakly*) Are you angry with me?

Mama (*Stands silently trembling as she looks down and notices she is on the wrong side of the railing. She looks up at the "White Ladies Room" sign and slowly works her way back to the "Colored" side. She feels completely lost*). No, mam. Excuse me please. (*With bitterness*) I just meant Hemsly works in the colored section of the shoe store. . . . He never once wanted to kill his self! (*She sits down on the bench and fumbles for her newspaper.*)

(*Silence.*)

Mrs. Carter (*Caught between anger and reason . . . she laughs nervously*). Well! Let's not be upset by this. It's entirely my fault you know. This whole thing is a completely controversial subject. (*Silence*) If it's too much for Jeff . . . well naturally I shouldn't discuss it with you. (*Approaching railing*) I'm sorry. Let *me* apologize.

Mama (*Keeps her eyes on the paper*). No need for that, mam.

(Silence.)

Mrs. Carter *(Painfully uncomfortable).* I've drifted away from . . . What started all of this?

Mama *(No comedy intended or allowed on this line).* Your brother, mam.

Mrs. Carter *(Trying valiantly to brush away the tension).* Yes. . . . Well I had to come down and sort of hold his hand over the reviews. He just thinks too much . . . and studies. He knows the Negro so well that sometimes our friends tease him and say he almost seems like . . . well you know. . . .

Mama. *(Tightly).* Yes'm.

Mrs. Carter *(Slowly walks over to the colored side near the top of the rail).* You know I try but it's really difficult to understand you people. However . . . I keep trying.

Mama *(Still tight).* Thank you, mam.

Mrs. Carter *(Retreats back to white side and begins to prove herself).* Last week . . . Why do you know what I did? I sent a thousand dollars to a Negro college for scholarships.

Mama. That was right kind of you.

Mrs. Carter *(Almost pleading).* I know what's going on in your mind . . . and what you're thinking is wrong. I've . . . I've . . . eaten with Negroes.

Mama. Yes, mam.

Mrs. Carter. *(Trying to find a straw).* . . . And there's Malcom! If it weren't for the guidance of Jeff he'd never written his poems. Malcom is a Negro.

Mama *(Freezing).* Yes, mam.

Mrs. Carter *(Gives up, crosses to her bench, opens her overnight bag and takes out a book and begins to read. She glances at Mama from time to time. Mama is deeply absorbed in her newspaper. Mrs. Carter closes her book with a bang . . . determined to penetrate the wall that Mama has built around her).* Why are you going to New York?

Mama *(Almost accusingly).* I got a daughter there.

Mrs. Carter. I lost my son in the war. *(Silence . . . Mama is ill at ease).* Your daughter . . . what is she doing . . . studying?

Mama. No'm. She's trying to get on the stage.

Mrs. Carter *(Pleasantly).* Oh . . . a singer?

Mama. No, mam. She's . . .

Mrs. Carter *(Warmly).* Your people have such a gift. I love spirituals . . . "Steal Away," "Swing Low, Sweet Chariot".

Mama. They are right nice. But Florence wants to act. Just say things in plays.

Mrs. Carter. A dramatic actress?

Mama. Yes, that's what it is. She been in a Colored moving picture, and a big show for two weeks on Broadway.

Mrs. Carter. The dear, precious child! . . . But this is funny . . . no! it's pathetic. She must be bitter . . . *really* bitter. Do you know what I do?

Mama. I can't rightly say.

Mrs. Carter. I'm an actress! A dramatic actress. . . . And I haven't really worked in six months. . . . And I'm pretty well known. . . . And everyone knows Jeff. I'd like to work. Of course, there are my committees, but you see, they don't need me. Not really . . . not even Jeff.

Mama. Now that's a shame.

Mrs. Carter. Your daughter . . . you must make her stop before she's completely unhappy. Make her stop!

Mama. Yes'm . . . why?

Mrs. Carter. I have the best of contacts and *I've* only done a few *broadcasts* lately. Of course, I'm not counting the things I just wouldn't do. Your daughter . . . make her stop.

Mama. A drama teacher told her she has real talent.

Mrs. Carter. A drama teacher! My dear woman, there are loads of unscrupulous whites up there that just hand out opinions for. . . .

Mama. This was a colored gentleman down here.

Mrs. Carter. Oh well! . . . And she went up there on the strength of that? This makes me very unhappy. (*Puts book away in case, and snaps lock.*)

(Silence)

Mama (*Getting an idea*). Do you really, truly feel that way, mam?

Mrs. Carter. I do. Please . . . I want you to believe me.

Mama. Could I ask you something?

Mrs. Carter. Anything.

Mama. You won't be angry mam?

Mrs. Carter (*Remembering*). I won't. I promise you.

Mama (*Gathering courage*). Florence is proud . . . but she's having it hard.

Mrs. Carter. I'm sure she is.

Mama. Could you help her out some, mam? Knowing all the folks you do . . . maybe. . . .

Mrs. Carter (*Rubs the outside of the case*). Well . . . it isn't that simple . . . but . . . you're very sweet. If I only could. . . .

Mama. Anything you did, I feel grateful. I don't like to tell it, but she can't even pay her rent and things. And she's used to my cooking for her. . . . I believe my girl goes hungry sometime up there . . . and yet she'd like to stay so bad.

Mrs. Carter (*Looks up, resting case on her knees*). How can I refuse? You seem like a good woman.

Mama. Always lived as best I knew how and raised my children up right. We got a fine family, mam.

Mrs. Carter. And I've no family at all. I've got to! It's clearly my duty. Jeff's books . . . guiding Malcom's poetry. . . . It isn't enough . . . oh I know it isn't! Have you ever heard of Melba Rugby?

Mama. No, mam. I don't know anybody much . . . except right here.

Mrs. Carter *(Brightening).* She's in California, but she's moving East again . . . hates California.

Mama. Yes'm.

Mrs. Carter. A most versatile woman. Writes, directs, acts . . . everything!

Mama. That's nice, mam.

Mrs. Carter. Well, she's uprooting herself and coming back to her first home . . . New York . . . to direct "Love Flowers" . . . it's a musical.

Mama. Yes'm.

Mrs. Carter. She's grand . . . helped so many people . . . and I'm sure she'll help your . . . what's her name.

Mama. Florence.

Mrs. Carter *(Turns back to bench, opens bag, takes out pencil and address book).* Yes, Florence. She'll have to *make* a place for her.

Mama. Bless you, mam.

Mrs. Carter *(Holds handbag steady on rail as she uses it to write on).* Now let's see . . . the best thing to do would be to give you the telephone number . . . since you're going there.

Mama. Yes'm.

Mrs. Carter *(Writing address on paper).* Your daughter will love her . . . and if she's a deserving girl. . . .

Mama *(Looking down as* Mrs. Carter *writes).* She's a good child. Never a bit of trouble. Except about her husband, and neither one of them could help that.

Mrs. Carter *(Stops writing, raises her head questioning).* Oh?

Mama. He got killed at voting time. He was a good man.

Mrs. Carter *(Embarrassed).* I guess that's worse than losing him in the war.

Mama. We all got our troubles passing through here.

Mrs. Carter *(Gives her the address).* Tell your dear girl to call this number about a week from now.

Mama. Yes, mam.

Mrs. Carter. Her experience won't matter with Melba. I know she'll understand. I'll call her too.

Mama. Thank you, mam.

Mrs. Carter. I'll just tell her . . . no heavy washing or ironing . . . just light cleaning and a little cooking . . . does she cook?

Mama. Mam? *(Slowly backs away from* Mrs. C. *and sits down on bench.)*

Mrs. Carter. Don't worry. That won't matter with Melba. *(Silence. Moves around rail to "Colored" side, leans over Mama.)* I'd take your daughter myself, but I've got Binnie. She's been with me for years, and I can't just let her go . . . can I?

Mama *(Looks at* Mrs. C. *closely)*.   No, mam.

Mrs. Carter.   Of course she must be steady. I couldn't ask Melba to take a fly-by-night. *(Touches* Mama's *arm.)* But she'll have her own room and bath, and above all . . . security.

Mama *(Reaches out, clutches* Mrs. C.'s *wrist almost pulling her off balance)*.   Child!

Mrs. Carter *(Frightened)*.   You're hurting my wrist.

Mama *(Looks down, realizes how tight she's clutching her, and releases her wrist)*.   I mustn't hurt you, must I.

Mrs. Carter *(Backs away rubbing her wrist)*.   It's all right.

Mama *(Rises)*.   You better get over on the other side of that rail. It's against the law for you to be here with me.

Mrs. Carter *(Frightened and uncomfortable)*.   If you think so.

Mama.   I don't want to break the law.

Mrs. Carter *(Keeps her eye on* Mama *as she drifts around railing to bench on her side. Gathers overnight bag)*.   I know I must look like a fright. The train should be along soon. When it comes, I won't see you until New York. These silly laws. *(Silence)* I'm going to powder my nose. *(Exits into "White Ladies" room.)*

Porter *(Singing offstage)*.

Mama *(Sits quietly, staring in front of her . . . then looks at the address for a moment . . . tears the paper into little bits and lets them flutter to the floor. She opens the suitcase, takes out notebook, an envelope and a pencil. She writes a few words on the paper.)*

Porter *(Enters with broom and dust pan)*.   Number 42 will be coming along in nine minutes. *(When* Mama *doesn't answer him, he looks up and watches her. She reaches in her bosom, unpins the check, smooths it out, places it in the envelope with the letter. She closes the suitcase)*. I said the train's coming. Where's the lady?

Mama.   She's in the *ladies'* room. You got a stamp?

Porter.   No. But I can get one out the machine. Three for a dime.

Mama *(Hands him the letter)*.   Put one on here and mail it for me.

Porter *(Looks at it)*.   Gee . . . you writing to Florence when you're going to see her?

Mama *(Picks up the shoe box and puts it back on the bench)*.   You want a good lunch? It's chicken and fruit.

Porter.   Sure . . . thank you . . . but won't you . . .

Mama *(Rises, paces up and down)*.   I ain't gonna see Florence for a long time. Might be never.

Porter.   How's that, Mrs. Whitney?

Mama.   She can be anything in the world she wants to be! That's her right. Marge can't make her turn back, Mrs. Carter can't make her turn back. "Lost My Lonely Way"! That's a book! People killing themselves 'cause they look white but be black. They just don't know do they, Mr. Brown?

Porter. Whatever happened don't you fret none. Life is too short.

Mama. Oh, I'm gonna fret plenty! You know what I wrote Florence?

Porter. No, mam. But you don't have to tell me.

Mama. I said "Keep trying." . . . Oh, I'm going home.

Porter. I'll take your bag. (*Picks up bag and starts out.*) Come on, Mrs. Whitney. (Porter *Exits.*)

Mama (*moves around to "White" side, stares at signs over door. Starts to knock on "White Ladies" door, changes her mind. As she turns to leave, her eye catches the railing; she approaches it gently, touches it, turns, exits.*) (*Stage is empty for about six or seven seconds. Sound of train whistle in distance. Slow curtain.*)

Study and Discussions Questions

1. What is the significance of the physical setting? Why a railway station waiting room? Trace the characters' movement between the "white" and "colored" sides.

2. Why does Mrs. Carter want Mama's approval so badly? What exactly are her attitudes toward black people? Trace the way those attitudes are revealed.

3. What is the source of the humor in the play? Why does Childress use humor with so serious a subject as racism?

4. What is the role of the porter in the play? Is he just there to help Childress convey information to the audience? What about Marge?

5. How did Florence's husband Jim die? What is the significance of this "minor" detail?

6. Why is the play called *Florence*, when Florence never appears on stage?

Writing Exercises

1. Analyze the conversations between Mama and Mrs. Carter in terms of the power relationships between them.

2. Does Mrs. Carter understand that Mama is asking her to help Florence find an *acting* job? Is the kind of job Mrs. Carter proposes an unconscious or a deliberate insult? Give evidence from the play to support your view.

3. Write a short imaginary review of Jeff's novel, *Lost My Lonely Way*.

4. What is the play saying about how equality for black people will and will not come about? Do you agree?

NONFICTION

MERIDEL LESUEUR   (b. 1900)

Meridel LeSueur was born in Iowa and attended high school in Kansas, but did not finish. She lived in an anarchist commune in New York City, worked briefly as an actress in Hollywood, and in the late 1920s began publishing journalism and fiction. Her political activism led, in the 1950s, to her blacklisting; the FBI intimidated publishers into rejecting her work. She was rediscovered by feminists in the 1970s, and a number of her earlier works are now in print. Among LeSueur's writings are a novel, The Girl *(1939; first published, 1978), and the story collections* Annunciation *(1935) and* Salute to Spring *(1940).*

Women on the Breadlines   (1932)

I am sitting in the city free employment bureau. It's the women's section. We have been sitting here now for four hours. We sit here every day, waiting for a job. There are no jobs. Most of us have had no breakfast. Some have had scant rations for over a year. Hunger makes a human being lapse into a state of lethargy, especially city hunger. Is there any place else in the world where a human being is supposed to go hungry amidst plenty without an outcry, without protest, where only the boldest steal or kill for bread, and the timid crawl the streets, hunger like the beak of a terrible bird at the vitals?

We sit looking at the floor. No one dares think of the coming winter. There are only a few more days of summer. Everyone is anxious to get work to lay up something for that long siege of bitter cold. But there is no work. Sitting in the room we all know it. That is why we don't talk much. We look at the floor dreading to see that knowledge in each other's eyes. There is a kind of humiliation in it. We look away from each other. We look at the floor. It's too terrible to see this animal terror in each other's eyes.

So we sit hour after hour, day after day, waiting for a job to come in. There are many women for a single job. A thin sharp woman sits inside a wire cage looking at a book. For four hours we have watched her looking at that book. She has a hard little eye. In the small bare room there are half a dozen women sitting on the benches waiting. Many come and go. Our faces are all familiar to each other, for we wait here every day.

This is a domestic employment bureau. Most of the women who come here are middle-aged, some have families, some have raised their families and are now alone, some have men who are out of work. Hard times and the man leaves to hunt for work. He doesn't find it. He drifts on. The woman probably doesn't hear from him for a long time. She expects it. She isn't surprised. She struggles alone to feed the many mouths. Sometimes she gets help from the charities. If she's clever she can get herself a good living from the charities, if she's naturally a lick spittle, naturally a little docile and cunning. If she's proud then she starves silently, leaving her children to find work, coming home after a day's searching to wrestle with her house, her children.

Some such story is written on the faces of all these women. There are young girls too, fresh from the country. Some are made brazen too soon by the city. There is a great exodus of girls from the farms into the city now. Thousands of farms have been vacated completely in Minnesota. The girls are trying to get work. The prettier ones can get jobs in the stores when there are any, or waiting on table, but these jobs are only for the attractive and the adroit. The others, the real peasants, have a more difficult time.

Bernice sits next to me. She is a Polish woman of thirty-five. She has been working in people's kitchens for fifteen years or more. She is large, her great body in mounds, her face brightly scrubbed. She has a peasant mind and finds it hard even yet to understand the maze of the city where trickery is worth more than brawn. Her blue eyes are not clever but slow and trusting. She suffers from loneliness and lack of talk. When you speak to her, her face lifts and brightens as if you had spoken through a great darkness, and she talks magically of little things as if the weather were magic, or tells some crazy tale of her adventures on the city streets, embellishing them in bright colors until they hang heavy and thick like embroidery. She loves the city anyhow. It's exciting to her, like a bazaar. She loves to go shopping and get a bargain, hunting out the places where stale bread and cakes can be had for a few cents. She likes walking the streets looking for men to take her to a picture show. Sometimes she goes to five picture shows in one day, or she sits through one the entire day until she knows all the dialog by heart.

She came to the city a young girl from a Wisconsin farm. The first thing that happened to her, a charlatan dentist took out all her good shining teeth and the fifty dollars she had saved working in a canning factory. After that she met men in the park who told her how to look out for herself, corrupting her peasant mind, teaching her to mistrust everyone. Sometimes now she forgets to mistrust everyone and gets taken in. They taught her to get what she could for nothing, to count her change, to go back if she found herself cheated, to demand her rights.

She lives alone in little rooms. She bought seven dollars' worth of second-hand furniture eight years ago. She rents a room for perhaps three dollars a month in an attic, sometimes in a cold house. Once the house where she stayed was condemned and everyone else moved out and she lived there all winter alone on the top floor. She spent only twenty-five dollars all winter.

She wants to get married but she sees what happens to her married friends, left with children to support, worn out before their time. So she stays single. She is virtuous. She is slightly deaf from hanging out clothes in winter. She had done people's washing and cooking for fifteen years and in that time saved thirty dollars. Now she hasn't worked steady for a year and she has spent the thirty dollars. She had dreamed of having a little house or a houseboat perhaps with a spot of ground for a few chickens. This dream she will never realize.

She has lost all her furniture now along with the dream. A married friend whose husband is gone gives her a bed for which she pays by doing a great deal of work for the woman. She comes here every day now sitting bewildered, her pudgy hands folded in her lap. She is hungry. Her great flesh has begun to hang in folds. She has been living on crackers. Sometimes a box of crackers lasts a week. She has a friend who's a baker and he sometimes steals the stale loaves and brings them to her.

A girl we have seen every day all summer went crazy yesterday at the YW. She went into hysterics, stamping her feet and screaming.

She hadn't had work for eight months. "You've got to give me something," she kept saying. The woman in charge flew into a rage that probably came from days and days of suffering on her part, because she is unable to give jobs, having none. She flew into a rage at the girl and there they were facing each other in a rage both helpless, helpless. This woman told me once that she could hardly bear the suffering she saw, hardly hear it, that she couldn't eat sometimes and had nightmares at night.

So they stood there, the two women, in a rage, the girl weeping and the woman shouting at her. In the eight months of unemployment she had gotten ragged, and the woman was shouting that she would not send her out like that. "Why don't you shine your shoes?" she kept scolding the girl, and the girl kept sobbing and sobbing because she was starving.

"We can't recommend you like that," the harassed YWCA woman said, knowing she was starving, unable to do anything. And the girls and the women sat docilely, their eyes on the ground, ashamed to look at each other, ashamed of something.

Sitting here waiting for a job, the women have been talking in low voices about the girl Ellen. They talk in low voices with not too much pity for her, unable to see through the mist of their own torment. "What happened to Ellen?" one of them asks. She knows the answer already. We all know it.

A young girl who went around with Ellen tells about seeing her last evening back of a cafe downtown, outside the kitchen door, kicking,

showing her legs so that the cook came out and gave her some food and
some men gathered in the alley and threw small coin on the ground for
a look at her legs. And the girl says enviously that Ellen had a swell
breakfast and treated her to one too, that cost two dollars.

A scrub woman whose hips are bent forward from stooping with hands
gnarled like watersoaked branches clicks her tongue in disgust. No one
saves their money, she says, a little money and these foolish young things
buy a hat, a dollar for breakfast, a bright scarf. And they do. If you've
ever been without money, or food, something very strange happens when
you get a bit of money, a kind of madness. You don't care. You can't
remember that you had no money before, that the money will be gone.
You can remember nothing but that there is the money for which you
have been suffering. Now here it is. A lust takes hold of you. You see
food in the windows. In imagination you eat hugely; you taste a thousand
meals. You look in windows. Colors are brighter; you buy something to
dress up in. An excitement takes hold of you. You know it is suicide but
you can't help it. You must have food, dainty, splendid food, and a bright
hat so once again you feel blithe, rid of that ratty gnawing shame.

"I guess she'll go on the street now," a thin woman says faintly, and
no one takes the trouble to comment further. Like every commodity now
the body is difficult to sell and the girls say you're lucky if you get fifty
cents.

It's very difficult and humiliating to sell one's body.

Perhaps it would make it clear if one were to imagine having to go
out on the street to sell, say, one's overcoat. Suppose you have to sell
your coat so you can have breakfast and a place to sleep, say, for fifty
cents. You decide to sell your only coat. You take it off and put it on
your arm. The street, that has before been just a street, now becomes a
mart, something entirely different. You must approach someone now and
admit you are destitute and are now selling your clothes, your most
intimate possessions. Everyone will watch you talking to the stranger
showing him your overcoat, what a good coat it is. People will stop and
watch curiously. You will be quite naked on the street. It is even harder
to try to sell one's self, more humiliating. It is even humiliating to try to
sell one's labor. When there is no buyer.

The thin woman opens the wire cage. There's a job for a nursemaid,
she says. The old gnarled women, like old horses, know that no one will
have them walk the streets with the young so they don't move. Ellen's
friend gets up and goes to the window. She is unbelievably jaunty. I
know she hasn't had work since last January. But she has a flare of life
in her that glows like a tiny red flame and some tenacious thing, perhaps
only youth, keeps it burning bright. Her legs are thin but the runs in her
old stockings are neatly mended clear down her flat shank. Two bright
spots of rouge conceal her pallor. A narrow belt is drawn tightly around

her thin waist, her long shoulders stoop and the blades show. She runs wild as a colt hunting pleasure, hunting sustenance.

It's one of the great mysteries of the city where women go when they are out of work and hungry. There are not many women in the bread line. There are no flop houses for women as there are for men, where a bed can be had for a quarter or less. You don't see women lying on the floor at the mission in the free flops. They obviously don't sleep in the jungle or under newspapers in the park. There is no law I suppose against their being in these places but the fact is they rarely are.

Yet there must be as many women out of jobs in cities and suffering extreme poverty as there are men. What happens to them? Where do they go? Try to get into the YW without any money or looking down at heel. Charities take care of very few and only those that are called "deserving." The lone girl is under suspicion by the virgin women who dispense charity.

I've lived in cities for many months broke, without help, too timid to get in bread lines. I've known many women to live like this until they simply faint on the street from privations, without saying a word to anyone. A woman will shut herself up in a room until it is taken away from her, and eat a cracker a day and be as quiet as a mouse so there are no social statistics concerning her.

I don't know why it is, but a woman will do this unless she has dependents, will go for weeks verging on starvation, crawling in some hole, going through the streets ashamed, sitting in libraries, parks, going for days without speaking to a living soul like some exiled beast, keeping the runs mended in her stockings, shut up in terror in her own misery, until she becomes too super-sensitive and timid to even ask for a job.

Bernice says even strange men she has met in the park have sometimes, that is in better days, given her a loan to pay her room rent. She has always paid them back.

In the afternoon the young girls, to forget the hunger and the deathly torture and fear of being jobless, try to pick up a man to take them to a ten-cent show. They never go to more expensive ones, but they can always find a man willing to spend a dime to have the company of a girl for the afternoon.

Sometimes a girl facing the night without shelter will approach a man for lodging. A woman always asks a man for help. Rarely another woman. I have known girls to sleep in men's rooms for the night on a pallet without molestation and be given breakfast in the morning.

It's no wonder these young girls refuse to marry, refuse to rear children. They are like certain savage tribes, who, when they have been conquered, refuse to breed.

Not one of them but looks forward to starvation for the coming winter. We are in a jungle and know it. We are beaten, entrapped. There is no way out. Even if there were a job, even if that thin acrid woman came and gave everyone in the room a job for a few days, a few hours, at thirty cents an hour, this would all be repeated tomorrow, the next day and the next.

Not one of these women but knows that despite years of labor there is only starvation, humiliation in front of them.

Mrs. Gray, sitting across from me, is a living spokesman for the futility of labor. She is a warning. Her hands are scarred with labor. Her body is a great puckered scar. She has given birth to six children, buried three, supported them all alive and dead, bearing them, burying them, feeding them. Bred in hunger they have been spare, susceptible to disease. For seven years she tried to save her boy's arm from amputation, diseased from tuberculosis of the bone. It is almost too suffocating to think of that long close horror of years of child-bearing, child-feeding, rearing, with the bare suffering of providing a meal and shelter.

Now she is fifty. Her children, economically insecure, are drifters. She never hears of them. She doesn't know if they are alive. She doesn't know if she is alive. Such subtleties of suffering are not for her. For her the brutality of hunger and cold. Not until these are done away with can those subtle feelings that make a human being be indulged.

She is lucky to have five dollars ahead of her. That is her security. She has a tumor that she will die of. She is thin as a worn dime with her tumor sticking out of her side. She is brittle and bitter. Her face is not the face of a human being. She has borne more than it is possible for a human being to bear. She is reduced to the least possible denominator of human feelings.

It is terrible to see her little bloodshot eyes like a beaten hound's fearful in terror.

We cannot meet her eyes. When she looks at any of us we look away. She is like a woman drowning and we turn away. We must ignore those eyes that are surely the eyes of a person drowning, doomed. She doesn't cry out. She goes down decently. And we all look away.

The young ones know though. I don't want to marry. I don't want any children. So they all say. No children. No marriage. They arm themselves alone, keep up alone. The man is helpless now. He cannot provide. If he propagates he cannot take care of his young. The means are not in his hands. So they live alone. Get what fun they can. The life risk is too horrible now. Defeat is too clearly written on it.

So we sit in this room like cattle, waiting for a nonexistent job, willing to work to the farthest atom of energy, unable to work, unable to get food and lodging, unable to bear children—here we must sit in this shame looking at the floor, worse than beasts at a slaughter.

It is appalling to think that these women sitting so listless in the room may work as hard as it is possible for a human being to work, may labor night and day, like Mrs. Gray wash streetcars from midnight to dawn and offices in the early evening, scrub for fourteen and fifteen hours a day, sleep only five hours or so, do this their whole lives, and never earn one day of security, having always before them the pit of the future. The endless labor, the bending back, the water-soaked hands, earning never more than a week's wages, never having in their hands more life than that.

It's not the suffering of birth, death, love that the young reject, but the suffering of endless labor without dream, eating the spare bread in bitterness, being a slave without the security of a slave.

Study and Discussion Questions

1. What does LeSueur suggest is specific to *women's* experience during the Great Depression?
2. What is the narrator's relation to the scene she describes?
3. List the characteristics of each of the following women: Bernice, Ellen, Mrs. Gray.
4. List examples of metaphor and simile in this essay. How do they contribute to the mood and the argument LeSueur is creating?
5. What is LeSueur's thesis in this essay?
6. Where are the men?
7. Characterize the relation of these women to each other.

Writing Exercises

1. Analyze the passage that begins "It is very difficult and humiliating to sell one's body" and ends "When there is no buyer." What series of analogies is LeSueur making in this passage?
2. To what extent has the situation of unemployed and poor women changed or not changed in the United States since LeSueur published this essay in 1932? What factors can you advance to account for this?
3. What emotional response did you have to "Women in the Breadlines"? What in particular evoked that response?

RICHARD WRIGHT   (1908–1960)

Son of sharecroppers, Richard Wright was born near Natchez, Mississippi, went to high school in Jackson, and then moved to Memphis, Tennessee, where he worked odd jobs and began to write. In 1927, he moved to Chicago, continued working at various menial jobs, and then, in the 1930s, joined the Federal Writer's Project there and in New York. Like many writers and intellectuals, Wright joined the Communist Party during the 1930s, but left it after several years. After World War II, he moved to Paris and continued to write. His works include the story collections Uncle Tom's Children *(1938) and* Eight Men *(1961), the novel* Native Son *(1940), and the autobiographies* Black Boy *(1945) and the posthumously published* American Hunger *(1977).*

The Man Who Went To Chicago (1945)

When I rose in the morning the temperature had dropped below zero. The house was as cold to me as the Southern streets had been in winter. I dressed, doubling my clothing. I ate in a restaurant, caught a streetcar, and rode south, rode until I could see no more black faces on the sidewalks. I had now crossed the boundary line of the Black Belt and had entered the territory where jobs were perhaps to be had from white folks. I walked the streets and looked into shop windows until I saw a sign in a delicatessen: PORTER WANTED.

I went in and a stout white woman came to me.

"Vat do you vant?" she asked.

The voice jarred me. She's Jewish, I thought, remembering with shame the obscenities I used to shout at Jewish storekeepers in Arkansas.

"I thought maybe you needed a porter," I said.

"Meester 'Offman, he eesn't here yet," she said. "Vill you vait?"

"Yes, ma'am."

"Seet down."

"No, ma'am, I'll wait outside."

"But eet's cold out zhere," she said.

"That's all right," I said.

She shrugged. I went to the sidewalk. I waited for half an hour in the bitter cold, regretting that I had not remained in the warm store, but unable to go back inside. A bald, stoutish white man went into the store and pulled off his coat. Yes, he was the boss man . . .

"Zo you vant a job?" he asked.

"Yes, sir," I answered, guessing at the meaning of his words.

"Vhere you vork before?"

"In Memphis, Tennessee."

"My brudder-in-law vorked in Tennessee vonce," he said.

I was hired. The work was easy, but I found to my dismay that I could not understand a third of what was said to me. My slow Southern ears were baffled by their clouded, thick accents. One morning Mrs. Hoffman asked me to go to a neighboring store—it was owned by a cousin of hers—and get a can of chicken *à la* king. I had never heard the phrase before and I asked her to repeat it.

"Don't you know nosing?" she demanded of me.

"If you would write it down for me, I'd know what to get," I ventured timidly.

"I can't vite!" she shouted in a sudden fury. "Vat kinda boy iss you?"

I memorized the separate sounds that she had uttered and went to the neighboring store.

"Mrs. Hoffman wants a can Cheek Keeng Awr Lar Keeng," I said slowly, hoping he would not think I was being offensive.

"All vite," he said, after staring at me a moment.

He put a can into a paper bag and gave it to me; outside in the street I opened the bag and read the label: Chicken à la King. I cursed, disgusted with myself. I knew those words. It had been her thick accent that had thrown me off. Yet I was not angry with her for speaking broken English; my English, too, was broken. But why could she not have taken more patience? Only one answer came to my mind. I was black and she did not care. Or so I thought . . . I was persisting in reading my present environment in the light of my old one. I reasoned thus: though English was my native tongue and America my native land, she, an alien, could operate a store and earn a living in a neighborhood where I could not even live. I reasoned further that she was aware of this and was trying to protect her position against me.

It was not until I had left the delicatessen job that I saw how grossly I had misread the motives and attitudes of Mr. Hoffman and his wife. I had not yet learned anything that would have helped me to thread my way through these perplexing racial relations. Accepting my environment at its face value, trapped by my own emotions, I kept asking myself what had black people done to bring this crazy world upon them?

The fact of the separation of white and black was clear to me; it was its effect upon the personalities of people that stumped and dismayed me. I did not feel that I was a threat to anybody; yet, as soon as I had grown old enough to think, I had learned that my entire personality, my aspirations, had long ago been discounted; that, in a measure, the very meaning of the words I spoke could not be fully understood.

And when I contemplated the area of No Man's Land into which the Negro mind in America had been shunted I wondered if there had ever been in all human history a more corroding and devastating attack upon the personalities of men than the idea of racial discrimination. In order to escape the racial attack that went to the roots of my life, I would have gladly accepted any way of life but the one in which I found myself. I would have agreed to live under a system of feudal oppression, not because I preferred feudalism but because I felt that feudalism made use of a limited part of a man, defined man, his rank, his function in society. I would have consented to live under the most rigid type of dictatorship, for I felt that dictatorships, too, defined the use of men, however degrading that use might be.

While working as a porter in Memphis I had often stood aghast as a friend of mine had offered himself to be kicked by the white men; but now, while working in Chicago, I was learning that perhaps even a kick was better than uncertainty . . . I had elected, in my fevered search for honorable adjustment to the American scene, not to submit and in doing so I had embraced the daily horror of anxiety, of tension, of eternal disquiet. I could now sympathize with—though I could never bring myself to approve—those tortured blacks who had given up and had gone to their white tormentors and had said: "Kick me, if that's all there is for me; kick me and let me feel at home, let me have peace!"

Color-hate defined the place of black life as below that of white life; and the black man, responding to the same dreams as the white man, strove to bury within his heart his awareness of this difference because it made him lonely and afraid. Hated by whites and being an organic part of the culture that hated him, the black man grew in turn to hate in himself that which others hated in him. But pride would make him hate his self-hate, for he would not want whites to know that he was so thoroughly conquered by them that his total life was conditioned by their attitude; but in the act of hiding his self-hate, he could not help but hate those who evoked his self-hate in him. So each part of his day would be consumed in a war with himself, a good part of his energy would be spent in keeping control of his unruly emotions, emotions which he had not wished to have, but could not help having. Held at bay by the hate of others, preoccupied with his own feelings, he was continuously at war with reality. He became inefficient, less able to see and judge the objective world. And when he reached that state, the white people looked at him and laughed and said:

"Look, didn't I tell you niggers were that way?"

To solve this tangle of balked emotion, I loaded the empty part of the ship of my personality with fantasies of ambition to keep it from toppling over into the sea of senselessness. Like any other American, I dreamed of going into business and making money; I dreamed of working for a firm that would allow me to advance until I reached an important position; I even dreamed of organizing secret groups of blacks to fight all whites . . . And if the blacks would not agree to organize, then they would have to be fought. I would end up again with self-hate, but it was now a self-hate that was projected outward upon other blacks. Yet I knew— with that part of my mind that the whites had given me—that none of my dreams were possible. Then I would hate myself for allowing my mind to dwell upon the unattainable. Thus the circle would complete itself.

Slowly I began to forge in the depths of my mind a mechanism that repressed all the dreams and desires that the Chicago streets, the newspapers, the movies were evoking in me. I was going through a second childhood; a new sense of the limit of the possible was being born in me. What could I dream of that had the barest possibility of coming true? I could think of nothing. And, slowly, it was upon exactly that nothingness that my mind began to dwell, that constant sense of wanting without having, of being hated without reason. A dim notion of what life meant to a Negro in America was coming to consciousness in me, not in terms of external events, lynchings, Jim Crowism, and the endless brutalities, but in terms of crossed-up feeling, of emotional tension. I sensed that Negro life was a sprawling land of unconscious suffering, and there were but few Negroes who knew the meaning of their lives, who could tell their story.

Word reached me that an examination for postal clerk was impending and at once I filed an application and waited. As the date for the examination drew near, I was faced with another problem. How could I get a free day without losing my job? In the South it would have been an unwise policy for a Negro to have gone to his white boss and asked for time to take an examination for another job. It would have implied that the Negro did not like to work for the white boss, that he felt he was not receiving just consideration and, inasmuch as most jobs that Negroes held in the South involved a personal, paternalistic relationship, he would have been risking an argument that might have led to violence.

I now began to speculate about what kind of man Mr. Hoffman was, and I found that I did not know him; that is, I did not know his basic attitude toward Negroes. If I asked him, would he be sympathetic enough to allow me time off with pay? I needed the money. Perhaps he would say: "Go home and stay home if you don't like this job!" I was not sure of him. I decided, therefore, that I had better not risk it. I would forfeit the money and stay away without telling him.

The examination was scheduled to take place on a Monday; I had been working steadily and I would be too tired to do my best if I took the examination without benefit of rest. I decided to stay away from the shop Saturday, Sunday, and Monday. But what could I tell Mr. Hoffman? Yes, I would tell him that I had been ill. No, that was too thin. I would tell him that my mother had died in Memphis and that I had gone down to bury her. That lie might work.

I took the examination and when I came to the store on Tuesday, Mr. Hoffman was astonished, of course.

"I didn't sink you vould ever come back," he said.

"I'm awfully sorry, Mr. Hoffman."

"Vat happened?"

"My mother died in Memphis and I had to go down and bury her," I lied.

He looked at me, then shook his head.

"Rich, you lie," he said.

"I'm not lying," I lied stoutly.

"You vanted to do somesink, zo you zayed ervay," he said shrugging.

"No, sir. I'm telling you the truth," I piled another lie upon the first one.

"No. You lie. You disappoint me," he said.

"Well, all I can do is tell you the truth," I lied indignantly.

"Vy didn't you use the phone?"

"I didn't think of it," I told a fresh lie.

"Rich, if your mudder die, you vould tell me," he said.

"I didn't have time. Had to catch the train," I lied yet again.

"Vhere did you get the money?"

"My aunt gave it to me," I said, disgusted that I had to lie and lie again.

"I don't vant a boy vat tells lies," he said.

"I don't lie," I lied passionately to protect my lies.

Mrs. Hoffman joined in and both of them hammered at me.

"Ve know. You come from ze Zouth. You feel you can't tell us ze truth. But ve don't bother you. Ve don't feel like people in ze Zouth. Ve treat you nice, don't ve?" they asked.

"Yes, ma'am," I mumbled.

"Zen vy lie?"

"I'm not lying," I lied with all my strength.

I became angry because I knew that they knew that I was lying. I had lied to protect myself, and then I had to lie to protect my lie. I had met so many white faces that would have violently disapproved of my taking the examination that I could not have risked telling Mr. Hoffman the truth. But how could I tell him that I had lied because I was so unsure of myself? Lying was bad, but revealing my own sense of insecurity would have been worse. It would have been shameful, and I did not like to feel ashamed.

Their attitudes had proved utterly amazing. They were taking time out from their duties in the store to talk to me, and I had never encountered anything like that from whites before. A Southern white man would have said: "Get to hell out of here!" or "All right, nigger. Get to work." But no white people had ever stood their ground and probed at me, questioned me at such length. It dawned upon me that they were trying to treat me as an equal, which made it even more impossible for me ever to tell them that I had lied, why I had lied. I felt that if I confessed I would be giving them a moral advantage over me that would have been unbearable.

"All vight, zay and vork," Mr. Hoffman said. "I know you're lying, but I don't care, Rich."

I wanted to quit. He had insulted me. But I liked him in spite of myself. Yes, I had done wrong; but how on earth could I have known the kind of people I was working for? Perhaps Mr. Hoffman would have gladly consented for me to take the examination; but my hopes had been far weaker than my powerful fears.

Working with them from day to day and knowing that they knew I had lied from fear crushed me. I knew that they pitied me and pitied the fear in me. I resolved to quit and risk hunger rather than stay with them. I left the job that following Saturday, not telling them that I would not be back, not possessing the heart to say good-by. I just wanted to go quickly and have them forget that I had ever worked for them.

After an idle week, I got a job as a dishwasher in a North Side cafe that had just opened. My boss, a white woman, directed me in unpacking barrels of dishes, setting up new tables, painting, and so on. I had charge of serving breakfast; in the late afternoon I carted trays of food to patrons in the hotel who did not want to come down to eat. My wages were fifteen dollars a week; the hours were long, but I ate my meals on the job.

The cook was an elderly Finnish woman with a sharp, bony face. There were several white waitresses. I was the only Negro in the café. The waitresses were a hard, brisk lot, and I was keenly aware of how their attitudes contrasted with those of Southern white girls. They had not been taught to keep a gulf between me and themselves; they were relatively free of the heritage of racial hate.

One morning as I was making coffee, Cora came forward with a tray loaded with food and squeezed against me to draw a cup of coffee.

"Pardon me, Richard," she said.

"Oh, that's all right," I said in an even tone.

But I was aware that she was a white girl and that her body was pressed closely against mine, an incident that had never happened to me before in my life, an incident charged with the memory of dread. But she was not conscious of my blackness or of what her actions would have meant in the South. And had I not been born in the South, her trivial act would have been as unnoticed by me as it was by her. As she stood close to me, I could not help thinking that if a Southern white girl had wanted to draw a cup of coffee, she would have commanded me to step aside so that she might not come in contact with me. The work of the hot and busy kitchen would have had to cease for the moment so that I could have taken my tainted body far enough away to allow the Southern white girl a chance to get a cup of coffee. There lay a deep, emotional safety in knowing that the white girl who was now leaning carelessly against me was not thinking of me, had no deep, vague, irrational fright that made her feel that I was a creature to be avoided at all costs.

One summer morning a white girl came late to work and rushed into the pantry where I was busy. She went into the women's room and changed her clothes; I heard the door open and a second later I was surprised to hear her voice:

"Richard, quick! Tie my apron!"

She was standing with her back to me and the strings of her apron dangled loose. There was a moment of indecision on my part, then I took the two loose strings and carried them around her body and brought them again to her back and tied them in a clumsy knot.

"Thanks a million," she said, grasping my hand for a split second, and was gone.

I continued my work, filled with all the possible meanings that the tiny, simple, human event could have meant to any Negro in the South where I had spent most of my hungry days.

I did not feel any admiration or any hate for the girls. My attitude was one of abiding and friendly wonder. For the most part I was silent with them, though I knew that I had a firmer grasp of life than most of them. As I worked I listened to their talk and perceived its puzzled, wandering, superficial fumbling with the problems and facts of life. There were many things they wondered about that I could have explained to them, but I never dared.

During my lunch hour, which I spent on a bench in a near-by park, the waitresses would come and sit beside me, talking at random, laughing, joking, smoking cigarettes. I learned about their tawdry dreams, their simple hopes, their home lives, their fear of feeling anything deeply, their sex problems, their husbands. They were an eager, restless, talkative, ignorant bunch, but casually kind and impersonal for all that. They knew nothing of hate and fear, and strove instinctively to avoid all passion.

I often wondered what they were trying to get out of life, but I never stumbled upon a clue, and I doubt if they themselves had any notion. They lived on the surface of their days; their smiles were surface smiles, and their tears were surface tears. Negroes lived a truer and deeper life than they, but I wished that Negroes, too, could live as thoughtlessly, serenely, as they. The girls never talked of their feelings; none of them possessed the insight or the emotional equipment to understand themselves or others. How far apart in culture we stood! All my life I had done nothing but feel and cultivate my feelings; all their lives they had done nothing but strive for petty goals, the trivial material prizes of American life. We shared a common tongue, but my language was a different language from theirs.

It was in the psychological distance that separated the races that the deepest meaning of the problem of the Negro lay for me. For these poor, ignorant white girls to have understood my life would have meant nothing short of a vast revolution in theirs. And I was convinced that what they needed to make them complete and grown-up in their living was the inclusion in their personalities of a knowledge of lives such as I lived and suffered containedly.

As I, in memory, think back now upon those girls and their lives I feel that for white America to understand the significance of the problem of the Negro will take a bigger and tougher America than any we have yet known. I feel that America's past is too shallow, her national character too superficially optimistic, her very morality too suffused with color hate for her to accomplish so vast and complex a task. Culturally the Negro represents a paradox: Though he is an organic part of the nation, he is excluded by the entire tide and direction of American culture. Frankly, it is felt to be right to exclude him, and it is felt to be wrong to admit him freely. Therefore if, within the confines of its present culture, the nation ever seeks to purge itself of its color hate, it will find itself at war with itself, convulsed by a spasm of emotional and moral confusion. If the nation ever finds itself examining its real relation to the Negro, it will find itself doing infinitely more than that; for the anti-Negro attitude of whites represents but a tiny part—though a symbolically significant one—

902   MONEY AND WORK

of the moral attitude of the nation. Our too-young and too-new America, lusty because it is lonely, aggressive because it is afraid, insists upon seeing the world in terms of good and bad, the holy and the evil, the high and the low, the white and the black; our America is frightened by fact, by history, by processes, by necessity. It hugs the easy way of damning those whom it cannot understand, of excluding those who look different; and it salves its conscience with a self-draped cloak of right-eousness. Am I damning my native land? No; for I, too, share these faults of character! And I really do not think that America, adolescent and cocksure, a stranger to suffering and travail, an enemy of passion and sacrifice, is ready to probe into its most fundamental beliefs.

I knew that not race alone, not color alone, but the daily values that gave meaning to life stood between me and those white girls with whom I worked. Their constant outwardlooking, their mania for radios, cars, and a thousand other trinkets, made them dream and fix their eyes upon the trash of life, made it impossible for them to learn a language that could have taught them to speak of what was in theirs or others' hearts. The words of their souls were the syllables of popular songs.

The essence of the irony of the plight of the Negro in America, to me, is that he is doomed to live in isolation, while those who condemn him seek the basest goals of any people on the face of the earth. Perhaps it would be possible for the Negro to become reconciled to his plight if he could be made to believe that his sufferings were for some remote, high, sacrificial end; but sharing the culture that condemns him, and seeing that a lust for trash is what blinds the nation to his claims, is what sets storms to rolling in his soul.

Though I had fled the pressure of the South, my outward conduct had not changed. I had been schooled to present an unalteringly smiling face and I continued to do so despite the fact that my environment allowed more open expression. I hid my feelings and avoided all relationships with whites that might cause me to reveal them.

Tillie, the Finnish cook, was a tall, ageless, red-faced, raw-boned woman with long snow-white hair, which she balled in a knot at the nape of her neck. She cooked expertly and was superbly efficient. One morning as I passed the sizzling stove, I thought I heard Tillie cough and spit, but I saw nothing; her face, obscured by steam, was bent over a big pot. My senses told me that Tillie had coughed and spat into that pot, but my heart told me that no human being could possibly be so filthy. I decided to watch her. An hour or so later I heard Tillie clear her throat with a grunt, saw her cough and spit into the boiling soup. I held my breath; I did not want to believe what I had seen.

Should I tell the boss lady? Would she believe me? I watched Tillie for another day to make sure that she was spitting into the food. She was; there was no doubt of it. But who would believe me if I told them what was happening? I was the only black person in the café. Perhaps they would think that I hated the cook. I stopped eating my meals there and bided my time.

The business of the café was growing rapidly and a Negro girl was hired to make salads. I went to her at once.

"Look, can I trust you?" I asked.

"What are you talking about?" she asked.

"I want you to say nothing, but watch that cook."

"For what?"

"Now, don't get scared. Just watch the cook."

She looked at me as though she thought I was crazy; and frankly, I felt that perhaps I ought not say anything to anybody.

"What do you mean?" she demanded.

"All right," I said. "I'll tell you. That cook spits in the food."

"What are you saying?" she asked aloud.

"Keep quiet," I said.

"Spitting?" she asked me in a whisper. "Why would she do that?"

"I don't know. But watch her."

She walked away from me with a funny look in her eyes. But half an hour later she came rushing to me, looking ill, sinking into a chair.

"Oh, God, I feel awful!"

"Did you see it?"

"She *is* spitting in the food!"

"What ought we do?" I asked.

"Tell the lady," she said.

"She wouldn't believe me," I said.

She widened her eyes as she understood. We were black and the cook was white.

"But I can't work here if she's going to do that," she said.

"Then you tell her," I said.

"She wouldn't believe me either," she said.

She rose and ran to the women's room. When she returned she stared at me. We were two Negroes and we were silently asking ourselves if the white boss lady would believe us if we told her that her expert white cook was spitting in the food all day long as it cooked on the stove.

"I don't know," she wailed, in a whisper, and walked away.

I thought of telling the waitresses about the cook, but I could not get up enough nerve. Many of the girls were friendly with Tillie. Yet I could not let the cook spit in the food all day. That was wrong by any human standard of conduct. I washed dishes, thinking, wondering; I served breakfast, thinking, wondering; I served meals in the apartments of patrons upstairs, thinking, wondering. Each time I picked up a tray of food I felt like retching. Finally the Negro salad girl came to me and handed me her purse and hat.

"I'm going to tell her and quit, goddamn," she said.

"I'll quit too, if she doesn't fire her," I said.

"Oh, she won't believe me," she wailed, in agony.

"You tell her. You're a woman. She might believe you."

Her eyes welled with tears and she sat for a long time; then she rose and went abruptly into the dining room. I went to the door and peered. Yes, she was at the desk, talking to the boss lady. She returned to the kitchen and went into the pantry; I followed her.

"Did you tell her?" I asked.

"Yes."

"What did she say?"

"She said I was crazy."

"Oh, God!" I said.

"She just looked at me with those gray eyes of hers," the girl said. "Why would Tillie do that?"

"I don't know," I said.

The boss lady came to the door and called the girl; both of them went into the dining room. Tillie came over to me; a hard cold look was in her eyes.

"What's happening here?" she asked.

"I don't know," I said, wanting to slap her across the mouth.

She muttered something and went back to the stove, coughed, and spat into a bubbling pot. I left the kitchen and went into the back areaway to breathe. The boss lady came out.

"Richard," she said.

Her face was pale. I was smoking a cigarette and I did not look at her.

"Is this true?"

"Yes, ma'am."

"It couldn't be. Do you know what you're saying?"

"Just watch her," I said.

"I don't know," she moaned.

She looked crushed. She went back into the dining room, but I saw her watching the cook through the doors. I watched both of them, the boss lady and the cook, praying that the cook would spit again. She did. The boss lady came into the kitchen and stared at Tillie, but she did not utter a word. She burst into tears and ran back into the dining room.

"What's happening here?" Tillie demanded.

No one answered. The boss lady came out and tossed Tillie her hat, coat, and money.

"Now, get out of here, you dirty dog!" she said.

Tillie stared, then slowly picked up her cat, coat, and the money; she stood a moment, wiped sweat from her forehead with her hand, then spat—this time on the floor. She left.

Nobody was ever able to fathom why Tillie liked to spit into the food.

Brooding over Tillie, I recalled the time when the boss man in Mississippi had come to me and had tossed my wages to me and said:

"Get out, nigger! I don't like your looks."

And I wondered if a Negro who did not smile and grin was as morally loathsome to whites as a cook who spat into the food.

The following summer I was called for temporary duty in the post office, and the work lasted into the winter. Aunt Cleo succumbed to a severe cardiac condition and, hard on the heels of her illness, my brother developed stomach ulcers. To rush my worries to a climax, my mother also became ill. I felt that I was maintaining a private hospital. Finally, the postoffice work ceased altogether and I haunted the city for jobs. But when I went into the streets in the morning I saw sights that killed my hope for the rest of the day. Unemployed men loitered in doorways with blank looks in their eyes, sat dejectedly on front steps in shabby clothing, congregated in sullen groups on street corners, and filled all the empty benches in the parks of Chicago's South Side.

Luck of a sort came when a distant cousin of mine, who was a superintendent for a Negro burial society, offered me a position on his staff as an agent. The thought of selling insurance policies to ignorant Negroes disgusted me.

"Well, if you don't sell them, somebody else will," my cousin told me. "You've got to eat, haven't you?"

During that year I worked for several burial and insurance societies that operated among Negroes, and I received a new kind of education. I found that the burial societies, with some exceptions, were mostly "rackets." Some of them conducted their business legitimately, but there were many that exploited the ignorance of their black customers.

I was paid under a system that netted me fifteen dollars for every dollar's worth of new premiums that I placed upon the company's books, and for every dollar's worth of old premiums that lapsed I was penalized fifteen dollars. In addition, I was paid a commission of ten per cent on total premiums collected, but during the Depression it was extremely difficult to persuade a black family to buy a policy carrying even a dime premium. I considered myself lucky if, after subtracting lapses from new business, there remained fifteen dollars that I could call my own.

This "gambling" method of remuneration was practiced by some of the burial companies because of the tremendous "turnover" in policyholders, and the companies had to have a constant stream of new business to keep afloat. Whenever a black family moved or suffered a slight reverse in fortune, it usually let its policy lapse and later bought another policy from some other company.

Each day now I saw how the Negro in Chicago lived, for I visited hundreds of dingy flats filled with rickety furniture and ill-clad children. Most of the policyholders were illiterate and did not know that their policies carried clauses severely restricting their benefit payments, and, as an insurance agent, it was not my duty to tell them.

After tramping the streets and pounding on doors to collect premiums, I was dry, strained, too tired to read or write. I hungered for relief and, as a salesman of insurance to many young black girls, I found it. There were many comely black housewives who, trying desperately to keep up their insurance payments, were willing to make bargains to escape paying a ten-cent premium. I had a long, tortured affair with one girl by paying her ten-cent premium each week. She was an illiterate black child with a baby whose father she did not know. During the entire period of my relationship with her, she had but one demand to make of me: she wanted me to take her to a circus. Just what significance circuses had for her, I was never able to learn.

After I had been with her one morning—in exchange for the dime premium—I sat on the sofa in the front room and began to read a book I had with me. She came over shyly.

"Lemme see that," she said.

"What?" I asked.

"That book," she said.

I gave her the book; she looked at it intently. I saw that she was holding it upside down.

"What's in here you keep reading?" she asked.

"Can't you really read?" I asked.

"Naw," she giggled. "You know I can't read."

"You can read *some*," I said.

"Naw," she said.

I stared at her and wondered just what a life like hers meant in the scheme of things, and I came to the conclusion that it meant absolutely nothing. And neither did my life mean anything.

"How come you looking at me that way for?"

"Nothing."

"You don't talk much."

"There isn't much to say."

"I wished Jim was here," she sighed.

"Who's Jim?" I asked, jealous. I knew that she had other men, but I resented her mentioning them in my presence.

"Just a friend," she said.

I hated her then, then hated myself for coming to her.

"Do you like Jim better than you like me?" I asked.

"Naw. Jim just likes to talk."

"Then why do you be with me, if you like Jim better?" I asked, trying to make an issue and feeling a wave of disgust because I wanted to.

"You all right," she said, giggling. "I like you."

"I could kill you," I said.

"What?" she exclaimed.

"Nothing," I said, ashamed.

"Kill me, you said? You crazy, man," she said.

"Maybe I am," I muttered, angry that I was sitting beside a human being to whom I could not talk, angry with myself for coming to her, hating my wild and restless loneliness.

"You oughta go home and sleep," she said. "You tired."

"What do you ever think about?" I demanded harshly.

"Lotta things."

"What, for example?"

"You," she said, smiling.

"You know I mean just one dime to you each week," I said.

"Naw, I thinka lotta you."

"Then what do you think?"

"'Bout how you talk when you talk. I wished I could talk like you," she said seriously.

"Why?" I taunted her.

"When you gonna take me to a circus?" she demanded suddenly.

"You ought to be in a circus," I said.

"I'd like it," she said, her eyes shining.

I wanted to laugh, but her words sounded so sincere that I could not.

"There's no circus in town," I said.

"I bet there is and you won't tell me 'cause you don't wanna take me," she said, pouting.

"But there's no circus in town, I tell you!"

"When will one come?"

"I don't know."

"Can't you read it in the papers?" she asked.

"There's nothing in the papers about a circus."

"There is," she said. "If I could read, I'd find it."

I laughed, and she was hurt.

"There *is* a circus in town," she said stoutly.

"There's no circus in town," I said. "But if you want to learn to read, then I'll teach you."

She nestled at my side, giggling.

"See that word?" I said, pointing.

"Yeah."

"That's an 'and,' " I said.

She doubled, giggling.

"What's the matter?" I asked.

She rolled on the floor, giggling.

"What's so funny?" I demanded.

"You," she giggled. "You so funny."

I rose.

"The hell with you," I said.

"Don't you go and cuss me now," she said. "I don't cuss you."

"I'm sorry," I said.

I got my hat and went to the door.

"I'll see you next week?" she asked.

"Maybe," I said.

When I was on the sidewalk, she called to me from a window.

"You promised to take me to a circus, remember?"

"Yes." I walked close to the window. "What is it you like about a circus?"

"The animals," she said simply.

I felt that there was a hidden meaning, perhaps, in what she had said, but I could not find it. She laughed and slammed the window shut.

Each time I left her I resolved not to visit her again. I could not talk to her; I merely listened to her passionate desire to see a circus. She was not calculating; if she liked a man, she just liked him. Sex relations were the only relations she had ever had; no others were possible with her, so limited was her intelligence.

Most of the other agents also had their bought girls and they were extremely anxious to keep other agents from tampering with them. One day a new section of the South Side was given to me as a part of my collection area, and the agent from whom the territory had been taken suddenly became very friendly with me.

"Say, Wright," he asked, "did you collect from Ewing on Champlain Avenue yet?"

"Yes," I answered, after consulting my book.

"How did you like her?" he asked, staring at me.

"She's a good-looking number," I said.

"You had anything to do with her yet?" he asked.

"No, but I'd like to," I said laughing.

"Look," he said. "I'm a friend of yours."

"Since when?" I countered.

"No, I'm really a friend," he said.

"What's on your mind?"

"Listen, that gal's sick," he said seriously.

"What do you mean?"

"She's got the clap," he said. "Keep away from her. She'll lay with anybody."

"Gee, I'm glad you told me," I said.

"You had your eye on her, didn't you?" he asked.

"Yes, I did," I said.

"Leave her alone," he said. "She'll get you down."

That night I told my cousin what the agent had said about Miss Ewing. My cousin laughed.

"That gal's all right," he said. "That agent's been fooling around with her. He told you she had a disease so that you'd be scared to bother her. He was protecting her from you."

That was the way the black women were regarded by the black agents. Some of the agents were vicious; if they had claims to pay to a sick black woman and if the woman was able to have sex relations with them, they would insist upon it, using the claims money as a bribe. If the woman refused, they would report to the office that the woman was a malingerer. The average black woman would submit because she needed the money badly.

As an insurance agent it was necessary for me to take part in one swindle. It appears that the burial society had originally issued a policy that was—from their point of view—too liberal in its provisions, and the officials decided to exchange the policies then in the hands of their clients for other policies carrying stricter clauses. Of course, this had to be done in a manner that would not allow the policyholder to know that his policy was being switched—that he was being swindled. I did not like it, but there was only one thing I could do to keep from being a party to it: I could quit and starve. But I did not feel that being honest was worth the price of starvation.

The swindle worked in this way. In my visits to the homes of the policyholders to collect premiums, I was accompanied by the superintendent who claimed to the policyholder that he was making a routine inspection. The policyholder, usually an illiterate black woman, would dig up her policy from the bottom of a trunk or chest and hand it to the superintendent. Meanwhile I would be marking the woman's premium book, an act which would distract her from what the superintendent was doing. The superintendent would exchange the old policy for a new one which was identical in color, serial number, and beneficiary, but which carried smaller payments. It was dirty work and I wondered how I could stop it. And when I could think of no safe way I would curse myself and the victims and forget about it. (The black owners of the burial societies were leaders in the Negro communities and were respected by whites.)

When I reached the relief station, I felt that I was making a public confession of my hunger. I sat waiting for hours, resentful of the mass of hungry people about me. My turn finally came and I was questioned by a middle-class Negro woman who asked me for a short history of my life. As I waited, I became aware of something happening in the room. The black men and women were mumbling quietly among themselves; they had not known one another before they had come here, but now their timidity and shame were wearing off and they were exchanging experiences. Before this they had lived as individuals, each somewhat afraid of the other, each seeking his own pleasure, each stanch in that degree of Americanism that had been allowed him. But now life had tossed them together, and they were learning to know the sentiments of their neighbors for the first time; their talking was enabling them to sense the collectivity of their lives, and some of their fear was passing.

Did the relief officials realize what was happening? No. If they had, they would have stopped it. But they saw their "clients" through the eyes of their profession, saw only what their "science" allowed them to see. As I listened to the talk, I could see black minds shedding many illusions. These people now knew that the past had betrayed them, had cast them out; but they did not know what the future would be like, did not know what they wanted. Yes, some of the things that the Communists said were true; they maintained that there came times in history when a ruling class could no longer rule. And now I sat looking at the beginnings of anarchy. To permit the birth of this new consciousness in these people was proof that those who ruled did not quite know what they were doing, assuming that they were trying to save themselves and their class. Had they understood what was happening, they would never have allowed millions of perplexed and defeated people to sit together for long hours and talk, for out of their talk was rising a new realization of life. And once this new conception of themselves had formed, no power on earth could alter it.

I left the relief station with the promise that food would be sent to me, but I also left with a knowledge that the relief officials had not wanted to give to me. I had felt the possibility of creating a new understanding of life in the minds of people rejected by the society in which they lived, people to whom the Chicago *Tribune* referred contemptuously as the "idle" ones, as though these people had deliberately sought their present state of helplessness.

Who would give these people a meaningful way of life? Communist theory defined these people as the molders of the future of mankind, but the Communist speeches I had heard in the park had mocked that definition. These people, of course, were not ready for a revolution; they had not abandoned their past lives by choice, but because they simply could not live the old way any longer. Now, what new faith would they embrace? The day I begged bread from the city officials was the day that showed me I was not alone in my loneliness; society had cast millions of others with me. But how could I be with them? How many understood what was happening? My mind swam with questions that I could not answer.

I was slowly beginning to comprehend the meaning of my environment; a sense of direction was beginning to emerge from the conditions of my life. I began to feel something more powerful that I could express. My speech and manner changed. My cynicism slid from me. I grew open and questioning. I wanted to know.

If I were a member of the class that rules, I would post men in all the neighborhoods of the nation, not to spy upon or club rebellious workers, not to break strikes or disrupt unions, but to ferret out those who no longer respond to the system under which they live. I would make it known that the real danger does not stem from those who seek to grab their share of wealth through force, or from those who try to defend their property through violence, for both of these groups, by their affirmative acts, support the values of the system under which they live. The millions that I would fear are those who do not dream of the prizes that the nation holds forth, for it is in them, though they may not know it, that a revolution has taken place and is biding its time to translate itself into a new and strange way of life.

I feel that the Negroes' relation to America is symbolically peculiar, and from the Negroes' ultimate reactions to their trapped state a lesson can be learned about America's future. Negroes are told in a language they cannot possibly misunderstand that their native land is not their own; and when, acting upon impulses which they share with whites, they try to assert a claim to their birthright, whites retaliate with terror, never pausing to consider the consequences should the Negroes give up completely. The whites never dream that they would face a situation far more terrifying if they were confronted by Negroes who made no claims at all than by those who are buoyed up by social aggressiveness. My knowledge of how Negroes react to their plight makes me declare that no man can possibly be individually guilty of treason, that an insurgent act is but a man's desperate answer to those who twist his environment so that he cannot fully share the spirit of his native land. Treason is a crime of the State.

Christmas came and I was once more called to the post office for temporary work. This time I met many young white men and we discussed world happenings, the vast armies of unemployed, the rising tide of radical action. I now detected a change in the attitudes of the whites I met; their privations were making them regard Negroes with new eyes, and, for the first time, I was invited to their homes.

When the work in the post office ended, I was assigned by the relief system as an orderly to a medical research institute in one of the largest and wealthiest hospitals in Chicago. I cleaned operating rooms, dog, rat, mice, cat, and rabbit pans, and fed guinea pigs. Four of us Negroes worked there and we occupied an underworld position, remembering that we must restrict ourselves—when not engaged upon some task—to the basement corridors, so that we would not mingle with white nurses, doctors, or visitors.

The sharp line of racial division drawn by the hospital authorities came to me the first morning when I walked along an underground corridor and saw two long lines of women coming toward me. A line of white girls marched past, clad in starched uniforms that gleamed white; their faces were alert, their step quick, their bodies lean and shapely, their shoulders erect, their faces lit with the light of purpose. And after them came a line of black girls, old, fat, dressed in ragged gingham, walking loosely, carrying tin cans of soap powder, rags, mops, brooms . . . I wondered what law of the universe kept them from being mixed? The sun would not have stopped shining had there been a few black girls in the first line, and the earth would not have stopped whirling on its axis had there been a few white girls in the second line. But the two lines I saw graded social status in purely racial terms.

Of the three Negroes who worked with me, one was a boy about my own age, Bill, who was either sleepy or drunk most of the time. Bill straightened his hair and I suspected that he kept a bottle hidden somewhere in the piles of hay which we fed to the guinea pigs. He did not like me and I did not like him, though I tried harder than he to conceal my dislike. We had nothing in common except that we were both black and lost. While I contained my frustration, he drank to drown his. Often I tried to talk to him, tried in simple words to convey to him some of my ideas, and he would listen in sullen silence. Then one day he came to me with an angry look on his face.

"I got it," he said.

"You've got what?" I asked.

"This old race problem you keep talking about," he said.

"What about it?"

"Well, it's this way," he explained seriously. "Let the government give every man a gun and five bullets, then let us all start over again. Make it just like it was in the beginning. The ones who come out on top, white or black, let them rule."

His simplicity terrified me. I had never met a Negro who was so irredeemably brutalized. I stopped pumping my ideas into Bill's brain for fear that the fumes of alcohol might send him reeling toward some fantastic fate.

The two other Negroes were elderly and had been employed in the institute for fifteen years or more. One was Brand, a short, black, morose bachelor; the other was Cooke, a tall, yellow, spectacled fellow who spent his spare time keeping track of world events through the Chicago *Tribune*. Brand and Cooke hated each other for a reason that I was never able to determine, and they spent a good part of each day quarreling.

When I began working at the institute, I recalled my adolescent dream of wanting to be a medical research worker. Daily I saw young Jewish boys and girls receiving instruction in chemistry and medicine that the average black boy or girl could never receive. When I was alone, I wandered and poked my fingers into strange chemicals, watched intricate machines trace red and black lines on ruled paper. At times I paused and stared at the walls of the rooms, at the floors, at the wide desks at which the white doctors sat; and I realized——with a feeling that I could never quite get used to——that I was looking at the world of another race.

My interest in what was happening in the institute amused the three other Negroes with whom I worked. They had no curiosity about "white folks' things," while I wanted to know if the dogs being treated for diabetes were getting well; if the rats and mice in which cancer had been induced showed any signs of responding to treatment. I wanted to know the principle that lay behind the Aschheim-Zondek tests that were made with rabbits, the Wassermann tests that were made with guinea pigs. But when I asked a timid question I found that even Jewish doctors had learned to imitate the sadistic method of humbling a Negro that the others had cultivated.

"If you know too much, boy, your brains might explode," a doctor said one day.

Each Saturday morning I assisted a young Jewish doctor in slitting the vocal cords of a fresh batch of dogs from the city pound. The object was to devocalize the dogs so that their howls would not disturb the patients in the other parts of the hospital. I held each dog as the doctor injected Nembutal into its veins to make it unconscious; then I held the dog's jaws open as the doctor inserted the scalpel and severed the vocal cords. Later, when the dogs came to, they would lift their heads to the ceiling and gape in a soundless wail. The sight became lodged in my imagination as a symbol of silent suffering.

To me Nembutal was a powerful and mysterious liquid, but when I asked questions about its properties I could not obtain a single intelligent answer. The doctor simply ignored me with:

"Come on. Bring me the next dog. I haven't got all day."

One Saturday morning, after I had held the dogs for their vocal cords to be slit, the doctor left the Nembutal on a bench. I picked it up, uncorked it, and smelled it. It was odorless. Suddenly Brand ran to me with a stricken face.

"What're you doing?" he asked.

"I was smelling this stuff to see if it had any odor," I said.

"Did you really smell it?" he asked me.

"Yes."

"Oh, God!" he exclaimed.

"What's the matter?" I asked.

"You shouldn't've done that!" he shouted.

"Why?"

He grabbed my arm and jerked me across the room.

"Come on!" he yelled, snatching open the door.

"What's the matter?" I asked.

"I gotta get you to a doctor 'fore it's too late," he gasped.

Had my foolish curiosity made me inhale something dangerous?

"But——Is it poisonous?"

"Run, boy!" he said, pulling me. "You'll fall dead."

Filled with fear, with Brand pulling my arm, I rushed out of the room, raced across a rear areaway, into another room, then down a long corridor. I wanted to ask Brand what symptoms I must expect, but we were running too fast. Brand finally stopped, gasping for breath. My heart beat wildly and my blood pounded in my head. Brand then dropped to the concrete floor, stretched out on his back, and yelled with laughter, shaking all over. He beat his fists against the concrete; he moaned, giggled, he kicked.

I tried to master my outrage, wondering if some of the white doctors had told him to play the joke. He rose and wiped tears from his eyes, still laughing. I walked away from him. He knew that I was angry and he followed me.

"Don't get mad," he gasped through his laughter.

"Go to hell," I said.

"I couldn't help it," he giggled. "You looked at me like you'd believe anything I said. Man, you was scared."

He leaned against the wall, laughing again, stomping his feet. I was angry, for I felt that he would spread the story. I knew that Bill and Cooke never ventured beyond the safe bounds of Negro living, and they would never blunder into anything like this. And if they heard about this, they would laugh for months.

"Brand, if you mention this, I'll kill you," I swore.

"You ain't mad?" he asked, laughing, staring at me through tears.

Sniffing, Brand walked ahead of me. I followed him back into the room that housed the dogs. All day, while at some task, he would pause and giggle, then smother the giggling with his hand, looking at me out of the corner of his eyes, shaking his head. He laughed at me for a week. I kept my temper and let him amuse himself. I finally found out the properties of Nembutal by consulting medical books; but I never told Brand.

One summer morning, just as I began work, a young Jewish boy came to me with a stop watch in his hand.

"Dr. _____ wants me to time you when you clean a room," he said. "We're trying to make the institute more efficient."

"I'm doing my work, and getting through on time," I said.

"This is the boss's order," he said.

"Why don't you work for a change?" I blurted, angry.

"Now, look," he said. "*This* is my work. Now *you* work."

I got a mop and pail, sprayed a room with disinfectant, and scrubbed at coagulated blood and hardened dog, rat, and rabbit feces. The normal temperature of a room was ninety, but, as the sun beat down upon the skylights, the temperature rose above a hundred. Stripped to my waist, I slung the mop, moving steadily like a machine, hearing the boy press the button on the stop watch as I finished cleaning a room.

"Well, how is it?" I asked.

"It took you seventeen minutes to clean that last room," he said. "That ought to be the time for each room."

"But that room was not very dirty," I said.

"You have seventeen rooms to clean," he went on as though I had not spoken. "Seventeen times seventeen make four hours and forty-nine minutes." He wrote upon a little pad. "After lunch, clean the five flights of stone stairs. I timed a boy who scrubbed one step and multiplied that time by the number of steps. You ought to be through by six."

"Suppose I want relief?" I asked.

"You'll manage," he said and left.

Never had I felt so much the slave as when I scoured those stone steps each afternoon. Working against time, I would wet five steps, sprinkle soap powder, and then a white doctor or a nurse would come along and, instead of avoiding the soapy steps, would walk on them and track the dirty water onto the steps that I had already cleaned. To obviate this, I cleaned but two steps at a time, a distance over which a ten-year-old child could step. But it did no good. The white people still plopped their feet down into the dirty water and muddied the other clean steps. If I ever really hotly hated unthinking whites, it was then. Not once during my entire stay at the institute did a single white person show enough courtesy to avoid a wet step. I would be on my knees, scrubbing, sweating, pouring out what limited energy my body could wring from my meager diet, and I would hear feet approaching. I would pause and curse with tense lips:

"These sonofabitches are going to dirty these steps again, goddamn their souls to hell!"

Sometimes a sadistically observant white man would notice that he had tracked dirty water up the steps, and he would look back down at me and smile and say:

"Boy, we sure keep you busy, don't we?"

And I would not be able to answer.

The feud that went on between Brand and Cooke continued. Although they were working daily in a building where scientific history was being made, the light of curiosity was never in their eyes. They were conditioned to their racial "place," had learned to see only a part of the whites and the white world; and the whites, too, had learned to see only a part of the lives of the blacks and their world.

Perhaps Brand and Cooke, lacking interests that could absorb them, fuming like children over trifles, simply invented their hate of each other in order to have something to feel deeply about. Or perhaps there was in them a vague tension stemming from their chronically frustrating way of life, a pain whose cause they did not know; and, like those devocalized dogs, they would whirl and snap at the air when their old pain struck them. Anyway, they argued about the weather, sports, sex, war, race, politics, and religion; neither of them knew much about the subjects they debated, but it seemed that the less they knew the better they could argue.

The tug of war between the two elderly men reached a climax one winter day at noon. It was incredibly cold and an icy gale swept up and down the Chicago streets with blizzard force. The door of the animal-filled room was locked, for we always insisted that we be allowed one hour in which to eat and rest. Bill and I were sitting on wooden boxes, eating our lunches out of paper bags. Brand was washing his hands at the sink. Cooke was sitting on a rickety stool, munching an apple and reading the Chicago *Tribune*.

Now and then a devocalized dog lifted his nose to the ceiling and howled soundlessly. The room was filled with many rows of high steel tiers. Perched upon each of these tiers were layers of steel cages containing the dogs, rats, mice, rabbits, and guinea pigs. Each cage was labeled in some indecipherable scientific jargon. Along the walls of the room were long charts with zigzagging red and black lines that traced the success or failure of some experiment. The lonely piping of guinea pigs floated unheeded about us. Hay rustled as a rabbit leaped restlessly about in its pen. A rat scampered around in its steel prison. Cooke tapped the newspaper for attention.

"It says here," Cooke mumbled through a mouthful of apple, "that this is the coldest day since 1888."

Bill and I sat unconcerned. Brand chuckled softly.

"What in hell you laughing about?" Cooke demanded of Brand.

"You can't believe what that damn *Tribune* says," Brand said.

"How come I can't?" Cooke demanded. "It's the world's greatest newspaper."

Brand did not reply; he shook his head pityingly and chuckled again.

"Stop that damn laughing at me!" Cooke said angrily.

"I laugh as much as I wanna," Brand said. "You don't know what you talking about. The *Herald-Examiner* says it's the coldest day since 1873."

"But the *Trib* oughta know," Cooke countered. "It's older'n that *Examiner*."

"That damn *Trib* don't know nothing!" Brand drowned out Cooke's voice.

"How in hell you know?" Cooke asked with rising anger.

The argument waxed until Cooke shouted that if Brand did not shut up he was going to "cut his black throat."

Brand whirled from the sink, his hands dripping soapy water, his eyes blazing.

"Take that back," Brand said.

"I take nothing back! What you wanna do about it?" Cooke taunted.

The two elderly Negroes glared at each other. I wondered if the quarrel was really serious, or if it would turn out harmlessly as so many others had done.

Suddenly Cooke dropped the Chicago *Tribune* and pulled a long knife from his pocket; his thumb pressed a button and a gleaming steel blade leaped out. Brand stepped back quickly and seized an ice pick that was stuck in a wooden board above the sink.

"Put that knife down," Brand said.

"Stay 'way from me, or I'll cut your throat," Cooke warned.

Brand lunged with the ice pick. Cooke dodged out of range. They circled each other like fighters in a prize ring. The cancerous and tubercular rats and mice leaped about in their cages. The guinea pigs whistled in fright. The diabetic dogs bared their teeth and barked soundlessly in our direction. The Aschheim-Zondek rabbits flopped their ears and tried to hide in the corners of their pens. Cooke now crouched and sprang forward with the knife. Bill and I jumped to our feet, speechless with surprise. Brand retreated. The eyes of both men were hard and unblinking; they were breathing deeply.

"Say, cut it out!" I called in alarm.

"Them damn fools is really fighting," Bill said in amazement.

Slashing at each other, Brand and Cooke surged up and down the aisles of steel tiers. Suddenly Brand uttered a bellow and charged into Cooke and swept him violently backward. Cooke grasped Brand's hand to keep the ice pick from sinking into his chest. Brand broke free and charged Cooke again, sweeping him into an animal-filled steel tier. The tier balanced itself on its edge for an indecisive moment, then toppled.

Like kingpins, one steel tier lammed into another, then they all crashed to the floor with a sound as of the roof falling. The whole aspect of the room altered quicker than the eye could follow. Brand and Cooke stood stock-still, their eyes fastened upon each other, their pointed weapons raised; but they were dimly aware of the havoc that churned about them.

The steel tiers lay jumbled; the doors of the cages swung open. Rats and mice and dogs and rabbits moved over the floor in wild panic. The Wassermann guinea pigs were squealing as though judgment day had come. Here and there an animal had been crushed beneath a cage.

All four of us looked at one another. We knew what this meant. We might lose our jobs. We were already regarded as black dunces; and if the doctors saw this mess they would take it as final proof. Bill rushed to the door to make sure that it was locked. I glanced at the clock and saw that it was 12:30. We had one half-hour of grace.

"Come on," Bill said uneasily. "We got to get this place cleaned."

Brand and Cooke stared at each other, both doubting.

"Give me your knife, Cooke," I said.

"Naw! Take Brand's ice pick *first*," Cooke said.

"The hell you say!" Brand said. "Take his knife *first*!"

A knock sounded at the door.

"Sssssh," Bill said.

We waited. We heard footsteps going away. We'll all lose our jobs, I thought.

Persuading the fighters to surrender their weapons was a difficult task, but at last it was done and we could begin to set things right. Slowly Brand stooped and tugged at one end of a steel tier. Cooke stooped to help him. Both men seemed to be acting in a dream. Soon, however, all four of us were working frantically, watching the clock.

As we labored we conspired to keep the fight a secret; we agreed to tell the doctors—if any should ask—that we had not been in the room during our lunch hour; we felt that that lie would explain why no one had unlocked the door when the knock had come.

We righted the tiers and replaced the cages; then we were faced with the impossible task of sorting the cancerous rats and mice, the diabetic dogs, the Aschheim-Zondek rabbits, and the Wassermann guinea pigs. Whether we kept our jobs or not depended upon how shrewdly we could cover up all evidence of the fight. It was pure guesswork, but we had to try to put the animals back into the correct cages. We knew that certain rats or mice went into certain cages, but we did not know *what* rat or mouse went into *what* cage. We did not know a tubercular mouse from a cancerous mouse—the white doctors had made sure that we would not know. They had never taken time to answer a single question; though we worked in the institute, we were as remote from the meaning of the experiments as if we lived in the moon. The doctors had laughed at what they felt was our childlike interest in the fate of the animals.

First we sorted the dogs; that was fairly easy, for we could remember the size and color of most of them. But the rats and mice and guinea pigs baffled us completely.

We put our heads together and pondered, down in the underworld of the great scientific institute. It was a strange scientific conference; the fate of the entire medical research institute rested in our ignorant, black hands.

We remembered the number of rats, mice, or guinea pigs—we had to handle them several times a day—that went into a given cage, and we supplied the number helter-skelter from those animals that we could catch running loose on the floor. We discovered that many rats, mice, and guinea pigs were missing—they had been killed in the scuffle. We solved that problem by taking healthy stock from other cages and putting them into cages with sick animals. We repeated this process until we were certain that, numerically at least, all the animals with which the doctors were experimenting were accounted for.

The rabbits came last. We broke the rabbits down into two general groups; those that had fur on their bellies and those that did not. We knew that all those rabbits that had shaven bellies—our scientific knowledge adequately covered this point because it was our job to shave the rabbits—were undergoing the Aschheim-Zondek tests. But in what pen did a given rabbit belong? We did not know. I solved the problem very simply. I counted the shaven rabbits; they numbered seventeen. I counted the pens labeled "Aschheim-Zondek," then proceeded to drop a shaven rabbit into each pen at random. And again we were numerically successful. At least white America had taught us how to count. . . .

Lastly we carefully wrapped all the dead animals in newspapers and hid their bodies in a garbage can.

At a few minutes to one the room was in order; that is, the kind of order that we four Negroes could figure out. I unlocked the door and we sat waiting, whispering, vowing secrecy, wondering what the reaction of the doctors would be.

Finally a doctor came, gray-haired, white-coated, spectacled, efficient, serious, taciturn, bearing a tray upon which sat a bottle of mysterious fluid and a hypodermic needle.

"My rats, please."

Cooke shuffled forward to serve him. We held our breath. Cooke got the cage which he knew the doctor always called for at that hour and brought it forward. One by one, Cooke took out the rats and held them as the doctor solemnly injected the mysterious fluid under their skins.

"Thank you, Cooke," the doctor murmured.

"Not at all, sir," Cooke mumbled with a suppressed gasp.

When the doctor had gone we looked at one another, hardly daring to believe that our secret would be kept. We were so anxious that we did not know whether to curse or laugh. Another doctor came.

"Give me A-Z rabbit number 14."

"Yes, sir," I said.

I brought him the rabbit and he took it upstairs to the operating room. We waited for repercussions. None came.

All that afternoon the doctors came and went. I would run into the room—stealing a few seconds from my step-scrubbing—and ask what progress was being made and would learn that the doctors had detected nothing. At quitting time we felt triumphant.

"They won't ever know," Cooke boasted in a whisper.

I saw Brand stiffen. I knew that he was aching to dispute Cooke's optimism, but the memory of the fight he had just had was so fresh in his mind that he could not speak.

Another day went by and nothing happened. Then another day. The doctors examined the animals and wrote in their little black books, in their big black books, and continued to trace red and black lines upon the charts.

A week passed and we felt out of danger. Not one question had been asked.

Of course, we four black men were much too modest to make our contribution known, but we often wondered what went on in the laboratories after that secret disaster. Was some scientific hypothesis, well on its way to validation and ultimate public use, discarded because of unexpected findings on that cold winter day? Was some tested principle given a new and strange refinement because of fresh, remarkable evidence? Did some brooding research worker—those who held stop watches and slopped their feet carelessly in the water of the steps I tried so hard to keep clean—get a wild, if brief, glimpse of a new scientific truth? Well, we never heard. . . .

I brooded upon whether I should have gone to the director's office and told him what had happened, but each time I thought of it I remembered that the director had been the man who had ordered the boy to stand over me while I was working and time my movements with a stop watch. He did not regard me as a human being. I did not share his world. I earned thirteen dollars a week and I had to support four people with it, and should I risk that thirteen dollars by acting idealistically? Brand and Cooke would have hated me and would have eventually driven me from the job had I "told" on them. The hospital kept us four Negroes as though we were close kin to the animals we tended, huddled together down in the underworld corridors of the hospital, separated by a vast psychological distance from the significant processes of the rest of the hospital—just as America had kept us locked in the dark underworld of

American life for three hundred years—and we had made our own code of ethics, values, loyalty.

Study and Discussion Questions

1. How many jobs does the narrator tell us about in "The Man Who Went to Chicago"? List and briefly describe each one.
2. What does the narrator learn (a) about himself and (b) about the world he lives in from each job experience?
3. One of the more insidious consequences of oppression is the way it affects the behavior and self-image of those who are oppressed. List examples Wright gives us of this phenomenon in "The Man Who Went to Chicago."
4. What insight does the narrator come to in the relief station?
5. What motivates the narrator in each case to (a) quit Hoffman's, (b) work as an insurance agent, and (c) keep quiet about the laboratory mishap?
6. What do the dogs without vocal cords symbolize?

Writing Exercises

1. How do you think a white person's work experiences would have been similar to and different from those of Wright's narrator?
2. List at least three aspects of Wright's criticism of white Americans' treatment of black Americans. Find evidence from "The Man Who Went to Chicago" to support each of your points.
3. Write about a job experience of your own in which you felt exploited, frustrated, and/or misunderstood.

AGNES SMEDLEY (1892–1950)

Agnes Smedley grew up in rural Missouri and in Colorado mining towns. She attended grade school, left home at a young age, worked at a variety of jobs, and studied for a year at a normal school in Arizona. In her twenties, she moved to New York City, and then to Germany, and became involved in a variety of political causes, including the birth control and India independence movements. In 1928 Smedley went to China as a correspondent for a German newspaper and traveled there covering the revolution until 1941, when illness forced her to return to the United States. Harassed by the FBI and others for her sympathies for the Chinese revolution, Smedley moved to England in 1949. Her books include Daughter of Earth *(1929), an autobiographical novel;* Chinese Destinies *(1933); and* Battle Hymn of China *(1943).*

Silk Workers   (1943)

Just as I arrived in Canton in the hot summer months of 1930, another General was killed by his bodyguard for the sake of the fifty Chinese dollars offered by a rival General. Such events had begun to strike me as sardonic. The Kwangtung Provincial Government was semi-independent, but in the hands of generals who took by violence what they considered their share in the loot of the south. They whirled around the city in bullet-proof cars with armed bodyguards standing on the running boards. Such was the spirit of the generals and of the officials whom they brought to power with them.

I interviewed them all and put no stock in what they said. They treated me magnificently, for foreign journalists seldom or never went south in the hot summer months. So I had a Government launch to myself, with an official guide to show me factories, paved roads, new waterworks and the Sun Yat-sen Memorial Hall. For truth I depended on Chinese university professors, an occasional newspaper reporter or editor, teachers and writers, the German Consul in Canton—and on my own eyes and ears.

The real reason I went south in the hottest part of the year was to study the lot of the millions of "silk peasants" in a silk industry which was rapidly losing its American markets to Japanese magnates. But I did not wish to see the silk regions as a guest of the powerful Canton Silk Guild, for the Guild, after all, was like a big laughing Buddha, naked to the waist, his fat belly hanging over his pajama belt. At last I found a group of Lingnan Christian University professors who were engaged in research in the industry. One young expert was leaving for the Shuntek silk region for a six weeks' inspection tour. I went with him to the Canton Silk Guild, where he argued with a suspicious Guild official until given permission to travel on Guild river steamers and enter the region in which millions of peasants toiled. There the millionaires of the South Seas had erected many large filatures; the spinners were all young women.

Next day the young expert and I boarded a river steamer. Some twenty or thirty Guild merchants were the only other passengers. The steamers had armor plating and machine-guns to protect the merchants from "bandits." The "bandits," I learned, were peasants who took to the highway for a part of each year in order to earn a living.

I once calculated that, if these "bandits" had attacked and captured our steamer, they would have secured enough food to feed a whole village for months. At meal times the merchants hunched over the tables, eating gargantuan meals and dropping the chicken bones on the floor. They talked of silk, money, markets, and of how much their firms were losing. The silk industry was indeed fighting for its life, but if there were losses, it clearly did not come out of the hides of these men. I pined a little for Jesse James.

My young escort was awed by these men, but when he spoke of the silk peasants or the girl filature workers, hostility and contempt crept into his voice. His particular hatred seemed to be the thousands of women spinners, and only with difficulty could I learn why. He told me that the women were notorious throughout China as Lesbians. They refused to marry, and if their families forced them, they merely bribed their husbands with a part of their wages and induced them to take concubines. The most such a married girl would do was bear one son; then she would return to the factory, refusing to live with her husband any longer. The Government had just issued a decree forbidding women to escape from marriage by bribery, but the women ignored it.

"They're too rich—that's the root of the trouble!" my young escort explained. "They earn as much as eleven dollars a month, and become proud and contemptuous." He added that on this money they also supported parents, brothers and sisters, and grandparents. "They squander their money!" he cried. "I have never gone to a picture theater without seeing groups of them sitting together, holding hands."

Until 1927, when they were forbidden, there had been Communist cells and trade unions in the filatures, he charged, and now these despicable girls evaded the law by forming secret "Sister Societies." They had even dared strike for shorter hours and higher wages. Now and then two or three girls would commit suicide together because their families were forcing them to marry.

For weeks my escort and I went by foot or small boat from village to village, from market town to market town. The fierce sun beat down upon us until our clothing clung to our bodies like a surgeon's glove and the perspiration wilted our hat bands and our shoes. At night we took rooms in village inns or pitched our camp beds under mosquito nets in family temples. All the roads and paths were lined with half-naked peasants bending low under huge baskets of cocoons swung from the ends of bamboo poles. Market towns reeked with the cocoons and hanks of raw silk piled up to the rafters in the warehouses. Every village was a mass of trays on which the silkworms fed, tended night and day by gaunt careworn peasants who went about naked to the waist.

At first curiously, then with interest, my escort began to translate for me as I questioned the peasants on their life and work. Their homes were bare huts with earthen floors, and the bed was a board covered by an old mat and surrounded by a cotton cloth, once white, which served as a mosquito net. There was usually a small clay stove with a cooking utensil or two, a narrow bench, and sometimes an ancient, scarred table. For millions this was home. A few owned several mulberry trees—for wealth was reckoned in trees. But almost all had sold their cocoon crops in advance in order to get money or food. If the crop failed, they were the losers. Wherever we traveled the story was the same: the silk peasants were held in pawn by the merchants and were never free from debt.

Only as we neared big market towns, in which silk filatures belched forth the stench of cocoons, did we come upon better homes and fewer careworn faces. The daughters of such families were spinners. It was then that I began to see what industrialism, bad as it had seemed elsewhere, meant to the working girls. These were the only places in the whole country where the birth of a baby girl was an occasion for joy, for here girls were the main support of their families. Consciousness of their worth was reflected in their dignified independent bearing. I began to understand the charges that they were Lesbians. They could not but compare the dignity of their positions with the low position of married women. Their independence seemed a personal affront to officialdom.

The hatred of my escort for these girls became more marked when we visited the filatures. Long lines of them, clad in glossy black jackets and trousers, sat before boiling vats of cocoons, their parboiled fingers twinkling among the spinning filaments. Sometimes a remark passed along their lines set a whole mill laughing. The face of my escort would grow livid.

"They call me a running dog of the capitalists, and you a foreign devil of an imperialist! They are laughing at your clothing and your hair and eyes!" he explained.

One evening the two of us sat at the entrance of an old family temple in the empty stone halls of which we had pitched our netted camp cots. On the other side of the canal rose the high walls of a filature, which soon began pouring forth black-clad girl workers, each with her tin dinner pail. All wore wooden sandals which were fastened by a single leather strap across the toes and which clattered as they walked. Their glossy black hair was combed back and hung in a heavy braid to the waist. At the nape of the neck the braid was caught in red yarn, making a band two or three inches wide—a lovely splash of color.

As they streamed in long lines over the bridge arching the canal and past the temple entrance, I felt I had never seen more handsome women.

I urged my young escort to interpret for me, but he refused, saying he did not understand their dialect. He was so irritated that he rose and walked toward the town. When he was gone, I went down the steps. A group of girls gathered around me and stared. I offered them some of my malt candy. There was a flash of white teeth and exclamations in a sharp staccato dialect. They took the candy, began chewing, then examined my clothing and stared at my hair and eyes. I did the same with them and soon we were laughing at each other.

Two of them linked their arms in mine and began pulling me down the flagstone street. Others followed, chattering happily. We entered the home of one girl and were welcomed by her father and mother and two big-eyed little brothers. Behind them the small room was already filled with other girls and curious neighbors. A candle burned in the center of a square table surrounded by crowded benches. I was seated in the place of honor and served the conventional cup of tea.

Then a strange conversation began. Even had I known the most perfect Mandarin, I could not have understood these girls, for their speech was different from that spoken in any other part of the country. I had studied Chinese spasmodically—in Manchuria, in Peking, in Shanghai—but each time, before I had more than begun, I had had to move on to new fields, and all that I had previously learned became almost useless. Shanghai had its own dialect, and what I had learned there aroused laughter in Peking and was utterly useless in the south. Only missionaries and consular officials could afford to spend a year in the Peking Language School. Journalists had to be here, there, and everywhere.

I therefore talked with the filature girls in signs and gestures. Did I have any children, they asked, pointing to the children. No? Not married either? They seemed interested and surprised. In explanation I unclamped my fountain pen, took a notebook from my pocket, tried to make a show of thinking, looked them over critically, and began to write. There was great excitement.

A man standing near the door asked me something in Mandarin and I was able to understand him. I was an American, a reporter, he told the crowded room. Yes, I was an intellectual—but was once a worker. When he interpreted this, they seemed to find it very hard to believe.

Girls crowded the benches and others stood banked behind them. Using my few words of Mandarin and many gestures, I learned that some of them earned eight or nine dollars a month, a few eleven. They worked ten hours a day—not eight, as my escort had said. Once they had worked fourteen.

My language broke down, so I supplemented it with crude pictures in my notebook. How did they win the ten-hour day? I drew a sketch of a filature with a big fat man standing on top laughing, then a second picture of the same with the fat man weeping because a row of girls stood holding hands all around the mill. They chattered over these drawings, then a girl shouted two words and all of them began to demonstrate a strike. They crossed their arms, as though refusing to work, while some rested their elbows on the table and lowered their heads, as though refusing to move. They laughed, began to link hands, and drew me into this circle. We all stood holding hands in an unbroken line, laughing. Yes, that was how they got the ten-hour day!

As we stood there, one girl suddenly began to sing in a high sweet voice. Just as suddenly she halted. The whole room chanted an answer. Again and again she sang a question and they replied, while I stood, excited, made desperate by the fact that I could not understand.

The strange song ended and they began to demand something of me. They wanted a song! The *Marseillaise* came to mind, and I sang it. They shouted for more and I tried the *Internationale*, watching carefully for any reaction. They did not recognize it at all. So, I thought, it isn't true that these girls had Communist cells!

A slight commotion spread through the room, and I saw that a man stood in the doorway holding a flute in his hand. He put it to his lips and it began to murmur softly. Then the sound soared and the high sweet voice of the girl singer followed. She paused. The flute soared higher and a man's voice joined it. He was telling some tale, and when he paused, the girl's voice answered. It was surely some ballad, some ancient song of the people, for it had in it the universal quality of folk-music.

In this way I spent an evening with people whose tongue I could not speak, and when I returned to my temple, many went with me, one lighting our way with a swinging lantern. I passed through the silent stone courtyards to my room and my bed. And throughout the night the village watchman beat his brass gong, crying the hours. His gong sounded first from a distance, passed the temple wall, and receded again, saying to the world that all was well.

I lay thinking of ancient things . . . of the common humanity, the goodness and unity of the common people of all lands.

Study and Discussion Questions

1. Compare the picture the "young expert" paints of the silk workers with what Smedley learns about them herself.
2. What does the expert mean when he says, "They're too rich—that's the root of the trouble"? How do doing important work and earning money shape the lives of these young women?
3. Why does Smedley take time to discuss the feuding generals, the young expert, and the silk merchants before getting to the heart of her story, meeting the silk workers?

Writing Exercises

1. What can we infer about Agnes Smedley from "Silk Workers"?
2. What can we infer about life in China in 1930 from this small glimpse?
3. Imagine a situation in your own society where a certain type of work that women usually do was recognized as essential to the economic well-being of the community. How might the lives of such women workers be different?

MONEY AND WORK: PAPER TOPICS

1. Discuss one or more works that deal with the experience of unemployment. Take into account and discuss the significance of social factors such as gender and historical context such as the Great Depression.

(Suggestions: Kromer, *Waiting for Nothing*; LeSueur, "Women on the Breadlines")

2. Discuss one or more works that depict work as a positive experience. What does the work depicted in them have in common? (Suggestions: Traven, "Assembly Line"; Smith, "The Bowl"; Frost, "Two Tramps in Mud Time")

3. Discuss one or more works that depict work as a problematic experience. What does the work depicted in them have in common? (Suggestions: Lawrence, "City Life"; Wright, "The Man Who Went to Chicago"; Roethke, "Dolor")

4. Discuss one or more works that explore the impact on the family of the need to make money. (Suggestions: Miller, *Death of a Salesman*; Olsen, "I Stand Here Ironing")

5. Discuss one or more works that explore the relationship between having money (and what money can buy) and individual self-image. (Suggestions: Smedley, "The Silk Workers"; Bambara, "The Lesson"; Hardy, "The Ruined Maid")

6. Discuss one or more works that dramatize encounters between individuals of different social classes. (Suggestions: Chute, "Tall Woman Love"; Brooks, "Bronzeville Woman in a Red Hat"; Childress, *Florence*; Walker, "Everyday Use")

7. There are many familiar sayings about work: "Many hands make light work"; "Man may work from sun to sun, but woman's work is never done"; "Work builds character"; and so on. Choose any such saying about work and show how a piece of writing in this section illustrates or disputes it.

8. Compare the kinds of work available to men and to women and discuss the consequences of the difference. You might, for example, look at Pitter, "Yorkshire Wife's Saga" and Phyllis McGinley, "View from a Suburban Window."

9. Discuss the relation between money and work in one or more writings. (Suggestions: Faulkner, "Spotted Horses"; Frost, "Two Tramps in Mud Time"; Traven, "Assembly Line")

10. Describe a day at work at either a job you liked or one you disliked. Write your description so that your overall attitude toward the job is clear in the details.

11. What images are used to present work, or workers, or the relation between them? Select one poem, story, play, or work of nonfiction and analyze it in detail, or else compare/contrast two or more works. (Suggestions: Grahn, "Ella, in a square apron on Highway 80"; LeSueur, "Women on the Breadlines")

PEACE AND WAR

The *Oxford English Dictionary* defines war as "hostile contention by means of armed forces, carried on between nations, states, or rulers, or between parties in the same nation or state." It defines peace as "freedom from, or cessation of, war or hostilities; that condition of a nation or community in which it is not at war with another."

It says something about the way we perceive the world and its possibilities that we define peace as the absence of war rather than war as the absence of peace. Apparently we think of war and conflict as more normal, or perhaps more interesting, than peace. Similarly, we often view narrative forms of literature like fiction and drama in terms of the initiation, acting out and resolution of conflict. It appears that we are more interested in and at home with conflict, stress, and tension than with serenity, stability, and peace. The literature about peace and war in this section reflects the fact that war as a subject has been written about far more often than peace. Peace appears to be a condition we take for granted or see, as dictionary definitions of the word suggest, as an absence of activity, as a negative state.

Yet peace, like a good marriage, takes work. "The planet is now as difficult to maintain as an intimate relationship," says a character in Marc Kaminsky's play *In the Traffic of a Targeted City*. In this view, peace is not static but active. The maintenance of peace requires positive effort. It is not achieved by neglect. It is a presence, not an absence. Perhaps if we changed our definitions of *peace* and *war*, conceptualizing and speaking about them differently, we might also begin to live those states of being differently.

"Nothing we do has the quickness, the sureness,/ the deep intelligence living at peace would have," writes Denise Levertov in her poem, "Life at War." War is stupid, slow, ungraceful. Certainly it is a breakdown of community and communication. Can we go so far as to say it is a form of social insanity? Many of the writers included in this section focus on the chaos of war, some portraying the nightmare of battle itself, as Black Elk does in "The Butchery at Wounded Knee" or as Wilfred Owen does in "Dulce et Decorum Est." Others look at the cost of war, at the wreckage of human lives in war's aftermath. Siegfried Sassoon's poem "Does It Matter?" and the excerpts from Ron Kovic's autobiographical *Born on the Fourth of July* and Marguerite Duras' *The War: A Memoir* are all concerned with people coming home from war, with those who are wounded not only physically, but psychologically and spiritually as well. Louise Erdrich's "The Red Convertible" offers an example of what used to be called "shellshock" and has come to be known, since the Vietnam War, as "post traumatic stress disorder." Research into this condition has shown that post traumatic stress disorder is also exactly what victims of rape and child abuse suffer. Is family life for a child or an ordinary city street for a woman potentially a war zone? Though the literature in this section does not take it up directly, this connection with child abuse and rape suggests that war is one end of a spectrum of institutionalized and sanctioned violence that has devastating consequences for human beings.

An issue the drama, prose, and poetry in this section does address very directly is the effect of war on civilian populations, as in Yōko Ōta's story, "Fireflies," and parts of Marc Kaminsky's *In the Traffic of a Targeted City*, both about the consequences of the atomic bombing of Hiroshima and Nagasaki. Donald Bartheleme's short story, "Report," uses chaos and disorder to satirize the reasoning, and its technological manifestations, of those who work for those who make war, while Henry Reed pushes order to its limits in "Naming of Parts," his satiric poem on boot camp training in weapons handling. And Ray Bradbury's elegiac science fiction story, "August 2026: There Will Come Soft Rains," tells of the gradual breakdown of a completely mechanized house, the only structure left standing after an atomic blast.

How do people deal with the memory of war and make the transition from war to peace? Lyman Lamartine, in "The Red Convertible," frantically tries to give his Vietnam veteran brother Henry some postwar purpose by providing him with an old car to restore. Rudyard Kipling points out in his 1890 poem "Tommy" that people often don't treat a soldier very well once the war is over. And finally, a New England village memorializes the American Civil War in Sara Orne Jewett's story, "Decoration Day."

Even in the midst of the inhumanity and insanity of war there are moments of human contact, peace, security, and beauty. Yevgeny Yevtushenko's poem "The Companion" tells how two children in the Soviet Union join together in 1941 to escape the German bombs. Though war is the setting of this poem, the subject is what the children learn from and about each other, about being male and female, about themselves, and about the strength of the human spirit. Babette Deutsch's poem "Dawn in Wartime" contrasts the speaker's memory of the day before, the "burned sore scabby face/ of the world," with what he now sees, the "immense marvel of morning/ rolling toward him all its uncreated hours."

Who suffers from war? Who profits? Marge Piercy's poem "The nine of cups" and Bertolt Brecht's "From a German War Primer" suggest that war and business are two aspects of the same phenomenon. "We fight and we die," Piercy writes, "for God, country and the dollar." Certainly it isn't the ordinary person who is profiting from war. Brecht remarks: "Among the conquered the common people / Starved. Among the conquerors / The common people starved too." In his 1967 speech "A Time to Break Silence," Martin Luther King, Jr. observes that the United States has been sending its poor, both black and white, to fight the poor in Southeast Asia. He speaks of "the cruel irony of watching Negro and white boys on TV screens as they kill and die together for a nation that has been unable to seat them together in the same schools. So we watch them in brutal solidarity burning the huts of a poor village. . . ."

Why do nations and the individuals in them go to war? Is it for patriotism and a dream of heroism, for glory and honor, as in Tennyson's

"The Charge of the Light Brigade"? Is it out of social responsibility and the joy of battle, as in the Papago Indian "War Song"? Or is it, as Yeats suggests in "An Irish Airman Foresees His Death," neither hate of the enemy nor love of country but a "lonely impulse of delight/ Drove to this tumult in the skies"? Wilfred Owen, in his World War I poem, "Dulce et Decorum Est," vividly contrasts the actual horror of war to the dreams of "desperate glory" on which children, especially young boys, are raised. Owen quotes the Roman poet Horace's phrase, "dulce et decorum est/ pro patria mori" (it is sweet and proper to die for one's country), and shows it to be a dangerous lie. Bob Dylan, in his protest song "With God on Our Side," suggests that we question our history books, which tell us that it is right (since God is with us) for Americans to die and to kill for our country. Not only the history books but much American popular culture has presented war as a glorious adventure justified by love of God and country, as those of us brought up on John Wayne movies can attest.

The drama, prose, and poetry in "Peace and War" range from Whitman's and Emerson's nostalgic memories of the American Revolution in "The Dying Veteran" and "Concord Hymn" respectively, through Ambrose Bierce's strange and haunting "An Occurrence at Owl Creek Bridge" set during the American Civil War to Black Elk's searing memory of the massacre at Wounded Knee. The literature spans the First and Second World Wars and their aftermath from British, American, Russian, Japanese and German perspectives; it includes portrayals of the Vietnam War and its repercussions. Among the other works are Bradbury's fantasy of a nuclear war, which might usefully be compared with accounts of the consequences of an actual nuclear attack, and Carolyn Forché's terrifying and surreal prose poem, "The Colonel," about a contemporary Central American military dictator. The perspectives on war that this literature offers range from glorification of wars past, through realistic accounts of the actual devastating experience of war for both soldiers and civilians, to antiwar protest literature. The mood ranges from nostalgia through horror and grief to very dark humor.

Reading about war can provoke an intense longing for peace. How can we think and live peace actively? How can we learn to see peace as a presence, not an absence? "I want strong peace, and delight,/ the wild good," writes Muriel Rukeyser in "Waking This Morning."

> today once more
> I will try to be non-violent
> one more day
> this morning, waking the world away
> in the violent day.

Nonviolence is a complex state of being we have to work at day by day, implies Rukeyser, and peace is something we have to make, the way we make bread or poetry or love.

FICTION

RAY BRADBURY   (b. 1920)

Born in Waukegan, Illinois, Ray Bradbury moved during his high school years to Los Angeles and has spent most of his life there. He began writing science fiction and fantasy stories for "pulp" magazines and his reputation grew after World War II, especially with the publication in 1950 of his collection, The Martian Chronicles. *He has written poetry, drama, and fiction of various kinds, but is best known for his science fiction, including the novels* Fahrenheit 451 *(1953) and* Something Wicked This Way Comes *(1962) and the story collections* The Illustrated Man *(1951) and* I Sing the Body Electric! *(1969).*

August 2026: There Will Come Soft Rains
(1950)

In the living room the voice-clock sang, *Tick-tock, seven o'clock, time to get up, time to get up, seven o'clock!* as if it were afraid that nobody would. The morning house lay empty. The clock ticked on, repeating and repeating its sounds into the emptiness. *Seven-nine, breakfast time, seven-nine!*

In the kitchen the breakfast stove gave a hissing sigh and ejected from its warm interior eight pieces of perfectly browned toast, eight eggs sunnyside up, sixteen slices of bacon, two coffees, and two cool glasses of milk.

"Today is August 4, 2026," said a second voice from the kitchen ceiling, "in the city of Allendale, California." It repeated the date three times for memory's sake. "Today is Mr. Featherstone's birthday. Today is the anniversary of Tilita's marriage. Insurance is payable, as are the water, gas, and light bills."

Somewhere in the walls, relays clicked, memory tapes glided under electric eyes.

Eight-one, tick-tock, eight-one o'clock, off to school, off to work, run, run, eight-one! But no doors slammed, no carpets took the soft tread of rubber heels. It was raining outside. The weather box on the front door sang quietly: "Rain, rain, go away; rubbers, raincoats for today . . ." And the rain tapped on the empty house, echoing.

Outside, the garage chimed and lifted its door to reveal the waiting car. After a long wait the door swung down again.

At eight-thirty the eggs were shriveled and the toast was like stone. An aluminum wedge scraped them into the sink, where hot water whirled them down a metal throat which digested and flushed them away to the distant sea. The dirty dishes were dropped into a hot washer and emerged twinkling dry.

Nine-fifteen, sang the clock, *time to clean.*

Out of warrens in the wall, tiny robot mice darted. The rooms were acrawl with the small cleaning animals, all rubber and metal. They thudded against chairs, whirling their mustached runners, kneading the rug nap, sucking gently at hidden dust. Then, like mysterious invaders, they popped into their burrows. Their pink electric eyes faded. The house was clean.

Ten o'clock. The sun came out from behind the rain. The house stood alone in a city of rubble and ashes. This was the one house left standing. At night the ruined city gave off a radioactive glow which could be seen for miles.

Ten-fifteen. The garden sprinklers whirled up in golden founts, filling the soft morning air with scatterings of brightness. The water pelted windowpanes, running down the charred west side where the house had been burned evenly free of its white paint. The entire west face of the house was black, save for five places. Here the silhouette in paint of a man mowing a lawn. Here, as in a photograph, a woman bent to pick flowers. Still farther over, their images burned on wood in one titanic instant, a small boy, hands flung into the air; higher up, the image of a thrown ball, and opposite him a girl, hands raised to catch a ball which never came down.

The five spots of paint—the man, the woman, the children, the ball—remained. The rest was a thin charcoaled layer.

The gentle sprinkler rain filled the garden with falling light.

Until this day, how well the house had kept its peace. How carefully it had inquired, "Who goes there? What's the password?" and, getting no answer from lonely foxes and whining cats, it had shut up its windows and drawn shades in an old-maidenly preoccupation with self-protection which bordered on a mechanical paranoia.

It quivered at each sound, the house did. If a sparrow brushed a window, the shade snapped up. The bird, startled, flew off! No, not even a bird must touch the house!

The house was an altar with ten thousand attendants, big, small, servicing, attending, in choirs. But the gods had gone away, and the ritual of the religion continued senselessly, uselessly.

Twelve noon.

A dog whined, shivering, on the front porch.

The front door recognized the dog voice and opened. The dog, once huge and fleshy, but now gone to bone and covered with sores, moved in and through the house, tracking mud. Behind it whirred angry mice, angry at having to pick up mud, angry at inconvenience.

For not a leaf fragment blew under the door but what the wall panels flipped open and the copper scrap rats flashed swiftly out. The offending dust, hair, or paper, seized in miniature steel jaws, was raced back to the burrows. There, down tubes which fed into the cellar, it was dropped into the sighing vent of an incinerator which sat like evil Baal in a dark corner.

The dog ran upstairs, hysterically yelping to each door, at last realizing, as the house realized, that only silence was here.

It sniffed the air and scratched the kitchen door. Behind the door, the stove was making pancakes which filled the house with a rich baked odor and the scent of maple syrup.

The dog frothed at the mouth, lying at the door, sniffing, its eyes turned to fire. It ran wildly in circles, biting at its tail, spun in a frenzy, and died. It lay in the parlor for an hour.

Two o'clock, sang a voice.

Delicately sensing decay at last, the regiments of mice hummed out as softly as blown gray leaves in an electrical wind.

Two-fifteen.

The dog was gone.

In the cellar, the incinerator glowed suddenly and a whirl of sparks leaped up the chimney.

Two thirty-five.

Bridge tables sprouted from patio walls. Playing cards fluttered onto pads in a shower of pips. Martinis manifested on an oaken bench with egg-salad sandwiches. Music played.

But the tables were silent and the cards untouched.

At four o'clock the tables folded like great butterflies back through the paneled walls.

Four-thirty.

The nursery walls glowed.

Animals took shape: yellow giraffes, blue lions, pink antelopes, lilac panthers cavorting in crystal substance. The walls were glass. They looked out upon color and fantasy. Hidden films clocked through well-oiled sprockets, and the walls lived. The nursery floor was woven to resemble a crisp, cereal meadow. Over this ran aluminum roaches and iron crickets, and in the hot still air butterflies of delicate red tissue wavered among the sharp aroma of animal spoors! There was the sound like a great matted yellow hive of bees within a dark bellows, the lazy bumble of a purring lion. And there was the patter of okapi feet and the murmur of a fresh jungle rain, like other hoofs, falling upon the summer-starched grass. Now the walls dissolved into distances of parched weed, mile on mile, and warm endless sky. The animals drew away into thorn brakes and water holes.

It was the children's hour.

Five o'clock. The bath filled with clear hot water.

Six, seven, eight o'clock. The dinner dishes manipulated like magic tricks, and in the study a click. In the metal stand opposite the hearth where a fire now blazed up warmly, a cigar popped out, half an inch of soft gray ash on it, smoking, waiting.

Nine o'clock. The beds warmed their hidden circuits, for nights were cool here.

Nine-five. A voice spoke from the study ceiling:

"Mrs. McClellan, which poem would you like this evening?"

The house was silent.

The voice said at last, "Since you express no preference, I shall select a poem at random." Quiet music rose to back the voice. "Sara Teasdale.[1] As I recall, your favorite. . . ."

"There will come soft rains and the smell of the ground,
And swallows circling with their shimmering sound;

And frogs in the pools singing at night,
And wild plum trees in tremulous white;

Robins will wear their feathery fire,
Whistling their whims on a low fence-wire;

And not one will know of the war, not one
Will care at last when it is done.

Not one would mind, neither bird nor tree,
If mankind perished utterly;

And Spring herself, when she woke at dawn
Would scarcely know that we were gone."

The fire burned on the stone hearth and the cigar fell away into a mound of quiet ash on its tray. The empty chairs faced each other between the silent walls, and the music played.

At ten o'clock the house began to die.

The wind blew. A falling tree bough crashed through the kitchen window. Cleaning solvent, bottled, shattered over the stove. The room was ablaze in an instant!

"Fire!" screamed a voice. The house lights flashed, water pumps shot water from the ceilings. But the solvent spread on the linoleum, licking,

---

[1] (1884–1933), American poet.

eating, under the kitchen door, while the voices took it up in chorus: "Fire, fire, fire!"

The house tried to save itself. Doors sprang tightly shut, but the windows were broken by the heat and the wind blew and sucked upon the fire.

The house gave ground as the fire in ten billion angry sparks moved with flaming ease from room to room and then up the stairs. While scurrying water rats squeaked from the walls, pistoled their water, and ran for more. And the wall sprays let down showers of mechanical rain.

But too late. Somewhere, sighing, a pump shrugged to a stop. The quenching rain ceased. The reserve water supply which had filled baths and washed dishes for many quiet days was gone.

The fire crackled up the stairs. It fed upon Picassos and Matisses in the upper halls, like delicacies, baking off the oily flesh, tenderly crisping the canvases into black shavings.

Now the fire lay in beds, stood in windows, changed the colors of drapes!

And then, reinforcements.

From attic trapdoors, blind robot faces peered down with faucet mouths gushing green chemical.

The fire backed off, as even an elephant must at the sight of a dead snake. Now there were twenty snakes whipping over the floor, killing the fire with a clear cold venom of green froth.

But the fire was clever. It had sent flame outside the house, up through the attic to the pumps there. An explosion! The attic brain which directed the pumps was shattered into bronze shrapnel on the beams.

The fire rushed back into every closet and felt of the clothes hung there.

The house shuddered, oak bone on bone, its bared skeleton cringing from the heat, its wire, its nerves revealed as if a surgeon had torn the skin off to let the red veins and capillaries quiver in the scalded air. Help, help! Fire! Run, run! Heat snapped mirrors like the first brittle winter ice. And the voices wailed Fire, fire, run, run, like a tragic nursery rhyme, a dozen voices, high, low, like children dying in a forest, alone, alone. And the voices fading as the wires popped their sheathings like hot chestnuts. One, two, three, four, five voices died.

In the nursery the jungle burned. Blue lions roared, purple giraffes bounded off. The panthers ran in circles, changing color, and ten million animals, running before the fire, vanished off toward a distant steaming river. . . .

Ten more voices died. In the last instant under the fire avalanche, other choruses, oblivious, could be heard announcing the time, playing music, cutting the lawn by remote-control mower, or setting an umbrella frantically out and in the slamming and opening front door, a thousand things happening, like a clock shop when each clock strikes the hour insanely before or after the other, a scene of maniac confusion, yet unity; singing, screaming, a few last cleaning mice darting bravely out to carry the horrid ashes away! And one voice, with sublime disregard for the situation, read poetry aloud in the fiery study, until all the film spools burned, until all the wires withered and the circuits cracked.

The fire burst the house and let it slam flat down, puffing out skirts of spark and smoke.

In the kitchen, an instant before the rain of fire and timber, the stove could be seen making breakfasts at a psychopathic rate, ten dozen eggs, six loaves of toast, twenty dozen bacon strips, which, eaten by fire, started the stove working again, hysterically hissing!

The crash. The attic smashing into kitchen and parlor. The parlor into cellar, cellar into sub-cellar. Deep freeze, armchair, film tapes, circuits, beds, and all like skeletons thrown in a cluttered mound deep under.

Smoke and silence. A great quantity of smoke.

Dawn showed faintly in the east. Among the ruins, one wall stood alone. Within the wall, a last voice said, over and over again and again, even as the sun rose to shine upon the heaped rubble and steam:

"Today is August 5, 2026, today is August 5, 2026, today is. . . ."

Study and Discussion Questions

1. Think about the Sara Teasdale poem that gives the story its title. How does it apply to the situation the story narrates?
2. Who is the main character of this story?
3. Summarize the story's plot. What does Bradbury use to move you from one event to the next?
4. Though there are no actual human beings in this story, list some of the traces or evidence of people.
5. What can this house do? What can't it do?

Writing Exercises

1. This is a rare example of a story without any human beings in it. How is that absence necessary to the meaning of this story?
2. Write about the significance and use of time in the story.
3. Bradbury writes: "The house was an altar with ten thousand attendants, big, small, servicing, attending, in choirs. But the gods had gone away, and the ritual of the religion continued senselessly, uselessly." Discuss this passage as a comment on our current relation to science and technology.

AMBROSE BIERCE (1842–1914?)

Ambrose Bierce was born in rural Meigs County, Ohio, worked as a printer's apprentice, and had only a year of formal education. After serving in the

*Union army in the Civil War, he moved to San Francisco, where he became
a well-known journalist. In 1897, he went to Washington, DC as a newspaper
correspondent and in 1913 left for Mexico, where he disappeared. His writing
includes* Tales of Soldiers and Civilians *(1891) and* The Cynic's Word Book
(1906), later retitled The Devil's Dictionary *(1911).*

An Occurrence at Owl Creek Bridge   (1892)

I

A man stood upon a railroad bridge in northern Alabama, looking down
into the swift water twenty feet below. The man's hands were behind
his back, the wrists bound with a cord. A rope closely encircled his neck.
It was attached to a stout cross-timber above his head and the slack fell
to the level of his knees. Some loose boards laid upon the sleepers
supporting the metals of the railway supplied a footing for him and his
executioners—two private soldiers of the Federal army, directed by a
sergeant who in civil life may have been a deputy sheriff. At a short
remove upon the same temporary platform was an officer in the uniform
of his rank, armed. He was a captain. A sentinel at each end of the bridge
stood with his rifle in the position known as "support," that is to say,
vertical in front of the left shoulder, the hammer resting on the forearm
thrown straight across the chest—a formal and unnatural position, enforcing an erect carriage of the body. It did not appear to be the duty of
these two men to know what was occurring at the centre of the bridge;
they merely blockaded the two ends of the foot planking that traversed
it.

Beyond one of the sentinels nobody was in sight; the railroad ran
straight away into a forest for a hundred yards, then, curving, was lost
to view. Doubtless there was an outpost farther along. The other bank
of the stream was open ground—a gentle acclivity topped with a stockade
of vertical tree trunks, loopholed for rifles, with a single embrasure through
which protruded the muzzle of a brass cannon commanding the bridge.
Midway of the slope between bridge and fort were the spectators—a
single company of infantry in line, at "parade rest," the butts of the rifles
on the ground, the barrels inclining slightly backward against the right
shoulder, the hands crossed upon the stock. A lieutenant stood at the
right of the line, the point of his sword upon the ground, his left hand
resting upon his right. Excepting the group of four at the centre of the
bridge, not a man moved. The company faced the bridge, staring stonily,
motionless. The sentinels, facing the banks of the stream, might have
been statues to adorn the bridge. The captain stood with folded arms,
silent, observing the work of his subordinates, but making no sign. Death

is a dignitary who when he comes announced is to be received with formal manifestations of respect, even by those most familiar with him. In the code of military etiquette silence and fixity are forms of deference.

The man who was engaged in being hanged was apparently about thirty-five years of age. He was a civilian, if one might judge from his habit, which was that of a planter. His features were good—a straight nose, firm mouth, broad forehead, from which his long, dark hair was combed straight back, falling behind his ears to the collar of his well-fitting frock-coat. He wore a mustache and pointed beard, but no whiskers; his eyes were large and dark gray, and had a kindly expression which one would hardly have expected in one whose neck was in the hemp. Evidently this was no vulgar assassin. The liberal military code makes provision for hanging many kinds of persons, and gentlemen are not excluded.

The preparations being complete, the two private soldiers stepped aside and each drew away the plank upon which he had been standing. The sergeant turned to the captain, saluted and placed himself immediately behind that officer, who in turn moved apart one pace. These movements left the condemned man and the sergeant standing on the two ends of the same plank, which spanned three of the cross-ties of the bridge. The end upon which the civilian stood almost, but not quite, reached a fourth. This plank had been held in place by the weight of the captain; it was now held by that of the sergeant. At a signal from the former the latter would step aside, the plank would tilt and the condemned man go down between two ties. The arrangement commended itself to his judgment as simple and effective. His face had not been covered nor his eyes bandaged. He looked a moment at his "unsteadfast footing," then let his gaze wander to the swirling water of the stream racing madly beneath his feet. A piece of dancing driftwood caught his attention and his eyes followed it down the current. How slowly it appeared to move! What a sluggish stream!

He closed his eyes in order to fix his last thoughts upon his wife and children. The water, touched to gold by the early sun, the brooding mists under the banks at some distance down the stream, the fort, the soldiers, the piece of drift—all had distracted him. And now he became conscious of a new disturbance. Striking through the thought of his dear ones was a sound which he could neither ignore nor understand, a sharp, distinct, metallic percussion like the stroke of a blacksmith's hammer upon the anvil; it had the same ringing quality. He wondered what it was, and whether immeasurably distant or near by—it seemed both. Its recurrence was regular, but as slow as the tolling of a death knell. He awaited each stroke with impatience and—he knew not why—apprehension. The intervals of silence grew progressively longer; the delays became maddening. With their greater infrequency the sounds increased in strength and sharpness. They hurt his ear like the thrust of a knife; he feared he would shriek. What he heard was the ticking of his watch.

He unclosed his eyes and saw again the water below him. "If I could free my hands," he thought, "I might throw off the noose and spring into the stream. By diving I could evade the bullets and, swimming vigorously, reach the bank, take to the woods and get away home. My home, thank God, is as yet outside their lines; my wife and little ones are still beyond the invader's farthest advance."

As these thoughts, which have here to be set down in words, were flashed into the doomed man's brain rather than evolved from it the captain nodded to the sergeant. The sergeant stepped aside.

II

Peyton Farquhar was a well-to-do planter, of an old and highly respected Alabama family. Being a slave owner and like other slave owners a politician he was naturally an original secessionist and ardently devoted to the Southern cause. Circumstances of an imperious nature, which it is unnecessary to relate here, had prevented him from taking service with the gallant army that had fought the disastrous campaigns ending with the fall of Corinth, and he chafed under the inglorious restraint, longing for the release of his energies, the larger life of the soldier, the opportunity for distinction. That opportunity, he felt, would come, as it comes to all in war time. Meanwhile he did what he could. No service was too humble for him to perform in aid of the South, no adventure too perilous for him to undertake if consistent with the character of a civilian who was at heart a soldier, and who in good faith and without too much qualification assented to at least a part of the frankly villainous dictum that all is fair in love and war.

One evening while Farquhar and his wife were sitting on a rustic bench near the entrance to his grounds, a gray-clad soldier rode up to the gate and asked for a drink of water. Mrs. Farquhar was only too happy to serve him with her own white hands. While she was fetching the water her husband approached the dusty horseman and inquired eagerly for news from the front.

"The Yanks are repairing the railroads," said the man, "and are getting ready for another advance. They have reached the Owl Creek bridge, put it in order and built a stockade on the north bank. The commandant has issued an order, which is posted everywhere, declaring that any civilian caught interfering with the railroad, its bridges, tunnels or trains will be summarily hanged. I saw the order."

"How far is it to the Owl Creek bridge?" Farquhar asked.

"About thirty miles."

"Is there no force on this side the creek?"

"Only a picket post half a mile out, on the railroad, and a single sentinel at this end of the bridge."

"Suppose a man—a civilian and student of hanging—should elude the picket post and perhaps get the better of the sentinel," said Farquhar, smiling, "what could he accomplish?"

The soldier reflected. "I was there a month ago," he replied. "I observed that the flood of last winter had lodged a great quantity of driftwood against the wooden pier at this end of the bridge. It is now dry and would burn like tow."

The lady had now brought the water, which the soldier drank. He thanked her ceremoniously, bowed to her husband and rode away. An hour later, after nightfall, he repassed the plantation, going northward in the direction from which he had come. He was a Federal scout.

III

As Peyton Farquhar fell straight downward through the bridge he lost consciousness and was as one already dead. From this state he was awakened—ages later, it seemed to him—by the pain of a sharp pressure upon his throat, followed by a sense of suffocation. Keen, poignant agonies seemed to shoot from his neck downward through every fibre of his body and limbs. These pains appeared to flash along well-defined lines of ramification and to beat with an inconceivably rapid periodicity. They seemed like streams of pulsating fire heating him to an intolerable temperature. As to his head, he was conscious of nothing but a feeling of fulness—of congestion. These sensations were unaccompanied by thought. The intellectual part of his nature was already effaced; he had power only to feel, and feeling was torment. He was conscious of motion. Encompassed in a luminous cloud, of which he was now merely the fiery heart, without material substance, he swung through unthinkable arcs of oscillation, like a vast pendulum. Then all at once, with terrible suddenness, the light about him shot upward with the noise of a loud plash; a frightful roaring was in his ears, and all was cold and dark. The power of thought was restored; he knew that the rope had broken and he had fallen into the stream. There was no additional strangulation; the noose about his neck was already suffocating him and kept the water from his lungs. To die of hanging at the bottom of a river!—the idea seemed to him ludicrous. He opened his eyes in the darkness and saw above him a gleam of light, but how distant, how inaccessible! He was still sinking, for the light became fainter and fainter until it was a mere glimmer. Then it began to grow and brighten, and he knew that he was rising toward the surface—knew it with reluctance, for he was now very comfortable. "To be hanged and drowned," he thought, "that is not so bad; but I do not wish to be shot. No; I will not be shot; that is not fair."

He was not conscious of an effort, but a sharp pain in his wrist apprised him that he was trying to free his hands. He gave the struggle his attention, as an idler might observe the feat of a juggler, without interest in the outcome. What splendid effort!—what magnificent, what superhuman strength! Ah, that was a fine endeavor! Bravo! The cord fell away; his arms parted and floated upward, the hands dimly seen on each side in the growing light. He watched them with a new interest as first one and then the other pounced upon the noose at his neck. They tore it away and thrust it fiercely aside, its undulations resembling those of a water-snake. "Put it back, put it back!" He thought he shouted these words to his hands, for the undoing of the noose had been succeeded by the direst pang that he had yet experienced. His neck ached horribly; his brain was on fire; his heart, which had been fluttering faintly, gave a great leap, trying to force itself out at his mouth. His whole body was racked and wrenched with an insupportable anguish! But his disobedient hands gave no heed to the command. They beat the water vigorously with quick, downward strokes, forcing him to the surface. He felt his head emerge; his eyes were blinded by the sunlight; his chest expanded convulsively, and with a supreme and crowning agony his lungs engulfed a great draught of air, which instantly he expelled in a shriek!

He was now in full possession of his physical senses. They were, indeed, preternaturally keen and alert. Something in the awful disturbance of his organic system had so exalted and refined them that they made record of things never before perceived. He felt the ripples upon his face and heard their separate sounds as they struck. He looked at the forest on the bank of the stream, saw the individual trees, the leaves and the veining of each leaf—saw the very insects upon them: the locusts, the brilliant-bodied flies, the gray spiders stretching their webs from twig to twig. He noted the prismatic colors in all the dewdrops upon a million blades of grass. The humming of the gnats that danced above the eddies of the stream, the beating of the dragon-flies' wings, the strokes of the water-spiders' legs, like oars which had lifted their boat—all these made audible music. A fish slid along beneath his eyes and he heard the rush of its body parting the water.

He had come to the surface facing down the stream; in a moment the visible world seemed to wheel slowly round, himself the pivotal point, and he saw the bridge, the fort, the soldiers upon the bridge, the captain, the sergeant, the two privates, his executioners. They were in silhouette against the blue sky. They shouted and gesticulated, pointing at him. The captain had drawn his pistol, but did not fire; the others were unarmed. Their movements were grotesque and horrible, their forms gigantic.

Suddenly he heard a sharp report and something struck the water smartly within a few inches of his head, spattering his face with spray. He heard a second report, and saw one of the sentinels with his rifle at his shoulder, a light cloud of blue smoke rising from the muzzle. The man in the water saw the eye of the man on the bridge gazing into his own through the sights of the rifle. He observed that it was a gray eye and remembered having read that gray eyes were keenest, and that all famous marksmen had them. Nevertheless, this one had missed.

A counter-swirl had caught Farquhar and turned him half round; he was again looking into the forest on the bank opposite the fort. The sound of a clear, high voice in a monotonous singsong now rang out behind him and came across the water with a distinctness that pierced and subdued all other sounds, even the beating of the ripples in his ears. Although no soldier, he had frequented camps enough to know the dread significance of that deliberate, drawling, aspirated chant; the lieutenant on shore was taking a part in the morning's work. How coldly and pitilessly—with what an even, calm intonation, presaging, and enforcing tranquillity in the men—with what accurately measured intervals fell those cruel words:

"Attention, company! . . . Shoulder arms! . . . Ready! . . . Aim! . . . Fire!"

Farquhar dived—dived as deeply as he could. The water roared in his ears like the voice of Niagara, yet he heard the dulled thunder of the volley and, rising again toward the surface, met shining bits of metal, singularly flattened, oscillating slowly downward. Some of them touched him on the face and hands, then fell away, continuing their descent. One lodged between his collar and neck; it was uncomfortably warm and he snatched it out.

As he rose to the surface, gasping for breath, he saw that he had been a long time under water; he was perceptibly farther down stream—nearer to safety. The soldiers had almost finished reloading; the metal ramrods flashed all at once in the sunshine as they were drawn from the barrels, turned in the air, and thrust into their sockets. The two sentinels fired again, independently and ineffectually.

The hunted man saw all this over his shoulder; he was now swimming vigorously with the current. His brain was as energetic as his arms and legs; he thought with the rapidity of lightning.

"The officer," he reasoned, "will not make that martinet's error a second time. It is as easy to dodge a volley as a single shot. He has probably already given the command to fire at will. God help me, I cannot dodge them all!"

An appalling plash within two yards of him was followed by a loud, rushing sound, *diminuendo*, which seemed to travel back through the air to the fort and died in an explosion which stirred the very river to its deeps! A rising sheet of water curved over him, fell down upon him, blinded him, strangled him! The cannon had taken a hand in the game. As he shook his head free from the commotion of the smitten water he heard the deflected shot humming through the air ahead, and in an instant it was cracking and smashing the branches in the forest beyond.

"They will not do that again," he thought; "the next time they will use a charge of grape. I must keep my eye upon the gun; the smoke will apprise me—the report arrives too late; it lags behind the missile. That is a good gun."

Suddenly he felt himself whirled round and round—spinning like a top. The water, the banks, the forests, the now distant bridge, fort and men—all were commingled and blurred. Objects were represented by their colors only; circular horizontal streaks of color—that was all he saw. He had been caught in a vortex and was being whirled on with a velocity of advance and gyration that made him giddy and sick. In a few moments he was flung upon the gravel at the foot of the left bank of the stream— the southern bank—and behind a projecting point which concealed him from his enemies. The sudden arrest of his motion, the abrasion of one of his hands on the gravel, restored him, and he wept with delight. He dug his fingers into the sand, threw it over himself in handfuls and audibly blessed it. It looked like diamonds, rubies, emeralds; he could think of nothing beautiful which it did not resemble. The trees upon the bank were giant garden plants; he noted a definite order in their arrangement, inhaled the fragrance of their blooms. A strange, roseate light shone through the spaces among their trunks and the wind made in their branches the music of æolian harps. He had no wish to perfect his escape—was content to remain in that enchanting spot until retaken.

A whiz and rattle of grapeshot among the branches high above his head roused him from his dream. The baffled cannoneer had fired him a random farewell. He sprang to his feet, rushed up the sloping bank, and plunged into the forest.

All that day he traveled, laying his course by the rounding sun. The forest seemed interminable; nowhere did he discover a break in it, not even a woodman's road. He had not known that he lived in so wild a region. There was something uncanny in the revelation.

By nightfall he was fatigued, footsore, famishing. The thought of his wife and children urged him on. At last he found a road which led him in what he knew to be the right direction. It was as wide and straight as a city street, yet it seemed untraveled. No fields bordered it, no dwelling anywhere. Not so much as the barking of a dog suggested human habitation. The black bodies of the trees formed a straight wall on both sides, terminating on the horizon in a point, like a diagram in a lesson in perspective. Overhead, as he looked up through this rift in the wood, shone great golden stars looking unfamiliar and grouped in strange constellations. He was sure they were arranged in some order which had a secret and malign significance. The wood on either side was full of singular noises, among which—once, twice, and again—he distinctly heard whispers in an unknown tongue.

His neck was in pain and lifting his hand to it he found it horribly swollen. He knew that it had a circle of black where the rope had bruised it. His eyes felt congested; he could no longer close them. His tongue was swollen with thirst; he relieved its fever by thrusting it forward from between his teeth into the cold air. How softly the turf had carpeted the untraveled avenue—he could no longer feel the roadway beneath his feet!

Doubtless, despite his suffering, he had fallen asleep while walking, for now he sees another scene—perhaps he has merely recovered from a delirium. He stands at the gate of his own home. All is as he left it, and all bright and beautiful in the morning sunshine. He must have traveled the entire night. As he pushes open the gate and passes up the wide white walk, he sees a flutter of female garments; his wife, looking fresh and cool and sweet, steps down from the veranda to meet him. At the bottom of the steps she stands waiting, with a smile of ineffable joy, an attitude of matchless grace and dignity. Ah, how beautiful she is! He springs forward with extended arms. As he is about to clasp her he feels a stunning blow upon the back of the neck; a blinding white light blazes all about him with a sound like the shock of a cannon—then all is darkness and silence!

Peyton Farquhar was dead; his body, with a broken neck, swung gently from side to side beneath the timbers of the Owl Creek bridge.

Study and Discussion Questions

1. How does Bierce work to make us think Farquhar's imagined escape is real? What hints are there along the way that it is in fact imaginary?
2. Trace Bierce's manipulation of point of view throughout the story. What does it accomplish? Why does Bierce narrate the events leading up to the hanging in a flashback in Part II rather than at the beginning of the story?
3. Characterize the way Bierce describes the hanging proceedings in the first two paragraphs. Compare it to the way he describes Farquhar's imaginary escape. What does this contrast in style suggest?
4. Why do you think Bierce, who himself volunteered to fight on the Union side in the Civil War, makes his hero a Southern planter, a slave owner, a supporter of the Confederates? How does this choice shape the kind of statement the story makes about war?

Writing Exercises

1. One critic has argued that the story makes fun of "the orthodox war yarn in which the hero's death or survival is noble and significant." Interpret the story taking this statement as your thesis. (You might begin by reexamining the characterization of Farquhar in Part II.)
2. How would you go about making a film of this story? How would you handle the shifts in point of view, the flashback, and the imaginary nature of Farquhar's escape? (If you've seen and remember a film version, discuss how well you think it does the job.)

SARAH ORNE JEWETT   (1849–1909)

Sarah Orne Jewett was born and grew up in South Berwick, Maine, and spent most of her life there. As a young girl, she traveled with her father, a country doctor, as he called on patients. She began publishing stories and sketches in the Atlantic Monthly *and other magazines and made a name for herself with her first collection,* Deephaven *(1877). The* Country of the Pointed Firs *(1896), a novel, is considered her most important work. Among her other writings are the novel* A Country Doctor *(1884) and the story collections* A White Heron *(1886) and* A Native of Winby *(1893).*

Decoration Day   (1892)

I

A week before the thirtieth of May, three friends—John Stover and Henry Merrill and Asa Brown—happened to meet on Saturday evening at Barton's store at the Plains. They were ready to enjoy this idle hour after a busy week. After long easterly rains, the sun had at last come out bright and clear, and all the Barlow farmers had been planting. There was even a good deal of ploughing left to be done, the season was so backward.

The three middle-aged men were old friends. They had been school-fellows, and when they were hardly out of their boyhood the war came on, and they enlisted in the same company, on the same day, and happened to march away elbow to elbow. Then came the great experience of a great war, and the years that followed their return from the South had come to each almost alike. These men might have been members of the same rustic household, they knew each other's history so well.

They were sitting on a low wooden bench at the left of the store door as you went in. People were coming and going on their Saturday night errands,—the post-office was in Barton's store,—but the friends talked on eagerly, without being interrupted, except by an occasional nod of recognition. They appeared to take no notice at all of the neighbors whom they saw oftenest. It was a most beautiful evening; the two great elms were almost half in leaf over the blacksmith's shop which stood across the wide road. Farther along were two small old-fashioned houses and the old white church, with its pretty belfry of four arched sides and a tiny dome at the top. The large cockerel on the vane was pointing a little south of west, and there was still light enough to make it shine bravely against the deep blue eastern sky. On the western side of the road, near the store, were the parsonage and the storekeeper's modern house, which had a French roof and some attempt at decoration, which the long-established Barlow people called gingerbread-work, and regarded with mingled pride and disdain. These buildings made the tiny village called Barlow Plains. They stood in the middle of a long narrow strip of level ground. They were islanded by green fields and pastures. There were hills beyond; the mountains themselves seemed very near. Scattered about on the hill slopes were farmhouses, which stood so far apart, with their clusters of out-buildings, that each looked lonely, and the pine woods above seemed to besiege them all. It was lighter on the uplands than it was in the valley, where the three men sat on their bench, with their backs to the store and the western sky.

"Well, here we be 'most into June, an' I 'ain't got a bush-bean above ground," lamented Henry Merrill.

"Your land's always late, ain't it? But you always catch up with the rest on us," Asa Brown consoled him. "I've often observed that your land, though early planted, was late to sprout. I view it there's a good week's difference betwixt me an' Stover an' your folks, but come first o' July we all even up."

" 'T is just so," said John Stover, taking his pipe out of his mouth, as if he had a good deal more to say, and then replacing it, as if he had changed his mind.

"Made it extry hard having that long wet spell. Can't none on us take no day off this season," said Asa Brown; but nobody thought it worth his while to respond to such evident truth.

"Next Saturday'll be the thirtieth o' May—that's Decoration Day, ain't it?—come round again. Lord! how the years slip by after you git to be forty-five an' along there!" said Asa again. "I s'pose some o' our folks'll go over to Alton to see the procession, same's usual. I've got to git one o' them small flags to stick on our Joel's grave, an' Mis' Dexter always counts on havin' some for Harrison's lot. I calculate to get 'em somehow. I must make time to ride over, but I don't know where the time's comin' from out o' next week. I wish the women folks would tend to them things. There's the spot where Eb Munson an' John Tighe lays in the poor-farm lot, an' I did mean certain to buy flags for 'em last year an' year before, but I went an' forgot it. I'd like to have folks that rode by notice 'em for once, if they was town paupers. Eb Munson was as darin' a man as ever stepped out to tuck o' drum."

"So he was," said John Stover, taking his pipe with decision and knocking out the ashes. "Drink was his ruin; but I wan't one that could be harsh with Eb, no matter what he done. He worked hard long's he could, too; but he wan't like a sound man, an' I think he took somethin' first not so much 'cause he loved it, but to kind of keep his strength up so's he could work, an' then, all of a sudden, rum clinched with him an' threw him. Eb was talkin' 'long o' me one day when he was about half full, an' says he, right out, 'I wouldn't have fell to this state,' says he, 'if I'd had me a home an' a little fam'ly; but it don't make no difference to nobody, and it's the best comfort I seem to have, an' I ain't goin' to do without it. I'm ailin' all the time,' says he, 'an' if I keep middlin' full, I make out to hold my own an' to keep along o' my work.' I pitied Eb. I says to him, 'You ain't goin' to bring no disgrace on us old army boys, be you, Eb?' an' he says no, he wan't. I think if he'd lived to get one o' them big fat pensions, he'd had it easier. Eight dollars a month paid his board, while he'd pick up what cheap work he could, an' then he got so that decent folks didn't seem to want the bother of him, an' so he come on the town."

"There was somethin' else to it," said Henry Merrill soberly. "Drink come natural to him, 't was born in him, I expect, an' there wan't nobody that could turn the divil out same's they did in Scriptur'. His father an' his gran'father was drinkin' men; but they was kind-hearted an' good neighbors, an' never set out to wrong nobody. 'T was the custom to drink in their day; folks was colder an' lived poorer in early times, an' that's how most of 'em kept a-goin'. But what stove Eb all up was his disapp-'intment with Marthy Peck—her forsakin' of him an' marryin' old John Down whilst Eb was off to war. I've always laid it up ag'inst her."

"So've I," said Asa Brown. "She didn't use the poor fellow right. I guess she was full as well off, but it's one thing to show judgment, an' another thing to have heart."

There was a long pause; the subject was too familiar to need further comment.

"There ain't no public sperit here in Barlow," announced Asa Brown, with decision. "I don't s'pose we could ever get up anything for Decoration Day. I've felt kind of 'shamed, but it always comes in a busy time; 't wan't no time to have it, anyway, right in late plantin'."

" 'Tain't no use to look for public sperit 'less you've got some yourself," observed John Stover soberly; but something had pleased him in the discouraged suggestion. "Perhaps we could mark the day this year. It comes on a Saturday; that ain't nigh so bad as bein' in the middle of the week."

Nobody made any answer, and presently he went on,—

"There was a time along back when folks was too nigh the war-time to give much thought to the bigness of it. The best fellows was them that had stayed to home an' worked their trades an' laid up money; but I don't know's it's so now."

"Yes, the fellows that stayed at home got all the fat places, an' when we come back we felt dreadful behind the times," grumbled Asa Brown. "I remember how 't was."

"They begun to call us heroes an' old stick-in-the-mud just about the same time," resumed Stover, with a chuckle. "We wa'n't no hand for strippin' woodland nor even tradin' hosses them first few years. I don' now why 't was we were so beat out. The best most on us could do was to sag right on to the old folks. Father he never wanted me to go to the war,—'t was partly his Quaker breed,—an' he used to be dreadful mortified with the way I hung round down here to the store an' loafed round a-talkin' about when I was out South, an' arguin' with folks that didn't know nothin', about what the generals done. There! I see me now just as he see me then; but after I had my boy-strut out, I took holt o' the old farm 'long o' father, an' I've made it bounce. Look at them old

meadows an' see the herd's grass that come off of 'em last year! I ain't
ashamed o' my place now, if I did go to the war."

"It all looks a sight bigger to me now than it did then," said Henry
Merrill. "Our goin' to the war, I refer to. We didn't sense it no more
than other folks did. I used to be sick o' hearin' their stuff about patriotism
and lovin' your country, an' them pieces o' poetry women folks wrote
for the papers on the old flag, an' our fallen heroes, an' them things;
they didn't seem to strike me in the right place; but I tell ye it kind o'
starts me now every time I come on the flag sudden,—it does so. A spell
ago—'long in the fall, I guess it was—I was over to Alton, an' there was
a fire company paradin'. They'd got the prize at a fair, an' had just come
home on the cars, an' I heard the band; so I stepped to the front o' the
store where me an' my woman was tradin', an' the company felt well,
an' was comin' along the street most as good as troops. I see the old flag
a-comin', kind of blowin' back, an' it went all over me. Somethin' worked
round in my throat; I vow I come near cryin'. I was glad nobody see
me."

"I'd go to war again in a minute," declared Stover, after an expressive
pause; "but I expect we should know better what we was about. I don'
know but we've got too many rooted opinions now to make us the best
o' soldiers."

"Martin Tighe an' John Tighe was considerable older than the rest, and
they done well," answered Henry Merrill quickly. "We three was the
youngest of any, but we did think at the time we knew the most."

"Well, whatever you may say, that war give the country a great start,"
said Asa Brown. "I tell ye we just begin to see the scope on 't. There
was my cousin, you know, Dan'l Evins, that stopped with us last winter;
he was tellin' me that one o' his coastin' trips he was into the port o'
Beaufort lo'din' with yaller-pine lumber, an' he roved into an old buryin'-
ground there is there, an' he see a stone that had on it some young
Southern fellow's name that was killed in the war, an' under it was, 'He
died for his country.' Dan'l knowed how I used to feel about them South
Car'lina goings on, an' I did feel kind o' red an' ugly for a minute, an'
then somethin' come over me, an' I says, 'Well, I don' know but what
the poor chap did, Dan Evins, when you come to view it all round.' "

The other men made no answer.

"Le's see what we can do this year. I don't care if we be a poor
han'ful," urged Henry Merrill. "The young folks ought to have the good
of it; I'd like to have my boys see somethin' different. Le's get together
what men there is. How many's left, anyhow? I know there was thirty-
seven went from old Barlow, three-months' men an' all."

"There can't be over eight now, countin' out Martin Tighe; he can't
march," said Stover. "No, 't ain't worth while." But the others did not
notice his disapproval.

"There's nine in all," announced Asa Brown, after pondering and
counting two or three times on his fingers. "I can't make us no more. I
never could carry figur's in my head."

"I make nine," said Merrill. "We'll have Martin ride, an' Jesse Dean too, if he will. He's awful lively on them canes o' his. An' there's Jo Wade with his crutch; he's amazin' spry for a short distance. But we can't let 'em go far afoot; they're decripped men. We'll make 'em all put on what they've got left o' their uniforms, an' we'll scratch round an' have us a fife an' drum, an' make the best show we can."

"Why, Martin Tighe's boy, the next to the oldest, is an excellent hand to play the fife!" said John Stover, suddenly growing enthusiastic. "If you two are set on it, let's have a word with the minister to-morrow, an' see what he says. Perhaps he'll give out some kind of a notice. You have to have a good many bunches o' flowers. I guess we'd better call a meetin', some few on us, an' talk it over first o' the week. 'T wouldn't be no great of a range for us to take to march from the old buryin'-ground at the meetin'-house here up to the poor-farm an' round by Deacon Elwell's lane, so's to notice them two stones he set up for his boys that was sunk on the man-o'-war. I expect they notice stones same's if the folks laid there, don't they?"

He spoke wistfully. The others knew that Stover was thinking of the stone he had set up to the memory of his only brother, whose nameless grave had been made somewhere in the Wilderness.

"I don't know but what they'll be mad if we don't go by every house in town," he added anxiously, as they rose to go home. " 'T is a terrible scattered population in Barlow to favor with a procession."

It was a mild starlit night. The three friends took their separate ways presently, leaving the Plains road and crossing the fields by foot-paths toward their farms.

II

The week went by, and the next Saturday morning brought fair weather. It was a busy morning on the farms—like any other; but long before noon the teams of horses and oxen were seen going home from work in the fields, and everybody got ready in haste for the great event of the afternoon. It was so seldom that any occasion roused public interest in Barlow that there was an unexpected response, and the green before the old white meeting-house was covered with country wagons and groups of people, whole families together, who had come on foot. The old soldiers were to meet in the church; at half past one the procession was to start, and on its return the minister was to make an address in the old burying-ground. John Stover had been first lieutenant in the war, so he was made captain of the day. A man from the next town had offered to drum for them, and Martin Tighe's proud boy was present with his fife. He had a great longing—strange enough in that peaceful, sheep-raising neighbor-hood—to go into the army; but he and his elder brother were the mainstay of their crippled father, and he could not be spared from the large household until a younger brother could take his place; so that all his fire and military zeal went for the present into martial tunes, and the fife was a safety-valve for his enthusiasm.

The army men were used to seeing each other; everybody knew everybody in the little country town of Barlow; but when one comrade after another appeared in what remained of his accoutrements, they felt the day to be greater than they had planned, and the simple ceremony proved more solemn than any one expected. They could make no use of their every-day jokes and friendly greetings. Their old blue coats and tarnished army caps looked faded and antiquated enough. One of the men had nothing left but his rusty canteen and rifle; but these he carried like sacred emblems. He had worn out all his army clothes long ago, because he was too poor when he was discharged to buy any others.

When the door of the church opened, the veterans were not abashed by the size and silence of the crowd. They came walking two by two down the steps, and took their places in line as if there were nobody looking on. Their brief evolutions were like a mystic rite. The two lame men refused to do anything but march as best they could; but poor Martin Tighe, more disabled than they, was brought out and lifted into Henry Merrill's best wagon, where he sat up, straight and soldierly, with his boy for driver. There was a little flag in the whip-socket before him, which flapped gayly in the breeze. It was such a long time since he had been seen out-of-doors that everybody found him a great object of interest, and paid him much attention. Even those who were tired of being asked to contribute to his support, who resented the fact of his having a helpless wife and great family; who always insisted that with his little pension and hopeless lameness, his fingerless left hand and failing sight, he could support himself and his household if he chose,—even those persons came forward now to greet him handsomely and with large approval. To be sure, he enjoyed the conversation of idlers, and his wife had a complaining way that was the same as begging, especially since her boys began to grow up and be of some use; and there were one or two near neighbors who never let them really want; so other people, who had cares enough of their own, could excuse themselves for forgetting him the year round, and even call him shiftless. But there were none to look askance at Martin Tighe on Decoration Day, as he sat in the wagon, with his bleached face like a captive's, and his thin, afflicted body. He stretched out his whole hand impartially to those who had remembered and those who had forgotten both his courage at Fredericksburg and his sorry need in Barlow.

Henry Merrill had secured the engine company's large flag in Alton, and now carried it proudly. There were eight men in line, two by two, and marching a good bit apart, to make their line the longer. The fife and drum struck up gallantly together, and the little procession moved away slowly along the country road. It gave an unwonted touch of color to the landscape,—the scarlet, the blue, between the new-ploughed fields and budding roadside thickets, between the wide dim ranges of the mountains, under the great white clouds of the spring sky. Such processions grow more pathetic year by year; it will not be so long now before wondering children will have seen the last. The aging faces of the men, the renewed comradeship, the quick beat of the hearts that remember, the tenderness of those who think upon old sorrows,—all these make the day a lovelier and a sadder festival. So men's hearts were stirred, they knew not why, when they heard the shrill fife and the incessant drum along the quiet Barlow road, and saw the handful of old soldiers marching by. Nobody thought of them as familiar men and neighbors alone,—they were a part of that army which had saved its country. They had taken their lives in their hands and gone out to fight for their country, plain John Stover and Jesse Dean and the rest. No matter if every other day in the year they counted for little or much, whether they were lame-footed and lagging, whether their farms were of poor soil or rich.

The little troop went in slender line along the road; the crowded country wagons and all the people who went afoot followed Martin Tighe's wagon as if it were a great gathering at a country funeral. The route was short, and the long, straggling line marched slowly; it could go no faster than the lame men could walk.

In one of the houses by the roadside an old woman sat by a window, in an old-fashioned black gown, and clean white cap with a prim border which bound her thin, sharp features closely. She had been for a long time looking out eagerly over the snowberry and cinnamon-rose bushes; her face was pressed close to the pane, and presently she caught sight of the great flag as it came down the road.

"Let me see 'em! I've got to see 'em go by!" she pleaded, trying to rise from her chair alone when she heard the fife, and the women helped her to the door, and held her so that she could stand and wait. She had been an old woman when the war began; she had sent sons and grandsons to the field; they were all gone now. As the men came by, she straightened her bent figure with all the vigor of youth. The fife and drum stopped suddenly; the colors lowered. She did not heed that, but her old eyes flashed and then filled with tears to see the flag going to salute the soldiers' graves. "Thank ye, boys; thank ye!" she cried, in her quavering voice, and they all cheered her. The cheer went back along the straggling line for old Grandmother Dexter, standing there in her front door between the lilacs. It was one of the great moments of the day.

The few old people at the poor-house, too, were waiting to see the show. The keeper's young son, knowing that it was a day of festivity, and not understanding exactly why, had put his toy flag out of the gable window, and there it showed against the gray clapboards like a gay flower. It was the only bit of decoration along the veterans' way, and they stopped and saluted it before they broke ranks and went out to the field corner beyond the poor-farm barn to the bit of ground that held the paupers' unmarked graves. There was a solemn silence while Asa Brown went to the back of Tighe's wagon, where such light freight was carried, and brought two flags, and he and John Stover planted them straight in the green sod. They knew well enough where the right graves were, for these had been made in a corner by themselves, with unwonted sentiment. And so Eben Munson and John Tighe were honored like the rest, both by their flags and by great and unexpected nosegays of spring flowers, daffies and flowering currant and red tulips, which lay on the graves already. John Stover and his comrade glanced at each other curiously while they stood singing, and then laid their own bunches of lilacs down and came away.

Then something happened that almost none of the people in the wagons understood. Martin Tighe's boy, who played the fife, had studied well his part, and on his poor short-winded instrument now sounded taps as well as he could. He had heard it done once in Alton at a soldier's funeral. The plaintive notes called sadly over the fields, and echoed back from the hills. The few veterans could not look at each other; their eyes brimmed up with tears; they could not have spoken. Nothing called back old army days like that. They had a sudden vision of the Virginian camp, the hillside dotted white with tents, the twinkling lights in other camps, and far away the glow of smouldering fires. They heard the bugle call from post to post; they remembered the chilly winter night, the wind in the pines, the laughter of the men. Lights out! Martin Tighe's boy sounded it again sharply. It seemed as if poor Eb Munson and John Tighe must hear it too in their narrow graves.

The procession went on, and stopped here and there at the little graveyards on the farms, leaving their bright flags to flutter through summer and winter rains and snows, and to bleach in the wind and sunshine. When they returned to the church, the minister made an address about the war, and every one listened with new ears. Most of what he said was familiar enough to his listeners; they were used to reading those phrases about the results of the war, the glorious future of the South, in their weekly newspapers; but there never had been such a spirit of patriotism and loyalty waked in Barlow as was waked that day by the poor parade of the remnant of the Barlow soldiers. They sent flags to all the distant graves, and proud were those households who claimed kinship with valor, and could drive or walk away with their flags held up so that others could see that they, too, were of the elect.

III

It is well that the days are long in the last of May, but John Stover had to hurry more than usual with his evening work, and then, having the longest distance to walk, he was much the latest comer to the Plains store, where his two triumphant friends were waiting for him impatiently on the bench. They also had made excuse of going to the post-office and doing an unnecessary errand for their wives, and were talking together so busily that they had gathered a group about them before the store. When they saw Stover coming, they rose hastily and crossed the road to meet him, as if they were a committee in special session. They leaned against the post-and-board fence, after they had shaken hands with each other solemnly.

"Well, we've had a great day, ain't we, John?" asked Henry Merrill. "You did lead off splendid. We've done a grand thing, now, I tell you. All the folks say we've got to keep it up every year. Everybody had to have a talk about it as I went home. They say they had no idea we should make such a show. Lord! I wish we'd begun while there was more of us!"

"That han'some flag was the great feature," said Asa Brown generously. "I want to pay my part for hirin' it. An' then folks was glad to see poor old Martin made o' some consequence."

"There was half a dozen said to me that another year they was goin' to have flags out, and trim up their places somehow or 'nother. Folks has feelin' enough, but you've got to rouse it," said Merrill.

"I have thought o' joinin' the Grand Army over to Alton time an' again, but it's a good ways to go, an' then the expense has been o' some consideration," Asa continued. "I don't know but two or three over there. You know, most o' the Alton men nat'rally went out in the rigiments t' other side o' the State line, an' they was in other battles, an' never camped nowheres nigh us. Seems to me we ought to have home feelin' enough to do what we can right here."

"The minister says to me this afternoon that he was goin' to arrange an' have some talks in the meetin'-house next winter, an' have some of us tell where we was in the South; an' one night 't will be about camp life, an' one about the long marches, an' then about the battles,—that would take some time,—an' tell all we could about the boys that was killed, an' their record, so they wouldn't be forgot. He said some of the folks must have the letters we wrote home from the front, an' we could make out quite a history of us. I call Elder Dallas a very smart man; he'd planned it all out a'ready, for the benefit o' the young folks, he said," announced Henry Merrill, in a tone of approval.

"I s'pose there ain't none of us but could add a little somethin'," answered John Stover modestly. " 'T would re'lly learn the young folks a good deal. I should be scared numb to try an' speak from the pulpit. That ain't what the Elder means, is it? Now I was one that had a good chance to see somethin' o' Washin'ton. I shook hands with President Lincoln, an' I always think I'm worth lookin' at for that, if I ain't for nothin' else. 'T was that time I was just out o' hospit'l, an' able to crawl about some. I've often told you how 't was I met him, an' he stopped an' shook hands an' asked where I'd been at the front an' how I was gettin' along with my hurts. Well, we'll see how 't is when winter comes. I never thought I had no gift for public speakin', 'less 't was for drivin' cattle or pollin' the house town-meetin' days. Here! I've got somethin' in mind. You needn't speak about it if I tell it to ye," he added suddenly. "You know all them han'some flowers that was laid on to Eb Munson's grave an' Tighe's? I mistrusted you thought the same thing I did by the way you looked. They come from Marthy Down's front yard. My woman told me when we got home that she knew 'em in a minute; there wa'n't nobody in town had that kind o' red flowers but her. She must ha' kind o' harked back to the days when she was Marthy Peck. She must have come over with 'em after dark, or else dreadful early in the mornin'."

Henry Merrill cleared his throat. "There ain't nothin' half-way 'bout Mis' Down," he said. "I wouldn't ha' spoken 'bout this 'less you had led right on to it; but I overtook her when I was gittin' towards home this afternoon, an' I see by her looks she was worked up a good deal; but we talked about how well things had gone off, an' she wanted to know what expenses we'd been put to, an' I told her; and she said she'd give five dollars any day I'd stop in for it. An' then she spoke right out. 'I'm alone in the world,' says she, 'and I've got somethin' to do with, an' I'd like to have a plain stone put up to Eb Munson's grave, with the number of his rigiment on it, an' I'll pay the bill. 'T ain't out o' Mr. Down's money,' she says; ' 't is mine, an' I want you to see to it.' I said I would, but we'd made a plot to git some o' them soldiers' headstones that's provided by the government. 'T was a shame it had been overlooked so long. 'No,' says she; 'I'm goin' to pay for Eb's myself.' An' I told her there wouldn't be no objection. Don't ary one o' you speak about it. 'T wouldn't be fair. She was real well-appearin'. I never felt to respect Marthy so before."

"We was kind o' hard on her sometimes, but folks couldn't help it. I've seen her pass Eb right by in the road an' never look at him when he first come home," said John Stover.

"If she hadn't felt bad, she wouldn't have cared one way or t' other," insisted Henry Merrill. " 'T ain't for us to judge. Sometimes folks has to get along in years before they see things fair. Come; I must be goin' home. I'm tired as an old dog."

"It seemed kind o' natural to be steppin' out together again. Strange we three got through with so little damage, an' so many dropped round us," said Asa Brown. "I've never been one mite sorry I went out in old A Company. I was thinkin' when I was marchin' to-day, though, that we should all have to take to the wagons before long an' do our marchin' on wheels, so many of us felt kind o' stiff. There's one thing,—folks won't never say again that we can't show no public sperit here in old Barlow."

Study and Discussion Questions

1. What indications do we get, especially in the first half of the story, that life in this small town is not so beautiful as its picturesque appearance might suggest?

2. What is the attitude in the town, before the parade, towards those who fought in the war? What is it after the parade? How does the structure of the story emphasize this change?

3. Late in Part I, Asa Brown says that a Southerner killed in the war has indeed "died for his country . . . when you come to view it all around." What does he mean?

4. At the beginning of Part II, we learn that Martin Tighe's son has "a great longing" to join the army, but cannot, because he must help support his father, who was crippled in the war. Does the irony of this undercut or reinforce the patriotic tone of the story?

5. What is the story saying about war?

Writing Exercises

1. Does "Decoration Day" ever become sentimental? If so, when? If not, how does Jewett avoid sentimentality?

2. Does this story about war suggest in any way (aside from the author's name) that a woman wrote it?

3. Describe what Marthy Peck Down might be feeling as she watches the parade.

Yōko Ōta   (1906–1963)

Yōko Ōta was born in Hiroshima, Japan, and moved to Tokyo, where she worked as a reporter and with a number of literary magazines. She was in Hiroshima when the United States dropped the atomic bomb on August 6, 1945. She survived to publish an account of what happened to her, the title of which translates as The City of Corpses.

Fireflies[1]

(1953)

I

Although I had visited the site the previous morning, I went again the next afternoon to see the stone walls of the ruined castle as they stood facing each other like the sleeves on a kimono.

Whether they used to be one of the castle gates or part of the solid rampart, I couldn't tell, since only the ruins remained. The obvious

---

[1] Translated by Kōichi Nakagawa.

assumption was that, unrealistic as it seemed, a section of the otherwise destroyed rampart still stood there.

It was past noon on a June day. I was standing between the two tall stone walls. The earth under my feet was shadowed as in a valley. The wall that I was facing appeared grotesque and on fire whenever I went back to see it. The surface of each stone in the wall, big and small alike, was burning in colors of brown, rusty vermilion and bright red. Summer grass was growing out of the cracks. Yellow flowers were blooming on the grass tips.

There was enough room for people to walk on the top of the wall. The grass and its flowers spread over the whole top. To me this giant wall seemed to brim with a kind of impressive beauty. One of the artists from Tokyo had been struck with the idea of engraving a poem in these burned stones. He wanted to carve the words written by a poet who had killed himself. I understood his intention well enough, and yet I knew about the nightmares that this place had seen.

I had never met the poet Tamiki Hara, but I had read the words written from his soul in "Requiem".

—Never live for yourself. Live only for the grief of the dead. I told myself again and again.—

—Pierce my body, Oh, Grief! Pierce my body, Countless Griefs!—

Several people came from Tokyo to select a place for a monument with Tamiki Hara's poetry engraved on it. I looked at a few places with them because, luckily or not, I had come to Hiroshima a couple of days before then. They all liked the radiation-burned stone wall, but I didn't. Only Tamiki Hara and I, with the eyes and souls we had in common, should be able to see the colors of the stone wall in the castle site. The eyes and souls of the visitors from Tokyo, who had never experienced the intense light of radiation, were different from ours.

To me the stones seemed to burn like balls of flame. Or I thought that the stones, retaining the rays of the midday sun, were actually hot. As I had done many times before, I passed my hand over the stone surfaces, feeling for some heat. They weren't hot, but there was a feeling of brittleness, as if they would soon crumble into fragments. The other sleeve of wall across the way, which had received the full force of the light of the bomb streaming down from the central part of the city, was burned a mottled shade of red. But the part of the wall where the surface had not been exposed to the direct light was not red. Rather, it seemed to be deteriorated and to have taken on the calm gray of a fossil. There was sand spilling out of its broken surface.

The wall was one and a half meters thick. If it had been a human body, it would have been burned up. I couldn't forget the scenes in which human faces had been burned exactly like this. I thought that the Tamiki Hara poetry monument, if erected here, might take on the same flaming color as the wall. Perhaps it was merely a morbid reaction. Come to think of it, wherever I happened to be in Hiroshima, although seven years had passed since the bombing, my eyes seemed to see only masses of fire and blood everywhere.

The shadow of dusk began to cover part of the stone walls. Evening clouds changed their shapes moment by moment. I thought about the poet who had had to take his own life and tried to relate his death to my own life and death. That was why I stood by the walls. But I had stood there too long, I realized, and I left. The place was deserted. By the moat was a slender willow tree, looking picturesque in its setting. It had caught my eye from the beginning, and I went and crouched down under it, because it looked like a good spot from which to sketch the walls. I put my drawing pad on my knees and opened it. I was not good at drawing, but I somehow managed to catch the shape of each stone in the walls. And then I started writing about the colors of the stones, the green grass, and the small yellow flowers. Two men came along. I saw the light of a cigarette. The men were carrying shovels on their shoulders.

They were probably workmen on their way back from cleaning up after the athletic exposition that had been held on the grounds of the castle site. The men squatted down at the edge of the moat and looked at me writing on my pad. Then they walked past me without a word. After they had passed, one of them turned around and asked inquiringly, "Lady?"—with a tone of sweetness—"what are you thinking about so seriously?"

The other man turned back, too, after walking a little way past me.

"Good evening," he said slowly, as if suddenly remembering the expression. I nearly burst out laughing.

"Good evening," I replied to their backs.

They both stopped and turned around again. Then they said from a distance, "You're not going to jump in the moat, are you? Leave a note behind? You're not going to kill yourself?"

"No, I'm not going to kill myself!"

The men walked away laughing. I had no intention of dying the way Tamiki Hara did. And yet, a lurking sense of death was always around me. I was trying to live, but on the other hand there was always the danger of death.

The sun was about to set. The stone walls were sinking into darkness. And yet I was able to make out each stone clearly, as if it were a living being.

I started back toward the makeshift shacks at the former military training ground, which was four or five streets from the downtown area. Turning my back on the stone walls, I began walking. It seemed as though those stone cliffs, turning into flames, were collapsing behind me. The feeling was not a false one. To me that was the ultimate truth.

II

While in Hiroshima, I was staying at my youngest sister Teiko's house. The place she lived in was not what you would normally call a "house".

I didn't know the right word for it—a shack, a barrack, some kind of little living unit appropriate to this devastated city.

I understood that it was a makeshift affair, and yet it was not only for temporary use because my sister had been living there for seven years since the war. And it didn't seem as though she was planning to move into a real house.

"Just once more in my lifetime I'd like to live in a house with running water," Teiko said. She was thirty-one years old.

"Don't sound so discouraged. Aren't there a lot of people who have moved out of these shacks and built new houses somewhere else?"

"No, almost none."

"Nobody? There are so many people here."

"I've never heard of it happening."

When the city was reduced to rubble, not a single house was left standing. The makeshift shacks were erected on the training ground, which was still strewn with the bones of numberless soldiers who had been burned to death there. It was strange to think of the shacks going up, a thousand of them in one corner of the training ground, built by the city for the relief of the survivors.

The facilities should have been able to house everybody, since the number of survivors was not that great. But because all the older houses had been destroyed, and because repatriates from abroad and discharged soldiers were pouring into the city, the shacks were soon filled up. Teiko, her husband, a junior high teacher, and her two-year-old daughter had managed to move into one of the units. That was at the end of 1946. The shack had two rooms, one designed to be floored with six tatami mats, the other with three mats. But at first the rooms were not even floored with mats because there were too many thieves and beggers around to make off with them. Teiko and her husband Soichi, with their little daughter tied onto her back, picked their way along a small path across the desolate army field, the cold wind sweeping over them, to go to the city housing office to pick up their tatami mats. Because all the huts were built to standardized dimensions, it didn't make any difference which mats and fixtures Teiko and Soichi picked out. They took nine tatami mats and a couple of wooden and glass doors and carried them back on their shoulders. None of the poorly-made tatami mats and doors fitted properly, so they had to wedge and stuff them into place as best they could.

There was no ceiling. The unfinished logs that served as beams formed a triangle that was open to view. Morning sunlight found its way between the wooden beams into the room. Here and there I could see the heads of nails and I felt as though I was lying in a log cabin in the mountains. There was a tiny toilet at the end of the open veranda. It looked like something built for children—you could imagine it pushing away any grownup who tried to use it. Inside were two rough boards placed over a shallow pot which was fully exposed to view.

And yet these were not slum dwellings. They were all separate units, with spaces in between, and there were rows and rows of them like so many long walls. No matter how harsh the circumstances, people can hardly be expected to put up with communal living for long. Here the occupants at least had their separate little roosts where they could guard their own particular secrets from one another. The lines and lines of small shacks were proof of this.

There was only one source of water for the occupants of the huts in Teiko's row and those opposite them. There had been a water outlet at the Army horse stables, but the pipe had been broken in the bombing. Until the water pipe was repaired, all the families in all one thousand shacks had gone all the way to Sakancho to get water, walking across the training grounds and over Aioi Bridge, right through the area where the bomb had burst. Now, however, the water pipe at the stables had been repaired, and Teiko and the others went back and forth from morning to night to draw water there, carrying their house keys in hand.

One rainy night I came back late. Since there was no real entrance, I could come into the hut from either the front or the back as I pleased. When I called out to Teiko from the back door, I heard someone inside pulling out a nail. Teiko looked at me with her large dark eyes. The corners of her mouth were scarred with keloid marks that stood out like welts. One step in from the outside was the three-mat living room. After I had changed into some dry clothes and sat down at the dilapidated table, my eyes were drawn to a number of slugs creeping around. Teiko put a light supper on the table and sat down across from me to pour the tea.

"Terrible slugs!" I said.

"Yes. We're trying to get rid of them but they just keep coming."

Soichi had rigged a clothes closet in one corner of the room. It didn't have a door but was hung with a tattered curtain. There was a small can full of thick salt water behind the curtain. Teiko took it out and, with a pair of cheap chopsticks, picked up the slugs and dropped them in the can one by one. It gave me a creepy feeling. The slugs slithered around in droves at the base of the sliding paper doors, which did not have the customary rain shutters to protect them. The slugs were even swarming around the legs of the table.

"Where do they come from in such numbers?"

"Every typhoon season we have a lot of rain and that huge area where the training ground was gets completely flooded. No way for the water to drain off. The floors are all rotting."

"Is it like this in all the houses?"

"Yes. They were all built at the same time. It's a miracle we've managed to stand it here for seven years. We just force ourselves to stay."

Because Teiko had once lived with a relative in Tokyo for six or seven years, she spoke Tokyo dialect with a Hiroshima accent.

"The roof is made of pressed paper tiles. We used to say we'd be lucky if it lasted three years."

"There weren't any slugs when I was here last time, were there? When did they start showing up?"

"About two years ago. They began by creeping around the kitchen sink and shelves, but last year it got like this. From the middle of the rainy season last year, they started slithering out one after another even in the other tatami room and climbing up the mosquito net. Mother got up any number of times in the middle of the night and threw them into the salt water can as fast as she could catch them with the chopsticks. It made me feel so sick I couldn't sleep right until fall came."

In the six-mat room, my mother and Teiko's two daughters were asleep. My mother was seventy-four. Teiko's older daughter was seven. The younger daughter had been born after the A-bomb, proof that Teiko's reproductive organs had not been impaired by the bomb. This gave our family some measure of relief. My mother, Tsuki, and Teiko's children were sleeping soundly with their heads together. I didn't feel hungry because of the slimy slugs creeping around under the table.

"I'm sorry I come back so late every night," I said to Teiko. "Shall we go to bed now?" Teiko was actually a half-sister, my mother's child by a different marriage.

"All right," Teiko said, but she did not leave the table.

"I want to talk to you when we have some free time."

"Me, too. I want to have a nice, long talk with you sometime. You always look so busy that I can't talk to you even those few times when you come back from Tokyo."

"Well, shall we talk tonight? But maybe you're sleepy?"

A slight smile crossed Teiko's face. When she was young, people considered her pretty, but now she looked worn out. Whenever she smiled, the scars around her lips became distorted and swollen. I had something I wanted to ask her when the chance came. I sat up straight and drank a sip of my tea, which by this time had gotten cold.

"What are you going to do from now on?" I asked, having no choice but to speak in vague terms, "Mother asked me to ask you about this too. When Soichi died, Yu took the trouble to come from Fukuoka, remember? And when Yu suggested that you marry again, you got all upset and wouldn't talk to him, didn't you?"

"My husband had just died! Nobody should have said such a thing to me at that time!"

"Of course, you're right. But maybe he was half joking, the way men do. Mother thinks she understands how you felt then, so she can't bring herself to talk to you about it. But you know, it's been three years."

"The time's gone by so fast!"

"How do you feel now? You know, women who've lost their husbands often say they'd rather remain single for the sake of the children. Do you feel that way too?"

Teiko is the kind who would say she did. And if she said she wanted to stay the way she was because of the children, we would all be in an awkward position.

"The way I feel. . . .," Teiko began weakly. "I don't think I could go on alone for the rest of my life, what with two children to raise."

"I know how you must feel. I think you should marry again."

"I guess I have no choice. I admire other women who go on alone, but I can't do it."

All of a sudden, tears came to my eyes. Teiko's confession brought on unexpected thoughts, because even though I was moved by her honest reply, the idea that someone like Teiko, a widow with two children, might be able to find happiness in a second marriage seemed to be, after all, only a dream. We speak of the hardships of a woman's lot, but this was the first time I had seen them spelled out in concrete terms in the life of one of my own flesh and blood.

"You know, those dark red stone walls you go to look at so often," said Teiko. "The ones where the Tamiki Hara monument is. I used to walk through there with Konomi on my way to work at the women's hall at the exposition."

Konomi was Teiko's second daughter. She was born shortly before Soichi died. Soichi had asked me to pick out a name for her so I sent the name I had chosen from Tokyo.

"You took Konomi with you to work? Didn't Mother take care of her?"

"At first she did. But then Kumi's eye infection began spreading to everyone else and for a while Mother almost lost her sight altogether. She went groping around the house and bumping into everything. It was too dangerous for Konomi to be here with them. Besides, Mother was in a bad mood, so I left Kumi with her and took the little one with me to work every day."

I was listening to her and nodding my head.

"I stood at the sales counter all day. It was a cheap place. There was a big board like a door laid on its side and I hung things like shoulder bags, cheap shoes, stationery goods and airplane models on it. I stood there all day. I hated selling models of war planes. Anyway, the customers were all busy complaining about the admission to the exposition being so expensive, so I couldn't sell very much."

"Did Konomi play all by herself?"

"She was just beyond the toddling stage, so she fell asleep right away. Of course, there was no real place for a child to sleep. I had to let her sleep right on the ground behind me."

Teiko paused in her narrative and then went on.

"It was a springtime exposition and very dusty, and a lot of country people came even though there wasn't much to see. When I was ready to leave and would go to pick up Konomi, she would be completely white with dust. A woman at one of the other counters felt sorry for us and the next day she lent me a reed mat for Konomi to sleep on."

I could picture the child sleeping innocently on the reed mat on the ground.

"After a little while, my eyes got infected too and I quit working before the exposition closed. I was all right but I felt terrible about the children, worse than I've ever felt before. And I was bitter about the death of my husband."

Soichi didn't die in the war. He wasn't even in Hiroshima when the bomb was dropped. He was in Kyushu, after having been drafted for the third time. The troops scheduled to go to Korea were massed at the tip of Kyushu, sitting around idle; they had no arms and there were no ships to take them across. Soichi was suffering from hemorrhoids. They had gotten worse after his second period of military service. He came back from a hospital in Kyushu a month after the war ended. His home was on Nomi Island in the Inland Sea and Teiko, her daughters and Mother and I had been waiting for him there. Then one day Soichi, wearing a dirty white robe and field cap, came strolling down the island path. Mother and I watched him come toward the house. He wasn't carrying anything in his hands.

"Other men brought back as many things as they could carry in their hands or on their backs. But Soichi didn't bring back anything at all—not even a can of food or a blanket!" Mother grumbled later when she came to see me in Tokyo.

"It was okay like that," I told her, but the dissatisfied look in her face did not disappear.

Then in October of 1949, Soichi suddenly coughed up blood and ran a continuous high fever. He died almost immediately. At that time, Mother was staying with me in Tokyo. Both Mother and I were sick and, though we several times bought train tickets, we were not well enough to leave for Hiroshima. Mother finally left Tokyo on the twentieth day after his death. I had seen her aging face change drastically as a result of the sorrow she felt for her daughter. In the space of twenty days the brightness went out of her face and she grew gaunt and faded.

Strictly speaking, Soichi was not a war casualty. However, deep inside her, Mother seemed to regard Soichi Ogura as one of those killed in action. I didn't mention this to Teiko and don't intend to until she becomes aware of it herself.

"Anyway, for the rest of my life I won't forget those burned stone walls where Mr. Hara's monument stands and how Konomi and I went back and forth through there all covered with dust. I agree with you when you say the place is 'carved with the seal of history.'"

"Those aren't my words," I blurted out. "I don't say such eloquent things. That's what Mr. A from Tokyo said."

"Aside from 'the seal of history', Mr. A said that every citizen of Hiroshima from every walk of life will go on passing back and forth between those walls forever. I liked that."

Teiko and I left the three-mat room.

"Oh, look at those slugs! What are things coming to!"

III

I was riding on a streetcar running southeast through the city bound for Ujina. With me was Makoto Kikawa, who had become famous as the first officially recognized victim of the A-bomb. Every day since I had come back to Hiroshima for the first time in three years, I had met with various people and listened to their stories about the aftermath of the bomb. With eyes full of tears, I used to go with somebody like Mr. Kikawa to call on other people. Mr. Kikawa's eyes always had a dark expression of cynicism, the kind possessed by people who have known great disappointment. They were deeply tinged with enmity.

At certain moments he would show a glimpse of the willful and conceited attitude common among famous people who have been spoiled by others. And yet, he understood all too well that people had made a show of him during his long hospitalization and had almost gotten pleasure out of examining his scarred body. I had seen his keloid-covered body only in a photograph. Of course, I couldn't ask him to let me see his body. In fact I would be afraid to look at it. But today we were going to Jiai, the city hospital, and it occurred to me that, if he took off his clothes in front of the doctor, I might be able to look at his radiation-torn body with a certain degree of detachment.

He kept one hand in his pocket. It was burned and deformed like a crab's claw.

"If we have time today, would you like to see Miss Mitsuko Takada?" he asked.

"Yes, I would. She lives near the hospital, doesn't she?"

"Right behind it."

"Is it all right to visit her without letting her know we're coming? I wonder what she does for a living."

"She worked shucking oysters during the winter. I hear she's running a little store now."

Kikawa knew a lot about people like Miss Takada who barely managed to survive in Hiroshima and who tried to live away from the public eye, as though they had done something bad. With some purpose in mind, he was making a list of the disabled, collecting their signatures.

"Miss Takada has the worst face I know of," he said in a matter-of-fact and emotionless tone. After all, for seven years since the end of the war he had seen A-bomb victims day after day and mingled with those who were in much worse condition than himself.

"I think Dr. Yamazaki will be surprised. I told him I'd bring you sometime, but he doesn't know it's today. He's been wanting to see you."

"Is that so?"

When I came to Hiroshima in 1945, shortly before the end of the war, I had an operation at Jiai Hospital. Dr. Yamazaki was working under the hospital director who operated on me. There was also a young doctor who appears under his real name in John Hersey's book *Hiroshima*.[2] Kikawa stayed in the hospital for six years after the war. He was there free of charge but he often quarreled with the doctors. He tried to organize the patients who had been wounded in the war into protesting the class discrimination reflected in the treatment given in this and other hospitals at the time. Once he made plans to escape from the hospital and go live under a bridge. But he had been operated on more than thirty times and he couldn't move around as he liked.

Kikawa had an ulterior motive in mind when he decided to go with me to Jiai Hospital. He felt bad about going there alone but he wanted to get a checkup. So it was convenient for him to visit the hospital with me because, in the past, I had gotten along quite well with all the doctors there. I, too, had another purpose in mind. One of my cousins, Taeko, had spent three and a half years in Jiai Hospital. She was a repatriate from Sariweon, Korea. I had never met her. Because both of her kidneys were tubercular, I thought that if I missed this chance, I would never be able to see my cousin's face.

The streetcar was moving through the central district of the city. We passed the bank whose stone steps had a human shadow burned into them. It was two hundred meters from ground zero. Near the bank was a new shopping street. From the window of the slowly moving streetcar, I looked at the faces of the strange men standing here and there on the streets. Their seemingly polished faces sported well-groomed beards. They were neatly dressed in bright colored clothes with shoes meticulously shined. These unknown men were a strange breed of Japanese. I had seen them, dressed in smart clothes, their bodies free of wounds, all over Hiroshima. And here and there, among the otherwise drab-looking passengers in the streetcar, were women full of vitality and without a scar, looking as though they must be these men's companions.

They wore the latest fashions and scattered through their wavy hair were dyed whirls of flaming red. I might have supposed that their hair had been burned by too much hair dryer, but in fact I had seen the same hair style many times before. From time to time, on the trains and streets, I had seen women with part of their hair in flames.

Makoto Kikawa and I got off the streetcar in front of Jiai Hospital.

IV

Kikawa took off his coat in the examining room for Dr. Yamazaki, head of the surgical department. He untied his crimson tie and then removed his shirt.

---

[2] American novelist (b. 1914); book appeared in 1946.

Item by item he took off his clothes, seeming very much accustomed to what he was doing. Like a machine, he was doing it automatically. Because his hands were deformed, they looked like monkey paws performing the actions. Yet he was quick, without hesitation. I couldn't look at his face, but my heart was gripped by a stifling indignation.

Probably neither the doctor nor Kikawa himself noticed how skilled his hands were, hands that for six years had learned to take off his clothes item by item so as to exhibit the body in front of countless viewers, Japanese and foreigners alike. I looked at Kikawa's stomach and back. Tears didn't come to my eyes. I was beyond tears. Part of the skin on his stomach had been grafted to his back. The scars left on his stomach had all turned to keloid. There was little skin left that could be used for grafting. I wished he would hurry up and put his clothes on again. I didn't want to look at his stomach and back any more. My purpose was not to look at the survivors in Hiroshima.

"Should I operate a couple more times?" Dr. Yamazaki asked Kikawa, who had just finished dressing.

"It's not necessary," said Kikawa with a laugh, waving his hand in a gesture of refusal. "I've had enough unless I get skin cancer."

Dr. Yamazaki avoided talking about skin cancer. He turned to me and said, "The other day a reporter came to see me from XX news agency." He mentioned the name of an American newspaper which had dispatched a correspondent.

"He wanted to ask me if I thought the Americans should use an A-bomb in the Korean War."

Dr. Yamazaki, Kikawa and I were sitting in casually arranged chairs in the small room that had been rebuilt after the bomb damage.

"I told him absolutely not! Dr. X was with me and he agreed it would be absolutely wrong. He got quite excited about it."

X was the young doctor that John Hersey had written about in *Hiroshima*.

"He asked me how I felt now about the Americans dropping the bomb on Hiroshima. I said maybe the bombing of Hiroshima couldn't have been helped if it was necessary to end the war. But since they must have been able to see the terrible damage from the air, they were absolutely wrong to drop the second bomb on Nagasaki. Then Dr. X got very angry again and said that both bombs were wrong, that dropping the first one on Hiroshima was absolutely wrong, too."

"Right! That's exactly right!" I blurted out. "It would have been wrong even to use it to end the war, but that wasn't why they used it. They used it in a hurry because they were afraid of losing their military balance of power with the Soviet Union. It was the first step in their present world policy."

"Do you know how many people were killed in Hiroshima?"

"How many?"

"Five hundred thousand."

I had seen the same figure somewhere else. It was in the newspaper in Hiroshima. I was not surprised that the figures from the newspaper and the hospital matched.

The doctor spread a piece of paper on the desk. He got a pencil and started drawing something. He drew a castle in the background of the picture. Beside the castle he wrote "divisional headquarters." I thought next he would sketch those stone walls attached to the castle and start writing Tamiki Hara's poetry there, but I was wrong. Instead, he drew several rectangles and put letters in each one.

"This is the army hospital, this is the second annex building, and this the first annex. Next to it is the artillery, and here are the first and second west units. And here is the transport corps. There must have been a couple of temporary hospitals, too."

The doctor, himself a victim of the A-bomb, announced in the candid manner of a surgeon, "Almost all the soldiers in this building that morning were killed instantly."

For a while I stared at the rectangle that the doctor had drawn on the white paper for the first west unit. One of my brothers-in-law had died there. None of his bones were recovered. As I remembered our childhood together, his shiny white teeth flashed through my mind.

"There were seven hundred thousand people in Hiroshima that day."

"That many? I thought there were only four hundred thousand and two-thirds of them were killed."

"The army personnel weren't included in the count. It was casually announced that such and such units were stationed in such and such places, and there were a lot of people going in and out at that time. At Mutual Benefit Hospital alone, there were five thousand people, and most of them were killed. The figure, five thousand reminds me that the Germans used a poison gas on the Ypres front for the first time during World War I. Five thousand soldiers were killed in three days as a result of the chlorine gas. Because it was such a cruel weapon, it became an international issue and then someone put forward a proposal to ban the use of poison gas."

Dr. Yamazaki spoke in a voice heavy with emotion. Then he added, "America didn't ratify the ban on poison gas at that time."

Kikawa had been resting his back against the window frame as he listened to Dr. Yamazaki. In a low, indifferent-sounding voice, he said, "The office at ground zero is now registering the names of A-bomb victims and putting together statistics. I hear they are surprised at the number of people who were killed."

The general assumption that two hundred thousand perished instantly was no exaggeration. However, that figure had for the sake of convenience been too quickly accepted as definitive. The figure was a miscalculation because all it meant was that some two hundred thousand people had died instantly. The citizens who failed to die that first day had died one after another in the days that followed. For months and years, people died in great numbers, until there were almost as many delayed deaths as there had been instantaneous deaths.

It had started raining. We decided to visit Mitsuko Takada at once.

"I'm not using my car, so why don't you take it?" the surgeon said. "Mr. Kikawa, you could go with her to Motomachi."

I decided to borrow Dr. Yamazaki's small car because of the rain. The thought of visiting my cousin came to mind for a moment, but there was no time to mention it. Kikawa and I drove through the rain in the small car.

At the foot of a bridge misty with rain, a makeshift wooden building, painted pale blue, came into view.

"There it is!"

Even before Kikawa pointed it out, I had guessed that it must be Mitsuko's house. It was a little bread and milk store, which had the friendly, inviting look peculiar to this town. From the car, I could see bread, candy, soft drinks and milk in a showcase in the middle of the dirt floor. Inside was a man in his fifties, his hair getting thin. I caught a glimpse of the back of a girl in a shabby, black dress, but she disappeared through a door in the rear of the store.

"She's changing her clothes," the elderly man said to me and smiled good-naturedly after Kikawa had spoken to him. Seating myself on a board at the foot of the entrance and holding the gift I had brought in my lap, I waited for the girl. Then she appeared and my breath stopped. This small girl must have been the one I saw in the black dress going inside.

It was not a girl but a monstrosity. Her deformed face and hands stood out even more grotesquely because she had put on her best clothes, a pure white blouse and a skirt with a flower pattern in crisp white. It seemed as though she was deliberately thrusting herself at me. Her face was expressionless and she didn't even greet me. I broke down weeping, slumped on the wooden board, shuddering but unable to stop my tears. I wished I could stand up, reach out to the monstrous body of the young woman and embrace it. However, Japanese people, and I especially, are not accustomed to expressing their emotions in that way.

I still couldn't stop weeping, sobbing loudly, my face pressed to the wooden board. The brazen instincts of the writer deserted me and I was no more than a plain, defenseless human being. The girl, standing motionless in the middle of the dirt floor, was observing me. Then she came nearer.

"It's all right. I've learned to accept it," Mitsuko said, and lifted me up in her arms. I was going to say, "Don't accept it!" but the words wouldn't come out. Still sobbing, I placed the gift in Mitsuko's hands. Her fingers were burned exactly the same as Kikawa's and they bent inward. The skin was shriveled and dark brown.

"I'm sorry," I said, continuing to cry. "I'm not a reporter, but because I'm a novelist I came here to ask you a few questions. I have a pad and pencil in my handbag. But I can't ask you anything today. . . ."

Mitsuko, who was young enough to be my daughter, said gently, "Would you like some milk?" She poured milk from a bottle into a glass and brought it to me with a straw. Kikawa, sitting in a chair, was drinking a bottle of soda pop. I was still feeling deeply depressed, and I thought I would become ill if I lived through many more tear-filled days like this one.

"Why don't you come inside and sit down and relax," Mitsuko said, seeming to open up to me, probably because I was crying so hard and because I had told her that I wouldn't ask her any questions. Pushing open a door, she led Kikawa and me into a room overlooking the river. The floor was tilted, the ceiling seemed about to fall in, and the walls were crumbling.

"Half of this house almost fell into the river that day. Later we pulled it back up and repaired it so we could at least sleep here," her father, the elderly man we had seen earlier, explained as he sat down beside me.

The mouth of an inlet near Ujina Bay was barely visible in the rain. Then he started talking about things I wanted to know.

"My daughter's face got like this when she was fourteen. I want her to have some operations or something as soon as possible, but she's only nineteen now. She's still a child and the doctor said it wouldn't be any good for her to have operations now while she's still growing. That's why we've put it off."

"Please give her the chance to have an operation as soon as possible, so she can get better, even a little. . . ."

"We raise oysters in Ujina Bay and every year the typhoons practically wipe them out. Oyster farming's our business, but if the beds are destroyed we have no way to get through the following year. So there's not enough money, even though we want her to have operations."

I wanted to get the conversation off such grim topics. Turning to Mitsuko, I asked, "About the oyster beds—can anyone farm oysters?"

Mitsuko, who had not shed a tear in my presence, replied in an ordinary tone of voice, with no trace of gloom.

"Oyster beds are like farm land—you buy so many lots. So you can't just go on and on buying lots."

Kikawa smiled. "So when they're wiped out, it's like losing a year's worth of crops. That's pretty bad!"

I leaned over the railing of the window for a while and gazed at the line where the sea and the river meet, my favorite kind of scenery. Then I drew a rough map showing how to get to Teiko's house and handed it to Mitsuko.

"I'll come again but please stop by when you feel like it."

"I will. I'll bring some fish from my father's catch," Mitsuko replied quickly.

The rain was coming down harder. Shortly after we had gotten into the car and started off, Kikawa asked thoughtfully, "What do you think about this idea? I'm planning to take the signatures of the A-bomb sufferers to General MacArthur's Headquarters in Tokyo.[3] Maybe they would contribute some money for rehabilitation. I want to go right away if possible."

"Don't do it!" I said, "The more you look to them for help, the more you'll be disappointed. If they had had any thought about the sufferings of A-bomb victims, they wouldn't have dropped such a thing in the first place!"

"You don't think it would work?"

I had in mind an article I'd read in a newspaper. It was about a women's group that organized a protest against the raising of electricity rates. They went to see the director of resources at General Headquarters and asked him to support the movement, but all he did was shout at them, "It's only been forty years since Japan first began using electricity. Electricity is a luxury for you! If you don't like the rate hike, then get some candles!" I didn't know whether that's actually what happened, but I told Kikawa the story anyway because it seemed symbolic to me.

"Is that so?" he said, "But I'll go at least once. Regardless of what happens, I intend to."

"I sometimes think I should take ten girls like Mitsuko Takada and stand them in line so those people could see their faces. But I don't know how they'd react."

The heavy rain continued to beat down on the small car.

V

Since I had been staying up late almost every night, I was still in bed a little before noon. Someone seemed to have come. I thought I heard the clear voice of a young woman calling from the dirt floored area, one step in from outside, that served as the entrance hall to Teiko's shack, and then I thought I heard my mother's voice. And yet after that the house was silent.

Teiko was not at home because of her work and Kumi was at school. I started dozing off again when I heard my mother sobbing. It sounded as though her chest were choked with pain. Her weeping continued for some time. Then she came and knelt down beside where I was sleeping.

"Miss Takada, the one you told me about, is here."

"All right."

I got up quickly and took off my night clothes. With my mother's help I folded up the bedding.

"You've told me about her, but what an awful face she has! So sad I couldn't help crying. . . ." She continued to weep as she put the bedding away. Mitsuko came in. She was wearing the same white skirt with the flower pattern that I had seen last time, along with a white jacket. Her

---

[3] Douglas MacArthur was in charge of the U.S. occupation of Japan after World War II.

outfit was very cheery. But her walk lacked the carefree ease common to young women her age. The radiation had burned and shriveled even her toes, so that Mitsuko walked like a cripple, with a tottering gait.

"I've brought you something you might like."

As soon as she came into the six-mat room and sat down, she untied the knot of the bundle she was carrying. With her twisted brown fingers, she pulled open the purple wrapping cloth.

"What is it?"

I unwrapped the newspaper from around the bundle, not expecting to find anything of great value. When I finally got it all open I discovered it was full of river crabs.

"My father and I caught them in the river and boiled them. Please eat them if you'd like."

"Thank you."

I remembered that my aunt had died suddenly at the age of twenty-nine after eating river crabs, but I could hardly tell Mitsuko that. Mitsuko said she was going to a Shochiku musical show today because she had gotten a ticket through the storekeepers' association she belonged to. The troupe was performing at the new culture center that had been built on a burned-out field in the old military ground.

"Miss Sacko Ozuki is performing with the troupe. The show starts at one o'clock, so I wanted to come to see you before that."

I felt odd when I thought of this girl's face among the audience watching Sacko Ozuki dance with the Shochiku troupe.

"Then why don't you have lunch here?"

"Thank you but I brought a box lunch. Still, maybe I won't go to the center. I guess I won't."

"Why not?"

"I don't feel like going anymore."

"You don't want to be stared at, is that it?"

I pressed ahead with more questions. I felt that I was trying to win the heart of a little girl. The calculations of the writer consciously rose in my mind. By making friends with this young girl, I'll be able to understand what's in the bottom of her heart. But, as though to transcend such calculations, my mind adopted a cool approach.

"I don't mind them looking at my face. I go alone to movie theaters without any hesitation and I walk proudly down the center of the main street," she said. It was a sad statement.

"At the spring festival held by the storekeepers' association this year, I got up on stage and danced. I knew it made the other people feel uneasy, but still I went up on the stage with this face. . . ."

She paused for a moment.

"I was dancing around, laughing and crying, and I thought I must look like a monkey or an ogre or something. Then the audience started crying out loud."

My eyes were full of tears. And yet Mitsuko's were dry. She didn't shed a single tear. She seemed to be trying to take revenge on somebody. Mitsuko talked in bursts, with short pauses in between.

"For a while I was going to church. I'd heard they would save people. But not people like me. Because we don't have any real intention of looking to them for help."

"So you quit going? Why?"

"A foreign lady was coming to the church and she always stared at my hands with a sorrowful expression on her face. And then she went to a lot of trouble and made a pair of gloves out of red yarn specially designed to fit my hands. After that, I quit going to church once and for all."

Two-year-old Konomi came in with a candy bowl full of rice crackers and put it down between Mitsuko and me. Konomi sat down and stared at Mitsuko's face without blinking.

"I guess there must be different kinds of foreign ladies. Another lady took a couple of pictures of me and then she turned aside and started looking for something in her handbag. She pulled out fifty or sixty yen and pressed it on me. I didn't want to take the money, but then her interpreter said I should because refusing it would be even ruder than accepting."

"Maybe they don't know anything about Japanese money."

"Yes, they do. Some people slip about twenty yen or more into my hand. They think I'm some kind of exhibition from the zoo. It's written on their faces."

As I grew accustomed to looking at her face, I realized that there was a certain expression in her eyes, where the skin around them was burned and stretched vertically. Her eyes were calm and seemed to be smiling gently.

"My eye is shining, isn't it?"

"Shining?"

"After that day, this eye shines more than the other. I can feel it myself."

Then, after being silent for a while, she said, "I want to be a gentle person."

"What would you like to do in the future?"

"I want to grow up fast and help people who're having a hard time. I wish I could be thirty years old right now. I keep thinking about it."

Mother fixed lunch for two. Konomi tried to lift up the table with a childish grunt. Mother and Konomi together brought in the food. Mitsuko spilled rice when she ate. Her lips were askew and the lower lip, having lost its natural shape, dropped in an unsightly fashion. Any kind of food was bound to drop out of her mouth. She had no choice but to push it down her throat as she ate. After eating only a little, she put her chopsticks down on the table.

"Don't you have to go to see Saeko Ozuki?"

"I don't feel like going today," she said. "If you don't mind, I'd rather spend some more time with you."

I took her for a walk. I had an impulse to take this monster-like Mitsuko and parade around town with her. And yet I found myself walking in the direction of the deserted places.

"Shall we go to the old castle site?"

"All right."

Between the rows of makeshift huts such as the one Teiko lived in, summer flowers were blooming here and there along the narrow paths. Every shack had flowers and vegetables growing in its fenced-in yard. They seemed to be a sign that people don't want to die but just want to go on living.

The water in the moat was stagnant and green, with duckweed floating on the surface. We came to the stone wall. The stones looked as though they were burning. They were on fire with bright and rusty reds, light greens and faint yellows burning in a melancholy fashion, like the printed cotton of olden times.

"Right here they're going to put up a monument to a poet who committed suicide."

"I read about him in the paper. Why did he commit suicide?"

"Nobody really understands about suicide. Some people say Tamiki Hara had suicidal tendencies anyway, even if he hadn't been terrified by memories of the bomb. Maybe they're right. But I can't help but think that Mr. Hara's suicide had something to do with the A-bomb," I added, as though talking to myself. "As long as 'Summer Flower', 'Requiem' and 'The Land of Heart's Desire' exist," I said, naming some of Tamiki Hara's works, "I have to think so."

"When the monument is erected," I said, "please come here sometime to see it. I can't come here that often from Tokyo."

"I'll certainly pay a visit on your behalf every August 6."

"The anniversary of his death is March 13th. Will you remember that for me?"

Mitsuko and I walked across the former training ground toward the downtown area. We came to the streetcar stop at Aioi Bridge. Without any real purpose in mind, we got on a streetcar.

I got back to Teiko's house after dark. The smell of grass filled the space between the rows of huts. I used the old horse trough as a landmark in finding my way to Teiko's shack. A firefly flickered in the grass.

The fireflies were not big enough to fly yet. I squatted down. Here and there the slender fireflies were flashing their lights in the clumps of grass. I picked one up.

"Mr. Soldier!" I said. "You must be the ghost of a dead soldier. Can't you break away? Shortly after you people died, the war ended. You're not soldiers anymore, so fly! Fly up high!"

I tried tossing the firefly high up into the air. It floated down lightly. Down in the grass, all the fireflies were glowing.

It seemed to me that it was not only the fireflies that were the ghosts of the dead soldiers. I came to feel the same about the slugs that slithered around the shack from evening till late at night. Even after Mother, Teiko and the children had fallen asleep, I was still awake. The three-mat room was like a house for slugs. I said to them, "You must have been soldiers. You come here every night because you have something you want to say. Can't you ever rest in peace?"

That is a frank expression of the way I felt.

Study and Discussion Questions

1. Why does the story begin with the tall stone walls of a ruined castle? What other things in the first section of the story come to be associated with the walls?
2. When and where is "Fireflies" set?
3. What does the narrator say about her sister's house where she is visiting; why does she keep mentioning the slugs?
4. List examples of fire imagery in the story.
5. Why does Ōta give her readers two separate examples of people physically affected by the atomic bomb? What is she doing with each example?
6. How does Mitsuko Takada, the young girl injured and disabled by radiation, feel about herself and her life? What is her response to the foreign woman who makes gloves for her and to the woman who gives her money?

Writing Exercises

1. What is the response of the narrator (who is a writer) to what she sees in Hiroshima—the physical setting, the people, her relatives? To what extent is she a part of it or detached from it? She says at one point, "the brazen instincts of the writer deserted me." What does she mean by this? Does she change in the course of the narrative?
2. Have you ever been disabled or physically challenged, even temporarily (by a broken arm or leg, for example)? Write about the experience.
3. Do you think the U.S. was justified in dropping atomic bombs on Hiroshima and Nagasaki? Write an argument for or against.
4. If, for the sake of argument, war is necessary, can you propose a way to engage in war that wouldn't make civilians (noncombatants) suffer?

LOUISE ERDRICH (b. 1954)

Daughter of a German immigrant and a Chippewa Indian, Louise Erdrich grew up in North Dakota and attended Dartmouth College and Johns Hopkins

University. *"The Red Convertible" is one of fourteen related stories that make up her first novel,* Love Medicine *(1984). Erdrich has also published a second novel,* The Beet Queen *(1986), and a volume of poetry,* Jacklight *(1984).*

The Red Convertible (1984)

I was the first one to drive a convertible on my reservation. And of course it was red, a red Olds. I owned that car along with my brother Henry Junior. We owned it together until his boots filled with water on a windy night and he bought out my share. Now Henry owns the whole car, and his younger brother Lyman (that's myself), Lyman walks everywhere he goes.

How did I earn enough money to buy my share in the first place? My one talent was I could always make money. I had a touch for it, unusual in a Chippewa. From the first I was different that way, and everyone recognized it. I was the only kid they let in the American Legion Hall to shine shoes, for example, and one Christmas I sold spiritual bouquets for the mission door to door. The nuns let me keep a percentage. Once I started, it seemed the more money I made the easier the money came. Everyone encouraged it. When I was fifteen I got a job washing dishes at the Joliet Café, and that was where my first big break happened.

It wasn't long before I was promoted to bussing tables, and then the short-order cook quit and I was hired to take her place. No sooner than you know it I was managing the Joliet. The rest is history. I went on managing. I soon become part owner, and of course there was no stopping me then. It wasn't long before the whole thing was mine.

After I'd owned the Joliet for one year, it blew over in the worst tornado ever seen around here. The whole operation was smashed to bits. A total loss. The fryalator was up in a tree, the grill torn in half like it was paper. I was only sixteen. I had it all in my mother's name, and I lost it quick, but before I lost it I had every one of my relatives, and their relatives, to dinner, and I also bought that red Olds I mentioned, along with Henry.

The first time we saw it! I'll tell you when we first saw it. We had gotten a ride up to Winnipeg, and both of us had money. Don't ask me why, because we never mentioned a car or anything, we just had all our money. Mine was cash, a big bankroll from the Joliet's insurance. Henry had two checks—a week's extra pay for being laid off, and his regular check from the Jewel Bearing Plant.

We were walking down Portage anyway, seeing the sights, when we saw it. There it was, parked, large as life. Really as *if* it was alive. I thought of the word *repose*, because the car wasn't simply stopped, parked, or whatever. That car reposed, calm and gleaming, a FOR SALE sign in its left front window. Then, before we had thought it over at all, the car belonged to us and our pockets were empty. We had just enough money for gas back home.

We went places in that car, me and Henry. We took off driving all one whole summer. We started off toward the Little Knife River and Mandaree in Fort Berthold and then we found ourselves down in Wakpala somehow, and then suddenly we were over in Montana on the Rocky Boys, and yet the summer was not even half over. Some people hang on to details when they travel, but we didn't let them bother us and just lived our everyday lives here to there.

I do remember this one place with willows. I remember I laid under those trees and it was comfortable. So comfortable. The branches bent down all around me like a tent or a stable. And quiet, it was quiet, even though there was a powwow close enough so I could see it going on. The air was not too still, not too windy either. When the dust rises up and hangs in the air around the dancers like that, I feel good. Henry was asleep with his arms thrown wide. Later on, he woke up and we started driving again. We were somewhere in Montana, or maybe on the Blood Reserve—it could have been anywhere. Anyway it was where we met the girl.

All her hair was in buns around her ears, that's the first thing I noticed about her. She was posed alongside the road with her arm out, so we stopped. That girl was short, so short her lumber shirt looked comical on her, like a nightgown. She had jeans on and fancy moccasins and she carried a little suitcase.

"Hop on in," says Henry. So she climbs in between us.

"We'll take you home," I says. "Where do you live?"

"Chicken," she says.

"Where the hell's that?" I ask her.

"Alaska."

"Okay," says Henry, and we drive.

We got up there and never wanted to leave. The sun doesn't truly set there in summer, and the night is more a soft dusk. You might doze off, sometimes, but before you know it you're up again, like an animal in nature. You never feel like you have to sleep hard or put away the world. And things would grow up there. One day just dirt or moss, the next day flowers and long grass. The girl's name was Susy. Her family really took to us. They fed us and put us up. We had our own tent to live in by their house, and the kids would be in and out of there all day and night. They couldn't get over me and Henry being brothers, we looked so different. We told them we knew we had the same mother, anyway.

One night Susy came in to visit us. We sat around in the tent talking of this thing and that. The season was changing. It was getting darker by that time, and the cold was even getting just a little mean. I told her it was time for us to go. She stood up on a chair.

"You never seen my hair," Susy said.

That was true. She was standing on a chair, but still, when she unclipped her buns the hair reached all the way to the ground. Our eyes opened. You couldn't tell how much hair she had when it was rolled up so neatly. Then my brother Henry did something funny. He went up to the chair and said, "Jump on my shoulders." So she did that, and her hair reached down past his waist, and he started twirling, this way and that, so her hair was flung out from side to side.

"I always wondered what it was like to have long pretty hair," Henry says. Well we laughed. It was a funny sight, the way he did it. The next morning we got up and took leave of those people.

On to greener pastures, as they say. It was down through Spokane and across Idaho then Montana and very soon we were racing the weather right along under the Canadian border through Columbus, Des Lacs, and then we were in Bottineau County and soon home. We'd made most of the trip, that summer, without putting up the car hood at all. We got home just in time, it turned out, for the army to remember Henry had signed up to join it.

I don't wonder that the army was so glad to get my brother that they turned him into a Marine. He was built like a brick outhouse anyway. We liked to tease him that they really wanted him for his Indian nose. He had a nose big and sharp as a hatchet, like the nose on Red Tomahawk, the Indian who killed Sitting Bull, whose profile is on signs all along the North Dakota highways. Henry went off to training camp, came home once during Christmas, then the next thing you know we got an overseas letter from him. It was 1970, and he said he was stationed up in the northern hill country. Whereabouts I did not know. He wasn't such a hot letter writer, and only got off two before the enemy caught him. I could never keep it straight, which direction those good Vietnam soldiers were from.

I wrote him back several times, even though I didn't know if those letters would get through. I kept him informed all about the car. Most of the time I had it up on blocks in the yard or half taken apart, because that long trip did a hard job on it under the hood.

I always had good luck with numbers, and never worried about the draft myself. I never even had to think about what my number was. But Henry was never lucky in the same way as me. It was at least three years before Henry came home. By then I guess the whole war was solved in the government's mind, but for him it would keep on going. In those years I'd put his car into almost perfect shape. I always thought of it as his car while he was gone, even though when he left he said, "Now it's yours," and threw me his key.

"Thanks for the extra key," I'd said. "I'll put it up in your drawer just in case I need it." He laughed.

When he came home, though, Henry was very different, and I'll say this: the change was no good. You could hardly expect him to change for the better, I know. But he was quiet, so quiet, and never comfortable sitting still anywhere but always up and moving around. I thought back to times we'd sat still for whole afternoons, never moving a muscle, just shifting our weight along the ground, talking to whoever sat with us, watching things. He'd always had a joke, then, too, and now you couldn't get him to laugh, or when he did it was more the sound of a man choking, a sound that stopped up the throats of other people around him. They got to leaving him alone most of the time, and I didn't blame them. It was a fact: Henry was jumpy and mean.

I'd bought a color TV set for my mom and the rest of us while Henry was away. Money still came very easy. I was sorry I'd ever bought it though, because of Henry. I was also sorry I'd bought color, because with black-and-white the pictures seem older and farther away. But what are you going to do? He sat in front of it, watching it, and that was the only time he was completely still. But it was the kind of stillness that you see in a rabbit when it freezes and before it will bolt. He was not easy. He sat in his chair gripping the armrests with all his might, as if the chair itself was moving at a high speed and if he let go at all he would rocket forward and maybe crash right through the set.

Once I was in the room watching TV with Henry and I heard his teeth click at something. I looked over, and he'd bitten through his lip. Blood was going down his chin. I tell you right then I wanted to smash that tube to pieces. I went over to it but Henry must have known what I was up to. He rushed from his chair and shoved me out of the way, against the wall. I told myself he didn't know what he was doing.

My mom came in, turned the set off real quiet, and told us she had made something for supper. So we went and sat down. There was still blood going down Henry's chin, but he didn't notice it and no one said anything, even though every time he took a bite of his bread his blood fell onto it until he was eating his own blood mixed in with the food.

While Henry was not around we talked about what was going to happen to him. There were no Indian doctors on the reservation, and my mom was afraid of trusting Old Man Pillager because he courted her long ago and was jealous of her husbands. He might take revenge through her son. We were afraid that if we brought Henry to a regular hospital they would keep him.

"They don't fix them in those places," Mom said; "they just give them drugs."

"We wouldn't get him there in the first place," I agreed, "so let's just forget about it."

Then I thought about the car.

Henry had not even looked at the car since he'd gotten home, though like I said, it was in tip-top condition and ready to drive. I thought the car might bring the old Henry back somehow. So I bided my time and waited for my chance to interest him in the vehicle.

One night Henry was off somewhere. I took myself a hammer. I went out to that car and I did a number on its underside. Whacked it up. Bent the tail pipe double. Ripped the muffler loose. By the time I was done with the car it looked worse than any typical Indian car that has been driven all its life on reservation roads, which they always say are like government promises—full of holes. It just about hurt me, I'll tell you that! I threw dirt in the carburetor and I ripped all the electric tape off the seats. I made it look just as beat up as I could. Then I sat back and waited for Henry to find it.

Still, it took him over a month. That was all right, because it was just getting warm enough, not melting, but warm enough to work outside.

"Lyman," he says, walking in one day, "that red car looks like shit."

"Well it's old," I says. "You got to expect that."

"No way!" says Henry. "That car's a classic! But you went and ran the piss right out of it, Lyman, and you know it don't deserve that. I kept that car in A-one shape. You don't remember. You're too young. But when I left, that car was running like a watch. Now I don't even know if I can get it to start again, let alone get it anywhere near its old condition."

"Well you try," I said, like I was getting mad, "but I say it's a piece of junk."

Then I walked out before he could realize I knew he'd strung together more than six words at once.

After that I thought he'd freeze himself to death working on that car. He was out there all day, and at night he rigged up a little lamp, ran a cord out the window, and had himself some light to see by while he worked. He was better than he had been before, but that's still not saying much. It was easier for him to do the things the rest of us did. He ate more slowly and didn't jump up and down during the meal to get this or that or look out the window. I put my hand in the back of the TV set, I admit, and fiddled around with it good, so that it was almost impossible now to get a clear picture. He didn't look at it very often anyway. He was always out with that car or going off to get parts for it. By the time it was really melting outside, he had it fixed.

I had been feeling down in the dumps about Henry around this time. We had always been together before. Henry and Lyman. But he was such a loner now that I didn't know how to take it. So I jumped at the chance one day when Henry seemed friendly. It's not that he smiled or anything. He just said, "Let's take that old shitbox for a spin." Just the way he said it made me think he could be coming around.

We went out to the car. It was spring. The sun was shining very bright. My only sister, Bonita, who was just eleven years old, came out and made us stand together for a picture. Henry leaned his elbow on the red car's windshield, and he took his other arm and put it over my shoulder, very carefully, as though it was heavy for him to lift and he didn't want to bring the weight down all at once.

"Smile," Bonita said, and he did.

That picture. I never look at it anymore. A few months ago, I don't know why, I got his picture out and tacked it on the wall. I felt good about Henry at the time, close to him. I felt good having his picture on the wall, until one night when I was looking at television. I was a little drunk and stoned. I looked up at the wall and Henry was staring at me. I don't know what it was, but his smile had changed, or maybe it was gone. All I know is I couldn't stay in the same room with that picture. I was shaking. I got up, closed the door, and went into the kitchen. A little later my friend Ray came over and we both went back into that room. We put the picture in a brown bag, folded the bag over and over tightly, then put it way back in a closet.

I still see that picture now, as if it tugs at me, whenever I pass that closet door. The picture is very clear in my mind. It was so sunny that day Henry had to squint against the glare. Or maybe the camera Bonita held flashed like a mirror, blinding him, before she snapped the picture. My face is right out in the sun, big and round. But he might have drawn back, because the shadows on his face are deep as holes. There are two shadows curved like little hooks around the ends of his smile, as if to frame it and try to keep it there—that one, first smile that looked like it might have hurt his face. He has his field jacket on and the worn-in clothes he'd come back in and kept wearing ever since. After Bonita took the picture, she went into the house and we got into the car. There was a full cooler in the trunk. We started off, east, toward Pembina and the Red River because Henry said he wanted to see the high water.

The trip over there was beautiful. When everything starts changing, drying up, clearing off, you feel like your whole life is starting. Henry felt it, too. The top was down and the car hummed like a top. He'd really put it back in shape, even the tape on the seats was very carefully put down and glued back in layers. It's not that he smiled again or even joked, but his face looked to me as if it was clear, more peaceful. It looked as though he wasn't thinking of anything in particular except the bare fields and windbreaks and houses we were passing.

The river was high and full of winter trash when we got there. The sun was still out, but it was colder by the river. There were still little clumps of dirty snow here and there on the banks. The water hadn't gone over the banks yet, but it would, you could tell. It was just at its limit, hard swollen, glossy like an old gray scar. We made ourselves a

fire, and we sat down and watched the current go. As I watched it I felt
something squeezing inside me and tightening and trying to let go all at
the same time. I knew I was not just feeling it myself; I knew I was
feeling what Henry was going through at that moment. Except that I
couldn't stand it, the closing and opening. I jumped to my feet. I took
Henry by the shoulders and I started shaking him. "Wake up," I says,
"wake up, wake up, wake up!" I didn't know what had come over me.
I sat down beside him again.

His face was totally white and hard. Then it broke, like stones break
all of a sudden when water boils up inside them.

"I know it," he says. "I know it. I can't help it. It's no use."

We start talking. He said he knew what I'd done with the car. It was
obvious it had been whacked out of shape and not just neglected. He
said he wanted to give the car to me for good now, it was no use. He
said he'd fixed it just to give it back and I should take it.

"No way," I says, "I don't want it."

"That's okay," he says, "you take it."

"I don't want it, though," I says back to him, and then to emphasize,
just to emphasize, you understand, I touch his shoulder. He slaps my
hand off.

"Take that car," he says.

"No," I say, "make me," I say, and then he grabs my jacket and rips
the arm loose. That jacket is a class act, suede with tags and zippers. I
push Henry backwards, off the log. He jumps up and bowls me over.
We go down in a clinch and come up swinging hard, for all we're worth,
with our fists. He socks my jaw so hard I feel like it swings loose. Then
I'm at his ribcage and land a good one under his chin so his head snaps
back. He's dazzled. He looks at me and I look at him and then his eyes
are full of tears and blood and at first I think he's crying. But no, he's
laughing. "Ha! Ha!" he says. "Ha! Ha! Take good care of it."

"Okay," I says, "okay, no problem. Ha! Ha!"

I can't help it, and I start laughing, too. My face feels fat and strange,
and after a while I get a beer from the cooler in the trunk, and when I
hand it to Henry he takes his shirt and wipes my germs off. "Hoof-and-
mouth disease," he says. For some reason this cracks me up, and so we're
really laughing for a while, and then we drink all the rest of the beers
one by one and throw them in the river and see how far, how fast, the
current takes them before they fill up and sink.

"You want to go on back?" I ask after a while. "Maybe we could snag
a couple nice Kashpaw girls."

He says nothing. But I can tell his mood is turning again.

"They're all crazy, the girls up here, every damn one of them."

"You're crazy too," I say, to jolly him up. "Crazy Lamartine boys!"

He looks as though he will take this wrong at first. His face twists,
then clears, and he jumps up on his feet. "That's right!" he says. "Crazier
'n hell. Crazy Indians!"

I think it's the old Henry again. He throws off his jacket and starts swinging his legs out from the knees like a fancy dancer. He's down doing something between a grouse dance and a bunny hop, no kind of dance I ever saw before, but neither has anyone else on all this green growing earth. He's wild. He wants to pitch whoopee! He's up and at me and all over. All this time I'm laughing so hard, so hard my belly is getting tied up in a knot.

"Got to cool me off!" he shouts all of a sudden. Then he runs over to the river and jumps in.

There's boards and other things in the current. It's so high. No sound comes from the river after the splash he makes, so I run right over. I look around. It's getting dark. I see he's halfway across the water already, and I know he didn't swim there but the current took him. It's far. I hear his voice, though, very clearly across it.

"My boots are filling," he says.

He says this in a normal voice, like he just noticed and he doesn't know what to think of it. Then he's gone. A branch comes by. Another branch. And I go in.

By the time I get out of the river, off the snag I pulled myself onto, the sun is down. I walk back to the car, turn on the high beams, and drive it up the bank. I put it in first gear and then I take my foot off the clutch. I get out, close the door, and watch it plow softly into the water. The headlights reach in as they go down, searching, still lighted even after the water swirls over the back end. I wait. The wires short out. It is all finally dark. And then there is only the water, the sound of it going and running and going and running and running.

Study and Discussion Questions

1. How does the tone of the story shift when Henry returns from Vietnam?
2. How has Henry changed now that he's back from Vietnam?
3. List the various ways that Erdrich gives us clues throughout "The Red Convertible" about how it will end.
4. What are the phases the car goes through? How do these stand for what Lyman and Henry are going through?
5. What does the description of Henry's picture tell us about Henry? About the narrator Lyman? Why is the picture incident placed where it is in the story?
6. Why do Henry and Lyman fight down by the river?
7. How does the first paragraph of the story manage to tell us exactly what the end of the story will be and yet not give that ending away?

Writing Exercises

1. Discuss the image of the red convertible's "drowning." Why does Lyman send the car into the water? Why do you think the car's lights are left on?

2. Are there any ways in which Erdrich suggests that being Native Americans shapes Henry's and Lyman's experience?
3. Pick one incident in the story—e.g., the visit to long-haired Susy in Alaska, or Henry's watching TV and biting through his lip—and discuss why you think Erdrich included it.

DONALD BARTHELME   (b. 1931)

Donald Barthelme was born in Philadelphia, grew up in Houston, and, after study at the University of Houston and service in the Army in Korea and Japan, moved to New York City in 1962. His short stories, frequently published in The New Yorker *magazine, are collected in* Unspeakable Practices, Unnatural Acts *(1968),* City Life *(1970),* Sadness *(1972), and other volumes. He has also published the novels* Snow White *(1967) and* The Dead Father *(1975).*

Report   (1968)

Our group is against the war. But the war goes on. I was sent to Cleveland to talk to the engineers. The engineers were meeting in Cleveland. I was supposed to persuade them not to do what they are going to do. I took United's 4:45 from LaGuardia arriving in Cleveland at 6:13. Cleveland is dark blue at that hour. I went directly to the motel, where the engineers were meeting. Hundreds of engineers attended the Cleveland meeting. I noticed many fractures among the engineers, bandages, traction. I noticed what appeared to be fracture of the carpal scaphoid in six examples. I noticed numerous fractures of the humeral shaft, of the os calcis, of the pelvic girdle. I noticed a high incidence of clay-shoveller's fracture. I could not account for these fractures. The engineers were making calculations, taking measurements, sketching on the black board, drinking beer, throwing bread, buttonholing employers, hurling glasses into the fireplace. They were friendly.

They were friendly. They were full of love and information. The chief engineer wore shades. Patella in Monk's traction, clamshell fracture by the look of it. He was standing in a slum of beer bottles and microphone cable. "Have some of this chicken à la Isambard Kingdom Brunel[1] the Great Ingineer," he said. "And declare who you are and what we can do for you. What is your line, distinguished guest?"

"Software," I said. "In every sense. I am here representing a small group of interested parties. We are interested in your thing, which seems

---

[1] 19th century British engineer.

to be functioning. In the midst of so much dysfunction, function is interesting. Other people's things don't seem to be working. The State Department's thing doesn't seem to be working. The U.N.'s thing doesn't seem to be working. The democratic left's thing doesn't seem to be working. Buddha's thing—"

"Ask us anything about our thing, which seems to be working," the chief engineer said. "We will open our hearts and heads to you, Software Man, because we want to be understood and loved by the great lay public, and have our marvels appreciated by that public, for which we daily unsung produce tons of new marvels each more life-enhancing than the last. Ask us anything. Do you want to know about evaporated thin-film metallurgy? Monolithic and hybrid integrated-circuit processes? The algebra of inequalities? Optimization theory? Complex high-speed micro-miniature closed and open loop systems? Fixed variable mathematical cost searches? Epitaxial deposition of semi-conductor materials? Gross interfaced space gropes? We also have specialists in the cuckooflower, the doctorfish, and the dumdum bullet as these relate to aspects of today's expanding technology, and they do in the damnedest ways."

I spoke to him then about the war. I said the same things people always say when they speak against the war. I said that the war was wrong. I said that large countries should not burn down small countries. I said that the government had made a series of errors. I said that these errors once small and forgivable were now immense and unforgivable. I said that the government was attempting to conceal its original errors under layers of new errors. I said that the government was sick with error, giddy with it. I said that ten thousand of our soldiers had already been killed in pursuit of the government's errors. I said that tens of thousands of the enemy's soldiers and civilians had been killed because of various errors, ours and theirs. I said that we are responsible for errors made in our name. I said that the government should not be allowed to make additional errors.

"Yes, yes," the chief engineer said, "there is doubtless much truth in what you say, but we can't possibly *lose* the war, can we? And stopping is losing, isn't it? The war regarded as a process, stopping regarded as an abort? We don't know *how* to lose a war. That skill is not among our skills. Our array smashes their array, that is what we know. That is the process. That is what is.

"But let's not have any more of this dispiriting downbeat counter-productive talk. I have a few new marvels here I'd like to discuss with you just briefly. A few new marvels that are just about ready to be gaped at by the admiring layman. Consider for instance the area of realtime online computer-controlled wish evaporation. Wish evaporation is going to be crucial in meeting the rising expectations of the world's peoples, which are as you know rising entirely too fast."

I noticed then distributed about the room a great many transverse fractures of the ulna. "The development of the pseudo-ruminant stomach for underdeveloped peoples," he went on, "is one of our interesting things you should be interested in. With the pseudoruminant stomach they can chew cuds, that is to say, eat grass. Blue is the most popular color worldwide and for that reason we are working with certain strains of your native Kentucky *Poa pratensis*, or bluegrass, as the staple input for the p/r stomach cycle, which would also give a shot in the arm to our balance-of-payments thing don't you know. . . ." I noticed about me then a great number of metatarsal fractures in banjo splints. "The kangaroo initiative . . . eight hundred thousand harvested last year . . . highest percentage of edible protein of any herbivore yet studied . . ."

"Have new kangaroos been planted?"

The engineer looked at me.

"I intuit your hatred and jealousy of our thing," he said. "The ineffectual always hate our thing and speak of it as anti-human, which is not at all a meaningful way to speak of our thing. Nothing mechanical is alien to me," he said (amber spots making bursts of light in his shades), "because I am human, in a sense, and if I think it up, then 'it' is human too, whatever 'it' may be. Let me tell you, Software Man, we have been damned forbearing in the matter of this little war you declare yourself to be interested in. Function is the cry, and our thing is functioning like crazy. There are things we could do that we have not done. Steps we could take that we have not taken. These steps are, regarded in a certain light, the light of our enlightened self-interest, quite justifiable steps. We could, of course, get irritated. We could, of course, *lose patience.*

"We could, of course, release thousands upon thousands of self-powered crawling-along-the-ground lengths of titanium wire eighteen inches long with a diameter of .0005 centimetres (that is to say, invisible) which, scenting an enemy, climb up his trouser leg and wrap themselves around his neck. We have developed those. They are within our capabilities. We could, of course, release in the arena of the upper air our new improved pufferfish toxin which precipitates an identity crisis. No special technical problems there. That is almost laughably easy. We could, of course, place up to two million maggots in their rice within twenty-four hours. The maggots are ready, massed in secret staging areas in Alabama. We have hypodermic darts capable of piebalding the enemy's pigmentation. We have rots, blights, and rusts capable of attacking his alphabet. Those are dandies. We have a hut-shrinking chemical which penetrates the fibres of the bamboo, causing it, the hut, to strangle its occupants. This operates only after 10 P.M., when people are sleeping. Their mathematics are at the mercy of a suppurating surd we have invented. We have a family of fishes trained to attack their fishes. We have the deadly testicle-destroying telegram. The cable companies are coöperating. We have a green substance that, well, I'd rather not talk about. We have a secret word that, if pronounced, produces multiple fractures in all living things in an area the size of four football fields."

"That's why—"

"Yes. Some damned fool couldn't keep his mouth shut. The point is that the whole structure of enemy life is within our power to *rend, vitiate, devour,* and *crush.* But that's not the interesting thing."

"You recount these possibilities with uncommon relish."

"Yes I realize that there is too much relish here. But *you* must realize that these capabilities represent in and of themselves highly technical and complex and interesting problems and hurdles on which our boys have expended many thousands of hours of hard work and brilliance. And that the effects are often grossly exaggerated by irresponsible victims. And that the whole thing represents a fantastic series of triumphs for the multi-disciplined problem-solving team concept."

"I appreciate that."

"We *could* unleash all this technology at once. You can imagine what would happen then. But that's not the interesting thing."

"What is the interesting thing?"

"The interesting thing is that we have *a moral sense.* It is on punched cards, perhaps the most advanced and sensitive moral sense the world has ever known."

"Because it is on punched cards?"

"It considers all considerations in endless and subtle detail," he said. "It even quibbles. With this great new moral tool, how can we go wrong? I confidently predict that, although we *could* employ all this splendid new weaponry I've been telling you about, *we're not going to do it.*"

"We're not going to do it?"

I took United's 5:44 from Cleveland arriving at Newark at 7:19. New Jersey is bright pink at that hour. Living things move about the surface of New Jersey at that hour molesting each other only in traditional ways. I made my report to the group. I stressed the friendliness of the engineers. I said, It's all right. I said, We have a moral sense. I said, *We're not going to do it.* They didn't believe me.

Study and Discussion Questions

1. Describe the chief engineer's attitude towards the war, towards technology, towards social problems, and towards morality.

2. What do the chief engineer's discussions of "wish evaporation" and the "pseudo-ruminant stomach" suggest about how he views the people of poor nations?

3. What kind of person is Software Man? What does he represent? What effect does his talk with the chief engineer have on him?

4. Reread the long paragraph in which the chief engineer describes the new weapons available. How are we supposed to react? What is the effect of the matter-of-fact tone in which these bizarre horrors are described?

5. "Report" was first published during the Vietnam war. What in the story points to that war in particular?

Writing Exercises

1. Discuss a product of modern technology that you find frightening.
2. Speculate on how high-technology weaponry changes the nature of war.

POETRY

WILFRED OWEN (1893–1918)

Wilfred Owen was born in Oswestry, England and attended the University of London, but had to leave for lack of money. He considered joining the priesthood, worked as a private tutor in France, and then came back to England in 1915 to enlist. He was killed at the front in 1918, a week before the Armistice that ended World War I. His Poems *appeared in 1920.*

Dulce Et Decorum Est[1]   (1920)

Bent double, like old beggars under sacks,
Knock-kneed, coughing like hags, we cursed through sludge,
Till on the haunting flares we turned our backs
And towards our distant rest began to trudge.
Men marched asleep. Many had lost their boots   5
But limped on, blood-shod. All went lame; all blind;
Drunk with fatigue; deaf even to the hoots
Of tired, outstripped Five–Nines[2] that dropped behind.

Gas! Gas! Quick boys!—An ecstasy of fumbling,
Fitting the clumsy helmets just in time;   10
But someone still was yelling out and stumbling
And flound'ring like a man in fire or lime . . .
Dim, through the misty panes and thick green light,
As under a green sea, I saw him drowning.

In all my dreams, before my helpless sight,   15
He plunges at me, guttering, choking, drowning.

If in some smothering dreams you too could pace
Behind the wagon that we flung him in,
And watch the white eyes writhing in his face,   20
His hanging face, like a devil's sick of sin;
If you could hear, at every jolt, the blood
Come gargling from the froth-corrupted lungs,
Obscene as cancer, bitter as the cud

---

[1] See last two lines for full quotation; from Horace: "It is sweet and proper to die for one's country."

[2] Gas shells.

Of vile, incurable sores on innocent tongues,—
My friend, you would not tell with such high zest   25
To children ardent for some desperate glory,
The old Lie: Dulce et decorum est
Pro patria mori.

Study and Discussion Questions

1. Who is speaking in the poem? Where is he? What is his past?
2. To whom is the poem addressed? Is it simply addressed to everyone?
3. List the various things the soldiers in general and the dying soldier in particular are compared to. What ironies do you find?

Writing Exercises

1. Which image in the poem strikes you most forcefully? Why?
2. Write your own critique (or defense) of the quote from Horace.

KOFI AWOONOR (b. 1935)

Kofi Awoonor was born in Wheta, Ghana and studied at the University of Ghana, the University of London, and the State University of New York at Stony Brook, where he has taught. He has also been Dean of Arts at the University of Cape Coast, Ghana and Ghana's Ambassador to Brazil. He has written fiction, drama, and several volumes of poetry, including Rediscovery *(1964),* Night of My Blood *(1971),* Ride Me, Memory *(1973), and* The House by the Sea *(1978).*

Song of War   (1961)

I shall sleep in white Calico;
War has come upon the sons of men
And I shall sleep in calico;
Let the boys go forward,
Kpli and his people should go forward;   5
Let the whiteman's guns boom,
We are marching forward;
We all shall sleep in calico.

When we start, the ground shall shake
The war is within our very huts;   10

Cowards should fall back
And live at home with the women;
They who go near our wives
While we are away in battle
Shall lose their calabashes when we come.   15

Where has it been heard before
That a snake has bitten a child
In front of its own mother?
The war is upon us:
It is within our very huts,   20
And the sons of men shall fight it.
Let the whiteman's guns boom,
And its smoke cover us.
We are fighting them to die.
We shall die on the battlefield;   25
We shall like death at no other place.
Our guns shall die with us,
And our sharp knives shall perish with us.
We shall die on the battlefield.

Study and Discussion Questions

1. What kind of war is this? Who is fighting whom?
2. What is the meaning of the repeated reference to sleeping in calico?
3. What makes the poem a "song" of war?

Writing Exercise

1. What is the speaker's attitude towards war and towards victory? How do you feel about this attitude?

BOB DYLAN (b. 1941)

Robert Zimmerman was born in Duluth, Minnesota and early in his singing career took the name "Dylan" from the poet Dylan Thomas. He began by singing the Depression songs of Woody Guthrie, but soon began composing and recording his own songs. Among his albums are The Times They Are A-Changin' *(1964),* John Wesley Harding *(1968), and* Blood on the Tracks *(1975).*

SONG: **With God on Our Side**   **(1963)**

Oh my name it is nothin'
My age it means less
The country I come from
Is called the Midwest
I's taught and brought up there   5
The laws to abide
And that land that I live in
Has God on its side.

Oh the history books tell it
They tell it so well   10
The cavalries charged
The Indians fell
The cavalries charged
The Indians died
Oh the country was young   15
With God on its side.

Oh the Spanish-American
War had its day
And the Civil War too
Was soon laid away   20
And the names of the heroes
I's made to memorize
With guns in their hands
And God on their side.

Oh the First World War, boys   25
It closed out its fate
The reason for fighting
I never got straight
But I learned to accept it
Accept it with pride   30
For you don't count the dead
When God's on your side.

When the Second World War
Came to an end
We forgave the Germans   35
And we were friends
Through they murdered six million

In the ovens they fried
The Germans now too
Have God on their side.   40

I've learned to hate Russians
All through my whole life
If another war starts
It's them we must fight
To hate them and fear them   45
To run and to hide
And accept it all bravely
With God on my side.

But now we got weapons
Of the chemical dust   50
If fire them we're forced to
Then fire them we must
One push of the button
And a shot the world wide
And you never ask questions   55
When God's on your side.

In a many dark hour
I've been thinkin' about this
That Jesus Christ
Was betrayed by a kiss   60
But I can't think for you
You'll have to decide
Whether Judas Iscariot
Had God on his side.

So now as I'm leavin'   65
I'm weary as Hell
The confusion I'm feelin'
Ain't no tongue can tell
The words fill my head
And fall to the floor   70
If God's on our side
He'll stop the next war.

Study and Discussion Questions

1. What wars does Dylan mention in this song? What future war does he
   fear?

2. What does it imply to say that God is on your side?
3. Why does Dylan bring in Jesus and Judas?
4. What does Dylan mean when he says in the last stanza: "the words fill my head / and fall to the floor"?

Writing Exercises

1. Pick any one of the wars Dylan mentions. What were you brought up to believe about it? If your beliefs have changed, what caused that to happen?
2. What does Dylan think of history and history books? Do you agree?
3. Compare the lyrics of "With God On Our Side" to a "patriotic" song such as "The Battle Hymn of the Republic." What is the argument each song is making? What are the assumptions underlying each?

DENISE LEVERTOV   (b. 1923)

Denise Levertov was born at Ilford, in England. Her mother was Welsh and her father a Russian Jew who became an Anglican priest. She was educated at home. Levertov worked as a nurse during World War II, moved to the United States in 1948, and in the 1960s became active in protests against the Vietnam War. Her poetry includes The Jacob's Ladder *(1961),* The Sorrow Dance *(1967),* Relearning the Alphabet *(1970),* Freeing the Dust *(1975), and* Candles in Babylon *(1982).*

Life at War   (1968)

The disasters numb within us
caught in the chest, rolling
in the brain like pebbles. The feeling
resembles lumps of raw dough

weighing down a child's stomach on baking day.   5
Or Rilke said it, 'My heart . . .
Could I say of it, it overflows
with bitterness . . . but no, as though

its contents were simply balled into
formless lumps, thus   10
do I carry it about.'
The same war

continues.
We have breathed the grits of it in, all our lives,
our lungs are pocked with it,   15
the mucous membrane of our dreams
coated with it, the imagination
filmed over with the gray filfth of it:

the knowledge that humankind,

delicate Man, whose flesh   20
responds to a caress, whose eyes
are flowers that perceive the stars,

whose music excels the music of birds,
whose laughter matches the laughter of dogs,
whose understanding manifests designs   25
fairer than the spider's most intricate web,

still turns without surprise, with mere regret
to the scheduled breaking open of breasts whose milk
runs out over the entrails of still-alive babies,
transformation of witnessing eyes to pulp-fragments,   30
implosion of skinned penises into carcass-gulleys.

We are the humans, men who can make;
whose language imagines *mercy*,
lovingkindness; we have believed one another
mirrored forms of a God we felt as good—   35

who do these acts, who convince ourselves
it is necessary; these acts are done
to our own flesh; burned human flesh
is smelling in Viet Nam as I write.

Yes, this is the knowledge that jostles for space   40
in our bodies along with all we
go on knowing of joy, of love;

our nerve filaments twitch with its presence
day and night,
nothing we say has not the husky phlegm of it in the saying,   45

nothing we do has the quickness, the sureness,
the deep intelligence living at peace would have.

Study and Discussion Question

1. What images does Levertov use to describe what war does?
2. What images does she use to describe what human beings are and can be?
3. What does Levertov mean when she writes: "these acts are done / to our own flesh."

Writing Exercises

1. Which one or more of the following best describes your initial response to this poem: despair, joy, nausea, pain, hope, disgust, shock, indifference? Why?
2. What does "living at peace" mean to you?
3. In a short paragraph, write what you see as the argument Levertov is making in this poem. That is, attempt to translate the poem into a brief, reasoned essay.

MARGARET ATWOOD   (b. 1939)

Margaret Atwood was born in Ottawa, Canada and educated at the University of Toronto and at Radcliffe College. She has taught in several Canadian universities and served as president of the Writer's Union of Canada. Her poetry includes Double Persephone *(1962),* Power Politics *(1973), and* True Stories *(1981). Among her novels are* The Edible Woman *(1969),* Surfacing *(1972), and* The Handmaid's Tale *(1985).*

At first I was given centuries   (1971)

At first I was given centuries
to wait in caves, in leather
tents, knowing you would never come back

Then it speeded up: only
several years between   5
the day you jangled off
into the mountains, and the day (it was

spring again) I rose from the embroidery
frame at the messenger's entrance.

That happened twice, or was it   10
more; and there was once, not so
long ago, you failed,
and came back in a wheelchair
with a moustache and a sunburn
and were insufferable.   15

Time before last though, I remember
I had a good eight months between
running alongside the train, skirts hitched, handing
you violets in at the window
and opening the letter; I watched   20
your snapshot fade for twenty years.

And last time (I drove to the airport
still dressed in my factory
overalls, the wrench
I had forgotten sticking out of the back   25
pocket; there you were,
zippered and helmeted, it was zero
hour, you said Be
Brave) it was at least three weeks before
I got the telegram and could start regretting.   30

But recently, the bad evenings
there are only seconds
between the warning on the radio and the
explosion; my hands
don't reach you   35

and on quieter nights
you jump up from
your chair without even touching your dinner
and I can scarcely kiss you goodbye
before you run out into the street and they shoot   40

Study and Discussion Questions

1. Who is speaking? To whom?
2. In what ways does the speaker change and in what ways remain the
   same?

3. Describe the progression of situations from stanza to stanza.
4. Who are "they" in the last line?

Writing Exercises

1. Can you identify any particular wars the speaker has lived through? What are the clues?
2. What is the mood of the poem? What feelings does it evoke as you read it?

E. E. CUMMINGS   (1894–1962)

Edward Estlin Cummings was born in Cambridge, Massachusetts. His father was a Harvard professor and congregational minister. After receiving his B.A. and M.A. at Harvard, Cummings left for France to become a volunteer ambulance driver in the war. His rebellious attitudes led to his internment for several months in a French prison camp as a suspected spy, an experience he described in The Enormous Room *(1922). In 1923, he left France for Greenwich Village, where he settled. His poetry includes* Tulips and Chimneys *(1923),* XLI Poems *(1925), is 5 *(1926),* and ViVa *(1931).*

"next to of course god america i   (1926)

"next to of course god america i
love you land of the pilgrims' and so forth oh
say can you see by the dawn's early my
country 'tis of centuries come and go
and are no more what of it we should worry   5
in every language even deafanddumb
thy sons acclaim your glorious name by gorry
by jingo by gee by gosh by gum
why talk of beauty what could be more beautiful than these heroic happy dead   10
who rushed like lions to the roaring slaughter
they did not stop to think they died instead
then shall the voice of liberty be mute?"

He spoke. And drank rapidly a glass of water

Study and Discussion Questions

1. Who is speaking in lines 1 to 13? What is the setting?
2. Identify the original sources of as many of the familiar phrases used as you can. Why does Cummings run them together?
3. Why has Cummings written this as a sonnet? What is the function of the last line?
4. Discuss the phrase "these heroic happy dead." What is the poem saying about war?

Writing Exercises

1. Restate as an argument the point the poem is making.
2. Write a similar parody, in prose or verse, of a different kind of speaker.

CAROLYN FORCHÉ (b. 1950)

Carolyn Forché was born in Detroit, was educated at Michigan State University and Bowling Green University, and has taught at a number of colleges. She worked as a journalist for the human rights organization Amnesty International in El Salvador and lived there for several years. She has published two books of poetry, Gathering the Tribes *(1976) and* The Country Between Us *(1981), and has translated* Flowers from the Volcano *(1982) by Salvadoran poet Claribel Alegria.*

The Colonel (1978)

What you have heard is true. I was in his house. His wife carried a tray of coffee and sugar. His daughter filed her nails, his son went out for the night. There were daily papers, pet dogs, a pistol on the cushion beside him. The moon swung bare on its black cord over the house. On the television was a cop show. It was in English. Broken bottles were embedded in the walls around the house to scoop the kneecaps from a man's legs or cut his hands to lace. On the windows there were gratings like those in liquor stores. We had dinner, rack of lamb, good wine, a gold bell was on the table for calling the maid. The maid brought green mangoes, salt, a type of bread. I was asked how I enjoyed the country. There was a brief commercial in Spanish. His wife took everything away. There was some talk then of how difficult it had become to govern. The parrot said hello on the terrace. The colonel told it to shut up, and pushed himself from the table. My friend said to me with his eyes: say nothing. The colonel returned with a sack used to bring groceries home. He spilled many human ears on the table. They were like dried peach halves. There is no other way to say this. He took one of them in his hands, shook it in our faces, dropped it into a water glass. It came alive there. I am tired of fooling around he said. As for the rights of anyone, tell your people they can go fuck themselves. He swept the ears to the floor with his arm and held the last of his wine in the air. Something for your poetry, no? he said. Some of the ears on the floor caught this scrap of his voice. Some of the ears on the floor were pressed to the ground.

Study and Discussion Questions

1. What is going on in the poem? Who is the colonel? Why is the speaker visiting him?
2. Characterize the speaker's tone. What does it suggest?
3. Why does Forché mention such commonplace details as the daily papers, the pet dogs, the colonel's daughter's filing her nails?
4. Why does the colonel have a sack of human ears? And why does he show them to the speaker? What is their symbolic significance?

Writing Exercises

1. How is this "prose poem" like poetry and how is it like prose? Why do you think Forché chose this form?
2. "On the television was a cop show. It was in English." What is the significance of this detail? Look into the recent history of El Salvador (Forché's subject) and discuss the poem in that context.

MURIEL RUKEYSER   (1913–1980)

Muriel Rukeyser was born in New York City and attended Vassar College and Columbia University. A social activist for most of her life, she protested Southern racism in the early 1930s as well as the Vietnam war and women's inequality forty years later, and was American president of P.E.N., an organization that supports the rights of writers around the world. Rukeyser's poetry includes Theory of Flight *(1935),* The Green Wave *(1948),* The Body of Waking *(1958),* The Speed of Darkness *(1968), and* Breaking Open *(1973).*

Waking This Morning   (1973)

Waking this morning,
a violent woman in the violent day
Laughing.

              Past the line of memory
along the long body of your life   5
in which move childhood, youth, your lifetime of touch,
eyes, lips, chest, belly, sex, legs, to the waves of the sheet.
I look past the little plant
on the city windowsill
to the tall towers bookshaped, crushed together in greed,   10
the river flashing flowing corroded,
the intricate harbor and the sea, the wars, the moon, the
   planets, all who people space
in the sun visible invisible.
African violets in the light   15
breathing, in a breathing universe.   I want strong peace, and
   delight,
the wild good.
I want to make my touch poems:
to find my morning, to find you entire   20
alive moving among the anti-touch people.

             I say across the waves of the air to you:
today once more
I will try to be non-violent
one more day   25
this morning, waking the world away
in the violent day.

Study and Discussion Questions

1. Why does the speaker call herself "a violent woman"?
2. What does she remember and see when she wakes up? Why those particular things?
3. To whom is the poem addressed?
4. What are "touch poems"?
5. Who are the "anti-touch people"?
6. What does the speaker of the poem want for herself?

Writing Exercise

1. Analyze Rukeyser's use of the word "violent" in this poem.

ANONYMOUS

Papago[1] War Song

Is it for me to eat what food I have
And all day sit idle?
Is it for me to drink the sweet water poured out
And all day sit idle?
Is it for me to gaze upon my wife   5
And all day sit idle?
Is it for me to hold my child in my arms
And all day sit idle?

My desire was uncontrollable.
It was the dizziness [of battle];   10
I ground it to powder and therewith I painted my face.

It was the drunkenness [of battle];
I ground it to powder and therewith I tied my hair in a war knot.   15
Then did I hold firm my well-covering shield and my hard-striking club.
Then did I hold firm my well-strung bow and my smooth, straight-flying
     arrows.
To me did I draw my far-striding sandals, and fast   20
I tied them.

Over the flat land did I then go striding,
Over the embedded stones did I then go stumbling,
Under the trees in the ditches did I go stooping,
Through the trees on the high ground did I go hurtling   25
Through the mountain gullies did I go brushing quickly.

In four halts did I reach the shining white eagle, my guardian,   30
And I asked power.
Then favorable to me he felt
And did bring forth his shining white stone.
Our enemy's mountains he made white as with moonlight   35
And brought them close,
And across them I went striding.

---

[1] Indians of the U.S. Southwest.

In four halts did I reach the blue hawk, my guardian,
And I asked power.
Then favorable to me he felt   40
And did bring forth his blue stone.
Our enemy waters he made white as with moonlight.
And around them I went striding.

There did I seize and pull up and make into a bundle   45
Those things which were my enemy's,
All kinds of seeds and beautiful clouds and beautiful winds.
Then came forth a thick stalk and a thick tassel,
And the undying seed did ripen.   50

This I did on behalf of my people.
Thus should you also think and desire,
All you my kinsmen.

RICHARD LOVELACE   (1618–1658)

To Lucasta, Going to the Wars   (1649)

Tell me not, sweet, I am unkind
That from the nunnery
Of thy chaste breast and quiet mind,
To war and arms I fly.

True, a new mistress now I chase,   5
The first foe in the field;
And with a stronger faith embrace
A sword, a horse, a shield.

Yet this inconstancy is such
As you too shall adore;   10
I could not love thee, dear, so much,
Loved I not honor more.

JOHN MILTON (1608–1674)

On the Late Massacre at Piemont[1] (1655)

Avenge, O Lord, thy slaughtered saints, whose bones
    Lie scattered on the Alpine mountains cold,
    Ev'n them who kept thy truth so pure of old
    When all our fathers worshiped stocks and stones,
Forget not; in thy book record their groans   5
    Who were thy sheep, and in their ancient fold
    Slain by the bloody Piemontese that rolled
    Mother with infant down the rocks. Their moans
The vales redoubled to the hills, and they
    To heav'n. Their martyred blood and ashes sow   10
    O'er all th' Italian fields, where still doth sway
The triple tyrant,[2] that from these may grow
    A hundredfold, who, having learnt thy way,
    Early may fly the Babylonian[3] woe.

RALPH WALDO EMERSON (1803–1882)

Concord Hymn (1837)

Sung At the Completion Of the Battle[4]
Monument, July 4, 1837

By the rude bridge that arched the flood,
    Their flag to April's breeze unfurled,
Here once the embattled farmers stood
    And fired the shot heard round the world.

The foe long since in silence slept;   5
    Alike the conqueror silent sleeps;

---

[1] In 1655, the Roman Catholic Duke of Savoy sent troops to massacre members of a Protestant religious community in northwestern Italy.

[2] The Pope.

[3] Protestants associated the Catholic Church with the corrupt city of Babylon, the destruction of which the Bible prophesies.

[4] Revolutionary War battle, Concord, Massachusetts.

And Time the ruined bridge has swept
    Down the dark stream which seaward creeps.

On this green bank, by this soft stream,
    We set to-day a votive stone;   10
That memory may their deed redeem,
    When, like our sires, our sons are gone.

Spirit, that made those heroes dare
    To die, and leave their children free,
Bid Time and Nature gently spare   15
    The shaft we raise to them and thee.

ALFRED LORD TENNYSON   (1809–1892)

The Charge of the Light Brigade[1]   (1854)

I

Half a league, half a league,
Half a league onward,
All in the valley of Death
    Rode the six hundred.
"Forward, the Light Brigade!   5
Charge for the guns!" he said.
Into the valley of Death
    Rode the six hundred.

II

"Forward, the Light Brigade!"
Was there a man dismay'd?   10
Not tho' the soldier knew
    Some one had blunder'd.
Theirs not to make reply,
Theirs not to reason why,
Theirs but to do and die.   15
Into the valley of Death
    Rode the six hundred.

---

[1] Reconnaissance cavalry.

III

Cannon to right of them,
Cannon to left of them,
Cannon in front of them   20
  Volley'd and thunder'd;
Storm'd at with shot and shell,
Boldly they rode and well,
Into the jaws of Death,
Into the mouth of hell   25
  Rode the six hundred.

IV

Flash'd all their sabres bare,
Flash'd as they turn'd in air
Sabring the gunners there,
Charging an army, while   30
  All the world wonder'd.
Plunged in the battery-smoke
Right thro' the line they broke;
Cossack and Russian
Reel'd from the sabre-stroke   35
  Shatter'd and sunder'd.
Then they rode back, but not,
  Not the six hundred.

V

Cannon to right of them,
Cannon to left of them,
Cannon behind them   40
  Volley'd and thunder'd;
Storm'd at with shot and shell,
While horse and hero fell,
They that had fought so well   45
Came thro' the jaws of Death,
Back from the mouth of hell,
All that was left of them,
  Left of six hundred.

VI

When can their glory fade?   50
O the wild charge they made!
  All the world wonder'd.
Honour the charge they made!

Honour the Light Brigade,
  Noble six hundred!   55

RUDYARD KIPLING   (1865–1936)
_____

Tommy   (1890)

I went into a public 'ouse to get a pint o' beer,
The publican 'e up an' sez, "We serve no red-coats here."
The girls be'ind the bar they laughed an' giggled fit to die,
I outs into the street again an' to myself sez I:
    O it's Tommy this, an' Tommy that, an' "Tommy, go away";   5
    But it's "Thank you, Mister Atkins,"[1] when the band begins to play—
    The band begins to play, my boys, the band begins to play,
    O it's "Thank you, Mister Atkins," when the band begins to
    play.   10

I went into a theatre as sober as could be,
They gave a drunk civilian room, but 'adn't none for me;
They sent me to the gallery or round the music-'alls,
But when it comes to fightin', Lord! they'll shove me in the stalls![2]
    For it's Tommy this, an' Tommy that, an' "Tommy, wait outside";
    But it's "Special train for Atkins" when the trooper's on the tide—
    The troopship's on the tide, my boys, the troopship's on the tide,
    O it's "Special train for Atkins" when the trooper's on the tide.

Yes, makin' mock o' uniforms that guard you while you sleep
Is cheaper than them uniforms, an' they're starvation cheap;
An' hustlin' drunken soldiers when they're goin' large a bit   25
Is five times better business than paradin' in full kit.
    Then it's Tommy this, an' Tommy that, an' "Tommy, 'ow's yer soul?"
    But it's "Thin red line of 'eroes" when the drums begin to
        roll—
    The drums begin to roll, my boys, the drums begin to roll,
    O it's "Thin red line of 'eroes" when the drums begin to roll.

_____
[1] Thomas Atkins, generic name for a British soldier.
[2] Cheap seats.

We aren't no thin red 'eroes, nor we aren't no blackguards too,
But single men in barricks, most remarkable like you;
An' if sometimes our conduck isn't all your fancy paints,   35
Why, single men in barricks don't grow into plaster saints;
> While it's Tommy this, an' Tommy that, an' "Tommy, fall be'ind,"
> But it's "Please to walk in front, sir," when there's trouble in the
>   wind—
>   40
> There's trouble in the wind, my boys, there's trouble in the wind,
> O it's "Please to walk in front, sir," when there's trouble in the wind.

You talk o'better food for us, an' schools, an' fires, an' all: 45
We'll wait for extry rations if you treat us rational.
Don't mess about the cook-room slops, but prove it to our face
The Widow's[3] Uniform is not the soldier-man's disgrace.
> For it's Tommy this, an' Tommy that, an' "Chuck him out, the brute!"
> But it's "Saviour of 'is country" when the guns begin to shoot;
> An' it's Tommy this, an' Tommy that, an' anything you please;
> An' Tommy ain't a bloomin' fool—you bet that Tommy sees!   55

WALT WHITMAN   (1819–1892)

The Dying Veteran   (1892)

(A Long Island incident—early part of the nineteenth century)

Amid these days of order, ease, prosperity,
Amid the current songs of beauty, peace, decorum,
I cast a reminiscence—(likely 'twill offend you,
I heard it in my boyhood;)—More than a generation since,
A queer old savage man, a fighter under Washington himself,   5
(Large, brave, cleanly, hot-blooded, no talker, rather spiritualistic,
Had fought in the ranks—fought well—had been all through the
     Revolutionary war,)
Lay dying—sons, daughters, church-deacons, lovingly tending him,
Sharping their sense, their ears, towards his murmuring, half-caught
     words:
"Let me return again to my war-days,
To the sights and scenes—to forming the line of battle,
To the scouts ahead reconnoitering,

---

[3] Queen's.

To the cannons, the grim artillery,   15
To the galloping aids, carrying orders,
To the wounded, the fallen, the heat, the suspense,
The perfume strong, the smoke, the deafening noise;
Away with your life of peace!—your joys of peace!
Give me my old wild battle-life again!"   20

MARGARET SACKVILLE   (1881–1963)

Nostra Culpa[1]   (1916)

We knew, this thing at least we knew,—the worth
Of life: this was our secret learned at birth.
We knew that Force the world has deified,
How weak it is. We spoke not, so men died.
Upon a world down-trampled, blood-defiled,   5
Fearing that men should praise us less, we smiled.

We knew the sword accursed, yet with the strong
Proclaimed the sword triumphant. Yea, this wrong
Unto our children, unto those unborn
We did, blaspheming God. We feared the scorn   10
Of men; men worshipped pride; so were they led,
We followed. Dare we now lament our dead?

Shadows and echoes, harlots! We betrayed
Our sons; because men laughed we were afraid.
That silent wisdom which was ours we kept   15
Deep-buried; thousands perished; still we slept.
Children were slaughtered, women raped, the weak
Down-trodden. Very quiet was our sleep.

Ours was the vision, but the vision lay
Too far, too strange; we chose an easier way.   20
The light, the unknown light, dazzled our eyes.—
Oh! sisters in our choice were we not wise?
When all men hated, could we pity or plead
For love with those who taught the Devil's creed?

---

[1] Our blame (Latin).

Reap we with pride the harvest! it was sown   25
By our own toil. Rejoice! it is our own.
This is the flesh we might have saved—our hands,
Our hands prepared these blood-drenched, dreadful lands.
What shall we plead? That we were deaf and blind?
We mothers and we murderers of mankind.   30

AMY LOWELL   (1874–1925)

Patterns   (1916)

I walk down the garden paths,
And all the daffodils
Are blowing, and the bright blue squills
I walk down the patterned garden-paths
In my stiff, brocaded gown.   5
With my powdered hair and jewelled fan,
I too am a rare
Pattern. As I wander down
The garden paths.

My dress is richly figured,   10
And the train
Makes a pink and silver stain
On the gravel, and the thrift
Of the borders.
Just a plate of current fashion,   15
Tripping by in high-heeled, ribboned shoes.
Not a softness anywhere about me,
Only whalebone and brocade.
And I sink on a seat in the shade
Of a lime tree. For my passion   20
Wars against the stiff brocade.
The daffodils and squills
Flutter in the breeze
As they please.
And I weep;   25
For the lime-tree is in blossom
And one small flower has dropped upon my bosom.

And the plashing of waterdrops
In the marble fountain
Comes down the garden-paths   30
The dripping never stops.
Underneath my stiffened gown
Is the softness of a woman bathing in a marble basin,
A basin in the midst of hedges grown
So thick, she cannot see her lover hiding,   35
But she guesses he is near,
And the sliding of the water
Seems the stroking of a dear
Hand upon her.
What is Summer in a fine brocaded gown!   40
I should like to see it lying in a heap upon the ground.
All the pink and silver crumpled up on the ground.

I would be the pink and silver as I ran along the paths,
And he would stumble after,
Bewildered by my laughter.   45
I should see the sun flashing from his sword-hilt and the
buckles on his shoes.
I would choose
To lead him in a maze along the patterned paths,
A bright and laughing maze for my heavy-booted lover.   50
Till he caught me in the shade,
And the buttons of his waistcoat bruised my body as he
clasped me,
Aching, melting, unafraid.
With the shadows of the leaves and the sundrops   55
And the plopping of the waterdrops,
All about us in the open afternoon—
I am very like to swoon
With the weight of this brocade,
For the sun sifts through the shade.   60

Underneath the fallen blossom
In my bosom,
Is a letter I have hid.
It was brought to me this morning by a rider from the Duke.   65
"Madam, we regret to inform you that Lord Hartwell
Died in action Thursday se'nnight."[1]
As I read it in the white, morning sunlight,
The letters squirmed like snakes.

---

[1] A week ago Thursday.

"Any answer, Madam?" said my footman.   70
"No," I told him.
"See that the messenger takes some refreshment.
No, no answer."
And I walked into the garden,
Up and down the patterned paths,   75
In my stiff, correct brocade.
The blue and yellow flowers stood up proudly in the sun,
Each one.
I stood upright too,
Held rigid to the pattern   80
By the stiffness of my gown.
Up and down I walked.
Up and down.

In a month he would have been my husband.   85
In a month, here, underneath this lime,
We would have broke the pattern;
He for me, and I for him,
He as Colonel, I as Lady,
On this shady seat.   90
He had a whim
That sunlight carried blessing.
And I answered, "It shall be as you have said."
Now he is dead.

In Summer and in Winter I shall walk   95
Up and down
The patterned garden-paths
In my stiff, brocaded gown.
The squills and daffodils
Will give place to pillared roses, and to asters, and to snow   100
I shall go
Up and down,
In my gown.
Gorgeously arrayed,   105
Boned and stayed.
And the softness of my body will be guarded from embrace
By each button, hook, and lace.
For the man who should loose me is dead,   110
Fighting with the Duke in Flanders,
In a pattern called a war.
Christ! What are patterns for?

MARINA TSVETAYEVA   (1892–1941)

'A white low sun'[1]   (1917)

A white low sun, low thunderclouds; and back
behind the kitchen-garden's white wall, graves.
On the sand, serried ranks of straw-stuffed forms
as large as men, hang from some cross-beam.

Through the staked fence, moving about, I see   5
a scattering: of soldiers, trees, and roads;
and an old woman standing by her gate
who chews on a black hunk of bread with salt.

What have these grey huts done to anger you,
my God? and why must so many be killed?   10
A train passed, wailing, and the soldiers wailed
as its retreating path got trailed with dust.

Better to die, or not to have been born,
than hear that plaining, piteous convict wail
about these beautiful dark eyebrowed women.   15
It's soldiers who sing these days. O Lord God.

SIEGFRIED SASSOON   (1886–1967)

Does it Matter?   (1918)

Does it matter?—losing your legs? . . .
For people will always be kind,
And you need not show that you mind
When the others come in after hunting
To gobble their muffins and eggs.   5

Does it matter?—losing your sight? . . .
There's such splendid work for the blind;

---

[1] Translated by David McDuff and Jon Silkin.

And people will always be kind,
As you sit on the terrace remembering
And turning your face to the light.   10

Do they matter?—those dreams from the pit? . . .
You can drink and forget and be glad,
And people won't say that you're mad;
For they'll know you've fought for your country
And no one will worry a bit.   15

WILLIAM BUTLER YEATS   **(1865–1939)**

An Irish Airman Foresees His Death   **(1919)**

I know that I shall meet my fate
Somewhere among the clouds above;
Those that I fight I do not hate,
Those that I guard I do not love;
My country is Kiltartan Cross,   5
My countrymen Kiltartan's poor,
No likely end could bring them loss
Or leave them happier than before.
Nor law, nor duty bade me fight,
Nor public men, nor cheering crowds,   10
A lonely impulse of delight
Drove to this tumult in the clouds;
I balanced all, brought all to mind,
The years to come seemed waste of breath,
A waste of breath the years behind   15
In balance with this life, this death.

E. E. CUMMINGS   **(1894–1962)**

---

my sweet old etcetera   **(1926)**

my sweet old etcetera
aunt lucy during the recent

war could and what
is more did tell you just
what everybody was fighting   5

for,
my sister

isabel created hundreds
(and
hundreds) of socks not to   10
mention shirts fleaproof earwarmers

etcetera wristers etcetera, my
mother hoped that

i would die etcetera
bravely of course my father used   15
to become hoarse talking about how it was
a privilege and if only he
could meanwhile my

self etcetera lay quietly
in the deep mud et   20

cetera
(dreaming,
et
    cetera, of
Your smile   25
eyes knees and of your Etcetera)

FEDERICO GARCÍA LORCA   (1898–1936)

Ballad of the Spanish Civil Guard[1]   (1938)

Their horses are black.
Black are their iron shoes.
On their capes shimmer stains

---

[1] National police force, organized along military lines and frequently used for political repression. Poem translated by Langston Hughes.

of ink and wax.
They have, and so they never weep,   5
skulls of lead.
With patent-leather souls
they come down the road.
Wherever they pass they spread
silences of thick rubber   10
and rears of fine sand.
They go by, if they wish to go,
concealing in their heads
a vague astronomy
of abstract pistols.   15

Oh, city of the gypsies!
On the corners, banners,
The moon and pumpkins
preserved with gooseberries.
Oh, city of the gypsies!   20
Who could see you and not remember you?
City of grief and of musk
with towers of cinnamon.
When the night that came
nightly came nightly,   25
the gypsies in their forges
made suns and arrows.
A horse with a mortal wound
went from one door to another.
Glass roosters crowed   30
toward Jerez de la Frontera.[2]
The naked wind turns
the corner in surprise
in the night-silver night
that nightly comes nightly.   35

San José and the Virgin
loose their castanets
and come looking for the gypsies
to see if they can find them.
The Virgin comes dressed   40
in her village finery
of chocolate paper
and necklaces of almonds.
San José swings his arms

---

[2] City in Southwest Spain known for its sherry and cognac.

under a silken cape.   45
Behind comes Pedro Domecq
With three sultans of Persia.

The half moon dreams
an ecstasy of cranes.
Banners and torches   50
invade the roof-tops.
In the looking glasses sob
dancers who have no hips.
Water and shadow, shadow and water
toward Jerez de la Frontera.   55
Oh, city of the gypsies!
On the corners, banners.
Put out your green lights
for the Civil Guards are coming.
Oh, city of the gypsies!   60
Who could see you and not remember you?
Leave her far off from the sea
with no combs for her hair.

Two by two they come
to the city of fiesta.   65
A rustle of *siemprevivas*[3]
invades their cartridge belts.
Two by two they come.
A night of double thickness.
To them the sky is nothing   70
but a window full of spurs.

Fear ran wild in a city
that multiplied its door.
Through them came forty Civil Guards
bent on pillage.   75
The clocks all stopped
and the cognac in the bottles
put on their November mask
to invite no suspicions.
A flight of screams unending   80
rose among the weather-vanes.
Sabers cut the air
that the horses trampled.

---

[3] Everlastings or immortelles, flowers that keep their shape and color when dried.

Through the dusky streets
old gypsy women   85
flew with drowsy nags
and crocks of money.
Up the steep streets
the sinister capes mount,
followed by fugitive   90
whirlwinds of scissors.

At the Gate of Belen
the gypsies gather.
San José, full of wounds,
shrouds a young maiden.   95
All through the night
stubborn guns sound sharply.
The Virgin treats the children
with drops of small saliva.

But the Civil Guard   100
advances sowing fires
where imagination burns
young and naked.
Rosa de los Camborios
sobs on her doorstep   105
with two breasts cut away
and put on a platter.
And other girls flee
pursued by their tresses
through the air where the roses   110
of black dust explode.
When the roof-tops are no more
than furrows on the earth,
dawn rocks her shoulders
in a long profile of stone.   115

Oh, city of the gypsies!
As the flames draw near
the Civil Guard goes off
down a tunnel full of silence.
Oh, city of the gypsies!   120
Who could see you and not remember you?
Let them look for you on my forehead,
game of the sand and the moon.

BERTOLT BRECHT   (1898–1956)

From a German War Primer[1]   (1938)

AMONGST THE HIGHLY PLACED
It is considered low to talk about food.
The fact is: they have
Already eaten.

The lowly must leave this earth   5
Without having tasted
Any good meat.

For wondering where they come from and
Where they are going
The fine evenings find them   10
Too exhausted.

They have not yet seen
The mountains and the great sea
When their time is already up.

If the lowly do not   15
Think about what's low
They will never rise.

THE BREAD OF THE HUNGRY HAS
ALL BEEN EATEN
Meat has become unknown. Useless   .   20
The pouring out of the people's sweat.
The laurel groves have been
Lopped down.
From the chimneys of the arms factories
Rises smoke.   25

THE HOUSE-PAINTER[2] SPEAKS OF
GREAT TIMES TO COME
The forests still grow.

---

[1] Translated by Lee Baxendall, H. R. Hays, Lesley Lendrum, and John Willett.
[2] Adolf Hitler was commonly believed to have once been a house painter.

The fields still bear
The cities still stand.
The people still breathe.   30

ON THE CALENDAR THE DAY IS NOT
YET SHOWN
Every month, every day
Lies open still. One of those days   35
Is going to be marked with a cross.

THE WORKERS CRY OUT FOR BREAD
The merchants cry out for markets.
The unemployed were hungry. The employed
Are hungry now.   40
The hands that lay folded are busy again.
They are making shells.

THOSE WHO TAKE THE MEAT FROM THE TABLE
Teach contentment.
Those for whom the contribution is destined   45
Demand sacrifice.
Those who eat their fill speak to the hungry
Of wonderful times to come.
Those who lead the country into the abyss
Call ruling too difficult   50
For ordinary men.

WHEN THE LEADERS SPEAK OF PEACE
The common folk know
That war is coming.

When the leaders curse war   55
The mobilisation order is already written out.

THOSE AT THE TOP SAY: PEACE
AND WAR
Are of different substance.
But their peace and their war   60
Are like wind and storm.

War grows from their peace
Like son from his mother

He bears
Her frightful features.   65

Their war kills
Whatever their peace
Has left over.

ON THE WALL WAS CHALKED:
They want war.   70
The man who wrote it
Has already fallen.

THOSE AT THE TOP SAY:
This way to glory.
Those down below say: 75
This way to the grave.

THE WAR WHICH IS COMING
Is not the first one. There were
Other wars before it.
When the last one came to an end   80
There were conquerors and conquered.
Among the conquered the common people
Starved. Among the conquerors
The common people starved too.

THOSE AT THE TOP SAY COMRADESHIP   85
Reigns in the army.
the truth of this is seen
In the cookhouse.
In their hearts should be
The selfsame courage. But   90
On their plates
Are two kinds of rations.

WHEN IT COMES TO MARCHING MANY DO NOT
KNOW
That their enemy is marching at their head.   95
The voice which gives them their orders
Is their enemy's voice and
The man who speaks of the enemy
Is the enemy himself.

IT IS NIGHT   100
The married couples
Lie in their beds. The young women
Will bear orphans.

GENERAL, YOUR TANK IS A POWERFUL VEHICLE
It smashes down forests and crushes a hundred men.   105
But it has one defect:
It needs a driver.

General, your bomber is powerful.
It flies faster than a storm and carries more than an elephant.
But it has one defect: 110
It needs a mechanic.

General, man is very useful.
He can fly and he can kill.
But he has one defect:
He can think.   115

BABETTE DEUTSCH   (1895–1982)

Dawn in Wartime   (1943)

Sunrise tumbling in like a surf,
A foam of petals, curling thousands, lightly crumbling
Away into light.
Waking to this, how could the eyes hold
The shape of night's barren island, the cold cliffs   5
Climbed in sleep, how
Recall the burned sore scabby
Face of the world?
Into that sea of light the spirit waded
Like a young child at morning on the beach,   10
Saw only those giant combers, soft as roses,
That mothy spume unfeathering into air.
Lingered there, as a child lingers
To smooth bastions of whitest sand,
To finger shells brighter than dogwood flowers,   15
To stand, quietly,

Watching the immense marvel of morning
Rolling toward him all its uncreated hours.

H. D. (HILDA DOOLITTLE) (1886–1961)

FROM **The Walls Do Not Fall** (1944)

[1]

An incident here and there,
and rails gone (for guns)
from your (and my) old town square:

mist and mist-grey, no colour,
still the Luxor bee, chick and hare   5
pursue unalterable purpose

in green, rose-red, lapis;
they continue to prophesy
from the stone papyrus:

there, as here, ruin opens   10
the tomb, the temple; enter,
there as here, there are no doors:

the shrine lies open to the sky,
the rain falls, here, there
sand drifts; eternity endures: 15

ruin everywhere, yet as the fallen roof
leaves the sealed room
open to the air,

so, through our desolation,
thoughts stir, inspiration stalks us   20
through gloom:

unaware, Spirit announces the Presence;
shivering overtakes us,
as of old, Samuel:

trembling at a known street-corner,   25
we know not nor are known;
the Pythian pronounces—we pass on

to another cellar, to another sliced wall
where poor utensils show
like rare objects in a museum;   30

Pompeii has nothing to teach us,
we know crack of volcanic fissure,
slow flow of terrible lava,

pressure on heart, lungs, the brain
about to burst its brittle case   35
(what the skull can endure!):

over us, Apocryphal fire,
under us, the earth sway, dip of a floor,
slope of a pavement

where men roll, drunk   40
with a new bewilderment,
sorcery, bedevilment:

the bone-frame was made for
no such shock knit within terror,
yet the skeleton stood up to it: 45

the flesh? it was melted away,
the heart burnt out, dead ember,
tendons, muscles shattered, outer husk dismembered,

yet the frame held:
we passed the flame: we wonder   50
what saved us? what for?

[14]

Yet we, the latter-day twice-born,
have our bad moments when

dragging the forlorn
husk of self after us,   55

we are forced to confess to
malaise and embarrassment;

we pull at this dead shell,
struggle but we must wait

till the new Sun dries off   60
the old-body humours;

awkwardly, we drag this stale
old will, old volition, old habit

about with us;
we are these people,   65

wistful, ironical, wilful,
who have no part in

new-world reconstruction,
in the confederacy of labour,

the practical issues of art   70
and the cataloguing of utilities:

O, do not look up
into the air,

you who are occupied
in the bewildering   75

sand-heap maze
of present-day endeavour;

you will be, not so much frightened
as paralysed with inaction,

and anyhow,   80
we have not crawled so very far

up our individual grass-blade
toward our individual star.

[33]

Let us measure defeat
in terms of bread and meat   85

and continents
in relative extent of wheat

fields; let us not teach
what we have learned badly

and not profited by;   90
let us not concoct

healing potions for the dead,
nor invent

new colours
for blind eyes.   95

[43]

Still the walls do not fall,
I do not know why;

there is zrr-hiss,
lightning in a not-known,

unregistered dimension;   100
we are powerless,

dust and powder fill our lungs
our bodies blunder

through doors twisted on hinges,
and the lintels slant   105

cross-wise;
we walk continually

on thin air
that thickens to a blind fog,

then step swiftly aside,   110
for even the air

is independable,
thick where it should be fine

and tenuous
where wings separate and open,   115

and the ether
is heavier than the floor,

and the floor sags
like a ship floundering;

we know no rule   120
of procedure,

we are voyagers, discoverers
of the not-known,

the unrecorded;
we have no map;   125

possibly we will reach haven,
heaven.

RANDALL JARRELL   (1914–1965)

The Death of the Ball Turret Gunner   (1945)

From my mother's sleep I fell into the State,
And I hunched in its belly till my wet fur froze.
Six miles from earth, loosed from its dream of life,
I woke to black flak and the nightmare fighters.
When I died they washed me out of the turret with a hose.   5

GWENDOLYN BROOKS   (b. 1917)

the white troops had their orders but
the Negroes looked like men[1]   (1945)

They had supposed their formula was fixed.
They had obeyed instructions to devise
A type of cold, a type of hooded gaze.
But when the Negroes came they were perplexed.
These Negroes looked like men. Besides, it taxed   5
Time and the temper to remember those
Congenital iniquities that cause
Disfavor of the darkness. Such as boxed
Their feelings properly, complete to tags—
A box for dark men and a box for Other—   10
Would often find the contents had been scrambled.
Or even switched. Who really gave two figs?
Neither the earth nor heaven ever trembled.
And there was nothing startling in the weather.

CLAUDE McKAY   (1890–1948)

Look Within   (1945)

Lord, let me not be silent while we fight
     In Europe Germans, Asia Japanese

---

[1] Brooks points out (in 1988) that the poem was published in 1945; she writes that the
word "Negro" is "no longer used by self-respecting Blacks."

For setting up a Fascist way of might
    While fifteen million Negroes on their knees
Pray for salvation from the Fascist yoke   5
    Of these United States. Remove the beam
(Nearly two thousand years since Jesus spoke)
    From your own eyes before the mote you deem
It proper from your neighbor's to extract!
    We bathe our lies in vapors of sweet myrrh,   10
And close our eyes not to perceive the fact!
    But Jesus said: You whited sepulchre,
Pretending to be uncorrupt of sin,
    While worm-infested, rotten through within!

HENRY REED   (b. 1914)

Naming of Parts   (1946)

To-day we have naming of parts. Yesterday,
We had daily cleaning. And to-morrow morning,
We shall have what to do after firing. But to-day,
To-day we have naming of parts. Japonica
Glistens like coral in all of the neighbouring gardens,   5
    And to-day we have naming of parts.

This is the lower sling swivel. And this
Is the upper sling swivel, whose use you will see,
When you are given your slings. And this is the piling swivel,   10
Which in your case you have not got. The branches
Hold in the gardens their silent, eloquent gestures,
    Which in our case we have not got.

This is the safety-catch, which is always released
With an easy flick of the thumb. And please do not let me   15
See anyone using his finger. You can do it quite easy
If you have any strength in your thumb. The blossoms
Are fragile and motionless, never letting anyone see
    Any of them using their finger.

And this you can see is the bolt. The purpose of this   20
Is to open the breech, as you see. We can slide it

Rapidly backwards and forwards: we call this
Easing the spring. And rapidly backwards and forwards
The early bees are assaulting and fumbling the flowers:
    They call it easing the Spring.   25

They call it easing the Spring: it is perfectly easy
If you have any strength in your thumb: like the bolt,
And the breech, and the cocking-piece, and the point of
balance,
Which in our case we have not got; and the almond-blossom   30
Silent in all of the gardens and the bees going backwards and forwards,
    For to-day we have naming of parts.

OWEN DODSON   (b. 1914)

Black Mother Praying   (1946)

My great God, You been a tenderness to me,
Through the thick and through the thin;
You been a pilla to my soul;
You been like the shinin light a mornin in the black dark,
A elevator to my spirit.   5

Now there's a fire in this land like a last judgment,
And I done sat down by the rivers of Babylon
And wept deep when I remembered Zion,
Seeing the water that can't quench fire
And the fire that burn up rivers.   10
Lord, I'm gonna say my say real quick and simple:

You know bout this war that's bitin the skies and gougin out the earth.
Last month, Lord, I bid my last boy away to fight.
I got all my boys fightin now for they country.
Didn't think bout it cept it were for freedom;   15
Didn't think cause they was black they wasn't American;
Didn't think a thing cept that they was my only sons,
And there was mothers all over the world
Sacrificin they sons like You let Yours be nailed
To the wood for men to behold the right.   20

Now I'm a black mother, Lord, I knows that now,
Black and burnin in these burnin times.
I can't hold my peace cause peace ain't fit to mention
When they's fightin right here in our streets
Like dogs—mongrel dogs and hill cats.   25
White is fightin black right here where hate abides like a cancer wound
And Freedom is writ big and crossed out:
Where, bless God, they's draggin us outta cars
In Texas and California, in Newark, Detroit,

Blood on the darkness, Lord, blood on the pavement,   30
Leavin us moanin and afraid.
What has we done?
Where and when has we done?
They's plantin the seeds of hate down in our bone marrow
When we don't want to hate.   35

We don't speak much in the street where I live, my God,
Nobody speak much, but we thinkin deep
Of the black sons in lands far as the wind can go,
Black boys fightin this war with them.

We thinkin deep bout they sisters stitchin airplane canvas,   40
And they old fathers plowin for wheat,
And they mothers bendin over washtubs,
They brothers at the factory wheels:
They all is bein body beat and spirit beat and heart sore and wonderin.

Listen, Lord, they ain't nowhere for black mothers to turn.   45
Won't You plant Your Son's goodness in this land
Before it too late?
Set Your stars of sweetness twinklin over us like winda lamps
Before it too late?
Help these men to see they losin while they winnin   50
Long as they allow theyselves to lynch in the city streets and
        on country roads?

When can I pray again,
View peace in my own parlor again?
When my sons come home   55
How can I show em my broken hands?
How can I show em they sister's twisted back?
How can I present they land to them?

How, when they been battlin in far places for freedom?
Better let em die in the desert drinkin sand   60
Or holdin onto water and shippin into death
Than they come back an see they sufferin for vain.

I done seen a man runnin for his life,
Runnin like the wind from a mob, to no shelter.
Where were a hidin place for him?   65
Saw a dark girl nine years old
Cryin cause her father done had
The light scratched from his eyes in the month of June.
Where the seein place for him?
A black boy lyin with his arms huggin the pavement in pain.   70
What he starin at?
Good people hands up, searched for guns and razors and pipes.
When they gonna pray again?

How, precious God, can I watch my son's eyes
When they hear this terrible?   75
How can I pray again when my tongue
Is near cleavin to the roof of my mouth?
Tell me, Lord, how?

Every time they strike us, they strikin Your Son;
Every time they shove us in, they cornerin they own children.   80
I'm gonna scream before I hope again.
I ain't never gonna hush my mouth or lay down this heavy, black,
          weary, terrible load
Until I fights to stamp my feet with my black sons
On a freedom solid rock and stand there peaceful   85
And look out into the star wilderness of the sky
And the land lyin about clean, and secure land,
And people not afraid again.

Lord, let us all see the golden wheat together,
Harvest the harvest together,   90
Touch the fulness and the hallelujah together.
                                        Amen.

GWENDOLYN BROOKS   (b. 1917)
_____

the sonnet-ballad   (1949)

Oh mother, mother, where is happiness?
They took my lover's tallness off to war,

Left me lamenting. Now I cannot guess
What I can use an empty heart-cup for.
He won't be coming back here any more.   5
Some day the war will end, but, oh, I knew
When he went walking grandly out that door
That my sweet love would have to be untrue.
Would have to be untrue. Would have to court
Coquettish death, whose impudent and strange   10
Possessive arms and beauty (of a sort)
Can make a hard man hesitate—and change.
And he will be the one to stammer, "Yes."
Oh mother, mother, where is happiness?

YEVGENY YEVTUSHENKO   (b. 1933)

The Companion[1]   (1954)

She was sitting on the rough embankment,
her cape too big for her tied on slapdash
over an odd little hat with a bobble on it,
her eyes brimming with tears of hopelessness.
An occasional butterfly floated down   5
fluttering warm wings onto the rails.
The clinkers underfoot were deep lilac.
We got cut off from our grandmothers
while the Germans were dive-bombing the train.
Katya was her name. She was nine.   10
I'd no idea what I could do about her,
but doubt quickly dissolved to certainty:
I'd have to take this thing under my wing;
—girls were in some sense of the word human,
a human being couldn't just be left.   15
The droning in the air and the explosions
receded farther into the distance,
I touched the little girl on her elbow.
'Come on. Do you hear? What are you waiting for?'
The world was big and we were not big,   20
and it was tough for us to walk across it.
She had galoshes on and felt boots,

---

[1] Translated by Robin Milner-Gulland and Peter Levi, S. J.

I had a pair of second-hand boots.
We forded streams and tramped across the forest;
each of my feet at every step it took   25
taking a smaller step inside the boot.
The child was feeble, I was certain of it.
'Boo-hoo,' she'd say. 'I'm tired,' she'd say.
She'd tire in no time I was certain of it,
but as things turned out it was me who tired.   30
I growled I wasn't going any further
and sat down suddenly beside the fence.
'What's the matter with you?' she said.
'Don't be so stupid! Put grass in your boots.
Do you want to eat something? Why won't you talk?   35
Hold this tin, this is crab.
We'll have refreshments. You small boys,
you're always pretending to be brave.'
Then out I went across the prickly stubble
marching beside her in a few minutes.   40
Masculine pride was muttering in my mind:
I scraped together strength and I held out
for fear of what she'd say. I even whistled.
Grass was sticking out from my tattered boots.
So on and on   45
we walked without thinking of rest
passing craters, passing fire,
under the rocking sky of '41
tottering crazy on its smoking columns.

BABETTE DEUTSCH   (1895–1982)

Disasters of War: Goya[1] at the Museum   (1959)

Streets opening like wounds: Madrid's. The thresh
Of resistance ends before a tumbled wall;
     The coward and the cursing sprawl
       Brotherly, one white heap of flesh
         Char-mouthed and boneyard black.   5
A woman, dragged off, howls—a lively sack
Of loot. An infant, fallen on its back,

---

[1] Francisco Jose de Goya (1746–1828), Spanish artist; created a series of etchings, "Disasters of War," after Napoleon's invasion of Spain.

Scowls from the stones at the Herodian[2] lark.
Light is the monster fattening on this dark.

If shadow takes cadavers for her chair,   10
Where fresh fires glare life lifts a wolfish snout.
    Bruised and abused by hope, the rout,
    Turning, is gunned across the square
    And scattered. Rope, knife, lead
Slice prayer short. A lolling head   15
Grins, as with toothache. Stubbornly, the dead
Thrust forward like a beggar's senseless claw.
What is scrawled there in acid? THIS I SAW.

Beyond the Madonnas and marbles, Goya's brute
Testament pits itself against the hush   20
    Of the blond halls, the urbane crush—
    Against the slat-eyed, the astute,
    Craning, against the guard, who yawns.
And pits itself in vain: this dark, these dawns,
Vomit of an old war, things the nightmare spawns   25
Are pictures at an exhibition. We
Look, having viewed too much, and cannot see.

ROBERT LOWELL   (1917–1977)

For the Union Dead   (1964)

"Relinquunt Omnia Servare Rem Publicam."[1]

The old South Boston Aquarium stands
in a Sahara of snow now. Its broken windows are boarded.
The bronze weathervane cod has lost half its scales.
The airy tanks are dry.

Once my nose crawled like a snail on the glass;   5
my hand tingled

---

[2] Herod, bloodthirsty king of Judea in Jesus's time.
[1] "They give up everything to serve the republic."

to burst the bubbles
drifting from the noses of the cowed, compliant fish.

My hand draws back. I often sigh still
for the dark downward and vegetating kingdom   10
of the fish and reptile. One morning last March,
I pressed against the new barbed and galvanized

fence on the Boston Common. Behind their cage,
yellow dinosaur steamshovels were grunting
as they cropped up tons of mush and grass   15
to gouge their underworld garage.

Parking spaces luxuriate like civic
sandpiles in the heart of Boston.
A girdle of orange, Puritan-pumpkin colored girders
braces the tingling Statehouse,   20

shaking over the excavations, as it faces Colonel Shaw[2]
and his bell-cheeked Negro infantry
on St. Gaudens' shaking Civil War relief,
propped by a plank splint against the garage's earthquake.

Two months after marching through Boston,   25
half the regiment was dead;
at the dedication,
William James could almost hear the bronze Negroes breathe.

Their monument sticks like a fishbone
in the city's throat.   30
Its Colonel is as lean
as a compass-needle.

He has an angry wrenlike vigilance,
a greyhound's gentle tautness;
he seems to wince at pleasure,   35
and suffocate for privacy.

He is out of bounds now. He rejoices in man's lovely,
peculiar power to choose life and die—

---

[2] Robert Gould Shaw, white, led a black regiment.

when he leads his black soldiers to death,
he cannot bend his back.   40

On a thousand small town New England greens,
the old white churches hold their air
of sparse, sincere rebellion; frayed flags
quilt the graveyards of the Grand Army of the Republic.

The stone statues of the abstract Union Soldier   45
grow slimmer and younger each year—
wasp-waisted, they doze over muskets
and muse through their sideburns . . .

Shaw's father wanted no monument
except the ditch,   50
where his son's body was thrown
and lost with his "niggers."

The ditch is nearer.
There are no statues for the last war here;
on Boylston Street, a commercial photograph   55
shows Hiroshima boiling

over a Mosler Safe, the "Rock of Ages"
that survived the blast. Space is nearer.
When I crouch to my television set,
the drained faces of Negro school-children rise like balloons.   60

Colonel Shaw
is riding on his bubble,
he waits
for the blessèd break.

The Aquarium is gone. Everywhere,   65
giant finned cars nose forward like fish;
a savage servility
slides by on grease.

DENISE LEVERTOV   **(b. 1923)**

What Were They Like?   (1966)

1) Did the people of Viet Nam
    use lanterns of stone?
2) Did they hold ceremonies
    to reverence the opening of buds?
3) Were they inclined to quiet laughter?   5
4) Did they use bone and ivory,
    jade and silver, for ornament?
5) Had they an epic poem?
6) Did they distinguish between speech and singing?

1) Sir, their light hearts turned to stone.   10
    It is not remembered whether in gardens
    stone lanterns illumined pleasant ways.
2) Perhaps they gathered once to delight in blossom,
    but after the children were killed
    there were no more buds.   15
3) Sir, laughter is bitter to the burned mouth.
4) A dream ago, perhaps. Ornament is for joy.
    All the bones were charred.
5) It is not remembered. Remember,
    most were peasants; their life   20
    was in rice and bamboo.
    When peaceful clouds were reflected in the paddies
    and the water buffalo stepped surely along terraces,
    maybe fathers told their sons old tales.
    When bombs smashed those mirrors   25
    there was time only to scream.
6) There is no echo yet
    of their speech which was like a song.
    It was reported their singing resembled
    the flight of moths in moonlight.   30
    Who can say? It is silent now.

LANGSTON HUGHES   **(1902–1967)**

Without Benefit of Declaration   (1967)

Listen here, Joe,
Don't you know

That tomorrow
You got to go
Out yonder where   5
The steel winds blow?

Listen here, kid,
It's been said
Tomorrow you'll be dead
Out there where   10
The rain is lead.

Don't ask me why.
Just go ahead and die.
Hidden from the sky
Out yonder you'll lie: 15
A medal to your family—
In exchange for
A guy.

Mama, don't cry.

MARY EMENY   (b. 1942)

Barbed Wire   (1968)

A girl glides gracefully down the path
    the wind enjoying her dress
    it dances in the wind
Wire catches—grace is lost

A spirit flies gleefully to the clouds   5
    the breeze evoking its dreams
    they play in the breeze
Wire catches—the spirit falls

A boy rides eagerly down the road
    his bicycle wheels singing with him   10
    they sing well together
Wire blocks—the song stops

A will strides glistening in the sun
   a rainbow setting its course
   it is set wisely   15
Wire blocks—the will rusts

A woman works deftly in the fields
   the earth giving much to her hands
   they know to work gently
Wire cuts—the earth bleeds   20

A heart goes openly to the street
   the neighbors sharing its fruit
   it lives in sharing
Wire cuts—the heart retreats

A man walks nobly in the land   25
   its soul directing his steps
   they know pride in walking
Wire snares—the soul hides

A mind looks searchingly to the sky
   an unknown testing its strength   30
   it grows in searching
Wire snares—the mind is bound.

ANONYMOUS[1]

Americans Are Not Beautiful   (ca. 1968)

They are called *My*,
Which my brother says means beautiful.
But they are not beautiful:
They have too much hair on their arms like monkeys,
They are tall like trees without branches,   5
Their eyes are green like eyes of boiled pigs
In the markets during the New Year.
Their hair is blond and not black,

---

[1] A Vietnamese girl, age 14, living in Saigon.

Their skin is pink and not brown,
Their cars frighten cyclists in the streets,   10
Their flying machines and their dragonflies
Drop death on people and animals
And make trees bare of their leaves.
Here, Americans are not beautiful.
"But they are,   15
In their faraway country"
My brother says.

SUSAN GRIFFIN   (b. 1943)

Song My[1]   (1971)

(Oh God, she said.)

It began a beautiful day by the sun up
And we sat in our grove of trees of smiles
Of morning eggs and toast and jam
and long talks, and baby babble   5
Becky sitting in her chair
spreading goo in her hair.

(Oh God, she said, look at the baby)

saying "hi" "ho" "ha" hi hi, goggydoggymamadada HI
and the light was coming through the window   10
through the handprints on the glass
making shadow patterns, and the cold day
was orange outside and they were muddling
in their underwear, getting dressed,
putting diapers on the baby,   15
slipping sandals on her feet.

---

[1] Scene of 1968 massacre by U.S. soldiers of unarmed Vietnamese villagers, also referred
to as the My Lai massacre.

(Oh God, she said, look at the baby
He has blood all over, she cried,)

Then the postman came,
And she went out on the steps   20
and got her magazine. They stood
by the stairs and looked, the baby
tugging at her skirt saying
mamamamama upupup mememe
and they looked at the pictures of Song My.   25

(Oh God, she said, look at the baby
He has blood all over, she cried,
Look at that woman's face, my God,
She knows she's going to get it.)

Going to get it, they knew   30
they were going to get it,
and it was a beautiful day,
the day that began in the fields
with the golden grain against the blue sky
the babies singing as if there were not   35
soldiers in the air.

MARGE PIERCY   (b. 1936)

The nine of cups[1]   (1972)

Not fat, not gross, just well fed and hefty he sits before what's his,
the owner, the ultimate consumer, the overlord.
No human kidneys can pump nine cups of wine through
but that's missing the point of having: possession is power   5
whether he owns apartment houses or herds of prime beef
or women's soft hands or the phone lines or the right to kill
or pieces of paper that channel men's working hours.

---

[1] A tarot card, signifying material good fortune.

He is not malcontent. He has that huge high-colored
healthy face you see on executives just massaged. 10
He eats lobster, he drinks aged scotch, he buys pretty women.
He buys men who write about how he is a servant of circumstance.
He buys armies to shoot peasants squatting on his oil.

He is your landlord: he shuts off the heat and the light and 15
    the water,
he shuts off air, he shuts off growth, he shuts off your sex.
He buys men who know geology for him, he buys men who
    count stars,
he buys women who paint their best dreams all over his ceiling. 20
He buys giants who grow for him and dwarfs who shrink
and he eats them all, he eats, he eats well,
he eats and twenty Bolivians starve, a division of labor.

You are in his cup, you float like an icecube, you sink like
    an onion. 25
Guilt is the training of his servants that we may serve harder.
His priests sell us penance for his guilt,
his psychiatrists whip our parents through our cold bowels,
his explainers drone of human nature and the human condition.

He is squatting on our heads laughing. He belches with health. 30
He feels so very good he rewards us with TV sets
which depict each one of us his servants sitting
just as fat and proud and ready to stomp
in front of the pile of tin cans we call our castle.

On the six o'clock news the Enemy attacks. 35
Then our landlord spares no expense to defend us,
for the hungry out there want to steal our TV sets.
He raises our taxes one hundred per cent
and sells us weapons and sends us out to fight.
We fight and we die, for god, country and the dollar 40
and then we come back home
and he raises the rent.

JANICE MIRIKITANI

Attack the Water (1973)

My first flash
on the newsprint/face

she could have been
obachan[1]
back then/just after   5
the camps[2]
when the land/dried/up
no water for months.
In town,
they would not sell   10
to japs.
we had to eat what
we could grow
that's only natural
when there is nothing   15
else
nothing
        else.

we ate rice with roots & rooster legs.

            Vietnamese woman   20
            her face etched old
            by newsprint/war
            mother/grandmother
            she has borne them all
            (have they all died?)   25

            flash!!

        "they are bombing the waterways

        "this new offensive
        which has previously/been/avoided/
        for humanitarian/reasons/   30
        will/seriously/jeopardize/
        their/food/situation."

Obachan
sitting
breathing heavily   35

---

[1] Grandmother.

[2] The United States government placed 110,000 Japanese-Americans in detention camps during World War II.

in the sun
watching her pet rabbits
(she loved them like children)
which one/
tonight?   40
i still remember her eyes
drawing the blood
like water.
And the rice—
there were maggots   45
in the rice.
no water
to flush/them/out.

      Up river
      bodies floated in My Chanh   50
      eyes eaten by crabs
      flushed onto the land—
      fly food.
      "They are attacking the water.
      when all else fails   55
      attack the water."

Obachan
would chew
the food first/spit

out maggots.   60
Grandchildren
ate the spit-flushed rice.

      when all else fails
      attack the water.

JUDY GRAHN   (b. 1940)

Vietnamese woman speaking to
an American soldier   (1978)

Stack your body
on my body

make
   life
make children play   5
in my jungle hair
make rice flare into my sky like
whitest flak
the whitest flash
my eyes have   10
    burned out
looking
press your swelling weapon
here
between us   if you   15
push it quickly I should
  come
to understand your purpose
what you bring us
what you call it   20
there
in your country

CAROLYN FORCHÉ   (b. 1950)

The Visitor   (1979)

In Spanish he whispers there is no time left.
It is the sound of scythes arcing in wheat,
the ache of some field song in Salvador.
The wind along the prison, cautious
as Francisco's hands on the inside, touching   5
the walls as he walks, it is his wife's breath
slipping into his cell each night while he
imagines his hand to be hers. It is a small country.

There is nothing one man will not do to another.

JUNE JORDAN   (b. 1936)

War Verse   (1985)

Something there is that sure must love a plane
No matter how many you kill with what kind of

bombs or how much blood you manage to spill
you never will hear the cries of pain

Something there is that sure must love a plane   5
The pilots are never crazy or mean
and bombing a hospital's quick and it's clean
and how could you call such precision insane?

Something there is that sure must love a plane!

DRAMA

MARC KAMINSKY   (b. 1943)

Marc Kaminsky was born in New York City and educated at Columbia University. He has taught English at the City University of New York, worked at a senior citizens center, run writing workshops, and been co-director of the Brookdale Institute for the Humanities, Arts, and Aging. He has written poetry, nonfiction, and drama. His book, The Road From Hiroshima *(1984) includes accounts by Hiroshima survivors.* In the Traffic of a Targeted City *premiered at the Theater for the New City in 1986.*

In the Traffic of a Targeted City   (1986)

CHARACTERS

New York:

Jonah, a sculptor
Walkman, a teenager
Joanna, a political activist
Uncle Max, a Holocaust survivor

Hiroshima:

Mother
Woman in White Kimono
Set-Chan
Nakajima Hiroshi, a poet
Townswoman
Nakajima's Wife
Misao, Nakajima's sister
Old Woman

Characters are played by two actors. Character definition is made by costume and lighting changes, as well as by changes in the actors' physical and vocal life.

SETTING

Japanese-like screens define the space of a New York studio, subway, office, cocktail party, bedroom and also several locations in Hiroshima. The screens have windows that can be opened and closed, a sliding door and one other entrance.

The set pieces consist of a bench and a stool; they are used to suggest a subway, an artist's stool and a Japanese desk. Shifts in lighting and music help to create the various locations.

The play takes place in New York today and Hiroshima, 1945.

As the audience enters, saxophone and piano music play over speakers. Jonah sits SR weaving together a network of wood slats with copper wire. He rolls up the slats, puts them aside, moves the ladder from UR to extreme DR (with slats) and exits. Lights to black. Music plays in darkness, finishes.

Music changes to saxophone clacks. Lights up DL on Walkman bopping on the subway. Sound changes to subway noise, then screech. Jonah enters DR and dresses hurriedly as:

Subway Announcement. Attention! Attention! We are holding this train due to a delay behind us! This is an express train making local stops. I repeat, this is a local train making express stops only. It is imperative that all passengers immediately proceed to . . . (words become unintelligible). . . .Please follow these instructions exactly. Thank you for your co-operation and patience.

Jonah *(has finished dressing and rushed to subway entrance).* What did he say? *(Walkman doesn't answer. Jonah sits, subway starts. Jonah looks at datebook.)*

It's amazing how little time there is in New York City! Men with briefcases on their laps do paperwork in the subway, thinking the whole time: In Tucson, maybe there there is time.

Women with ladles in their hands and telephones in their necks are talking to Kansas: In Grandmother's time there was time, but in these renovated brownstones there isn't any left.

I'm no different from anybody else. I run across a lot of women in the course of a week. In offices, in parties, in bed, they are all depressed.

(They lean as subway stops, Walkman exits.)

There's no time for supper. The men are grabbing a slice of pizza on Forty-Second Street.

The women are making up before a make-up exam at the New School.[1]

There is no time to transplant the bride's veil.

There is no time because there are dirty socks in the hamper.

There are 10,000 mile tune-ups, there are friends from Boston, there is snow, there are innuendos, there are taxes, dentists, dissertations, parking meters, bonuses, transfers, cousins and ice cream or fortune cookies.

(Subway stops. Joanna enters, sits.)

There are three important relationships.

(They lean as subway starts.)

There are twenty-five people ahead of you waiting to be tested for herpes.

There are children fracturing common daylight in prism studies, they all want to do well on the rainbow exam.

There is software and geology, there is the shortage of French brie, there are stamps, there is fluorescent lighting, there is the bartender who takes forever to serve you.

There are people who push six when you are trying to get to the ground floor.

There is the subway conductor who presides over husbands who are getting left behind.

There are usually benefits, there are often stop signs, there are long lines at the teller's window every Friday, there is Susan Sontag's[2] new book on authenticity, and this week there are dress rehearsals and tomatoes on sale.

There is no time because there is Marlon Brando[3] at the Trans Lux East and the general disposition of everything to run down, be reviewed, or require sleep.

(They lean as subway stops.)

There is no time because it takes so much time to think of all this and to feel depressed about it and to go through with it.

---

[1] The New School for Social Research, a university in New York City.

[2] (b. 1933), American critic.

[3] (b. 1924), American movie actor.

(They lean as subway starts.)

       Datebooks don't seem to help.
       No matter how ingeniously the men and women of New York
fold and pack their hours, they can't take everything with them
in a seven-day week.
       They spread out their calendars before them like generals.
They move love into the position occupied by the Soho opening
to make room for the piano.
       They drop pottery, juggle basketball, cancel dance, advance
Spanish, they wake up, they go to sleep, they miss appointments
with their therapists, forty-five minutes does not leave them enough
time for breakfast. They get finished with sex in time to walk the
dog.

(They lean as subway stops.)

       I would like to open my closets and show you what lack of
time has done to my shoes and make you see what happens when
there is no time in the courtrooms and in the heads of households.

(He turns to her and speaks. She doesn't hear him.)

       I would like to touch the back of your head with a strong
pair of feelings.
       I would like to massage your eyes, neck and temples until
the tension leaves you and you start to cry.
       But I know you don't have time for this, and I too have to
be getting on.

(They lean as subway starts.)

*(Joanna has been reading a book. Jonah looks over her shoulder. She catches
him; he goes back to his datebook. She looks over to see what he is reading
and becomes very interested. He catches her; she goes back to her book. They
both lean over and read the other's book. They catch each other and laugh.
As the train comes to a stop, she gives him her book, and then, as she goes
off, she swipes his datebook. The door shuts before he can catch her. He starts
to read the book she gave him. A very long screech is heard. There is a
blackout. The lights come back up in silence. Jonah goes back to the book.
Live chords are heard, and a woman in a kimono appears behind a screen.*

She speaks what Jonah is reading. She is carrying a blanket that appears to
have a baby inside it.)

Mother: It happened something like an electric short
                   a bluish-white light
                   blanked out everything
                   there was noise more than the ground beneath me
                   could take I felt great heat
                   even inside the house
                   I was underneath the destroyed house
                   I thought: a bomb
                   has fallen directly upon me our house
                   has been directly hit I became furious
                   roof tiles and walls everything black covering me
                   I screamed from all around I heard screaming
                   then I felt a kind of danger
                   unable to do anything by my own power
                   I didn't know where I was or what I was under
                   I thought: I'm going to die.

(The woman disappears. Jonah slams the book shut. Blackout, music and lights
up on Uncle Max in hat, overcoat, with cane.)

Uncle Max: I alone survived:

                   my wife
                   couldn't abandon
                   her furniture

                   my son was
                   determined to finish his book
                   on Wagner[4]

                   Father couldn't believe
                   the ministers in black leather
                   were death

                   my friend
                   buried his circumcised dread
                   in the little hours you rent in hotel rooms

---

[4] Richard Wagner (1813–1883), German composer.

but I
who found the consolations of daily life
insufficient, I alone

survived.

(Uncle Max removes his hat and straightens up to reveal Jonah, who removes and hangs up his coat and hat as he speaks.)

Jonah. That's what my Great Uncle Max told me last Friday. Every other Friday we meet in the park and we talk. He makes me ask myself— and I hate the question—"What can I be in this wretched time?"

(Jonah crosses DR to his "studio" and examines his ladder sculpture until there is a beep of a phone answering-machine. Joanna's voice as phone message comes over speaker.)

Joanna. Hi. My name is Joanna Green. I'm the one who stole your datebook this morning on the subway. You certainly are a busy fellow. But your datebook says you're free tonight. I'm going to be at a meeting of Artists for a Nuclear Free Harbor at 7:30, 225 Lafayette Street. You could meet me there, and I can give you the book back, and we could use your help. I hope to see you there. Oh—I hope you read the book I gave you. I'd like to know what you think of it.

(Jonah puts sculpture away and picks up book. As he reads, a woman in a long white kimono enters behind him, carrying a lantern. She speaks what he is reading.)

Woman: A great river runs through Hiroshima
and every year
we bring lanterns
inscribed with the names of the family dead

and light them and set them afloat—
lanterns
that carry the dead
vows of the living who will never forget

them and the way they died—
and for miles
the full breadth of the river is one
mass of flames.

(She hangs the lantern UC. It will remain there throughout the play. She turns her back to the audience.)

Jonah *(reading).* August 10, 1945.

Along the main road out
of Hiroshima
all the shutters were closed.
So the wounded walked on

or lay down in front of the houses
that no cry
would open.
But at a dry-goods store

on this side of Mitaki Station
they found
a woman who had managed to sneak inside
and die in one of their closets.

The owner, annoyed
at this disagreeable consequence,
dragged the body out by its feet
which were bare

and filthy.
And his wife was distraught
and he was scandalized
when they saw

the corpse dressed in their
daughter's best
summer kimono—a wonderful
piece of work

which they instantly tore
off the dead body,
only to find
that it had no underwear on.

And they could feel only
how unlucky they were
till the priest came
and explained what had probably happened.

She must have been burnt out
of her home—a girl
of no more than sixteen years—
who fled

all the way from the city,
looking for something
to hide her nakedness
even before she sought water.

(Woman tears off her kimono slowly, turns downstage and walks as she describes):

There was no light at all every time
an oildrum exploded
the ground shook huge pillars
of smoke went up they broke

into a run they ran
a few feet then went back
to their dead walk
their eyes closed

they swayed to and fro pushed
they staggered in any direction
they were carried by the long lines leaving
Hiroshima

covered with black rain
with chalky ash there wasn't one
who wasn't bleeding the hands
the face the feet the anus

from any place it is possible
to bleed they bled
their mouths their eyes I am
still with them I see them

like walking ghosts their arms
bent forward like this
they had a special way of walking—
very slowly—like this—

if only
there were one or two of them!

but wherever I walked
I met these people

many of them
died along the road—
I myself
was one of them.

*(Music and ghost walk continue until phone rings. Blackout. Music. Lights up
on Jonah UC with the book.)*

Jonah: What is to be done?
          The time given to me on earth
          is already half gone

          I have little to waste
          on public causes
          and I dislike the righteous ones
          who wave aside my nuances.

(Joanna enters with datebook, shakes hands with Jonah.)

Joanna: I don't know how many nights
          I lay awake with an aching conscience—like you
          I wasted days, months, asking:
          what is to be done?

*(She hands him datebook, he hands her Hiroshima book; during the following
they pass the two books back and forth. Jonah ends up with both.)*

Jonah: Look, I am
          an artist. I mean:
          my days are eaten up
          with putting bread on the table

          my nights with putting on paper
          what my life has given me
          to make known, my friends
          complain they don't see me

          enough, and I also yearn
          for them, and a few hours

of ceasing to drop
through these bottomless weeks

in this speeded-up, well-planned
rampantly efficient absence
of time—

Joanna: We have a hall to rent. Posters
          to print. Money to raise.

Jonah: Where will I fit
          more tasks? how can I commit
          more hours—

Joanna: Come back when you are tired
          of being agitated. And don't think
          I'm promising you peace
          of mind. The exhilaration

          of working to save the planet
          will pass quickly enough.
          Immersed in routine tasks, you
          won't feel particularly ennobled.

          Nor will you feel despairing.
          You will simply know: you
          are doing what must be done.
          But this will be enough

          to allow you to remain fully conscious—
          even of the anguish at the bottom
          of oceans
          in these deadening times.

Jonah: But this will be enough.

          to allow me to remain fully conscious—
          even of the anguish at the bottom
          of oceans
          in these deadening times.

(She exits. Jonah opens Hiroshima book. Voice of **Nakajima** is heard over
speakers.)

Yoshiko! Nanae! Misa!
If you are here among this pile of bones,
move your fingers a little,
so that I can tell it is you—
I will take you home for proper burial.

(Lights down on Jonah. Up on Walkman UC.)

Walkman: In History
the teacher asked us:
How do you prepare
for nuclear war?
Can it be done?
He divided the class

into two teams
and had us debate
the issue.
At the end we voted.
Mostly everyone
voted no.

And my heart
was racing
so fast I didn't think
I'd be able to
talk
maybe what I wanted

to say
was stupid
but how could they
raise their arms
and vote no
so calmly?

Listen, I said,
I made a tape
exactly 26 minutes long
it took me weeks
to pick out the top 8 songs
of my life.

I'll tell you something
I cried

when I had to leave out
"Like a Virgin."
But there just wasn't time
for everything.

And I carry this
tape with me everywhere I go.
So people can prepare
and they do, everyone
does in his own way.

When the warning comes
I'll put on my headphones
and turn on
my tape
and let the music blast off

let it take my mind
off the earth
and go to my feet
and I'll just start walking on air
till I meet the bomb.

(Walkman dances to the music on her headphones, exits as lights fade on her and come up on Jonah. Nakajima's voice comes over speakers.)

Even those
who looked like they were going to be spared
were not spared.

One by one
those who escaped with light injuries
began to sicken.

Nosebleeds, bloody vomit, bleeding
from the vagina,
bloodspots under the skin—

with these signs
the bomb took up its second life
among us. Without privacy

we open every fold
of our bodies to anyone
who happens to be looking,

> hundreds of times a day, looking
> for the hidden spot that tells
> how soon
>
> each of us is going to turn the mulberry
> color of worms
> and die.

Jonah (*interrupts voice*). There are taxes, dentists, dissertations, parking meters, bonuses, transfers, cousins, and ice cream or fortune cookies. There are three important relationships. . . .

(*Woman in long dark kimono appears upstage, speaks*)

Set-Chan: Her voice under the burning house
saying:

> Mother will come after you, Set-chan,
> so you go away first.
> Now quickly. Quickly.
>
> Forty-one years have passed
> walking
>   and lying down
>
> alone
> or in the arms of any man
> I hear my mother shouting at me:
>
> you go away
> quickly!

(*Blackout. Lights up on Jonah pacing and Joanna sitting on stool DR.*)

Joanna: Tell!

Jonah: I was born in 1943

Joanna: Grew up in the traffic
of a targeted city.

Jonah: With chalk. And asphalt.
Home and second
base were manhole

                        covers. I played
                        in the intervals
                        between oncoming cars.

Joanna: At school?

Jonah: Aquired
               the basic skills.

Joanna: And a stainless steel
               chain around the neck.

Jonah: I learned: this
               was a first aquisition
               of status.

Joanna: And it is the necklace
               that soldiers wear
               into battle.

Jonah: I loved
               its silveriness

               and the clattering
               sound of running
               the name plate

               along its string
               of tiny
               ball bearings. I

               put them into my mouth
               and pulled them taut
               like a horse's bit.

Joanna: A nervous habit.

Jonah: My teachers
               tried to break me

               of this. So I started
               to finger my chain
               as if it were both

               my rosary
               and my worry beads

Joanna: No one explained it
              to you.

Jonah: But I knew:
              my name
              and my charred remains

              could be separated
              and thanks
              to the dog tag

              I would be sent
              to the correct parents
              for burial.

(Fifties-style rock and roll music begins. Jonah speaks, then sings as Joanna joins him singing in the style of a 50's doo-wop song.)

Jonah: Oh air raid drills of the early fifties!
              sublime minutes
              when Linda Brandon and I
              huddled under our desk chairs—
              my first taste of romantic love!

Jonah:	**Joanna:**
I remember how hushed the room was	The grotto of love
we were taken by surprise	The grotto of love
every time the teacher	The grotto of love
whispered it breathlessly—	
"Take cover!"	cover cover cover
	cover cover cover. . .
and we dove into a cave	
a cave of arms, our own	
and those of our desk chairs—	
two virginal bodies in the fifth grade	two virginal bodies in the fifth grade
I knew you had nothing on	The grotto of love
under your dress	The grotto of love
when you brushed against me	
and your straight black hair	
fell across my arm	
and a sheet of flame ran across my skin	and a sheet of flame ran across my skin

Oooooo. . . .
The grotto—   The grotto. . .
Room 417! What a place
for a love-grotto!
      —of love.   . . .of love.

(The music continues; Jonah and Joanna dance a slow jitterbug.)

Joanna *(while dancing):*
    Under every highway
    At the mouth

    Of every tunnel
    We drive into the dark

    Half-believing
    We'll never get out of it

    We grew up knowing
    What no generation before us

    Could know: the planet
    Is now as difficult

    To maintain as an intimate
    Relationship.

Jonah: Are you always this serious?

Joanna: You want fun? Go bowling. Don't get your hopes up on me.

Jonah: I only meant—it must be hell for you, living in some imaginary Hiroshima.

Joanna: It isn't imaginary. It happened. It could happen again. Hiroshima—New York. We're commuters.

(Blackout. Lights up on Uncle Max UC.)

Uncle Max: There were heroes: first
    and foremost were those with the courage
    to see in time.

I was not with them. Blinded
by humility. Or what I once called humility.
And by love. Or what passed

in our world for love. My attachment
to those who looked at the mask of evil
and called it a human face.

I thought: Who are you
to move against the weight
of their judgement?

And I thought: You will be crushed.
I thought: Who
will listen to you?

And even if
your nightmares are the real
news

who
will repair the damage if you
awaken the sleepwalkers?

So when the officials told us
to pack our bags
and come to the terminal

I, too,
took my place
quietly, in line.

(Blackout. Jonah and Joanna appear DR with cocktails. Music as at a party.)

Joanna: Everyone's running around
                   Hungry to be saved

                   Vitamin C, Jesus, jogging

Jonah: Oral worship of the foot

Joanna: Each day we commit ourselves
                   To another regimen

Jonah: Muktananda[5]

Joanna: juice fasts

Jonah: changing
          Apartments

Joanna: partners

Jonah: or genders

Joanna: We go geneological and hunt
          For roots

Jonah: Make a latter-day communion
          With ethnic food

Joanna: Or return to librium

Jonah: Or the Ph.D. program
          In industrial psychology

Joanna: With a little cocaine, a little
          Real estate speculation

Jonah: Or the Lubavitcher Rebbe[6]

          The Moonie[7] kids
          Greet us with roses

          Under every highway
          At the mouth

          Of every tunnel

Joanna: We drive into the dark

          Half-believing
          We'll never get out of it.

          We grew up knowing
          What no generation before us

---

[5] Swami Paramhamsa Muktananda (b. 1908), guru popular in the United States.

[6] Leader of Jewish sect.

[7] Member of cult led by Sun Myung Moon.

Could know: the planet
Is now as difficult

To maintain as an intimate
Relationship

Joanna: And we go through
One enlightening experience

After another, hoping
Each time

To take final vows—
We, who are no good

At long-term affairs

(They kiss. Joanna exits. Jonah crosses DR. Nakajima's voice is heard over the speakers.)

Nakajima *(over speakers):* Yoshiko! Nanae! Misa!

Yoshiko *(over speakers):* Where are your daughters? In good health?

Jonah: Joanna, do you ever think about having children?

(The Hibakusha Mother enters in short kimono, carrying blanket/baby.)

Mother: I am still on the road to the doctor's house
carrying my baby
in my arms
thinking: he is going to survive

He was five months old
and all I could give him was gruel—
thin gruel
there were no spots on his body

A week after the bomb fell
he began to look better
I was pleased—
he was the only one I had left

and while we were on the road
to the doctor's house
he died
I found two big spots on his bottom

I am always on the road to the doctor.

(She crosses to Jonah and hands him the folded blanket. He begins to unfold it.)

Joanna *(over speakers):*   Something meant for use. A shadow passport.
This is your chance.

(Jonah unfolds the blanket completely to reveal a kimono jacket and the Hiroshima book. Jonah hesitates, then puts on kimono, kneels Japanese-style and picks up the book—the same one Joanna gave him on the subway. As he does this, the Mother folds the blanket and sets it DL with a pair of Japanese sandals. An air raid siren is heard; Jonah, as Nakajima Hiroshi, runs DL to his desk.)

Nakajima: The screeching alarm bells
and rattle
of antiaircraft fire

woke me at three this morning.
The enemy planes
had already passed over

our house and were dropping
incendiary bombs
in the distance.

At my desk, my hands
tremble. I can do nothing
but helplessly record

these events
in a journal I have to keep
hidden.

If I live
to have grandchildren
ask me about the war

I will tell them:
it wasn't possible to write
let alone publish

the truth. To speak
sometimes meant
never to speak again.

Hiroshima, New Year's Day, 1945.

After the all clear
my daughters went up to Gobenden shrine
to pray.

Today the temple bells
that signal the end of the year
did not sound.

And it began to snow
just before dawn.
Bit by bit, in unison, the sky

and the earth became one
color, and the seven rivers froze
From the hills at Futaba-no-sato

I looked down at Hiroshima
and I saw the many
bridges of the city

bleed
into the white
rivers

and the rivers meld
with the unaccustomed whiteness
of the streets

and the sun breaks
through
onto this field of lost edges

turning it
into a blinding
sheet of light.

(A Woman in a short kimono appears behind a window. She appears at doors and windows during the next section.)

Woman: What can this mean, snowfall
in January?

Nakajima: They walked side by side
with their heads bowed, speaking
in whispers:

old and young, walking
home from the factories, across
Aioi Bridge.

Woman: When was the last time
this happened?

Nakajima. *(in the voice of a naive young man):*
Snow
on the Inland Sea?

Woman: In
the warmth of our winter?

Nakajima: The old ones tried to remember
details of the storm
that befell their grandparents—

The young ones insisted:

Woman: It is not a sign
that some catastrophe will come
before the year is out.

Nakajima: In whispers, the questions.
In whispers, the answers
the repetitions. . . .

Woman: It is an omen
that the B-29's will continue
to pass

over Hiroshima without dropping
their load.

Both: Our luck will hold good.

Nakajima: Listening
                     as always to the conversations
                     among which I walk

                     I measure the intervals
                     between these exchanges of
                     the correct views.

                     Each day they get longer.
                     The list
                     Of things we dare not say

                     has gotten so huge
                     it blots out nearly all discussion.
                     Once we had victories

                     of the Imperial Army
                     to talk about.
                     Then there was rationing

                     then factory work
                     then the black market
                     then the air raids

                     but all that is used up.
                     Today we have snow in January.

Both (*singing*): the war has gone on too long
                     our luck can't hold

                     holidays can't be told
                     apart from days of hunger
                     and every day beaten

                     into nightmare by the erratic
                     air-raid warnings and lack
                     of sleep

                     the endless drills and hours
                     of "volunteer labor"—nothing exists now
                     but the war.

(She exits. Nakajima folds blanket and lays it out as a tablecloth.)

Nakajima: May 7, 1945.

                     This morning—six small clams.
                     I dug them
                     out of the sand under Miyuki Bridge.

                     My daughters
                     foraged for wild plants
                     near the banks of the Ota
                     but even their secret place
                     was picked clean.

                     So my wife set out
                     with our youngest one's
                     best summer kimono—
                     the last fine piece of
                     anything we had to trade.

Nakajima's Wife: *(enters with a tray of dishes to be used later for dinner)*:
                                          I sold it

                     for a cake of bean curd
                     two Chinese cabbages
                     six carrots, a bunch of spinach
                     and four eggplants—

                     all this
                     because my sister Misao arrived
                     from Tokyo today

                     and we didn't want her
                     coming under our roof
                     without a proper welcome.

(He crosses UC. Misao, dressed in short kimono, enters. They bow.)

Nakajima: Three steps
                     out of the train
                     as she embraced me
                     Misao whispered:

Misao: Do you still eat here
                     in Hiroshima?

                                          (They cross DR, Misao kneels.)

Nakajima: We walked
for miles beyond the city
and in a scorched field

where only the crows
could overhear us
I answered, "No."   *(Nakajima kneels, they lean to-*
                                     ward each other.)

Misao: My husband   *(Misao pulls back, looks around*
was not captured   *to see if they are being watched,*
he is dead   *and leans back to Nakajima. She*
                                    speak-sings this section.)

and our house
destroyed
after the latest raid

Tokyo
is a plain of broken objects
I have nothing

not even a photograph
to place on a family altar
nothing

remains of my life
in Tokyo
my daughter was seized

by the Kempei-tai[8]
for making defeatist remarks
marched into a meadow

made to sit down
and pummeled
from early morning

until late at night.
Don't think I believe   *(Her tone of voice changes.)*
that Japan will lose the war.

Nakajima: Misao! I'm your brother!   *(He reaches to comfort her.)*

(They rise and move to the blanket.)

---

[8] Secret Police.

Nakajima: I ushered her into   *(They remove shoes.)*
our house
ceremoniously

Misao: We sat down formally *(She begins to set places at the table.)*
on our heels.

Nakajima: My sister Misao, my brother Kyoji,   *(He walks around*
my daughters Yoshiko, Nanae, Misa,   *the table indi-*
my wife and I.   *cating the places*
                                       where each will
Our daughters served the meal: *sit, then kneels.)*

Misao: A tempura   *(She lays out serving dishes.)*
of eggplant and cabbage,
a bit of bean curd, broiled
with salt, two
raw slices of carrot—

Nakajima: a great luxury—

Misao: and a bowl of barley.

Nakajima: The clams—

Misao: six
little reminders
of days of peace—

Nakajima: were beautifully displayed—

Misao: three apiece—

Nakajima: on the plates
of my sister and brother.

And so we entered the circle
of the comfort of food.   *(They reach for chopsticks.)*
But Yoshiko could not
contain herself! She asked:

Misao: Where is your daughter?
In good health?

                                 (Her chopstick drops.)

Nakajima: Misao answered:

Misao: In Tokyo.

Nakajima: For one night let us forget
the war:

I have something
which can draw
out forgotten feelings

and give us a taste of
how we will live
when it ends.   *(He exits, returns with tray
of sake and two cups.)*

Nakajima: Sake!—homemade—
that I managed to lay my hands on.
To our health   *(He pours glass for
Misao, she pours
one for him.)*

and to the health of everyone here.
Two glasses of this
will get you quite happy   *(They clink glasses,
drink.)*

and if you think you are happy—   *(She pours him an-
then you are—in a way—   other glass, they
happy. One by one   clink again, drink.)*

we drank to each other's health:
sister and brother and brother
and sister-in-law and wife

and daughters and aunt and nieces
and uncle and parents—
all gathered at one table.

That night
while we were together
again

it seemed as though a line
had been drawn
around my house

and for as long as we sat there
banqueting
the war couldn't come in.

July 1st, 1945.   *(Shift in music.)*

Misao: Used up the last of our salt   *(She hurriedly puts dishes back*
with tonight's meal.   *on tray.)*

Nakajima: At sundown we crawled
into our bedrolls, hoping
to get some rest   *(He extinguishes the lan-*
before the air raid sirens. . .   *tern and unfolds the*
                                     blanket to a bed.)
our fatigue   *(Air siren is heard.)*
is so vast
it has gotten the better of

our fears. We yearn
for one thing only: a night
of sleep.   *(She exits with tray,*
                                      comes back and gets

Misao: Let them   *under blanket.)*
get it over with!
We've been at it so long—

let it come! tonight!
let the worst of it
be finished!

(Nakajima embraces her as light fades slowly to black and then comes up on Jonah and Joanna in a similar embrace.)

Joanna: If I shriek
who will hear me
if I don't
break the silence
            who will
hear me
if I speak normal
words in the normal
order

who will hear me

if I tell
what they saw and heard on the road
from Hiroshima

will I disturb
the dead

will I
be a merchant of their disaster

if I fail
who will forgive me

(*Lights down to black and then up on Nakajima and Misao in original embrace.*)

Nakajima: August 6th, 1945.

(*They get up as in morning. He kneels at his desk. As she hands him a cup of tea, there is a blinding flash and a blackout. During the following poem, which is heard in the voice of Nakajima over the speakers, there is a series of "tableaux vivants." In each one, the lights come up slowly on the image and then there is a blinding flash and a blackout:*

> *Set-chan at the window.
> *Nakajima, reaching through the door to light the lantern.
> *Misao, offering a bowl of rice.
> *Uncle Max and Joanna, arm-in-arm.
> *Walkman, dancing*

Nakajima (*over speakers*):
          A terrible flash
          rushed from east to west
          and became everywhere
          at once

          there was a wave
          of heat
          that reached under my clothes
          and scorched my skin

          it passed
          the sky held its breath
          trees broke
          into flame

          there was a blank
          in time
          then a huge boom
          came thundering

          toward the mountain
          a violent rush of air

took my body
and flung it against the ground

my hair tangled in branches
a wall of wind
pressed my being
into the earth

there was a silence
then a series
of shattering sounds
a mass of clouds

rose
and climbed rapidly into the sky
a column of boiling
clouds

spread and climbed, erupted
unfolded sideways, constantly
changing shape and color
climbed higher and wider

then burst
at the summit
and put out a monstrous head
that loomed over everything

I looked out
over a ledge of rock
and what I felt then
and what I feel now

I can't explain
it was not shock
or horror
I became mute with

I could see streets
in the distance
a few buildings
standing

here and there
but Hiroshima didn't exist

I saw
Hiroshima did not exist.

(*Lights up on Jonah and Joanna in bed. Joanna wakes as from a nightmare. She speaks the following, initially as a nightmare, then more and more as a young Japanese girl. Jonah puts on Nakajima's kimono and listens.*)

Joanna: Not aware
of what I was doing
I jumped
down to the train track and braced
myself against it

somebody fell on top of me, screaming
a stream of pebbles lashed my face
trying to scream
my tongue fought an eerie
weight and I couldn't
hear me

though I lay there shrieking with all
my strength

I found
I had stuffed a handkerchief into my mouth
and covered my eyes and ears
with my hands

I tried to open
my eyes
I thought: Lord
why have you blinded me?
I thought: this is happening
in a dream

there wasn't a soul on the platform

but their shoes! hundreds
of shoes, left
and right separated, confused
with clogs, strewn
among sandals and slippers

half buried
under hoods and parasols—

only the shoes and hats, shorn
of their people!

like headstones and footstones

and I
the only one left?

leaving Yokogawa Station
I couldn't make out the road.

I walked through what had once been
a house

shreds of someone's daily routine—
a clock, an ironing board, a photograph
Of a sailor carrying a boy on his back—

pieces of white blouse and mattress
hanging
from telegraph poles

Anyone here?

I realized I
was together with the dead
woman in her bedroom

only we weren't really inside the house

all the walls between outside
and inside missing

fire beginning to fan out before me
around me

everywhere was out-of-doors
and cemetery.

One thing consoled me: my watch
was still ticking
it was 8:31! Only sixteen minutes
since the blast

I began counting my footsteps
timing my progress.

8:50 A.M near Yokogawa Station:

Again
it came back to me: the sensation
this is happening in a dream—

the thatched roof on fire

the peasant and his wife
were carrying
a great laquered chest of drawers
they got stuck
in the doorway

no matter how they turned
and angled it
they couldn't come through

so they stood facing each other

the man taking a half-step to the left, slowly
the woman to the right
then back again
as if in a trance

a slow, solemn, mesmerizing dance
in the open doorway
as the cottage burned

nobody stopped to help them.

9:15 A.M., crossing Misasa Bridge:

From a distance
I could see only the woman, lying
on her side
half-blocking
the other end of the bridge

and the refugees, as they approached
her, hesitated

one turned back
and ran toward the burning city

"What is it?" I cried

but she didn't answer

"You'll get past this," I told myself
"if you don't look!"

but after counting a hundred steps
afraid
something bad was about to happen
I dropped my hands

and a baby girl
was undoing the buttons
of her mother's blouse

I drew close
and I saw
her clutch at the breasts of a corpse
she looked up at me
terrified

What could I possibly do for her?

"Go on," I said to my legs
"step over the body
and go on."

9:20 A.M., on the other side:

A girl my age
was standing with vacant eyes in the middle
of the road
the great wound in her forehead
like a pomegranate
cracked open

instinctively
I ran
my fingers across the skin
of my face

when I looked
down at my hands
there was blood on them

so I got the mirror
out of my emergency kit

and located
a small cut on my eyebrow

which I washed with spittle

then I
did up my hair
in a handkerchief
neatly
and went on.

9:40 A.M. at the bank of the Nagatsuka:

I was wearing a white blouse
with a blue pattern
miraculously it was free
of dirt
and it
didn't get torn

everyone else
was in rags and hurt
a woman
with the flesh of her side scooped out
and her ribs exposed
seeing me thread my way through the crowd
in my nice clothes
asked, "Can you help me?"

but a man came between us
and admonished her, saying, "Everyone
has the same pain as you.
Endure it
and we will find shelter."

4:30 P.M.

I reached my aunt's village

and I went to the river
to wash my clothes

the moment
I dipped my blouse in the water
it fell apart.

(She weeps. Jonah/Nakajima embraces her, as before.)

Jonah: Are you always this serious?

Joanna: You want fun? Go bowling.

Jonah: If I shriek
who will hear me
if I don't
break the silence
    who will
hear me
if I speak normal
words in the normal
order

who will hear me

if I put myself on the road
from Hiroshima
and tell what I hear and see

will I disturb
the dead

will I
be a merchant of our disaster

if I fail
who will forgive me

(Blackout. Lights up on Nakajima DC. Boogie woogie piano plays underneath.)

Nakajima: Instead of the usual rations
each of us was given seven cartons of
Wrigley's Spearmint Gum

we chewed
until the sugar was out of it
then spit it out

unfolding and working through
new sticks
at the rate of fifty an hour

I watched refugees
walk along, dropping
rubbery pellets

and silver
gum wrappers, ceaselessly
chewing.

When would they give us rice?
No one asked.
But how hopefully we greeted

each convoy of jeeps! the GIs beeped
in their good-natured way

there was a chorus of
"Hi!
How are you?"

and lines of frightened
beggars
immediately formed—

they were barraged with
Wrigley's
with a shower of

thousands of packs
of spearmint chewing
gum.

Already
the American century was carpeting Japan
with peculiar abundance

the road to the A-bomb ward
was now paved
with silver.

(Nakajima has picked up Jonah's shoes, and dances with them to the music.)

Nakajima *(over speakers)*:
          When the moment came
          I bent down
          and removed the shoes from the feet
          of a woman not yet

dead.
Glass scattered on the road—
in bare feet
I would never have escaped

On the day I forget her
eyes
and begin to live
at peace with my memories

I will not recognize what
I am, pure
as a bone, and all my words
lies.

Nakajima: And I ask myself:
will I ever again find anything
to celebrate?

Then I remember:

on the outskirts of the ruined city
all the houses collapsed
suddenly I was greeted by
dragonflies
flitting this way and that, so quickly, above
emerald fields
of rice

And I hated myself, realizing
that even on the day of horrors
I rejoiced!

(Old Woman appears at door in long white kimono. She sings.)

Old Woman: I still keep two pillows
on your side of the bed
but instead of puffing them up every morning
my hands sink into them

and put back the impression
your head left
when you slipped noiselessly into the day
I was still asleep

when the bomb fell
and all that remained
of your body
was this hollow place.

Anyone who might have seen you die
also evaporated
I have no thought
of anything now but you.

You must have gone
from driving full speed across Aioi Bridge
to death
in an instant.

My hands sink into them
and put back the impression
your head left
when you slipped noiselessly into the day.

(Lights out on Old Woman. During next poem, Nakajima removes kimono, puts on Jonah's shirt. Joanna enters and sits, peeling an orange into a bowl.)

Nakajima: I had a visitor.
He told me
he was a scrivener
he told me
he was sorry for talking too much
and he told me
this story:

In Danbara Shin-machi
he came
upon four women at the side of the road
and he wouldn't have stopped
but
they were sitting in a circle
they were sitting and facing each other
in a circle
and this
struck him as a remarkable thing

more than that—
an act of resistance
something

like meditation
like women
in a temple courtyard

so he was drawn to them
and their eyes
unlike the eyes of other victims
their eyes were open
they were

looking into each other's eyes

and this
more than anything else he saw that day
kept death from ascendancy
everywhere

He asked one of them where her home was

she said, "This is my home.
I am Yoshiko, oldest daughter
of the poet
Nakajima Hiroshi. If you meet my father
tell him not to waste time
looking for me
or Nanae or Misa or Aunt Misao.
We are all going to die
right here."

The others nodded in agreement

then the tears came
and he was helpless before them

Yoshiko said, "If you would shield us
from the sun
if you would find a way to shield us
from the wind
it would make us quite happy."

*(He builds a lean-to
with the ladder, the
slats and a piece of the
bench left onstage from
the bombing section.)*

So he built them a lean-to
of straw mats
and a few sheets of corrugated steel

and he went inside
and sat with them for a while

in his lunch box—three ripe tomatoes
which he sliced into halves
and he squeezed the juice onto the lips
and into the mouths
of my daughters   *(He hangs Na-*
                                         kajima's kimono
and though they could barely swallow   *over the lean-to.)*
each one mumbled
"Oishii! delicious!"

(Joanna crosses to Jonah and embraces him. The voice of Nakajima comes over speakers with other voices, singing.)

Rains will fall on the ruins
of the castle
as before

and trees will respond
each with its own kind of leaves
applauding the sun.

(While the song is playing, Joanna brings Jonah a slice of orange. He eats it as they look at lean-to.)

Jonah *(as song finishes):* Delicious!   *(They look at each other. Blackout)*

(Uncle Max enters UC.)

Uncle Max: No one told us: no

not the shoes you wore
to the state opera house

but the old boots
in the back of the closet—

and even then
you probably won't survive.

Here, retired admirals
speak against the arms race.

Scientists proclaim their warnings
on television.

You ask: How could we
go to our deaths like sleepwalkers?

But you of all people
should not ask.

(Jonah removes Uncle Max's hat and coat, takes down lantern. Joanna enters with the blanket and lays it out like the table near the lean-to.)

Jonah: A great river runs through Hiroshima

Both: and every year
we bring lanterns
inscribed with the names of the family dead

(He places lantern on blanket and they kneel.)

and light them and set them afloat.

(He lights lantern.)

Joanna: In Danbara Shin-machi
he came
upon four women by the side of the road
and he wouldn't have stopped
but
they were sitting in a circle

Jonah: they were sitting and facing each other
in a circle

Joanna: and this
struck him as a remarkable thing

Jonah: more than that—
an act of resistance

Joanna: And their eyes

Jonah: unlike the eyes of other victims

Both: their eyes were open

Jonah: they were sitting and
              looking into each other's eyes

Joanna: and this
              more than anything else he saw that day

Both: kept death from ascendancy
              everywhere.

Study Questions

1. What are the two settings of the play? What point is Kaminsky making by intersecting and juxtaposing these places and times?
2. How and why is there little or no time in New York City?
3. Who is Uncle Max? Why is he in the play?
4. Are there elements of humor in this play? Give two or three examples. How does humor function in the play?
5. What does the title of the play mean to you?
6. Why do Jonah and Joanna put on kimonos halfway through the play?
7. Why are the four women sitting at the side of the road seen as engaging in "an act of resistance"?

Writing Exercises

1. "The planet/ is now as difficult/ to maintain as an intimate/ relationship." What does this comment mean in the context of the play? Do you agree or disagree? Why?
2. Select one of the following and write about its significance in the play: the subway in New York City, the river in Hiroshima, Nakajima's family dinner, the road from Hiroshima, Wrigley's spearmint chewing gum, shoes.
3. Select a pair of juxtaposed speeches and discuss how their placement next to each other heightens meaning. Example: Walkman's speech about preparing for nuclear war by making a tape of favorite songs and the speech soon after by Nakajima which begins: "even those/ who looked like they were going to be spared/ were not spared."

NONFICTION

BLACK ELK (1863–1950)

Black Elk was a Sioux medicine man and second cousin to Sioux leader Crazy Horse. In 1930 and again in 1931, John G. Neihardt, poet and student of Native American history, visited Black Elk. The medicine man, with his son Ben acting as translator, recounted his life story to Neihardt. From a stenographic transcript of Black Elk's account, Neihardt pieced together a chronological narrative, which he published in 1932 as Black Elk Speaks. *"The Butchering at Wounded Knee" is one of the later chapters of that oral history.*

The Butchering at Wounded Knee[1]   (1932)

That evening before it happened, I went in to Pine Ridge and heard these things, and while I was there, soldiers started for where the Big Foots were. These made about five hundred soldiers that were there next morning. When I saw them starting I felt that something terrible was going to happen. That night I could hardly sleep at all. I walked around most of the night.

In the morning I went out after my horses, and while I was out I heard shooting off toward the east, and I knew from the sound that it must be wagon-guns (cannon) going off. The sounds went right through my body, and I felt that something terrible would happen.

When I reached camp with the horses, a man rode up to me and said: "Hey-hey-hey! The people that are coming are fired on! I know it!"

I saddled up my buckskin and put on my sacred shirt. It was one I had made to be worn by no one but myself. It had a spotted eagle outstretched on the back of it, and the daybreak star was on the left shoulder, because when facing south that shoulder is toward the east. Across the breast, from the left shoulder to the right hip, was the flaming rainbow, and there was another rainbow around the neck, like a necklace, with a star at the bottom. At each shoulder, elbow, and wrist was an eagle feather; and over the whole shirt were red streaks of lightning. You will see that this was from my great vision, and you will know how it protected me that day.

---

[1] South Dakota scene of the 1890 massacre described here.

I painted my face all red, and in my hair I put one eagle feather for the One Above.

It did not take me long to get ready, for I could still hear the shooting over there.

I started out alone on the old road that ran across the hills to Wounded Knee. I had no gun. I carried only the sacred bow of the west that I had seen in my great vision. I had gone only a little way when a band of young men came galloping after me. The first two who came up were Loves War and Iron Wasichu. I asked what they were going to do, and they said they were just going to see where the shooting was. Then others were coming up, and some older men.

We rode fast, and there were about twenty of us now. The shooting was getting louder. A horseback from over there came galloping very fast toward us, and he said: "Hey-hey-hey! They have murdered them!" Then he whipped his horse and rode away faster toward Pine Ridge.

In a little while we had come to the top of the ridge where, looking to the east, you can see for the first time the monument and the burying ground on the little hill where the church is. That is where the terrible thing started. Just south of the burying ground on the little hill a deep dry gulch runs about east and west, very crooked, and it rises westward to nearly the top of the ridge where we were. It had no name, but the Wasichus sometimes call it Battle Creek now. We stopped on the ridge not far from the head of the dry gulch. Wagon guns were still going off over there on the little hill, and they were going off again where they hit along the gulch. There was much shooting down yonder, and there were many cries, and we could see cavalrymen scattered over the hills ahead of us. Cavalrymen were riding along the gulch and shooting into it, where the women and children were running away and trying to hide in the gullies and the stunted pines.

A little way ahead of us, just below the head of the dry gulch, there were some women and children who were huddled under a clay bank, and some cavalrymen were there pointing guns at them.

We stopped back behind the ridge, and I said to the others: "Take courage. These are our relatives. We will try to get them back." Then we all sang a song which went like this:

A thunder being nation I am, I have said.
A thunder being nation I am, I have said.
You shall live.
You shall live.
You shall live.
You shall live.

Then I rode over the ridge and the others after me, and we were crying: "Take courage! It is time to fight!" The soldiers who were guarding our relatives shot at us and then ran away fast, and some more cavalrymen on the other side of the gulch did too. We got our relatives and sent them across the ridge to the northwest where they would be safe.

I had no gun, and when we were charging, I just held the sacred bow out in front of me with my right hand. The bullets did not hit us at all.

We found a little baby lying all alone near the head of the gulch. I could not pick her up just then, but I got her later and some of my people adopted her. I just wrapped her up tighter in a shawl that was around her and left her there. It was a safe place, and I had other work to do.

The soldiers had run eastward over the hills where there were some more soldiers, and they were off their horses and lying down. I told the others to stay back, and I charged upon them holding the sacred bow out toward them with my right hand. They all shot at me, and I could hear bullets all around me, but I ran my horse right close to them, and then swung around. Some soldiers across the gulch began shooting at me too, but I got back to the others and was not hurt at all.

By now many other Lakotas, who had heard the shooting, were coming up from Pine Ridge, and we all charged on the soldiers. They ran eastward toward where the trouble began. We followed down along the dry gulch, and what we saw was terrible. Dead and wounded women and children and little babies were scattered all along there where they had been trying to run away. The soldiers had followed along the gulch, as they ran, and murdered them in there. Sometimes they were in heaps because they had huddled together, and some were scattered all along. Sometimes bunches of them had been killed and torn to pieces where the wagon guns hit them. I saw a little baby trying to suck its mother, but she was bloody and dead.

There were two little boys at one place in this gulch. They had guns and they had been killing soldiers all by themselves. We could see the soldiers they had killed. The boys were all alone there, and they were not hurt. These were very brave little boys.

When we drove the soldiers back, they dug themselves in, and we were not enough people to drive them out from there. In the evening they marched off up Wounded Knee Creek, and then we saw all that they had done there.

Men and women and children were heaped and scattered all over the flat at the bottom of the little hill where the soldiers had their wagon-guns, and westward up the dry gulch all the way to the high ridge, the dead women and children and babies were scattered.

When I saw this I wished that I had died too, but I was not sorry for the women and children. It was better for them to be happy in the other world, and I wanted to be there too. But before I went there I wanted to have revenge. I thought there might be a day, and we should have revenge.

After the soldiers marched away, I heard from my friend, Dog Chief, how the trouble started, and he was right there by Yellow Bird when it happened. This is the way it was:

In the morning the soldiers began to take all the guns away from the Big Foots, who were camped in the flat below the little hill where the monument and burying ground are now. The people had stacked most of their guns, and even their knives, by the tepee where Big Foot was lying sick. Soldiers were on the little hill and all around, and there were soldiers across the dry gulch to the south and over east along Wounded Knee Creek too. The people were nearly surrounded, and the wagon-guns were pointing at them.

Some had not yet given up their guns, and so the soldiers were searching all the tepees, throwing things around and poking into everything. There was a man called Yellow Bird, and he and another man were standing in front of the tepee where Big Foot was lying sick. They had white sheets around and over them, with eyeholes to look through, and they had guns under these. An officer came to search them. He took the other man's gun, and then started to take Yellow Bird's. But Yellow Bird would not let go. He wrestled with the officer, and while they were wrestling, the gun went off and killed the officer. Wasichus and some others have said he meant to do this, but Dog Chief was standing right there, and he told me it was not so. As soon as the gun went off, Dog Chief told me, an officer shot and killed Big Foot who was lying sick inside the tepee.

Then suddenly nobody knew what was happening, except that the soldiers were all shooting and the wagon-guns began going off right in among the people.

Many were shot down right there. The women and children ran into the gulch and up west, dropping all the time, for the soldiers shot them as they ran. There were only about a hundred warriors and there were nearly five hundred soldiers. The warriors rushed to where they had piled their guns and knives. They fought soldiers with only their hands until they got their guns.

Dog Chief saw Yellow Bird run into a tepee with his gun, and from there he killed soldiers until the tepee caught fire. Then he died full of bullets.

It was a good winter day when all this happened. The sun was shining. But after the soldiers marched away from their dirty work, a heavy snow began to fall. The wind came up in the night. There was a big blizzard, and it grew very cold. The snow drifted deep in the crooked gulch, and it was one long grave of butchered women and children and babies, who had never done any harm and were only trying to run away.

Study and Discussion Questions

1. What is the narrator's tone? Does it change?
2. How is the narrative structured?

3. In the narrative, what is the significance of ritual? Of the natural environment?

Writing Exercises

1. What can we infer from "The Butchering at Wounded Knee" about the Native Americans' way of life?
2. Do some research on the history of Native Americans in the United States. What light does it shed on the narrative?
3. In recent decades, many have chosen to call themselves "Native Americans" rather than "Indians." Why do you think that is?

MARGUERITE DURAS (b. 1914)

Marguerite Duras was born near Saigon in French Indochina (Vietnam) where her parents were teaching. She moved to Paris before she was twenty, and has remained there since. During World War II, she worked with the Resistance against the Nazi occupation of France. Much of her fiction, drama, and nonfiction has been translated into English, including The Vice-Consul *(1968) and* The Lover *(1984). She also wrote the screenplay for* Hiroshima, Mon Amour *(1960).*

FROM The War: A Memoir[1]   (1944)

I heard stifled cries on the stairs, a stir, a clatter of feet. Then doors banging and shouts. It was them. It was them, back from Germany.

I couldn't stop myself—I started to run downstairs, to escape into the street. Beauchamp and D. were supporting him under the arms. They'd stopped on the first-floor landing. He was looking up.

I can't remember exactly what happened. He must have looked at me and recognized me and smiled. I shrieked no, that I didn't want to see. I started to run again, up the stairs this time. I was shrieking, I remember that. The war emerged in my shrieks. Six years without uttering a cry. I found myself in some neighbors' apartment. They forced me to drink some rum, they poured it into my mouth. Into the shrieks.

I can't remember when I found myself back with him again, with him, Robert L. I remember hearing sobs all over the house; that the tenants stayed for a long while out on the stairs; that the doors were left open.

---

[1] Translated by Barbara Bray.

I was told later that the concierge had put decorations up in the hall to welcome him, and that as soon as he'd gone by she tore them all down and shut herself up alone in her lodge to weep.

In my memory, at a certain moment, the sounds stop and I see him. Huge. There before me. I don't recognize him. He looks at me. He smiles. Lets himself be looked at. There's a supernatural weariness in his smile, weariness from having managed to live till this moment. It's from this smile that I suddenly recognize him, but from a great distance, as if I were seeing him at the other end of a tunnel. It's a smile of embarrassment. He's apologizing for being here, reduced to such a wreck. And then the smile fades, and he becomes a stranger again. But the knowledge is still there, that this stranger is he, Robert L., totally.

He wanted to see around the apartment again. We supported him, and he toured the rooms. His cheeks creased, but didn't release his lips; it was in his eyes that we'd seen his smile. In the kitchen he saw the clafoutis we'd made for him. He stopped smiling. "What is it?" We told him. What was it made with? Cherries—it was the height of the season. "May I have some?" "We don't know, we'll have to ask the doctor." He came back into the sitting room and lay down on the divan. "So I can't have any?" "Not yet." "Why?" "There have been accidents in Paris already from letting deportees eat too soon after they got back from the camps."

He stopped asking questions about what had happened while he was away. He stopped seeing us. A great, silent pain spread over his face because he was still being refused food, because it was still as it had been in the concentration camp. And, as in the camp, he accepted it in silence. He didn't see that we were weeping. Nor did he see that we could scarcely look at him or respond to what he said.

The doctor came. He stopped short with his hand on the door handle, very pale. He looked at us, and then at the form on the divan. He didn't understand. And then he realized: the form wasn't dead yet, it was hovering between life and death, and he, the doctor, had been called in to try to keep it alive. The doctor came into the room. He went over to the form and the form smiled at him. The doctor was to come several times a day for three weeks, at all hours of the day and night. Whenever we were too afraid we called him and he came. He saved Robert L. He too was caught up in the passionate desire to save Robert L. from death. He succeeded.

We smuggled the clafoutis out of the house while he slept. The next day he was feverish and didn't talk about food any more.

If he had eaten when he got back from the camp his stomach would have been lacerated by the weight of the food, or else the weight would have pressed on the heart, which had grown enormous in the cave of his emaciation. It was beating so fast you couldn't have counted its beats, you couldn't really say it was beating—it was trembling, rather, as if from terror. No, he couldn't eat without dying. But he couldn't go on not eating without dying. That was the problem.

The fight with death started very soon. We had to be careful with it, use care, tact, skill. It surrounded him on all sides. And yet there was still a way of reaching him. It wasn't very big, this opening through which to communicate with him, but there was still life in him, scarcely more than a splinter, but a splinter just the same. Death unleashed its attack. His temperature was 104.5° the first day. Then 105°. Then 106°. Death was doing all it could. 106°: his heart vibrated like a violin string. Still 106°, but vibrating. The heart, we thought—it's going to stop. Still 106°. Death deals cruel knocks, but the heart is deaf. This can't go on, the heart will stop. But no.

Gruel, said the doctor, a teaspoonful at a time. Six or seven times a day we gave him gruel. Just a teaspoonful nearly choked him, he clung to our hands, gasped for air, and fell back on the bed. But he swallowed some. Six or seven times a day, too, he asked to go to the toilet. We lifted him up, supported him under the arms and knees. He must have weighed between eighty-two and eighty-four pounds: bone, skin, liver, intestines, brain, lungs, everything—eighty-four pounds for a body five feet ten inches tall. We sat him on the edge of the sanitary pail, on which we'd put a small cushion: the skin was raw where there was no flesh between it and the joints. *(The elbows of the little Jewish girl of seventeen from the Faubourg du Temple stick through the skin on her arms. Probably because she's so young and her skin so fragile, the joint is outside instead of in, sticking out naked and clean. She suffers no pain either from her joints or from her belly, from which all her genital organs have been taken out one by one at regular intervals.)* Once he was sitting on his pail he excreted in one go, in one enormous, astonishing gurgle. What the heart held back the anus couldn't: it let out all that was in it. Everything, or almost everything, did the same, even the fingers, which no longer kept their nails, but let them go too. But the heart went on holding back what it contained. The heart. And then there was the head. Gaunt but sublime, it emerged alone from that bag of bones, remembering, relating, recognizing, asking for things. And talking. Talking. The head was connected to the body by the neck, as heads usually are, but the neck was so withered and shrunken—you could circle it with one hand—that you wondered how life could pass through it; a spoonful of gruel almost blocked it. At first the neck was at right angles to the shoulders. Higher up, the neck was right inside the skeleton, joined on at the top of the jaws and winding around the ligaments like ivy. You could see the vertebrae through it, the carotid arteries, the nerves, the pharynx, and the blood passing through: the skin had become like cigarette paper. So, he excreted this dark green, slimy, gushing thing, a turd such as no one had ever seen before. When he'd finished we put him back to bed. He lay for a long time with his eyes half shut, prostrated.

For seventeen days the turd looked the same. It was inhuman. It separated him from us more than the fever, the thinness, the nailless fingers, the marks of SS blows. We gave him gruel that was golden yellow, gruel for infants, and it came out of him dark green like slime from a swamp. After the sanitary pail was closed you could hear the bubbles bursting as they rose to the surface inside. Viscous and slimy, it was almost like a great gob of spit. When it emerged the room filled with a smell, not of putrefaction or corpses—did his body still have the where-withal to make a corpse?—but rather of humus, of dead leaves, of dense undergrowth. It was a somber smell, dark reflection of the dark night from which he was emerging and which we would never know. (*I leaned against the shutters, the street went by below, and as they didn't know what was going on in the room I wanted to tell them that here, in this room above them, a man had come back from the German camps, alive.*)

Of course he'd rummaged in trashcans for food, he'd eaten wild plants, drunk water from engines. But that didn't explain it. Faced with this strange phenomenon we tried to find explanations. We thought that perhaps there, under our very eyes, he was consuming his own liver or spleen. How were we to know? How were we to know what strangeness that belly still contained, what pain?

For seventeen whole days that turd still looks the same. For seventeen days it's unlike anything ever known. Every one of the seven times he excretes each day, we smell it, look at it, but can't recognize it. For seventeen days we hide from him that which comes out of him, just as we hide from him his own legs and feet and whole unbelievable body.

We ourselves never got used to seeing them. You couldn't get used to it. The incredible thing was that he was still alive. Whenever anyone came into the room and saw that shape under the sheets, they couldn't bear the sight and averted their eyes. Many went away and never came back. He never noticed our horror, not once. He was happy, he wasn't afraid any more. The fever bore him up. For seventeen days.

One day his temperature drops.

After seventeen days, death grows weary. In the pail his excretion doesn't bubble any more, it becomes liquid. It's still green, but it smells more human, it smells human. And one day his temperature drops—he's been given twelve liters of serum, and one morning his temperature drops. He's lying on his nine cushions, one for the head, two for the forearms, two for the arms, two for the hands, and two for the feet. For no part of his body could bear its own weight; the weight had to be swathed in down and immobilized.

And then, one morning, the fever leaves him. It comes back, but abates again. Comes back again, not quite so high, and falls again. And then one morning he says, "I'm hungry."

Hunger had gone as his temperature rose. It came back when the fever abated. One day the doctor said, "Let's try—let's try giving him something to eat. We can begin with meat extract. If he can take that, keep on giving it, but at the same time give him all kinds of other food, just small amounts at first, increasing the quantity just a little every three days."

I spend the morning going around to all the restaurants in Saint-Germain-des-Prés trying to find a meat-juice extractor. I find one in a fashionable restaurant. They say they can't lend it. I say it's for a political deportee who's very ill, it's a matter of life and death. The woman thinks for a minute and says, "I can't lend it to you, but I can rent it to you for a thousand francs a day." I leave my name and address and a deposit. The Saint-Benoît restaurant sells me the meat at cost price.

He digested the meat extract without any difficulty, so after three days he began to take solid food.

His hunger grew from what it fed on. It grew greater and greater, became insatiable.

It took on terrifying proportions.

We didn't serve him food. We put the dishes in front of him and left him and he ate. Methodically, as if performing a duty, he was doing what he had to do to live. He ate. It was an occupation that took up all his time. He would wait for food for hours. He would swallow without knowing what he was eating. Then we'd take the food away and he'd wait for it to come again.

He has gone and hunger has taken his place. Emptiness has taken his place. He is giving to the void, filling what was emptied: those wasted bowels. That's what he's doing. Obeying, serving, ministering to a mysterious duty. How does he know what to do about hunger? How does he perceive that this is what he has to do? He knows with a knowledge that has no parallel.

He eats a mutton chop. Then he gnaws the bone, eyes lowered, concentrating on not missing a morsel of meat. Then he takes a second chop. Then a third. Without looking up.

He's sitting in the shade in the sitting room near a half-open window, in an armchair, surrounded by his cushions, his stick beside him. His legs look like crutches inside his trousers. When the sun shines you can see through his hands.

Yesterday he made enormous efforts to gather up the breadcrumbs that had fallen on his trousers and on the floor. Today he lets a few lie.

We leave him alone in the room while he's eating. We don't have to help him now. His strength has come back enough for him to hold a spoon or a fork. But we still cut up the meat for him. We leave him alone with the food. We try not to talk in the adjoining rooms. We walk on tiptoe. We watch him from a distance. He's performing a duty. He has no special preference for one dish over another. He cares less and less. He crams everything down. If the dishes don't come fast enough, he sobs and says we don't understand.

Yesterday afternoon he stole some bread out of the refrigerator. He steals. We tell him to be careful, not to eat too much. Then he weeps.

I used to watch him from the sitting-room door. I didn't go in. For two weeks, three, I watched him eat with unremitting pleasure. I couldn't get used to it either. Sometimes his pleasure made me weep too. He didn't see me. He'd forgotten me.

Strength is coming back.

I start to eat again too, and to sleep. I put on some weight. We're going to live. Like him I haven't been able to eat for seventeen days. Like him I haven't slept for seventeen days, or at least that's what I think. In fact, I've slept for two or three hours a day. I fall asleep anywhere. And wake in terror. It's awful, every time I think he's died while I was asleep. I still have that slight fever at night. The doctor who comes to see him is worried about me, too. He prescribes injections. The needle breaks in the muscle in my thigh, my muscles are knotted, as if tetanized. The nurse won't give me any more injections. Lack of sleep gives me eye trouble. I have to hold on to the furniture when I walk, the ground seems to slope away from me, I'm afraid of falling. We eat the meat from which we extracted the juice. It's like paper or cotton wool. I don't cook any more, except coffee. I feel very close to the death I wished for. It's a matter of indifference to me; I don't even think about its being a matter of indifference. My identity has gone. I'm just she who is afraid when she wakes. She who wills in his stead, for him. I exist in that will, that desire, and even when Robert L. is at death's door it's inexpressibly strong because he is still alive. When I lost my younger brother and my baby I lost pain too. It was without an object, so to speak: it was built on the past. But now there is hope, and pain is implanted in hope. Sometimes I'm amazed I don't die; a cold blade plunged deep into the living flesh, night and day, and you survive.

Strength is coming back.

We were informed by telephone. For a month we kept the news from him. It was only after he'd got some of his strength back, while he was staying at Verrières-le-Buisson at a convalescent home for deportees, that we told him of the death of his younger sister, Marie-Louise L. It was at night. His youngest sister and I were there. We said, "There's something we've been keeping from you." He said, "Marie-Louise is dead." We stayed together in the room till daylight, without speaking about her, without speaking. I vomited. I think we all did. He kept saying, "Twenty-four years old." Sitting on the bed, his hands on his stick, not weeping.

More strength came back. Another day I told him we had to get a divorce, that I wanted a child by D., that it was because of the name the child would bear. He asked if one day we might get together again. I said no, that I hadn't changed my mind since two years ago, since I'd met D. I said that even if D. hadn't existed I wouldn't have lived with him again. He didn't ask me my reasons for leaving. I didn't tell him what they were.

One time we're at Saint-Jorioz on Lake Annecy, in a rest home for deportees. It's a roadside hotel with a restaurant attached. It's in August 1945. It's there we hear about Hiroshima. He's got some of his weight back. But he hasn't the strength to carry it. He walks with that stick: I can see it now, a thick stick, made of some dark wood. Sometimes it's as if he'd like to lash out with it, hit walls, furniture, doors—not people, no, but all the things he meets. D. is there by Lake Annecy too. We haven't any money to go to hotels where we'd have to pay.

I don't see him as near to us during that trip to Savoy. He's surrounded by strangers, he's still alone, he doesn't say what he's thinking. He's hidden. He's dark. Then by the side of the road one morning that huge headline: Hiroshima.

It's as if he'd like to lash out, as if he's blinded by a rage through which he has to pass before he can live again. After Hiroshima I think he talks to D. D. is his best friend, Hiroshima is perhaps the first thing outside his own life that he sees or reads about.

Another time, it was before Savoy, he was standing among the tables outside the Café Flore. It was very sunny. He wanted to go to the Flore "to see," he said. The waiters came up and greeted him. And it's at that moment that I see him now, shouting, banging on the ground with his stick. I'm afraid he's going to smash the windows. The waiters look at him in consternation, almost in tears, speechless. And then I see him sit down, and sit there for a long while in silence.

Then more time went by.

It was the first summer of the peace—1946.

It was a beach in Italy, between Leghorn and La Spezia.

A year and four months have gone by since he came back from the camps. He's known about his sister, he's known about our separation, for many months.

He's there, on the beach, he's watching some people approach. I don't know who. The way he looked at things, his way of seeing—that was what died first in the German image of his death I had while I was waiting for him in Paris. Sometimes he stays a long while without saying anything, looking at the ground. He still can't get used to the death of his younger sister: twenty-four years old, blind, her feet frostbitten, in the last stages of consumption, flown from Ravensbrück to Copenhagen and dead on the day she arrived, the day of the armistice. He never mentions her, never utters her name.

He wrote a book on what he thought he had experienced in Germany. It was called *The Human Race*. Once the book was written, finished, published, he never spoke of the German concentration camps again. Never uttered the words again. Never again. Nor the title of the book.

. . .

It's a day when the *libeccio*, the southwest wind, is blowing.
   In the light that goes with the wind, the idea that he's dead ends.

I'm lying down beside Ginetta. We've climbed up the slope from the beach and gone deep in among the reeds. We've undressed. We've just emerged from the coolness of our swim; the sun blazes down on the coolness without yet reaching it. The skin offers good protection. On my skin, beneath my ribs, in a hollow, I can see my heart beating. I'm hungry.

The others have stayed on the beach. They're playing football. All except Robert L. Not yet.

Above the reeds you can see the snowy sides of the marble quarries of Carrara. Above them are higher mountains, sparkling white. Nearer, on the other side, you can see Mount Marcello, just over the estuary of La Magra. You can't see the village of Mount Marcello, only the hill, the groves of fig trees, and right at the top the dark sides of the pines.

We can hear them; they're laughing. Especially Elio. Ginetta says, "Listen to him—he's like a child."
   Robert L. isn't laughing. He's lying under an umbrella. He still can't bear the sun. He watches the others playing.

The wind can't get through the reeds, but it brings us the sounds from the beach. It's terribly hot.
   Ginetta takes two halves of lemon out of her bathing cap and gives me one. We squeeze the lemon over our open mouths. It runs down our throats drop by drop, reaches our hunger, and makes us feel its depth and strength. Ginetta says lemon is the fruit you need when it's as hot as this. She says, "Look at the lemons on the plain around Carrara—see how huge they are, they've got thick skins that keep them cool in the sun, they have as much juice as oranges, but they've got a harsh taste."

We can still hear the players. But Robert L.—we still can't hear him. It's in that silence that the war's still there, flowing across the sand and through the wind.

Ginetta says, "I'm sorry I didn't know you when you were waiting for Robert to come back." She says she thinks he looks well, but as if he tires easily. She notices it especially when he walks or swims, from his slowness, his painful slowness. But as she didn't know him before, she says she can't be sure. But she's afraid he may never be as strong again as he was before the camps.

At the name, Robert L., I weep. I still weep. I shall weep all my life. Ginetta apologizes and is silent.

Every day she thinks I'm going to be able to talk about him, and still I can't. But that day I tell her I think I shall be able to one day. And that I've already written something about that return. Tried to say something about that love. That it was then, by his deathbed, that I knew him, Robert L., best, that I understood forever what made him himself, himself alone and nothing and no one else in the world. Then I spoke of Robert L.'s special grace here below, of his own peculiar grace which carried him through the camps—the intelligence, the love, the reading, the politics, and all the inexpressible things of all the days; that grace peculiar to him but made up equally of the despair of all.

The heat became too unbearable. We put on our swimsuits again and ran down across the beach and straight into the sea. Ginetta swam far out. I stayed near the shore.

The *libeccio* had stopped blowing. Or else it was another day with no wind.

Or else it was another year. Another summer. Another day with no wind.

The sea was blue, even there before our eyes, and there weren't any waves, just a very gentle swell, a breath in a deep sleep. The others stopped playing and squatted down on their towels in the sand. He stood up and walked over to the sea. I came near the edge. I looked at him. He saw me looking. He blinked his eyes behind his glasses and smiled at me, giving little shakes of his head, as you do when you're laughing at someone. And I knew he knew, knew that every hour of every day I was thinking, "He didn't die in the concentration camp."

Study and Discussion Questions

1. What is Robert L's physical condition when he arrives home from the concentration camp?
2. How do people react to him? For what reasons?
3. What is Robert L's relation to food? How does that change?
4. Though the subject is Robert L, what sense do we get of the narrator as a person?

Writing Exercises

1. "Six years without uttering a cry." Why does the protagonist cry now that the war is over and her husband is back?
2. Trace the stages of Robert L's physical and mental healing.
3. What emotional response(s) did you have to this memoir? What details in particular evoked those responses?

RON KOVIC (b. 1946)

Ron Kovic was born on July 4, 1946 and grew up in Massapequa, New York, where he was a high school athlete. Impressed by a Marine recruiter who came to his school, he enlisted, fought in Vietnam, and was seriously wounded. After returning to the United States, he studied briefly at Hofstra University and soon became active in Vietnam Veterans Against the War.

FROM **Born on the Fourth of July**   (1976)

I

The blood is still rolling off my flak jacket from the hole in my shoulder and there are bullets cracking into the sand all around me. I keep trying to move my legs but I cannot feel them. I try to breathe but it is difficult. I have to get out of this place, make it out of here somehow.

Someone shouts from my left now, screaming for me to get up. Again and again he screams, but I am trapped in the sand.

Oh get me out of here, get me out of here, please someone help me! Oh help me, please help me. Oh God oh Jesus! "Is there a corpsman?" I cry. "Can you get a corpsman?"

There is a loud crack and I hear the guy begin to sob. "They've shot my fucking finger off! Let's go, sarge! Let's get outta here!"

"I can't move," I gasp. "I can't move my legs! I can't feel anything!"

I watch him go running back to the tree line.

"Sarge, are you all right?" Someone else is calling to me now and I try to turn around. Again there is the sudden crack of a bullet and a boy's voice crying. "Oh Jesus! Oh Jesus Christ!" I hear his body fall in back of me.

I think he must be dead but I feel nothing for him, I just want to live. I feel nothing.

And now I hear another man coming up from behind, trying to save me. "Get outta here!" I scream. "Get the fuck outta here!"

A tall black man with long skinny arms and enormous hands picks me up and throws me over his shoulder as bullets begin cracking over our heads like strings of firecrackers. Again and again they crack as the sky swirls around us like a cyclone. "Motherfuckers motherfuckers!" he screams. And the rounds keep cracking and the sky and the sun on my face and my body all gone, all twisted up dangling like a puppet's, diving again and again into the sand, up and down, rolling and cursing, gasping for breath. "Goddamn goddamn motherfuckers!"

And finally I am dragged into a hole in the sand with the bottom of my body that can no longer feel, twisted and bent underneath me. The black man runs from the hole without ever saying a thing. I never see his face. I will never know who he is. He is gone. And others now are in the hole helping me. They are bandaging my wounds. There is fear in their faces.

"It's all right," I say to them. "Everything is fine."

Someone has just saved my life. My rifle is gone and I don't feel like finding it or picking it up ever again. The only thing I can think of, the only thing that crosses my mind, is living. There seems to be nothing in the world more important than that.

Hundreds of rounds begin to crash in now. I stare up at the sky because I cannot move. Above the hole men are running around in every direction. I see their legs and frightened faces. They are screaming and dragging the wounded past me. Again and again the rounds crash in. They seem to be coming in closer and closer. A tall man jumps in, hugging me to the earth.

"Oh God!" he is crying. "Oh God please help us!"

The attack is lifted. They are carrying me out of the hole now—two, three, four men—quickly they are strapping me to a stretcher. My legs dangle off the sides until they realize I cannot control them. "I can't move them," I say, almost in a whisper. "I can't move them." I'm still carefully sucking the air, trying to calm myself, trying not to get excited, not to panic. I want to live. I keep telling myself, Take it slow now, as they strap my legs to the stretcher and carry my wounded body into an Amtrac packed with other wounded men. The steel trapdoor of the Amtrac slowly closes as we begin to move to the northern bank and back across the river to the battalion area.

Men are screaming all around me. "Oh God get me out of here!" "Please help!" they scream. Oh Jesus, like little children now, not like marines, not like the posters, not like that day in the high school, this is for real. "Mother!" screams a man without a face. "Oh I don't want to die!" screams a young boy cupping his intestines with his hands. "Oh please, oh no, oh God, oh help! Mother!" he screams again.

We are moving slowly through the water, the Amtrac rocking back and forth. We cannot be brave anymore, there is no reason. It means nothing now. We hold on to ourselves, to things around us, to memories, to thoughts, to dreams. I breathe slowly, desperately trying to stay awake.

The steel trapdoor is opening. I see faces. Corpsmen, I think. Others, curious, looking in at us. Air, fresh, I feel, I smell. They are carrying me out now. Over wounded bodies, past wounded screams. I'm in a helicopter now lifting above the battalion area. I'm leaving the war. I'm going to live. I am still breathing, I keep thinking over and over, I'm going to live and get out of here.

They are shoving tubes and needles in my arms. Now we are being packed into planes. I begin to believe more and more as I watch the other wounded packed around me on shelves that I am going to live.

I still fight desperately to stay awake. I am in an ambulance now rushing to some place. There is a man without any legs screaming in pain, moaning like a little baby. He is bleeding terribly from the stumps that were once his legs, thrashing his arms wildly about his chest, in a semiconscious daze. It is almost too much for me to watch.

I cannot take much more of this. I must be knocked out soon, before I lose my mind. I've seen too much today, I think. But I hold on, sucking the air. I shout then curse for him to be quiet. "My wound is much worse than yours!" I scream. "You're lucky," I shout, staring him in the eyes. "I can feel nothing from my chest down. You at least still have part of your legs. Shut up!" I scream again. "Shut the fuck up, you goddamned baby!" He keeps thrashing his arms wildly above his head and kicking his bleeding stumps toward the roof of the ambulance.

The journey seems to take a very long time, but soon we are at the place where the wounded are sent. I feel a tremendous exhilaration inside me. I have made it this far. I have actually made it this far without giving up and now I am in a hospital where they will operate on me and find out why I cannot feel anything from my chest down anymore. I know I am going to make it now. I am going to make it not because of any god, or any religion, but because *I* want to make it, *I* want to live. And I leave the screaming man without legs and am brought to a room that is very bright.

"What's your name?" the voice shouts.

"Wh-wh-what?" I say.

"What's your name?" the voice says again.

"K-K-Kovic," I say.

"No!" says the voice. "I want your name, rank, and service number. Your date of birth, the name of your father and mother."

"Kovic. Sergeant. Two-oh-three-oh-two-six-one, uh, when are you going to . . ."

"Date of birth!" the voice shouts.

"July fourth, nineteen forty-six. I was born on the Fourth of July. I can't feel . . ."

"What religion are you?"

"Catholic," I say.

"What outfit did you come from?"

"What's going on? When are you going to operate?" I say.

"The doctors will operate," he says. "Don't worry," he says confidently. "They are very busy and there are many wounded but they will take care of you soon."

He continues to stand almost at attention in front of me with a long clipboard in his hand, jotting down all the information he can. I cannot understand why they are taking so long to operate. There is something very wrong with me, I think, and they must operate as quickly as possible. The man with the clipboard walks out of the room. He will send the priest in soon.

I lie in the room alone staring at the walls, still sucking the air, determined to live more than ever now.

The priest seems to appear suddenly above my head. With his fingers he is gently touching my forehead, rubbing it slowly and softly. "How are you," he says.

"I'm fine, Father." His face is very tired but it is not frightened. He is almost at ease, as if what he is doing he has done many times before.

"I have come to give you the Last Rites, my son."

"I'm ready, Father," I say.

And he prays, rubbing oils on my face and gently placing the crucifix to my lips. "I will pray for you," he says.

"When will they operate?" I say to the priest.

"I do not know," he says. "The doctors are very busy. There are many wounded. There is not much time for anything here but trying to live. So you must try to live my son, and I will pray for you."

Soon after that I am taken to a long room where there are many doctors and nurses. They move quickly around me. They are acting very competent. "You will be fine," says one nurse calmly.

"Breathe deeply into the mask," the doctor says.

"Are you going to operate?" I ask.

"Yes. Now breathe deeply into the mask." As the darkness of the mask slowly covers my face I pray with all my being that I will live through this operation and see the light of day once again. I want to live so much. And even before I go to sleep with the blackness still swirling around my head and the numbness of sleep, I begin to fight as I have never fought before in my life.

I awake to the screams of other men around me. I have made it. I think that maybe the wound is my punishment for killing the corporal and the children. That now everything is okay and the score is evened up. And now I am packed in this place with the others who have been wounded like myself, strapped onto a strange circular bed. I feel tubes going into my nose and hear the clanking, pumping sound of a machine. I still cannot feel any of my body but I know I am alive. I feel a terrible pain in my chest. My body is so cold. It has never been this weak. It feels so tired and out of touch, so lost and in pain. I can still barely breathe. I look around me, at people moving in shadows of numbness. There is the man who had been in the ambulance with me, screaming louder than ever, kicking his bloody stumps in the air, crying for his mother, crying for his morphine.

Directly across from me there is a Korean who has not even been in the war at all. The nurse says he was going to buy a newspaper when he stepped on a booby trap and it blew off both his legs and his arm. And all that is left now is this slab of meat swinging one arm crazily in the air, moaning like an animal gasping for its last bit of life, knowing that death is rushing toward him. The Korean is screaming like a madman at the top of his lungs. I cannot wait for the shots of morphine. Oh, the morphine feels so good. It makes everything dark and quiet. I can rest. I can leave this madness. I can dream of my back yard once again.

When I wake they are screaming still and the lights are on and the clock, the clock on the wall, I can hear it ticking to the sound of their screams. I can hear the dead being carted out and the new wounded being brought in to the beds all around me. I have to get out of this place.

"Can I call you by your first name?" I say to the nurse.

"No. My name is Lieutenant Wiecker."

"Please, can I . . ."

"No," she says. "It's against regulations."

I'm sleeping now. The lights are flashing. The black pilot is next to me. He says nothing. He stares at the ceiling all day long. He does nothing but that. But something is happening now, something is going wrong over there. The nurse is shouting for the machine, and the corpsman is crawling on the black man's chest, he has his knees on his chest and he's pounding it with his fists again and again.

"His heart has stopped!" screams the nurse.

Pounding, pounding, he's pounding his fist into his chest. "Get the machine!" screams the corpsman.

The nurse is pulling the machine across the hangar floor as quickly as she can now. They are trying to put curtains around the whole thing, but the curtains keep slipping and falling down. Everyone, all the wounded who can still see and think, now watch what is happening to the pilot, and it is happening right next to me. The doctor hands the corpsman a syringe, they are laughing as the corpsman drives the syringe into the pilot's chest like a knife. They are talking about the Green Bay Packers and the corpsman is driving his fist into the black man's chest again and again until the black pilot's body begins to bloat up, until it doesn't look like a body at all anymore. His face is all puffy like a balloon and saliva rolls slowly from the sides of his mouth. He keeps staring at the ceiling and saying nothing. "The machine! The machine!" screams the doctor, now climbing on top of the bed, taking the corpsman's place. "Turn on the machine!" screams the doctor.

He grabs a long suction cup that is attached to the machine and places it carefully against the black man's chest. The black man's body jumps up from the bed almost arcing into the air from each bolt of electricity, jolting and arcing, bloating up more and more.

"I'll bet on the Packers," says the corpsman.

"Green Bay doesn't have a chance," the doctor says, laughing.

The nurse is smiling now, making fun of both the doctor and the corpsman. "I don't understand football," she says.

They are pulling the sheet over the head of the black man and strapping him onto the gurney. He is taken out of the ward.

The Korean civilian is still screaming and there is a baby now at the end of the ward. The nurse says it has been napalmed by our own jets. I cannot see the baby but it screams all the time like the Korean and the young man without any legs I had met in the ambulance.

I can hear a radio. It is the Armed Forces radio. The corpsman is telling the baby to shut the hell up and there is a young kid with half his head blown away. They have brought him in and put him where the black pilot has just died, right next to me. He has thick bandages wrapped all around his head till I can hardly see his face at all. He is like a vegetable— a nineteen-year-old vegetable, thrashing his arms back and forth, babbling and pissing in his clean white sheets.

"Quit pissin' in your sheets!" screams the corpsman. But the nineteen-year-old kid who doesn't have any brains anymore makes the corpsman very angry. He just keeps pissing in the sheets and crying like a little baby.

There is a Green Beret sergeant calling for his mother. Every night now I hear him. He has spinal meningitis. He will be dead before this evening is over.

The Korean civilian does not moan anymore. He does not wave his one arm and two fingers above his head. He is dead and they have taken him away too.

There is a nun who comes through the ward now with apples for the wounded and rosary beads. She is very pleasant and smiles at all of the wounded. The corpsman is reading a comicbook, still cursing at the baby. The baby is screaming and the Armed Forces radio is saying that troops will be home soon. The kid with the bloody stumps is getting a morphine shot.

There is a general walking down the aisles now, going to each bed. He's marching down the aisles, marching and facing each wounded man in his bed. A skinny private with a Polaroid camera follows directly behind him. The general is dressed in an immaculate uniform with shiny shoes. "Good afternoon, marine," the general says. "In the name of the President of the United States and the United States Marine Corps, I am proud to present you with the Purple Heart, and a picture," the general says. Just then the skinny man with the Polaroid camera jumps up, flashing a picture of the wounded man. "And a picture to send to your folks."

He comes up to my bed and says exactly the same thing he has said to all the rest. The skinny man jumps up, snapping a picture of the general handing the Purple Heart to me. "And here," says the general, "here is a picture to send home to your folks." The general makes a sharp left face. He is marching to the bed next to me where the nineteen-year-old kid is still pissing in his pants, babbling like a little baby.

"In the name of the President of the United States," the general says. The kid is screaming now almost tearing the bandages off his head, exposing the parts of his brain that are still left. ". . . I present you with the Purple Heart. And here," the general says, handing the medal to the nineteen-year-old vegetable, the skinny guy jumping up and snapping a picture, "here is a picture . . .," the general says, looking at the picture the skinny guy has just pulled out of the camera. The kid is still pissing in his white sheets. ". . . And here is a picture to send home. . . ." The general does not finish what he is saying. He stares at the nineteen-year-old for what seems a long time. He hands the picture back to his photographer and as sharply as before marches to the next bed.

"Good afternoon, marine," he says.

The kid is still pissing in his clean white sheets when the general walks out of the room.

I am in this place for seven days and seven nights. I write notes on scraps of paper telling myself over and over that I will make it out of here, that I am going to live. I am squeezing rubber balls with my hands to try to get strong again. I write letters home to Mom and Dad. I dictate them to a woman named Lucy who is with the USO. I am telling Mom and Dad that I am hurt pretty bad but I have done it for America and that it is worth it. I tell them not to worry. I will be home soon.

The day I am supposed to leave has come. I am strapped in a long frame and taken from the place of the wounded. I am moved from hangar to hangar, then finally put on a plane, and I leave Vietnam forever.

II

The bus turned off a side street and onto the parkway, then into Queens where the hospital was. For the first time on the whole trip everyone was laughing and joking. He felt himself begin to wake up out of the nightmare. This whole area was home to him—the streets, the parkway, he knew them like the back of his hand. The air was fresh and cold and the bus rocked back and forth. "This bus sucks!" yelled a kid. "Can't you guys do any better than this? I want my mother, I want my mother."

The pain twisted into his back, but he laughed with the rest of them— the warriors, the wounded, entering the gates of St. Albans Naval Hospital. The guard waved them in and the bus stopped. He was the last of the men to be taken off the bus. They had to carry him off. He got the impression that he was quite an oddity in his steel frame, crammed inside it like a flattened pancake.

They put him on the neuro ward. It was sterile and quiet. I'm with the vegetables again, he thought. It took a long while to get hold of a nurse. He told her that if they didn't get the top of the frame off his back he would start screaming. They took it off him and moved him back downstairs to another ward. This was a ward for men with open wounds. They put him there because of his heel, which had been all smashed by the first bullet, the back of it blown completely out.

He was now in Ward 1-C with fifty other men who had all been recently wounded in the war—twenty-year-old blind men and amputees, men without intestines, men who limped, men who were in wheelchairs, men in pain. He noticed they all had strange smiles on their faces and he had one too, he thought. They were men who had played with death and cheated it at a very young age.

He lay back in his bed and watched everything happen all around him. He went to therapy every day and worked very hard lifting weights. He had to build up the top of his body if he was ever going to walk again. In Da Nang the doctors had told him to get used to the idea that he would have to sit in a wheelchair for the rest of his life. He had accepted it, but more and more he was dreaming and thinking about walking. He prayed every night after the visitors left. He closed his eyes and dreamed of being on his feet again.

Sometimes the American Legion group from his town came in to see him, the men and their wives and their pretty daughters. They would all surround him in his bed. It would seem to him that he was always having to cheer them up more than they were cheering him. They told him he was a hero and that all of Massapequa was proud of him. One time the commander stood up and said they were even thinking of naming a street after him. But the guy's wife was embarrassed and made her husband shut up. She told him the commander was kidding—he tended to get carried away after a couple of beers.

After he had been in the hospital a couple of weeks, a man appeared one morning and handed him a large envelope. He waited until the man had gone to open it up. Inside was a citation and a medal for Conspicuous Service to the State of New York. The citation was signed by Governor Rockefeller. He stuck the envelope and all the stuff in it under his pillow.

None of the men on the wards were civilian yet, so they had reveille at six o'clock in the morning. All the wounded who could get on their feet were made to stand in front of their beds while a roll call was taken. After roll call they all had to make their beds and do a general clean-up of the entire ward—everything from scrubbing the floors to cleaning the windows. Even the amputees had to do it. No one ever bothered him, though. He usually slept through the whole thing.

Later it would be time for medication, and afterward one of the corpsmen would put him in a wheelchair and push him to the shower room. The corpsman would leave him alone for about five minutes, then pick his body up, putting him on a wooden bench, his legs dangling, his toes barely touching the floor. He would sit in the shower like that every morning watching his legs become smaller and smaller, until after a month the muscle tone had all but disappeared. With despair and frustration he watched his once strong twenty-one-year-old body become crippled and disfigured. He was just beginning to understand the nature of his wound. He knew now it was the worst he could have received without dying or becoming a vegetable.

More and more he thought about what a priest had said to him in Da Nang: "Your fight is just beginning. Sometimes no one will want to hear what you're going through. You are going to have to learn to carry a great burden and most of your learning will be done alone. Don't feel frightened when they leave you. I'm sure you will come through it all okay."

I am in a new hospital now. Things are very different than in the last place. It is quiet in the early morning. There is no reveille here. The sun is just beginning to come in through the windows and I can hear the steady dripping of the big plastic bags that overflow with urine onto the floor. The aide comes in the room, a big black woman. She goes to Willey's bed across from me, almost stepping in the puddle of urine. She takes the cork out of the metal thing in his neck and sticks the long rubber tube in, then clicks on the machine by the bed. There is a loud sucking slurping sound. She moves the rubber tube around and around until it sucks all the stuff out of his lungs. After she is done she puts the cork back in his throat and leaves the room.

There are people talking down at the end of the hall. The night shift is getting ready to go home. They are laughing very loud and flushing the toilets, cursing and telling jokes, black men in white uniforms walking past my door. I shut my eyes. I try to get back into the dream I was having. She is so pretty, so warm and naked lying next to me. She kisses me and begins to unbutton my hospital shirt. "I love you," I hear her say. "I love you." I open my eyes. Something strange is tickling my nose.

It is Tommy the enema man and today is my day to get my enema. "Hey Kovic," Tommy is saying. "Hey Kovic, wake up, I got an enema for you."

She kisses my lips softly at first, then puts her tongue into my mouth. I am running my hands through her hair and she tells me that she loves that. She is unbuttoning my trousers now and her small hand is working itself deep down into my pants. I keep driving my tongue into her more furiously than ever. We have just been dancing on the floor, I was dancing very funny like a man on stilts, but now we are making love and just above me I hear a voice trying to wake me again.

"Kovic! I have an enema for you. Come on. We gotta get you outta here."

I feel myself being lifted. Tommy and another aide, a young black woman, pick me up, carefully unhooking my tube. They put my body into the frame, tying my legs down with long white twisted sheets. They lay another big sheet over me. The frame has a long metal bar that goes above my head. My rear end sticks out of a slit that I lie on.

"Okay," shouts Tommy in his gravel voice. "This one's ready to go."

The aide pushes me into the line-up in the hallway. There are frames all over the place now, lined up in front of the blue room for their enemas. It is the Six o'Clock Special. There are maybe twenty guys waiting by now. It looks like a long train, a long assembly line of broken, twisted bodies waiting for deliverance. It is very depressing, all these bodies, half of them asleep, tied down to their frames with their rear ends sticking out. All these bodies bloated, waiting to be released. Every third day I go for my enema and wait with the long line of men shoved against the green hospital wall. I watch the dead bodies being pushed into the enema room, then finally myself.

It is a small blue room and they cram us into it like sardines. Tommy runs back and forth placing the bedpans under our rear ends, laughing and joking, a cigarette dangling from the corner of his mouth. "Okay, okay, let's go!" he shouts. There is a big can of soapy water above each man's head and a tube that comes down from it. Tommy is jumping all around and whistling like a little kid, running to each body, sticking the rubber tubes up into them. He is jangling the pans, undoing little clips on the rubber tubes and filling the bellies up with soapy water. Everyone is trying to sleep, refusing to admit that this whole thing is happening to them. A couple of the bodies in the frames have small radios close to their ears. Tommy keeps running from one frame to the other, changing the rubber gloves on his hands and squirting the tube of lubricant onto his fingers, ramming his hands up into the rear ends, checking each of the bodies out, undoing the little clips. The aide keeps grabbing the bedpans and emptying all the shit into the garbage cans, occasionally missing and splattering the stuff on the floor. She places the empty pans in a machine and closes it up. There is a steam sound and the machine opens with all the bedpans as clean as new.

Oh God, what is happening to me? What is going on here? I want to get out of this place! All these broken men are very depressing, all these bodies so emaciated and twisted in these bedsheets. This is a nightmare. This isn't like the poster down by the post office where the guy stood with the shiny shoes; this is a concentration camp. It is like the pictures of all the Jews that I have seen. This is as horrible as that. I want to scream. I want to yell and tell them that I want out of this. All of this, all these people, this place, these sounds, I want out of this forever. I am only twenty-one and there is still so much ahead of me, there is so much ahead of me.

I am wiped clean and pushed past the garbage cans. The stench is terrible. I try to breathe through my mouth but I can't. I'm trapped. I have to watch, I have to smell. I think the war has made me a little mad—the dead corporal from Georgia, the old man that was shot in the village with his brains hanging out. But it is the living deaths I am breathing and smelling now, the living deaths, the bodies broken in the same war that I have come from.

I am outside now in the narrow hallway. The young black woman is pushing my frame past all the other steel contraptions. I look at her face for a moment, at her eyes, as she pushes my frame up against another. I can hear the splashing of water next door in the shower room. The sun has come up in the Bronx and people are walking through the hallways. They can look into all the rooms and see the men through the curtains that never close. It is as if we are a bunch of cattle, as if we do not really count anymore.

They push me into the shower. The black woman takes a green plastic container and squirts it, making a long thin white line from my head to my legs. She is turning on the water, and after making sure it is not too hot she hoses me down.

It's like a car wash, I think, it's just like a big car wash, and I am being pushed and shoved through with the rest of them. I am being checked out by Tommy and hosed off by the woman. It is all such a neat, quick process. It is an incredible thing to run twenty men through a place like this, to clean out the bodies of twenty paralyzed men, twenty bloated twisted men. It is an incredible feat, a stupendous accomplishment, and Tommy is a master. Now the black woman is drying me off with a big white towel and shoving me back into the hallway.

Oh get me back into the room, get me back away from these people who are walking by me and making believe like all the rest that they don't know what's happening here, that they can't figure out that this whole thing is crazy. Oh God, oh God help me, help me understand this place. There goes the nurse and she's running down the hall, hitting the rubber mat that throws open the big green metal door with the little windows with the wire in them. Oh nurse please help me nurse, my stomach is beginning to hurt again like it does every time I come out of this place and my head is throbbing, pounding like a drum. I want to get out of this hall where all of you are walking past me. I want to get back into my bed where I can make believe this never happened. I want to go to sleep and forget I ever got up this morning.

I never tell my family when they come to visit about the enema room. I do not tell them what I do every morning with the plastic glove, or about the catheter and the tube in my penis, or the fact that I can't ever make it hard again. I hide all that from them and talk about the other, more pleasant things, the things they want to hear. I ask Mom to bring me *Sunrise at Campobello,* the play about the life of Franklin Roosevelt— the great crisis he had gone through when he had been stricken with polio and the comeback he had made, becoming governor, then president of the United States. There are things I am going through here that I know she will never understand.

I feel like a big clumsy puppet with all his strings cut. I learn to balance and twist in the chair so no one can tell how much of me does not feel or move anymore. I find it easy to hide from most of them what I am going through. All of us are like this. No one wants too many people to know how much of him has really died in the war.

Study and Discussion Questions

1. Why does Kovic spend so much time describing the physical condition of *other* men in the hospital?
2. Why might he find it so disturbing that the hospital staff joke while they try to save the man whose heart has stopped?
3. Near the end, Kovic describes the shower he and the others are given as "like a car wash." What is the significance of this comparison?
4. Trace the changes in tense and person ("I" versus "he"). What is the effect?
5. Why do you think Kovic titled his book *Born on the Fourth of July*?

Writing Exercises

1. Discuss the meaning and significance of Kovic's last sentence: "No one wants too many people to know how much of him has really died in the war."
2. Discuss the various ways the hospital, as an institution, denies Kovic's suffering as an individual. Why is it this way?

MARTIN LUTHER KING, JR.   (1929–1968)

Martin Luther King was born in Atlanta, Georgia, attended segregated schools, and enrolled at Morehouse College at age fifteen. He preached in his father's Baptist church, earned a Ph.D. in theology at Boston University, and, in 1954, was appointed pastor of a church in Montgomery, Alabama. The next year, he led a boycott by blacks of segregated buses, and two years later became president of a new civil rights organization, the Southern Christian Leadership Conference. In the 1960s, he led voter registration drives, helped organize a massive march on Washington in 1963 (at which he delivered his speech, "I Have a Dream"), and engaged in other forms of nonviolent protest. In 1968, in Memphis, Tennessee, working to support striking sanitation workers, he was killed by a sniper. His books include Stride Toward Freedom *(1958),* Why We Can't Wait *(1964), and* Trumpet of Conscience *(1968).*

FROM **A Time to Break Silence**[1] (1967)

IMPORTANCE OF VIETNAM

Since I am a preacher by trade, I suppose it is not surprising that I have seven major reasons for bringing Vietnam into the field of my moral vision. There is at the outset a very obvious and almost facile connection between the war in Vietnam and the struggle I, and others, have been waging in America. A few years ago there was a shining moment in that struggle. It seemed as if there was a real promise of hope for the poor— both black and white—through the poverty program. There were experiments, hopes, new beginnings. Then came the buildup in Vietnam and I watched the program broken and eviscerated as if it were some idle political plaything of a society gone mad on war, and I knew that America would never invest the necessary funds or energies in rehabilitation of its poor so long as adventures like Vietnam continued to draw men and skills and money like some demonic destructive suction tube. So I was increasingly compelled to see the war as an enemy of the poor and to attack it as such.

Perhaps the more tragic recognition of reality took place when it became clear to me that the war was doing far more than devastating the hopes of the poor at home. It was sending their sons and their brothers and their husbands to fight and to die in extraordinarily high proportions relative to the rest of the population. We were taking the black young men who had been crippled by our society and sending them eight thousand miles away to guarantee liberties in Southeast Asia which they had not found in southwest Georgia and East Harlem. So we have been repeatedly faced with the cruel irony of watching Negro and white boys on TV screens as they kill and die together for a nation that has been unable to seat them together in the same schools. So we watch them in brutal solidarity burning the huts of a poor village, but we realize that they would never live on the same block in Detroit. I could not be silent in the face of such cruel manipulation of the poor.

My third reason moves to an even deeper level of awareness, for it grows out of my experience in the ghettos of the North over the last three years—especially the last three summers. As I have walked among the desperate, rejected and angry young men I have told them that Molotov cocktails and rifles would not solve their problems. I have tried to offer them my deepest compassion while maintaining my conviction that social change comes most meaningfully through nonviolent action. But they asked—and rightly so—what about Vietnam? They asked if our own

---

[1] Speech delivered April 4, 1967 at the Riverside Church in New York City to Clergy and Laity Concerned, a group opposing the war in Vietnam.

nation wasn't using massive doses of violence to solve its problems, to bring about the changes it wanted. Their questions hit home, and I knew that I could never again raise my voice against the violence of the oppressed in the ghettos without having first spoken clearly to the greatest purveyor of violence in the world today—my own government. For the sake of those boys, for the sake of this government, for the sake of the hundreds of thousands trembling under our violence, I cannot be silent.

For those who ask the question, "Aren't you a civil rights leader?" and thereby mean to exclude me from the movement for peace, I have this further answer. In 1957 when a group of us formed the Southern Christian Leadership Conference, we chose as our motto: "To save the soul of America." We were convinced that we could not limit our vision to certain rights for black people, but instead affirmed the conviction that America would never be free or saved from itself unless the descendants of its slaves were loosed completely from the shackles they still wear. In a way we were agreeing with Langston Hughes,[2] that black bard of Harlem, who had written earlier:

O, yes,
I say it plain,
America never was America to me,
And yet I swear this oath—
America will be!

Now, it should be incandescently clear that no one who has any concern for the integrity and life of America today can ignore the present war. If America's soul becomes totally poisoned, part of the autopsy must read Vietnam. It can never be saved so long as it destroys the deepest hopes of men the world over. So it is that those of us who are yet determined that America *will* be are led down the path of protest and dissent, working for the health of our land.

As if the weight of such a commitment to the life and health of America were not enough, another burden of responsibility was placed upon me in 1964; and I cannot forget that the Nobel Prize for Peace was also a commission—a commission to work harder than I had ever worked before for "the brotherhood of man." This is a calling that takes me beyond national allegiances, but even if it were not present I would yet have to live with the meaning of my commitment to the ministry of Jesus Christ. To me the relationship of this ministry to the making of peace is so obvious that I sometimes marvel at those who ask me why I am speaking against the war. Could it be that they do not know that the good news was meant for all men—for Communist and capitalist, for their children and ours, for black and for white, for revolutionary and conservative? Have they forgotten that my ministry is in obedience to the one who loved his enemies so fully that he died for them? What then can I say to the "Vietcong" or to Castro or to Mao as a faithful minister of this

---

[2] (1902–1967), American writer. See pp. 753.

one? Can I threaten them with death or must I not share with them my life?

Finally, as I try to delineate for you and for myself the road that leads from Montgomery[3] to this place I would have offered all that was most valid if I simply said that I must be true to my conviction that I share with all men the calling to be a son of the living God. Beyond the calling of race or nation or creed is this vocation of sonship and brotherhood, and because I believe that the Father is deeply concerned especially for his suffering and helpless and outcast children, I come tonight to speak for them.

This I believe to be the privilege and the burden of all of us who deem ourselves bound by allegiances and loyalties which are broader and deeper than nationalism and which go beyond our nation's self-defined goals and positions. We are called to speak for the weak, for the voiceless, for victims of our nation and for those it calls enemy, for no document from human hands can make these humans any less our brothers.

STRANGE LIBERATORS

And as I ponder the madness of Vietnam and search within myself for ways to understand and respond to compassion my mind goes constantly to the people of that peninsula. I speak now not of the soldiers of each side, not of the junta in Saigon, but simply of the people who have been living under the curse of war for almost three continuous decades now. I think of them too because it is clear to me that there will be no meaningful solution there until some attempt is made to know them and hear their broken cries.

They must see Americans as strange liberators. The Vietnamese people proclaimed their own independence in 1945 after a combined French and Japanese occupation, and before the Communist revolution in China. They were led by Ho Chi Minh. Even though they quoted the American Declaration of Independence in their own document of freedom, we refused to recognize them. Instead, we decided to support France in its reconquest of her former colony.

Our government felt then that the Vietnamese people were not "ready" for independence, and we again fell victim to the deadly Western arrogance that has poisoned the international atmosphere for so long. With that tragic decision we rejected a revolutionary government seeking self-determination, and a government that had been established not by China (for whom the Vietnamese have no great love) but by clearly indigenous forces that included some Communists. For the peasants this new government meant real land reform, one of the most important needs in their lives.

---

[3] Alabama city where King led 1955 boycott to integrate city buses.

For nine years following 1945 we denied the people of Vietnam the right of independence. For nine years we vigorously supported the French in their abortive effort to recolonize Vietnam.

Before the end of the war we were meeting eighty per cent of the French war costs. Even before the French were defeated at Dien Bien Phu, they began to despair of the reckless action, but we did not. We encouraged them with our huge financial and military supplies to continue the war even after they had lost the will. Soon we would be paying almost the full costs of this tragic attempt at recolonization.

After the French were defeated it looked as if independence and land reform would come again through the Geneva agreements. But instead there came the United States, determined that Ho should not unify the temporarily divided nation, and the peasants watched again as we supported one of the most vicious modern dictators—our chosen man, Premier Diem. The peasants watched and cringed as Diem ruthlessly routed out all opposition, supported their extortionist landlords and refused even to discuss reunification with the north. The peasants watched as all this was presided over by U.S. influence and then by increasing numbers of U.S. troops who came to help quell the insurgency that Diem's methods had aroused. When Diem was overthrown they may have been happy, but the long line of military dictatorships seemed to offer no real change—especially in terms of their need for land and peace.

The only change came from America as we increased our troop commitments in support of governments which were singularly corrupt, inept and without popular support. All the while the people read our leaflets and received regular promises of peace and democracy—and land reform. Now they languish under our bombs and consider us—not their fellow Vietnamese—the real enemy. They move sadly and apathetically as we herd them off the land of their fathers into concentration camps where minimal social needs are rarely met. They know they must move or be destroyed by our bombs. So they go—primarily women and children and the aged.

They watch as we poison their water, as we kill a million acres of their crops. They must weep as the bulldozers roar through their areas preparing to destroy the precious trees. They wander into the hospitals, with at least twenty casualties from American firepower for one "Vietcong"-inflicted injury. So far we may have killed a million of them—mostly children. They wander into the towns and see thousands of the children, homeless, without clothes, running in packs on the streets like animals. They see the children degraded by our soldiers as they beg for food. They see the children selling their sisters to our soldiers, soliciting for their mothers.

What do the peasants think as we ally ourselves with the landlords and as we refuse to put any action into our many words concerning land reform? What do they think as we test out our latest weapons on them, just as the Germans tested out new medicine and new tortures in the concentration camps of Europe? Where are the roots of the independent Vietnam we claim to be building? Is it among these voiceless ones?

We have destroyed their two most cherished institutions: the family and the village. We have destroyed their land and their crops. We have cooperated in the crushing of the nation's only non-Communist revolutionary political force—the unified Buddhist church. We have supported the enemies of the peasants of Saigon. We have corrupted their women and children and killed their men. What liberators!

Now there is little left to build on—save bitterness. Soon the only solid physical foundations remaining will be found at our military bases and in the concrete of the concentration camps we call fortified hamlets. The peasants may well wonder if we plan to build our new Vietnam on such grounds as these? Could we blame them for such thoughts? We must speak for them and raise the questions they cannot raise. These too are our brothers.

Perhaps the more difficult but no less necessary task is to speak for those who have been designated as our enemies. What of the National Liberation Front—that strangely anonymous group we call VC or Communists? What must they think of us in America when they realize that we permitted the repression and cruelty of Diem which helped to bring them into being as a resistance group in the south? What do they think of our condoning the violence which led to their own taking up of arms? How can they believe in our integrity when now we speak of "aggression from the north" as if there were nothing more essential to the war? How can they trust us when now we charge them with violence after the murderous reign of Diem and charge them with violence while we pour every new weapon of death into their land? Surely we must understand their feelings even if we do not condone their actions. Surely we must see that the men we supported pressed them to their violence. Surely we must see that our own computerized plans of destruction simply dwarf their greatest acts.

How do they judge us when our officials know that their membership is less than twenty-five percent Communist and yet insist on giving them the blanket name? What must they be thinking when they know that we are aware of their control of major sections of Vietnam and yet we appear ready to allow national elections in which this highly organized political parallel government will have no part? They ask how we can speak of free elections when the Saigon press is censored and controlled by the military junta. And they are surely right to wonder what kind of new government we plan to help form without them—the only party in real touch with the peasants. They question our political goals and they deny the reality of a peace settlement from which they will be excluded. Their questions are frighteningly relevant. Is our nation planning to build on political myth again and then shore it up with the power of new violence?

Here is the true meaning and value of compassion and nonviolence when it helps us to see the enemy's point of view, to hear his questions, to know his assessment of ourselves. For from his view we may indeed see the basic weaknesses of our own condition, and if we are mature, we may learn and grow and profit from the wisdom of the brothers who are called the opposition.

So, too, with Hanoi. In the north, where our bombs now pummel the land, and our mines endanger the waterways, we are met by a deep but understandable mistrust. To speak for them is to explain this lack of confidence in Western words, and especially their distrust of American intentions now. In Hanoi are the men who led the nation to independence against the Japanese and the French, the men who sought membership in the French commonwealth and were betrayed by the weakness of Paris and the willfulness of the colonial armies. It was they who led a second struggle against French domination at tremendous costs, and then were persuaded to give up the land they controlled between the thirteenth and seventeenth parallels as a temporary measure at Geneva. After 1954 they watched us conspire with Diem to prevent elections which would have surely brought Ho Chi Minh to power over a united Vietnam, and they realized they had been betrayed again.

When we ask why they do not leap to negotiate, these things must be remembered. Also it must be clear that the leaders of Hanoi considered the presence of American troops in support of the Diem regime to have been the initial military breach of the Geneva agreements concerning foreign troops, and they remind us that they did not begin to send in any large number of supplies or men until American forces had moved into the tens of thousands.

Hanoi remembers how our leaders refused to tell us the truth about the earlier North Vietnamese overtures for peace, how the president claimed that none existed when they had clearly been made. Ho Chi Minh has watched as America has spoken of peace and built up its forces, and now he has surely heard of the increasing international rumors of American plans for an invasion of the north. He knows the bombing and shelling and mining we are doing are part of traditional pre-invasion strategy. Perhaps only his sense of humor and of irony can save him when he hears the most powerful nation of the world speaking of aggression as it drops thousands of bombs on a poor weak nation more than eight thousand miles away from its shores.

At this point I should make it clear that while I have tried in these last few minutes to give a voice to the voiceless on Vietnam and to understand the arguments of those who are called enemy, I am as deeply concerned about our troops there as anything else. For it occurs to me that what we are submitting them to in Vietnam is not simply the brutalizing process that goes on in any war where armies face each other and seek to destroy. We are adding to the process of death, for they must know after a short period there that none of the things we claim to be fighting for are really involved. Before long they must know that their government has sent them into a struggle among Vietnamese, and the more sophisticated surely realize that we are on the side of the wealthy and the secure while we create a hell for the poor.

Somehow this madness must cease. We must stop now. I speak as a child of God and brother to the suffering poor of Vietnam. I speak for those whose land is being laid waste, whose homes are being destroyed, whose culture is being subverted. I speak for the poor of America who are paying the double price of smashed hopes at home and death and corruption in Vietnam. I speak as a citizen of the world, for the world as it stands aghast at the path we have taken. I speak as an American to the leaders of my own nation. The great initiative in this war is ours. The initiative to stop it must be ours.

Study and Discussion Questions

1. What are King's "seven major reasons for bringing Vietnam into the field of [his] moral vision"?
2. What does he mean when he calls Americans the "strange liberators"?
3. Why does he have a number of paragraphs composed entirely or mostly of questions? From whose perspective are these questions asked? Is there an ethical or moral purpose behind this rhetorical device? Is it effective?
4. What are the assumptions underlying his argument that the United States must stop military involvement in Vietnam?

Writing Exercises

1. Select one paragraph in this speech and analyze it in detail. What is the main point or thesis of the paragraph? What are the supporting evidence and secondary points?
2. Pick a contemporary political issue and adapt and apply King's argument to it.
3. If you were to construct an argument against King's position in "A Time to Break Silence," what would your major points be? Come up with at least five.

PEACE AND WAR: PAPER TOPICS

1. Compare the descriptions of battle in two or more works. (Suggestions: Owen, "Dulce et Decorum Est"; Black Elk, "The Butchering at Wounded Knee"; Tennyson, "The Charge of the Light Brigade")
2. Pick two works, one supporting and one opposing war, that seem to be in dialogue with each other and analyze the argument implicit (or explicit) in each and the literary devices used to persuade the reader. (Suggestions: Emerson, "Concord Hymn"; Dylan, "With God on Our Side")

3. Discuss the way people cope with the memory of war. (Suggestions: Erdrich, "The Red Convertible"; Jewett, "Decoration Day"; Whitman, "The Dying Veteran")

4. Discuss the consequences of war for individuals or communities in one or more works. (Suggestions: Kovic, *Born on the Fourth of July*; Duras, *The War: A Memoir*; Ota, "Fireflies"; H.D., "The Walls Must Fall")

5. Discuss in one or more works the various strategies for survival used by people involved, either willingly or unwillingly, in war. (Suggestions: Kaminsky, *In the Traffic of a Targeted City*; Yevtuskenko, "The Companion"; Grahn, "Vietnamese Woman Speaking to an American Soldier")

6. Analyze one or more works that explore why people go to war. (Suggestions: Yeats, "An Irish Airman Foresees His Death"; "Papago War Song"; Lovelace, "For Lucasta, on Going to the Wars")

7. Choose two or more works whose subject is the same war and compare their perspectives on that war.

8. Is there a difference between male and female perspectives on war? Support your argument with reference to at least two works by men and at least two works by women.

9. Analyze in detail the way one work conveys the fragility of peace. (Suggestions: Kaminsky, *In The Traffic of a Targeted City*; Rukeyser, "Waking This Morning")

10. Discuss the way an individual's race or social class affects his or her relation to war in one or more works.

11. Discuss the psychology of those who make war, as depicted in one or more works. (Suggestions: Barthelme, "Report"; Dylan, "With God On Our Side"; Reed, "Naming of Parts")

12. Analyze how formal elements such as character, setting, point of view, and sequencing of events make meaning in one or more works. (Suggestions: Bradbury, "August 2026: There Will Come Soft Rains"; Bierce, "An Occurrence at Owl Creek Bridge"; Kaminsky, *In the Traffic of a Targeted City*)

VARIETIES OF PROTEST

Fundamentally, to protest means to say "no." The stories, essays, speeches, poems, plays and songs in this section present a vivid and extensive variety of ways to say no to injustice, oppression, and lack of choice. Some of the protests written about here succeed; some don't. In some cases we don't know the outcome. Some are protests by groups of people; others come from individuals. Many concern issues touched upon throughout this anthology: slavery and its legacy of racism; poor working conditions, low pay, job discrimination and other forms of economic oppression; sexism and heterosexism; war. What characterizes the selections here is that they are as much about the act of protest as they are about the issues protested.

With a few exceptions, these literary works are from the United States. The fact that our national history began in protest and that the United States was founded in revolution with proclamations of equality and justice for all is the irony at the center of several of the selections included here. In his famous speech, "I Have a Dream," delivered at the 1963 March on Washington for Jobs and Freedom, Martin Luther King, Jr. sees the Constitution and Declaration of Independence as promissory notes which America has defaulted on where black Americans are concerned. In 1855, John Greenleaf Whittier, in his abolitionist poem "For Righteousness' Sake," writes that "The brave old strife the fathers saw/ For Freedom calls for men again" and worries that his own era has become complacent and indifferent to injustice, "dull and mean."

Because slavery and racism have been our most glaring national shame, a great deal of American protest literature has been concerned with these issues. The 1757 selection from the *Journal* of Quaker writer and preacher John Woolman records powerful arguments against slavery from a time when few white Americans had begun to question its morality. In an excerpt from one of the few slave narratives by a woman, *Incidents in the Life of a Slave Girl*, Harriet Jacobs writes about the suffering she endured to escape from slavery. Margaret Walker's prose poem, "For My People," written almost a hundred years after Jacobs's narrative, details Walker's love for her people, her sense of their suffering, America's continuing history of racism, and how far we have yet to go. Barbara Deming, arrested as a civil rights protestor in the 1960s, describes in "Prison Notes" her time in jail and how it solidified her political commitment.

Many of the issues protested overlap. Though we are often conscious of a weary yearning to reduce their complexity to manageable proportions, life and literature are rarely simple. Harriet Jacobs is oppressed both because she is a woman and because she is black. Thoreau is protesting war as well as slavery in "Civil Disobedience." In Sophocles's play, Antigone's protest against King Creon occurs on at least four fronts: female against male, youth against age, the rights of the individual against the power of the state, religious against secular priorities. Nadine Gordimer's story, "Something for the Time Being," about one white married couple and one black married couple whose lives briefly intersect, is as much about sexual politics as it is about the politics of race and class in South Africa. Judy Grahn's long and complex poem, "A Woman Is Talking To Death," touches upon war and violence, and also upon race, class and gender oppression as well as the protest against homophobia which is at its center. For Grahn in this poem, protest takes the form of commitment and engagement rather than a turning away from those who are oppressed; she redefines heroism as involvement, cowardice as detachment. Love in all its forms—physical, emotional, spiritual and political—is, she concludes, "the resistance that tells death he will starve for lack of the fat of us." On the other hand, Alexander Pope, speaking from the comfortable position of privilege, implies in an excerpt from his eighteenth-century poem, *An Essay on Man*, that all protest is inappropriate, even a bit vulgar: "Whatever IS—is RIGHT."

The forms the protests take, from individual acts of conscience to demonstrations, strikes, and riots, are as various as the issues protested. The title character of Herman Melville's short story, "Bartleby the Scrivener," engages in passive resistance throughout the fable, his verbal leitmotif a polite "I would prefer not to." Though what exactly Bartleby is protesting is only hinted at in the story, we can clearly see the impact of the tactic of passive resistance on the people around him, particularly on the narrator. Thoreau, in his essay "Civil Disobedience," and John Woolman, in his autobiographical *Journal*, both write about individual acts of resistance. Thoreau would undoubtedly agree with Woolman's argument that people must act out of conscience whether or not current law and custom support them. "It is the duty of all to be firm in that which they certainly know is right for them." Thoreau spends a night in jail for refusing to pay taxes to a government that supports slavery and the Mexican-American War, though he does tell us he is released the next morning when someone pays his taxes for him. That, however, is not his concern. Woolman not only argues against slavery, but describes his own individual acts of resistance, how he acts out his convictions by refusing to write wills for people who own slaves and uses that refusal as an occasion to argue with individual slave owners. Two centuries later, Pat Parker in "Where Will You Be?" prods the individual conscience of each one of her readers who might refuse to stand up and be counted.

More indirect forms of protest occur in Pamela Zoline's short story, "The Heat Death of the Universe," and Adrienne Rich's poem, "The Trees." Both focus on a crisis for the female protagonist or persona, where either a breakdown or a breakthrough is possible. In each case, the image of suddenly mobile or out-of-control vegetation becomes a metaphor for the changes going on inside the main character or speaker. In Sylvia Plath's poem "Mushrooms," which takes as its text the beatitude, "blessed are the meek, for they shall inherit the earth," whimsy turns sinister as more and more of the mushrooms pop their featureless heads above ground. All three of these pieces were written by married American women in the years immediately preceeding the contemporary wave of feminism. How angry are these women, we might ask, and why are they displacing their anger onto plants?

Speaking of anger, Alan Sillitoe's "The Loneliness of the Long-distance Runner" (1959) gives us an unabashed, undiluted, angry working-class view of the British class system. For the first-person narrator of this piece, a Borstal (reform school) boy, the world is divided into "us" and "them." Because he is a good runner, "they" try to bribe him to win a race for them with the carrot of class mobility. He muses:

> I realized it might be possible to do such a thing, run for money, trot for wages on piece work at a bob a puff rising bit by bit to a guinea a gasp and retiring through old age at thirty-two because of lace-curtain lungs, a football heart, and legs like varicose beanstalks. But I'd have a wife and car and get my grinning long-distance clock in the papers and have a smashing secretary to answer piles of letters sent by tarts who'd mob me when they saw who I was as I pushed my way into Woolworth's for a packet of razor blades and a cup of tea.

His ultimate protest against his situation is clever, cynical, effective— and costs him. It is an individual protest, but made in the context of his self-definition as a member of a social class.

The contrasts between individual and collective protest, between working within the system and changing it, between charitable and political action inform Dorothy Canfield Fisher's 1915 short story, "A Drop in the Bucket." A New England spinster rescues a single mother and her children from the city tenements and is seen as crazy by her conservative small-town community and as misguided—a provider of bandaids for a case of social gangrene—by the revolutionary who has unwittingly provoked her into action. Her particular form of protest is to give up her own middle-class comfort and solitude in order to share what she has with a family who has less. An important question is where in this story the writer's sympathy lies and whether the story's title is ironic.

A few of the selections eulogize or memorialize people who spent their lives, and sometimes died, trying to make the world a better place. Robert Hayden's poem "Frederick Douglass" eulogizes a black leader who worked for his people's rights. So does Susan Griffin's poem "I Like to Think of Harriet Tubman," but specifically in the context of Tubman's relevance as a hero for the contemporary women's movement. Pablo Neruda's "Ode to Federico García Lorca" is a tribute to a Spanish poet who used his art to protest injustice during the Spanish Civil War. He was executed barely a year after Neruda's ode to him was written. We might compare Neruda's poem to Lorca's own "Ballad of the Spanish Civil Guard" in the Peace and War section. Even in translation, we can see how Neruda's poem evokes Lorca's language and imagery, his "black-draped orange-tree voice."

The question of violent versus nonviolent means of protest is raised in several of these selections. Langston Hughes, in "Harlem," suggests through a brilliant series of images that oppression too long repressed is bound eventually to explode, and Gwendolyn Brooks's poem "Riot" focuses on just such an outbreak of violence. James Alan McPherson's story, "A Loaf of Bread," traces the consequences and suggests the power of an organized nonviolent protest, and Martin Luther King, Jr.'s speech, "I Have a Dream," urges black Americans, despite their impatience and despite the violence that has been directed against them, to follow the path of nonviolent civil disobedience. Lake Sagaris's "The March," set in Chile under the dictator Pinochet, shows the cost of protest for one woman. If riots are one form of collective protest, union activism is another and usually gentler form, though the resistance to union organizing has often been violently confrontational. The union song "Solidarity Forever" urges workers toward a consciousness of economic injustice and of their potential strength in acting together.

Finally, the movement from individual to group action and the question of the appropriateness of violence as a mode of protest is the subject of Susan Glaspell's early twentieth-century play, *Trifles*, about a woman who (perhaps) has killed her husband and about two women who (may) decide to support her. Originally published as a short story with the title "A Jury of Her Peers," *Trifles* is a deliberately provocative work of art, raising disturbing questions about the relations between women and men, about where our loyalties ultimately lie, about whether law and justice are identical, and about who has the right and who has the power to judge another. *Trifles* is built on the careful consideration of ethical choices. So are most of the works included in this section, probably because protest is the crossroads of conviction and action.

FICTION

HERMAN MELVILLE (1819–1891)

Herman Melville was born in New York City into a wealthy family whose fortunes declined with the bankruptcy and death of his father. Melville left school at fifteen, clerked in a bank, farmed, taught, worked as a cabin boy on a ship to Liverpool, sailed on a whaler, lived in the South Sea islands, and enlisted on a Navy frigate. Typee (1846), Omoo (1847), and other early novels based on his adventures were very popular, while what is now considered his major work, Moby Dick (1851), marked the beginning of the fast decline of his reputation. Melville lived for over a decade on a farm in Massachusetts, where he became friends with Nathaniel Hawthorne, and then returned to New York to take a job as a customs inspector, where he worked in obscurity for nineteen years. His writing was rediscovered in the early 1920s. Among his other important works of fiction are Pierre (1852), The Piazza Tales (1856), and Billy Budd (1891).

Bartleby, The Scrivener

A Story of Wall Street   (1853)

I am a rather elderly man. The nature of my avocations, for the last thirty years, has brought me into more than ordinary contact with what would seem an interesting and somewhat singular set of men, of whom, as yet, nothing, that I know of, has ever been written—I mean, the law-copyists, or scriveners. I have known very many of them, professionally and privately, and, if I pleased, could relate divers histories, at which good-natured gentlemen might smile, and sentimental souls might weep. But I waive the biographies of all other scriveners, for a few passages in the life of Bartleby, who was a scrivener, the strangest I ever saw, or heard of. While, of other law-copyists, I might write the complete life, of Bartleby nothing of that sort can be done. I believe that no materials exist, for a full and satisfactory biography of this man. It is an irreparable loss to literature. Bartleby was one of those beings of whom nothing is ascertainable, except from the original sources, and, in his case, those are very small. What my own astonished eyes saw of Bartleby, *that* is all I know of him, except, indeed, one vague report, which will appear in the sequel.

Ere introducing the scrivener, as he first appeared to me, it is fit I make some mention of myself, my employés, my business, my chambers, and general surroundings; because some such description is indispensable to an adequate understanding of the chief character about to be presented. Imprimis: I am a man who, from his youth upward, has been filled with a profound conviction that the easiest way of life is the best. Hence, though I belong to a profession proverbially energetic and nervous, even to turbulence, at times, yet nothing of that sort have I ever suffered to invade my peace. I am one of those unambitious lawyers who never addresses a jury, or in any way draws down public applause; but, in the cool tranquillity of a snug retreat, do a snug business among rich men's bonds, and mortgages, and title-deeds. All who know me, consider me an eminently *safe* man. The late John Jacob Astor, a personage little given to poetic enthusiasm, had no hesitation in pronouncing my first grand point to be prudence; my next, method. I do not speak it in vanity, but simply record the fact, that I was not unemployed in my profession by the late John Jacob Astor; a name which, I admit, I love to repeat; for it hath a rounded and orbicular sound to it, and rings like unto bullion. I will freely add, that I was not insensible to the late John Jacob Astor's good opinion.

Some time prior to the period at which this little history begins, my avocations had been largely increased. The good old office, now extinct in the State of New York, of a Master in Chancery, had been conferred upon me. It was not a very arduous office, but very pleasantly remunerative. I seldom lose my temper; much more seldom indulge in dangerous indignation at wrongs and outrages; but, I must be permitted to be rash here, and declare, that I consider the sudden and violent abrogation of the office of Master in Chancery, by the new Constitution, as a—premature act; inasmuch as I had counted upon a life-lease of the profits, whereas I only received those of a few short years. But this is by the way.

My chambers were upstairs, at No. — Wall Street. At one end, they looked upon the white wall of the interior of a spacious skylight shaft, penetrating the building from top to bottom.

This view might have been considered rather tame than otherwise, deficient in what landscape painters call 'life.' But, if so, the view from the other end of my chambers offered, at least, a contrast, if nothing more. In that direction, my windows commanded an unobstructed view of a lofty brick wall, black by age and everlasting shade; which wall required no spy-glass to bring out its lurking beauties, but, for the benefit of all near-sighted spectators, was pushed up to within ten feet of my window panes. Owing to the great height of the surrounding buildings, and my chambers being on the second floor, the interval between this wall and mine not a little resembled a huge square cistern.

At the period just preceding the advent of Bartleby, I had two persons as copyists in my employment, and a promising lad as an office-boy. First, Turkey; second, Nippers; third, Ginger Nut. These may seem names, the like of which are not usually found in the Directory. In truth, they were nicknames, mutually conferred upon each other by my three clerks, and were deemed expressive of their respective persons or characters. Turkey was a short, pursy[1] Englishman, of about my own age—that is, somewhere not far from sixty. In the morning, one might say, his face was of a fine florid hue, but after twelve o'clock, meridian—his dinner hour—it blazed like a grate full of Christmas coals; and continued blazing—but, as it were, with a gradual wane—till six o'clock, P.M., or thereabouts; after which, I saw no more of the proprietor of the face, which, gaining its meridian with the sun, seemed to set with it, to rise, culminate, and decline the following day, with the like regularity and undiminished glory. There are many singular coincidences I have known in the course of my life, not the least among which was the fact, that, exactly when Turkey displayed his fullest beams from his red and radiant countenance, just then, too, at that critical moment, began the daily period when I considered his business capacities as seriously disturbed for the remainder of the twenty-four hours. Not that he was absolutely idle, or averse to business, then; far from it. The difficulty was, he was apt to be altogether too energetic. There was a strange, inflamed, flurried, flighty recklessness of activity about him. He would be incautious in dipping his pen into his inkstand. All his blots upon my documents were dropped there after twelve o'clock, meridian. Indeed, not only would he be reckless, and sadly given to making blots in the afternoon, but, some days, he went further, and was rather noisy. At such times, too, his face flamed with augmented blazonry, as if cannel coal had been heaped on anthracite. He made an unpleasant racket with his chair; spilled his sand-box; in mending his pens, impatiently split them all to pieces, and threw them on the floor in a sudden passion; stood up, and leaned over his table, boxing his papers about in a most indecorous manner, very sad to behold in an elderly man like him. Nevertheless, as he was in many ways a most valuable person to me, and all the time before twelve o'clock, meridian, was the quickest, steadiest creature, too, accomplishing a great deal of work in a style not easily to be matched—for these reasons, I was willing to overlook his eccentricities, though, indeed, occasionally, I remonstrated with him. I did this very gently, however, because, though the civilest, nay, the blandest and most reverential of men in the morning, yet, in the afternoon, he was disposed, upon provocation, to be slightly rash with his tongue—in fact, insolent. Now, valuing his morning services as I did, and resolved not to lose them—yet, at the same time, made uncomfortable by his inflamed ways after twelve o'clock—and being a man of peace, unwilling by my admonitions to call forth unseemly retorts from him, I took upon me, one Saturday noon (he was always worse on Saturdays) to hint to him, very kindly, that, perhaps, now that he was growing old, it might be well to abridge his labours; in short, he need

---

[1] Short-winded; fat.

not come to my chambers after twelve o'clock, but, dinner over, had best go home to his lodgings, and rest himself till tea-time. But no; he insisted upon his afternoon devotions. His countenance became intolerably fervid, as he oratorically assured me—gesticulating with a long ruler at the other end of the room—that if his services in the morning were useful, how indispensable, then, in the afternoon?

'With submission, sir,' said Turkey, on this occasion, 'I consider myself your right-hand man. In the morning I but marshal and deploy my columns; but in the afternoon I put myself at their head, and gallantly charge the foe, thus'—and he made a violent thrust with the ruler.

'But the blots, Turkey,' intimated I.

'True; but, with submission, sir, behold these hairs! I am getting old. Surely, sir, a blot or two of a warm afternoon is not to be severely urged against gray hairs. Old age—even if it blot the page—is honourable. With submission, sir, we *both* are getting old.'

This appeal to my fellow-feeling was hardly to be resisted. At all events, I saw that go he would not. So, I made up my mind to let him stay, resolving, nevertheless, to see to it that, during the afternoon, he had to do with my less important papers.

Nippers, the second on my list, was a whiskered, sallow, and, upon the whole, rather piratical-looking young man, of about five-and-twenty. I always deemed him the victim of two evil powers—ambition and indigestion. The ambition was evinced by a certain impatience of the duties of a mere copyist, an unwarrantable usurpation of strictly professional affairs, such as the original drawing up of legal documents. The indigestion seemed betokened in an occasional nervous testiness and grinning irritability, causing the teeth to audibly grind together over mistakes committed in copying; unnecessary maledictions, hissed, rather than spoken, in the heat of business; and especially by a continual discontent with the height of the table where he worked. Though of a very ingenious mechanical turn, Nippers could never get this table to suit him. He put chips under it, blocks of various sorts, bits of pasteboard, and at last went so far as to attempt an exquisite adjustment, by final pieces of folded blotting-paper. But no invention would answer. If, for the sake of easing his back, he brought the table lid at a sharp angle well up toward his chin, and wrote there like a man using the steep roof of a Dutch house for his desk, then he declared that it stopped the circulation in his arms. If now he lowered the table to his waistbands, and stooped over it in writing, then there was a sore aching in his back. In short, the truth of the matter was, Nippers knew not what he wanted. Or, if he wanted anything, it was to be rid of a scrivener's table altogether. Among the manifestations of his diseased ambition was a fondness he had for receiving visits from certain ambiguous-looking fellows in seedy coats, whom he called his clients. Indeed, I was aware that not only was he, at times, considerable of a ward-politician, but he occasionally did a little business at the Justices' courts, and was not unknown on the steps of the Tombs.[2] I have good reason to believe, however, that one individual who called upon him at my chambers, and who, with a grand air, he insisted was his client, was no other than a dun, and the alleged title-deed, a bill. But, with all his failings, and the annoyances he caused me, Nippers, like his compatriot Turkey, was a very useful man to me; wrote a neat, swift hand; and, when he chose, was not deficient in a gentlemanly sort of deportment. Added to this, he always dressed in a gentlemanly sort of way; and so, incidentally, reflected credit upon my chambers. Whereas, with respect to Turkey, I had much ado to keep him from being a reproach to me. His clothes were apt to look oily, and smell of eating-houses. He wore his pantaloons very loose and baggy in summer. His coats were execrable; his hat not to be handled. But while the hat was a thing of indifference to me, inasmuch as his natural civility and deference, as a dependent Englishman, always led him to doff it the moment he entered the room, yet his coat was another matter. Concerning his coats, I reasoned with him; but with no effect. The truth was, I suppose, that a man with so small an income could not afford to sport such a lustrous face and a lustrous coat at one and the same time. As Nippers once observed, Turkey's money went chiefly for red ink. One winter day, I presented Turkey with a highly respectable-looking coat of my own—a padded gray coat, of a most comfortable warmth, and which buttoned straight up from the knee to the neck. I thought Turkey would appreciate the favour, and abate his rashness and obstreperousness of afternoons. But no; I verily believe that buttoning himself up in so downy and blanket-like a coat had a pernicious effect upon him—upon the same principle that too much oats are bad for horses. In fact, precisely as a rash, restive horse is said to feel his oats, so Turkey felt his coat. It made him insolent. He was a man whom prosperity harmed.

Though, concerning the self-indulgent habits of Turkey, I had my own private surmises, yet, touching Nippers, I was well persuaded that, whatever might be his faults in other respects, he was, at least, a temperate young man. But, indeed, nature herself seemed to have been his vintner, and, at his birth, charged him so thoroughly with an irritable, brandy-like disposition, that all subsequent potations were needless. When I consider how, amid the stillness of my chambers, Nippers would sometimes impatiently rise from his seat, and stooping over his table, spread his arms wide apart, seize the whole desk, and move it, and jerk it, with a grim, grinding motion on the floor, as if the table were a perverse voluntary agent, intent on thwarting and vexing him, I plainly perceive that, for Nippers, brandy-and-water were altogether superfluous.

It was fortunate for me that, owing to its peculiar cause—indigestion—the irritability and consequent nervousness of Nippers were mainly observable in the morning, while in the afternoon he was comparatively mild. So that, Turkey's paroxysms only coming on about twelve o'clock,

---

[2] New York City prison.

I never had to do with their eccentricities at one time. Their fits relieved each other, like guards. When Nipper's was on, Turkey's was off; and *vice versa*. This was a good natural arrangement, under the circumstances.

Ginger Nut, the third on my list, was a lad, some twelve years old. His father was a carman, ambitious of seeing his son on the bench instead of a cart, before he died. So he sent him to my office, as student at law, errand-boy, cleaner and sweeper, at the rate of one dollar a week. He had a little desk to himself, but he did not use it much. Upon inspection, the drawer exhibited a great array of the shells of various sorts of nuts. Indeed, to this quick-witted youth, the whole noble science of the law was contained in a nut-shell. Not the least among the employments of Ginger Nut, as well as one which he discharged with the most alacrity, was his duty as cake and apple purveyor for Turkey and Nippers. Copying law-papers being proverbially a dry, husky sort of business, my two scriveners were fain to moisten their mouths very often with Spitzenbergs, to be had at the numerous stalls nigh the Custom House and Post Office. Also, they sent Ginger Nut very frequently for that peculiar cake—small, flat, round, and very spicy—after which he had been named by them. Of a cold morning, when business was but dull, Turkey would gobble up scores of these cakes, as if they were mere wafers—indeed, they sell them at the rate of six or eight for a penny—the scrape of his pen blending with the crunching of the crisp particles in his mouth. Of all the fiery afternoon blunders and flurried rashnesses of Turkey, was his once moistening a ginger-cake between his lips, and clapping it on to a mortgage, for a seal. I came within an ace of dismissing him then. But he mollified me by making an oriental bow, and saying—'With submission, sir, it was generous of me to find you in[3] stationery on my own account.'

Now my original business—that of a conveyancer and title-hunter, and drawer-up of recondite documents of all sorts—was considerably increased by receiving the master's office. There was now great work for scriveners. Not only must I push the clerks already with me, but I must have additional help.

In answer to my advertisement, a motionless young man one morning stood upon my office threshold, the door being open, for it was summer. I can see that figure now—pallidly neat, pitiably respectable, incurably forlorn! It was Bartleby.

After a few words touching his qualifications, I engaged him, glad to have among my corps of copyists a man of so singularly sedate an aspect, which I thought might operate beneficially upon the flighty temper of Turkey, and the fiery one of Nippers.

I should have stated before that ground-glass folding-doors divided my premises into two parts, one of which was occupied by my scriveners, the other by myself. According to my humour, I threw open these doors, or closed them. I resolved to assign Bartleby a corner by the folding-

---

[3] To supply you with.

doors, but on my side of them, so as to have this quiet man within easy call, in case any trifling thing was to be done. I placed his desk close up to a small side-window in that part of the room, a window which originally had afforded a lateral view of certain grimy back-yards and bricks, but which, owing to subsequent erections, commanded at present no view at all, though it gave some light. Within three feet of the panes was a wall, and the light came down from far above, between two lofty buildings, as from a very small opening in a dome. Still further to a satisfactory arrangement, I procured a high green folding-screen, which might entirely isolate Bartleby from my sight, though not remove him from my voice. And thus, in a manner, privacy and society were conjoined.

At first, Bartleby did an extraordinary quantity of writing. As if long famishing for something to copy, he seemed to gorge himself on my documents. There was no pause for digestion. He ran a day and night line, copying by sun-light and by candle-light. I should have been quite delighted with his application, had he been cheerfully industrious. But he wrote on silently, palely, mechanically.

It is, of course, an indispensable part of a scrivener's business to verify the accuracy of his copy, word by word. Where there are two or more scriveners in an office, they assist each other in this examination, one reading from the copy, the other holding the original. It is a very dull, wearisome, and lethargic affair. I can readily imagine that, to some sanguine temperaments, it would be altogether intolerable. For example, I cannot credit that the mettlesome poet, Byron, would have contentedly sat down with Bartleby to examine a law document of, say, five hundred pages, closely written in a crimpy hand.

Now and then, in the haste of business, it had been my habit to assist in comparing some brief document myself, calling Turkey or Nippers for this purpose. One object I had, in placing Bartleby so handy to me behind the screen, was, to avail myself of his services on such trivial occasions. It was on the third day, I think, of his being with me, and before any necessity had arisen for having his own writing examined, that, being much hurried to complete a small affair I had in hand, I abruptly called to Bartleby. In my haste and natural expectancy of instant compliance, I sat with my head bent over the original on my desk, and my right hand sideways, and somewhat nervously extended with the copy, so that, immediately upon emerging from his retreat, Bartleby might snatch it and proceed to business without the least delay.

In this very attitude did I sit when I called to him, rapidly stating what it was I wanted him to do—namely, to examine a small paper with me. Imagine my surprise, nay, my consternation, when, without moving from his privacy, Bartleby, in a singularly mild, firm voice, replied, 'I would prefer not to.'

I sat a while in perfect silence, rallying my stunned faculties. Immediately it occurred to me that my ears had deceived me, or Bartleby had entirely misunderstood my meaning. I repeated my request in the clearest tone I could assume; but in quite as clear a one came the previous reply, 'I would prefer not to.'

'Prefer not to,' echoed I, rising in high excitement, and crossing the room with a stride. 'What do you mean? Are you moon-struck? I want you to help me compare this sheet here—take it,' and I thrust it toward him.

'I would prefer not to,' said he.

I looked at him steadfastly. His face was leanly composed; his gray eye dimly calm. Not a wrinkle of agitation rippled him. Had there been the least uneasiness, anger, impatience, or impertinence in his manner; in other words, had there been anything ordinarily human about him, doubtless I should have violently dismissed him from the premises. But as it was, I should have as soon thought of turning my pale plaster-of-paris bust of Cicero out of doors. I stood gazing at him a while, as he went on with his own writing, and then reseated myself at my desk. This is very strange, thought I. What had one best do? But my business hurried me. I concluded to forget the matter for the present, reserving it for my future leisure. So calling Nippers from the other room, the paper was speedily examined.

A few days after this, Bartleby concluded four lengthy documents, being quadruplicates of a week's testimony taken before me in my High Court of Chancery. It became necessary to examine them. It was an important suit, and great accuracy was imperative. Having all things arranged, I called Turkey, Nippers, and Ginger Nut, from the next room, meaning to place the four copies in the hands of my four clerks, while I should read from the original. Accordingly, Turkey, Nippers, and Ginger Nut had taken their seats in a row, each with his document in his hand, when I called to Bartleby to join this interesting group.

'Bartleby! quick, I am waiting.'

I heard a slow scrape of his chair legs on the uncarpeted floor, and soon he appeared standing at the entrance of this hermitage.

'What is wanted?' said he mildly.

'The copies, the copies,' said I hurriedly. 'We are going to examine them. There'—and I held toward him the fourth quadruplicate.

'I would prefer not to,' he said, and gently disappeared behind the screen.

For a few moments I was turned into a pillar of salt, standing at the head of my seated column of clerks. Recovering myself, I advanced toward the screen, and demanded the reason for such extraordinary conduct.

'Why do you refuse?'

'I would prefer not to.'

With any other man I should have flown outright into a dreadful passion, scorned all further words, and thrust him ignominiously from my presence. But there was something about Bartleby that not only strangely disarmed me, but, in a wonderful manner, touched and disconcerted me. I began to reason with him.

'These are your own copies we are about to examine. It is labour saving to you, because one examination will answer for your four papers. It is common usage. Every copyist is bound to help examine his copy. Is it not so? Will you not speak? Answer!'

'I prefer not to,' he replied in a flute-like tone. It seemed to me that, while I had been addressing him, he carefully revolved every statement that I made; fully comprehended the meaning; could not gainsay the irresistible conclusion; but, at the same time, some paramount consideration prevailed with him to reply as he did.

'You are decided, then, not to comply with my request—a request made according to common usage and common sense?'

He briefly gave me to understand, that on that point my judgment was sound. Yes: his decision was irreversible.

It is not seldom the case that, when a man is browbeaten in some unprecedented and violently unreasonable way, he begins to stagger in his own plainest faith. He begins, as it were, vaguely to surmise that, wonderful as it may be, all the justice and all the reason is on the other side. Accordingly, if any disinterested persons are present, he turns to them for some reinforcement for his own faltering mind.

'Turkey,' said I, 'what do you think of this? Am I not right?'

'With submission, sir,' said Turkey, in his blandest tone, 'I think that you are.'

'Nippers,' said I, 'what do *you* think of it?'

'I think I should kick him out of the office.'

(The reader, of nice perceptions, will here perceive that, it being morning, Turkey's answer is couched in polite and tranquil terms, but Nipper's replies in ill-tempered ones. Or, to repeat a previous sentence, Nipper's ugly mood was on duty, and Turkey's off.)

'Ginger Nut,' said I, willing to enlist the smallest suffrage in my behalf, 'what do *you* think of it?'

'I think, sir, he's a little *luny*,' replied Ginger Nut, with a grin.

'You hear what they say,' said I, turning toward the screen, 'come forth and do your duty.'

But he vouchsafed no reply. I pondered a moment in sore perplexity. But once more business hurried me. I determined again to postpone the consideration of this dilemma to my future leisure. With a little trouble we made out to examine the papers without Bartleby, though at every page or two Turkey deferentially dropped his opinion, that this proceeding was quite out of the common; while Nippers, twitching in his chair with a dyspeptic nervousness, ground out, between his set teeth, occasional hissing maledictions against the stubborn oaf behind the screen. And for his (Nippers's) part, this was the first and the last time he would do another man's business without pay.

Meanwhile Bartleby sat in his hermitage, oblivious to everything but his own peculiar business there.

Some days passed, the scrivener being employed upon another lengthy work. His late remarkable conduct led me to regard his ways narrowly. I observed that he never went to dinner; indeed, that he never went anywhere. As yet I had never, of my personal knowledge, known him to be outside of my office. He was a perpetual sentry in the corner. At about eleven o'clock though, in the morning, I noticed that Ginger Nut would advance toward the opening in Bartleby's screen, as if silently beckoned thither by a gesture invisible to me where I sat. The boy would then leave the office, jingling a few pence, and reappear with a handful of ginger-nuts, which he delivered in the hermitage, receiving two of the cakes for his trouble.

He lives, then, on ginger-nuts, thought I; never eats a dinner, properly speaking; he must be a vegetarian, then; but no; he never eats even vegetables, he eats nothing but ginger-nuts. My mind then ran on in reveries concerning the probable effects upon the human constitution of living entirely on ginger-nuts. Ginger-nuts are so called, because they contain ginger as one of their peculiar constituents, and the final flavouring one. Now, what was ginger? A hot, spicy thing. Was Bartleby hot and spicy? Not at all. Ginger, then, had no effect upon Bartleby. Probably he preferred it should have none.

Nothing so aggravates an earnest person as a passive resistance. If the individual so resisted be of a not inhumane temper, and the resisting one perfectly harmless in his passivity, then, in the better moods of the former, he will endeavour charitably to construe to his imagination what proves impossible to be solved by his judgment. Even so, for the most part, I regarded Bartleby and his ways. Poor fellow! thought I, he means no mischief; it is plain he intends no insolence; his aspect sufficiently evinces that his eccentricities are involuntary. He is useful to me. I can get along with him. If I turn him away, the chances are he will fall in with some less-indulgent employer, and then he will be rudely treated, and perhaps driven forth miserably to starve. Yes. Here I can cheaply purchase a delicious self-approval. To befriend Bartleby; to humour him in his strange wilfulness, will cost me little or nothing, while I lay up in my soul what will eventually prove a sweet morsel for my conscience. But this mood was not invariable with me. The passiveness of Bartleby sometimes irritated me. I felt strangely goaded on to encounter him in new opposition—to elicit some angry spark from him answerable to my own But, indeed, I might as well have essayed to strike fire with my knuckles against a bit of Windsor soap. But one afternoon the evil impulse in me mastered me, and the following little scene ensued:—

'Bartleby,' said I, 'when those papers are all copied, I will compare them with you.'

'I would prefer not to.'

'How? Surely you do not mean to persist in that mulish vagary?'

No answer.

I threw open the folding-doors near by, and, turning upon Turkey and Nippers, exclaimed:

'Bartleby a second time says, he won't examine his papers. What do you think of it, Turkey?'

It was afternoon, be it remembered. Turkey sat glowing like a brass boiler; his bald head steaming; his hands reeling among his blotted papers.

'Think of it?' roared Turkey; 'I think I'll just step behind his screen, and black his eyes for him!'

So saying, Turkey rose to his feet and threw his arms into a pugilistic position. He was hurrying away to make good his promise, when I detained him, alarmed at the effect of incautiously rousing Turkey's combativeness after dinner.

'Sit down, Turkey,' said I, 'and hear what Nippers has to say. What do you think of it, Nippers? Would I not be justified in immediately dismissing Bartleby?'

'Excuse me, that is for you to decide, sir. I think his conduct quite unusual, and, indeed, unjust, as regards Turkey and myself. But it may only be a passing whim.'

'Ah,' exclaimed I, 'you have strangely changed your mind, then—you speak very gently of him now.'

'All beer,' cried Turkey; 'gentleness is effects of beer—Nippers and I dined together to-day. You see how gentle *I* am, sir. Shall I go and black his eyes?'

'You refer to Bartleby, I suppose. No, not to-day, Turkey,' I replied; 'pray, put up your fists.'

I closed the doors, and again advanced toward Bartleby. I felt additional incentives tempting me to my fate. I burned to be rebelled against again. I remembered that Bartleby never left the office.

'Bartleby,' said I, 'Ginger Nut is away; just step around to the Post Office, won't you? (it was but a three minutes' walk), and see if there is anything for me.'

'I would prefer not to.'

'You *will* not?'

'I *prefer* not.'

I staggered to my desk, and sat there in a deep study. My blind inveteracy returned. Was there any other thing in which I could procure myself to be ignominiously repulsed by this lean, penniless wight?—my hired clerk? What added thing is there, perfectly reasonable, that he will be sure to refuse to do?

'Bartleby!'

No answer.

'Bartleby,' in a louder tone.

No answer.

'Bartleby,' I roared.

Like a very ghost, agreeably to the laws of magical invocation, at the third summons, he appeared at the entrance of his hermitage.

'Go to the next room, and tell Nippers to come to me.'

'I prefer not to,' he respectfully and slowly said, and mildly disappeared.

'Very good, Bartleby,' said I, in a quiet sort of serenely-severe self-possessed tone, intimating the unalterable purpose of some terrible retribution very close at hand. At the moment I half intended something of the kind. But upon the whole, as it was drawing toward my dinner-hour, I thought it best to put on my hat and walk home for the day, suffering much from perplexity and distress of mind.

Shall I acknowledge it? The conclusion of this whole business was, that it soon became a fixed fact of my chambers, that a pale young scrivener, by the name of Bartleby, had a desk there; that he copied for me at the usual rate of four cents a folio (one hundred words); but he was permanently exempt from examining the work done by him, that duty being transferred to Turkey and Nippers, out of compliment, doubtless, to their superior acuteness; moreover, said Bartleby was never, on any account, to be dispatched on the most trivial errand of any sort; and that even if entreated to take upon him such a matter, it was generally understood that he would 'prefer not to'—in other words, that he would refuse point-blank.

As days passed on, I became considerably reconciled to Bartleby. His steadiness, his freedom from all dissipation, his incessant industry (except when he chose to throw himself into a standing revery behind his screen), his great stillness, his unalterableness of demeanour under all circumstances, made him a valuable acquisition. One prime thing was this—*he was always there*—first in the morning, continually through the day, and the last at night. I had a singular confidence in his honesty. I felt my most precious papers perfectly safe in his hands. Sometimes, to be sure, I could not, for the very soul of me, avoid falling into sudden spasmodic passions with him. For it was exceeding difficult to bear in mind all the time those strange peculiarities, privileges, and unheard-of exemptions, forming the tacit stipulations on Bartleby's part under which he remained in my office. Now and then, in the eagerness of dispatching pressing business, I would inadvertently summon Bartleby, in a short, rapid tone, to put his finger, say, on the incipient tie of a bit of red tape with which I was about compressing some papers. Of course, from behind the screen the usual answer, 'I prefer not to,' was sure to come; and then, how could a human creature, with the common infirmities of our nature, refrain from bitterly exclaiming upon such perverseness—such unreasonableness. However, every added repulse of this sort which I received only tended to lessen the probability of my repeating the inadvertence.

Here it must be said, that according to the custom of most legal gentlemen occupying chambers in densely populated law-buildings, there were several keys to my door. One was kept by a woman residing in the attic, which person weekly scrubbed and daily swept and dusted my apartments. Another was kept by Turkey for convenience sake. The third I sometimes carried in my own pocket. The fourth I knew not who had.

Now, one Sunday morning I happened to go to Trinity Church, to hear a celebrated preacher, and finding myself rather early on the ground I thought I would walk round to my chambers for a while. Luckily I had my key with me; but upon applying it to the lock, I found it resisted by something inserted from the inside. Quite surprised, I called out; when to my consternation a key was turned from within; and thrusting his lean visage at me, and holding the door ajar, the apparition of Bartleby appeared, in his shirt-sleeves, and otherwise in a strangely tattered dishabille, saying quietly that he was sorry, but he was deeply engaged just then, and— preferred not admitting me at present. In a brief word or two, he moreover added, that perhaps I had better walk round the block two or three times, and by that time he would probably have concluded his affairs.

Now, the utterly unsurmised appearance of Bartleby, tenanting my law-chambers of a Sunday morning, with his cadaverously gentlemanly nonchalance, yet withal firm and self-possessed, had such a strange effect upon me, that incontinently I slunk away from my own door, and did as desired. But not without sundry twinges of impotent rebellion against the mild effrontery of this unaccountable scrivener. Indeed, it was his wonderful mildness chiefly, which not only disarmed me, but unmanned me as it were. For I consider that one, for the time, is a sort of unmanned when he tranquilly permits his hired clerk to dictate to him, and order him away from his own premises. Furthermore, I was full of uneasiness as to what Bartleby could possibly be doing in my office in his shirt-sleeves, and in an otherwise dismantled condition of a Sunday morning. Was anything amiss going on? Nay, that was out of the question. It was not to be thought of for a moment that Bartleby was an immoral person. But what could he be doing there?—copying? Nay again, whatever might be his eccentricities, Bartleby was an eminently decorous person. He would be the last man to sit down to his desk in any state approaching to nudity. Besides, it was Sunday; and there was something about Bartleby that forbade the supposition that he would by any secular occupation violate the proprieties of the day.

Nevertheless, my mind was not pacified; and full of a restless curiosity, at last I returned to the door. Without hindrance I inserted my key, opened it, and entered. Bartleby was not to be seen. I looked round anxiously, peeped behind his screen; but it was very plain that he was gone. Upon more closely examining the place, I surmised that for an indefinite period Bartleby must have ate, dressed, and slept in my office, and that, too, without plate, mirror, or bed. The cushioned seat of a rickety old sofa in one corner bore the faint impress of a lean, reclining form. Rolled away under his desk, I found a blanket; under the empty grate a blacking box and brush; on a chair, a tin basin, with soap and a ragged towel; in a newspaper a few crumbs of ginger-nuts and a morsel of cheese. Yes, thought I, it is evident enough that Bartleby has been making his home here, keeping bachelor's hall all by himself. Immediately then the thought came sweeping across me, what miserable friendlessness and loneliness are here revealed! His poverty is great; but his solitude, how horrible! Think of it. Of a Sunday, Wall Street is deserted as Petra; and every night of every day it is an emptiness. This building, too, which of week-days hums with industry and life, at nightfall echoes with sheer vacancy, and all through Sunday is forlorn. And here Bartleby makes his home; sole spectator of a solitude which he has seen all-populous—a sort of innocent and transformed Marius brooding among the ruins of Carthage!

For the first time in my life a feeling of overpowering stinging melancholy seized me. Before, I had never experienced aught but a not unpleasing sadness. The bond of a common humanity now drew me irresistibly to gloom. A fraternal melancholy! For both I and Bartleby were sons of Adam. I remembered the bright silks and sparkling faces I had seen that day, in gala trim, swan-like sailing down the Mississippi of Broadway; and I contrasted them with the pallid copyist, and thought to myself, Ah, happiness courts the light, so we deem the world is gay; but misery hides aloof, so we deem that misery there is none. These sad fancyings—chimeras, doubtless, of a sick and silly brain—led on to other and more special thoughts, concerning the eccentricities of Bartleby. Presentiments of strange discoveries hovered round me. The scrivener's pale form appeared to me laid out, among uncaring strangers, in its shivering winding-sheet.

Suddenly I was attracted by Bartleby's closed desk, the key in open sight left in the lock.

I mean no mischief, seek the gratification of no heartless curiosity, thought I; besides, the desk is mine, and its contents, too, so I will make bold to look within. Everything was methodically arranged, the papers smoothly placed. The pigeon-holes were deep, and removing the files of documents, I groped into their recesses. Presently I felt something there, and dragged it out. It was an old bandanna handkerchief, heavy and knotted. I opened it, and saw it was a savings-bank.

I now recalled all the quiet mysteries which I had noted in the man. I remembered that he never spoke but to answer; that, though at intervals he had considerable time to himself, yet I had never seen him reading—no, not even a newspaper; that for long periods he would stand looking out, at his pale window behind the screen, upon the dead brick wall; I was quite sure he never visited any refectory or eating-house; while his pale face clearly indicated that he never drank beer like Turkey, or tea and coffee even, like other men; that he never went anywhere in particular that I could learn; never went out for a walk, unless, indeed, that was the case at present; that he had declined telling who he was, or whence he came, or whether he had any relatives in the world; that though so thin and pale, he never complained of ill health. And more than all, I remembered a certain unconscious air of pallid—how shall I call it?—of pallid haughtiness, say, or rather an austere reserve about him, which had positively awed me into my tame compliance with his eccentricities, when I had feared to ask him to do the slightest incidental thing for me, even though I might know, from his long-continued motionlessness, that behind his screen he must be standing in one of those dead-wall reveries of his.

Revolving all these things, and coupling them with the recently discovered fact, that he made my office his constant abiding-place and home, and not forgetful of his morbid moodiness; revolving all these things, a prudential feeling began to steal over me. My first emotions had been those of pure melancholy and sincerest pity; but just in proportion as the forlornness of Bartleby grew and grew to my imagination, did that same melancholy merge into fear, that pity into repulsion. So true it is, and so terrible, too, that up to a certain point the thought or sight of misery enlists our best affections; but, in certain special cases, beyond that point it does not. They err who would assert that invariably this is owing to the inherent selfishness of the human heart. It rather proceeds from a certain hopelessness of remedying excessive and organic ill. To a sensitive being, pity is not seldom pain. And when at last it is perceived that such pity cannot lead to effectual succour, common-sense bids the soul be rid of it. What I saw that morning persuaded me that the scrivener was the victim of innate and incurable disorder. I might give alms to his body; but his body did not pain him; it was his soul that suffered, and his soul I could not reach.

I did not accomplish the purpose of going to Trinity Church that morning. Somehow, the things I had seen disqualified me for the time from church-going. I walked homeward, thinking what I would do with Bartleby. Finally, I resolved upon this—I would put certain calm questions to him the next morning, touching his history, etc., and if he declined to answer them openly and unreservedly (and I supposed he would prefer not), then to give him a twenty-dollar bill over and above whatever I might owe him, and tell him his services were no longer required; but that if in any other way I could assist him, I would be happy to do so, especially if he desired to return to his native place, wherever that might be, I would willingly help to defray the expenses. Moreover, if, after reaching home, he found himself at any time in want of aid, a letter from him would be sure of a reply.

The next morning came.

'Bartleby,' said I, gently calling to him behind his screen.

No reply.

'Bartleby,' said I, in a still gentler tone, 'come here; I am not going to ask you to do anything you would prefer not to do—I simply wish to speak to you.'

Upon this he noiselessly slid into view.

'Will you tell me, Bartleby, where you were born?'

'I would prefer not to.'

'Will you tell me *anything* about yourself?'

'I would prefer not to.'

'But what reasonable objection can you have to speak to me? I feel friendly toward you.'

He did not look at me while I spoke, but kept his glance fixed upon my bust of Cicero, which, as I then sat, was directly behind me, some six inches above my head.

'What is your answer, Bartleby?' said I, after waiting a considerable time for a reply, during which his countenance remained immovable, only there was the faintest conceivable tremor of the white attenuated mouth.

'At present I prefer to give no answer,' he said, and retired into his hermitage.

It was rather weak in me, I confess, but his manner, on this occasion, nettled me. Not only did there seem to lurk in it a certain calm disdain, but his perverseness seemed ungrateful, considering the undeniable good usage and indulgence he had received from me.

Again I sat ruminating what I should do. Mortified as I was at his behaviour, and resolved as I had been to dismiss him when I entered my office, nevertheless I strangely felt something superstitious knocking at my heart, and forbidding me to carry out my purpose, and denouncing me for a villain if I dared to breathe one bitter word against this forlornest of mankind. At last, familiarly drawing my chair behind his screen, I sat down and said: 'Bartleby, never mind, then, about revealing your history; but let me entreat you, as a friend, to comply as far as may be with the usages of this office. Say now, you will help to examine papers to-morrow or next day: in short, say now, that in a day or two you will begin to be a little reasonable:—say so, Bartleby.'

'At present I would prefer not to be a little reasonable,' was his mildly cadaverous reply.

Just then the folding-doors opened, and Nippers approached. He seemed suffering from an unusually bad night's rest, induced by severer indigestion than common. He overheard those final words of Bartleby.

'*Prefer not*, eh?' gritted Nippers—'I'd *prefer* him, if I were you, sir,' addressing me—'I'd *prefer* him; I'd give him preferences, the stubborn mule! What is it, sir, pray, that he *prefers* not to do now?'

Bartleby moved not a limb.

'Mr. Nippers,' said I, 'I'd prefer that you would withdraw for the present.'

Somehow, of late, I had got into the way of involuntarily using this word 'prefer' upon all sorts of not exactly suitable occasions. And I trembled to think that my contact with the scrivener had already and seriously affected me in a mental way. And what further and deeper aberration might it not yet produce? This apprehension had not been without efficacy in determining me to summary measures.

As Nippers, looking very sour and sulky, was departing, Turkey blandly and deferentially approached.

'With submission, sir,' said he, 'yesterday I was thinking about Bartleby here, and I think that if he would but prefer to take a quart of good ale every day, it would do much toward mending him, and enabling him to assist in examining his papers.'

'So you have got the word too,' said I, slightly excited.

'With submission, what word, sir,' asked Turkey, respectfully crowding himself into the contracted space behind the screen, and by so doing, making me jostle the scrivener. 'What word, sir?'

'I would prefer to be left alone here,' said Bartleby, as if offended at being mobbed in his privacy.

'*That's* the word, Turkey,' said I—'*that's* it.'

'Oh, *prefer*? oh yes—queer word. I never use it myself. But, sir, as I was saying, if he would but prefer—'

'Turkey,' interrupted I, 'you will please withdraw.'

'Oh certainly, sir, if you prefer that I should.'

As he opened the folding-door to retire, Nippers at his desk caught a glimpse of me, and asked whether I would prefer to have a certain paper copied on blue paper or white. He did not in the least roguishly accent the word prefer. It was plain that it involuntarily rolled from his tongue. I thought to myself, surely I must get rid of a demented man, who already has in some degree turned the tongues, if not the heads of myself and clerks. But I thought it prudent not to break the dismission at once.

The next day I noticed that Bartleby did nothing but stand at his window in his dead-wall revery. Upon asking him why he did not write, he said that he had decided upon doing no more writing.

'Why, how now? what next?' exclaimed I, 'do no more writing?'

'No more.'

'And what is the reason?'

'Do you not see the reason for yourself?' he indifferently replied.

I looked steadfastly at him, and perceived that his eyes looked dull and glazed. Instantly it occurred to me, that his unexampled diligence in copying by his dim window for the first few weeks of his stay with me might have temporarily impaired his vision.

I was touched. I said something in condolence with him. I hinted that of course he did wisely in abstaining from writing for a while; and urged him to embrace that opportunity of taking wholesome exercise in the open air. This, however, he did not do. A few days after this, my other clerks being absent, and being in a great hurry to dispatch certain letters by the mail, I thought that having nothing else earthly to do, Bartleby would surely be less inflexible than usual, and carry these letters to the Post Office. But he blankly declined. So, much to my inconvenience, I went myself.

Still added days went by. Whether Bartleby's eyes improved or not, I could not say. To all appearance, I thought they did. But when I asked him if they did, he vouchsafed no answer. At all events, he would do no copying. At last, in reply to my urgings, he informed me that he had permanently given up copying.

'What!' exclaimed I; 'suppose your eyes should get entirely well—better than ever before—would you not copy then?'

'I have given up copying,' he answered, and slid aside.

He remained as ever, a fixture in my chamber. Nay—if that were possible—he became still more of a fixture than before. What was to be done? He would do nothing in the office; why should he stay there? In plain fact, he had now become a millstone to me, not only useless as a necklace, but afflictive to bear. Yet I was sorry for him. I speak less than truth when I say that, on his own account, he occasioned me uneasiness. If he would but have named a single relative or friend, I would instantly have written, and urged their taking the poor fellow away to some convenient retreat. But he seemed alone, absolutely alone in the universe. A bit of wreck in the mid-Atlantic. At length, necessities connected with my business tyrannised over all other considerations. Decently as I could, I told Bartleby that in six days' time he must unconditionally leave the office. I warned him to take measures, in the interval, for procuring some other abode. I offered to assist him in this endeavour, if he himself would but take the first step toward a removal. 'And when you finally quit me, Bartleby,' added I, 'I shall see that you go not away entirely unprovided. Six days from this hour, remember.'

At the expiration of that period, I peeped behind the screen, and lo! Bartleby was there.

I buttoned up my coat, balanced myself; advanced slowly toward him, touched his shoulder, and said, 'The time has come; you must quit this place; I am sorry for you; here is money; but you must go.'

'I would prefer not,' he replied, with his back still toward me.

'You *must*.'

He remained silent.

Now I had an unbounded confidence in this man's common honesty. He had frequently restored to me sixpences and shillings carelessly dropped upon the floor, for I am apt to be very reckless in such shirt-button affairs. The proceeding, then, which followed will not be deemed extraordinary.

'Bartleby,' said I, 'I owe you twelve dollars on account; here are thirty-two; the odd twenty are yours—Will you take it?' and I handed the bills toward him.

But he made no motion.

'I will leave them here, then,' putting them under a weight on the table. Then taking my hat and cane and going to the door, I tranquilly turned and added—'After you have removed your things from these offices, Bartleby, you will of course lock the door—since everyone is now gone for the day but you—and if you please, slip your key underneath the mat, so that I may have it in the morning. I shall not see you again; so good-bye to you. If, hereafter, in your new place of abode, I can be of any service to you, do not fail to advise me by letter. Good-bye, Bartleby, and fare you well.'

But he answered not a word; like the last column of some ruined temple, he remained standing mute and solitary in the middle of the otherwise deserted room.

As I walked home in a pensive mood, my vanity got the better of my pity. I could not but highly plume myself on my masterly management in getting rid of Bartleby. Masterly I call it, and such it must appear to any dispassionate thinker. The beauty of my procedure seemed to consist in its perfect quietness. There was no vulgar bullying, no bravado of any sort, no choleric hectoring, and striding to and fro across the apartment, jerking out vehement commands for Bartleby to bundle himself off with his beggarly traps. Nothing of the kind. Without loudly bidding Bartleby depart—as an inferior genius might have done—I *assumed* the ground that depart he must; and upon that assumption built all I had to say. The more I thought over my procedure, the more I was charmed with it. Nevertheless, next morning, upon awakening, I had my doubts—I had somehow slept off the fumes of vanity. One of the coolest and wisest hours a man has, is just after he awakes in the morning. My procedure seemed as sagacious as ever—but only in theory. How it would prove in practice—there was the rub. It was truly a beautiful thought to have assumed Bartleby's departure; but, after all, that assumption was simply my own, and none of Bartleby's. The great point was, not whether I had assumed that he would quit me, but whether he would prefer so to do. He was more a man of preferences than assumptions.

After breakfast, I walked down town, arguing the probabilities *pro* and *con*. One moment I thought it would prove a miserable failure, and Bartleby would be found all alive at my office as usual; the next moment it seemed certain that I should find his chair empty. And so I kept veering about. At the corner of Broadway and Canal Street, I saw quite an excited group of people standing in earnest conversation.

'I'll take odds he doesn't,' said a voice as I passed.

'Doesn't go?—done!' said I; 'put up your money.'

I was instinctively putting my hand in my pocket to produce my own, when I remembered that this was an election day. The words I had overheard bore no reference to Bartleby, but to the success or non-success of some candidate for the mayoralty. In my intent frame of mind, I had, as it were, imagined that all Broadway shared in my excitement, and were debating the same question with me. I passed on, very thankful that the uproar of the street screened my momentary absent-mindedness.

As I had intended, I was earlier than usual at my office door. I stood listening for a moment. All was still. He must be gone. I tried the knob. The door was locked. Yes, my procedure had worked to a charm; he indeed must be vanished. Yet a certain melancholy mixed with this: I was almost sorry for my brilliant success. I was fumbling under the door-mat for the key, which Bartleby was to have left there for me, when accidentally my knee knocked against a panel, producing a summoning sound, and in response a voice came to me from within—'Not yet; I am occupied.'

It was Bartleby.

I was thunderstruck. For an instant I stood like the man who, pipe in mouth, was killed one cloudless afternoon long ago in Virginia, by summer lightning; at his own warm open window he was killed, and remained leaning out there upon the dreamy afternoon, till someone touched him, when he fell.

'Not gone!' I murmured at last. But again obeying that wondrous ascendency which the inscrutable scrivener had over me, and from which ascendency, for all my chafing, I could not completely escape, I slowly went downstairs and out into the street, and while walking round the block, considered what I should next do in this unheard-of perplexity. Turn the man out by an actual thrusting I could not; to drive him away by calling him hard names would not do; calling in the police was an unpleasant idea; and yet, permit him to enjoy his cadaverous triumph over me—this, too, I could not think of. What was to be done? or, if nothing could be done, was there anything further that I could *assume* in the matter? Yes, as before I had prospectively assumed that Bartleby would depart, so now I might retrospectively assume that departed he was. In the legitimate carrying out of this assumption, I might enter my office in a great hurry, and pretending not to see Bartleby at all, walk straight against him as if he were air. Such a proceeding would in a singular degree have the appearance of a home-thrust. It was hardly possible that Bartleby could withstand such an application of the doctrine of assumptions. But upon second thoughts the success of the plan seemed rather dubious. I resolved to argue the matter over with him again.

'Bartleby,' said I, entering the office, with a quietly severe expression, 'I am seriously displeased. I am pained, Bartleby. I had thought better of you. I had imagined you of such a gentlemanly organisation, that in any delicate dilemma a slight hint would suffice—in short, an assumption. But it appears I am deceived. Why,' I added, unaffectedly starting, 'you have not even touched that money yet,' pointing to it, just where I had left it the evening previous.

He answered nothing.

'Will you, or will you not, quit me?' I now demanded in a sudden passion, advancing close to him.

'I would prefer *not* to quit you,' he replied, gently emphasizing the *not*.

'What earthly right have you to stay here? Do you pay any rent? Do you pay my taxes? Or is this property yours?'

He answered nothing.

'Are you ready to go on and write now? Are your eyes recovered? Could you copy a small paper for me this morning? or help examine a few lines? or step round to the Post Office? In a word, will you do anything at all, to give a colouring to your refusal to depart the premises?'

He silently retired into his hermitage.

I was now in such a state of nervous resentment that I thought it but prudent to check myself at present from further demonstrations. Bartleby and I were alone. I remembered the tragedy of the unfortunate Adams and the still more unfortunate Colt[4] in the solitary office of the latter; and how poor Colt, being dreadfully incensed by Adams, and imprudently permitting himself to get wildly excited, was at unawares hurried into his fatal act—an act which certainly no man could possibly deplore more than the actor himself. Often it had occurred to me in my ponderings upon the subject, that had that altercation taken place in the public street, or at a private residence, it would not have terminated as it did. It was the circumstance of being alone in a solitary office, upstairs, of a building entirely unhallowed by humanising domestic associations—an uncarpeted office, doubtless, of a dusty, haggard sort of appearance—this it must have been, which greatly helped to enhance the irritable desperation of the hapless Colt.

But when this old Adam of resentment rose in me and tempted me concerning Bartleby, I grappled him and threw him. How? Why, simply by recalling the divine injunction: 'A new commandment give I unto you, that ye love one another.' Yes, this it was that saved me. Aside from higher considerations, charity often operates as a vastly wise and prudent principle—a great safeguard to its possessor. Men have committed murder for jealousy's sake, and anger's sake, and hatred's sake, and selfishness' sake, and spiritual pride's sake; but no man, that ever I heard of, ever committed a diabolical murder for sweet charity's sake. Mere self-interest, then, if no better motive can be enlisted, should, especially with high-tempered men, prompt all beings to charity and philanthropy. At any rate, upon the occasion in question, I strove to drown my exasperated feelings toward the scrivener by benevolently construing his conduct. Poor fellow, poor fellow! thought I, he don't mean anything; and besides, he has seen hard times, and ought to be indulged.

I endeavoured, also, immediately to occupy myself, and at the same time to comfort my despondency. I tried to fancy, that in the course of the morning, at such time as might prove agreeable to him, Bartleby, of his own free accord, would emerge from his heritage and take up some decided line of march in the direction of the door. But no. Half-past twelve o'clock came; Turkey began to glow in the face, overturn his inkstand, and become generally obsteperous; Nippers abated down into quietude and courtesy; Ginger Nut munched his noon apple; and Bartleby remained standing at his window in one of his profoundest dead-wall reveries. Will it be credited? Ought I to acknowledge it? That afternoon I left the office without saying one further word to him.

Some days now passed, during which, at leisure intervals, I looked a little into 'Edwards on the Will,' and 'Priestley on Necessity.'[5] Under the

---

[4] In 1841, John C. Colt struck and killed Samuel Adams in a fight.

[5] American theologian Jonathan Edwards and English scientist Joseph Priestly both argued against the existence of free will.

circumstances, those books induced a salutary feeling. Gradually I slid into the persuasion that these troubles of mine, touching the scrivener, had been all predestinated from eternity, and Bartleby was billeted upon me for some mysterious purpose of an all-wise Providence, which it was not for a mere mortal like me to fathom. Yes, Bartleby, stay there behind your screen, thought I; I shall persecute you no more; you are harmless and noiseless as any of these old chairs; in short, I never feel so private as when I know you are here. At last I see it, I feel it; I penetrate to the predestinated purpose of my life. I am content. Others may have loftier parts to enact; but my mission in this world, Bartleby, is to furnish you with office-room for such period as you may see fit to remain.

I believe that this wise and blessed frame of mind would have continued with me, had it not been for the unsolicited and uncharitable remarks obtruded upon me by my professional friends who visited the rooms. But thus it often is, that the constant friction of illiberal minds wears out at last the best resolves of the more generous. Though to be sure, when I reflected upon it, it was not strange that people entering my office should be struck by the peculiar aspect of the unaccountable Bartleby, and so be tempted to throw out some sinister observations concerning him. Sometimes an attorney, having business with me, and calling at my office, and finding no one but the scrivener there, would undertake to obtain some sort of precise information from him touching my whereabouts; but without heeding his idle talk, Bartleby would remain standing immovable in the middle of the room. So after contemplating him in that position for a time, the attorney would depart, no wiser than he came.

Also, when a reference was going on, and the room full of lawyers and witnesses, and business driving fast, some deeply occupied legal gentleman present, seeing Bartleby wholly unemployed, would request him to run round to his (the legal gentleman's) office and fetch some papers for him. Thereupon, Bartleby would tranquilly decline, and yet remain idle as before. Then the lawyer would give a great stare, and turn to me. And what could I say? At last I was made aware that all through the circle of my professional acquaintance, a whisper of wonder was running round, having reference to the strange creature I kept at my office. This worried me very much. And as the idea came upon me of his possibly turning out a long-lived man, and keep occupying my chambers, and denying my authority; and perplexing my visitors; and scandalising my professional reputation; and casting a general gloom over the premises; keeping soul and body together to the last upon his savings (for doubtless he spent but half a dime a day), and in the end perhaps outlive me, and claim possession of my office by right of his perpetual occupancy: as all these dark anticipations crowded upon me more and more, and my friends continually intruded their relentless remarks upon the apparition in my room; a great change was wrought in me. I resolved to gather all my faculties together, and forever rid me of this intolerable incubus.

Ere revolving any complicated project, however, adapted to this end, I first simply suggested to Bartleby the propriety of his permanent departure. In a calm and serious tone, I commended the idea to his careful and mature consideration. But, having taken three days to meditate upon it, he appraised me, that his original determination remained the same; in short, that he still preferred to abide with me.

What shall I do? I now said to myself, buttoning up my coat to the last button. What shall I do? what ought I to do? what does conscience say I *should* do with this man, or, rather, ghost. Rid myself of him, I must; go, he shall. But how? You will not thrust him, the poor, pale, passive mortal—you will not thrust such a helpless creature out of your door? you will not dishonour yourself by such cruelty? No, I will not, I cannot do that. Rather would I let him live and die here, and then mason up his remains in the wall. What, then, will you do? For all your coaxing, he will not budge. Bribes he leaves under your own paperweight on your table; in short, it is quite plain that he prefers to cling to you.

Then something severe, something unusual must be done. What! surely you will not have him collared by a constable, and commit his innocent pallor to the common jail? And upon what ground could you procure such a thing to be done?—a vagrant, is he? What! he a vagrant, a wanderer, who refuses to budge? It is because he will *not* be a vagrant, then, that you seek to count him *as* a vagrant. That is too absurd. No visible means of support; there I have him. Wrong again: for indubitably he *does* support himself, and that is the only unanswerable proof that any man can show of his possessing the means so to do. No more, then. Since he will not quit me, I must quit him. I will change my offices; I will move elsewhere, and give him fair notice, that if I find him on my new premises I will then proceed against him as a common trespasser.

Acting accordingly, next day I thus addressed him: 'I find these chambers too far from the City Hall; the air is unwholesome. In a word, I propose to remove my offices next week, and shall no longer require your services. I tell you this now, in order that you may seek another place.'

He made no reply, and nothing more was said.

On the appointed day I engaged carts and men, proceeded to my chambers, and, having but little furniture, everything was removed in a few hours. Throughout, the scrivener remained standing behind the screen, which I directed to be removed the last thing. It was withdrawn; and, being folded up like a huge folio, left him the motionless occupant of a naked room. I stood in the entry watching him a moment, while something from within me upbraided me.

I re-entered, with my hand in my pocket—and—and my heart in my mouth.

'Good-bye, Bartleby; I am going—good-bye, and God some way bless you; and take that,' slipping something in his hand. But it dropped upon the floor, and then—strange to say—I tore myself from him whom I had so longed to be rid of.

Established in my new quarters, for a day or two I kept the door locked, and started at every footfall in the passages. When I returned to my rooms, after any little absence, I would pause at the threshold for an instant, and attentively listen ere applying my key. But these fears were needless. Bartleby never came nigh me.

I thought all was going well, when a perturbed-looking stranger visited me, inquiring whether I was the person who had recently occupied rooms at No. — Wall Street.

Full of forebodings, I replied that I was.

'Then, sir,' said the stranger, who proved a lawyer, 'you are responsible for the man you left there. He refuses to do any copying; he refuses to do anything; he says he prefers not to; and he refuses to quit the premises.'

'I am very sorry, sir,' said I, with assumed tranquillity, but an inward tremor, 'but, really, the man you allude to is nothing to me—he is no relation or apprentice of mine, that you should hold me responsible for him.'

'In mercy's name, who is he?'

'I certainly cannot inform you. I know nothing about him. Formerly I employed him as a copyist; but he has done nothing for me now for some time past.'

'I shall settle him, then—good morning, sir.'

Several days passed, and I heard nothing more; and, though I often felt a charitable prompting to call at the place and see poor Bartleby, yet a certain squeamishness, of I know not what, withheld me.

All is over with him, by this time, thought I, at last, when, through another week, no further intelligence reached me. But, coming to my room the day after, I found several persons waiting at my door in a high state of nervous excitement.

'That's the man—here he comes,' cried the foremost one, whom I recognized as the lawyer who had previously called upon me alone.

'You must take him away, sir, at once,' cried a portly person among them, advancing upon me, and whom I knew to be the landlord of No. — Wall Street. 'These gentlemen, my tenants, cannot stand it any longer; Mr. B—,' pointing to the lawyer, 'has turned him out of his room, and he now persists in haunting the building generally, sitting upon the banisters of the stairs by day, and sleeping in the entry by night. Everybody is concerned; clients are leaving the offices; some fears are entertained of a mob; something you must do, and that without delay.'

Aghast at this torrent, I fell back before it, and would fain have locked myself in my new quarters. In vain I persisted that Bartleby was nothing to me—no more than to anyone else. In vain—I was the last person known to have anything to do with him, and they held me to the terrible account. Fearful, then, of being exposed in the papers (as one person present obscurely threatened), I considered the matter, and, at length, said, that if the lawyer would give me a confidential interview with the scrivener, in his (the lawyer's) own room, I would, that afternoon, strive my best to rid them of the nuisance they complained of.

Going upstairs to my old haunt, there was Bartleby silently sitting upon the banister at the landing.

'What are you doing here, Bartleby?' said I.

'Sitting upon the banister,' he mildly replied.

I motioned him into the lawyer's room, who then left us.

'Bartleby,' said I, 'are you aware that you are the cause of great tribulation to me, by persisting in occupying the entry after being dismissed from the office?'

No answer.

'Now one of two things must take place. Either you must do something, or something must be done to you. Now what sort of business would you like to engage in? Would you like to re-engage in copying for someone?'

'No; I would prefer not to make any change.'

'Would you like a clerkship in a dry-goods store?'

'There is too much confinement about that. No, I would not like a clerkship; but I am not particular.'

'Too much confinement,' I cried, 'why, you keep yourself confined all the time!'

'I would prefer not to take a clerkship,' he rejoined, as if to settle that little item at once.

'How would a bar-tender's business suit you? There is no trying of the eyesight in that.'

'I would not like it at all; though, as I said before, I am not particular.'

His unwonted wordiness inspirited me. I returned to the charge.

'Well, then, would you like to travel through the country collecting bills for the merchants? That would improve your health.'

'No, I would prefer to be doing something else.'

'How, then, would going as a companion to Europe, to entertain some young gentleman with your conversation—how would that suit you?'

'Not at all. It does not strike me that there is anything definite about that. I like to be stationary. But I am not particular.'

'Stationary you shall be, then,' I cried, now losing all patience, and, for the first time in all my exasperating connection with him, fairly flying into a passion. 'If you do not go away from these premises before night, I shall feel bound—indeed, I *am* bound—to—to quit the premises myself!' I rather absurdly concluded, knowing not with what possible threat to try to frighten his immobility into compliance. Despairing of all further efforts, I was precipitately leaving him, when a final thought occurred to me—one which had not been wholly unindulged before.

'Bartleby,' said I, in the kindest tone I could assume under such exciting circumstances, 'will you go home with me now—not to my office, but my dwelling—and remain there till we can conclude upon some convenient arrangement for you at our leisure? Come, let us start now, right away.'

'No; at present I would prefer not to make any change at all.'

I answered nothing; but, effectually dodging everyone by the suddenness and rapidity of my flight, rushed from the building, ran up Wall Street toward Broadway, and, jumping into the first omnibus, was soon removed from pursuit. As soon as tranquillity returned, I distinctly perceived that I had now done all that I possibly could, both in respect to the demands of the landlord and his tenants, and with regard to my own desire and sense of duty, to benefit Bartleby, and shield him from rude persecution. I now strove to be entirely carefree and quiescent; and my conscience justified me in the attempt; though, indeed, it was not so successful as I could have wished. So fearful was I of being again hunted out by the incensed landlord and his exasperated tenants, that, surrendering my business to Nippers, for a few days, I drove about the upper part of the town and through the suburbs, in my rockaway; crossed over to Jersey City and Hoboken, and paid fugitive visits to Manhattanville and Astoria. In fact, I almost lived in my rockaway for the time.

When again I entered my office, lo, a note from the landlord lay upon the desk. I opened it with trembling hands. It informed me that the writer had sent to the police, and had Bartleby removed to the Tombs as a vagrant. Moreover, since I knew more about him than anyone else, he wished me to appear at that place, and make a suitable statement of the facts. These tidings had a conflicting effect upon me. At first I was indignant; but, at last, almost approved. The landlord's energetic, summary disposition had led him to adopt a procedure which I do not think I would have decided upon myself; and yet, as a last resort, under such peculiar circumstances, it seemed the only plan.

As I afterward learned, the poor scrivener, when told that he must be conducted to the Tombs, offered not the slightest obstacle, but, in his pale, unmoving way, silently acquiesced.

Some of the compassionate and curious bystanders joined the party; and headed by one of the constables arm in arm with Bartleby, the silent procession filed its way through all the noise, and heat, and joy of the roaring thoroughfares at noon.

The same day I received the note, I went to the Tombs, or, to speak more properly, the Halls of Justice. Seeking the right officer, I stated the purpose of my call, and was informed that the individual I described was, indeed, within. I then assured the functionary that Bartleby was a perfectly honest man, and greatly to be compassionated, however unaccountably eccentric. I narrated all I knew, and closed by suggesting the idea of letting him remain in as indulgent confinement as possible, till something less harsh might be done—though, indeed, I hardly knew what. At all events, if nothing else could be decided upon, the almshouse must receive him. I then begged to have an interview.

Being under no disgraceful charge, and quite serene and harmless in all his ways, they had permitted him freely to wander about the prison, and, especially, in the enclosed grass-platted yards thereof. And so I found him there, standing all alone in the quietest of the yards, his face toward a high wall, while all around, from the narrow slits of the jail windows, I thought I saw peering out upon him the eyes of murderers and thieves.

'Bartleby!'

'I know you,' he said, without looking round—'and I want nothing to say to you.'

'It was not I that brought you here, Bartleby,' said I, keenly pained at his implied suspicion. 'And to you, this should not be so vile a place. Nothing reproachful attaches to you by being here. And see, it is not so sad a place as one might think. Look, there is the sky, and here is the grass.'

'I know where I am,' he replied, but would say nothing more, and so I left him.

As I entered the corridor again, a broad meat-like man, in an apron, accosted me, and, jerking his thumb over his shoulder, said, 'Is that your friend?'

'Yes.'

'Does he want to starve? If he does, let him live on the prison fare, that's all.'

'Who are you?' asked I, not knowing what to make of such an unofficially speaking person in such a place.

'I am the grub-man. Such gentlemen as have friends here, hire me to provide them with something good to eat.'

'Is this so?' said I, turning to the turnkey.

He said it was.

'Well, then,' said I, slipping some silver into the grub-man's hands (for so they called him), 'I want you to give particular attention to my friend there; let him have the best dinner you can get. And you must be as polite to him as possible.'

'Introduce me, will you?' said the grub-man, looking at me with an expression which seemed to say he was all impatience for an opportunity to give a specimen of his breeding.

Thinking it would prove of benefit to the scrivener, I acquiesced; and, asking the grub-man his name, went up with him to Bartleby.

'Bartleby, this is a friend; you will find him very useful to you.'

'Your sarvant, sir, your sarvant,' said the grub-man, making a low salutation behind his apron. 'Hope you find it pleasant here, sir; nice grounds—cool apartments—hope you'll stay with us some time—try to make it agreeable. What will you have for dinner to-day?'

'I prefer not to dine to-day,' said Bartleby, turning away. 'It would disagree with me; I am unused to dinners.' So saying, he slowly moved to the other side of the enclosure, and took up a position fronting the dead-wall.

'How's this?' said the grub-man, addressing me with a stare of astonishment. 'He's odd, ain't he?'

'I think he is a little deranged,' said I sadly.

'Deranged? deranged is it? Well, now, upon my word, I thought that friend of yourn was a gentleman forger; they are always pale and genteel-like, them forgers. I can't help pity 'em—can't help it, sir. Did you know Monroe Edwards?' he added touchingly, and paused. Then, laying his hand piteously on my shoulder, sighed, 'he died of consumption at Sing-Sing. So you weren't acquainted with Monroe?'

'No, I was never socially acquainted with any forgers. But I cannot stop longer. Look to my friend yonder. You will not lose by it. I will see you again.'

Some few days after this, I again obtained admission to the Tombs, and went through the corridors in quest of Bartleby; but without finding him.

'I saw him coming from his cell not long ago,' said a turnkey, 'maybe he's gone to loiter in the yards.'

So I went in that direction.

'Are you looking for the silent man?' said another turnkey, passing me. 'Yonder he lies—sleeping in the yard there. 'Tis not twenty minutes since I saw him lie down.'

The yard was entirely quiet. It was not accessible to the common prisoners. The surrounding walls, of amazing thickness, kept off all sounds behind them. The Egyptian character of the masonry weighed upon me with its gloom. But a soft imprisoned turf grew under foot. The heart of the eternal pyramids, it seemed, wherein, by some strange magic, through the clefts, grass-seed, dropped by birds, had sprung.

Strangely huddled at the base of the wall, his knees drawn up, and lying on his side, his head touching the cold stones, I saw the wasted Bartleby. But nothing stirred. I paused; then went close up to him; stooped over, and saw that his dim eyes were open; otherwise he seemed profoundly sleeping. Something prompted me to touch him. I felt his hand, when a tingling shiver ran up my arm and down my spine to my feet.

The round face of the grub-man peered upon me now. 'His dinner is ready. Won't he dine to-day, either? Or does he live without dining?'

'Lives without dining,' said I, and closed the eyes.

'Eh!—He's asleep, ain't he?'

'With kings and counsellors,' murmured I.

* * *

There would seem little need for proceeding further in this history. Imagination will readily supply the meagre recital of poor Bartleby's interment. But, ere parting with the reader, let me say, that if this little narrative has sufficiently interested him, to awaken curiosity as to who Bartleby was, and what manner of life he led prior to the present narrator's making his acquaintance, I can only reply, that in such curiosity I fully share, but am wholly unable to gratify it. Yet here I hardly know whether I should divulge one little item of rumour, which came to my ear a few months after the scrivener's decease. Upon what basis it rested I could never ascertain; and hence, how true it is I cannot now tell. But, inasmuch as this vague report has not been without a certain suggestive interest to me, however sad, it may prove the same with some others; and so I will briefly mention it. The report was this: that Bartleby had been a subordinate clerk in the Dead Letter Office at Washington, from which he had been suddenly removed by a change in the administration. When I think over this rumour, hardly can I express the emotions which seize me. Dead letters! does it not sound like dead men? Conceive a man by nature and misfortune prone to a pallid hopelessness, can any business seem more fitted to heighten it than that of continually handling these dead letters, and assorting them for the flames? For by the cartload they are annually burned. Sometimes from out the folded paper the pale clerk takes a ring—the finger it was meant for, perhaps, moulders in the grave; a bank-note sent in swiftest charity—he whom it would relieve, nor eats nor hungers any more; pardon for those who died despairing; hope for those who died unhoping; good tidings for those who died stifled by unrelieved calamities. On errands of life, these letters speed to death.

Ah, Bartleby! Ah, humanity!

Study and Discussion Questions

1. Why do you think the narrator says that knowing something about himself, his employees, his business, and his physical setting "is indispensible to an adequate understanding" of Bartleby?
2. What does the narrator say about himself? Do his encounters with Bartleby change him? How?
3. What words does the narrator use to introduce Bartleby?
4. What does Bartleby actually say in the course of this story?
5. Chart the stages of Bartleby's withdrawal.
6. Where did Bartleby work, according to rumor, before he came to work for the narrator? Does that sufficiently explain his attitude?
7. What purpose do Nippers, Ginger Nuts, and Turkey serve in the story?
8. Is this simply a story about an elaborate suicide?

Writing Exercises

1. "Nothing so aggravates an earnest person as passive resistance." Imagine that someone you work with or live with suddenly began to say nothing but, 'I would prefer not to." How would you respond? Try narrating the story of a day (or part of a day) with this person.
2. What does the narrator give as his motives for his treatment of Bartleby? Do you agree, or do you think there are other things going on?
3. How strange a creature is Bartleby? Make a case that his behavior makes more sense than anyone else's in the story.

4. Act a bit like Bartleby. (Maybe you already do.) Try mild, yet steadfast passive resistance for part of a day and take note of people's reactions, including your own reaction to behaving unconventionally. Write about what you discover.

PAMELA ZOLINE (b. 1941)

Pamela Zoline was born in Chicago and educated at the Slade School of Fine Art in London. She now lives in Telluride, Colorado, where she works as a painter and an environmental activist as well as a writer. She has published Annika and the Wolves *(1985), a children's book, and* The Heat Death of the Universe and Other Stories *(1988).*

The Heat Death of the Universe (1967)

1. ONTOLOGY: That branch of metaphysics which concerns itself with the problems of the nature of existence or being.

2. Imagine a pale blue morning sky, almost green, with clouds only at the rims. The earth rolls and the sun appears to mount, mountains erode, fruits decay, the Foraminifera adds another chamber to its shell, babies' fingernails grow as does the hair of the dead in their graves, and in egg timers the sands fall and the eggs cook on.

3. Sarah Boyle thinks of her nose as too large, though several men have cherished it. The nose is generous and performs a well-calculated geometric curve, at the arch of which the skin is drawn very tight and a faint whiteness of bone can be seen showing through, it has much the same architectural tension and sense of mathematical calculation as the day after Thanksgiving breastbone on the carcass of turkey; her maiden name was Sloss, mixed German, English and Irish descent; in grade school she was very bad at playing softball and, besides being chosen last for the team, was always made to play center field, no one could ever hit to center field; she loves music best of all the arts, and of music, Bach, J.S.; she lives in California, though she grew up in Boston and Toledo.

4. BREAKFAST TIME AT THE BOYLES' HOUSE ON LA FLORIDA STREET, ALAMEDA, CALIFORNIA, THE CHILDREN DEMAND SUGAR FROSTED FLAKES.
With some reluctance Sarah Boyle dishes out Sugar Frosted Flakes to her children, already hearing the decay set in upon the little milk-white

teeth, the bony whine of the dentist's drill. The dentist is a short, gentle man with a moustache who sometimes reminds Sarah of an uncle who lives in Ohio. One bowl per child.

5. If one can imagine it considered as an abstract object, by members of a totally separate culture, one can see that the cereal box might seem a beautiful thing. The solid rectangle is neatly joined and classical in proportions, on it are squandered wealths of richest colors, virgin blues, crimsons, dense ochres, precious pigments once reserved for sacred paintings and as cosmetics for the blind faces of marble gods. Giant size. Net Weight 16 ounces, 250 grams. "They're tigeriffic!" says Tony the Tiger. The box blatts promises: Energy, Nature's Own Goodness, an endless pubescence. On its back is a mask of William Shakespeare to be cut out, folded, worn by thousands of tiny Shakespeares in Kansas City, Detroit, Tucson, San Diego, Tampa. He appears at once more kindly and somewhat more vacant than we are used to seeing him. Two or more of the children lay claim to the mask, but Sarah puts off that Solomon's decision until such time as the box is empty.

6. A notice in orange flourishes states that a Surprise Gift is to be found somewhere in the package, nestled amongst the golden flakes. So far it has not been unearthed, and the children request more cereal than they wish to eat, great yellow heaps of it, to hurry the discovery. Even so, at the end of the meal, some layers of flakes remain in the box and the Gift must still be among them.

7. There is even a Special Offer of a secret membership, code and magic ring; these to be obtained by sending in the box top with 50¢.

8. Three offers on one cereal box. To Sarah Boyle this seems to be oversell. Perhaps something is terribly wrong with the cereal and it must be sold quickly, got off the shelves before the news breaks. Perhaps it causes a special, cruel Cancer in little children. As Sarah Boyle collects the bowls printed with bunnies and baseball statistics, still slopping half full of milk and wilted flakes, she imagines *in her mind's eye* the headlines, "Nation's Small Fry Stricken, Fate's Finger Sugar Coated, Lethal Sweetness Socks Tots."

9. Sarah Boyle is a vivacious and intelligent young wife and mother, educated at a fine Eastern college, proud of her growing family which keeps her busy and happy around the house.

10. BIRTHDAY.
Today is the birthday of one of the children. There will be a party in the late afternoon.

11. CLEANING UP THE HOUSE. ONE.

Cleaning up the kitchen. Sarah Boyle puts the bowls, plates, glasses and silverware into the sink. She scrubs at the stickiness on the yellow-marbled formica table with a blue synthetic sponge, a special blue which we shall see again. There are marks of children's hands in various sizes printed with sugar and grime on all the table's surfaces. The marks catch the light, they appear and disappear according to the position of the observing eye. The floor sweepings include a triangular half of toast spread with grape jelly, bobby pins, a green band-aid, flakes, a doll's eye, dust, dog's hair and a button.

12. Until we reach the statistically likely planet and begin to converse with whatever green-faced, teleporting denizens thereof—considering only this shrunk and communication-ravaged world—can we any more postulate a separate culture? Viewing the metastasis of Western Culture, it seems progressively less likely. Sarah Boyle imagines a whole world which has become like California, all topographical imperfections sanded away with the sweet-smelling burr of the plastic surgeon's cosmetic polisher; a world populace dieting, leisured, similar in pink and mauve hair and rhinestone shades. A land Cunt Pink and Avocado Green, brassiered and girdled by monstrous complexities of Super Highways, a California endless and unceasing, embracing and transforming the entire globe, California, California!

13. INSERT ONE. ON ENTROPY.

ENTROPY: A quantity introduced in the first place to facilitate the calculations, and to give clear expressions to the results of thermodynamics. Changes of entropy can be calculated only for a reversible process, and may then be defined as the ratio of the amount of heat taken up to the absolute temperature at which the heat is absorbed. Entropy changes for actual irreversible processes are calculated by postulating equivalent theoretical reversible changes. The entropy of a system is a measure of its degree of disorder. The total entropy of any isolated system can never decrease in any change; it must either increase (irreversible process) or remain constant (reversible process). The total entropy of the Universe therefore is increasing, tending toward a maximum, corresponding to complete disorder of the particles in it (assuming that it may be regarded as an isolated system). See *Heat Death of the Universe*.

14. CLEANING UP THE HOUSE. TWO.

Washing the baby's diapers. Sarah Boyle writes notes to herself all over the house; a mazed wild script larded with arrows, diagrams, pictures; graffiti on every available surface in a desperate/heroic attempt to index, record, bluff, invoke, order and placate. On the fluted and flowered white plastic lid of the diaper bin she has written in Blushing Pink Nitetime lipstick a phrase to ward off fumey ammoniac despair: "The nitrogen cycle is the vital round of organic and inorganic exchange on earth. The sweet breath of the Universe." On the wall by the washing machine are Yin and Yang signs, mandalas and the words, "Many young wives feel trapped. It is a contemporary sociological phenomenon which may be explained in part by a gap between changing living patterns and the accommodation of social services to these patterns." Over the stove she had written "Help, Help, Help, Help, Help."

15. Sometimes she numbers or letters the things in a room, writing the assigned character on each object. There are 819 separate moveable objects in the living room, counting books. Sometimes she labels objects with their names, or with false names, thus on her bureau the hair brush is labeled HAIR BRUSH, the cologne, COLOGNE, the hand cream, CAT. She is passionately fond of children's dictionaries, encyclopedias, ABCs and all reference books, transfixed and comforted at their simulacra of a complete listing and ordering.

16. On the door of a bedroom are written two definitions from reference books, "GOD: An object of worship"; "HOMEOSTASIS: Maintenance of constancy of internal environment."

17. Sarah Boyle washes the diapers, washes the linen, Oh Saint Veronica, changes the sheets on the baby's crib. She begins to put away some of the toys, stepping over and around the organizations of playthings which still seem inhabited. There are various vehicles, and articles of medicine, domesticity and war; whole zoos of stuffed animals, bruised and odorous with years of love; hundreds of small figures, plastic animals, cowboys, cars, spacemen, with which the children make sub and supra worlds in their play. One of Sarah's favorite toys is the Baba, the wooden Russian doll which, opened, reveals a smaller but otherwise identical doll which opens to reveal, etc., a lesson in infinity at least to the number of seven dolls.

18. Sarah Boyle's mother has been dead for two years. Sarah Boyle thinks of music as the formal articulation of the passage of time, and of Bach as the most poignant rendering of this. Her eyes are sometimes the color of the aforementioned kitchen sponge. Her hair is natural spaniel brown; months ago on an hysterical day she dyed it red, so now it is two-toned with a stripe in the middle, like the painted walls of slum buildings or old schools.

19. INSERT TWO. HEAT DEATH OF THE UUNIVERSE.

The second law of thermodynamics can be interpreted to mean that the ENTROPY of a closed system tends toward a maximum and that its available ENERGY tends toward a minimum. It has been held that the Universe constitutes a thermodynamically closed system, and if this were true it would mean that a time must finally come when the Universe "unwinds" itself, no energy being available for use. This state is referred to as the "heat death of the Universe." It is by no means certain, however, that the Universe can be considered as a closed system in this sense.

20. Sarah Boyle pours out a Coke from the refrigerator and lights a cigarette. The coldness and sweetness of the thick brown liquid make her throat ache and her teeth sting briefly, sweet juice of my youth, her eyes glass with the carbonation, she thinks of the Heat Death of the Universe. A logarithmic of those late summer days, endless as the Irish serpent twisting through jeweled manuscripts forever, tail in mouth, the heat pressing, bloating, doing violence. The Los Angeles sky becomes so filled and bleached with detritus that it loses all color and silvers like a mirror, reflecting back the fricasseeing earth. Everything becoming warmer and warmer, each particle of matter becoming more agitated, more excited until the bonds shatter, the glues fail, the deodorants lose their seals. She imagines the whole of New York City melting like a Dali into a great chocolate mass, a great soup, the Great Soup of New York.

21. CLEANING UP THE HOUSE. THREE.
Beds made. Vacuuming the hall, a carpet of faded flowers, vines and leaves which endlessly wind and twist into each other in a fevered and permanent ecstasy. Suddenly the vacuum blows instead of sucks, spewing marbles, dolls' eyes, dust, crackers. An old trick. "Oh my god," says Sarah. The baby yells on cue for attention/changing/food. Sarah kicks the vacuum cleaner and it retches and begins working again.

22. AT LUNCH ONLY ONE GLASS OF MILK IS SPILLED.
At lunch only one glass of milk is spilled.

23. The plants need watering, Geranium, Hyacinth, Lavender, Avocado, Cyclamen. Feed the fish, happy fish with china castles and mermaids in the bowl. The turtle looks more and more unwell and is probably dying.

24. Sarah Boyle's blue eyes, how blue? Bluer far and of a different quality than the Nature metaphors which were both engine and fuel to so much of precedent literature. A fine, modern, acid, synthetic blue; the shiny cerulean of the skies on postcards sent from lush subtropics, the natives grinning ivory ambivalent grins in their dark faces; the promising, fat, unnatural blue of the heavy tranquillizer capsule; the cool, mean blue of that fake kitchen sponge; the deepest, most unbelievable azure of the tiled and mossless interiors of California swimming pools. The chemists in their kitchens cooked, cooled and distilled this blue from thousands of colorless and wonderfully constructed crystals, each one unique and nonpareil; and now that color hisses, bubbles, burns in Sarah's eyes.

25. INSERT THREE. ON LIGHT.

LIGHT: Name given to the agency by means of which a viewed object influences the observer's eyes. Consists of electromagnetic radiation within the wavelength range 4×10^{-5} cm. to 7×10^{-5} cm. approximately; variations in the wavelength produce different sensations in the eye, corresponding to different colors. See color vision.

26. LIGHT AND CLEANING THE LIVING ROOM.

All the objects (819) and surfaces in the living room are dusty, gray common dust as though this were the den of a giant, molting mouse. Suddenly quantities of waves or particles of very strong sunlight speed in through the window, and everything incandesces, multiple rainbows. Poised in what has become a solid cube of light, like an ancient insect trapped in amber, Sarah Boyle realizes that the dust is indeed the most beautiful stuff in the room, a manna for the eyes. Duchamp, that father of thought, has set with fixative some dust which fell on one of his sculptures, counting it as part of the work. "That way madness lies, says Sarah," says Sarah. The thought of ordering a household on Dada principles balloons again. All the rooms would fill up with objects, newspapers and magazines would compost, the potatoes in the rack, the canned green beans in the garbage can would take new heart and come to life again, reaching out green shoots toward the sun. The plants would grow wild and wind into a jungle around the house, splitting plaster, tearing shingles, the garden would enter in at the door. The goldfish would die, the birds would die, we'd have them stuffed; the dog would die from lack of care, and probably the children—all stuffed and sitting around the house, covered with dust.

27. INSERT FOUR. DADA.

DADA (Fr., hobby-horse) was a nihilistic precursor of Surrealism, invented in Zurich during World War I, a product of hysteria and shock lasting from about 1915 to 1922. It was deliberately anti-art and anti-sense, intended to outrage and scandalize, and its most characteristic production was the reproduction of the *Mona Lisa* decorated with a moustache and the obscene caption LHOOQ (read: *elle a chaud au cul*) "by" Duchamp. Other manifestations included Arp's collages of colored paper cut out at random and shuffled, ready-made objects such as the bottle drier and the bicycle wheel "signed" by Duchamp, Picabia's drawings of bits of machinery with incongruous titles, incoherent poetry, a lecture given by 38 lecturers in unison, and an exhibition in Cologne in 1920, held in an annex to a café lavatory, at which a chopper was provided for spectators to smash the exhibits with—which they did.

28. TIME PIECES AND OTHER MEASURING DEVICES.

In the Boyle house there are four clocks; three watches (one a Mickey Mouse watch which does not work); two calendars and two engagement books; three rulers; a yard stick; a measuring cup; a set of red plastic measuring spoons which includes a tablespoon, a teaspoon, a one-half teaspoon, one-fourth teaspoon and one-eighth teaspoon; an egg timer; an oral thermometer and a rectal thermometer; a Boy Scout compass; a barometer in the shape of a house, in and out of which an old woman and an old man chase each other forever without fulfilment; a bathroom scale; an infant scale; a tape measure which can be pulled out of a stuffed felt strawberry; a wall on which the children's heights are marked; a metronome.

29. Sarah Boyle finds a new line in her face after lunch while cleaning the bathroom. It is as yet hardly visible, running from the midpoint of her forehead to the bridge of her nose. By inward curling of her eyebrows she can etch it clearly as it will come to appear in the future. She marks another mark on the wall where she has drawn out a scoring area. Face Lines and Other Limitations of Mortality, the heading says. There are thirty-two marks, counting this latest one.

30. Sarah Boyle is a vivacious and witty young wife and mother, educated at a fine Eastern college, proud of her growing family which keeps her happy and busy around the house, involved in many hobbies and community activities, and only occasionally given to obsessions concerning Time/Entropy/Chaos and Death.

31. Sarah Boyle is never quite sure how many children she has.

32. Sarah thinks from time to time; Sarah is occasionally visited with this thought; at times this thought comes upon Sarah, that there are things to be hoped for, accomplishments to be desired beyond the mere reproductions, mirror reproduction of one's kind. The babies. Lying in bed at night sometimes the memory of the act of birth, always the hue and texture of red plush theater seats, washes up; the rending which always, at a certain intensity of pain, slipped into landscapes, the sweet breath of the sweating nurse. The wooden Russian doll has bright, perfectly round red spots on her cheeks, she splits in the center to reveal a doll smaller but in all other respects identical with round bright red spots on her cheeks, etc.

33. How fortunate for the species, Sarah muses or is mused, that children are as ingratiating as we know them. Otherwise they would soon be salted off for the leeches they are, and the race would extinguish itself in a fair sweet flowering, the last generations' massive achievement in the arts and pursuits of high civilization. The finest women would have their tubes tied off at the age of twelve, or perhaps refrain altogether from the Act of Love? All interests would be bent to a refining and perfecting of each febrile sense, each fluid hour, with no more cowardly

investment in immortality via the patchy and too often disappointing vegetables of one's own womb.

34. INSERT FIVE. LOVE.

LOVE: a typical sentiment involving fondness for, or attachment to, an object, the idea of which is emotionally colored whenever it arises in the mind, and capable, as Shand has pointed out, of evoking any one of a whole gamut of primary emotions, according to the situation in which the object is placed, or represented; often, and by psychoanalysts always, used in the sense of *sex-love* or even *lust* (q.v.).

35. Sarah Boyle has at times felt a unity with her body, at other times a complete separation. The mind/body duality considered. The time/space duality considered. The male/female duality considered. The matter/energy duality considered. Sometimes, at extremes, her Body seems to her an animal on a leash, taken for walks in the park by her Mind. The lamp posts of experience. Her arms are lightly freckled, and when she gets very tired the places under her eyes become violet.

36. Housework is never completed, the chaos always lurks ready to encroach on any area left unweeded, a jungle filled with dirty pans and the roaring of giant stuffed toy animals suddenly turned savage. Terrible glass eyes.

37. SHOPPING FOR THE BIRTHDAY CAKE.

Shopping in the supermarket with the baby in front of the cart and a larger child holding on. The light from the ice-cube-tray-shaped fluorescent lights is mixed blue and pink and brighter, colder, and cheaper than daylight. The doors swing open just as you reach out your hand for them, Tantalus, moving with a ghastly quiet swing. Hot dogs for the party. Potato chips, gum drops, a paper table cloth with birthday designs, hot dog buns, catsup, mustard, picalilli, balloons, instant coffee Continental style, dog food, frozen peas, ice cream, frozen lima beans, frozen broccoli in butter sauce, paper birthday hats, paper napkins in three colors, a box of Sugar Frosted Flakes with a Wolfgang Amadeus Mozart mask on the back, bread, pizza mix. The notes of a just graspable music filter through the giant store, for the most part bypassing the brain and acting directly on the liver, blood and lymph. The air is delicately scented with aluminum. Half and half cream, tea bags, bacon, sandwich meat, strawberry jam. Sarah is in front of the shelves of cleaning products now, and the baby is beginning to whine. Around her are whole libraries of objects, offering themselves. Some of that same old hysteria that had incarnadined her hair rises up again, and she does not refuse it. There is one moment when she can choose direction, like standing on a chalk drawn X, a hot cross bun, and she does not choose calm and measure. Sarah Boyle begins to pick out, methodically, deliberately and with a careful ecstasy, one of every cleaning product which the store sells. Window Cleaner, Glass Cleaner, Brass Polish, Silver Polish, Steel Wool, eighteen different brands of Detergent, Disinfectant, Toilet Cleanser, Water Softener, Fabric Softener, Drain Cleanser, Spot Remover, Floor Wax, Furniture Wax, Car Wax, Carpet Shampoo, Dog Shampoo, Shampoo for people with dry, oily and normal hair, for people with dandruff, for people with gray hair. Tooth Paste, Tooth Powder, Denture Cleaner, Deodorants, Antiperspirants, Antiseptics, Soaps, Cleansers, Abrasives, Oven Cleansers, Makeup Removers. When the same products appear in different sizes Sarah takes one of each size. For some products she accumulates whole little families of containers: a giant Father bottle of shampoo, a Mother bottle, an Older Sister bottle just smaller than the Mother bottle, and a very tiny Baby Brother bottle. Sarah fills three shopping carts and has to have help wheeling them all down the aisles. At the check-out counter her laughter and hysteria keep threatening to overflow as the pale blonde clerk with no eyebrows like the *Mona Lisa* pretends normality and disinterest. The bill comes to $57.53 and Sarah has to write a check. Driving home, the baby strapped in the drive-a-cot and the paper bags bulging in the back seat, she cries.

38. BEFORE THE PARTY.

Mrs. David Boyle, mother-in-law of Sarah Boyle, is coming to the party of her grandchild. She brings a toy, a yellow wooden duck on a string, made in Austria; the duck quacks as it is pulled along the floor. Sarah is filling paper cups with gum drops and chocolates, and Mrs. David Boyle sits at the kitchen table and talks to her. She is talking about several things, she is talking about her garden which is flourishing except for a plague of rare black beetles, thought to have come from Hong Kong, which are undermining some of the most delicate growths at the roots, and feasting on the leaves of other plants. She is talking about a sale of household linens which she plans to attend on the following Tuesday. She is talking about her neighbor who has cancer and is wasting away. The neighbor is a Catholic woman who had never had a day's illness in her life until the cancer struck, and now she is, apparently, failing with dizzying speed. The doctor says her body's chaos, chaos, cells running wild all over, says Mrs. David Boyle. When I visited her she hardly *knew* me, can hardly *speak*, can't keep herself *clean*, says Mrs. David Boyle.

39. Sometimes Sarah can hardly remember how many cute, chubby little children she has.

40. When she used to stand out in center field far away from the other players, she used to make up songs and sing them to herself.

41. She thinks of the end of the world by ice.

42. She thinks of the end of the world by water.

43. She thinks of the end of the world by nuclear war.

44. There must be more than this, Sarah Boyle thinks, from time to time. What could one do to justify one's passage? Or less ambitiously, to change, even in the motion of the smallest mote, the course and circulation of the world? Sometimes Sarah's dreams are of heroic girth, a new symphony using laborotories of machinery and all invented instruments, at once giant in scope and intelligible to all, to heal the bloody breach; a series of paintings which would transfigure and astonish and calm the frenzied art world in its panting race; a new novel that would refurbish language. Sometimes she considered the mystical, the streaky and random, and it seems that one change, no matter how small, would be enough. Turtles are supposed to live for many years. To carve a name, date and perhaps a word of hope upon a turtle's shell, then set him free to wend the world, surely this one act might cancel out absurdity?

45. Mrs. David Boyle has a faint moustache, like Duchamp's *Mona Lisa*.

46. THE BIRTHDAY PARTY.
Many children, dressed in pastels, sit around the long table. They are exhausted and overexcited from games fiercely played, some are flushed and wet, others unnaturally pale. This general agitation, and the paper party hats they wear, combine to make them appear a dinner party of debauched midgets. It is time for the cake. A huge chocolate cake in the shape of a rocket and launching pad and covered with blue and pink icing is carried in. In the hush the birthday child begins to cry. He stops crying, makes a wish and blows out the candles.

47. One child will not eat hot dogs, ice cream or cake, and asks for cereal. Sarah pours him out a bowl of Sugar Frosted Flakes, and a moment later he chokes. Sarah pounds him on the back and out spits a tiny green plastic snake with red glass eyes, the Surprise Gift. All the children want it.

48. AFTER THE PARTY THE CHILDREN ARE PUT TO BED.
Bath time. Observing the nakedness of children, pink and slippery as seals, squealing as seals, now the splashing, grunting and smacking of cherry flesh on raspberry flesh reverberate in the pearl tiled steamy cubicle. The nakedness of children is so much more absolute than that of the mature. No musky curling hair to indicate the target points, no knobbly clutch of plane and fat and curvature to ennoble this prince of beasts. All well-fed naked children appear edible, Sarah's teeth hum in her head with memory of bloody feastings, prehistory. Young humans appear too like the young of other species for smugness, and the comparison is not even in their favor, they are much the most peeled and unsupple of those young. Such pinkness, such utter nuded pinkness; the orifices neatly

incised, rimmed with a slightly deeper rose, the incessant demands for breast time milks of many sorts.

49. INSERT SIX. WEINER ON ENTROPY.

In Gibbs' Universe order is least probable, chaos most probable. But while the Universe as a whole, if indeed there is a whole Universe, tends to run down, there are local enclaves whose direction seems opposed to that of the Universe at large and in which there is a limited and temporary tendency for organization to increase. Life finds its home in some of these enclaves.

50. Sarah Boyle imagines, in her mind's eye, cleaning and ordering the whole world, even the Universe. Filling the great spaces of Space with a marvelous sweet smelling, deep cleansing foam. Deodorizing rank caves and volcanoes. Scrubbing rocks.

51. INSERT SEVEN. TURTLES.

Many different species of carnivorous Turtles live in the fresh waters of the tropical and temperate zones of various continents. Most Northerly of the European Turtles (extending as far as Holland and Lithuania) is the European Pond Turtle (*Emys orbicularis*). It is from 8 to 10 inches long and may live a hundred years.

52. CLEANING UP AFTER THE PARTY.

Sarah is cleaning up after the party. Gum drops and melted ice cream surge off paper plates, making holes in the paper tablecloth through the printed roses. A fly has died a splendid death in a pool of strawberry ice cream. Wet jelly beans stain all they touch, finally becoming themselves colorless, opaque white like flocks of tamed or sleeping maggots. Plastic favors mount half-eaten pieces of blue cake. Strewn about are thin strips of fortune papers from the Japanese poppers. Upon them are printed strangely assorted phrases selected by apparently unilingual Japanese. Crowds of delicate yellow people spending great chunks of their lives in producing these most ephemeral of objects, and inscribing thousands of fine papers with absurd and incomprehensible messages. "The very hairs of your head are all numbered," reads one. Most of the balloons have popped. Someone has planted a hot dog in the daffodil pot. A few of the helium balloons have escaped their owners and now ride the ceiling. Another fortune paper reads, "Emperor's horses meet death worse, numbers, numbers."

53. She is very tired, violet under the eyes, mauve beneath the eyes. Her uncle in Ohio used to get the same marks under his eyes. She goes to the kitchen to lay the table for tomorrow's breakfast, then she sees that in the turtle's bowl the turtle is floating, still, on the surface of the water. Sarah Boyle pokes at it with a pencil but it does not move. She

stands for several minutes looking at the dead turtle on the surface of the water. She is crying again.

54. She begins to cry. She goes to the refrigerator and takes out a carton of eggs, white eggs, extra large. She throws them one by one onto the kitchen floor which is patterned with strawberries in squares. They break beautifully. There is a Secret Society of Dentists, all moustached, with Special Code and Magic Rings. She begins to cry. She takes up three bunny dishes and throws them against the refrigerator, they shatter, and then the floor is covered with shards, chunks of partial bunnies, an ear, an eye here, a paw; Stockton, California, Acton, California, Chico, California, Redding, California, Glen Ellen, California, Cadix, California, Angels Camps, California, Half Moon Bay. The total ENTROPY of the Universe therefore is increasing, tending toward a maximum, corresponding to complete disorder of the particles in it. She is crying, her mouth is open. She throws a jar of grape jelly and it smashes the window over the sink. Her eyes are blue. She begins to open her mouth. It has been held that the Universe constitutes a thermodynamically closed system, and if this were true it would mean that a time must finally come when the Universe "unwinds" itself, no energy being available for use. This state is referred to as the "Heat Death of the Universe." Sarah Boyle begins to cry. She throws a jar of strawberry jam against the stove, enamel chips off and the stove begins to bleed. Bach had twenty children, how many children has Sarah Boyle? Her mouth is open. Her mouth is opening. She turns on the water and fills the sinks with detergent. She writes on the kitchen wall, "William Shakespeare has Cancer and lives in California." She writes, "Sugar Frosted Flakes are the Food of the Gods." The water foams up in the sink, overflowing, bubbling onto the strawberry floor. She is about to begin to cry. Her mouth is opening. She is crying. She cries. How can one ever tell whether there are one or many fish? She begins to break glasses and dishes, she throws cups and cooking pots and jars of food which shatter and break and spread over the kitchen. The sand keeps falling, very quietly, in the egg timer. The old man and woman in the barometer never catch each other. She picks up eggs and throws them into the air. She begins to cry. She opens her mouth. The eggs arch slowly through the kitchen, like a baseball, hit high against the spring sky, seen from far away. They go higher and higher in the stillness, hesitate at the zenith, then begin to fall away slowly, slowly, through the fine, clear air.

Study and Discussion Questions

1. How does Sarah Boyle spend her day?
2. What function do the "Inserts" have in the story?
3. How many children does Sarah Boyle have?

4. Find examples of irony in the story.
5. List instances in the story of the passing of time.
6. Why do you think one of Sarah's favorite toys is the Russian Baba doll?
7. How does Zoline use color in this story? Find some examples.
8. What happens to Sarah Boyle in the supermarket?
9. In the last paragraph, Sarah Boyle "begins to cry." What else does she do and where do you think it is leading?

Writing Exercises

1. Why do you think Zoline tells this story in numbered paragraphs?
2. Write a short character sketch of Sarah Boyle.
3. Choose any one of the paragraphs, analyze it, and discuss its function in the development of the story.
4. Is Sarah Boyle's life a "closed system"? (See paragraph 19.) If so, how? If not, where are the potential or actual openings?
5. Is Sarah Boyle crazy or has she just become sane?
6. Write a postcript to this story. What is Sarah Boyle going to do next? You might set your postcript immediately after the time of the story or you might set it a few years later.

JAMES ALAN McPHERSON   (b. 1943)

James Alan McPherson was born in Savannah, Georgia, attended segregated schools there, and went on to Morris Brown College in Atlanta and to Harvard Law School. He has worked as a journalist and taught literature at several universities. His stories are collected in Hue and City *(1969) and in* Elbow Room *(1977), which won a Pulitzer Prize.*

A Loaf of Bread   (1977)

It was one of those obscene situations, pedestrian to most people, but invested with meaning for a few poor folk whose lives are usually spent outside the imaginations of their fellow citizens. A grocer named Harold Green was caught red-handed selling to one group of people the very same goods he sold at lower prices at similar outlets in better neighborhoods. He had been doing this for many years, and at first he could not understand the outrage heaped upon him. He acted only from habit, he insisted, and had nothing personal against the people whom he served. They were his neighbors. Many of them he had carried on the cuff during hard times. Yet, through some mysterious access to a television station, the poor folk were now empowered to make grand denunciations of the grocer. Green's children now saw their father's business being picketed on the Monday evening news.

No one could question the fact that the grocer had been overcharging the people. On the news even the reporter grimaced distastefully while reading the statistics. His expression said, "It is my job to report the news, but sometimes even I must disassociate myself from it to protect my honor." This, at least, was the impression the grocer's children seemed to bring away from the television. Their father's name had not been mentioned, but there was a close-up of his store with angry black people, and a few outraged whites, marching in groups of three in front of it. There was also a close-up of his name. After seeing this, they were in no mood to watch cartoons. At the dinner table, disturbed by his children's silence, Harold Green felt compelled to say, "I am not a dishonest man." Then he felt ashamed. The children, a boy and his older sister, immediately left the table, leaving Green alone with his wife. "Ruth, I am not dishonest," he repeated to her.

Ruth Green did not say anything. She knew, and her husband did not, that the outraged people had also picketed the school attended by their children. They had threatened to return each day until Green lowered his prices. When they called her at home to report this, she had promised she would talk with him. Since she could not tell him this, she waited for an opening. She looked at her husband across the table.

"I did not make the world," Green began, recognizing at once the seriousness in her stare. "My father came to this country with nothing but his shirt. He was exploited for as long as he couldn't help himself. He did not protest or picket. He put himself in a position to play by the rules he had learned." He waited for his wife to answer, and when she did not, he tried again. "I did not make this world," he repeated. "I only make my way in it. Such people as these, they do not know enough to not be exploited. If not me, there would be a Greek, a Chinaman, maybe an Arab or a smart one of their own kind. Believe me, I deal with them. There is something in their style that lacks the patience to run a concern such as mine. If I closed down, take my word on it, someone else would do what has to be done."

But Ruth Green was not thinking of his leaving. Her mind was on other matters. Her children had cried when they came home early from school. She had no special feeling for the people who picketed, but she did not like to see her children cry. She had kissed them generously, then sworn them to silence. "One day this week," she told her husband, "you will give free, for eight hours, anything your customers come in to buy. There will be no publicity, except what they spread by word of mouth. No matter what they say to you, no matter what they take, you will remain silent." She stared deeply into him for what she knew was there. "If you refuse, you have seen the last of your children and myself."

Her husband grunted. Then he leaned toward her. "I will not knuckle under," he said. "I will *not* give!"

"We shall see," his wife told him.

The black pickets, for the most part, had at first been frightened by the audacity of their undertaking. They were peasants whose minds had long before become resigned to their fate as victims. None of them, before now, had thought to challenge this. But now, when they watched themselves on television, they hardly recognized the faces they saw beneath the hoisted banners and placards. Instead of reflecting the meekness they all felt, the faces looked angry. The close-ups looked especially intimidating. Several of the first pickets, maids who worked in the suburbs, reported that their employers, seeing the activity on the afternoon news, had begun treating them with new respect. One woman, midway through the weather report, called around the neighborhood to disclose that her employer had that very day given her a new china plate for her meals. The paper plates, on which all previous meals had been served, had been thrown into the wastebasket. One recipient of this call, a middle-aged woman known for her bashfulness and humility, rejoined that her husband, a sheet-metal worker, had only a few hours before been called "Mister" by his supervisor, a white man with a passionate hatred of color. She added the tale of a neighbor down the street, a widow-woman named Murphy, who had at first been reluctant to join the picket; this woman now was insisting it should be made a daily event. Such talk as this circulated among the people who had been instrumental in raising the issue. As news of their victory leaked into the ears of others who had not participated, they received all through the night calls from strangers requesting verification, offering advice, and vowing support. Such strangers listened, and then volunteered stories about indignities inflicted on them by city officials, policemen, other grocers. In this way, over a period of hours, the community became even more incensed and restless than it had been at the time of the initial picket.

Soon, the man who had set events in motion found himself a hero. His name was Nelson Reed, and all his adult life he had been employed as an assembly-line worker. He was a steady husband, the father of three children, and a deacon in the Baptist church. All his life he had trusted in God and gotten along. But now something in him capitulated to the reality that came suddenly into focus. "I was wrong," he told people who called him. "The onliest thing that matters in this world is *money*. And when was the last time you seen a picture of Jesus on a dollar bill?" This line, which he repeated over and over, caused a few callers to laugh nervously, but not without some affirmation that this was indeed the way things were. Many said they had known it all along. Others argued that although it was certainly true, it was one thing to live without money and quite another to live without faith. But still most callers laughed and said, "You right. You *know* I know you right. Ain't it the truth, though?"

Only a few people, among them Nelson Reed's wife, said nothing and looked very sad.

Why they looked sad, however, they would not communicate. And anyone observing their troubled faces would have to trust his own intuition. It is known that Reed's wife, Betty, measured all events against the fullness of her own experience. She was skeptical of everything. Brought to the church after a number of years of living openly with a jazz musician, she had embraced religion when she married Nelson Reed. But though she no longer believed completely in the world, she nonetheless had not fully embraced God. There was something in the nature of Christ's swift rise that had always bothered her, and something in the blood and vengeance of the Old Testament that was mellowing and refreshing. But she had never communicated these thoughts to anyone, especially her husband. Instead, she smiled vacantly while others professed leaps of faith, remained silent when friends spoke fiercely of their convictions. The presence of this vacuum in her contributed to her personal mystery; people said she was beautiful, although she was not outwardly so. Perhaps it was because she wished to protect this inner beauty that she did not smile now, and looked extremely sad, listening to her husband on the telephone.

Nelson Reed had no reason to be sad. He seemed to grow more energized and talkative as the days passed. He was invited by an alderman, on the Tuesday after the initial picket, to tell his story on a local television talk show. He sweated heavily under the hot white lights and attempted to be philosophical. "I notice," the host said to him, "that you are not angry at this exploitative treatment. What, Mr. Reed, is the source of your calm?" The assembly-line worker looked unabashedly into the camera and said, "I have always believed in *Justice* with a capital *J*. I was raised up from a baby believin' that God ain't gonna let nobody go *too* far. See, in *my* mind God is in charge of *all* the capital letters in the alphabet of this world. It say in the Scripture He is Alpha and Omega, the first and the last. He is just about the *onliest* capitalizer they is." Both Reed and the alderman laughed. "Now, when *men* start to capitalize, they gets *greedy*. They put a little *j* in *joy* and a littler one in *justice*. They raise up a big *G* in *Greed* and a big *E* in *Evil*. Well, soon as they commence to put a little *g* in *God*, you can expect some kind of reaction. The Savior will just raise up the *H* in *Hell* and go on from there. And that's just what I'm doin', giving these sharpies *HELL* with a big *H*" The talk show host laughed along with Nelson Reed and the alderman After the taping they drank coffee in the back room of the studio and talked about the sad shape of the world.

Three days before he was to comply with his wife's request, Green, the grocer, saw this talk show on television while at home. The words of Nelson Reed sent a chill through him. Though Reed had attempted to be philosophical, Green did not perceive the statement in this light. Instead, he saw a vindictive-looking black man seated between an ambitious alderman and a smug talk-show host. He saw them chatting comfortably about the nature of evil. The cameraman had shot mostly close-ups, and Green could see the set in Nelson Reed's jaw. The color of Reed's face was maddening. When his children came into the den, the grocer was in a sweat. Before he could think, he had shouted at them and struck the button turning off the set. The two children rushed from the room screaming. Ruth Green ran in from the kitchen. She knew why he was upset because she had received a call about the show; but she said nothing and pretended ignorance. Her children's school had been picketed that day, as it had the day before. But both children were still forbidden to speak of this to their father.

"Where do they get so much power?" Green said to his wife. "Two days ago, nobody would have cared. Now, everywhere, even in my home, I am condemned as a rascal. And what do I own? An airline? A multi-national? Half of South America? *No!* I own three stores, one of which happens to be in a certain neighborhood inhabited by people who cost me money to run it." He sighed and sat upright on the sofa, his chubby legs spread wide. "A cab driver has a meter that clicks as he goes along. I pay extra for insurance, iron bars, pilfering by customers and employees. Nothing clicks. But when I add a little overhead to my prices, suddenly everything clicks. But for someone else. When was there last such a world?" He pressed the palms of both hands to his temples, suggesting a bombardment of brain-stinging sounds.

This gesture evoked no response from Ruth Green. She remained standing by the door, looking steadily at him. She said, "To protect yourself, I would not stock any more fresh cuts of meat in the store until after the giveaway on Saturday. Also, I would not tell it to the employees until after the first customer of the day has begun to check out. But I would urge you to hire several security guards to close the door promptly at seven-thirty, as is usual." She wanted to say much more than this, but did not. Instead she watched him. He was looking at the blank gray television screen, his palms still pressed against his ears. "In case you need to hear again," she continued in a weighty tone of voice, "I said two days ago, and I say again now, that if you fail to do this you will not see your children again for many years."

He twisted his head and looked up at her. "What is the color of these people?" he asked.

"Black," his wife said.

"And what is the name of my children?"

"Green."

The grocer smiled. "There is your answer," he told his wife. "Green is the only color I am interested in."

His wife did not smile. "Insufficient," she said.

"The world is mad!" he moaned. "But it is a point of sanity with me to not bend. I will not bend." He crossed his legs and pressed one hand firmly atop his knee. "*I will not bend,*" he said.

"We will see," his wife said.

Nelson Reed, after the television interview, became the acknowledged leader of the disgruntled neighbors. At first a number of them met in the kitchen at his house; then, as space was lacking for curious newcomers, a mass meeting was held on Thursday in an abandoned theater. His wife and three children sat in the front row. Behind them sat the widow Murphy, Lloyd Dukes, Tyrone Brown, Les Jones—those who had joined him on the first picket line. Behind these sat people who bought occasionally at the store, people who lived on the fringes of the neighborhood, people from other neighborhoods come to investigate the problem, and the merely curious. The middle rows were occupied by a few people from the suburbs, those who had seen the talk show and whose outrage at the grocer proved much more powerful than their fear of black people. In the rear of the theater crowded aging, old-style leftists, somber students, cynical young black men with angry grudges to explain with inarticulate gestures. Leaning against the walls, and huddled near the doors at the rear, tape-recorder-bearing social scientists looked as detached and serene as bookies at the track. Here and there, in this diverse crowd, a politician stationed himself, pumping hands vigorously and pressing his palms gently against the shoulders of elderly people. Other visitors passed out leaflets, buttons, glossy color prints of men who promoted causes, the familiar and obscure. There was a hubbub of voices, a blend of the strident and the playful, the outraged and the reverent, lending an undercurrent of ominous energy to the assembly.

Nelson Reed spoke from a platform on the stage, standing before a yellowed, shredded screen that had once reflected the images of matinee idols. "I don't mind sayin' that I have always been a sucker," he told the crowd. "All my life I have been a sucker for the words of Jesus. Being a natural-born fool, I just ain't never had the *sense* to learn no better. Even right today, while the whole world is sayin' wrong is right and up is down, I'm so dumb I'm *still* steady believin' what is wrote in the Good Book. . . ."

From the audience, especially the front rows, came a chorus singing, "Preach!"

"I have no doubt," he continued in a low baritone, "that it's true what is writ in the Good Book: 'The last shall be first and the first shall be last.' I don't know about y'all, but I have *always* been the last. I never wanted to be the first, but sometimes it look like the world get so bad that them that's holdin' onto the tree of life is the onliest ones left when God commence to blowin' dead leafs off the branches."

"Now you preaching," someone called.

In the rear of the theater a white student shouted an awkward "Amen."

Nelson Reed began walking across the stage to occupy the major part of his nervous energy. But to those in the audience, who now hung on his every word, it looked as though he strutted. "All my life," he said,

"I have claimed to be a man without earnin' the right to call myself that. You know, the *average* man ain't really a man. The average man is a *boot-licker*. In fact, the *average* man would *run away* if he found hisself standing alone facin' down a adversary. I have done that *too many a time* in my life! But *not no more*. Better to be *once* was than *never* was a man. I will tell you tonight, there is somethin' *wrong* in being average. *I intend to stand up!* Now, if your average man that ain't really a man stand up, two things gonna happen: *One,* he g'on bust through all the weights that been place on his head, and, *two,* he g'on feel a lot of pain. But that same hurt is what make things fall in place. That, and gettin' your hands on one of these slick four-flushers tight enough so's you can squeeze him and say, 'No *more!*' You do that, you g'on hurt some, but *you won't be average no more* . . ."

"No *more!*" a few people in the front rows repeated.

"I say *no more!*" Nelson Reed shouted.

"*No more! No more! No more!*" The chant rustled through the crowd like the rhythm of an autumn wind against a shedding tree.

Then people laughed and chattered in celebration.

As for the grocer, from the evening of the television interview he had begun to make plans. Unknown to his wife, he cloistered himself several times with his brother-in-law, an insurance salesman, and plotted a course. He had no intention of tossing steaks to the crowd. "And why should I, Tommy?" he asked his wife's brother, a lean, bald-headed man named Thomas. "I don't cheat anyone. I have never cheated anyone. The businesses I run are always on the up-and-up. So why should I pay?"

"Quite so," the brother-in-law said, chewing an unlit cigarillo. "The world has gone crazy. Next they will say that people in my business are responsible for prolonging life. I have found that people who refuse to believe in death refuse also to believe in the harshness of life. I sell well by saying that death is a long happiness. I show people the realities of life and compare this to a funeral with dignity, *and* the promise of a bundle for every loved one salted away. When they look around hard at life, they usually buy."

"So?" asked Green. Thomas was a college graduate with a penchant for philosophy.

"So," Thomas answered. "You must fight to show these people the reality of both your situation and theirs. How would it be if you visited one of their meetings and chalked out, on a blackboard, the dollars and cents of your operation? Explain your overhead, your security fees, all the additional expenses. If you treat them with respect, they might understand."

Green frowned. "That I would never do," he said. "It would be admission of a certain guilt."

The brother-in-law smiled, but only with one corner of his mouth. "Then you have something to feel guilty about?" he asked.

The grocer frowned at him. *"Nothing!"* he said with great emphasis.
"So?" Thomas said.

This first meeting between the grocer and his brother-in-law took place on Thursday, in a crowded barroom.

At the second meeting, in a luncheonette, it was agreed that the grocer should speak privately with the leader of the group, Nelson Reed. The meeting at which this was agreed took place on Friday afternoon. After accepting this advice from Thomas, the grocer resigned himself to explain to Reed, in as finite detail as possible, the economic structure of his operation. He vowed to suppress no information. He would explain everything: inventories, markups, sale items, inflation, balance sheets, specialty items, overhead, and that mysterious item called profit. This last item, promising to be the most difficult to explain, Green and his brother-in-law debated over for several hours. They agreed first of all that a man should not work for free, then they agreed that it was unethical to ruthlessly exploit. From these parameters, they staked out an area between fifteen and forty percent, and agreed that someplace between these two borders lay an amount of return that could be called fair. This was easy, but then Thomas introduced the factor of circumstance. He questioned whether the fact that one serviced a risky area justified the earning of profits closer to the forty-percent edge of the scale. Green was unsure. Thomas smiled. "Here is a case that will point out an analogy," he said, licking a cigarillo. "I read in the papers that a family wants to sell an electric stove. I call the home and the man says fifty dollars. I ask to come out and inspect the merchandise. When I arrive I see they are poor, have already bought a new stove that is connected, and are selling the old one for fifty dollars because they want it out of the place. The electric stove is in good condition, worth much more than fifty. But because I see what I see I offer forty-five."

Green, for some reason, wrote down this figure on the back of the sales slip for the coffee they were drinking.

The brother-in-law smiled. He chewed his cigarillo. "The man agrees to take forty-five dollars, saying he has had no other calls. I look at the stove again and see a spot of rust. I say I will give him forty dollars. He agrees to this, on condition that I myself haul it away. I say I will haul it away if he comes down to thirty. You, of course, see where I am going."

The grocer nodded. "The circumstances of his situation, his need to get rid of the stove quickly, placed him in a position where he has little room to bargain?"

"Yes," Thomas answered. "So? Is it ethical, Harry?"

Harold Green frowned. He had never liked his brother-in-law, and now he thought the insurance agent was being crafty. "But," he answered, "this man does not *have* to sell! It is his choice whether to wait for other calls. It is not the fault of the buyer that the seller is in a hurry. It is the right of the buyer to get what he wants at the lowest price possible. That is the rule. That has *always* been the rule. And the reverse of it applies to the seller as well."

"Yes," Thomas said, sipping coffee from the Styrofoam cup. "But suppose that in addition to his hurry to sell, the owner was also of a weak soul. There are, after all, many such people." He smiled. "Suppose he placed no value on the money?"

"Then," Green answered, "your example is academic. Here we are not talking about real life. One man lives by the code, one man does not. Who is there free enough to make a judgment?" He laughed. "Now you see," he told his brother-in-law. "Much more than a few dollars are at stake. If this one buyer is to be condemned, then so are most people in the history of the world. An examination of history provides the only answer to your question. This code will be here tomorrow, long after the ones who do not honor it are not."

They argued fiercely late into the afternoon, the brother-in-law leaning heavily on his readings. When they parted, a little before 5:00 P.M., nothing had been resolved.

Neither was much resolved during the meeting between Green and Nelson Reed. Reached at home by the grocer in the early evening, the leader of the group spoke coldly at first, but consented finally to meet his adversary at a nearby drugstore for coffee and a talk. They met at the lunch counter, shook hands awkwardly, and sat for a few minutes discussing the weather. Then the grocer pulled two gray ledgers from his briefcase. "You have for years come into my place," he told the man. "In my memory I have always treated you well. Now our relationship has come to this." He slid the books along the counter until they touched Nelson Reed's arm.

Reed opened the top book and flipped the thick green pages with his thumb. He did not examine the figures. "All I know," he said, "is over at your place a can of soup cost me fifty-five cents, and two miles away at your other store for white folks you chargin' thirty-nine cents." He said this with the calm authority of an outraged soul. A quality of condescension tinged with pity crept into his gaze.

The grocer drummed his fingers on the counter top. He twisted his head and looked away, toward shelves containing cosmetics, laxatives, toothpaste. His eyes lingered on a poster of a woman's apple red lips and milk white teeth. The rest of the face was missing.

"Ain't no use to hide," Nelson Reed said, as to a child. "*I* know you wrong, *you* know you wrong, and before I finish, *everybody in this city* g'on know you wrong. God don't *like* ugly." He closed his eyes and gripped the cup of coffee. Then he swung his head suddenly and faced the grocer again. "Man, why you want to *do* people that way?" he asked. "We human, same as you."

"Before *God!*" Green exclaimed, looking squarely into the face of Nelson Reed. "Before God!" he said again. "*I am not an evil man!*" These last words sounded more like a moan as he tightened the muscles in his throat to lower the sound of his voice. He tossed his left shoulder as if adjusting the sleeve of his coat, or as if throwing off some unwanted weight. Then he peered along the countertop. No one was watching. At the end of the counter the waitress was scrubbing the coffee urn. "Look at these figures, please," he said to Reed.

The man did not drop his gaze. His eyes remained fixed on the grocer's face.

"All right," Green said. "Don't look. I'll tell you what is in these books, believe me if you want. I work twelve hours a day, one day off per week, running my business in three stores. I am not a wealthy person. In one place, in the area you call white, I get by barely by smiling lustily at old ladies, stocking gourmet stuff on the chance I will build a reputation as a quality store. The two clerks there cheat me; there is nothing I can do. In this business you must be friendly with everybody. The second place is on the other side of town, in a neighborhood as poor as this one. I get out there seldom. The profits are not worth the gas. I use the loss there as a write-off against some other properties." he paused. "Do you understand write-off?" he asked Nelson Reed.

"Naw," the man said.

Harold Green laughed. "What does it matter?" he said in a tone of voice intended for himself alone. "In this area I will admit I make a profit, but it is not so much as you think. But I do not make a profit here because the people are black. I make a profit because a profit is here to be made. I invest more here in window bars, theft losses, insurance, spoilage; I deserve to make more here than at the other places." He looked, almost imploringly, at the man seated next to him. "You don't accept this as the right of a man in business?"

Reed grunted. "Did the bear shit in the woods?" he said.

Again Green laughed. He gulped his coffee awkwardly, as if eager to go. Yet his motions slowed once he had set the coffee cup down on the blue plastic saucer. "Place yourself in *my* situation," he said, his voice high and tentative. "If *you* were running my store in this neighborhood, what would be *your* position? Say on a profit scale of fifteen to forty percent, at what point in between would you draw the line?"

Nelson Reed thought. He sipped his coffee and seemed to chew the liquid. "Fifteen to forty?" he repeated.

"Yes."

"I'm a churchgoin' man," he said. "Closer to fifteen than to forty."

"How close?"

Nelson Reed thought. "In church you tithe ten percent."

"In restaurants you tip fifteen," the grocer said quickly.

"All right," Reed said. "Over fifteen."

"How much over?"

Nelson Reed thought.

"Twenty, thirty, thirty-five?" Green chanted, leaning closer to Reed. Still the man thought.

"Forty? Maybe even forty-five or fifty?" the grocer breathed in Reed's ear. "In the supermarkets, you know, they have more subtle ways of accomplishing such feats."

Reed slapped his coffee cup with the back of his right hand. The brown liquid swirled across the counter top, wetting the books. "*Damn this!*" he shouted.

Startled, Green rose from his stool.

Nelson Reed was trembling. "I ain't *you*," he said in a deep baritone. "I ain't the *supermarket* neither. All I is is a poor man that works *too* hard to see his pay slip through his fingers like rainwater. All I know is you done *cheat* me, you done *cheat* everybody in the neighborhood, and we organized now to get some of it *back!*" Then he stood and faced the grocer. "My daddy sharecropped down in Mississippi and bought in the company store. He owed them twenty-three years when he died. I paid off five of them years and then run away to up here. Now, I'm a deacon in the Baptist church. I raised my kids the way my daddy raise me and don't bother nobody. Now come to find out, after all my runnin', they done lift that *same company store* up out of Mississippi and slip it down on us here! Well, my daddy was a *fighter*, and if he hadn't owed all them years he would of raise him some hell. Me, I'm steady my daddy's child, plus I got seniority in my union. I'm a free man. Buddy, don't you know *I'm gonna raise me some hell!*"

Harold Green reached for a paper napkin to sop the coffee soaking into his books.

Nelson Reed threw a dollar on top of the books and walked away.

"I *will* not do it!" Harold Green said to his wife that same evening. They were in the bathroom of their home. Bending over the face bowl, she was washing her hair with a towel draped around her neck. The grocer stood by the door, looking in at her. "I will not bankrupt myself tomorrow," he said.

"I've been thinking about it, too," Ruth Green said, shaking her wet hair. "You'll do it, Harry."

"Why should I?" he asked. "You won't leave. You know it was a bluff. I've waited this long for you to calm down. Tomorrow is Saturday. This week has been a hard one. Tonight let's be realistic."

"Of course you'll do it," Ruth Green said. She said it the way she would say "Have some toast." She said, "You'll do it because you want to see your children grow up."

"And for what other reason?" he asked.

She pulled the towel tighter around her neck. "Because you are at heart a moral man."

He grinned painfully. "If I am, why should I have to prove it to *them?*"

"Not them," Ruth Green said, freezing her movements and looking in the mirror. "Certainly not them. By no means them. They have absolutely nothing to do with this."

"Who, then?" he asked, moving from the door into the room. "Who else should I prove something to?"

His wife was crying. But her entire face was wet. The tears moved secretly down her face.

"Who else?" Harold Green asked.

It was almost 11:00 P.M. and the children were in bed. They had also cried when they came home from school. Ruth Green said, "For yourself, Harry. For the love that lives inside your heart."

All night the grocer thought about this.

Nelson Reed also slept little that Friday night. When he returned home from the drugstore, he reported to his wife as much of the conversation as he could remember. At first he had joked about the exchange between himself and the grocer, but as more details returned to his conscious mind he grew solemn and then bitter. "He ask me to put myself in *his* place," Reed told his wife. "Can you imagine that kind of gumption? I never cheated nobody in my life. All my life I have lived on Bible principles. I am a deacon in the church. I have work all my life for other folks and I don't even own the house I live in." He paced up and down the kitchen, his big arms flapping loosely at his sides. Betty Reed sat at the table, watching. "This here's a low-down, ass-kicking world," he said. "I swear to God it is! All my life I have lived on principle and I ain't got a dime in the bank. Betty," he turned suddenly toward her, "don't you think I'm a fool?"

"Mr. Reed," she said. "Let's go on to bed."

But he would not go to bed. Instead, he took the fifth of bourbon from the cabinet under the sink and poured himself a shot. His wife refused to join him. Reed drained the glass of whiskey, and then another, while he resumed pacing the kitchen floor. He slapped his hands against his sides. "I think I'm a fool," he said. "Ain't got a dime in the bank, ain't got a pot to *pee* in or a wall to pitch it over, and that there *cheat* ask me to put myself inside *his* shoes. Hell, I can't even *afford* the kind of shoes he wears." He stopped pacing and looked at his wife.

"Mr. Reed," she whispered, "tomorrow ain't a work day. Let's go to bed."

Nelson Reed laughed, the bitterness in his voice rattling his wife. "The *hell* I will!" he said.

He strode to the yellow telephone on the wall beside the sink and began to dial. The first call was to Lloyd Dukes, a neighbor two blocks away and a lieutenant in the organization. Dukes was not at home. The second call was to McElroy's Bar on the corner of 65th and Carroll, where Stanley Harper, another of the lieutenants, worked as a bartender. It was Harper who spread the word, among those men at the bar, that the organization would picket the grocer's store the following morning. And all through the night, in the bedroom of their house, Betty Reed was awakened by telephone calls coming from Lester Jones, Nat Lucas, Mrs.

Tyrone Brown, the widow-woman named Murphy, all coordinating the time when they would march in a group against the store owned by Harold Green. Betty Reed's heart beat loudly beneath the covers as she listened to the bitterness and rage in her husband's voice. On several occasions, hearing him declare himself a fool, she pressed the pillow against her eyes and cried.

The grocer opened later than usual this Saturday morning, but still it was early enough to make him one of the first walkers in the neighborhood. He parked his car one block from the store and strolled to work. There were no birds singing. The sky in this area was not blue. It was smog-smutted and gray, seeming on the verge of a light rain. The street, as always, was littered with cans, papers, bits of broken glass. As always the garbage cans overflowed. The morning breeze plastered a sheet of newspaper playfully around the sides of a rusted garbage can. For some reason, using his right foot, he loosened the paper and stood watching it slide into the street and down the block. The movement made him feel good. He whistled while unlocking the bars shielding the windows and door of his store. When he had unlocked the main door he stepped in quickly and threw a switch to the right of the jamb, before the shrill sound of the alarm could shatter his mood. Then he switched on the lights. Everything was as it had been the night before. He had already telephoned his two employees and given them the day off. He busied himself doing the usual things—hauling milk and vegetables from the cooler, putting cash in the till—not thinking about the silence of his wife, or the look in her eyes, only an hour before when he left home. He had determined, at some point while driving through the city, that today it would be business as usual. But he expected very few customers.

The first customer of the day was Mrs. Nelson Reed. She came in around 9:30 A.M. and wandered about the store. He watched her from the checkout counter. She seemed uncertain of what she wanted to buy. She kept glancing at him down the center aisle. His suspicions aroused, he said finally, "Yes, may I help you, Mrs. Reed?" His words caused her to jerk, as if some devious thought had been perceived going through her mind. She reached over quickly and lifted a loaf of whole wheat bread from the rack and walked with it to the counter. She looked at him and smiled. The smile was a broad, shy one, that rare kind of smile one sees on virgin girls when they first confess love to themselves. Betty Reed was a woman of about forty-five. For some reason he could not comprehend, this gesture touched him. When she pulled a dollar from her purse and laid it on the counter, an impulse, from no place he could locate with his mind, seized control of his tongue. "Free," he told Betty Reed. She paused, then pushed the dollar toward him with a firm and determined thrust of her arm. "Free," he heard himself saying strongly, his right palm spread and meeting her thrust with absolute force. She clutched the loaf of bread and walked out of his store.

The next customer, a little girl, arriving well after 10:30 A.M., selected a candy bar from the rack beside the counter. "Free," Green said cheerfully. The little girl left the candy on the counter and ran out of the store.

At 11:15 A.M. a wino came in looking desperate enough to sell his soul. The grocer watched him only for an instant. Then he went to the wine counter and selected a half-gallon of medium-grade red wine. He shoved the jug into the belly of the wino, the man's sour breath bathing his face. "Free," the grocer said. "But you must not drink it in here."

He felt good about the entire world, watching the wino through the window gulping the wine and looking guiltily around.

At 11:25 A.M. the pickets arrived.

Two dozen people, men and women, young and old, crowded the pavement in front of his store. Their signs, placards, and voices denounced him as a parasite. The grocer laughed inside himself. He felt lighthearted and wild, like a man drugged. He rushed to the meat counter and pulled a long roll of brown wrapping paper from the rack, tearing it neatly with a quick shift of his body resembling a dance step practiced fervently in his youth. He laid the paper on the chopping block and with the black-inked, felt-tipped marker scrawled, in giant letters, the word Free. This he took to the window and pasted in place with many strands of Scotch tape. He was laughing wildly. "Free!" he shouted from behind the brown paper. "Free! Free! Free! Free! Free! Free!" He rushed to the door, pushed his head out, and screamed to the confused crowd, "Free!" Then he ran back to the counter and stood behind it, like a soldier at attention.

They came in slowly.

Nelson Reed entered first, working his right foot across the dirty tile as if tracking a squiggling worm. The others followed: Lloyd Dukes dragging a placard, Mr. and Mrs. Tyrone Brown, Stanley Harper walking with his fists clenched, Lester Jones with three of his children, Nat Lucas looking sheepish and detached, a clutch of winos, several bashful nuns, ironic-smiling teenagers and a few students. Bringing up the rear was a bearded social scientist holding a tape recorder to his chest. "Free!" the grocer screamed. He threw up his arms in a gesture that embraced, or dismissed, the entire store. "All free!" he shouted. He was grinning with the grace of a madman.

The winos began grabbing first. They stripped the shelf of wine in a matter of seconds. Then they fled, dropping bottles on the tile in their wake. The others, stepping quickly through this liquid, soon congealed it into a sticky, blood-like consistency. The young men went for the cigarettes and luncheon meats and beer. One of them had the prescience to grab a sack from the counter, while the others loaded their arms swiftly, hugging cartons and packages of cold cuts like long-lost friends. The students joined them, less for greed than for the thrill of the experience. The two nuns backed toward the door. As for the older people, men and women, they stood at first as if stuck to the wine-smeared floor. Then Stanley

Harper, the bartender, shouted, "The man said *free*, y'all heard him." He paused. "Didn't you say *free* now?" he called to the grocer.

"I said free," Harold Green answered, his temples pounding.

A cheer went up. The older people began grabbing, as if the secret lusts of a lifetime had suddenly seized command of their arms and eyes. They grabbed toilet tissue, cold cuts, pickles, sardines, boxes of raisins, boxes of starch, cans of soup, tins of tuna fish and salmon, bottles of spices, cans of boned chicken, slippery cans of olive oil. Here a man, Lester Jones, burdened himself with several heads of lettuce, while his wife, in another aisle, shouted for him to drop those small items and concentrate on the gourmet section. She herself took imported sardines, wheat crackers, bottles of candied pickles, herring, anchovies, imported olives, French wafers, an ancient, half-rusted can of paté, stocked, by mistake, from the inventory of another store. Others packed their arms with detergents, hams, chocolate-coated cereal, whole chickens with hanging asses, wedges of bologna and salami like squashed footballs, chunks of cheeses, yellow and white, shriveled onions, and green peppers. Mrs. Tyrone Brown hung a curve of pepperoni around her neck and seemed to take on instant dignity, much like a person of noble birth in possession now of a long sought-after gem. Another woman, the widow Murphy, stuffed tomatoes into her bosom, holding a half-chewed lemon in her mouth. The more enterprising fought desperately over the three rusted shopping carts, and the victors wheeled these along the narrow aisles, sweeping into them bulk items—beer in six-packs, sacks of sugar, flour, glass bottles of syrup, toilet cleanser, sugar cookies, prune, apple and tomato juices—while others endeavored to snatch the carts from them. There were several fistfights and much cursing. The grocer, standing behind the counter, hummed and rang his cash register like a madman.

Nelson Reed, the first into the store, followed the nuns out, empty-handed.

In less than half an hour the others had stripped the store and vanished in many directions up and down the block. But still more people came, those late in hearing the news. And when they saw the shelves were bare, they cursed soberly and chased those few stragglers still bearing away goods. Soon only the grocer and the social scientist remained, the latter stationed at the door with his tape recorder sucking in leftover sounds. Then he too slipped away up the block.

By 12:10 P.M. the grocer was leaning against the counter, trying to make his mind slow down. Not a man given to drink during work hours, he nonetheless took a swallow from a bottle of wine, a dusty bottle from beneath the wine shelf, somehow overlooked by the winos. Somewhat recovered, he was preparing to remember what he should do next when he glanced toward a figure at the door. Nelson Reed was standing there, watching him.

"All gone," Harold Green said. "My friend, Mr. Reed, there is no more." Still the man stood in the doorway, peering into the store.

The grocer waved his arms about the empty room. Not a display case had a single item standing. "All gone," he said again, as if addressing a stupid child. "There is nothing left to get. You, my friend, have come back too late for a second load. I am cleaned out."

Nelson Reed stepped into the store and strode toward the counter. He moved through wine-stained flour, lettuce leaves, red, green, and blue labels, bits and pieces of broken glass. He walked toward the counter.

"All day," the grocer laughed, not quite hysterically now, "all day long I have not made a single cent of profit. The entire day was a loss. This store, like the others, is *bleeding* me." He waved his arms about the room in a magnificent gesture of uncaring loss. "Now do you understand?" he said. "Now will you put yourself in my shoes? I have nothing here. Come, now, Mr. Reed, would it not be so bad a thing to walk in my shoes?"

"Mr. Green," Nelson Reed said coldly. "My wife bought a loaf of bread in here this mornin'. She forgot to pay you. I, myself, have come here to pay you your money."

"Oh," the grocer said.

"I think it was brown bread. Don't that cost more than white?"

The two men looked away from each other, but not at anything in the store.

"In my store, yes," Harold Green said. He rang the register with the most casual movement of his finger. The register read fifty-five cents.

Nelson Reed held out a dollar.

"And two cents tax," the grocer said.

The man held out the dollar.

"After all," Harold Green said. "We are all, after all, Mr. Reed, in debt to the government."

He rang the register again. It read fifty-seven cents.

Nelson Reed held out a dollar.

Study and Discussion Questions

1. What kind of person is Harold Green? Why does he refuse for so long to "bend"? When he finally gives his groceries away, why does he keep shouting "free"?
2. What kind of person is Nelson Reed? Why does he emerge as a leader of the protest? Why does he persist?
3. How do the attitudes of Ruth Green and Betty Reed towards the conflict differ from those of their husbands? Why?
4. Characterize the narrator's attitude towards the events narrated.
5. What is the significance of Green and his brother-in-law's discussion of business ethics? What does it reveal about Green?
6. At the end, why does Reed insist on paying for the loaf of bread? Why doesn't Green refuse the money? What does the ending mean?

Writing Exercises

1. At their meeting, Green tells Reed: "I do not make a profit here because the people are black. I make a profit because a profit is here to be made." Explain the distinction Green is trying to make. Does it make sense? What does Green's statement suggest about the society he lives in?

2. What do you think of Green's method (forced on him by his wife) of making amends? Can you think of a better way? Can amends be made?

NADINE GORDIMER   (b. 1923)

Nadine Gordimer was born in South Africa and lives in its capital, Johannesburg. She was educated in private schools and attended the University of Witwatersrand for a year. She has been a leading white critic of apartheid, the system of racial separation and white supremacy that structures life in South Africa, and some of her writings have been banned by the government. Her fiction includes the novels The Lying Days *(1953),* Burger's Daughter *(1979), and* July's People *(1981), and the short story collections* Friday's Footprint *(1960) and* Livingstone's Companions *(1972).*

Something for the Time Being   (1960)

He thought of it as discussing things with her, but the truth was that she did not help him out at all. She said nothing, while she ran her hand up the ridge of bone behind the rim of her child-sized yellow-brown ear, and raked her fingers tenderly into her hairline along the back of her neck as if feeling out some symptom in herself. Yet her listening was very demanding; when he stopped at the end of a supposition or a suggestion, her silence made the stop inconclusive. He had to take up again what he had said, carry it—where?

'Ve vant to give you a tsance, but you von't let us,' he mimicked; and made a loud glottal click, half-angry, resentfully amused. He knew it wasn't because Kalzin Brothers were Jews that he had lost his job at last, but just because he had lost it, Mr Solly's accent suddenly presented to him the irresistibly vulnerable. He had come out of prison nine days before, after spending three months as an awaiting-trial prisoner in a political case that had just been quashed—he was one of those who would not accept bail. He had been in prison three or four times since 1952; his wife Ella and the Kalzin Brothers were used to it. Until now, his employers had always given him his job back when he came out. They were importers of china and glass and he was head packer in a team of black men who ran the dispatch department. 'Well, what the hell, I'll get something else,' he said. 'Hey?'

She stopped the self-absorbed examination of the surface of her skin for a slow moment and shrugged, looking at him.

He smiled.

Her gaze loosened hold like hands falling away from grasp. The ends of her nails pressed at small imperfections in the skin of her neck. He drank his tea and tore off pieces of bread to dip in it; then he noticed the tin of sardines she had opened and sopped up the pale matrix of oil in which ragged flecks of silver were suspended. She offered him more tea, without speaking.

They lived in one room of a decent, three-roomed house belonging to someone else; it was better for her that way, since he was often likely to have to be away for long stretches. She worked in a factory that made knitted socks; there was no one at home to look after their one child, a girl, and the child lived with a grandmother in a dusty, peaceful village a day's train-journey from the city.

He said, dismissing it as of no importance, 'I wonder what chance they meant? You can imagine. I don't suppose they were going to give me an office with my name on it.' He spoke as if she would appreciate the joke. She had known when she married him that he was a political man; she had been proud of him because he didn't merely want something for himself, like the other young men she knew, but everything, and for *the people*. It had excited her, under his influence, to change her awareness of herself as a young black girl to awareness of herself as belonging to the people. She knew that everything wasn't like something—a hand-out, a wangled privilege, a trinket you could hold. She would never get something from him.

Her hand went on searching over her skin as if it must come soon, come anxiously, to the flaw, the sickness, the evidence of what was wrong with her; for on this Saturday afternoon all these things that she knew had deserted her. She had lost her wits. All that she could understand was the one room, the child growing up far away in the mud house, and the fact that you couldn't keep a job if you kept being away from work for weeks at a time.

'I think I'd better look up Flora Donaldson,' he said. Flora Donaldson was a white woman who had set up an office to help political prisoners. 'Sooner the better. Perhaps she'll dig up something for me by Monday. It's the beginning of the month.'

He got on all right with those people. Ella had met Flora Donaldson once; she was a pretty white woman who looked just like any white woman who would automatically send a black face round to the back door, but she didn't seem to know that she was white and you were black.

He pulled the curtain that hung across one corner of the room and took out his suit. It was a thin suit, of the kind associated with holiday-makers in American clothing advertisements, and when he was dressed in it, with a sharp-brimmed grey hat tilted slightly back on his small head, he looked a wiry, boyish figure, rather like one of those boy-men who sing and shake before a microphone, and whose clothes admirers try to touch as a talisman.

He kissed her good-bye, obliging her to put down, the lowering of a defence, the piece of sewing she held. She had cleared away the dishes from the table and set up the sewing-machine, and he saw that the shapes of cut material that lay on the table were the parts of a small girl's dress.

She spoke suddenly. 'And when the next lot gets tired of you?'

'When that lot gets tired of me, I'll get another job again, that's all.'

She nodded, very slowly, and her hand crept back to her neck.

'Who was that?' Madge Chadders asked.

Her husband had been out into the hall to answer the telephone.

'Flora Donaldson. I wish you'd explain to these people exactly what sort of factory I've got. It's so embarrassing. She's trying to find a job for some chap, he's a skilled packer. There's no skilled packing done in my workshop, no skilled jobs at all done by black men. What on earth can I offer the fellow? She says he's desperate and anything will do.'

Madge had the broken pieces of a bowl on a newspaper spread on the Persian carpet. 'Mind the glue, darling! There, just next to your foot. Well, anything is better than nothing. I suppose it's someone who was in the Soganiland sedition case. Three months awaiting trial taken out of their lives, and now they're chucked back to fend for themselves.'

William Chadders had not had any black friends or mixed with coloured people on any but master-servant terms until he married Madge, but his views on the immorality and absurdity of the colour bar were sound; sounder, she often felt, than her own, for they were backed by the impersonal authority of a familiarity with the views of great thinkers, saints and philosophers, with history, political economy, sociology and anthropology. She knew only what she felt. And she always did something, at once, to express what she felt. She never measured the smallness of her personal protest against the establishment she opposed; she marched with Flora and eight hundred black women in a demonstration against African women being forced to carry passes; outside the university where she had once been a student, she stood between sandwich-boards bearing messages of mourning because a Bill had been passed closing the university, for the future, to all but white students; she had living in the house for three months a young African who wanted to write and hadn't the peace or space to get on with it in a location. She did not stop to consider the varying degree of usefulness of the things she did, and if others pointed this out to her and suggested that she might make up her mind to throw her weight on the side either of politics or philanthropy, she was not resentful but answered candidly that there was so little it was possible to do that she simply took any and every chance to get off her chest her disgust at the colour bar. When she had married William Chadders, her friends had thought that her protestant activities would stop; they underestimated not only Madge, but also William, who, although he was a wealthy businessman, subscribed to the view of absolute personal freedom as strictly as any bohemian. Besides he was not fool enough to want to change in any way the person who had enchanted him just as she was.

She reacted upon him, rather than he upon her; she, of course, would not hesitate to go ahead and change anybody. (But why not? she would have said, astonished. If it's to the good?) The attitude she sought to change would occur to her as something of independent existence, she would not see it as a cell in the organism of personality, whose whole structure would have to regroup itself round the change. She had the boldness of being unaware of these consequences.

William did not carry a banner in the streets, of course; he worked up there, among his first principles and historical precedents and economic necessities, but now they were translated from theory to practice of an anonymous, large-scale and behind-the-scenes sort—he was the brains and part of the money in a scheme to get Africans some economic power besides consumer power, through the setting up of an all-African trust company and investment corporation. A number of Madge's political friends, both white and black (like her activities, her friends were mixed, some political, some do-gooders), thought this was putting the middle-class cart before the proletarian horse, but most of the African leaders welcomed the attempt as an essential backing to popular movements on other levels—something to count on outside the unpredictability of mobs. Sometimes it amused Madge to think that William, making a point at a meeting in a boardroom, fifteen floors above life in the streets, might achieve in five minutes something of more value than she did in all her days of turning her hand to anything—from sorting old clothes to roneo-ing[1] a manifesto or driving people during a bus boycott. Yet this did not knock the meaning out of her own life, for her; she knew that she had to see, touch and talk to people in order to care about them, that's all there was to it.

Before she and her husband dressed to go out that evening she finished sticking together the broken Chinese bowl and showed it to him with satisfaction. To her, it was whole again. But it was one of a set, that had belonged together, and whose unity had illustrated certain philosophical concepts. William had bought them long ago, in London; for him, the whole set was damaged for ever.

He said nothing to her, but he was thinking of the bowls when she said to him as they drove off, 'Will you see that chap, on Monday, yourself?'

He changed gear deliberately, attempting to follow her out of his preoccupation. But she said, 'The man Flora's sending. What was his name?'

---

[1] A form of duplicating.

He opened his hand on the steering wheel, indicating that the name escaped him.

'See him yourself?'

'I'll have to leave it to the works manager to find something for him to do,' he said.

'Yes, I know. But see him yourself, too?'

Her anxious voice made him feel very fond of her. He turned and smiled at her suspiciously. 'Why?'

She was embarrassed at his indulgent manner. She said, frank and wheedling, 'Just to show him. You know. That you know about him and it's not much of a job.'

'All right,' he said. 'I'll see him myself.'

He met her in town straight from the office on Monday and they went to the opening of an exhibition of paintings and on to dinner and to see a play, with friends. He had not been home at all, until they returned after midnight. It was a summer night and they sat for a few minutes on their terrace, where it was still mild with the warmth of the day's sun coming from the walls in the darkness, and drank lime juice and water to quench the thirst that wine and the stuffy theatre had given them. Madge made gasps and groans of pleasure at the release from the pressures of company and noise. Then she lay quiet for a while, her voice lifting now and then in fragments of unrelated comment on the evening—the occasional chirp of a bird that has already put its head under its wing for the night.

By the time they went in, they were free of the evening. Her black dress, her ear-rings and her bracelets felt like fancy-dress; she shed the character and sat on the bedroom carpet, and, passing her, he said, 'Oh— that chap of Flora's came today, but I don't think he'll last. I explained to him that I didn't have the sort of job he was looking for.'

'Well, that's all right, then,' she said enquiringly. 'What more could you do?'

'Yes,' he said, deprecating. 'But I could see he didn't like the idea much. It's a cleaner's job; nothing for him. He's an intelligent chap. I didn't like having to offer it to him.'

She was moving about her dressing table, piling out upon it the contents of her handbag. 'Then I'm sure he'll understand. It'll give him something for the time being, anyway, darling. You can't help it if you don't need the sort of work he does.'

'Huh, he won't last. I could see that. He accepted it, but only with his head. He'll get fed up. Probably won't turn up tomorrow. I had to speak to him about his Congress[2] button, too. The works manager came to me.'

'What about his Congress button?' she said.

He was unbuttoning his shirt and his eyes were on the unread evening paper that lay folded on the bed. 'He was wearing one,' he said inattentively.

---

[2] African National Congress, South African anti-apartheid organization.

'I know, but what did you have to speak to him about it for?'

'He was wearing it in the workshop all day.'

'Well, what about it?' She was sitting at her dressing-table, legs spread, as if she had sat heavily and suddenly. She was not looking at him, but at her own face.

He gave the paper a push and drew his pyjamas from under the pillow. Vulnerable and naked, he said authoritatively, 'You can't wear a button like that among the men in the workshop.'

'Good heavens,' she said, almost in relief, laughing, backing away from the edge of tension, chivvying him out of a piece of stuffiness. 'And why can't you?'

'You can't have someone clearly representing a political organization like Congress.'

'But he's not there *representing* anything, he's there as a workman?' Her mouth was still twitching with something between amusement and nerves.

'Exactly.'

'Then why can't he wear a button that signifies his allegiance to an organization in his private life outside the workshop? There's no rule about not wearing tie-pins or club buttons or anything, in the workshop, is there?'

'No, there isn't, but that's not quite the same thing.'

'My dear William,' she said, 'it is exactly the same. It's nothing to do with the works manager whether the man wears a Rotary button, or an Elvis Presley button, or an African National Congress button. It's damn all his business.'

'No, Madge, I'm sorry,' William said, patient, 'but it's not the same. I can give the man a job because I feel sympathetic towards the struggle he's in, but I can't put him in the workshop as a Congress man. I mean that wouldn't be fair to Fowler. That I can't do to Fowler.' He was smiling as he went towards the bathroom, but his profile, as he turned into the doorway, was incisive.

She sat on at her dressing-table, pulling a comb through her hair, dragging it down through knots. Then she rested her face on her palms, caught sight of herself and became aware, against her fingers, of the curving shelf of bone, like the lip of a strong shell, under each eye. Everyone has his own intimations of mortality. For her, the feel of the bone beneath the face, in any living creature, brought her the message of the skull. Once hollowed out of this, outside the world, too. For what it's worth. It's worth a lot, the world, she affirmed, as she always did, life rising at once in her as a fish opens its jaws to a fly. It's worth a lot; and she sighed and got up with the sigh.

She went into the bathroom and sat down on the edge of the bath. He was lying there in the water, his chin relaxed on his chest, and he smiled at her. She said, 'You mean you don't want Fowler to know.'

'Oh,' he said, seeing where they were again. 'What is it I don't want Fowler to know?'

'You don't want your partner to know that you slip black men with political ideas into your workshop. Cheeky kaffir agitators. Specially a man who's been in jail for getting people to defy the government!—What was his name; you never said?'

'Daniel something. I don't know. Mongoma or Ngoma. Something like that.'

A line like a cut appeared between her eyebrows. 'Why can't you remember his name?' Then she went on at once, 'You don't want Fowler to know what you think, do you? That's it? You want to pretend you're like him, you don't mind the native in his place. You want to pretend that to please Fowler. You don't want Fowler to think you're cracked or Communist or whatever it is that good-natured, kind, jolly rich people like old Fowler think about people like us.'

'I couldn't have less interest in what Fowler thinks outside our board-room. And inside it, he never thinks about anything but how to sell more earth-moving gear.'

'I don't mind the native in his place. You want him to think you go along with all that.' She spoke aloud, but she seemed to be telling herself rather than him.

'Fowler and I run a factory. Our only common interest is the efficient running of that factory. Our *only* one. The factory depends on a stable, satisfied black labour-force, and that we've got. Right, you and I know that the whole black wage standard is too low, right, we know that they haven't a legal union to speak for them, right, we know that the conditions they live under make it impossible for them really to be stable. All that. But the fact is, so far as accepted standards go in this crazy country, they're a stable, satisfied labour-force with better working conditions than most. So long as I'm a partner in a business that lives by them, I can't officially admit an element that represents dissatisfaction with their lot.'

'A green badge with a map of Africa on it,' she said.

'If you make up your mind not to understand, you don't, and there it is,' he said indulgently.

'You give him a job but you make him hide his Congress button.'

He began to soap himself. She wanted everything to stop while she inquired into things, she could not go on while a remark was unexplained or a problem unsettled, but he represented a principle she subscribed to but found so hard to follow, that life must go on, trivially, commonplace, the trailing hem of the only power worth clinging to. She smoothed the film of her nightgown over the shape of her knees, over and over, and presently she said, in exactly the flat tone of statement that she had used before, the flat tone that was the height of belligerence in her, 'He can say and do what he likes, he can call for strikes and boycotts and anything he likes, outside the factory, but he mustn't wear his Congress button at work.'

He was standing up, washing his body that was full of scars; she knew them all, from the place on his left breast where a piece of shrapnel had gone in, all the way back to the place under his arm where he had torn himself on barbed wire as a child. 'Yes, of course, anything he likes.'

'Anything except his self-respect,' she grumbled to herself. 'Pretend, pretend. Pretend he doesn't belong to a political organization. Pretend he doesn't want to be a man. Pretend he hasn't been to prison for what he believes.' Suddenly she spoke to her husband: 'You'll let him have anything except the one thing worth giving.'

They stood in uncomfortable proximity to each other, in the smallness of the bathroom. They were at once aware of each other as people who live in intimacy are only when hostility returns each to the confines of himself. He felt himself naked before her, where he had stepped out onto the towelling mat, and he took a towel and slowly covered himself, pushing the free end in round his waist. She felt herself an intrusion and, in silence, went out.

Her hands were tingling as if she were coming round from a faint. She walked up and down the bedroom floor like someone waiting to be summoned, called to account. I'll forget about it, she kept thinking, very fast, I'll forget about it again. Take a sip of water. Read another chapter. Don't call a halt. Let things flow, cover up, go on.

But when he came into the room with his wet hair combed and his stranger's face, and he said, 'You're angry,' it came from her lips, a black bird in the room, before she could understand what she had released— 'I'm not angry. I'm beginning to get to know you.'

Ella Mngoma knew he was going to a meeting that evening and didn't expect him home early. She put the paraffin lamp on the table so that she could see to finish the child's dress. It was done, buttons and all, by the time he came in at half past ten.

'Well, now we'll see what happens. I've got them to accept, *in principle*, that in future we won't take bail. You should have seen Ben Tsolo's face when I said that we lent the government our money interest-free when we paid bail. That really hit him. That was language he understood.' He laughed, and did not seem to want to sit down, the heat of the meeting still upon him. '*In principle.* Yes, it's easy to accept in principle. We'll see.'

She pumped the primus[3] and set a pot of stew to warm up for him. 'Ah, that's nice.' He saw the dress. 'Finished already?' And she nodded vociferously in pleasure; but at once she noticed his forefinger run lightly along the braid round the neck, and the traces of failure that were always at the bottom of her cup tasted on her tongue again. Probably he was not even aware of it, or perhaps his instinct for what was true—the plumb

---

[3] Portable oil stove.

line, the coin with the right ring—led him absently to it, but the fact was that she had botched the neck.

She had an almost Oriental delicacy about not badgering him and she waited until he had washed and sat down to eat before she asked, 'How did the job go?'

'Oh that,' he said. 'It went.' He was eating quickly, moving his tongue strongly round his mouth to marshal the bits of meat that escaped his teeth. She was sitting with him, feeling, in spite of herself, the rest of satisfaction in her evening's work. 'Didn't you get it?'

'It got *me*. But I got loose again, all right.'

She watched his face to see what he meant. 'They don't want you to come back tomorrow?'

He shook his head, no, no, no, to stem the irritation of her suppositions. He finished his mouthful and said, 'Everything very nice. Boss takes me into his office, apologizes for the pay, he knows it's not the sort of job I should have and so forth. So I go off and clean up in the assembly shop. Then at lunchtime he calls me into the office again: they don't want me to wear my A.N.C. badge at work. Flora Donaldson's sympathetic white man, who's going to do me the great favour of paying me three pounds a week.' He laughed. 'Well, there you are.'

She kept on looking at him. Her eyes widened and her mouth tightened; she was trying to prime herself to speak, or was trying not to cry. The idea of tears exasperated him and he held her with a firm, almost belligerently inquiring gaze. Her hand went up round the back of her neck under her collar, anxiously exploratory. 'Don't do that!' he said. 'You're like a monkey catching lice.'

She took her hand down swiftly and broke into trembling, like a sweat. She began to breathe hysterically. 'You couldn't put it in your pocket, for the day,' she said wildly, grimacing at the bitterness of malice towards him.

He jumped up from the table. 'Christ! I knew you'd say it! I've been waiting for you to say it. You've been wanting to say it for five years. Well, now it's out. Out with it. Spit it out!' She began to scream softly as if he were hitting her. The impulse to cruelty left him and he sat down before his dirty plate, where the battered spoon lay among bits of gristle and potato-eyes. Presently he spoke. 'You come out and you think there's everybody waiting for you. The truth is, there isn't anybody. You think straight in prison because you've got nothing to lose. Nobody thinks straight, outside. They don't want to hear you. What are you all going to do with me, Ella? Send me back to prison as quickly as possible? Perhaps I'll get a banishment order next time. That'd do. That's what you've got for me. I must keep myself busy with that kind of thing.'

He went over to her and said, in a kindly voice, kneading her shoulder with spread fingers, 'Don't cry. Don't cry. You're just like any other woman.'

Study and Discussion Questions

1. Compare Madge's attitudes towards injustice and protest with those of her husband William. How are their differences suggested by the relation of each to the broken Chinese bowl? How might you explain the differences?

2. Compare Daniel's and Ella's attitudes towards injustice and protest. How might you explain these differences? What is the significance of the story's title?

3. How are the two marital conflicts similar and how are they different? What do the two men have in common? The two women?

4. Compare the environments, the physical contexts of the two couples' arguments.

5. Why does Gordimer begin and end the story with the black couple and yet devote more time to the white couple? Who would you guess her primary audience is?

Writing Exercises

1. Daniel Mngoma says: "You think straight in prison because you've got nothing to lose. Nobody thinks straight, outside." Discuss the story in light of this remark.

2. Who is right, Daniel or Ella?

LAKE SAGARIS (b. 1956?)

Lake Sagaris was born in Santiago, Chile, and teaches language and translation there. She has published poetry and fiction in Chile, the United States, and Canada, and is translating an anthology of Canadian literature into Spanish.

The March   (1983)

She started up out of her sleep, like a mother who has lost her child. She rubbed her eyes with unaccustomed force and looked around her, feeling the unusual silence of the place. Where was she? Shreds of dreams and memory clung to her and she had trouble knowing which was which.

She stared at the canvas walls, hastily put together, eyes of light peering at her through the holes. Then she remembered something. Tito! Where was he?

She scrambled up off the floor and only then did she realize how stiff and bruised she felt. What had happened? She went outside. The tent crouched with a hundred others, grey, weatherbeaten, huddled together as if a wolf were stalking the horizon.

A shadow of voices murmuring, the clatter of pots and pans and the smell of beans for breakfast (the same odor which had followed them from home to here, the big city, the capital, the President's house . . . ah, that was it, the President). But where was Tito? Her dark-eyed, skinny son, with two dimples so deep it looked like his smile had been nailed on. Indeed, his three-year-old eyes expressed an anguish that made his smile unreal, irrelevant.

"Tito!" she cried. "Tito! Where are you? Come here." A gust of empty wind darted past her, but nothing more, no answer, no footsteps, no voices whispered in the dry canvas, hot under the midday sun.

She saw her old shawl, now a clumsy tent door, and remembered trying to decide whether to take it or not. She heard Chavela's voice calling her: "Rosamaría! Ven pu'h! Nos vamos ahora mismo,"[1] and she remembered grabbing Tito's hand and hurrying after her friend.

That was it, of course. That's why there was no one here. They had risen early to go downtown to see the President, to tell him everything, to ask for help.

'But I went with them,' she thought, confused. With little Tito beside me, his thin legs agile as a spider's even though he's only three years old.

She remembered the time he'd gone wandering and got locked behind the heavy wooden door where they parked the mine vehicles. Less than a year old and he'd pulled and crawled his way up the door. She had turned at the sound of his plaintive "ma—ma," only to see his head disappear abruptly as he lost his grip and fell.

She could hear him crying as she threw herself against the rough boards, trying to get to him. And then she was rolling on the ground, her son beside her, the security guard who had opened the door laughing down at them. His laughter was rain-fresh. She looked at her wandering son and she too began to laugh. A sudden smile chased the tears from Tito's face.

He's a tough one, she thought proudly, as hard and dark as the coal they tear from the mines, with the same fire glowering inside.

Perhaps this is a dream, she thought. Perhaps they had only just arrived and, exhausted from the long march she was sleeping, dreaming. But she remembered the morning. Where had they all gone? Where had they taken the morning?

She looked down the dusty road that stumbled uncertainly into the city and remembered Chavela: "Ya, Rosamaría. Ven acá.[2] We're going to see the president. We're going to explain about the strike, the prices, the company store, how the children. . . ."

---

[1] Come on, already! We're going right now.

[2] Now, Rosamaría. Come here.

While she listened to her friend's confident voice, she watched his thin legs flash in the sun as he kicked a stone down the hill, and ran after it.

Dreaming or waking she walks down the hill and with each step the city moves toward her, its paved streets hold her feet, the hot air burns her face, she sees again the people's eyes, turned toward them, this raggle-taggle mob of women and children who've come to see the President, come to explain why the strike, why the men won't go back to work until the company—

"Tito," she calls. And searches among the dirty children playing on the cracked sidewalk. Tito, she calls again, unconsciously tracing the same route, following the morning, Chavela, her son's legs, the sturdy arms and backs of neighbors and friends, the white blouses clouded with dust, the dark hair streaked with grey and a hunger for justice hidden behind the wrinkled mouths, cared for by the rough hands, like a weak child, all the more loved because its time is so short.

Asleep, or awake, she follows the memory of movements down the main street toward the palace, remembers her husband's grey, gritty kiss, his eyes red from coal dust and lack of sleep, alive with something she'd never seen before. There was exhaustion, attraction, and something new, surprise, as if she were a stranger, this woman, this wife, who suddenly left the daily ticking of their life to go out and meet the President, to argue for justice for her husband, her son, for all the miners on strike. And Tito marched along beside her, or rode majestic on her broad shoulders. She remembered her husband watching her, that new expression on his face, on all the strikers' faces, their husbands, their brothers, their fathers, waiting at home for the women who left for the city.

And here she was, dreaming awake in the city, her hand full of the memory of Tito's hand, her eyes full of the memory of all those backs and steady arms, heads held high, marching to the palace gates, calling the President, calling and calling, a hundred voices, a hundred women's voices, the children laughing, a thousand voices crying out for their daily bread, not pleading, not begging, claiming the daily bread earned in the daily struggle in the mines. She had never been down a mine, but she knew it intimately. Her husband filled their house with it every night, and took it away with him when he went to work every morning.

But the road she was traveling stopped abruptly in a wooden barricade, guarded by soldiers.

"Where are you going?" one asked, stepping in front of her, his machine gun cradled in his arms.

"I want my son," she said. "We came by here. I remember."

He looked at her. A shadow crossed his face. He pushed her away.

"Move along, lady. The road to the palace is closed. You can't pass."

She had been at the end of the long line of women. Tito had wandered off; she remembered seeing him kick a stone and run and then a line of soldiers, and then the thunder of bullets as if the whole world had caved in. And she was running toward her son, and someone beside her fell and clutched her leg. Chavela grabbed her arm and dragged her away screaming, from the President, the shiny clean palace, the soldiers calmly firing. Chavela fell and she had run and run and run, forgetting everything except the time Tito fell off the wooden door, the security guard laughing, his gun a toy in friendly hands, Tito's dimples so deep, like two nails, his hands, the time Tito fell before the soldiers, his dimples obliterated by the sharp teeth of hungry bullets, chewing his face until it was nothing but blood and grey, spongy thoughts that might have been love or mother or one day the mine—

And she was running toward him, ducking under the barricade, past police cars, tanks, ambulances, somewhere here her son, Chavela, she had to take them home, she had to tell the President, she had to tell the men on strike, the President—! the company—!

The machine gun fire.

And no more memories. No more dreams.

Study and Discussion Questions

1. Give examples of how the writer foreshadows what we will come to know later in the story.
2. What emotional state is the narrator in?
3. What function is served in the story by the episode where Tito is "locked behind the heavy wooden door where they parked the mine vehicles"?
4. Why do the women and children go to see the president?
5. How does the narrator's husband feel about her going on the march? How does *she* feel about it?
6. What has in fact happened in this story?

Writing Exercises

1. How does Sagaris distort time in this story? Why do you think she does this?
2. What was your emotional response to this story as you read it?

DOROTHY CANFIELD FISHER   (1879–1958)

Dorothy Canfield Fisher was born in Lawrence, Kansas and studied at Ohio State University, at the Sorbonne, and at Columbia University, from which she received a Ph.D. in comparative literature. She moved with new husband John Fisher to Vermont in 1907, but traveled to Rome in 1912, where she witnessed the innovative teaching methods of Maria Montessori. Fisher lived

in Europe during World War I, where she worked with an ambulance corps,
produced books for the blind, and aided refugees. Among her books, some
published under the name Dorothy Canfield, are the novels The Squirrel Cage
(1912), The Bent Twig *(1915), and* The Deepening Stream *(1930); the story*
collections Hillsboro People *(1915) and* The Real Motive *(1916); and two*
books on the Montessori method.

A Drop in the Bucket   (1913)

There is no need to describe in detail the heroine of this tale, because
she represents a type familiar to all readers of the conventional New-
England-village dialect story. She was for a long time the sole inhabitant
of Hillsboro, who came up to the expectations of our visiting friends from
the city, on the lookout for Mary Wilkins[1] characters. We always used to
take such people directly to see Cousin Tryphena, as dwellers in an Italian
city always take their foreign friends to see their one bit of ruined city
wall or the heap of stones which was once an Inquisitorial torture chamber,
never to see the new water-works or the modern, sanitary hospital.

On the way to the other end of the street, where Cousin Tryphena's
tiny, two-roomed house stood, we always laid bare the secrets of her
somnolent, respectable, unprofitable life; we always informed our visitors
that she lived and kept up a social position on two hundred and fifteen
dollars a year, and that she had never been further from home than to
the next village. We always drew attention to her one treasure, the fine
Sheraton sideboard that had belonged to her great-grandfather, old Priest
Perkins; and, when we walked away from the orderly and empty house,
we were sure that our friends from the city would always exclaim with
great insight into character, "What a charmingly picturesque life! Isn't she
perfectly delicious!"

Next door to Cousin Tryphena's minute, snow-white house is a forlorn
old building, one of the few places for rent in our village, where nearly
everyone owns his own shelter. It stood desolately idle for some time,
tumbling to pieces almost visibly, until, one day, two years ago, a burly,
white-bearded tramp stopped in front of it, laid down his stick and bundle,
and went to inquire at the neighbor's if the place were for rent, then
moved in with his stick and bundle and sent away for the rest of his
belongings, that is to say, an outfit for cobbling shoes. He cut a big
wooden boot out of the side of an empty box, painted it black with axle-
grease and soot, hung it up over the door, and announced himself as
ready to do all the cobbling and harness-repairing he could get . . . and
a fine workman he showed himself to be.

---

[1] Mary E. Wilkins Freeman. See "A Mistaken Charity" on p. 148.

We were all rather glad to have this odd new member of our community settle down among us . . . all, that is, except Cousin Tryphena, who was sure, for months afterward, that he would cut her throat some night and steal away her Sheraton sideboard. It was an open secret that Putnam, the antique-furniture dealer in Troy, had offered her two hundred and fifty dollars for it. The other women of the village, however, not living alone in such dangerous proximity to the formidable stranger, felt reassured by his long, white beard, and by his great liking for little children.

Although, from his name, as from his strong accent, it was evident that old Jombatiste belonged, by birth, to our French-Canadian colony, he never associated himself with that easy-going, devoutly Catholic, law-abiding, and rather unlettered group of our citizens. He allied himself with quite another class, making no secret of the fact that he was an out-and-out Socialist, Anti-clerical, Syndicalist, Anarchist, Nihilist. . . . We in Hillsboro are not acute in distinguishing between the different shades of radicalism, and never have been able exactly to place him, except that, beside his smashing, loudly-voiced theories, young Arthur Robbins' Progressivism sounds like old Martin Pelham's continued jubilation over the Hayes campaign.[2]

The central article of Jombatiste's passionately held creed seemed to be that everything was exactly wrong, and that, while the Socialist party was not nearly sweeping enough in its ideas, it was, as yet, the best means for accomplishing the inevitable, righteous overturning of society. Accordingly, he worked incessantly, not only at his cobbling, but at any odd job he could find to do, lived the life of an anchorite, went in rags, ate mainly crackers and milk, and sent every penny he could save to the Socialist Headquarters. We knew about this not only through his own trumpeting of the programme of his life, but because Phil Latimer, the postmaster, is cousin to us all and often told us about the money-orders, so large that they must have represented almost all the earnings of the fanatical old shoemaker.

And yet he was never willing to join in any of our charitable enterprises, although his ardent old heart was evidently as tender as it was hot. Nothing threw him into such bellowing fury as cruelty. He became the terror of all our boys who trapped rabbits, and, indeed, by the sole influence of his whirlwind descents upon them, and his highly illegal destruction of their traps, he practically made that boyish pastime a thing of the past in Hillsboro. Somehow, though the boys talked mightily about how they'd have the law of dirty, hot-tempered old Jombatiste, nobody cared really to face him. He had on tap a stream of red-hot vituperation astonishingly varied for a man of his evident lack of early education. Perhaps it came from his incessant reading and absorption of Socialist and incendiary literature.

---

[2] Probably a reference to Rutherford B. Hayes, who was elected president in 1876 even though his opponent had the greater popular vote.

He took two Socialist newspapers, and nobody knows how many queer little inflammatory magazines from which he read aloud selections to anyone who did not run away.

Naturally enough, from his point of view, he began with his neighbor, fastidious Cousin Tryphena.

What Cousin Tryphena did not know about the way the world outside of Hillsboro was run would have made a complete treatise on modern civilization. She never took a newspaper, only borrowing, once in a while, the local sheet to read the news items from Greenford, where she had some distant cousins; and, though she occasionally looked at one of the illustrated magazines, it was only at the pictures.

It is therefore plain that old Jombatiste could not have found a worse listener for his bellowed statements that ninety per cent. of the money of this country was in the hands of two per cent. of the population; that the franchise was a farce because the government was controlled by a Wall Street clique; and that any man who could not earn a good living for his family had a moral right to shoot a millionaire. For the most part, Cousin Tryphena counted her tatting stitches and paid not the least attention to her malcontent neighbor. When she did listen, she did not believe a word he said. She had lived in Hillsboro for fifty-five years and she knew what made people poor. It was shiftlessness. There was always plenty of work to be had at the brush-back factory for any man who had the sense and backbone to keep at it. If they *would* stop work in deer-week to go hunting, or go on a spree Town-meeting day, or run away to fish, she'd like to know what business they had blaming millionaires because they lost their jobs. She did not expound her opinions of these points to Jombatiste because, in the first place, she despised him for a dirty Canuck, and, secondly, because opinions seemed shadowy and unsubstantial things to her. The important matters were to make your starch clear and not to be late to church.

It is proverbial that people who are mostly silent often keep for some time a reputation for more wisdom than is theirs. Cousin Tryphena unconsciously profited in the estimation of her neighbor by this fact of psychology. Old Jombatiste had thundered his per cents. of the distribution of capital for many months before he discovered that he was on the wrong track.

Then, one winter day, as Cousin Tryphena was hanging out her washing, he ran over to her, waving his favorite magazine. He read her a paragraph from it, striking the paper occasionally for emphasis with his horny, blackened, shoemaker's hand, and following her as she moved along the clothes-lines—

"And it is thus definitely *proved*," he shouted in conclusion, "that Senator Burlingame was in the pay of J. D. Darby, when he held up the Rouse Workingman's Bill in the Senate Committee. . . ." He stopped and glared triumphantly at his neighbor. A rare impulse of perversity rose in Cousin Tryphena's unawakened heart. She took a clothes-pin out of her mouth and asked with some exasperation, "Well, what *of* it!" a comment on his information which sent the old man reeling back as though she had struck him.

In the conversation which followed, old Jombatiste, exploring at last Cousin Tryphena's mind, leaned giddily over the abyss of her ignorance of political economy and sociology, dropping one exploring plummet after another into its depths, only to find them fathomless. He went shakily back to his own house, silenced for once.

But, although for the first time he neglected work to do it, he returned to the attack the next day with a new weapon. He made no more remarks about industrial slavery, nor did he begin, as was his wont, with the solemnly enunciated axiom, "Wealth comes from labor alone!" He laid down, on the Sheraton sideboard, an armful of his little magazines, and settled himself in a chair, observing with a new comprehension how instinctively Cousin Tryphena reached for her tatting as he began to read aloud. He read the story of a man who was burned to death in molten steel because his employers did not install a rather expensive safety device, and who left a young widow and three children. These tried to earn their livings by making artificial flowers. They could earn, all of them working together, three cents an hour. When the last dollar of the dead father's savings was used up, and there was talk of separating the family so that the children could be put in an asylum, the mother drowned the three little ones and herself after them. Cousin Tryphena dropped her tatting, her country-bred mind reeling. "Didn't she have any *folks* to help her out?"

Jombatiste explained that she came from East Poland, so that her folks, if indeed she had any, were too far away to be of use. He struck one fist inside his palm with a fierce gesture, such as he used when he caught a boy trapping, and cried, ". . . and that in a country that produces three times the food it consumes." For the first time, a statistical statement awoke an echo in Cousin Tryphena's atrophied brain.

Old Jombatiste read on, this time about a girl of seventeen, left by her parents' death in charge of a small brother. She had been paid twenty cents for making crocheted lace which sold for a dollar and a half. By working twelve hours a day, she had been able to make forty-seven cents. Seeing her little brother grow pale from lack of food, she had, in desperation, taken the first, the awfully decisive first step downward, and had almost at once thereafter vanished, drawn down by the maelstrom of vice. The little brother, wild with grief over his sister's disappearance, had been taken to an orphan asylum where he had since twice tried to commit suicide.

Cousin Tryphena sat rigid, her tatting fallen to the floor, her breath coming with difficulty. It is impossible for the average modern mind, calloused by promiscuous reading, to conceive the effect upon her primitive organism of this attack from the printed page. She not only did not dream that these stories might not be true, they seemed as real to her as though she had seen the people. There was not a particle of blood in her haggard face.

Jombatiste read on . . . the story of a decent, ambitious man, employed in a sweatshop tailoring establishment, who contracted tuberculosis from the foul air, and who dragged down with him, in his agonizing descent to the very depths of misery, a wife and two children. He was now dead, and his wife was living in a corner of a moldy, damp basement, a pile of rags the only bed for her and her children, their only heat what fire the mother could make out of paper and rubbish picked up on the streets.

Cousin Tryphena's horrified eyes fell on her well-blacked stove, sending out the aromatic breath of burning white-birch sticks. She recoiled from it with a shudder.

Jombatiste read on, the story of the woman who, when her three sons died in an accident due to negligence on their employer's part . . . he read no more that day, for Cousin Tryphena put her gray head down on the center-table and wept as she never had done in her life. Jombatiste rose softly and tiptoed out of the room.

The tap-tap-tap of his hammer rang loud and fast the rest of that day. He was exulting over having aroused another bourgeois from the sleep of greasy complacency. He had made a convert. To his dire and utter pennilessness, Cousin Tryphena's tiny income seemed a fortune. He had a happy dream of persuading her to join him in his weekly contributions to the sacred funds! As he stood at midnight, in the open door, for the long draught of fresh air he always took before turning in on his pile of hay, he heard in the wood on the hill back of the house the shrill shriek of a trapped rabbit. He plowed furiously out through the deep snow to find it, gave the tortured animal a merciful death, carried the trap back to the river and threw it in with a furious splash. He strode home under the frosty stars, his dirty shirt open over his corded, old neck, his burning heart almost content. He had done a good day's work.

Early the next morning, his neighbor came to his door, very white, very hollow-eyed, evidently with a sleepless night back of her, and asked him for the papers he had read from. Jombatiste gave them to her in a tactful silence. She took them in one shaking hand, drawing her shawl around her wrinkled face with the other, and went back through the snow to her own house.

By noon that day, everyone in the village was thrilling with wild surmise. Cousin Tryphena had gone over to Graham and Sanders', asked to use their long-distance telephone and had telephoned to Putnam to come and get her sideboard. After this strange act, she had passed Albert Graham, then by chance alone in the store, with so wild a mien that he had not ventured to make any inquiries. But he took pains to mention the matter to everyone who happened to come in, that morning; and, by dinner-time, every family in Hillsboro was discussing over its pie the possibility that the well-known *queer streak*, which had sent several of

Cousin Tryphena's ancestors to the asylum, was suddenly making its appearance in her.

I was detained, that afternoon, and did not reach her house until nearly four; and I was almost the last to arrive. I found Cousin Tryphena very silent, her usually pale face very red, the center of a group of neighbors who all at once began to tell me what had happened. I could make nothing out of their incoherent explanations. . . . "Trypheny was crazy . . . she'd ought to have a guardeen . . . that Canuck shoemaker had addled her brains . . . there'd ought to be a law against that kind of newspaper. . . . Trypheny was goin' like her great-aunt, Lucilly, that died in the asylum. . . ." I appealed directly to Cousin Tryphena for information as to what the trouble was.

"There ain't any trouble's I know of," she answered in a shaking voice. "I've just heard of a widow-woman, down in the city, who's bringin' up her two children in the corner of a basement where the green mold stands out on the wall, and I'm goin' down to fetch her an' the children up here to live with me . . . them an' a little orphan boy as don't like the 'sylum where they've put him—"

Somebody broke in on her to cry, "Why, Trypheny, you simple old critter, that's four people! Where you goin' to put 'em in this little tucked-up place?"

Cousin Tryphena answered doggedly and pointedly, "Your own grandmother, Rebecca Mason, brought up a family of seven in a house no bigger than this, and no cellar."

"But how, . . ." another voice exclaimed, "air you goin' to get enough for 'em to eat? You ain't got but barely enough for yourself!"

Cousin Tryphena paled a little, "I'm a good sewer, I could make money sewing . . . and I could do washings for city-folks, summer-times. . . ." Her set mouth told what a price she paid for this voluntary abandonment of the social standing that had been hers by virtue of her idleness. She went on with sudden spirit, "You all act as though I was doin' it to spite you and to amuse myself! I don't *want* to! When I think of my things I've kept so nice always, I'm *wild* . . . but how can I help it, now I know about 'em! I didn't sleep a wink last night. I'll go clean crazy if I don't do something! I saw those three children strugglin' in the water and their mother a-holdin' on 'em down, and then jumpin' in herself—Why, I give enough milk to the *cat* to keep a baby . . . what else can I do?"

I was touched, as I think we all were, by her helpless simplicity and ignorance, and by her defenselessness against this first vision of life, the vision which had been spared her so long, only to burst upon her like a forest-fire. I had an odd fancy that she had just awakened after a sleep of half a century.

"Dear Cousin Tryphena," I said as gently as I could, "you haven't had a very wide experience of modern industrial or city conditions and there are some phases of this matter which you don't take into consideration." Then I brought out the old, wordy, eminently reasonable arguments we all use to stifle the thrust of self-questioning: I told her that it was very likely that the editor of that newspaper had invented, or at least greatly exaggerated those stories, and that she would find on investigation that no such family existed.

"I don't see how that lets me out of *lookin'* for them," said Cousin Tryphena.

"Well, at least," I urged, "don't be in such a hurry about it. Take time to think it over! Wait till—"

"Wait!" cried Cousin Tryphena. "Why, another one may be jumpin' in the river this minute! If I'd ha' had the money, I'd ha' gone on the noon train!"

At this point, the man from Putnam's came with a team from our livery to carry away the Sheraton sideboard. Cousin Tryphena bore herself like a martyr at the stake, watching, with dry eyes, the departure of her one certificate to dear gentility and receiving with proud indifference the crisp bills of a denomination most of us had never seen before.

"You won't need all that just to go down to the city," I remonstrated.

She stopped watching the men load her shining old treasure into the wagon and turned her anguished eyes to me. "They'll likely be needing clothes and things."

I gave up. She had indeed thought it all out.

It was time for us to go home to prepare our several suppers and we went our different ways, shaking our heads over Tryphena's queerness. I stopped a moment before the cobbler's open door, watched him briskly sewing a broken halter and telling a folk-tale to some children by his knee. When he finished, I said with some acerbity, "Well, Jombatiste, I hope you're satisfied with what you've done to poor old Miss Tryphena . . . spoiling the rest of her life for her!"

"Such a life, Madame," said Jombatiste dryly, "ought to be spoiled, the sooner the better."

"She's going to start for the city to-morrow," I said, supposing of course that he had heard the news.

Jombatiste looked up very quickly. "For what goes she to the city?"

"Why . . . she's gone daft over those bogie-stories of yours . . . she's looked the list over and picked out the survivors, the widow of the man who died of tuberculosis, and so on, and she's going to bring them back here to share her luxurious life."

Jombatiste bounded into the air as if a bomb had exploded under him, scattering his tools and the children, rushing past me out of the house and toward Cousin Tryphena's. . . . As he ran, he did what I have never seen anyone do, out of a book; he tore at his bushy hair and scattered handfuls in the air. It seemed to me that some sudden madness had struck our dull little village, and I hastened after him to protect Cousin Tryphena.

She opened the door in answer to his battering knocks, frowned, and began to say something to him, but was fairly swept off her feet by the torrent of his reproaches. . . . "How dare you take the information I give you and use it to betray your fellow-man! How do you *dare* stand there, so mealy-mouthed, and face me, when you are planning a cowardly attack on the liberty of your country! You call yourself a nurse . . . what would you think of a mother who hid an ulcer in her child's side from the doctor because it did not look pretty! What *else* are you planning to do? What would you think of a nurse who put paint and powder on her patient's face, to cover up a filthy skin disease? What else are you planning to do . . . you with your plan to put court-plaster over one pustule in ten million and thinking you are helping cure the patient! You are planning simply to please yourself, you cowardly . . . and you are an idiot too. . . ." He beat his hands on the door-jambs, ". . . if you had the money of forty millionaires, you couldn't do anything in that way . . . how many people are you thinking to help . . . two, three . . . maybe four! But there are hundreds of others . . . why, I could read you a thousand stories of worse—"

Cousin Tryphena's limit had been reached. She advanced upon the intruder with a face as excited as his own. . . . "Jombatiste Ramotte, if you ever dare to read me another such story, I'll go right out and jump in the Necronsett River!"

The mania which had haunted earlier generations of her family looked out luridly from her eyes.

I felt the goose-flesh stand out on my arms, and even Jombatiste's hot blood was cooled. He stood silent an instant.

Cousin Tryphena slammed the door in his face.

He turned to me with a bewilderment almost pathetic, so tremendous was it. . . . "Did you hear that . . . what sort of logic do you call—"

"Jombatiste," I counseled him, "if you take my advice, you'll leave Miss Tryphena alone after this."

Cousin Tryphena started off on her crack-brained expedition, the very next morning, on the six-thirty train. I happened to be looking out sleepily and saw her trudging wearily past our house in the bleak gray of our mountain dawn, the inadequate little, yellow flame of her old-fashioned lantern like a glowworm at her side. It seemed somehow symbolical of something, I did not know what.

It was a full week before we heard from her, and we had begun really to fear that we would never see her again, thinking that perhaps, while she was among strangers, her unsettled mind might have taken some new fancy which would be her destruction.

That week Jombatiste shut the door to his house. The children reported that he would not even let them in, and that they could see him through the window stitching away in ominous silence, muttering to himself.

Eight days after Cousin Tryphena had gone away, I had a telegram from her, which read, "Build fires in both my stoves to-morrow afternoon."

The dark comes early in the mountains, and so, although I dare say there was not a house in the village without a face at the pane after the late evening train came up, none of us saw anything but our usual impenetrable December darkness. That, too, seemed, to my perhaps overwrought consciousness of the problem, highly suggestive of the usual course of our lives. At least, I told myself, Cousin Tryphena had taken her absurd little lantern and gone forth.

The next morning, soon after breakfast, I set off for the other end of the street. Cousin Tryphena saw me coming and opened the door. She did not smile, and she was still very pale, but I saw that she had regained her self-control. "Come right in," she said, in rather a tense voice, and, as I entered she added, in our rustic phrase for introduction, "Make you 'quainted with my friend, Mrs. Lindstrom. She's come up from the city to stay with me. And this is her little boy, Sigurd, and this is the baby."

Blinking somewhat, I shook hands with a small, stoop-shouldered woman, in a new, ready-made dress, with abundant yellow hair drawn back from the thinnest, palest, saddest little face I had ever seen. She was holding an immaculately clean baby, asleep, its long golden lashes lying on cheeks as white and sunken as her own. A sturdily built boy of about six scrambled up from where he lay on the floor, playing with the cat, and gave me a hand shyly, hanging down his head. His mother had glanced up at me with a quick, shrinking look of fright, the tears starting to her eyes.

Cousin Tryphena was evidently afraid that I would not take her cue and sound the right note, for she went on hastily, "Mrs. Lindstrom has been real sick and kind o' worried over the baby, so's she's some nervous. I tell her Hillsboro air is thought very good for people's nerves. Lots of city folks come here in summer time, just for that. Don't you think Sigurd is a real big boy for only six and a half? He knows his letters too! He's goin' to school as soon as we get settled down. I want you should bring over those alphabet blocks that your Peggy doesn't use any more—"

The other woman was openly crying now, clinging to her benefactress' hand and holding it against her cheek as she sobbed.

My heroic old cousin patted her hair awkwardly, but kept on talking in her matter-of-fact manner, looking at me sternly as though defying me to show, by look or word, any consciousness of anything unusual in the situation; and we fell at once, she and I, into a commonplace conversation about the incidents of the trip up.

When I came away, half an hour later, Cousin Tryphena slipped a shawl over her head and came down the walk with me to the gate. I was much affected by what seemed to me the dramatically fitting outcome of my old kinswoman's Quixotism. I saw Cousin Tryphena picturesquely as the Happy Fool of old folk-lore, the character who, through his very lack of worldly wisdom, attains without effort all that self-seeking folks try for in vain. The happy ending of her adventure filled me with a cheerful wonder at the ways of Providence, which I tried to pass on to her in the exclamation, "Why, Cousin Tryphena, it's like a story-book!

You're going to *enjoy* having those people. The woman is as nice as she can be, and that's the brightest little boy! He's as smart as a whip!"

I was aware that the oddness of Cousin Tryphena's manner still persisted even now that we were alone. She sighed heavily and said, "I don't sleep much better nights now I've done it!" Then facing me, "I hadn't ought to have brought them up here! I just did it to please myself! Once I saw 'em . . . I wanted 'em!"

This seemed to me the wildest possible perversion of the Puritan instinct for self-condemnation and, half-vexed, I attempted some expostulation.

She stopped me with a look and gesture Dante might have had, "You ain't seen what I've seen."

I was half-frightened by her expression but tried to speak coolly. "Why, was it as bad as that paper said?" I asked.

She laid her hand on my arm, "Child, it was nothing like what the paper said . . . it was so much worse!"

"Oh . . ." I commented inadequately.

"I was five days looking for her . . . they'd moved from the address the paper give. And, in those five days, I saw so many others . . . *so many others* . . ." her face twitched. She put one lean old hand before her eyes. Then, quite unexpectedly, she cast out at me an exclamation which made my notion of the pretty picturesqueness of her adventure seem cheap and trivial and superficial. "Jombatiste is right!" she cried to me with a bitter fierceness: "Everything is wrong! Everything is wrong! If I can do anything, I'd ought to do it to help them as want to smash everything up and start over! What good does it do for me to bring up here just these three out of all I saw . . ." Her voice broke into pitiful, self-excusing quavers, "but when I saw them . . . the baby was so sick . . . and little Sigurd is so cunning . . . he took to me right away, came to me the first thing . . . this morning he wouldn't pick up his new rubbers off the floor for his mother, but, when I asked him, he did, right off . . . you ought to have seen what he had on . . . such rags . . . such dirt . . . and 'twan't her fault either! She's . . . why she's like *any*body . . . like a person's cousin they never happened to see before . . . why, they were all *folks!*" she cried out, her tired old mind wandering fitfully from one thing to another.

"You didn't find the little boy in the asylum?" I asked.

"He was dead before I got there," she answered.

"Oh . . .!" I said again, shocked, and then tentatively, "Had he . . .?"

"I don't know whether he had or not," said Cousin Tryphena, "I didn't ask. I didn't want to know. I know too much now!" She looked up fixedly at the mountain line, high and keen against the winter sky, "Jombatiste is right," she said again unsparingly, "I hadn't ought to be enjoying them . . . their father ought to be alive and with them. He was willing to work all he could, and yet he . . . here I've lived for fifty-five years and never airned my salt a single day. What was I livin' on? The stuff these folks ought to ha' had to eat . . . them and the Lord only knows how many more besides! Jombatiste is right . . . what I'm doin' now is only a drop in the bucket!"

She started from her somber reverie at the sound of a childish wail from the house. . . . "That's Sigurd . . . I *knew* that cat would scratch him!" she told me with instant, breathless agitation, as though the skies were falling, and darted back. After a moment's hesitation I, too, went back and watched her bind up with stiff, unaccustomed old fingers the little scratched hand, watched the frightened little boy sob himself quiet on her old knees that had never before known a child's soft weight, saw the expression in her eyes as she looked down at the sleeping baby and gazed about the untidy room so full of life, which had always been so orderly and so empty.

She lifted the little boy up higher so that his tousled yellow hair rested against her bosom. He put an arm around her neck and she flushed with pleasure like a girl; but, although she held him close to her with a sudden wistful tenderness, there was in her eyes a gloomy austerity which forbade me to sentimentalize over the picture she made.

"But, Cousin Tryphena," I urged, "it *is* a drop in the bucket, you know, and that's something!"

She looked down at the child on her knee, she laid her cheek against his bright hair, but she told me with harsh, self-accusing rigor, "'Tain't right for me to be here alive enjoying that dead man's little boy."

.   .   .   .   .   .

That was eighteen months ago. Mrs. Lindstrom is dead of consumption; but the two children are rosy and hearty and not to be distinguished from the other little Yankees of the village. They are devotedly attached to their Aunt Tryphena and rule her despotically.

And so we live along, like a symbol of the great world, bewildered Cousin Tryphena toiling lovingly for her adopted children, with the memory of her descent into hell still darkening and confusing her kind eyes; Jombatiste clothing his old body in rags and his soul in flaming indignation as he batters hopefully at the ramparts of intrenched unrighteousness . . . and the rest of us doing nothing at all.

Study and Discussion Questions

1. How are Cousin Tryphena and Jombatiste different and how are they alike?
2. What is the narrator's attitude towards Tryphena and towards Jombatiste? How does it change?
3. Tryphena's family insanity is frequently cited to explain her behavior. What does this suggest about those who offer such explanations?
4. On several occasions, the narrator compares Tryphena and Jombatiste to characters in fiction. How do such comparisons function in the story?
5. What are the sources of comedy in the story? Why does Fisher take a comic approach with this rather serious material?

Writing Exercises

1. Why does Tryphena's planned act of charity so enrage Jombatiste? What do you think of his argument against charity?
2. Discuss your own responses to human suffering due to social injustice when you see or learn about it. You might describe and analyze a particular instance.

ALAN SILLITOE (b. 1928)

Alan Sillitoe was born in Nottingham, England and at fourteen had to leave school to work. He held jobs in a bicycle plant and a plywood mill, and as a lathe operator. While serving in the Royal Air Force in Malaya, he began reading seriously, and soon began to write. His first novel, Saturday Night and Sunday Morning *(1958), brought him immediate recognition, and he followed it with* The Loneliness of the Long-distance Runner *(1959), a story collection, and* The General *(1960), a second novel. He has written a number of other books of fiction, as well as poetry and drama.*

The Loneliness of the Long-distance Runner　　(1959)

As soon as I got to Borstal[1] they made me a long-distance cross-country runner. I suppose they thought I was just the build for it because I was long and skinny for my age (and still am) and in any case I didn't mind it much, to tell you the truth, because running had always been made much of in our family, especially running away from the police. I've always been a good runner, quick and with a big stride as well, the only trouble being that no matter how fast I run, and I did a very fair lick even though I do say so myself, it didn't stop me getting caught by the cops after that bakery job.

You might think it a bit rare, having long-distance cross-country runners in Borstal, thinking that the first thing a long-distance cross-country runner would do when they set him loose at them fields and woods would be to run as far away from the place as he could get on a bellyful of Borstal slumgullion—but you're wrong, and I'll tell you why. The first thing is that them bastards over us aren't as daft as they most of the time look, and for another thing I'm not so daft as I would look if I tried to make a break for it on my long-distance running, because to abscond and then

---

[1] Reform school.

get caught is nothing but a mug's game, and I'm not falling for it. Cunning is what counts in this life, and even that you've got to use in the slyest way you can; I'm telling you straight: they're cunning, and I'm cunning. If only 'them' and 'us' had the same ideas we'd get on like a house on fire, but they don't see eye to eye with us and we don't see eye to eye with them, so that's how it stands and how it will always stand. The one fact is that all of us are cunning, and because of this there's no love lost between us. So the thing is that they know I won't try to get away from them: they sit there like spiders in that crumbly manor house, perched like jumped-up jackdaws on the roof, watching out over the drives and fields like German generals from the tops of tanks. And even when I jog-trot on behind a wood and they can't see me anymore they know my sweeping-brush head will bob along that hedge-top in an hour's time and that I'll report to the bloke on the gate. Because when on a raw and frosty morning I get up at five o'clock and stand shivering my belly off on the stone floor and all the rest still have another hour to snooze before the bells go, I slink downstairs through all the corridors to the big outside door with a permit running-card in my fist, I feel like the first and last man on the world, both at once, if you can believe what I'm trying to say. I feel like the first man because I've hardly got a stitch on and am sent against the frozen fields in a shimmy and shorts—even the first poor bastard dropped on to the earth in midwinter knew how to make a suit of leaves, or how to skin a pterodactyl for a topcoat. But there I am, frozen stiff, with nothing to get me warm except a couple of hours' long-distance running before breakfast, not even a slice of bread-and-sheepdip. They're training me up fine for the big sports day when all the pig-faced snotty-nosed dukes and ladies—who can't add two and two together and would mess themselves like loonies if they didn't have slavies to beck-and-call—come and make speeches to us about sports being just the thing to get us leading an honest life and keep our itching finger-ends off them shop locks and safe handles and hairgrips to open gas meters. They give us a bit of blue ribbon and a cup for a prize after we've shagged ourselves out running or jumping, like race horses, only we don't get so well looked-after as race horses, that's the only thing.

So there I am, standing in the doorway in shimmy and shorts, not even a dry crust in my guts, looking out at frosty flowers on the ground. I suppose you think this is enough to make me cry? Not likely. Just because I feel like the first bloke in the world wouldn't make me bawl. It makes me feel fifty times better than when I'm cooped up in that dormitory with three hundred others. No, it's sometimes when I stand there feeling like the *last* man in the world that I don't feel so good. I feel like the last man in the world because I think that all those three hundred sleepers behind me are dead. They sleep so well I think that every scruffy head's kicked the bucket in the night and I'm the only one left, and when I look out into the bushes and frozen ponds I have the feeling that it's going to get colder and colder until everything I can see, meaning my red arms as well, is going to be covered with a thousand miles of ice, all the earth, right up to the sky and over every bit of land and sea. So I try to kick this feeling out and act like I'm the first man on earth. And that makes me feel good, so as soon as I'm steamed up enough to get this feeling in me, I take a flying leap out of the doorway, and off I trot.

I'm in Essex. It's supposed to be a good Borstal, at least that's what the governor said to me when I got here from Nottingham. "We want to trust you while you are in this establishment," he said, smoothing out his newspaper with lily-white workless hands, while I read the big words upside down: *Daily Telegraph*. "If you play ball with us, we'll play ball with you." (Honest to God, you'd have thought it was going to be one long tennis match.) "We want hard honest work and we want good athletics," he said as well. "And if you give us both these things you can be sure we'll do right by you and send you back into the world an honest man." Well, I could have died laughing, especially when straight after this I hear the barking sergeant-major's voice calling me and two others to attention and marching us off like we was Grenadier Guards. And when the governor kept saying how 'we' wanted you to do this, and 'we' wanted you to do that, I kept looking round for the other blokes, wondering how many of them there was. Of course, I knew there were thousands of them, but as far as I knew only one was in the room. And there *are* thousands of them, all over the poxeaten country, in shops, offices, railway stations, cars, houses, pubs—In-law blokes like you and them, all on the watch for Out-law blokes like me and us—and waiting to 'phone for the coppers as soon as we make a false move. And it'll always be there, I'll tell you that now, because I haven't finished making all my false moves yet, and I dare say I won't until I kick the bucket. If the In-laws are hoping to stop me making false moves they're wasting their time. They might as well stand me up against a wall and let fly with a dozen rifles. That's the only way they'll stop me, and a few million others. Because I've been doing a lot of thinking since coming here. They can spy on us all day to see if we're pulling our puddings and if we're working good or doing our 'athletics' but they can't make an X-ray of our guts to find out what we're telling ourselves. I've been asking myself all sorts of questions, and thinking about my life up to now. And I like doing all this. It's a treat. It passes the time away and don't make Borstal seem half so bad as the boys in our street used to say it was. And this long-distance running lark is the best of all, because it makes me think so good that I learn things even better than when I'm on my bed at night. And apart from that, what with thinking so much while I'm running I'm getting to be one of the best runners in the Borstal. I can go my five miles round better than anybody else I know.

So as soon as I tell myself I'm the first man ever to be dropped into the world, and as soon as I take that first flying leap out into the frosty grass of an early morning when even birds haven't the heart to whistle,

I get to thinking, and that's what I like. I go my rounds in a dream, turning at lane or footpath corners without knowing I'm turning, leaping brooks without knowing they're there, and shouting good morning to the early cow-milker without seeing him. It's a treat, being a long-distance runner, out in the world by yourself with not a soul to make you bad-tempered or tell you what to do or that there's a shop to break and enter a bit back from the next street. Sometimes I think that I've never been so free as during that couple of hours when I'm trotting up the path out of the gates and turning by that bare-faced, big-bellied oak tree at the lane end. Everything's dead, but good, because it's dead before coming alive, not dead after being alive. That's how I look at it. Mind you, I often feel frozen stiff at first. I can't feel my hands or feet or flesh at all, like I'm a ghost who wouldn't know the earth was under him if he didn't see it now and again through the mist. But even though some people would call this frost-pain suffering if they wrote about it to their mams in a letter, I don't, because I know that in half an hour I'm going to be warm, that by the time I get to the main road and am turning on to the wheatfield footpath by the bus stop I'm going to feel as hot as a potbellied stove and as happy as a dog with a tin tail.

It's a good life, I'm saying to myself, if you don't give in to coppers and Borstal-bosses and the rest of them bastard-faced In-laws. Trot-trot-trot. Puff-puff-puff. Slap-slap-slap go my feet on the hard soil. Swish-swish-swish as my arms and side catch the bare branches of a bush. For I'm seventeen now, and when they let me out of this—if I don't make a break and see that things turn out otherwise—they'll try to get me in the army, and what's the difference between the army and this place I'm in now? They can't kid me, the bastards. I've seen the barracks near where I live, and if there weren't swaddies on guard outside with rifles you wouldn't know the difference between their high walls and the place I'm in now. Even though the swaddies come out at odd times a week for a pint of ale, so what? Don't I come out three mornings a week on my long-distance running, which is fifty times better than boozing. When they first said that I was to do my long-distance running without a guard pedalling beside me on a bike I couldn't believe it; but they called it a progressive and modern place, though they can't kid me because I know it's just like any other Borstal, going by the stories I've heard, except that they let me trot about like this. Borstal's Borstal no matter what they do; but anyway I moaned about it being a bit thick sending me out so early to run five miles on an empty stomach, until they talked me round to thinking it wasn't so bad—which I knew all the time—until they called me a good sport and patted me on the back when I said I'd do it and that I'd try to win them the Borstal Blue Ribbon Prize Cup For Long Distance Cross Country Running (All England). And now the governor talks to me when he comes on his rounds, almost as he'd talk to his prize race horse, if he had one.

"All right, Smith?" he asks.

"Yes, sir," I answer.

He flicks his grey moustache: "How's the running coming along?"

"I've set myself to trot round the grounds after dinner just to keep my hand in, sir," I tell him.

The pot-bellied pop-eyed bastard gets pleased at this: "Good show. I know you'll get us that cup," he says.

And I swear under my breath: "Like boggery, I will." No, I won't get them that cup, even though the stupid tash-twitching bastard has all his hopes in me. Because what does his barmy hope mean? I ask myself. Trot-trot-trot, slap-slap-slap, over the stream and into the wood where it's almost dark and frosty-dew twigs sting my legs. It don't mean a bloody thing to me, only to him, and it means as much to him as it would mean to me if I picked up the racing paper and put my bet on a hoss I didn't know, had never seen, and didn't care a sod if I ever did see. That's what it means to him. And I'll lose that race, because I'm not a race horse at all, and I'll let him know it when I'm about to get out— if I don't sling my hook even before the race. By Christ I will. I'm a human being and I've got thoughts and secrets and bloody life inside me that he doesn't know is there, and he'll never know what's there because he's stupid. I suppose you'll laugh at this, me saying the governor's a stupid bastard when I know hardly how to write and he can read and write and add-up like a professor. But what I say is true right enough. He's stupid, and I'm not, because I can see further into the likes of him than he can see into the likes of me. Admitted, we're both cunning, but I'm more cunning and I'll win in the end even if I die in gaol at eighty-two, because I'll have more fun and fire out of my life than he'll ever get out of his. He's read a thousand books I suppose, and for all I know he might even have written a few, but I know for a dead cert, as sure as I'm sitting here, that what I'm scribbling down is worth a million to what he could ever scribble down. I don't care what anybody says, but that's the truth and can't be denied. I know when he talks to me and I look into his army mug that I'm alive and he's dead. He's as dead as a doornail. If he ran ten yards he'd drop dead. If he got ten yards into what goes on in my guts he'd drop dead as well—with surprise. At the moment it's dead blokes like him as have the whip-hand over blokes like me, and I'm almost dead sure it'll always be like that, but even so, by Christ, I'd rather be like I am—always on the run and breaking into shops for a packet of fags and a jar of jam—than have the whip-hand over somebody else and be dead from the toe nails up. Maybe as soon as you get the whip-hand over somebody you do go dead. By God, to say that last sentence has needed a few hundred miles of long-distance running. I could no more have said that at first than I could have took a million-pound note from my back pocket. But it's true, you know, now I think of it again, and has always been true, and always will be true, and I'm surer of it every time I see the governor open that door and say Goodmorning lads.

As I run and see my smoky breath going out into the air as if I had ten cigars stuck in different parts of my body I think more on the little speech the governor made when I first came. Honesty. Be honest. I laughed so much one morning I went ten minutes down in my timing because I had to stop and get rid of the stitch in my side. The governor was so worried when I got back late that he sent me to the doctor's for an X-ray and heart check. Be honest. It's like saying: Be dead, like me, and then you'll have no more pain of leaving your nice slummy house for Borstal or prison. Be honest and settle down in a cosy six pounds a week job. Well, even with all this long-distance running I haven't yet been able to decide what he means by this, although I'm just about beginning to— and I don't like what it means. Because after all my thinking I found that it adds up to something that can't be true about me, being born and brought up as I was. Because another thing people like the governor will never understand is that I *am* honest, that I've never been anything else but honest, and that I'll always be honest. Sounds funny. But it's true because I know what honest means according to me and he only knows what it means according to him. I think my honesty is the only sort in the world, and he thinks his is the only sort in the world as well. That's why this dirty great walled-up and fenced-up manor house in the middle of nowhere has been used to coop-up blokes like me. And if I had the whip-hand I wouldn't even bother to build a place like this to put all the cops, governors, posh whores, penpushers, army officers, Members of Parliament in; no, I'd stick them up against a wall and let them have it, like they'd have done with blokes like us years ago, that is, if they'd ever known what it means to be honest, which they don't and never will so help me God Almighty.

I was nearly eighteen months in Borstal before I thought about getting out. I can't tell you much about what it was like there because I haven't got the hang of describing buildings or saying how many crumby chairs and slatted windows make a room. Neither can I do much complaining, because to tell you the truth I didn't suffer in Borstal at all. I gave the same answer a pal of mine gave when someone asked him how much he hated it in the army. "I didn't hate it," he said. "They fed me, gave me a suit, and pocket-money, which was a bloody sight more than I ever got before, unless I worked myself to death for it, and most of the time they wouldn't let me work but sent me to the dole office twice a week." Well, that's more or less what I say. Borstal didn't hurt me in that respect, so since I've got no complaints I don't have to describe what they gave us to eat, what the dorms were like, or how they treated us. But in another way Borstal does something to me. No, it doesn't get my back up, because it's always been up, right from when I was born. What it does do is show me what they've been trying to frighten me with. They've got other things as well, like prison and, in the end, the rope. It's like me rushing up to thump a man and snatch the coat off his back when, suddenly, I pull up because he whips out a knife and lifts it to stick me like a pig if I come too close. That knife is Borstal, clink, the rope. But once you've seen the knife you learn a bit of unarmed combat. You have to, because you'll never get that sort of knife in your own hands, and this unarmed combat doesn't amount to much. Still, there it is, and you keep on rushing up to this man, knife or not, hoping to get one of your hands on his wrist and the other on his elbow both at the same time, and press back until he drops the knife.

You see, by sending me to Borstal they've shown me the knife, and from now on I know something I didn't know before: that it's war between me and them. I always knew this, naturally, because I was in Remand Homes as well and the boys there told me a lot about their brothers in Borstal, but it was only touch and go then, like kittens, like boxing-gloves, like dobbie. But now that they've shown me the knife, whether I ever pinch another thing in my life again or not, I know who my enemies are and what war is. They can drop all the atom bombs they like for all I care: I'll never call it war and wear a soldier's uniform, because I'm in a different sort of war, that they think is child's play. The war they think is war is suicide, and those that go and get killed in war should be put in clink for attempted suicide because that's the feeling in blokes' minds when they rush to join up or let themselves be called up. I know, because I've thought how good it would be sometimes to do myself in and the easiest way to do it, it occurred to me, was to hope for a big war so's I could join up and get killed. But I got past that when I knew I already was in a war of my own, that I was born into one, that I grew up hearing the sound of 'old soldiers' who'd been over the top at Dartmoor, half-killed at Lincoln, trapped in no-man's-land at Borstal, that sounded louder than any Jerry bombs. Government wars aren't my wars; they've got nowt to do with me, because my own war's all that I'll ever be bothered about. I remember when I was fourteen and I went out into the country with three of my cousins, all about the same age, who later went to different Borstals, and then to different regiments, from which they soon deserted, and then to different gaols where they still are as far as I know. But anyway, we were all kids then, and wanted to go out to the woods for a change, to get away from the roads of stinking hot tar one summer. We climbed over fences and went through fields, scrumping a few sour apples on our way, until we saw the wood about a mile off. Up Colliers' Pad we heard another lot of kids talking in high-school voices behind a hedge. We crept up on them and peeped through the brambles, and saw they were eating a picnic, a real posh spread out of baskets and flasks and towels. There must have been about seven of them, lads and girls sent out by their mams and dads for the afternoon. So we went on our bellies through the hedge like crocodiles and surrounded them, and then dashed into the middle, scattering the fire and batting their tabs and snatching up all there was to eat, then running off over Cherry Orchard fields into the wood, with a man chasing us who'd come up while we were ransacking their picnic. We got away all right, and had a good feed into the bargain, because we'd been clambed to death and couldn't wait long enough to get our chops ripping into them thin lettuce and ham sandwiches and creamy cakes.

Well, I'll always feel during every bit of my life like those daft kids should have felt before we broke them up. But they never dreamed that what happened was going to happen, just like the governor of this Borstal who spouts to us about honesty and all that wappy stuff don't know a bloody thing, while I know every minute of my life that a big boot is always likely to smash any nice picnic I might be barmy and dishonest enough to make for myself. I admit that there've been times when I've thought of telling the governor all this so as to put him on his guard, but when I've got as close as seeing him I've changed my mind, thinking to let him either find out for himself or go through the same mill as I've gone through. I'm not hard-hearted (in fact I've helped a few blokes in my time with the odd quid, lie, fag, or shelter from the rain when they've been on the run) but I'm boggered if I'm going to risk being put in the cells just for trying to give the governor a bit of advice he don't deserve. If my heart's soft I know the sort of people I'm going to save it for. And any advice I'd give the governor wouldn't do him the least bit of good; it'd only trip him up sooner than if he wasn't told at all, which I suppose is what I want to happen. But for the time being I'll let things go on as they are, which is something else I've learned in the last year or two. (It's a good job I can only think of these things as fast as I can write with this stub of pencil that's clutched in my paw, otherwise I'd have dropped the whole thing weeks ago.)

By the time I'm half-way through my morning course, when after a frost-bitten dawn I can see a phlegmy bit of sunlight hanging from the bare twigs of beech and sycamore, and when I've measured my half-way mark by the short-cut scrimmage down the steep bush-covered bank and into the sunken lane, when still there's not a soul in sight and not a sound except the neighing of a piebald foal in a cottage stable that I can't see, I get to thinking the deepest and daftest of all. The governor would have a fit if he could see me sliding down the bank because I could break my neck or ankle, but I can't not do it because it's the only risk I take and the only excitement I ever get, flying flat-out like one of them pterodactyls from the 'Lost World' I once heard on the wireless, crazy like a cut-balled cockerel, scratching myself to bits and almost letting myself go but not quite. It's the most wonderful minute because there's not one thought or word or picture of anything in my head while I'm going down. I'm empty, as empty as I was before I was born, and I don't let myself go, I suppose, because whatever it is that's farthest down inside me don't want me to die or hurt myself bad. And it's daft to think deep, you know, because it gets you nowhere, though deep is what I am when I've passed this half-way mark because the long-distance run of an early morning makes me think that every run like this is a life—a little life, I know—but a life as full of misery and happiness and things happening as you can ever get really around yourself—and I remember that after a lot of these runs I thought that it didn't need much know-how to tell how a life was going to end once it had got well started. But as usual I was wrong, caught first by the cops and then by my own bad brain, I could never trust myself to fly scot-free over these traps, was always tripped up sooner or later no matter how many I got over to the good without even knowing it. Looking back I suppose them big trees put their branches to their snouts and gave each other the wink, and there I was whizzing down the bank and not seeing a bloody thing.

II

I don't say to myself: "You shouldn't have done the job and then you'd have stayed away from Borstal"; no, what I ram into my runner-brain is that my luck had no right to scram just when I was on my way to making the coppers think I hadn't done the job after all. The time was autumn and the night foggy enough to set me and my mate Mike roaming the streets when we should have been rooted in front of the telly or stuck into a plush posh seat at the pictures, but I was restless after six weeks away from any sort of work, and well you might ask me why I'd been bone-idle for so long because normally I sweated my thin guts out on a milling-machine with the rest of them, but you see, my dad died from cancer of the throat, and mam collected a cool five hundred in insurance and benefits from the factory where he'd worked, "for your bereavement," they said, or words like that.

Now I believe, and my mam must have thought the same, that a wad of crisp blue-back fivers ain't a sight of good to a living soul unless they're flying out of your hand into some shopkeeper's till, and the shopkeeper is passing you tip-top things in exchange over the counter, so as soon as she got the money, mam took me and my five brothers and sisters out to town and got us dolled-up in new clothes. Then she ordered a twenty-one-inch telly, a new carpet because the old one was covered with blood from dad's dying and wouldn't wash out, and took a taxi home with bags of grub and a new fur coat. And do you know—you wain't believe me when I tell you—she'd still near three hundred left in her bulging handbag the next day, so how could any of us go to work after that? Poor old dad, he didn't get a look in, and he was the one who'd done the suffering and dying for such a lot of lolly.

Night after night we sat in front of the telly with a ham sandwich in one hand, a bar of chocolate in the other, and a bottle of lemonade between our boots, while mam was with some fancy-man upstairs on the new bed she'd ordered, and I'd never known a family as happy as ours was in that couple of months when we'd got all the money we needed. And when the dough ran out I didn't think about anything much, but just roamed the streets—looking for another job, I told mam—hoping I suppose to get my hands on another five hundred nicker so's the nice life we'd got used to could go on and on for ever. Because it's surprising how quick you can get used to a different life. To begin with, the adverts on the telly had shown us how much more there was in the world to buy than we'd ever dreamed of when we'd looked into shop windows but hadn't seen all there was to see because we didn't have the money to buy it with anyway. And the telly made all these things seem twenty times better than we'd ever thought they were. Even adverts at the cinema were cool and tame, because now we were seeing them in private at home. We used to cock our noses up at things in shops that didn't move, but suddenly we saw their real value because they jumped and glittered around the screen and had some pasty-faced tart going head over heels to get her nail-polished grabbers on to them or her lipstick lips over them, not like the crumby adverts you saw on posters or in newspapers as dead as doornails; these were flickering around loose, half-open packets and tins, making you think that all you had to do was finish opening them before they were yours, like seeing an unlocked safe through a shop window with the man gone away for a cup of tea without thinking to guard his lolly. The films they showed were good as well, in that way, because we couldn't get our eyes unglued from the cops chasing the robbers who had satchel-bags crammed with cash and looked like getting away to spend it—until the last moment. I always hoped they would end up free to blow the lot, and could never stop wanting to put my hand out, smash into the screen (it only looked a bit of rag-screen like at the pictures) and get the copper in a half-nelson so's he'd stop following the bloke with the money-bags. Even when he'd knocked off a couple of bank clerks I hoped he wouldn't get nabbed. In fact I wished more than ever he wouldn't because it meant the hot-chair if he did, and I wouldn't wish that on anybody no matter what they'd done, because I'd read in a book where the hot-chair worn't a quick death at all, but that you just sat there scorching to death until you were dead. And it was when these cops were chasing the crooks that we played some good tricks with the telly, because when one of them opened his big gob to spout about getting their man I'd turn the sound down and see his mouth move like a goldfish or mackerel or a minnow mimicking what they were supposed to be acting—it was so funny the whole family nearly went into fits on the brand-new carpet that hadn't yet found its way to the bedroom. It was the best of all though when we did it to some Tory telling us about how good his government was going to be if we kept on voting for them— their slack chops rolling, opening and bumbling, hands lifting to twitch moustaches and touching their buttonholes to make sure the flower hadn't wilted, so that you could see they didn't mean a word they said, especially with not a murmur coming out because we'd cut off the sound. When the governor of the Borstal first talked to me I was reminded of those times so much that I nearly killed myself trying not to laugh. Yes, we played so many good stunts on the box of tricks that mam used to call us the Telly Boys, we got so clever at it.

My pal Mike got let off with probation because it was his first job—anyway the first they ever knew about—and because they said he would never have done it if it hadn't been for me talking him into it. They said I was a menace to honest lads like Mike—hands in his pockets so that they looked stone-empty, head bent forward as if looking for half-crowns to fill 'em with, a ripped jersey on and his hair falling into his eyes so that he could go up to women and ask them for a shilling because he was hungry—and that I was the brains behind the job, the guiding light when it came to making up anybody's mind, but I swear to God I worn't owt like that because really I ain't got no more brains than a gnat after hiding the money in the place I did. And I—being cranky like I am—got sent to Borstal because to tell you the honest truth I'd been to Remand Homes before—though that's another story and I suppose if ever I tell it it'll be just as boring as this one is. I was glad though that Mike got away with it, and I only hope he always will, not like silly bastard me.

So on this foggy night we tore ourselves away from the telly and slammed the front door behind us, setting off up our wide street like slow tugs on a river that'd broken their hooters, for we didn't know where the housefronts began what with the perishing cold mist all around. I was snatched to death without an overcoat: mam had forgotten to buy me one in the scrummage of shopping, and by the time I thought to remind her of it the dough was all gone. So we whistled 'The Teddy Boys Picnic' to keep us warm, and I told myself that I'd get a coat soon if it was the last thing I did. Mike said he thought the same about himself, adding that he'd also get some brand-new glasses with gold rims, to wear instead of the wire frames they'd given him at the school clinic years ago. He didn't twig it was foggy at first and cleaned his glasses every time I pulled him back from a lamp-post or car, but when he saw the lights on Alfreton Road looking like octopus eyes he put them in his pocket and didn't wear them again until we did the job. We hadn't got two ha-pennies between us, and though we weren't hungry we wished we'd got a bob or two when we passed the fish and chip shops because the delicious sniffs of salt and vinegar and frying fat made our mouths water. I don't mind telling you we walked the town from one end to the other and if our eyes worn't glued to the ground looking for lost wallets and watches they was swivelling around house windows and shop doors in case we saw something easy and worth nipping into.

Neither of us said as much as this to each other, but I know for a fact that that was what we was thinking. What I don't know—and as sure as I sit here I know I'll never know—is which of us was the first bastard to latch his peepers on to that baker's backyard. Oh yes, it's all right me telling myself it was me, but the truth is that I've never known whether it was Mike or not, because I do know that I didn't see the open window until he stabbed me in the ribs and pointed it out. "See it?" he said.

"Yes," I told him, "so let's get cracking."

"But what about the wall though?" he whispered, looking a bit closer.

"On your shoulders," I chipped in.

His eyes were already up there: "Will you be able to reach?" It was the only time he ever showed any life.

"Leave it to me," I said, ever-ready. "I can reach anywhere from your ham-hock shoulders."

Mike was a nipper compared to me, but underneath the scruffy draught-board jersey he wore were muscles as hard as iron, and you wouldn't think to see him walking down the street with glasses on and hands in pockets that he'd harm a fly, but I never liked to get on the wrong side of him in a fight because he's the sort that don't say a word for weeks on end—sits plugged in front of the telly, or reads a cowboy book, or just sleeps—when suddenly BIFF—half kills somebody for almost nothing at all, such as beating him in a race for the last Football Post on a Saturday night, pushing in before him at a bus stop, or bumping into him when he was day-dreaming about Dolly-on-the-Tub next door. I saw him set on a bloke once for no more than fixing him in a funny way with his eyes, and it turned out that the bloke was cockeyed but nobody knew it because he'd just that day come to live in our street. At other times none of these things would matter a bit, and I suppose the only reason why I was pals with him was because I didn't say much from one month's end to another either.

He puts his hands up in the air like he was being covered with a Gatling-Gun, and moved to the wall like he was going to be mowed down, and I climbed up him like he was a stile or step-ladder, and there he stood, the palms of his upshot maulers flat and turned out so's I could step on 'em like they was the adjustable jack-spanner under a car, not a sound of a breath nor a shiver of a flinch coming from him. I lost no time in any case, took my coat from between my teeth, chucked it up to the glass-topped wall (where the glass worn't too sharp because the jags had been worn down by years of accidental stones) and was sitting astraddle before I knew where I was. Then down the other side, with my legs rammed up into my throat when I hit the ground, the crack coming about as hard as when you fall after a high parachute drop, that one of my mates told me was like jumping off a twelve-foot wall, which this must have been. Then I picked up my bits and pieces and opened the gate for Mike, who was still grinning and full of life because the hardest part of the job was already done. "I came, I broke, I entered," like that clever-dick Borstal song.

I didn't think about anything at all, as usual, because I never do when I'm busy, when I'm draining pipes, looting sacks, yaling locks, lifting latches, forcing my bony hands and lanky legs into making some-thing move, hardly feeling my lungs going in-whiff and out-whaff, not realizing whether my mouth is clamped tight or gaping, whether I'm hungry, itching from scabies, or whether my flies are open and flashing dirty words like muck and spit into the late-night final fog. And when I don't know anything about all this then how can I honest-to-God say I think of anything at such times? When I'm wondering what's the best way to get a window open or how to force a door, how can I be thinking or have anything on my mind? That's what the four-eyed white-smocked bloke with the note-book couldn't understand when he asked me questions for days and days after I got to Borstal; and I couldn't explain it to him then like I'm writing it down now; and even if I'd been able to maybe he still wouldn't have caught on because I don't know whether I can understand it myself even at this moment, though I'm doing my best you can bet.

So before I knew where I was I was inside the baker's office watching Mike picking up that cash box after he'd struck a match to see where it was, wearing a tailor-made fifty-shilling grin on his square crew-cut nut as his paws closed over the box like he'd squash it to nothing. "Out," he suddenly said, shaking it so's it rattled. "Let's scram."

"Maybe there's some more," I said, pulling half a dozen drawers out of a rollertop desk.

"No," he said, like he'd already been twenty years in the game, "this is the lot," patting his tin box, "this is it."

I pulled out another few drawers, full of bills, books and letters. "How do you know, you loony sod?"

He barged past me like a bull at a gate. "Because I do."

Right or wrong, we'd both got to stick together and do the same thing. I looked at an ever-loving babe of a brand-new typewriter, but knew it was too traceable, so blew it a kiss, and went out after him. "Hang on," I said, pulling the door to, "we're in no hurry."

"Not much we aren't," he says over his shoulder.

"We've got months to splash the lolly," I whispered as we crossed the yard, "only don't let that gate creak too much or you'll have the narks tuning-in."

"You think I'm barmy?" he said, creaking the gate so that the whole street heard.

I don't know about Mike, but now I started to think, of how we'd get back safe through the streets with that money-box up my jumper. Because he'd clapped it into my hand as soon as we'd got to the main road, which might have meant that he'd started thinking as well, which only goes to show how you don't know what's in anybody else's mind unless you think about things yourself. But as far as my thinking went at that moment it wasn't up to much, only a bit of fright that wouldn't budge not even with a hot blow-lamp, about what we'd say if a copper asked us where we were off to with that hump in my guts.

"What is it?" he'd ask, and I'd say: "A growth." "What do you mean, a growth, my lad?" he'd say back, narky like. I'd cough and clutch myself like I was in the most tripe-twisting pain in the world, and screw my eyes up like I was on my way to the hospital, and Mike would take my arm like he was the best pal I'd got. "Cancer," I'd manage to say to Narker, which would make his slow punch-drunk brain suspect a thing or two. "A lad of your age?" So I'd groan again, and hope to make him feel a real bully of a bastard, which would be impossible, but anyway: "It's in the family. Dad died of it last month, and I'll die of it next month by the feel of it." "What, did he have it in the guts?" "No, in the throat. But it's got me in the stomach." Groan and cough. "Well, you shouldn't be out like this if you've got cancer, you should be in the hospital." I'd get ratty now: "That's where I'm trying to go if only you'd let me and stop asking so many questions. Aren't I, Mike?" Grunt from Mike as he unslung his cosh. Then just in time the copper would tell us to get on our way, kind and considerate all of a sudden, saying that the outpatient department of the hospital closes at twelve, so hadn't he better call us a taxi? He would if we liked, he says, and he'd pay for it as well. But we tell him not to bother, that he's a good bloke even if he is a copper, that we know a short cut anyway. Then just as we're turning a corner he gets it into his big batchy head that we're going the opposite way to the hospital, and calls us back. So we'd start to run . . . if you can call all that thinking.

Up in my room Mike rips open that money-box with a hammer and chisel, and before we know where we are we've got seventy-eight pounds fifteen and fourpence ha'penny *each* lying all over my bed like tea spread out on Christmas Day: cake and trifle, salad and sandwiches, jam tarts and bars of chocolate: all shared and shared alike between Mike and me because we believed in equal work and equal pay, just like the comrades my dad was in until he couldn't do a stroke anymore and had no breath left to argue with. I thought how good it was that blokes like that poor baker didn't stash all his cash in one of the big marble-fronted banks that take up every corner of the town, how lucky for us that he didn't trust them no matter how many millions of tons of concrete or how many iron bars and boxes they were made of, or how many coppers kept their blue pop-eyed peepers glued on to them, how smashing it was that he believed in money-boxes when so many shopkeepers thought it old-fashioned and tried to be modern by using a bank, which wouldn't give a couple of sincere, honest, hardworking, conscientious blokes like Mike and me a chance.

Now you'd think, and I'd think, and anybody with a bit of imagination would think, that we'd done as clean a job as could ever be done, that, with the baker's shop being at least a mile from where we lived, and with not a soul having seen us, and what with the fog and the fact that we weren't more than five minutes in the place, that the coppers should never have been able to trace us. But then, you'd be wrong, I'd be wrong, and everybody else would be wrong, no matter how much imagination was diced out between us.

Even so, Mike and I didn't splash the money about, because that would have made people think straightaway that we'd latched on to something that didn't belong to us. Which wouldn't do at all, because even in a street like ours there are people who love to do a good turn for the coppers, though I never know why they do. Some people are so mean-gutted that even if they've only got tuppence more than you and they think you're the sort that would take it if you have half the chance, they'd get you put inside if they saw you ripping lead out of a lavatory, even if it weren't their lavatory—just to keep their tuppence out of your reach. And so we didn't do anything to let on about how rich we were, nothing like going down town and coming back dressed in brand-new Teddy boy suits and carrying a set of skiffle-drums like another pal of ours who'd done a factory office about six months before. No, we took the odd bobs and pennies out and folded the notes into bundles and stuffed them up the drainpipe outside the door in the backyard. "Nobody'll ever think of looking for it there," I said to Mike. "We'll keep it doggo for a week or two, then take a few quid a week out till it's all gone. We might be thieving bastards, but we're not green."

Some days later a plain-clothes dick knocked at the door. And asked for me. I was still in bed, at eleven o'clock, and had to unroll myself from the comfortable black sheets when I heard mam calling me. "A man to see you," she said. "Hurry up, or he'll be gone."

I could hear her keeping him at the back door, nattering about how fine it had been but how it looked like rain since early this morning—and he didn't answer her except to snap out a snotty yes or no. I scrambled into my trousers and wondered why he'd come—knowing it was a copper because 'a man to see you' always meant just that in our house—and if I'd had any idea that one had gone to Mike's house as well at the same time I'd have twigged it to be because of that hundred and fifty quid's worth of paper stuffed up the drainpipe outside the back door about ten inches away from that plain-clothed copper's boot, where mam still talked to him thinking she was doing me a favour, and I wishing to God she'd ask him in, though on second thoughts realizing that that would seem more suspicious than keeping him outside, because they know we hate their guts and smell a rat if they think we're trying to be nice to them. Mam wasn't born yesterday, I thought, thumping my way down the creaking stairs.

I'd seen him before: Borstal Bernard in nicky-hat, Remand Home Ronald in rowing-boat boots, Probation Pete in a pit-prop mackintosh, three-months clink in collar and tie (all this out of a Borstal skiffle-ballad that my new mate made up, and I'd tell you it in full but it doesn't belong in this story), a 'tec who'd never had as much in his pockets as that drainpipe had up its jackses. He was like Hitler in the face, right down to the paint-brush tash, except that being six-foot tall made him seem worse. But I straightened my shoulders to look into his illiterate blue eyes—like I always do with any copper.

Then he started asking me questions, and my mother from behind said: "He's never left that television set for the last three months, so you've got nowt on him, mate. You might as well look for somebody else, because you're wasting the rates you get out of my rent and the income-tax that comes out of my pay-packet standing there like that"—which was a laugh because she'd never paid either to my knowledge, and never would, I hoped.

"Well, you know where Papplewick Street is, don't you?" the copper asked me, taking no notice of mam.

"Ain't it off Alfreton Road?" I asked him back, helpful and bright.

"You know there's a baker's half-way down on the left-hand side, don't you?"

"Ain't it next door to a pub, then?" I wanted to know.

He answered me sharp: "No, it bloody well ain't." Coppers always lose their tempers as quick as this, and more often than not they gain nothing by it. "Then I don't know it," I told him, saved by the bell.

He slid his big boot round and round on the doorstep. "Where were you last Friday night?" Back in the ring, but this was worse than a boxing match.

I didn't like him trying to accuse me of something he wasn't sure I'd done. "Was I at that baker's you mentioned? Or in the pub next door?"

"You'll get five years in Borstal if you don't give me a straight answer," he said, unbuttoning his mac even though it was cold where he was standing.

"I was glued to the telly, like mam says," I swore blind. But he went on and on with his looney questions: "Have you got a television?"

The things he asked wouldn't have taken in a kid of two, and what else could I say to the last one except: "Has the aerial fell down? Or would you like to come in and see it?"

He was liking me even less for saying that. "We know you weren't listening to the television set last Friday, and so do you, don't you?"

"P'raps not, but I was *looking* at it, because sometimes we turn the sound down for a bit of fun." I could hear mam laughing from the kitchen, and I hoped Mike's mam was doing the same if the cops had gone to him as well.

"We know you weren't in the house," he said, starting up again, cranking himself with the handle. They always say 'We' 'We', never 'I' 'I'—as if they feel braver and righter knowing there's a lot of them against only one.

"I've got witnesses," I said to him. "Mam for one. Her fancy-man, for two. Ain't that enough? I can get you a dozen more, or thirteen altogether, if it was a baker's that got robbed."

"I don't want no lies," he said, not catching on about the baker's dozen. Where do they scrape cops up from anyway? "All I want is to get from you where you put that money."

Don't get mad, I kept saying to myself, don't get mad—hearing mam setting out cups and saucers and putting the pan on the stove for bacon.

I stood back and waved him inside like I was a butler. "Come and search the house. If you've got a warrant."

"Listen, my lad," he said, like the dirty bullying jumped-up bastard he was, "I don't want too much of your lip, because if we get you down to the Guildhall you'll get a few bruises and black-eyes for your trouble." And I knew he wasn't kidding either, because I'd heard about all them sort of tricks. I hoped one day though that him and all his pals would be the ones to get the black-eyes and kicks; you never knew. It might come sooner than anybody thinks, like in Hungary. "Tell me where the money is, and I'll get you off with probation."

"What money?" I asked him, because I'd heard that one before as well.

"You know what money."

"Do I look as though I'd know owt about money?" I said, pushing my fist through a hole in my shirt.

"The money that was pinched, that you know all about," he said. "You can't trick me, so it's no use trying."

"Was it three-and-eightpence ha'penny?" I asked.

"You thieving young bastard. We'll teach you to steal money that doesn't belong to you."

I turned my head around: "Mam," I called out, "get my lawyer on the blower, will you?"

"Clever, aren't you?" he said in a very unfriendly way, "but we won't rest until we clear all this up."

"Look," I pleaded, as if about to sob my socks off because he'd got me wrong, "it's all very well us talking like this, it's like a game almost, but I wish you'd tell me what it's all about, because honest-to-God I've just got out of bed and here you are at the door talking about me having pinched a lot of money, money that I don't know anything about."

He swung around now as if he'd trapped me, though I couldn't see why he might think so. "Who said anything about money? I didn't. What made you bring money into this little talk we're having?"

"It's you," I answered, thinking he was going barmy, and about to start foaming at the chops, "you've got money on the brain, like all policemen. Baker's shops as well."

He screwed his face up. "I want an answer from you: where's that money?"

But I was getting fed-up with all this. "I'll do a deal."

Judging by his flash-bulb face he thought he was suddenly on to a good thing. "What sort of a deal?"

So I told him: "I'll give you all the money I've got, one and fourpence ha'penny, if you stop this third-degree and let me go in and get my breakfast. Honest, I'm clambed to death. I ain't had a bite since yesterday. Can't you hear my guts rollin'?"

His jaw dropped, but on he went, pumping me for another half hour. A routine check-up, as they say on the pictures. But I knew I was winning on points.

Then he left, but came back in the afternoon to search the house. He didn't find a thing, not a French farthing. He asked me questions again and I didn't tell him anything except lies, lies, lies, because I can go on doing that forever without batting an eyelid. He'd got nothing on me and we both of us knew it, otherwise I'd have been down at the Guildhall in no time, but he kept on keeping on because I'd been in a Remand Home for a high-wall job before; and Mike was put through the same mill because all the local cops knew he was my best pal.

When it got dark me and Mike were in our parlour with a low light on and the telly off, Mike taking it easy in the rocking chair and me slouched out on the settee, both of us puffing a packet of Woods. With the door bolted and curtains drawn we talked about the dough we'd crammed up the drainpipe. Mike thought we should take it out and both of us do a bunk to Skegness or Cleethorpes for a good time in the arcades, living like lords in a boarding house near the pier, then at least we'd both have had a big beano before getting sent down.

"Listen, you daft bleeder," I said, "we aren't going to get caught at all, *and* we'll have a good time, later." We were so clever we didn't even go out to the pictures, though we wanted to.

In the morning old Hitler-face questioned me again, with one of his pals this time, and the next day they came, trying as hard as they could to get something out of me, but I didn't budge an inch. I know I'm showing off when I say this, but in me he'd met his match, and I'd never give in to questions no matter how long it was kept up. They searched the house a couple of times as well, which made me think they thought they really had something to go by, but I know now that they hadn't, and that it was all buckshee speculation. They turned the house upside down and inside out like an old sock, went from top to bottom and front to back but naturally didn't find a thing. The copper even poked his face up the front-room chimney (that hadn't been used or swept for years) and came down looking like Al Jolson so that he had to swill himself clean at the scullery sink. They kept tapping and pottering around the big aspidistra plant that grandma had left to mam, lifting it up from the table to look under the cloth, putting it aside so's they could move the table and get at the boards under the rug—but the big headed stupid ignorant bastards never once thought of emptying the soil out of the plant pot, where they'd have found the crumpled-up money-box that we'd buried the night we did the job. I suppose it's still there, now I think about it, and I suppose mam wonders now and again why the plant don't prosper like it used to—as if it could with a fistful of thick black tin lapped around its guts.

The last time he knocked at our door was one wet morning at five minutes to nine and I was sleep-logged in my crumby bed as usual. Mam had gone to work that day so I shouted for him to hold on a bit, and then went down to see who it was. There he stood, six-feet tall and sopping wet, and for the first time in my life I did a spiteful thing I'll never forgive myself for: I didn't ask him to come in out of the rain, because I wanted him to get double pneumonia and die. I suppose he could have pushed by me and come in if he'd wanted, but maybe he'd got used to asking questions on the doorstep and didn't want to be put off by changing his ground even though it was raining. Not that I don't like being spiteful because of any barmy principle I've got, but this bit of spite, as it turned out, did me no good at all. I should have treated him as a brother I hadn't seen for twenty years and dragged him in for a cup of tea and a fag, told him about the picture I hadn't seen the night before, asked him how his wife was after her operation and whether they'd shaved her moustache off to make it, and then sent him happy and satisfied out by the front door. But no, I thought, let's see what he's got to say for himself now.

He stood a little to the side of the door, either because it was less wet there, or because he wanted to see me from a different angle, perhaps having found it monotonous to watch a bloke's face always telling lies from the same side. "You've been identified," he said, twitching raindrops from his tash. "A woman saw you and your mate yesterday and she swears blind you are the same chaps she saw going into that bakery."

I was dead sure he was still bluffing, because Mike and I hadn't even seen each other the day before, but I looked worried. "She's a menace then to innocent people, whoever she is, because the only bakery I've been in lately is the one up our street to get some cut-bread on tick for mam."

He didn't bit on this. "So now I want to know where the money is"— as if I hadn't answered him at all.

"I think mam took it to work this morning to get herself some tea in the canteen." Rain was splashing down so hard I thought he'd get washed away if he didn't come inside. But I wasn't much bothered, and went on: "I remember I put it in the telly-vase last night—it was my only one-and-three and I was saving it for a packet of tips this morning—and I nearly had a jibbering black fit just now when I saw it had gone. I was reckoning on it for getting me through today because I don't think life's worth living without a fag, do you?"

I was getting into my stride and began to feel good, twigging that this would be my last pack of lies, and that if I kept it up for long enough this time I'd have the bastards beat: Mike and me would be off to the coast in a few weeks time having the fun of our lives, playing at penny football and latching on to a couple of tarts that would give us all they were good for. "And this weather's no good for picking-up fag-ends in the street," I said, "because they'd be sopping wet. Course, I know you could dry 'em out near the fire, but it don't taste the same you know, all said and done. Rainwater does summat to 'em that don't bear thinkin' about: it turns 'em back into hoss-tods without the taste though."

I began to wonder, at the back of my brainless eyes, why old copper-lugs didn't pull me up sharp and say he hadn't got time to listen to all this, but he wasn't looking at me anymore, and all my thoughts about Skegness went bursting to smithereens in my sludgy loaf. I could have dropped into the earth when I saw what he'd fixed his eyes on.

He was looking at *it*, an ever-loving fiver, and I could only jabber: "The one thing is to have some real fags because new hoss-tods is always better than stuff that's been rained on and dried, and I know how you feel about not being able to find money because one-and-three's one-and-three in anybody's pocket, and naturally if I see it knocking around I'll get you on the blower tomorrow straightaway and tell you where you can find it."

I thought I'd go down in a fit: three green-backs as well had been washed down by the water, and more were following, lying flat at first after their fall, then getting tilted at the corners by wind and rainspots as if they were alive and wanted to get back into the dry snug drainpipe out of the terrible weather, and you can't imagine how I wished they'd be able to. Old Hitler-face didn't know what to make of it but just kept staring down and down, and I thought I'd better keep on talking, though I knew it wasn't much good now.

"It's a fact, I know, that money's hard to come by and half-crowns don't get found on bus seats or in dustbins, and I didn't see any in bed last night because I'd 'ave known about it, wouldn't I? You can't sleep with things like that in the bed because they're too hard, and anyway at first they're. . . ." It took Hitler-boy a long time to catch on; they were beginning to spread over the yard a bit, reinforced by the third colour of a ten-bob note, before his hand clamped itself on to my shoulder.

III

The pop-eyed potbellied governor said to a pop-eyed potbellied Member of Parliament who sat next to his pop-eyed potbellied whore of a wife that I was his only hope for getting the Borstal Blue Ribbon Prize Cup For Long Distance Cross Country Running (All England), which I was, and it set me laughing to myself inside, and I didn't say a word to any potbellied pop-eyed bastard that might give them real hope, though I knew the governor anyway took my quietness to mean he'd got that cup already stuck on the bookshelf in his office among the few other mildewed trophies.

"He might take up running in a sort of professional way when he gets out," and it wasn't until he'd said this and I'd heard it with my own flap-tabs that I realized it might be possible to do such a thing, run for money, trot for wages on piece work at a bob a puff rising bit by bit to a guinea a gasp and retiring through old age at thirty-two because of lace-curtain lungs, a football heart, and legs like varicose beanstalks. But I'd have a wife and car and get my grinning long-distance clock in the papers and have a smashing secretary to answer piles of letters sent by tarts who'd mob me when they saw who I was as I pushed my way into Woolworth's for a packet of razor blades and a cup of tea. It was something to think about all right, and sure enough the governor knew he'd got me when he said, turning to me as if I would at any rate have to be consulted about it all: "How does this matter strike you, then, Smith, my lad?"

A line of potbellied pop-eyes gleamed at me and a row of goldfish mouths opened and wiggled gold teeth at me, so I gave them the answer they wanted because I'd hold my trump card until later. "It'd suit me fine, sir," I said.

"Good lad. Good show. Right spirit. Splendid."

"Well," the governor said, "get that cup for us today and I'll do all I can for you. I'll get you trained so that you whack every man in the Free World." And I had a picture in my brain of me running and beating everybody in the world, leaving them all behind until only I was trot-trotting across a big wide moor alone, doing a marvellous speed as I ripped between boulders and reed-clumps, when suddenly: CRACK! CRACK!—bullets that can go faster than any man running, coming from a copper's rifle planted in a tree, winged me and split my gizzard in spite of my perfect running, and down I fell.

The potbellies expected me to say something else. "Thank you, sir." I said.

Told to go, I trotted down the pavilion steps, out on to the field because the big cross-country was about to begin and the two entries from Gunthorpe had fixed themselves early at the starting line and were ready to move off like white kangaroos. The sports ground looked a treat: with big tea-tents all round and flags flying and seats for families—empty because no mam or dad had known what opening day meant—and boys still running heats for the hundred years, and lords and ladies walking from stall to stall, and the Borstal Boys Brass Band in blue uniforms; and up on the stands the brown jackets of Hucknall as well as our own grey blazers, and then the Gunthorpe lot with short sleeves rolled. The blue sky was full of sunshine and it couldn't have been a better day, and all of the big show was like something out of Ivanhoe that we'd seen on the pictures a few days before.

"Come on, Smith," Roach the sports master called to me, "we don't want you to be late for the big race, eh? Although I dare say you'd catch them up if you were." The others catcalled and grunted at this, but I took no notice and placed myself between Gunthorpe and one of the Aylesham trusties, dropped on my knees and plucked a few grass blades to such on the way round. So the big race it was, for them, watching from the grandstand under a fluttering Union Jack, a race for the governor, that he had been waiting for, and I hoped he and all the rest of his pop-eyed gang were busy placing big bets on me, hundred to one to win, all the money they had in their pockets, all the wages they were going to get for the next five years, and the more they placed the happier I'd be. Because here was a dead cert going to die on the big name they'd built for him, going to go down dying with laughter whether it choked him or not. My knees felt the cool soil pressing into them, and out of my eye's corner I saw Roach lift his hand. The Gunthorpe boy twitched before the signal was given; somebody cheered too soon; Medway bent forward; then the gun went, and I was away.

We went once around the field and then along a half-mile drive of elms, being cheered all the way, and I seemed to feel I was in the lead as we went out by the gate and into the lane, though I wasn't interested enough to find out. The five-mile course was marked by splashes of whitewash gleaming on gateposts and trunks and stiles and stones, and a boy with a waterbottle and bandage-box stood every half-mile waiting for those that dropped out or fainted. Over the first stile, without trying, I was still nearly in the lead but one; and if any of you want tips about running, never be in a hurry, and never let any of the other runners know you are in a hurry even if you are. You can always overtake on long-distance running without letting the others smell the hurry in you; and when you've used your craft like this to reach the two or three up front then you can do a big dash later that puts everybody else's hurry in the shade because you've not had to make haste up till then. I ran to a steady jog-trot rhythm, and soon it was so smooth that I forgot I was running, and I was hardly able to know that my legs were lifting and falling and my arms going in and out, and my lungs didn't seem to be working at all, and my heart stopped that wicked thumping I always get at the beginning of a run. Because you see I never race at all; I just run, and somehow I know that if I forget I'm racing and only jog-trot along until I don't know I'm running I always win the race. For when my eyes recognize that I'm getting near the end of the course—by seeing a stile or cottage corner—I put on a spurt, and such a fast big spurt it is because I feel that up till then I haven't been running and that I've used up no energy at all. And I've been able to do this because I've been thinking; and I wonder if I'm the only one in the running business with this system of forgetting that I'm running because I'm too busy thinking; and I wonder if any of the other lads are on to the same lark, though I know for a fact that they aren't. Off like the wind along the cobbled footpath and rutted lane, smoother than the flat grass track on the field and better for thinking because it's not too smooth, and I was in my element that afternoon knowing that nobody could beat me at running but intending to beat myself before the day was over. For when the governor talked to me of being honest when I first came in he didn't know what the word meant or he wouldn't have had me here in this race, trotting along in shimmy and shorts and sunshine. He'd have had me where I'd have had him if I'd been in his place: in a quarry breaking rocks until he broke his back. At least old Hitler-face the plain-clothes dick was honester than the governor, because he at any rate had had it in for me and I for him, and when my case was coming up in court a copper knocked at our front door at four o'clock in the morning and got my mother out of bed when she was paralytic tired, reminding her she had to be in court at dead on half past nine. It was the finest bit of spite I've ever heard of, but I would call it honest, the same as my mam's words were honest when she really told that copper what she thought of him and called him all the dirty names she'd ever heard of, which took her half an hour and woke the terrace up.

I trotted on along the edge of a field bordered by the sunken lane, smelling green grass and honeysuckle, and I felt as though I came from a long line of whippets trained to run on two legs, only I couldn't see a toy rabbit in front and there wasn't a collier's cosh behind to make me keep up the pace. I passed the Gunthorpe runner whose shimmy was already black with sweat and I could just see the corner of the fenced-up copse in front where the only man I had to pass to win the race was going all out to gain the half-way mark. Then he turned into a tongue of trees and bushes where I couldn't see him anymore, and I couldn't see anybody, and I knew what the loneliness of the long-distance runner running across country felt like, realizing that as far as I was concerned this feeling was the only honesty and realness there was in the world and I knowing it would be no different ever, no matter what I felt at odd times, and no matter what anybody else tried to tell me. The runner behind me must have been a long way off because it was so quiet, and there was even less noise and movement than there had been at five o'clock of a frosty winter morning. It was hard to understand, and all I knew was that you had to run, run, run, without knowing why you were running, but on you went through fields you didn't understand and into woods that made you afraid, over hills without knowing you'd been up and down, and shooting across streams that would have cut the heart out of you had you fallen into them. And the winning post was no end to it, even though crowds might be cheering you in, because on you had to go before you got your breath back, and the only time you stopped really was when you tripped over a tree trunk and broke your neck or fell into a disused well and stayed dead in the darkness forever. So I thought: they aren't going to get me on this racing lark, this running and trying to win, this jog-trotting for a bit of blue ribbon, because it's not the way to go on at all, though they swear blind that it is. You should think about nobody and go your own way, not on a course marked out for you by people holding mugs of water and bottles of iodine in case you fall and cut yourself so that they can pick you up—even if you want to stay where you are—and get you moving again.

On I went, out of the wood, passing the man leading without knowing I was going to do so. Flip-flap, flip-flap, jog-trot, jog-trot, crunchslap-crunchslap, across the middle of a broad field again, rhythmically running in my greyhound effortless fashion, knowing I had won the race though it wasn't half over, won it if I wanted it, could go on for ten or fifteen or twenty miles if I had to and drop dead at the finish of it, which would be the same, in the end, as living an honest life like the governor wanted me to. It amounted to: win the race and be honest, and on trot-trotting I went, having the time of my life, loving my progress because it did me good and set me thinking which by now I liked to do, but not caring at all when I remembered that I had to win this race as well as run it. One of the two, I had to win the race or run it, and I knew I could do both because my legs had carried me well in front—now coming to the short cut down the bramble bank and over the sunken road—and would carry me further because they seemed made of electric cable and easily alive to keep on slapping at those ruts and roots, but I'm not going to win because the only way I'd see I came in first would be if winning meant that I was going to escape the coppers after doing the biggest bank job of my life, but winning means the exact opposite, no matter how they try to kill or kid me, means running right into their white-gloved wall-barred hands and grinning mugs and staying there for the rest of my natural long life of stone-breaking anyway, but stone-breaking in the way I want to do it and not in the way they tell me.

Another honest thought that comes is that I could swing left at the next hedge of the field, and under its cover beat my slow retreat away from the sports ground winning post. I could do three or six or a dozen miles across the turf like this and cut a few main roads behind me so's they'd never know which one I'd taken; and maybe on the last one when it got dark I could thumb a lorry-lift and get a free ride north with somebody who might not give me away. But no, I said I wasn't daft didn't I? I won't pull out with only six months left, and besides there's nothing I want to dodge and run away from; I only want a bit of my own back on the In-laws and Potbellies by letting them sit up there on their big posh seats and watch me lose this race, though as sure as God made me I know that when I do lose I'll get the dirtiest crap and kitchen jobs in the months to go before my time is up. I won't be worth a threpp'ny-bit to anybody here, which will be all the thanks I get for being honest in the only way I know. For when the governor told me to be honest it was meant to be in his way not mine, and if I kept on being honest in the way he wanted and won my race for him he'd see I got the cushiest six months still left to run; but in my own way, well, it's not allowed, and if I find a way of doing it such as I've got now then I'll get what-for in every mean trick he can set his mind to. And if you look at it in my way, who can blame him? For this is war—and ain't I said so?—and when I hit him in the only place he knows he'll be sure to get his own back on me for not collaring that cup when his heart's been set for ages on seeing himself standing up at the end of the afternoon to clap me on the back as I take the cup from Lord Earwig or some such chinless wonder with a name like that. And so I'll hit him where it hurts a lot, and he'll do all he can to get his own back, tit for tat, though I'll enjoy it most because I'm hitting first, and because I planned it longer. I don't know why I think these thoughts are better than any I've ever had, but I do, and I don't care why. I suppose it took me a long time to get going on all this because I've had no time and peace in all my bandit life, and now my thoughts are coming pat and the only trouble is I often can't stop, even when my brain feels as if it's got cramp, frostbite and creeping paralysis all rolled into one and I have to give it a rest by slap-dashing down through the brambles of the sunken lane. And all this is another uppercut I'm getting in first at people like the governor, to show how—if I can—his races are never won even though some bloke always comes unknowingly in first, how in the end the governor is going to be doomed while blokes like me will take the pickings of his roasted bones and dance like maniacs around his Borstal's ruins. And so this story's like the race and once again I won't bring off a winner to suit the governor; no, I'm being honest like he told me to, without him knowing what he means, though I don't suppose he'll ever come in with a story of his own, even if he reads this one of mine and knows who I'm talking about.

I've just come up out of the sunken lane, kneed and elbowed, thumped and bramble-scratched, and the race is two-thirds over, and a voice is going like a wireless in my mind saying that when you've had enough of feeling good like the first man on earth of a frosty morning, and you've known how it is to be taken bad like the last man on earth on a summer's afternoon, then you get at last to being like the only man on earth and don't give a bogger about either good or bad, but just trot on with your slippers slapping the good dry soil that at least would never do you a bad turn. Now the words are like coming from a crystal-set that's broken down, and something's happening inside the shell-case of my guts that bothers me and I don't know why or what to blame it on, a grinding near my ticker as though a bag of rusty screws is loose inside me and I shake them up every time I trot forward. Now and again I break my rhythm to feel my left shoulder-blade by swinging a right hand across my chest as if to rub the knife away that has somehow got stuck there. But I know it's nothing to bother about, that more likely it's caused by too much thinking that now and again I take for worry. For sometimes I'm the greatest worrier in the world I think (as you twigged I'll bet from me having got this story out) which is funny anyway because my mam don't know the meaning of the word so I don't take after her; though dad had a hard time of worry all his life up to when he filled his bedroom with hot blood and kicked the bucket that morning when nobody was in the house. I'll never forget it, straight I won't, because I was the one that found him and I often wished I hadn't. Back from a session on the fruit-machines at the fish-and-chip shop, jingling my three-lemon loot to a nail-dead house, as soon as I got in I knew something was wrong, stood leaning my head against the cold mirror above the mantelpiece trying not to open my eyes and see my stone-cold clock—because I knew I'd gone as white as a piece of chalk since coming in as if I'd been got at by a Dracula-vampire and even my penny-pocket winnings kept quiet on purpose.

Gunthorpe nearly caught me up. Birds were singing from the briar hedge, and a couple of thrushies flew like lightning into some thorny bushes. Corn had grown high in the next field and would be cut down soon with scythes and mowers; but I never wanted to notice much while running in case it put me off my stroke, so by the haystack I decided to leave it all behind and put on such a spurt, in spite of nails in my guts, that before long I'd left both Gunthorpe and the birds a good way off; I wasn't far now from going into that last mile and a half like a knife through margarine, but the quietness I suddenly trotted into between two pickets was like opening my eyes underwater and looking at the pebbles on a stream bottom, reminding me again of going back that morning to the house in which my old man had croaked, which is funny because I hadn't thought about it at all since it happened and even then I didn't brood much on it. I wonder why? I suppose that since I started to think on these long-distance runs I'm liable to have anything crop up and pester at my tripes and innards, and now that I see my bloody dad behind each grass-blade in my barmy runner-brain I'm not so sure I like to think and that it's such a good thing after all. I choke my phlegm and keep on running anyway and curse the Borstal-builders and their athletics—flappity-flap, slop-slop, crunchslap-crunchslap-crunchslap—who've maybe got their own back on me from the bright beginning by sliding magic-lantern slides into my head that never stood a chance before. Only if I take whatever comes like this in my runner's stride can I keep on keeping on like my old self and beat them back; and now I've thought on this far I know I'll win, in the crunchslap end. So anyway after a bit I went upstairs one step at a time not thinking anything about how I should find dad and what I'd do when I did. But now I'm making up for it by going over the rotten life mam led him ever since I can remember, knocking-on with different men even when he was alive and fit and she not caring whether he knew it or not, and most of the time he wasn't so blind as she thought and cursed and roared and threatened to punch her tab, and I had to stand up to stop him even though I knew she deserved it. What a life for all of us. Well, I'm not grumbling, because if I did I might just as well win this bleeding race, which I'm not going to do, though if I don't lose speed I'll win it before I know where I am, and then where would I be?

Now I can hear the sportsground noise and music as I head back for the flags and the lead-in drive, the fresh new feel of underfoot gravel going against the iron muscles of my legs. I'm nowhere near puffed despite that bag of nails that rattles as much as ever, and I can still give a big last leap like gale-force wind if I want to, but everything is under control and I know now that there ain't another long-distance cross-country running runner in England to touch my speed and style. Our doddering bastard of a governor, our half-dead gangrened gaffer is hollow like an empty petrol drum, and he wants me and my running life to give him glory, to put in him blood and throbbing veins he never had, wants his potbellied pals to be his witnesses as I gasp and stagger up to his winning post so's he can say: "My Borstal gets that cup, you see. I win my bet, because it pays to be honest and try to gain the prizes I offer to my lads, and they know it, have known it all along. They'll always be honest now, because I made them so." And his pals will think: "He trains his lads to live right, after all; he deserves a medal but we'll get him made a Sir"— and at this very moment as the birds come back to whistling I can tell myself I'll never care a sod what any of the chinless spineless In-laws think or say. They've seen me and they're cheering now and loudspeakers set around the field like elephant's ears are spreading out the big news that I'm well in the lead, and can't do anything else but stay there. But I'm still thinking of the Out-law death my dad died, telling the doctors to scat from the house when they wanted him to finish up in hospital (like a bleeding guinea-pig, he raved at them). He got up in bed to throw them out and even followed them down the stairs in his shirt though he was no more than skin and stick. They tried to tell him he'd want some drugs but he didn't fall for it, and only took the pain-killer that mam and I got from a herb-seller in the next street. It's not till now that I know what guts he had, and when I went into the room that morning he was lying on his stomach with the clothes thrown back, looking like a skinned rabbit, his grey head resting just on the edge of the bed, and on the floor must have been all the blood he'd had in his body, right from his toe-nails up, for nearly all of the lino and carpet was covered in it, thin and pink.

And down the drive I went, carrying a heart blocked up like Boulder Dam across my arteries, the nail-bag clamped down tighter and tighter as though in a woodwork vice, yet with my feet like birdwings and arms like talons ready to fly across the field except that I didn't want to give anybody that much of a show, or win the race by accident. I smell the hot dry day now as I run towards the end, passing a mountain-heap of grass emptied from cans hooked on to the fronts of lawnmowers pushed by my pals; I rip a piece of tree-bark with my fingers and stuff it in my mouth, chewing wood and dust and maybe maggots as I run until I'm nearly sick, yet swallowing what I can of it just the same because a little birdie whistled to me that I've got to go on living for at least a bloody sight longer yet but that for six months I'm not going to smell that grass or taste that dusty bark or trot this lovely path. I hate to have to say this but something bloody-well made me cry, and crying is a thing I haven't bloody-well done since I was a kid of two or three. Because I'm slowing down now for Gunthorpe to catch me up, and I'm doing it in a place just where the drive turns in to the sportsfield—where they can see what I'm doing, especially the governor and his gang from the grandstand, and I'm going so slow I'm almost marking time. Those on the nearest seats haven't caught on yet to what's happening and are still cheering like mad ready for when I make that mark, and I keep on wondering when the bleeding hell Gunthorpe behind me is going to nip by on to the field because I can't hold this up all day, and I think Oh Christ it's just my rotten luck that Gunthorpe's dropped out and that I'll be here for half an hour before the next bloke comes up, but even so, I say, I won't budge, I won't go for that last hundred yards if I have to sit down cross-legged on the grass and have the governor and his chinless wonders pick me up and carry me there, which is against their rules so you can bet they'd never do it because they're not clever enough to break the rules—like I would be in their place—even though they are their own. No, I'll show him what honesty means if it's the last thing I do, though I'm sure he'll never understand because if he and all them like him did it'd mean they'd be on my side which is impossible. By God I'll stick this out like my dad stuck out his pain and kicked them doctors down the stairs: if he had guts for that then I've got guts for this and here I stay waiting for Gunthorpe or Aylesham to bash that turf and go right slap-up against that bit of clothes-line stretched across the winning post. As for me, the only time I'll hit that clothes-line will be when I'm dead and a comfortable coffin's been got ready on the other side. Until then I'm a long-distance runner, crossing country all on my own no matter how bad it feels.

The Essex boys were shouting themselves blue in the face telling me to get a move on, waving their arms, standing up and making as if to run at that rope themselves because they were only a few yards to the side of it. You cranky lot, I thought, stuck at that winning post, and yet I knew they didn't mean what they were shouting, were really on my side and always would be, not able to keep their maulers to themselves, in and out of cop-shops and clink. And there they were now having the time of their lives letting themselves go in cheering me which made the governor think they were heart and soul on his side when he wouldn't have thought any such thing if he'd had a grain of sense. And I could hear the lords and ladies now from the grandstand, and could see them standing up to wave me in: "Run!" they were shouting in their posh voices. "Run!" But I was deaf, daft and blind, and stood where I was, still tasting the bark in my mouth and still blubbing like a baby, blubbing now out of gladness that I'd got them beat at last.

Because I heard a roar and saw the Gunthorpe gang throwing their coats up in the air and I felt the pat-pat of feet on the drive behind me getting closer and closer and suddenly a smell of sweat and a pair of lungs on their last gasp passed me by and went swinging on towards that rope, all shagged out and rocking from side to side, grunting like a Zulu that didn't know any better, like the ghost of me at ninety when I'm heading for that fat upholstered coffin. I could have cheered him myself: "Go on, go on, get cracking. Knot yourself up on that piece of tape." But he was already there, and so I went on, trot-trotting after him until I got to the rope, and collapsed, with a murderous sounding roar going up through my ears while I was still on the wrong side of it.

It's about time to stop; though don't think I'm not still running, because I am, one way or another. The governor at Borstal proved me right; he didn't respect my honesty at all; not that I expected him to, or tried to explain it to him, but if he's supposed to be educated then he should have more or less twigged it. He got his own back right enough, or thought he did, because he had me carting dustbins about every morning from the big full-working kitchen to the garden-bottoms where I had to empty them; and in the afternoon I spread out slops over spuds and carrots growing in the allotments. In the evenings I scrubbed floors, miles and miles of them. But it wasn't a bad life for six months, which was another thing he could never understand and would have made it grimmer if he could, and it was worth it when I look back on it, considering all the thinking I did, and the fact that the boys caught on to me losing the race on purpose and never had enough good words to say about me, or curses to throw out (to themselves) at the governor.

The work didn't break me; if anything it made me stronger in many ways, and the governor knew, when I left, that his spite had got him nowhere. For since leaving Borstal they tried to get me in the army, but I didn't pass the medical and I'll tell you why. No sooner was I out, after that final run and six-months hard, that I went down with pleurisy, which means as far as I'm concerned that I lost the governor's race all right, and won my own twice over, because I know for certain that if I hadn't raced my race I wouldn't have got this pleurisy, which keeps me out of khaki but doesn't stop me doing the sort of work my itchy fingers want to do.

I'm out now and the heat's switched on again, but the rats haven't got me for the last big thing I pulled. I counted six hundred and twenty-eight pounds and am still living off it because I did the job all on my own, and after it I had the peace to write all this, and it'll be money enough to keep me going until I finish my plans for doing an even bigger snatch, something up my sleeve I wouldn't tell to a living soul. I worked out my systems and hiding-places while pushing scrubbing-brushes around them Borstal floors, planned my outward life of innocence and honest work, yet at the same time grew perfect in the razor-edges of my craft for what I knew I had to do once free; and what I'll do again if netted by the poaching coppers.

In the meantime (as they say in one or two books I've read since, useless though because all of them ended on a winning post and didn't teach me a thing) I'm going to give this story to a pal of mine and tell him that if I do get captured again by the coppers he can try and get it put into a book or something, because I'd like to see the governor's face when he reads it, if he does, which I don't suppose he will; even if he did read it though I don't think he'd know what it was all about. And if I don't get caught the bloke I give this story to will never give me away; he's lived in our terrace for as long as I can remember, and he's my pal. That I do know.

Study and Discussion Questions

1. What are the different kinds of loneliness Smith feels in the course of the story?
2. What are the different kinds of honesty Smith talks about?
3. Who is "us"? Who is "them"? What does Smith mean when he says, "they've shown me the knife"?
4. What does the narrator take pride in?
5. "I know every minute of my life that a big boot is always likely to smash any nice picnic I might be barmy and dishonest enough to make for myself." How does this sentence express Smith's philosophy of life? Where does his outlook come from?
6. How does the description of his father's death shed light on Smith's ideas? Why does it come where it does in the story?
7. What does Smith's family do when they collect the insurance money for his father's death? How do you feel about that?
8. Why does having the "whip hand" make you dead, according to Smith?
9. What does Smith give up through his protest? What does he gain?
10. Give instances of how Smith's running and his thinking go together.

Writing Exercises

1. What are the differences between the image of life as a race and the image of life as a run? What does making it a race do to the running?
2. Have you ever protested something, or have you ever regretted not protesting something? Either way, write about why you did what you did when you were faced with the decision.
3. Speculate on Sillitoe's attitude toward Smith. Cite evidence from the story to support your remarks.

POETRY

PAUL LAURENCE DUNBAR   (1872–1906)

Paul Laurence Dunbar was born in Dayton, Ohio, the son of former slaves. He graduated high school, but could not afford college, and instead worked as an elevator operator. With his own money, he published his first two books of poetry, Oak and Ivy *(1893) and* Majors and Minors *(1895). The latter attracted critical attention and he was able to find a major publisher for* Lyrics of Lowly Life *(1896). He became the first black American poet to win national recognition. While the public preferred his dialect poems, Dunbar preferred those, like "We Wear the Mask," written in literary English. His later work included* Lyrics of the Heathside *(1899),* Lyrics of Love and Laughter *(1903),* Lyrics of Sunshine and Shadow *(1905), and several novels.*

We Wear the Mask   (1896)

We wear the mask that grins and
    lies,
It hides our cheeks and shades our
    eyes,—
This debt we pay to human guile;   5
With torn and bleeding hearts we
    smile,
And mouth with myriad subtleties.

Why should the world be over-
    wise,   10
In counting all our tears and
    sighs?
Nay, let them only see us, while
    We wear the mask.   15

We smile, but, O great Christ,
    our cries
To thee from tortured souls arise.
We sing, but oh the clay is vile
Beneath our feet, and long the
    mile;   20
But let the world dream other-
    wise,
    We wear the mask!

Study and Discussion Questions

1. Whom does "we" refer to?
2. What does the mask hide?
3. Why "let the world dream otherwise"?
4. To what extent is the poem itself still masked?

Writing Exercises

1. What can we infer, from this poem, about the situation of black people in the United States in the 1890s?
2. Is the poem out of date? Explain.

MARGARET WALKER (b. 1915)

Margaret Walker was born in Birmingham, Alabama. Her father was a minister and her mother a musicologist. After graduating Northwestern University, she worked for the WPA Writer's Project in Chicago and then studied at the University of Iowa. Walker has taught English at Jackson State College and directed the Institute for the Study of History, Life, and Culture of Black People there. Her writings include the novel Jubilee *(1966) and the poetry collections* For My People *(1942),* Prophets for a New Day *(1970), and* October Journey *(1973).*

For My People   (1942)

For my people everywhere singing their slave songs repeatedly: their
        dirges and their ditties and their blues and jubilees, praying their
        prayers nightly to an unknown god, bending their knees humbly
        to an unseen power;

For my people lending their strength to the years, to the gone years and
        the now years and the maybe years, washing ironing cooking
        scrubbing sewing mending hoeing plowing digging planting pruning
        patching dragging along never gaining never reaping never knowing
        and never understanding;

For my playmates in the clay and dust and sand of Alabama backyards
        playing baptizing and preaching and doctor and jail and soldier
        and school and mama and cooking and playhouse and concert and
        store and hair and Miss Choomby and company;

For the cramped bewildered years we went to school to learn to know the reasons why and the answers to and the people who and the places where and the days when, in memory of the bitter hours when we discovered we were black and poor and small and different and nobody cared and nobody wondered and nobody understood;

For the boys and girls who grew in spite of these things to be man and woman, to laugh and dance and sing and play and drink their wine and religion and success, to marry their playmates and bear children and then die of consumption and anemia and lynching;

For my people thronging 47th Street in Chicago and Lenox Avenue in New York and Rampart Street in New Orleans, lost disinherited dispossessed and happy people filling the cabarets and taverns and other people's pockets needing bread and shoes and milk and land and money and something—something all our own;

For my people walking blindly spreading joy, losing time being lazy, sleeping when hungry, shouting when burdened, drinking when hopeless, tied and shackled and tangled among ourselves by the unseen creatures who tower over us omnisciently and laugh;

For my people blundering and groping and floundering in the dark of churches and schools and clubs and societies, associations and councils and committees and conventions, distressed and disturbed and deceived and devoured by money-hungry glory-craving leeches, preyed on by facile force of state and fad and novelty, by false prophet and holy believer;

For my people standing staring trying to fashion a better way from confusion, from hypocrisy and misunderstanding, trying to fashion a world that will hold all the people, all the faces, all the adams and eves and their countless generations;

Let a new earth rise. Let another world be born. Let a bloody peace be written in the sky. Let a second generation full of courage issue forth; let a people loving freedom come to growth. Let a beauty full of healing and a strength of final clenching be the pulsing in our spirits and our blood. Let the martial songs be written, let the dirges disappear. Let a race of men now rise and take control.

Study and Discussion Questions

1. Why the repetition of the phrase "for my people"? What effect does it have on you?
2. What is the poet doing in the final stanza?
3. What is the mood of this poem?
4. Who are Walker's people and what are their strengths?
5. Chart the historical progression in the poem.

Writing Exercises

1. What associations does the phrase "a bloody peace" bring to your mind?
2. Write a stanza for your people (even if they are Walker's people too).

SUSAN GRIFFIN   (b. 1943)

Susan Griffin was born in California, graduated from San Francisco State University, and has worked as a waitress, a teacher, a house painter, and a switchboard operator to support her writing and her daughter. Her writings include poetry, Dear Sky *(1971) and* Like the Iris of an Eye *(1976); radio drama,* Voices *(1975); and nonfiction,* Woman and Nature *(1978) and Pornography and Silence *(1981).*

I Like to Think of Harriet Tubman[1]   (1976)

I like to think of Harriet Tubman.
Harriet Tubman who carried a revolver,
who had a scar on her head from a rock thrown
by a slave-master (because she
talked back), and who   5
had a ransom on her head
of thousands of dollars and who
was never caught, and who
had no use for the law
when the law was wrong,   10
who defied the law. I like
to think of her.
I like to think of her especially

---

[1] (1820?–1913), an escaped slave and leader of the Underground Railroad, which helped slaves flee.

when I think of the problem of
feeding children.   15

The legal answer
to the problem of feeding children
is ten free lunches every month,
being equal, in the child's real life,
to eating lunch every other day.   20
Monday but not Tuesday.
I like to think of the President
eating lunch Monday, but not
Tuesday.
And when I think of the President   25
and the law, and the problem of
feeding children, I like to
think of Harriet Tubman
and her revolver.

And then sometimes   30
I think of the President
and other men,
men who practice the law,
who revere the law,
who make the law,   35
who enforce the law,
who live behind
and operate through
and feed themselves
at the expense of   40
starving children
because of the law.

Men who sit in paneled offices
and think about vacations
and tell women   45
whose care it is
to feed children
not to be hysterical
not to be hysterical as in the word
hysterikos, the greek for   50
womb suffering,
not to suffer in their
wombs,
not to care,

not to bother the men   55
because they want to think
of other things
and do not want
to take the women seriously.
I want them   60
to take women seriously.

I want them to think about Harriet Tubman,
and remember,
remember she was beat by a white man
and she lived   65
and she lived to redress her grievances,
and she lived in swamps
and wore the clothes of a man
bringing hundreds of fugitives from
slavery, and was never caught,   70
and led an army,
and won a battle,
and defied the laws
because the laws were wrong, I want men
to take us seriously.   75
I am tired wanting them to think
about right and wrong.
I want them to fear.
I want them to feel fear now
as I have felt suffering in the womb, and   80
I want them
to know
that there is always a time
there is always a time to make right
what is wrong,   85
there is always a time
for retribution
and that time
is beginning.

Study and Discussion Questions

1. Why is it Harriet Tubman the speaker likes to think of?
2. What is the speaker's attitude toward the law?
3. How is she subverting traditional notions of how a woman should behave?

4. What is the role of repetition in the poem? What phrases are repeated, and why?

Writing Exercise

1. Discuss a law you feel ought to be changed and why it has not been changed.

ADRIENNE RICH (b. 1929)

Adrienne Rich was born in Baltimore; she graduated from Radcliffe College in 1951 and that same year her first book of poetry, A Change of World, *won the Yale Younger Poets Award. Rich was involved with the antiwar movement in the late 1960s, and since 1970 has been an increasingly important spokesperson for the women's movement. She taught English in the Open Admissions Program at City College, then at Douglass College and in 1979 moved to rural western Massachusetts to edit the lesbian-feminist journal* Sinister Wisdom. *Her writings include the poetry* Snapshots of a Daughter-in-Law (1963), Diving Into the Wreck (1973), *and* The Dream of a Common Language (1978); *and the nonfiction* Of Woman Born: Motherhood as Experience and Institution (1976), On Lies, Secrets, and Silence (1979), *and* Blood, Bread, and Poetry (1986).

The Trees   (1963)

The trees inside are moving out into the forest,
the forest that was empty all these days
where no bird could sit
no insect hide
no sun bury its feet in shadow   5
the forest that was empty all these nights
will be full of trees by morning.

All night the roots work
to disengage themselves from the cracks
in the veranda floor.   10
The leaves strain toward the glass
small twigs stiff with exertion
long-cramped boughs shuffling under the roof
like newly discharged patients
half-dazed, moving   15
to the clinic doors.

I sit inside, doors open to the veranda
writing long letters
in which I scarcely mention the departure
of the forest from the house.   20
The night is fresh, the whole moon shines
in a sky still open
the smell of leaves and lichen
still reaches like a voice into the rooms.
My head is full of whispers   25
which tomorrow will be silent.

Listen. The glass is breaking.
The trees are stumbling forward
into the night. Winds rush to meet them.
The moon is broken like a mirror,   30
its pieces flash now in the crown
of the tallest oak.

Study and Discussion Questions

1. What happens in each stanza?
2. Describe the persona of the poem, her mood and state of mind, and her relation to the trees.
3. Why is she "writing long letters" in which she scarcely mentions "the departure / of the forest from the house"?
4. Where are the trees going? And why?

Writing Exercises

1. Write a version of one of those letters the speaker mentions.
2. In reality, of course, trees don't pick up their roots and depart. What do the trees stand for?

MARGE PIERCY (b. 1936)

Marge Piercy was born in Detroit, Michigan, and attended the University of Michigan and Northwestern University. She has been an activist in the civil rights movement, in Students for a Democratic Society, and in the women's movement. Piercy's poetry includes Breaking Camp *(1968),* To Be of Use *(1973),* The Moon Is Always Female *(1980), and* Circles on the Water *(1982), and she has written a number of novels, among them* Small Changes *(1973),* Woman on the Edge of Time *(1976), and* Gone to Soldiers *(1987).*

What's that smell in the kitchen?   (1980)

All over America women are burning dinners.
It's lambchops in Peoria; it's haddock
in Providence; it's steak in Chicago
tofu delight in Big Sur; red
rice and beans in Dallas.   5
All over America women are burning
food they're supposed to bring with calico
smile on platters glittering like wax.
Anger sputters in her brainpan, confined
but spewing out missiles of hot fat.   10
Carbonized despair presses like a clinker
from a barbecue against the back of her eyes.
If she wants to grill anything, it's
her husband spitted over a slow fire.
If she wants to serve him anything   15
it's a dead rat with a bomb in its belly
ticking like the heart of an insomniac.
Her life is cooked and digested,
nothing but leftovers in Tupperware.
Look, she says, once I was roast duck   20
on your platter with parsley but now I am Spam.
Burning dinner is not incompetence but war.

Study and Discussion Questions

1. Why a "calico smile"?
2. What do the four lines before the last line mean?
3. Why the panoramic opening? Why the repetition of "All over America"?

Writing Exercise

1. What other instances can you imagine where it is "not incompetence but war"?

MERVYN MORRIS   (b. 1937)

Mervyn Morris was born in Kingston, Jamaica and attended Munro College in Jamaica and then Oxford University on a Rhodes Scholarship. He teaches English at the University of the West Indies and has edited two anthologies

of Caribbean literature. His poetry includes The Pond *(1973),* On Holy Week
(1976), and Shadowboxing *(1979).*

The Early Rebels   **(1973)**

Time and the changing passions played them tricks,
Killing the shop-soiled resolutions dead.
Gone are the early angry promises
Of rich men squeezed, of capitalists bled.
More adult honesties have straightened ties   5
And brushed the dinner-jackets clean,
Maturer minds have smelt out fallacies
And redefined what thinkers mean.

Hope drives a chromium symbol now
And smiles a toothpaste passion to the poor,   10
With colder eloquence explaining how
The young were foolish when they swore
They'd see those dunghills dank and dreary
All replaced by bright new flats:
Good sense was never youthful fury   15
And rash young promises by brats. . . .

"Let's drink a loyal toast to dedication:
We mean the same but youth is past;
We are the fathers of our nation,
The thinking leaders come at last.   20
Cheers for the faith of simple minds,
Cheers for the love of humble friends;
Love does not alter when it finds
That we have redefined its ends."

Study and Discussion Questions

1. How does Morris keep us aware that he is being ironic?
2. What do the last two lines mean?
3. Is there any clue in the poem as to *why* these people have changed?

Writing Exercise

1. Why might it often be easier to be a rebel when young?

ALLEN GINSBERG   (b. 1926)

Allen Ginsberg was born in Paterson, New Jersey, where his father was a high school English teacher and unsuccessful poet. Ginsberg attended Columbia University and, in the early 1950s, moved to San Francisco and began his relationship with poet Peter Orlovsky. City Lights Bookstore published Howl *in 1956, which established Ginsberg as a major "Beat" poet. In the 1960s, he studied Buddhism, gave wild poetry readings, and became an increasingly outspoken social critic. His poetry includes* Kaddish *(1961),* Reality Sandwiches *(1963),* Planet News *(1968),* Mind Breaths *(1977), and* Collected Poems *(1985).*

America   (1956)

America I've given you all and now I'm nothing.
America two dollars and twentyseven cents January 17, 1956.
I can't stand my own mind.
America when will we end the human war?
Go fuck yourself with your atom bomb.   5
I don't feel good don't bother me.
I won't write my poem till I'm in my right mind.
America when will you be angelic?
When will you take off your clothes?
When will you look at yourself through the grave?   10
When will you be worthy of your million Trotskyites?
America why are your libraries full of tears?
America when will you send your eggs to India?
I'm sick of your insane demands.
When can I go into the supermarket and buy what I need with my good
        looks?
America after all it is you and I who are perfect not the next world.
Your machinery is too much for me.
You made me want to be a saint.
There must be some other way to settle this argument.   20
Burroughs[1] is in Tangiers I don't think he'll come back it's sinister.
Are you being sinister or is this some form of practical joke?
I'm trying to come to the point.
I refuse to give up my obsession.
America stop pushing I know what I'm doing.   25
America the plum blossoms are falling.
I haven't read the newspapers for months, everyday somebody goes on
        trial for murder.
America I feel sentimental about the Wobblies.
America I used to be a communist when I was a kid I'm not sorry. 30

---

[1] William Burroughs (b. 1914), American novelist.

I smoke marijuana every chance I get.
I sit in my house for days on end and stare at the roses in the closet.
When I go to Chinatown I get drunk and never get laid.
My mind is made up there's going to be trouble.
You should have seen me reading Marx.   35
My psychoanalyst thinks I'm perfectly right.
I won't say the Lord's Prayer.
I have mystical visions and cosmic vibrations.
America I still haven't told you what you did to Uncle Max after he came
    over from Russia.   40

I'm addressing you.
Are you going to let your emotional life be run by Time Magazine?
I'm obsessed by Time Magazine.
I read it every week.
Its cover stares at me every time I slink past the corner candystore.   45
I read it in the basement of the Berkeley Public Library.
It's always telling me about responsibility. Businessmen are serious.
    Movie producers are serious. Everybody's serious but me.
It occurs to me that I am America.
I am talking to myself again.   50

Asia is rising against me.
I haven't got a chinaman's chance.
I'd better consider my national resources.
My national resources consist of two joints of marijuana millions of genitals
    an unpublishable private literature that jetplanes 1400 miles
    an hour and twentyfive-thousand mental institutions.
I say nothing about my prisons nor the millions of underprivileged who
    live in my flowerpots under the light of five hundred suns.
I have abolished the whorehouses of France, Tangiers is the next to go.
My ambition is to be President despite the fact that I'm a Catholic.

America how can I write a holy litany in your silly mood?
I will continue like Henry Ford my strophes are as individual as his
    automobiles more so they're all different sexes.
America I will sell you strophes $2500 apiece $500 down on your old
    strophe
America free Tom Mooney²   65
America save the Spanish Loyalists
America Sacco & Vanzetti must not die

----

² American Wobbly, jailed on murder charges in 1916 and pardoned over twenty years
later.

America I am the Scottsboro boys.[3]

America when I was seven momma took me to Communist Cell meetings
they sold us garbanzos a handful per ticket a ticket costs a nickel
and the speeches were free everybody was angelic and sentimental
about the workers it was all so sincere you have no idea what a
good thing the party was in 1835 Scott Nearing was a grand old
man a real mensch Mother Bloor the Silk-strikers' Ewig-Weibliche
made me cry I once saw the Yiddish orator Israel Amter plain.[4]
Everybody must have been a spy.   75

America you don't really want to go to war.

America it's them bad Russians.

Them Russians them Russians and them Chinamen. And them Russians.

The Russia wants to eat us alive. The Russia's power mad. She wants to
take our cars from out our garages.

Her wants to grab Chicago. Her needs a Red *Reader's Digest*. Her wants
our auto plants in Siberia. Him big bureaucracy running our fil-
lingstations.

That no good. Ugh. Him make Indians learn read. Him need big black
niggers. Hah. Her make us all work sixteen hours a day. Help.

America this is quite serious.

America this is the impression I get from looking in the television set.

America is this correct?

I'd better get right down to the job.   90

It's true I don't want to join the Army or turn lathes in precision parts
factories, I'm nearsighted and psychopathic anyway.

America I'm putting my queer shoulder to the wheel.

Study and Discussion Questions

1. Why does Ginsberg keep repeating the word "America"?
2. What is the argument the speaker is having with America?
3. Why do you think Ginsberg chooses to address his poem to America
   rather than, say, to us, about America?
4. List the qualities of America as portrayed in this poem.
5. Characterize the speaker of the poem.
6. The speaker says, "Everybody's serious but me." How does he mean
   that? Do you agree with him?
7. What does he mean in the last line about putting his "queer shoulder
   to the wheel"? Has he undergone a change of attitude during the poem?

---

[3] Nine black youths convicted on flimsy evidence, in 1931, of raping two white women.

[4] Nearing, Bloor, Amter were American leftists. Ewig-Weibliche means "the eternal feminine."

Writing Exercises

1. Find a copy of Whitman's "Song of Myself," read some of it, and compare Ginsberg's "America" to it. You might look at line length and rhythm, and at the two poets' sense of themselves as Americans.
2. Write a series of lines, each one beginning "America," that expresses your own relationship to the United States.

ALEXANDER POPE   (1688–1744)

FROM **An Essay on Man**   (1733)

Cease then, nor ORDER imperfection name:
Our proper bliss depends on what we blame.
Know thy own point: this kind, this due degree
Of blindness, weakness, Heaven bestows on thee.
Submit—In this, or any other sphere,   5
Secure to be as blest as thou canst bear:
Safe in the hand of one disposing Power,
Or in the natal, or the mortal hour.
All Nature is but art, unknown to thee;
All chance, direction, which thou canst not see;   10
All discord, harmony not understood;
All partial evil, universal good:
And, spite of pride, in erring reason's spite,
One truth is clear: Whatever IS, is RIGHT.

JOHN GREENLEAF WHITTIER   (1807–1892)

For Righteousness' Sake   (1855)

Inscribed to friends under arrest for treason against the slave power.

The age is dull and mean. Men creep,
    Not walk; with blood too pale and tame
    To pay the debt they owe to shame;
Buy cheap, sell dear; eat, drink, and sleep
    Down-pillowed, deaf to moaning want;   5

Pay tithes for soul-insurance; keep
  Six days to Mammon, one to Cant.

In such a time, give thanks to God,
  That somewhat of the holy rage
  With which the prophets in their age   10
On all its decent seemings trod,
  Has set your feet upon the lie,
That man and ox and soul and clod
  Are market stock to sell and buy!

The hot words from your lips, my own,   15
  To caution trained, might not repeat;
  But if some tares among the wheat
Of generous thought and deed were sown,
  No common wrong provoked your zeal;
The silken gauntlet that is thrown   20
  In such a quarrel rings like steel.

The brave old strife the fathers saw
  For Freedom calls for men again
  Like those who battled not in vain
For England's Charter, Alfred's law;[1]   25
  And right of speech and trial just
Wage in your name their ancient war
  With venal courts and perjured trust.

God's ways seem dark, but, soon or late,
  They touch the shining hills of day;   30
  The evil cannot brook delay,
The good can well afford to wait.
  Give ermined knaves their hour of crime;
Ye have the future grand and great,
  The safe appeal of Truth to Time!   35

RALPH CHAPLIN   **(1887–1961)**

SONG: **Solidarity Forever**   **(1915)**

When the union's inspiration through the workers' blood shall run,
There can be no power greater anywhere beneath the sun.

---

[1] The Magna Carta (1215), charter of English liberties; Alfred the Great (849–899), King of Wessex, instituted many reforms.

Yet what force on earth is weaker than the feeble strength of one?
But the union makes us strong.

       Solidarity forever!   5
       Solidarity forever!
       Solidarity forever!
       For the union makes us strong.

Is there aught we hold in common with the greedy parasite
Who would lash us into serfdom and would crush us with his might?
Is there anything left for us but to organize and fight?   10
For the union makes us strong.

It is we who plowed the prairies; built the cities where they trade;
Dug the mines and built the workshops; endless miles of railroad laid.
Now we stand, outcast and starving, 'mid the wonders we have made;
But the union makes us strong.   15

All the world that's owned by idle drones, is ours and ours alone.
We have laid the wide foundations; built it skyward stone by stone.
It is ours, not to slave in, but to master and to own,
While the union makes us strong.

They have taken untold millions that they never toiled to earn.   20
But without our brain and muscle not a single wheel can turn.
We can break their haughty power; gain our freedom while we learn
That the union makes us strong.

In our hands is placed a power greater than their hoarded gold;   25
Greater than the might of armies, magnified a thousand-fold.
We can bring to birth the new world from the ashes of the old,
For the union makes us strong.

WILLIAM BUTLER YEATS   (1865–1939)

Easter 1916[1]   (1916)

I HAVE met them at close of day
Coming with vivid faces

---

[1] Date of uprising by a group of Irish nationalists; some are referred to in the second stanza and four are named near the end of the poem.

From counter or desk among grey
Eighteenth-century houses.
I have passed with a nod of the head 5
Or polite meaningless words,
Or have lingered awhile and said
Polite meaningless words,
And thought before I had done
Of a mocking tale or a gibe 10
To please a companion
Around the fire at the club,
Being certain that they and I
But lived where motley is worn:
All changed, changed utterly: 15
A terrible beauty is born.

That woman's days were spent
In ignorant good-will,
Her nights in argument
Until her voice grew shrill. 20
What voice more sweet than hers
When, young and beautiful,
She rode to harriers?
This man had kept a school
And rode our wingèd horse; 25
This other his helper and friend
Was coming into his force;
He might have won fame in the end,
So sensitive his nature seemed,
So daring and sweet his thought. 30
This other man I had dreamed
A drunken, vainglorious lout.
He had done most bitter wrong
To some who are near my heart,
Yet I number him in the song; 35
He, too, has resigned his part
In the casual comedy;
He, too, has been changed in his turn,
Transformed utterly:
A terrible beauty is born. 40

Hearts with one purpose alone
Through summer and winter seem
Enchanted to a stone
To trouble the living stream.
The horse that comes from the road, 45

The rider, the birds that range
From cloud to tumbling cloud,
Minute by minute they change;
A shadow of cloud on the stream
Changes minute by minute;   50
A horse-hoof slides on the brim,
And a horse plashes within it;
The long-legged moor-hens dive,
And hens to moor-cocks call;
Minute by minute they live: 55
The stone's in the midst of all.

Too long a sacrifice
Can make a stone of the heart.
O when may it suffice?
That is Heaven's part, our part   60
To murmur name upon name,
As a mother names her child
When sleep at last has come
On limbs that had run wild.
What is it but nightfall?   65
No, no, not night but death;
Was it needless death after all?
For England may keep faith
For all that is done and said.
We know their dream; enough   70
To know they dreamed and are dead;
And what if excess of love
Bewildered them till they died?
I write it out in a verse—
MacDonagh and MacBride   75
And Connolly and Pearse
Now and in time to be,
Wherever green is worn,
Are changed, changed utterly:
A terrible beauty is born.   80

CLAUDE McKAY   (1890–1948)

If We Must Die   (1922)

If we must die, let it not be like hogs
Hunted and penned in an inglorious spot,

While round us bark the mad and hungry dogs,
Making their mock at our accursed lot.
If we must die, O let us nobly die,　　　　　　　　　　　　5
So that our precious blood may not be shed
In vain; then even the monsters we defy
Shall be constrained to honor us though dead!
O kinsmen! we must meet the common foe!
Though far outnumbered let us show us brave,　　　　　10
And for their thousand blows deal one deathblow!
What though before us lies the open grave?
Like men we'll face the murderous, cowardly pack,
Pressed to the wall, dying, but fighting back!

E.E. CUMMINGS　　　　　　　　　　　　　　　　**(1894–1962)**

---

i sing of Olaf glad and big　　　　　　　**(1935)**

i sing of Olaf glad and big
whose warmest heart recoiled at war:
a conscientious object-or

his wellbelovéd colonel(trig
westpointer most succinctly bred)　　　　　　　　　5
took erring Olaf soon in hand;
but—though an host of overjoyed
noncoms(first knocking on the head
him)do through icy waters roll
that helplessness which others stroke　　　　　　　10
with brushes recently employed
anent this muddy toiletbowl,
while kindred intellects evoke
allegiance per blunt instruments—
Olaf(being to all intents　　　　　　　　　　　15
a corpse and wanting any rag
upon what God unto him gave)
responds, without getting annoyed
"I will not kiss your fucking flag"

straightway the silver bird looked grave　　　　　20
(departing hurriedly to shave)

but—though all kinds of officers
(a yearning nation's blueeyed pride)
their passive prey did kick and curse
until for wear their clarion   25
voices and boots were much the worse,
and egged the firstclassprivates on
his rectum wickedly to tease
by means of skilfully applied
bayonets roasted hot with heat—   30
Olaf(upon what were once knees)
does almost ceaselessly repeat
"there is some shit I will not eat"

our president, being of which
assertions duly notified   35
threw the yellowsonofabitch
into a dungeon, where he died

Christ(of His mercy infinite)
i pray to see; and Olaf,too

preponderatingly because   40
unless statistics lie he was
more brave than me:more blond than you.

PABLO NERUDA   (1904–1973)

Ode to Federico García Lorca[1]   (1935)

If I could weep with fear in a solitary house,
if I could take out my eyes and eat them,
I would do it for your black-draped orange-tree voice
and for your poetry that comes forth shouting.

Because for you they paint hospitals bright blue,   5
and schools and sailors' quarters grow,
and wounded angels are covered with feathers,

---

[1] (1899–1936), Spanish poet and playwright, executed by the Fascists during the Spanish Civil War. Poem translated by Donald D. Walsh.

and nuptial fish are covered with scales,
and hedgehogs go flying to the sky:
for you tailorshops with their black skins   10
fill up with spoons and blood,
and swallow red ribbons and kiss each other to death,
and dress in white.

When you fly dressed as a peach tree,
when you laugh with a laugh of hurricaned rice,   15
when to sing you shake arteries and teeth,
throat and fingers,
I could die for how sweet you are,
I could die for the red lakes
where in the midst of autumn you live   20
with a fallen steed and a bloodied god,
I could die for the cemeteries
that pass like ash-gray rivers
with water and tombs,
at night, among drowned bells: 25
rivers as thick as wards
of sick soldiers, that suddenly grow
toward death in rivers with marble numbers
and rotted crowns, and funeral oils:
I could die to see you at night   30
watching the sunken crosses go by,
standing and weeping,
because before death's river you weep
forlornly, woundedly,
you weep weeping, your eyes filled   35
with tears, with tears, with tears.

If at night, wildly alone, I could
gather oblivion and shadow and smoke
above railroads and steamships,
with a black funnel,   40
biting the ashes,
I would do it for the tree in which you grow,
for the nests of golden waters that you gather,
and for the vine that covers your bones,
revealing to you the secret of the night.   45

Cities with a smell of wet onions
wait for you to pass singing raucously,
and silent sperm boats pursue you,

and green swallows nest in your hair,
and also snails and weeks,   50
furled masts and cherry trees
definitively walk about when they glimpse
your pale fifteen-eyed head
and your mouth of submerged blood.

If I could fill town halls with soot   55
and, sobbing, tear down clocks,
it would be to see when to your house
comes summer with its broken lips,
come many people with dying clothes,
come regions of sad splendor,   60
come dead plows and poppies,
come gravediggers and horsemen,
come planets and maps with blood,
come owls covered with ashes,
come masked men dragging damsels   65
pierced by great knives,
come roots, veins, hospitals,
springs, ants,
comes night with the bed where
a solitary hussar is dying among the spiders,   70
comes a rose of hatred and pins,
comes a yellowish vessel,
comes a windy day with a child,
come I with Oliverio, Norah,
Vicente Aleixandre, Delia,   75
Maruca, Malva, Marina, María Luisa, and Larco,
the Blond, Rafael, Ugarte,
Cotapos, Rafael Alberti,
Carlos, Bebé, Manolo Altolaguirre,
Molinari,   80
Rosales, Concha Méndez,
and others that slip my mind.

Come, let me crown you, youth of health
and butterflies, youth pure
as a black lightningflash perpetually free,   85
and just between you and me,
now, when there is no one left among the rocks,
let us speak simply, man to man:
what are verses for if not for the dew?

What are verses for if not for that night   90
in which a bitter dagger finds us out, for that day,
for that dusk, for that broken corner
where the beaten heart of man makes ready to die?

Above all at night,
at night there are many stars,   95
all within a river
like a ribbon next to the windows
of houses filled with the poor.

Someone of theirs has died, perhaps
they have lost their jobs in the offices,   100
in the hospitals, in the elevators,
in the mines,
human beings suffer stubbornly wounded
and there are protests and weeping everywhere:
while the stars flow within an endless river   105
there is much weeping at the windows,
the thresholds are worn away by the weeping,
the bedrooms are soaked by the weeping
that comes wave-shaped to bite the carpets.

Federico,   110
you see the world, the streets,
the vinegar,
the farewells in the stations
when the smoke lifts its decisive wheels
toward where there is nothing but some   115
separations, stones, railroad tracks.

There are so many people asking questions
everywhere.
There is the bloody blindman, and the angry one, and the
disheartened one,   120
and the wretch, the thorn tree,
the bandit with envy on his back.

That's the way life is, Federico, here you have
the things that my friendship can offer you,
the friendship of a melancholy manly man.   125
By yourself you already know many things,
and others you will slowly get to know.

W. H. AUDEN   (1907–1973)

The Unknown Citizen   (1940)

(To JS/07/M/378
This Marble Monument
Is Erected by the State)

He was found by the Bureau of Statistics to be
One against whom there was no official complaint,
And all the reports on his conduct agree
That, in the modern sense of an old-fashioned word, he was a saint, 5
For in everything he did he served the Greater Community.
Except for the War till the day he retired
He worked in a factory and never got fired,
But satisfied his employers, Fudge Motors Inc.
Yet he wasn't a scab or odd in his views,   10
For his Union reports that he paid his dues,
(Our report on his Union shows it was sound)
And our Social Psychology workers found
That he was popular with his mates and liked a drink.
The Press are convinced that he bought a paper every day   15
And that his reactions to advertisements were normal in every way.
Policies taken out in his name prove that he was fully insured,
And his Health-card shows he was once in hospital but left it cured. 20
Both Producers Research and High-Grade Living declare
He was fully sensible to the advantages of the Instalment Plan
And had everything necessary to the Modern Man,
A phonograph, a radio, a car and a frigidaire.
Our researchers into Public Opinion are content   25
That he held the proper opinions for the time of year;
When there was peace, he was for peace; when there was war, he went.
He was married and added five children to the population,
Which our Eugenist says was the right number for a parent of   30
    his generation,
And our teachers report that he never interfered with their education.
Was he free? Was he happy? The question is absurd:
Had anything been wrong, we should certainly have heard.   35

ROBERT HAYDEN   (1913–1980)

Frederick Douglass[1]   (1947)

When it is finally ours, this freedom, this liberty, this beautiful
and terrible thing, needful to man as air,
usable as earth; when it belongs at last to all,
when it is truly instinct, brain matter, diastole, systole,
reflex action; when it is finally won; when it is more   5
than the gaudy mumbo jumbo of politicians:
this man, this Douglass, this former slave, this Negro
beaten to his knees, exiled, visioning a world
where none is lonely, none hunted, alien,
this man, superb in love and logic, this man   10
shall be remembered. Oh, not with statues' rhetoric,
not with legends and poems and wreaths of bronze alone,
but with the lives grown out of his life, the lives
fleshing his dream of the beautiful, needful thing.

LANGSTON HUGHES   (1902–1967)

Harlem   (1951)

What happens to a dream deferred?

Does it dry up
like a raisin in the sun?
Or fester like a sore—
And then run?   5
Does it stink like rotten meat?
Or crust and sugar over—
like a syrupy sweet?

Maybe it just sags
like a heavy load.   10

Or does it explode?

---

[1] Escaped slave, abolitionist, writer (1817?–1895).

SYLVIA PLATH (1932–1963)

Mushrooms (1959)

Overnight, very
Whitely, discreetly,
Very quietly

Our toes, our noses
Take hold on the loam,   5
Acquire the air.

Nobody sees us,
Stops us, betrays us;
The small grains make room.

Soft fists insist on   10
Heaving the needles,
The leafy bedding,

Even the paving.
Our hammers, our rams,
Earless and eyeless,   15

Perfectly voiceless,
Widen the crannies,
Shoulder through holes. We

Diet on water,
On crumbs of shadow,   20
Bland-mannered, asking

Little or nothing.
So many of us!
So many of us!

We are shelves, we are   25
Tables, we are meek,
We are edible,

Nudgers and shovers
In spite of ourselves.
Our kind multiplies: 30

We shall by morning
Inherit the earth.
Our foot's in the door.

WOLE SOYINKA   (b. 1934)

Telephone Conversation   (1960)

The price seemed reasonable, location
Indifferent. The landlady swore she lived
Off premises. Nothing remained
But self-confession. 'Madam,' I warned,
'I hate a wasted journey—I am African.'   5
Silence. Silenced transmission of
Pressurized good-breeding. Voice, when it came,
Lipstick coated, long gold-rolled
Cigarette-holder pipped. Caught I was, foully.
'HOW DARK?' . . . I had not misheard . . . 'ARE YOU LIGHT   10
OR VERY DARK?' Button B. Button A. Stench
Of rancid breath of public hide-and-speak.
Red booth. Red pillar-box. Red double-tiered
Omnibus squelching tar. It *was* real! Shamed
By ill-mannered silence, surrender   15
Pushed dumbfoundment to beg simplification.
Considerate she was, varying the emphasis—
'ARE YOU DARK? OR VERY LIGHT?' Revelation came.
'You mean—like plain or milk chocolate?'
Her assent was clinical, crushing in its light   20
Impersonality. Rapidly, wave-length adjusted,
I chose. 'West African sepia'—and as afterthought,
'Down in my passport.' Silence for spectroscopic
Flight of fancy, till truthfulness clanged her accent
Hard on the mouthpiece. 'WHAT'S THAT?' conceding   25
'DON'T KNOW WHAT THAT IS.' 'Like brunette.'
'THAT'S DARK, ISN'T IT?' 'Not altogether.
Facially, I am brunette, but madam, you should see
The rest of me. Palm of my hand, soles of my feet

Are a peroxide blonde. Friction, caused—   30
Foolishly madam—by sitting down, has turned
My bottom raven black—One moment madam!'—sensing
Her receiver rearing on the thunderclap
About my ears—'Madam,' I pleaded, 'wouldn't you rather
See for yourself?'   35

RAY DUREM   (1915–1963)

To the pale poets   (1962)

I know I'm not sufficiently obscure
to please the critics, nor devious enough.
Imagery escapes me.
I cannot find those mild and precious words
to clothe the carnage.   5
Blood is blood and murder's murder.
What's a lavender word for lynch?

Come, you pale poets, wan, refined, and dreamy—
here is a black woman working out her guts
in a white man's kitchen   10
for little money and no glory.
How should I tell that story?
There is a black boy, blacker still from death,
face down in the cold Korean mud.
Come on with your effervescent jive,   15
explain to him why he ain't alive.

Reword our specific discontent
into some plaintive melody,
a little whine, a little whimper,
not too much—and no rebellion,   20
God, no! Rebellion's much too corny.
You deal with finer feelings,
very subtle—an autumn leaf
hanging from a tree—
            I see a body.   25

HELEN CHASIN   (b. 1938)

Alabama, 1964   (1968)

At home, lounging on page one,
fatback necks screwed
in an occasional slow swivel,
they stare from wirephotos as if they knew me
and spit suggestions like jets of tobacco.   5
They are casual, but ready for action.
(I would fold and sag
into dying—disappointed, rabbitty.)
Last night they moved into
a Boston minister: 10
his chipped skull and smashed breathing
bear witness to trouble in Selma.
He lies wrapped up in Birmingham
in very critical condition.
I am afraid, but bandaged in bulletins.   15
The early news mentions the *cruelty*
of breakthrough, as if
militant in our hope but knowing how things are
we should expect to pay in bodies.

VICTOR HERNANDEZ CRUZ   (b. 1949)

today is a day of great joy   (1969)

when they stop poems
in the mail & clap
their hands & dance to
them
when women become pregnant   5
by the side of poems
the strongest sounds making
the river go along

it is a great day

as poems fall down to   10
movie crowds   in restaurants
in bars

when poems start to
knock down walls to
choke politicians   15
when poems scream &
begin to break the air

that is the time of
true poets   that is
the time of greatness   20

a true poet aiming
poems & watching things
fall to the ground

it is a great day.

GWENDOLYN BROOKS   (b. 1917)

Riot   (1969)

> A riot is the language of the unheard.
> —Martin Luther King

John Cabot, out of Wilma, once a Wycliffe,
all whitebluerose below his golden hair,
wrapped richly in right linen and right wool,
almost forgot his Jaguar and Lake Bluff;
almost forgot Grandtully (which is The   5
Best Thing That Ever Happened To Scotch);
        almost
forgot the sculpture at the Richard Gray
and Distelheim; the kidney pie at Maxim's,
the Grenadine de Boeuf at Maison Henri.   10

Because the Negroes were coming down the street.

Because the Poor were sweaty and unpretty
(not like Two Dainty Negroes in Winnetka)
and they were coming toward him in rough ranks.   15
In seas. In windsweep. They were black and loud.
And not detainable. And not discreet.

Gross. Gross. *"Que tu es grossier!"*[1] John Cabot
itched instantly beneath the nourished white
that told his story of glory to the World.   20
"Don't let It touch me! the blackness! Lord!" he whispered
to any handy angel in the sky.

But, in a thrilling announcement, on It drove
and breathed on him: and touched him. In that breath   25
the fume of pig foot, chitterling and cheap chili,
malign, mocked John. And, in terrific touch, old
averted doubt jerked forward decently,
cried "Cabot! John! You are a desperate man,   30
and the desperate die expensively today."

John Cabot went down in the smoke and fire
and broken glass and blood, and he cried "Lord!
Forgive these nigguhs that know not what they do."   35

PEGGY SEEGER   (b. 1935)

SONG: **I'm Gonna Be an Engineer**   (1970)

When I was a little girl, I wished I was a boy,
I tagged along behind the gang and wore my corduroys,
Everybody said I only did it to annoy
But I was gonna be an engineer.
    Mamma told me, "Can't you be a lady?   5
    Your duty is to make me the mother of a pearl.
    Wait until you're older, dear, and maybe
    You'll be glad that you're a girl.

---

[1] "How crude you are!"

DAINTY AS A DRESDEN STATUE.
GENTLE AS A JERSEY COW. 10
SMOOTH AS SILK, GIVES CREAMY MILK
LEARN TO COO, LEARN TO MOO,
THAT'S WHAT YOU DO TO BE A LADY NOW—

When I went to school I learned to write and how to read,
Some history, geography, and home economy. 15
And typing is a skill that every girl is sure to need,
To while away the extra time until the time to breed,
And then they had the nerve to say, "What would you like to be?"
I says, "I'm gonna be an engineer!"
   No, you only need to learn to be a lady, 20
   The duty isn't yours for to try and run the world,
   An engineer could never have a baby!
   Remember, dear, that you're a girl.

SHE'S SMART (FOR A WOMAN).
I WONDER HOW SHE GOT THAT WAY? 25
YOU GET NO CHOICE, YOU GET NO VOICE,
JUST STAY MUM, PRETEND YOU'RE DUMB
AND THAT'S HOW YOU COME TO BE A LADY TODAY—

Then Jimmy come along and we set up a conjugation,
We were busy every night with loving recreation. 30
I spent my day at work so HE could get his education,
Well, now he's an engineer.
   He says, "I know you'll always be a lady,
   It's the duty of my darling to love me all her life,
   Could an *engineer* look after or obey me? 35
   Remember, dear, that you're my wife."

Well, as soon as Jimmy got a job, I began again,
Then, happy at my turret-lathe a year or so, and then:
The morning that the twins were born, Jimmy says to them,
"Kids, your mother *was* an engineer." 40
   You owe it to the kids to be a lady,
   Dainty as a dishrag, faithful as a chow,
   Stay at home, you got to mind the baby,
   Remember you're a mother now.

Well, every time I turn around it's something else to do, 45
It's cook a meal, mend a sock, sweep a floor or two,

I listen in to Jimmy Young, it makes me want to spew,
I WAS GONNA BE AN ENGINEER!
   Don't I really wish that I could be a lady?
   I could do the lovely things that a lady's 'sposed to do,   50
   I wouldn't even mind, if only they would pay me,
   And I could be a person too.

   WHAT PRICE—FOR A WOMAN?
   YOU CAN BUY HER FOR A RING OF GOLD.
   TO LOVE AND OBEY (WITHOUT ANY PAY)   55
   YOU GET A COOK AND A NURSE (FOR BETTER OR WORSE)
   YOU DON'T NEED A PURSE WHEN THE LADY IS SOLD.

Ah, but now that times are harder and my Jimmy's got the sack,
I went down to Vicker's, they were glad to have me back,
But I'm a third-class citizen, my wages tell me that,   60
And I'm a first-class engineer.
   The boss he says, "We pay you as a lady,
   You only got the job 'cause I can't afford a man,
   With you I keep the profits high as may be,
   You're just a cheaper pair of hands."   65

   YOU GOT ONE FAULT—YOU'RE A WOMAN.
   YOU'RE NOT WORTH THE EQUAL PAY.
   A BITCH OR A TART, YOU'RE NOTHING BUT HEART,
   SHALLOW AND VAIN, YOU GOT NO BRAIN,
   YOU EVEN GO DOWN THE DRAIN LIKE A LADY TODAY—   70

Well, I listened to my mother and I joined a typing-pool,
I listened to my lover and I put him through his school,
But if I listen to the boss, I'm just a bloody fool
And an underpaid engineer!
   I been a sucker ever since I was a baby,   75
   As a daughter, as a wife, as a mother and a "dear"—
   But I'll fight them as a woman, not a lady,
   Fight them as an engineer!

JUDY GRAHN   (b. 1940)

A Woman Is Talking To Death   (1973)

One
Testimony in trials that never got heard

my lovers teeth are white geese flying above me
my lovers muscles are rope ladders under my hands

we were driving home slow   5
my lover and I, across the long Bay Bridge,
one February midnight, when midway
over in the far left lane, I saw a strange scene:

one small young man standing by the rail,
and in the lane itself, parked straight across   10
as if it could stop anything, a large young
man upon a stalled motorcycle, perfectly
relaxed as if he'd stopped at a hamburger stand;
he was wearing a peacoat and levis, and
he had his head back, roaring, you   15
could almost hear the laugh, it
was so real.

"Look at that fool," I said, "in the
middle of the bridge like that," a very
womanly remark.   20

Then we heard the meaning of the noise
of metal on a concrete bridge at 50
miles an hour, and the far left lane
filled up with a big car that had a
motorcycle jammed on its front bumper, like   25
the whole thing would explode, the friction
sparks shot up bright orange for many feet
into the air, and the racket still sets
my teeth on edge.

When the car stopped we stopped parallel   30
and Wendy headed for the callbox while I
ducked across those 6 lanes like a mouse
in the bowling alley. "Are you hurt?" I said,
the middle-aged driver had the greyest black face,
"I couldn't stop, I couldn't stop, what happened?"   35

Then I remembered. "Somebody," I said, "was *on*
the motorcycle," I ran back,
one block? two blocks? the space for walking
on the bridge is maybe 18 inches, whoever

engineered this arrogance, in the dark   40
stiff wind it seemed I would
be pushed over the rail, would fall down
screaming onto the hard surface of
the bay, but I did not, I found the tall young man
who thought he owned the bridge, now lying on   45
his stomach, head cradled in his broken arm.

He had glasses on, but somewhere he had lost
most of his levis, where were they?
and his shoes. Two short cuts on his buttocks,
that was the only mark except his thin white   50
seminal tubes were all strung out behind; no
child left *in* him; and he looked asleep.

I plucked wildly at his wrist, then put it
down; there were two long haired women
holding back the traffic just behind me   55
with their bare hands, the machines came
down like mad bulls, I was scared, much
more than usual, I felt easily squished
like the earthworms crawling on a busy
sidewalk after the rain; *I wanted to*   60
leave. And met the driver, walking back.

"The guy is dead." I gripped his hand,
the wind was going to blow us off the bridge.

"Oh my God," he said, "haven't I had enough
trouble in my life?" He raised his head,   65
and for a second was enraged and yelling,
at the top of the bridge—"I was just driving
home!" His head fell down. "My God, and
now I've killed somebody."

I looked down at my own peacoat and levis,   70
then over at the dead man's friend, who
was bawling and blubbering, what they would
call hysteria in a woman. "It isn't possible"
he wailed, but it was possible, it was
indeed, accomplished and unfeeling, snoring   75
in its peacoat, and without its levis on.

He died laughing: that's a fact.

I had a woman waiting for me,
in her car and in the middle of the bridge,
I'm frightened, I said.   80
I'm afraid, he said, stay with me,
please don't go, stay with me, be
my witness—"No," I said, "I'll be your
witness—later," and I took his name
and number, "but I can't stay with you,   85
I'm too frightened of the bridge, besides
I have a woman waiting
and no license—
and no tail lights—"
So I left—   90
as I have left so many of my lovers.

we drove home
shaking, Wendy's face greyer
than any white person's I have ever seen.
maybe he beat his wife, maybe he once
drove taxi, and raped a lover   95
of mine—how to know these things?
we do each other in, that's a fact.

who will be my witness?
death wastes our time with drunkenness
and depression   100
death, who keeps us from our
lovers.
he had a woman waiting for him,
I found out when I called the number
days later   105

"Where is he" she said, "he's disappeared."
He'll be all right" I said, "*we* could
have hit the guy as easy as anybody, it
wasn't anybody's fault, they'll know that,"
women so often say dumb things like that,   110
they teach us to be sweet and reassuring,
and say ignorant things, because we dont invent
the crime, the punishment, the bridges

that same week I looked into the mirror
and nobody was there to testify,
how clear, an unemployed queer woman
makes no witness at all,
nobody at all was there for
those two questions: what does
she do, and who is she married to?

115

120

I am the woman who stopped on the bridge
and this is the man who was there
our lovers teeth are white geese flying
above us, but we ourselves are
easily squished.

125

keep the women small and weak
and off the street, and off the
bridges, that's the way, brother
one day I will leave you there,
as I have left you there before,
working for death.

130

we found out later
what we left him to.
Six big policemen answered the call,
all white, and no child *in* them.
they put the driver up against his car
and beat the hell out of him.
What did you kill that poor kid for?
you mutherfucking nigger.
that's a fact.

135

140

Death only uses violence
when there is any kind of resistance,
the rest of the time a slow
weardown will do.

They took him to 4 different hospitals
til they got a drunk test report to fit their
case, and held him five days in jail
without a phone call.
how many lovers have we left.

145

there are as many contradictions to the game,   150
as there are players.
a woman is talking to death,
though talk is cheap, and life takes a long time
to make
right. He got a cheesy lawyer   155
who had him cop a plea, 15 to 20
instead of life
Did I say life?

the arrogant young man who thought he
owned the bridge, and fell asleep on it   160
he died laughing: that's a fact.
the driver sits out his time
off the street somewhere,
does he have the most vacant of
eyes, will he die laughing?   165

Two
They don't have to lynch the women anymore

death sits on my doorstep
cleaning his revolver
death cripples my feet and sends me out   170
to wait for the bus alone,
then comes by driving a taxi.

the woman on our block with 6 young children
has the most vacant of eyes
death sits in her bedroom, loading   175
his revolver

they don't have to lynch the women
very often anymore, although
they used to—the lord and his men
went through the villages at night, beating &   180
killing every woman caught
outdoors.
the European witch trials took away
the independent people; two different villages
—after the trials were through that year—   185
had left in them, each—

one living woman:
one

What were those other women up to? had they
run over someone? stopped on the wrong bridge?   190
did they have teeth like
any kind of geese, or children
in them?

Three
This woman is a lesbian be careful   195

In the military hospital where I worked
as a nurse's aide, the walls of the halls
were lined with howling women
waiting to deliver
or to have some parts removed.   200
One of the big private rooms contained
the general's wife, who needed
a wart taken off her nose.
we were instructed to give her special attention
not because of her wart or her nose   205
but because of her husband, the general.

as many women as men die, and that's a fact.

At work there was one friendly patient, already
claimed, a young woman burnt apart with X-ray,
she had long white tubes instead of openings;   210
rectum, bladder, vagina—I combed her hair, it
was my job, but she took care of me as if
nobody's touch could spoil her.

ho ho death, ho death
have you seen the twinkle in the dead woman's eye?   215

when you are a nurse's aide
someone suddenly notices you
and yells about the patient's bed,
and tears the sheets apart so you
can do it over, and over   220

while the patient waits
doubled over in her pain
for you to make the bed *again*
and no one ever looks at you,
only at what you do not do   225

Here, general, hold this soldier's bed pan
for a moment, hold it for a year—
then we'll promote you to making his bed.
we believe you wouldn't make such messes

if you had to clean up after them.   230

that's a fantasy.
this woman is a lesbian, be careful.

When I was arrested and being thrown out
of the military, the order went out: dont anybody
speak to this woman, and for those three   235
long months, almost nobody did; the dayroom, when
I entered it, fell silent til I had gone; they
were afraid, they knew the wind would blow
them over the rail, the cops would come,
the water would run into their lungs.   240
Everything I touched
was spoiled. They were my lovers, those
women, but nobody had taught us to swim.
I drowned, I took 3 or 4 others down
when I signed the confession of what we   245
had done   together.

No one will ever speak to me again.

I read this somewhere; I wasn't there:
in WW II the US army had invented some floating
amphibian tanks, and took them over to   250
the coast of Europe to unload them,
the landing ships all drawn up in a fleet,
and everybody watching. Each tank had a
crew of 6 and there were 25 tanks.
The first went down the landing planks   255
and sank, the second, the third, the
fourth, the fifth, the sixth went down

and sank. They weren't supposed
to sink, the engineers had
made a mistake. The crews looked around   260
wildly for the order to quit,
but none came, and in the sight of
thousands of men, each 6 crewmen
saluted his officers, battened down
his hatch in turn and drove into the   265
sea, and drowned, until all 25 tanks
were gone. did they have vacant
eyes, die laughing, or what? what
did they talk about, those men,
as the water came in?   270

was the general their lover?

Four
A Mock Interrogation

Have you ever held hands with a woman?

Yes, many times—women about to deliver, women about to   275
have breasts removed, wombs removed, miscarriages, women
having epileptic fits, having asthma, cancer, women having
breast bone marrow sucked out of them by nervous or indifferent interns, women with heart condition, who were
vomiting, overdosed, depressed, drunk, lonely to the point   280
of extinction: women who had been run over, beaten up,
deserted, starved. women who had been bitten by rats; and
women who were happy, who were celebrating, who were
dancing with me in large circles or alone, women who were
climbing mountains or up and down walls, or trucks or roofs   285
and needed a boost up, or I did; women who simply wanted
to hold my hand because they liked me, some women who
wanted to hold my hand because they liked me better than
anyone.

These were many women?   290

Yes. many.

What about kissing? Have you kissed any women?

I have kissed many women.

When was the first woman you kissed with serious feeling?

The first woman ever I kissed was Josie, who I had loved at　　　295
such a distance for months. Josie was not only beautiful,
she was tough and handsome too. Josie had black hair and
white teeth and strong brown muscles. Then she dropped
out of school unexplained. When she came back she came
back for one day only, to finish the term, and there was a　　　300
child in her. She was all shame, pain, and defiance. Her eyes
were dark as the water under a bridge and no one would
talk to her, they laughed and threw things at her. In the
afternoon I walked across the front of the class and looked
deep into Josie's eyes and I picked up her chin with my　　　305
hand, because I loved her, because nothing like her trouble
would ever happen to me, because I hated it that she was
pregnant and unhappy, and an outcast. We were thirteen.

You didn't kiss her?

How does it feel to be thirteen and having a baby?　　　310

You didn't actually kiss her?

Not in fact.

You have kissed other women?

Yes, many, some of the finest women I know, I have kissed.
women who were lonely, women I didn't know and didn't　　　315
want to, but kissed because that was a way to say yes we are
still alive and loveable, though separate, women who recognized a loneliness in me, women who were hurt, I confess to
kissing the top of a 55 year old woman's head in the snow in
boston, who was hurt more deeply than I have ever been　　　320
hurt, and I wanted her as a very few people have wanted
me—I wanted her and me to own and control and run the
city we lived in, to staff the hospital I knew would mistreat

her, to drive the transportation system that had betrayed
her, to patrol the streets controlling the men who would 325
murder or disfigure or disrupt us, not accidently with
machines, but on purpose, because we are not allowed out
on the street alone—

Have you ever committed any indecent acts with women?

Yes, many. I am guilty of allowing suicidal women to die 330
before my eyes or in my ears or under my hands because I
thought I could do nothing, I am guilty of leaving a prostitute who held a knife to my friend's throat to keep us from
leaving, because we would not sleep with her, we thought
she was old and fat and ugly; I am guilty of not loving her 335
who needed me; I regret all the women I have not slept with
or comforted, who pulled themselves away from me for lack
of something I had not the courage to fight for, for us, our
life, our planet, our city, our meat and potatoes, our love.
These are indecent acts, lacking courage, lacking a certain 340
fire behind the eyes, which is the symbol, the raised fist, the
sharing of resources, the resistance that tells death he will
starve for lack of the fat of us, our extra. Yes I have committed acts of indecency with women and most of them were
acts of omission. I regret them bitterly. 345

Five
Bless this day oh cat our house

"I was allowed to go
3 places, growing up," she said—
"3 places, no more. 350
there was a straight line from my house
to school, a straight line from my house
to church, a straight line from my house
to the corner store."
her parents thought something might happen to her. 355
but nothing ever did.

my lovers teeth are white geese flying above me
my lovers muscles are rope ladders under my hands
we are the river of life and the fat of the land
death, do you tell me I cannot touch this woman? 360

if we use each other up
on each other
that's a little bit less for you
a little bit less for you, ho
death, ho ho death. 365

Bless this day oh cat our house
help me be not such a mouse
death tells the woman to stay home
and then breaks in the window.

I read this somewhere, I wasn't there: 370
In feudal Europe, if a woman committed adultery
her husband would sometimes tie her
down, catch a mouse and trap it
under a cup on her bare belly, until
it gnawed itself out, now are you 375
afraid of mice?

Six
Dressed as I am, a young man once called
me names in Spanish

a woman who talks to death 380
is a dirty traitor

inside a hamburger joint and
dressed as I am, a young man once called me
names in Spanish
then he called me queer and slugged me. 385
first I thought the ceiling had fallen down
but there was the counterman making a ham
sandwich, and there was I spread out on his
counter.

For God's sake I said when 390
I could talk, this guy is beating me up
can't you call the police or something,
can't you stop him? he looked up from
working on his sandwich, which was *my*
sandwich, I had ordered it. He liked 395

the way I looked. "There's a pay phone
right across the street" he said.

I couldn't listen to the Spanish language
for weeks afterward, without feeling the
most murderous of urges, the simple   400
association of one thing to another,
so damned simple.

The next day I went to the police station
to become an outraged citizen
Six big policemen stood in the hall,   405
all white and dressed as they do
they were well pleased with my story, pleased
at what had gotten beat out of me, so
I left them laughing, went home fast
and locked my door.   410
For several nights I fantasized the scene
again, this time grabbing a chair
and smashing it over the bastard's head,
killing him. I called him a spic, and
killed him. My face healed, his didn't   415
no child *in* me.

now when I remember I think:
maybe *he* was Josie's baby.
all the chickens come home to roost,
all of them.   420

Seven
Death and disfiguration

One Christmas eve my lovers and I
we left the bar, driving home slow
there was a woman lying in the snow   425
by the side of the road. She was wearing
a bathrobe and no shoes, where were
her shoes? she had turned the snow
pink, under her feet. she was an Asian
woman, didnt speak much English, but   430
she said a taxi driver beat her up
and raped her, throwing her out of his
car.

what on earth was she doing there
on a street she helped to pay for
but doesn't own?   435
doesn't she know to stay home?

I am a pervert, therefore I've learned
to keep my hands to myself in public
but I was so drunk that night,
I actually did something loving   440
I took her in my arms, this woman,
until she could breathe right, and
my friends who are perverts too
they touched her too
we all touched her.   445
"You're going to be all right"
we lied. She started to cry
"I'm 55 years old" she said
and that said everything.   450

Six big policemen answered the call
no child *in* them.
they seemed afraid to touch her,
then grabbed her like a corpse and heaved her
on their metal stretcher into the van   455
crashing and clumsy.
She was more frightened than before.
they were cold and bored.
'don't leave me' she said.
'she'll be all right' they said.   460
we left, as we have left all of our lovers
as all lovers leave all lovers
much too soon to get the real loving done.

Eight
a mock interrogation   465

Why did you get into the cab with him, dressed as you are?

I wanted to go somewhere.

Did you know what the cab driver might do
if you got into the cab with him?

I just wanted to go somewhere.   470

How many times did you
get into the cab with him?

I dont remember.

If you dont remember, how do you know it happened to
you?   475

Nine
Hey you death

ho and ho poor death
our lovers teeth are white geese flying above us
our lovers muscles are rope ladders under our hands   480
even though no women yet go down to the sea in ships
except in their dreams.

only the arrogant invent a quick and meaningful end
for themselves, of their own choosing.
everyone else knows how very slow it happens   485
how the woman's existence bleeds out her years,
how the child shoots up at ten and is arrested and old
how the man carries a murderous shell within him
and passes it on.

we are the fat of the land, and   490
we all have our list of casualties

to my lovers I bequeath
the rest of my life

I want nothing left of me for you, ho death
except some fertilizer   495
for the next batch of us
who do not hold hands with you
who do not embrace you
who try not to work for you
or sacrifice themselves or trust   500
or believe you, ho ignorant
death, how do you know
we happened to you?

wherever our meat hangs on our own bones
for our own use   505
your pot is so empty

death, ho death
you shall be poor

PAT PARKER   (b. 1944)

What Will You Be?   (1978)

Boots are being polished
Trumpeters clean their horns
Chains and locks forged
The crusade has begun.

Once again flags of Christ   5
are unfurled in the dawn
and cries of soul saviors
sing apocalyptic on air waves.

Citizens, good citizens all
parade into voting booths   10
and in self-righteous sanctity
X away our right to life.

I do not believe as some
that the vote is an end,
I fear even more   15
It is just a beginning.

So I must make assessment
Look to you and ask:
Where will you be
when they come?   20

They will not come
a mob rolling
through the streets,
but quickly and quietly
move into our homes   25
and remove the evil,
the queerness,
the faggotry,
the perverseness

from their midst.
They will not come
clothed in brown,
and swastikas, or
bearing chest heavy with
gleaming crosses.   35
The time and need
for ruses are over.
They will come
in business suits
to buy your homes   40
and bring bodies to
fill your jobs.
They will come in robes
to rehabilitate
and white coats   45
to subjugate
and where will you be
when they come?

Where will we *all be*
when the come?   50
And they will come—

they will come
because we are
defined as opposite-
perverse   55
and we are perverse.

Every time we watched
a queer hassled in the
streets and said nothing—
It was an act of perversion.   60

Everytime we lied about
the boyfriend or girlfriend
at coffee break—
It was an act of perversion.

Everytime we heard,   65
"I don't mind gays
but why must they
be blatant?" and said nothing—
It was an act of perversion.

Everytime we let a lesbian mother   70
lose her child and did not fill
the courtrooms—
It was an act of perversion.

Everytime we let straights
make out in our bars while   75
we couldn't touch because
of laws—
It was an act of perversion.

Everytime we put on the proper
clothes to go to a family   80
wedding and left our lovers
at home—
It was an act of perversion.

Everytime we heard
"Who I go to bed with   85
is my personal choice-
It's personal not political"
and said nothing—
It was an act of perversion.

Everytime we let straight relatives   90
bury our dead and push our
lovers away—
It was an act of perversion.

And they will come.
They will come for
the perverts   95

& it won't matter
if you're
        homosexual, not a faggot
        lesbian, not a dyke   100
        gay, not queer
It won't matter
if you
        own your business
        have a good job   105
        or are on S.S.I.[1]
It won't matter

---

[1] Supplemental Security Income, government support for the aged, blind, and disabled.

if you're
    Black
    Chicano   110
    Native American
    Asian
    or White
It won't matter
if you're from   115
    New York
    or Los Angeles
    Galveston
    or Sioux Falls
It won't matter   120
if you're
    Butch, or Fem
    Not into roles
    Monogamous
    Non Monagamous   125
It won't matter
If you're
    Catholic
    Baptist
    Atheist   130
    Jewish
    or M.C.C.[2]

They will come
They will come
to the cities   135
and to the land
to your front rooms
and in *your* closets.

They will come for
the perverts   140
and where will
you be
When they come?

---

[2] Metropolitan Community Church, a gay and lesbian church.

CAROLYN FORCHÉ   (b. 1950)

Selective Service   (1981)

We rise from the snow where we've
lain on our backs and flown like children,
from the imprint of perfect wings and cold gowns,
and we stagger together wine-breathed into town
where our people are building   5
their armies again, short years after
body bags, after burnings. There is a man
I've come to love after thirty, and we have
our rituals of coffee, of airports, regret.
After love we smoke and sleep   10
with magazines, two shot glasses
and the black and white collapse of hours.
In what time do we live that it is too late
to have children? In what place
that we consider the various ways to leave?   15
There is no list long enough
for a selective service card shriveling
under a match, the prison that comes of it,
a flag in the wind eaten from its pole
and boys sent back in trash bags.   20
We'll tell you. You were at that time
learning fractions. We'll tell you
about fractions. Half of us are dead or quiet
or lost. Let them speak for themselves
We lie down in the fields and leave behind   25
the corpses of angels.

DRAMA

SOPHOCLES (496?–406 B.C.)

Born into a wealthy family in Athens, Sophocles was a major figure in Athenian life, a general and a priest as well as a playwright. His tragedies won many first prizes in the annual drama festivals; he introduced the full use of a third actor, which allowed for more dramatic complexity. Of his 123 plays, only seven survive, among them Antigone, Oedipus the King, Electra, and Oedipus at Colonus, the last written when he was almost ninety.

Antigone[1]   (ca. 441 B.C.)

PERSONS REPRESENTED

> ANTIGONE
> ISMENE
> EURYDICE
> CREON
> HAIMON
> TEIRESIAS
> A SENTRY
> A MESSENGER
> CHORUS

SCENE: *Before the palace of Creon, King of Thebes. A central double door, and two lateral doors. A platform extends the length of the façade, and from this platform three steps lead down into the "orchestra" or chorus-ground.* TIME: *dawn of the day after the repulse of the Argive army from the assault on Thebes.*

PROLOGUE

Antigone *and* Ismene *enter from the central door of the Palace.*

---

[1] An English version by Dudley Fitts and Robert Fitzgerald.

Antigone.

Ismenê, dear sister,
You would think that we had already suffered enough
For the curse on Oedipus:[2]
I cannot imagine any grief
That you and I have not gone through. And now—   5
Have they told you of the new decree of our King Creon?

Ismene.

I have heard nothing: I know
That two sisters lost two brothers, a double death
In a single hour; and I know that the Argive army   10
Fled in the night; but beyond this, nothing.

Antigone.

I thought so. And that is why I wanted you
To come out here with me. There is something we must do.

Ismene.

Why do you speak so strangely?   15

Antigone.

Listen, Ismenê:
Creon buried our brother Eteoclês
With military honors, gave him a soldier's funeral,
And it was right that he should; but Polyneicês,
Who fought as bravely and died as miserably,—   20
They say that Creon has sworn
No one shall bury him, no one mourn for him,
But his body must lie in the fields, a sweet treasure
For carrion birds to find as they search for food.
That is what they say, and our good Creon is coming here   25
To announce it publicly; and the penalty—
Stoning to death in the public square!
                    There it is,
And now you can prove what you are: 30
A true sister, or a traitor to your family.

Ismene.

Antigonê, you are mad! What could I possibly do?

---

[2] Oedipus, father of Antigone, Ismene, Polyneices, and Eteocles, was King of Thebes. Unknowingly, he killed his father and married his mother. Upon learning what he had done, he put out his eyes and went into exile. Heirs to the throne, Polyneices and Eteocles eventually quarreled. Eteocles drove out Polyneices, but Polyneices returned to attack Thebes, and both brothers died in battle. Creon became king and ordered that Polyneices's body be left unburied.

Antigone.

You must decide whether you will help me or not.

Ismene.

I do not understand you. Help you in what?

Antigone.

Ismenê, I am going to bury him. Will you come?   35

Ismene.

Bury him! You have just said the new law forbids it.

Antigone.

He is my brother. And he is your brother, too.

Ismene.

But think of the danger! Think what Creon will do!

Antigone.

Creon is not strong enough to stand in my way.

Ismene.

Ah sister!   40
Oedipus died, everyone hating him
For what his own search brought to light, his eyes
Ripped out by his own hand; and Iocastê died,
His mother and wife at once: she twisted the cords
That strangled her life; and our two brothers died,   45
Each killed by the other's sword. And we are left:
But oh, Antigonê,
Think how much more terrible than these
Our own death would be if we should go against Creon   50
And do what he has forbidden! We are only women,
We cannot fight with men, Antigonê!
The law is strong, we must give in to the law
In this thing, and in worse. I beg the Dead
To forgive me, but I am helpless: I must yield   55
To those in authority. And I think it is dangerous business
To be always meddling.

Antigone.

                    If that is what you think,
I should not want you, even if you asked to come.   60
You have made your choice, you can be what you want to be
But I will bury him; and if I must die,
I say that this crime is holy: I shall lie down

With him in death, and I shall be as dear   65
To him as he to me.

                   It is the dead,
Not the living, who make the longest demands:
We die for ever . . .

                   You may do as you like,   70
Since apparently the laws of the gods mean nothing to you.

Ismene.

They mean a great deal to me; but I have no strength
To break laws that were made for the public good.

Antigone.

That must be your excuse, I suppose. But as for me,   75
I will bury the brother I love.

Ismene.

                   Antigonê,
I am so afraid for you!

Antigone.

               You need not be:
You have yourself to consider, after all.   80

Ismene.

But no one must hear of this, you must tell no one!
I will keep it a secret, I promise!

Antigone.

                Oh tell it! Tell everyone!
Think how they'll hate you when it all comes out
If they learn that you knew about it all the time!   85

Ismene.

So fiery! You should be cold with fear.

Antigone.

Perhaps. But I am doing only what I must.

Ismene.

But can you do it? I say that you cannot.

Antigone.

Very well: when my strength gives out, I shall do no more.   90

Ismene.

Impossible things should not be tried at all.

Antigone.

Go away, Ismenê:
I shall be hating you soon, and the dead will too,
For your words are hateful. Leave me my foolish plan:
I am not afraid of the danger; if it means death,   95
It will not be the worst of deaths—death without
honor.

Ismene.

Go then, if you feel that you must.
You are unwise,
But a loyal friend indeed to those who love you.   100

Exit into the Palace. Antigone goes off, L. Enter the Chorus.

PARODOS[3]

Chorus.

Strophe 1

Now the long blade of the sun, lying
Level east to west, touches with glory
Thebes of the Seven Gates. Open, unlidded
Eye of golden day! O marching light
Across the eddy and rush of Dircê's stream,[4]   5
Striking the white shields of the enemy
Thrown headlong backward from the blaze of morning!

Choragos.[5]

Polyneicês their commander
Roused them with windy phrases,   10
He the wild eagle screaming
Insults above our land,
His wings their shields of snow,
His crest their marshalled helms.

Chorus.

Antistrophe 1

Against our seven gates in a yawning ring   15
The famished spears came onward in the night;

---

[3] Sung by the Chorus upon entering.

[4] Near Thebes.

[5] Leader of the Chorus.

But before his jaws were sated with our blood,
Or pinefire took the garland of our towers,
He was thrown back; and as he turned, great Thebes—
No tender victim for his noisy power—   20
Rose like a dragon behind him, shouting war.

   Choragos.
For God hates utterly
The bray of bragging tongues;
And when he beheld their smiling,
Their swagger of golden helms,   25
The frown of his thunder blasted
Their first man from our walls.

  Chorus.
                                  Strophe 2
We heard his shout of triumph high in the air
Turn to a scream; far out in a flaming arc
He fell with his windy torch, and the earth struck him.   30
And others storming in fury no less than his
Found shock of death in the dusty joy of battle.

  Choragos.
Seven captains at seven gates
Yielded their clanging arms to the god   35
That bends the battle-line and breaks it.
These two only, brothers in blood,
Face to face in matchless rage,
Mirroring each the other's death,
Clashed in long combat.   40

  Chorus.
                              Antistrophe 2
But now in the beautiful morning of victory
Let Thebes of the many chariots sing for joy!
With hearts for dancing we'll take leave of war:
Our temples shall be sweet with hymns of praise,
And the long night shall echo with our chorus.   45

   SCENE I

  Choragos.
But now at last our new King is coming:
Creon of Thebes, Menoikeus' son.
In this auspicious dawn of his reign

What are the new complexities
That shifting Fate has woven for him?   5
What is his counsel? Why has he summoned
The old men to hear him?

Enter Creon *from the Palace, C. He addresses the* Chorus *from the top step.*

Creon.

Gentlemen: I have the honor to inform you that our Ship of State, which
   recent storms have threatened to destroy, has come safely to harbor at
   last, guided by the merciful wisdom of Heaven. I have summoned you
   here this morning because I know that I can depend upon you: your
   devotion to King Laïos was absolute; you never hesitated in your duty
   to our late ruler Oedipus; and when Oedipus died, your loyalty was
   transferred to his children. Unfortunately, as you know, his two sons,
   the princes Eteoclês and Polyneicês, have killed each other in battle;
   and I, as the next in blood, have succeeded to the full power of the
   throne.

I am aware, of course, that no Ruler can expect complete loyalty from
   his subjects until he has been tested in office. Nevertheless, I say to
   you at the very outset that I have nothing but contempt for the kind
   of Governor who is afraid, for whatever reason, to follow the course
   that he knows is best for the State; and as for the man who sets private
   friendship above the public welfare,—I have no use for him, either. I
   call God to witness that if I saw my country headed for ruin, I should
   not be afraid to speak out plainly; and I need hardly remind you that
   I would never have any dealings with an enemy of the people. No
   one values friendship more highly than I; but we must remember that
   friends made at the risk of wrecking our Ship are not real friends at
   all.

These are my principles, at any rate, and that is why I have made the
   following decision concerning the sons of Oedipus: Eteoclês, who died
   as a man should die, fighting for his country, is to be buried with full
   military honors, with all the ceremony that is usual when the greatest
   heroes die; but his brother Polyneicês, who broke his exile to come
   back with fire and sword against his native city and the shrines of his
   fathers' gods, whose one idea was to spill the blood of his blood and
   sell his own people into slavery—Polyneicês, I say, is to have no burial:
   no man is to touch him or say the least prayer for him; he shall lie
   on the plain, unburied; and the birds and the scavenging dogs can do
   with him whatever they like.

This is my command, and you can see the wisdom behind it. As long as
   I am King, no traitor is going to be honored with the loyal man. But
   whoever shows by word and deed that he is on the side of the State,—

he shall have my respect while he is living, and my reverence when
he is dead.

Choragos.
If that is your will, Creon son of Menoikeus,
You have the right to enforce it: we are yours.

Creon.
That is my will. Take care that you do your part.   60

Choragos.
We are old men: let the younger ones carry it out.

Creon.
I do not mean that: the sentries have been appointed.

Choragos.
Then what is it that you would have us do?

Creon.
You will give no support to whoever breaks this law.

Choragos.
Only a crazy man is in love with death!   65

Creon.
And death it is; yet money talks, and the wisest
Have sometimes been known to count a few coins
      too many.

Enter Sentry *from L.*

Sentry.
I'll not say that I'm out of breath from running, King, because every time
I stopped to think about what I have to tell you, I felt like going back.
And all the time a voice kept saying, "You fool, don't you know you're
walking straight into trouble?"; and then another voice: "Yes, but if
you let somebody else get the news to Creon first, it will be even
worse than that for you!" But good sense won out, at least I hope it
was good sense, and here I am with a story that makes no sense at
all; but I'll tell it anyhow, because, as they say, what's going to happen's
going to happen, and—

Creon.
Come to the point. What have you to say?

Sentry.
I did not do it. I did not see who did it. You must not punish me for
what someone else has done.

Creon.
A comprehensive defense! More effective, perhaps,   85
If I knew its purpose. Come: what is it?

Sentry.
A dreadful thing . . . I don't know how to put it—

Creon.
Out with it!

Sentry.
          Well, then;
The dead man—
                    Polyneicês—   90

Pause. The Sentry *is overcome, fumbles for words. Creon* waits impassively.

                    out there—
                              someone,—
New dust on the slimy flesh!

Pause. No sign from Creon

Someone has given it burial that way, and   95
Gone . . .

Long pause. Creon finally speaks with deadly control:

Creon.
And the man who dared do this?

Sentry.
                    I swear I
Do not know! You must believe me!
                              Listen:
The ground was dry, not a sign of digging, no,   100
Not a wheeltrack in the dust, no trace of anyone.
It was when they relieved us this morning: and one of them,
The corporal, pointed to it.

                              There it was,   105
The strangest—
                    Look:
The body, just mounded over with light dust: you see?
Not buried really, but as if they'd covered it
Just enough for the ghost's peace. And no sign   110
Of dogs or any wild animal that had been there.

And then what a scene there was! Every man of us
Accusing the other: we all proved the other man did it,
We all had proof that we could not have done it.
We were ready to take hot iron in our hands,   115
Walk through fire, swear by all the gods,
It was not I!
I do not know who it was, but it was not I!

Creon's *rage has been mounting steadily, but the* Sentry *is too intent upon
his story to notice it*

And then, when this came to nothing, someone said
A thing that silenced us and made us stare   120
Down at the ground: you had to be told the news,
And one of us had to do it! We threw the dice,
And the bad luck fell to me. So here I am,
No happier to be here than you are to have me:
Nobody likes the man who brings bad news.   125

   Choragos.
I have been wondering, King: can it be that the gods have done this?

   Creon. *Furiously*
Stop!
Must you doddering wrecks
Go out of your heads entirely? "The gods!"   130
Intolerable!
The gods favor this corpse? Why? How had he served them?
Tried to loot their temples, burn their images,
Yes, and the whole State, and its laws with it!   135
Is it your senile opinion that the gods love to honor bad men?
A pious thought!—
                    No, from the very beginning
There have been those who have whispered together,   140
Stiff-necked anarchists, putting their heads together,

Scheming against me in alleys. These are the men,
And they have bribed my own guard to do this thing.

Money!
                                        Sententiously
There's nothing in the world so demoralizing as money.   145
Down go your cities,
Homes gone, men gone, honest hearts corrupted,
Crookedness of all kinds, and all for money!
                                        To Sentry
                                    But you—!
I swear by God and by the throne of God,   150
The man who has done this thing shall pay for it!
Find that man, bring him here to me, or your death
Will be the least of your problems: I'll string you up
Alive, and there will be certain ways to make you
Discover your employer before you die;   155
And the process may teach you a lesson you seem to have missed:
The dearest profit is sometimes all too dear:
That depends on the source. Do you understand me?
A fortune won is often misfortune.   160

   Sentry.
King, may I speak?

   Creon.
Your very voice distresses me.

   Sentry.
Are you sure that it is my voice, and not your conscience?

   Creon.
By God, he wants to analyze me now!   165

   Sentry.
It is not what I say, but what has been done, that hurts you.

   Creon.
You talk too much.

   Sentry.
Maybe; but I've done nothing.

Creon.
Sold your soul for some silver: that's all you've done.   170

Sentry.
How dreadful it is when the right judge judges wrong!

Creon.
Your figures of speech
May entertain you now; but unless you bring me the man,
You will get little profit from them in the end.   175

Exit Creon *into the Palace.*

Sentry.
"Bring me the man"—!
I'd like nothing better than bringing him the man!
But bring him or not, you have seen the last of me here.
At any rate, I am safe!   180

Exit Sentry

ODE I

Chorus.
Strophe 1

Numberless are the world's wonders, but none
More wonderful than man; the stormgray sea
Yields to his prows, the huge crests bear him high;
Earth, holy and inexhaustible, is graven
With shining furrows where his plows have gone
Year after year, the timeless labor of stallions.   5

Antistrophe 1

The lightboned birds and beasts that cling to cover,
The lithe fish lighting their reaches of dim water,
All are taken, tamed in the net of his mind;
The lion on the hill, the wild horse windy-maned,   10
Resign to him; and his blunt yoke has broken
The sultry shoulders of the mountain bull.

Strophe 2

Words also, and thought as rapid as air,

He fashions to his good use; statecraft is his,
And his the skill that deflects the arrows of snow,   15
The spears of winter rain: from every wind
He has made himself secure—from all but one:
In the late wind of death he cannot stand.

                                            Antistrophe 2

O clear intelligence, force beyond all measure!
O fate of man, working both good and evil!   20
When the laws are kept, how proudly his city stands!
When the laws are broken, what of his city then?
Never may the anárchic man find rest at my hearth,
Never be it said that my thoughts are his thoughts.

SCENE II

Re-enter Sentry *leading* Antigone.

Choragos.
What does this mean? Surely this captive woman
Is the Princess, Antigonê. Why should she be taken?

Sentry.
Here is the one who did it! We caught her
In the very act of burying him.—Where is Creon?

Choragos.
Just coming from the house.   5

Enter Creon, C.

Creon.
                          What has happened?
Why have you come back so soon?

Sentry. *Expansively*
                          O King,
A man should never be too sure of anything:
I would have sworn   10
That you'd not see me here again: your anger
Frightened me so, and the things you threatened me with;
But how could I tell then
That I'd be able to solve the case so soon?   15

No dice-throwing this time: I was only too glad to come!

Here is this woman. She is the guilty one:
We found her trying to bury him.
Take her, then; question her; judge her as you will.   20
I am through with the whole thing now, and glád óf it.

Creon.
But this is Antigonê! Why have you brought her here?

Sentry.
She was burying him, I tell you!   25

Creon. *Severely*

                                   Is this the truth?

Sentry.
I saw her with my own eyes. Can I say more?

Creon.
The details: come, tell me quickly!

Sentry.
                                   It was like this:
After those terrible threats of yours, King,   30
We went back and brushed the dust away from the body.
The flesh was soft by now, and stinking,
So we sat on a hill to windward and kept guard.
No napping this time! We kept each other awake.   35
But nothing happened until the white round sun
Whirled in the center of the round sky over us:
Then, suddenly,
A storm of dust roared up from the earth, and the sky
Went out, the plain vanished with all its trees   40
In the stinging dark. We closed our eyes and endured it.
The whirlwind lasted a long time, but it passed;
And then we looked, and there was Antigonê!

I have seen   45
A mother bird come back to a stripped nest, heard
Her crying bitterly a broken note or two
For the young ones stolen. Just so, when this girl
Found the bare corpse, and all her love's work wasted,
She wept, and cried on heaven to damn the hands   50
That had done this thing.

                    And then she brought more dust
And sprinkled wine three times for her brother's ghost.

We ran and took her at once. She was not afraid,
Not even when we charged her with what she had done.   55
She denied nothing.
                    And this was a comfort to me,
And some uneasiness: for it is a good thing
To escape from death, but it is no great pleasure   60
To bring death to a friend.
                    Yet I always say
There is nothing so comfortable as your own safe skin!

Creon. *Slowly, dangerously*
And you, Antigonê,
You with your head hanging,—do you confess this thing?   65

Antigone.
I do. I deny nothing.

Creon.
To Sentry:
                    You may go.
                                        Exit Sentry

                              To Antigone:
    Tell me, tell me briefly:
Had you heard my proclamation touching this matter?   70

Antigone.
It was public. Could I help hearing it?

Creon.
And yet you dared defy the law.

Antigone.
                    I dared.
It was not God's proclamation. That final Justice
That rules the world below makes no such laws.   75

Your edict, King, was strong,
But all your strength is weakness itself against
The immortal unrecorded laws of God.
They are not merely now: they were, and shall be,
Operative for ever, beyond man utterly.   80

I knew I must die, even without your decree:
I am only mortal. And if I must die
Now, before it is my time to die,
Surely this is no hardship: can anyone
Living, as I live, with evil all about me,   85
Think Death less than a friend? This death of mine
Is of no importance; but if I had left my brother
Lying in death unburied, I should have suffered.
Now I do not.

             You smile at me. Ah Creon,   90
Think me a fool, if you like; but it may well be
That a fool convicts me of folly.

Choragos.

Like father, like daughter: both headstrong, deaf to reason!
She has never learned to yield.   95

Creon.

                She has much to learn.
The inflexible heart breaks first, the toughest iron
Cracks first, and the wildest horses bend their necks
At the pull of the smallest curb.

                 Pride? In a slave?   100
This girl is guilty of a double insolence,
Breaking the given laws and boasting of it.
Who is the man here,
She or I, if this crime goes unpunished?
Sister's child, or more than sister's child,   105
Or closer yet in blood—she and her sister
Win bitter death for this!

                  To servants:
           Go, some of you,
Arrest Ismenê. I accuse her equally.
Bring her: you will find her sniffling in the house there.   110

Her mind's a traitor: crimes kept in the dark
Cry for light, and the guardian brain shudders;
But how much worse than this
Is brazen boasting of barefaced anarchy!

Antigone.

Creon, what more do you want than my death?   115

Creon.

                     Nothing.
That gives me everything.

Antigone.

Then I beg you: kill me.
This talking is a great weariness: your words
Are distasteful to me, and I am sure that mine   120
Seem so to you. And yet they should not seem so:
I should have praise and honor for what I have done.
All these men here would praise me
Were their lips not frozen shut with fear of you.

Bitterly
                                                                    125
Ah the good fortune of kings,
Licensed to say and do whatever they please!

Creon.

You are alone here in that opinion.

Antigone.

No, they are with me. But they keep their tongues in leash.

Creon.

Maybe. But you are guilty, and they are not.   130

Antigone.

There is no guilt in reverence for the dead.

Creon.

But Eteoclês—was he not your brother too?

Antigone.

My brother too.

Creon.

And you insult his memory?

Antigone.

Softly
The dead man would not say that I insult it.   135

Creon.

He would: for you honor a traitor as much as him.

Antigone.

His own brother; traitor or not, and equal in blood.

Creon.

He made war on his country. Eteoclês defended it.

Antigone.
Nevertheless, there are honors due all the dead.

Creon.
But not the same for the wicked as for the just.   140

Antigone.
Ah Creon, Creon,
Which of us can say what the gods hold wicked?

Creon.
An enemy is an enemy, even dead.

Antigone.
It is my nature to join in love, not hate.

Creon.   *Finally losing patience*
Go join them, then; if you must have your love,   145
Find it in hell!

Choragos.
But see, Ismenê comes:

Enter Ismene, *guarded*

Those tears are sisterly, the cloud
That shadows her eyes rains down gentle sorrow.

Creon.
You too, Ismenê,   150
Snake in my ordered house, sucking my blood
Stealthily—and all the time I never knew
That these two sisters were aiming at my throne!
                                             Ismenê,
Do you confess your share in this crime, or deny it?
Answer me.   155

Ismene.
Yes, if she will let me say so. I am guilty.

Antigone.
Coldly
No, Ismenê. You have no right to say so.
You would not help me, and I will not have you help me.   160

Ismene.
But now I know what you meant; and I am here
To join you, to take my share of punishment.

Antigone.
The dead man and the gods who rule the dead
Know whose act this was. Words are not friends.

Ismene.
Do you refuse me, Antigonê? I want to die with you: 165
I too have a duty that I must discharge to the dead.

Antigone.
You shall not lessen my death by sharing it.

Ismene.
What do I care for life when you are dead?

Antigone.
Ask Creon. You're always hanging on his opinions.

Ismene.
You are laughing at me. Why, Antigonê?   170

Antigone.
It's a joyless laughter, Ismenê.

Ismene.
                              But can I do nothing?

Antigone.
Yes. Save yourself. I shall not envy you.
There are those who will praise you; I shall have honor, too.   175

Ismene.
But we are equally guilty!

Antigone.
                    No more, Ismenê.
You are alive, but I belong to Death.

Creon.   *To the* Chorus:
Gentlemen, I beg you to observe these girls:
One has just now lost her mind; the other,   180
It seems, has never had a mind at all.

Ismene.
Grief teaches the steadiest minds to waver, King.

Creon.
Yours certainly did, when you assumed guilt with the guilty!

Ismene.
But how could I go on living without her?   185

Creon.
                                    You are.
She is already dead.

Ismene.
                    But your own son's bride!

Creon.
There are places enough for him to push his plow.
I want no wicked women for my sons!   190

Ismene.
O dearest Haimon, how your father wrongs you!

Creon.
I've had enough of your childish talk of marriage!

Choragos.
Do you really intend to steal this girl from your son?

Creon.
No; Death will do that for me.

Choragos.
                    Then she must die?   195

Creon. *Ironically*
You dazzle me.
            —But enough of this talk!

To Guards:

You, there, take them away and guard them well:
For they are but women, and even brave men run
When they see Death coming.   200

Exeunt Ismene, Antigone, *and* Guards

ODE II

Chorus.

Strophe 1

Fortunate is the man who has never tasted God's vengeance!
Where once the anger of heaven has struck, that house is shaken
For ever: damnation rises behind each child   5
Like a wave cresting out of the black northeast,
When the long darkness under sea roars up
And bursts drumming death upon the windwhipped sand.

Antistrophe 1

I have seen this gathering sorrow from time long past   10
Loom upon Oedipus' children: generation from generation
Takes the compulsive rage of the enemy god.
So lately this last flower of Oedipus' line
Drank the sunlight! but now a passionate word   15
And a handful of dust have closed up all its beauty.

Strophe 2

    What mortal arrogance
    Transcends the wrath of Zeus?
Sleep cannot lull him, nor the effortless long months
Of the timeless gods: but he is young for ever,   20
And his house is the shining day of high Olympos.
    All that is and shall be,
    And all the past, is his.
No pride on earth is free of the curse of heaven.

Antistrophe 2   25

    The straying dreams of men
    May bring them ghosts of joy:

But as they drowse, the waking embers burn them;
Or they walk with fixed éyes, as blind men walk.
But the ancient wisdom speaks for our own time:
   Fate works most for woe   30
   With Folly's fairest show.
Man's little pleasure is the spring of sorrow.

SCENE III

Choragos.
But here is Haimon, King, the last of all your sons.
Is it grief for Antigonê that brings him here,
And bitterness at being robbed of his bride?

Enter Haimon

Creon.
We shall soon see, and no need of diviners.

                       —Son,   5
You have heard my final judgment on that girl:
Have you come here hating me, or have you come
With deference and with love, whatever I do?

Haimon.
I am your son, father. You are my guide.
You make things clear for me, and I obey you.   10
No marriage means more to me than your continuing wisdom.

Creon.
Good. That is the way to behave: subordinate
Everything else, my son, to your father's will.
This is what a man prays for, that he may get   15
Sons attentive and dutiful in his house,
Each one hating his father's enemies,
Honoring his father's friends. But if his sons
Fail him, if they turn out unprofitably,
What has he fathered but trouble for himself   20
And amusement for the malicious?
                         So you are right
Not to lose your head over this woman.
Your pleasure with her would soon grow cold, Haimon,
And then you'd have a hellcat in bed and elsewhere.   25

Let her find her husband in Hell!
Of all the people in this city, only she
Has had contempt for my law and broken it.

Do you want me to show myself weak before the people?   30
Or to break my sworn word? No, and I will not.
The woman dies.
I suppose she'll plead "family ties." Well, let her.
If I permit my own family to rebel,
How shall I earn the world's obedience?   35
Show me the man who keeps his house in hand,
He's fit for public authority.
                              I'll have no dealings
With law-breakers, critics of the government: 40
Whoever is chosen to govern should be obeyed—
Must be obeyed, in all things, great and small,
Just and unjust! O Haimon,
The man who knows how to obey, and that man only,
Knows how to give commands when the time comes.   45
You can depend on him, no matter how fast
The spears come: he's a good soldier, he'll stick it out.

Anarchy, anarchy! Show me a greater evil!
This is why cities tumble and the great houses rain down,   50
This is what scatters armies!

No, no: good lives are made so by discipline.
We keep the laws then, and the lawmakers,
And no woman shall seduce us. If we must lose,
Let's lose to a man, at least! Is a woman stronger than we?   55

Choragos.
Unless time has rusted my wits,
What you say, King, is said with point and dignity.

Haimon. *Boyishly earnest*
Father:
Reason is God's crowning gift to man, and you are right.   60
To warn me against losing mine. I cannot say—
I hope that I shall never want to say!—that you
Have reasoned badly. Yet there are other men
Who can reason, too; and their opinions might be helpful.   65
You are not in a position to know everything
That people say or do, or what they feel:
Your temper terrifies them—everyone
Will tell you only what you like to hear.   70

But I, at any rate, can listen; and I have heard them
Muttering and whispering in the dark about this girl.
They say no woman has ever, so unreasonably,
Died so shameful a death for a generous act:
"She covered her brother's body. Is this indecent?   75
She kept him from dogs and vultures. Is this a crime?
Death?—She should have all the honor that we can give her!"

This is the way they talk out there in the city.

You must believe me: 80
Nothing is closer to me than your happiness.
What could be closer? Must not any son
Value his father's fortune as his father does his?
I beg you, do not be unchangeable:
Do not believe that you alone can be right.   85
The man who thinks that,
The man who maintains that only he has the power
To reason correctly, the gift to speak, the soul—
A man like that, when you know him, turns out empty.   90

It is not reason never to yield to reason!

In flood time you can see how some trees bend,
And because they bend, even their twigs are safe,
While stubborn trees are torn up, roots and all.   95
And the same thing happens in sailing:
Make your sheet fast, never slacken,—and over you go,
Head over heels and under: and there's your voyage.
Forget you are angry! Let yourself be moved!
I know I am young; but please let me say this: 100
The ideal condition
Would be, I admit, that men should be right by instinct;
But since we are all too likely to go astray,
The reasonable thing is to learn from those who can teach.   105

Choragos.
You will do well to listen to him, King,
If what he says is sensible. And you, Haimon,
Must listen to your father.—Both speak well.

Creon.
You consider it right for a man of my years and experience   110
to go to school to a boy?

Haimon.

It is not right

If I am wrong. But if I am young, and right,

What does my age matter?   115

Creon.

You think it right to stand up for an anarchist?

Haimon.

Not at all. I pay no respect to criminals.

Creon.

Then she is not a criminal?

Haimon.

The City would deny it, to a man.

Creon.

And the City proposes to teach me how to rule?   120

Haimon.

Ah. Who is it that's talking like a boy now?

Creon.

My voice is the one voice giving orders in this City!

Haimon.

It is no City if it takes orders from one voice.

Creon.

The State is the King!

Haimon.

Yes, if the State is a desert.   125

Pause

Creon.

This boy, it seems, has sold out to a woman.

Haimon.

If you are a woman: my concern is only for you.

Creon.

So? Your "concern"! In a public brawl with your father!

Haimon.

How about you, in a public brawl with justice?   130

Creon.

With justice, when all that I do is within my rights?

Haimon.

You have no right to trample God's right.

Creon. *Completely out of control*
Fool, adolescent fool! Taken in by a woman!

Haimon.

You'll never see me taken in by anything vile.

Creon.

Every word you say is for her!   135

Haimon. *Quietly, darkly*
                                    And for you.
And for me. And for the gods under the earth.

Creon.

You'll never marry her while she lives.

Haimon.

Then she must die.—But her death will cause another.

Creon.
Another?   140
Have you lost your senses? Is this an open threat?

Haimon.

There is no threat in speaking to emptiness.

Creon.

I swear you'll regret this superior tone of yours!
You are the empty one!

Haimon.

                                    If you were not my father,   145
I'd say you were perverse.

Creon.

You girlstruck fool, don't play at words with me!

Haimon.
I am sorry. You prefer silence.

Creon.
                   Now, by God—!   150
I swear, by all the gods in heaven above us,
You'll watch it, I swear you shall!
                      To the Servants:
                  Bring her out!
Bring the woman out! Let her die before his eyes!
Here, this instant, with her bridegroom beside her!

Haimon.
Not here, no; she will not die here, King.   155
And you will never see my face again.
Go on raving as long as you've a friend to endure you.

Exit Haimon

Choragos.
Gone, gone.
Creon, a young man in a rage is dangerous!

Creon.
Let him do, or dream to do, more than a man can.   160
He shall not save these girls from death.

Choragos.
                      These girls?
You have sentenced them both?

Creon.
                 No, you are right.
I will not kill the one whose hands are clean.   165

Choragos.
But Antigonê?

Creon. *Somberly*
            I will carry her far away
Out there in the wilderness, and lock her
Living in a vault of stone. She shall have food,
As the custom is, to absolve the State of her death.   170
And there let her pray to the gods of hell:
They are her only gods:

Perhaps they will show her an escape from death,
Or she may learn,
                    though late,
That piety shown the dead is pity in vain.   175

Exit Creon

ODE III

Chorus.

                                        Strophe

Love, unconquerable
Waster of rich men, keeper
Of warm lights and all-night vigil
In the soft face of a girl:
Sea-wanderer, forest-visitor!   5
Even the pure Immortals cannot escape you,
And mortal man, in his one day's dusk,
Trembles before your glory.

                                   Antistrophe

Surely you swerve upon ruin
The just man's consenting heart,   10
As here you have made bright anger
Strike between father and son—
And none has conquered but Love!
A girl's glánce wórking the will of heaven:
Pleasure to her alone who mocks us,   15
Merciless Aphroditê.

SCENE IV

Choragos.

                         As Antigone *enters guarded*
But I can no longer stand in awe of this,
Nor, seeing what I see, keep back my tears.
Here is Antigonê, passing to that chamber
Where all find sleep at last.

Antigone.

Strophe 1   5

Look upon me, friends, and pity me
Turning back at the night's edge to say
Good-by to the sun that shines for me no longer;
Now sleepy Death
Summons me down to Acheron, that cold shore:
There is no bridesong there, nor any music.   10

Chorus.

Yet not unpraised, not without a kind of honor,
You walk at last into the underworld;
Untouched by sickness, broken by no sword.
What woman has ever found your way to death?

Antigone.

Antistrophe 1   15

How often I have heard the story of Niobê,
Tantalos' wretched daughter, how the stone
Clung fast about her, ivy-close: and they say
The rain falls endlessly
And sifting soft snow; her tears are never done.
I feel the loneliness of her death in mine.   20

Chorus.

But she was born of heaven, and you
Are woman, woman-born. If her death is yours,
A mortal woman's, is this not for you
Glory in our world and in the world beyond?

Antigone.

Strophe 2   25

You laugh at me. Ah, friends, friends,
Can you not wait until I am dead? O Thebes,
O men many-charioted, in love with Fortune,
Dear springs of Dircê, sacred Theban grove,
Be witnesses for me, denied all pity,
Unjustly judged! and think a word of love   30
For her whose path turns
Under dark earth, where there are no more tears.

Chorus.

You have passed beyond human daring and come at last
Into a place of stone where Justice sits.   35
I cannot tell
What shape of your father's guilt appears in this.

Antigone.

Antistrophe 2

You have touched it at last: that bridal bed
Unspeakable, horror of son and mother mingling:
Their crime, infection of all our family!   40
O Oedipus, father and brother!
Your marriage strikes from the grave to murder mine.
I have been a stranger here in my own land:
All my life
The blasphemy of my birth has followed me.   45

Chorus.

Reverence is a virtue, but strength
Lives in established law: that must prevail.
You have made your choice,
Your death is the doing of your conscious hand.

Antigone.

Epode

Then let me go, since all your words are bitter,   50
And the very light of the sun is cold to me.
Lead me to my vigil, where I must have
Neither love nor lamentation; no song, but silence.

Creon *interrupts impatiently*

Creon.

If dirges and planned lamentations could put off death,
Men would be singing for ever.   55

[To the Servants:
Take her, go!
You know your orders: take her to the vault
And leave her alone there. And if she lives or dies,
That's her affair, not ours: our hands are clean.   60

Antigone.

O tomb, vaulted bride-bed in eternal rock,
Soon I shall be with my own again
Where Persephonê welcomes the thin ghosts underground:
And I shall see my father again, and you, mother,
And dearest Polyneicês—   65
                        dearest indeed
To me, since it was my hand

That washed him clean and poured the ritual wine:
And my reward is death before my time!   70

And yet, as men's hearts know, I have done no wrong.
I have not sinned before God. Or if I have,
I shall know the truth in death. But if the guilt
Lies upon Creon who judged me, then, I pray,
May his punishment equal my own.   75

Choragos.
                                        O passionate heart,
Unyielding, tormented still by the same winds!

Creon.
Her guards shall have good cause to regret their delaying.

Antigone.
Ah! That voice is like the voice of death!   80

Creon.
I can give you no reason to think you are mistaken.

Antigone.
Thebes, and you my fathers' gods,
And rulers of Thebes, you see me now, the last
Unhappy daughter of a line of kings,
Your kings, led away to death. You will remember   85
What things I suffer, and at what men's hands,
Because I would not transgress the laws of heaven.

To the Guards, simply:
Come: let us wait no longer.

                                        Exit Antigone, L., *guarded*

ODE IV

Chorus.
                                                        Strophe 1

All Danaê's beauty was locked away
In a brazen cell where the sunlight could not come:
A small room, still as any grave, enclosed her.
Yet she was a princess too,
And Zeus in a rain of gold poured love upon her.   5
O child, child,

No power in wealth or war
Or tough sea-blackened ships
Can prevail against untiring Destiny!

Antistrophe 1

And Dryas' son[6] also, that furious king,   10
Bore the god's prisoning anger for his pride:
Sealed up by Dionysos in deaf stone,
His madness died among echoes.
So at the last he learned what dreadful power
His tongue had mocked: 15
For he had profaned the revels,
And fired the wrath of the nine
Implacable Sisters that love the sound of the flute.[7]

Strophe 2

And old men tell a half-remembered tale
Of horror done where a dark ledge splits the sea   20
And a double surf beats on the gráy shóres:
How a king's new woman, sick
With hatred for the queen he had imprisoned,
Ripped out his two sons' eyes with her bloody hands
While grinning Arês watched the shuttle plunge   25
Four times: four blind wounds crying for revenge,[8]

Antistrophe 2

Crying, tears and blood mingled.—Piteously born,
Those sons whose mother was of heavenly birth!
Her father was the god of the North Wind
And she was cradled by gales,   30
She raced with young colts on the glittering hills
And walked untrammeled in the open light:
But in her marriage deathless Fate found means
To build a tomb like yours for all her joy.

SCENE V

Enter blind Teiresias, *led by a boy. The opening speeches of* Teiresias *should be in singsong contrast to the realistic lines of* Creon.

---

[6] Lycurgus, King of Thrace.

[7] The nine Muses.

[8] Reference to Eidothea, wife of King Phineas.

Teiresias.
This is the way the blind man comes, Princes, Princes,
Lock-step, two heads lit by the eyes of one.

Creon.
What new thing have you to tell us, Old Teiresias?

Teiresias.
I have much to tell you: listen to the prophet, Creon.

Creon.
I am not aware that I have ever failed to listen.   5

Teiresias.
Then you have done wisely, King, and ruled well.

Creon.
I admit my debt to you. But what have you to say?

Teiresias.
This, Creon: you stand once more on the edge of fate.

Creon.
What do you mean? Your words are a kind of dread.

Teiresias.
Listen, Creon:
I was sitting in my chair of augury, at the place   10
Where the birds gather about me. They were all a-chatter,
As is their habit, when suddenly I heard
A strange note in their jangling, a scream, a   15
Whirring fury; I knew that they were fighting,
Tearing each other, dying
In a whirlwind of wings clashing. And I was afraid.
I began the rites of burnt-offering at the altar,
But Hephaistos failed me: instead of bright flame,   20
There was only the sputtering slime of the fat thighflesh
Melting: the entrails dissolved in gray smoke,
The bare bone burst from the welter. And no blaze!

This was a sign from heaven. My boy described it,   25
Seeing for me as I see for others.

I tell you, Creon, you yourself have brought
This new calamity upon us. Our hearths and altars
Are stained with the corruption of dogs and carrion birds   30

That glut themselves on the corpse of Oedipus' son.
The gods are deaf when we pray to them, their fire
Recoils from our offering, their birds of omen
Have no cry of comfort, for they are gorged
With the thick blood of the dead.   35
                              O my son,
These are no trifles! Think: all men make mistakes,
But a good man yields when he knows his course is wrong,
And repairs the evil. The only crime is pride.   40

Give in to the dead man, then: do not fight with a corpse—
What glory is it to kill a man who is dead?
Think, I beg you:
It is for your own good that I speak as I do.   45
You should be able to yield for your own good.

Creon.
It seems that prophets have made me their especial province.
All my life long
I have been a kind of butt for the dull arrows   50
Of doddering fortune-tellers!
                              No, Teiresias:
If your birds—if the great eagles of God himself
Should carry him stinking bit by bit to heaven,
I would not yield. I am not afraid of pollution: 55
No man can defile the gods.
                              Do what you will,
Go into business, make money, speculate
In India gold or that synthetic gold from Sardis,
Get rich otherwise than by my consent to bury him.   60
Teiresias, it is a sorry thing when a wise man
Sells his wisdom, lets out his words for hire!

Teiresias.
Ah Creon! Is there no man left in the world—

Creon.
To do what?—Come, let's have the aphorism!

Teiresias.
No man who knows that wisdom outweighs any wealth?   65

Creon.
As surely as bribes are baser than any baseness.

Teiresias.
You are sick, Creon! You are deathly sick!

Creon.
As you say: it is not my place to challenge a prophet.

Teiresias.
Yet you have said my prophecy is for sale. 70

Creon.
The generation of prophets has always loved gold.

Teiresias.
The generation of kings has always loved brass.

Creon.
You forget yourself! You are speaking to your King.

Teiresias.
I know it. You are a king because of me.

Creon.
You have a certain skill; but you have sold out. 75

Teiresias.
King, you will drive me to words that—

Creon.
                                        Say them, say them!
Only remember: I will not pay you for them.

Teiresias.
No, you will find them too costly.

Creon.
                                        No doubt. Speak: 80
Whatever you say, you will not change my will.

Teiresias.
Then take this, and take it to heart!
The time is not far off when you shall pay back
Corpse for corpse, flesh of your own flesh.
You have thrust the child of this world into living night, 85
You have kept from the gods below the child that is theirs:
The one in a grave before her death, the other,
Dead, denied the grave. This is your crime: 90

And the Furies and the dark gods of Hell
Are swift with terrible punishment for you.

Do you want to buy me now, Creon?

                         Not many days,
And your house will be full of men and women weeping.   95
And curses will be hurled at you from far
Cities grieving for sons unburied, left to rot
Before the walls of Thebes.

These are my arrows, Creon: they are all for you.   100

                                 To Boy:
But come, child: lead me home.
Let him waste his fine anger upon younger men.
Maybe he will learn at last
To control a wiser tongue in a better head.

Exit Teiresias

   Choragos.
The old man has gone, King, but his words   105
Remain to plague us. I am old, too,
But I cannot remember that he was ever false.

   Creon.
That is true. . . . It troubles me.
Oh it is hard to give in! but it is worse
To risk everything for stubborn pride.   110

   Choragos.
Creon: take my advice.

   Creon.
                What shall I do?

   Choragos.
Go quickly: free Antigonê from her vault
And build a tomb for the body of Polyneicês.

   Creon.
You would have me do this?   115

   Choragos.
                Creon, yes!

And it must be done at once: God moves
Swiftly to cancel the folly of stubborn men.

Creon.
It is hard to deny the heart! But I
Will do it: I will not fight with destiny.   120

Choragos.
You must go yourself, you cannot leave it to others.

Creon.
     I will go.
—Bring axes, servants:
Come with me to the tomb. I buried her, I
Will set her free.   125
       Oh quickly!
My mind misgives—
The laws of the gods are mighty, and a man must serve them
To the last day of his life!   130

Exit Creon

PAEAN

Choragos.
                            Strophe 1

God of many names

Chorus.
           O Iacchos
              son
of Kadmeian Sémelê
           O born of the Thunder!   5
Guardian of the West
            Regent
of Eleusis' plain
          O Prince of maenad Thebes
and the Dragon Field by rippling Ismenos: 10

Choragos.
                         Antistrophe 1

God of many names

Chorus.

the flame of torches
flares on our hills
                the nymphs of Iacchos
dance at the spring of Castalia: 15

From the vine-close mountain
                        come ah come in ivy:
Evohé evohé![9] sings through the streets of Thebes

Choragos.

                                        Strophe 2
God of many names

Chorus.

                Iacchos of Thebes   20
heavenly Child
                of Sémelê bride of the Thunderer!
The shadow of plague is upon us:
                        come   25
with clement feet
                oh come from Parnasos
down the long slopes
                        across the lamenting water

Choragos.

                                        Antistrophe 2
Iô Fire! Chorister of the throbbing stars!
O purest among the voices of the night!   30
Thou son of God, blaze for us!

Chorus.
Come with choric rapture of circling Maenads
Who cry *Iô Iacche!*
                God of many names!

ÉXODOS[10]

Enter Messenger, *L.*

_____

[9] "Come forth; come forth!"
[10] Concluding scene.

Messenger.
Men of the line of Kadmos, you who live
Near Amphion's citadel:[11]
                    I cannot say
Of any condition of human life "This is fixed,
This is clearly good, or bad". Fate raises up,   5
And Fate casts down the happy and unhappy alike:
No man can foretell his Fate.
                    Take the case of Creon:
Creon was happy once, as I count happiness:
Victorious in battle, sole governor of the land,   10
Fortunate father of children nobly born.
And now it has all gone from him! Who can say
That a man is still alive when his life's joy fails?
He is a walking dead man. Grant him rich,
Let him live like a king in his great house: 15
If his pleasure is gone, I would not give
So much as the shadow of smoke for all he owns.

Choragos.
Your words hint at sorrow: what is your news for us?

Messenger.
They are dead. The living are guilty of their death.

Choragos.
Who is guilty? Who is dead? Speak!   20

Messenger.
                    Haimon.
Haimon is dead; and the hand that killed him
Is his own hand.

Choragos.
          His father's? or his own?

Messenger.
His own, driven mad by the murder his father had done.   25

Choragos.
Teiresias, Teiresias, how clearly you saw it all!

Messenger.
This is my news: you must draw what conclusions you can from it.

----

[11] Thebes.

Choragos.
But look: Eurydicê, our Queen:
Has she overheard us? 30

Enter Eurydice *from the Palace, C.*

Eurydice.
I have heard something, friends:
As I was unlocking the gate of Pallas' shrine,
For I needed her help today, I heard a voice
Telling of some new sorrow. And I fainted 35
There at the temple with all my maidens about me.
But speak again: whatever it is, I can bear it:
Grief and I are no strangers.

Messenger.
                              Dearest Lady,
I will tell you plainly all that I have seen. 40
I shall not try to comfort you: what is the use,
Since comfort could lie only in what is not true?
The truth is always best.
                         I went with Creon
To the outer plain where Polyneicês was lying, 45
No friend to pity him, his body shredded by dogs.
We made our prayers in that place to Hecatê
And Pluto, that they would be merciful. And we bathed
The corpse with holy water, and we brought 50
Fresh-broken branches to burn what was left of it,
And upon the urn we heaped up a towering barrow
Of the earth of his own land.
                              When we were done, we ran
To the vault where Antigonê lay on her couch of stone. 55
One of the servants had gone ahead,
And while he was yet far off he heard a voice
Grieving within the chamber, and he came back
And told Creon. And as the King went closer, 60
The air was full of wailing, the words lost,
And he begged us to make all haste. "Am I a prophet?"
He said, weeping, "And must I walk this road,
The saddest of all that I have gone before? 65
My son's voice calls me on. Oh quickly, quickly!
Look through the crevice there, and tell me
If it is Haimon, or some deception of the gods!"

We obeyed; and in the cavern's farthest corner
We saw her lying: 70
She had made a noose of her fine linen veil
And hanged herself. Haimon lay beside her,
His arms about her waist, lamenting her,
His love lost under ground, crying out
That his father had stolen her away from him.   75

When Creon saw him the tears rushed to his eyes
And he called to him: "What have you done, child?
    Speak to me.
What are you thinking that makes your eyes so strange?   80
O my son, my son, I come to you on my knees!"
But Haimon spat in his face. He said not a word,
Staring—
            And suddenly drew his sword
And lunged. Creon shrank back, the blade missed;   85
    and the boy,
Desperate against himself, drove it half its length
Into his own side, and fell. And as he died
He gathered Antigonê close in his arms again,
Choking, his blood bright red on her white cheek.   90
And now he lies dead with the dead, and she is his
At last, his bride in the houses of the dead.

Exit Eurydice *into the Palace*

  Choragos.
She has left us without a word. What can this mean?

  Messenger.
It troubles me, too; yet she knows what is best,
Her grief is too great for public lamentation,   95
And doubtless she has gone to her chamber to weep
For her dead son, leading her maidens in his dirge.

  Choragos.
It may be so: but I fear this deep silence

Pause

Messenger.
I will see what she is doing. I will go in.

Exit Messenger *into the Palace*

Enter Creon *with attendants, bearing* Haimon's *body*

Choragos.
But here is the King himself: oh look at him,   100
Bearing his own damnation in his arms.

Creon.
Nothing you say can touch me any more.
My own blind heart has brought me
From darkness to final darkness. Here you see
The father murdering, the murdered son—   105
And all my civic wisdom!

Haimon my son, so young, so young to die,
I was the fool, not you; and you died for me.

Choragos.
That is the truth; but you were late in learning it.

Creon.
This truth is hard to bear. Surely a god   110
Has crushed me beneath the hugest weight of heaven,
And driven me headlong a barbaric way
To trample out the thing I held most dear.

The pains that men will take to come to pain!

Enter Messenger *from the Palace*

Messenger.
The burden you carry in your hands is heavy,   115
But it is not all: you will find more in your house.

Creon.
What burden worse than this shall I find there?

Messenger.
The Queen is dead.

Creon.

O port of death, deaf world,
Is there no pity for me? And you, Angel of evil,   120
I was dead, and your words are death again.
Is it true, boy? Can it be true?
Is my wife dead? Has death bred death?

Messenger.

You can see for yourself.

The doors are opened, and the body of Eurydice *is disclosed within.*

Creon.

Oh pity!
All true, all true, and more than I can bear!   125
O my wife, my son!

Messenger.

She stood before the altar, and her heart
Welcomed the knife her own hand guided,
And a great cry burst from her lips for Megareus[12] dead,   130
And for Haimon dead, her sons; and her last breath
Was a curse for their father, the murderer of her sons.
And she fell, and the dark flowed in through her closing eyes.

Creon.

O God, I am sick with fear.   135
Are there no swords here? Has no one a blow for me?

Messenger.

Her curse is upon you for the deaths of both.

Creon.

It is right that it should be. I alone am guilty.
I know it, and I say it. Lead me in,
Quickly, friends.   140
I have neither life nor substance. Lead me in.

Choragos.

You are right, if there can be right in so much wrong.
The briefest way is best in a world of sorrow.

---

[12] Son of Creon, killed in the attack on Thebes.

Creon.

Let it come, 145
Let death come quickly, and be kind to me.
I would not ever see the sun again.

Choragos.

All that will come when it will; but we, meanwhile,
Have much to do. Leave the future to itself.

Creon.

All my heart was in that prayer!

Choragos.

Then do not pray any more: the sky is deaf. 150

Creon.

Lead me away. I have been rash and foolish.
I have killed my son and my wife.
I look for comfort; my comfort lies here dead.
Whatever my hands have touched has come to nothing. 155
Fate has brought all my pride to a thought of dust.

As Creon *is being led into the house, the* Choragos *advances and speaks directly to the audience*

Choragos.

There is no happiness where there is no wisdom;
No wisdom but in submission to the gods.
Big words are always punished,
And proud men in old age learn to be wise. 160

Study and Discussion Questions

1. Summarize the tragedies which have befallen Antigone and Ismene prior to the opening dialogue.
2. What are Antigone's principles? Ismene's?
3. What are Creon's stated reasons, and what are his motives, for: (a) forbidding burial of Polyneices, (b) punishing the law breaker, and (c) exiling Antigone?
4. What does Creon assume everyone else's motives are?
5. How is time important to what happens in the play?

6. Under what conditions does Antigone say she would have obeyed Creon's decree?
7. Are there any hints that the gods are on Antigone's side in the conflict?
8. What is the situation of each of the main characters at the end of the play?
9. Antigone and Creon have at least four areas of conflict: youth versus age, female versus male, the individual versus the state, the religious versus the secular. Give examples from the play for each of these conflicts.

Writing Exercises

1. The title of a classical tragedy is usually the name of the tragic figure, whose flaw brings his or her downfall. How is the situation more complicated in this play? What would you say Antigone's flaw is? What is the flaw of the other candidate for tragic hero of the play?
2. Choose one choral ode and discuss its purpose and effect within the play.
3. How are Creon and Antigone alike? Analyze some passages where you see their similarities.
4. Discuss how Haimon manipulates language in his speech to his father in Scene III.
5. Is Antigone's decision to protest Creon's decree and be honest and open about her actions a case of going too far? Is she courageous and admirable or just plain crazy? Take a position and argue it using evidence from the play.

SUSAN GLASPELL (1882–1948)

Susan Glaspell was born in Davenport, Iowa, worked briefly as a journalist, and then began writing fiction full time. She moved to Greenwich Village in 1911, soon married, and together with her husband founded the Provincetown Playhouse, a small, experimental, and soon influential theater group on Cape Cod in Massachusetts. Among her plays (several, like Trifles, *written expressly for the Provincetown Playhouse) are* Suppressed Desires *(1914),* The Verge *(1921), and* Alison's House *(1930), for which she won a Pulitzer Prize. In addition to her plays, she published ten novels and about forty short stories.*

Trifles   (1916)

CHARACTERS

GEORGE HENDERSON, *County Attorney*
HENRY PETERS, *Sheriff*
LEWIS HALE, *A Neighboring Farmer*
MRS. PETERS
MRS. HALE

SCENE: *The kitchen in the now abandoned farmhouse of* John Wright, *a gloomy kitchen, and left without having been put in order—unwashed pans under the sink, a loaf of bread outside the bread-box, a dish-towel on the table—other signs of incompleted work. At the rear the outer door opens and the* Sheriff *comes in followed by the* County Attorney *and* Hale. *The* Sheriff *and* Hale *are men in middle life, the* County Attorney *is a young man; all are much bundled up and go at once to the stove. They are followed by the two women—the* Sheriff's *wife first; she is a slight wiry woman, a thin nervous face.* Mrs. Hale *is larger and would ordinarily be called more comfortable looking, but she is disturbed now and looks fearfully about as she enters. The women have come in slowly, and stand close together near the door.*

County Attorney. [*Rubbing his hands.*] This feels good. Come up to the fire, ladies.
Mrs. Peters. [*After taking a step forward.*] I'm not—cold.
Sheriff. [*Unbuttoning his overcoat and stepping away from the stove as if to mark the beginning of official business.*] Now, Mr. Hale, before we move things about, you explain to Mr. Henderson just what you saw when you came here yesterday morning.
County Attorney. By the way, has anything been moved? Are things just as you left them yesterday?
Sheriff. [*Looking about.*] It's just the same. When it dropped below zero last night I thought I'd better send Frank out this morning to make a fire for us—no use getting pneumonia with a big case on, but I told him not to touch anything except the stove—and you know Frank.
County Attorney. Somebody should have been left here yesterday.
Sheriff. Oh—yesterday. When I had to send Frank to Morris Center for that man who went crazy—I want you to know I had my hands full yesterday. I knew you could get back from Omaha by today and as long as I went over everything here myself—
County Attorney. Well, Mr. Hale, tell just what happened when you came here yesterday morning.
Hale. Harry and I had started to town with a load of potatoes. We came along the road from my place and as I got here I said, "I'm going to

see if I can't get John Wright to go in with me on a party telephone."
I spoke to Wright about it once before and he put me off, saying folks
talked too much anyway, and all he asked was peace and quiet—I
guess you know about how much he talked himself; but I thought
maybe if I went to the house and talked about it before his wife,
though I said to Harry that I didn't know as what his wife wanted
made much difference to John—

County Attorney. Let's talk about that later, Mr. Hale. I do want to
talk about that, but tell now just what happened when you got to the
house.

Hale. I didn't hear or see anything; I knocked at the door, and still it
was all quiet inside. I knew they must be up, it was past eight o'clock.
So I knocked again, and I thought I heard somebody say, "Come in."
I wasn't sure, I'm not sure yet, but I opened the door—this door
[Indicating the door by which the two women are still standing] and there
in that rocker—*[pointing to it]* sat Mrs. Wright.

They all look at the rocker.

County Attorney. What—was she doing?

Hale. She was rockin' back and forth. She had her apron in her hand
and was kind of—pleating it.

County Attorney. And how did she—look?

Hale. Well, she looked queer.

County Attorney. How do you mean—queer?

Hale. Well, as if she didn't know what she was going to do next. And
kind of done up.

County Attorney. How did she seem to feel about your coming?

Hale. Why, I don't think she minded—one way or other. She didn't pay
much attention. I said, "How do, Mrs. Wright, it's cold, ain't it?" And
she said, "Is it?"—and went on kind of pleating at her apron. Well, I
was surprised; she didn't ask me to come up to the stove, or to set
down, but just sat there, not even looking at me, so I said, "I want
to see John." And then she—laughed. I guess you would call it a laugh.
I thought of Harry and the team outside, so I said a little sharp: "Can't
I see John?" "No," she says, kind o' dull like. "Ain't he home?" says
I. "Yes," says she, "he's home." "Then why can't I see him?" I asked
her, out of patience. "'Cause he's dead," says she. *"Dead?"* says I. She
just nodded her head, not getting a bit excited, but rockin' back and
forth. "Why—where is he?" says I, not knowing what to say. She just
pointed upstairs—like that *[himself pointing to the room above]*. I got
up, with the idea of going up there. I walked from there to here—
then I says, "Why, what did he die of?" "He died of a rope round his
neck," says she, and just went on pleatin' at her apron. Well, I went

out and called Harry. I thought I might—need help. We went upstairs and there he was lyin'—

County Attorney. I think I'd rather have you go into that upstairs, where you can point it all out. Just go on now with the rest of the story.

Hale. Well, my first thought was to get that rope off. It looked . . . *[Stops, his face twitches]* . . . but Harry, he went up to him, and he said, "No, he's dead all right, and we'd better not touch anything." So we went back down stairs. She was still sitting that same way. "Has anybody been notified?" I asked. "No," says she, unconcerned. "Who did this, Mrs. Wright?" said Harry. He said it business-like— and she stopped pleatin' of her apron. "I don't know," says she. "You don't *know*?" says Harry. "No," says she. "Weren't you sleepin' in the bed with him?" says Harry. "Yes," says she, "but I was on the inside." "Somebody slipped a rope round his neck and strangled him and you didn't wake up?" says Harry. "I didn't wake up," she said after him. We must 'a looked as if we didn't see how that could be, for after a minute she said, "I sleep sound." Harry was going to ask her more questions but I said maybe we ought to let her tell her story first to the coroner, or the sheriff, so Harry went fast as he could to Rivers' place, where there's a telephone.

County Attorney. And what did Mrs. Wright do when she knew that you had gone for the coroner?

Hale. She moved from that chair to this one over here *[Pointing to a small chair in the corner]* and just sat there with her hands held together and looking down. I got a feeling that I ought to make some conversation, so I said I had come in to see if John wanted to put in a telephone, and at that she started to laugh, and then she stopped and looked at me—scared. *[The County Attorney, who has had his notebook out, makes a note.]* I dunno, maybe it wasn't scared. I wouldn't like to say it was. Soon Harry got back, and then Dr. Lloyd came, and you, Mr. Peters, and so I guess that's all I know that you don't.

County Attorney. *[Looking around.]* I guess we'll go upstairs first—and then out to the barn and around there. *[To the Sheriff.]* You're convinced that there was nothing important here—nothing that would point to any motive.

Sheriff. Nothing here but kitchen things.

The County Attorney, *after again looking around the kitchen, opens the door of a cupboard closet. He gets up on a chair and looks on a shelf. Pulls his hand away, sticky.*

County Attorney. Here's a nice mess.

The women draw nearer.

Mrs. Peters. *[To the other woman.]* Oh, her fruit; it did freeze. *[To the Lawyer.]* She worried about that when it turned so cold. She said the fire'd go out and her jars would break.

Sheriff. Well, can you beat the women! Held for murder and worryin' about her preserves.

County Attorney. I guess before we're through she may have something more serious than preserves to worry about.

Hale. Well, women are used to worrying over trifles.

The two women move a little closer together.

County Attorney. *[With the gallantry of a young politician.]* And yet, for all their worries, what would we do without the ladies? *[The women do not unbend. He goes to the sink, takes a dipperful of water from the pail and pouring it into a basin, washes his hands. Starts to wipe them on the roller-towel, turns it for a cleaner place.]* Dirty towels! *[Kicks his foot against the pans under the sink.]* Not much of a housekeeper, would you say, ladies?

Mrs. Hale. *[Stiffly.]* There's a great deal of work to be done on a farm.

County Attorney. To be sure. And yet *[With a little bow to her]* I know there are some Dickson county farmhouses which do not have such roller towels.

He gives it a pull to expose its full length again.

Mrs. Hale. Those towels get dirty awful quick. Men's hands aren't always as clean as they might be.

County Attorney. Ah, loyal to your sex, I see. But you and Mrs. Wright were neighbors. I suppose you were friends, too.

Mrs. Hale. *[Shaking her head.]* I've not seen much of her of late years. I've not been in this house—it's more than a year.

County Attorney. And why was that? You didn't like her?

Mrs. Hale. I liked her all well enough. Farmers' wives have their hands full, Mr. Henderson. And then—

County Attorney. Yes—?

Mrs. Hale. *[Looking about.]* It never seemed a very cheerful place.

County Attorney. No—it's not cheerful. I shouldn't say she had the homemaking instinct.

Mrs. Hale. Well, I don't know as Wright had, either.

County Attorney. You mean that they didn't get on very well?

Mrs. Hale. No, I don't mean anything. But I don't think a place'd be any cheerfuller for John Wright's being in it.

County Attorney. I'd like to talk more of that a little later. I want to get the lay of things upstairs now.

He goes to the left, where three steps lead to a stair door.

Sheriff. I suppose anything Mrs. Peters does'll be all right. She was to take in some clothes for her, you know, and a few little things. We left in such a hurry yesterday.

County Attorney. Yes, but I would like to see what you take, Mrs. Peters, and keep an eye out for anything that might be of use to us.

Mrs. Peters. Yes, Mr. Henderson.

The women listen to the men's steps on the stairs, then look about the kitchen.

Mrs. Hale. I'd hate to have men coming into my kitchen, snooping around and criticising.

She arranges the pans under sink which the Lawyer *had shoved out of place.*

Mrs. Peters. Of course it's no more than their duty.

Mrs. Hale. Duty's all right, but I guess that deputy sheriff that came out to make the fire might have got a little of this on. *[Gives the roller towel a pull.]* Wish I'd thought of that sooner. Seems mean to talk about her for not having things slicked up when she had to come away in such a hurry.

Mrs. Peters. *[Who has gone to a small table in the left rear corner of the room, and lifted one end of a towel that covers a pan.]* She had bread set.

Stands still.

Mrs. Hale. *[Eyes fixed on a loaf of bread beside the breadbox, which is on a low shelf at the other side of the room. Moves slowly toward it.]* She was going to put this in there. *[Picks up loaf, then abruptly drops it. In a manner of returning to familiar things.]* It's a shame about her fruit. I wonder if it's all gone. *[Gets up on the chair and looks.]* I think there's some here that's all right, Mrs. Peters. Yes—here; *[Holding it toward the window]* this is cherries, too. *[Looking again.]* I declare I believe that's the only one. *[Gets down, bottle in her hand. Goes to the sink and wipes it off on the outside.]* She'll feel awful bad after all her hard work in the hot weather. I remember the afternoon I put up my cherries last summer.

*She puts the bottle on the big kitchen table, center of the room. With a
sigh, is about to sit down in the rocking-chair. Before she is seated realizes
what chair it is; with a slow look at it, steps back. The chair which she
has touched rocks back and forth.*

Mrs. Peters. Well, I must get those things from the front room closet.
[*She goes to the door at the right, but after looking into the other room,
steps back.*] You coming with me, Mrs. Hale? You could help me carry
them.

They go in the other room; reappear, Mrs. Peters *carrying a dress and
skirt,* Mrs. Hale *following with a pair of shoes.*

Mrs. Peters. My, it's cold in there.

She puts the clothes on the big table, and hurries to the stove.

Mrs. Hale. [*Examining the skirt.*] Wright was close. I think maybe that's
why she kept so much to herself. She didn't even belong to the Ladies
Aid. I suppose she felt she couldn't do her part, and then you don't
enjoy things when you feel shabby. She used to wear pretty clothes
and be lively, when she was Minnie Foster, one of the town girls
singing in the choir. But that—oh, that was thirty years ago. This all
you was to take in?

Mrs. Peters. She said she wanted an apron. Funny thing to want, for
there isn't much to get you dirty in jail, goodness knows. But I suppose
just to make her feel more natural. She said they was in the top drawer
in this cupboard. Yes, here. And then her little shawl that always hung
behind the door. [*Opens stair door and looks.*] Yes, here it is.

Quickly shuts door leading upstairs.

Mrs. Hale. [*Abruptly moving toward her.*] Mrs. Peters?
Mrs. Peters. Yes, Mrs. Hale?
Mrs. Hale. Do you think she did it?
Mrs. Peters. [*In a frightened voice.*] Oh, I don't know.
Mrs. Hale. Well, I don't think she did. Asking for an apron and her
little shawl. Worrying about her fruit.
Mrs. Peters. [*Starts to speak, glances up, where footsteps are heard in the
room above. In a low voice.*] Mr. Peters says it looks bad for her. Mr.
Henderson is awful sarcastic in a speech and he'll make fun of her
sayin' she didn't wake up.

Mrs. Hale. Well, I guess John Wright didn't wake when they was slipping that rope under his neck.

Mrs. Peters. No, it's strange. It must have been done awful crafty and still. They say it was such a—funny way to kill a man, rigging it all up like that.

Mrs. Hale. That's just what Mr. Hale said. There was a gun in the house. He says that's what he can't understand.

Mrs. Peters. Mr. Henderson said coming out that what was needed for the case was a motive; something to show anger, or—sudden feeling.

Mrs. Hale. *[Who is standing by the table.]* Well, I don't see any signs of anger around here. *[She puts her hand on the dish towel which lies on the table, stands looking down at table, one half of which is clean, the other half messy.]* It's wiped to here. *[Makes a move as if to finish work, then turns and looks at loaf of bread outside the breadbox. Drops towel. In that voice of coming back to familiar things.]* Wonder how they are finding things upstairs. I hope she had it a little more red-up there. You know, it seems kind of *sneaking.* Locking her up in town and then coming out here and trying to get her own house to turn against her!

Mrs. Peters. But Mrs. Hale, the law is the law.

Mrs. Hale. I s'pose 'tis. *[Unbuttoning her coat.]* Better loosen up your things, Mrs. Peters. You won't feel them when you go out.

Mrs. Peters *takes off her fur tippet, goes to hang it on hook at back of room, stands looking at the under part of the small corner table.*

Mrs. Peters. She was piecing a quilt.

She brings the large sewing basket and they look at the bright pieces.

Mrs. Hale. It's log cabin pattern. Pretty, isn't it? I wonder if she was goin' to quilt it or just knot it?

Footsteps have been heard coming down the stairs. The Sheriff *enters followed by* Hale *and the* County Attorney.

Sheriff. They wonder if she was going to quilt it or just knot it!

The men laugh, the women look abashed.

County Attorney. *[Rubbing his hands over the stove]* Frank's fire didn't do much up there, did it? Well, let's go out to the barn and get that cleared up.

The men go outside.

Mrs. Hale. *[Resentfully.]* I don't know as there's anything so strange, our takin' up our time with little things while we're waiting for them to get the evidence. *[She sits down at the big table smoothing out a block with decision.]* I don't see as it's anything to laugh about.

Mrs. Peters. *[Apologetically.]* Of course they've got awful important things on their minds.

Pulls up a chair and joins Mrs. Hale at the table.

Mrs. Hale. *[Examining another block.]* Mrs. Peters, look at this one. Here, this is the one she was working on, and look at the sewing! All the rest of it has been so nice and even. And look at this! It's all over the place! Why, it looks as if she didn't know what she was about!

After she has said this they look at each other, then start to glance back at the door. After an instant Mrs. Hale has pulled at a knot and ripped the sewing.

Mrs. Peters. Oh, what are you doing, Mrs. Hale?

Mrs. Hale. *[Mildly.]* Just pulling out a stitch or two that's not sewed very good. *[Threading a needle.]* Bad sewing always make me fidgety.

Mrs. Peters. *[Nervously.]* I don't think we ought to touch things.

Mrs. Hale. I'll just finish up this end. *[Suddenly stopping and leaning forward.]* Mrs. Peters?

Mrs. Peters. Yes, Mrs. Hale?

Mrs. Hale. What do you suppose she was so nervous about?

Mrs. Peters. Oh—I don't know. I don't know as she was nervous. I sometimes sew awful queer when I'm just tired. *[Mrs. Hale starts to say something, looks at Mrs. Peters, then goes on sewing.]* Well I must get these things wrapped up. They may be through sooner than we think. *[Putting apron and other things together.]* I wonder where I can find a piece of paper, and string.

Mrs. Hale. In that cupboard, maybe.

Mrs. Peters. *[Looking in cupboard.]* Why, here's a bird-cage. *[Holds it up.]* Did she have a bird, Mrs. Hale?

Mrs. Hale. Why, I don't know whether she did or not—I've not been here for so long. There was a man around last year selling canaries cheap, but I don't know as she took one; maybe she did. She used to sing real pretty herself.

Mrs. Peters. *[Glancing around.]* Seems funny to think of a bird here. But she must have had one, or why would she have a cage? I wonder what happened to it.

Mrs. Hale. I s'pose maybe the cat got it.

Mrs. Peters. No, she didn't have a cat. She's got that feeling some people have about cats—being afraid of them. My cat got in her room and she was real upset and asked me to take it out.

Mrs. Hale. My sister Bessie was like that. Queer, ain't it?

Mrs. Peters. [*Examining the cage.*] Why, look at this door. It's broke. One hinge is pulled apart.

Mrs. Hale. [*Looking too.*] Looks as if someone must have been rough with it.

Mrs. Peters. Why, yes.

She brings the cage forward and puts it on the table.

Mrs. Hale. I wish if they're going to find any evidence they'd be about it. I don't like this place.

Mrs. Peters. But I'm awful glad you came with me, Mrs. Hale. It would be lonesome for me sitting here alone.

Mrs. Hale. It would, wouldn't it? [*Dropping her sewing.*] But I tell you what I do wish, Mrs. Peters. I wish I had come over sometimes when *she* was here. I—[*Looking around the room*]—wish I had.

Mrs. Peters. But of course you were awful busy, Mrs. Hale—your house and your children.

Mrs. Hale. I could've come. I stayed away because it weren't cheerful— and that's why I ought to have come. I—I've never liked this place. Maybe because it's down in a hollow and you don't see the road. I dunno what it is, but it's a lonesome place and always was. I wish I had come over to see Minnie Foster sometimes. I can see now—

Shakes her head.

Mrs. Peters. Well, you mustn't reproach yourself, Mrs. Hale. Somehow we just don't see how it is with other folks until—something comes up.

Mrs. Hale. Not having children makes less work—but it makes a quiet house, and Wright out to work all day, and no company when he did come in. Did you know John Wright, Mrs. Peters?

Mrs. Peters. Not to know him; I've seen him in town. They say he was a good man.

Mrs. Hale. Yes—good; he didn't drink, and kept his word as well as most, I guess, and paid his debts. But he was a hard man, Mrs. Peters. Just to pass the time of day with him—[*Shivers.*] Like a raw wind that gets to the bone. [*Pauses, her eye falling on the cage.*] I should think she would 'a wanted a bird. But what do you suppose went with it?

Mrs. Peters. I don't know, unless it got sick and died.

She reaches over and swings the broken door, swings it again, both women watch it.

Mrs. Hale.　You weren't raised round here, were you? [Mrs. Peters *shakes her head.*] You didn't know—her?

Mrs. Peters.　Not till they brought her yesterday.

Mrs. Hale.　She—come to think of it, she was kind of like a bird herself— real sweet and pretty, but kind of timid and—fluttery. How—she— did—change. [*Silence; then as if struck by a happy thought and relieved to get back to every day things.*] Tell you what, Mrs. Peters, why don't you take the quilt in with you? It might take up her mind.

Mrs. Peters.　Why, I think that's a real nice idea, Mrs. Hale. There couldn't possibly be any objection to it, could there? Now, just what would I take? I wonder if her patches are in here—and her things.

They look in the sewing basket.

Mrs. Hale.　Here's some red. I expect this has got sewing things in it. [*Brings out a fancy box.*] What a pretty box. Looks like something somebody would give you. Maybe her scissors are in here. [*Opens box. Suddenly puts her hand to her nose.*] Why—[Mrs. Peters *bends nearer, then turns her face away.*] There's something wrapped up in this piece of silk.

Mrs. Peters.　Why, this isn't her scissors.

Mrs. Hale.　[*Lifting the silk.*] Oh, Mrs. Peters—its—

Mrs. Peters bends closer.

Mrs. Peters.　It's the bird.

Mrs. Hale.　[*Jumping up.*] But, Mrs. Peters—look at it! It's neck! Look at its neck! It's all—other side *to.*

Mrs. Peters.　Somebody—wrung—its—neck.

Their eyes meet. A look of growing comprehension, of horror. Steps are heard outside. Mrs. Hale *slips box under quilt pieces, and sinks into her chair. Enter* Sheriff *and* County Attorney. Mrs. Peters *rises.*

County Attorney.　[*As one turning from serious things to little pleasantries.*] Well, ladies, have you decided whether she was going to quilt it or knot it?

Mrs. Peters.　We think she was going to—knot it.

County Attorney. Well, that's interesting, I'm sure. *[Seeing the birdcage.]* Has the bird flown?

Mrs. Hale. *[Putting more quilt pieces over the box.]* We think the—cat got it.

County Attorney. *[Preoccupied.]* Is there a cat?

Mrs. Hale *glances in a quick covert way at* Mrs. Peters.

Mrs. Peters. Well, not *now*. They're superstitious, you know. They leave.

County Attorney. *[To* Sheriff Peters, *continuing an interrupted conversation.]* No sign at all of anyone having come from the outside. Their own rope. Now let's go up again and go over it piece by piece. *[They start upstairs.]* It would have to have been someone who knew just the—

Mrs. Peters *sits down. The two women sit there not looking at one another, but as if peering into something and at the same time holding back. When they talk now it is in the manner of feeling their way over strange ground, as if afraid of what they are saying, but as if they can not help saying it.*

Mrs. Hale. She liked the bird. She was going to bury it in that pretty box.

Mrs. Peters. *[In a whisper.]* When I was a girl—my kitten—there was a boy took a hatchet, and before my eyes—and before I could get there— *[Covers her face an instant.]* If they hadn't held me back I would have— *[Catches herself, looks upstairs where steps are heard, falters weakly]*—hurt him.

Mrs. Hale. *[With a slow look around her.]* I wonder how it would seem never to have had any children around. *[Pause.]* No, Wright wouldn't like the bird—a thing that sang. She used to sing. He killed that, too.

Mrs. Peters. *[Moving uneasily.]* We don't know who killed the bird.

Mrs. Hale. I knew John Wright.

Mrs. Peters. It was an awful thing was done in this house that night, Mrs. Hale. Killing a man while he slept, slipping a rope around his neck that choked the life out of him.

Mrs. Hale. His neck. Choked the life out of him.

Her hand goes out and rests on the bird-cage.

Mrs. Peters. *[With rising voice.]* We don't know who killed him. We don't *know*.

Mrs. Hale. *[Her own feeling not interrupted.]* If there'd been years and years of nothing, then a bird to sing to you, it would be awful—still, after the bird was still.

Mrs. Peters. *[Something within her speaking.]* I know what stillness is. When we homesteaded in Dakota, and my first baby died—after he was two years old, and me with no other then—

Mrs. Hale. *[Moving.]* How soon do you suppose they'll be through, looking for the evidence?

Mrs. Peters. I know what stillness is. *[Pulling herself back.]* The law has got to punish crime, Mrs. Hale.

Mrs. Hale. *[Not as if answering that.]* I wish you'd seen Minnie Foster when she wore a white dress with blue ribbons and stood up there in the choir and sang. *[A look around the room.]* Oh, I *wish* I'd come over here once in a while! That was a crime! That was a crime! Who's going to punish that?

Mrs. Peters. *[Looking upstairs.]* We mustn't—take on.

Mrs. Hale. I might have known she needed help! I know how things can be—for women. I tell you, it's queer, Mrs. Peters. We live close together and we live far apart. We all go through the same things—it's all just a different kind of the same thing. *[Brushes her eyes, noticing the bottle of fruit, reaches out for it.]* If I was you I wouldn't tell her her fruit was gone. Tell her it *ain't.* Tell her it's all right. Take this in to prove it to her. She—she may never know whether it was broke or not.

Mrs. Peters. *[Takes the bottle, looks about for something to wrap it in; takes petticoat from the clothes brought from the other room, very nervously begins winding this around the bottle. In a false voice.]* My, it's a good thing the men couldn't hear us. Wouldn't they just laugh! Getting all stirred up over a little thing like a—dead canary. As if that could have anything to do with—with—wouldn't they *laugh!*

The men are heard coming down stairs.

Mrs. Hale. *[Under her breath.]* Maybe they would—maybe they wouldn't.

County Attorney. No, Peters, it's all perfectly clear except a reason for doing it. But you know juries when it comes to women. If there was some definite thing. Something to show—something to make a story about—a thing that would connect up with this strange way of doing it—

The women's eyes meet for an instant. Enter Hale from outer door.

Hale. Well, I've got the team around. Pretty cold out there.

County Attorney. I'm going to stay here a while by myself. [*To the Sheriff.*] You can send Frank out for me, can't you? I want to go over everything. I'm not satisfied that we can't do better.

Sheriff. Do you want to see what Mrs. Peters is going to take in?

The Lawyer *goes to the table, picks up the apron, laughs.*

County Attorney. Oh, I guess they're not very dangerous things the ladies have picked out. [*Moves a few things about, disturbing the quilt pieces which cover the box. Steps back.*] No, Mrs. Peters doesn't need supervising. For that matter, a sheriff's wife is married to the law. Ever think of it that way, Mrs. Peters?

Mrs. Peters. Not—just that way.

Sheriff. [*Chuckling.*] Married to the law. [*Moves toward the other room.*] I just want you to come in here a minute, George. We ought to take a look at these windows.

County Attorney. [*Scoffingly.*] Oh, windows!

Sheriff. We'll be right out, Mr. Hale.

Hale *goes outside. The* Sheriff *follows the* County Attorney *into the other room. Then* Mrs. Hale *rises, hands tight together, looking intensely at* Mrs. Peters, *whose eyes make a slow turn, finally meeting* Mrs. Hale's. *A moment* Mrs. Hale *holds her, then her own eyes point the way to where the box is concealed. Suddenly* Mrs. Peters *throws back quilt pieces and tries to put the box in the bag she is wearing. It is too big. She opens box, starts to take bird out, cannot touch it, goes to pieces, stands there helpless. Sound of a knob turning in the other room.* Mrs. Hale *snatches the box and puts it in the pocket of her big coat. Enter* County Attorney *and* Sheriff.

County Attorney. [*Facetiously.*] Well, Henry, at least we found out that she was not going to quilt it. She was going to—what is it you call it, ladies?

Mrs. Hale. [*Her hand against her pocket.*] We call it—knot it, Mr. Henderson.

CURTAIN

Study and Discussion Questions

1. Characterize Minnie Wright and John Wright. What was their marriage like?

2. List the series of clues that lead Mrs. Hale and Mrs. Peters to conclude that Minnie Wright murdered her husband. Do the broken bird cage and the dead canary have any significance in the play beyond their role as clues?

3. Trace the various signs throughout the play that the men and the women see things differently.

4. Early on, Sheriff Peters says, "Nothing here but kitchen things," meaning that the men should look elsewhere for clues. Find other examples of irony in the play. Is there a pattern to the ironies?

5. Compare Mrs. Hale and Mrs. Peters. Which one changes more over the course of the play, and how? Trace the signs and the causes of the growing empathy the two women feel with Minnie Wright.

6. What are some of the conflicts in this drama? Is any one primary?

7. What has Glaspell lost and what has she gained by shaping the play so that we never meet either John or Minnie Wright?

Writing Exercises

1. Glaspell rewrote *Trifles* as a short story, which she titled "A Jury of Her Peers." Would that have made a better or worse title for the play? Does it change the emphasis? Explain.

2. Try to imagine a play with the same plot, but with the gender of every character reversed and with male-oriented clues that men see but women don't. Would such a play make sense? Would it have the same impact as *Trifles*?

3. Write an entry or two for the journal you imagine Minnie Wright might have kept.

4. Suppose the canary was found and Minnie Wright was convicted and about to be sentenced. Write a speech she might address to the court explaining why she killed her husband.

5. Were Mrs. Hale and Mrs. Peters justified in covering up the murder of John Wright? Explain.

NONFICTION

JOHN WOOLMAN (1720–1772)

John Woolman was born in a small southern New Jersey Quaker community and worked on his father's farm and as a tailor's apprentice. In his twenties, he began traveling up and down the East Coast preaching. He opposed slavery and argued for the redistribution of wealth. Among his writings are Some Considerations on the Keeping of Negroes *(1754),* A Plea for the Poor *(1763), and his* Journal, *which he kept for over fifteen years and which was first published in 1774, shortly after his death.*

FROM The Journal of John Woolman   (1774)

Scrupling to do writings relative to keeping slaves has been a means of sundry small trials to me, in which I have so evidently felt my own will set aside that I think it good to mention a few of them. Tradesmen and retailers of goods, who depend on their business for a living, are naturally inclined to keep the good-will of their customers; nor is it a pleasant thing for young men to be under any necessity to question the judgment or honesty of elderly men, and more especially of such as have a fair reputation. Deep-rooted customs, though wrong, are not easily altered; but it is the duty of all to be firm in that which they certainly know is right for them. A charitable, benevolent man, well acquainted with a negro, may, I believe, under some circumstances, keep him in his family as a servant, on no other motives than the negro's good; but man, as man, knows not what shall be after him, nor hath he any assurance that his children will attain to that perfection in wisdom and goodness necessary rightly to exercise such power; hence it is clear to me, that I ought not to be the scribe where wills are drawn in which some children are made masters over others during life.

About this time an ancient man of good esteem in the neighborhood came to my house to get his will written. He had young negroes, and I asked him privately how he purposed to dispose of them. He told me; I then said, "I cannot write thy will without breaking my own peace," and respectfully gave him my reasons for it. He signified that he had a choice that I should have written it, but as I could not, consistently with my conscience, he did not desire it, and so he got it written by some other person. A few years after, there being great alterations in his family, he came again to get me to write his will. His negroes were yet young, and his son, to whom he intended to give them, was, since he first spoke to me, from a libertine become a sober young man, and he supposed that I would have been free on that account to write it. We had much friendly talk on the subject, and then deferred it. A few days after he came again and directed their freedom, and I then wrote his will.

Near the time that the last-mentioned Friend[1] first spoke to me, a neighbor received a bad bruise in his body and sent for me to bleed him, which having done, he desired me to write his will. I took notes, and amongst other things he told me to which of his children he gave his young negro. I considered the pain and distress he was in, and knew not how it would end, so I wrote his will, save only that part concerning his slave, and carrying it to his bedside read it to him. I then told him in a friendly way that I could not write any instruments by which my fellow-creatures were made slaves, without bringing trouble on my own mind. I let him know that I charged nothing for what I had done, and desired to be excused from doing the other part in the way he proposed. We then had a serious conference on the subject; at length, he agreeing to set her free, I finished his will.

* * *

Soon after I entered this province[2] a deep and painful exercise came upon me, which I often had some feeling of, since my mind was drawn toward these parts, and with which I had acquainted my brother before we agreed to join as companions. As the people in this and the Southern Provinces live much on the labor of slaves, many of whom are used hardly, my concern was that I might attend with singleness of heart to the voice of the true Shepherd, and be so supported as to remain unmoved at the faces of men.

As it is common for Friends on such a visit to have entertainment free of cost, a difficulty arose in my mind with respect to saving my money by kindness received from what appeared to me to be the gain of oppression. Receiving a gift, considered as a gift, brings the receiver under obligations to the benefactor, and has a natural tendency to draw the obliged into a party with the giver. To prevent difficulties of this kind, and to preserve the minds of judges from any bias, was that Divine prohibition: "Thou shalt not receive any gift; for a gift blindeth the wise, and perverteth the words of the righteous." (Exod. xxiii. 8.) As the disciples were sent forth without any provision for their journey, and our Lord said the workman is worthy of his meat, their labor in the gospel was considered as a reward for their entertainment, and therefore not received as a gift; yet, in regard to my present journey, I could not see my way clear in that respect. The difference appeared thus: the entertainment the

---

[1] Quaker.
[2] Maryland.

disciples met with was from them whose hearts God had opened to receive them, from a love to them and the truth they published; but we, considered as members of the same religious society, look upon it as a piece of civility to receive each other in such visits; and such reception, at times, is partly in regard to reputation, and not from an inward unity of heart and spirit. Conduct is more convincing than language, and where people, by their actions, manifest that the slave-trade is not so disagreeable to their principles but that it may be encouraged, there is not a sound uniting with some Friends who visit them.

The prospect of so weighty a work, and of being so distinguished from many whom I esteemed before myself, brought me very low, and such were the conflicts of my soul that I had a near sympathy with the Prophet, in the time of his weakness, when he said: "If thou deal thus with me, kill me, I pray thee, if I have found favor in thy sight." (Num. xi. 15.) But I soon saw that this proceeded from the want of a full resignation to the Divine will. Many were the afflictions which attended me, and in great abasement, with many tears, my cries were to the Almighty for his gracious and fatherly assistance, and after a time of deep trial I was favored to understand the state mentioned by the Psalmist more clearly than ever I had done before; to wit: "My soul is even as a weaned child." (Psalm cxxxi. 2.) Being thus helped to sink down into resignation, I felt a deliverance from that tempest in which I had been sorely exercised, and in calmness of mind went forward, trusting that the Lord Jesus Christ, as I faithfully attended to him, would be a counsellor to me in all difficulties, and that by his strength I should be enabled even to leave money with the members of society where I had entertainment, when I found that omitting it would obstruct that work to which I believed he had called me. As I copy this after my return, I may here add, that oftentimes I did so under a sense of duty. The way in which I did it was thus: when I expected soon to leave a Friend's house where I had entertainment, if I believed that I should not keep clear from the gain of oppression without leaving money, I spoke to one of the heads of the family privately, and desired them to accept of those pieces of silver, and give them to such of their negroes as they believed would make the best use of them; and at other times I gave them to the negroes myself, as the way looked clearest to me. Before I came out, I had provided a large number of small pieces for this purpose and thus offering them to some who appeared to be wealthy people was a trial both to me and them. But the fear of the Lord so covered me at times that my way was made easier than I expected; and few, if any, manifested any resentment at the offer, and most of them, after some conversation, accepted of them.

* * *

A Friend at whose house we breakfasted setting us a little on our way, I had conversation with him, in the fear of the Lord, concerning his slaves, in which my heart was tender; I used much plainness of speech with him, and he appeared to take it kindly. We pursued our journey without appointing meetings, being pressed in my mind to be at the Yearly Meeting in Virginia. In my travelling on the road, I often felt a cry rise from the centre of my mind, thus: "O Lord, I am a stranger on the earth, hide not thy face from me." On the 11th, we crossed the rivers Patowmack and Rapahannock, and lodged at Port Royal. On the way we had the company of a colonel of the militia, who appeared to be a thoughtful man. I took occasion to remark on the difference in general betwixt a people used to labor moderately for their living, training up their children in frugality and business, and those who live on the labor of slaves; the former, in my view, being the most happy life. He concurred in the remark, and mentioned the trouble arising from the untoward, slothful disposition of the negroes, adding that one of our laborers would do as much in a day as two of their slaves. I replied, that free men, whose minds were properly on their business, found a satisfaction in improving, cultivating, and providing for their families; but negroes, laboring to support others who claim them as their property, and expecting nothing but slavery during life, had not the like inducement to be industrious.

After some further conversation I said, that men having power too often misapplied it; that though we made slaves of the negroes, and the Turks made slaves of the Christians, I believed that liberty was the natural right of all men equally. This he did not deny, but said the lives of the negroes were so wretched in their own country that many of them lived better here than there. I replied, "There is great odds in regard to us on what principle we act"; and so the conversation on that subject ended. I may here add that another person, some time afterwards, mentioned the wretchedness of the negroes, occasioned by their intestine wars, as an argument in favor of our fetching them away for slaves. To which I replied, if compassion for the Africans, on account of their domestic troubles, was the real motive of our purchasing them, that spirit of tenderness being attended to, would incite us to use them kindly, that, as strangers brought out of affliction, their lives might be happy among us. And as they are human creatures, whose souls are as precious as ours, and who may receive the same help and comfort from the Holy Scriptures as we do, we could not omit suitable endeavors to instruct them therein; but that while we manifest by our conduct that our views in purchasing them are to advance ourselves, and while our buying captives taken in war animates those parties to push on the war, and increase desolation amongst them, to say they live unhappily in Africa is far from being an argument in our favor. I further said, the present circumstances of these provinces to me appear difficult; the slaves look like a burdensome stone to such as burden themselves with them; and that if the white people retain a resolution to prefer their outward prospects of gain to all other considerations, and do not act conscientiously toward them as fellow-creatures, I believe that burden will grow heavier and heavier, until times change in a way disagreeable to us. The person appeared very serious, and owned that in considering their condition and the manner of their treatment in these provinces he had sometimes thought it might be just in the Almighty so to order it.

Study and Discussion Questions

1. What does Woolman *do* to act out his antislavery convictions?
2. What struggles does he go through with himself in order to act?
3. How do people respond to him?
4. In the third section of this excerpt from his journal, Woolman argues with a militia colonel about the rationale for slaveholding. What are the Colonel's arguments? What are Woolman's arguments?

Writing Exercises

1. Write about a time you acted out of a belief in what you thought was right. What was the situation? What were your feelings? What response did you receive from others? How do you feel about it in retrospect?
2. Woolman writes, "It is the duty of all to be firm in that which they certainly know is right for them." Do you agree or disagree? What about law? What about expediency? What about inconvenience?

HENRY DAVID THOREAU   (1817–1862)

Henry David Thoreau was born in Concord, Massachusetts, educated at Harvard, and with his brother ran a private school for a number of years. He became close friends with Ralph Waldo Emerson and for two years chose to live in a hut in the woods on land Emerson owned near Walden Pond. In 1846, he spent a night in jail for refusing to pay taxes he felt supported injustice. He later worked as a painter, carpenter, and mason, and traveled frequently into the woods of New England and Canada. Among his writings are A Week on the Concord and Merrimack Rivers *(1849), "Resistance to Civil Government" (1849), later know as "Civil Disobedience," and* Walden *(1854).*

Civil Disobedience   (1849)

I heartily accept the motto,—"That government is best which governs least;"[1] and I should like to see it acted up to more rapidly and systematically. Carried out, it finally amounts to this, which also I believe,—"That government is best which governs not at all;" and when men are prepared for it, that will be the kind of government which they will have. Government is at best but an expedient; but most governments are usually, and all governments are sometimes, inexpedient. The objections which have been brought against a standing army, and they are many and weighty, and deserve to prevail, may also at last be brought against a standing government. The standing army is only an arm of the standing government. The government itself, which is only the mode which the people have chosen to execute their will, is equally liable to be abused and perverted before the people can act through it. Witness the present Mexican war,[2] the work of comparatively a few individuals using the standing government as their tool; for, in the outset, the people would not have consented to this measure.

This American government,—what is it but a tradition, though a recent one, endeavoring to transmit itself unimpaired to posterity, but each instant losing some of its integrity? It has not the vitality and force of a single living man; for a single man can bend it to his will. It is a sort of wooden gun to the people themselves; and, if ever they should use it in earnest as a real one against each other, it will surely split. But it is not the less necessary for this; for the people must have some complicated machinery or other, and hear its din, to satisfy that idea of government which they have. Governments show thus how successfully men can be imposed on, even impose on themselves, for their own advantage. It is excellent, we must all allow; yet this government never of itself furthered any enterprise, but by the alacrity with which it got out of its way. It does not keep the country free. It does not settle the West. It does not educate. The character inherent in the American people has done all that has been accomplished; and it would have done somewhat more, if the government had not sometimes got in its way. For government is an expedient by which men would fain succeed in letting one another alone; and, as has been said, when it is most expedient, the governed are most let alone by it. Trade and commerce, if they were not made of India rubber, would never manage to bounce over the obstacles which legislators are continually putting in their way; and, if one were to judge these men wholly by the effects of their actions, and not partly by their intentions, they would deserve to be classed and punished with those mischievous persons who put obstructions on the railroads.

---

[1] On the masthead of the *United States Magazine and Democratic Review*.

[2] 1846–1848; begun with the annexation of Texas by the United States; seen by many critics as an attempt to extend slavery to the West.

But, to speak practically and as a citizen, unlike those who call them-selves no-government men, I ask for, not at once no government, but *at once* a better government. Let every man make known what kind of government would command his respect, and that will be one step toward obtaining it.

After all, the practical reason why, when the power is once in the hands of the people, a majority are permitted, and for a long period continue, to rule, is not because they are most likely to be in the right, nor because this seems fairest to the minority, but because they are physically the strongest. But a government in which the majority rule in all cases cannot be based on justice, even as far as men understand it. Can there not be a government in which majorities do not virtually decide right and wrong, but conscience?—in which majorities decide only those questions to which the rule of expediency is applicable? Must the citizen ever for a moment, or in the least degree, resign his conscience to the legislator? Why has every man a conscience, then? I think that we should be men first, and subjects afterward. It is not desirable to cultivate a respect for the law, so much as for the right. The only obligation which I have a right to assume, is to do at any time what I think right. It is truly enough said, that a corporation has no conscience; but a corporation of conscientious men is a corporation *with* a conscience. Law never made men a whit more just; and, by means of their respect for it, even the well-disposed are daily made the agents of injustice. A common and natural result of an undue respect for law is, that you may see a file of soldiers, colonel, captain, corporal, privates, powder-monkeys and all, marching in admirable order over hill and dale to the wars, against their wills, aye, against their common sense and consciences, which makes it very steep marching indeed, and produces a palpitation of the heart. They have no doubt that it is a damnable business in which they are concerned; they are all peaceably inclined. Now, what are they? Men at all? or small moveable forts and magazines, at the service of some unscrupulous man in power? Visit the Navy Yard, and behold a marine, such a man as an American government can make, or such as it can make a man with its black arts, a mere shadow and reminiscence of humanity, a man laid out alive and standing, and already, as one may say, buried under arms with funeral accompaniments, though it may be

> "Not a drum was heard, nor a funeral note,
>   As his corse to the ramparts we hurried;
> Not a soldier discharged his farewell shot
>   O'er the grave where our hero we buried."[3]

The mass of men serve the State thus, not as men mainly, but as machines, with their bodies. They are the standing army, and the militia,

---

[3] From "The Burial of Sir John Moore at Corunna," by Charles Wolfe.

jailers, constables, *posse comitatus,* &c. In most cases there is no free exercise whatever of the judgment or of the moral sense; but they put themselves on a level with wood and earth and stones; and wooden men can perhaps be manufactured that will serve the purpose as well. Such command no more respect than men of straw, or a lump of dirt. They have the same sort of worth only as horses and dogs. Yet such as these even are commonly esteemed good citizens. Others, as most legislators, politicians, lawyers, ministers, and office-holders, serve the State chiefly with their heads; and, as they rarely make any moral distinctions, they are as likely to serve the devil, without intending it, as God. A very few, as heroes, patriots, martyrs, reformers in the great sense, and *men,* serve the State with their consciences also, and so necessarily resist it for the most part; and they are commonly treated by it as enemies. A wise man will only be useful as a man, and will not submit to be "clay," and "stop a hole to keep the wind away,"[4] but leave that office to his dust at least:—

> "I am too high-born to be propertied,
> To be a secondary at control,
> Or useful serving-man and instrument
> To any sovereign state throughout the world."[5]

He who gives himself entirely to his fellow-men appears to them useless and selfish; but he who gives himself partially to them is pronounced a benefactor and philanthropist.

How does it become a man to behave toward this American government to-day? I answer that he cannot without disgrace be associated with it. I cannot for an instant recognize that political organization as *my* government which is the *slave's* government also.

All men recognize the right of revolution; that is, the right to refuse allegiance to and to resist the government, when its tyranny or its inefficiency are great and unendurable. But almost all say that such is not the case now. But such was the case, they think, in the Revolution of '75. If one were to tell me that this was a bad government because it taxed certain foreign commodities brought to its ports, it is most probable that I should not make an ado about it, for I can do without them: all machines have their friction; and possibly this does enough good to counterbalance the evil. At any rate, it is a great evil to make a stir about it. But when the friction comes to have its machine, and oppression and robbery are organized, I say, let us not have such a machine any longer. In other words, when a sixth of the population of a nation which has undertaken to be the refuge of liberty are slaves, and a whole country is unjustly overrun and conquered by a foreign army, and subjected to military law, I think that it is not too soon for honest men to rebel and

---

[4] From William Shakespeare, *Hamlet,* V, i, 236–37.

[5] From William Shakespeare, *King John,* V, ii, 79–82.

revolutionize. What makes this duty the more urgent is the fact, that the country so overrun is not our own, but ours is the invading army.

Paley,[6] a common authority with many on moral questions, in his chapter on the "Duty of Submission to Civil Government," resolves all civil obligation into expediency; and he proceeds to say, "that so long as the interest of the whole society requires it, that is, so long as the established government cannot be resisted or changed without public inconveniency, it is the will of God that the established government be obeyed, and no longer."—"This principle being admitted, the justice of every particular case of resistance is reduced to a computation of the quantity of the danger and grievance on the one side, and of the probability and expense of redressing it on the other." Of this, he says, every man shall judge for himself. But Paley appears never to have contemplated those cases to which the rule of expediency does not apply, in which a people, as well as an individual, must do justice, cost what it may. If I have unjustly wrested a plank from a drowning man, I must restore it to him though I drown myself. This, according to Paley, would be inconvenient. But he that would save his life, in such a case, shall lose it. This people must cease to hold slaves, and to make war on Mexico, though it cost them their existence as a people.

In their practice, nations agree with Paley; but does any one think that Massachusetts does exactly what is right at the present crisis?

"A drab of state, a cloth-o'-silver slut,
To have her train borne up, and her soul trail in the dirt."[7]

Practically speaking, the opponents to a reform in Massachusetts are not a hundred thousand politicians at the South, but a hundred thousand merchants and farmers here, who are more interested in commerce and agriculture than they are in humanity, and are not prepared to do justice to the slave and to Mexico, *cost what it may*. I quarrel not with far-off foes, but with those who, near at home, co-operate with, and do the bidding of those far away, and without whom the latter would be harmless. We are accustomed to say, that the mass of men are unprepared; but improvement is slow, because the few are not materially wiser or better than the many. It is not so important that many should be as good as you, as that there be some absolute goodness somewhere; for that will leaven the whole lump. There are thousands who are *in opinion* opposed to slavery and to the war, who yet in effect do nothing to put an end to them; who, esteeming themselves children of Washington and Franklin, sit down with their hands in their pockets, and say that they know not what to do, and do nothing; who even postpone the question of freedom to the question of free-trade, and quietly read the prices-current along

---

[6] William Paley (1743–1805), British philosopher.

[7] From Cyril Tourneur, *The Revenger's Tragedie* (1607), IV, iv, 71–72.

with the latest advices from Mexico, after dinner, and, it may be, fall asleep over them both. What is the price-current of an honest man and patriot to-day? They hesitate, and they regret, and sometimes they petition; but they do nothing in earnest and with effect. They will wait, well disposed, for others to remedy the evil, that they may no longer have it to regret. At most, they give only a cheap vote, and a feeble countenance and God-speed, to the right, as it goes by them. There are nine hundred and ninety-nine patrons of virtue to one virtuous man; but it is easier to deal with the real possessor of a thing than with the temporary guardian of it.

All voting is a sort of gaming, like chequers or backgammon, with a slight moral tinge to it, a playing with right and wrong, with moral questions; and betting naturally accompanies it. The character of the voters is not staked. I cast my vote, perchance, as I think right; but I am not vitally concerned that that right should prevail. I am willing to leave it to the majority. Its obligation, therefore, never exceeds that of expediency. Even voting *for the right* is *doing* nothing for it. It is only expressing to men feebly your desire that it should prevail. A wise man will not leave the right to the mercy of chance, nor wish it to prevail through the power of the majority. There is but little virtue in the action of masses of men. When the majority shall at length vote for the abolition of slavery, it will be because they are indifferent to slavery, or because there is but little slavery left to be abolished by their vote. *They* will then be the only slaves. Only *his* vote can hasten the abolition of slavery who asserts his own freedom by his vote.

I hear of a convention to be held at Baltimore, or elsewhere, for the selection of a candidate for the Presidency, made up chiefly of editors, and men who are politicians by profession; but I think, what is it to any independent, intelligent, and respectable man what decision they may come to, shall we not have the advantage of his wisdom and honesty, nevertheless? Can we not count upon some independent votes? Are there not many individuals in the country who do not attend conventions? But no: I find that the respectable man, so called, has immediately drifted from his position, and despairs of his country, when his country has more reason to despair of him. He forthwith adopts one of the candidates thus selected as the only *available* one, thus proving that he is himself *available* for any purposes of the demagogue. His vote is of no more worth than that of any unprincipled foreigner or hireling native, who may have been bought. Oh for a man who is a *man*, and, as my neighbor says, has a bone in his back which you cannot pass your hand through! Our statistics are at fault: the population has been returned too large. How many *men* are there to a square thousand miles in this country? Hardly one. Does not America offer any inducement for men to settle here? The American has dwindled into an Odd Fellow,—one who may be known by the development of his organ of gregariousness, and a manifest lack of intellect and cheerful self-reliance; whose first and chief concern, on coming into the world, is to see that the alms-houses are in good repair; and, before yet he has lawfully donned the virile garb, to collect a fund for the support of the widows and orphans that may be; who, in short, ventures to live only by the aid of the mutual insurance company, which has promised to bury him decently.

It is not a man's duty, as a matter of course, to devote himself to the eradication of any, even the most enormous wrong; he may still properly have other concerns to engage him; but it is his duty, at least, to wash his hands of it, and, if he gives it no thought longer, not to give it practically his support. If I devote myself to other pursuits and contemplations, I must first see, at least, that I do not pursue them sitting upon another man's shoulders. I must get off him first, that he may pursue his contemplations too. See what gross inconsistency is tolerated. I have heard some of my townsmen say, "I should like to have them order me out to help put down an insurrection of the slaves, or to march to Mexico,—see if I would go;" and yet these very men have each, directly by their allegiance, and so indirectly, at least, by their money, furnished a substitute. The soldier is applauded who refuses to serve in an unjust war by those who do not refuse to sustain the unjust government which makes the war; is applauded by those whose own act and authority he disregards and sets at nought; as if the State were penitent to that degree that it hired one to scourge it while it sinned, but not to that degree that it left off sinning for a moment. Thus, under the name of order and civil government, we are all made at last to pay homage to and support our own meanness. After the first blush of sin, comes its indifference; and from immoral it becomes, as it were, *un*moral, and not quite unnecessary to that life which we have made.

The broadest and most prevalent error requires the most disinterested virtue to sustain it. The slight reproach to which the virtue of patriotism is commonly liable, the noble are most likely to incur. Those who, while they disapprove of the character and measures of a government, yield to it their allegiance and support, are undoubtedly its most conscientious supporters, and so frequently the most serious obstacles to reform. Some are petitioning the State to dissolve the Union, to disregard the requisitions of the President. Why do they not dissolve it themselves,—the union between themselves and the State,—and refuse to pay their quota into its treasury? Do not they stand in the same relation to the State, that the State does to the Union? And have not the same reasons prevented the State from resisting the Union, which have prevented them from resisting the State?

How can a man be satisfied to entertain an opinion merely, and enjoy *it?* Is there any enjoyment in it, if his opinion is that he is aggrieved? If you are cheated out of a single dollar by your neighbor, you do not rest satisfied with knowing that you are cheated, or with saying that you are cheated, or even with petitioning him to pay you your due; but you take effectual steps at once to obtain the full amount, and see that you are never cheated again. Action from principle,—the perception and the performance of right,—changes things and relations; it is essentially revolutionary, and does not consist wholly with any thing which was. It not only divides states and churches, it divides families; aye, it divides the *individual*, separating the diabolical in him from the divine.

Unjust laws exist: shall we be content to obey them, or shall we endeavor to amend them, and obey them until we have succeeded, or shall we transgress them at once? Men generally, under such a government as this, think that they ought to wait until they have persuaded the majority to alter them. They think that, if they should resist, the remedy would be worse than the evil. But it is the fault of the government itself that the remedy *is* worse than the evil. *It* makes it worse. Why is it not more apt to anticipate and provide for reform? Why does it not cherish its wise minority? Why does it cry and resist before it is hurt? Why does it not encourage its citizens to be on the alert to point out its faults, and *do* better than it would have them? Why does it always crucify Christ, and excommunicate Copernicus and Luther, and pronounce Washington and Franklin rebels?

One would think, that a deliberate and practical denial of its authority was the only offense never contemplated by government; else, why has it not assigned its definite, its suitable and proportionate penalty? If a man who has no property refuses but once to earn nine shillings for the State, he is put in prison for a period unlimited by any law that I know, and determined only by the discretion of those who placed him there; but if he should steal ninety times nine shillings from the State, he is soon permitted to go at large again.

If the injustice is part of the necessary friction of the machine of government, let it go, let it go: perchance it will wear smooth,—certainly the machine will wear out. If the injustice has a spring, or a pulley, or a rope, or a crank, exclusively for itself, then perhaps you may consider whether the remedy will not be worse than the evil; but if it is of such a nature that it requires you to be the agent of injustice to another, then, I say, break the law. Let your life be a counter friction to stop the machine. What I have to do is to see, at any rate, that I do not lend myself to the wrong which I condemn.

As for adopting the ways which the State has provided for remedying the evil, I know not of such ways. They take too much time, and a man's life will be gone. I have other affairs to attend to. I came into this world, not chiefly to make this a good place to live in, but to live in it, be it good or bad. A man has not every thing to do, but something; and because he cannot do *every thing*, it is not necessary that he should do *something* wrong. It is not my business to be petitioning the governor or the legislature any more than it is theirs to petition me; and, if they should not hear my petition, what should I do then? But in this case the State has provided no way: its very Constitution is the evil. This may seem to be harsh and stubborn and unconciliatory; but it is to treat with the utmost kindness and consideration the only spirit that can appreciate or deserves it. So is all change for the better, like birth and death which convulse the body.

I do not hesitate to say, that those who call themselves abolitionists should at once effectually withdraw their support, both in person and property, from the government of Massachusetts, and not wait till they constitute a majority of one, before they suffer the right to prevail through them. I think that it is enough if they have God on their side, without waiting for that other one. Moreover, any man more right than his neighbors, constitutes a majority of one already.

I meet this American government, or its representative the State government, directly, and face to face, once a year, no more, in the person of its tax-gatherer; this is the only mode in which a man situated as I am necessarily meets it; and it then says distinctly, Recognize me; and the simplest, the most effectual, and, in the present posture of affairs, the indispensablest mode of treating with it on this head, of expressing your little satisfaction with and love for it, is to deny it then. My civil neighbor, the tax-gatherer, is the very man I have to deal with,—for it is, after all, with men and not with parchment that I quarrel,—and he has voluntarily chosen to be an agent of the government. How shall he ever know well what he is and does as an officer of the government, or as a man, until he is obliged to consider whether he shall treat me, his neighbor, for whom he has respect, as a neighbor and well-disposed man, or as a maniac and disturber of the peace, and see if he can get over this obstruction to his neighborliness without a ruder and more impetuous thought or speech corresponding with his action? I know this well, that if one thousand, if one hundred, if ten men whom I could name,—if ten *honest* men only,—aye, if *one* HONEST man, in this State of Massachusetts, *ceasing to hold slaves*, were actually to withdraw from this copartnership, and be locked up in the county jail therefor, it would be the abolition of slavery in America. For it matters not how small the beginning may seem to be: what is once well done is done for ever. But we love better to talk about it: that we say is our mission. Reform keeps many scores of newspapers in its service, but not one man. If my esteemed neighbor, the State's ambassador,[8] who will devote his days to the settlement of the question of human rights in the Council Chamber, instead of being threatened with the prisons of Carolina, were to sit down the prisoner of Massachusetts, that State which is so anxious to foist the sin of slavery upon her sister,—though at present she can discover only an act of inhospitality to be the ground of a quarrel with her,—the Legislature would not wholly waive the subject the following winter.

Under a government which imprisons any unjustly, the true place for a just man is also a prison. The proper place to-day, the only place which

---

[8] Samuel Hoar (1778–1856), sent by the state of Massachusetts to South Carolina to help black sailors from Massachusetts who were taken from their ships there, was evicted from Charleston by the South Carolina legislature.

Massachusetts has provided for her freer and less desponding spirits, is in her prisons, to be put out and locked out of the State by her own act, as they have already put themselves out by their principles. It is there that the fugitive slave, and the Mexican prisoner on parole, and the Indian come to plead the wrongs of his race, should find them; on that separate, but more free and honorable ground, where the State places those who are not *with* her but *against* her,—the only house in a slave-state in which a free man can abide with honor. If any think that their influence would be lost there, and their voices no longer afflict the ear of the State, that they would not be as an enemy within its walls, they do not know by how much truth is stronger than error, nor how much more eloquently and effectively he can combat injustice who has experienced a little in his own person. Cast your whole vote, not a strip of paper merely, but your whole influence. A minority is powerless while it conforms to the majority; it is not even a minority then; but it is irresistible when it clogs by its whole weight. If the alternative is to keep all just men in prison, or give up war and slavery, the State will not hesitate which to choose. If a thousand men were not to pay their tax-bills this year, that would not be a violent and bloody measure, as it would be to pay them, and enable the State to commit violence and shed innocent blood. This is, in fact, the definition of a peaceable revolution, if any such is possible. If the tax-gatherer, or any other public officer, asks me, as one has done, "But what shall I do?" my answer is, "If you really wish to do any thing, resign your office." When the subject has refused allegiance, and the officer has resigned his office, then the revolution is accomplished. But even suppose blood should flow. Is there not a sort of blood shed when the conscience is wounded? Through this wound a man's real manhood and immortality flow out, and he bleeds to an everlasting death. I see this blood flowing now.

I have contemplated the imprisonment of the offender, rather than the seizure of his goods,—though both will serve the same purpose,—because they who assert the purest right, and consequently are most dangerous to a corrupt State, commonly have not spent much time in accumulating property. To such the State renders comparatively small service, and a slight tax is wont to appear exorbitant, particularly if they are obliged to earn it by special labor with their hands. If there were one who lived wholly without the use of money, the State itself would hesitate to demand it of him. But the rich man—not to make any invidious comparison—is always sold to the institution which makes him rich. Absolutely speaking, the more money, the less virtue; for money comes between a man and his objects, and obtains them for him; and it was certainly no great virtue to obtain it. It puts to rest many questions which he would otherwise be taxed to answer; while the only new question which it puts is the hard but superfluous one, how to spend it. Thus his moral ground is taken from under his feet. The opportunities of living are diminished in proportion as what are called the "means" are increased. The best thing a man can do for his culture when he is rich is to endeavour to carry out those schemes which he entertained when he was poor. Christ answered the Herodians according to their condition. "Show me the tribute-money," said he;—and one took a penny out of his pocket;—If you use money which has the image of Cæsar on it, and which he has made current and valuable, that is, *if you are men of the State*, and gladly enjoy the advantages of Cæsar's government, then pay him back some of his own when he demands it; "Render therefore to Cæsar that which is Cæsar's, and to God those things which are God's,"—leaving them no wiser than before as to which was which; for they did not wish to know.

When I converse with the freest of my neighbors, I perceive that, whatever they may say about the magnitude and seriousness of the question, and their regard for the public tranquility, the long and the short of the matter is, that they cannot spare the protection of the existing government, and they dread the consequences of disobedience to it to their property and families. For my own part, I should not like to think that I ever rely on the protection of the State. But, if I deny the authority of the State when it presents its tax-bill, it will soon take and waste all my property, and so harass me and my children without end. This is hard. This makes it impossible for a man to live honestly and at the same time comfortably in outward respects. It will not be worth the while to accumulate property; that would be sure to go again. You must hire or squat somewhere, and raise but a small crop, and eat that soon. You must live within yourself, and depend upon yourself, always tucked up and ready for a start, and not have many affairs. A man may grow rich in Turkey even, if he will be in all respects a good subject of the Turkish government. Confucius said,—"If a State is governed by the principles of reason, poverty and misery are subjects of shame; if a State is not governed by the principles of reason, riches and honors are the subjects of shame." No: until I want the protection of Massachusetts to be extended to me in some distant southern port, where my liberty is endangered, or until I am bent solely on building up an estate at home by peaceful enterprise, I can afford to refuse allegiance to Massachusetts, and her right to my property and life. It costs me less in every sense to incur the penalty of disobedience to the State, than it would to obey. I should feel as if I were worth less in that case.

Some years ago, the State met me in behalf of the church, and commanded me to pay a certain sum toward the support of a clergyman whose preaching my father attended, but never I myself. "Pay it," it said, "or be locked up in the jail." I declined to pay. But, unfortunately, another man saw fit to pay it. I did not see why the schoolmaster should be taxed to support the priest, and not the priest the schoolmaster; for I was not the State's schoolmaster, but I supported myself by voluntary subscription. I did not see why the lyceum should not present its tax-bill, and have the State to back its demand, as well as the church. However, at the request of the selectmen, I condescended to make some such statement as this in writing:—"Know all men by these presents, that I, Henry Thoreau, do not wish to be regarded as a member of any incorporated society which I have not joined." This I gave to the town-clerk; and he has it. The State, having thus learned that I did not wish to be regarded as a member of that church, has never made a like demand on me since; though it said that it must adhere to its original presumption that time. If I had known how to name them, I should then have signed off in detail from all the societies which I never signed on to; but I did not know where to find a complete list.

I have paid no poll-tax for six years. I was put into a jail once on this account, for one night; and, as I stood considering the walls of solid stone, two or three feet thick, the door of wood and iron, a foot thick, and the iron grating which strained the light, I could not help being struck with the foolishness of that institution which treated me as if I were mere flesh and blood and bones, to be locked up. I wondered that it should have concluded at length that this was the best use it could put me to, and had never thought to avail itself of my services in some way. I saw that, if there was a wall of stone between me and my townsmen, there was a still more difficult one to climb or break through, before they could get to be as free as I was. I did not for a moment feel confined, and the walls seemed a great waste of stone and mortar. I felt as if I alone of all my townsmen had paid my tax. They plainly did not know how to treat me, but behaved like persons who are underbred. In every threat and in every compliment there was a blunder; for they thought that my chief desire was to stand the other side of that stone wall. I could not but smile to see how industriously they locked the door on my meditations, which followed them out again without let or hinderance, and *they* were really all that was dangerous. As they could not reach me, they had resolved to punish my body; just as boys, if they cannot come at some person against whom they have a spite, will abuse his dog. I saw that the State was half-witted, that it was timid as a lone woman with her silver spoons, and that it did not know its friends from its foes, and I lost all my remaining respect for it, and pitied it.

Thus the State never intentionally confronts a man's sense, intellectual or moral, but only his body, his senses. It is not armed with superior wit or honesty, but with superior physical strength. I was not born to be forced. I will breathe after my own fashion. Let us see who is the strongest. What force has a multitude? They only can force me who obey a higher law than I. They force me to become like themselves. I do not hear of *men* being *forced* to live this way or that by masses of men. What sort of life were that to live? When I meet a government which says to me, "Your money or your life," why should I be in haste to give it my money? It may be in a great strait, and not know what to do: I cannot help that. It must help itself; do as I do. It is not worth the while to snivel about it. I am not responsible for the successful working of the machinery of society. I am not the son of the engineer. I perceive that, when an acorn and a chestnut fall side by side, the one does not remain inert to make way for the other, but both obey their own laws, and spring and grow and flourish as best they can, till one, perchance, overshadows and destroys the other. If a plant cannot live according to its nature, it dies; and so a man.

The night in prison was novel and interesting enough. The prisoners in their shirt-sleeves were enjoying a chat and the evening air in the door-way, when I entered. But the jailer said, "Come, boys, it is time to lock up;" and so they dispersed, and I heard the sound of their steps returning into the hollow apartments. My room-mate was introduced to me by the jailer, as "a first-rate fellow and a clever man." When the door was locked, he showed me where to hang my hat, and how he managed matters there. The rooms were whitewashed once a month; and this one, at least, was the whitest, most simply furnished, and probably the neatest apartment in the town. He naturally wanted to know where I came from, and what brought me there; and, when I had told him, I asked him in my turn how he came there, presuming him to be an honest man, of course; and, as the world goes, I believe he was. "Why," said he, "they accuse me of burning a barn; but I never did it." As near as I could discover, he had probably gone to bed in a barn when drunk, and smoked his pipe there; and so a barn was burnt. He had the reputation of being a clever man, had been there some three months waiting for his trial to come on, and would have to wait as much longer; but he was quite domesticated and contented, since he got his board for nothing, and thought that he was well treated.

He occupied one window, and I the other; and I saw, that if one stayed there long, his principal business would be to look out the window. I had soon read all the tracts that were left there, and examined where former prisoners had broken out, and where a grate had been sawed off, and heard the history of the various occupants of that room; for I found that even here there was a history and a gossip which never circulated beyond the walls of the jail. Probably this is the only house in the town where verses are composed, which are afterward printed in a circular form, but not published. I was shown quite a long list of verses which were composed by some young men who had been detected in an attempt to escape, who avenged themselves by singing them.

I pumped my fellow-prisoner as dry as I could, for fear I should never see him again; but at length he showed me which was my bed, and left me to blow out the lamp.

It was like travelling into a far country, such as I had never expected to behold, to lie there for one night. It seemed to me that I never had heard the town-clock strike before, nor the evening sounds of the village; for we slept with the windows open, which were inside the grating. It was to see my native village in the light of the middle ages, and our Concord was turned into a Rhine stream, and visions of knights and castles passed before me. They were the voices of old burghers that I heard in the streets. I was an involuntary spectator and auditor of whatever was done and said in the kitchen of the adjacent village-inn,—a wholly new and rare experience to me. It was a closer view of my native town. I was fairly inside of it. I never had seen its institutions before. This is one of its peculiar institutions; for it is a shire town. I began to comprehend what its inhabitants were about.

In the morning, our breakfasts were put through the hole in the door, in small oblong-square tin pans, made to fit, and holding a pint of chocolate, with brown bread, and an iron spoon. When they called for the vessels again, I was green enough to return what bread I had left; but my comrade seized it, and said that I should lay that up for lunch or dinner. Soon after, he was let out to work at haying in a neighboring field, whither he went every day, and would not be back till noon; so he bade me good-day, saying that he doubted if he should see me again.

When I came out of prison,—for some one interfered, and paid the tax,—I did not perceive that great changes had taken place on the common, such as he observed who went in a youth, and emerged a tottering and gray-headed man; and yet a change had to my eyes come over the scene,—the town, and State, and country,—greater than any that mere time could effect. I saw yet more distinctly the State in which I lived. I saw to what extent the people among whom I lived could be trusted as good neighbors and friends; that their friendship was for summer weather only; that they did not greatly purpose to do right; that they were a distinct race from me by their prejudices and superstitions, as the Chinamen and Malays are; that, in their sacrifices to humanity, they ran no risks, not even to their property; that, after all, they were not so noble but they treated the thief as he had treated them, and hoped, by a certain outward observance and a few prayers, and by walking in a particular straight though useless path from time to time, to save their souls. This may be to judge my neighbors harshly; for I believe that most of them are not aware that they have such an institution as the jail in their village.

It was formerly the custom in our village, when a poor debtor came out of jail, for his acquaintances to salute him, looking through their fingers, which were crossed to represent the grating of a jail window, "How do ye do?" My neighbors did not thus salute me, but first looked at me, and then at one another, as if I had returned from a long journey. I was put into jail as I was going to the shoemaker's to get a shoe which was mended. When I was let out the next morning, I proceeded to finish my errand, and, having put on my mended shoe, joined a huckleberry party, who were impatient to put themselves under my conduct; and in half an hour,—for the horse was soon tackled,—was in the midst of a huckleberry field, on one of our highest hills, two miles off; and then the State was nowhere to be seen.

This is the whole history of "My Prisons."[9]

I have never declined paying the highway tax, because I am as desirous of being a good neighbor as I am of being a bad subject; and, as for supporting schools, I am doing my part to educate my fellow-countrymen now. It is for no particular item in the tax-bill that I refuse to pay it. I simply wish to refuse allegiance to the State, to withdraw and stand aloof from it effectually. I do not care to trace the course of my dollar, if I could, till it buys a man, or a musket to shoot one with,—the dollar is innocent,—but I am concerned to trace the effects of my allegiance. In fact, I quietly declare war with the State, after my fashion, though I will still make what use and get what advantage of her I can, as is usual in such cases.

If others pay the tax which is demanded of me, from a sympathy with the State, they do but what they have already done in their own case, or rather they abet injustice to a greater extent than the State requires. If they pay the tax from a mistaken interest in the individual taxed, to save his property or prevent his going to jail, it is because they have not considered wisely how far they let their private feelings interfere with the public good.

This, then, is my position at present. But one cannot be too much on his guard in such a case, lest his action be biassed by obstinacy, or an undue regard for the opinions of men. Let him see that he does only what belongs to himself and to the hour.

I think sometimes, Why, this people mean well; they are only ignorant; they would do better if they knew how: why give your neighbors this pain to treat you as they are not inclined to? But I think, again, this is no reason why I should do as they do, or permit others to suffer much greater pain of a different kind. Again, I sometimes say to myself, When many millions of men, without heat, without ill-will, without personal feeling of any kind, demand of you a few shillings only, without the possibility, such is their constitution, of retracting or altering their present demand, and without the possibility, on your side, of appeal to any other millions, why expose yourself to this overwhelming brute force? You do not resist cold and hunger, the winds and the waves, thus obstinately; you quietly submit to a thousand similar necessities. You do not put your head into the fire. But just in proportion as I regard this as not wholly a brute force, but partly a human force, and consider that I have relations to those millions as to so many millions of men, and not of mere brute

---

[9] Reference to *Le Mie Prigioni* (1832), prison memoirs of Silvio Pellico.

or inanimate things, I see that appeal is possible, first and instantaneously, from them to the Maker of them, and, secondly, from them to themselves. But, if I put my head deliberately into the fire, there is no appeal to fire or to the Maker of fire, and I have only myself to blame. If I could convince myself that I have any right to be satisfied with men as they are, and to treat them accordingly, and not according, in some respects, to my requisitions and expectations of what they and I ought to be, then, like a good Mussulman and fatalist, I should endeavor to be satisfied with things as they are, and say it is the will of God. And, above all, there is this difference between resisting this and a purely brute or natural force, that I can resist this with some effect; but I cannot expect, like Orpheus, to change the nature of the rocks and trees and beasts.

I do not wish to quarrel with any man or nation. I do not wish to split hairs, to make fine distinctions, or set myself up as better than my neighbors. I seek rather, I may say, even an excuse for conforming to the laws of the land. I am but too ready to conform to them. Indeed I have reason to suspect myself on this head; and each year, as the tax-gatherer comes round, I find myself disposed to review the acts and position of the general and state governments, and the spirit of the people, to discover a pretext for conformity. I believe that the State will soon be able to take all my work of this sort out of my hands, and then I shall be no better a patriot than my fellow-countrymen. Seen from a lower point of view, the Constitution, with all its faults, is very good; the law and the courts are very respectable; even this State and this American government are, in many respects, very admirable and rare things, to be thankful for, such as a great many have described them; but seen from a point of view a little higher, they are what I have described them; seen from a higher still, and the highest, who shall say what they are, or that they are worth looking at or thinking of at all?

However, the government does not concern me much, and I shall bestow the fewest possible thoughts on it. It is not many moments that I live under a government, even in this world. If a man is thought-free, fancy-free, imagination-free, that which *is not* never for a long time appearing *to be* to him, unwise rulers or reformers cannot fatally interrupt him.

I know that most men think differently from myself; but those whose lives are by profession devoted to the study of these or kindred subjects, content me as little as any. Statesmen and legislators, standing so completely within the institution, never distinctly and nakedly behold it. They speak of moving society, but have no resting-place without it. They may be men of a certain experience and discrimination, and have no doubt invented ingenious and even useful systems, for which we sincerely thank them; but all their wit and usefulness lie within certain not very wide limits. They are wont to forget that the world is not governed by policy and expediency. Webster never goes behind government, and so cannot speak with authority about it. His words are wisdom to those legislators who contemplate no essential reform in the existing government; but for thinkers, and those who legislate for all time, he never once glances at the subject. I know of those whose serene and wise speculations on this theme would soon reveal the limits of his mind's range and hospitality. Yet, compared with the cheap professions of most reformers, and the still cheaper wisdom and eloquence of politicians in general, his are almost the only sensible and valuable words, and we thank Heaven for him. Comparatively, he is always strong, original, and, above all, practical. Still his quality is not wisdom, but prudence. The lawyer's truth is not Truth, but consistency, or a consistent expediency. Truth is always in harmony with herself, and is not concerned chiefly to reveal the justice that may consist with wrong-doing. He well deserves to be called, as he has been called, the Defender of the Constitution. There are really no blows to be given by him but defensive ones. He is not a leader, but a follower. His leaders are the men of '87.[10] "I have never made an effort," he says, "and never propose to make an effort; I have never countenanced an effort, and never mean to countenance an effort, to disturb the arrangement as originally made, by which the various States came into the Union." Still thinking of the sanction which the Constitution gives to slavery, he says, "Because it was a part of the original compact,—let it stand." Notwithstanding his special acuteness and ability, he is unable to take a fact out of its merely political relations, and behold it as it lies absolutely to be disposed of by the intellect,—what, for instance, it behoves a man to do here in America to-day with regard to slavery, but ventures, or is driven, to make some such desperate answer as the following, while professing to speak absolutely, and as a private man,—from which what new and singular code of social duties might be inferred?—"The manner," says he, "in which the government of those States where slavery exists are to regulate it, is for their own consideration, under their responsibility to their constituents, to the general laws of propriety, humanity, and justice, and to God. Associations formed elsewhere, springing from a feeling of humanity, or any other cause, have nothing whatever to do with it. They have never received any encouragement from me, and they never will."

They who know of no purer sources of truth, who have traced up its stream no higher, stand, and wisely stand, by the Bible and the Constitution, and drink at it there with reverence and humility; but they who behold where it comes trickling into this lake or that pool, gird up their loins once more, and continue their pilgrimage toward its fountain-head.

No man with a genius for legislation has appeared in America. They are rare in the history of the world. There are orators, politicians, and eloquent men, by the thousand; but the speaker has not yet opened his mouth to speak, who is capable of settling the much-vexed questions of the day. We love eloquence for its own sake, and not for any truth which

---

[10] Those who wrote the Constitution.

it may utter, or any heroism it may inspire. Our legislators have not yet learned the comparative value of free-trade and of freedom, of union, and of rectitude, to a nation. They have no genius or talent for comparatively humble questions of taxation and finance, commerce and manufactures and agriculture. If we were left solely to the wordy wit of legislators in Congress for our guidance, uncorrected by the seasonable experience and the effectual complaints of the people, America would not long retain her rank among the nations. For eighteen hundred years, though perchance I have no right to say it, the New Testament has been written; yet where is the legislator who has wisdom and practical talent enough to avail himself of the light which it sheds on the science of legislation?

The authority of government, even such as I am willing to submit to,— for I will cheerfully obey those who know and can do better than I, and in many things even those who neither know nor can do so well,—is still an impure one: to be strictly just, it must have the sanction and consent of the governed. It can have no pure right over my person and property but what I concede to it. The progress from an absolute to a limited monarchy, from a limited monarchy to a democracy, is a progress toward a true respect for the individual. Is a democracy, such as we know it, the last improvement possible in government? Is it not possible to take a step further towards recognizing and organizing the rights of man? There will never be a really free and enlightened State, until the State comes to recognize the individual as a higher and independent power, from which all its own power and authority are derived, and treats him accordingly. I please myself with imagining a State at last which can afford to be just to all men, and to treat the individual with respect as a neighbor; which even would not think it inconsistent with its own repose, if a few were to live aloof from it, not meddling with it, nor embraced by it, who fulfilled all the duties of neighbors and fellow-men. A State which bore this kind of fruit, and suffered it to drop off as fast as it ripened, would prepare the way for a still more perfect and glorious State, which also I have imagined, but not yet anywhere seen.

Study and Discussion Questions

1. What is wrong, according to Thoreau, with the very concept of government?
2. How does Thoreau characterize and what is his objection to a standing army?
3. Define *expediency*. Define *justice*.
4. What two injustices supported by the U.S. government is Thoreau protesting?
5. What is Thoreau's opinion of majority rule?
6. How do we support and help maintain government policies, according to Thoreau?

7. In Thoreau's philosophy, where does responsibility reside?
8. How does Thoreau tell us he personally protests injustice?
9. What does Thoreau say about his night in jail?
10. How does he feel about his home town after spending a night in its jail?
11. Someone else pays Thoreau's tax and he is let out of jail; a couple of hours later he is picking berries in a field. Does this undermine his argument, or is this irrelevant?
12. How is Thoreau "free"? Give some examples from the essay.
13. What are the lower, higher, and highest points of view to which Thoreau refers?
14. Where, according to Thoreau, ought power ultimately be located?

Writing Exercises

1. List some ways in which Thoreau's position in "Civil Disobedience" is idealistic and ways in which it is practical. Would you say he is more idealistic or more practical? Why?
2. Early in "Civil Disobedience," Thoreau says, "The only obligation which I have a right to assume is to do at any time what I think right." Do you agree with him or not? Take an example from your own experience to support your argument.
3. Take Thoreau's position and apply it to a current issue of conscience, expediency, and justice.
4. "Under a government which imprisons any unjustly, the true place for a just man is also a prison," writes Thoreau. What rights would *you* be willing to go to prison to defend?

HARRIET JACOBS   (1813–1897)

Harriet Ann Jacobs was born into slavery. When she was six, her mother died, and her mistress took her into her house to work and taught her to read and write. When Jacobs was twelve, her mistress died, and Jacobs was inherited by a three-year-old child, whose father, "Dr. Flint" in the narrative, harassed her sexually. Her only protector was her grandmother, a freed slave. After hiding from Flint for years and eventually escaping to the North, Jacobs wrote an account of her life and, with the encouragement and editing help of abolitionist Lydia Maria Child, she published it as Incidents in the Life of a Slave Girl *under the pseudonym Linda Brent. After the Civil War, she worked for a while in Washington, DC, helping to resettle black refugees.*

FROM **Incidents in the Life of a Slave Girl**

(1861)

V

THE TRIALS OF GIRLHOOD

During the first years of my service in Dr. Flint's family, I was accustomed to share some indulgences with the children of my mistress. Though this seemed to me no more than right, I was grateful for it, and tried to merit the kindness by the faithful discharge of my duties. But I now entered on my fifteenth year—a sad epoch in the life of a slave girl. My master began to whisper foul words in my ear. Young as I was, I could not remain ignorant of their import. I tried to treat them with indifference or contempt. The master's age, my extreme youth, and the fear that his conduct would be reported to my grandmother, made him bear this treatment for many months. He was a crafty man, and resorted to many means to accomplish his purposes. Sometimes he had stormy, terrific ways, that made his victims tremble; sometimes he assumed a gentleness that he thought must surely subdue. Of the two, I preferred his stormy moods, although they left me trembling. He tried his utmost to corrupt the pure principles my grandmother had instilled. He peopled my young mind with unclean images, such as only a vile monster could think of. I turned from him with disgust and hatred. But he was my master. I was compelled to live under the same roof with him—where I saw a man forty years my senior daily violating the most sacred commandments of nature. He told me I was his property; that I must be subject to his will in all things. My soul revolted against the mean tyranny. But where could I turn for protection? No matter whether the slave girl be as black as ebony or as fair as her mistress. In either case, there is no shadow of law to protect her from insult, from violence, or even from death; all these are inflicted by fiends who bear the shape of men. The mistress, who ought to protect the helpless victim, has no other feelings towards her but those of jealousy and rage. The degradation, the wrongs, the vices, that grow out of slavery, are more than I can describe. They are greater than you would willingly believe. Surely, if you credited one half the truths that are told you concerning the helpless millions suffering in this cruel bondage, you at the north would not help to tighten the yoke. You surely would refuse to do for the master, on your own soil, the mean and cruel work which trained bloodhounds and the lowest class of whites do for him at the south.

Every where the years bring to all enough of sin and sorrow; but in slavery the very dawn of life is darkened by these shadows. Even the little child, who is accustomed to wait on her mistress and her children, will learn, before she is twelve years old, why it is that her mistress hates such and such a one among the slaves. Perhaps the child's own mother is among those hated ones. She listens to violent outbreaks of jealous passion, and cannot help understanding what is the cause. She will become prematurely knowing in evil things. Soon she will learn to tremble when she hears her master's footfall. She will be compelled to realize that she is no longer a child. If God has bestowed beauty upon her, it will prove her greatest curse. That which commands admiration in the white woman only hastens the degradation of the female slave. I know that some are too much brutalized by slavery to feel the humiliation of their position; but many slaves feel it most acutely, and shrink from the memory of it. I cannot tell how much I suffered in the presence of these wrongs, nor how I am still pained by the retrospect. My master met me at every turn, reminding me that I belonged to him, and swearing by heaven and earth that he would compel me to submit to him. If I went out for a breath of fresh air, after a day of unwearied toil, his footsteps dogged me. If I knelt by my mother's grave, his dark shadow fell on me even there. The light heart which nature had given me became heavy with sad forebodings. The other slaves in my master's house noticed the change. Many of them pitied me; but none dared to ask the cause. They had no need to inquire. They knew too well the guilty practices under that roof; and they were aware that to speak of them was an offence that never went unpunished.

I longed for some one to confide in. I would have given the world to have laid my head on my grandmother's faithful bosom, and told her all my troubles. But Dr. Flint swore he would kill me, if I was not as silent as the grave. Then, although my grandmother was all in all to me, I feared her as well as loved her. I had been accustomed to look up to her with a respect bordering upon awe. I was very young, and felt shamefaced about telling her such impure things, especially as I knew her to be very strict on such subjects. Moreover, she was a woman of a high spirit. She was usually very quiet in her demeanor; but if her indignation was once roused, it was not very easily quelled. I had been told that she once chased a white gentleman with a loaded pistol, because he insulted one of her daughters. I dreaded the consequences of a violent outbreak; and both pride and fear kept me silent. But though I did not confide in my grandmother, and even evaded her vigilant watchfulness and inquiry, her presence in the neighborhood was some protection to me. Though she had been a slave, Dr. Flint was afraid of her. He dreaded her scorching rebukes. Moreover, she was known and patronized by many people; and he did not wish to have his villainy made public. It was lucky for me that I did not live on a distant plantation, but in a town not so large that the inhabitants were ignorant of each other's affairs. Bad as are the laws and customs in a slaveholding community, the doctor, as a professional man, deemed it prudent to keep up some outward show of decency.

O, what days and nights of fear and sorrow that man caused me! Reader, it is not to awaken sympathy for myself that I am telling you truthfully what I suffered in slavery. I do it to kindle a flame of compassion in your hearts for my sisters who are still in bondage, suffering as I once suffered.

I once saw two beautiful children playing together. One was a fair white child; the other was her slave, and also her sister. When I saw them embracing each other, and heard their joyous laughter, I turned sadly away from the lovely sight. I foresaw the inevitable blight that would fall on the little slave's heart. I knew how soon her laughter would be changed to sighs. The fair child grew up to be a still fairer woman. From childhood to womanhood her pathway was blooming with flowers, and overarched by a sunny sky. Scarcely one day of her life had been clouded when the sun rose on her happy bridal morning.

How had those years dealt with her slave sister, the little playmate of her childhood? She, also, was very beautiful; but the flowers and sunshine of love were not for her. She drank the cup of sin, and shame, and misery, whereof her persecuted race are compelled to drink.

In view of these things, why are ye silent, ye free men and women of the north? Why do your tongues falter in maintenance of the right? Would that I had more ability! But my heart is so full, and my pen is so weak! There are noble men and women who plead for us, striving to help those who cannot help themselves. God bless them! God give them strength and courage to go on! God bless those, every where, who are laboring to advance the cause of humanity!

XVII

THE FLIGHT

"$300 REWARD! Ran away from the subscriber, an intelligent, bright, mulatto girl, named Linda, 21 years of age. Five feet four inches high. Dark eyes, and black hair inclined to curl; but it can be made straight. Has a decayed spot on a front tooth. She can read and write, and in all probability will try to get to the Free States. All persons are forbidden, under penalty of the law, to harbor or employ said slave. $150 will be given to whoever takes her in the state, and $300 if taken out of the state and delivered to me, or lodged in jail.

DR. FLINT"

XXI

THE LOOPHOLE OF RETREAT

A small shed had been added to my grandmother's house years ago. Some boards were laid across the joists at the top, and between these boards and the roof was a very small garret, never occupied by any thing but rats and mice. It was a pent roof, covered with nothing but shingles, according to the southern custom for such buildings. The garret was only nine feet long and seven wide. The highest part was three feet high, and sloped down abruptly to the loose board floor. There was no admission for either light or air. My uncle Phillip, who was a carpenter, had very skilfully made a concealed trap-door, which communicated with the store-room. He had been doing this while I was waiting in the swamp. The storeroom opened upon a piazza. To this hole I was conveyed as soon as I entered the house. The air was stifling; the darkness total. A bed had been spread on the floor. I could sleep quite comfortably on one side; but the slope was so sudden that I could not turn on the other without hitting the roof. The rats and mice ran over my bed; but I was weary, and I slept such sleep as the wretched may, when a tempest has passed over them. Morning came. I knew it only by the noises I heard; for in my small den day and night were all the same. I suffered for air even more than for light. But I was not comfortless. I heard the voices of my children. There was joy and there was sadness in the sound. It made my tears flow. How I longed to speak to them! I was eager to look on their faces; but there was no hole, no crack, through which I could peep. This continued darkness was oppressive. It seemed horrible to sit or lie in a cramped position day after day, without one gleam of light. Yet I would have chosen this, rather than my lot as a slave, though white people considered it an easy one; and it was so compared with the fate of others. I was never cruelly overworked; I was never lacerated with the whip from head to foot; I was never so beaten and bruised that I could not turn from one side to the other; I never had my heel-strings cut to prevent my running away; I was never chained to a log and forced to drag it about, while I toiled in the fields from morning till night; I was never branded with hot iron, or torn by bloodhounds. On the contrary, I had always been kindly treated, and tenderly cared for, until I came into the hands of Dr. Flint. I had never wished for freedom till then. But though my life in slavery was comparatively devoid of hardships, God pity the woman who is compelled to lead such a life!

My food was passed up to me through the trap-door my uncle had contrived; and my grandmother, my uncle Phillip, and aunt Nancy would seize such opportunities as they could, to mount up there and chat with me at the opening. But of course this was not safe in the daytime. It must all be done in darkness. It was impossible for me to move in an erect position, but I crawled about my den for exercise. One day I hit my head against something, and found it was a gimlet. My uncle had left it sticking there when he made the trap-door. I was as rejoiced as Robinson Crusoe could have been at finding such a treasure. It put a lucky thought into my head. I said to myself, "Now I will have some light. Now I will see my children." I did not dare to begin my work during the daytime, for fear of attracting attention. But I groped round;

and having found the side next the street, where I could frequently see my children, I stuck the gimlet in and waited for evening. I bored three rows of holes, one above another; then I bored out the interstices between. I thus succeeded in making one hole about an inch long and an inch broad. I sat by it till late into the night, to enjoy the little whiff of air that floated in. In the morning I watched for my children. The first person I saw in the street was Dr. Flint. I had a shuddering, superstitious feeling that it was a bad omen. Several familiar faces passed by. At last I heard the merry laugh of children, and presently two sweet little faces were looking up at me, as though they knew I was there, and were conscious of the joy they imparted. How I longed to *tell* them I was there!

My condition was now a little improved. But for weeks I was tormented by hundreds of little red insects, fine as a needle's point, that pierced through my skin, and produced an intolerable burning. The good grandmother gave me herb teas and cooling medicines, and finally I got rid of them. The heat of my den was intense, for nothing but thin shingles protected me from the scorching summer's sun. But I had my consolations. Through my peeping-hole I could watch the children, and when they were near enough, I could hear their talk. Aunt Nancy brought me all the news she could hear at Dr. Flint's. From her I learned that the doctor had written to New York to a colored woman, who had been born and raised in our neighborhood, and had breathed his contaminating atmosphere. He offered her a reward if she could find out any thing about me. I know not what was the nature of her reply; but he soon after started for New York in haste, saying to his family that he had business of importance to transact. I peeped at him as he passed on his way to the steamboat. It was a satisfaction to have miles of land and water between us, even for a little while; and it was a still greater satisfaction to know that he believed me to be in the Free States. My little den seemed less dreary than it had done. He returned, as he did from his former journey to New York, without obtaining any satisfactory information. When he passed our house next morning, Benny[1] was standing at the gate. He had heard them say that he had gone to find me, and he called out, "Dr. Flint, did you bring my mother home? I want to see her." The doctor stamped his foot at him in a rage, and exclaimed, "Get out of the way, you little damned rascal! If you don't, I'll cut off your head."

Benny ran terrified into the house, saying, "You can't put me in jail again. I don't belong to you now." It was well that the wind carried the words away from the doctor's ear. I told my grandmother of it, when we had our next conference at the trap-door; and begged of her not to allow the children to be impertinent to the irascible old man.

Autumn came, with a pleasant abatement of heat. My eyes had become accustomed to the dim light, and by holding my book or work in a certain position near the aperture I contrived to read and sew. That was a great

---

[1] Her son, whose father, Mr. Sands, is white.

relief to the tedious monotony of my life. But when winter came, the cold penetrated through the thin shingle roof, and I was dreadfully chilled. The winters there are not so long, or so severe, as in northern latitudes; but the houses are not built to shelter from cold, and my little den was peculiarly comfortless. The kind grandmother brought me bed-clothes and warm drinks. Often I was obliged to lie in bed all day to keep comfortable; but with all my precautions, my shoulders and feet were frostbitten. O, those long, gloomy days, with no object for my eye to rest upon, and no thoughts to occupy my mind, except the dreary past and the uncertain future! I was thankful when there came a day sufficiently mild for me to wrap myself up and sit at the loophole to watch the passers by. Southerners have the habit of stopping and talking in the streets, and I heard many conversations not intended to meet my ears. I heard slave-hunters planning how to catch some poor fugitive. Several times I heard allusions to Dr. Flint, myself, and the history of my children, who, perhaps, were playing near the gate. One would say, "I wouldn't move my little finger to catch her, as old Flint's property," Another would say, "I'll catch *any* nigger for the reward. A man ought to have what belongs to him, if he *is* a damned brute." The opinion was often expressed that I was in the Free States. Very rarely did any one suggest that I might be in the vicinity. Had the least suspicion rested on my grandmother's house, it would have been burned to the ground. But it was the last place they thought of. Yet there was no place, where slavery existed, that could have afforded me so good a place of concealment.

Dr. Flint and his family repeatedly tried to coax and bribe my children to tell something they had heard said about me. One day the doctor took them into a shop, and offered them some bright little silver pieces and gay handkerchiefs if they would tell where their mother was. Ellen[2] shrank away from him, and would not speak; but Benny spoke up, and said, "Dr. Flint, I don't know where my mother is. I guess she's in New York; and when you go there again, I wish you'd ask her to come home, for I want to see her; but if you put her in jail, or tell her you'll cut her head off, I'll tell her to go right back."

XXIX

PREPARATIONS FOR ESCAPE

I hardly expect that the reader will credit me, when I affirm that I lived in that little dismal hole, almost deprived of light and air, and with no space to move my limbs, for nearly seven years. But it is a fact; and to me a sad one, even now; for my body still suffers from the effects of that long imprisonment, to say nothing of my soul. Members of my family,

---

[2] Her daughter.

now living in New York and Boston, can testify to the truth of what I say.

Countless were the nights that I sat late at the little loophole scarcely large enough to give me a glimpse of one twinkling star. There, I heard the patrols and slave-hunters conferring together about the capture of runaways, well knowing how rejoiced they would be to catch me.

Season after season, year after year, I peeped at my children's faces, and heard their sweet voices, with a heart yearning all the while to say, "Your mother is here." Sometimes it appeared to me as if ages had rolled away since I entered upon that gloomy, monotonous existence. At times, I was stupefied and listless; at other times I became very impatient to know when these dark years would end, and I should again be allowed to feel the sunshine, and breathe the pure air.

After Ellen left us, this feeling increased. Mr. Sands had agreed that Benny might go to the north whenever his uncle Phillip could go with him; and I was anxious to be there also, to watch over my children, and protect them so far as I was able. Moreover, I was likely to be drowned out of my den, if I remained much longer; for the slight roof was getting badly out of repair, and uncle Phillip was afraid to remove the shingles, lest some one should get a glimpse of me. When storms occurred in the night, they spread mats and bits of carpet, which in the morning appeared to have been laid out to dry; but to cover the roof in the daytime might have attracted attention. Consequently, my clothes and bedding were often drenched; a process by which the pains and aches in my cramped and stiffened limbs were greatly increased. I revolved various plans of escape in my mind, which I sometimes imparted to my grandmother, when she came to whisper with me at the trap-door. The kind-hearted old woman had an intense sympathy for runaways. She had known too much of the cruelties inflicted on those who were captured. Her memory always flew back at once to the sufferings of her bright and handsome son, Benjamin, the youngest and dearest of her flock. So, whenever I alluded to the subject, she would groan out, "O, don't think of it, child. You'll break my heart." I had no good old aunt Nancy now to encourage me; but my brother William and my children were continually beckoning me to the north.

And now I must go back a few months in my story. I have stated that the first of January was the time for selling slaves, or leasing them out to new masters. If time were counted by heart-throbs, the poor slaves might reckon years of suffering during that festival so joyous to the free. On the New Year's day preceding my aunt's death, one of my friends, named Fanny, was to be sold at auction, to pay her master's debts. My thoughts were with her during all the day, and at night I anxiously inquired what had been her fate. I was told that she had been sold to one master, and her four little girls to another master, far distant; that she had escaped from her purchaser, and was not to be found. Her mother was the old Aggie I have spoken of. She lived in a small tenement belonging to my grandmother, and built on the same lot with her own house. Her dwelling was searched and watched, and that brought the patrols so near me that I was obliged to keep very close in my den. The hunters were somehow eluded; and not long afterwards Benny accidentally caught sight of Fanny in her mother's hut. He told his grandmother, who charged him never to speak of it, explaining to him the frightful consequences; and he never betrayed the trust. Aggie little dreamed that my grandmother knew where her daughter was concealed, and that the stooping form of her old neighbor was bending under a similar burden of anxiety and fear; but these dangerous secrets deepened the sympathy between the two old persecuted mothers.

My friend Fanny and I remained many weeks hidden within call of each other; but she was unconscious of the fact. I longed to have her share my den, which seemed a more secure retreat than her own; but I had brought so much trouble on my grandmother, that it seemed wrong to ask her to incur greater risks. My restlessness increased. I had lived too long in bodily pain and anguish of spirit. Always I was in dread that by some accident, or some contrivance, slavery would succeed in snatching my children from me. This thought drove me nearly frantic, and I determined to steer for the North Star at all hazards. At this crisis, Providence opened an unexpected way for me to escape. My friend Peter came one evening, and asked to speak with me. "Your day has come, Linda," said he. "I have found a chance for you to go to the Free States. You have a fortnight to decide." The news seemed too good to be true; but Peter explained his arrangements, and told me all that was necessary was for me to say I would go. I was going to answer him with a joyful yes, when the thought of Benny came to my mind. I told him the temptation was exceedingly strong, but I was terribly afraid of Dr. Flint's alleged power over my child, and that I could not go and leave him behind. Peter remonstrated earnestly. He said such a good chance might never occur again; that Benny was free, and could be sent to me; and that for the sake of my children's welfare I ought not to hesitate a moment. I told him I would consult with uncle Phillip. My uncle rejoiced in the plan, and bade me go by all means. He promised, if his life was spared, that he would either bring or send my son to me as soon as I reached a place of safety. I resolved to go, but thought nothing had better be said to my grandmother till very near the time of departure. But my uncle thought she would feel it more keenly if I left her so suddenly. "I will reason with her," said he, "and convince her how necessary it is, not only for your sake, but for hers also. You cannot be blind to the fact that she is sinking under her burdens." I was not blind to it. I knew that my concealment was an ever-present source of anxiety, and that the older she grew the more nervously fearful she was of discovery. My uncle talked with her, and finally succeeded in persuading her that it was absolutely necessary for me to seize the chance so unexpectedly offered.

The anticipation of being a free woman proved almost too much for my weak frame. The excitement stimulated me, and at the same time bewildered me. I made busy preparations for my journey, and for my son to follow me. I resolved to have an interview with him before I went, that I might give him cautions and advice, and tell him how anxiously I should be waiting for him at the north. Grandmother stole up to me as often as possible to whisper words of counsel. She insisted upon my writing to Dr. Flint, as soon as I arrived in the Free States, and asking him to sell me to her. She said she would sacrifice her house, and all she had in the world, for the sake of having me safe with my children in any part of the world. If she could only live to know *that* she could die in peace. I promised the dear old faithful friend that I would write to her as soon as I arrived, and put the letter in a safe way to reach her; but in my own mind I resolved that not another cent of her hard earnings should be spent to pay rapacious slaveholders for what they called their property. And even if I had not been unwilling to buy what I had already a right to possess, common humanity would have prevented me from accepting the generous offer, at the expense of turning my aged relative out of house and home, when she was trembling on the brink of the grave.

I was to escape in a vessel; but I forbear to mention any further particulars. I was in readiness, but the vessel was unexpectedly detained several days. Meantime, news came to town of a most horrible murder committed on a fugitive slave, named James. Charity, the mother of this unfortunate young man, had been an old acquaintance of ours. I have told the shocking particulars of his death, in my description of some of the neighboring slaveholders. My grandmother, always nervously sensitive about runaways, was terribly frightened. She felt sure that a similar fate awaited me, if I did not desist from my enterprise. She sobbed, and groaned, and entreated me not to go. Her excessive fear was somewhat contagious, and my heart was not proof against her extreme agony. I was grievously disappointed, but I promised to relinquish my project.

When my friend Peter was apprised of this, he was both disappointed and vexed. He said, that judging from our past experience, it would be a long time before I had such another chance to throw away. I told him it need not be thrown away; that I had a friend concealed near by, who would be glad enough to take the place that had been provided for me. I told him about poor Fanny, and the kind-hearted, noble fellow, who never turned his back upon any body in distress, white or black, expressed his readiness to help her. Aggie was much surprised when she found that we knew her secret. She was rejoiced to hear of such a chance for Fanny, and arrangements were made for her to go on board the vessel the next night. They both supposed that I had long been at the north, therefore my name was not mentioned in the transaction. Fanny was carried on board at the appointed time, and stowed away in a very small cabin. This accommodation had been purchased at a price that would pay for a voyage to England. But when one proposes to go to fine old England, they stop to calculate whether they can afford the cost of the pleasure; while in making a bargain to escape from slavery, the trembling victim is ready to say, "Take all I have, only don't betray me!"

The next morning I peeped through my loophole, and saw that it was dark and cloudy. At night I received news that the wind was ahead, and the vessel had not sailed. I was exceedingly anxious about Fanny, and Peter too, who was running a tremendous risk at my instigation. Next day the wind and weather remained the same. Poor Fanny had been half dead with fright when they carried her on board, and I could readily imagine how she must be suffering now. Grandmother came often to my den, to say how thankful she was I did not go. On the third morning she rapped for me to come down to the storeroom. The poor old sufferer was breaking down under her weight of trouble. She was easily flurried now. I found her in a nervous, excited state, but I was not aware that she had forgotten to lock the door behind her, as usual. She was exceedingly worried about the detention of the vessel. She was afraid all would be discovered, and then Fanny, and Peter, and I, would all be tortured to death, and Phillip would be utterly ruined, and her house would be torn down. Poor Peter! If he should die such a horrible death as the poor slave James had lately done, and all for his kindness in trying to help me, how dreadful it would be for us all! Alas, the thought was familiar to me, and had sent many a sharp pang through my heart. I tried to suppress my own anxiety, and speak soothingly to her. She brought in some allusion to aunt Nancy, the dear daughter she had recently buried, and then she lost all control of herself. As she stood there, trembling and sobbing, a voice from the piazza called out, "Whar is you, aunt Marthy?" Grandmother was startled, and in her agitation opened the door, without thinking of me. In stepped Jenny, the mischievous housemaid, who had tried to enter my room, when I was concealed in the house of my white benefactress. "I's bin huntin ebery whar for you, aunt Marthy," said she. "My missis wants you to send her some crackers." I had slunk down behind a barrel, which entirely screened me, but I imagined that Jenny was looking directly at the spot, and my heart beat violently. My grandmother immediately thought what she had done, and went out quickly with Jenny to count the crackers locking the door after her. She returned to me, in a few minutes, the perfect picture of despair. "Poor child!" she exclaimed, "my carelessness has ruined you. The boat ain't gone yet. Get ready immediately, and go with Fanny. I ain't got another word to say against it now; for there's no telling what may happen this day."

Uncle Phillip was sent for, and he agreed with his mother in thinking that Jenny would inform Dr. Flint in less than twenty-four hours. He advised getting me on board the boat, if possible; if not, I had better keep very still in my den, where they could not find me without tearing the house down. He said it would not do for him to move in the matter, because suspicion would be immediately excited; but he promised to communicate with Peter. I felt reluctant to apply to him again, having implicated him too much already; but there seemed to be no alternative. Vexed as Peter had been by my indecision, he was true to his generous nature, and said at once that he would do his best to help me, trusting I should show myself a stronger woman this time.

He immediately proceeded to the wharf, and found that the wind had shifted, and the vessel was slowly beating down stream. On some pretext of urgent necessity, he offered two boatmen a dollar apiece to catch up with her. He was of lighter complexion than the boatmen he hired, and when the captain saw them coming so rapidly, he thought officers were pursuing his vessel in search of the runaway slave he had on board. They hoisted sails, but the boat gained upon them, and the indefatigable Peter sprang on board.

The captain at once recognized him. Peter asked him to go below, to speak about a bad bill he had given him. When he told his errand, the captain replied, "Why, the woman's here already; and I've put her where you or the devil would have a tough job to find her."

"But it is another woman I want to bring," said Peter. "*She* is in great distress, too, and you shall be paid any thing within reason, if you'll stop and take her."

"What's her name?" inquired the captain.

"Linda," he replied.

"That's the name of the woman already here," rejoined the captain. "By George! I believe you mean to betray me."

"O!" exclaimed Peter, "God knows I wouldn't harm a hair of your head. I am too grateful to you. But there really *is* another woman in great danger. Do have the humanity to stop and take her!"

After a while they came to an understanding. Fanny, not dreaming I was any where about in that region, had assumed my name, though she called herself Johnson. "Linda is a common name," said Peter, "and the woman I want to bring is Linda Brent."

The captain agreed to wait at a certain place till evening, being handsomely paid for his detention.

Of course, the day was an anxious one for us all. But we concluded that if Jenny had seen me, she would be too wise to let her mistress know of it; and that she probably would not get a chance to see Dr. Flint's family till evening, for I knew very well what were the rules in that household. I afterwards believed that she did not see me; for nothing ever came of it, and she was one of those base characters that would have jumped to betray a suffering fellow being for the sake of thirty pieces of silver.

I made all my arrangements to go on board as soon as it was dusk. The intervening time I resolved to spend with my son. I had not spoken to him for seven years, though I had been under the same roof, and seen him every day, when I was well enough to sit at the loophole. I did not dare to venture beyond the storeroom; so they brought him there, and locked us up together, in a place concealed from the piazza door. It was an agitating interview for both of us. After we had talked and wept together for a little while, he said, "Mother, I'm glad you're going away. I wish I could go with you. I knew you was here; and I have been *so* afraid they would come and catch you!"

I was greatly surprised, and asked him how he had found it out.

He replied, "I was standing under the eaves, one day, before Ellen went away, and I heard somebody cough up over the wood shed. I don't know what made me think it was you, but I did think so. I missed Ellen, the night before she went away; and grandmother brought her back into the room in the night; and I thought maybe she'd been to see *you*, before she went, for I heard grandmother whisper to her, 'Now go to sleep; and remember never to tell.' "

I asked him if he ever mentioned his suspicions to his sister. He said he never did; but after he heard the cough, if he saw her playing with other children on that side of the house, he always tried to coax her round to the other side, for fear they would hear me cough, too. He said he had kept a close lookout for Dr. Flint, and if he saw him speak to a constable, or a patrol, he always told grandmother. I now recollected that I had seen him manifest uneasiness, when people were on that side of the house, and I had at the time been puzzled to conjecture a motive for his actions. Such prudence may seem extraordinary in a boy of twelve years, but slaves, being surrounded by mysteries, deceptions, and dangers, early learn to be suspicious and watchful, and prematurely cautious and cunning. He had never asked a question of grandmother, or uncle Phillip, and I had often heard him chime in with other children, when they spoke of my being at the north.

I told him I was now really going to the Free States, and if he was a good, honest boy, and a loving child to his dear old grandmother, the Lord would bless him, and bring him to me, and we and Ellen would live together. He began to tell me that grandmother had not eaten any thing all day. While he was speaking, the door was unlocked, and she came in with a small bag of money, which she wanted me to take. I begged her to keep a part of it, at least, to pay for Benny's being sent to the north; but she insisted, while her tears were falling fast, that I should take the whole. "You may be sick among strangers," she said, "and they would send you to the poorhouse to die." Ah, that good grandmother!

For the last time I went up to my nook. Its desolate appearance no longer chilled me, for the light of hope had risen in my soul. Yet, even with the blessed prospect of freedom before me, I felt very sad at leaving forever that old homestead, where I had been sheltered so long by the dear old grandmother; where I had dreamed my first young dream of love; and where, after that had faded away, my children came to twine themselves so closely round my desolate heart. As the hour approached for me to leave, I again descended to the storeroom. My grandmother and Benny were there. She took me by the hand, and said, "Linda, let us pray." We knelt down together, with my child pressed to my heart, and my other arm round the faithful, loving old friend I was about to leave forever. On no other occasion has it ever been my lot to listen to so fervent a supplication for mercy and protection. It thrilled through my heart, and inspired me with trust in God.

Peter was waiting for me in the street. I was soon by his side, faint in body, but strong of purpose. I did not look back upon the old place, though I felt that I should never see it again.

Study and Discussion Questions

1. To whom, and for what purpose, is Jacobs writing? How do her audience and her purpose shape the language she uses?
2. How might the excerpt here be different if it were written, instead, for other former slaves?
3. Of her seven years hiding in the garret, Jacobs writes: "my body still suffers from the effects of that long imprisonment, to say nothing of my soul." In what way do you think her "soul" still suffers?

Writing Exercises

1. Write a journal entry Jacobs might have written one day while hiding in the garret.
2. Write a journal entry Jacobs might have written on the boat heading north.

MARTIN LUTHER KING, JR.   (1929–1968)*

I Have a Dream   (1963)

I am happy to join with you today[1] in what will go down in history as the greatest demonstration for freedom in the history of our nation.

Fivescore years ago, a great American, in whose symbolic shadow we stand today, signed the Emancipation Proclamation. This momentous decree came as a great beacon light of hope to millions of Negro slaves

---

* A brief biography of Martin Luther King, Jr. appears on page 1113.
[1] August 28, 1963, at a civil rights demonstration in Washington, DC.

who had been seared in the flames of withering injustice. It came as a joyous daybreak to end the long night of their captivity.

But one hundred years later, the Negro still is not free; one hundred years later, the life of the Negro is still sadly crippled by the manacles of segregation and the chains of discrimination; one hundred years later, the Negro lives on a lonely island of poverty in the midst of a vast ocean of material prosperity; one hundred years later, the Negro is still languished in the corners of American society and finds himself in exile in his own land.

So we've come here today to dramatize a shameful condition. In a sense we've come to our nation's capital to cash a check. When the architects of our republic wrote the magnificent words of the Constitution and the Declaration of Independence, they were signing a promissory note to which every American was to fall heir. This note was the promise that all men, yes, black men as well as white men, would be guaranteed the unalienable rights of life, liberty, and the pursuit of happiness.

It is obvious today that America has defaulted on this promissory note in so far as her citizens of color are concerned. Instead of honoring this sacred obligation, America has given the Negro people a bad check; a check which has come back marked "insufficient funds." We refuse to believe that there are insufficient funds in the great vaults of opportunity of this nation. And so we've come to cash this check, a check that will give us upon demand the riches of freedom and the security of justice.

We have also come to this hallowed spot to remind America of the fierce urgency of now. This is no time to engage in the luxury of cooling off or to take the tranquilizing drug of gradualism. Now is the time to make real the promises of democracy; now is the time to rise from the dark and desolate valley of segregation to the sunlit path of racial justice; now is the time to lift our nation from the quicksands of racial injustice to the solid rock of brotherhood; now is the time to make justice a reality for all God's children. It would be fatal for the nation to overlook the urgency of the moment. This sweltering summer of the Negro's legitimate discontent will not pass until there is an invigorating autumn of freedom and equality.

Nineteen sixty-three is not an end, but a beginning. And those who hope that the Negro needed to blow off steam and will now be content, will have a rude awakening if the nation returns to business as usual.

There will be neither rest nor tranquility in America until the Negro is granted his citizenship rights. The whirlwinds of revolt will continue to shake the foundations of our nation until the bright day of justice emerges.

But there is something that I must say to my people who stand on the warm threshold which leads into the palace of justice. In the process of gaining our rightful place we must not be guilty of wrongful deeds.

Let us not seek to satisfy our thirst for freedom by drinking from the cup of bitterness and hatred. We must forever conduct our struggle on the high plane of dignity and discipline. We must not allow our creative protest to degenerate into physical violence. Again and again we must rise to the majestic heights of meeting physical force with soul force.

The marvelous new militancy which has engulfed the Negro community must not lead us to a distrust of all white people, for many of our white brothers, as evidenced by their presence here today, have come to realize that their destiny is tied up with our destiny and they have come to realize that their freedom is inextricably bound to our freedom. This offense we share mounted to storm the battlements of injustice must be carried forth by a biracial army. We cannot walk alone.

And as we walk, we must make the pledge that we shall always march ahead. We cannot turn back. There are those who are asking the devotees of civil rights, "When will you be satisfied?" We can never be satisfied as long as the Negro is the victim of the unspeakable horrors of police brutality.

We can never be satisfied as long as our bodies, heavy with fatigue of travel, cannot gain lodging in the motels of the highways and the hotels of the cities. We cannot be satisfied as long as the Negro's basic mobility is from a smaller ghetto to a larger one.

We can never be satisfied as long as our children are stripped of their selfhood and robbed of their dignity by signs stating "for whites only." We cannot be satisfied as long as a Negro in Mississippi cannot vote and a Negro in New York believes he has nothing for which to vote. No, we are not satisfied, and we will not be satisfied until justice rolls down like waters and righteousness like a mighty stream.

I am not unmindful that some of you have come here out of excessive trials and tribulation. Some of you have come fresh from narrow jail cells. Some of you have come from areas where your quest for freedom left you battered by the storms of persecution and staggered by the winds of police brutality. You have been the veterans of creative suffering. Continue to work with the faith that unearned suffering is redemptive.

Go back to Mississippi; go back to Alabama; go back to South Carolina; go back to Georgia; go back to Louisiana; go back to the slums and ghettos of the northern cities, knowing that somehow this situation can, and will be changed. Let us not wallow in the valley of despair.

So I say to you, my friends, that even though we must face the difficulties of today and tomorrow, I still have a dream. It is a dream deeply rooted in the American dream that one day this nation will rise up and live out the true meaning of its creed—we hold these truths to be self-evident, that all men are created equal.

I have a dream that one day on the red hills of Georgia, sons of former slaves and sons of former slave-owners will be able to sit down together at the table of brotherhood.

I have a dream that one day, even the state of Mississippi, a state sweltering with the heat of injustice, sweltering with the heat of oppression, will be transformed into an oasis of freedom and justice.

I have a dream my four little children will one day live in a nation where they will not be judged by the color of their skin but by content of their character. I have a dream today!

I have a dream that one day, down in Alabama, with its vicious racists, with its governor having his lips dripping with the words of interposition and nullification, that one day, right there in Alabama, little black boys and black girls will be able to join hands with little white boys and white girls as sisters and brothers. I have a dream today!

I have a dream that one day every valley shall be exalted, every hill and mountain shall be made low, the rough places shall be made plain, and the crooked places shall be made straight and the glory of the Lord will be revealed and all flesh shall see it together.

This is our hope. This is the faith that I go back to the South with.

With this faith we will be able to hew out of the mountain of despair a stone of hope. With this faith we will be able to transform the jangling discords of our nation into a beautiful symphony of brotherhood.

With this faith we will be able to work together, to pray together, to struggle together, to go to jail together, to stand up for freedom together, knowing that we will be free one day. This will be the day when all of God's children will be able to sing with new meaning—"my country 'tis of thee; sweet land of liberty; of thee I sing; land where my fathers died, land of the pilgrim's pride; from every mountain side, let freedom ring"—and if America is to be a great nation, this must become true.

So let freedom ring from the prodigious hilltops of New Hampshire.

Let freedom ring from the mighty mountains of New York.

Let freedom ring from the heightening Alleghenies of Pennsylvania.

Let freedom ring from the snow-capped Rockies of Colorado.

Let freedom ring from the curvaceous slopes of California.

But not only that.

Let freedom ring from Stone Mountain of Georgia.

Let freedom ring from Lookout Mountain of Tennessee.

Let freedom ring from every hill and molehill of Mississippi, from every mountainside, let freedom ring.

And when we allow freedom to ring, when we let it ring from every village and hamlet, from every state and city, we will be able to speed up that day when all of God's children—black men and white men, Jews and Gentiles, Catholics and Protestants—will be able to join hands and to sing in the words of the old Negro spiritual, "Free at last, free at last; thank God Almighty, we are free at last."

Study and Discussion Questions

1. What does King mean by the metaphor of the promissory note and the "bad check"?

2. King has two audiences, white Americans and black Americans. What is he saying to each audience and what is directed to both?
3. How does King define the American Dream in this speech?
4. List the parts of *his* dream.
5. How is the last of the paragraphs that begin "I have a dream" different from the preceding ones?

Writing Exercises

1. Gather some examples of the way King uses repetition in this speech. What effect does the repetition have? Read the speech aloud.
2. How much civil rights progress has been made in the years since King made this speech? Give examples of what has changed and what has not.
3. Should ministers and other religious leaders be politically active? Argue for or against.

BARBARA DEMING   (1917–1984)

Barbara Deming was born in New York City and attended Bennington College and Western Reserve University. A civil rights, antiwar, feminist, and gay activist, she was for some years an editor of Liberation *magazine. Her fiction, poetry, and essays on politics, theater, and film appeared in the* New Yorker, Nation, Paris Review, *and other publications. Among her books are* Prison Notes *(1966),* Wash Us and Comb Us *(1972), and* We Cannot Live Without Our Lives *(1974).*

FROM **Prison Notes**   (1966)

II

We are not let out of our cage, day or night. There is no mess hall in this jail; my one meal is shoved to me in a tin plate along the floor under the door's lowest bar. (Usually: baloney, which I leave; grits; black-eyed peas; a slightly bitter diced vegetable which I suppose is turnips.) Our toilet is there in the cell. (If a guard comes by while one of us is sitting on it, we hold up a coat for a screen.) There is no prison yard. We get our only exercise climbing up and down from the top bunks. (And Erica, with determination, once a day, stands in the narrow space between the bunks and touches her toes with her hands, brings up her knees to her chin a few times.) Here we are. We sit on our bunks or we lie on our bunks.

We sit and listen to the life about us in the jail. We can see from our cage only the corridor outside and, through the row of dirty windows, the alley, the brick wall. But to our ears the prison lies open—except for one distant room, "the hole," all on one floor. Acoustics play strange tricks and it's hard to locate exactly from where it is the voices come; but we can shout back and forth to the men in our group—even to Ray and Ronnie and Tyrone, in a segregated cell because they're Negroes. We don't shout very often, because it takes a lot of energy. But Ray, several times a day, sings out to us: "Oh-oh free-dom! Oh-oh free-dom!" Sometimes we join in, sometimes we just let his single voice roll down the corridors, round the various corners, into all the cells.

Now and then the other prisoners call to us. Most often they call to Yvonne. Something in her voice intrigues them.

"Eevon!"

"What?"

"Do you have any cigarettes?"

"No—I'm sorry."

"Alright."

When Candy arrives, they call as often to her—intrigued by her name, of course, and by her youth: she is only seventeen.

"Candy, you there? You alright, baby?"

"Yes, I'm fine. Thank you."

"Alright."

But mostly they call back and forth to one another—teasing, cursing, or appealing. Or they talk or groan to themselves.

We talk among ourselves, too, but for long stretches we sit in silence, listening. I look at my friends and see their faces marked by a kind of awe. I recognise it. I remember suddenly the night in which I left jail after my first brief imprisonment in New York—bailed out, to my surprise, in the middle of the night. I remember walking away, up Greenwich Avenue, turning and turning to look back at the high gloomy building there—my feet, in spite of me, dragging, drawn to retrace my steps and at least touch the walls of the prison; turning to touch it with my eyes, and wondering, as I lingered, at the strength of my feeling that I was walking away from something of which I was deeply a part.

We sit and listen to the cries, the groans, the curses. Who hasn't at some time uttered that groan, uttered essentially that curse—of one estranged from others and from his own groped-for life? Those who have thrown us in here wanted to dispose of us. But instead of throwing us out of society as they would have liked, they have admitted us, by their act, into its inmost room. Here are men and women at their weakest; here, too, society confesses itself at a loss. These are people with whom it has been unable to cope, whom it has been unable to sustain.

A cop unlocks the heavy door of our cell and pushes in with us a pretty curly-haired young woman who's been arrested for drunkenness. She presses her body against the bars, as he retreats, shrieking after him. She pulls off one of her pretty white cowgirl boots and begins to bang at the bars with it in a helpless tantrum. The paper drinking cups we've lined up there spill to the floor and roll. Our underclothes which we've washed and hung there to dry are scattered too. A button goes flying off her boot into the corridor. We try to calm her, ask her questions about herself. She quiets down for a moment but then begins to rage again: "I'll kill them all, kill them all!" She takes a bobbie pin from her hair and reaching around the door, begins frantically to try to pick its lock. We point out that it's hopeless, laugh at her gently, and she finally begins to laugh too, her tantrum dissolving—though she picks away for a little while still. Leaning against one of the bunks, then, she tells us about herself: "I was married at fourteen. . . . Seven miserable years with him. . . . I'm nothing but a whore, I suppose. . . . I called my mother the other day; she sounded just like my enemy"; turning her eyes on us, lost, shining: "I never had any kind of life."

In the cell next to us for a while is a young travelling salesman, member of a fly-by-night company that's been doing something illegal in town. After he has told us with good humor of how, if our peace walk came through his town and "started a ruckus," he'd just as soon shoot us "as anyone"—"A kid I won't shoot, but if it's a grownup I don't care if it's a man or a woman"—he goes on to describe his manner of life to us a little, to tell us of the good times he and the others in his company have, as they move in a group from one motel to another—"We don't know till we jump where we go." "We have a ball—lying in bed and ordering chicken dinners, and watching television, each with a girl on call too of course." "Saturday night the boss doles out our money. . . . We shower up and go to the honky-tonk. . . . Everybody gets drunk." The recitation of his joys is almost as sad as the recitation of the young woman's sorrows; he is so hectically eager to have us believe in them.

One night two cops come to unlock our door and steer into the cell a drunken weeping woman, huge as a sow—with pendulous belly, pendulous chins. Tears run from the corners of her eyes and black rivulets of snuff from the corners of her mouth. She stands blindly in the small space between the bunks, staring at us, confused; then sinks—like a mountain sinking into the sea—onto a lower bunk we've quickly cleared. We take off her shoes for her. She reaches out her hand suddenly toward me and I take it and she begins to tell us about herself. "I am so old. . . . My husband . . . doesn't love me . . . my grandchildren . . . ashamed of me. . . . I'd like to be pretty like all of you. . . . I am so old." We ask her how old she is. Fifty. We tell her that isn't old. One of us asks, why doesn't she see a doctor if it bothers her to be fat. She's been to see a doctor. "He laughed at me." Have we anything to eat? Have we any snuff?

In the distance a Negro woman begins to cry: "Oh my baby! Let me go home to my baby! Oh help!"

The fat woman grips my hand more tightly. What are we in for? We tell her about our walk. "You didn't walk with niggers, did you?" she asks, frightened. "They have more than whites do, you know it—better schools, better everything. I have a cook, she's a nigger, and she says she wouldn't want things different." Her eyes implore us. Suddenly she falls asleep.

She wakes, turning in bed, groaning. "Have you really walked all this way?" And then—in a voice that's almost a whisper, "Girls, I want to ask you something—Did you ever do anything you were so ashamed of you didn't know what to do?" Yvonne tells her, "No, I believe you do things because you can't help it." She whispers to us, "Do you think it's very wrong to go with a young boy? My husband . . . doesn't love me . . . One day . . . I just couldn't stand it any more . . . The boy was only twenty-one . . . I got him to drive into the country. . . . We went into the back room of a church." She ends, her voice flat, "He couldn't do anything." The tears begin to run from her eyes again.

We stare at each other, helpless; and I stare again at all the names scratched on these walls: BOBBY. LINDA. JIMMY. DAVID. RUFUS. Over the toilet, someone has scratched an arrow and THIS WAY OUT. High up in the corner of the wall next to which the woman lies, in letters slanting down, someone has scratched: FOR GOD SO LOVED THE WORLD . . .

I remember suddenly a woman in the Macon jail—Evelyn—in and out constantly for drinking. A handsome restless woman, she moves to and fro about the room (in Macon's jail there is space in which to move), conversing with herself when not with us, to keep up her spirits; making a kind of bitter fun of herself and of her plight. A plane passes close overhead and we all stop what we're doing to listen to it. Evelyn raises her arms—marked with dark bruises where the cops have been rough with her—and cries out: "Mr. pilot! Mr. pilot! Here I am! Help me! Take me away!" The plane passes on, high overhead, the humming of its motor growing fainter. "Mr. pilot!" she cries. "Oh come back, come back, don't leave me! Come back and get me, Mr. pilot!" She throws herself upon her cot—"Mr. pilot! Mr. pilot!"—half laughing, half weeping loudly— "Oh don't abandon me!" We laugh too, we almost weep too. Her comic cry is the cry of almost all in here, and a cry everybody knows, the cry in uttering which Jesus took on the flesh of every person born: "My God, my God, why hast thou forsaken me?" I remember again the first hours I ever spent in jail—in the New York Women's House of Detention. We have been questioned, fingerprinted, photographed, and searched one two three four five times. The elevator doors open and we step out into the ward to which we've been assigned. The doors open and the scene explodes upon us—explodes within us. The clamor of bedlam bursts in our ears: wild giggles, shrieks of rage, distracted pratings. The motions of bedlam meet our eyes. It is the hour just after dinner; the women have not yet been locked in two's in their cramped cells for the night. They wander in the halls like lost spirits, some of them dejected, heads hanging, others running here and there, others clinging together, amorous—timid about this, some of them, some of them eager to be noticed. They roll their eyes in our direction to see who we are. "Where did they pick *them* up? Look, look." And there also bursts upon us the strong smell of the place— disinfectant, bad cooking, sweat, urine, and something more than this: that special distillation of the flesh of those who are miserable, the smell, simply, of human desperation.

We have missed the dinner hour but are given a hasty meal by ourselves in the mess hall, while a prisoner sloshes a mop about the place. On each tin plate a very sticky mass of macaroni and a large turd which we decide is a fish ball. The stuff is hard to swallow; we dump most of it into the garbage pail which stands in the hall. Then it's time for all to be locked in their cells. I'm given a cell with one of my fellow pacifists. Two cots, side by side, a toilet (an empty bottle floats in it), a tiny basin with cold water and no stopper. During the day the one cot can be pushed under the other; when they're side by side, no floor space remains. We talk a little, then try to settle down. This jail provides sheets but they are the size of crib sheets, don't stretch the length of the mattresses. I feel in spite of myself that I share the bed with prisoner after prisoner who has slept here before me, sweated on this mattress, wept on it, exhaled her despair, been sick, been incontinent. I have undressed and put on the knee-length prison nightgown allotted me, but I decide now to put back on my underclothes and my skirt. And I try to curl up so that no part of me touches the mattress itself. And as my flesh shrinks from the touch of certain things here, my spirit shrinks from contact with the life about me. The prisoners are calling to one another from their row of cells. Much of the language is slang and unfamiliar, but the cries sound to me lewd and abandoned. I think with despair: See to what a hardly human condition the human being can be reduced. In a delirium of depression, I begin to laugh. My companion has turned her face to the wall. A guard yells at the women to stop their racket—there's supposed to be no talking after a certain hour. The place hushes for a moment. Then some giggling begins. Suddenly there is a shriek: "What's this in my goddam bed? Matron, turn on the light, turn on the light!" "It's probably Mickey the mouse," someone calls; "Old Mickey never fails." There is more giggling, and a great deal of commotion in that cell. Then another hush.

Then suddenly from the cell across from me a woman imitates the plaintive rather delicate miowwing of a cat. A pause. MOO! MOO!—sad and low. And from another dark cell, staccato: OINK OINK! A trembling BAA! BAA! echoes the length of the corridor. And then a rooster's voice bursts the air in prolonged fireworks: COCK A DOODLE DOODLE DOO-DLE DOODLE DOODLE DOO!

My depression is scattered. I feel all at once light of heart, and no longer set apart in spirit from these others, able to feel for them only pity and distaste.

Someone calls, "Goodnight, Joan," and someone, "Goodnight, Lola."

"Goodnight, Doris!"

"Goodnight, Cookie!"

"Goodnight, Toots!"

My cell mate is sitting bolt upright, smiling, and I guess from her look that her feelings now are something like mine. She's a young college girl, very bright and very grave with heavy glasses, a somewhat peaked look. We nod at each other mutely, and she lies down again in bed.

I sit there, leaning my head against the wall, listening. From the small window over the toilet, sounds of traffic far below enter our cell—very clear. Down the corridor I hear the small sounds of prisoners turning in bed, or stirring, sighing. I sit there a long time, a peculiar joy rising in me, my sense of distance from all the others here more and more dissolving, a sense of kinship with them waking in me more and more. I reach out and grasp one of the bars of the cage with my hand. I have only to remember that gesture—. I feel a queer stirring in me and it is as though my heart first bursts the bars that are my ribs and then bursts the bars of this cell, and then travels with great lightness and freedom down the corridor and into each stinking cell, acknowledging: Yes, we are all of us one flesh. This motion of my heart seems, in fact, so very physical that when I hear my companion suddenly turn in her bed, I decide abruptly: this disturbance in the air may frighten her. I call it back into its cage, and sit trembling.

I hear a little sound from her. Is she weeping? I whisper, "Are you alright?"

She whispers, "Oh yes, oh yes! You?"

I whisper, "Yes."

We lie now in our cage in Albany, Georgia. Candy and Mary have been arrested, too, and are with us. There are eight of us, and four bunks. We've asked for two extra mattresses and been given them, and they're on the floor. Three people lie there, closely side by side, legs under one bunk, heads half under the other. The third person has her coat over her head, because she lies right next the toilet. I lie alone on a lower bunk tonight; it's my turn to stretch out. From the bunk above me, Edie's thin foot dangles in the air; and in the crack between that bunk and the wall, Erica's square hand is visible. I'm not always as sure which limb belongs to whom.

We lie and listen to the cries, the groans, the curses. We are all of us wakeful tonight, but heavy-headed too. No window has been opened for a long time and the air is thick. A cop has just taken a bottle of corn liquor off someone he's brought in and poured the stuff out in the corridor. The fumes of this spread, too. The man who's been brought in is screaming, "Oh get me out of here, get me out of here!" After Jesus, dying on the

Cross, cried out that he felt abandoned, the rocky foundations of Hell are supposed to have been tumbled out of place; and before he ascended into Heaven he went down into Hell, to gather all those spirits who wanted to be gathered.

I think: Let the foundations of every jail that exists be tumbled out of place. Let these Hells be harrowed; let them be emptied. I think of all the men and women cast, for a time, into this damnation, and marked by it. I think of their troublesome return to society. I think of the senseless attempt to build Heaven more securely by creating Hell. The one region can never be shut off from the other. I remember Debs' statement: "While there is a criminal element, I am of it; while there is a soul in prison, I am not free"—not a sentimental statement but a simple statement of fact. I think: The only way to build "the beloved community" is to seek again and again not how to cast out but how to gather, is to attempt to imitate Jesus' action. I remember Evelyn again, whom we met in Macon's jail. "We need more company," she'd said at one point: "I'm going to ride the broom." A battered broom stood leaning against the wall in a corner and she straddled it and trotted energetically back and forth the length of the room. This was supposed to be a kind of magic to bring more company in. I think: Yes, ride the broom, ride the broom! Ride it until you've ridden *all* in who are outside! For if any live in Hell, then all do. "We are members one of another." Let them all know this place. When they know it, let them cry out. Then let the walls fall!

Study and Discussion Questions

1. Why is Deming in prison? Why has she been in prison before?
2. Deming writes that the first time she was ever in prison, she felt, upon leaving, that she was "walking away from something of which I was deeply a part." What does she mean?
3. Characterize her relationship to the "regular" prisoners, those not there for political reasons. Does it change? What does she have and not have in common with them? What does she learn from her interaction with them?
4. Prison, she writes, is society's "inmost room," a place where "society confesses itself at a loss." What does this mean?
5. Discuss the meaning of the second half of the last paragraph.

Writing Exercises

1. Deming quotes Eugene V. Debs—"While there is a criminal element, I am of it; while there is a soul in prison, I am not free"—and calls this "not a sentimental statement but a simple statement of fact." What does she mean? Do you agree?
2. Is there anything you would be willing to go to prison to protest?

VARIETIES OF PROTEST: PAPER TOPICS

1. Discuss the imagery of anger and protest in one or more works. (Suggestions: Plath, "Mushrooms"; Rich, "The Trees"; Zoline, "The Heat Death of the Universe")

2. Discuss one or more works that are themselves protests in spite of the fact that they are about protests which seem to fail. (Suggestions: Sagaris, "The March"; Melville, "Bartleby the Scrivener")

3. Discuss one or more works that deal with protests motivated more by personal conviction than by desire for change, that is, where the impetus for the protest originates in idealism rather than pragmatism. (Suggestions: Woolman, *Journal*; Thoreau, "Civil Disobedience"; Sophocles, *Antigone*)

4. "Nothing so aggravates an earnest person as passive resistance," says the narrator in "Bartleby the Scrivener." Discuss the effectiveness of passive resistance as a tactic in one or more works. (Suggestions: Melville, "Bartleby"; Thoreau, "Civil Disobedience")

5. Discuss one or more works that deal either with protest around an issue of concern to you, or a kind of protest you might consider engaging in.

6. Compare the dynamics of individual protest versus group protest using two works. (Suggestions: McPherson, "A Loaf of Bread"; cummings, "I sing of Olaf glad and big"; Sillitoe, "The Loneliness of the Long-distance Runner"; Deming, "Prison Notes")

7. Discuss one or more works in which the act of protest clearly grows out of the immediate circumstances of a character's life. (Suggestions: Zoline, "The Heat Death of the Universe"; Jacobs, *Incidents in the Life of a Slave Girl*; Glaspell, *Trifles*)

8. Select one of the works in this section, state what the writer's stance is toward the issue that is the subject of the work, and analyze the way in which the writer uses formal techniques to make her or his point. How effective are these techniques? (Suggestions: King, "A Time to Break Silence"; Gordimer, "Something for the Time Being"; Parker, "Where Will You Be?")

HOW FICTION WORKS

A good way to begin discussing fiction might be to look at some. The following is more a sketch than a fully developed short story, but it raises a number of important questions about how fiction works.

PAULETTE CHILDRESS WHITE

Alice

Alice. Drunk Alice. Alice of the streets. Of the party. Of the house of dark places. From whom without knowing I hid love all my life behind remembrances of her house where I went with Momma in the daytime to borrow things, and we found her lounging in the front yard on a dirty plastic lawn chair drinking warm beer from the can in a little brown bag where the flies buzzed in and out of the always-open door of the house as we followed her into the cool, dim rank-smelling rooms for what it was we'd come. And I fought frowns as my feet caught on the sticky gray wooden floor but looked up to smile back at her smile as she gave the dollar or the sugar or the coffee to Momma who never seemed to notice the floor or the smell or Alice.

Alice, tall like a man, with soft wooly hair spread out in tangles like a feathered hat and her face oily and her legs ashy, whose beauty I never quite believed because she valued it so little but was real. Real like wild flowers and uncut grass, real like the knotty sky-reach of a dead tree. Beauty of warm brown eyes in a round dark face and of teeth somehow always white and clean and of lips moist and open, out of which rolled the voice and the laughter, deep and breathless, rolling out the strong and secret beauty of her soul.

Alice of the streets. Gentle walking on long legs. Close-kneed. Careful. Stopping sometimes at our house on her way to unknown places and other people. She came wearing loose, flowered dresses and she sat in our chairs rubbing the too-big knees that sometimes hurt, and we gathered, Momma, my sisters and I, to hear the beautiful bad-woman talk and feel the rolling laughter, always sure that she left more than she came for. I accepted the tender touch of her hands on my hair or my face or my arms like favors I never returned. I clung to the sounds of her words and the light of her smiles like stolen fruit.

Alice, mother in a house of dark places. Of boys who fought each other and ran cursing through the wild back rooms where I did not go alone but sometimes with Alice when she caught them up and knuckled their heads and made them cry or hugged them close to her saying funny things to tease them into laughter. And of the oldest son, named for his father, who sat twisted into a wheelchair by sunny windows in the front where she stayed with him for hours giving him her love, filling him with her laughter and he sat there—his words strained, difficult but soft and warm like the sun from the windows.

Alice of the party. When there was not one elsewhere she could make one of the evenings when her husband was not storming the dim rooms in drunken fits or lying somewhere in darkness filling the house with angry grunts and snores before the days he would go to work. He sat near her drinking beer with what company was there—was always sure to come—greedy for Alice and her husband, who leaned into and out of each other, talking hard and laughing loud and telling lies and being real. And there were rare and wondrously wicked times when I was caught there with Daddy who was one of the greedy ones and could not leave until the joy-shouting, table-slapping arguments about God and Negroes, the jumping up and down, the bellowing "what about the time" talks, the boasting and reeling of people drunk with beer and laughter and the ache of each other was over and the last ones sat talking sad and low, sick with themselves and too much beer. I watched Alice growing tired and ill and thought about the boys who had eaten dinners of cake and soda pop from the corner store, and I struggled to despise her for it against the memory of how, smiling they'd crept off to their rooms and slept in peace. And later at home, I, too, slept strangely safe and happy, hugging the feel of that sweet fury in her house and in Alice of the party.

Alice, who grew older as I grew up but stayed the same while I grew beyond her, away from her. So far away that once, on a clear early morning in the spring, when I was eighteen and smart and clean on my way to work downtown in the high-up office of my government job, with eyes that would not see I cut off her smile and the sound of her voice calling my name. When she surprised me on a clear spring morning, on her way somewhere or from somewhere in the streets and I could not see her beauty, only the limp flowered dress and the tangled hair and the face puffy from too much drinking and no sleep, I cut off her smile. I let my eyes slide away to say without speaking that I had grown beyond her. Alice, who had no place to grow in but was deep in the soil that fed me.

It was eight years before I saw Alice again and in those eight years Alice had buried her husband and one of her boys and lost the oldest son to the county hospital where she traveled for miles to take him the sun and her smiles. And she had become a grandmother and a member of the church and cleaned out her house and closed the doors. And in those eight years I had married and become the mother of sons and did not always keep my floors clean or my hair combed or my legs oiled and I learned to like the taste of beer and how to talk bad-woman talk. In those eight years life had led me to the secret laughter.

Alice, when I saw her again, was in black, after the funeral of my brother, sitting alone in an upstairs bedroom of my mother's house, her face dusted with brown powder and her gray-streaked hair brushed back into a neat ball and her wrinkled hands rubbing the tight-stockinged, tumor-filled knees and her eyes quiet and sober when she looked at me where I stood at the top of the stairs. I had run upstairs to be away from the smell of food and the crowd of comforters come to help bury our dead when I found Alice sitting alone in black and was afraid to smile remembering how I'd cut off her smile when I thought I had grown beyond her and was afraid to speak because there was too much I wanted to say.

Then Alice smiled her same smile and spoke my name in her same voice and rising slowly from the tumored knees said, "Come on in and sit with me." And for the very first time I did.

Let's begin with a deceptively simple question: Who's telling the story? Although Paulette Childress White's name appears above the title, we cannot easily know whether White is recounting her own experiences or instead writing a fictional account of a fictional "I" who knew a fictional "Alice." Were the teller of the story (the "I") an obvious lunatic, say, or a creature from another galaxy, we might deduce that this "I" isn't the author Paulette Childress White; but since we cannot be certain, we can simply avoid the question by calling the voice telling the story the narrator.

The choice of narrator is central in any piece of fiction. Had Alice herself narrated, for example, we readers might have seen things quite differently—more emphasis, perhaps, on those painful knees; physical description of the present narrator (let's call her June) rather than of Alice; and, most important, Alice's thoughts rather than those of her young friend.

White also might have chosen to avoid an "I" or first-person narrator altogether, by telling the story instead in a disembodied voice that described, perhaps dispassionately, what happened to two individuals, Alice and June, each referred to in the third person, that is, as "she." By choosing the narrator she did, White has made the story at least as much about June as about Alice. And if we look more carefully—at the sixth sentence in the story, for example, where we find the phrase "without knowing"—we can be even more precise and say that the narrator is not June as she was growing up, knowing Alice, but rather an older June *remembering* her changing relationship to Alice. Thus, through her choice and construction of narrator, White has made this a story about what a young woman growing up learned, though unaware of it at the time, from her encounters with a woman named Alice.

Having understood the function of the particular narrator White has created, we can see more clearly that this seemingly rambling sketch has a plot. Plot is not simply a sequence of events but a web of relationships between those events. Central to most plots is conflict of some kind and early on the story establishes a conflict between two different attitudes toward Alice, "Alice. . . . from whom without knowing I hid love all my life behind remembrances of her house." The narrator can still see the "dirty plastic lawn chair," Alice drinking "warm beer from the can in a little brown bag," the flies buzzing, the "cool, dim rank-smelling rooms," but also, "her smile." Drawn to Alice's warmth, energy, and love, yet repelled by the sloppiness she cannot understand, June has strongly conflicting feelings towards this "beautiful bad-woman." As a child, June is at once attracted and made nervous by Alice's relaxed sensuality. She sees Alice's lapses as mother and homemaker not as evidence of the great burden her situation places on her, or as natural consequences of her engaging spontaneity, but as a moral failing. She observes that Alice's sons eat dinners of "cake and soda pop from the corner store," but also how happy they seem, and has to "struggle to despise her." At eighteen, dressed up and on the way to the government job she is so proud of, June runs into a bedraggled Alice and snubs her, refuses to return her smile. Eight years later, confident, settled, herself an overburdened mother, but also attuned now to "the secret laughter," she sees Alice again, and for the first time fully appreciates, understands, and loves her. So while we have a character sketch of Alice, the plot centers around June.

"Alice" has a rather simple plot, but White makes the story rich with emotion through her use of language, her style. The sixth sentence of the first paragraph, for example, through its length, its rhythm, its easy flow, helps create a mood of dream-like remembering, as the adult narrator gathers her past impressions of Alice. White also effectively uses many well-chosen details to create a picture of Alice: her "too-big knees that sometimes hurt," her "teeth somehow always white and clean," her "lips moist and open," the warm beer she drank "from the can in a little brown bag," and later "her limp flowered dress" and "tangled hair."

White also uses comparisons, or similes, to help us understand June's feelings towards Alice. To say that Alice's beauty is "real like wild flowers and uncut grass, real like the knotty sky-reach of a dead tree" is to communicate very concisely something rather complicated. When the narrator says "I clung to the sounds of her words and the light of her smiles like stolen fruit," we can readily imagine her ambivalence. By the time we reach the end, when June was "afraid to speak because there was too much I wanted to say," White doesn't have to *tell* us what June wanted to say because she has already shown us—made us share those feelings.

Something else shown rather than told is the social dimension of "Alice," the relationship of its characters and their situations to their society and to such social categories as gender, race, and class. That Paulette Childress

White is a woman may be obvious; that she is black may be less obvious; but consideration of both facts can help us see more in the story. Perhaps above all else, "Alice" portrays a relationship between two *women*. For all her spirit and energy, Alice is worn down by the responsibility of caring for a husband and sons, including one in a wheelchair, responsibilities that fall on her because she is a woman in a society that assigns nurturing to women. In rejecting Alice, June may be rejecting what she fears will be her own fate as a married woman. The government job she holds so proudly (and it is on the way to this job that she so cruelly snubs Alice) represents her hope that she might avoid that fate. Later, a mother herself, experiencing many of the pressures of that role (her own floors are not always clean; now she, too, relaxes with a beer sometimes) June has a fuller and more sympathetic understanding of Alice, "who had no place to grow in," and also a grateful understanding of how much the example of Alice's strength nurtured her as she was growing up. So the reconciliation at the end is more than just a reconciliation between two people; it is a reconciliation between two women, who have a special understanding because of the difficulties and, most important, the joys (that "secret laughter") that they share.

The ending of "Alice" represents a reconciliation also between two *black* people or, put another way, between June and the black community towards which she felt so ambivalent while growing up. This may be subtler than the feminism of the story, but there is enough evidence, especially in the descriptions of Alice in the second paragraph, for us to infer that the characters are black, even without knowing that the author is. Though White never spells this out, the poverty, and the many losses Alice experiences—a son and husband dead, another son in the county hospital—are surely related in some way to her status as a black person in a racist society. And just as that government job represents June's hope for escape from the suffering she sees in her community (government jobs were among the few possible avenues out of poverty for black Americans in recent decades), her reconciliation with Alice at the end represents a reconciliation with her community, a fuller acceptance of her roots and of herself.

Now this might seem like "reading things into the story." But we interpret whenever we read and think about fiction. Other readings of "Alice" are of course possible; the point, if we want to share our interpretations with others, is to offer evidence. Our interpretations will inevitably depend not only on what the author has written but on who we are. A racist and sexist reader of "Alice," for example, might see it as a story about the eternal laziness of black women: Alice drinks too much, neglects her children and her housekeeping responsibilities, creates her own problems; June has a chance to better herself (the government gives her a job, after all) but eventually becomes just like Alice. This, too, is a reading of the story, though a quite perverse reading, one that seems to ignore a great deal of what White has written, perhaps most of all her efforts to make Alice so sympathetic a character.

We can never say with any finality that one reading is the correct reading, but with an understanding of the ways writers work to shape our responses, a community of readers, through discussion, through argument, can begin to distinguish a careful and persuasive reading from one that simply ignores what the author has written. The following more general discussion of how fiction works is designed to help.*

POINT OF VIEW

A writer attempts to shape our responses to characters and events by telling a story from a particular angle or perspective, much as a film maker through positioning of the camera shapes our responses to a film. In fiction, as the discussion of "Alice" suggested, a writer's construction of a narrator—that is, the **point of view**—is central to our experience as readers.

Narrators are commonly categorized as either nonparticipant or participant narrators. A **nonparticipant narrator** always speaks in the third person, referring to characters by name and as "he" or "she," never as "I." This kind of narrative voice may develop a personality of its own (humorous, sarcastic, solemn, and so on) but does not belong to any character in the fictional world it creates. A nonparticipant narrator may comment on the action in the story but never participates in it.

Nonparticipant narrators are usually labeled according to how much they know, how much they tell us. An **omniscient narrator** knows not only what is happening everywhere but what everyone is thinking. Such a narrator can provide us with broad overviews ("Smithville has been for decades the dullest town in the state"), can describe events involving various characters ("While Joe slept peacefully, his younger brother, across town, was buying a gun"), and can dip into the minds of any number of characters to tell us their thoughts ("Carol wondered whether her investigation of Joe's murder would lead to a front page story"). An omniscient narrator is an artifice—no individual could know so much—but an artifice that readers adapt to quickly and that writers find an extremely flexible instrument for storytelling.

A **limited omniscient narrator** (or **selective omniscient narrator**) is also a third-person narrator, a disembodied voice, but one that has access to the inner thoughts of only one character and focuses on the experiences and perceptions of that single character, sometimes a character in the

---

* Paulette Childress White (b. 1948) grew up and went to high school in Detroit, Michigan. She began art school, but could not afford to continue. She married and she wrote poems and stories while raising children, eventually publishing her poetry, which includes *Love Poem to a Black Junkie* (1975) and *The Watermelon Dress* (1983). "Alice," her first published story, appeared in *Essence* in 1977.

thick of the story's action, sometimes one on the periphery, more observer than actor. Since in reality we have immediate access to the thoughts of only one person, ourself, the limited omniscient point of view can often give us a strong sense of intimacy, an **identification** with the character through whose consciousness events are filtered. If the narrative, or a section of it, consists entirely of this character's thoughts, as if spoken aloud to himself or herself, then we have an **interior monologue;** and if these thoughts are presented not as a logical sequence of statements but as a seeming jumble of thought fragments and sensory perceptions in an effort to create a strong sense of the character's inner reality, then we have **stream of consciousness** writing. (Both the interior monologue and stream of consciousness writing, by the way, can also be used with participant narrators.)

A third type of nonparticipant narrator is the **objective narrator,** a third-person narrator that describes characters from the outside only, never revealing their thoughts. Since readers want and need to know what characters are thinking, the burden on this kind of "fly-on-the-wall" narrator, as it is often called, is to describe characters' appearance, speech, and actions in a way that enables us to *infer* their thoughts. An objective narrator is sometimes also called a **dramatic narrator,** since *dialogue—* what characters say—often becomes, as in drama, the key element in revealing their thoughts.

A **participant narrator** is a character in the story as well as the teller of the story. Such a narrator describes a fictional world of which he or she is a part and therefore, like the narrator of "Alice," says "I." This "I" may be central to the action, or a minor character, more witness than actor. Like the limited omniscient narrator, the first-person participant narrator enters into the mind of only one character, himself or herself. Use of a participant narrator can mean a loss of flexibility; all that the writer can present directly to the reader are the words of a single character. But a participant narrator can also create a certain intimacy and drama; as we read we may feel as if a person (rather than a disembodied voice, as with a nonparticipant narrator) is speaking directly to us.

When a writer reveals to us what a character is thinking, how a character sees the world, we develop an attitude toward that character's thinking. Depending on the writer's language, the nature and logic of that character's views, their relation to events and other characters in the story, we may identify with that character and find his or her views sensible, reasonable, persuasive, or we may feel distant from that character and question those views. When we have a participant narrator, often a child or other innocent, and we understand the implications of what is happening better than that narrator does, we have a **naive narrator.** If the narrator comes to conclusions we as readers know are wrong, we can speak of an **unreliable narrator.**

A writer can put distance between us and a participant narrator quite quickly. Fyodor Dostoevsky's novel *Notes from Underground* opens like this: "I am a sick man. . . . I am a spiteful man. I am an unattractive man." Then, a few paragraphs later, after describing his nasty, spiteful behavior as a government official, the narrator tells us: "I was lying when I said just now that I was a spiteful official. I was lying from spite." Whether we decide this narrator is toying with us or insane (or both), it doesn't take much talk like this to alienate us from him. Though the entire novel is narrated by this character, from his point of view, though we see only what he chooses to show us and have access to no one's thoughts but his, we scarcely identify with him. Instead we watch him from an emotional distance, with morbid fascination.

A nonparticipant narrator can also distance us from the character whose thoughts are revealed. "After the Party," a short story by Tess Slesinger, begins like this:

> Mrs Colborne had given three cocktail parties a week in honor of various celebrities, ever since her nervous breakdown back in 1930. The doctor had told her then, when she was convalescing, that she must get interested in something; he suggested dancing (she felt she was too old), social work (but she shuddered, she had had dreadful experiences, really dreadful), writing a novel, going round the world, being psychoanalyzed in Vienna, studying economics in London, taking a course in sculpture, endowing a hospital, adopting a baby, breeding dogs, Christian Science (he was very broad), collecting early clocks, marrying again (oh dear no, Mrs Colborne said, that was as bad as social work), starting a publishing house, running an interior decorating shop, moving to the country, or learning to hand-paint china.

The entire story is told from Mrs. Colborne's point of view. Though we have ample access to her thoughts, we don't really *share* them. Slesinger has quickly and deftly led us to see Mrs. Colborne in a way that she does not see herself, that is, to see her as foolish.

With participant and with limited omniscient, nonparticipant narrators, writers shape our attitude towards events and characters not only by controlling distance between reader and character but also by the choice of *which* character's thoughts to reveal, and when. A story, say, of a domestic dispute culminating in a woman leaving her husband would obviously look very different from her point of view than from his; unless there were significant distancing we would tend to sympathize with the character through whose eyes we saw events most often. A good way to begin figuring out the significance of point of view in a work of fiction is to ask yourself the following: What attitude is the writer trying to create towards the character whose thoughts are revealed? And how would the story be different if narrated from a different point of view?

PLOT

A **plot** is a sequence of fictional events arranged in a meaningful pattern. A fictional plot is usually based on or driven by **conflict,** that is, opposition or antagonism between two elements. There may be conflict between two individuals, between two groups of people, between an individual and society, even between two tendencies within an individual. Conflict in a work of fiction is often complex and may consist of two or more constituent conflicts, whether sequentially or simultaneously. In "Fire and Cloud," a short story by Richard Wright, there is conflict between the black and white communities in a small Southern town. At the same time, there is conflict within the heart of black leader Reverend Taylor between his impulse to try to help his people through compliance with the whites who rule the town and his growing awareness that only militant action offers any real hope. The larger conflict is not resolved, but the conflict within Taylor is, through his painful but also liberating decision to defy the white leaders he's feared and cowered before for so long.

We can often gain much insight into the meaning of a story by looking at the shape of its plot. A happy ending, for example, can have very different implications than an unhappy ending. A happy ending can tie everything together neatly, and help us forget whatever conflict set the plot in motion; an unhappy ending can be messier, leaving conflicts unresolved, questions unanswered, problems continuing. The social criticism of Alan Sillitoe's story "The Loneliness of the Long-distance Runner" (p. 1208), for example, would be seriously undermined if, at the end, its troubled, angry, rebellious working-class hero were to get a good job, become a success, move up the social ladder, and settle down as a happy, comfortable, well-fed family man. We needn't go so far as this hero does (he calls the few books he's read "useless" because "all of them ended on a winning post and didn't teach me a thing") but we can see the potential significance of a happy ending, especially an easy one. In "Fire and Cloud," on the other hand, an upbeat ending seems to strengthen the story's social criticism, for it suggests there is an alternative to accommodation and despair—not only for Reverend Taylor but for anyone confronted with injustice.

Not just the ending of a story but the whole sequencing of events helps shape its meaning. Imagine a plot about a married couple, Sue and Al, which consists of three major incidents: they fight at home over a trivial matter; Sue has an angry dispute at work with a coworker over a minor misunderstanding; Al goes to a bar and drinks heavily. A great deal, of course, would depend on point of view and other matters, but we can probably make the following comparisons with some confidence. If the sequence of events were Al's drinking, then the quarrel at home, then Sue's blow-up at work, we might assume (in the absence of evidence to the contrary) a certain causality—that Al's drinking led to the quarrel, which upset Sue and made her testy at work; we might have a story, then, about the evils of drink. If, instead, the **sequence** were Sue's dispute at work, then the fight at home, then Al's drinking in the bar, we might infer that Sue's difficulties at work led to her fight with Al which in turn led to his drinking—a story, perhaps, about the toll jobs can take on people, or, with an antifeminist slanting, a story about what happens when women work outside the home. Alternatively, if the fight came first, say at breakfast, and then simultaneously Sue went off to trouble at work and Al went off to whiskey in the bar, we might have a story about the difficulties of marriage and the unhappiness it can cause for both partners.

Staying with this last time sequence—the fight at home, then work and drink simultaneously—we might speculate on what difference the *order of narration* might make. Were the drinking to come last, we might expect (assuming, say, an omniscient narrator that revealed Sue's and Al's thoughts similarly) to sympathize more fully with Al than with Sue, as the story would come to a close with him alone in the bar with his thoughts. On the other hand, were the story to end with Sue, frustrated and miserable at work, we might see it more as her story than his.

Use of **flashback,** in which the chronological flow of a narrative is interrupted to narrate a scene that occurred earlier, might change our relative sympathy towards the two characters in other ways. Suppose that we read first about Sue's dispute at work, then, in a flashback, read about the fight between Al and Sue earlier that morning, and then, finally, read about Al's drinking after the fight. While the story might devote equal time to Al's drinking and Sue's difficulties at work, we would read about Al's drinking with knowledge of its cause (the fight at breakfast) and thus with more sympathy, while we would read about Sue's testiness at work *without* knowledge of its cause (for this knowledge would only come later in the story) and possibly just think her an irritable person. On the other hand, if the story began with Al's drinking, flashed back to the fight at breakfast, and then moved on to the fight's repercussions for Sue at work, we would probably sympathize more fully with her. And since Sue and Al are, after all, fighting, it certainly matters with whom we sympathize.

These are just a few of the ways that plot structure can shape our attitudes towards characters and events in fiction. Other and more complicated kinds of plot are obviously possible, including plots without discernible causality, the point of which might be that what happens to us in life is random and meaningless. (We'd certainly get bored reading more than a few stories with such plots.) Sometimes, too, parallels and contrasts between incidents, rather than links of causality, can be the key to a story's meaning. But however a work of fiction is structured, a good step towards understanding its meanings is to chart its plot.

CHARACTER

Characterization, the means a writer uses to reveal what a character is like, can take many forms. With an omniscient or limited omniscient narrator, a writer can describe a character directly: "Harry Smythe was too confident for his own good. . . ." But with a participant narrator, characterization can be more complicated: "I have always been an honest person. . . . Albert, who got the promotion that rightfully was mine, is a sneak and a hypocrite." As readers we would have to weigh assertions like these against other evidence.

Writers can not only tell but also show us what their characters are like. We can come to know characters through what they do, or don't do: bravery or cowardice, for example, or generosity or selfishness are easily demonstrated through action. We can learn about characters through what they say and, if we are privy to their thoughts, through what they think. In addition, we can learn about them from what *other* characters say and think about them. And, of course, a combination of elements can reveal character; we may, for example, understand characters' hypocrisy only by observing the discrepancy between their actions and their words. Finally, we can sometimes find clues to what characters are like in incidental ways, through their appearance, perhaps, or even their name; in fiction, unlike life, someone named Knightly (as in Jane Austen's novel *Emma*) is likely to be of noble character, while someone named Jesse B. Simple (as in Langston Hughes's sketches) will probably turn out to be, ironically, a sophisticated social critic.

Fictional characters are usually labeled as either **major** or **minor characters.** Major characters are at the center of the plot and usually drawn in detail; minor characters are peripheral, sketched quickly. The most important character in a work of fiction we call the **protagonist,** and if the primary conflict is between that character and another, we call the latter the **antagonist.** Major characters tend to be complex (or "round," to use novelist E. M. Forster's term); minor characters tend to be simpler, often one-dimensional, or "flat." Major characters, because they often have conflicting tendencies within them, are more likely to be *dynamic*, that is to change somehow in the course of a work of fiction; minor characters, too simply drawn to embody conflict, tend to be *static*.

Discussion of flat characters leads to the issue of **stereotypes.** Fiction often relies on simple characterization and, in short fiction, even the central character may not be very fully developed. Consequently, we will often find characters outlined quickly, based on a single defining trait and sometimes on commonly held assumptions about particular kinds of individuals: the lonely spinster, the manly hunter, the mad scientist, and so on. Stereotyping can be useful, for it allows a writer to sketch a character in a few quick strokes, with confidence that most readers will fill in the details in a predictable way. But since we tend to see fiction as representative, as embodying in specific characters general truths about human beings, such stereotyped characters can also reinforce our worst prejudices, particularly about oppressed groups in society. It is one thing for a writer to portray an accountant as dull or a professor as absent-minded, and quite another to use such stereotypes as the shrewish wife or the dumb blue-collar worker or the lazy welfare recipient. Of course writers often create characters *against* type, as, for example, in Doris Lessing's story, "Our Friend Judith" (p. 133), in which traditional assumptions about a "spinster" are proven quite wrong.

LANGUAGE AND TONE

A careful look, sentence by sentence, at the language of a work of fiction—the words chosen and the way they are put together—can often help us understand what that work means. Writers labor to make language serve their purposes, to produce the effects they desire, and what is distinctive about the language of a writer or a work we call **style.**

One aspect of style, one important use of language in fiction, is the **metaphor.** In James Baldwin's story, "Sonny's Blues" (p. 96)1, the narrator, a school teacher in Harlem, uses metaphor to describe the boys in his class, boys without much future: "they were growing up with a rush and their heads bumped abruptly against the low ceiling of their actual possibilities." The implicit comparison or metaphor (an *explicit* comparison is called a **simile**) is between (1) growing up, through no fault of your own, with little chance of success; and (2) bumping your head on a low ceiling as you grow taller. It makes vivid and real, in few words, the painful nature of the trap these boys are in.

Metaphors are one way writers use language to shape our attitude towards characters and events, that is, one way they establish **tone.** The tone of the quote from "Sonny's Blues" is primarily sympathetic. There are other kinds of tone. The novel *Maggie: A Girl of the Streets,* by Stephen Crane, begins like this:

> A very little boy stood upon a heap of gravel for the honor of Rum Alley. He was throwing stones at howling urchins from Devil's Row, who were circling madly about the heap and pelting at him.
>
> His infantile countenance was livid with fury. His small body was writhing in the delivery of great, crimson oaths.

The tone here is mocking; Crane is making fun of the almost grotesque spectacle he is describing. The "honor" being fought for is the honor of "Rum Alley," fought for not by knights or soldiers but by "howling urchins." Crane's language is **ironic,** in that he is saying one thing (that the boys are fighting for honor) and meaning another (that Rum Alley is hardly the place to find honor).

Irony often joins with comedy and also scorn, as in the tone of the following passage, the opening of "Slave on the Block," a story by Langston Hughes:

They were people who went in for Negroes—Michael and Anne—the Carraways. But not in the social-service, philanthropic sort of way, no. They saw no use in helping a race that was already too charming and naive and lovely for words. Leave them unspoiled and just enjoy them, Michael and Anne felt. So they went in for the Art of Negroes—the dancing that had such jungle life about it, the songs that were so simple and fervent, the poetry that was so direct, so real. They never tried to influence that art, they only bought it and raved over it, and copied it. For they were artists, too.

Hughes, like Crane, is making fun of his characters, though with far less sympathy. Hughes does not need to spell out his attitude towards the Carraways; his language creates a distinct tone of mockery. "They saw no use in helping a race that was already too charming and naive and lovely for words." Both through their actions (buying art) and what are implicitly their thoughts ("too . . . lovely for words") we see the superficiality and phoniness of the Carraways' admiration for black people. By the time we get to the last sentence ("they were artists, too") its irony comes through with clarity and force.

Tone serves a different function in the opening of "Dotson Gerber Resurrected," a short story by Hal Bennett:

> We saw the head of Mr. Dotson Gerber break ground at approximately nine o'clock on a bright Saturday morning in March out near our collard patch, where Poppa had started to dig a well and then filled it in. Of course, none of us knew then that the shock of red hair and part of a head sprouting from the abandoned well belonged to Mr. Dotson Gerber, who'd been missing from his farm since early last fall.

Here the language is deliberately matter-of-fact. Bennet wants us to accept this unlikely event as real, so his narrator describes it very simply, flatly, as if there were no reason in the world not to believe it. The narrator moves quickly past the fantastic part, the head breaking ground, to a series of quite ordinary details—the time, the day, the month, and so on. He draws us in further, towards acceptance of this bizarre event, by starting the second sentence with "Of course." This not only sustains the matter-of-factness of his tone, but also says to us that he's not the type who'd try to put one over on us—he'd never claim they *recognized* the head.

The opening of *The American* (1877), a novel by Henry James, illustrates another use of language, and a very different style:

> On a brilliant day in May, in the year 1868, a gentleman was reclining at his ease on the great circular divan which at that period occupied the centre of the Salon Carré, in the Museum of the Louvre.

The commodious ottoman has since been removed, to the extreme regret of all weak-kneed lovers of the fine arts; but the gentleman in question had taken serene possession of its softest spot, and, with his head thrown back and his legs outstretched, was staring at Murillo's beautiful moon-borne Madonna in profound enjoyment of his posture.

James's language here creates a strong sense of social class. It is not just the scene described that does this, but the way it is described, the implicit assumption that the reader understands, without explanation, references to "the Salon Carré" and "Murillo's . . . moon-borne Madonna," references most familiar in James's day to a small class of people who could afford to travel to Paris. The length and the slow pace of the sentences, too, suggest a world of refined leisure; their stately rhythms surround the reader with the sense of a stable, established aristocratic order.

Compare this now to the opening of *Waiting for Nothing* (p. 713), Tom Kromer's autobiographical novel about a young man, jobless and hungry, during the Great Depression:

It is night. I am walking along this dark street, when my foot hits a stick. I reach down and pick it up. I finger it. It is a good stick, a heavy stick. One sock from it would lay a man out.

The difference here lies not just in the setting, the street rather than the Louvre, but in the language used to describe the scene. The words are everyday words, mostly of one syllable (unlike James's), and expressions such as "this dark street" and "sock" are colloquial rather than formal English. The sentences are short and grammatically simple; their broken rhythms create a sense of almost reflex behavior, a focus on immediate survival, unlike the leisurely, contemplative atmosphere James's language creates.

These are just a few of the ways the particular language of a work of fiction shapes our reading experience. Slow down and examine a passage or two as you read—perhaps an opening passage or one that somehow grabs you—and see if you can figure out what the writer is up to.

THEME AND SYMBOL

Fiction is specific. It tells of specific characters in specific places doing specific things. But, if it is to interest us very much, it should also be in some sense general, with implications beyond the confines of the imaginary world it creates. What we can abstract from the specifics of a work of fiction—its central idea or statement, what it is *about*—we call its **theme**. Since fiction is often complex and open-ended, formulating the theme of a work of fiction is not simple. One reader might argue that "Alice" is

basically about appreciating when adults people we did not appreciate
when we were children. Another might see its theme as the ultimate
connectedness of all women. Trying to distill a theme from a work of
fiction raises important questions about its essential meaning and is therefore an important step in coming to understand it.

This complex embodiment of the general in the specific is also the basis
of literary symbolism. A **symbol** is an object (or person, setting, event)
that suggests meanings beyond its literal meaning in a work of literature.
Some symbols are widely used and conventional such as a rose to symbolize love, a physical wound to symbolize an emotional one; some are
specific to a particular work. Generally, a symbol, especially a noncon-
ventional symbol, is open ended; that is, we cannot give it one precise
meaning. Much of the value of symbols in fiction lies in their open-
endedness, their complexity, but also in their economy and in the emotional
power of indirection, that is, of suggesting without saying.

In Tess Slesinger's story, "Mother to Dinner" (p. 457), for example, a
thunderstorm at the end suggests the coming clash the narrator fears
when her husband and mother eat dinner together, as well as her own
emotional turmoil as she struggles with conflicting loyalties and desires.
In Ralph Ellison's "Battle Royal" (p. 62), for the amusement of the white
leaders of a Southern town, a group of young black men fight each other
blindfolded for a cash prize. They are then set to scrambling for coins
and bills on a rug, which turns out to be electrified and sends them
lurching and twitching across the floor. Though these grotesque games
function on a realistic level to divide and humiliate the young men, they
also have symbolic implications—about the nature of white promises,
about the perils of trying to get ahead, about the plight of the black
community. In "The Paradise of Bachelors and the Tartarus of Maids," a
story by Herman Melville, the narrator visits a paper factory, which has
drained the life out of the young women who toil there. The factory is
described in terms that parallel pregnancy and childbirth, and these descriptions suggest on a symbolic level something complicated and disturbing about the relationship between human life and the technology
that is supposed to serve it.

Symbols appear often in fiction, but it is very easy to overemphasize
their importance, treating a story as if it were a puzzle, its solution the
discovery and explanation of symbols. Most things in fiction are *not*
symbolic. Writers usually highlight their symbols, whether through repetition or positioning, and a predominantly symbolic interpretation of most
works of fiction makes sense only if it fits together with and enriches
interpretation based on character, plot, and point of view. Interpretations
which reduce everything to abstraction and symbolism ignore the essential
value of fiction as the representation of lived human experience.

Symbolism returns us to the question of what "correctness" in interpreting fiction means. There is no perfect or even best interpretation of

a story; no amount of care, persistence, and intelligence in examining plot, character, point of view, or symbolism will lead us to an ultimate interpretation. Fictional texts cannot have meanings totally independent of readers; the act of reading is, in a sense, an interaction between story and reader; jointly they create its meaning.

Thus fiction can have different meanings for different individuals, cultures, or eras. In the eyes of some critics, Herman Melville's novel *Billy Budd* sanctions Captain Vere's hanging of the naive hero Billy, who has impulsively struck and unintentionally killed an evil man; they see as its theme the necessity of enforcing the law. But for others, the novel is about the utter injustice of this hanging, the essential difference between justice and law. For some readers, Mark Twain's *The Adventures of Huckleberry Finn* is a deeply racist novel; for others, it is a profound attack on racism. And in any number of classic novels and stories, recent feminist critics have found the theme of men's and women's roles where earlier readers have found studies of money or science or war.

But, again, none of this is to say that anything goes, that any reaction represents a valid interpretation. Interpretation, as opposed to reaction, should be rooted in evidence and informed by an understanding of how fiction works. It takes some effort, but trying to persuade others of the rightness of your interpretation is one of the many pleasures of reading fiction.

HOW POETRY WORKS

Poems are like dreams; in them you put what you don't
know you know.

Adrienne Rich

If I read a book and it makes my whole body so
cold no fire can ever warm me, I know that it is
poetry. If I feel physically as if the top of my head
were taken off, I know that it's poetry.

Emily Dickinson

As imagination bodies forth
The forms of things unknown, the poet's pen
Turns them to shapes and gives to airy nothing
a local habitation and a name.

William Shakespeare

Poetry is "imaginary gardens with real toads in them."

Marianne Moore

Poetry is the spontaneous overflow of powerful feelings
. . . emotion recollected in tranquility.

William Wordsworth

The joy and function of poetry is, and was, the
celebration of man, which is also the celebration of
God.

Dylan Thomas

Poetry is not a turning loose of emotion, but an escape
from emotion; it is not the expression of personality, but
an escape from personality.

T. S. Eliot

. . . a door opens, a door shuts. In between you
have had a glimpse: a garden, a person, a rainstorm,
a dragonfly, a heart, a city . . . So a poem takes
place.

Sylvia Plath

A poem should not mean but be.

Archibald Macleish

Blood is blood and murder's murder.
What's a lavender word for lynch?
Come, you pale poets, wan, refined and dreamy—
here is a black woman working out her guts
in a white man's kitchen
for little money and no glory.
How should I tell that story?

Ray Durem

I have always maintained that the writer's task has nothing
to do with mystery or magic, and that the poet's, at least,
must be a personal effort for the benefit of all. The closest
thing to poetry is a loaf of bread or a ceramic dish or a
piece of wood lovingly carved, even if by clumsy hands.

Pablo Neruda

A poem is not its words or images, any more than
a symphony is its notes or a river its drops of water.
Poetry depends on the moving relations within itself.
It is an art that lives in time, expressing and evoking
the moving relation between the individual consciousness and the world. The work that a poem
does is a transfer of human energy, and I think human
energy may be defined as consciousness, the capacity
to make change in existing conditions.

Muriel Rukeyser

Reading poetry is rather like learning how to ride a bicycle without
holding on to the handlebars. Poetry is a heightened, concentrated, intense
and sometimes more complicated language than prose, the way riding a
bicycle on balance alone is a more intense, heightened, concentrated and
initially more complicated way of riding a bicycle. Since we have grown
up in a time and a culture which emphasizes prose, we have more
familiarity with prose and generally find it easier to read. Had we grown
up in a different time and place, we might have been reading, and even
writing, poetry from the time we began to learn to use language. Since
most of us haven't had that experience, reading poetry with grace and
ease is a skill we have to learn as adults. Reading this chapter and
practicing on the poems included in this anthology should give you the

necessary training and open up the genre for you. One more analogy to riding a bicycle: as you learn to read poetry, you need both to trust your developing skills and have the courage to take risks. You may have to pick yourself up from the ground and dust yourself off a couple of times while you're learning. However, the ride is usually worth it.

WHAT IS POETRY?

Read again through the definitions at the beginning of this chapter, which various poets from Shakespeare to Muriel Rukeyser have given of poetry. Poetry is imaginative, as both Shakespeare and Adrienne Rich remark. A poem is concerned with emotion, though as Wordsworth and Eliot suggest, it is emotion shaped, controlled, and contained in form. A poem often says something significant; it attempts to achieve beauty. Of course, what is significant and beautiful is open to discussion and may change with time and place. Poetry is generally more concentrated than prose. A word can stand for a phrase, a phrase for a sentence, a line for a paragraph. If you try to paraphrase a poem, "translate" it into prose, your translation will tend to be longer and looser than the poem itself. Poetry is melodic and rhythmic, as concerned with sound as it is with content. Historically connected to music, song, and dance, poetry has often been an integral part of ritual, from the Elysian mysteries of Hellenic Greece to the celebration of the Catholic mass. A good bit of the Bible is poetry, including the love poem "The Song of Solomon," part of which we have included in this book (p. 515).

Poetry is specific, particular, and concrete; as William Carlos Williams remarks, "No ideas but in things." Poetry is concerned with ideas and insights, but it usually expresses these through sense-oriented language. Poetry is often built around images, representations of sensory experience. For Eliot, the image is an "objective correlative" of a complex combination of idea and emotion. Milton in the seventeenth century wrote that the language of poetry is "simple, sensuous and impassioned." For Muriel Rukeyser, poetry is an expression of the connection and tension between self and world; so are other forms of writing, but poetry often accomplishes this connection in a more intense and rhythmic way. Poetry is playful and often joyful in its use of language, even if the mood of the poem is somber. Poetry is mysterious and often seems more connected to the subconscious than does prose. Perhaps this is what Adrienne Rich means when she says "poems are like dreams": because the concentrated language of poetry can short circuit or disrupt the usual relations of syntax, or because poetry is more associative than strictly logical.

KINDS OF POETRY

Though poetry ranges from limerick to epic, there is general agreement about three major categories of poetry: *lyric*, *dramatic*, and *narrative*.

A **lyric poem** is fairly short and subjective, usually expressing the emotions and thoughts of one person, the speaker of the poem. Originally written to be sung to the accompaniment of a lyre, lyrics are often strongly melodic. Hymn, song, sonnet, ode, elegy, pastoral, and perhaps haiku are all types of lyrics. Here is a late nineteenth-century lyric poem, Christina Rossetti's "A Birthday," in which the melodic element is very clear and striking.

A Birthday

My heart is like a singing bird
  Whose nest is in a watered shoot;
My heart is like an apple-tree
  Whose boughs are bent with thickset fruit;

My heart is like a rainbow shell
  That paddles in a halcyon sea;
My heart is gladder than all these
  Because my love is come to me.

Raise me a dais of silk and down;
  Hang it with vair and purple dyes;
Carve it in doves and pomegranates,
  And peacocks with a hundred eyes;

Work it in gold and silver grapes,
  In leaves and silver fleurs-de-lys;
Because the birthday of my life
  Is come, my love is come to me.

But a lyric poem need not be as celebratory as "A Birthday." Edna St. Vincent Millay's four-line lyric, "Grown-Up," is a rueful recognition that adult life is not so exciting achieved as it was anticipated.

Grown-Up

Was it for this I uttered prayers,
And sobbed and cursed and kicked the stairs,
That now, domestic as a plate,
I should retire at half-past eight?

Though entirely different in mood, what both these lyrics have in common is that they express, through image and event, an individual state of mind.

Dramatic poetry employs dramatic form or dramatic technique, such as the dramatic monologue of T. S. Eliot's "The Love Song of J. Alfred Prufrock" (p. 165), which assumes an audience and draws that audience into the poem in the opening lines: "Let us go then, you and I, / When the evening is spread out against the sky." Poems which have more characters than simply the lyric speaker of the poem, and poems which use dialogue between characters or which stress conflict between characters, whether the characters directly speak or not, may be dramatic poems. There is a fine line between dramatic poetry and *poetic drama*, as suggested by such "plays" as Sylvia Plath's radio play *Three Women* (p. 209) and ntozake shange's "choreopoem" *for colored girls who have considered suicide / when the rainbow is enuf* (p. 623), both of which are written in verse form as juxtaposed dramatic monologues.

A **narrative poem** tells a story. It may be short or long, simple or complex. **Epics,** long poems such as Homer's *Odyssey*, which tell the story of a hero and/or of a nation or race are narrative poems. **Ballads,** which tell a story in a form intended to be sung, are also narrative poems. Bob Dylan's "With God on Our Side" (p. 990) is an example of a ballad. Anne Sexton's "Briar Rose" (p. 199), also a narrative, retells in verse for contemporary readers the Sleeping Beauty fairy tale. The title of Susan Griffin's "This Is the Story of a Day in the Life of a Woman Trying" (p. 781) makes her narrative intent clear. Judy Grahn's "A Woman Is Talking To Death" (p. 1270) has lyric and dramatic elements, but is finally more a narrative poem, a species of epic perhaps, with a number of smaller stories in the form of flashbacks set inside one framing story.

Though many poems can be classified as either lyric, dramatic or narrative, much modern and contemporary poetry merges types or lives on the boundaries between them. So, while it is helpful to know that these three types of poetry exist and what their major characteristics are, it doesn't do to see them as rigid categories into which each poem must fit. As Wallace Stevens once wrote, "All poetry is experimental poetry." The word *poet* comes from a Greek word that means "maker" or "creator." Poets are constantly experimenting, playing, or, as Ezra Pound remarked, "making it new," and in the process invigorating language and perception.

IMAGERY

An **image** is a literal and particular representation of an experience or object perceived through the senses. It is presented in language in such a way that we can see, hear, smell, taste, touch it, or feel it move in our imagination.

Several things could happen in this poem.
Plums could appear, on a pewter plate.
A dead red hare, hung by one foot.
A vase of flowers. Three shallots.

A man could sing, in a burgundy robe
with a gold belt tied in a square knot.
Someone could untie the knot.
A woman could toss a gold coin.

In these opening stanzas of Martha Collins's "Several Things" (p. 560), the poet presents us with a handful of images on which she will work a number of changes in the course of the poem. She also shares with us her sense of the playfulness of poetry, its imaginative creative quality, the process by which one makes a poem from images. A number of our senses are engaged in these lines. In "plums could appear, on a pewter plate," we see the plums, red or perhaps darker, on the dull silver color of the plate. It could be that our sense of touch is evoked, if we have ever handled the cold, heavy smoothness of pewter. Perhaps our sense of taste is stimulated by the memory of a tartly sweet ripe plum. The image "A man could sing, in a burgundy robe / with a gold belt tied in a square knot" evokes our sense of hearing as we imagine the man singing. More directly, the burgundy robe is richly visual and reminds us of the plums in the preceding stanza. The "gold belt tied in a square knot" is particularly visual and our eyes move, like a camera, from the man as a whole to the belt at his waist—which in the next line someone (perhaps the woman tossing a gold coin) unties. As you will see when you read the entire poem, "Several Things" was originally inspired by a recipe.

Also concerned in part with food, the following two stanzas from John Keats's long poem "The Eve of St. Agnes" practically knock you over with their lush sensuality:

The Eve of St. Agnes

And still she slept an azure-lidded sleep,
  In blanched linen, smooth, and lavender'd.
While he from forth the closet brought a heap
  Of candied apple, quince, and plum, and gourd;
With jellies soother than the creamy curd,
  And lucent syrops, tinct with cinnamon;
Manna and dates, in argosy transferr'd
  From Fez; and spiced dainties, every one,
From silken Samarcand to cedar'd Lebanon.

These delicates he heap'd with glowing hand
On golden dishes and in baskets bright
Of wreathed silver: sumptuous they stand
In the retired quiet of the night,
Filling the chilly room with perfume light.—
'And now, my love, my seraph fair, awake!
'Thou art my heaven, and I thine eremite:
'Open thine eyes, for meek St. Agnes' sake,
'Or I shall drowse beside thee, so my soul doth ache.'

Though this poem, first published in 1820, contains a number of words
we might need to look up in the dictionary, still the imagery evoking the
senses of sight, smell, taste, touch, and, through its absence, sound is,
even on first reading, as seductive as the scene. Try listing which sense
or senses each image in the first stanza evokes. You might also try a
short "sensual" poem of your own, using two or three of the senses. If
the idea of writing a whole poem sounds too intimidating, try a series of
loosely connected lines, each one containing a single image based on one
sense—sound, perhaps, or taste or touch.

   Moving from the elaboration of Keats to the economy of Ezra Pound,
look at Pound's compact poem, "In a Station of the Metro," which presents
us with two images we are meant to hold in our minds simultaneously:

In a Station of the Metro

The apparition of these faces in the crowd;
Petals on a wet, black bough.

That's it. Pound defined an image as "an intellectual and emotional complex
in a instant of time." Here he gives us an insight that might be paraphrased
in this way: "I was standing in the subway station in Paris one night
and it occurred to me that the white and somewhat ghostly faces of
people waiting for the train looked the way apple blossoms look against
a tree branch after a rainstorm." Paraphrasing a poem is often a useful
first step in understanding its literal meaning, but the paraphrase clearly
doesn't have the economical power of the poem itself.

   We are fortunate in the case of this poem to have what the poet himself
said about it. What follows is not a paraphrase, which is a prose rendering
of a completed poem, but a description of the process by which the poem
was created:

   Three years ago in Paris I got out of a "metro" train at La Concorde,
   and saw suddenly a beautiful face, and then another and another,
   and then a beautiful child's face, and then another beautiful woman,

and I tried all that day to find words for what this had meant to me, and I could not find any words that seemed to me worthy, or as lovely as that sudden emotion. And that evening, as I went home along the Rue Raynouard, I was still trying, and I found, suddenly, the expression. I do not mean that I found words, but there came an equation . . . not in speech, but in little splotches of color. It was just that—a "pattern," or hardly a pattern, if by "pattern" you mean something with a "repeat" in it. But it was a word, the beginning, for me, of a language in color . . .

The "one-image poem" is a form of super-position, that is to say it is one idea set on top of another. I found it useful in getting out of the impasse in which I had been left by my metro emotion. I wrote a thirty-line poem, and destroyed it because it was what we call work "of second intensity." Six months later I made a poem half that length; a year later I made the following *hokku* [haiku] - like sentence:—

The apparition of these faces in the crowd;
Petals on a wet, black bough.

I dare say it is meaningless unless one has drifted into a certain vein of thought. In a poem of this sort one is trying to record the precise instant when a thing outward and objective transforms itself, or darts into a thing inward and subjective.

Pound and other early twentieth-century poets such as H.D. (Hilda Doolittle), Carl Sandburg, Amy Lowell, D. H. Lawrence, and William Carlos Williams were part of the Imagist movement, which flourished in the second decade of this century. In rebellion against what they saw as the conventionality and tiredness of late nineteenth-century poetry, the Imagists published three anthologies that, as it turned out, revolutionized modern poetry. Their major objectives were: 1) to use the language of common speech, but always to employ the exact word; 2) to avoid cliches; 3) to create rhythms as expressions of mood; that is, rather than use strict forms such as the sonnet, they preferred free verse, in which the rhythm of the poem arises organically from the mood and emotion of the poem; 4) to allow absolute freedom in choice of subject—a red wheelbarrow was just as appropriately poetic as Keats's "lucent syrops, tinct with cinnamon"; 5) to present an image concretely, definitely, specifically, clearly, even harshly if necessary; 6) to work for concentration and economy, which they felt were the essence of poetry; and 7) to suggest rather than to tell. The Imagists were influenced by the economy and emphasis on image of Japanese and Chinese poetry, especially forms like the **haiku** (or *hokku*), a poem of seventeen syllables in three lines of five, seven, and five syllables, the intent of which is to create a picture which evokes emotion and often a spiritual insight. Though two lines instead of three, and two syllables over the official seventeen, "In a Station of the Metro" is heavily influenced by the haiku form. The Imagists lasted barely ten years as an organized movement or school of poetry, but perhaps because their number included several of the major modern poets, the influence of their example and theory is still a major force in contemporary British and American poetry.

FIGURATIVE LANGUAGE

Look back for a minute at Christina Rossetti's "A Birthday." While the second stanza of that poem is simply sensual and imagistic, the first stanza is built from a series of three similes. Her heart, she writes, is like a singing bird, like an apple tree, like a rainbow shell. A **simile** is a direct comparison or stated similarity between apparently unrelated things. The signal of a simile is the presence of "like" or "as." If we say, "his thoughts were like clouds passing across a clear blue sky," we are connecting two unrelated things—thoughts and clouds—and further we are suggesting or implying that the human mind is like the sky. This simile asks the reader to think about his or her own memory or experience of seeing clouds moving across a clear blue sky and then to apply that memory to "thoughts." Often a simile gives us a clearer sense of something unfamiliar or less easily described by comparing it to something we are more familiar with. If to you, "clouds passing across a clear blue sky" suggests good weather, a benign mood, and serenity without stagnation, then you can get a sense quickly, without longwinded explanation, of this person's state of mind.

Langston Hughes's "Harlem" is a short poem built mostly on a series of similes.

Harlem

What happens to a dream deferred?

Does it dry up
like a raisin in the sun?
Or fester like a sore—
And then run?
Does it stink like rotten meat?
Or crust and sugar over—
Like a syrupy sweet?

Maybe it just sags
like a heavy load.

Or does it explode?

Written in the early 1950s, "Harlem" is an attempt to present the mood of a community the way "clouds passing across a clear blue sky" might present one person's state of mind. The concept Hughes explores here is the "dream deferred," the American dream of justice and equality for all, which for black Americans has been postponed far too long. Hughes's opening question, "What happens to a dream deferred?" is answered by a series of similes, several also in question form, each of which expands and deepens our sense of the controlling phrase, "a dream deferred." The deferred dream, Hughes writes, is like a dried up raisin, like a festering sore, like stinking, rotten meat, like a sugary, dried up sweet, like a sagging load. In the last line, *Or does it explode?* Hughes only implies the final simile, leaving the particular form of the explosion (volcanic? atomic?) to our imaginations. The rhetorical effect of the implied simile here is, oddly, more powerful and frightening than if Hughes had given it to us directly. Note also that in "Harlem" all of our senses are engaged—sight, touch, smell, hearing, taste and motion. We'll come back to his poem in the section on sound.

A **metaphor** is a simile with "like" or "as" left out. That is, one thing is compared to or identified with another by being spoken of as though it *were* that object. In "A Woman Is Talking to Death," Judy Grahn writes: "My lover's teeth are white geese flying above me / My lover's muscles are rope ladders under my hands." Vivid, strong, perhaps even harsh in the Imagists' sense, Grahn deliberately avoids here a soft, vague romanticism in speaking about love. Metaphor can also work in a negative way, as when Edna St. Vincent Millay (p. 499) defines love by what it is not.

Love is not all: it is not meat nor drink
Nor slumber nor a roof against the rain;
Nor yet a floating spar to men that sink
And rise and sink and rise and sink again

A poem built entirely on one extended metaphor is Ted Hughes's "The Lovepet" (p. 510), which presents love as a stray and starving animal a man and woman have adopted. On the image level of the poem, which is also the literal level, the lovepet gradually and voraciously eats the couple out of house and home and more. On the conceptual level, the poem charts the disintegration of a marriage. Here is one section of "The Lovepet":

It ate the faces of their children
They gave it their photograph albums they gave it their records
It ate the color of the sun
They gave it a thousand letters they gave it money

It ate their future complete it waited for them
Staring and starving
They gave it screams it had gone too far
It ate into their brains
It ate the roof
It ate lonely stone it ate wind crying famine
It went furiously off.

Related to simile and metaphor but less easy to identify is the **symbol,** usually something with sensual and literal reality which stands for or suggests something else, often an abstract idea or complex of ideas. The eagle on the back of a quarter, to take a simple example, is a symbol for the United States. We can see metaphor becoming a complex symbol in Shakespeare's sonnet #73, in which three images—autumn trees, twilight, and a dying fire—convey the poet's sense of aging.

LXXIII

That time of year thou mayst in me behold
When yellow leaves, or none, or few, do hang
Upon those boughs which shake against the cold.
Bare ruin'd choirs, where late the sweet birds sang.
In me thou see'st the twilight of such day
As after sunset fadeth in the west;
Which by and by black night doth take away,
Death's second self, that seals up all in rest.
In me thou see'st the glowing of such fire,
That on the ashes of his youth doth lie,
As the death-bed whereon it must expire,
Consum'd with that which it was nourish'd by.
This thou perceiv'st, which makes thy love more strong,
To love that well which thou must leave ere long.

Personification gives human qualities or attributes to animals, ideas, or inanimate objects. Ted Hughes's "The Lovepet" is *not* an example of personification, because the animal, though it stands for the human emotion of love, retains animal qualities. On the other hand, John Donne's seventeenth-century poem, "The Sun Rising" (p. 516), makes the sun into a silly interfering busybody who demonstrates his skewed sense of priorities by bringing an end to the night the poet has been spending with his beloved.

Busy old fool, unruly sun.
Why dost thou thus,

Through windows, and through curtains call on us?
Must to thy motions lovers' seasons run?
   Saucy pedantic wretch, go chide
   Late school-boys, and sour prentices,
 Go tell court-huntsmen, that the King will ride
 Call country ants to harvest offices;
 Love, all alike, no season knows, nor clime,
 Nor hours, days, months, which are the rags of time.

Here the poem is a speech—"go away, please"—addressed to the sun, who is not only personified but made symbolic of time passing. Personification also characterizes Theodore Roethke's "Dolor," a portrait in shades of gray of a bureaucratic age. Unlike Donne's poem, Roethke's describes rather than addresses the objects personified. "I have known," he writes, and "I have seen . . ." Here is the whole poem:

Dolor

I have known the inexorable sadness of pencils,
Neat in their boxes, dolor of pad and paper-weight,
All the misery of manila folders and mucilage,
Desolation in immaculate public places,
Lonely reception room, lavatory, switchboard,
The unalterable pathos of basin and pitcher,
Ritual of multigraph, paper-clip, comma,
Endless duplication of lives and objects.
And I have seen dust from the walls of institutions,
Finer than flour, alive, more dangerous than silica,
Sift, almost invisible, through long afternoons of tedium,
Dropping a fine film on nails and delicate eyebrows,
Glazing the pale hair, the duplicate grey standard faces.

Roethke consciously mixes up people and objects in this poem. He endows the objects with human attributes and emotions: pencils are sad, manila folders miserable, public places desolate. People, on the other hand, are objectified. Their "duplicate grey standard faces," like statues, collect dust through the "long afternoons of tedium." The use of personification of objects and objectification of persons in "Dolor" makes a poignant and powerful statement about what it is like to work in an office and what it is like to live in an age of office work.

THE SOUND OF A POEM

Poetry is as much an oral as it is a visual form. It is meant to be read aloud and to be heard. The history of poetry—from ritual chants through

Homeric epics to medieval lyrics sung to musical accompaniment, to contemporary poet Nikki Giovanni's recorded performances with choral backup—is a history of words spoken and sung. Only recently in human history has poetry reached its audience primarily as a written form. Even today, poets generally perform their work, giving poetry readings and making recordings of their poems. It is almost always helpful in understanding a poem to hear how the poet reads the poem, what words he or she emphasizes, where the pauses come, what kind of mood comes across in the tone of voice. A student once commented on Sylvia Plath's "Daddy": "When I first read this poem, I thought it was a very angry poem. When I heard Sylvia Plath read it, I wanted to cry. Underneath the anger in this poem is an insoluble pain . . ." Listening to a recording of Plath reading "Daddy," the student was able to add another dimension to her understanding of that poem.

Often we do not have access to the poet's own voice (certainly we don't with pre-twentieth-century poets like Shakespeare or Donne), but poetry is written in such a way as to give us cues as to how to read the poem ourselves. The visual arrangement of lines on the page, where the lines break, where the **stanzas** (poetic paragraphs) begin and end, and how punctuation is used all tell us very specifically how to translate the poem from sight into sound. Where, for example, do we pause, and for how long? The end of a line, even if there is no punctuation there, calls for a small, sometimes almost imperceptible, pause. A comma asks for a slightly longer pause, a semi-colon slightly longer, a colon or a dash slightly longer than a semi-colon, and a period or a question mark asks for a full pause. A stanza break emphasizes a pause. Here is Langston Hughes's "Harlem" again.

Harlem

What happens to a dream deferred?

    Does it dry up
    like a raisin in the sun?
    Or fester like a sore—
    And then run?
    Does it stink like rotten meat?
    Or crust and sugar over—
    like a syrupy sweet?

    Maybe it just sags
    like a heavy load.

Or does it explode?

The way the words, lines and stanzas are arranged in this poem tells you how to read it. The first line, "What happens to a dream deferred?" is set off and emphasized in three ways. First, it is a stanza by itself, which is like a one-sentence paragraph in prose—a separate and discreet unit of meaning that the writer wants to emphasize. Second, it is a complete grammatical unit, a question. Third, it is set off from the rest of the poem because it is three spaces closer to the left margin. Since the whole question is contained in one line, it is read as one breath unit, with no breaks.

The second stanza of "Harlem" consists of four similes, all in the form of questions. Note how Hughes asks you to read them in a way that varies the rhythm and makes them more interesting than if he had used the same format four times in a row.

> Does it dry up
> like a raisin in the sun?

Since there is no punctuation after "up," the pause between lines is quite short. The second simile

> Or fester like a sore—
> And then run?

asks for a substantially longer pause between lines, signaled by the dash. Hughes varies this again in the following simile, "Does it stink like rotten meat?" in which the question is in one line, has no pause and therefore moves more quickly. The fourth simile ("or crust and sugar over— / like a syrupy sweet") then slows the reader down again, picking up the form used in the second simile, the dash at the end of the line.

Hughes then moves to a stanza of two lines, still one simile but this time not phrased as a question.

> Maybe it just sags
> like a heavy load.

If you read those two lines aloud, you will see that putting the verb "sags" at the end of the line emphasizes the word and gives it more force. Try reading it as a sentence with no pause, then again as two lines the way the poet has directed you to.

Finally, "Harlem" ends with a one-line question, *Or does it explode?* Hughes emphasizes this possibility by making it the last line of the poem, by putting it in italics, and by making it the only one-line stanza except for the first—"What happens to a dream deferred?"—thus visually relating those two, the question and that particular answer, in our minds. "Harlem" is clearly a warning about what could happen if a whole group's dreams continue to be ignored. However, Hughes manages, through his visual and sound structure, to argue in a way that makes most readers more likely to listen than if he had come right out and stated his political point bluntly. Putting the explosion in the form of a question, with its rising inflection, startles the reader initially less than if the poet had used a declarative form.

Rhyme, Resonance, and Repetition

Let us consider the sounds of words and the sound patterns that poets build between words to set a mood, convey an emotion, and make connections between images and ideas. The sound patterns of a poem are sometimes obvious and sometimes subtle, but if you look for them you will find them. Read the poem aloud, more than once; listen and look for the patterns your ear hears and your eye sees on the page. Write a list of everything you notice about the sound of the poem. How do the sounds and the sound patterns parallel and reinforce the images, ideas, and theme of the poem? You may have the beginnings of an essay here, but we're getting ahead of ourselves. First let's think about rhyme, resonance, and repetition.

How much **rhyme** is used, where and how it is used have varied considerably in the history of poetry. Rhyme was not too important in English poetry before Chaucer in the fourteenth century and it is used considerably less strictly in twentieth-century poetry than in the three centuries preceding our own.

A good example of the strict use of **end rhyme** is in Shakespeare's Sonnet #73 quoted earlier, "That time of year thou mayst in me behold." A **sonnet** is a fourteen-line poem, generally written in iambic pentameter (see following section on meter), which follows a set **rhyme scheme** or pattern in the rhymes at the end of lines. The **Shakespearian** or **English sonnet** has three **quatrains** or groups of four lines, followed by a **couplet**, or two-line unit. The rhyme scheme is *abab* for the first quatrain, *cdcd* for the second, *efef* for the third, and *gg* for the final couplet. Each letter of the alphabet identifies a particular rhyme, so each quatrain in this type of sonnet has two rhymes in alternating lines and, in addition, the two lines of the final couplet rhyme. The couplet often comments on or sums up the poem.

Another type of sonnet is the **Italian** or **Petrarchan sonnet,** divided into one octave of eight lines, rhyming *abbaabba*, and a sestet of six lines, rhyming *cdecde, cdccdc,* or *cdedce.* Often the octave raises a question or presents a narrative and the sestet answers the question or interprets the narrative to make a more abstract point. Milton's "On the Late Massacre in Piemont" (p. 1001) is an Italian sonnet.

Twentieth-century poets are not particularly wedded to strict rhyme schemes like the sonnet, and tend more often to write in **free verse,** a cadenced rhythmic form which varies from poem to poem, arising organically from the subject, images, issues and mood of a particular poem in the process of creation. Still, a number of modern and contemporary poets do use end rhyme, though sometimes more subtly and less strictly than pre-twentieth-century poets. Let's look again at Ezra Pound's haiku-like poem, this time paying attention not to the images but to the sounds.

In a Station of the Metro

The apparition of these faces in the crowd;
Petals on a wet, black bough.

The end of each line, "crowd" and "bough," are examples of **assonance** or repetition of similar vowel sounds (here "ow") in stressed syllables, though the consonants differ. The last word in the title of this poem, "Metro," *almost* rhymes with "crowd" and "bough." When the rhyming words have almost the same sound, a **slant rhyme** has occurred.

Rhyme happens inside lines as well as at the end of lines. Even more subtle than slant rhyme, **internal rhyme** can give a poem much of its musical quality. In Pound's poem, "station" and "faces" rhyme because of the assonance of the long "a" sound, and "apparition" repeats the "tion" (shun) sound in "station." We can also see (and hear) Pound making use of **alliteration** or repetition of initial letters of a word, most often consonants. Here "black bough" is an example of alliteration.

If a poem is working the way a poet wants it to, these sound patterns or *resonance* help carry and reinforce the meaning and feeling of the poem. Read these last five lines of Marge Piercy's poem, "The woman in the ordinary" (p. 540), about a young woman on the verge of breaking out of her rut to become whatever she has the potential to become.

In her bottled up is a woman peppery as curry,
a yam of a woman of butter and brass,
compounded of acid and sweet like a pineapple,
like a handgrenade set to explode,
like goldenrod ready to bloom.

Though this poem does not rely on end rhyme at all, notice how the images and the meaning of the poem are reinforced in these lines by various devices of sound. The images are spicy and bold: curry, peppery; brass, acid—examples of internal rhyme. Piercy uses an abundance of alliteration with "p" and "b" sounds—bottled, peppery, butter, brass, pineapple, explode, bloom. "P" and "b" are called "plosive" sounds because, in order to make them, you must close your lips and blow the air that carries the sound forcefully at the closed lips, "exploding" them open. Try it. Piercy's use of literally explosive sounds reinforces her explosively growing images and theme. Another pattern in these lines, not quite so striking, is the use of nasal sounds like "m" and "n" in such words as woman, yam, compounded, pineapple, handgrenade, bloom. You might want to think about what effect this second pattern of sound has and how it works together with the pattern of plosives.

Other frequently repeated sounds include the liquid "l" and "r." Keats's repetition of the liquid "l" in the two stanzas from "The Eve of St. Agnes" quoted earlier have much to do with the luscious luxurious effect of that poem. "S" is a sibilant sound and a number of "s" words together make a hissing sound. Langston Hughes employs many "s" words in "Harlem"— raisin, sun, fester, sore, stink, crust, sugar, syrupy, sweet, sags—which make an ominous hissing undercurrent (rather like the burning fuse of a bomb) to his other major sound in "Harlem," the hard sound of air stopped behind the teeth in "d" and "t"—dream deferred, dry, rotten, load, explode. We have **onomatopoeia** when a word imitates a natural sound, for example, if "a snake hissed and its passing rustled the grass." In this sentence, the word "hissed" imitates the sound it stands for and is strictly onomatopoetic; all the other "s" sounds reinforce the hissing and also imitate the slithering sound the snake makes as (we hope) it slides away. While Piercy's and Hughes's use of sound to reinforce sense is not always strictly onomatopoetic, it extends our sense of the possibilities of that probably too narrowly defined term.

A poet can repeat whole phrases or lines to achieve a desired effect. Christina Rossetti's "A Birthday," quoted in full earlier, uses *repetition* in three ways. In the first stanza, every other line begins "My heart is . . . ." The first three pairs of lines are similes; the fourth concludes: "My heart is gladder than all these / Because my love is come to me." In the second stanza, Rossetti uses an imperative verb form three times—hang it, carve it, work it—and though the particular verb changes, the imperative form is repeated. Finally, in the last two lines of the second stanza, she picks up a phrase from the end of her first stanza, so that both stanzas end with the same phrase, "my love is come to me," emphasizing what is, after all, the occasion for this joyful poem.

Producing a very different effect than Rossetti's poem is Muriel Rukeyser's "Waiting for Icarus," which uses repetition throughout. The poem is a contemporary retelling of the Greek myth about the young man who borrowed his father's wings and flew disastrously close to the sun—but from the point of view of the woman who waits for him, increasingly disgruntled, on the shore.

Waiting for Icarus

He said he would be back and we'd drink wine together
He said that everything would be better than before

He said we were on the edge of a new relation
He said he would never again cringe before his father
He said that he was going to invent full-time
He said he loved me that going into me
He said was going into the world and the sky
He said the wax was the best wax
He said Wait for me here on the beach
He said Just don't cry

I remember the gulls and the waves
I remember the islands going dark on the sea
I remember the girls laughing
I remember they said he only wanted to get away from me
I remember mother saying: Inventors are like poets, a trashy lot
I remember she told me those who try out inventions are worse
I remember she added: Women who love such are the worst of all

I have been waiting all day, or perhaps longer.
I would have liked to try those wings myself.
It would have been better than this.

"Waiting for Icarus" moves from what the speaker of the poem remembers "he" said to what she remembers "they" (the girls, her mother) said to, finally, a tentative assertion of her own voice and identity in the last three lines of the poem. These three lines, it should be noted, are the only ones to which the poet puts a period. And though the rest of each line in the poem is varied enough so that the poem itself remains interesting, the initial repetition in each line is meant to be monotonous, to replicate the boredom of waiting, of being a passive spectator and listener rather than part of the action.

One final example of repetition, this time of a single word, comes from the opening of the narrative poem "Rain" by William Carpenter (p. 207).

A man stood in the rain outside his house.
Pretty soon, the rain soaked through
his jacket and shirt. He might have
gone in, but he wanted to be wet, to be
really wet, so that it finally got through
his skin and began raining on the rooftops
of the small city that the man always carried
inside him, a city where it hadn't rained
for thirty years, only now the sky darkened
and tremendous drops fell in the thick dust
of the streets.

Rain, rain, raining, rained. The repetition of various forms of "rain" builds, after a while, into the kind of relentless (but happy) downpour the man is experiencing. Two other uses of repetition in this passage are worth noting: the repetition of a phrase, as in "he wanted to be wet, to be / really wet" and "in the small city that the man always carried / inside him, a city where. . ."; and, in the last three lines, the powerful use of "d" and "t" sounds to create an effect of pounding rain: "the sky darkened / and tremendous drops fell in the thick dust / of the streets." Try writing a short poem, say five to twelve lines, in which you use a sound pattern to create a mood.

Meter

The rhythmic and recurrent pattern of stressed and unstressed syllables in a poem is called its **meter.** Each unit of this pattern, which will have either two or three syllables, is called a **foot.** The number of feet in a line of poetry gives you the meter. In English, the most frequently used foot is **iambic,** which has two syllables, with the accent on the second ($\smile$ $\diagup$). The most common poetic line in English is **iambic pentameter,** composed of five iambs, or ten syllables in a pattern of alternating unstressed and stressed syllables.

Not marble, nor the gilded monuments
Of princes, shall outlive this powerful rime;
But you shall shine more bright in these contents
Than unswept stone, besmear'd with sluttish time.

This first quatrain of Shakespeare's sonnet 50 is in iambic pentameter and its **scansion** is as follows:

$$\smile \; \diagup \; \smile \; \diagup \; \diagup \; \smile \; \diagup \; \smile \; \diagup$$

$$\smile \; \diagup \; \smile \; \smile \; \diagup \; \smile \; \diagup \; \smile \; \diagup$$

$$\smile \; \diagup \; \smile \; \diagup \; \smile \; \diagup \; \smile \; \diagup \; \smile \; \diagup$$

$$\smile \; \diagup \; \smile \; \diagup \; \smile \; \diagup \; \smile \; \diagup \; \diagup$$

A particular type of iambic pentameter is **blank verse** or *unrhymed iambic pentameter,* which we can see in these opening four lines of Robert Frost's "Mending Wall."

Sŏmethĭng theře iś thăt doésń't loɼe ă waĺl,

Thăt seńds the fŕozeň-gróund-sẅell úndeř iť

Ańd spiĺls the úppeř bóuldeřs iń the sún,

Ańd makes gaṕs évĕn tẃo căn paśs ăbreást.

As well as in lyric poems, blank verse is frequently used in dramatic
poems and in poetic drama. It is, for example, characteristic of Shakespearian drama.

Here is a list of terms used to describe meter:

FOOT	EXAMPLE
iamb/iambic (˘ ´)	ĕx-plóde
trochee/trochaic (´ ˘)	wrít-ĕr
spondee/spondaic (´ ´)	huḿ-drúm
anapest/anapestic (˘ ˘ ´)	ăf-tĕr-nóon
dactyl/dactylic (´ ˘ ˘)	týpe-wrĭt-ĕr

LINE LENGTH

monometer: one foot
dimeter: two feet
trimeter: three feet
tetrameter: four feet
pentameter: five feet
hexameter: six feet
heptameter: seven feet
octameter: eight feet

Scansion

To scan a poem is to divide the lines into feet and mark the unstressed
and stressed syllables. In this way we can determine the overall meter of
the poem. Keep in mind that scansion is not an exact science and that
generally what you will be getting is an approximation.

Look at this first stanza of Roethke's sixteen-line poem, "My Papa's
Waltz" (p. 193).

Thĕ whískĕy ón yoŭr breáth

Coŭld máke ă smáll bŏy dízzў;

Bŭt Í hŭng ón lĭke deáth:

Sŭch wáltzĭng wás nŏt eásў.

If we read these four lines aloud and put the accents where they would be in ordinary speech, it is not too hard to mark which syllables are stressed and which are unstressed. It is helpful to begin by looking at a two or three syllable word. We know, for example, that "whiskey" is stressed on the first syllable and this gives us a clue as to how to stress the surrounding syllables. The pattern here is the most commonly found pattern in English, iambic. There are three iambs in the first line, and also in the third. The second and fourth lines each contain three iambs, plus an extra unstressed syllable at the end. Overall, the meter of this poem is iambic trimeter. The lines move regularly and quickly, rather like the breathless waltzing (in three-quarter time) that the poet is describing. The trimeter or count of three replicates the time of a waltz; the iambic pattern replicates the waltz's rise and fall.

Poets quite deliberately choose the meter of a poem to fit the theme and mood. Look at the very different first two lines of "Dolor," another poem by Theodore Roethke.

Í hăve knówn the iňéxorăble sádnešs ŏf péncils,

Neát ĭn thĕir bóxĕs, dólŏr ŏf pád aňd pápĕr-wĕight

In this thirteen-line poem, Roethke alternates between anapestic (⌣ ⌣ ‐) and dactylic (‐ ⌣ ⌣) lines. The first line has four anapestic feet with an extra unstressed syllable at the end. The second line has a dactyl, a trochee, a dactyl, a trochee, and a dactyl, adding up to five feet. Roethke alternates between anapestic tetrameter and dactylic pentameter in "Dolor." But when you've said that, what have you got besides a mouthful of terminology? What scanning this poem can tell you is that Roethke is primarily using a longer foot (of three syllables rather than the two he employs in "My Papa's Waltz") and that this longer foot, combined with the longer line (four or five feet in "Dolor" instead of three as in "My Papa's Waltz"), gives this poem a longer, slower, more drawn out and perhaps more mournful rhythm. That each line reverses the previous one (unstressed then stressed syllables in the first line; stressed followed by unstressed in the second) makes reading the poem laborious work for the reader, in contrast to the fast and easy spinning dancing rhythm of "My Papa's Waltz." Roethke's choice of meter in "Dolor" fits precisely the mood and subject of that poem, the tedium of office work.

A NOTE ON TONE

A poem might be joyful, gloomy, bitter, celebratory, angry, ironic, distanced, intimate, playful, comic, or something else. The **tone** or mood of a poem is both our sense of the attitude or emotion of the poet and the mood the poem evokes in us. We are all more or less skilled at picking up mood when someone speaks to us. In a piece of writing we cannot hear the speaker's tone of voice, in the literal sense of that phrase, so we must rely on other clues: the sound of the poem, the images, the statement the poem makes and/or the story it tells. A consideration of tone and mood is quite helpful in interpreting a poem. Ask yourself what the writer's attitude is toward the subject of the poem, toward the audience, toward the *persona* or speaker of the poem. In the two previous Theodore Roethke poems, the meter gave us valuable evidence to back up our sense of the quite different tones of "Dolor" and "My Papa's Waltz."

THE SPEAKER OF THE POEM

The speaker of the poem is not identical to the poet. Often the poet creates a **persona** (from the Latin for "mask") who speaks the poem in the first person ("I"). This is usually a single character, like Prufrock in T. S. Eliot's "The Love Song of J. Alfred Prufrock," or the unnamed woman, weary of waiting, in Muriel Rukeyser's "Waiting for Icarus." Gwendolyn Brooks's short poem about a group of high school dropouts has a communal *persona*.

We Real Cool

> The Pool Players.
> Seven at the Golden Shovel.

We real cool. We
Left school. We

Lurk late. We
Strike straight. We

Sing sin. We
Thin gin. We

Jazz June. We
Die soon.

In "We Real Cool," the speaker(s) of the poem are clearly not identical with the poet. We know there are seven of them. Since they are hanging out at a pool hall and have "left school," we suspect they are adolescents. And we can probably assume, since this poem was written in 1960, that the seven are male. In fact, Brooks confirms this in comments on the poem.

There are many cases, however, in which the speaker of the poem is less clearly differentiated from the poet, as in Roethke's "My Papa's Waltz," which is written as though it were the poet's memory of his own childhood. As a general rule, it is safest, in thinking and writing about poetry (or fiction), to assume that the speaker of a poem (or the first-person narrator of a story) is a *creation* of the writer and, like the setting, sound, images, and mood, is a result of choices the writer has made in the service of the whole effect she or he is working to create.

To whom is the poem spoken? The speaker of John Donne's "The Sun Rising" is addressing himself to the rising sun, which he personifies as a "busy old fool." In Roethke's "My Papa's Waltz," the speaker of the poem is talking to his father or, more probably, to his memory of his father. Langston Hughes's "Harlem" seems to be addressed directly to the reader. The series of questions that make up the poem is a series of rhetorical hooks that snag our attention. Many poems, primarily descriptive, don't seem addressed to anyone specific. For example, Marge Piercy's "The woman in the ordinary" describes a person; Ezra Pound's "In a Station of the Metro" describes a scene.

THE WORLD OF THE POEM

The speaker of a poem doesn't exist in a vacuum but is in interaction or tension with the world of the poem. Like a story, a poem has a setting which may be physical, social, or both. It is often helpful to list or to describe the characteristics of a poem's world as part of your analysis or explication of a poem. Here is Adrienne Rich's Poem XI from *Twenty-One Love Poems*:

XI.

Every peak is a crater. This is the law of volcanoes,
making them eternally and visibly female.
No height without depth, without a burning core,
though our straw soles shred on the hardened lava.
I want to travel with you to every sacred mountain
smoking within like the sibyl stooped over her tripod,
I want to reach for your hand as we scale the path,
to feel your arteries glowing in my clasp,
never failing to note the small, jewel-like flower

unfamiliar to us, nameless till we rename her,
that clings to the slowly altering rock—
that detail outside ourselves that brings us to ourselves,
was here before us, knew we would come, and sees beyond us.

The physical setting of this poem is the slope of a volcano. There appear to be two people in the poem, two women who are climbing the sides of the volcano. What is the relation or the tension here between the speaker of the poem and the world of the poem? Poem XI is about a journey, a mode in which writers since Homer have expressed the tension between self and world. The two people on this journey, it is important to note, seem to be in harmony. If they were fighting with each other all the way up the mountain, the tone and meaning of the poem would be quite different.

We can see the particular quality and degree of the tension between speaker and physical setting in the line "though our straw soles shred on the hardened lava." The journey is arduous and wearing but not dangerous or life-threatening. This is a journey of self-discovery, we might guess, since the travelers are women and the volcano is defined as female in the first two lines. How do we know the two people in the poem are women? Since the poet, Adrienne Rich, is female we probably have to assume, given the absence of any evidence to the contrary, that the speaker of the poem is also female. And since everything that is given gender in the poem is female—the volcano, the sibyl, the "small, jewel-like flower," we can assume that the speaker's traveling companion is also female. As it turns out, this is an intensely female poem and *Twenty-One Love Poems* is a series of poems about a relationship between two women.

The journey of the poem is both physical and metaphysical. The two travelers are climbing the volcano; they are also learning about themselves, noting "the detail outside ourselves that brings us to ourselves." There is a carefully wrought tension in this poem between opposites: peak is set against crater, height against depth, straw soles against hardened lava, the flower against "the slowly altering rock" to which it clings. The poem is a journey from duality toward unity, toward a place where inside and outside meet. The process of this journey is in part accomplished through perception and language. The central mystery of the poem, "the small, jewel-like flower / unfamiliar to us," is given meaning through language, is "nameless till we rename her." Not all poems demonstrate so clearly the importance of setting and the relation between setting and speaker; nevertheless, this is almost always a useful area to explore in reading and writing about a poem.

THE WORLD AND THE POEM

Not only is there a set of relations or tensions within a poem, but, like any other work of literature, a poem is in a certain tension with the time, place, and person who produced it and with the time, place, and person who reads it. A diagram of that set of relations might look something like this collection of overlapping circles:

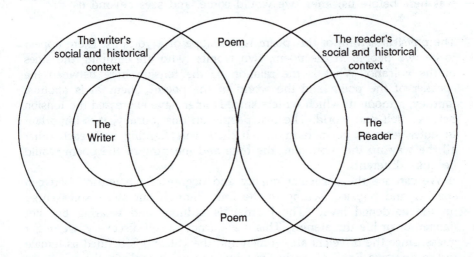

Though a poem, like any work of literature, should be able to stand on its own, it can deepen our understanding and enjoyment of the poem to know something about the life of the writer. The important social, political, and philosophical issues of the poet's era, what writers might have influenced her or him, what kind of poetry was customarily written at that time, and where in the writing career of the poet this particular poem was written are factors which enhance our understanding of the poem. Similarly, our interpretation of a poem and the resonance a poem has for us have something to do with who we are and when and where and how we are living. If you are male and eighteen years old, you might have a different emotional response to Gwendolyn Brooks's "We Real Cool" than if you are thirty-five years old and female. You might read the poem differently depending on whether you are black or white, middle class or working class. We come to a poem with all the baggage of our personal biography and the beliefs of our community and historical period.

Does this imply that a poem means anything we want it to mean? Or that all the analytical tools previously discussed are unimportant? No, what it means is simply that a poem is multidimensional and living. More than anything else, a poem is a communication, across space and time, between the person who wrote it and the person who reads it. "You can tear a poem apart to see what makes it technically tick," writes Dylan Thomas,

and say to yourself, when the works are laid out before you, the vowels, the consonants, the rhymes and rhythms, "Yes, this is *it.*

This is why the poem moves me so. It is because of the craftmanship." But you're back again where you began. You're back with the mystery of having been moved by words. The best craftmanship always leaves holes and gaps in the works of the poem so that something that is *not* in the poem can creep, crawl, flash, or thunder in.

Perhaps the best way to learn how to read a poem is to write some poetry, enough to learn through experience that poetic craft is a matter of making choices and that writing well is a combination of sweat, skill, and luck out of which, sometimes, something magical happens.

HOW DRAMA WORKS

As we did in "How Fiction Works," let's begin with an example, this time the opening of Arthur Miller's 1949 play, *Death of a Salesman*. The passage we will examine represents only about 5 percent of the whole play, but it lays the groundwork for much of what is to come and illustrates a number of important general points about how drama works. Turn now to page 793 and read carefully, as far as the italicized sentence one third down that begins *"On Willy's last line . . . ."* Then return to this page and continue reading.

After the play's title and list of characters, we encounter the *stage directions*, which clearly set drama apart from other literary genres. Most fiction, for example, is written entirely in the past tense ("It was a dark and stormy night . . ."), but the stage directions of a play are in the present tense (*"A melody is heard . . ."*)—a hint of the immediacy of drama, even drama on the page rather than on stage. In general, stage directions are aimed primarily at people putting on a play. Descriptions of the set, fairly elaborate in this case, can help someone design and build that set. Physical descriptions of characters (Willy is *"past sixty years of age, dressed quietly"*) can help in the selection of actors, in the design of their costumes, and in the acting. Psychological descriptions of characters (*"Linda . . . has developed an iron repression of her exceptions to Willy's behavior"*) can help actors conceptualize their roles, speak their lines, and hold and move their faces and their bodies.

But stage directions are also essential to *readers* of a play. It is often tempting to skim through or skip over stage directions, especially if they are long, and get right to the dialogue, to "the play itself." But if, instead, we read stage directions carefully, and try to visualize what an actual performance of the play might look like, we will come much closer to the experience of seeing such a performance and perhaps even capture some of its excitement.

A close look at the opening of *Death of a Salesman* should suggest how important stage directions can be for readers. The directions begin with stark contrast: the flute music, *"telling of grass and trees and the horizon,"* against the *"towering, angular shapes"* of the apartment buildings with their *"angry glow of orange."* The *"small, fragile-seeming home"* is surrounded by *"a solid vault of apartment houses."* This creates a sense of entrapment, of external, rather ominous forces closing in on a peaceful but vulnerable center, much as Willy Loman's dream and life, we learn later, are the victims of forces beyond his control.

The set described seems to *suggest* a home rather than reproduce one realistically on stage. There is some furniture, but no fixtures; the setting is largely transparent; walls can be walked through. Willy's *"imaginings"* of the past are to be acted out at the front of the stage, with actors stepping freely through walls; but to portray the *"present,"* actors will treat the wall-lines as solid walls and enter and exit only through a door. The stage directions suggest—and the play bears this out—that Willy will live much of his life in his imagination and that stage action will flow smoothly between imaginary scenes and scenes of present "reality." What is done quite easily in fiction—movement back and forth between actual experience and what takes place only in a character's mind—can be more difficult in drama, and Miller has created a rather complex scheme for doing the job.

Seeing the play in performance we would quickly get used to the idea that walls are not always walls and that the same actors can represent both the present and the past, both external reality and the world inside Willy's head. Reading the play is both more difficult and easier than seeing it. Visualizing what is on the page takes effort, but our imagination, if aroused, is even more flexible than Miller's set.

The stage directions in a play represent the writer's only real chance to speak directly to readers. The rest of the play consists simply of what characters say, that is, of dialogue. Though stage directions contain narrative elements (*"She is taking off his shoes"*), basically, there is no narrator in drama. The story is not told, the plot is not related by one controlling voice, as in fiction. The story, in a sense, seems to tell itself. We watch and listen to what characters are doing and saying if we *see* a play; we read what seems like a transcript of what characters are doing and saying if we *read* a play.

In fiction, a narrator may prepare us for the main action by quickly summarizing events that have led up to it and by relating the personal histories of its main characters. But in drama, we generally have only the characters' own words. (Miller helps us a little with his description in the opening stage directions of Linda and Willy's relationship, but this is very brief and, of course, in performance, would not be spoken.) The action of *Death of a Salesman* begins in the middle of things—Willy has just dragged himself into the house—but we quickly learn a great deal about him and his family. The dialogue, especially in early scenes, not only moves the action forward, but also provides us with important information about the characters.

We learn, among other things, that Willy is having trouble with his job. He's getting tired, and finding it difficult to keep his mind on the present. His boss, son of the man he once worked for, is younger and doesn't appreciate him. Willy is concerned that one of his sons, Biff, a young man of great promise back in high school, is now a farm hand, a failure in his father's eyes. More than concerned, he's angry, and yet he also loves Biff and is proud of him. Deeply conflicted in his feelings towards Biff, Willy refers to him as "a lazy bum" and then, a moment later, insists that "there's one thing about Biff—he's not lazy." We suspect Willy has been counting on his son's life somehow to compensate for his own, and though we haven't yet met Biff, we can imagine that the pressure of Willy's expectations has taken its toll on him.

Willy is frustrated, rude, and irritable; he snaps repeatedly at Linda, his wife. When she buys American cheese, instead of the usual Swiss, he takes it as a personal affront, an attack on his authority and dignity. Linda worries about him and seems to do everything in her power to calm and comfort him, downplaying his problems ("Maybe it's your glasses"), offering suggestions and criticism only gently, suffering his rudeness *"with infinite patience."* Unlike Willy, she's not concerned about her son's income and status so much as about his feelings; she just wants Biff and Willy to get along with each other.

Willy cares very much about money and status, yet has little of either and seems ashamed of his son. He is trapped, as is Linda, and escapes into *"reminiscences,"* which is just what the staging dramatizes—the sense of external forces closing like a trap, and the contrast between a difficult present and memories of an idealized past. So by the time that Willy complains, near the end of the scene, of being "boxed . . . in" by the apartments around him, the full significance of his words should be clear, as should the irony of his talk of living in "the greatest country in the world."

In a short scene, which lasts perhaps ten minutes on stage, we've learned a great deal (much more, indeed, than has been spelled out here), not only about several characters in the play, but about some of the conflicts that drive the plot: conflict between Willy and Biff, conflict between reminiscence and present reality, conflict between Willy and his world. So even though the title of the play has more or less already told us what ultimately happens to Willy, we arrive at the transition to the next scene (*"Biff and Happy raise themselves up in their beds"*) eager to learn what happens next and rather well informed about the people it will happen to.

DRAMA ON STAGE AND ON THE PAGE

A good way to begin a more general discussion of how drama works is to pursue further the difference between seeing and reading a play. Perhaps the most striking thing about a play performed on stage is the presence of live actors. Lines spoken aloud have an impact that words on the page do not; this is why we often read aloud, whether to others or to ourselves, passages that we find especially moving or meaningful.

Anger, or despair, or delight in an actor's voice can communicate emotion to us in a way that words on a page cannot. And actors can move as well as speak. In many of Shakespeare's plays, heroes and villains flash their swords and daggers; in Ibsen's *A Doll's House* (p. 563), Nora performs a frenzied tarantella; in shange's *for colored girls who have considered suicide / when the rainbow is enuf* (p. 623), subtitled "a choreopoem," seven women dramatize their pain and their joy through dance. Even from the back row, live theater can be impressive.

A set described in written stage directions is usually described only once, but a set on stage stands continuously before us, constantly shaping our responses. In plays from other cultures and historical periods, a set (as well as props and costumes) can help draw us in to that place and time. The use of space itself, even on the barest stage, can also affect us in important ways. We may notice, when reading, that stage directions place two lovers physically far apart as they discuss their problems, but it is quite another thing to see half the width of the stage gaping between them for the duration of the scene, making tangible the emotional distance they are feeling. Visual impact is essential to drama on stage.

The presence of an audience also makes drama seen different from drama read. Dramatic performance is a communal art; its roots are in religion and ritual. To a large extent, members of the audience experience a play not as separate individuals, but as a community, even if a community of strangers. Anyone who has seen a funny movie alone in a theater, or nearly alone, has no doubt felt the emptiness of the surrounding seats, the absence of a community of viewers. The kind of collective response we experience when we see a play is what we miss when we read a play.

Live drama also excites an audience because each performance is, in some sense, unique, its success uncertain. Will the actors remember all their lines? Will this be an exceptional performance? Will the audience, through its response, perhaps even inspire the actors to their best performance ever? The effect of the audience may be more obvious, say, at a rock concert; an audience may communicate its pleasure or displeasure to the actors more conspicuously at a comic than at a tragic play; but even when the audience's response is subtle, it does influence the actors' performance and helps shape the theatrical event. Reading a play, on the other hand, our response is ours alone.

The point, of course, is not that we shouldn't bother to read drama, but that we need to keep the nature of live drama in mind as we do read. When possible, we ought to read plays—or at least key scenes, or lines—aloud, preferably with others, but alone if necessary, so we can feel the sound of a human voice speaking lines meant to be spoken. And if we have the chance, and the money, we ought to see live performances of plays we are reading.

But there are certain advantages to reading rather than seeing a play. If we care, for example, about the playwright's intentions, the printed text is usually a more objective guide than any performance. A performance, after all, is an interpretation, and even the most elaborately detailed stage directions cannot fully spell out how a playwright envisions the play on stage. The stage directions of *Death of a Salesman* say nothing, for example, about Willy Loman's height, and clearly the play would be different if he were 5'2" than if he were a foot taller. A director cannot avoid interpreting; even casting Willy Loman as a man of average height would represent one interpretation rather than another. Sometimes a playwright directs his or her own play, and these rare productions are usually paid special attention. But short of that, the play in print probably represents the closest we can come to the original voice of its author.

Reading can also provide a good first approach to a difficult play. The rich language, dense with meaning, of poet Sylvia Plath's radio play, *Three Women* (p. 209), or of Shakespeare's *King Lear* (p. 221) can take time to assimilate, and in the case of *Lear*, most of us need the help of footnotes to understand an English very different from today's. But even with plays that do not seem difficult at first glance, plays such as *Death of a Salesman* or Alice Childress's *Florence* (p. 876), where the language is conversational, reading allows us to stop the action and think over what's been happening, something impossible to do in a theater. Though reading a play may afford us a less intense emotional experience than seeing that play performed, it may offer a fuller intellectual experience; we may feel less, but we are more likely to understand what we feel.

The fact that most plays are written to be performed shapes the texts we read in ways that may not be obvious. Theater audiences need to be kept awake and interested; if they find a play dull, it may close quickly, a serious blow to the playwright, who may then find it difficult to get future plays produced. So plays generally have strong plots and often rely rather heavily on suspense. Fiction, by contrast, can easily digress from the main line of action to develop a mood or dwell on the subtleties of a character's psyche. But in most drama, plot is central, and events must keep unfolding in order to move that plot forward.

Playwrights face other constraints when constructing their plots that writers of fiction do not face. Plot in drama is generally linear; since audiences will see events on stage one after another, they tend to assume that these events take place in that same order. Flashbacks, common in fiction, are more difficult to manage in drama—thus the complicated stage directions at the start of *Death of a Salesman*. Since sets can be expensive and take some effort to change (though modern technology has made this easier), plays that use realistic sets usually do not take place, for example, on mountain tops or at sea, and tend to avoid frequent changes of location. For similar reasons of practicality, realistic plays usually avoid scenes that directly involve animals or small children. In fiction, the stroke of a pen can put thirty people in a room, talking and eating hors d'oeuvres. But in drama, the limited size of the stage, and of the budget (not to mention the trouble an audience might have understanding an individual character speaking against the chatter of the others) make this quite difficult. None of the many constraints that performance puts on playwriting are absolute, of course, but they help to explain why playwrights so often write scenes of two or three or four characters in a room together talking.

CHANGING STAGE CONVENTIONS

In different historical periods, playwrights have faced different constraints within which they had to work. Or, to put it in positive terms, they have found different technical devices available to them for creating dramatic reality. If a dramatic technique or device—the **soliloquy,** for example, in which a character, alone on stage, speaks his or her private thoughts aloud to the audience—is widely used in a particular period and has become accepted and readily understood by audiences, we call it a **convention.** Theatrical conventions have changed over the years and what may have seemed to audiences in one period like a perfectly clear and reasonable way of depicting reality on stage might well have seemed artificial and perhaps even confusing to audiences in another. Though we may feel uncomfortable with dramatic conventions that differ significantly from those of our own time, in order to understand and appreciate what we read, we should know something about them.

Classical Greek theater, in particular the fifth century B.C. theater of Sophocles's *Antigone* (p. 1290), was very different from the theater of today. Plays were performed outdoors, in a large semicircular amphitheater, before an audience of tens of thousands. Actors stood in front of a painted scene building, wearing oversized masks that made them visible to a large audience and functioned as megaphones to project their voices. In the **orchestra,** a circular area between the actors and the audience, stood the **chorus,** fifteen men who, between scenes, danced solemnly and chanted commentary on the main action. Key events, such as Antigone's burial of her brother and, later, her own death, often took place offstage and were reported by messengers. The time a play covered was, by convention, usually less than a day, often only a few hours; plots were constructed around a short period of intense action, the prelude to which audiences already knew or learned about indirectly.

The Elizabethan theater, for which Shakespeare wrote, used a roofed stage that projected into an audience of perhaps two thousand. Nearly surrounding the stage and stacked up in balconies and galleries in a rather compact building, the audience were all physically quite close to the actors, so that conventions such as the **aside** (in which a character speaks directly to the audience, unheard by the other actors on stage), as well as the soliloquy, seemed quite natural. There were few props and no scenery. For the most part, characters on stage created a sense of place through their words, as in *King Lear*, when Edgar begins a scene saying, "Here, father, take the shadow of this tree." The absence of scenery allowed for rapid shifting of scene from place to place. Together with rather free manipulation of time—minutes or weeks could elapse between scenes, and even years between acts—this created great flexibility and made possible considerable complexity of plot.

The **realistic theater,** which began in the nineteenth century in Europe, attempted to reproduce as faithfully as possible the reality of daily life as it might appear to an observer. The **box set** of the realistic stage consisted of a rectangular room with one wall missing so that the audience could see in. The room was fully furnished, as the opening stage directions of Ibsen's *A Doll's House* suggest, and every effort was made, down to the smallest detail, to make the room appear like an actual room. In line with the desired illusion that the members of the audience were invisible observers of real life, characters never addressed the audience in soliloquies or asides, and they spoke in what seemed to be the language of everyday life, not in the poetry of Sophocles's or Shakespeare's noble personages. Events were linked together with discernibly credible causality, for plots, like sets and characters, had, above all, to maintain the appearance of reality.

Theater since Ibsen has been characterized primarily by the variety of its conventions. Some plays, staged with all the attention to physical detail of a work by Ibsen, have tried to imitate surface reality directly; others, performed on bare stages, have called upon the audience to imagine the physical setting; and still others, like *Death of a Salesman,* taking a middle course, have used props and sets as much to suggest as to construct the physical environment of the play's action. Most twentieth-century plays use actors in a realistic way: characters behave as if unaware of the audience's presence. But in Marc Kaminsky's *In the Traffic of a Targeted City* (p. 1046), for example, characters frequently deliver soliloquies. And in the work of German playwright Bertolt Brecht, a number of techniques such as song, text projected onto the stage area, and self-consciously theatrical acting are used in order to break down the illusion of reality so that the audience will not become absorbed in events on stage, but will instead think critically about them. Twentieth-century playwrights tend to draw on whatever conventions suit their dramatic purposes.

It is tempting to view theatrical conventions we are accustomed to, particularly realistic conventions, as somehow less artificial, more natural than those we are not used to, such as the soliloquies and asides in *King Lear* or the Chorus in *Antigone.* But how natural is it, after all, for a group of actors in a box-like room on a stage to hold private conversations and pretend not to be aware that the audience is watching? One might very well argue that Shakespearean actors, who openly acknowledge the presence of the audience by addressing it in asides and soliloquies, are behaving more naturally than actors in realistic drama. While different conventions have different implications—they shape what a playwright can and cannot do, and how it is to be done—*all* conventions are artificial. Those we are accustomed to tend to be transparent; we do not even notice them most of the time. But unfamiliar conventions can easily seem artificial, even foolish. We will get the most out of the drama we read if we ask ourselves the same question about all conventions: How does the playwright use them to shape the meaning of the play?

PLOT AND CHARACTER

An essential element in plays, whatever their conventions, is **plot.** The plot of a play, like the plot of a work of fiction, is a sequence of events arranged in a meaningful pattern. The plot of many plays follows a traditional pattern: **exposition,** in which characters, relationships, setting are introduced; then **rising action,** in which matters begin getting complicated, conflict develops; then **climax,** a turning point or moment of decision, when dramatic intensity peaks; then **falling action,** in which the consequences of the climactic events unfold; and, finally, **denouement,** in which action comes to a meaningful end. This pattern is followed more closely in *Antigone* and *King Lear* than, say, in *Death of a Salesman;* and it bears little relationship at all to plays like *for colored girls who have considered suicide / when the rainbow is enuf* and *In the Traffic of a Targeted City.* So while we might want to look for this pattern to help us understand how plays are structured, we should not insist on finding it.

Many plays are best understood in terms of multiple plots. In Sylvia Plath's *Three Women,* for example, three voices narrate three different experiences: giving birth to a much-wanted child, having a miscarriage, and delivering an unwanted baby to be given up for adoption. The three narratives, which intercut one another, represent three independent events, three separate plots, but they create meaning through their juxtaposition. In Marc Kaminsky's *In the Traffic of a Targeted City,* action takes place alternately, as the stage directions indicate, *"in New York today and Hiroshima, 1945."* Though the two sets of events remain separate, what happens in Hiroshima clearly shapes the lives of the characters in New York today, and also suggests what their future might be.

Plays often employ a **subplot,** in which a second plot, though connected to, is also clearly subordinated to the main plot. In *King Lear,* for example, Gloucester, like Lear, learns only too late which of his children is truly devoted. Here, the main plot (Lear's) and the subplot (Gloucester's) intersect at points, but their similarities and differences as separate plots also shape the play's meaning. In *A Doll's House,* Mrs. Linden's developing relationship with Krogstad, as well as her past history, provide a number of important contrasts to Nora's stifling marriage to Helmer and help shape the statement the play is making about marriage and women's roles.

Events that have occurred before the moment at which the play's action begins can also serve as a sort of second plot that complicates the meaning of the main plot. The past events that Willy Loman's onstage reminiscences gradually reveal in *Death of a Salesman* provide an often painful contrast with the events unfolding in the present and help us understand their significance. The hero of *Krapp's Last Tape* (p. 356) replays tape-recorded journal entries he made as a younger man, so that past and present plot are interwoven in meaningful ways. In Susan Glaspell's *Trifles* (p. 1334), past events prove especially significant. These past events are neither acted on stage nor narrated on tape; they are merely described by various characters and revealed through objects left behind; but they make themselves felt very strongly in the present. The bold action Mrs. Hale and Mrs. Peters take at the end of the play is very much inspired by the boldness of Minnie Foster in the story they have pieced together of her actions in the past. Of course, plotting can get much more complicated than this, but the point to emphasize again is that plot consists not simply of events but of their meaningful arrangement. A step towards understanding that meaning can be to ask how a play would be different if the same events were arranged differently for an audience, that is, fashioned into a different plot.

It is difficult to imagine plot in drama without **character,** and in much drama, as in much fiction, what happens to characters grows out of what kind of people they are. It is not uncommon in fiction, particularly in long works of fiction that trace the entire life of a central character, for plot to shape character significantly; the central figure, from childhood on perhaps, goes through a number of formative experiences that help determine what kind of person he or she becomes. But drama usually begins in the middle of things; characters have already become more or less what they are, and their interactions, perhaps with external events as well as with each other, sets a plot in motion. A character's nature may be gradually *revealed* over the course of a play, but it is unlikely to change fundamentally.

Characters in drama, like characters in fiction, can be **major characters** (most central to the plot, fully developed, complex) or **minor characters** (on the periphery, sketchily drawn, rather one-dimensional); original characters (generally, they are major not minor characters) or **stock characters** (that is, easily recognized "types"); and **protagonist** (the main character, the hero) or **antagonist** (opponent to the protagonist). Categorization is not always easy, though; critics still debate, for example, whether Antigone or Creon is the protagonist of Sophocles's *Antigone*.

Though stage directions and the list of characters (the **dramatis personae**) at the start of a play may sometimes describe characters for a reader directly, most characterization in drama—far more so than in fiction—is indirect. Character in drama can be revealed through what characters say, through what they do, through what others say to and about them, and, sometimes, through what they say to audiences in soliloquies and asides. As readers, we need to compare and evaluate carefully all sorts of revelations of character, including such clues as physical appearance and name (Krapp, or Willy Loman, for example).

A NOTE ON TRAGEDY AND COMEDY

Tragedy is defined by character as well as by plot. Generally, tragedy involves a hero or protagonist of great social importance, such as a king or prince, who, often because of a flaw such as excessive pride, makes a decision and acts in a way that ultimately brings about his or her death. The hero usually dies after gaining new understanding that comes too late to alter his or her fate. Lear, out of vanity and stubbornness, gives his kingdom to two flattering daughters and sets in motion a chain of events that leads to his death, though only after he has come to a fuller understanding of his world. In *Antigone,* the matter is more complicated, for while Antigone may be flawed by zealousness and does die, Creon is flawed as well and, unlike Antigone, comes to a new understanding before the end. Which character we view as protagonist (and thus as tragically flawed) may have less to do with the structure of the play itself than with where our individual sympathies lie, whether with the ruler Creon or with the rebel Antigone. In *Death of a Salesman,* Arthur Miller tries to make what he called "the common man" the subject of tragedy. "I don't say he's a great man," Willy's wife Linda says at one point, ". . . but he's a human being, and a terrible thing is happening to him. So attention must be paid." But whether Willy Loman achieves the stature we tend to associate with tragedy, or whether he is more pathetic than tragic, is certainly open to question.

Comedy, generally, differs from tragedy in that its hero is more likely to be a young lover than an old noble; it ends in a marriage or other joyful event, not death; its overall mood is playful, not somber; and it appeals to our intellect more than to our emotions. Though many plays fit one of these definitions quite well, most modern plays squirm uncomfortably if we try to force them into the comic or the tragic mold. In *A Doll's House,* for example, though Nora eventually comes to a new understanding of herself and her world, the play does not end with her death, as in tragedy, but, in a sense, with her rebirth. On the other hand, though the play's ending is basically a positive one, the concluding event is not marriage, as in comedy, but the end of a marriage.

While *King Lear* and other tragedies make use of **comic relief,** humorous interludes that provide escape from and also an intensifying contrast to the overall mood of tragedy, modern plays often mix comic elements much more thoroughly with the material of tragedy. For example, Jonah and Joanna, in an early scene of *In the Traffic of a Targeted City,* dance a jitterbug as they discuss their fears of nuclear holocaust. And Krapp, old, alone, compulsively eating bananas and playing his tapes, is at once funny and pathetic, a combination not uncommon in **Theater of the Absurd.** Absurdist plays, like those of Samuel Beckett, portray human existence as meaningless, hopeless, irrational, and the individual as ultimately isolated and alienated. Yet these plays are often grotesquely funny, their humor in stark contrast to the horror of their underlying message.

Though the mood, the hero, and the structure of many recent plays may be difficult to categorize as simply tragic or comic, tragic and comic elements are central to most drama, and the concepts of tragedy and comedy can often provide a useful starting point for the analysis of a play.

DRAMA AND SOCIAL CRITICISM

Plays often picture human suffering in various forms, but they differ considerably in what they suggest about the causes and the necessity of such suffering. Tragedy has traditionally portrayed suffering as part of the nature of things. Though the action of a flawed protagonist may precipitate disaster, we come to feel that such disaster is inevitable. Modern readers may look to the psychology of Creon or Antigone for explanations, but for Sophocles's original audiences, fate (that is, the gods) played an essential role in bringing catastrophe. As the daughter of Oedipus, Antigone shares his curse, for, as the Chorus explains, "Where once the anger of heaven has struck, that house is shaken / For ever." Similarly, when Lear rages upon the heath against the violent storm, he is raging against an inexorable force, against his inescapable fate; the structure and feel of *The Tragedy of King Lear* are of inevitability.

Nora's suffering in *A Doll's House* comes across as far from inevitable, its ultimate cause not cosmic but social. Nora does not die at the end of the play, but rather, through her own action, alters the course of her life in a positive way. This is drama of social criticism, its message that the status of women in society should and can be improved. The play is a far cry from *Antigone*, which, however we view it, is not a plea for stricter child-rearing or better training of kings.

Drama of social criticism since Ibsen has worked in a variety of ways to suggest that change is necessary and possible. *In the Traffic of a Targeted City* gives voice to the victims of Hiroshima, juxtaposes their experiences with the frantic pursuit of trivial activities by today's New Yorkers, and thus impresses on us the urgency of preventing nuclear war. The traditionally realistic *Florence* presents a black woman's encounter with a white woman that dramatizes the subtlety and pervasiveness of racism and the protagonist's new-found determination to resist it. *for colored girls who have considered suicide / when the rainbow is enuf*, blending poetry and dance in dramatic form, protests racism and sexism, and at the same time affirms the value and necessity of sisterhood and strength. Even *Death of a Salesman*, though it ends with the death of its protagonist, can be read more as social criticism than as tragedy of inevitability, for Willy is the victim of the flawed society that produced him. He has swallowed whole an American Dream that could never deliver what it promised and he suffers for his misplaced faith in a business world that discards him when he proves unprofitable. "Business is business," Howard explains coldly as he fires Willy.

In *Trouble in Mind,* a play Alice Childress wrote several years after *Florence,* black protagonist Wiletta Mayer insists, even at the risk of losing her job, that the script of a play she is acting in be revised because she feels the play is telling a lie about her people. Her actions dramatize quite effectively the importance of the social interpretation of drama. A play always embodies a perspective, be it critical or uncritical, consistent or perhaps contradictory, on the social order; and though we may disagree about what that perspective is, trying to understand it is an essential part of reading and interpreting drama.

A NOTE ON FILM AND TELEVISION

Film is frequently studied along with literature and can usefully be compared with drama, though it also shares certain characteristics with fiction, poetry, and even nonfiction. Like drama in performance, film creates an image to be seen and heard by an audience, though generally what is seen plays the more important role in film and what is heard (in particular, the dialogue) plays the more important role in drama. Like drama, film—however "real" it may seem—also relies on conventions, such as the use of music (romantic, ominous, lighthearted, and so on) to help create a mood even when no conceivable source for that music exists within the world of the film. Unlike drama, though, film does not have to choose between variety and surface realism in settings; film can shift rapidly and repeatedly to new physical locations, thus combining, in a sense, the flexibility of the Elizabethan stage with the faithful reproduction of appearances of the realistic stage.

Film shares with fiction rather than with drama the ability to embody point of view, for the camera, in some ways like the narrator in a work of fiction, continuously controls what we see and how we see it. A scene, for example, of a Civil War battle shot from a distance (a **long shot**) might lead us to concentrate on the question of which side is winning, while a **close-up** of the face of one soldier in that battle might instead emphasize fear and suffering, that is, the human cost of war. And a **zoom shot** that began at a distance and gradually moved in to focus on one face might make a point about the relationship between these two aspects of war.

Camera angle as well as distance can shape a viewer's response to a film. A scene of a political leader delivering an impassioned speech, for example, if shot fairly close and from a low angle (so that the viewer looked up at the politician) might create an image, perhaps a menacing one, of great personal power. On the other hand, a scene of a person sitting alone in a room, if shot from a high angle (looking down) might create an image of weakness and vulnerability. Film can also shape a viewer's response through **cutting,** that is through instantaneous changes from one perspective or scene to another (made by attaching together pieces of film shot separately). In a scene, for example, of a disagreement over a raise between a manager and a low-paid employee, a quick cut to a shot of the manager's diamond pinky ring might help us take sides. Similarly, repeated cutting back and forth (or **cross cutting**) between a husband watching television and a wife scrubbing pots and pans would make an unmistakable point.

There is obviously a great deal more to say about the wide variety of techniques available to film makers (and most introductory film books explore the technical side of film making in detail), but it is also worth noting that in general making films is business, usually big business. A Hollywood film costs millions of dollars to produce and millions more to advertise, so artistic considerations easily give way to commercial ones. The romantic image of the artist aflame with a vision and beholden only to his or her muse bears little resemblance to the work of a Hollywood film maker hoping to sell a film to a mass audience. For this reason, some of the best as well as the most innovative American films today come from "independent" film makers, working with small budgets and outside Hollywood.

Television uses many of the same techniques as film, though we find, for example, fewer long shots and more close-ups on television because of the smaller size of the screen. Like film, television is shaped significantly by commercial considerations; network executives, and thus everyone else involved, watch the ratings very closely. Creators of television series face numerous external constraints. Each episode of a series, for example, must be the same length and must be divided into segments, themselves of more or less prescribed length, which end at moments of excitement or suspense so that viewers will keep watching despite commercial interruption. Major characters in a series cannot die, no matter how much danger they find themselves in, if they are to appear again the following week. And writers have to come up with twenty-six episodes a year. So it is not surprising that many series—even those that begin with great promise—settle quickly into tired formulas.

From time to time plays are produced for television. As with film versions of plays, some of these consist simply of a stage performance recorded on videotape or film, and they offer us a convenient way of seeing a play. Others move the play off the stage, outdoors if a scene calls for it; they keep the original dialogue but use the camera as expressively as in any film or television show. In plays made for television, in the work of independent video artists, and in other productions that depart from the weekly routine, we can sometimes glimpse the still largely untapped potential of the medium.

HOW NONFICTION WORKS

You might be asking yourself why nonfiction is included in an anthology called *Literature and Society*. What is literature, and is nonfictional prose literature? Some people define literature primarily in evaluative terms, as writing which achieves a certain level of excellence regardless of its form. But how do we decide what is excellent and what is not; and, further, who decides? Others label as literature only that writing which is imaginative or "creative." But imagination can take many forms, not all of them clearly or entirely poetic, fictional, or dramatic. The speaker in Judy Syfers's "Why I Want a Wife" (p. 671) imagines herself out of the role of wife, with which she is obviously intimately familiar, and into the role of possessor of a wife—one whose social expectations might include having someone to cook and clean up after her, to bear and raise her children, to act as hostess and secretary and, in general, to make her life easier. Clearly a work of imagination, "Why I Want a Wife" is just as clearly neither a story, a poem, nor a play, but a satiric essay.

Many works of nonfiction use techniques we have already become acquainted with in the sections on How Fiction Works, How Poetry Works, and How Drama Works: narration, figurative language, dramatic scenes, dialogue, character sketches and character development, sensual and rhythmic language. Literature, it seems to us, includes any writing that: (1) takes itself seriously as writing and persuades its readers to take it seriously; and (2) pays decided attention to matters of language and of form, being as concerned with how it says something as with what is said. Two further considerations, more open to disagreement and debate, are that literature should move us in some way, have an emotional effect on us, and that it should have lasting value.

The typical news story in the daily paper is very probably not literature. It is ephemeral, not meant to last. It is written to a formula—who, what, where, when, how, and, maybe, if there's space, why—and even if the individual reporter is a good writer, one task of the news editor is to smooth out flair and originality and to shape that writing into a style consistent with the rest of the paper's writing. Editorial and feature writing are, of course, another matter, and Meridel LeSueur's "Women on the Breadlines" (p. 888) is an example of reportage that we can be reasonably secure in calling literature. Written during the Great Depression as an exposé to bring the situation of unemployed women to the attention of a nation focused on finding jobs for men, the piece uses fictional devices like narration, character sketch, and creation of setting; poetic devices like metaphor and simile; and dramatic devices like dialogue and scene to construct an essay that both informs and persuades.

> So we sit hour after hour, day after day, waiting for a job to come in. There are many women for a single job. A thin sharp woman sits inside a wire cage looking at a book. For four hours we have watched her looking at that book. She has a hard little eye. In the small bare room there are half a dozen women sitting on the benches waiting. Many come and go. Our faces are all familiar to each other, for we wait here every day.

This paragraph early in LeSueur's essay provides a setting and begins to introduce us to some of the people who inhabit that setting. The description of the "small bare room" and the women in it, including the first-person narrator who is both a participant and an observer, is written in such a way as to evoke a particular atmosphere or mood—of tedium, endurance, passivity, and perhaps a growing desperation. What makes "Women on the Breadlines" an essay rather than a story is LeSueur's emphasis on developing an idea and an argument. Throughout she mixes narration with persuasion, using the characters, anecdotes, and atmosphere as evidence for her argument that women too are out of work and suffering, that their invisibility is in part due to their socialization as women and is mirrored in media, government, and popular ignorance of their condition. After telling us about one woman, Bernice, who has lived on crackers for weeks, she writes: "A woman will shut herself up in a room until it is taken away from her, and eat a cracker a day and be as quiet as a mouse so there are no social statistics concerning her." The individual women LeSueur describes in vivid detail serve as representative types. She continually moves from the particular to the general, from the specific to the abstract, each detail a piece of evidence in the construction and development of her thesis. This method of argument is already clear in her opening sentences:

> I am sitting in the city free employment bureau. It's the women's section. We have been sitting here now for four hours. We sit here every day, waiting for a job. There are no jobs.

While LeSueur's rhetorical intent breaks through her narration often enough to make classifying this piece as an essay not too difficult, some prose lives quite congenially and unrepentantly on the line between fiction and nonfiction. Richard Wright's "The Man Who Went to Chicago" (p. 893) has been variously classified as fiction and nonfiction during its publishing history. Published by Wright as a separate fictional piece in the 1940s, it finally ended up in an expanded version as part of *American Hunger*, the posthumous second volume of his autobiography. Writing about his experience with several different jobs in Chicago during the Depression, Wright sometimes lets his narration launch him into an impassioned argument against American racism. Is this essay or autobiography? How much did Wright shape, combine, and rearrange events, details, and characters? How much is "truth" and how much "fiction"? The question of truth also arises with Maxine Hong Kingston's "No Name Woman" (p. 364), the first of five sections of *The Woman Warrior*, her account of growing up Chinese-American. This book won the National Book Critics Circle award as best work of nonfiction in 1976, yet the piece consists of "stories" spiraling out of other "stories." We bring up these examples not in order to confuse, but to suggest that while labeling and categorizing can be useful, they also have their limits. Writers are adventurers and explorers who constantly cross and expand the mapped boundaries of form. This fact is nowhere clearer than in nonfictional prose, a category which seems to include everything in prose left over after we have separated out works of fiction and drama.

TYPES OF NONFICTIONAL PROSE

It is possible to name and describe two broad categories of nonfictional prose—*narrative nonfictional prose* and *rhetorical nonfictional prose*—though the dividing lines are fuzzy and a work of nonfictional prose may succeed in being both at once. **Narrative nonfictional prose** recounts an event or sequence of events. It moves in time, either in simple chronological sequence or in a more complex pattern. **Diaries** and **journals** are most often simple chronologies of events and introspection recorded sequentially. A diary is usually more intimate, personal and private, whereas a journal tends to be a more public form, as much concerned with the world as it is with the self writing. The brief section we include from eighteenth-century Quaker John Woolman's *Journal* (p. 1349) recounts his daily struggles to follow his conscience and act on his antislavery beliefs. The austerity of Quaker belief made the journal, because it was nonfictional, one of the few literary forms permissible to members of this religious group. The kind of **letters** people write to friends and acquaintances are often narrative, and collections of letters, especially by well-known people, are often published and read with interest. **Epistles** are more formal and public letters, written by individuals or groups, which address philosophical or political issues and tend to be rhetorical as often as narrative.

Perhaps the most varied and enjoyable form of narrative nonfictional prose is the **autobiography** or **memoir.** The memoir tends to emphasize well-known personalities or events the writer has known or witnessed, whereas autobiography centers on the life of the writer. French writer Marguerite Duras, in *The War: A Memoir* (p. 1093), tells of the arrival home of her husband from a concentration camp at the end of World War II. Though the incident described is personal, it is the war itself and its effects on people's lives which is the organizing principle of Duras' book.

We have included several autobiographical selections: Richard Wright's "The Man Who Went to Chicago," Black Elk's "The Butchering at Wounded Knee" (p. 1089), Maxine Hong Kingston's "No Name Woman," Barbara Deming's "Prison Notes" (p. 1388), and excerpts from Harriet Jacobs's *Incidents in the Life of a Slave Girl* (p. 1371), Ron Kovic's *Born on the Fourth of July* (p. 1102), and Audre Lorde's *Zami* (p. 374). Each of these works narrates and meditates upon an event or series of events crucial in retrospect in the life of the writer—from Kingston's and Lorde's memories of the beginning of puberty, to Ron Kovic's account of his physical and emotional devastation after being wounded in Vietnam, to Black Elk's description of the defeat of his people. To say that the mode of writing in these autobiographical selections is primarily narrative does not mean that there is no persuasive intent in the writing. Harriet Jacobs, for example, hoped that by describing her own considerable suffering as a slave, she would move her white readers to support the antislavery cause. Barbara Deming's account of her stay in jail as a civil rights activist deliberately raises questions about whether there is much difference between being in jail or out of jail in an unjust society.

Rhetoric is the art and skill of persuasion, and **rhetorical nonfictional prose** presents facts and ideas in such a way as to persuade a reader of the truth, or at least the likelihood, of the writer's position. Just as persuasion may be found in narrative nonfictional prose, so narrative elements are often part of rhetorical nonfictional prose. Image, anecdote, character sketch, and descriptions of places may contribute to the development of an idea or an argument. The earlier discussion of Meridel LeSueur's "Women on the Breadlines" points out how she uses a variety of narrative techniques to move her readers closer to the position she is advocating. "Women on the Breadlines," and also Agnes Smedley's "The Silk Workers" (p. 920), are **journalistic essays,** examples of reportage which go beyond the simple reporting of events to take and support a position.

Alongside narrative and rhetorical writing are two other modes of nonfictional prose: the **descriptive** and the **expository.** Descriptive writing tells readers what a person or object or place looks like, or feels, smells, tastes, or sounds like. Expository writing explains, provides readers with information—how a watch works, what "neurosis" means, how to read nonfictional prose. But in writing considered literature, a work that is exclusively descriptive or expository is somewhat rare; description most often appears in the service of narration and exposition in the service of persuasion. So we find it more useful to talk of descriptive and expository *elements* in nonfictional writing.

Whether narrative or rhetorical, most nonfictional prose pieces could also be called **essays,** a term originating in a French verb meaning "to try" or "to attempt." The essay can be divided into the **informal essay,** relatively more personal or subjective, more tentative, not meant to be the last word on a subject, relaxed in tone and form, often more dependent on the techniques of fiction, poetry, and drama; and the **formal essay,** more dignified and serious in tone, more objective and distanced from reader and subject, more formally structured. Scientific treatises, much traditional historical writing, and a good deal of literary criticism are written in a more formal mode. Most of the essays included in this anthology would be classified as informal. Your own papers about literature are frequently essays and, depending on your temperament and your topic, they may lie anywhere on the spectrum from informal to formal.

STRATEGIES OF NONFICTIONAL PROSE

The passage by Virginia Woolf on "Shakespeare's Sister" (p. 667), Henry David Thoreau's "Civil Disobedience" (p. 1353) and Judy Syfers's "Why I Want a Wife" are examples of **political essays;** each writer has a definite political position for (or against) which she or he is arguing. Woolf uses the method of comparison and contrast to imagine what the chances of becoming a writer would have been for a young woman in Shakespeare's time. "Let me imagine, since facts are so hard to come by, what would have happened had Shakespeare had a wonderfully gifted sister, called Judith, let us say." In "Civil Disobedience," Thoreau mixes personal narration (the story of how he went to jail for not paying his taxes) with an argument about why it is immoral to pay taxes when they will be used for immoral purposes—in this case, to support war and the institution of slavery. Then Thoreau moves to the next level of his argument to try to persuade us each to know what our convictions are and to act out of them. One way of characterizing Thoreau's rhetorical method is as concentric circles of argument, each one opening out into a further level of abstraction, but with a kernel of personal narration at the very center to anchor his theorizing. In a sense, the form of Thoreau's writing reflects his ethics—no one else can tell us what is right; each person must act (and write) out of personal experience and conviction.

Syfers's much shorter essay uses humor as a strategy to keep us reading in the face of any initial resistance we might have to her topic. The relentless repetition of the phrase "I want a wife," combined with vivid detail from her own experiences as a wife, carry us along with the writer so that by the time she concludes, "My god, who wouldn't want a wife?" we are inclined to agree with her. Syfers's use of repetition as a rhetorical strategy is more common in oral than in written forms and is a technique we encounter frequently in poetry. Repetition is also often used in sermons and speeches because repetition of important ideas or emotions is crucial to retention of content in situations where the audience doesn't have a text that they can reread. In addition, repetition creates a rhythm in spoken prose which in turn creates a mood shared communally, holding an audience's attention and moving them toward a particular conclusion. The Reverend Martin Luther King, Jr.'s powerful and moving speeches were influenced by the rhetorical form of the sermon, especially as it developed in the black church in America. His two speeches included here, "I Have a Dream" (p. 1384) and "A Time to Break Silence" (p. 1113), as well as Sojourner Truth's "Ain't I a Woman" (p. 670), are examples of particularly effective oral rhetoric. The reader of the text of a speech needs to remember that, like poetry, a speech is meant to be heard and that reading some or all of it aloud can be an aid to understanding. While much modern writing envisions an individual reader, speeches, like drama, imagine a communal audience. In any piece of writing, and especially in any rhetorical piece of writing, it is useful to think about the audience the writer had in mind. In considering a speech, its time and place and occasion can be crucial in your interpretation of its meaning. For example, Sojourner Truth's redefinition of "woman" makes more sense when you know she was a black woman in the middle of the nineteenth century speaking to an audience primarily of white women and men about women's place and women's rights.

Like any other piece of writing, a work of nonfictional prose needs to be able to stand on its own and make sense to us as a separate entity. However, an essay, like a poem, a story, or a play, may be in part working out of or challenging a literary, philosophical, or political tradition, or be responding to contemporary social or biographical events. Researching and keeping in mind historical factors such as the time, place, and occasion of a piece of writing, literary factors such as its place in the writer's overall work, and biographical factors such as what else was going on in the writer's life at that time can provide a valuable context for the text itself. Especially in the case of rhetorical nonfictional prose, it is useful to discover, if we can, what other writers have said about the same subject, for often an essay will be a response to another essay or a contribution to an argument being carried on by a number of people in a given period.

Finally, a note on one more form of nonfictional prose included in this anthology: the **parable,** an illustrative story that teaches a lesson, points a moral, or answers a question. We are probably familiar with such Biblical parables as those of Jonah and the whale, the Prodigal Son, and the endlessly divisible loaves and fishes. Aristophanes' speech, from Plato's *Symposium* (p. 663), is a parable about human sexuality and love. You might consider writing a short parable of your own on a subject important to you.

In reading and writing about nonfictional prose, it may make sense to look for the **theme** of the work if the piece is primarily narrative or to look for the **thesis** of the work if it is primarily rhetorical or persuasive. What does the work as a whole add up to? What was the writer's intent or purpose in writing it? What is your response to the work, and do you think yours is the response the writer wanted? How does the writer develop either the theme or the thesis? What are its stages? What are its elements? What does the writer use to build an argument, present an idea, provide an experience for us to share?

One of the best ways to understand any type of writing is to attempt (or essay) it yourself, to experience the craft of writing in that mode from the inside. This is true of fiction, poetry, and drama, though with the last you might content yourself with a short scene rather than a whole play. In essaying nonfictional prose, you might try writing a short autobiographical sketch, centered perhaps on one significant incident in your life. Or you could tell your life story from the perspective created by a particular focus, such as social class, race, or gender. Or you could argue your position on a topic by using an anecdote or extended metaphor (image) to present your main point. The chapter "Literature and the Writing Process" is constructed to help train you in a variety of approaches to a particular type of writing—nonfictional prose that has a literary text as its subject. The works of nonfictional prose included in *Literature and Society* can stimulate your thinking and serve as models for your own writing about literature, ideas, experience, and beliefs.

CREDITS

INDEX OF FIRST LINES
OF POEMS

INDEX OF AUTHORS
AND TITLES

INDEX OF LITERARY TERMS